CONTENTS

P9-BYZ-563

THE OFFICIAL VISITOR GUIDE

Fodor's National Parks of the West

SECOND EDITION

Everything to **see and do** in America's western parks | **Maps and itineraries** for park-to-park driving tours | Where to **stay and eat** near the parks | Plus **field guides** to national-park flora and fauna

Fodor's Travel Publications
New York Toronto London Sydney Auckland
www.fodors.com

NATIONAL PARK
FOUNDATION

Fodor's National Parks of the West

Editor: Constance Jones

Editorial Contributors: Jean Arthur (Glacier), Gina Bacon (Pacific Northwest), Michele Bardsley (Death Valley, Great Basin), Tom Griffith (The Mountains and the Plains, Badlands, Wind Cave), Marilyn Haddrill (The Desert Southwest, Big Bend, Carlsbad Caverns, Guadalupe Mountains), Cynthia Hirschfield (Black Canyon of the Gunnison, Rocky Mountain), Mara Levin (Saguaro), Janet Lowe (Visiting the National Parks of the West, Canyon Country, Arches/Canyonlands, Bryce Canyon, Capitol Reef, Zion), Eric Lucas (Crater Lake, Mt. Rainier, North Cascades, Olympic), Diana Lambdin Meyer (Theodore Roosevelt, Mesa Verde), Candy Moulton (Grand Teton, Yellowstone), Marty Olmstead (Lassen Volcanic, Redwood), Nina Rubin (Desert Southwest, Pacific Northwest), John Vlahides (California Classics, Sequoia/Kings Canyon, Yosemite), Kim Westerman (Grand Canyon, Petrified Forest), Bobbi Zane (Channel Islands, Joshua Tree)

Maps: Maryland Cartographics, Mapping Specialists, *cartographers;* Bob Blake and Rebecca Baer, *map editors*

Design: Siobhan O'Hare

Production/Manufacturing: Angela L. McLean

Photos: Pacific Northwest chapter and field guide of Canyon Country chapter, Corbis. Kodak boxes, Siobhan O'Hare. All other photos, Photodisc.

Special Sales

This book is available for special discounts for bulk purchases for sales promotions or premiums. Special editions, including personalized covers, excerpts of existing books, and corporate imprints, can be created in large quantities for special needs. For more information, write to Special Markets/Premium Sales, 1745 Broadway, MD 6-2, New York, New York 10019 or e-mail *specialmarkets@randomhouse.com*.

An Important Tip & An Invitation

Although all prices, opening times, and other details in this book are based on information supplied to us at press time, changes occur all the time in the travel world, and Fodor's cannot accept responsibility for facts that become outdated or for inadvertent errors or omissions. So **always confirm information when it matters,** especially if you're making a detour to visit a specific place. Your experiences—positive and negative—matter to us. If we have missed or misstated something, **please write to us.** We follow up on all suggestions. Contact the National Parks of the West editor at editors@fodors.com or c/o Fodor's at 1745 Broadway, New York, NY 10019.

PRINTED IN THE UNITED STATES OF AMERICA

10 9 8 7 6 5 4 3 2 1

Great National Park Trips

Of all the things that went wrong with Clark Griswold's vacation, one stands out: The theme park he had driven across the country to visit was closed when he got there. Clark, the suburban bumbler played by Chevy Chase in 1983's hilarious *National Lampoon's Vacation*, is fictional, of course. But his story is poignantly true. Although most Americans get only two precious weeks of vacation a year, many set off on their journeys with surprisingly little guidance. Many travelers are inspired to visit our national parks by friends and family or wait to get travel information until they arrive at the park, where they receive a park map and maybe a park newspaper. It makes no sense to spend priceless vacation time in the visitor center parking lot reading about the park, when you could be out seeing it up close and personal.

Congratulate yourself on picking up this guide. Studying it—before you leave home—is the best possible first step toward making sure your national park vacation fulfills your every dream.

Inside you'll find all the tools you need to plan a perfect trip to the national parks of the American West. In the dozens of parks and towns we describe, you'll find thousands of places to explore. So you'll always know what's around the next bend. And with the practical information we provide, you can easily call to confirm the details that matter and study up on what you'll want to see and do, before you leave home.

By all means, when you plan your trip, allow yourself time to make a few detours. Because as wonderful as it is to visit sights you've read about, it's the serendipitous experiences that often prove the most memorable: the hiking trail that passes a waterfall too small to have a name, the lone picnic table hidden in a grove of cottonwoods along an unmarked spur road. As you roll along the park roads, use the book to find out more about the features announced by roadside signs. Consider turning off at the next scenic overlook. And always remember: In this great country of ours, there's an adventure around every corner.

HOW TO USE THIS BOOK

There's never been a better time to visit the national parks of the American West. This book contains everything you need to know in order to plan and enjoy your trip to our country's greatest scenic wonders. Whether you are a family on summer vacation, a retiree traveling the country by RV, a college student on break, or anyone at all who wants to be immersed in nature—and our nation's heritage—on a grand scale, the book that you hold in your hands is indispensable. Get ready to drive some of the most beautiful roads you'll ever see, to pause in wonder at the scenic turnouts, and to learn about the magnificent western landscape and the creatures that inhabit it. You can hike trails through forests and deserts, take ranger-led tram tours, dine in historic lodges, and sleep under the stars. Whatever your interests, this book will help you take the vacation of a lifetime.

What's Inside

For each of the national parks of the West we have gathered comprehensive information on everything within the park and on the towns and attractions nearby. We have included as many sights, activities, lodging, and dining options, and practical details as space allows, focusing on delivering to you the kind of in-depth, first-hand knowledge that you won't get anywhere else. First, "Visiting the National Parks of the West" introduces you to the national park experience and provides tips on how to make the most of your visit. Then, five distinct sections of the book are devoted to the parks in each of the five regions of the West: the Pacific Northwest, California, the mountains and plains, canyon country, and the desert Southwest.

REGIONAL DRIVING TOURS AND FIELD GUIDES

Whether you are trying to decide which part of the West to explore or have already chosen a destination, the opening of each regional section can answer your questions. There's a general description of the area and the parks within it, detailed information on driving, suggestions on when to visit, weather and climate facts, and tips on what to pack. An excellent trip-planning tool is the driving tour (or two) mapped out for each region. It's an efficient yet adventurous itinerary for your road trip, complete with recommendations on which routes to take for a great drive, interesting places to stop along the way, and where to spend each night. Every driving tour is accompanied by a handy map showing all the important highways, cities, and attractions. At the end of each regional section, a concise field guide will help you identify and understand the ecosystems, flora, fauna, geology, and topographical features that you will see as you drive through the region and visit its parks.

Where to Find It Park by Park

Between the introductory material and the field guide, the national parks are presented in alphabetical order within the regional sections. Coverage of each park is detailed and comprehensive and is arranged in a logical, easy-to-use format. Scattered in the margins are fun facts and insider's tips to enrich your park experience.

INTRODUCTION

Here you'll get your first glimpse of what the park is all about. You will get the scoop on the best times to visit and on festivals and seasonal events, as well as on the towns nearby and how to get more information about them. You'll also find a list of books and other publications about the park, which can whet your appetite before your trip and help you understand and enjoy the park while you are there.

EXPLORING THE PARK

This section gives you the lowdown on the park, including basics such as fees, getting around, and what to do in an emergency. We outline a couple of itineraries that can help you make the best use of your time in the park, whether you are staying just one day or longer. Of course, we've included a detailed map. Extensive listings of park attractions—ranger-led programs, specialty tours, scenic drives, visitor centers, scenic overlooks—follow. Each listing gives a description of the activity or facility, plus the where, when, and how much of it. Sports and other outdoor activities have a section of their own. From bicycling to snowmobiling, we let you know what your options are and how you can get in on the fun. Individual hiking trails, bird-watching spots, marinas, and other venues are described and their precise locations given.

OUTFITTERS

Riding a trail on horseback, rafting down a stretch of river, or casting a fishing line lets you immerse yourself in a national park in ways that mere sightseeing misses. Outfitters in communities near most of the parks are ready to share with you their special ways of getting to know the great outdoors. Some of them lead expeditions of a few hours or several days in length, others provide lessons in technique, and some rent or sell the sports equipment you will need. Not only do these outfitters serve the park, many of them can also guide you to state recreation areas, rock-climbing sites, or ski slopes near the park.

ATTRACTIONS NEARBY

Under this heading are all kinds of things to see and do near the park, from museums and monuments to wildlife preserves and water parks. You'll learn about scenic highways, area tours, and places to enjoy outdoor activities and sports from four-wheeling to hot-air ballooning.

DINING

Eating in and around most of the West's national parks is a fairly straightforward affair involving lots of good old American food, but you do find the occasional exceptions. This section tells you everywhere you can get a meal in the park and where you can picnic if you bring your own. We also list plenty of restaurants in the towns near the park. Each review tells you what to expect of the restaurants, including type of cuisine, reservations policy, seasonal closings, and price range of entrées.

LODGING

The national parks of the West are home to some of the country's most distinctive and historic hotels. In this section you will find reviews of all the lodgings available inside the park and of many hotels, inns, motels, and B&B's nearby. The reviews describe the lodgings and detail their facilities (such as hot tubs and refrigerators) and policies (such as seasonal closings and whether pets are allowed). We let you know where you may have to reserve far in advance, and we give the price range for double rooms at each property.

CAMPING AND RV FACILITIES

For many visitors, camping is a central part of the national park experience. If you are one such person you will find all you need to know right here. We list most of the developed, frontcountry campgrounds as well as many primitive and backcountry sites. You'll learn what each campground has to offer, including such facilities as showers and fire grates, strategies for getting a campsite in each park, seasonal closings, and how much you will pay for the pleasure of camping out. We also explain the park's backcountry camping opportunities and policies for permits and fire safety.

SHOPPING

Whether you need to stock up on snacks or buy a gift for your nephew, you can look in this section to find out where to fill your shopping needs, both in and near the park.

ESSENTIAL INFORMATION

Coverage of each park concludes with a listing of traveler's services available in and near the park. Look here to find out the location of the nearest ATM, service station, or post office.

Important Tip

Although all prices, opening times, and other details in this book are based on information supplied to us at this writing, changes occur all the time in the travel world, and Fodor's cannot accept responsibility for facts that become outdated or for inadvertent errors or omissions. So always confirm information when it matters, especially if you are making a detour to visit a specific place.

Let Us Hear From You

Keeping a travel guide fresh and up-to-date is a big job, and we welcome any and all comments. We'd love to have your thoughts on places we've listed, and we're interested in hearing about your own special finds. Our guides are thoroughly updated for each new edition, and we're always adding new information, so your feedback is vital. Contact the National Parks of the West editor at editors@fodors.com or c/o Fodor's at 1745 Broadway, New York, NY 10019. We look forward to hearing from you. And in the meantime, have a wonderful trip.

THE EDITORS

Fodor's National Parks of the West

SECOND EDITION

NATIONAL PARK
FOUNDATION

Visiting the National Parks of the West

"We need the tonic of wilderness," wrote Henry David Thoreau in the 19th century. Led by Thoreau and Ralph Waldo Emerson, a literary movement called transcendentalism swept through America in the mid-1800s. By experiencing nature, the transcendentalists believed, people could gain a heightened awareness of beauty and of their place in the universe. Emerson wrote: "To the body and mind which have been cramped by noxious work or company, nature is medicinal and restores their tone. The tradesman, the attorney comes out of the din and craft of the street and sees the sky and the woods, and is a man again. In their eternal calm, he finds himself." Thoreau agreed that ". . . a taste for the beautiful is most cultivated out of doors."

The influx of white settlers in the West, accompanied by the growth of the railroad and the finality of U.S. military campaigns against the Indians, appeared to signal the end of America's untamed wilderness. Interest in preserving scenic lands and ancient archaeological sites out West emerged, along with a national sense of responsibility for the wilderness. By 1916 the Interior Department was responsible for 14 national parks and 21 national monuments. On August 25 of that year, President Woodrow Wilson approved legislation creating the National Park Service within the Interior Department. The mission of this new agency was "to conserve the scenery and the natural and historic objects and the wild life therein and to provide for the enjoyment of the same in such manner and by such means as will leave them unimpaired for the enjoyment of future generations."

Almost all of the first national parks in America were in the West. Yellowstone, designated in 1872, was the first and is the oldest national park in the world. Yosemite, along with Sequoia, is the second-oldest national park. Today, a visit to a western national park is a grand adventure. You may see landscapes vastly different from your home and may encounter deer, elk, moose, eagles, hawks, or falcons. Children may see their first snake in a national park or learn what a marmot is. If you're traveling from a large metropolitan area you might be amazed by the starry sky, and you may see the Milky Way for the first time. And you'll find something else. We have come to count on the national parks as a sanctuary, not only for the animals who live there but for ourselves. The national parks are a place to escape from the hectic, fast-paced life of the city and to remember there was a time when technology didn't change in the blink of an eye. In the great parks of the West we are reminded of who we are and what is important in the grand scheme of life. For a few days or a few moments, these protected lands give us the opportunity to be quiet and reflect upon the universe. No doubt Mr. Emerson and Mr. Thoreau smile from their graves.

THE FUTURE OF THE PARKS OF THE WEST

When Congress set aside the Grand Canyon as a national park in 1919, members could not possibly have known that someday nearly 5 million people would visit it each year. Yosemite, Yellowstone, Olympic, and Rocky Mountain national parks receive more than 3 million visitors annually. Glacier, Grand Teton, and Zion top 2 million visitors, and Bryce Canyon, Death Valley, and Mount Rainier welcome more than 1 million guests each year. As more people visit the parks, more services are needed to accommodate them. Motels, restaurants, markets, and gift shops crowd the boundaries of the national parks. More visitation threatens wildlife. Plants take a beating from foot traffic and from vehicle exhaust. Traffic jams are as common in some parks as they are on city freeways. Some parks have begun to address the problem of overcrowding by closing their roads to private vehicles and running shuttles during the busiest times of year.

The popularity of the parks has had some negative consequences. Certain animals, such as bison, elk, moose, and bighorn sheep, were protected, but predators such as wolves and mountain lions were trapped and shot. Forest fires were suppressed and fish populations were manipulated to enhance sportfishing for the enjoyment of recreationists. As a result the ecosystems of many parks have been thrown out of balance, threatening the very thing the national parks were intended to protect. Conservationists have spearheaded movements to reintroduce species that were indigenous to the parks a century ago, but ranchers protest that wolves and coyotes take their livestock. Citizens of the towns that have encroached on the parks worry that mountain lions or other predators might pose a danger to children or pets.

Even as the parks face such problems, they are handicapped by budget cuts. Year after year park programs disappear: there are not enough rangers to present campfire talks, campgrounds close, and many parks operate with skeleton crews in spite of visitation statistics that topple previous records. The future of the parks is uncertain, but it is certain that there's no place on Earth like Arches National Park. There's no where else in the world to see the ancient bristlecone pine than Great Basin National Park. There are few places other than Mesa Verde to see the ancestral homelands of ancient Native Americans, and Old Faithful only erupts in one place on the planet.

Park Basics

Contacts and Resources: National Park Service Headquarters. | 1849 C St. NW, Washington, DC 20240 | 202/208–6843 | www.nps.gov.

Intermountain Region. | 12795 Alameda Pkwy., Denver, CO 80225 | 303/969–2500.

Pacific West Region. | One Jackson Center, 1111 Jackson St., Suite 700, Oakland, CA 94607 | 510/817–1300 | www.nps.gov/pwro.

National Park Reservation Service. You can make reservations for tours and campsites at many of the parks through this office. | Box 1600 Cumberland MD 21502 | 800/365–2267 | reservations.nps.gov.

National Park Foundation. This nonprofit partner of the National Park Service raises support from corporations, foundations, and individuals to protect and enhance the national parks. | 11 Dupont Circle NW, Suite 600 Washington, DC 20036 | 202/238–4200 | fax 202/234–3103 | www.nationalparks.org.

National Parks Conservation Association. Founded in 1919, this organization is America's only private, nonprofit advocacy organization dedicated solely to protecting, preserving, and enhancing the National Park System. A library of national park information, including fact sheets, congressional testimony, and press releases, is available on the Web site.

| 1300 19th St. NW, Suite 300, Washington, DC 20036 | 800/628–7275 | fax 202/659–0650 | www.npca.org.

Fees and Passes: Most parks charge admission of $10–$20 for a pass that's good for a week. Some parks also offer annual passes. Inquire at the visitor center to determine if the park you are interested in offers such a pass.

Golden Access Passport. This free, lifetime pass will admit you to all national parks, monuments, historic sites, recreation areas, and national wildlife refuges if you are a U.S. citizen who is blind or permanently disabled. Rules for admission are the same as for the Golden Age Passport. You can obtain the pass in person at any national parks administered site that charges an entrance fee. You will be asked to provide proof of permanent medical disability or eligibility for disability benefits.

Golden Age Passport. If you are a U.S. citizen over the age of 62 you can obtain this free, lifetime entrance pass to all national parks, monuments, historic sites, recreation areas, and national wildlife refuges. The pass admits you and any passengers in your private vehicle to the site and provides a 50% discount on federal use fees for facilities and services such as camping, swimming, parking, boat launching, and tours. In some cases only you and not your companions receive the discount. The Golden Age Passport is nontransferable and it does not reduce or cover fees for special recreation permits or any fees charged by concessionaires. There's a one-time $10 processing fee to receive this pass and you must show identification such as a birth certificate or passport. You can purchase it at any national park where an entrance fee is charged, at park visitor centers, or from the National Park Foundation.

Golden Eagle Pass. For $15 you can purchase a Golden Eagle hologram to affix to your National Parks Pass. Your upgraded pass will cover entrance fees at all NPS-administered sites and sites managed by the U.S. Fish and Wildlife Service, the U.S. Forest Service, and the Bureau of Land Management (BLM). Rules of admittance are the same as those for the National Parks Pass; the Golden Eagle expires when the parks pass expires. Purchase the Golden Eagle Pass at most national park sites, Fish and Wildlife sites, and BLM fee stations.

National Parks Pass. This pass admits you and any passengers in your private vehicle to any national park, national monument, national recreation area or other NPS-administered site in the United States. If the park charges a per-person admission fee the pass admits you, your spouse, your children, and your parents when you arrive together. The $50 annual pass is nontransferable and does not cover or reduce fees for camping, parking, tours, or concessions. You can purchase it at any national park where an entrance fee is charged, at park visitor centers, or from the National Park Foundation.

Making the Most of Your Park Visit

There's nothing quite like setting off for a vacation in one of America's western national parks. For many, it's a once-in-a-lifetime opportunity to see lands that lie far from the urban centers where they live. In spite of increased numbers of visitors to the national parks, these national treasures still give the gift of wilderness and adventure. Who could not be excited about a mule ride into the bottom of a mile-deep canyon, or a ferry ride with the potential of seeing a whale emerge from the water? How many opportunities in life are there to walk across a glacier or creep underneath the earth in caverns? Untold rewards are waiting in the national parks of the West.

Planning Your Visit

The success of any trip depends on a combination of good luck and good planning. A little forethought can go a long way toward making your national parks vacation memorable for all the right reasons.

Each year the National Park Foundation, in cooperation with the National Park Service and Kodak, holds a photo contest to select the image to be used on the National Parks Pass. You can get information about this contest by contacting the National Parks Foundation | 1101 17th St., NW, Suite 102, Washington, DC 20036 | www.nationalparks.org.

WHICH PARK?

With more than 30 western national parks to choose from, all of them as gorgeous and rewarding as the next, it's difficult to choose where in the West to go. First, consider the type of vacation you want to have. Do you want to see lush temperate forests? Rugged mountain ranges? Wide-open deserts? Do you dream of camping in the wilderness, hiking deep into the backcountry on little-used trails, and not encountering another living soul? Select a less-visited park that offers lots of hiking opportunities, such as Canyonlands or North Cascades. Are you traveling with children, but would still like to hike? Select a park where the trails aren't so challenging as to discourage the younger members of your group, perhaps Petrified Forest or Guadalupe Mountains. If wildlife viewing is a priority, Rocky Mountain or the Channel Islands might fit the bill. And if the West's greatest hits are on your wish list, Yellowstone, Yosemite, and the Grand Canyon are a few obvious choices.

To refine your selection consider the time of year you will be traveling—climate can have a great impact on your visit. Parks at high elevation, such as Great Basin, Crater Lake, or Grand Teton may have limited services and access from late fall through early spring. Conversely, unless you like serious heat summer is not the best time to visit parks like Death Valley, Big Bend, or Arches. Now think about your schedule: if you have a limited amount of time, select the most accessible parks—those close to a major interstate or the airport where you'll begin your road trip. Saguaro, Mt. Rainier, or Joshua Tree, for instance, fall into this category. See how many other parks are in the general vicinity and study the driving tours in this book to help you plan an efficient loop.

COPING WITH THE CROWDS

The best way to cope with the crowds in national parks is to avoid them altogether. Most parks have high and low seasons, and you can certainly have a more serene time if you visit in low season. If you don't want to come when many park facilities and nearby amenities may be closed, you might consider visiting during a shoulder season. But if you, like many people, do not have the luxury of traveling in off-season, don't hesitate to take your trip anyway and simply enjoy the many activities and the people you'll meet on the trails, in the campgrounds, and at the lodges. You don't have to resign yourself to a substandard peak-season experience: rise early to hit the trails or the most popular sites. Ride park shuttles to beat the traffic and eliminate parking hassles. Venture into the backcountry during the peak hours of the day to spend some time alone.

NATIONAL PARK LODGES

The lodges of the national parks of the West have a long and rich history. Many were constructed during the early development of the national park system, by railroad companies who were promoting tourism to the area. Many have remarkable rustic architecture. A stay at a national park lodge is still as exciting and romantic as it was in the early years. You can't beat the spectacular setting; lodges often overlook some of the best scenery in the park. Many parks have newer lodges, some designed for functional economy and others to provide the grand experience of the historic lodges. New or old, the park lodges often have viewing decks, patios, or outdoor dining that put you right in the middle of the wilderness you came to see. Each of the lodges has at least one restaurant, and some have elegant dining rooms and cozy bars. Room rates range from very reasonable to very expensive and reservations can be hard to come by. Most in-park lodging companies accept reservations up to a year in advance, so you should reserve as early as possible. Sometimes you can pick up a cancellation right before you arrive at the park.

BRINGING THE KIDS

A visit to any of America's western national parks can be among your children's most lasting memories. To make the trip as fun for them (and you!) as possible, invite your children to help with the planning. Go on-line or open a picture book to see which parks most interest your little ones. Once you've decided where to go, pick up a kid-friendly book about your destination so your children can find out about the things they'll see there, and bring home story books that are set in the West. Buy colored pencils and paper and have the kids draw pictures of the animals they might see in the park. If they've never been camping and you're planning on sleeping under the stars, set up the tent at home before you go so they aren't frightened when you do pitch your tent in the park. A new backpack stocked with trail food and their own canteen, flashlight, and journal will get your children excited about the expedition. Make sure you pack appropriate footwear and clothing, for there's no surer vacation spoiler than a cold kid with blistered feet.

Once you arrive at the park, leave the computer games and portable CD players in the car. Unencumbered by the trappings of ordinary life, you have a great opportunity to teach your children respect for nature. Remind them not to pick flowers, collect rocks, or break off tree branches as they walk the trails. Challenge them to see how many tracks they can find in the sand and to guess what animals or bugs left them—better yet, buy an animal-track book to help them identify the marks they see. Let your children lead your hike so they can set the pace. Sign them up for Junior Ranger programs, a wonderful way to introduce them to the natural and cultural history of the region. If you've got a teenager in tow, find active, hands-on national park activities. Challenging hikes or bike rides, river paddling or white-water trips, or watching rock climbers scale towering walls will intrigue your teen. And whatever your children's ages, above all encourage them to be quiet in the national parks. Point out that noise will scare away birds and animals that may be waiting just around the corner. Help them to appreciate the solitude and peace that so many people seek in these treasured lands.

PETS
Generally, pets are allowed only in developed areas of the national parks, including drive-in campgrounds and picnic areas, but they must be kept on a leash at all times. With the exception of guide dogs, pets are not allowed inside buildings, on most trails, on beaches, or in the backcountry. They also may be prohibited in areas controlled by concessionaires. Some of the parks have kennels, but before you decide to bring your pet with you to a national park, call ahead for information.

VISITOR CENTERS AND RANGER PROGRAMS
A stop at the visitor center is essential—and not just for the bathroom. Take a few moments to look at the exhibits that explain the geology, wildlife, history, and archaeology of the park, and you will find that your visit to the park will be greatly enriched. Most parks have an orientation video or slide show that gives you an overview of what you'll see during your visit; this can help you plan your approach to the park. Most visitor centers have a bookstore that sells books, maps, and guidebooks—often difficult to find anywhere else—that can help you understand what you see in the park. Pick up inexpensive bird and plant lists so you can identify species while you walk the trails. As the park's hub of information, the visitor center has a complete list of park services, campgrounds, facilities, and programs. Take advantage of this resource. The rangers on duty are always thrilled to share their knowledge with interested visitors. They can give you trail advice, driving directions, and the current weather forecast. Don't pass up ranger programs like campfire talks, guided hikes, and the like. The men and women who wear the "flat hat" know their park through and through and are full of stories that can make the park come alive.

PARK TRANSPORTATION
It might be difficult to give up the independence of driving your own vehicle, but there's a much more relaxing way to visit many of the national parks of the west. If you leave your car behind and take a park shuttle whenever you can, you won't get stuck in a long line of vehicles waiting to park at the popular overlooks. Shuttles run frequently and make

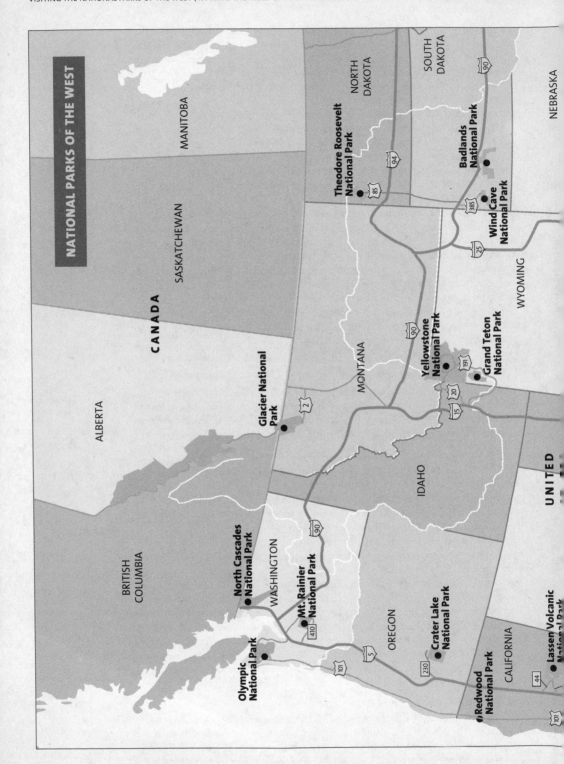

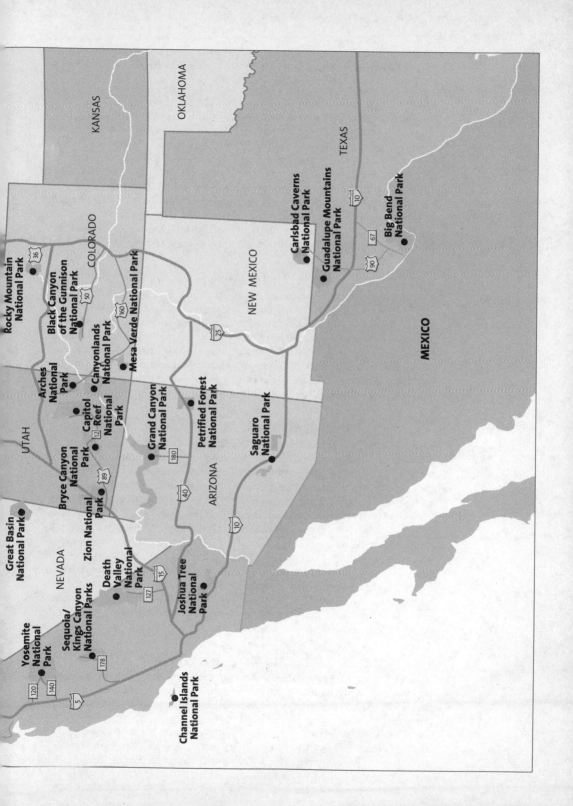

If your vacation is to include a lot of hiking, take two different pairs of boots and alternate wearing them so that neither has a chance to rub a blister or bruise. Never wear new boots on your hiking vacation; break them in before you leave home.

lots of stops, so you'll be able to get most everywhere you want to go in a timely manner. At some parks you have no choice but to take the shuttle, but even where it's still optional give the shuttle a try and enjoy a less stressful visit.

SCENIC DRIVES AND NATURE WALKS

Everybody's heard of the visitor to the Grand Canyon, or Yosemite, or Yellowstone, who drives up to an overlook, rolls down the window, takes a picture, and drives away. Don't miss out on a great experience by falling into that sad category. Take some time to put down the video camera and get to know the park you have traveled so far to see. If you're on a shuttle, get out at every stop to smell the air and walk to the overlook. Read the interpretive displays that discuss landmarks in the distance or the significance of a geologic formation. If you're driving, go slowly and observe the trees, the colors, the birds and butterflies that flutter by. Hike as many trails as you can. Listen to the silence, get rained on, and sniff the flowers. Sit by a lake for an hour. That's what the national parks have been saved for—your enjoyment. If you give yourself the time to soak up the park, you'll have a rare and wonderful trip.

OUTDOOR ACTIVITIES AND SPORTS

There is no better way to get to know a national park than to get up close and personal with the rocks, the lakes, the bats, the cacti, and the rivers. Dare to hike the tough trail or run the rapids, to bike a back road or snowshoe through the woods. Your senses will be heightened and you'll breathe deeper when you get dirt under your fingernails and grass stains on your jeans. You'll be *in* the park more truly and thoroughly when you pit your body against nature's challenges. Of course, don't push yourself too far. Even if you just take a walk across a field or dip your toe in a stream you'll become a part of the park, and you'll wonder how you ever lived without the experience.

CAMPING

There's nothing quite like sleeping out under the stars, roasting marshmallows over an open fire, and waking to the clear blue skies of the West. In the national parks you can pitch your tent in some of the West's most famous landscapes. It seems like everyone wants to experience this idyllic setting, so national park campgrounds are often full in busy seasons. Most of the developed, front-country national park campgrounds do not accept reservations, so bone up on the camping situation in your destination and learn the tricks for securing a campsite. Frequently, you must arrive at the campground between 10 and 11 AM to get a site, and all the sites will be grabbed by noon. If you're a tent camper and don't want to listen to the hum of generators, look for tent-only campgrounds or campgrounds accessed by roads that cannot accommodate RVs. Likewise, if you're an RV camper make sure the park offers the kind of hookups and dump stations that you need to make your stay enjoyable. And, tent or RV, respect the campground's quiet times and help keep the national park camping experience as it was meant to be. Evening curfews on generators and noise are enforced so that all campers can enjoy the quiet that is one of the prizes of the national parks.

Playing It Safe in the Parks

In spite of modern facilities and developments in many of the West's national parks, visiting these remote, rugged areas is still an adventure into a little bit of the unknown. The park service has done everything possible to make sure your visit is safe, but you venture into these last enclaves of the truly wild West at your own risk. Park brochures, Web sites, and newspapers give detailed information on safety precautions at each national park—be sure to read these. Pay attention to safety postings on signs and bulletin boards throughout the park, and stop by the visitor center or ranger station before you set out into more remote areas. If you're planning on using backcountry areas of the parks, check ahead of time to see if you need permits or reservations. It's not uncommon to make backcountry reservations as far as a year ahead of time at some national parks. The National Park Service wants you to immerse yourself in the park experience, and park personnel will always encourage you to get out on the trails and get a glimpse of the wildlife. By following a few simple guidelines and arriving at the parks prepared, you can maximize not only your safety but your enjoyment as well.

INTRODUCTION
PARK BASICS
MAKING THE
MOST OF YOUR
PARK VISIT
PLAYING IT SAFE
IN THE PARKS
RESPECTING
YOUR PARKS

KNOW BEFORE YOU GO

A few minutes of research before your national park adventure can eliminate many unpleasant surprises. The pages that follow include detailed information on weather, driving conditions, hiking trails, and other park features. The National Park Service Web site offers comprehensive tips on how to visit each park. Additionally, local visitor bureaus can educate you about the area you're planning to visit. Read up and make informed decisions about your trip. Make note of rainy seasons or weather that may restrict your mobility on park back roads. Winter comes early and stays late at many of the West's national parks, and trails and roads within these parks may close. Likewise, summer temperatures in some Western parks can exceed 100°F for weeks on end. Not only is a visit less than fun in these temperatures, physical exertion can be dangerous. Consider factors beyond the weather, too. If you have your heart set on hiking with the kids, for instance, choose a park where the trails are suitable for less experienced hikers. Your family will thank you for your thorough research.

BE PREPARED

Preparedness for your expedition into the national parks involves more than research. Start by creating a packing list well before your departure date. A basic first aid kit is always a good idea: a first-aid manual, aspirin (or acetaminophen or ibuprofen), adhesive bandages, butterfly bandages, sterile gauze pads, 1-inch wide adhesive tape, an elastic bandage, antibacterial ointment, antiseptic cream, antihistamines, razor blades, tweezers, a needle, scissors, calamine lotion, and moleskin for blisters. Also on your packing list should be an ample supply of any prescription medications you may take, as pharmacies and physicians may be few and far between in Western areas. Insect repellent and sunscreen should make their way into your suitcase, as should a broad-brimmed hat for sun protection (especially for kids), not only in the desert but at higher elevations where the air is clear and thin. Layered clothing is pretty much the rule throughout the West. Weather changes suddenly and dramatically, so you may need to add or remove layers of clothing to be more comfortable. Include rain gear in your suitcase and remember to take it on the trail with you. Gloves, a warm hat, and long underwear are advised if you're traveling to higher elevations, or in the spring, fall, or winter throughout the West. And always bring appropriate boots and footwear for everyone in your group.

If you're traveling to higher elevations from lower elevations, be prepared to experience a difference in your stamina level. If you plan on doing some hiking on your trip, prepare at home. Get out and walk, run, or add a backpack with some weight to your daily workout. When you get to the parks, your body may need time to acclimate to higher elevations. If you aren't used to hiking at elevation you can't expect to get out the first day and enjoy an 8-mi hike at 9,000 ft with the same exuberance you do at 1,000 ft. Likewise, make sure your vehicle is ready for the great American road trip. Have your oil changed, belts and fluid levels checked, and tires properly rotated and balanced before you hit the road. Check to see that your spare tire is in good repair. Take an extra key in the event you lock your keys inside your vehicle. If you're traveling in fall, winter, or spring, purchase a set of chains for your vehicle so you can get over snowy mountain passes when necessary. Bring your cell phone on the road, even though you may lose the signal in remote areas, canyons, or mountains. Determine if you need extra gasoline or water while traveling in backcountry areas.

Once you're happily meandering through the national parks, never attempt risky activities alone. Take time to register at trailheads so park personnel know where you are. Don't

It is customary to tip guides employed by the concessionaires who provide tour services. River rafting, horseback riding, four-wheel-drive touring, and scenic boat tours are examples of activities that call for tipping. Typical gratuities are $10–$20 per person per day.

take on activities that are beyond your fitness level. And always drink plenty of water. Dehydration kills, especially in the desert West. Bring along water bottles and a pack to carry them. Remember to keep children well-hydrated, as they are especially prone to dehydration. Always take along high-protein snacks like nuts and energy bars. Granola, dried fruit, and hard vegetables such as celery and carrots are also great snacks for a hike.

GETTING HELP

Don't put yourself or your family at risk: seek medical attention immediately in the event of any illness, injury, or other emergency. Within the national parks, dial 911. Telephones are most often located at campgrounds, museums, and other visitor service areas. Depending on the dispatcher's instructions, stay where you are or proceed directly to the visitor center, ranger station, or a park concessionaire. If you are in the backcountry or on a trail and cannot reach help quickly, dial 911 if you have a cell phone that works, and ask other visitors to go for help.

Respecting Your Parks

America's national parks were set aside to preserve some of the most outstanding landscapes in the world. It is imperative that we continue to treat these national treasures as rare and fragile vestiges of a lost world. Our children, their children, and all those who follow deserve to see the national parks as we see them today.

TAKE ONLY PICTURES, LEAVE ONLY FOOTPRINTS

Each year as more and more people visit the national parks, keeping them clean, undamaged, quiet, and wild becomes more and more difficult. You can help ensure that the parks remain a refuge for animals and people alike simply by following a few guidelines.

- Always place litter in appropriate containers. Don't drop any kind of refuse, including cigarette butts, on trails. Try to pick up what other, less careful visitors, have left behind.
- As you hike through the parks, remain quiet and encourage your companions—especially your children—to do the same so they do not disturb others.
- Never feed animals. Not only is this not healthy for them, it habituates them to human food and makes them more aggressive and thus dangerous to future visitors.
- Whenever you encounter animals allow them space. Remember, you are in their home. Harassing or approaching wild animals will cause them to flee, possibly causing injury and definitely using up vital energy reserves they need for mating, raising their young, and winter survival. Teach your children not to chase lizards, snakes, deer, birds, or other animals that live in the parks.
- Every rock, flower, and stick of wood inside the national parks is protected. Do not take anything out of a national park. If you are tempted to take "just one" rock, imagine what would happen if every visitor did the same: many millions of rocks would disappear from the national parks each year. Besides, there are stiff penalties if you are caught.
- Many of the West's national parks preserve Native American villages, artifacts, and rock art as well as old cowboy camps, mines, and evidence of early pioneers. The people who created these legacies are gone, and now the traces they left behind are disappearing at an alarming rate as well. Never touch rock art; the oil in your skin can destroy it. Do not go into dwellings unless specifically allowed by the National Park Service. Do not move or take artifacts—leave these treasures untouched for future generations. Damaging archaeological sites is illegal and punishable by stiff fines or even imprisonment.

STAY ON THE TRAIL

There are many good reasons to stay on designated trails while hiking in the national parks.
- Staying on marked trails minimizes your risk of getting lost. You can easily become disoriented in unfamiliar terrain. Panic can set in quickly if you suddenly spin around and realize that everything looks the same and that you can't tell the difference between one tree or canyon and the next.

- When you're in a national park, you're in the homeland of animals who rely on the area for a safe habitat. People rambling through the canyons, mountains, or riparian areas unchecked can do untold damage to wildlife habitat, not to mention frightening them.
- Leaving the trail can cause erosion on creek and river banks and disturb soils where plants need to grow to stabilize the area.
- Throughout the large region of canyon country and extending into other deserts, the ground supports biological soil crusts that are actually living colonies of creatures. If destroyed, these colonies take decades to repair. In the meantime, plants can't grow and the area becomes a blowing sand pile.
- Stay out of creeks, rivers, and potholes—they are water sources for animals. Very small quantities of pollutants can make springs, ponds, and potholes unusable. Suntan lotions and vehicle lubricants can harm aquatic life, eggs, or larvae that may be invisible to the naked eye. Carry your own drinking water and leave the wild water for the wild critters. Don't camp near water sources. You will frighten away birds and animals who drink there and also risk destroying plants where they nest.

FIRE SAFETY

There's nothing quite like a campfire to complete the outdoors experience. So you can enjoy this time-honored tradition, most national park campgrounds include fire pits or grates where you can build fires. Never build fires in the backcountry; one breath of wind can carry a cinder for miles and plant it on dry grasslands. Check with the visitor center for rules governing wood collection; most parks do not allow the collection of wood. Don't build a fire when you're alone, and never leave your fire unattended. Clear the ground around the fireplace so that wind cannot blow sparks into dry leaves or grass. Always keep your fire inside the pit, and keep a pot of water or sand near your fire. Throw your used matches into the fire. Never cook in your tent or a poorly ventilated area. When finished, be sure the fire is out cold, meaning you can touch it with your bare hands.

The Pacific Northwest

Nature's most imposing creations dominate the national parks of the Pacific Northwest— towering trees and surging rivers, glaciers draping massive volcanic peaks, mist-shrouded shores pounded by Pacific breakers. Here you'll find many of the continental United States' superlatives: the largest volcano, Mount Rainier; the deepest lake, Crater Lake; the most glaciers, in the North Cascades; the biggest firs and cedars, at Olympic National Park; and the tallest trees of all, in Redwood National and State parks. Each park is visually sensational and spiritually bracing—and they hold living evidence of the forces that made them, from the underlying Pacific Rim tectonic ferment to the ocean-borne climatic symphony overhead.

Impressive as all that is, each of these parks offers gentler, more subtle rewards as well. Mist rolls through moss-draped trees in the Olympic rain forest. Bumblebees visit lily trumpets at timberline in the North Cascades. Tart huckleberries ripen in the August sun on the shoulders of Rainier. Indigo-shouldered Steller's jays flash in the open woods at Crater Lake, and orchids gild the forest floor in the sun-dappled depths of the redwoods. Spectacular as the Pacific Northwest's obvious sights are, you'll gain the finest memories by looking and listening both quietly and closely.

Rules of the Road

License Requirements: To drive unrestricted in California and Oregon, you must be at least 18 years old and have a valid driver's license. To drive in Washington you must be at least 16 years old and have a valid driver's license. Non-U.S. residents should have a license whose text is in the Roman alphabet; an international license is recommended but not required. Drivers must carry proof of insurance.

Right Turn on Red: Unless otherwise indicated, a right turn at a red light is permitted, after a complete stop, in California, Oregon, and Washington. A left turn at a red light is allowed onto a one-way street.

Seat Belt and Helmet Laws: Seat belts must be worn by all vehicle occupants in California, Oregon, and Washington. There are no exceptions. Children under 60 pounds or 6 years of age must be secured in an approved child safety or booster seat in the back seat of the vehicle. Helmets are required for all motorcycle riders in all three states.

Speed Limits: The rural interstate speed limit in California, Oregon, and Washington is 70 mph. On urban freeways, U.S. highways, and major state highways, speed limits vary from 55 to 65 mph.

For More Information: California Department of Motor Vehicles | 800/777–0133. **California Highway Patrol** | 916/657–7202. **Oregon Driver and Motor Vehicles Services** | 503/945–5000. **Washington Traffic Safety Commission** | 360/753–6197.

Pacific Northwest Driving Tour
FROM THE NORTH CASCADES TO REDWOOD

Distance: 1,724 mi   Time: 12–13 days
Breaks: Overnight in Yakima, Mount Rainier National Park, Port Angeles, and Olympic National Park, WA; Florence, Crater Lake National Park, and Ashland, OR; and Eureka and Mendocino, CA.

This comprehensive 12-day tour covers many miles and sites. You'll see plenty of scenery from your car window, but be sure to get out of your car to explore subtler features of each park. After all, you haven't really seen an old-growth forest until you've smelled the sun-warmed bark of a 1,000-year-old tree.

The one-way tour travels from north to south here, but you can just as well start in California and go up by reversing the order. Note that many of the overnight stops require reservations far in advance—up to six months for midsummer dates at Paradise Inn in Rainier, Lake Crescent Lodge, and Lake Quinault Lodge in Olympic, and up to one year for Crater Lake Lodge.

❶ Start in Sedro-Woolley, where you can pick up information about **North Cascades National Park** at park headquarters. From Sedro-Woolley, it's a 45-minute drive on Route 20 to the entrance of the park. You can take your first stroll through an old-growth forest from the visitor center in Newhalem. Devote the rest of the day to driving through the **Cascades** on Route 20, stopping at various overlooks. Exit the park and continue through the **Methow Valley.** Head south on Route 20, then Route 153, then U.S. 97, then I–82 (just over 300 mi total) to **Yakima,** where you should stay the night.

❷ On the morning of day two, take U.S. 12 west from Yakima 102 mi to Ohanapecosh, the southern entrance to **Mount Rainier National Park.** If time allows, take the 35-mi three-hour drive on Sunrise Road, which reveals the "back" (northeast) side of Rainier. A room at the Paradise Inn is your base for the next two nights. Mount Rainier is worth the next full day of your trip. Take advantage of one of the frequent ranger-led activities exploring the alpine Cascades habitat, and don't miss a hike to Panorama Point near the foot of the **Muir Snowfield** to see panoramic views of the Puget Sound and the glaciers and high ridges of Rainier overhead. After dinner at the inn, watch the sunset's alpenglow on the peak from the back porch.

❸ On day four, follow routes 706 and 7 to U.S. 12 from Paradise, heading west to I–5. When you reach the interstate, you can take a detour south to spend the day visiting the **Mount St. Helens National Volcanic Monument** to see first-hand the destruction caused from the 1980 volcanic eruption, or head north on I–5 to Olympia, where you should pick up

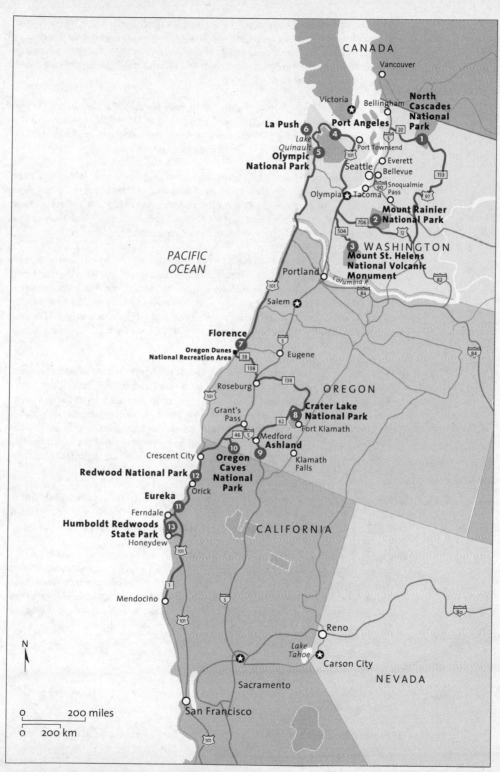

CANADA

Vancouver

Victoria

Bellingham

North Cascades National Park

La Push **6**

Port Angeles

4

Lake Quinault

Port Townsend

20

1

5

Olympic National Park

Everett

Bellevue

Seattle

153

97

Snoqualmie Pass

90

Olympia Tacoma

Mount Rainier National Park

706

2

PACIFIC OCEAN

504

12

3

Mount St. Helens National Volcanic Monument

W A S H I N G T O N

Portland

Columbia R.

82

84

Salem

Florence **7**

Oregon Dunes National Recreation Area

38

5

Eugene

84

138

O R E G O N

Roseburg

101

138

Crater Lake National Park

Grant's Pass

62

8

Fort Klamath

46 5

10

Medford

Ashland

9

Crescent City

Oregon Caves National Park

Klamath Falls

Redwood National Park **12**

Orick

Eureka

Ferndale

11

Humboldt Redwoods State Park **13**

Honeydew

C A L I F O R N I A

101

Mendocino

1

5

80

Reno

Lake Tahoe

Carson City

N E V A D A

Sacramento

San Francisco

101

N

0   200 miles

0   200 km

U.S. 101 north to ❹ **Port Angeles,** a distance of 116 mi (three hours) from the junction of U.S. 12 and I–5. The highway winds through scenic Puget Sound countryside, skirting the Olympic foothills, and periodically dipping down to the waterfront. If you're up for a two-hour side trip, head to Port Townsend, a charming Victorian town, for lunch. Have dinner and spend the night in Port Angeles.

❺ The next morning, launch into a full day at **Olympic National Park.** Head back to Port Angeles for the evening. Start day six with a drive west on U.S. 101 for 25 mi to **Lake Crescent.** Head up Sol Duc Road to the hot springs resort and spend a couple of hours soaking in the baths. Stay the night in the famed Lake Crescent Lodge.

❻ From Lake Crescent the next morning, go to Forks via U.S. 101 and on to **La Push** via Route 110 (45 mi). Here, an hour-long lunchtime stroll to **Second or Third Beach** will offer a taste of the wild Pacific coastline. Back on 101, head south to **Lake Quinault,** a distance from Lake Crescent of 98 mi. Check into the Lake Quinault Lodge, then drive up the river 6 mi to one of the rain forest trails through the lush Quinault Valley.

❼ Leave Lake Quinault early on day eight for the long but scenic drive south on 101 through the Washington coastal foothills and along the famous Oregon Coast. Here the road winds through coastal spruce forests, periodically rising on headlands to offer Pacific Ocean panoramas. Numerous overlooks invite more leisurely contemplation of the wave-tossed shore. Once in Oregon, small seaside resort towns beckon with cafés, shops, and inns. Your final stop is the charming village of **Florence,** 290 mi (6–8 hours) from Lake Quinault, where you can spend the night.

❽ From Florence, take 101 south to Reedsport, Routes 38 and 138 west to Sutherlin, I–5 south to Roseburg, and Route 138 west again to **Crater Lake National Park,** 180 mi total. Once you leave the misty, cliff-strewn Oregon Coast, your route ascends into coastal rain forest, crosses inland valleys and pastures, and climbs again to montane woodlands, with the peaks of Cascades popping up in the distance as you climb. Once inside the park, you can continue along Rim Drive for another half hour for excellent views of the lake. Overnight in the park or in Fort Klamath. The following morning, take the lake boat tour and a hike through the surrounding forest.

❾ In the afternoon, head south on Route 62 to I–5, and on to **Ashland,** 83 mi and about two hours from Crater Lake. Plan to stay the night in Ashland, a lovely city with many superb B&Bs. Have dinner and attend one of the **Oregon Shakespeare Festival** productions.

❿ On day 10, head back north on I–5 from Ashland to Grants Pass, then turn south on U.S. 199 as it winds down the Illinois River valley and narrow Smith River Canyon. At Cave Junction, 67 mi from Ashland, you can take a three-hour side-trip to **Oregon Caves National Monument.** Once in California, be sure to stop at **Jedediah Smith Redwoods State Park,** about 100 mi from Ashland, for your first taste of the giant sequoias. After a short stroll take U.S. 199 west another 5 mi to get back on U.S. 101 going south.

⓫ **Eureka,** 168 mi from Ashland, is a good spot to spend the night.

⓬ Spend day 11 of your trip in **Redwood National Park,** and the several adjacent state parks, walking among the giant trees and hiking the trails down to the Pacific shore. Spend another night in Eureka.

⓭ The final morning, head south early on U.S. 101, the famous **Redwood Highway,** for the next 100 mi. Be sure to check out some of the old-fashioned tourist attractions along the way, such as the various drive-through trees—they're corny but fun, and examples of an almost extinct tourist culture of the mid-20th century. Leave the highway to visit **Humboldt Redwoods State Park.** Its scenic driving route, Avenue of the Giants, parallels U.S. 101 for 21 mi, winding through redwood groves where 1,000-year-old trees grow right at the asphalt's edge. Stop for the night in the coastal town of **Mendocino,** a distance from Eureka of 140 mi. From here it's an easy jaunt to the **Wine Country** of Napa and Sonoma, or down to **San Francisco.**

When to Visit

It's a myth that it rains all the time in the Pacific Northwest. But like most myths there is an element of truth within it—it rains often, especially from September to June. That's why (along with school calendars) these parks are inundated by visitors during the three months when they are not usually inundated by rain, and at the high-elevation mountain parks, snow. Rainier, Olympic, and Redwood receive up to 90% of their visitors from Memorial Day to Labor Day; Crater Lake and North Cascades are even more subject to this phenomenon, as they are both basically closed by snow from October through May. Pick your annoyance, in other words: the likelihood of crowds, or the probability of rain. The best months to compromise between the two factors are May and September, though in Rainier and Olympic, the high country will still be mostly snowed in during May. The occasional Indian summer in October is pleasant, but storms, while infrequent, are intense. If you are deterred by crowds, take heart—there are those who believe that visiting a rain forest in the rain is an essential part of the experience.

CLIMATE

The West Coast is the world capital of microclimates—simply moving a few miles can make a great difference. In the redwood zone, for instance, the weather can be 60°F and cloudy in Eureka, but 90°F and clear 30 mi away at Weott, in the heart of Humboldt Redwoods State Park. On Mount Rainier, it can be 35°F with snow flurries at Paradise, but 60°F and partly cloudy 18 mi away at Ashford. On the Olympic Peninsula, Forks is frequently beset by rain when Port Angeles is not. But in general, the climate along the west coast is maritime—meaning it is mild, with highs above 75°F rare in summer, and lows below 30°F rare in winter. The farther inland you go, or the higher in elevation, the more temperature variation there is. Persistent rain is usually confined to November through March. In spring you can expect moderate rainfall, with temperatures in the 50s; summer gets the least rainfall and warm, sunny, 70°F days; fall remains mild, with temperatures in the 60s and 50s through the end of October, in the 40s in November, and with occasional storms; and winter temperatures hover in the lower 40s, sometimes dipping to freezing, with most days doused in rain. Of course, above 1,000 ft or so, frost, snow, and much colder temperatures move in late October through April. The year-round ocean temperature of 50°F–60°F varies little from the Monterey Peninsula all the way to Vancouver Island.

What to Pack

As much as it seems like a cliché to suggest being prepared for anything, that's the case in all these parks, any time of year, with the exception of Redwood. In June, July, and August you might need only shorts and T-shirts, even at the highest elevations on Rainier and in Olympic. On the other hand, anywhere above 3,000 ft, it can (and does) snow every month of the year. Most experienced Pacific Northwest travelers rely on jeans, shorts, T-shirts, windbreakers, and rain gear. Add a wool sweater or two, warm socks, and waterproof footwear (duck boots are the standard), and you'll be prepared for everything up to a full-scale snowstorm. You can leave your coats, ties, and dresses at home. Formal wear is not necessary in most Northwest hotels or restaurants. If you prefer to advertise that you're a tourist, wear bright-colored polyester fabrics.

Bring sunglasses, sun screen, and hats; if the sky's clear, the sun is fierce, especially at high elevation. Remember to include a day pack for each person in your party; it's essential even for short hikes. Emergency gear that should be in the day-pack includes a compass, rain poncho, fire-starting material, extra food, a water bottle, a flashlight, and a good knife. Toss in your binoculars to spot whales, sea lions, eagles, and other avian species. ASA 200–400 film is the best choice for gray or rainy days. Bring a couple of rolls of ASA 100 film for use on the sunniest days at the beach or on a mountaintop.

CRATER LAKE NATIONAL PARK
SOUTHWESTERN OREGON

Route 62, 75 mi northeast of I–5 and 30 mi northwest of U.S. 97; Route 138, 87 mi east of I–5 and 15 mi west of U.S. 97.

The pure, untrammeled blue of Crater Lake defies easy description, but it never fails to astound at first sight. The 21-square-mi lake was created 7,700 years ago after the eruption of Mount Mazama. Days after the eruption, the mountain collapsed in on an underground chamber emptied of lava. Rain and snowmelt filled the caldera, creating a sapphire-blue lake so clear that sunlight penetrates to a depth of 400 ft (the lake's depth is 1,943 ft). Today it's both the clearest and deepest lake in the United States, and the world's seventh deepest. Aside from the breathtaking sight of the lake, the 183,224-acre park is a geologic marvel, evincing the aftermaths of volcanic activity everywhere, including huge cinder cones, pumice deserts and old lava flows.

Native Americans witnessed Mount Mazama's collapse and kept the event alive in their oral traditions. In 1853 three gold prospectors happened upon the lake, the first white explorers to see it. Forgotten during the gold rush, Crater Lake was finally brought to national attention in the 1870s and 1880s by the photographs of pioneer photographer Peter Britt. Oregon's only national park joined the national park system in 1902, after years of dedicated campaigning by William Gladstone Steel. Steel first heard of the lake when he was a Kansas farm boy in 1870. After a visit in 1885, he dedicated his life to preserving it, overcoming opposition from ranchers and timber interests. Crater Lake Lodge, built in the early 20th century, is considered one of the country's most glorious national park lodges. Lake views from the lodge, which is perched right on the caldera rim, are sensational.

PUBLICATIONS
Crater Lake National Park: A Global Treasure, by former park rangers Ann and Myron Sutton, celebrates the park's first 100 years with stunning photography, charts, and drawings. Ron Warfield's *A Guide to Crater Lake National Park and The Mountain That Used to Be* gives a useful and lushly illustrated overview of Crater Lake's history and physical features. The National Park Service uses Stephen Harris's *Fire Mountains of the West* in its ranger training; the detailed handbook covers Cascade Range geology. *Wildflowers of the Olympics and Cascades,* by Charles Stewart, is an easy-to-use guide to the area's flora and fauna. Pick up a copy of the park newspaper, *Reflections,* upon arrival.

These books, and a mail-order catalog of books and maps about the park, are available from the **Crater Lake Natural History Association.** | Box 157, Crater Lake, OR 97604 | 541/594-3110 | www.nps.gov/crla/nha.htm.

When to Visit
Although it never closes per se, most of the park is only accessible in late June/early July through mid-October. The rest of the year, snow closes all park roadways and entrances except Highway 62 and the access road to Rim Village from Mazama Village. Rim Drive is typically closed because of heavy snowfall from mid-October to mid-July, and icy condi-

tions can be encountered any month of the year, particularly in early morning. Crater Lake receives more snowfall—an annual average of 44 ft—than any other national park except for Mount Rainier. For a real-time view of weather conditions at the rim, log onto the Crater Lake Lodge crater cam at www.craterlakelodges.com/cratercam.htm.

SCENERY AND WILDLIFE

The park's elk and deer are reclusive, but can sometimes be seen at dusk and dawn feeding at forest's edge. Black bears and pine martins, a cousin of the short-tailed weasel, also call Crater Lake home. Birds are more commonly seen in the summer in the pine and fir forests below the lake.

HIGH AND LOW SEASON

High season for the park is July and August. September and early October—which can be delightful months, weather-wise, bring much smaller crowds. From October through June, virtually the entire park closes due to heavy snowfall and freezing temperatures. The road is kept open just to the rim in winter, except during severe weather.

Average High/Low Temperature (°F) and Monthly Precipitation (in inches, rain/snow)

	JAN.	FEB.	MAR.	APR.	MAY	JUNE
CRATER LAKE	32/20	34/19	35/23	38/24	48/31	51/40
	10.7/106	8.4/88	8.0/87	4.9/45	3.4/21	2.3/4

	JULY	AUG.	SEPT.	OCT.	NOV.	DEC.
	59/44	66/47	55/42	50/34	39/21	33/20
	0.8/0	1.2/0	2.1/3	5.2/22	9.7/64	11.4/93

FESTIVALS AND SEASONAL EVENTS
WINTER

Dec.: **Snowflake Festival.** Every winter a week of holiday season–inspired activities—including a gingerbread house contest—culminates in a night parade, with floats and regional bands drawing 40,000 people to downtown Klamath Falls. | 541/884–5193 or 800/445–6728.

Feb.: **Klamath Basin Bald Eagle Conference.** Nature enthusiasts from around the world flock to the Oregon Institute of Technology in Klamath Falls each February for the nation's oldest birding festival. | 541/884–5193 or 800/445–6728.

Feb.–Nov.: **Oregon Shakespeare Festival.** More than 100,000 Bard-loving fanatics descend on Ashland (89 mi from Crater Lake) for this well-known event. Its accomplished repertory company mounts some of the finest Shakespeare productions you're likely to see this side of Stratford-upon-Avon— plus works by Ibsen, Williams, and contemporary playwrights. The festival traces its roots to the Chautauqua Movement of the late 19th century, which brought arts and culture to rural areas across the country. Plays run 10 months of the year in three theaters; the peak season is July, August, and September. | 541/482–4331.

Nearby Towns

Three small cities serve as gateways to Crater Lake—each a 1½- to 2-hour drive to the park. Klamath Lake, the largest freshwater lake in Oregon, is anchored at its south end by the city of **Klamath Falls,** population 20,000. With year-round sunshine, Klamath Falls is home to acres of parks and marinas from which to enjoy water sports and bird-watching. Reminders of the city's pioneer past live on in local museums and commemorative parks. The city has basic visitor services, including an airport. **Roseburg's** location

EDGINESS

There is only one safe way to reach Crater Lake's edge: the Cleetwood Cove Trail from the north rim. The rest of the inner caldera is steep and composed of loose gravel, basalt, and pumice—extremely dangerous, in other words. That's why all hiking and climbing are strictly prohibited inside the rim, and rangers will issue citations for violations.

at the west edge of the southern Cascades led to its status as a timber industry center—the heart of the town's economy still—but its site along the Umpqua River has also drawn fishermen here for years. The small town spreads along the banks of the South Umpqua and enjoys sunny, warm summers. **Ashland,** one of the premier destinations in the Northwest, is a charming small city set in the foothills of the Siskiyou Mountains. The foundation of the city's appeal is its famed Shakespeare Festival and its dozens of fine small inns, shops, and restaurants.

INFORMATION

Ashland Chamber of Commerce | 110 E. Main St., Box 1360, Ashland, 97520 | 541/482–3486 | www.ashlandchamber.com. **Klamath County Chamber of Commerce** | 507 Main St., Klamath Falls, 97603 | 541/884–5193 | www.klamath.org. **Klamath County Department of Tourism** | 507 Main St., Box 1867, Klamath Falls, 97601 | 541/884–5193 or 800/445–6728 | www.klamathcounty.net. **Roseburg Visitors and Convention Bureau** | 410 S.E. Spruce St., Box 1262, Roseburg, 97470 | 541/672–9731 or 800/444–9584 | www.visitroseburg.com.

Exploring Crater Lake

PARK BASICS

Contacts and Resources: Crater Lake National Park | Box 7, Crater Lake, OR 97604 | 541/594–3090 | www.nps.gov/crla.

Hours: Crater Lake National Park is open 24 hours a day year-round; however, snow closes most park roadways October through June.

Fees: Entrance to the park costs $10 per vehicle; it's good for seven days.

Getting Around: Virtually everyone who comes to the park makes the 33-mi circle of the crater on Rim Drive, which is open roughly mid-June to mid-October. The road is narrow, winding, and hilly, so to take in the scenery it's imperative that you pull off at some of the 30 overlooks. Icy conditions are possible any time of year; even in dry weather, the complete circle takes up to two hours.

Permits: Backcountry campers and hikers must obtain a free wilderness permit for all overnight trips at Rim Visitor Center or Steel Information Center.

Public Telephones and Rest Rooms: There are public telephones and rest rooms at Steel Information Center, Rim Village, Crater Lake Lodge, and the Mazama Village complex. There are also rest rooms at the top and bottom of Cleetwood Cove Trail and many picnic areas.

Accessibility: All the overlooks along Rim Drive are accessible to those with impaired mobility, as are Crater Lake Lodge, the facilities at Rim Village, and Steel Information Center. A half-dozen accessible campsites are available at Mazama Campground.

Emergencies: Dial 911 for all emergencies in the park. Park police are based at park headquarters, next to Steel Information Center.

Lost and Found: The park's lost and found is at the ranger station next to Steel Information Center.

Good Tours

CRATER LAKE IN ONE DAY

Begin your tour at **Steel Information Center,** where interpretive displays and a short video introduce you to the story of the lake's formation and its unique characteristics. Then begin your circumnavigation of the crater's rim by heading northeast on **Rim Drive,** allowing an hour to stop at various overlooks—be sure to check out the Phantom Ship rock formation in the lake below—before you reach **Cleetwood Cove Trail** trailhead, the

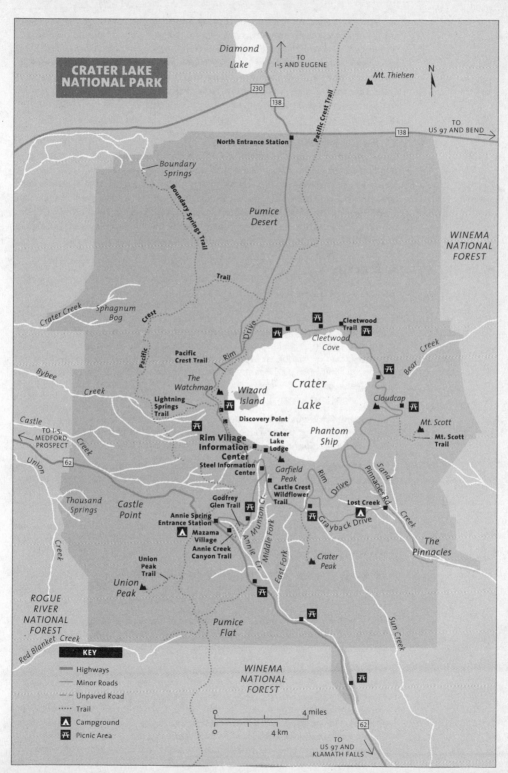

CRATER LAKE
NATIONAL PARK

Diamond Lake

TO
I-5 AND EUGENE

230

138

Pacific Crest Trail

Mt. Thielsen

N

TO
US 97 AND BEND

138

North Entrance Station

Boundary Springs

Boundary Spring Trail

Pumice Desert

WINEMA NATIONAL FOREST

Trail

Crater Creek

Sphagnum Bog

Crest

Pacific

Pacific Crest Trail

Rim

Drive

Cleetwood Trail

Cleetwood Cove

Bear Creek

Bybee

Creek

The Watchman

Lightning Springs Trail

Wizard Island

Crater Lake

Discovery Point

Cloudcap

Mt. Scott

Castle

TO I-5,
MEDFORD,
PROSPECT

Creek

Union

62

Rim Village Information Center

Steel Information Center

Crater Lake Lodge

Phantom Ship

Mt. Scott Trail

Thousand Springs

Castle Point

Godfrey Glen Trail

Annie Spring Entrance Station

Mazama Village

Annie Creek Canyon Trail

Munson Ck.

Annie Ck.

Middle Fork

East Fork

Garfield Peak

Castle Crest Wildflower Trail

Rim

Drive

Grayback Drive

Lost Creek

Sand

Creek

Pinnacles Rd.

The Pinnacles

Union Peak Trail

Union Peak

Crater Peak

ROGUE RIVER NATIONAL FOREST

Red Blanket Creek

Pumice Flat

Sun Creek

WINEMA NATIONAL FOREST

62

TO
US 97 AND
KLAMATH FALLS

KEY

Highways
Minor Roads
Unpaved Road
Trail
Campground
Picnic Area

0 ⟼ 4 miles

0 ⟼ 4 km

only safe and legal access to the lake. Hike down the trail to reach the dock, and hop aboard one of the concessionaire **tour boats** for an almost-two-hour tour around the lake.

Back on Rim Drive, continue around the lake, stopping at **The Watchman** for a short but steep hike to this peak above the rim, which affords not only a splendid view of the lake, but a broad vista of the surrounding southern Cascades. Wind up your visit at **Crater Lake Lodge**—allow an hour just to wander the lobby of the 1915 structure perched on the rim. Dinner at the lodge restaurant, overlooking the lake and the Cascade sunset, caps the day.

CRATER LAKE IN TWO DAYS

Follow the itinerary described above, adding in a trip to **Wizard Island** for a picnic lunch. Wind up the day with a meal and a night's stay at Crater Lake Lodge.

The next morning, head back eastward on Rim Drive, turning off at **Pinnacles Road** for a short side-trip to view an unusual formation of hoodoos in a mountainside canyon. Then follow Rim Drive north to the **Mount Scott** trailhead. This 5-mi round-trip hike gains 1,000 ft, taking you to the park's highest point. Check out the 360-degree view of the Cascades and the Great Basin high desert before heading back to the lodge for dinner.

Attractions

PROGRAMS AND TOURS

Boat Tours. The most extensively used guided tours in Crater Lake are on the water, aboard launches that carry 49 passengers on a one-hour, 45-minute tour accompanied by a ranger. The boats circle the lake and make a brief stop at Wizard Island, where you can get off if you like. The first of nine tours leaves the dock at 10 AM; the last departs at 4:30 PM. After Labor Day, the schedule is reduced. To get to the dock you must hike down Cleetwood Cove Trail, a 1-mi walk that drops 700 ft. Rest rooms are available at the top and bottom of the Cleetwood Trail. | Cleetwood Cove Trail, off north Rim Dr., 10 mi from Rim Village | 541/594–3090 | $20 | July–mid-Sept., daily.

Evening Campfire Programs. Park rangers and naturalists discuss topics ranging from volcanic activity to the legend of Sasquatch. | Mazama Campground amphitheater, Mazama Village near Annie Spring entrance station | 541/594–3090 | July–Sept., daily at dusk.

Interpretive Walks. Park rangers lead interpretive walks and natural history discussions. | Crater Lake Lodge, 565 Rim Village Dr., just east of Rim Visitor Center | 541/594–3090 | July–Sept., daily.

Introduction to Crater Lake. Rangers give a 10–15 minute talk about the origins of Crater Lake and are well prepared to answer questions. | Sinnott Memorial Overlook, Rim Visitor Center, Rim Dr. on the south side of the lake, 4.5 mi north of Annie Spring entrance station | 541/594–3090 | July–Sept., daily.

Junior Ranger Program. Youngsters can learn from a ranger about volcanoes, Crater Lake, and the unique environment of the southern Cascades. Junior Ranger booklets and badges are available at Steel Information Center and Rim Visitor Center. | 541/594–3090.

Sunset Hikes. Rangers lead sunset hikes to the top of The Watchman in July and August. Consult park bulletin boards for the exact times for hike departures, and bring a flashlight. | Meet at Watchman Trail parking lot, west Rim Dr., 2.5 mi from Rim Village | 541/594–3090.

SCENIC DRIVES

★ **Rim Drive.** The 33-mi loop around the lake is the main scenic route, affording views of the lake and its cliffs from every conceivable angle. The drive alone takes up to two hours. Frequent stops at viewpoints and short hikes can stretch this to half a day. Rim Drive is typically closed because of heavy snowfall from mid-October to mid-June, and icy conditions can be encountered any month of the year, particularly in early morning. Along Rim Drive are many scenic turnouts and picnic areas. Two of the best spots are on the north side of the lake, between Llao Rock and Cleetwood Cove, where the cliffs are nearly vertical. | Rim Drive leads from Annie Springs entrance station to Rim Village, where the drive circles around the rim; it's about 4.5 mi from the entrance station to Rim Village. From the north entrance at Route 230, it's 10 mi on the North Crater Lake access road to where it joins Rim Drive.

Pinnacles Road. Off Rim Drive, this 7-mi trip southeast scoots along Sand Creek Canyon with its exotic volcanic landscape and ends up at The Pinnacles, a canyon full of spires and hoodoos composed of hardened ash deposits. | Rim Dr., 9 mi east of Steel Information Center.

SIGHTS TO SEE

Cloudcap Overlook. The highest road-access overlook on the Crater Lake rim, Cloudcap has a westward view across the lake to Wizard Island; and an eastward view of Mount Scott, the volcanic cone that is the park's highest point, just 2 mi from the overlook. | 2 mi off Rim Dr., 13 mi northeast of Steel Information Center.

★ **Crater Lake Lodge.** First built in 1915, this classic log-and-stone structure was erected too hastily to withstand Crater Lake's extreme winters. The entire lodge has since been restored, with only the original lodgepole pine pillars, beams, and stone fireplaces and abutments remaining. Its grand lobby has leather furniture, Pendleton wool throws, and rustic trimmings such as mounted animals. The lodge porch, which overlooks the lake, offers an unmatched view. | Rim Village just east of Rim Visitor Center.

Discovery Point. This overlook marks the spot at which prospectors first spied the lake in 1853. Wizard Island is just northeast, close to shore. | Rim Dr., 1.5 mi north of Rim Village.

Mazama Village. In summer a campground, motor inn, amphitheater, gas station, post office, and small store are open here. | Mazama Village Rd. near Annie Spring entrance station | 541/830–8700 | www.nps.gov/crla | June–Sept., daily 8–6.

Phantom Ship Overlook. From this point you can get a close look at Phantom Ship, a rock formation that resembles a small boat. | Rim Dr., 7 mi northeast of Steel Information Center.

Pinnacles Overlook. Ascending from the banks of Sand and Wheeler creeks, unearthly spires of eroded ash resemble the peaks of fairy tale castles. Once upon a time, the road continued east to a former entrance. A path now replaces the old road and follows the rim of Sand Creek (and more views of pinnacles) to where the entrance arch still stands. | 5 mi northeast of Steel Information Center.

Rim Visitor Center. In summer you can obtain park information here, take a ranger-led tour, or stop into the nearby Sinnott Memorial, with a small museum and a 900-ft view down to the lake's surface. In winter snowshoe walks are offered on weekends and holidays. The Rim Village Gift Store and Cafeteria are the only services open in winter. | Rim Dr. on the south side of the lake, 7 mi north of Annie Spring entrance station | 541/594–3090 | www.nps.gov/crla | Late June–Sept., daily 9:30–5.

Steel Information Center. This is part of the park headquarters, with rest rooms and a first-aid station. There's a small post office here and shop that sells books, maps, and postcards. In the auditorium, an ongoing 18-minute film, *The Crater Lake Story*, describes Crater Lake's formation. | Rim Dr., 4 mi north of Annie Spring entrance station | 541/594–3100 | www.nps.gov/crla | Mid-April–Nov., daily 9–5; Nov.–mid-Apr., daily 10–4.

Sun Notch. It's a moderate 0.25-mi hike through wildflowers and dry meadow to this overlook of Crater Lake and Phantom Ship. Mind the steep edges. | E. Rim Dr., 4 mi northeast of Steel Information Center.

★ **Wizard Island.** To get here you've got to hike down Cleetwood Cove Trail (and back up upon your return) and board the tour boat for a 1 3/4-hour ride. Plan to picnic. | Cleetwood Cove Trail, Wizard Island dock | 541/594–3090 | Late June–mid-Sept., daily.

CRATER LAKE
NATIONAL PARK

EXPLORING
ATTRACTIONS NEARBY
DINING
LODGING
CAMPING AND RV
FACILITIES
SHOPPING
ESSENTIAL
INFORMATION

Sports and Outdoor Activities

No off-road driving or bicycling is permitted in the park because of the fragile alpine and volcanic soils. No private craft are allowed on the lake, no bicycle or boat rentals are available, and hiking and rock climbing are strictly prohibited within the caldera.

BICYCLING

Rim Drive. Although no designated bike route exists, vehicle traffic is generally slow-moving along the 33-mi Rim Drive. The road is at an average elevation of 7,000 ft, and some portions are steep and narrow, so this ride is not for casual cyclists. The shoulder is dangerously small, so use extreme caution.

BIRD-WATCHING

Clark's nutcracker and Steller's and gray jays are found throughout the park, and ravens strut and croak near almost all rim viewpoints. Keen observers on the lake rim are likely to spot raptors such as eagles, hawks, and falcons soaring in the updrafts. Songbirds are most often seen in the lower-elevation woods below the caldera rim. Listen for the hoots of northern spotted owls at night.

FISHING

Fishing is allowed in the lake, but many find it more frustrating than pleasurable. In such a massive body of water, the problem is finding the fish. Try your luck near the Cleetwood Cove boat dock or take poles on the boat tour and fish off Wizard Island. Rainbow trout and kokanee salmon lurk in Crater Lake's aquamarine depths, some growing to monster lunker size. You don't need a state fishing license, but remember to use only artificial bait to protect the lake's pristine waters.

HIKING

Annie Creek Canyon Trail. Annie Creek is strenuous but still easy compared with some of the steep rim hikes, such as that of the Cleetwood Trail. The 2-mi loop threads through Annie Creek Canyon, giving views of the narrow cleft scarred by volcanism. This is a good spot to look for flowers and deer. | Mazama Campground, Mazama Village Rd., near Annie Spring entrance station.

Boundary Springs Trail. If you're up for a challenge, consider a trip along this 8-mi trail. Easing down the gradually sloping northwestern shoulders of the old Mount Mazama, the path angles toward Pumice Desert and ends up at Boundary Springs, one of the sources of the Rogue River. Expect 3–4 hours of hiking each way. To avoid the return trip, many hikers arrange to be picked up at Lake West, a campground outside the park that is easily accessible via Route 230. | Pacific Crest Trail parking lot, north access road 2 mi north of Rim Dr., 8 mi south of the park's north entrance station.

Castle Crest Wildflower Trail. The 1-mi creek-side loop in the upper part of Munson Valley is one of the park's flatter and less demanding hikes, with only some uneven ground of which to be mindful. In July the wildflowers are in full bloom. | Across the street from Steel Information Center parking lot, Rim Dr.

Cleetwood Cove Trail. This 1-mi strenuous hike descends 700 ft down nearly vertical cliffs along the lake to the boat dock. Allow 1½ hours round-trip. | Cleetwood Cove trailhead, N. Rim Dr., 11 mi north of Rim Village.

Godfrey Glen Trail. Between Steel Information Center and the Castle Crest Wildflower Trail, take the road down Munson Valley, and you will reach the parking area for this 2-mi loop. It'll take you through an excellent example of what geologists term a hanging valley—the place where one valley hangs over a lower valley, with a cliff and a waterfall between them. Deer are frequently seen here, and the flowers are plentiful. | 2 mi off Rim Dr., 2.4 mi south of Steel Information Center.

★ **Mount Scott Trail.** The 2.5-mi trail takes you to the park's highest point, the top of Mount Scott, at 8,929 ft. It will take the average hiker 90 minutes to make the steep uphill trek and about 45 minutes to get down. The trail starts at an elevation of about 7,450 ft, so the climb is not extreme but does get steep in spots. The view of the lake is wonderful, and views to the east and south of the broad Klamath Basin are equally spectacular. Mount Scott is the oldest volcanic cone of Mount Mazama. | 14 mi east of Steel Information Center, across E. Rim Dr. from the road to Cloudcap Overlook.

Pacific Crest Trail. You can join up with the Pacific Crest Trail, which extends from Mexico to Canada, and winds through the park for more than 30 mi. For this prime backcountry experience of the park, catch the trail about a mile east of the north entrance road, where it shadows the road along the west rim of the lake for about 6 mi, then descends down Dutton Creek to the Mazama Village area. An on-line brochure offers further details. | Pacific Crest Trail parking lot, north access road 2 mi north of Rim Dr., 8 mi south of the park's north entrance station | www.nps.gov/crla/brochures/pct.htm.

The Watchman Trail. While numerous overlooks along Rim Drive provide car-bound visitors many perspectives on Crater Lake, the best short hike is to this one. Though it's less than a mile each way, the trail climbs more than 400 ft—not counting the steps up to the actual lookout. | Watchman Overlook, 3.7 mi northwest of Rim Village on W. Rim Dr.

SKIING

There are no maintained ski trails in the park, although some backcountry trails are marked with blue diamonds or snow poles. Most cross-country skiers park at Rim Village and follow a portion of West Rim Drive as best they can toward Wizard Island Overlook (4 mi). The road is plowed to Rim Village, but it may be closed temporarily by severe storms. Snow tires and chains are essential. The park's on-line brochure (available at | www.nps.gov/crla/brochures/skiing.htm) lists additional trails and their length and difficulty.

SNOWMOBILING

Snowmobiling is allowed only on the 9-mi stretch of the north entrance road up to its junction with Rim Drive. Some adventurous cross-country skiers ride snowmobiles to the remote north rim to ski that area or the large, flat Pumice Desert.

SWIMMING

Swimming is allowed in the lake, but it's not usually advised. Made up entirely of snowmelt, Crater Lake is very cold—about 45°F to 62°F during summer. When swimming takes place it's in a lagoon on Wizard Island or at Cleetwood Cove, but even then it's only appealing when the air temperature rises above 80°F, which is another rare occurrence. On the other hand, how many people can say they've taken a dip in the deepest lake in the United States?

Outfitters

Diamond Lake Resort. The closest outfitter to the park rents snowmobiles by the hour, half day, or full day; plus cross-country skis and fishing equipment. Expect to leave a credit card deposit. | Rte. 138, 25 mi north of Crater Lake, Diamond Lake | 541/793–3333 or 800/733–7593 | Dec.–Apr., daily 8–6.

Attractions Nearby

Sights to See

Collier Memorial State Park and Logging Museum. The museum, 30 mi north of Klamath Falls, has a historical log-cabin exhibit and a display of antique logging equipment dating to the 1880s. The park also has picnic areas and a campground. | 46000 U.S. 97, Chilo-

CRATER LAKE NATIONAL PARK

EXPLORING
ATTRACTIONS NEARBY
DINING
LODGING
CAMPING AND RV FACILITIES
SHOPPING
ESSENTIAL INFORMATION

quin | 541/783–2471 | www.collierloggingmuseum.org | Free | May–Oct., daily 8–8; Nov.–Apr., daily 8–4.

★ **Klamath Basin National Wildlife Refuge Complex.** Sometimes as many as 1,000 bald eagles make Klamath Basin their rest stop, amounting to the largest wintering concentration of these birds in the contiguous United States. The largest number of migratory birds also congregate in the Klamath Basin, 24 mi south of Klamath Falls on the California–Oregon border. Although winter is eagle season, dozens of different birds can be seen here any time of year. Call for a seasonal viewing appointment. | 4009 Hill Rd., 20 mi south of Klamath Falls via U.S. 97 or Rte. 39, Tulelake, CA | 530/667–2231 | www.klamathnwr.org | Free (fee for tours) | Weekdays 8–4:30; weekends 10–4.

Klamath County Museum. Covering the wildlife, geology, anthropology, and history of the Klamath Basin, the museum is notable for its dioramas that depict local birds in their natural habitat. The museum organization also runs the Senator Baldwin Hotel Museum in Klamath Falls and the nearby Fort Klamath Museum. From June to September, a $1 ticket buys a narrated trolley ride that runs from the county museum to the hotel. | 1451 Main St., Klamath Falls | 541/883–4208 | $3 | Tues.–Sat. 8:30–5:30.

Mount Bailey Snowcat Skiing. If you're an expert downhill skier or snowboarder and crave solitude, this is the ski-guide service for you. Heated Sno-Cats deliver you to the summit of Mount Bailey, an 8,300-ft peak not far from Crater Lake, where you can attack the virgin powder on 4 mi of runs, with a vertical drop of 3,000 ft. The excursions are limited to 12 skiers a day. Tours leave from Diamond Lake Resort, which has three restaurants, a bar, lodgings, Nordic trails, and downhill and Nordic ski rentals. | 218 Aspen La., Rte. 138, 25 mi north of Crater Lake, Diamond Lake | 541/793–3348 or 800/446–4555 | www.mountbailey. com | $220 | Dec.–Apr., daily 7–5.

Oregon Caves National Monument. The marble caves, large calcite formations, and huge underground rooms that are the main attraction here are quite rare in the West. The surrounding valley holds an old-growth forest with some of the state's largest trees. | Caves Highway (Rte. 46), Cave Junction | 541/592–2100 | www.nps.gov/orca | $7.50 | Late May–mid-Sept., daily 9–7; mid-Mar.–late May and mid-Sept.–Dec., daily 10–4.

Dining

In Crater Lake

Dining Room at Crater Lake Lodge. Contemporary. This restaurant serves ambitious fare in upscale surroundings. The room itself is magnificent, with a large stone fireplace and views out over the clear blue waters of Crater Lake. The supper menu includes fresh Pacific Northwest seafood, pasta, steak, lamb, and duck. Select from a diverse selection of regional wines and microbrews. | Crater Lake Lodge, Rim Village, east of Rim Visitor Center | 541/594–2255 | Reservations essential | $14–$28 | MC, V | Closed mid-Oct.–mid-May.

Llao Rock Cafeteria. American/Casual. It's family-style dining at this barnlike cafeteria, where hamburgers and sandwiches constitute the bulk of the menu. Try a rice bowl as an alternative to the standard American fare. | Rim Dr. on the south side of the lake, 4.5 mi north from Annie Spring entrance station | 541/594–2255 | $3–$6 | MC, V.

Picnic Areas.
   Godfrey Glen Trail. Abuzz in summer with songbirds, squirrels, chipmunks, and other forest denizens, the small canyon in which this picnic area is nestled has a south-facing, protected location. The half-dozen picnic tables are in a small meadow; there are a few fire grills, and a pit toilet. | On Rim Dr., 1 mi east of Annie Spring entrance station.
   Rim Drive. Perhaps a half dozen picnic-area turnouts encircle the lake. All have good views, but they can get very windy. Most have pit toilets, and a few have fire grills. There is no running water at any of them. | Rim Dr.

Rim Village. This is the only park picnic area with running water. The tables are set behind the visitor center, and most have some view of the lake below. There are also flush toilets inside the visitor center. | Rim Dr. on the south side of the lake, 7 mi north of Annie Spring entrance station.

Route 62. Set in the fir, spruce, and pine forests of the Cascades' dry side, the three picnic areas along Route 62 provide tables, some fire grills, and pit toilets, although no drinking water. Picnickers who mind traffic noise should head farther into the park. | Rte. 62; 2, 4, and 7 mi southeast of Annie Spring entrance station.

Vidae Falls. In the upper reaches of Sun Creek, the four picnic tables here enjoy the sound of the small but close-by falls across the road. There is a vault toilet, and a couple of fire grills. | Rim Dr., 2.5 mi east of Steel Information Center, between the turnoffs for Crater Peak and Lost Creek.

Wizard Island. The park's best picnic venue is on Wizard Island; to avail yourself of this experience you've got to pack a picnic lunch and book yourself on one of the early morning boat tour departures, reserving space on an afternoon return. There are no formal picnic areas and just pit toilets, but there are plenty of sunny, protected spots where you can have a quiet meal and appreciate the astounding scene that surrounds you.

Watchman Restaurant. American. The all-you-can-eat buffet here is a casual alternative to the dinners served at Lodge's more formal Dining Room, although you'll still have a lake view. You'll find salads, soups, a potato bar, a taco bar, and entrées like salmon, Salisbury steak, and chicken. | Crater Lake Lodge, Rim Village, east of Rim Visitor Center | 541/594–2255 | $12 | MC, V | Closed mid-Oct.–mid-May.

Near the Park

Bella Union. American. Sophisticated pub food at this unpretentious restaurant in an 1870s saloon includes fresh fish—familiar species and more exotic ones like Hawaiian opah and mako shark—that's flown in daily. Another specialty is Tennessee quail wrapped in peppered bacon. Pastas are handmade. Vast pizzas, heaping salads, and gargantuan sandwiches round out the menu. | 170 California St., Jacksonville | 541/899–1770 | $8–$21 | AE, D, MC, V.

Chateaulin. French. One of southern Oregon's most romantic restaurants occupies an ivy-covered storefront a block from the Oregon Shakespeare Festival center, where chef David Taub dispenses French food, local wine, and impeccable service with equal facility. Try the pan-roasted rack of lamb or the Black Angus filet mignon. | 50 E. Main St., Ashland | 541/482–2264 | $14–$33 | AE, D, MC, V | No lunch.

Rocky Point Resort. American. The setting is what draws diners to this restaurant poised on a point overlooking Upper Klamath Lake. Guests lucky enough to snag a window table spend as much time ogling the lake and mountain views as they do the menu, which offers a mainstream selection of steaks, sandwiches and seafood. From November through May, the restaurant is only open on weekends, and then just for dinner. | 28121 Rocky Point Rd., Klamath Falls | 541/356–2287 | Reservations essential | $12–$25 | AE, MC, V.

Thai Pepper. Thai. With an interior filled with local art, rattan, linen, and crystal, it feels like a French café in downtown Bangkok. The Indonesian chef/owner turns out some of the best Thai food in town. | 84 N. Main St., Ashland | 541/482–8058 | $10–$18 | AE, DC, MC, V | No lunch Sat.–Thurs.

Winchester Country Inn. Continental. The menu is small but imaginative in the restaurant at this inn that dates to 1886. High-windowed dining rooms set among manicured gardens radiate a feeling of casual elegance. Menu items are seasonal and include such specialties as wine-poached seafood, and filet mignon with anise, lemon zest, and crushed red pepper. Sunday brunch shines with the inn's signature homemade scones. | 35 S. 2nd St., Ashland | 541/488–1113 | $16–$22 | AE, D, MC, V | No lunch. Closed Mon. Nov.–May.

CRATER LAKE
NATIONAL PARK

EXPLORING
ATTRACTIONS NEARBY
DINING
LODGING
CAMPING AND RV
FACILITIES
SHOPPING
ESSENTIAL
INFORMATION

Lodging

In Crater Lake

★ **Crater Lake Lodge.** This historic 1915 lodge is on the rim of the caldera and has views of the lake. Ponderosa pine columns, gleaming wood floors, and stone fireplaces grace the common areas, and the contemporary furnishings blend in perfectly. The lodge was rebuilt to restore its national park lodge grandeur, and is now considered one of the finest examples of its type. Rooms with views of the lake are coveted; but reservations for these start to fill up a year in advance. Dinner and lodging packages are the best bargain. 2 restaurants, picnic area. No a/c, no room phones. No room TVs. No smoking. | Rim Village, east of Rim Visitor Center | 541/594–3090, 541/830–8700 (for reservations) | fax 541/594–2622 | www.craterlakelodges.com | 71 rooms | $123–$238 | D, MC, V | Closed mid-Oct.–mid-May.

Mazama Village Motor Inn. In a wooded area 7 mi south of the lake, this complex is made up of several A-frame buildings. It has minimal but adequate accommodations—although all fill up fast—and all the rooms have two queen beds and a private bath. A convenience store and gas station are nearby in the village. No room phones. No room TVs. | Mazama Village, near Annie Spring entrance station | 541/830-8700 | fax 541/594–2622 | 40 rooms | $103 | D, MC, V | Closed mid-Oct.–May.

Near the Park

Best Western Klamath Inn. You will be staying right on Klamath Lake at this property, which is within 1 mi of the Jefferson Square Mall and only 0.25 mi from the fairgrounds. The back of the inn has tables and chairs for outdoor relaxing. In-room data ports, some in-room hot tubs, microwaves, refrigerators. Cable TV. Indoor pool. Some pets allowed. | 4061 S. 6th St., Klamath Falls | 541/882–1200 | fax 541/882–2729 | www.bestwestern.com | 52 rooms | $55–$75 | AE, D, DC, MC, V.

Cimarron Motor Inn. This is the largest lodging facility in Klamath Falls. It's near restaurants and shopping. Microwaves, refrigerators. Cable TV. Pool. Business services. Some pets allowed (fee). | 3060 S. 6th St., Klamath Falls | 541/882–4601 or 800/742–2648 | fax 541/882–6690 | 164 rooms | $55–$75 | AE, D, DC, MC, V.

Red Lion Inn. The rooms in this chain hotel are bright and comfortable. It's across the street from the Klamath County Event Center and near a good French restaurant, Chez Nous. Restaurant. In-room data ports, some in-room hot tubs, some microwaves, some refrigerators. Cable TV. Pool. Outdoor hot tub. Bar. Laundry facilities, laundry service. | 3612 S. 6th St., Klamath Falls | 541/882–8864 | fax 541/884–2046 | www.redlion.com | 100 rooms, 8 suites | $79–$89 | AE, D, DC, MC, V.

Running Y Ranch Resort. This 3,600-acre ranch on the Caledonia Marsh 7 mi west of town is on the Pacific Flyway and sees flocks of swan, geese, and ducks each spring and fall. The vaulted ceilings, stone floors, and stone fireplace with a tall chimney in the lobby complement the lodge's rustic stained-wood exterior. Rooms have either forest or golf-course views. The 18-hole course is one of the best in Oregon. Restaurant. Some kitchenettes. Tennis court. Indoor pool. Exercise equipment, hot tub, spa. Boating. Bicycles. Basketball, hiking, horseback riding. | 5391 Running Y Rd., Klamath Falls | 541/850–5500 or 888/850–0275 | fax 541/885–3194 | 73 rooms, 6 suites, 13 town homes | $115 rooms, $199–$249 town homes, $229 suites | AE, D, MC, V.

Camping and RV Facilities

In Crater Lake

Lost Creek Campground. The small, remote sites here are usually available on a daily basis. In July and August arrive early to secure a spot. Lost Creek is for tent campers only;

RVs must stay at Mazama. Flush toilets. Drinking water. Fire grates. | 16 sites | Grayback Dr. and Pinnacles Rd. | 541/594-3090 | Reservations not accepted | $10 | July–mid-Sept.

Mazama Campground. Crater Lake National Park's major visitor accommodation, aside from the famed lodge on the rim, is set well below the lake caldera in the pine and fir forest of the Cascades. Not far from the main access road (Route 62), its virtues involve convenience more than outdoor serenity. However, adjacent hiking trails lead away from the roadside bustle. About half the spaces are pull-throughs, some with electricity, but no hookups are available. The best tent spots are on some of the outer loops above Annie Creek Canyon. Flush toilets. Dump station. Drinking water, guest laundry, showers. Fire grates. Public telephone. | 217 sites | Mazama Village, near Annie Spring entrance station | 541/594-2255 or 541/830-8700 | Reservations not accepted | $16–$21 | MC, V | Mid-June–mid-Oct.

Near the Park

Collier Memorial State Park. The large campground is near an outdoor logging museum, a pioneer village, hiking trailheads, Williamson River and trout fishing, and a 4-corral primitive horse camp. Naturalists lead hikes along the river. Flush toilets. Full hookups, dump station. Drinking water, guest laundry, showers. Picnic tables. Public telephone. | 68 sites, 50 with full hookups | U.S. 97, 30 mi north of Klamath Falls, Chiloquin | 541/783-2471 or 800/551-6949 | Reservations not accepted | www.oregonstateparks.org | $11–$17 | Mid-Apr.–Oct. 31.

Jackson F. Kimball State Park. This park, 3 mi north of Fort Klamath, is at the headwaters of the Wood River next to a spring-fed lagoon. You'll find good fishing and a campground with a handful of rustic sites. Pit toilets. Fire pits. | 10 RV sites | Rte. 232, 3 mi north of Fort Klamath, Fort Klamath | 541/783-2471 or 800/551-6949 | Reservations not accepted | www.oregonstateparks.org | $6 | Mid-Apr.–Oct. 31.

Shopping

Camper's Service Store. The park's only store is small, but carries food supplies and such camping necessities as stove fuel, firewood, and lantern mantels. Also available are coin-operated laundry and showers. | Mazama Village Rd., near Annie Spring entrance station | 541/594-2255 | Closed Nov.–May.

Diamond Lake Resort. The resort's shop has basic food supplies and fishing tackle. | Rte. 138, 25 mi north of Crater Lake | 541/793-3333 or 800/733-7593.

Rim Village Gift Store. The shop has Northwest and volcano-theme mementoes, books, postcards, and T-shirts. | Rim Dr. on the south side of the lake, 4.5 mi north of Annie Spring entrance station | 541/594-2255.

Essential Information

All park and visitor facilities at Crater Lake are located within a few miles of each other at Mazama Village near Route 62, at Steel Information Center, and at Rim Village and Crater Lake Lodge. Except for a few picnic areas and overlooks, the rest of the park is completely undeveloped.

ATMS: Village Gift Shop | Mazama Village Rd., near Annie Spring entrance station | Closed Nov.–late May.

AUTOMOBILE SERVICE STATIONS: Mazama Village | Mazama Village, near Annie Spring entrance station | 541/594-3090 | Closed Nov.–late May.

POST OFFICE: Steel Information Center | Crater Lake Post Office, Rim Dr., Crater Lake, 97604 | 541/594-3090.

MOUNT RAINIER NATIONAL PARK

SOUTHWESTERN WASHINGTON

Nisqually entrance: Rte. 706, 14 mi east of Rte. 7. Ohanapecosh entrance: Rte. 123, 5 mi north of U.S. 12. White River entrance: Rte. 410, 3 mi north of Chinook and Cayuse passes.

Like a mysterious white-clad woman, often veiled in clouds even when the surrounding forests and fields are bathed in sunlight, Mount Rainier is the centerpiece of its name-sake park. At one time an unbroken wilderness stretched for hundreds of miles in every direction around this summit, but today the park is an oasis of wilderness in a sea of clear cuts and encroaching suburban sprawl. Its 235,612 acres were preserved by President McKinley in 1899, who proclaimed Mount Rainier the nation's fifth national park. Today, its cathedral-like groves of Douglas-fir, western hemlock, and western red-cedar—some more than 1,000 years old—preserve vestiges of the grandeur of the Pacific Northwest's old-growth forests. Water and lush greenery are everywhere in the park, and dozens of thundering waterfalls, accessible from the road or by a short hike, fill the air with mist. The impressive volcanic peak, visible in good weather for 200 mi, stands at an elevation of 14,411 ft, making it the fifth highest in the lower 48 states. One of the most conspicuous mountains on Earth from a distance, Rainier is so massive that its summit is often obscured by its own shoulders. When the summit is visible—from up-close vantage points such as Paradise and Sunrise—the views are breathtaking. More than 2 million visitors a year return home with a lifelong memory of the image.

At Mount Rainier you will find not only silent forests and sensational alpine scenery, but geological and climatic forces evident in few other places. Rainier is an episodically active volcano, quiescent recently but bound to erupt again: steam vents are still active at its summit. With more than two dozen major glaciers, the mountain holds the largest glacial system in the lower 48. The winter tempests that bring the snow so much resemble those of the Himalayas that Everest expeditions train here. But that's on the mountain's face above 10,000 ft; most visitors see a much more benign place with a spirit unmatched anywhere else.

PUBLICATIONS

The park office distributes a useful, free four-page guide for those planning overnight trips in the backcountry, "Wilderness Trip Planner: A Hiker's Guide to the Wilderness of Mount Rainier National Park." The free, quarterly *Tahoma* newsletter lists current information on roads, campgrounds, and the like; it's available at visitor centers. The best general guide to the park, *A Traveler's Companion to Mount Rainier National Park*, is available through the Northwest Interpretative Association (NWIA). NWIA also offers a list of books and park publications, the "Catalogue of Books and Maps—Mount Rainier National Park." William H. Moir's *Forests of Mount Rainier* is a fine overview if you're interested in the flora, fauna, and geology of the park. Other recommended trailside companions are *Cascade and Olympic Natural History*, by Daniel Matthews; *Mount Rainier: The Story Behind the Scenery*, a colorful backgrounder by Ray Snow; and *Wilderness Above the Sound*, an illustrated history by Arthur Martinson. For a concise and useful map and guide to Rainier's trail system, buy *50 Hikes in Mount Rainier National Park*, by Ira Spring and Harvey Manning, published by Seattle's famed Mountaineers. If you're curious about glaciers, Carolyn Driedger's pamphlet "Visitor's Guide to Mount Rainier's Glaciers" will give you an easy-to-understand explanation of the forces that continue to shape the mountain. *Timberline: Mountain and Arctic Forest Frontier*, by Stephen Arno and Ramona Hammerly, is a comprehensive guide to alpine ecology.

When to Visit

SCENERY AND WILDLIFE

Rainier is the Puget Sound's weather vane: if you can see it, the weather is going to be fine. Visitors are most likely to see the summit in July, August, and September. True to its name, Paradise is often sunny during periods when the lowlands are under a cloud layer. The other nine months of the year, Rainier's summit gathers lenticular clouds whenever a Pacific storm approaches, and once it vanishes from view, not only is it impossible to see the peak, it's time to haul out rain gear.

Wildflower season in the meadows at and above timberline is mid-July through August, depending on the exposure (southern earlier, northern later) and the preceding winter's snowfall. Most of the park's higher-elevation trails are not snow-free until late June. You are not as likely to see Rainier's wildlife—deer, elk, black bears, cougars, and other mountain creatures—as often as you might at other parks, such as Olympic. As always, the best times are at dawn and dusk, when animals can often be spotted at forest's edge. Fawns are born to the park's does in May, and the bugling of bull elk on the high ridges can be heard in late September and October, especially on the park's eastern side.

HIGH AND LOW SEASON

Crowds are heaviest in July, August, and September, when the parking lots at Paradise and Sunrise often fill before noon. During this period campsites are reserved months in advance, and other lodgings are reserved as much as a year ahead. Washington's rare periods of clear winter weather bring lots of residents up to Paradise for cross-country skiing.

Average High/Low Temperature (°F) and Monthly Precipitation (in inches)

	JAN.	FEB.	MAR.	APR.	MAY	JUNE
MOUNT RAINIER	35/24	40/27	44/28	50/31	57/36	65/42
	10.80	9.20	7.30	5.60	4.10	3.70
	JULY	AUG.	SEPT.	OCT.	NOV.	DEC.
	72/46	73/47	66/42	56/36	41/30	35/26
	1.70	2.30	4.30	6.70	11.50	13.70

FESTIVALS AND SEASONAL EVENTS

WINTER

Feb.: **White Pass Winter Carnival.** A giant snow castle is the main attraction at this carnival held in White Pass, on the Cascade Crest on U.S. 2. Activities include live music, a fireworks display, face painting and plenty of games for children. | 509/672–3101.

FALL

Sept.: **Puyallup Fair.** One of the largest state fairs in the nation brings 17 days of top entertainment, animals, food, rodeo, exhibits, and rides to Puyallup. | 253/841–5045.

Oct.: **Lark at the Mountain Music Festival.** Folk, jazz, and bluegrass are all part of this three-day celebration, held in Ashford on the first weekend in October. The festival is free and encourages family attendance. | 877/886–4662.

Nearby Towns

Ashford sits astride an ancient trail across the Cascades used by the Yakama Indians to trade with the coastal tribes of western Washington. The town began as a logging railway terminal; today, it's the main gateway to Mount Rainier, the only year-round access to the park, and caters to visitors with lodges, restaurants, groceries, and gift shops.

MOUNT RAINIER
NATIONAL PARK

EXPLORING
ATTRACTIONS NEARBY
DINING
LODGING
CAMPING AND RV
FACILITIES
SHOPPING
ESSENTIAL
INFORMATION

Surrounded by Cascade peaks, **Packwood** is a pretty mountain village on U.S. 12, below White Pass. Between Mount Rainier and Mount St. Helens, it's a perfect jumping-off point for local wilderness areas. From Randle to the west, a road runs through National Forest land to the east side of Mount St. Helens and the Windy Ridge Viewpoint, the best place from which to observe the destruction wrought by the 1980 eruption, and the dramatic renewal of the natural landscape.

INFORMATION

Destination Packwood Association | Box 64, Packwood, 98361 | 360/494–2223 or 800/963-7898 | www.destinationpackwood.com. **Mount Rainier Business Association** | Box 214, Ashford, 98304 | 360/569–0910 or 877/617–9950 | www.mt-rainier.com.

Exploring Mount Rainier

PARK BASICS

Contacts and Resources: The park service provides numerous free fliers, brochures, and maps covering various aspects of Mount Rainier ecology, geology, history, trails, camping, and climbing opportunities. To get copies of these write or call the superintendent. **Mount Rainier National Park** | Tahoma Woods, Star Route, Ashford, WA 98304 | 360/569–2211 | www.nps.gov/mora.

Hours: Mount Rainier is open 24 hours a day. Entrance gates at Nisqually (Longmire), Stevens Canyon (Ohanapecosh), and White River are staffed in daylight hours year-round. During off-hours you can buy passes at the entrance gates from machines that accept credit and debit cards.

Fees: Entrance fee is $10 per vehicle, which covers everyone in the vehicle for seven days. Motorcycles and bicycles pay $5. Annual passes are available for $30.

Getting Around: The major roads that reach Mount Rainier National Park—Routes 410, 706 and 123—are paved and well-maintained state highways. However, as they reach Rainier, they become mountain roads and wind up and down many steep slopes. Cautious driving is essential. Vehicles hauling large loads should gear down, especially on downhill sections. Even drivers of passenger cars should take care not to overheat brakes by constant use. Because they traverse the shoulders of a mountain with tempestuous weather, these roads are subject to storms any time of year—even in midsummer—and are almost always being repaired in summer from winter damage and washouts. Expect to encounter road-work delays several times if you are circumnavigating the mountain.

The side roads that wind their way into the park's western slope are all narrower, unpaved, and subject to frequent flooding and washouts. All but Carbon River Road and Route 706 to Paradise are closed by snow in winter. During this time, however, Carbon River Road tends to flood near the park boundary. (Route 410 is open to the Crystal Mountain access road entrance.) Cayuse Pass usually opens in late April; the Westside Road, Paradise Valley Road, and Stevens Canyon Road usually open in May; Chinook Pass, Mowich Lake Road, and White River Road, late May; and Sunrise Road, late June. All these dates are subject to weather fluctuations.

All off-road vehicle use—4X4 vehicles, ATVs, motorcycles, snowmobiles—is prohibited in Mount Rainier National Park. See the activities section for a description of limited snowmobile use areas.

Permits: Climbing permits are $30 per person per climb or glacier trek. Wilderness use permits, which must be obtained for all backcountry trips, are free; but cost $20 per party for advance reservations.

Public Telephones and Rest Rooms: Public telephones and rest rooms are located at all park visitor centers (Sunrise, Ohanapecosh, and Paradise), National Park Inn at Longmire, and Paradise Inn at Paradise.

Accessibility: The only trail in the park that is fully accessible to those with impaired mobility is Kautz Creek Trail, a half-mile boardwalk that leads to a splendid view of the mountain. Parts of the Trail of the Shadows at Longmire, and the Grove of the Patriarchs at Ohanapecosh, are accessible. The campgrounds at Cougar Rock, Ohanapecosh and Sunshine Point have several accessible sites. All the main visitor centers, as well as National Park Inn at Longmire, are accessible.

Emergencies: For all park emergencies, dial 911.

Lost and Found: The park's lost-and-found is at the park administrative center at Longmire.

Good Tours

MOUNT RAINIER IN ONE DAY

The best way to get a complete overview of Mount Rainier in a day or less is to enter via Nisqually and begin your tour by browsing in **Longmire Museum.** The 0.5-mi **Trail of the Shadows nature loop** acquaints you with the environment in and around Longmire Meadow and the overgrown ruins of Longmire Springs Hotel.

From Longmire, the road climbs northeast into the mountains toward Paradise. Take a moment to explore gorgeous **Christine Falls,** just north of the road 1.5 mi past Cougar Rock Campground, and **Narada Falls,** 3 mi farther on; both are spanned by graceful stone footbridges. Fantastic mountain views, alpine meadows crosshatched with nature trails, a welcoming lodge and restaurant, and the excellent **Henry M. Jackson Memorial Visitor Center** combine to make lofty Paradise the primary goal of most park visitors. One outstanding (but challenging) way to explore the high country is to hike the 5 mi round-trip **Skyline Trail** to Panorama Point, which rewards you with stunning 360-degree views.

Continue eastward 21 mi and leave your car for an hour to explore the incomparable, thousand-year-old **Grove of the Patriarchs,** a small, protected island where a 1.5-mi nature trail leads through towering Douglas fir, cedar, and hemlock. Afterward, turn your car north toward White River and **Sunrise Visitor Center,** from where you can watch the alpenglow fade from Mount Rainier's domed summit.

MOUNT RAINIER IN TWO DAYS

More strenuous hiking adds immeasurably to your Rainier experience on a two-day tour of the park, namely because the more you hike, the closer you can get to views of Rainier's stunning glaciers. Remember to carry day-packs with emergency gear—food, compass, warm and water-resistant clothing—on all hikes.

Start the first day at the southern park entrance (Ohanapecosh) with an early morning stroll through the **Grove of the Patriarchs,** an easy 1.5-mi walk among gargantuan old-growth Douglas-firs. Then it's back in the car for the 30 mi, one-hour drive up **Routes 123–410** to Sunrise, a winding, scenic route that leads first through old-growth forest along the Ohanapecosh and White River valleys, then up the steep ridge-side to Sunrise. Here, **Sunrise Nature Trail** is an easy 1.5-mi loop through mountain meadows, with good views of the Cascades and Rainier. Have a bite to eat at the Sunrise snack shop, then hop back in the car for the 30-mi, 45-minute drive back to the Grove of the Patriarchs, then head west on Route 706 to Paradise. Expansive vistas of the Cascade foothills and Puget Sound basin accompany you along the way. Check in to **Paradise Inn;** after dinner, head out on one of the area's many short trails to watch the sunset wash the peak above.

On your second day, pack a picnic lunch and head west on Route 706 about 5 mi, toward Longmire, to the **Van Trump Park** trailhead at Christine Falls. The first stretch of the hike, 5 mi, gains 2,200 ft, and the average hiker can make it up in three to four hours. The "park" is a vast expanse of meadows covered with wildflowers in July and August; snowmelt freshets plunge through little gullies, and on clear days the view of southern Puget

MOUNT RAINIER
NATIONAL PARK

EXPLORING
ATTRACTIONS NEARBY
DINING
LODGING
CAMPING AND RV
FACILITIES
SHOPPING
ESSENTIAL
INFORMATION

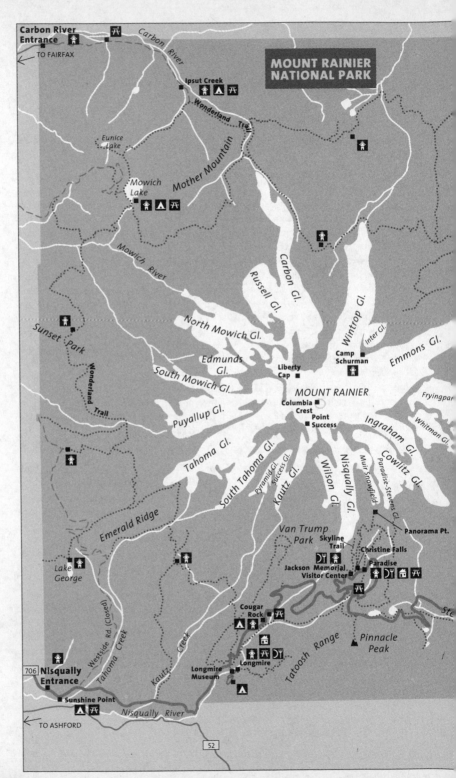

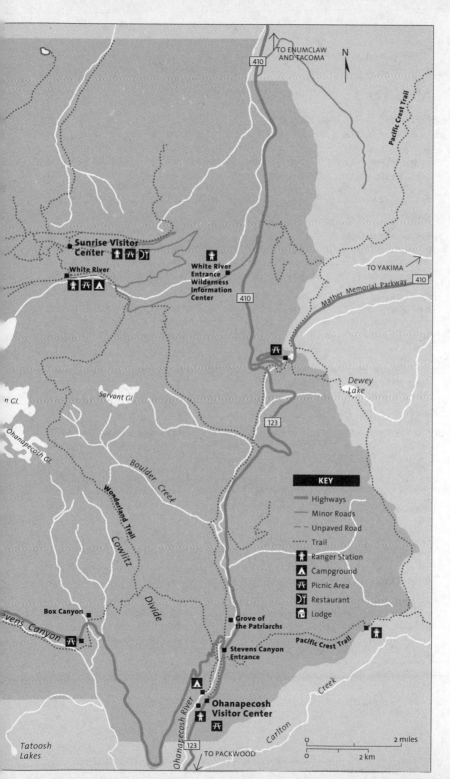

TO ENUMCLAW
AND TACOMA

410

N

Pacific Crest Trail

Sunrise Visitor Center 🚹 🎋 🍴

White River 🚹 🎋 ⛺

White River Entrance Wilderness Information Center 🚹

410

TO YAKIMA

Mather Memorial Parkway 410

🎋

Dewey Lake

Sarvant Gl.

n Gl.

Ohanapecosh Gl.

123

Boulder Creek

Wonderland Trail

Cowlitz

Divide

Box Canyon 🎋

Stevens Canyon

Grove of the Patriarchs

Stevens Canyon Entrance

Pacific Crest Trail

🚹

Ohanapecosh Visitor Center 🚹 🎋

⛺

Tatoosh Lakes

123

TO PACKWOOD

Ohanapecosh River

Carlton Creek

KEY

▬▬	Highways
──	Minor Roads
─ ─	Unpaved Road
⋯⋯	Trail
🚹	Ranger Station
⛺	Campground
🎋	Picnic Area
🍴	Restaurant
🏠	Lodge

0   2 miles

0   2 km

MOUNT RAINIER NATIONAL PARK

EXPLORING
ATTRACTIONS NEARBY
DINING
LODGING
CAMPING AND RV FACILITIES
SHOPPING
ESSENTIAL INFORMATION

Sound is sensational. After lunch, if your stamina permits, walk another mile of trail to **Mildred Point,** with splendid views of Kautz Glacier looming above.

The hike back down takes one to two hours. Back in your car, head down Route 706 4 mi to Longmire, to wind up your visit at **Longmire Museum and Visitor Center.**

Attractions

PROGRAMS AND TOURS

★ **Alpine Meadow Walks.** Rangers lead visitors from Jackson Memorial Visitor Center and Sunrise visitor center on paved or gravel paths to point out wildflowers and explain the fragile nature of the alpine meadow ecology. For exact schedules, consult bulletin boards at visitor centers, ranger stations, and campgrounds. | Jackson Memorial visitor center or Sunrise visitor center | 360/569–2211 Ext. 2328 (Jackson Memorial visitor center), 360/663–2425 (Sunrise visitor center) | Free | June–Sept., hours and days vary according to staffing schedules.

★ **Ancient Forest Walks.** Park naturalists help visitors learn to identify the different rain-forest trees and plants. For exact schedules, consult bulletin boards at visitor centers, ranger stations, and campgrounds. | Ohanapecosh visitor center: Rte. 123, 11 mi north of Packwood | 360/569–6046 | Free | June–Sept., hours and days vary according to staffing schedules.

Gray Line Bus Tours. This company conducts sightseeing tours of Seattle, and one-day and longer tours from Seattle to Mount Rainier and Olympic national parks, Mount St. Helens, the North Cascades, and the Washington Wine Country (Yakima Valley). | 4500 Marginal Way SW, Seattle | 206/624–5077 or 800/426–7532 | fax 206/626–5209 | www.graylineofseattle.com | Call for prices and schedules.

Junior Ranger Program. Children ages 6–12 follow a pamphlet that helps them find and identify the park's natural features, from glaciers to glacier lilies. The pamphlet is available at all ranger stations and visitor centers. | July 4–Aug.

SCENIC DRIVES

★ **Chinook Pass Road.** Route 410 (the highway to Yakima) follows the eastern edge of the park to Chinook Pass, where it climbs the steep, 5,432-ft pass via a series of switchbacks. At its top, you'll see broad views of Rainier and the east slope of the Cascades.

★ **Mowich Lake Road.** In the northwest corner of the park, this 24-mi mountain road begins in Wilkeson and heads up the Rainier foothills to Mowich Lake, traversing beautiful mountain meadows along the way. Mowich Lake is a pleasant spot for a picnic, and has a peaceful walk-in campground.

Paradise Road. This 9 mi stretch of Route 706 winds its way up the mountain's southwest flank from Longmire to Paradise. It takes you from lowland forest to ever-expanding vistas of the mountain above. Visit on a weekday if possible, especially in peak summer months, when the road is packed with cars. The route is open year-round.

Route 123 and Stevens Canyon Road. At Chinook Pass you can pick up Route 123 south to its junction with Stevens Canyon Road. Take this road west to its junction with the Paradise–Nisqually entrance road, which runs west through Longmire and exits the park at Nisqually. It winds among valley-floor rain forest and uphill slopes. Vistas of Puget Sound and the Cascade Range appear at numerous points along the way.

Sunrise Road. This popular (read: crowded) scenic road carves its way 11 mi up Sunrise Ridge from the White River Valley on the northeast side of the park. As you top the ridge you have sweeping views of the surrounding lowlands below. The road is open late June to October.

SIGHTS TO SEE

★ **Grove of the Patriarchs.** Protected from the periodic fires that swept surrounding areas, this small island of 1,000-year-old trees is one of Mount Rainier National Park's most memorable features. A 1.5-mi loop trail heads over a small bridge through lush old-growth forest of Douglas fir, cedar, and hemlock. | Rte. 123, west of the Stevens Canyon entrance.

Jackson Memorial Visitor Center. High on the mountain's southern flank, the center houses exhibits on geology, mountaineering, glaciology, winter storms, and alpine ecology. Multimedia programs repeat at half-hour intervals. Many trails surrounding the Paradise area wind through mountain meadows and up to the foot of Muir Snowfield. This is the park's most popular visitor destination, and quite crowded in summer. | Rte. 123, 1 mi north of Ohanapecosh at the high point of Rte. 706 | 360/569–2211 Ext. 2328 | May–mid-Oct., daily; Nov.–Apr., weekends and holidays.

★ **Longmire Museum and Visitor Center.** Glass cases preserve plants and animals from the park, including a large, friendly looking stuffed cougar, inside this museum. Historical photographs and geographical displays provide a worthwhile overview of the park's history. The visitor center, next door to the museum, has some perfunctory exhibits on the surrounding forest and its inhabitants, as well as pamphlets and information about park activities. | Rte. 706, 17 mi from Ashford | 360/569–2211 Ext. 3314 | Free | Daily 9–4:15.

Ohanapecosh Visitor Center. Near the Grove of the Patriarchs you can learn about the region's dense old-growth forests through interpretive displays and videos. | Rte. 123, 11 mi north of Packwood | 360/569–6046 | Late May–Oct., daily 9–6.

Sunrise Visitor Center. Exhibits at this center explain the region's sparser alpine and subalpine ecology. A network of nearby loop trails lead you through alpine meadows and forest to overlooks that afford broad views of the Cascades and Rainier. Evening programs are offered at White River Campground on Thursday through Saturday nights in summer. | Sunrise Road, 15 mi from the White River park entrance | 360/663–2425 | Early July–Labor Day, daily 9–6.

Sports and Outdoor Activities

BICYCLING

Bicycling is not a prime activity in the park. Bikes are allowed, but only on constructed roads; your best bets are usually Westside Road, which is closed to vehicles 3 mi up from Route 706, and Carbon River Road, which is subject to flooding and carries little vehicle traffic. Off-road mountain biking is prohibited. Park roads are narrow, winding, and, in summer, extremely crowded with cars. Bike rentals are not available within the park.

BIRD-WATCHING

★ Watch for kestrels, red-tailed hawks, and, occasionally, golden eagles on snags in the lowland forests. Rarely seen, but also present at Rainier, are great horned owls, spotted owls, and screech owls. Iridescent rufous hummingbirds flit from blossom to blossom in the drowsy summer lowlands, and sprightly water ouzels flutter in the many forest creeks. Raucous Steller's jays and gray jays scold passersby from trees, often darting boldly down to steal morsels from unguarded picnic tables. At higher elevations, look for the pure white plumage of the white-tailed ptarmigan as it hunts for seeds and insects in winter. Waxwings, vireos, nuthatches, sapsuckers, warblers, flycatchers, larks, thrushes, siskins, tanagers, and finches are common throughout the park in every season but winter.

BOATING

Nonmotorized boating is permitted on all lakes inside the park except Frozen, Ghost, Reflection, and Tipsoo lakes. Mowich Lake, in the northwest corner of the park, is the only lake easily accessible to canoes and kayaks. There are no boat rentals inside the park.

FISHING

Fishing in Rainier's unstocked lakes and rivers is apt to be an unproductive experience; the park isn't known for its fishing, but you're welcome to try. Small rainbow and cutthroat trout are the main quarry, and park rangers encourage "fishing for fun," with barbless hooks.

MOUNT RAINIER
NATIONAL PARK

EXPLORING
ATTRACTIONS NEARBY
DINING
LODGING
CAMPING AND RV
FACILITIES
SHOPPING
ESSENTIAL
INFORMATION

*Fay Fuller was the
first woman to
climb Mount
Rainier, reaching
the summit in
August 1890.
Bowing to the
social mores of the
time, she did so in
long pants and
hoop skirt. Later
that decade Fuller
was one of the
leaders of the
campaign to
declare Mount
Rainier a national
park, which
Congress did on
March 2, 1899.*

No license is required, but seasonal regulations are enforced. The Ohanapecosh River and its tributaries are open to fly-fishing only. If you're planning on fly-fishing, remember that only artificial flies are allowed.

HIKING

★ It's almost impossible to experience the blissful beauty of the alpine environment or the hushed serenity of the old-growth forest without getting out of your car and walking. Numerous hiking trails in and around Mount Rainier afford plenty of opportunities to experience the true nature of the park, ranging from low-key one-hour strolls to weeks-long traverses around the mountain.

Although the mountain can seem remarkably benign on calm summer days, hiking Rainier is not a city-park stroll. Each year, lives are lost on the mountain, and dozens of hikers and trekkers lose their way and must be rescued. Weather that approaches cyclonic levels can appear quite suddenly, any month of the year. With the possible exception of the short loop hikes listed below, all visitors venturing far from vehicle access points should carry day-packs with warm clothing, food, and other emergency supplies.

Nisqually Vista Trail. Equally popular in summer and winter, this trail is a 1.25-mi round-trip through subalpine meadows to an overlook point for Nisqually Glacier. In winter, the snow-covered, gradually sloping trail is a favorite venue for cross-country skiers. In summer, listen for the shrill alarm calls of the area's marmots. | Jackson Memorial visitor center, Rte. 123, 1 mi north of Ohanapecosh, at the high point of Rte. 706.

Skyline Trail. This 5-mi loop, one of the highest trails in the park, beckons day-trippers with a vista of alpine ridges and, in summer, meadows filled with brilliant flowers and birds. At 6,800-ft, Panorama Point, the spine of the Cascade Range, spreads away to the east, and Nisqually Glacier grumbles its way downslope. | Jackson Memorial visitor center, Rte. 123, 1 mi north of Ohanapecosh at the high point of Rte. 706.

Sourdough Ridge Self-Guiding Trail. The mile-long loop of this easy trail takes you through the delicate subalpine meadows near the Sunrise visitor center. A gradual climb to the ridge top yields magnificent views of Mount Rainier and the more distant volcanic cones of Mounts Baker, Adams, Glacier, and Hood. | Sunrise visitor center, Sunrise Road, 15 mi from the White River park entrance.

Trail of the Shadows. This 0.5-mi trek is notable for its glimpses of meadowland ecology, its colorful soda springs (don't drink the water), James Longmire's old homestead cabin, and the foundation of the old Longmire Springs Hotel, which was destroyed around 1900. | Rte. 706, 10 mi east of Nisqually entrance.

Van Trump Park Trail. You gain an exhilarating 2,200 ft while hiking through a vast expanse of meadow with views of southern Puget Sound. The 5-mi trail provides good footing, and the average hiker can make it up in three to four hours. | Rte. 706 at Christine Falls, 4.4 mi east of Longmire.

Wonderland Trail. All other Mount Rainier hikes pale in comparison to this stunning 93-mi trek, which completely encircles the mountain. The trail passes through all the major life zones of the park, from the old-growth forests of the lowlands to the alpine meadows and goat-haunted glaciers of the highlands. Be sure to pick up a mountain-goat sighting card from a ranger station or information center to help in the park's ongoing effort to learn more about these elusive animals. Wonderland is a rugged trail; elevation gains and losses totaling 3,500 ft are common in a day's hike, which averages 8 mi. Most hikers start out from either Longmire or Sunrise and take 10–14 days to cover the 93-mi route. Snow lingers on the high passes well into June (sometimes July), and you can count on rain any time of the year. Campsites are wilderness trailside areas with pit toilets and water that must be purified before drinking. Only hardy, well-equipped, and experienced wilderness trekkers should attempt this trip, but those who do will be amply rewarded. Wilderness permits are required and reservations are strongly recommended. | Longmire visitor center, Rte. 706, 17 mi from Ashford; Sunrise visitor center, Sunrise Rd., 15 mi from the White River park entrance.

HORSEBACK RIDING

Horseback riding is permitted on nearly 75 of the park's 240 mi of maintained trails, most of which are accessible from mid-July to September. Parties with horses may use four backcountry camps: Deer Creek, Mowich River, North Puyallup River, and Three Lakes. Neither saddle nor pack animals are permitted in auto campgrounds, picnic grounds, or within 100 yards of trail shelters or campsites. A horse trail map is available at ranger stations. There are no horse rentals or guided rides inside the park.

MOUNTAIN CLIMBING

★ Climbing Mount Rainier is not for amateurs; each year, climbers die on the mountain, and many climbers become lost and must be rescued. Near-catastrophic weather can appear quite suddenly, any month of the year. If you're experienced in technical, high-elevation snow, rock, and ice field adventuring, Mount Rainier can be a memorable experience. Experienced climbers can fill out a climbing card at the Paradise, White River, or Carbon River ranger stations and lead their own groups of two or more. Climbers must register with a ranger before leaving and check out upon return. There's a $15 per person fee for a single trip, or a $25 annual climbing fee. This applies to anyone venturing above 10,000 ft, or onto one of Rainier's glaciers.

Rainier Mountaineering Inc. The highly regarded concessionaire, cofounded by Himalayan adventurer Lou Whittaker, makes climbing the Queen of the Cascades an adventure open to anyone in good health and physical condition. The company teaches the fundamentals of mountaineering at one-day classes held during climbing season, from late May through early September. Participants in these classes are evaluated on their fitness for the climb; they must be able to withstand a 16-mi round-trip with a 9,000-ft gain in elevation. Winter ski programs are also offered. | Jackson Memorial visitor center, Rte. 123, 1 mi north of Ohanapecosh, at the high point of Rte. 706, Paradise | 888/892–5462 | www.rmguides.com | $771 (three-day summit climb package).

SKIING

Mount Rainier is a major Nordic ski center. Although trails are not groomed, those around Paradise are extremely popular. If you want to ski with fewer people, try the trails in and around the Ohanapecosh–Stevens Canyon area, which are just as beautiful and, because of their more-easterly exposure, slightly less subject to the rains that can douse the Longmire side, even in the dead of winter. You should never ski on the plowed main roads, especially in the Paradise area—the snowplow operator can't see you. No rentals are available on the eastern side of the park.

Longmire Ski Touring Center. Equipment rentals are available at this outfitter, adjacent to the National Park Inn at Longmire. | Longmire | 360/569–2411 | Late Nov.–early Apr., daily 9–5.

SNOWMOBILING

Snowmobiling is allowed on the east side of the park between the Stevens Canyon entrance and Box Canyon, and between the park's northern boundary on Route 410 and the White River Campground. Snowmobiles are also permitted along Westside Road, from its junction with the main park road, to Round Pass. Contact a park ranger at the Longmire Museum for maps and additional snowmobile information.

SNOWSHOEING

★ Deep snows make Mount Rainier a snowshoeing capital. The network of trails in the Paradise area makes it the best choice for snowshoers. The park's east side roads, Highways 123 and 410, are unplowed and provide another good snowshoeing venue, although you must share the main parts of the road with snowmobilers.

MOUNT RAINIER
NATIONAL PARK

EXPLORING
ATTRACTIONS NEARBY
DINING
LODGING
CAMPING AND RV
FACILITIES
SHOPPING
ESSENTIAL
INFORMATION

Mount Rainier Guest Services Ski Shop. Snowshoeing equipment is available for rent at this outfitter, adjacent to the National Park Inn. | Longmire | 360/569–2411 | Late Nov.–early Apr., daily 9–5.

Snowshoe Walks. Park rangers lead snowshoe walks that start at Jackson Memorial visitor center at Paradise and cover 1.2 mi in about two hours. Check park publications for exact dates. | 1 mi north of Ohanapecosh on Rte. 123, at the high point of Rte. 706 | 360/569–2211 Ext. 2328 | Free | Late Dec.–Apr, weekends and holidays.

SWIMMING

There are 62 lakes and countless streams and rivers within the park, and all are fed by snowmelt. Unless your tolerance for bone-chilling cold equals that of a walrus, it's best to avoid Rainier's waters. Reflection Lake, Frozen Lake, and Tipsoo Lake are closed to swimming.

Attractions Nearby

★ **Coldwater Ridge Visitor Center.** Exhibits at this multimillion-dollar facility document the great blast of Mount St. Helens and its effects on the surrounding 150,000 acres—which were devastated but are in the process of a remarkable recovery. A 0.25-mi trail leads from the visitor center to Coldwater Lake, which has a recreation area. | Rte. 504, 43 mi east of I–5 | 360/274–2131 | Free | Daily 10–6.

Crystal Mountain Ski Area. Washington State's biggest and best-known ski area is also open in summer for chairlift rides that afford sensational views of Rainier and the Cascades. | Crystal Mountain Boulevard, off Rte. 410, Crystal Mountain | 360/663–2265 | www.crystalmt.com | $15 | Memorial Day–Labor Day, weekends and holidays 10–4.

Federation Forest State Park. One of the last undisturbed old-growth groves of Douglas fir along the Cascade Front, this 619-acre park on the banks of the White River is awe-inspiring—and disturbing, when you consider how many Douglas firs have been lost. Aside from a forest trail, there's a small picnic area and interpretive display. | Rte. 410, 2 mi west of Greenwater | 360/663–2207 | Free | May–Labor Day, daily 8–dusk.

★ **Goat Rocks Wilderness.** The crags in Gifford Pinchot National Forest, south of Mount Rainier, are aptly named: you often see mountain goats, especially when you hike into the backcountry. Goat Lake is a particularly good spot for viewing these elusive creatures. You can see the goats without backpacking by taking Forest Road 2140 south from U.S. 12 near Packwood to Stonewall Ridge (ask for exact directions in Packwood, or ask a National Forest Ranger). The goats will be on Stonewall Ridge looming up ahead of you. | 10600 N.E. 51st St. Circle, Vancouver; wilderness entrance points along U.S. 12, 2–10 mi east of White Pass | 360/891–5000 | fax 360/891–5045 | www.fs.fed.us/gpnf | Free | Call for weather conditions.

Johnston Ridge Observatory. With the most spectacular views of the crater and lava dome of Mount St. Helens, this observatory also has exhibits that interpret the geology of the mountain and explain how scientists monitor an active volcano. | Rte. 504, 53 mi east of I–5, Mount St. Helens | 360/274–2140 | Free | Daily 10–6.

★ **Mount Rainier Scenic Railroad.** Beginning at Elbe, 11 mi west of Ashford, the train takes you southeast through lush forests and across scenic bridges. In all it covers 14 mi of incomparable beauty. Seasonal theme trips, such as the Halloween Ghost Train and the Christmastime Snowball Express, are also available. | Rte. 7, Elbe | 888/783–2611 | www.mrsr.com | $12 | Memorial Day–July 4, weekends; early July–Labor Day, daily; remainder of Sept., weekends; Dec. (Snowball Express), weekends. Call for hrs.

Mount St. Helens Visitor Center. This facility, one of three visitor centers along Route 504 on the west side of the mountain, has exhibits documenting the eruption, plus a walkthrough volcano. | Rte. 504, 5 mi east of I–5, Silver Lake | 360/274–2100 | Free | Daily 9–6.

★ **Northwest Trek Wildlife Park.** One of the pioneers in modern zoo operation, this park consists of large, natural enclosures in which native animals such as elk, caribou, moose, and deer roam free. Five miles of nature trails that meander near enclosures and the hands-on "Cheney Discovery Center" provide an up-close experience with wildlife. Hop on a tram for a narrated tour of the park or go on a tour in which you accompany keepers while they feed the wildlife. | Rte. 161, about 35 mi west of Mount Rainier National Park, Eatonville | 360/832–6122 | www.nwtrek.org | $8.75 | Mid-Feb.–Oct., daily 9:30–6; Nov.–mid-Feb., Fri.–Sun. 9:30–6.

Dining

In Mount Rainier

★ **National Park Inn.** Contemporary. Photos of Mount Rainier taken by some of the Northwest's top photographers adorn the walls of this inn's large dining room—a bonus on the many days the mountain refuses to show itself. Meals, served family-style, are simple but tasty: maple hazelnut chicken, tenderloin tip stir-fry, and grilled red snapper with black bean sauce and corn relish. For breakfast, don't miss the home-baked cinnamon rolls with cream-cheese frosting. | Longmire | 360/569–2411 | Reservations not accepted | $10–$24 | MC, V.

★ **Paradise Inn.** Continental. Where else can you get a decent Sunday brunch in a historic heavy-timbered lodge halfway up a mountain? Tall, many-paned windows provide terrific views of Rainier, and the warm glow of native wood permeates the large dining room. The lunch menu is simple and healthy—grilled salmon, salads, and the like. For dinner, there's nothing like a hearty plate of the inn's signature bourbon buffalo meat loaf. | Paradise | 360/569–2413 | Reservations not accepted | $12–$25 | MC, V | Closed Oct.–late May.

Picnic Areas. The picnic areas at Mount Rainier are justly famous, especially in summer, when wildflowers fill the meadows and friendly yellow pine chipmunks dart hopefully about in search of handouts. All these areas are open July through September only.

    Carbon River Picnic Ground. You'll find a half-dozen tables in the woods, near the park's northwest boundary. | Carbon River Rd., 1.5 mi east of park entrance.

    Paradise Picnic Area. Great views on clear days is the main attraction here. After picnicking at Paradise, you can take an easy hike to one of the numerous waterfalls in the area—Sluiskin, Myrtle, or Narada, to name a few. | Rte. 706, 11 mi east of Longmire.

    Sunrise Picnic Area. Set in an alpine meadow, with wildflowers in July and August, this picnic area provides expansive views of the mountain and surrounding ranges in good weather. | Sunrise Rd., 11 mi west of the White River entrance.

    Sunshine Point Picnic Area. At the Sunshine Point campground, a small group of picnic tables occupies an open meadow along the burbling Nisqually River. | Rte 706, 1 mi east of the Nisqually entrance.

Near the Park

★ **Alexander's Country Inn.** American. Without a doubt, this classic, woodsy Northwest country inn built in 1912 serves some of the best food in the area. Ceiling fans and wooden booths lining the walls make it look like a country kitchen. Try the steak or trout (freshly caught from the pond on the grounds); the homemade bread is fantastic, and the blueberry pie is a must for dessert. You can dine inside or outside on a patio overlooking the trout pond and a waterfall. The Inn can prepare box lunches for adventurers upon request. | 37515 Rte. 706, Ashford | 360/569–2300 or 800/654–7615 | $11–$22 | MC, V | Closed Nov.–Mar., Mon.–Thurs.

Scaleburgers. American/Casual. Seven miles south of Ashford, this restaurant began as a state weigh station in 1939. Since then, it's evolved into a popular spot for hamburgers, fries, milkshakes, and ice cream made from only the finest of ingredients. You eat outside

STEAMY DOINGS

Despite its blanket of ice and snow above 8,000 ft, Mount Rainier is a live volcano. Hikers to the summit who take part in a mountaineering ritual—enjoying a "dip" in the steam vents at 14,000 ft—are reminded of Rainier's thermal underpinnings: the mountain occasionally emits a small burst of carbon dioxide through one of various vents.

on tables overlooking the hills and scenic railroad. | 54109 Mountain Hwy. E, Elbe | 360/569–2247 | $3–$4 | No credit cards.

Lodging

In Mount Rainier

The Mount Rainier area is remarkably bereft of quality lodging, which may be a result of its proximity to Seattle and that accommodations here have never had to work hard to reach full occupancy in summer. The two national park lodges, at Longmire and Paradise, are attractive and well maintained, and ooze considerable history and charm—especially Paradise Inn—but unless you've made summer reservations a year in advance, getting a room is a challenge. There are dozens of motels and cabin complexes near the park entrances, but the vast majority are plain, overpriced, or downright dilapidated. With just a few exceptions, you're better off camping.

★ **National Park Inn.** A large stone fireplace takes pride of place in the common room at this otherwise generic country inn, one of only two in the park. Such rustic details as wrought-iron lamps and antique bentwood headboards adorn the rooms. The inn is the only year-round lodging in the park. Restaurant. No a/c, no room phones. No room TVs. | Longmire Visitor Complex, Rte. 706, 10 mi east of Nisqually entrance | 360/569–2275 | fax 360/569–2770 | www.guestservices.com/rainier | 25 rooms | $87–$159 | AE, D, DC, MC, V.

★ **Paradise Inn.** With its hand-carved Alaskan cedar logs, burnished parquet floors, stone fireplaces, Indian rugs, and glorious mountain views, this 1917 inn is a sterling example of National Park lodge architecture. Its small, sparsely furnished rooms have thin walls and showers that can run cold, but it's hard to beat the inn's alpine setting on the flanks of Rainier. In addition to the full-service dining room, there's a small snack bar and a snug lounge. Restaurant. Bar. No a/c, no room phones. No room TVs. | Rte. 706, 11 mi east of Longmire | 360/569–2275 | fax 360/569–2770 | www.guestservices.com/rainier | 117 rooms (88 with bath) | $82–$169 | MC, V | Closed Nov.–mid-May.

Near the Park

★ **Alexander's Country Inn.** Right down to the fairy-tale turret, Alexander's is Victorian in every detail; it was built in 1912. There's no lack of modern comforts, however. A large hot tub overlooks the trout pond out back, and a second-floor sitting room has a fireplace, stained-glass doors, and complimentary evening wine. The inn also includes two separate three-bedroom ranch houses next door, the Forest House and the Chalet. The Chalet has the same country-quaint qualities found in the Inn; the spartan Forest House has a private moss-covered backyard. The inn is 4 mi east of Ashford. Restaurant. Hot tub. Fishing. | 37515 Rte. 706, Ashford | 360/569–2300 or 800/654–7615 | 12 rooms, 2 guest houses | $89–$145 | MC, V.

Cowlitz River Lodge. This comfortable two-story family motel provides simple clean, quiet rooms. Cable TV. Hot tub. | 13069 U.S. 12, Packwood | 360/494–4444 | fax 360/494–2075 | 32 rooms | $57–$73 | AE, MC, V.

★ **Inn of Packwood.** Mount Rainier and the Cascade Mountains tower above this inn surrounded by lawns at the center of Packwood. Pine paneling and furniture lend the rooms a rustic, country charm. You can swim in an indoor heated pool beneath skylights or picnic beneath a weeping willow. Picnic area. Some kitchenettes, some microwaves, some refrigerators. Cable TV. Pool. Hot tub. | 13032 U.S. 12, Packwood | 360/494–5500 | www.innofpackwood.com | 34 rooms | $50–$145 | MC, V.

Mountain Meadows Inn Bed and Breakfast at Mount Rainier. Antiques, Native American baskets, and a collection of John Muir memorabilia adorn the living room of this homey inn, 6 mi southwest from Mount Rainier National Park. Each unit in the modern cottage has its own private entrance and kitchen. Pond. Hot tub. No a/c, no room phones. No room

TVs. No smoking. | 28912 Rte. 706, Ashford | 360/569–2788 | www.mt-rainier.net | 6 rooms, 3 efficiencies | $85–$140 | MC, V | BP.

Nisqually Lodge. Built in 1989, this motor lodge 2 mi east of Ashford has a faux Swiss-chalet feel, with a big stone fireplace, exposed beams, and lots of knotty pine in the lobby. Although it's decorated with budget furniture and institutionlike amenities, the lodge retains an airy, comfortable atmosphere. Hot tub. | 31609 Rte. 706, Ashford | 360/569–8804 | 24 rooms | $89–$129 | AE, DC, MC, V | CP.

Randle Motel. No-frills, comfortable accommodations fill this motor inn, conveniently adjacent to restaurants and stores, in the center of Randle. Each room comes furnished with a double bed. Some pets allowed. No a/c, no room phones. | 9780 U.S. 12, Randle | 360/497–5346 | 10 rooms | $35–$45 | MC, V.

★ **Wellspring.** In the woodlands outside Ashford, the accommodations here include tastefully designed log cabins, a tree house, and a room in a greenhouse. Rooms are individually decorated: a queen-size feather bed suspended by ropes beneath a skylight highlights the Nest Room; the Tatoosh room has a huge stone fireplace and can accommodate up to 10 people. Also available are a variety of spa-like amenities. This collection of units is the creation of a massage therapist, and is the only property of its kind in the area. Some kitchenettes, some microwaves, some refrigerators. Pond. Hot tub, outdoor hot tub, massage, sauna, spa. Hiking. No room phones. No room TVs. No smoking. | 54922 Kernehan Rd., Ashford | 360/569–2514 | 5 rooms, 6 cabins, 1 cottage | $79–$129 | MC, V.

Whittaker's Bunkhouse. This vintage-1912 motel once housed loggers and millworkers. In those days it was nicknamed "The place to stop on the way to the Top." In the early 1990s, famed climber Lou Whittaker bought and renovated the facility. Now, as then, it's a comfortable hostelry, with inexpensive single bunks as well as larger private rooms. Restaurant. Hot tub. | 30205 Rte. 706, Ashford | 360/569–2439 | 20 rooms | $30–$100 | MC, V.

Camping and RV Facilities

In Mount Rainier

There are five drive-in campgrounds in the park—Cougar Rock, Ipsut Creek, Ohanapecosh, Sunshine Point, and White River—with almost 700 campsites for tents and RVs. None of the park campgrounds has hot water or RV hookups; showers are available at Jackson Memorial visitor center.

For backcountry camping you must obtain a free wilderness permit at one of the visitor centers. Primitive sites are spaced at 7- or 8-mi intervals along the Wonderland Trail. A copy of "Wilderness Trip Planner: A Hiker's Guide to the Wilderness of Mount Rainier National Park," available from any of the park's four visitor centers or through the superintendent's office, is an invaluable guide if you're planning overnight backcountry stays. Advance reservations are available for specific wilderness campsites, May–September, for $20. For more information, call the Wilderness Information Center at 360/569–4453.

★ **Cougar Rock Campground.** This very popular, secluded, heavily wooded campground with an amphitheater is one of the first campgrounds to fill up. Group sites can be reserved for $3 per person, per night, with a minimum of 12 people per group. Reservations are accepted for summer only. Flush toilets. Dump station. Drinking water. Fire grates. Ranger station. | 173 sites | 2.5 mi north of Longmire | 800/365–2267 or 301/722–1257 | http://reservations.nps.gov | $15 | Late May–mid-Oct.

Ipsut Creek Campground. The quietest park campground in the northwest corner of the park is also the most difficult to reach. In the middle of a wet, green, and rugged wilderness, this campground is near many self-guided trails. It's theoretically open year-round, though the gravel Carbon River Road that leads to it is subject to flooding and potential

MOUNT RAINIER
NATIONAL PARK

EXPLORING
ATTRACTIONS NEARBY
DINING
LODGING
**CAMPING AND RV
FACILITIES**
SHOPPING
ESSENTIAL
INFORMATION

closure at any time. Running water (non-potable). Fire grates. | 31 sites | Carbon River Rd., 4 mi east of the Carbon River entrance | 360/569–2211 | Free | Reservations not accepted.

★ **Mowich Lake Campground.** This is Rainier's only lakeside campground, at 4,959 ft, and is by national park standards quite peaceful and secluded. It's accessible only by 5 mi of convoluted gravel roads, which are subject to weather damage and potential closure at any time. A ranger station is adjacent, and sites are walk-in. Pit toilets. Fire grates, picnic tables. | 30 sites | Mowich Lake Rd., 6 mi east of the park boundary | 360/568–2211 | Free | Reservations not accepted | Mid-July–Nov.

★ **Ohanapecosh Campground.** In the southeast corner of the park, this lush, green campground has a visitor center, amphitheater, and self-guided trail. It's one of the first campgrounds to open up. Reservations are accepted for summer only. Flush toilets. Dump station. Drinking water. Fire grates. Ranger station. | 189 sites | Ohanapecosh Visitor Center, Rte 123, 1.5 mi north of park boundary | 301/722–1257 or 800/365–2267 | http://reservations.nps.gov | $15 | May–late Oct.

Sunshine Point Campground. This is a pleasant, partly wooded riverside campground near the river, and one of the first campgrounds to fill up. Drinking water. Fire grates. | 18 sites | 5 mi past the Nisqually entrance | 360/569–2211 | $10 | Reservations not accepted.

White River Campground. At an elevation of 4,400 ft, White River is one of the highest and least-wooded campground in the park. Here you can enjoy campfire programs, self-guided trails, and partial views of Mount Rainier's summit. Flush toilets. Drinking water. Fire grates. Ranger station. | 112 sites | 5 mi past White River entrance | 360/569-2211 | $10 | Reservations not accepted | Late June–mid-Sept.

Near the Park

★ **La Wis Wis Campground.** Alongside a small creek in Gifford Pinchot National Forest, this Forest Service campground is a few miles from the Ohanapecosh gateway to Rainier. Drinking water. Grills, picnic tables. | 100 sites | U.S. 12, 7 mi northeast of Packwood, then 0.5 mi west on Forest Service Road 1272 | 360/494–5515 | $12 | No credit cards.

Mounthaven Resort. Amid tall firs, this small, RV-only campground resort is just west of the national park boundary. Recreation includes volleyball, badminton, and horseshoes. Flush toilets. Full hookups. Drinking water, guest laundry, showers. Fire pits, grills, picnic tables. Electricity, public telephone. | 19 sites | Rte. 706, Ashford | 360-569-2594 or 800/456–9380 | $20 | MC, V.

Packwood RV Park. This large complex in Packwood provides grassy sites in the foothills of Mount Rainier. Flush toilets. Full hookups. Drinking water, showers. Grills, picnic tables. Electricity, public telephone. | 88 sites, 77 with hookups | U.S. 12, Packwood | 360/494–5145 | $20 | MC, V.

Shopping

Eatonville Market. This is the best place for park visitors to stock up before entering Rainier. Aside from a wide selection of groceries, the market sells espresso drinks, videos, and handmade sausage. | 210 Center St., Eatonville | 360/832–4551.

General Store at Longmire's National Park Inn. The store inside this historic inn stocks food, gifts, camping supplies including firewood, and other basic necessities. | Longmire Visitor Complex | 360/569–2411.

Paradise Inn. The inn's gift shop sells souvenirs, knickknacks, postcards, and guidebooks. | Rte. 706, 11 mi east of Longmire | 360/569–2275 | Closed Nov.–Apr.

Plaza Market. This minimart stocks picnic and camping supplies, snacks, and sundries such as film. | 201 Center St., Eatonville | 360/832–6151.

MOUNT RAINIER CAMPGROUNDS

	Total # of sites	# of RV sites	# of hook-ups	Drive-to sites	Hike-to sites	Flush toilets	Pit toilets	Drinking water	Showers	Fire grates/pits	Swimming	Boat access	Playground	Dump station	Ranger station	Public telephone	Reservation possible	Daily fee per site	Dates open
INSIDE THE PARK																			
Cougar Rock	173	173	0	•		•		•		•				•	•		•	$15	May–Oct.
Ipsut	30	0	0	•			•			•								Free	Y/R
Mowich Lake	30	0	0		•		•			•	•				•			Free	Jul.–Nov.
Ohanapecosh	188	188	0	•		•		•		•			•	•	•	•	•	$15	May–Oct.
Sunshine Point	18	18	0	•			•	•		•								$10	Y/R
White River	112	112	0	•		•		•		•					•	•		$10	Jun.–Sep.
NEAR THE PARK																			
La Wis Wis Campground	100	80	0	•	•			•									•	$14–$28	May–Oct.
Mounthaven Resort	19	19	19	•		•		•	•	•						•	•	$20	Y/R
Packwood RV Park	88	88	77	•		•		•	•							•	•	$20	Y/R

* In summer only   ** Reservation fee charged   Y/R=Year-round
UL=Unlimited   ULP=Unlimited primitive   LD=Labor Day   MD=Memorial Day

Essential Information

ATMS (24-HOUR): There are no ATMs in the park. Numerous ATMs are available at stores, gas stations, and bank branches in Ashford, Packwood, and Eatonville. In Ashford there is an ATM at Ashford Valley Grocery and Suver's General Store. **First Community Bank** | 121 Washington Ave. N, Eatonville | 360/832–7200. **Key Bank** | 101 Center St. E, Eatonville | 360/832–6125.

AUTOMOBILE SERVICE STATIONS: Gas and auto service is not available in Mount Rainier National Park. Ashford and Packwood, with several stations each, are the closest outlets. **Mill Town Chevron** | 236 Center St. E, Eatonville | 360/832–6476.

POST OFFICES: The National Park Inn Post Office | Longmire, 98304 | No phone. **Paradise Inn Post Office** | Jackson Memorial Visitor Center, Paradise, 98304 | No phone.

NORTH CASCADES NATIONAL PARK

NORTHERN WASHINGTON

Route 20, 65 mi east of I–5.

Countless snow-clad mountain spires dwarf narrow glacial valleys in one of America's least-developed national parks. Considered by some the most spectacular mountain scenery in the lower 48 states, the untrammeled expanse covers 505,000 acres of rugged mountain terrain and is home to more than 700 glaciers. Only one road (Route 20, the North Cascades Highway) gives access to the park, and it's closed by snow half the year. The highway passes through a strip of Ross Lake National Recreation Area, between the North and South units of North Cascades National Park. Grizzly bears and wolves are believed to inhabit the North Cascades, along with deer, elk, black bears, mountain lions, bald eagles and other endemic Pacific Northwest wildlife. The area's lowlands include spectacular old-growth forests, and the adjacent Ross Lake and Lake Chelan National Recreation Areas (administered by the park) are popular, remote summer getaways. Because the park itself is completely wilderness, our coverage includes attractions in the adjacent national recreation areas, particularly in the beautiful and secluded Stehekin Valley.

PUBLICATIONS

Contact the Northwest Interpretive Association for a comprehensive catalog of books, guides, maps, and other materials covering the North Cascades. Especially popular are the various hiking guides, such as *Best Easy Day Hikes in the North Cascades* and *100 Hikes in the North Cascades*. **Northwest Interpretive Association** | 810 Rte. 20, Sedro-Woolley, 98284 | 360/856–5700 Ext. 291 or 515 | www.nwpubliclands.com.

When to Visit

Although the lowland sections of the park are open year-round, snow closes the North Cascades Highway each fall, usually in November, and it does not fully reopen until late April. Exact dates depend on snow conditions. Summer is short and glorious in the North Cascades high country, extending from snowmelt (late May to July, depending on the elevation and the amount of snow) to early September. During this brief period wildflowers paint the mountain meadows, hummingbirds and songbirds pepper the forest air, and even the high ridges are pleasantly warm. Autumn brings crisp nights and many cool sunny days, when the flowers turn to seed and the leaves turn colors.

SCENERY AND WILDLIFE

The spectacular, craggy peaks of the North Cascades—often likened to the Alps—are a breathtaking sight in any season. However, they are most often and easily seen in July, August, and September, when the usual spate of incoming Pacific storms moderates. Even in summer, valleys can start the day shrouded in fog; the best time to drive the highway west-to-east is afternoon. A morning start is a good choice coming the other way from Winthrop. The most sensational scenery, however, is reached by hiking to one of the high park passes or mountain lookouts. Although some trails are switchbacked, they are all very steep. Still, a hike rewards you with a view that's virtually unmatched in the continental United States, with literally dozens of snowcapped crags visible.

Bald eagles are present year-round along the Skagit River and the various lakes, although in December, hundreds flock to the Skagit to feed on a rare winter salmon run; they remain through January. Black bears are often seen in spring and early summer along the roadsides in the high country, feeding on new green growth. Deer and elk can often be seen in early morning and late evening, grazing and browsing at forest's edge.

HIGH AND LOW SEASON

Summer is peak season for the North Cascades, especially on the alpine stretches of Route 20—and up here, summer begins in July and ends around Labor Day. Summer weekends and holidays can be quite crowded, with space at a premium at the best overlooks and the Cascade Pass trailhead. The North Cascades Highway is a popular autumn drive in September and October, when the changing leaves (on larches, the only conifer that sheds its leaves, as well as aspen, vine maple, huckleberry and cottonwood) make a colorful show. The lowland forest areas, such as the complex around Newhalem, can be visited almost any time of year. They can be quite wonderful and uncrowded in early spring or late autumn on mild, rainy days, when you can experience the weather that makes old-growth forest possible.

Average High/Low Temperature (°F) and Monthly Precipitation (in inches)

	JAN.	FEB.	MAR.	APR.	MAY	JUNE
MARBLEMOUNT, WA	39/30	43/32	49/34	56/38	64/43	70/49
	9.50	9.10	7.10	4.90	3.40	2.60
	JULY	AUG.	SEPT.	OCT.	NOV.	DEC.
	76/52	76/53	69/49	57/42	45/36	39/31
	1.90	2.00	3.80	7.70	10.30	10.80

FESTIVALS AND SEASONAL EVENTS
WINTER

Dec.: **Upper Skagit Bald Eagle Festival.** Honoring the national bird, hundreds of which gather along the river in winter, this festival includes Native American music and dancing, bluegrass workshops, an arts-and-crafts show, as well as a "get acquainted" session with several live birds in Concrete. | 360/853–7009 | www.skagiteagle.org.

Jan.: **Freeze Yer Buns Fest.** Celebrate the cold with a snowmobile drag race, a fun run, and a snowman building contest in Twisp. | 509/997–2926.

SPRING

Apr.: **Skagit Valley Tulip Festival.** The lower valley (mostly west of Interstate 5 near Mount Vernon) is ablaze with tulips, daffodils, and other flowering bulbs in bloom at growers' farms. The open house event brings huge crowds (and traffic to a crawl) on weekends. | 360/428–5959 | www.tulipfestival.org.

Nearby Towns

Capital of the scenic Methow Valley, **Winthrop** endeavors to combine Western tradition with modern sophistication. The town's pioneer storefront appearance (consciously adopted in the '70s as a theme) belies its somewhat more modern outlook; it's a cross-country skiing center, and hosts an impressive blues festival each summer. Many of the valley's 3,000 residents are urban escapees who've come for a simpler life. **Twisp,** a town a few miles down the valley from Winthrop, is an agricultural center in the midst of vast hayfields; though it does have a few restaurants and motels.

Sedro-Woolley (pronounced "ceedro wooley"), a former logging and steel-mill town, has a bit of an old downtown and a smattering of Tarheel culture (as it was settled by pioneer loggers and farmers from North Carolina). Its setting in the pastoral farmland of the Skagit Valley is pretty, and the national park headquarters are here. Basic visitor services, including food, lodging and supplies, are available here and upriver in **Concrete** and **Marblemount.** Marblemount is also a former logging town now depending on outdoor recreation for its fortunes. Fishermen, campers, hikers, bird-watchers, and hunters come and go from the town's collection of motels, cafés, and stores. Once an apple-growing center—some of the apple-box posters most highly prized by collectors depict its early-20th century orchards—**Chelan** has become one of Washington state's most popular resort communities. Perched at Lake Chelan's foot beneath the eastern foothills of the Cascades, it's where Seattleites come in early summer to bask in sun and escape the clouds and drizzle back home.

INFORMATION

Lake Chelan Chamber of Commerce | 102 E. Johnson, Chelan, WA 98816 | 800/424–3526 | www.lakechelan.com. **North Cascades Chamber of Commerce** | 59831 Route 20, Marblemount | Box 175, Marblemount, WA 98267 | 360/873–2106 or 877/875–2448 | www.marblemount.com. **Sedro-Woolley Chamber of Commerce** | 714-B Metcalf St., Sedro-Woolley, 98284 | 360/835–1582 or 888/225–8365 | fax 360/855–1582 | www.sedro-woolley.com. **Twisp Visitor Information Center and Chamber of Commerce** | 201 South Methow Valley Hwy., Twisp, 98856 | 509/997–2926 | fax 509/997–2164 | www.twispinfo.com. **Winthrop Chamber of Commerce** | Box 39, Winthrop, 98862 | 888/463–8469 | www.winthropwashington.com.

Exploring North Cascades

PARK BASICS

Contacts and Resources: North Cascades National Park | North Cascades NPS Complex, 810 Rte. 20, Sedro-Woolley, 98284 | 360/856–5700 | www.nps.gov/noca.

Hours: The park never closes, but access is limited by snow in winter. Note that Route 20 (North Cascades Highway), the major access to the park, is partially closed from mid-November to mid-April.

Fees: A Northwest Forest Pass, required for use of various park and National Forest facilities, such as trailheads, is $5 per vehicle for one calendar day or $30 for one year. A free wilderness permit is required for all overnight stays in the backcountry.

Getting Around: The only road into the park is Cascade River Road, a narrow two-lane mostly gravel road that provides access from Marblemount to the Cascade Pass trailhead.

Chelan Air. On-demand service to Stehekin and back is available by floatplane; the very scenic flight takes about 45 minutes each way from Chelan. | Box W, Chelan, 98816 | 509/682–5555 | www.chelanairways.com | $120 round-trip.

Lady of the Lake II. This Lake Chelan vessel can give you a lift to the lakeshore trails and will pick you up again at a prearranged time. Aboard the *Lady* you can get transportation to Stehekin and other lakefront communities, as well as the eastern end of the national park itself, which can be reached only by boat, floatplane, or hiking. The Lake Chelan Boat

Company also operates an ultra-fast catamaran on various schedules depending on the time of year. | 1418 W. Woodin Ave., Chelan | 509/682–4584 | www.ladyofthelake.com | $25–$89 round-trip.

Valley Shuttles. Vans provide access to Stehekin Valley Road. In mid-May there's service to the Lower Valley (Stehekin Valley to High Bridge); come June you can get a lift to the Upper Valley (High Bridge to Glory Mountain). For $1, hop on the "Bakery Special" for a ride from Stehekin Landing to the Stehekin Pastry Co. Reservations are strongly recommended for most tours but are not needed for the bakery run. | 360/856–5700 Ext. 340 then press 14 | $6–$24 | www.nps.gov/noca/focus/focus.htm | No credit cards | Mid-May–mid-Oct.

Permits: A Northwest Forest Pass, $5 per day or $30 annual, is required for hiking in North Cascades National Park, Ross Lake National Recreation Area, and most areas of Mount Baker-Snoqualmie National Forest. A free wilderness permit is required for overnight backcountry activities; you can acquire one at the Wilderness Information Center in Marblemount or at park ranger stations. Backcountry permits are issued in person only.

Public Telephones and Rest Rooms: Public telephones and rest rooms are found at the North Cascades Visitor Center and Skagit Information Center in Newhalem; and at the Purple Point Information Center and North Cascades Stehekin Lodge in Stehekin.

Accessibility: All visitor centers along North Cascades Highway, including the main facility in Newhalem, are accessible to those with mobility impairments. Accessible hikes along the highway include Sterling Munro, River Loop, and Rock Shelter, three short trails into lowland old-growth forest, all at Mile 120 along Route 20 near Newhalem; and the Happy Creek Forest Trail at Mile 134.

Emergencies: Dial 911 for all emergencies.

Lost and Found: The park's lost and found is at the visitor center in Newhalem.

NORTH CASCADES
NATIONAL PARK

EXPLORING
ATTRACTIONS NEARBY
DINING
LODGING
CAMPING AND RV
FACILITIES
SHOPPING
ESSENTIAL
INFORMATION

Good Tours

NORTH CASCADES IN ONE DAY

Although a simple drive through the mountains seems short shrift for a national park, this drive, along the **North Cascades Highway,** is one of the most memorable in the United States. The best approach is from Winthrop, westbound; traffic is a little lighter this direction, and morning fog is less common on the Cascades' east slope. Start in Winthrop as early as 8 AM, heading up the valley; after Mazama the road climbs quickly to **Washington Pass,** the highway's highest point. The overlook here affords a sensational vantage of the North Cascades maze of peaks.

From here, the highway crosses **Rainy Pass,** another good vantage point, and then drops into the west slope valleys. Old-growth forest begins to appear; after about an hour, you reach **Gorge Creek Falls overlook,** and a view of a 242-ft cascade. Continue west to Newhalem. Stop here for lunch; afterward, a half-hour stroll along the **Trail of the Cedars** will introduce you to the ancient forest ecosystem. In the afternoon, take one of the trails from **North Cascades Visitor Center** for a hike. From here, it's an hour drive down the Skagit Valley to Sedro-Woolley; be sure to watch for bald eagles along the river in winter.

NORTH CASCADES IN THREE DAYS

Advance NPS shuttle bus reservations and a Northwest Forest Pass are essential for this trip. Call the Purple Point Information Center at 360/856–5700 Ext. 340, then Ext. 14.

A moderate six- to seven-hour hike (12 mi) to Glory Mountain makes this two-day trip a true North Cascades experience. Start with an early morning departure from Sedro-Woolley or Marblemount, driving up the Cascade River Road to the **Cascade Pass** Trailhead, about 45 minutes (23 mi), on a mostly gravel road. Here, outfitted with complete day packs (be sure to include essentials for overnight survival just in case), head up the

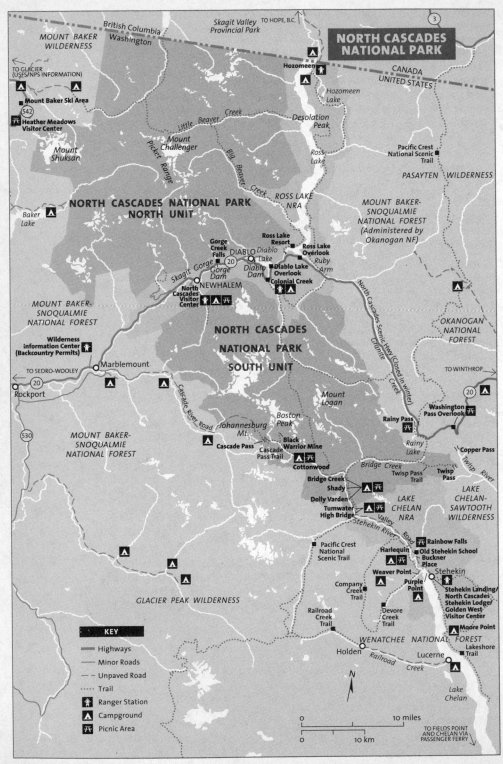

NORTH CASCADES NATIONAL PARK

KEY
- Highways
- Minor Roads
- Unpaved Road
- Trail
- Ranger Station
- Campground
- Picnic Area

0 — 10 miles
0 — 10 km

N

switchbacked trail to the pass, taking time to enjoy the many wildflowers painting the mountain meadows. At the top, the panorama of Cascade peaks—including nearby Johannesburg Mountain, draped with glaciers—is unmatched. Heading down the other side you've crossed into the upper Stehekin Valley; down the valley, you can catch a National Park Service shuttle bus ($6) at Glory Mountain for a scenic ride into **Stehekin** to spend the night or two at Stehekin Valley Ranch. If you want a true rustic experience, choose one of their tent cabins—or the beautiful Silver Bay Inn on Lake Chelan. In the morning, catch the bus back to the **Buckner Homestead** pioneer farm and orchard. After you've explored the area, the National Park Service shuttle will return you to the trailhead to hike the 12 mi back up over the pass.

Attractions

PROGRAMS AND TOURS

In summer, daily programs, which usually include walks and talks for adults and forest walks and games for children, take place at the visitor center in Newhalem, and the Purple Point Information Center in Stehekin; schedules vary widely and are posted on bulletin boards.

North Cascades Institute (NCI). NCI offers classes, field trips, seminars, and wilderness adventures that range from forest ecology to backpack trips to Cascades hot springs. Call for information as schedules, locations, and fees vary widely. | 810 Rte. 20, Sedro-Woolley | 360/856–5700 Ext. 209 | www.ncascades.org.

SCENIC DRIVE

★ **North Cascades Highway.** Route 20, the North Cascades Highway, traverses Ross Lake National Recreation Area, which lies between the North and South units of North Cascades National Park. East of Ross Lake, several pullouts offer great lake views and the snow-capped peaks surrounding it. The whitish rocks in the road cuts are limestone and marble. Meadows along this stretch of the highway are covered with wildflowers from June to September; nearby slopes are golden and red with fall foliage from late September through October. The pinnacle point of this stretch is 5,477-ft-high Washington Pass, east of which the road drops down to the Methow Valley. The pass, and this section of the highway, is closed in winter, usually from November to April, depending on snowfall and avalanche conditions.

SIGHTS TO SEE

Buckner Homestead. Founded in 1912, this pioneer farm includes an apple orchard, farmhouse, barn, and many ranch buildings, which are slowly being restored by the National Park Service. | Stehekin Valley Rd., 3.5 mi from Stehekin Landing, Stehekin | 360/856–5700 Ext. 340 then press 14 | June–Sept., daily.

Diablo Dam. From the tour center in Diablo, Seattle City Lights operates a 2½-hour tour that takes you across Diablo Dam by motor-coach and then on a boat cruise of Diablo Lake. Purchase snacks at the Skagit General Store or pack a picnic lunch for the trip. Due to increased security, there is no longer public access to Ross Powerhouse, the Incline Railway, or Diablo Dam (except on the tour). | 500 Newhalem St., Rockport | 206/684–3030 | $17 | www.ci.seattle.wa.us/light/tours/skagit | June–Sept. Tours depart daily at 9:45 and 12:45.

Gorge Powerhouse/Ladder Creek Falls and Rock Gardens. A powerhouse is a powerhouse, but the rock gardens overlooking Ladder Creek Falls, 7 mi west of Diablo, are beautiful and inspiring. | Rte. 20, 2 mi east of North Cascades Visitor Center, Newhalem | 206/684–3030 | www.ci.seattle.wa.us/light/tours/skagit | $5 | Mid-June–Oct., daily.

North Cascades National Park Headquarters. This is the major administrative center for the park complex, and a good place to pick up passes and permits, as well as to obtain information about current conditions. | 810 Rte. 20, Sedro-Woolley | 360/856–5700 | www.nps.gov/noca | Mid-Oct.–mid-May, weekdays 8–4:30; mid-May–mid-Oct., daily 8–4:30.

NORTH CASCADES
NATIONAL PARK

EXPLORING
ATTRACTIONS NEARBY
DINING
LODGING
CAMPING AND RV
FACILITIES
SHOPPING
ESSENTIAL
INFORMATION

North Cascades Visitor Center. This is the major visitor facility for the park complex, with an extensive series of displays on the natural features of the surrounding landscape. You can learn about the history and value of old-growth trees, the many creatures that depend on the rain forest ecology, and the effects of human activity. Park rangers frequently conduct programs; check bulletin boards for schedules. | Rte. 20, Newhalem | 206/386–4495 | 9–5, extended hrs in July and August.

Purple Point Information Center. Rangers here offer guidance on hiking, camping, and other local activities. This is a good place to pick up permits and passes. Maps and concise displays explain the complicated ecology of the valley, which encompasses in its length virtually every ecosystem in the Northwest. Hours vary in spring and fall. | Stehekin Valley Rd., 0.25 mi north of Stehekin Landing, Stehekin | 360/856–5700 Ext. 340 then Ext. 14 | Mid-Mar.–mid-Oct., daily 8:30–5.

Stehekin. One of the most beautiful, and most secluded, valleys in the Pacific Northwest, Stehekin, which was homesteaded by very hardy souls in the late 19th century, is not really a town but a small community set at the northwest end of Lake Chelan. There is no road to it; access is by boat, floatplane, or hiking only. Limited facilities serve a maximum of about 200 visitors during summer peak season. Year-round residents enjoy a wilderness lifestyle—there are barely two dozen cars in the whole valley, outside communication is iffy, especially in winter, and all supplies arrive once or twice a week by boat.

Sports and Outdoor Activities

HIKING

Dozens of trails wind their way from the lowland valleys into old-growth forest, and then up into the national park highlands. Note that group treks are limited to 12 persons.

★ **Cascade Pass.** Perhaps the most popular park hike, this much-traveled, moderate switch-backed 3.7-mi trail leads to a divide from which dozens of peaks can be seen. From here there are trails for exploring in several directions from the pass. The meadows here are covered with alpine wildflowers in July and early August. On sunny summer weekends and holidays, the pass parking lot can fill up; it's best to arrive before noon. The trip up and back will take the average hiker less than four hours, but allow plenty of extra time at the summit for admiring the wildflowers and gawking at the surrounding peaks. Listen for the sound of ice falling from hanging glaciers on Johannesburg Mountain. Northwest Forest Pass needed. | At the end of Cascade River Rd., 14 mi from Marblemount.

Rainy Pass. This easy and accessible 1-mi paved trail leads to Rainy Lake, a waterfall, and glacier-view platform. | Rte. 20, 38 mi from visitor center at Newhalem.

★ **River Loop.** One of the most notable hikes in the park, this 1.8-mi handicapped accessible trail loops through stands of huge, old-growth firs and cedars, dipping down to the Skagit River and out onto a riverside gravel bar. | Near visitor center.

Thornton Lakes Trail. A 5-mi climb into an alpine basin with two pretty lakes, this steep and strenuous hike takes about five–six hours round-trip. After about 2 mi, you'll break out onto an open ridge with views of Mount Triumph, Teebone Ridge, and the Skagit Valley. Northwest Forest Pass needed. | Rte. 20, 3 mi west of Newhalem.

★ **Trail of the Cedars.** Only 0.5 mi long, this trail winds its way through one of the finest surviving stand of old-growth Western red cedar in Washington state. Some of the trees on the path are more than 1,000 years old. | Near visitor center.

RAFTING

On a scenic half-day raft trip, you can traverse the lower section of the Stehekin River, which winds through cottonwood and pine forest on its way to Lake Chelan.

Stehekin Valley Ranch. Guided trips on the class III river leave from here. | Stehekin Valley Rd., 3.5 mi from Stehekin Landing, Stehekin | 509/682–4677 or 800/536–0745 | $45 | June–Sept.

ROCK CLIMBING

Thousands of climbers and mountaineers have honed their skills on the craggy, sheer faces here. Famed ascents include Mount Shuksan on the park's north side, and Johannesburg Mountain, above Cascade Pass in the south section. These climbs are not for amateurs: the rock tends to be loose, the numerous snowfields and glaciers present many hazards, and the weather can be highly temperamental. Climbers must get a free backcountry permit, and are urged to register with park rangers at Sedro-Woolley headquarters, or call the Wilderness Information Center for more information at 360/873–4500 Ext. 39.

Attractions Nearby

Sights to See

★ **Lake Chelan.** This 55-mi-long fjord, Washington's deepest lake, is surrounded by mountains that rise ever higher as your boat penetrates deeper into them. There is no road that runs the length of the lake, so a boat or floatplane is the only way to see the whole thing. Several resorts line the eastern (and warmer) shore of the lake. The western end, at Stehekin, reaches Lake Chelan National Recreation Area. | Alt. 97, Chelan | 360/856–5700 Ext. 340, then 14 | www.nps.gov/lach | Free | Daily.

Mount Baker Ski Area. You can snowboard and ski downhill or cross-country 17 mi east of the town of Glacier, from roughly November to the end of April. The area is famed for setting a world snowfall record in the winter of 1998–99. Ski and snowboard equipment are available. | Mount Baker Hwy. 542, 62 mi east of Bellingham, Mount Baker | 360/734–6771, 360/671–0211 for snow reports | www.mtbaker.us | All-day lift ticket weekends and holidays $36, weekdays $29 | Nov.–April.

Stehekin Boat Co. Come aboard to tour Lake Chelan. Voyages range from high-speed catamaran jaunts up-lake in 2 hours, to leisurely 4½-hour cruises that allow thorough inspection of the changing scenery as it goes by. Although most summer passengers are tourists, these are also working boats that haul supplies, mail, and even cars and construction material up-lake to Stehekin. The vessel will also drop you at lakeshore trailheads and pick you up later. | 1418 Woodin Ave., Chelan | 509/682–4584 or 509/682–2224 | fax 509/682–8026 | www.ladyofthelake.com | $25–$89 | Daily; call for schedule.

Dining

In North Cascades

Except for the facilities at Stehekin, the park has no restaurants.

Picnic Areas. Developed picnic areas at Rainy Pass (Route 20, 38 mi east of the park visitor center) and Washington Pass (42 mi east) each have a half-dozen picnic tables, drinking water, and pit toilets. The vistas of surrounding peaks are sensational at these two overlooks. There are also picnic facilities near the visitor center in Newhalem, and at Colonial Creek Campground 10 mi east of the visitor center on Route 20.

Stehekin Pastry Company. Café. Stehekin Pastry Company is one of the most popular valley attractions, offering fresh-baked muffins, rolls, pastries, and breads. In the afternoon and evening, stop by for ice cream or a slice of pie on the porch. | Stehekin Valley Rd., about 2 mi from Stehekin Landing, on the way to Rainbow Falls, Stehekin | 509/682–4677 | $2–$4 | No credit cards | Closed Oct.–June.

A SENATOR'S
LEGACY

*Credit the
persistence of a
powerful senator
for the existence of
North Cascades
National Park.
Timber, mining,
and hydropower
interests blocked all
early attempts to
create the park—
until former U.S.
Senator Henry
"Scoop" Jackson
made it a personal
goal. He pushed the
park authorization
act through
Congress in 1968,
helped by Supreme
Court Justice
William O. Douglas,
a Washington
native.*

Stehekin Valley Ranch. American. Meals at this classic guest ranch include hearty breakfasts of omelets, hash browns, and pancakes; the buffet dinners include steak, ribs, hamburgers, salad, beans and dessert. Transportation from Stehekin Landing is included. | Stehekin Valley Rd., 9 mi north of Stehekin Landing, Stehekin | 509/682–4677 or 800/536–0745 | $11–$20 | No credit cards | Closed Oct.–mid-June.

Near North Cascades

Buffalo Run Restaurant. American. Game meats such as buffalo, venison, elk, and ostrich are the specialty here, where "Dine on the Wild Side" is the motto. The menu also has a few vegetarian dishes. | 60084 Rte. 20, Marblemount | 360/873–2461 | $13–$20 | AE, D, MC, V.

Dining Room at Sun Mountain Lodge. Contemporary. Every table here offers great scenery. The good food centers around seafood and meat, with an emphasis on fresh local ingredients. Dishes such as line-caught king salmon with roasted asparagus and morels and rack of lamb stuffed with aged goat cheese and preserved lemon give this menu panache. Breakfast is also served. | Patterson Lake Rd., Winthrop | 509/996–2211 | $16–$30 | AE, DC, MC, V.

Duck Brand Cantina, Bakery and Hotel. American/Casual. This modern roadhouse was built to resemble a frontier-style hotel—and it works. It serves good, square meals at reasonable prices, ranging from omelets at breakfast to burritos and pasta dishes. The freshly baked cinnamon rolls and berry pies are excellent. | 248 Riverside Ave., Winthrop | 509/996–2192 | $8–$17 | AE, D, DC, MC, V.

Ferry Street Grill and Bar. American/Casual. Everything is homemade at this popular historic downtown eatery. Rise and shine for home-style breakfasts—omelets are a specialty, but the big seller is the biscuits and gravy. The dinner menu covers steaks, ribs, and pastas, plus hand-tossed pizzas. | 208 Ferry St., Sedro-Woolley | 360/855–2210 | $7–$15 | MC, V | Closed Sun.

Twisp River Pub. American. Salmon, steak, and duck are some of the menu's upscale offerings, but you can get bratwurst and burgers, too. The brewery serves as many as eight of its own beers plus a number of wines. | 201 N.E. Methow Valley Hwy., Twisp | 509/997–6822 | $6–$15 | AE, D, DC, MC, V.

Lodging

In North Cascades

There are no accommodations inside North Cascades National Park itself, as the entire park proper is wilderness. Reservations at Stehekin Valley lodgings are imperative.

North Cascades Stehekin Lodge. A classic log lodge with functional rooms, this place has a dining room, lobby with fireplace, and a porch overlooking the lake. Some of the bigger, lake-view rooms have kitchenettes and sleep up to six people. The lodge dining room is one of two dinner-service facilities in the valley. You can only get to the lodge via the *Lady of the Lake* ferry, float plane, or hiking. Restaurant. Some kitchenettes. Laundry facilities. | About 5 mi south of Stehekin Landing on Lake Chelan | Box 457, Stehekin Landing, Chelan 98816 | 509/682–4494 | www.stehekin.com | 38 rooms | $92–$136 | D, MC, V.

Silver Bay Inn. A charming inn perched on a private little slip of land at the head of Lake Chelan, Silver Bay has two cabins and a guest house that can house up to six people. Aside from hiking, canoeing and swimming are available—or you can just sit in a lawn chair by the lake, reading. Boating. Hiking. | Silver Bay Rd., Box 85, Stehekin | 509/682–2212 or 800/555–7781 | www.silverbayinn.com | 2 cabins | $185 | AE, MC, V.

Stehekin Valley Ranch. Nestled along pretty meadows at the edge of pine forest, this classic guest ranch has tent cabins with bunk beds and kerosene lamps—how much more genuine can you get? There are also five cabins with baths. Horseback riding, hiking, river rafting and other activities pass the time in the blissfully peaceful valley. Shuttles provide transportation to and from Stehekin Landing, from June through early October. Restaurant. Hiking, horseback riding. | Stehekin Valley Rd., 9 mi north of Stehekin Landing, Stehekin | 509/682–4677 or 800/536–0745 | www.courtneycountry.com | 27 tent cabins, 5 cabins | $150–$170 | No credit cards | Closed Oct.–mid-June | FAP.

Near North Cascades

Clark's Skagit River Resort. The Clark Family runs this rambling resort at the western entrance to the North Cascades, near Rockport. Cabins, a bed-and-breakfast, camping, and RV sites are available on 125 lush acres along the Skagit River. A meal at the resort's Roadhouse Restaurant is a must. Be sure to have a slice of Tootsie Clark's homemade pie, especially pecan, wild blackberry, or mincemeat made from local elk. Tootsie remains a link to the area's pioneer past—her grandmother arrived in these woods in 1888 by Indian canoe and started a roadhouse above present-day Marblemount. | 58468 Rte. 20, Rockport | 360/873–2250 or 800/273–2606 | www.northcascades.com | 32 cabins, 4 B&B rooms with shared bath, 5 trailers, 30 RV sites, 15 tent sites | $69–$129 | MC, V.

Chewuch Inn. This inn sits on 4 acres surrounded by the North Cascade Mountains just 0.3 mi south of Winthrop. The rooms are individually appointed with furnishings that reflect the rustic environment; murals ornament many of the walls. When you're not exploring the mountains, relax in front of your fireplace, or work out the kinks of ranch life with yoga classes offered three days per week. Some kitchenettes. In-room VCRs. Hot tub. Hiking, horseback riding. No room phones. No smoking. | 223 White Ave., Winthrop | 509/996–3107 or 800/747–3107 | www.chewuchinn.com | 8 rooms, 6 cabins | $65–$125 | AE, D, MC, V.

Freestone Inn. More than 2 million acres of forest surround this resort, 15 mi northwest of Winthrop. Rough hewn logs and rocks form the major building components of the inn and its lakefront lodges. The guestrooms have fireplaces and decks that overlook Freestone Lake. Restaurant. Some kitchenettes, some microwaves, some refrigerators. Lake. Fishing. Bicycles. Hiking. Shops. No a/c in some rooms. No smoking. | 17798 Rte. 20, Mazama | 509/996–3906 or 800/639–3809 | fax 509/996–3907 | www.freestoneinn.com | 21 rooms, 15 cabins, 2 cottages | $190–$460 | AE, D, DC, MC, V.

Methow Valley Inn. Guest rooms in this 1912 house are appointed with antiques and quilt-covered iron beds. The great room downstairs has a gigantic stone fireplace in front of a leather sofa. Fresh flowers in the rooms and complimentary seasonal fruits from an organic garden are some of the ways the proprietors will pamper you. No a/c, no room phones. No kids under 12. No smoking. | 234 E. 2nd Ave., Twisp | 509/997–2253 | www.methowvalleyinn. com | 7 rooms (4 with private bath) | $89–$109 | MC, V.

South Bay Bed and Breakfast. Standing above Lake Whatcom, 20 mi north of Sedro-Woolley and 20 mi southeast of Bellingham, this Craftsman-style house has exquisite views of the lake and mountains, and the surrounding undeveloped park areas create a secluded environment that is bursting with wildlife. Of the five tastefully furnished rooms, four have fireplaces and hot tubs. All have lake views. In-room hot tubs. Boating. Fishing. Bicycles. No a/c, no room phones. No room TVs. No smoking. | 4095 S. Bay Dr., Sedro-Woolley | 360/595–2086 or 877/595–2086 | fax 360/595–1043 | www.southbaybb.com | 5 rooms | $135–$150 | MC, V | BP.

Sun Mountain Lodge. This hilltop lodge has great views of the surrounding Cascade Mountains and Methow Valley. Some guest rooms have views of Mount Gardner or Mount Robinson. The cabins are 1.5 mi below on the Patterson lakefront. Restaurant, picnic area, room service. Some kitchenettes, some refrigerators. Tennis court. 2 pools. Exercise equipment, hot tub. Bicycles. Hiking, horseback riding. Cross-country skiing. Bar. Children's programs (ages 4–10), playground. Business services. | Patterson Lake Rd., Winthrop | 509/996–2211 or 800/572–0493 | fax 509/996–3133 | www.sunmountainlodge.com | 102 rooms; 13 cabins | $115–$255, $155–$340 cabins | AE, DC, MC, V.

NORTH CASCADES
NATIONAL PARK

EXPLORING
ATTRACTIONS NEARBY
DINING
LODGING
CAMPING AND RV
FACILITIES
SHOPPING
ESSENTIAL
INFORMATION

Camping and RV Facilities

In North Cascades

Lake Chelan National Recreation Area. Many backcountry camping areas, from the Lower Valley and up, are accessible via park shuttles or by boat and require free backcountry permits. Three boat-in lakeside grounds (with 12 sites) require a $5 per day Forest Service dock permit. Requests for group camps may be made in writing only. Everything you bring must be able to be hung on bear wires, so rethink those big coolers. Purple Point, the most popular campground, with seven tent-only sites, has bear boxes and is closest to transportation and shower facilities. Pit toilets. Drinking water. Bear boxes. | 63 tent sites | Stehekin Landing, NPS, Box 7, Stehekin, WA 98852 | 360/856–5700 Ext. 360 then Ext.14 | www.nps.gov/noca/focus/focus5.htm | Free | Reservations not accepted | No credit cards.

Ross Lake National Recreation Area. The National Park Service maintains three upper Skagit Valley campgrounds near Newhalem. | 360/856–5700 Ext. 515 | www.nps.gov/noca/pphtml/camping.html | Reservations not accepted | No credit cards.

Colonial Creek Campground. In a valley setting amid old-growth forest, this campground is close to Route 20 services and Diablo Lake. A boat ramp affords easy access to the lake, and several hiking trails that lead into the park begin at the campground. Flush toilets. Dump station. Drinking water. Fire grates, picnic tables. | 130 tent sites, 32 RV sites | 10 mi east of Newhalem on Rte. 20 | $12 | Mid-May–Sept.

Goodell Creek Campground. This forested site lies across the river from Newhalem Creek Campground, near the visitor center. It's somewhat more primitive than Newhalem Creek, with pit toilets and no campground programs. No water is available in winter. Pit toilets. Drinking water. Fire grates, picnic tables. | 21 tent sites | Rte. 20, 0.5 mi west of park visitor center turnoff | 360/873–4590 | $10, free mid-Oct.–mid-Apr.

Newhalem Creek Campground. With three loops, a small amphitheater, a playground, and a regular slate of ranger programs in summer, Newhalem Creek is the main North Cascades park complex campground. Perched on a bench above the Skagit River, in old-growth forest, it is adjacent to the visitor center, and close to several trails that access the river and the surrounding second-growth forest. Flush toilets. Dump station. Drinking water. Fire grates, picnic tables. Public telephone. Ranger station. Play area. | 111 RV sites | Rte. 20, along the access road to the park's main visitor center | 360/873–4590 | $12 | Mid-May–mid-Oct.

Near North Cascades

National Forest Service. The service maintains a number of campgrounds in the North Cascades region, ranging from small, fairly primitive spots at the end of gravel access roads to larger facilities along state highways. | 509/996–4000.

Rockport State Park. The park's camping area, in an old-growth Douglas fir grove, has 5 mi of hiking trails. Eight sites are walk-in from the nearby parking lot. The park is at the foot of Sauk Mountain; a trail leads to the top of the 5,400-ft peak. Flush toilets. Dump station. Drinking water, showers. Fire grates. | 8 tent sites, 50 RV sites with full hookups | Rte. 20, 25 mi west of Newhalem | phone/fax 360/853–8461 | 800/452–5687 | www.parks.wa.gov | $10–$21, $6 per additional vehicle | Reservations not accepted | Apr.–Oct.

Shopping

Skagit General Store. You can buy groceries, snacks, camping supplies, and souvenirs here, including carvings, posters, and natural history books. The store has quite a history of its own: it opened in 1922 as a commissary for workers during construction of the Gorge Dam. Don't miss the homemade fudge. | Rte. 20, Mile 120, next to the visitor center, Newhalem | 206/386–4489 | Closed Oct.–Apr.

The House That Jack Built. This community cooperative opened in the late 1970s. Here you'll find T-shirts, cards, jewelry, and crafts made by Stehekin Valley residents. | Stehekin Landing, Stehekin | No phone | Closed Oct.–Apr.

Essential Information

ATMS (24-HOUR): There are no ATMs in the park. Marblemount, west of the park, and Winthrop, east of the park along Route 20, have several banks with 24-hour ATMs.

AUTOMOBILE SERVICE STATIONS: There are no gas or service stations available between Marblemount and Mazama. Marblemount has several gas and service stations.

POST OFFICES: There are no post offices in the park. The nearest is in Marblemount. **Marblemount Post Office** | 60096 Rte. 20, Marblemount, 98267 | 360/873–2125.

OLYMPIC NATIONAL PARK

WESTERN WASHINGTON

U.S. 101, 89 mi west of I–5 exit 88 via U.S. 12, or 121 mi north of I–5 exit 104. From Seattle, Washington State ferry (Seattle–Bainbridge or Edmonds–Kingston route) to Route 305 or Route 3, then Route 104 to U.S. 101.

Wave-stung ocean shore, mossy, misty river valleys, and craggy peaks add up to one magnificent wilderness in Olympic National Park. The park's west slope holds the most scenic temperate rain forests in the Northwest, studded with huge spruces, firs, and cedars. The roadless interior of the park is an empire of glacier-draped mountains, almost as difficult to traverse as it was a century ago. The separate coastal unit protects a rugged 65-mi stretch of stunning shoreline. Bald eagles, osprey, blue heron, hawks, and hundreds of smaller birds soar Olympic's skies. Black bears, cougars, deer and elk, and numerous smaller animals thrive in the park's forests, and its near-shore waters hold migrating whales, sea lions, sea otters, seals, and many other Pacific denizens. One of the largest (922,651 acres), most remote and least developed national parks in the United States, Olympic draws 3.4 million visitors annually, most of whom visit the six major entry points where roads penetrate a few miles into the park. But even in the most congested spots you're quite likely to see wildlife—and certain to see the Pacific Northwest as it appeared 150 years ago when settlers first arrived.

PUBLICATIONS

Robert L. Wood's *Olympic Mountain Trail Guide* is a bible for both day hikers and those planning longer excursions, and by far the most detailed guide to all of the park's trails. Stephen Whitney's *A Field Guide to the Cascades and Olympics* is an excellent trailside reference covering more than 500 plant and animal species found in the park. Rowland W. Tabor's *Geology of Olympic National Park* provides a detailed history of the forces that shape the Olympic Peninsula and guides geophiles to geologic points of interest within the park. Robert Steelquist's *The Olympics: A Wilderness Trilogy* is a lavishly illustrated coffee-table book.

The park service publishes a wide variety of free fliers on specific aspects of the park, including "Suggested Day Hikes," "Facilities and Services," "Climate and Seasons," and brief guides to the rain forest, flora and fauna, and notable sights in the park. The park's newspaper, the *Bugler*, is a seasonal up-to-date guide to activities and opportunities in Olympic National Park. You can pick these up at the visitor centers, or write to the park superintendent.

Olympic National Park was originally preserved to protect the elk that had been hunted nearly to extinction for their teeth, which were used as watch fobs.

A handy mail-order catalog of books and maps of the park is available from the **Northwest Interpretive Association.** | 3002 Mount Angeles Rd., Port Angeles | 360/565–3195 | http://nwpubliclands.com.

When to Visit

SCENERY AND WILDLIFE

You need good weather to enjoy Olympic's most popular panoramas such as Hurricane Ridge north to Vancouver Island or the seascape at Ruby Beach. Clear skies are common early July–mid-September, and quite possibly in May, June, and October. However, the misty, rain-splashed allure that truly represents the area's character adds indelible atmosphere to the rain forest valleys and the Pacific coastline, even if it obscures distant views. Rain is possible any time of year, but most common November–May.

Many of Olympic's larger wild animals—elk, bear, deer, mountain goats—are most often seen by roadsides and meadow edges at dawn or dusk. While visiting Hurricane Ridge, you'll almost always see goats on the road up and deer at the visitor center during the day. Bears are most commonly seen in May and June, and in fall when they prowl berry patches. Elk summer in the high country and return to lowland valleys in autumn. You must keep in mind that all wild animals are just that—wild—and both people and animals benefit by keeping their distance.

HIGH AND LOW SEASON

June through September are peak months, when more than 75% of visitors visit the park. Its most popular sites, such as Hurricane Ridge, can approach capacity by 10 AM. Crowds are much lighter in May and October, both of which have favorable weather. Winter brings persistent cloudiness, frequent rain and chilly temperatures; crowds are almost nonexistent from Thanksgiving to Easter. On weekends, Hurricane Ridge draws visitors for skiing, snowshoeing, and snow play.

Average High/Low Temperature (°F) and Monthly Precipitation (in inches)

	JAN.	FEB.	MAR.	APR.	MAY	JUNE
OLYMPIC	45/33	48/35	51/36	55/39	60/44	65/48
	4.00	2.60	2.00	1.30	1.00	0.80

	JULY	AUG.	SEPT.	OCT.	NOV.	DEC.
	68/50	69/51	66/48	58/42	50/37	45/34
	00	0.80	1.20	2.30	4.00	4.40

FESTIVALS AND SEASONAL EVENTS

SPRING

Apr.: **Rainfest.** A celebration of arts and crafts inspired by the huge annual rainfall of 100+ inches takes place mid-April, in downtown Forks. | 800/443–6757.

May: **Irrigation Festival.** A more-than-a-century-old event, this is a celebration of the lack of rain in Sequim, which lies in the rain shadow of the Olympic Mountains. See an antique car show, logging demonstrations, arts and crafts, dancing, parade, live music, and more. | 360/683–6197.

Juan de Fuca Festival of the Arts. Port Angeles comes alive each May with four days of music, dance, and theater from around the world, as well as children's programs. | 360/457-5411.

SUMMER

June–Aug.: **Centrum Summer Arts Festival.** A former aircraft hangar in Port Townsend is the arena for this summer-long music and performance festival, whose concerts range from blues to folk. | 360/385–3102.

June–Sept.: **Olympic Music Festival.** Led by the Philadelphia String Quartet, some of the country's most prestigious summer classical music festivals take place in (and around) a barn near Port Townsend. | 206/527–8839.

July: **Fourth of July Celebration.** A salmon bake, a parade, a demolition derby, and arts and crafts exhibits are some of the events at Forks' four-day-long Independence Day festival. | 800/443–6757.

FALL

Sept.: **Historic Homes Tour.** Dozens of Port Townsend's finest Victorian homes are open to the public during this annual event. | 360/385–2722.

Wooden Boat Festival. The weekend after Labor Day brings hundreds of antique boats, and their fans, to a local marina in Port Townsend. | 360/385–3628.

Oct.: **Forks Heritage Days.** Logging skills contests, parades, pancake breakfasts, and other events are devoted to Forks' pioneer past. | 800/443–6757.

Nearby Towns

While most Olympic Peninsula towns have evolved from their once-total reliance on timber, **Forks** remains one of the Northwest's logging capitals. Washington state's wettest town (100 inches or more of rain a year), it is a small (3,500 residents), friendly place with a modicum of visitor facilities, proud of the distinctiveness its heritage and isolation engender, and steadily adding tourism and recreation to its economic base. Not long ago **Port Angeles** was a timber mill town, its livelihood far more dependent on using the Olympic Peninsula's forests than on preserving them. Since timber harvest slowdowns have shut mills and idled workers, the town of 19,000 focuses on its status as the main gateway to Olympic National Park and Victoria, BC. Set along a bench above the Strait of Juan de Fuca, looking north to Vancouver Island, it has an enviably scenic site and is filled with attractive, Craftsman-style homes. The Pacific Northwest has its very own "Banana Belt" in the waterfront community of **Sequim.** The town of 6,000 is located in the rain shadow of the Olympics and receives only 16 inches of rain per year (compared to the 40 inches that drench the Hoh Rain Forest just 40 mi away).

INFORMATION

Forks Chamber of Commerce Visitor Center | 1411 S. Forks Ave. (U.S. 101), Forks, 98331 | 800/443–6757 | www.forkswa.com. **Port Angeles Chamber of Commerce Visitor Center** | 121 E. Railroad Ave., Port Angeles, 98362 | 360/452–2363 | www.cityofpa.com. **Sequim-Dungeness Chamber of Commerce** | Box 907, Sequim 98382 | 360/693-6197 or 800/737-8462 | www.cityofsequim.com.

Exploring Olympic

PARK BASICS

Contacts and Resources: Olympic National Park | 600 East Park Ave., Port Angeles, 98362 | 360/565–3130 | www.nps.gov/olym.

OLYMPIC
NATIONAL PARK

EXPLORING
ATTRACTIONS NEARBY
DINING
LODGING
CAMPING AND RV FACILITIES
SHOPPING
ESSENTIAL INFORMATION

A NEW FRONTIER

In 1890, the Seattle Press financed an expedition to cross the Olympic mountains. Five adventurers headed up the Elwha River by boat—in winter!—and, after an almost impossible four-month trek through chilly water and deep snow, crossed a divide into the Quinault valley and reached the Pacific shore.

Hours: Park entrances are open 24 hours year-round; gate kiosk hours (for buying passes) vary widely according to season and location, but most kiosks are staffed during daylight hours.

Fees: Vehicle admission fee is $10, each individual $5 (for a seven-day pass). An annual pass costs $30. Parking at Ozette, the trailhead for one of the park's most popular hikes, is $1 per day.

Getting Around: U.S. 101 essentially encircles the main section of Olympic National Park, and a number of roads lead from the highway into the park's mountains and toward the park's beaches. You can reach U.S. 101 via I–5 at Olympia, via Route 12 at Aberdeen, or via Route 104 from the Washington State ferry terminals at Bainbridge or Kingston. The ferries are the most direct route to the Olympic area from Seattle. Most routes provide service roughly once an hour, but lines can be lengthy on holiday and summer weekends. Fares vary according to the route, the size of your vehicle, and the number of passengers. Call Washington State ferries at 800/843–3779 or 206/464–6400 for information. You can enter the park at a number of points. Access roads do not penetrate far into the park, which is 95% wilderness. Most follow river valleys, affording few open views. Except on paved roads, motorized vehicles are prohibited throughout Olympic National Park.

Permits: The required overnight wilderness permit, available at visitor centers and ranger stations, costs $5 for registration of your party for up to 14 days, plus $2 per person per night. A frequent-hiker pass is $30 per year. Fishing in freshwater streams and lakes within Olympic National Park does not require a Washington state fishing license; however, anglers must acquire a salmon-steelhead punch card when fishing for those species. Ocean fishing and shellfish and seaweed harvesting require licenses, which are available at sporting goods and outdoor supply stores.

Public Telephones: Public telephones are at the Olympic National Park visitor center, Hoh River Rain Forest visitor center, and the four lodging properties within the park—Lake Crescent, Kalaloch, and Sol Duc Hot Springs. Fairholm General Store also has a phone.

Rest Rooms: There are public rest rooms at visitor centers, interpretive centers, and ranger stations within the park, as well as picnic grounds, campgrounds, and the four lodging properties within the park—Lake Quinault, Lake Crescent, Kalaloch, and Sol Duc Hot Springs.

Accessibility: Wheelchair-accessible facilities are distributed throughout Olympic National Park, including trails at Elwha Valley (Madison Falls, 0.25 mi of Elwha River trail), Hurricane Ridge (Meadow Loop, 1.5 mi of Hurricane Hill trail), Sol Duc Valley (Salmon Cascades Trail), Hoh Rain Forest (Mini-Rain Forest Trail), and Quinault Valley (Maple Glades and Kestner Homestead trails). You'll also find accessible trails at the Olympic National Park visitor center (Living Forest trail), Lake Crescent (Moments in Time, and part of Marymere Falls and Spruce Railroad trails), and at Staircase (Big Cedar Tree and River Viewpoint trails). Short trails enable access to Rialto Beach and Ruby Beach, barring any storm-tossed logs and pebbles.

Campgrounds with accessible facilities, including rest rooms, campsites, picnic tables and amphitheaters, are Fairholm, Heart O' the Hills, Hoh, Kalaloch, Mora, and Sol Duc. Most other campgrounds have accessible rest rooms, except Dosewallips, Graves Creek and Ozette. The National Park visitor center in Port Angeles is fully accessible, as are the centers at Hoh Rain Forest and Hurricane Ridge. Kalaloch Lodge, Lake Crescent Lodge and Sol Duc Hot Springs Resort have accessible facilities that include one or more rooms, restaurant and lodge.

Emergencies: For all park emergencies, dial 360/565–3000 (7 AM–midnight in summer, 7–5:30 off season); after hours dial 911. Park rangers are on duty during daylight hours at Port Angeles visitor center, Hoh Rain Forest visitor center, and Hurricane Ridge visitor center.

Other ranger stations are staffed daily in summer, staff levels permitting; schedules vary in off-season.

Lost and Found: The park's lost-and-found is at the main visitor center in Port Angeles.

Good Tours

OLYMPIC IN ONE DAY

In midsummer, when 18 hours of daylight bathes Olympic National Park and sunset paints the northwest sky past 11 PM, a one-day whirlwind tour can expose an energetic visitor to all three of the park's facets—rain forest, Pacific beach, alpine meadow. Start your day with an early breakfast at **Lake Quinault Lodge,** heading out as early as 7 AM to drive up the **South Shore Road** into the Quinault valley. Keep a watchful eye for deer and elk browsing along the forest edge, arriving a half-hour later at the **Graves Creek Nature Trail.** Meandering among Sitka spruce, Douglas fir, black cottonwood, red alder and bigleaf maple, this trail is at its best with a touch of early morning mist sifting through the trees. Pause for a moment to push aside the forest duff and note how poor the underlying soil is, leached by the constant rains. Returning along the **North Shore Road,** stop at the Quinault Rain Forest Interpretive Trail to learn about the delicate interdependence among rain, sun and fire, plant and animal, which rain forests need to thrive. Head west to U.S. 101, turning north toward Forks. The highway passes through the **Quinault Indian Reservation,** reaching the ocean just past Queets. At **Ruby Beach,** a quick stop to walk down to the beach yields the first glimpse of the sea stacks and headlands that dominate the coast from here north to Cape Flattery.

Returning inland, the highway crosses huge expanses of clear-cuts on National Forest land; the damage wrought by erosion can be seen along gullies and road cuts. Forks, which you'll reach around noon, is a good lunch stop. The **Forks Timber Museum** delineates the traditional perspective on forest products industries in this area. From Forks it's a 20-minute drive down the Sol Duc River to **La Push.** While you're here, stroll down to the surf's edge on one of the three separate beaches and beachcomb a while; watch for sea stars, abalone shells and, in spring and fall, migrating whales offshore. First Beach is the closest to the road, and the smallest beach; Second and Third beaches are about 0.75-mi and 1.5-mi trails, respectively.

After returning to Forks, the drive east along 101 passes through intermittent patches of forest and clear-cut, until you return to the park along the upper Sol Duc. The road winds along the shore to glistening **Lake Crescent,** climbing the foothills to reach **Port Angeles.** After dinner here, head up the **Hurricane Ridge Road,** topping out at the visitor center about 7 or 8 PM. A short hike (3-mi round-trip, takes 1.5 hours) brings you to **Hurricane Hill,** a 5,757-ft promontory from which the panorama north to Vancouver Island, and south into the heart of the park, is magnificent. Using a map and compass, it's possible to pinpoint the tip of Mount Olympus 12 mi south. By now the summer sun is churning into the Pacific to the northwest, invariably painting half the sky vermilion and lavender. Be sure to head back down to the parking lot before dark.

OLYMPIC IN THREE DAYS

Start at **Port Angeles,** heading up to **Hurricane Ridge** early to beat the crowds and watch the sun climb up over the easterly ridges. Then head west on 101 to **Lake Crescent,** stopping for a (bracing but quite worthwhile) swim at East Beach, which faces south into the sun. Have lunch at the **Lake Crescent Lodge,** and then drive up the Sol Duc Road, stopping to spy salmon jumping at **Salmon Cascades.** Wind up the afternoon at **Sol Duc Hot Springs Resort,** allowing time for long soaks both before and after dinner.

On the morning of day two, head on through Forks and out the La Push Road, stopping at the **Third Beach trailhead** about 11 mi from Forks. It's a 15-minute hike down to the beach, but you'll want to spend a couple hours strolling the sand, maybe even hiking

OLYMPIC
NATIONAL PARK

EXPLORING
ATTRACTIONS NEARBY
DINING
LODGING
CAMPING AND RV
FACILITIES
SHOPPING
ESSENTIAL
INFORMATION

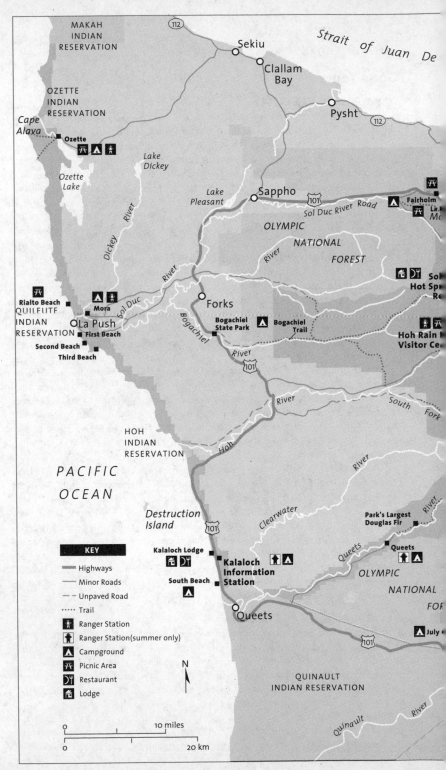

MAKAH
INDIAN
RESERVATION

Strait of Juan De

Sekiu

Clallam
Bay

Pysht

OZETTE
INDIAN
RESERVATION

Cape
Alava

Ozette

Lake
Dickey

Lake
Pleasant

Sappho

Fairholm

Sol Duc River Road

Ozette
Lake

Dickey River

River

OLYMPIC

NATIONAL

FOREST

Sol Duc River

River

Sol
Hot Sp
Re

Rialto Beach

Mora

QUILEUTE

INDIAN
RESERVATION

La Push

First Beach

Second Beach

Third Beach

Sol Duc

Bogachiel

River

Forks

Bogachiel
State Park

Bogachiel
Trail

Hoh Rain
Visitor Ce

River

River

South Fork

HOH
INDIAN
RESERVATION

Hoh

PACIFIC
OCEAN

Destruction
Island

Clearwater River

Park's Largest
Douglas Fir

Queets

River

OLYMPIC

NATIONAL

FOR

KEY

Highways

Minor Roads

Unpaved Road

Trail

Ranger Station

Ranger Station(summer only)

Campground

Picnic Area

Restaurant

Lodge

Kalaloch Lodge

South Beach

Kalaloch
Information
Station

Queets

July

N

QUINAULT
INDIAN RESERVATION

Quinault River

0   10 miles
|_____|_____|
0   20 km

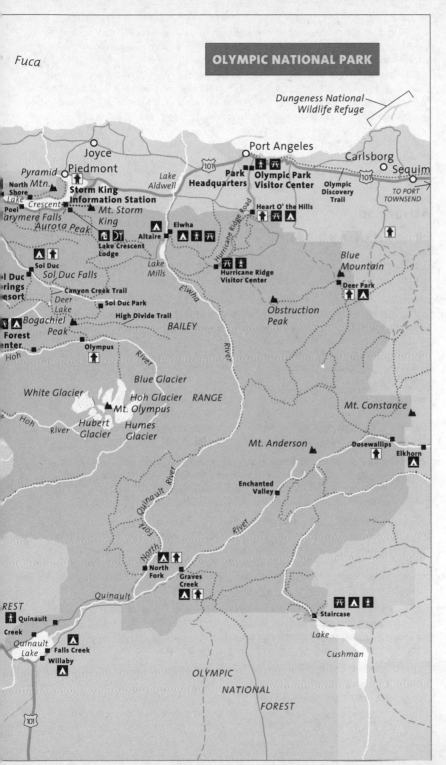

OLYMPIC NATIONAL PARK

Fuca

Dungeness National
Wildlife Refuge

Joyce

Port Angeles

Carlsborg

Sequim

Pyramid
Mtn.
Piedmont
Park
Headquarters
Olympic Park
Visitor Center
Olympic
Discovery
Trail

North
Shore
Lake
Storm King
Information Station
Lake
Aldwell

TO PORT
TOWNSEND

Poel
Crescent

Mt. Storm
King

Heart O' the Hills

arymere Falls

Aurora Peak

Altaire

Elwha

Hurricane Ridge Road

Blue
Mountain

l Duc
rings
esort

Sol Duc

Lake Crescent
Lodge

Lake
Mills

Deer Park

Sol Duc Falls

Canyon Creek Trail

Elwha
River

Hurricane Ridge
Visitor Center

Deer
Lake

Sol Duc Park

High Divide Trail

Obstruction
Peak

BAILEY

Bogachiel
Peak

Forest
nter.

Olympus

River

Mt. Constance

Hoh

Blue Glacier

White Glacier

Hoh Glacier

RANGE

Hoh
River

Mt. Olympus

Hubert
Glacier

Humes
Glacier

Mt. Anderson

Dosewallips

Elkhorn

Quinault River

Enchanted
Valley

River

North Fork

North
Fork

Graves
Creek

REST

Quinault

Creek

Quinault
Lake

Falls Creek

Willaby

Quinault

Staircase

Lake

Cushman

OLYMPIC

NATIONAL

FOREST

OLYMPIC
NATIONAL PARK

EXPLORING
ATTRACTIONS NEARBY
DINING
LODGING
CAMPING AND RV
FACILITIES
SHOPPING
ESSENTIAL
INFORMATION

up and over **Taylor Point,** the headland to the south. Be sure to look for sea otters in the kelp beds just offshore. After a picnic lunch on the beach, head back to Forks and south on 101, stopping for a swim at **Bogachiel State Park** if it's a warm day. Wind up the day with dinner and a room at **Kalaloch Lodge.**

The third day is for rain forest exploration. Start by heading south on 101, then up North Shore Road at Lake Quinault to stop at the **Quinault Rain Forest Interpretive Nature Trail** to learn about the delicate balance of the rain forest ecology. Then head up Quinault River Road to the **Graves Creek trailhead**—watch for elk along the road—and a half-day hike up the Quinault valley, an easy, pleasant stroll in old-growth fir, cedar, and hemlock forest. Stop for another picnic lunch, but this time look for a downed cedar log along the river to use as a picnic table. Very dedicated and energetic hikers who make an early start can climb out of rain forest into alpine territory about 10 mi up the trail. However far you go, head back in late afternoon to wind up the day at **Lake Quinault Lodge.**

Attractions

PROGRAMS AND TOURS

Many park campgrounds host summertime programs such as evening campfire talks. Schedules vary widely, according to sunset times and park staffing. For up-to-date information, check with the park's main visitor center in Port Angeles.

★**Beach Walks.** Beach walks at Kalaloch and Rialto Beach are scheduled according to tides and posted on bulletin boards at the beach trailhead parking lots and at nearby campgrounds and visitor centers. You can access Kalaloch beach at six major trailheads. | Kalaloch Beach: 2 mi south of the Kalaloch Information Station to 8 mi north; Rialto Beach: Rte. 110, 14 mi west of Forks, 1 mi west of Mora Ranger Station | 360/962–2283 Kalaloch Beach, 360/374–5460 Rialto Beach | Free | Schedules vary according to tides, seasons, and park staffing levels.

Children's Activities. Heart O' the Hills Campground has children's activities ranging from guided nature walks to evening campfire talks. Consult campground bulletin boards for exact schedules. | 3 mi south of the main visitor center, Port Angeles | 360/565–3130 | Free | Schedules vary according to seasons and park staffing levels.

★**Junior Ranger Program.** This program provides children with an activity booklet that explains tide pools, wildlife activities, and Native American lore. On completion of assigned activities, children receive a badge. Booklets are available at park visitor centers, information centers, and most ranger stations. | 360/565–3130 | Small donation requested.

Olympic Park Institute. The institute runs seminars on various aspects of park ecology, history, native culture, and arts such as writing, painting, and photography. It also organizes one- to five-day hiking and guided backpacking trips in summer and fall, as well as whale- and bird-watching in spring. Classes are led by wildlife experts, local artists, and park rangers. | 111 Barnes Point Rd., Port Angeles | 360/928–3720 or 800/775–3720 | $12–$290 | Late March–early Nov.

★**Rain Forest Walks.** Park naturalists describe the obvious rain forest features such as old-growth cedars and firs, and the not-so-obvious such as the tree-dwelling lichens that extract nitrogen from the atmosphere and ultimately transfer it to the forest soil. | Hoh River Road, 18 mi east of U.S. 101 | 360/565–3130 | Free | Schedules vary according to seasons and park staffing levels.

SCENIC DRIVES

Port Angeles to Fairholm. The last 10 mi of U.S. 101 between these towns winds along Lake Crescent. Although it's actually at a fairly low elevation, the long, gem-clear lake amid mountain ridges seems like a high-mountain scene.

★ **Port Angeles Visitor Center to Hurricane Ridge.** Climbing steeply to 5,242 ft, from thick fir forest in the foothills and subalpine meadow below the ridge to alpine meadow at the top, this is the premier scenic drive in Olympic National Park. However, the route's popularity often means road congestion, especially in summer. Along the way, ever-larger panoramas of the mountains ahead and the Strait of Juan de Fuca behind reveal themselves. At the top, the visitor center at Hurricane Ridge has some truly spectacular views of the heart of the mountains and across the Strait of Juan de Fuca. (Backpackers note wryly that you have to hike a long way in other parts of the park to get the kinds of views you can drive to at Hurricane Ridge.) Hurricane Ridge also has an uncommonly fine display of wildflowers in spring and summer, including columbines, monkey flowers, geum, lupine, larkspur, avalanche lily, glacier lily, fireweed, and wild sweet pea.

Rain Forest Drives. The best rain forest drives are up Lake Quinault River Road, Hoh River Road, and the Queet. All three have long passages through rain forest, including stretches of moss-draped maples and alders.

Ruby Beach to Queets. On this shore-hugging stretch of U.S. 101, periodic views of the Pacific and long expanses of coastal spruce forest unfold.

Strait of Juan de Fuca National Scenic Byway The Strait of Juan de Fuca Highway (Rte. 112) hugs the shoreline of a glacial fjord that connects Puget Sound to the Pacific Ocean. The 61-mi drive takes about two hours.

SIGHTS TO SEE

★ **Hoh Rain Forest.** South of Forks, an 18-mi spur road leads from U.S. 101 to Hoh Rain Forest, with spruce and hemlock trees soaring to heights of more than 200 ft. Alders and big-leaf maples are so densely covered with moss that they look more like shaggy prehistoric animals than trees. The visitor center has information that explains how the forest functions and has short trails leading among the trees. Watch for elk browsing in shaded glens. | Upper Hoh Rd., 18 mi east of U.S. 101 | 360/565–3130 | Sept.–May, often unstaffed.

★ **Hurricane Ridge.** The panoramic view from this 5,200-ft-high ridge encompasses the Olympic range, the Strait of Juan de Fuca, and Vancouver Island. Guided tours are given in summer along the many paved and unpaved trails, where wildflowers and wildlife such as deer and marmots flourish. This most popular spot in the park is often packed on summer days and weekends. | Hurricane Ridge Road, 17 mi south of Port Angeles | 360/565–3130 | Visitor center daily 10–5.

Kalaloch. With a lodge, huge campground, miles of beach to stroll, and easy access from the highway, which parallels the coast here, this is one of the park's most popular visitor spots. Keen-eyed beachcombers may spot sea otters just offshore; they were reintroduced here in 1970. | U.S. 101, 32 mi northwest of Lake Quinault | 360/962–2283.

Lake Crescent. Almost everyone who visits the park sees Lake Crescent, as the highway winds along its south shore. The cold, clear blue, mountain-ringed lake is unlike some of the tannic-water lakes on the west side of the park, and has long been a popular summer getaway for swimming, boating, and fishing. | U.S. 101, 16 mi west of Port Angeles | 360/928–3380.

★ **Lake Quinault.** Glimmering Lake Quinault is the first landmark you reach when driving the west-side loop of 101. Here are the famed historic lodge, several public and private campgrounds, the lake itself, and a scenic loop drive, which circles the lake and heads up both mountain forks of the Quinault River. The rain forest is at its densest and wettest here, with moss-draped maples and alders and towering spruces, firs, and hemlocks. Popular nature trails wind through the woods at several spots in the valley. | U.S. 101, 42 mi north of Aberdeen | 360/288–2444 | Ranger-Information station, May–Sept., daily 8–5.

La Push. At the mouth of Quileute River, La Push is the tribal center of the Quileute Indians. In fact, the town's name is a variation on the French *la bouche,* which means "the mouth".

OLYMPIC
NATIONAL PARK

EXPLORING
ATTRACTIONS NEARBY
DINING
LODGING
CAMPING AND RV
FACILITIES
SHOPPING
ESSENTIAL
INFORMATION

Offshore rock spires known as sea stacks dot the coast here, and you may catch a glimpse of bald eagles nesting in the nearby cliffs. | Rte. 110, 14 mi west of Forks.

★ **Ozette.** This small town, home of a coastal tribe, is the trailhead for two of the park's better one-day hikes. Three-mile trails lead over boardwalks through swampy wetland and coastal old-growth forest to the ocean shore and uncrowded beach. The northernmost trail reaches shore at Cape Alava, westernmost point in the continental United States. Lake Ozette is a deep glacial impoundment, the third largest in Washington state, popular for canoeing and kayaking. The boardwalk trails are often slippery in wet weather. | At the end of Hoko-Ozette Rd., 26 mi southwest of Rte. 112 west of Sekiu | 360/963–2725 | Ranger station Sept.–May, often unstaffed.

Second and Third Beaches. During low tide, the tide pools here brim with life, and you can walk out to some sea stacks. Gray whales play offshore during their annual spring migration, and most of the year the waves are great for surfing and kayaking (if you bring a wet suit). This is the car-accessible site most like the spectacular wilderness coast that stretches 50 mi northward from here. | U.S. 101, 32 mi north of Lake Quinault | 360/374–5460.

Sol Duc. Sol Duc Valley is one of those magical, serene places where all the Northwest's virtues seem at hand—lush lowland forest, a sparkling, cheery river, salmon runs, and quiet hiking trails. The popular Sol Duc Hot Springs (open to both resort guests and day visitors) and adjacent resort have been attracting visitors for more than a century. | Sol Duc Rd. south of U.S. 101, 1 mi past the west end of Lake Crescent | 360/374–6925.

Staircase. Unlike the forests of the park's south and west sides, Douglas fir is the dominant tree here on the east slope of the Olympic Mountains. Fire has played an important role in creating the majestic forest here, a role the Staircase Ranger Station explains in interpretive exhibits. | At end of Rte. 119, 15 mi from U.S. 101 at Hoodsport | 360/877–5569.

Sports and Outdoor Activities

BEACHCOMBING

★ Engage your soul as well as your body by observing tide pools, keeping your eyes peeled for sea otters, seals, eagles, and other shoreline denizens, and just generally letting your mind relax. However, beachcombers need to be alert for wave-rolled logs—which periodically shift, sometimes even when struck by fairly small waves—and the rare but highly hazardous rogue waves, which can be two or three times as large as regular surf. Best and most easily accessible nonwilderness beaches are Rialto; First and Second near Mora and La Push; Ruby Beach; and Beach 4 and 2 in the Kalaloch stretch.

BICYCLING

The Quinault Valley, Queets River, Hoh River, and Sol Duc River roads have bike paths through old-growth forest. U.S. 101, which carries very heavy truck and RV traffic, is not recommended for leisure bicycling.

CLIMBING

Mount Olympus and other peaks in the park are very popular with climbers, partly because they are rugged and quite challenging, but not overly high (Olympus, the tallest, tops out at 7,965 ft). Do get expert advice from rangers before setting out. The mountains are steep, the landscape is broken up by escarpments and ridges, and there are bridgeless creeks and rivers to cross. It's easy to take a fall or to get lost (which happens every year to inexperienced hikers and climbers). All climbers are asked to register with park officials before setting out.

FISHING

Rainbow and cutthroat trout are found in the park's streams and lakes. Salmon ply the rivers and shores; a special Washington state punch card is needed to fish for anadromous fish. The Bogachiel, Hoh, Quinault, Skokomish, and Dosewallips rivers are world-famed steelhead streams. Fishing regulations vary throughout the park; check regulations for each location. Licenses are available from sporting goods and outdoor supply stores.

HIKING

★ Many of the park's most precious treasures are accessible only on foot. Wilderness beaches provide the park's most unusual hiking experience: an opportunity to explore a green Pacific coastline essentially unaltered by humans. Raccoons waddle from the forest to pluck dinner from the tide pools; bald eagles stoop over fantastic tangles of bleached drift-logs, the bones of ancient forests. Entry points are La Push, Rialto Beach, and Cape Alava. Advance preparation is essential; it's imperative that hikers learn to read and understand tide tables lest they be trapped by the ocean.

Inside the park, it's backpacking that reveals its deepest facets. The trailheads embedded in the long, forested river valleys provide perfect warm-ups for the intense climbs into alpine country that await after 6–12 mi of walking. The Elwha, Dosewallips, Skokomish, Quinault, Hoh, and Sol Duc valleys all have developed trails that wend their way upstream, finally climbing into high passes and a glacier-rimmed alpine basin where they link up with each other. Hikes up to two weeks are possible. A wilderness use permit ($5) is required for all overnight backcountry visits. Contact the park's Wilderness Information Center.

Olympic National Park abounds in short exploratory walks showcasing various aspects of the park. Every campground and road-end in the park has short, established, and relatively easy trails suitable for one- to six-hour hikes.

Boulder Creek Trail. A popular day hike is the 5-mi round-trip walk up Boulder Creek from the Elwha River to Olympic Hot Springs, a half-dozen pools of varying temperatures (some of which are clothing-optional). | End of the Elwha River Road, 4 mi south of Altaire campground.

Cape Alva Trail. Beginning at Ozette, this 3-mi trail leads from forest to wave-tossed headlands. Be careful of the often slippery boardwalks. | End of the Hoko-Ozette Road, 26 mi south of Rte. 112, west of Sekiu.

Graves Creek Trail. This 6-mi moderately strenuous climb winds from lowland rain forest to alpine territory at Sundown Pass. A fiord halfway up is often impassable in May and June. | End of south Quinault Valley Road, 23 mi east of U.S. 101.

High Divide Trail. A 9-mi hike in the park's high country defines this trail, which includes some strenuous climbing on its last 4 mi before it tops out at a small alpine lake. A return loop along High Divide wends its way an extra mile through alpine territory with sensational views of Olympic peaks. This trail is only for dedicated hikers in good shape, properly equipped. | End of Sol Duc River Road, 13 mi south of U.S. 101.

Hoh Valley Trail. Leaving from the Hoh Visitor Center, this rain forest jaunt takes you into the Hoh Valley, wending its way through deep cedar/fir forests, along open meadows where elk roam in winter, and through moss-draped stands of maple and alder. | Hoh Visitor Center, 18 mi east of U.S. 101.

Hurricane Ridge. A 0.25-mi alpine loop, most of it wheelchair-accessible, leads through wildflower meadows overlooking numerous vistas of the interior Olympic peaks to the south and the Strait of Juan de Fuca panorama to the north. | Hurricane Ridge visitor center, Hurricane Ridge Road, 17 mi south of Port Angeles.

Sol Duc Trail. This 3-mi stroll along the Sol Duc River traverses dense, north-slope cedar and fir rain forest to Sol Duc Falls, a small but scenic cataract at which spawning salmon can sometimes be seen. | Sol Duc Rd., 11 mi south of U.S. 101.

KAYAKING AND CANOEING

Lake Crescent, Lake Ozette, and Lake Quinault are all open to kayaking and canoeing. Ozette, a large lake with road access only at one corner, is an opportunity for overnight

OLYMPIC
NATIONAL PARK

EXPLORING
ATTRACTIONS NEARBY
DINING
LODGING
CAMPING AND RV
FACILITIES
SHOPPING
ESSENTIAL
INFORMATION

trips, although only experienced canoe and kayak handlers should travel far from the put-in, as fierce storms occasionally strike, even in summer.

Fairholm General Store. Rowboats, canoes, kayaks, and motorboats are available to rent for day use on Lake Crescent. The store is on the west end of the lake, 27 mi west of Port Angeles. | U.S. 101, Fairholm | 360/928–3020 | $10–$70 | D, MC, V | May–Sept., daily 9–6.

Log Cabin Resort. Log Cabin's rental operations and boat dock afford easy access to Crescent Lake's quieter northeast section. It's on the lake's east arm. | Piedmont Road, off U.S. 101, 17 mi west of Port Angeles | 360/928–3325 | $10–$30 | MC, V | May–Sept., daily 9–6.

SKIING AND SNOWSHOEING

The best conditions for winter sports in the park are from mid-December through late March. The most popular route for day mushers is the 1.5-mi Hurricane Hill road, west of the visitor center parking area. A marked snow–play area with trails and gentle hills has been set aside near the visitor center for cross-country skiers, snowshoers, inner tubers, and children. For recorded road and weather information November–April, call 360/565–3131. Ski and snowshoe rentals ($12–$35) are available at the visitor center.

SWIMMING

Lake Crescent has the park's nicest freshwater beach, East Beach on the north shore. Although visitors are warned that the Pacific is cold and treacherous (and it can be), hardy souls do go in at Kalaloch, La Push, and along the wilderness shores. The park's rivers, virtually all of which arise in glacial basins, are bracingly cold.

Attractions Nearby

7 Cedars Casino. The Jamestown S'Klallam tribe's enormous yet oddly subdued casino has blackjack, roulette, and slots—in addition to live entertainment. One end of the casino is devoted to bingo. The tribe also runs an art gallery and gift shop. | 270756 U.S. 101, Sequim | 360/683–7777 | www.7cedarscasino.com | Weekdays 10 AM–2 AM, weekends 10 AM–3 AM.

Clallam County Historical Museum. Temporarily housed in the Clallam County Federal Building, the museum presents an engaging exhibition detailing the lifestyles and history of Port Angeles's Native American and Anglo communities. Plans are underway for the museum to move into Port Angeles' Carnegie Library (1220 Lawrence St.) in early 2004. | 138 W. 1st St., Port Angeles | 360/452–2662 | Free | Weekdays 10–4.

★**Dungeness Spit.** Sheltering the bay from the crashing surf, this 8-mi spit (one of the longest in the world) extends to the Dungeness Lighthouse, in operation since 1867. The finger of land is also a temporary home to at least 30,000 migratory waterfowl each year (spring and fall are the best viewing times, but many species live here in summer). | Kitchen Rd., 4 mi west of Sequim | 360/457–8451 | $3 | Wildlife refuge daily dawn–dusk, campground Feb.–Sept.

Heritage & Underground Tours. Port Angeles has seen many changes to its downtown since the late 1800s, one of the most remarkable of which is the lifting of the flood-prone town in 1914. Dirt was brought in to raise the streets by 10 to 14 ft; some buildings were hoisted onto pilings and others turned their former ground floors into basements. On a walking tour you can see remnants of the underground district that was created, complete with subterranean sidewalks and a former brothel. | 121 Railroad Ave., Port Angeles | 360/452–2363 Ext. 101 | $8 | Mon.–Sat. 10–2.

★**Jamestown S'Klallam Village.** An Indian village, not a reservation, on the beach north of Sequim Bay, this site has been occupied by S'Klallams for thousands of years. The S'Klallams had been driven out by early settlers and relocated to the Skokomish Reservation on the Hood Canal, but in 1874, tribal leader James Balch, followed by 130 S'Klallam, regained the site by paying hard cash for it. The S'Klallam have lived here ever since. A gallery sells regional arts and crafts. | U.S. 101, 4 mi south of Sequim | Free | Daily.

★ **Olympic Discovery Trail.** Eventually, 100 mi of nonmotorized trail will lead from Port Townsend west to the Pacific Coast. As of this writing, 32 mi of the trail are complete (a few miles near Port Townsend, a few miles near Sequim, and around 20 mi near and in Port Angeles). The trail has been conceived as the northern portion of a trail that will eventually encircle the entire Olympic Peninsula. | 360/457–8451 | www.olympicdiscoverytrail. com | Free.

Port Angeles Fine Arts Center. A small but surprisingly sophisticated museum is tucked away inside the former home of artist and publisher Esther Barrows Webster, one of Port Angeles's most energetic citizens. Outdoor sculpture and trees surround the center, which has panoramic views of the city and harbor. Exhibitions emphasize the works of emerging and well-established Pacific Northwest artists in various media. | 1203 E. Lauridsen Blvd., Port Angeles | 360/457–3532 | Free | Thurs.–Sun. 11–5, and by appointment.

Sequim Bay State Park. Protected by a sand spit 4 mi southwest of Sequim on Sequim Bay, this woodsy inlet park has picnic tables, campsites, hiking trails, tennis courts, and a boat ramp. | U.S. 101, Sequim | 360/683–4235 | www.parks.wa.gov | Free, camping $15–$21 | Daily 8–dusk.

Dining

In Olympic

★ **Kalaloch Lodge.** American. You can count on finding fresh seafood and well-aged beef at this popular seaside resort, just within the southern boundary of the park's coastal strip. The menu changes seasonally, but it's hard to go wrong with the local oysters, crab, and salmon, often served baked or broiled with a simple lemon-butter sauce. Dinner is also served in the upstairs cocktail lounge—which, like the restaurant, has unobstructed ocean views. | U.S. 101, Kalaloch | 360/962–2271 | $12–$23 | AE, MC, V.

★ **Lake Crescent Lodge.** American. Part of the original 1916 lodge (21 mi west of Port Angeles), the fir-paneled dining room overlooks the lake; you also won't find a better spot for a spectacular view of the sunset. A variety of seafood entrées complement the classic American dishes. | 416 Lake Crescent Rd., Port Angeles | 360/928–3211 | $15–$25 | AE, D, DC, MC, V | Closed mid-Oct.–mid-Apr.

Picnic Areas. All Olympic National Park campgrounds have adjacent picnic areas with tables, some shelters, and rest rooms but no cooking facilities. The same is true for major visitor centers such as Hoh Rain Forest. Drinking water is available at ranger stations, interpretive centers, and inside campgrounds.

East Beach Picnic Area. Set on a grassy meadow overlooking Lake Crescent, this popular swimming spot has six picnic tables and vault toilets. | U.S. 101, 17 mi west of Port Angeles, at the far east end of Lake Crescent.

La Poel Picnic Area. Tall firs lean over a tiny gravel beach at this small picnic area, with five picnic tables and a splendid view of Pyramid Mountain across Lake Crescent. | U.S. 101, 22 mi west of Port Angeles.

North Shore Picnic Area. Beneath Pyramid Mountain lies this picnic site along the north shore of Lake Crescent. A steep trail leads from the picnic ground to the top of Pyramid. Facilities include eight picnic tables and a vault toilet. | North Shore Rd., 3 mi east of Fairholm.

Rialto Beach Picnic Area. Relatively secluded at the end of the road from Forks, this is one of the premier day-use areas in the park's Pacific Coast segment. This site has 12 picnic tables, fire grills, and vault toilets. | Rte. 110, 14 mi west of Forks.

Sol Duc Hot Springs Resort. American. The attractive fir-and-cedar paneled dining room serves unpretentious and healthful meals (breakfast, lunch, and dinner) drawing on the best of the Northwest: salmon, crab, fresh vegetables, and fruit. | Soleduck Rd. and U.S. 101,

OLYMPIC
NATIONAL PARK

EXPLORING
ATTRACTIONS NEARBY
DINING
LODGING
CAMPING AND RV
FACILITIES
SHOPPING
ESSENTIAL
INFORMATION

Port Angeles | 360/327–3583 | fax 360/327–3398 | $11–$17 | AE, D, MC, V | Closed mid-Oct.– mid-May.

Near the Park

Bella Italia. Café. Traditional Italian cuisine is served with a smile in a warm candlelit set- ting. Get into the spirit of Italy with the espresso-smoked duck breast or warm up after a day of beach combing with a steaming bowl of cioppino prepared with fresh-caught seafood. They also serve Sunday brunch. | 118 E. 1st St., Port Angeles | 360/457–5442 | $9– $20 | AE, D, DC, MC, V | No lunch.

C'est Si Bon. French. The Olympic Peninsula's most elegant dining room exudes a playful ambience, with its bold red walls and large European oil paintings. The food is ambitiously French but sometimes uneven in quality. The wine list is superb. A romantic balcony over- looks the room with four small tables, and views of the rose garden and the Olympic Moun- tains add to the allure. | 23 Cedar Park Dr., Port Angeles | 360/452–8888 | $19–$25 | AE, D, DC, MC, V | Closed Mon. No lunch.

★ **Fountain Café.** Café. Artwork and creative knickknacks fill this small, funky café. Old stan- dards such as oysters Dorado remain by popular demand, but plenty of innovative regional dishes pepper the menu. Look for seafood and pasta specialties with imaginative twists such as smoked salmon in light cream sauce with hint of scotch. | 920 Washington St., Port Townsend | 360/385–1364 | Reservations not accepted | $11–$20 | MC, V | Closed Tues. in winter.

Khu Larb Thai. Thai. In the land of crab shacks and roadside burger stands, ethnic food can be spotty in quality, but not here. Some of the state's best Thai food is prepared at this unassuming restaurant, which also has a location in Sequim. Taking advantage of local bounty, the kitchen turns out fresh seafood with dishes like salmon with garlic sauce, or tender fresh halibut with curry sauce. The restaurant's signature black rice pudding is a dessert way beyond the usual coconut ice cream of mainstream Thai menus. | 225 Adams St., Port Townsend | 360/385–5023 | $8–$18 | AE, MC, V | Closed Mon.

La Casita. Mexican. This family-run Mexican restaurant overlooking Port Angeles harbor leans heavily on old standbys and combination plates, but what sets it apart is its artful use of local fish. Try the seafood chimichanga, a crisp-fried burrito filled with Dungeness crab, bay shrimp, fresh cod, Monterey jack cheese, tomato, and chilies. | 203 E. Front St., Port Angeles | 360/452–2289 | $7–$14 | AE, D, MC, V.

★ **Marina Restaurant.** American/Casual. With tremendous views of John Wayne Marina and Sequim Bay, this family restaurant is a fun place to watch the ships placidly sail by. The menu includes seafood, pasta, salads, and sandwiches, but the emphasis is on steak, especially prime rib, which is served on Saturday night. | 2577 W. Sequim Bay Rd., Sequim | 360/681–0577 | $11–$18 | AE, D, MC, V | Closed Tues. in winter.

Oak Table Café. American/Casual. Focusing primarily on breakfast dishes, this restaurant imparts an inventive flair to such traditional items as pancakes, waffles, and eggs. Try the eggs Benny, a toasted English muffin topped with country sausage, a poached egg, and blanket of homemade mushroom sauce served with fresh-grated potato pancakes. Although breakfast is served all day, a lunch menu includes burgers, salads, and sandwiches. | 292 W. Bell St., Sequim | 360/683–2179 | $6–$9 | AE, D, MC, V | No dinner.

Salal Café. American. Ample breakfasts are served around the clock on Sunday at this infor- mal, brightly lit restaurant known for its hearty morning meals of omelets and pancakes. The lunch menu consists of standard American fare, with plenty of vegetarian options. Dinners are more exotic, with such entrées as tofu Stroganoff, mushroom risotto with oys- ters, and curried sea scallops. Try to get a table in the glassed-in back room, which faces a plant-filled courtyard. | 634 Water St., Port Townsend | 360/385–6532 | Reservations not accepted | $6–$15 | No credit cards | No dinner Tues. or Thurs.

★ **Shanghai Restaurant.** Chinese. The peninsula's best Chinese food is served here. Highlights include specialties from Szechuan and Hunan, most ranging from spicy to volcanic. Popular favorites are the gingery kung pao shrimp, fresh salmon smothered in brown oyster sauce and brought sizzling to your table, and Shanghai's signature hot-and-sour soup. | 265 Point Hudson, Port Townsend | 360/385–4810 | $6–$10 | D, DC, MC, V.

Smoke House Restaurant. Steak. Since 1975, this restaurant has operated as a smoke-house, serving such popular items as smoked salmon. Steak is a specialty, and the prime rib is especially delicious. The interior, with its rough paneled walls and pictures of the local scenery, exude a rustic warmth, perfectly matching the surrounding countryside. | 193161 U.S. 101, Forks | 360/374–6258 | $10–$20 | D, MC, V | No lunch weekends.

★ **Three Crabs.** Seafood. An institution since 1958, this large crab shack on the beach, 5 mi north of Sequim, specializes in Dungeness's famed specialty. Although you can have clawed creatures served many ways, because these crabs are so fresh, it's best to have them the simple way: with lemon and butter. One crab fills the plate and is more than enough for an entire meal. The large menu also accommodates nonseafood eaters and children. The ambience is vaguely nautical, with knotty-pine walls and views of New Dungeness Bay. | 11 Three Crabs Rd., Sequim | 360/683–4264 | $10–$22 | MC, V | Closed Tues. in winter.

Toga's International Cuisine. Eclectic. Toga's serves an eclectic collection of dishes, ranging from German to Pacific Rim, including crabmeat Rockefeller, aged prime rib, traditional Swiss cheese fondue (with 24-hour notice), and New Zealand rack of lamb. Windows open to a view of the Olympic Mountains. You can dine inside or in the open air on the patio, with wooden chairs and umbrellas. | 122 W. Lauridsen Blvd., Port Angeles | 360/452–1952 | Reservations essential | $16–$26 | MC, V | Closed Sun.–Mon.

Lodging

In Olympic

★ **Kalaloch Lodge.** On a low bluff overlooking the Pacific, just inside the southern boundary of Olympic's coastal strip, sits this cedar-sided two-story lodge. The informal lodge has eight rooms; in addition, 40 small cabins and a modern 10-room minimotel, Sea Crest House, straggle southward along the crest. The cabins are unadorned and rustic, but comfortable; most have terrific ocean views and fireplaces. Decor tends toward knotty pine and earth tones, with deep comfortable couches looking seaward out of picture windows. Cabins 1 through 16 and the Macy and Overly cabins have the best ocean views. Restaurant. Kitchenettes. Library. No room phones. No room TVs. | U.S. 101, HC 80, Box 1100, Forks | 360/962–2271 | 18 rooms, 40 cabins | $89–$258 | AE, MC, V.

★ **Lake Crescent Lodge.** Deep in the forest at the foot of Mount Storm King, with a broad veranda and picture windows framing a view of the brilliant aquamarine waters, historic Lake Crescent Lodge has been beguiling visitors to the peninsula since 1916. There are 30 motel rooms, 17 modern cabins, and five lodge rooms, all but the latter with private bath. The grand old, two-story cedar-shingle lodge has an acceptable restaurant and a lively lounge; rooms are clean, functional, and heavy on hand-rubbed wood. Four of the cabins have fireplaces; all have small, private porches. Restaurant. Boating. No room phones. No room TVs. | Barnes Point, south side of Lake Crescent (follow signs from U.S. 101), HC 62, Box 11, Port Angeles | 360/928–3211 | www.lakecrescentlodge.com | 35 rooms, 17 cabins (5 rooms share 2 baths) | $50–$175 | AE, DC, MC, V | Closed Nov.–late Apr.

★ **Lake Quinault Lodge.** Set on a perfect glacial lake in the midst of the Olympic National Forest, the lodge is within walking distance of spectacular old-growth forests and Lake Quinault, where there's abundant salmon and trout fishing. The complex consists of a medium-size central lodge with 33 rooms, 16 fireplace units attached to the lodge, and 43 units in the lakeside addition, a half block away on the lake. The main lodge was built in 1926 of cedar shingles. Though rooms are sparsely furnished and lack the sophistication of the

OLYMPIC
NATIONAL PARK

EXPLORING
ATTRACTIONS NEARBY
DINING
LODGING
CAMPING AND RV
FACILITIES
SHOPPING
ESSENTIAL
INFORMATION

grand lobby, all have antique furniture and a large stone fireplace, and most have views of the lawns and lake beyond. The restaurant is excellent, and there's an old-fashioned, lively bar. Hiking and jogging trails begin right across the street. Restaurant. Pool. Hot tub, sauna. Boating. Bar. | South Shore Rd. (follow signs from U.S. 101), Box 7, Quinault | 360/288–2900 or 800/562–6672 | 92 rooms | $89–$129 | AE, MC, V.

Log Cabin Resort. Amid an idyllic setting at the northeast end of Lake Crescent sits this rustic hostelry. Settle into one of the A-frame chalet units, standard cabins, "camping cabins" (wooden tents with shared bathroom), motel units, or RV sites, which include full hookups. Some rooms have full kitchens. Twelve of the units are on the lake. You can rent paddleboats or kayaks to use by the day. Restaurant. Dock. Fishing. Laundry facilities. | 3183 E. Beach Rd., Port Angeles | 360/928–3325 | 28 units, 4 cabins, 40 RV | $59–$129 | D, MC, V | Closed Nov.–Mar.

★ **Sol Duc Hot Springs Resort.** This resort lies deep in the brooding forest along the Sol Duc River, surrounded by 5,000-ft mountains. Bubbling, steaming sulfur springs fill the three large outdoor pools, which range from 98°F to 106°F. Nearby is a swimming pool, filled with slightly warmed glacial runoff. The resort was built in 1910; a 1988 renovation added fresh paint and bathrooms to each unit. Rooms are functional, even spartan, but after a day's hiking in the rugged Seven Lakes Basin nearby, a dip in the pool, and dinner at the surprisingly sophisticated restaurant in the lodge, you'll hardly notice. Restaurant. Some kitchenettes. Pool. Bar. | Sol Duc River Rd. (follow signs from U.S. 101 between Forks and Port Angeles), Box 2169, Port Angeles | 360/327–3583 | 32 rooms, 6 cabins | $112–$132 | AE, D, MC, V | Closed Oct.–mid-May.

Near the Park

★ **Colette's Bed and Breakfast.** On a gorgeous waterfront property overlooking the Strait of Juan de Fuca, 10 mi east of Port Angeles, sits this contemporary B&B. The rooms, which overlook the water, have contemporary luxury furnishings with a range of modern amenities. Eagles, fox, and deer are some of the animals you can meet while strolling through the expansive grounds with planted perennial gardens and more than 200 rhododendrons. In-room hot tubs, refrigerators. Cable TV, in-room VCRs. No kids under 15. No smoking. | 339 Finn Hall Rd., Port Angeles | 360/457–9197 | fax 360/452–0711 | www.colettes.com | 5 rooms | $175–$235 | MC, V | BP.

Domaine Madeleine. This delightfully comfortable B&B sits among bluff-top trees above the Strait of Juan de Fuca, and has some great views of the Vancouver Island mountains to the north and Mount Baker to the far northeast. Picnic area. In-room data ports, in-room hot tubs, some microwaves, some refrigerators. Cable TV, in-room VCRs. Business services. No kids under 12. No smoking. | 146 Wildflower La., Port Angeles | 360/457–4174 | fax 360/457–3037 | www.domainemadeleine.com | 5 rooms | $174–$195 | AE, D, MC, V | BP.

★ **Dungeness Panorama Bed and Breakfast.** As you would expect from its name, unbeatable views of the Olympic Mountains, the strait, and bay encircle this B&B. The furnishings are built around a French provincial theme, reflecting the background of the proprietors. The bay is only a short walk from the backyard. Each suite has its own fireplace and deck overlooking the water. Room service. Kitchenettes, microwaves, refrigerators. In-room VCRs. No kids under 12. No smoking. | 630 Marine Dr., Sequim | 360/683–4503 | www.awaterview.com | 2 suites | $95–$125 | No credit cards | BP.

Fort Worden State Park Conference Center. The 330-acre Fort Worden was built as a late-19th-century gun emplacement to guard the mouth of the Puget Sound. Its mighty cannons are long gone, and enterprising souls have now turned the 32 spacious Victorian homes on officer's row into one of the more memorable lodgings on the Olympic Peninsula. The houses have a spare charm and are furnished with antique reproductions. The old fort is a magical place for children, with an artillery museum, a bronze foundry, a marine science center, a dirigible hangar, and a graceful old lighthouse. It's 1 mi north of Port Townsend. Restaurant. Kitchenettes. | 200 Battery Way, Port Townsend | 360/344–4400 | 2 1-bedroom houses, 10 2-bedroom houses, 19 larger houses, 80 campsites with full hookups | $102–$359 houses; $22 campsites | D, MC, V.

Greywolf. This snug B&B in a Northwest hilltop farmhouse overlooks Dungeness Valley and Sequim Bay. Its rooms are theme-oriented and enhanced by antiques. Picnic area. Cable TV, in-room VCRs. Exercise equipment, hot tub. Business services. No a/c, no phones in some rooms. No kids under 12. No smoking. | 395 Keeler Rd., Sequim | 360/683–5889 or 800/914–9653 | fax 360/683–1487 | www.greywolfinn.com | 5 rooms | $75–$125 | AE, D, MC, V.

Groveland Cottage. A cozy Victorian farmhouse built in 1886, this country B&B is adorned with stained glass windows and a mix of period furnishings and modern pieces. Picnic area. In-room hot tubs, some kitchenettes. Cable TV, in-room VCRs. Library. Business services. No a/c. No kids under 12. No smoking. | 4861 Sequim-Dungeness Way, Dungeness | 360/683–3565 or 800/879–8859 | fax 360/683–5181 | www.sequimvalley.com | 4 rooms, 1 cottage | $80–$110 | AE, D, MC, V.

★ **James House.** Considered by many to be the state's premier B&B, this century-old house has unrivaled views of the sound. Sumptuous furnishings and the impeccable hospitality of its owners justify the inn's reputation. Library. No smoking. | 1238 Washington St., Port Townsend | 360/385–1238 or 800/385–1238 | 11 rooms | $125–$195 | AE, MC, V.

Miller Tree Inn Bed and Breakfast. Originally a farmhouse, this B&B is bordered on two sides by pasture land. The inn's many windows make the rooms bright, cheerful places to relax amid the assortment of antiques, knickknacks, and quilts. A porch and back deck allow for summer lounging. Hot tub. No a/c, no room phones. No TV in some rooms. No smoking. | 654 E. Division St., Forks | 360/374–6806 or 800/943–6563 | fax 360/374–6807 | www.millertreeinn.com | 7 rooms | $95–$135 | D, MC, V | CP.

Quality Inn. South of town, at the green edge of the Olympic Mountain foothills, this inn has views of the mountains and the harbor. Some kitchenettes, some microwaves, refrigerators. Cable TV. No a/c. | 101 E. 2nd St., Port Angeles | 360/457–9434 or 800/858–3812 | fax 360/457–5915 | 51 rooms | $69–$169 | AE, D, DC, MC, V.

Tudor Inn. High enough uphill from the ferry landing to avoid the bustle, this renovated 1910 inn provides a quiet and peaceful retreat. A colonial British theme dominates the decor and furnishings, down to the marble-top dressers and brass beds and collection of classic Kipling tales in the wood-paneled library. Library. No a/c, no room phones. No room TVs. No kids under 12. No smoking. | 1108 S. Oak, Port Angeles | 360/452–3138 | www.tudorinn.com | 5 rooms | $90–$145 | AE, D, MC, V | BP.

OLYMPIC
NATIONAL PARK

EXPLORING
ATTRACTIONS NEARBY
DINING
LODGING
CAMPING AND RV
FACILITIES
SHOPPING
ESSENTIAL
INFORMATION

Camping and RV Facilities

In Olympic

The best and most popular accommodations at Olympic are the 17 campgrounds, which range from primitive backcountry sites reached only by grueling hikes, to paved handicapped-accessible trailer parks with toilets and nightly naturalist programs. Olympic has about 925 vehicle-accessible campsites. There are no showers or RV hookups at park campgrounds, and some are open in summer only. No credit cards or reservations are accepted at any of the campgrounds; almost all space is allocated strictly on a first-come, first-served basis. On summer weekends, plan to arrive by Thursday night if possible.

More intrepid hikers camp on the park's wilderness beaches or virtually anywhere in the mountain and forest areas of the park. All overnight use in the park's backcountry requires a wilderness use permit ($5 registration per party for up to 14 days, plus $2 per person per night), which you can obtain from the visitor center. You must choose a site at least 0.5 mi inside the park. In the park's wilderness areas, reservations are required to camp in the coastal area near Ozette, from Duc Point to Yellow Banks.

Altaire Campground. This small campground sits amid an old-growth forest by the river in the rather narrow Elwha River Valley. A popular trail leads downstream from the campground. Flush toilets. Drinking water. Fire grates. | 30 sites | Elwha River Road, 8 mi south of U.S. 101 | No phone | $10 | Apr.–Oct.

Deer Park Campground. At 5,400 ft in the eastern edge of the park, this is the only drive-to alpine campground in the park. The access road is steep and winding, and half the distance is gravel. RVs are prohibited. Pit toilets. Drinking water. Fire grates. | 14 sites | Deer Park (Blue Mountain) Road, 21 mi south of U.S. 101 | No phone | $8 | May–Sept.

★ **Dosewallips Campground.** Now walk-in only due to a road washout, this small remote campground lies beneath Mount Constance, one of the most conspicuous peaks in the park. The campground is in old-growth forest along the river. It is popular with hikers, and also with hunters in the fall. Pit toilets. Fire grates. | 30 sites | Dosewallips River Rd., 15 mi west of Brinnon | No phone | Free | May–Oct.

Elwha Campground. The larger of the Elwha Valley's two campgrounds is one of Olympic's year-round facilities, with two campsite loops in an old-growth forest. Flush toilets. Drinking water. Fire grates. Public telephone. Ranger station. | 41 sites | Elwha River Road, 7 mi south of U.S. 101 | No phone | $10.

★ **Fairholm Campground.** One of just three lakeside campgrounds in the park, Fairholm is at the most popular end of Lake Crescent, near the resort of the same name, a major swimming beach. Flush toilets. Dump station. Drinking water. Fire grates. Public telephone. Swimming (lake). | 87 sites | U.S. 101, 28 mi west of Port Angeles, on the west end of Lake Crescent | No phone | $10 | Apr.–Oct.

Graves Creek Campground. At the junction of its namesake creek and the east fork of the Quinault, this campground lies deep in an old-growth rain forest. The access road includes an 11-mi stretch of gravel prone to washouts. Nearby is the trailhead for one of the park's best alpine day hikes. Flush toilets. Drinking water. Fire grates. Ranger station. | 30 sites | South Quinault Valley Rd., 22 mi east of U.S. 101 | No phone | $10 | Apr.–Oct.

Heart O' the Hills Campground. At the foot of Hurricane Ridge in a grove of tall firs, this popular and crowded year-round campground offers a regular slate of campground programs in summer. The price is a distinct lack of the peace and calm most people expect in a national park. Flush toilets. Drinking water. Fire grates. Public telephone. Ranger station. | 105 sites | Hurricane Ridge Road, 4 mi south of the main park visitor center in Port Angeles | No phone | $10.

★ **Hoh Campground.** Crowds flock to this deep rain forest campground, which provides visitors with a quintessential old-growth forest experience—moss-draped maples, towering spruce trees, morning mist, and the damp climate that makes it all possible. Flush toilets. Dump station. Drinking water. Fire grates. Public telephone. Ranger station. | 89 sites | Hoh River Rd., 17 mi east of U.S. 101 | No phone | $10.

July Creek Campground. This walk-in campground overlooks Lake Quinault and the rugged mountains beyond. Lake access is less than 100 yards away. Pit toilets. Drinking water (no water in winter). Fire grates. Swimming (lake). | 28 sites | North Shore Rd., 3 mi east of U.S. 101 | No phone | $10.

Kalaloch Campground. Kalaloch is the biggest and most popular Olympic campground. Its vantage of the Pacific is duplicated at no other campground anywhere on the park's coastal stretch, although the campsites themselves are set back in the spruce fringe. The campground is open year-round, and you can reserve up to five months in advance to camp here mid-June–early September. Flush toilets. Dump station. Drinking water. Fire grates. Public telephone. Ranger station (nearby). | 177 sites | U.S. 101, 1/2-mi north of the Kalaloch Information Station | Reservations 800/365-2267 | $12–$16.

★ **Mora Campground.** Along the Quillayute estuary, this campground doubles as a popular staging point for hikes northward, up the coast's wilderness stretch. The nearby Bogachiel and Sol Duc rivers are famed steelhead streams in winter. Flush toilets. Dump station. Drinking water. Fire grates. Public telephone. Ranger station. | 94 sites (1 walk-in) | Rte. 110, 13 mi west of Forks | No phone | $10.

North Fork Campground. The park's smallest campground is for self-sufficient travelers who want to enjoy the rain forest in peace and quiet. It's deep, wet woods here; RVs are not advised. Pit toilets. Fire grates. Ranger station. | 7 sites | North Quinault Valley Rd., 19 mi east of U.S. 101 | No phone | $10 | May–Sept.

★ **Ozette Campground.** Hikers heading to Cape Alava, a scenic promontory that's the westernmost point in the lower 48 states, use this lakeshore campground as a jumping-off point. At 3 mi from the Pacific Coast, this campground sits almost at sea level. Beware of the danger of flooding. There's a boat launch and a small beach. Pit toilets. Fire grates. Ranger station. | 15 sites | Hoko-Ozette Rd., 26 mi south of Rte. 112 | No phone | $10.

Queets Campground. Amid lush old-growth forests in the southwestern corner of the park, near the park's largest Douglas fir tree, this campground is not suitable for camp trailers or RVs. There's no water. Pit toilets. Fire grates. Ranger station. | 20 sites | Queets River Rd., 12 mi east of U.S. 101 | No phone | $8 | Apr.–Oct.

Sol Duc Campground. Sol Duc resembles virtually all Olympic campgrounds except for one distinguishing feature—the famed hot springs are a short walk away. The nearby Sol Duc River has several spots where visitors can watch spawning salmon work their way upstream. Flush toilets. Dump station. Drinking water. Fire grates. Public telephone. Ranger station. Swimming (hot springs). | 80 sites | Sol Duc Rd., 11 mi south of U.S. 101 | No phone | $12 | May–Oct.

South Beach Campground. The first campground travelers reach as they enter the park's coastal stretch from the south, this is basically an overflow campground for the more popular and better-equipped Kalaloch a few miles north. Campsites are set in the spruce fringe, just back from the beach itself. There is no water. Pit toilets. Fire grates. | 50 sites | U.S. 101, 2 mi south of the Kalaloch information station at the southern boundary of the park | No phone | $8 | Apr.–Oct.

Staircase Campground. In deep woods away from the river, this campground provides a popular jumping-off point for hikes into the Skokomish River Valley and the Olympic high country. Flush toilets. Drinking water. Fire grates. Public telephone. Ranger station. | 56 sites | Rte. 119, 16 mi northwest of U.S. 101 | No phone | $10.

Near the Park

Bogachiel State Park Campground. Famed for steelhead fishing (mostly in winter) the Bogachiel River is the centerpiece of this quiet, forested state park. Boating (no motors), swimming and fishing, and hiking in the rain forest are popular draws. Flush toilets. Drinking water, showers. Grills, picnic tables. Electricity, public telephone. Swimming (river). | 42 sites, 6 with hookups | 6 mi south of Forks on U.S. 101 | 360/374–6356 | $10–$21 tents and RVs | No credit cards.

★ **Conestoga Quarters RV Park Campground.** Off U.S. 101, partly surrounded by a fir forest, this compact RV park provides a shuttle van to take you into Port Angeles to facilities such as the Victoria ferry. The park also offers pet care while you tour the park. All of the sites have hookups; eight sites have phones. Flush toilets. Full hookups. Drinking water, showers. Grills, picnic tables. Electricity, public telephone. Play area. | 8 tent sites, 34 RV sites | 40 Sieberts Creek Rd., Port Angeles | 360/452–4637 or 800/808–4637 | $12 tents, $23 RVs | D, MC, V.

Forks 101 RV Park Campground. In the rain forest outside Forks, this campground is popular with fishermen and mushroom pickers in spring and fall. Flush toilets. Full hookups.

OLYMPIC
NATIONAL PARK

EXPLORING
ATTRACTIONS NEARBY
DINING
LODGING
**CAMPING AND RV
FACILITIES**
SHOPPING
ESSENTIAL
INFORMATION

OLYMPIC CAMPGROUNDS

	Total # of sites	# of RV sites	# of hook-ups	Drive-to sites	Hike-to sites	Flush toilets	Pit toilets	Drinking water	Showers	Fire grates/pits	Swimming	Boat access	Playground	Dump station	Ranger station	Public telephone	Reservation possible	Daily fee per site	Dates open
Altaire	30	30	0	•		•		•		•								$10	Apr.–Oct.
Deer Park	14	0	0	•			•	•		•								$8	May–Sep.
Dosewallips	30	0	0	•			•			•								Free	May–Oct.
Elwha	41	41	0	•		•		•		•						•	•	$10	Apr.–Oct.
Fairholm	88	88	0	•		•		•		•	•	•	•	•		•		$10	Apr–Oct.
Graves Creek	30	30	0	•		•		•		•						•	•	$10	Apr.–Oct.
Heart o' the Hills	105	105	0	•		•		•		•					•	•	•	$10	Y/R
Hoh	89	89	0	•		•		•		•				•	•	•		$10	Y/R
July Creek	28	0	0		•		•	•*		•	•							$10	Y/R
Kalaloch	177	177	0	•		•		•		•			•	•	•	•	•	$12–$16	Y/R
Mora	94	94	0	•	•	•		•		•				•	•	•		$10	Y/R
North Fork	7	0	0	•			•			•						•		Free	May–Oct.
Ozette	15	15	0	•		•				•	•	•				•		$10	May–Oct.
Queets	20	0	0	•			•			•						•		$8	May–Oct.
Sol Duc	80	80	0	•		•		•		•	•			•	•	•		$12	May–Oct.
South Beach	50	50	0	•			•			•								$8	Apr.–Oct.
Staircase	56	59	0	•		•		•		•						•	•	$10	Y/R

* In summer only   ** Reservation fee charged   Y/R=Year-round
UL=Unlimited   ULP=Unlimited primitive   LD=Labor Day   MD=Memorial Day

Drinking water, showers. Grills, picnic tables. Electricity, public telephone. | 50 sites, 36 full hookups | 901 S. Forks Ave. (U.S. 101), Forks | 360/374–5073 or 800/962–9964 | $22 | MC, V.

Hoh River Resort Campground. Spruce trees shade this all-around sportsman's hangout along the Hoh River, 20 mi south of Forks; fishing and hiking are nearby. Flush toilets. Full hookups. Drinking water, showers. Grills, picnic tables. Electricity, public telephone. General store. | 13 sites with hookups, 7 tent sites | 175443 U.S. 101, Forks | 360/374–5566 | $15 tents, $18 RVs | MC, V.

★ **Lake Quinault Rain Forest Resort Village Campground.** Sprawled on the south shore of Lake Quinault, this campground has ample recreation facilities, including beaches, canoes, ball fields, and horseshoes. Flush toilets. Full hookups. Drinking water, showers. Grills, picnic tables. Electricity, public telephone. General store. | 30 sites | S. Shore Rd., 3.5 mi east of U.S. 101, Lake Quinault | 360/288–2535 or 800/255–6936 | $18 RVs and tents | MC, V.

Lonesome Creek RV Park. A mile of sandy beach abuts this shoreside resort in La Push. Horseshoe pits and beachcombing occupy guests; the store sells Native American arts. Flush toilets. Full hookups. Drinking water, showers. Grills, picnic tables. Electricity, public telephone. General store. | 55 sites, 42 with hookups | 490 Ocean Dr., La Push | 360/374–4338 | $34 | MC, V.

Peabody Creek RV Park. Set along a creek, this campground is within Port Angeles and close to the waterfront, but calm and relatively secluded. Shops, ferries, and restaurants are within walking distance; eight sites have phones. Pet sitting is available. Flush toilets. Full hookups. Drinking water, showers. Grills, picnic tables. Electricity, public telephone. Play area. | 44 sites, 36 full hookups | 127 S. Lincoln St., Port Angeles | 360/457–7092 or 800/392–2361 | $23 | MC, V.

★ **Port Angeles KOA.** This KOA "gold" campground includes an outdoor heated pool and hot tub, cable TV, a mini-golf course, and access to a nearby regular golf course. Flush toilets. Full hookups. Drinking water, guest laundry, showers. Grills, picnic tables. Electricity, public telephone. Play area, swimming (pool). | 90 sites, 18 full hookups, 55 partial hookups (water and electric); 17 tent sites | 80 O'Brien Rd., Port Angeles | 360/457–5916 or 800/562–7558 | $26 tents, $37 RVs | AE, MC, V.

Salt Creek RV Park. Adjacent to a golf course development, this large park offers every conceivable campground amenity, including nightly security patrols and an on-site store. Quiet hours are 10 PM to 8 AM. Flush toilets. Full hookups. Drinking water, guest laundry, showers. Grills, picnic tables. Electricity, public telephone. Play area. | 51 sites, all with hookups | 53802 Rte. 122 W, Port Angeles | 360/928–2488 | $20 | AE, MC, V.

Salt Creek and Tongue Point Recreation Area. Swimming in fresh and saltwater, fishing, hiking, and beachcombing provide bountiful activity at this Clallam Count park. It is located along a creek, near where Fort Hayden once guarded the coastline. There are no hookups. Flush toilets. Drinking water, showers. Grills, picnic tables. Public telephone. Play area, swimming (river, ocean). | 90 sites | 13 mi west of Port Angeles on Rte. 112, 3 mi north on Camp Hayden Rd. | 360/928–3441 | $10 | No credit cards | May–Oct.

Essential Information

ATMS (24-HOUR): Bank of America | 481 S. Forks Ave. (U.S. 101), Forks. **Washington Mutual Bank** | 101 W. Front St., Port Angeles. **Washington Mutual Bank** | 680 W. Washington St., Sequim.

AUTOMOBILE SERVICE STATIONS: Port Angeles and Forks have numerous gas stations and auto repair facilities. **Fairholm General Store** | On U.S. 101 at the west end of Lake Crescent | 360/928–3020. **Port Angeles Chevron** | 402 Marine Dr. | 360/457–6350. **Toni's Texaco** | E. 5th St. and S. Lincoln | 360/457–3623.

OLYMPIC
NATIONAL PARK

EXPLORING
ATTRACTIONS NEARBY
DINING
LODGING
CAMPING AND RV
FACILITIES
SHOPPING
**ESSENTIAL
INFORMATION**

GROWING OLD

Redwood National Park has 45% of all California's old-growth redwood forests. Of the original 3,125 square mi (2 million acres) in the Redwoods Historic Range, only 4% remain following the logging that began in 1850; 1% is privately owned and managed, and the other 3% is on public land.

POST OFFICES: **Forks Post Office** | 61 S. Spartan Ave., Forks, 98331 | 360/374–6303. **Port Angeles Post Office** | 424 E. 1st Ave., Port Angeles, 98362 | 360/452–9275.

REDWOOD NATIONAL PARK

NORTHERN CALIFORNIA

22 mi north of Trinidad on U.S. 101

Soaring to more than 300 ft, the coastal redwoods that give this park its name are miracles of efficiency, some surviving hundreds of years (a few can live for more than 2,000 years). They glean nutrients from the rich alluvial flats at their feet as well as from the moisture and nitrogen trapped in their uneven canopy. Their huge, thick-barked trunks can hold thousands of gallons of water, reservoirs that have helped them withstand centuries of firestorms.

Redwood National Park was created in 1968 along a thin 50-mi-long strip of California coastline. Ten years later it was expanded to provide a "buffer" forest to protect the redwoods. Today the park is a World Heritage Site and International Biosphere Reserve, and it surrounds Prairie Creek Redwoods State Park, Jedediah Smith Redwoods State Park, Del Norte Coast Redwoods State Park, and former timberlands.

PUBLICATIONS

Joseph Brown's *Monarchs of the Mist* is a brief and readable history of the coast redwood and the parks. Richard Rasp's *Redwood: The Story Behind the Scenery* is a photo essay on the forest. Bill Schneider uses simple text and enchanting watercolors to describe big trees to small readers in *The Tree Giants*.

When to Visit

SCENERY AND WILDLIFE

Ocean, rain forest, and mountains crowd each other here. Although the sand verbena and evening primrose that grow along beaches are charming, the park's major draw is, of course, the coast redwood. These magnificent trees are 500 to 700 years old—still a good 1,200 years younger than the oldest of the giant sequoias found in central California's Sierra Nevada. In the higher, drier elevations, redwoods give way to Douglas fir, oak, red alder, and madrone.

In the backcountry, you might spot mountain lions, black bears, black-tail deer, river otters, beavers, and minks. Rivers and streams are filled with several varieties of salmon and trout. Along the coast, you may see gray whales, seals, and sea lions. And thanks to the area's location along the Pacific Flyway, an amazing 402 species of bird have been sighted here.

HIGH AND LOW SEASON

Campers and hikers flock to the park from mid-June to early September, the driest and busiest months. In winter, frequent rains and nasty potholes are trade-offs for a crowd-free visit. Temperatures vary widely throughout the park, with marked differences between the foggy coastal lowland and the interior's higher altitude.

Average High/Low Temperatures (°F) and Monthly Precipitation (in inches)

	JAN.	FEB.	MAR.	APR.	MAY	JUNE
REDWOOD	53/36	56/38	57/38	59/39	63/41	66/46
	9.80	8.50	9.30	4.90	2.80	1.20
	JULY	AUG.	SEPT.	OCT.	NOV.	DEC.
	68/48	69/48	70/46	66/42	57/40	52/37
	0.30	0.90	1.60	4.60	9.90	10.90

FESTIVALS AND SEASONAL EVENTS

WINTER

Feb.: **World Championship Crab Races.** Held on President's Day Weekend in Crescent City, this one-day event features races of locally caught crabs and an all-out chow down. | 800/343–8300.

SPRING

Mar.: **Redwood Coast Dixieland Jazz Festival.** Eureka's jazz festival draws thousands of music-lovers and performers from around the country. | 707/445–3378 or 707/442–3738.

Aleutian Goose Festival. The hordes of geese that nest each spring on the offshore rocks are the focus of this three-day Crescent City celebration, which includes art exhibits and outings to the birds' habitats. | 707/465–0888.

May: **Kinetic Sculpture Race.** A cross between a science fair and the Tour de France, this three-day, 38-mi race of human-powered, wheeled sculptures starts in Arcata and ends in Ferndale. | 707/786–9259.

SUMMER

June: **U.S. National Jet Boat Races.** Testosterone levels rise during this two-day display of speed and splashing on the Klamath River. | 800/200–2335.

Aug.: **Klamath Salmon Festival.** Klamath hosts this two-day Native American celebration held by the local Yurok tribe. | 707/482–7165.

Del Norte County Fair. Crescent City's four-day festival includes a carnival. | 707/464–9556.

FALL

Oct.: **Noll Longboard Classic.** Held on Crescent City's wide South Beach, this two-day competition brings more than 200 participants to California's northernmost surfing outpost. | 707/465–4400 | www.noll.net.

Nearby Towns

Crescent City, north of the park, is Del Norte County's largest town (pop. 5,000) and home to the Redwood National and State Park Headquarters. Though it curves around a beautiful stretch of ocean and radiates small-town charm, rain and bone-chilling fog often prevail. Roughly 60 mi south of Crescent City, **Arcata** began life in 1850 as a base camp for miners and lumberjacks. Today this town of 16,000 residents is also home to the 7,500 students of Humboldt State University. Activity centers around Arcata Plaza, which is surrounded by restored buildings. Pick up the "Victorian Walking Tour" map at the chamber of commerce. **Eureka,** south of Arcata, may be filled with strip malls, but this city of 27,000 residents has some history. In 1850 it was a place to stock up on mining supplies; indeed, it was named after a gold miner's hearty exclamation. Old Town has a new waterfront boardwalk, a few good restaurants and shops, and the chamber of commerce has a free driving map to Victorian homes.

INFORMATION

Arcata Chamber of Commerce | 1635 Heindon Rd., Arcata, 95521-5800 | 707/822–3619 | www.arcata.com/chamber. **Crescent City/Del Norte County Chamber of Commerce** | 1001 Front St., Crescent City, 95531 | 707/464–3174 or 800/343–8300 | www.northerncalifornia. net. **Eureka/Humboldt County Convention and Visitors Bureau** | 1034 2nd St., Eureka, 95501-0541 | 707/443–5097 or 800/346–3482 | www.redwoodvisitor.org.

Exploring Redwood

Park Basics

Contacts and Resources: Crescent City Information Center | 1111 2nd St., Crescent City, 95531 | 707/464–6101 Ext. 5064 | www.nps.gov/redw. **Hiouchi Information Center** | U.S. 199, Hiouchi, 95531 | 707/464–6101 Ext. 5067. **Redwood Information Center** | U.S. 101, Orick, 95555 | 707/464–6101 Ext. 5265.

Hours: The park is open year round, 24 hours a day. The Crescent City visitor center is open daily 9–5 from March to late December and Monday–Saturday 9–5 from late December through February. The Orick center has hours weekdays 9–5 year-round, and the one in Hiouchi is open weekdays 9–5 from mid-June through mid-September.

Fees: Admission to the national park portion of Redwood National and State Parks is free. There's a $4 day-use fee to enter one or all of the state parks.

Getting Around: U.S. 101 runs north–south along the park, and U.S. 199 cuts east–west through its northern portion. Access routes off 101 include Bald Hills Road, Davison Road, Newton B. Drury Scenic Parkway, Coastal Drive, Requa Road, and Enderts Beach Road. From 199 take South Fork Road to Howland Hill Road. Speed limits vary throughout the park, and many roads aren't paved. Winter rains can turn them into obstacle courses; sometimes they're closed completely. In the dry summer season, most vehicles can pass along these routes, though RVs and trailers aren't permitted on some routes or beyond certain points on others.

Permits: To visit Tall Trees Grove, you must get a free permit at the Redwood Information Center in Orick.

Public Telephones: There are phones at the Crescent City and Redwood visitor centers.

Rest Rooms: You'll find rest rooms at all the visitor centers and state park campgrounds and at some picnic areas. There's also a rest room at the wayside station in Elk Meadow on Davison Road.

Accessibility: Park maps indicate which camping, picnic, and other areas are wheelchair accessible. Such spots include all the visitor centers as well as Crescent Beach, Crescent Beach Overlook, Lagoon Creek, Klamath Overlook, High Bluff Overlook, Gold Bluffs Beach, Stone Lagoon, Dolason Praier, Big Tree Wayside, and Lost Man Creek.

Emergencies: In an emergency call 911 or go to the nearest visitor center.

Lost and Found: To find whatever you've lost, head to the nearest visitor center.

Good Tours

REDWOOD IN ONE DAY

Take U.S. 101 south from Crescent City, making a left on Elk Valley Road and a right at the Stout Grove sign onto the 12-mi-long **Howland Hill Road** (trailers and RVs should avoid this one-lane gravel route). About 10 mi into the drive, you'll reach **Stout Grove,** where a flat, 1-mi loop leads along the Smith River and past the Stout Tree, one of the park's largest redwoods. Two miles farther, Howland Hill Road runs into U.S. 199, where you should turn left. If it's summertime, visit the **Hiouchi Information Center** and its gift shop. Head up to **Walker Road,** an unpaved route through redwood forest that provides access to the Smith River and some short hiking trails. Retrace your path on Walker Road and turn west onto U.S. 199; follow it for a couple of miles before turning south onto **Elk Valley Road,** which leads to the coast and U.S. 101. Drive south about 2 mi from Crescent City and stop for a picnic lunch at **Crescent Beach.** (From here, trailers should return to U.S. 101 to continue south.) Continue south about 2 mi to the end of Enderts Beach Road and the **Crescent Beach Overlook.** A 1-mi hike on **Enderts Beach Trail** takes you to the shore. Another 0.5 mi leads to a camping area where five sites have beach access. Stay overnight at the camp, at the Mill Creek campground (drive east into Del Norte Coast Redwoods State Park via U.S. 101), or in Crescent City, roughly 30 minutes north.

REDWOOD IN TWO DAYS

Spend the first day as described above. The next day head south on U.S. 101. About a mile south of Klamath, detour onto the 8-mi-long, partially paved **Coastal Drive,** which loops north before reaching the ocean. Along the way, you'll pass the old **Douglas Memorial Bridge,** destroyed in the 1964 flood. Coastal Drive turns south above Flint Ridge (trailers should turn off at Alder Camp Road). In less than a mile you'll reach the **World War II Radar Station,** which looks like a farmhouse. Continue south to the intersection with Alder Camp Road, stopping at the **High Bluff Overlook.**

Coastal Drive segues into **Newton B. Drury Scenic Parkway.** You can turn left to continue south (or return north) on U.S. 101, or stay on the parkway, which leads to the **Prairie Creek Visitor Center**—a good place to visit the rest room and have a picnic lunch. Head north less than a mile and drive out unpaved **Cal-Barrel Road,** which leads east from the parkway through redwood forests. Return to the parkway, continue south about 2 mi, and turn west on **Davison Road.** Like Cal-Barrel, it's unpaved and inadvisable for trailers. In about 30 minutes you'll reach **Gold Bluffs Beach.** Turn right and drive north to the terminus at **Fern Canyon.**

Return to the parkway, which is U.S. 101 as well, and continue south to the turnoff for Redwood National Park. To visit the **Tall Trees Grove,** continue a couple of miles south to the **Redwood Information Center** and pick up free permits. Return to the turnoff for **Bald Hills Road,** a steep road that doesn't allow trailers or RVs (park them at the trailhead or the information center). If you visit the grove, allow about four hours round-trip from the information center. You could also bypass the turnoff to the grove and continue south on Bald Hills Road to 3,097-ft **Schoolhouse Peak.**

Attractions

PROGRAMS AND TOURS

Field Seminars. State park rangers and other experts conduct one-day and overnight seminars with an emphasis on natural history. Activities include kayaking, a banana slug derby, a candlelight celebration of the woods, and star-gazing. The programs often sell out in advance. | 707/464–6101 Ext. 5095 | $30–$70.

Junior Ranger Program. The state parks run these programs on summer mornings. Rangers instruct children ages 7–12 on bird identification, outdoor survival skills, and more. | 707/464–6101 Ext. 5095 | Free.

Ranger Talks. From Memorial Day through Labor Day, state park rangers regularly lead discussions on the redwoods, tide pools, geology, and Native American culture. Pick up a schedule at one of the visitor centers. | 707/464–6101 Ext. 5095 | Free.

SCENIC DRIVES

★ **Coastal Drive.** This 8-mi, partially paved road takes about 45 minutes to drive one-way. Along the way are stands of redwoods as well as close-up views of the Klamath River and expansive panoramas of the Pacific. There are picnic tables at several ocean overlooks. From here you'll find access to the Flint Ridge section of the Coastal Trail.

Howland Hill Road/Stout Grove. Take your time driving 10 mi along Mill Creek through old-growth redwoods and past the Smith River. Trailers aren't advised to follow this route.

Newton B. Drury Scenic Parkway/Big Tree Wayside. This 10-mi route cuts through Prairie Creek Redwoods State Park and old-growth redwoods. Just north of the park's visitor center you can make the 0.8-mi walk to Big Tree Wayside and observe Roosevelt elk in the prairie.

REDWOOD NATIONAL PARK

EXPLORING
ATTRACTIONS NEARBY
DINING
LODGING
CAMPING AND RV FACILITIES
SHOPPING
ESSENTIAL INFORMATION

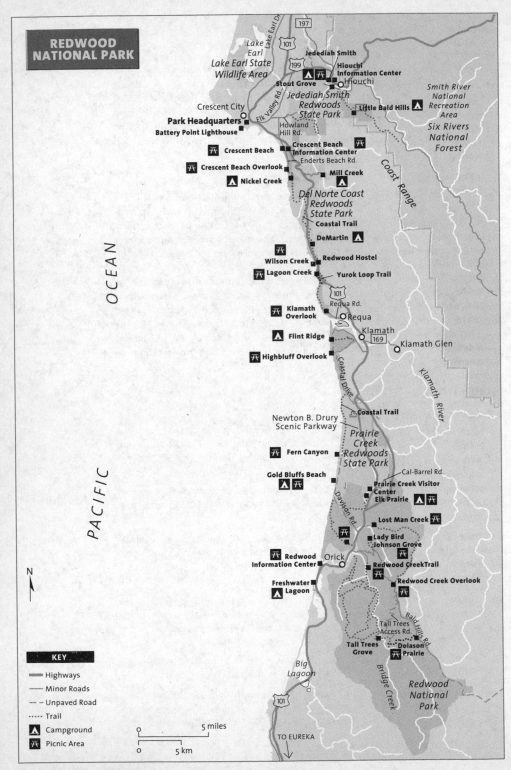

REDWOOD NATIONAL PARK

Lake Earl
Lake Earl State
Wildlife Area

Jedediah Smith
Hiouchi Information Center
Hiouchi
Stout Grove
Jedediah Smith Redwoods State Park
Crescent City
Park Headquarters
Battery Point Lighthouse
Howland Hill Rd.
Crescent Beach
Crescent Beach Information Center
Enderts Beach Rd.
Crescent Beach Overlook
Mill Creek
Nickel Creek
Del Norte Coast Redwoods State Park
Little Bald Hills
Smith River National Recreation Area
Six Rivers National Forest
Coast Range
Coastal Trail
DeMartin
Wilson Creek
Redwood Hostel
Lagoon Creek
Yurok Loop Trail
Klamath Overlook
Requa Rd.
Requa
Klamath
Klamath Glen
Flint Ridge
Highbluff Overlook
Coastal Drive
Klamath River
Coastal Trail
Newton B. Drury Scenic Parkway
Prairie Creek Redwoods State Park
Fern Canyon
Cal-Barrel Rd.
Gold Bluffs Beach
Prairie Creek Visitor Center
Elk Prairie
Davison Rd.
Lost Man Creek
Lady Bird Johnson Grove
Redwood Information Center
Orick
Redwood Creek Trail
Redwood Creek Overlook
Freshwater Lagoon
Bald Hill Rd.
Tall Trees Access Rd.
Tall Trees Grove
Dolason Prairie
Big Lagoon
Bridge Creek
Redwood National Park
TO EUREKA

OCEAN
PACIFIC

N

KEY
Highways
Minor Roads
Unpaved Road
Trail
Campground
Picnic Area

5 miles
5 km

SIGHTS TO SEE

Crescent Beach Overlook. The scenery here includes ocean views and, perhaps, a glimpse of a whale. Picnicking is also possible. The overlook is known as a good spot to see gray whales that migrate here November–December and March–April. | 2 mi south of Crescent City off Enderts Beach Rd.

Fern Canyon. Enter another world and be surrounded by 60-ft canyon walls covered with sword, maidenhair, and five-finger ferns. Allow an hour to explore the 0.25-mi long vertical garden along a 1.5-mi round-trip trail, which ends at a mining town abandoned after the Gold Rush. From the north end of Gold Bluffs Beach it's an easy walk, although you must wade across a small stream several times. | 10 mi east of Prairie Creek visitor center, via Newton B. Drury Scenic Pkwy. (U.S. 101) and Davison Rd.

Lady Bird Johnson Grove. This section of the park was dedicated by, and named for, the former first lady. A 1-mi, wheelchair accessible nature loop follows an old logging road through a mature redwood forest. Allow 45 minutes to complete the trail. | 5 mi east of Redwood Information Center, along U.S. 101 and Bald Hills Rd.

Redwoods State Parks. The three state parks have miles of trails that lead to magnificent redwood groves and overlooks with views of sea lion colonies and migrating whales. Birds inhabit bluffs, lagoons, and offshore rocks. All three parks are open year-round and have ranger programs for children, as well as ranger-led talks. Admission is $4 per day.

Del Norte Coast Redwoods State Park. Seven miles southeast of Crescent City via U.S. 101, this park contains 15 memorial redwood groves. The growth extends down steep slopes almost to the shore. | Crescent City Information Center, 1111 2nd St., off U.S. 101, Crescent City | 707/464–6101 Ext. 5064 | www.parks.ca.gov | Daily 9–5.

Jedediah Smith Redwoods State Park. Home to the Stout Memorial Grove, this park is named after a trapper who, in 1826, became the first white man to explore northern California's interior. You'll find 20 mi of hiking and nature trails and a visitor center here. The park is 2 mi west of Hiouchi and 9 mi east of Crescent City off U.S. 199. | Jedediah Smith Information Center, U.S. 199, Hiouchi | 707/464–6101 Ext. 5113 | www.parks.ca.gov | Late May– late Sept., daily 9–5 | Hiouchi Information Center, U.S. 199, Hiouchi | 707/464–6101 Ext. 5067 | www.parks.ca.gov | Mid-June–mid-Sept., daily 9–5.

Prairie Creek Redwoods State Park. Spectacular redwoods and lush ferns make up this park 3 mi north of Orick and 50 mi south of Crescent City. Extra space has been paved alongside the parklands, providing fine places to observe herds of Roosevelt elk in adjoining meadows. | Prairie Creek Information Center, Newton B. Drury Scenic Pkwy. | 707/464– 6101 Ext. 5300 | Mar.–Oct., daily 9–5; Nov.–Feb., daily 10–4 | Redwood Information Center, U.S. 101, Orick | 707/464–6101 Ext. 5265 | Daily 9–5.

★ **Tall Trees Grove.** From the Redwood Information Center, you can get a free permit to make the drive up the steep 17-mi Tall Trees Access Road (the last 6 mi are gravel) to the grove's trailhead. Access to the popular grove is first-come, first-served. A maximum of 40 permits are handed out each day. A 3-mi round-trip trail leads to the world's first-, third-, and fifth-tallest redwoods. | Access road is 10 mi drive east of Redwood Information Center, via U.S. 101 and Bald Hills Rd.

Sports and Outdoor Activities

BICYCLING

Besides the roadways, you can bike on several trails. Good bets include the 11-mi Lost Man Creek Trail, which has a pleasant dismount-and-walk section through Lady Bird Johnson Grove; the 13-mi round-trip Coastal Trail (Last Chance Section), which travels through the dense slopes of foggy redwood forests, but is easy enough to be suitable for children; and the 19-mi, single-track Ossagon Trail Loop, where you're likely to spy elk as you cruise through

REDWOOD
NATIONAL PARK

EXPLORING
ATTRACTIONS NEARBY
DINING
LODGING
CAMPING AND RV
FACILITIES
SHOPPING
ESSENTIAL
INFORMATION

redwoods before ending up oceanside for the last leg of the trail. You can rent mountain bikes from Lunker's in Hiouchi (*see* Outfitters, *below*).

BIRD-WATCHING

Many rare and striking winged specimens inhabit the area, including brown pelicans, great blue herons, pileated woodpeckers, spotted owls, and marbled murrelets.

Yurok Loop Trail. Beginning at the Lagoon Creek picnic area, this 1-mi round-trip trail has good bird-watching opportunities. Visit in spring to enjoy a riot of wildflowers. You'll need 45 minutes to follow the trail. | Just off U.S. 101, 14 mi south of Crescent City visitor center.

FISHING

Both deep-sea and freshwater fishing are popular sports here. Anglers often stake out sections of the Klamath and Smith rivers in their search for salmon and trout. (Note that fishing licenses are required for both ocean and river fishing.) Less serious anglers can go crabbing or clamming on the coast. Lunker's in Hiouchi sells and rents gear and supplies; you can also connect with a fishing guide there (*see* Outfitters, *below*).

Coast True Value. This is a good place to get licenses ($17.35–$29.40) for both river and ocean fishing. | 900 N. Crest Dr., Crescent City | 707/464–3535.

HIKING

The almost 120 mi of trails in Redwood National and State Parks are rated according to six classifications of difficulty, based on steepness, the number of switchbacks, and the length. For a complete review of the park's trails, buy a trail map at any visitor center.

★ **Coastal Trail.** Although this trail runs along the park's entire 70-mi length, smaller sections—of varying degrees of difficulty—are accessible via frequent, well-marked trailheads. The somewhat difficult DeMartin section leads past 5 mi of mature redwoods and through prairie. Those who feel up to a real workout will be well rewarded with the brutal but stunning Flint Ridge section, a 4.5-mi stretch of steep grades and numerous switchbacks that leads past redwoods and Marshall Pond. The 4-mi-long Hidden Beach section connects the Lagoon Creek picnic area with Klamath Overlook and provides coastal views and whale-watching opportunities. | Flint Ridge trailhead: Douglas Bridge parking area, north end of Coastal Dr.

West Ridge–Friendship Ridge–James Irvine Loop. For a moderately strenuous trek, try this 12.5-mi loop. The West Ridge segment passes redwoods looming above a carpet of ferns. The Friendship Ridge portion slopes down toward the coast through forests of spruce and hemlock. The James Irvine Trail portion winds along a small creek and amid old-growth redwoods. | Prairie Creek Redwoods State Park information center, off Newton B. Drury Scenic Pkwy.

KAYAKING

With many miles of often shallow rivers and streams in the area, kayaking is a popular pastime in the park. You can rent an inflatable kayak from Lunker's in Hiouchi (*see* Outfitters, *below*); they will also shuttle you to and from a put-in point on the Smith River.

SWIMMING

Though the Pacific Ocean may seem inviting, the pounding surf and rip currents are so deadly that rangers suggest you never swim in the ocean, even if it appears calm. Its waters are cold, but the Smith River is a good place for a dip or an inner tube ride.

WHALE WATCHING

There are several good vantage points for whale-watching, including Crescent Beach Overlook, the Redwood Information Center in Orick, and points along the Coastal Drive. Late November through January are usually good months to see their southward migrations and February through April are good for observing the return trip, during which the whales generally pass closer to shore.

Outfitters

Lunker's. You can buy bait, rent fishing gear (including a boat), and arrange for a fishing guide ($175) here. You can also rent mountain bikes for $25 a day and, in summer, inflatable and hard shell kayaks for $20 a day; another $10 gets you transportation to and from a put-in point on the Smith River (make reservations a day or two in advance). Lunker's is open daily except for parts of September and October as well as April and May; call ahead in these months. | 2095 U.S. 199, Hiouchi | 707/458–4704 or 800/248–4704 | Early Sept.– late May 8–5; Memorial Day–Labor Day 6–6.

Attractions Nearby

Sights to See

Battery Point Lighthouse. At low tide from April through September, you can walk from the pier across the ocean floor to this working lighthouse, which was built in 1856. It houses a museum with nautical artifacts and photographs of shipwrecks, and even a resident ghost. In peak season, call ahead for guided tours. | A St., Crescent City | 707/464–3089 | $2 | Apr.–Sept., Tues.–Sun. at low tide.

★ **California Western Railroad Skunk Train.** Following the same coastal route between Fort Bragg and Willits since 1885, the Skunk Train crosses some 30 bridges and passes through two tunnels. The gas-powered locomotive replaced the steam engine on this train in 1925. Locals say, "You can smell 'em before you can see 'em." Hence, the nickname. You can take a full- or half-day trip. | 100 W. Laurel St., Fort Bragg | 707/964–6371 or 800/777–5865 | www.skunktrain.com | $35–$45 | Mar.–Nov.

Humboldt State University Natural History Museum. A 60-gallon tide pool tank, 500-million-year-old fossils, a birds of the redwoods exhibit, a saber-toothed cat skeleton, butterflies, and Pacific seashells are among this museum's features. | 1315 G St., Arcata | 707/826–4479 | $2 donation | Tues.–Sat. 10–5.

Mendocino Coast Botanical Gardens. Formal flower gardens, pine forests, 100 species of birds, and 80 species of mushrooms fill the lush grounds here, the only public garden in the continental states that's on the ocean. Frozen treats and light fare are available from April through September. | 18220 N. Rte. 1, Fort Bragg | 707/964–4352 | www.gardenbythesea.org | $7.50 | Mar.–Oct., daily 9–5; Nov.–Feb., daily 9–4.

★ **Northcoast Marine Mammal Center.** This nonprofit organization rescues and rehabilitates stranded, sick, or injured seals, sea lions, dolphins, porpoises, and whales. Here you can see the rescued creatures and learn about marine mammals and coastal ecosystems. | 242 Howe Dr., Crescent City | 707/465–6265 | www.northcoastmarinemammal.org | Free | Daily 8 AM– 9 PM; feeding times at 8 AM, noon, 4 PM, and 8 PM.

Ocean World. The centerpiece of this aquarium is a huge reef tank. Other highlights include a touchable tide pool, river otter exhibit, shark petting tank, tours, and performances by trained sea lions. | 304 U.S. 101 S, Crescent City | 707/464–4900 | $6 | Daily 8 AM–9 PM.

Sequoia Park and Zoo. You get a taste of nature, both native and exotic, in this 50-acre, redwood-filled zoo that opened in 1907. The most famous resident is Bill, the third-oldest chimpanzee in captivity, who was born in 1946. There's also an aviary, a garden, and a snack shop. | Glatt and W Sts., Eureka | 707/442–6552 | www.eurekawebs.com/zoo | $2 donation | Oct.–Apr., Tues.–Sun. 10–5; May–Sept., Tues.–Sun. 10–7.

REDWOOD
NATIONAL PARK

EXPLORING
**ATTRACTIONS
NEARBY**
DINING
LODGING
CAMPING AND RV
FACILITIES
SHOPPING
ESSENTIAL
INFORMATION

CAT TACTICS

Mountain lions, or cougars, are rarely seen in the parks, and no attacks on humans have been reported. If you happen upon such a cat, stand up and face it, picking up any young children and slowly backing away. Don't run, crouch, bend over, turn your back on, or take your eyes off the lion. If it attacks, shout loudly and fight back aggressively.

Dining

In Redwood

Picnic Areas. There are no restaurants in the park, but a brief glance at a park-service map will tell you Redwood has more than a dozen picnic grounds, some of them quite small. All grounds have picnic tables; some have toilets.

Crescent Beach. This beach has a grassy picnic area with tables, fire pits, and rest rooms. There's an overlook south of the beach. | 2 mi south of Crescent City visitor center, on Enderts Beach Rd.

Elk Prairie. In addition to many elk, this spot has a campground, a nature trail, and a ranger station. | On Newton B. Drury Scenic Pkwy. in Prairie Creek Redwoods State Park.

Gold Bluffs Beach. Fern Canyon is nearby this spot on a beach where Roosevelt elk stroll. | End of Davison Rd., off U.S. 101 in Prairie Creek Redwoods State Park.

High Bluff. This picnic area's sunsets and whale-watching are unequaled. A 0.5-mi trail leads from here to the beach. | On Coastal Dr. about 2 mi from U.S. 101, south of Golden Bear Bridge over the Klamath River via Alder Camp Rd.

Jedediah Smith. Old-growth coast redwoods provide shade and scenery at the picnic areas in this campground. | 8 mi east of Crescent City on U.S. 199.

Lagoon Creek. Here, you can beachcomb, fish the freshwater lagoon, or hike along a trail. | Off U.S. 101, 14 mi south of Crescent City visitor center.

Near the Parks

Apple Peddler. American. This busy eatery serves breakfast around the clock, plus burgers, steaks, and seasonal seafood. | 308 U.S. 101 S, Crescent City | 707/464–5630 | $10–$15 | D, MC, V.

★ **Good Harvest Cafe.** Vegetarian. Not only does the Good Harvest have a funky atmosphere, but it serves the best breakfasts in town. A lunch menu of salads, hamburgers, and sandwiches is served after 11 AM, and an espresso bar is open all day long. | 700 Northcrest Dr., Crescent City | 707/465–6028 | $5–$10 | D, DC, MC, V | No dinner.

When traveling in the West, always keep your gas tank as full as possible. There are long stretches—many more than 100 mi—between gas stations, and large areas inhabited by no one at all.

Harbor View Grotto. Seafood. The fish comes straight from the boat, into this casual eatery's kitchen, and onto your plate. Not surprisingly, the dining room has large windows overlooking the Pacific. Note that the white two-story building off U.S. 101 is marked only by a neon RESTAURANT sign—keep your eyes open. | 150 Starfish Way, Crescent City | 707/464–3815 | $13–$21 | D, MC, V.

Headlands Coffee House. Café. Musicians perform nightly at this local haunt. Along with coffee and sweets, you can order lasagna, soups, stews, and Italian-style panini for lunch or dinner. Belgian waffles are a breakfast (served from 7 AM daily) favorite. | 120 E. Laurel St., Fort Bragg | 707/964–1987 | $8–$12 | D, MC, V.

Humboldt Brewing Co. American. This laid-back watering hole caters to a college crowd with burgers, sandwiches, and microbrews. There's live music on weekends. | 856 10th St., Arcata | 707/826–2739 | Reservations not accepted | $7–$16 | AE, D, MC, V.

Palms Cafe. American. Dishes at this funky diner have memorable names: the Vagabond (a bacon burger with cheese), the Long Hand (steak and two eggs), Salesman's Sandwich (French dip), and Old Hen on the Nest (chicken strips, fries, and toast). It's no bastion of haute cuisine, but it's a good place to join the locals for an old-fashioned meal. | 121030 U.S. 101, Orick | 707/488–3381 | $9–$15 | AE, D, DC, MC, V.

★ **Samoa Cookhouse.** American. Loggers and miners have dined at this landmark for more than a century. The giant restaurant serves up hearty meals at long wooden tables. The fixed menu consists of a soup or a salad, an entrée (meat loaf or fried chicken), a side dish (scalloped potatoes or corn), and dessert. | 79 Cookhouse La., Eureka | 707/442–1659 | $14 | AE, D, MC, V.

The Wharf. Continental. From the dining room you can enjoy harbor views while feasting on fresh seafood—from Pacific red snapper to Dungeness crab—or prime rib. At lunch you can sit out on the patio under a big green umbrella. | 780 N. Harbor Dr., Fort Bragg | 707/964–4283 | $15–$23 | D, MC, V.

Lodging

In Redwood

Hostels International–Redwood. Travelers of all ages are welcome at this vintage 1908 Edwardian-style hostel. Perks include an enthusiastic staff and an oceanside location, but beware the 10–5 lockout and the 11 PM curfew. There are three dorm rooms and three private rooms; bring a sleeping bag or plan to rent a sheet. A wood-burning stove warms the common room, and kitchen and laundry facilities are available. | 14480 U.S. 101, Klamath | phone/fax 707/482–8265 | fax 707/482–4665 | www.norcalhostels.com | 34 beds | $16–$42 | MC, V.

Near the Parks

Colonial Inn. Built as a residence in 1912 and converted to a hotel in the 1940s, this inn is an arts and crafts marvel. Rooms have individual furnishings and original artwork in keeping with the Craftsman style; two rooms have wood-burning fireplaces. Cable TV, in-room VCRs. Some pets allowed (fee). No room phones. No smoking. | 533 E. Fir St., Fort Bragg | 707/964–1384 or 877/964–1384 | fax 707/964–4571 | www.colonialinnfortbragg.com | 10 rooms | $80–$140 | No credit cards.

★ **Cornelius Daly Inn.** In the heart of Eureka's historic area, this three-story B&B was built in 1905 as the home of department store magnate Cornelius Daly. Period touches include Victorian gardens, ornate floral wallpaper, a ballroom, and many antiques. Innkeepers Donna and Bob Gafford serve complimentary refreshments in the afternoon. Four rooms have wood-burning fireplaces; some rooms share a bath. Dining room, picnic area. In-room VCRs. Laundry facilities. Business services. No room phones. No smoking. | 1125 H St., Eureka | 707/445–3638 or 800/321–9656 | fax 707/444–3636 | www.dalyinn.com | 5 rooms, 2 suites | $90–$160 | AE, D, MC, V.

Curly Redwood Lodge. A single redwood tree produced the 57,000 ft of lumber used to build this lodge in 1957. Furnishings make the most of that tree, with paneling, platform beds, and built-in dressers. Cable TV. No smoking. | 701 Redwood Hwy. S, Crescent City | 707/464–2137 | fax 707/464–1655 | www.curlyredwoodlodge.com | 36 rooms, 3 suites | $41–$65 | AE, DC, MC, V.

Eureka Inn. Swing dances take place in the vast lobby of this 1922 Tudor-style hotel. Past guests have included Winston Churchill, Cornelius Vanderbilt, Jr., Shirley Temple, Bill Cosby, Steven Spielberg, and Mickey Mantle. 2 restaurants. Cable TV. Pool. Hot tub, sauna. 2 bars. Business services. Airport shuttle. Some pets allowed. | 518 7th St., Eureka | 707/442–6441 or 800/862–4906 | fax 707/442–0637 | www.eurekainn.com | 95 rooms, 9 suites | $99–$145 rooms | AE, D, DC, MC, V.

Grey Whale. Every guest room in this 1915 four-story B&B has a bath and views of the garden, town, hills, or ocean. Some rooms have fireplaces, and one has a hot tub. There's a fireside lounge and a recreation area with a pool table. Restaurant. Library. Business services. No smoking. | 615 N. Main St., Fort Bragg | 707/964–0640 or 800/382–7244 | fax 707/964–4408 | www.greywhaleinn.com | 13 rooms, 1 suite | $98–$165 rooms | AE, D, MC, V.

Harbor Lite Lodge. At a mere 0.25 mi from the beach, the lodge's location is a main selling point. Many rooms overlook the Noyo River and the fishing village, and others have a wood-burning stove. Refrigerators. Cable TV. Sauna. | 120 N. Harbor Dr., Fort Bragg | 707/964–0221 or 800/643–2700 | fax 707/964–8748 | www.harborlitelodge.com | 79 rooms | $77–$142 | AE, D, DC, MC, V.

SLEEP STOPS

You can camp anywhere along Redwood Creek's gravel bars between the first seasonal bridge and no closer than within 0.25 mi of Tall Trees Grove. Backpackers with proper permits can collect up to 50 pounds of dead and down wood per day per campsite.

Hiouchi Motel. This spartan but reliable motel near the Smith River and Jedediah Smith State Park makes plain its purpose by proudly advertising plenty of freezer space for your catch. Still, it's not a bad little place for a nonfishing family to use as base while exploring the surrounding redwoods. Restaurant. | 2097 U.S. 199, Hiouchi | 707/458–3041 | fax 707/458–4312 | 17 rooms | $60 | D, MC, V.

★ **Hotel Arcata.** At this 1915 hotel, sun-drenched rooms are small but quaint, with antique accents, floral curtains, and claw-foot tubs. The tiled lobby has gold chandeliers. Restaurant. Hair salon. Business services. | 708 9th St., Arcata | 707/826–0217 or 866/446–8244 | fax 707/826–1737 | www.hotelarcata.com | 32 rooms | $66–$132 | AE, D, DC, MC, V.

Palms Motel and Cafe. This little motel and the adjacent Palms Cafe are equally endearing, and ideal for a genuine road trip experience. The motel is noted for its namesake palm tree, which sprouts from the roof, and its funky exterior trompe l'oeil mural. The furniture and decor are eclectic, and all rooms have citrus-themed paintings. Cool off with a dip in the enclosed pool. Restaurant. Pool. | 121130 U.S. 101 S, Orick | 707/488–3381 | 18 rooms | $55–$60 | AE, D, MC, V.

Surf and Sand Lodge. Paths lead 150 ft from this motel to the rocky shore. The six least expensive rooms don't have views, but the fancier second-story rooms have hot tubs and fireplaces. All of the rooms have extras such as coffeemakers, hair dryers, and binoculars. Some in-room hot tubs, some kitchenettes, refrigerators. Cable TV. Business services. | 1131 N. Main St., Fort Bragg | 707/964–9383 or 800/964–0184 | fax 707/964–0314 | www.surfsandlodge.com | 30 rooms | $89–$175 | AE, D, DC, MC, V.

Camping and RV Facilities

Within a 30-minute drive of Redwood National and State Parks there are nearly 60 public and private camping facilities. Of the five primitive areas in Redwood, only one—Freshwater Lagoon—is a drive-in site. Although you don't need a permit and the camping is free at the four hike-in primitive sites, stop at a ranger station to inquire about availability. Redwood also has four developed campgrounds, but none of them has RV hookups.

In Redwood

DeMartin Campground. This primitive hike-in area occupies a grassy prairie with a panoramic ocean view. Pit toilets. Drinking water. Fire pits, picnic tables. | 10 sites | 3 mi from Coastal Trail along U.S. 101 | 800/444–7275 | Free.

Elk Prairie Campground. Adjacent to a prairie and old-growth redwoods, this campground is popular with Roosevelt elk. To park here, RVs can be no longer than 27 ft, trailers no longer than 24 ft. Flush toilets. Dump station. Drinking water, showers. Bear boxes, fire pits, picnic tables. Public telephone. Ranger station. | On Newton B. Drury Scenic Pkwy. in Prairie Creek Redwoods State Park | 800/444–7275 | 75 RV or tent sites | $15 | AE, D, MC, V.

BEAR BUSTING

Bears are common sights in the parks. To reduce your likelihood of an unpleasant encounter, keep a clean camp. Food odors entice bears, so store food in airtight containers and use bear-proof lockers if available; otherwise, lock food in the trunk of your car.

Flint Ridge Campground. In old-growth forest with excellent wildlife viewing opportunities, this primitive site is accessible from two trailheads along Coastal Drive: from the west, it's a 0.5-mi hike; from the east, it's 4.5 mi. Pit toilets. Bear boxes, fire pits, picnic tables. | On Coastal Trail south of Klamath River estuary | 800/444–7275 | 10 sites | Free.

Freshwater Lagoon Campground. There's an unlimited number of primitive sites along a strip of sand on the west shoulder of U.S. 101, with the ocean on one side and the lagoon on the other. Car and tent camping are permitted, though most sites are taken by RVs and trailers. The area is not officially run by the park service. Pit toilets. Showers. Fire pits, grills, picnic tables. | 0.25 mi south of Redwood Information Center on U.S. 101 | 707/464–6101 Ext. 5265 | $10, $3 for bikers and hikers | Reservations not accepted | AE, D, MC, V.

Gold Bluffs Beach Campground. You can camp in tents or RVs right on the beach at this Prairie Creek Redwoods State Park campground near Fern Canyon. Keep your eyes open

REDWOOD CAMPGROUNDS

	Total # of sites	# of RV sites	# of hook-ups	Drive-to sites	Hike-to sites	Flush toilets	Pit toilets	Drinking water	Showers	Fire grates/pits	Swimming	Boat access	Playground	Dump station	Ranger station	Public telephone	Reservation possible	Daily fee per site	Dates open
INSIDE THE PARK																			
DeMartin	10	0	0		•		•	•		•								Free	Y/R
Flint Ridge	10	0	0	•			•			•								Free	Y/R
Freshwater Lagoon	ULP	ULP	0	•			•			•								$10	Y/R
Little Bald Hills	5	0	0	•			•	•		•								Free	Y/R
Nickel Creek	5	0	0	•			•			•								Free	Y/R
INSIDE STATE PARKS																			
Elk Prairie	75	75	0	•		•		•	•	•				•	•	•	•*	$15	Y/R
Gold Bluffs Beach	9	25	0	•		•		•	•	•								$15	Y/R
Jedediah Smith	106	106	0	•		•		•	•	•	•	•		•	•	•	•*	$15	Y/R
Mill Creek	145	145	0	•		•		•	•	•				•			•*	$15	Y/R
NEARBY																			
Hiouchi Hamlet R.V. Resort	129	120	0	•		•			•	•				•		•	•	$23	Y/R

* In summer only   ** Reservation fee charged   Y/R=Year-round
UL=Unlimited   ULP=Unlimited primitive   LD=Labor Day   MD=Memorial Day

for Roosevelt elk. Note that RVs must be less than 24-ft long and 8-ft wide, and trailers aren't allowed on the access road. Flush toilets. Drinking water, showers. Fire pits, picnic tables. | At end of Davison Rd., 5 mi north of Redwood Information Center off U.S. 101 | 800/444–7275 | 29 tent sites, 25 RV sites | $15 | Reservations not accepted | AE, D, MC, V.

Jedediah Smith Campground. This is one of the few places to camp—in tents or RVs—within groves of old-growth redwood forest. The length limit on RVs is 36 ft; for trailers it's 31 ft. Flush toilets. Dump station. Drinking water, showers. Bear boxes, fire pits, picnic tables. Public telephone. Ranger station. Play area, swimming (river). | 8 mi northeast of Crescent City on U.S. 199 | 800/444–7275 | 106 RV or tent sites | $15 | AE, D, MC, V.

Little Bald Hills Campground. You can hike, bike, or horseback ride the 4.5-mi through old-growth forest and prairies lined with fir and pine to this primitive area and its ridge-top vistas. There's a corral and horse troughs. Pit toilets. Drinking water. Bear boxes, fire pits, picnic tables. | East end of Howland Hill Rd. | 800/444–7275 | 5 sites | Free.

Mill Creek Campground. Mill Creek is the largest of the state park campgrounds. Flush toilets. Dump station. Drinking water, showers. Bear boxes, fire pits, picnic tables. | West of U.S. 101, 7 mi south of Crescent City | 800/444–7275 | 145 tent and RV sites | $12 | AE, D, MC, V | Apr.–late Sept.

Nickel Creek Campground. An easy hike gets you to this primitive site, which is near tide pools and has great ocean views. Pit toilets. Bear boxes, fire pits, picnic tables. | On Coastal Trail 0.5 mi from end of Enderts Beach Rd. | 800/444–7275 | 5 sites | Free.

Near the Parks

Hiouchi Hamlet R.V. Resort. When it's time to get away from the coastal wind and fog you can take your RV inland. In summer, activities include kayaking and hiking as well as trout fishing; in winter, you can fish for salmon and steelhead on the Smith River. Fishing permits and kayak rentals are available nearby. Flush toilets. Full hookups, dump station. Drinking water, guest laundry, showers. Fire pits, grills, picnic tables. | 4 mi east of Crescent City on U.S. 199 | 707/458–3321 or 800/722–9468 | 9 tent sites, 120 RV sites | $23 | No credit cards.

Shopping

The visitor centers in Orick and Prairie Creek have gift shops that are open year-round. Although there are no general stores inside the park, more than two dozen grocery stores dot the map in the small towns surrounding it.

Orick Market. If you're in the southern half of the park, you can stop at this small market for sundries, liquor, ice, tackle, and some groceries. | 121175 U.S. 101, Orick | 707/488–3225.

Rite Aid Drugstore. In addition to cosmetics and prescription and over-the-counter medicines, this store sells hardware, auto parts, sporting equipment, and camera supplies. | 575 M St., Crescent City | 707/465–3981.

Safeway. Just off U.S. 101 in Crescent City, the 24-hour supermarket is a good place to stock up on groceries. | 475 M St., Crescent City | 707/465–3353.

Essential Information

ATMS: Bank of America | 240 H St., Crescent City | 800/237–8052. **Washington Mutual** | 803 3rd St., Crescent City | 707/464–4106.

AUTOMOBILE SERVICE STATIONS: Crescent City Chevron | 315 U.S. 101 S, Crescent City | 707/465–3825. **Pete's Auto and Marine** | 1305 2nd St., Crescent City | 707/464–2538.

POST OFFICE: Crescent City Post Office | 751 2nd St., Crescent City, 95531 | 707/464–2151.

FIELD GUIDE: PACIFIC NORTHWEST

Ecological Communities

Alpine zone. Thrashed by winter storms of hurricane strength and snowbound until June or July, the alpine zone of the Cascade Mountains is a place where summer is brief but glorious. At timberline, where the larches and high-country firs give way to open meadows, there are lilies, columbines, paintbrush, penstemons, and bluebells blanketing the ground in a vivid tapestry. Marmots whistle, bumblebees poke into blossoms, and hawks and eagles soar in the thermal currents. By the end of August, the seedheads dry, shrubs such as huckleberry begin to turn crimson and purple, and bull elk racks reach their height and lose their velvet. By the time the elks bugle in late September the first storms are swirling in the North Pacific and the entire ecosystem begins a nine-month hibernation under snow that can pile 20 ft deep. It's one of the harshest, and most beautiful, environments on earth.

Pacific shore. South-flowing currents of cold water bring remarkable uniformity to the Pacific Coast climate and habitat. From Eureka, California to Vancouver Island there's a near-uniform ecosystem consisting of spruce, cedar, and hemlock trees; and salal, salmonberry, and thimbleberry undergrowth. The shore itself is a long stretch of rocky headlands and sea stacks interspersed with gray-sand and pebble beaches, especially along the wilderness coast of Olympic National Park. Oregon's coast has the most sand dunes. Harbor seals and California sea lions are common, especially in estuaries, harbors, and river mouths, where they find and eat salmon. The intertidal zone exposed at low tide holds a colorful array of anemones, starfish, mussels, and barnacles, and is a delight for visitors of all ages to explore—taking care not to damage the fragile creatures therein.

Temperate rain forest. The maritime rain forests of the Pacific Northwest depend in large part on the fierce winter rainstorms that drop more than 100 inches of rain on the rain forest valleys of the Olympic Peninsula and the west slopes of the Cascades. In summer, long days at this northerly latitude provide plenty of energy for growth (even if filtered through clouds), and the mild coastal climate adds a long growing season. The region is, in effect, a cool greenhouse. Summer temperatures hover around 70°F; winter temperatures rarely drop below 20°F. As a result, temperate rain forests contain more biotic matter (plant and animal material), by weight than any other habitat on Earth. The trees are redwood, Douglas fir, western red cedar, western hemlock, big-leaf maple, and red alder. The understory is a jungle of shrubs that thrive in low light, such as salmonberry, skunk cabbage, and devil's club; slightly drier locales hold huckleberries. Symbiotic hangers-on (literally) in the rain forest range from the mosses of the lower canopy to the rarely seen flying squirrels that spend almost their whole lives without touching ground. Although the above-ground forest seems lush and rich, the soil in the Northwest's temperate rain forest is quite rocky and shallow. Volcanic in origin, it is leached by the constant winter rain; biologists have discovered that most of the forest's essential nitrogen supply is produced by mosses and lichens that grow in the canopy.

Fauna

BIRDS

Bald eagle. The Northwest is one of the strongholds where America's national symbol survived its mid-20th-century brush with extinction. With a wingspan of up to 8 ft, the bald eagle is as large as any North American bird except the condor. It likes to roost in cottonwoods, but will usually nest in conifers such as Douglas fir, and it's most often seen near water. This eagle thrives on the salmon and waterfowl of the Pacific coast. Some lowland populations are year-round residents, while others migrate as far north as Alaska. The bald eagle does not develop its distinctive white head and tail until maturity at five years. Its late winter mid-air courting dance is sensational.

Rufous hummingbird. A flash of carmine, a sharp chittering cry, and a steep dive— these are the hallmarks of the West Coast hummingbird. Aggressive enough that it has been known to "dive-bomb" people near a food source (such as a feeder), the rufous spends winter in California and summer (April to September) as far north as the Alaska panhandle, nourishing itself with flower nectar and small insects.

Steller's jay. The midnight-blue cap (head and shoulders) of this West Coast bird distinguishes it from the blue jay of the Rockies. While it is not shy, it isn't inclined to steal food like the gray jay familiar to most who have camped in the West.

FISH

Pacific salmon. Four species of salmon are born in and return to Northwest rivers— Chinook (king), the largest at up to 60 pounds; coho (silver), the most widely sought by anglers; pinks; and chum. Most rivers and streams in the national parks are the scene of salmon runs; the best viewing sites are in Olympic National Park. Salmon remain in freshwater until they are about a year old, migrating then to the ocean to feed and grow, and returning to spawn in the fresh waters of their birth after two years. A separate species, steelhead, is considered a trout, and is the only one that sometimes spawns more than once. All Pacific salmon are descended from rainbow trout.

Sunflower starfish. These distinctive orange stars, found in tide pools and sometimes above water at low tide, grow quite large, adding arms with age. Some specimens may have 16 arms and spread 2 ft. Starfish feed on oysters and clams, prying open the shells to get at the meat inside.

MAMMALS

Black bear. *Ursus americanus*, one of the most common animals in the Northwest forests, thrives on the region's spring greens and summertime berries. The black bear grows up to 6 ft long and 600 pounds, but is usually smaller. It can be cinnamon-colored, but is not as large as a brown bear (grizzly). You may see the black bear along roadsides, especially in early summer. *Never* approach or feed a bear.

Black-tailed deer. A subspecies of the common Western mule deer, the black-tail is slightly smaller but no less numerous. It is most often seen at the forest edge at dusk and dawn. Mature bucks have racks 1–4 ft long.

Gray whale. Once on the verge of extinction, the California gray whale population is back to relatively healthy numbers, thanks to federal protection laws. The midsize baleen (bottom-feeding) whale grows to almost 50 ft and migrates along the Pacific coast to the Gulf of Alaska in spring, returning in fall. Often seen within a couple miles of shore in March and April, the gray whale can be recognized by its spout. Unlike the humpback and the orca, it rarely breaches.

Marmot. You know you're in the high country when you hear the distinctive, piercing whistle of the marmot, a denizen of rocky slopes near and above timberline. The hoary marmot of the Pacific Northwest is a chunky animal, about 2 ft long. The Olympic marmot, found only on its namesake peninsula, is a separate species. Marmot, especially the tail, was a favorite prospector delicacy.

Roosevelt elk. The Pacific coast variety of elk is slightly shorter, stockier, and more inclined to browse—eat small plants and brush, as well as grass—than the more numerous Rocky Mountain elk. The imminent disappearance of this magnificent creature prompted Theodore Roosevelt to declare its Olympic Mountains habitat a national monument in 1909, thus the elk's name. Mature bulls reach 5 ft at the shoulder and their mating calls, or bugles, resound from the high ridges in September and October.

Seals and sea lions. The harbor seal and California sea lion, close cousins, both prowl the waters of the Pacific coast. The sea lion is larger, usually 6–7 ft in length; the seal grows to 4–5 ft. Difficult to distinguish in the water, especially at a distance, the two species differ chiefly in that the seal does not have ears, and the sea lion has a longer snout. Both feed on fish. Sea lions consume so much salmon in some areas that they are considered a pest by fishermen. The raucous barking of sea lions on buoys, docks, and rock perches can carry a mile or more and is one of the most common sounds of the Pacific coast.

Flora

FLOWERS

Glacier lily. Look for the low-growing, pendant yellow trumpets of this lily at the edges of receding snowbanks in the highlands of North Cascades, Mount Rainier, and Olympic national parks.

Tiger lily. The vivid, cheery, orange-red trumpets of this native Northwest lily attracted hybridizers, and today it's one of the ancestors of some common garden lilies. Look for its 2-ft stems at the forest edge in the mid- and upper elevations of the Cascades.

SHRUBS

Devil's club. Long, sharp thorns mark the stems of this shrub, which is common in the boggy ground of rain forest valleys. It grows 6–10 ft tall, with huge leaves to gather what little light penetrates to the forest floor.

Huckleberry. Both red and dark-blue forms of the huckleberry, a relative of the blueberry, are found in and around the temperate rain forests of the Northwest. The bushes grow 2–8 ft in height, often in the understory of old-growth forest. If you're looking for bears, the place to find them is a huckleberry patch in August.

Poison oak. Similar to poison ivy, the three-lobed leaves of this shrub are distinctive—and memorable to anyone who has experienced the itchy, blistering rash that contact with them causes. Found in drier locales along the Pacific coast, poison oak turns a most attractive crimson-auburn in late summer and fall.

Salmonberry. The pink blossoms of salmonberries announce the arrival of spring along the Pacific coast from Mendocino to Alaska, drawing rufous hummingbirds north. Orange and reddish berries follow in June. Salmonberry thickets grow in rain forest valleys wherever light penetrates, reaching 8 ft in height and an impenetrable thickness.

TREES

Big-leaf maple. The sizeable leaves that mark the Northwest's largest deciduous tree are sometimes more than a foot across (usually on saplings). Common to lowland valleys such as the Hoh, Queets, and Quinault in Olympic National Park, big-leaf maples can grow to 100 ft, with trunks up to 5 ft in diameter.

Black cottonwood. Tall and straight unlike its plains cousin, the Pacific coast cotton-wood lines almost every river from Northern California to the Yukon. It can reach heights of 80 ft; only the mature tree develops the black, furrowed bark that gives the cottonwood its name. The branches, lined with heart-shaped leaves, are a favorite perch for bald eagles and ospreys. Some inland tribes used the wood for canoes.

Douglas fir. Craggy, deeply lobed reddish bark marks the maritime Northwest's most famous tree. Although it grows throughout the West (and can adapt to dry landscapes) Douglas fir reaches its greatest heights on the west slopes of the Cascades and Olympics, where it can grow to 300 ft high and 11 ft in diameter. It and ponderosa pine are America's two most significant timber species. Old-growth Douglas fir lumber, now very expensive, is so hard that nails cannot be driven into it.

Red alder. The reddish inner bark of this ubiquitous lowland tree gives it its name. A relative of aspen, alder grows in dense thickets along stream-courses from northern California to southeast Alaska; its wood was traditionally used by coastal Native Americans to roast salmon, and is now used for furniture.

Redwood. Redwoods are the tallest and most admired of the West Coast's giant trees. The dark-amber bark, graceful spire shape, and incredible size and age of the trees lend redwood groves a cathedral-like air unmatched in any other forest. Redwoods grow only in the coastal ranges from Big Sur to southern Oregon, and are highly dependent on moisture from the intense winter rains and the summer morning coastal fog.

Sitka spruce. The near-shore forest of the Northwest is composed mainly of this dense-canopied tree that can reach 10 ft in diameter. Its light wood was once used for airplane frames (the reason that the Boeing Company started up in Seattle) and is now valued for musical instruments such as guitars and pianos.

Vine maple. The slender, whiplike stems of this small tree make it seem like a shrub. Found at the edge of clearings in Douglas fir groves, vine maple is unremarkable 10 months of the year. Late August through early October, however, its leaves turn incandescent shades of crimson, maroon, and burgundy, making it the most conspicuous rain forest tree in autumn.

Western red cedar. There's almost no end to the uses coastal Natives made of cedar—the bark yielded clothing, rope, fish-nets and baskets; the wood made planks for housing; entire trunks were carved into canoes. The huge, pyramidal base of the red cedar helps to hold the tree fast in the wet ground it prefers. The tops of old red cedars are almost always snapped off by storms, and the side branches that spring up create the "candelabra" appearance. Red cedars can reach 20 ft in diameter and surpass 1,000 years in age. Highly valued for decking and roofing material, most available old-growth cedar has been cut, and second-growth wood is not nearly as rot-resistant.

Geology and Terrain

Two huge forces shaped the Northwest landscape—glaciation, both local and during ice ages; and the tectonic dynamism of the Pacific Rim, whose earthquakes and volcanic eruptions are almost constant events on the geologic time scale. Most of the Pacific coast is relatively young, its volcanoes less than a million years old. The Cascade Range is also just a teenager in geological time.

Caldera. Although it is the largest and deepest example, the bowl-shaped depression in which Crater Lake lies is only one of many along the Pacific Rim. Created when volcanoes blow their tops, small caldera remnants lie atop Mount Rainier and Mount Baker, and a bigger one remains on Mount St. Helens, where its side blew out in 1980.

Glacial valley. The steep-sided, tunnel-shape valleys that wrinkle the Cascades are the result of glacial carving that occurred during the most recent ice ages 15,000 and 35,000 years ago. Excellent examples are the Stehekin Valley in the Lake Chelan National Recreation Area, the Carbon River Valley on the northwest side of Mount Rainier National Park, and the Elwha Valley on the north side of Olympic National Park.

Glaciers. Heavy snow compacted by centuries of accumulation forms the distinctive blue, dense ice of a glacier. Incremental movement, usually inches a year, is what distinguishes a glacier from a snowfield; most of the glaciers in the continental United States are in Washington and Oregon, and most are receding due to global warming.

Sea stacks. Perched offshore, from San Francisco to Vancouver, Canada, sea stacks are rock headlands and pinnacles. They are composed of basalt and other volcanic material and have been separated from the mainland by the Pacific's erosive force. Some West Coast sea stacks rise more than 100 ft above the surf, and with breakers surging onto and around them, they are highly photogenic. Some of the best are found from Eureka, CA to Port Orford, OR; and from Queets to Neah Bay, WA. Sea caves and arches are rarer.

Volcanoes. The volcanoes of the West Coast—including Mount Rainier, Crater Lake, Mount Hood, and Mount Baker—are not, as commonly believed, dormant. Instead, most are described as "episodically active," as Mount St. Helens was in 1980. Most of the Northwest's volcanoes are much younger than a million years old. The mountains themselves are composed of basalt and pumice.

California Classics

It's impossible to exaggerate the majesty and awe-inspiring beauty of California's national parks. Giant glaciated river canyons, vast scorching deserts, and tiny fog-shrouded islands lie within several hours of the state's largest metropolitan areas. Though you can reach them in half a day, you'll feel a world away from civilization by the time you approach the parks. At 14,494 ft, Mount Whitney in Sequoia National Park is the highest point in the continental United States. If you're brave enough to summit her craggy peak, you'll spot the lowest point on the continent, in Death Valley 282 ft below sea level. West of Mount Whitney's ridgeline, 2,000-year-old stands of giant sequoia dwarf people, and still farther west, the Channel Islands support species of plants and animals found nowhere else on earth. Follow the Sierra crest to Yosemite, and you see the world's largest granite monolith, the continent's highest waterfall, and the Sierra Nevada's largest subalpine meadow, which explodes with wildflowers every summer. Near the Oregon border, the Mount Lassen volcano, which erupted 1914–21, is a living labora-tory for geologists. There is no way to speak of the national parks of California without using superlatives. As you explore the state's ever-changing terrain, you will come to under-stand that no matter how many times you return, you'll never be able to see it all.

Rules of the Road

California highways present drivers with every imaginable challenge. Wintertime rains on the coast occasionally wash out portions of Route 1, heavy snows close some roads over the Sierra Nevada for months at a time, and rush–hour traffic on freeways around urban areas can slow to a crawl. Proper preparation is a must. Because of great varia-tions in temperature between the valleys and the mountains, particularly in summer, your vehicle can take a beating. Keep it in good mechanical order, with all fluids topped off, and ensure that your tires have the necessary tread depth and are properly inflated. Make sure your spare tire is in good condition, too. If you are driving to the mountains in winter, check road conditions before you depart and, unless you have a four-wheel-

In This Chapter

Channel Islands National Park • Death Valley National Park • Lassen Volcanic National Park • Sequoia and Kings Canyon National Parks • Yosemite National Park

drive vehicle with all-season tires, always carry chains—they are available at some gas stations and most auto-supply stores in the foothills—and learn how to install and remove them yourself.

License Requirements: To drive in California, you must have a valid driver's license. Non-U.S. residents should have a license whose text is in the Roman alphabet, though it need not be in English; an international license is strongly recommended but not required. Remember, if the police can't easily read or interpret your foreign driver's license, they may question its validity. Drivers must carry proof of insurance.

Right Turn on Red: Unless otherwise indicated, a right turn at a red light is allowed after you come to a full stop. A left turn at a red light is allowed only from a one-way street onto another one-way street.

Seat Belt/Helmet Laws: Seat belts are required for all passengers and the driver at all times. Children must sit in approved child safety seats or booster seats until they are 6 years old or weigh 60 pounds. Operators of single-track vehicles such as motorcycles must always wear a helmet.

Speed Limits: The speed limit on many rural highways is 70 mph. Freeway speed limits are 55–65 mph.

For More Information: California Department of Motor Vehicles | 800/777–0133. **California Highway Patrol** | 916/657–7202. **Caltrans Highway Information Line** | 800/427–7623 or 916/445–1534.

California Classics Driving Tour
FROM LASSEN VOLCANIC TO CHANNEL ISLANDS

Distance: 1,600–2,200 mi   Time: 8–11 days
Breaks: Overnight in Lassen Volcanic National Park, Mineral, or Red Bluff; Tahoe City; Yosemite National Park or Mariposa Kings Canyon or Sequoia national parks; Bakersfield or Lake Isabella; Death Valley National Park; Barstow or Los Angeles; and Ventura.

Most of California's national parks require a full day or more to visit. By staying at each one for two or more nights, you can get a sense of what makes them special. You may wish to shorten the driving tour by traveling on I–5 between Los Angeles and San Francisco. Though it runs through the agricultural Central Valley and can be extremely foggy in winter and scorching hot in summer (and not all that interesting to tourists), it is by far the fastest route. Route 1 takes 12 hours; U.S. 101, nine hours; and I–5, six hours. If you do travel the coast, stop at Hearst Castle (reservations for tours are essential; call 805/927–2020 or 800/444–4445). Monterey, Carmel, and Santa Barbara, also along the coast, are beautiful places to stay and dine.

Beginning in San Francisco gives you the option of going first to either Mount Lassen or to Yosemite. In summer, make Lassen your first stop. In winter, Route 89 through the park is closed due to snow, so skip Lassen and go directly to Yosemite.

❶ From **San Francisco,** take I–80 east to I–505 north to I–5 north, and continue to Red Bluff, the western gateway to Lassen Volcanic National Park. Spend the night in the park, in **Mineral,** or in **Red Bluff.** If you're taking the tour in winter, or if you prefer to skip Lassen, then leave San Francisco via the Bay Bridge and follow I–580 east to I–205 east to I–5 north. Two miles after entering I–5, exit the freeway onto Route 120 east and follow it to Yosemite. The drive takes about four hours and is approximately 200 mi from the city.

PERNICIOUS PLANT

From the coastal areas to elevations of 5,000 ft, watch out for poison oak. Leaves grow in clusters of three, are red in fall and green in summer, and have an oily sheen. If you come into contact with them, wash with hot soap and water or with Tecnu, an over-the-counter soap made specifically to counteract the effects of poison oak. There is no poison ivy in California.

② To reach **Lassen Volcanic National Park** from Red Bluff, turn east on Route 36 for 47 mi, then north on Route 89. Enter the park through the southwest entrance. As you wind your way up the mountains, note that this is where the Sierra meet the Cascades; plant and animal species unique to each co-exist here. Near the road's highest point, tiny Lake Helen is still frozen well into August, hinting at the area's harsh and snowy winters. At the northwest entrance station, continue north to the junction with Route 44 at Old Station. Go east on Route 44 through Lassen National Forest. At the junction with Route 36, turn west toward Lake Almanor. When the road intersects with Route 89, turn south. The loop through and around the park is approximately 125 mi and, without stops, takes about three hours. Add time to see the park. Spend another night in or near Lassen.

③ The next day, drive south on Route 89 for three hours and about 150 mi to **Lake Tahoe,** where you can spend an enjoyable afternoon and stay for the night. The town of Tahoe City on the northwest shore has accommodations ranging from rustic vacation cottages to small hotel-style resorts.

④ Early on the morning of day four, take Route 89 through the spectacular scenery along the west shore of the lake. Route 89 ends at U.S. 395 about 85 mi or 2¹/₂ hours from Tahoe City. (In winter, Route 89 along the southwest shore of the lake may be closed for avalanche control immediately following a snowstorm, and it will certainly be closed over Monitor Pass, just west of U.S. 395, for the entire season. At these times, take Route 28 around the north and east shores of the lake to U.S. 50 east to U.S. 395 south.) Turn south on U.S. 395 and drive 60 mi through the high-mountain desert of the eastern Sierra to Route 120. Drive west on Route 120 and enter **Yosemite National Park** through its eastern gate. The 60-mi crossing over the high country takes you over Tioga Pass. At 9,941 ft, this is the highest stretch of road in California. Upon reaching Tuolumne Meadows, stop for lunch and see the carpet of wildflowers that stretches across the huge alpine meadow. Follow Route 120 to the turn-off for Yosemite Valley, and drive through the Valley to view its huge granite monoliths from up close. Traffic through the park can move slowly in summer; plan on two full hours to reach the Valley from the eastern gate. In winter, Route 120 from the east is closed, so approach the Valley from the west via Route 120 or Route 140. If you can secure a reservation, stay the night in Yosemite Valley or Wawona. Otherwise, book a room in Mariposa, 40 mi to the west on Route 140.

⑤ Spend the next day and night in Yosemite, then on day six leave Yosemite Valley on Route 41 south and drive 100 mi, or about two hours, to Fresno and the turn-off for Route 180 east. Ahead 50 mi, you'll reach the entrance to **Kings Canyon National Park.** Follow Route 180 (summer only) along the Kings River and its giant granite canyon, well over a mile deep at some points. Stop along the way at pull-outs for long vistas of some of the highest mountains in the United States. (In winter, you'll have to head south on the Generals Highway.)

⑥ Double back to the Generals Highway and continue south to **Sequoia National Park,** where some of the world's oldest and largest trees stand. Driving the winding, 40-mi-long Generals Highway takes about two hours. Book in advance and stay for two nights in either of the two parks. Spend the intervening day exploring the parks.

⑦ On day eight leave Sequoia via the southern entrance and follow Route 198 about 23 mi to Route 65 south, where you'll turn left and head 60 mi toward Bakersfield. Route 65 ends at Route 99 south; get on the freeway, go one exit to Route 204 (Golden State Avenue), and turn onto Route 178 east. Follow Route 178 through the southern tip of the Sequoia National Forest, and about 35 mi from Bakersfield, you'll reach **Lake Isabella,** the reservoir that catches the water from the Kern River, the major drainage for snow melting off the peaks in Sequoia National Park. The trip from Sequoia to the lake should take three hours.

8 Continue east on Route 178 for about 55 mi, where the road joins U.S. 395 north. Turn north on U.S. 395 and travel about 80 mi to Route 190 east, where you'll turn right and continue 60 mi to **Death Valley National Park.** Vast expanses of desert and mountain ranges extend as far as the eye can see, and you'll find the lowest point on the continent here, at 282 ft below sea level. Summer heat is brutal, and all safety precautions should be taken. Plan on spending the night here, but be sure to secure reservations in advance; this isolated area is not a place to wander around looking for a room. From Lake Isabella, the trip should take three to four hours, so expect an eight-hour, 400-mi day of driving from Sequoia National Park. Alternatively, stop in Bakersfield for the night, or camp at Lake Isabella, and make the trip the next day. If you make the trip in one shot, spend two nights in Death Valley and explore the park for a full day. If you stop for the night between Sequoia and Death Valley, get an early start so you can spend most of the day in the park, then overnight there.

9 Leave Death Valley early in the morning on day 10. Travel east on Route 190 to Death Valley Junction and turn south onto Route 127, passing **Mojave National Preserve.** Drive 115 mi through the Mojave Desert to I–15, then travel south 60 mi on the interstate to **Barstow,** where you can stop for lunch. The town is nothing special, but you can visit **Rainbow Basin National Natural Landmark** and take a short hike through a landscape of colored sedimentary rock; it's 8 mi north of town. The trip from Death Valley to Barstow should take around four hours. From Barstow, head south on I–15 for 70 mi to I–10, where you'll turn west and drive about 20 mi. Be prepared for speeding cars and the always-busy freeways of the Los Angeles Basin. Pay attention: Los Angeles's freeway system uses both names and numbers, and sometimes the route number changes but the name of the freeway does not.

10 To skirt north of L.A., take I–210 (Foothill Freeway) west for 24 mi to Route 134 (Ventura Freeway) west. Approximately 12 mi ahead, Route 134 will merge with U.S. 101 north. Though the road numbers change, you will remain on the Ventura Freeway for approximately 50 mi to **Ventura,** one of the gateway cities to Channel Islands National Park. From Barstow, plan on five hours' travel time. This is a scenic, but long day's drive through the desert from Death Valley, and you may wish to break the trip into two days by spending the night in Barstow or Los Angeles. If you drive straight through you'll be spending two nights in Ventura and if not, you'll spend one.

11 The seaside community of Ventura is home to many beaches and the **Channel Islands National Park** visitor center. Many folks stop at the visitor center but don't actually make it out to the islands. If you're planning to visit the islands themselves, you'll need a reservation for the boat. Otherwise you can go to the docks and, if you're lucky, catch a glimpse of them from shore. As they are often obscured by fog or mist, you may be unable to spot them.

Your tour of the classic California parks ends in Ventura. If you plan to head back to San Francisco you have a delightful drive still ahead of you. Following U.S. 101 north you'll pass **12 San Luis Obispo,** home of Mission San Luis Obispo de Tolosa, the County Historical Museum, and the kitschy and garish Madonna Inn. From San Luis Obispo you can continue north either on scenic but slow Route 1 (Pacific Coast Highway) or on speedy but nondescript U.S. 101. Either way, it's about 230 mi to San Francisco. Along the way, stop in **13 Monterey and Carmel,** where you can have lunch and visit the Monterey Bay Aquarium or the Carmel Mission. Plan the rest of your drive back to San Francisco carefully so as to avoid rush hour in San Jose, usually 4 PM–7 PM.

When to Visit

Many of California's national parks are in the Sierra Nevada mountain range, so it's best to plan a visit between April and October. Heavy snows in winter close many roads and the cloud ceiling may not lift for days, obstructing the views for which many of these parks are famous. Still, if you must come between November and March you'll have the parks almost to yourself, and will be free to enjoy the quiet that the off-season brings. And winter is perhaps the best time to see Death Valley, since summertime temperatures can exceed 110°F. The ideal time for visiting any of the parks is spring or fall, when temperatures are mild and crowds few.

CLIMATE

If you're traveling to California in summer, you can expect high humidity and cool temperatures on the coast (highs in the upper 60s); scorching heat and low humidity in the inland valleys (highs in the upper 90s); and warm days and cool nights in the mountains (highs in the low-80s). From the coast to the lower foothills, wintertime temperatures rarely drop below freezing, but the air is damp and cool. The rainiest months are from December through March.

What to Pack

Layers of lightweight clothing are optimal year-round in California, except in the mountains where you'll need heavier outerwear in winter. Pack a windbreaker, sweater, long-sleeved shirt, short-sleeved shirt, bathing suit, cotton pants, hiking shorts, and a sun hat. If you plan to hike, sturdy boots that support your ankles are best. As nighttime temperatures can drop to near freezing in the mountains and fog enshrouds the coast for much of the summer, it may be helpful to pack long underwear. Bring a comfortable pair of sandals or sneakers to wear in the car. If you're going to Death Valley, protect yourself from sunburn and dehydration by wearing lightweight clothing that covers your arms and legs, and always wear a hat to avoid sunstroke.

Wintertime brings rain to the coast and snow to the mountains. You'll need a rain jacket and waterproof foot gear, and if you're traveling to high elevations, carry a wool cap, long underwear, warm socks, a thick sweater, gloves, and a ski parka. For hiking, a pair of nylon gators is helpful to keep your pants from getting wet with snow. On the coast, layers of medium-weight clothing are better than thick sweaters and heavy jackets, since it can get quite warm in the middle of the day. Lightweight layers are enough for the desert during the day, but at night the desert is very cold so you'll need a heavy sweater, a warm hat, thick socks, long underwear, and gloves.

At any time of year, sunglasses and sunscreen are essential. Always bring lots of water and snacks, since distances between the parks are long and there are few services in the mountains and deserts.

CHANNEL ISLANDS NATIONAL PARK

SOUTHERN CALIFORNIA

In the Santa Barbara Channel, south of Santa Barbara and southwest of Oxnard and Ventura. In Ventura, follow Harbor Boulevard south to Ventura Marina. In Oxnard, take Victoria Avenue to Channel Islands Marina. In Santa Barbara, follow Carrillo to Santa Barbara Marina.

The mountains that mark Channel Islands National Park are clearly visible against the blue sky on brilliantly clear days. But more often than not they are hidden behind a thin veil of mist, totally obscuring them from view. Most of the 12 million people who live in Southern California have never seen them, let alone experienced the splendid wilderness they protect. Northwest of Los Angeles, the Channel Islands range in size from 1-square-mi Santa Barbara to 96-square-mi Santa Cruz. They protect many native plants and animals found nowhere else on the planet. If you visit East Anacapa, you'll walk through a nesting area of western gulls. If you're lucky enough to get to windswept San Miguel you might have a chance to see as many as 30,000 pinnipeds (seals and sea lions) camped out on the beach. Kayakers have an opportunity to paddle with the seals, while snorkelers and divers will move through some of the world's richest kelp forests. Even traveling on an excursion boat will give you a chance to visit the sea lions, spot a brown pelican, or watch a whale spout.

PUBLICATIONS

In the Channel Islands visitor center you can find a handful of books about this little-known gem, including *California's Channel Islands: 1001 Questions Answered* by Marla Daily and *Channel Islands National Park* by Tim Hauf. In addition, *Island of the Blue Dolphins* by Scott O'Dell is a good book to get kids acquainted with the park.

When to Visit

SCENERY AND WILDLIFE

Sometimes called the North American Galapagos, the Channel Islands are home to species found nowhere else on Earth. Mammals such as the island fox, birds like the island scrub jay, and plants like the Santa Barbara live-forever make their homes on one or more of the islands. Other species, such as the Santa Rosa Torrey pine and the island oak have evolved differently from their counterparts on the mainland. It all adds up to a living laboratory not unlike the one naturalist Charles Darwin discovered off the coast of South America 200 years ago.

HIGH AND LOW SEASON

Relatively few people visit Channel Islands, so crowds are rarely a problem. About 620,000 visitors are recorded each year, and most of those never venture beyond the visitor center in Ventura. Summer and fall—when winds are calm and the weather is warm—are the ideal times for water sports in the Channel Islands. You must be prepared for fog, high winds, and rough seas any time of the year.

CHANNEL ISLANDS
NATIONAL PARK

EXPLORING
ATTRACTIONS NEARBY
DINING
LODGING
CAMPING AND RV
FACILITIES
SHOPPING
ESSENTIAL
INFORMATION

Average High/Low Temperature (°F) and Monthly Precipitation (in inches)

	JAN.	FEB.	MAR.	APR.	MAY	JUNE
CHANNEL	66/44	66/45	66/46	68/48	69/51	71/55
ISLANDS	3.00	3.10	2.40	0.90	0.10	0.00

	JULY	AUG.	SEPT.	OCT.	NOV.	DEC.
	74/57	75/59	75/57	74/53	70/48	66/44
	0.00	0.10	0.40	0.30	2.00	2.00

FESTIVALS AND SEASONAL EVENTS
WINTER

Dec.: **Channel Islands Harbor Parade of Lights.** A celebration of the islands' natural beauty, this evening parade on the water has been a tradition since 1965. | 805/985–4852.

Jan.–Mar.: **Celebration of the Whale.** This annual event held in Channel Islands Harbor celebrates the migration of the gray whale. Highlights include

**UNTRAMMELED
ISLANDS**

*You'll find plenty
of solitude on the
islands. Fewer than
30,000 people set
foot on all of them
in the course of a
year.*

marine-related exhibits from the national park, whale-watching trips,
an open-air art festival, and children's crafts and entertainment. | 805/
985–4852.

SPRING

Mar.: **Spring Flower Viewing.** Displays of the native plants of Channel Islands
are found on the islands and at Channel Islands visitor center in Ventura.
| 805/658–5730.

May: **California Strawberry Festival.** Celebrate Oxnard's cash crop with strawberries prepared more ways than you could imagine—strawberry short-
cake, strawberry jam, strawberry tarts, and even strawberry pizza. | 805/
385–4739 or 888/288–9242.

SUMMER

July: **Salsa Festival.** Things get spicy at this annual event that celebrates
everything salsa—music, dancing, and condiment. Festivities take place
at 5th and B streets in Oxnard. | 805/289–4875.

Aug.: **Hueneme Beach Festival.** Hit the beach for this family-oriented celebration in Port Hueneme. There are games, live music, and a swimming con-
test for the area's lifeguards. | 323/655–2010.

FALL

Oct.: **Ventura Kinetic Sculpture Race.** Getting there is more than half the fun
in this light-hearted competition between home-constructed people-
powered vehicles. | 805/652–0000.

Taste of Ventura County Food and Wine Festival. Sample fine fare from
30 regional restaurants, then wash it down with vintages from 25 wineries.
| 800/333–2989.

Nearby Towns

**PERSONAL
PROTECTION**

*Be prepared for
high winds, fog,
and rough seas any
time of year. High
winds can come
without notice,
particularly on the
outer islands of
Santa Rosa and San
Miguel. Carry a
warm jacket and
wear sunscreen,
sunglasses, and a
wide-brim hat that
you can tie to your
head.*

With a population of more than 100,000, **Ventura** is the main gateway to Channel Islands
National Park. It's a classic California beach town filled with interesting restaurants, a
wide range of accommodations, and miles of clean, white beaches. The first inhabitants
were the Chumash people, who also once populated the Channel Islands. South of
Ventura is **Oxnard,** a community of 162,000 boasting a busy harbor and uncrowded
beaches. The first European to visit the area was Spanish explorer Juan Rodriguez Cabrillo,
who called it the "land of everlasting summers." It's surrounded by vast fields where broc-
coli, lettuce, and strawberries are grown. The U. S. arrival point for many of the world's
most famous luxury cars, **Port Hueneme** (pronounced "why-nee-mee") is the only major
port for international shipping between Los Angeles and San Francisco. This quiet beach
town is also home of the U.S. Navy Civil Engineer Corps, which is why you'll find the Seabee
Museum in this little town of 22,000. Known for its Spanish ambiance, **Santa Barbara**
has a beautiful waterfront set against a backdrop of towering mountains. Here you'll
find glistening palm-lined beaches, white-washed adobe structures with red-tile roofs,
and plenty of genteel charm.

INFORMATION

Oxnard Convention and Visitors Bureau | 200 W. 7th St., Oxnard, 93030-7154 | 805/385–
7545 or 800/269–6273 | www.oxnardtourism.com. **Port Hueneme Chamber of Commerce**
| 220 N. Market St., Port Hueneme, 93041 | 805/488–2023 | www.huenemechamber.com.
Santa Barbara Conference and Visitors Bureau and Film Commission | 1601 Anacapa St.,
Santa Barbara, 93101-1909 | 805/966–9222 or 800/549–5133 | www.santabarbaraca.com.

Ventura Visitors and Convention Bureau | 89 S. California St., Suite C, Ventura, 93001 | 805/648–2075 or 800/333–2989 | www.ventura-usa.com.

Exploring Channel Islands

PARK BASICS

Contacts and Resources: Channel Islands Visitor Center | 1901 Spinnaker Dr., Ventura, CA 93001 | 805/658–5730 | www.nps.gov/chis | Daily 8:30–5.

Hours: The islands are open every day of the year. Channel Islands visitor center is closed Thanksgiving and Christmas.

Fees: There is no fee to enter Channel Islands National Park, but there is a $7.35-per-day campground use fee. The cost of taking a boat to the park varies depending on individual operators.

Getting Around: Private vehicles are not permitted on the islands. Transportation to and from the mainland is provided by private companies; the following are the three official park concessionaires. Most scheduled day trips are to a single island, so island-hopping is not an option unless you charter a boat or take a multi-day trip.

Channel Islands Aviation. Channel Islands Aviation provides charter flights from Camarillo Airport, about 10 mi east of Oxnard, to an airstrip on Santa Rosa. You can spend as little as an hour or close to a full day on the island. | 305 Durley Ave., Camarillo | 805/987–1301 | www.flycia.com | $106 per person.

Island Packers. Sailing from Oxnard and Ventura, this company heads to Anacapa and Santa Cruz daily in summer, less frequently the rest of the year. Island Packers also visits the other islands three to four times a month and provides transportation for campers. | 3600 S. Harbor Blvd., Oxnard | 805/642–1393 | 1691 Spinnaker Dr., Ventura | 805/642–1393 | www.islandpackers.com | $32–$62.

Truth Aquatics. If you want to depart the mainland from Santa Barbara, Truth Aquatics serves all the park's islands for single-day voyages or multiple-day overnight trips, when you can sleep on board the 65' twin-engine single-hull vessels, or camp on the islands. They also offer scuba-diving tours. | 301 W. Cabrillo Blvd., Santa Barbara | 805/962–1127 | www.truthaquatics.com | $60–$75 for day trips, add $10 per night for camping; onboard all-inclusive overnight trips average $130 per day.

Permits: Permits are not required to visit Channel Islands except at Middle Anacapa. Boaters who want to land on the Nature Conservancy preserve on Santa Cruz Island should call 949/263–0933 Ext. 36, or visit www.tnccalifornia.org; allow 15 days to process your application. To hike on San Miguel, call 805/658–5711. Anglers require a state fishing license. For details, call the California Department of Fish and Game at 916/653–7664.

Accessibility: Channel Islands visitor center is fully accessible. The islands themselves have few facilities and are not easy to navigate by individuals in wheelchairs or those with limited mobility.

Public Telephones: Public telephones are available near Channel Islands visitor center. There are no public phones on the islands.

Rest Rooms: Public rest rooms are available at Channel Islands visitor center and at the campgrounds on all five islands.

Emergencies: In the event of an emergency, contact a park ranger on patrol or call 911.

Lost and Found: The park's lost-and-found is at Channel Islands visitor center.

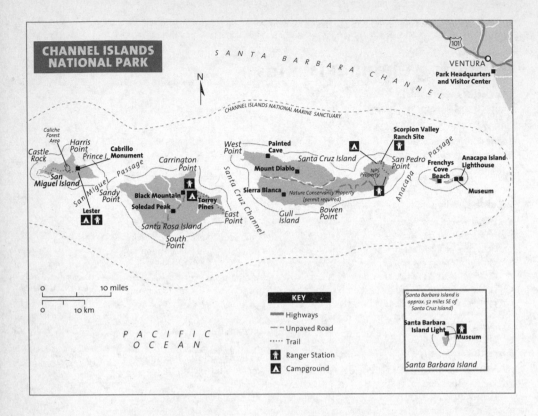

Good Tours

CHANNEL ISLANDS IN ONE DAY

If you have just one day to visit Channel Islands National Park, view the exhibits at the **visitor center** in Ventura and cruise over to **East Anacapa,** where you'll have sweeping views of the mainland—provided it's not too foggy. Hiking is the primary activity here, especially in spring where there are fields of sunny coreopsis flowers. Wander through western gull rookeries or peer down from steep cliffs and watch the antics of sea lions and seals.

CHANNEL ISLANDS IN TWO OR THREE DAYS

If you have two days to explore Channel Islands, on the first day check out the **visitor center** in Ventura, then take a full- or half-day cruise out to **Anacapa,** where you can explore the island on foot or by kayak. Return to the mainland and overnight at one of the lodgings in the nearby towns. On the second day board a boat bound for Scorpion Anchorage on **Santa Cruz Island,** where you'll find a nice white-sand beach for kayaking, snorkeling, or sunbathing. You can also visit the historic ranch here or hike to **Cavern Point** to admire sweeping coastal vistas and scan the horizon for migrating gray whales. Alternately, on the second day you can take a cruise to **Santa Rosa Island,** which includes a boat ride through the spectacular **Painted Cave** at the northwestern end of Santa Cruz Island.

Programs and Tours

Interpreting the Language of the Park. Presentations by different rangers focus on the park's rich history. Rangers discuss everything from tide pools and marine life to human and cultural history. Presented at the Channel Islands visitor center. | 1901 Spinnaker Rd., Ventura | 805/658–5730 | www.nps.gov/chis | Free | Weekends and holidays 3 PM.

Tidepool Talk. Explore the area's marine habitat without getting your feet wet. Rangers show how animals and plants adapt to the harsh condition found in tidal pools of the Channel Islands. At the Channel Islands visitor center. | 1901 Spinnaker Rd., Ventura | 805/658–5730 | www.nps.gov/chis | Weekends and holidays at 11 AM.

Underwater Video Program. Divers armed with video cameras explore the undersea world of the kelp forest off Anacapa Island. Images are transmitted to monitors located on the dock at Landing Cove and in the main visitor center. You'll see what the divers are seeing: bright red sea stars, spiny sea urchins, brilliant orange garibaldis. | Landing Cove, Anacapa Island | Summer, Tue. and Thurs., 2 PM | Free.

SIGHTS TO SEE

★ **Anacapa Island.** Although most people think of it as an island, Anacapa comprises three narrow islets. Although the tips of these volcanic formations nearly touch, they are inaccessible from each other except by boat. Here you'll find towering cliffs, isolated sea caves, and natural bridges such as Arch Rock, one of the best-known symbols of Channel Islands National Park. Wildlife viewing is the reason most people come to Anacapa, particularly in summer when the seagull chicks are crying for food and sea lions and seals are lounging on the beaches. Almost all visitors head to East Anacapa, the park's most popular destination. A limited number of boats travel to Frenchy's Cove on West Anacapa, where there's a pristine tide pool. The rest of West Anacapa is closed to protect nesting brown pelicans.

Displaying the original crystal and brass lens from the nearby lighthouse and other interesting items, the compact **museum** tells the history of the island. Summer visitors can also learn about the nearby kelp forest from rangers. | East Anacapa | No phone | Daily.

San Miguel Island. The westernmost of the Channel Islands, San Miguel is frequently battered by storms sweeping across the North Pacific. The 15-square-mi island's wild, windswept landscape is lush with vegetation. Point Bennett at the western tip of the island offers one of the world's most spectacular wildlife displays when more than 30,000 pinnipeds hit the beach. Explorer Juan Rodriguez Cabrillo was the first European to visit this island; he claimed it for Spain in 1542. Legend holds that Cabrillo died on the island; no one knows where he's buried, but there's a memorial to him on a bluff above Cuyler Harbor.

Santa Barbara Island. At about 1-square-mi, Santa Barbara is the smallest of the Channel Islands. It's also the southernmost island in the chain, separated from the others by nearly 40 mi. Roughly triangular in shape, its steep cliffs are topped by twin peaks. The island was visited in 1602 by explorer Sebastian Vizcaino, who named it in honor of Saint Barbara. Each spring the island treats visitors to a brilliant display of yellow coreopsis and many other wildflowers. The cliffs here offer a perfect nesting spot for the Xantus' murrelet, a rare seabird.

With exhibits on the region's natural history, the small **museum** is a great place to learn about the wildlife on and around the islands. | Santa Barbara Island | No phone | Daily.

Santa Cruz Island. Five miles west of Anacapa, 96-square-mi Santa Cruz is the largest of the Channel Islands. The National Park Service manages the eastern part of the island; the rest is owned by The Nature Conservancy, which requires a permit to land. When your boat drops you off on the 70 mi of craggy coastline you'll find two rugged mountain ranges with peaks soaring to 2,000 ft and deep canyons traversed by steams. This varied environment is home to a remarkable array of species—more than 600 plants, 140 land birds, 11 mammals, five reptiles, three amphibians. Bird-watchers will want to look for the endemic scrub jay, found nowhere else in the world. Although the Chumash occupied the island for 8,000 years, the first European to visit was Gaspar Portola in 1769.

CHANNEL ISLANDS
NATIONAL PARK

EXPLORING
ATTRACTIONS NEARBY
DINING
LODGING
CAMPING AND RV
FACILITIES
SHOPPING
ESSENTIAL
INFORMATION

IN THE POOL

The tide pools at Channel Islands are some of the most interesting in Southern California. At certain times of the year at Frenchy's Cove on West Anacapa you can get close up and personal with anemones, sea stars, urchins, limpets, periwinkles, barnacles, and mussels.

★ The largest and deepest sea cave in the world, **Painted Cave,** lies along the northwest coast of Santa Cruz. Named for the colorful lichen that cover its walls, Painted Cave is nearly 0.25-mi long and 100 ft wide. In spring, a waterfall cascades over the entrance. Kayakers may encounter seals or sea lions cruising alongside their boats inside the cave.

Remnants of a dozen Chumash villages can be seen here. The largest of these villages, at the eastern end of the island, occupied the area now called **Scorpion Ranch.** The Chumash mined extensive chert deposits on the island for tools to produce "shell-bead money," which they traded with people on the mainland. Remnants of the ranching era can also be seen in the massive adobe ovens that produced bread for the entire island.

Santa Rosa Island. Located between Santa Cruz and San Miguel, Santa Rosa is the second largest of the Channel Islands. The island has a relatively low profile, broken by a central mountain range rising to 1,589 ft. The coastal areas range from broad sandy beaches to sheer cliffs. The island is home to about 500 species of plants, including the rare Torrey pine. Three unusual mammals—the endemic island fox, spotted skunk, and deer mouse—are among those that make their home here. They hardly compare to the mammoths that once roamed the island; a nearly complete skeleton of a 6-ft-tall pygmy mammoth was unearthed here in 1994.

On this island once stood the historic **Vail and Vickers Ranch,** which raised cattle on the island for 160 years. You can see what the operation was like by viewing the historic ranch buildings, barns, equipment, and the wooden pier from which cattle were brought onto the island.

Visitor Center. You can get a good taste of the Channel Islands without even leaving the mainland. In a small tide pool you can watch brilliant orange garibaldis cruise around and blood starfish cling to rocks. You'll see quite a bit about the region's natural history, including a full-size replica of the pygmy mammoth skeleton fossil that was unearthed on Santa Rosa in 1994. The visitor center also has a small bookstore and is staffed by rangers and knowledgeable volunteers. | 1901 Spinnaker Dr., Ventura | 805/658–5730 | www.nps.gov/chis | Daily 8:30–5.

Sports and Outdoor Activities

HIKING

As no vehicles are allowed on the islands, hiking is the only way to explore their natural beauty. Santa Cruz has the most hiking opportunities, from a 0.25-mi stroll to the historic ranch to a strenuous 8-mi off-trail hike to an 1,808-ft peak. Terrain on most islands ranges from flat to moderately hilly. Hikes labeled as strenuous typically involve scrambling over rocks and loose terrain. High winds can present challenges on San Miguel any time of the year. No special equipment is needed, but you must carry your own water and food. Sun protection is always advisable.

Cavern Point. This moderate 2-mi hike takes you to the bluffs northwest of Scorpion harbor on Santa Cruz, where you'll capture magnificent coastal views and see pods of migrating gray whales from December through March. | Santa Cruz Campground.

Cuyler Harbor Beach. This easy walk takes you along a 2-mi-long white sand beach on San Miguel. Sometimes the eastern section is cut off by high tides. | San Miguel Campground.

East Point. This strenuous 12-mi hike along beautiful white-sand beaches yields the opportunity to see rare Torrey pines. Some beaches are closed between March and September, so you'll have to remain on the road for portions of this hike. | Santa Rosa Campground.

Elephant Seal Cove. This moderate to strenuous walk takes you across Santa Barbara to a point where you can view magnificent elephant seals from steep cliffs. | Landing Cove.

Historic Ranch. This easy 0.5-mi walk on Santa Cruz Island takes you to a historic ranch where you can see remnants of a cattle ranch. | Scorpion Beach.

★ **Inspiration Point.** This 1.5-mi hike along flat terrain takes in most of East Anacapa. There are great views from Inspiration Point and Cathedral Cove. | Landing Cove.

Lester Ranch. This short but strenuous 2-mi hike leads up a spectacular canyon filled with waterfalls and lush native plants. At the end of a steep climb to the top of a peak you'll be rewarded with views of the historic Lester Ranch and the Cabrillo Monument. (If you plan to hike beyond the Lester Ranch, you'll need a hiking permit; call 805/658–5730.) | San Miguel Campground.

Point Bennett. Rangers conduct 15-mi hikes across San Miguel to Point Bennett, where more than 30,000 pinnipeds (three different species) can be seen. | San Miguel Campground.

★ **Prisoners Harbor.** Taking in quite a bit of Santa Cruz, this moderate to strenuous 3-mi trail to Pelican Cove is one of the best hikes in the park. You must secure a permit, as it takes you through Nature Conservancy property. | Prisoners Harbor.

Water Canyon. Starting at Santa Rosa Campground, this 2-mi walk along a white-sand beach includes some exceptional beachcombing. Frequent strong winds can change this from an easy hike to a fairly strenuous excursion, so be prepared. If you extend your walk into Water Canyon, you'll follow animal paths to a lush canyon full of native vegetation. | Santa Rosa Campground.

KAYAKING

Although hiking can bring you to some breathtaking heights, more remote parts of Channel Islands are accessible only by a sea kayak. Some of the best kayaking in the park can be found on Anacapa, Santa Barbara, and the eastern tip of Santa Cruz. Anacapa has plenty of sea caves, tide pools, and even natural bridges you can paddle beneath. Santa Barbara's steep cliffs provide nesting sites for brown pelicans, cormorants, and storm petrels. Here you'll find one of the world's largest colonies of Xantus' murrelets. You can also get up close and personal with seals and sea lions. Santa Cruz has plenty of secluded beaches you can explore, as well as seabird nesting sites and seal and sea lion rookeries. You may land at any of the islands, but permits are required for the western side of Santa Cruz. There are no public moorings around the islands, so it's recommended that one person stay aboard the boat at all times. Outfitters offer tours year-round, but high seas may cause cancellation of trips between December and March. The operators listed below hold permits from the National Parks Service to conduct kayak tours. If you choose a different company, verify that it holds the proper permits.

Aquasports. This highly regarded company offers guided one-, two-, and three-day trips to Scorpion Landing on Santa Cruz and one-day trips to Santa Barbara Island for kayakers ranging from beginners to experts. Cross-channel passage, instruction, equipment, and guides are included. | 111 Verona Ave., Goleta | 800/773–2309 or 805/968–7231 | www.islandkayaking.com | Call for times and dates | $175–$330.

Channel Islands Kayak Center. This company rents kayaks and offers one-day guided kayak and snorkeling trips. Excursions include transportation, equipment, and guides. | 3600 Harbor Blvd., Oxnard | 805/984–5995 | www.cikayak.com | $160.

Paddle Sports. You can take a one-day trip to Santa Cruz Island, which includes equipment, instruction, and transportation across the channel. In summer, there's a morning day camp for kids, who can learn about kayaking and marine life. | 117B Harbor Way, Santa Barbara | 805/899–4925 | www.paddlesportsofsantabarbara.com | $179 for day trips, $140 for a week of children's day camp.

DIVING

Some of the best snorkeling and diving in the world can be found in the cool waters surrounding Channel Islands. Each island provides an entirely different experience. In the relatively warm water around Anacapa and eastern Santa Cruz, photographers can

CHANNEL ISLANDS
NATIONAL PARK

EXPLORING
ATTRACTIONS NEARBY
DINING
LODGING
CAMPING AND RV
FACILITIES
SHOPPING
ESSENTIAL
INFORMATION

GULLS IN TRAINING

Thousands of western gulls hatch each summer on Anacapa then fly off to the mainland, where they spend about four years learning all their bad habits. Then they return to the island to roost and have chicks of their own.

get great shots of rarely seen giant black bass among the kelp forests. Here you'll also find a reef covered with red brittle starfish. If you're an experienced diver, you might swim among five species of seals and sea lions or try your hand at spearing rockfish or halibut near San Miguel and Santa Rosa.

Truth Aquatics. Trips to Santa Cruz, San Miguel, and Santa Rosa lasting a day or more can be arranged through this Santa Barbara operator. You live aboard the boats on multi-day trips, with all meals provided. | 301 Cabrillo Blvd., Santa Barbara | 805/962–1127 | www.truthaquatics.com | $79–$590.

WHALE WATCHING

In July and August, humpback and blue whales feed off the north shore of Santa Rosa. From late-December to April, up to 10,000 gray whales pass through the Santa Barbara Channel on their way from Alaska to Mexico.

Island Packers. Three-hour tours leave several times daily to watch the migration of whales in the channel. Depending on the season, you can take either a three-hour tour or an all-day tour from either Oxnard or Ventura. | 3600 S. Harbor Blvd., Oxnard | 805/642–1393 | 1691 Spinnaker Dr., Ventura | 805/642–1393 | www.islandpackers.com | $24–$58.

Attractions Nearby

Albinger Archaeological Museum. You can follow the course of more than three millennia of human history in the region through the archaeological exhibits on display at this small museum. Dating back to 1600 BC, relics on display include those left behind by people who lived here hundreds of years before the Chumash people arrived in the 16th century. | 113 E. Main St., Ventura | 805/648–5823 or 805/653–0323 | Free | June–Aug., Wed.–Sun. 10–4; Sept.–May, Wed.–Fri. 10–4.

Channel Islands Harbor. More than 2,500 boats are moored in nine marinas at this classic seaside harbor in Oxnard. You can rent paddleboats, sailboats, scuba and snorkeling gear, or bicycles from shops along the docks. You'll find shopping at Fisherman's Wharf, Harbor Landing, and the Marine Emporium. The harbor is also the venue for a huge Sunday morning farmers market. | 3900 Pelican Way, Oxnard | 805/985–4852 | www.oxnardtourism.com | Free | Daily.

El Presidio State Historic Park. One of four military strongholds established by the Spanish along the California coast, it protected the region from 1782 to 1846. The guardhouse, called *El Cuartel,* one of the two original structures that remain, is the oldest building owned by the state. | 123 El Cañon Perdido St., Santa Barbara | 805/965–0093 | www.sbthp.org/home. htm | Free | Daily 10:30–4:30.

Outdoors Santa Barbara Visitor Center. This small visitor center provides maps and other information about Channel Islands National Park, Channel Islands National Marine Sanctuary, and Los Padres National Forest. The same building houses the Santa Barbara Maritime Museum. | 113 Harbor Dr., Santa Barbara | 805/884–1475 | Usually daily 11–6; call to confirm.

Santa Barbara Museum of Natural History. A 72-foot skeleton of a blue whale is one of the eye-catching exhibits at this small museum in Santa Barbara. Eleven halls hold a variety of exhibits, including one on the history of the Chumash people who once inhabited the Channel Islands. | 2559 Puesta del Sol Rd., Santa Barbara | 805/682–4711 | www. sbnature.org | $6 | Daily 10–5.

Seabee Museum. This warehouse-size collection of naval memorabilia is from the construction work done by the U.S. Navy Civil Engineer Corps from World War II to the Vietnam War. This group built the landing strips, airports, housing, roads and facilities the troops used while fighting the wars. For security reasons, the general public must make advance arrangements to visit the museum. | 1000 23rd Ave., Port Hueneme | 805/982–1249 reser-

vations; 805/982–5165 museum | www.ncbc.navfac.navy.mil/cecmuseum | Free | Wed. and
Fri., by appointment only.

Ventura County Maritime Museum. This museum holds an internationally renowned collection of model ships dating back to 1650 (including rare prisoner-of-war models made of whale bone), and rotating exhibits of maritime art. | 2731 S. Victoria Ave., Oxnard | 805/984–6260 | $3 | Daily 11–5.

Dining

In Channel Islands

There are no restaurants on any of the Channel Islands. However, you can pick up picnic supplies on the mainland or purchase some items on the boats to the islands.

Picnic Areas. Picnic tables are available on all the islands except San Miguel. You can also picnic on the beaches of Santa Cruz, Santa Rosa, and San Miguel. High winds are always a possibility on Santa Rosa and San Miguel.

Near the Park

Andria's Seafood. Seafood. Place your order at the counter, then take a table in the comfortable dining room or out on the patio that overlooks the harbor. This family-oriented restaurant specializes in fish and chips (made with angel shark) and homemade clam chowder. | 1449 Spinnaker Dr., Ventura | 805/654–0546 | $8–$15 | No credit cards.

Brophy Bros. American. The outdoor tables at this casual restaurant in the harbor have perfect views of the marina and mountains. A fine place for lunch and dinner, Brophy's serves enormous, exceptionally fresh fish dishes. Try the seafood salad. If there's a wait, they give you a pager; you can stroll along the waterfront until the pager beeps that your table's ready. | 119 Harbor Way, Santa Barbara | 805/966–4418 | $14–$18 | AE, MC, V.

Cabo Seafood Grill and Cantina. Mexican. A crowd of locals-in-the-know gathers at this lively restaurant and bar close to downtown for South of the Border seafood specialties served with fresh handmade tortillas. The rainbow-hued dining rooms and patio are casual and cheery. If you're not a seafood fan, try the *carne asada* (marinated strips of beef) or one of the large combination plates. | 1041 S. Oxnard Blvd., Oxnard | 805/487–6933 | $6–$15 | AE, D, DC, MC, V.

Montecito Café. Contemporary. This upscale yet casual and relatively affordable restaurant serves contemporary cuisine such as grilled chicken breast with roasted Anaheim chilies and smoked salmon on goat cheese pancakes. The salads and lamb dishes are particularly inventive. | 1295 Coast Village Rd., Montecito (3 mi east of Santa Barbara) | 805/969–3392 | $10–$18 | AE, MC, V.

71 Palm. French. In a 1910 house, this refined restaurant has wooden floors and trim, lace curtains, and a fireplace. For an appetizer try the innovative potato caviar (boiled red potatoes hollowed out and filled with caviar); for dinner there's grilled salmon on a potato pancake or New Zealand rack of lamb Provençale. You can sit indoors or out. | 71 N. Palm St., Ventura | 805/653–7222 | Closed Sun. No lunch Sat. | $15–$27 | AE, D, DC, MC, V.

The Whale's Tail. American. This popular seafood house in Channel Islands Harbor includes a casual upstairs shellfish bar with indoor/outdoor seating and a more formal main dining room downstairs. Practically all the tables let in waterfront views. Fresh fish is delivered to the restaurant's dock daily. | 3950 Bluefin Circle, Oxnard | 805/985–2511 | Reservations essential | $15–$21 | AE, MC, V.

THE LEGACY OF AN OIL SPILL

Many consider the publicity that surrounded the 1969 oil spill in the Santa Barbara Channel as the beginning of the modern environmental movement. An accident on an offshore oil drilling platform dumped 200,000 gallons of crude into the ocean. The resulting 800-square-mi oil slick killed thousands of marine mammals and seabirds. The first Earth Day was held the following year, and the movement to protect the fragile islands began.

Lodging

Near the Park

Casa Via Mar Inn and Tennis Club. Flowers tumble out of the clay pots that line the balconies at this cozy Spanish-style hotel. Relax by the pool or play a few games of tennis on the well-kept courts. Beaches are 1.5 mi to the west. Kitchenettes. Cable TV, in-room VCRs. 6 tennis courts. Pool. Hot tub. Business services. | 377 W. Channel Islands Blvd., Port Hueneme | 805/984–6222 | fax 805/984–9490 | www.casaviamar.com | 74 rooms | $69–$81 | AE, D, DC, MC, V | CP.

Channel Islands Inn and Suites. This hacienda-style hotel is set amid soaring palm trees. Spacious, modern rooms are filled with shaker- and mission-style furnishings. In-room data ports, minibars, microwaves, refrigerators. Cable TV, in-room VCRs. Pool. Gym, hot tub. Laundry facilities. | 1001 E. Channel Islands Blvd., Oxnard, 93033 | 805/487–7755 or 800/344–5998 | fax 805/486–1374 | www.channelislandsinn.com | 92 rooms | $89 | AE, D, DC, MC, V | BP.

Clocktower Inn. Set in a former firehouse, this historic hotel in the heart of downtown Ventura sits next to Mission San Buenaventura, the Historical Museum, and many boutique shops. Rooms are done up in soft Southwestern colors, and many have private patios, fireplaces, carved headboards, desks, leather chairs, and armoires. Restaurant, room service. Cable TV with movies. No-smoking rooms. | 181 E. Santa Clara, Ventura | 805/652–0141 or 800/727–1027 | www.clocktowerinn.com | 50 rooms | $73–$116 | AE, D, DC, MC, V | CP.

Fess Parker's Doubletree Resort. Occupying 24 of Santa Barbara's most stunning beachfront acres, this Mediterranean-style hotel consists of gleaming white buildings with red-tile roofs. Many of the rooms have private patios or balconies. 2 restaurants, room service. In-room data ports. Cable TV with movies. Putting green, tennis court. Pool. Exercise equipment, hair salon, massage. Basketball. Bar. Laundry facilities. Business services. Airport shuttle, parking (fee). Some pets allowed. | 633 E. Cabrillo Blvd., Santa Barbara | 805/564–4333 or 800/222–8733 | fax 805/564–4964 | www.fpdtr.com | 337 rooms, 23 suites | $225–$425 | AE, D, DC, MC, V.

Glenborough Inn. This charming B&B is made up of four separate bungalows built a century ago. Each of the rooms has its own distinctive details; the Craftsman Room, for example, has dark-wood paneling and a tile fireplace, while the Nouveau Suite has a Franklin stove and a window seat overlooking the well-kept gardens. Several rooms have hot tubs outside on a private patio. Some in-room hot tubs, some refrigerators. Cable TV, in-room VCRs. Hot tub. Business services. No a/c in some rooms. No smoking. | 1327 Bath St., Santa Barbara | 805/966–0589 or 800/962–0589 | fax 805/564–8610 | www.glenboroughinn.com | 7 rooms, 9 suites, 1 cottage | $120–$300 | AE, D, DC, MC, V | BP.

Inn By The Harbor. Tropical gardens surround this hotel, making you feel far from the crowds. Rooms, appointed with pine furniture, overlook the enclosed sundeck where you'll find a pool and hot tub. Rooms with full kitchens are a good deal for families. There are milk and cookies, and wine and cheese in the evening. The beach and harbor are three blocks away. Some kitchens, some microwaves, some refrigerators. Cable TV. Pool. Hot tub. Laundry facilities. Free parking. No a/c. | 433 W. Montecito St., Santa Barbara | 805/963–7851 or 800/626–1986 | fax 805/962–9428 | www.sbhotels.com/harbor.htm | 42 rooms, 1 suite | $142–$172 | AE, D, DC, MC, V | CP.

★ **San Ysidro Ranch.** You can feel equally at home in jeans and cowboy boots or designer jackets at this romantic hideaway, where John and Jackie Kennedy spent their honeymoon. Guest cottages, all with down comforters and wood-burning stoves or fireplaces, are scattered among 14 acres of orange trees and flower beds. Many cottages have private outdoor spas, and one has its own pool. Hiking trails crisscross 500 acres of open space surrounding the property. The Stonehouse Restaurant and Plow & Angel Bistro are Santa

Barbara institutions. Dining room, room service. In-room data ports, some in-room hot tubs, refrigerators. Cable TV, in-room VCRs. Driving range, 2 tennis courts. Pool, wading pool. Gym, massage. Hiking. Bar. Playground. Business services. Some pets allowed (fee). No Smoking. | 900 San Ysidro La., Santa Barbara | 805/969–5046 or 800/368–6788 | fax 805/565–1995 | www.sanysidroranch.com | 23 rooms, 15 suites | $399–$599 | AE, DC, MC, V | 2-day minimum stay on weekends, 3-day minimum on holiday weekends.

Camping and RV Facilities

In Channel Islands

Camping is the best way to experience the natural beauty and isolation of Channel Islands. Not tied to the tour schedules, you'll have plenty of time to explore mountain trails, snorkel in the kelp forests, or kayak into sea caves. Campsites are primitive with no water (except at Santa Rosa and Santa Cruz Scorpion) or electricity; enclosed camp stoves must be used. You must carry all your gear and pack out all trash. Campers must arrange transportation to the islands prior to reserving a camp site. To reserve, call 800/365–2267 up to five months in advance.

Del Norte Campground. This campground on Santa Cruz, the newest on the islands, offers backpackers sweeping ocean views from its 1,500-foot perch. It's accessed via a 3.5-mi hike through a series of canyons and ridges. Pit toilets. Picnic tables. | 4 sites | Scorpion Beach landing | 800/365–2267 | http://reservations.nps.gov | $10.

East Anacapa Campground. You'll have to walk 0.5 mi and ascend more than 150 steps to reach this open treeless camping area above Cathedral Cove. Pit toilets. Picnic tables. Ranger station. | 7 sites | East Anacapa landing | 800/365–2267 | http://reservations.nps.gov | $10.

San Miguel Campground. Accessed by a steep 1-mi hike through a lush canyon, this campground is on the site of the Lester Ranch. Nearby you'll find the Cabrillo Monument. Strong winds and thick fog are common on this remote island. Pit toilets. Picnic tables. Ranger station. | 9 sites | Cuyler Harbor landing | 800/365–2267 | http://reservations.nps.gov | $10.

Santa Barbara Campground. This seldom-visited campground perched on a cliff above Landing Cove is reached via a challenging 0.5-mi uphill climb. Three-day trips are permitted. Pit toilets. Picnic tables. Ranger station. | 8 sites | Landing Cove | 800/365–2267 | http://reservations.nps.gov | $10.

★ **Santa Cruz Scorpion Campground.** In a grove of eucalyptus trees, this campground is near the historic buildings of Scorpion Ranch. This campground is accessed via an easy, 0.5-mi, flat trail from Scorpion Beach landing. Pit toilets. Drinking water. Picnic tables. | 40 sites | Scorpion Beach landing | 800/365–2267 | http://reservations.nps.gov | $10.

Santa Rosa Campground. Backcountry beach camping for kayakers is available on this island. It's a 1.5-mi flat walk to the campground. There's a spectacular view of Santa Cruz Island across the water. Pit toilets. Drinking water. Picnic tables. | 15 sites | Bechers Bay landing | http://reservations.nps.gov | 800/365–2267 | $10.

NEAR THE PARK

McGrath State Beach. Set along the banks of the Santa Clara River, this lush campground is in one of the state's best bird-watching areas. A nature trail leads to the Santa Clara Estuary Natural Preserve. This park fills up in summer, so make reservations well in advance. Flush toilets. Dump station. Drinking water. Fire pits, picnic tables. Ranger station. | 174 sites | Off Harbor Blvd., 5 mi south of Ventura | 805/654–4744 or 800/444–7275 | www.parks.ca.gov | $13–$16.

CHANNEL ISLANDS CAMPGROUNDS

	Total # of sites	# of RV sites	# of hook-ups	Drive-to sites	Hike-to sites	Flush toilets	Pit toilets	Drinking water	Showers	Fire grates/pits	Swimming	Boat access	Playground	Dump station	Ranger station	Public telephone	Reservation possible	Daily fee per site	Dates open
INSIDE THE PARK																			
Del Norte	4	0	0		•		•										$10	Y/R
East Anacapa	7	0	0		•		•								•		•	$10	Y/R
Santa Cruz	40	0	0		•		•	•									•	$10	Y/R
San Miguel	9	0	0		•		•								•		•	$10	Y/R
Santa Barbara	8	0	0		•		•								•		•	$10	Y/R
Santa Rosa	15	0	0		•		•	•									•	$10	Y/R
NEAR THE PARK																			
McGrath State Beach	174	174	0	•		•		•		•	•				•		•	$13–16	Y/R
Refugio State Beach	80	80	0	•		•		•		•	•					•	•	$12–15	Y/R
Ventura Beach RV Resort	144	144	144	•		•		•	•	•			•	•		•	•	$38–44	Y/R

* In summer only   ** Reservation fee charged   Y/R=Year-round
UL=Unlimited   ULP=Unlimited primitive   LD=Labor Day   MD=Memorial Day

Refugio State Beach. Here, in a protected cove lined with palm trees, you can head out for a swim—the surf is less than a 5-minute walk from the camping area—and bike or hike along the bluff. This campground is wheelchair accessible. Advance reservations are needed in summer. Flush toilets. Drinking water. Fire pits. Public telephone. General store, ranger station. Swimming (ocean). | 80 sites | U.S. 101 at Refugio Rd., 17 mi west of Santa Barbara | 805/986–1033 or 800/444–7275 | www.parks.ca.gov (park info); www.reserveamerica.com (reservations) | $12–$15.

Ventura Beach RV Resort. Shaded by lots of trees, this attractive campground features large, grassy pull-through spaces. There's plenty for families to do together, including riding bikes, playing checkers, and tossing horseshoes. For the adults there's an outdoor hot tub and even karaoke on summer weekends. Flush toilets. Full hookups, dump station. Drinking water, guest laundry, showers. Fire pits, picnic tables, food service. Electricity, public telephone. General store. Play area, swimming (pool). | 144 RV sites, 38 tent sites | 800 W. Main St., Ventura | 805/643–9137 | fax 805/643–7479 | $44 RV sites, $38 tent sites.

Shopping

State Street. The commercial hub of Santa Barbara, State Street is a joy to shop. Chic malls, quirky storefronts, antiques emporia, elegant boutiques, and funky thrift shops line the thoroughfare. | State St. between Cabrillo Blvd. and Sola St., Santa Barbara.

Essential Information

ATMS (24-HOUR): Santa Barbara Bank and Trust | 583 W. Channel Islands Blvd. (near Channel Islands Harbor), Port Hueneme | 805/965–5594. **Santa Barbara Bank and Trust** | 1960 Cliff Dr., Santa Barbara | 805/965–5594.

AUTOMOBILE SERVICE STATIONS: Bill Burke's Channel Islands Chevron | 1960 Victoria Ave., Oxnard | 805/985–1592. **Texaco** | 134 S. Milpas St., Santa Barbara | 805/965–2249.

POST OFFICES: Santa Barbara Main Post Office | 836 Anacapa St., Santa Barbara, 93102 | 805/564–2226 or 800/275–8777. **Oxnard Main Post Office** | 1961 North C St., Oxnard, 93030 | 805/278–7615 or 800/275–8777. **Ventura Main Post Office.** | 675 E. Santa Clara St., Ventura, 93001 | 805/643–8057 or 800/275–8777.

DEATH VALLEY NATIONAL PARK
SOUTHWESTERN CALIFORNIA

Rte. 190, 18 mi northwest of Rte. 127.

The desert is no Disneyland. With its scorching summer heat and vast, sparsely populated tracts of land, it's not often at the top of the list when most people assemble their "must-see" list of California attractions. But the natural riches of Death Valley (the largest national park outside Alaska) are overwhelming: rolling waves of sand dunes, black cinder cones thrusting up hundreds of feet from a blistered desert floor, riotous sheets of wildflowers, bizarrely shaped Joshua trees basking in the orange glow of a sunset, and an abundant silence that is both dramatic and startling. A single car speeding down an empty road can sound as loud as a low-flying airplane. If the heat gets to be too much, relief can be found around the oasis at Furnace Creek, where warm-water springs support vegetation such as salt cedars and palms. People come here to play golf and tennis, to swim, and to dine. Warm, dry winters attract a large contingent of senior citizens, who drive their motor homes or pull their trailers to Furnace Creek for stays of up to a month.

Long before the invention of the RV, Furnace Creek was home to four successive Native American cultures. White travelers looking for a shortcut to the California gold fields accidentally stumbled into the valley, and eventually prospectors came looking for

**DEATH VALLEY
NATIONAL PARK**

EXPLORING
ATTRACTIONS NEARBY
DINING
LODGING
CAMPING AND RV
FACILITIES
SHOPPING
ESSENTIAL
INFORMATION

gold and silver. In 1873 borax, the so-called white gold of the desert, was discovered in Death Valley. Twenty-mule teams operated from 1883 to 1889, carrying the borax out of the valley. Officials of the Pacific Coast Borax Company brought the beauty of Death Valley to the attention of the National Park Service, and on February 11, 1933, President Hoover signed a proclamation creating Death Valley National Monument. Further recognizing Death Valley's unique geology and biology, Congress approved the landmark Desert Protection Act in October 1994. This made the national monument a national park and increased its size by 1.3 million acres. All of Death Valley—just under 3.4 million acres (5,300 square mi)—is now within park boundaries.

PUBLICATIONS

The Death Valley Natural History Association sells a variety of books on the area and publishes a pamphlet outlining a self-guided tour of Golden Canyon, which costs 50¢ and is available from the association or the bookstore at the visitor center. The association also sells a waterproof, tear-proof topographical map of the entire park, ideal for back-country exploration and hiking, for $10. Additional topo maps covering select areas are $4.75 each and available at the visitor center or from the **Death Valley Natural History Association** (760/786–2146 or 800/478–8564).

When to Visit

Spring, fall, and winter are the best seasons to tour the desert. Winters are generally mild, but summers can be brutal. Room rates drop as the temperatures rise. Early morning is the best time to visit sights and avoid crowds, but some museums don't open until 10. If you schedule your arrival for late afternoon, you can drop by the visitor centers just before closing hours to line up an itinerary for the next day. Plan indoor activities for midday during hotter months. Because relatively few people visit the desert, many attractions have limited hours of access.

SCENERY AND WILDLIFE

There's a general misconception that Death Valley National Park consists of mile upon endless mile of flat desert sands, scattered cacti, and an occasional cow skull. Many people don't realize that across the valley floor from Badwater—the lowest point in the Western Hemisphere—Telescope Peak towers 11,049 ft above sea level. The extreme topography of Death Valley is a lesson in geology. Two hundred million years ago seas covered the area, depositing layers of sediment and fossils. Between 3.5 million and 5 million years ago faults in the Earth's crust and volcanic activity pushed and folded the ground, causing mountain ranges to rise and the valley floor to drop. The valley was then filled periodically by lakes, which eroded the surrounding rocks into fantastic formations and deposited the salts that now cover the floor of the basin.

Most animal life in Death Valley is found near the limited sources of water. The bighorn sheep spends most of its time in the secluded upper reaches of the park's rugged canyons and ridges. Coyotes can often be seen lazing in the shade next to the golf course and have been known to run onto the fairways to steal a golf ball. The only native fish in the park is the pupfish, which grows to slightly longer than 1 inch. In winter, when the water is cold, the fish lie dormant in the bottom mud, becoming active again in spring. Because they are wary of large moving shapes, you must stand quietly over a pool at Salt Creek to see them.

Botanists say there are more than 1,000 species of plants here (21 of which exist nowhere else in the world), though many annual plants lie dormant as seeds for all but a few months in spring, when rains trigger a bloom. The rest congregate around limited sources of water. Most of the low-elevation vegetation grows around the oases at Furnace Creek and Scotty's Castle, where oleanders, palms, and salt cedar grow. At the higher elevations you will find piñon, juniper, and bristlecone pine.

HIGH AND LOW SEASON

Some summer visitors to the park are disappointed if they don't arrive on the hottest day of the year, since seeing nature at its most extreme is precisely what attracts many people. However, most of the park's one million annual visitors still come between late fall and early spring, taking advantage of moderate temperatures and the lack of rainfall. During these cooler months you will need to book a room in advance, but don't worry: the park never feels crowded. Although precipitation in the valley averages less than 2 inches annually, rainfall here can be a dramatic occurrence. Because there's little vegetation to soak up the rain and keep soil together, flash floods are common; sections of roadway can be flooded or washed away. The wettest month of the year is February, when the park receives an average of 0.3 inch of rain. You can check the park's daily weather report on-line at www.nps.gov/deva/morning.htm.

Average High/Low Temperature (°F) and Monthly Precipitation (in inches)

	JAN.	FEB.	MAR.	APR.	MAY	JUNE
DEATH VALLEY	65/39	73/46	81/54	88/62	100/72	110/81
	0.2	0.3	0.2	0.1	0	0

	JULY	AUG.	SEPT.	OCT.	NOV.	DEC.
	116/88	113/86	106/81	91/62	75/48	66/40
	0.1	0.1	0.1	0.1	0.2	0.2

FESTIVALS AND SEASONAL EVENTS

SPRING

Mar.: **Diaz Lake Trout Derby.** The eastern Sierra is one of the best places in the state for trout fishing. The first Saturday of the month, you can take a shot at the "big one" in this fully stocked lake at 3,700 ft above sea level and 3 mi south of Lone Pine. Prizes are awarded for all age groups. Admission is free. | 760/876–4444.

FALL

Nov.: **Death Valley 49er Encampment Days.** Originally a centennial celebration held in 1949 to honor the area's first European visitors, this event annually draws thousands of people to the park from around the world. The weeklong celebration includes art shows, organized seminars and walks, demonstrations, and dances. | www.deathvalley49ers.org.

Shoshone Old West Days. Just outside of Death Valley National Park, an annual festival here celebrates Wild West heritage with live music, arts and crafts, competitions and contests, children's activities, and plenty of hot and hearty food. | 760/852–4524.

Nearby Towns

Founded at the turn-of-the-20th-century, **Beatty** sits 16 mi east of the California-Nevada border. The small town has a number of services for travelers entering the park from the east. Named for a single pine tree found at the bottom of the canyon of the same name, **Lone Pine** is where you'll find Mount Whitney, the highest peak in the Continental U.S., at 14,494 ft. You'll find several motels and restaurants here, as well as a Hollywood icon: the nearby Alabama Hills have been used in many movies and TV scenes, including segments in *The Lone Ranger.* Unincorporated **Shoshone,** a very small town at the edge of Death Valley, started out as a mining town. Miners lived nearby in small caves dynamited out of the rock.

Beatty Chamber of Commerce | 119 E. Main St., Beatty, NV 89003 | 775/553–2424 | www. governet.net/nv/as/bea. **Death Valley Chamber of Commerce** | 118 S. Rte. 127, Box 157, Shoshone, 92384 | 760/852–4524 | fax 760/852–4414 | www.deathvalleychamber.org. **Lone Pine Chamber of Commerce** | 126 S. Main St., Box 749, Lone Pine, 93545 | 760/876–4444 or 877/253–8981 | www.lonepinechamber.org. **Shoshone Development** | Box 67, Shoshone, 92384 | 760/852–4224 | fax 760/852–4250 | www.shoshonevillage.com.

Exploring Death Valley

Death Valley National Park covers 5,310 square mi, ranges from 6 to 60 mi wide, and measures 140 mi north to south. Within the park, the Panamint Range parallels Death Valley to the west, the Amargosa Range to the east. Minerals and ores in the rugged, barren mountains turn them shades that range from green to yellow to brown to white to black. Scores of alluvial fans spread across the valley floor, which is composed of alkali flats and sand dunes.

Believe everything you've ever heard about desert heat—it can be brutal. The dry air wicks moisture from the body without causing a sweat, so remember to drink plenty of water. Bring sunglasses, a hat, and sufficient clothing to block the sun's rays or the wind. In morning and evening, particularly in spring and fall, the temperature ranges from cool and crisp to pleasantly warm and dry. In several places within the park it's possible to drive to an elevation higher than 5,000 ft, where the air temperature is generally 15 to 20 degrees cooler than on the valley floor. Winds are common, especially at higher elevations at sunrise and sunset.

PARK BASICS

Contacts and Resources: Death Valley National Park | Box 579, Death Valley, 92328 | 760/786–2331, 760/786–3225 TDD | fax 760/786–3283 | www.nps.gov/deva. **Death Valley Natural History Association** | Box 188, Death Valley, 92328 | 760/786–2146 or 800/478–8564.

Hours: Most facilities within the park remain open year-round, daily 8–6.

Fees: The entrance fee is $10 per vehicle and $5 for those entering on foot, bus, bike, or motorcycle. The payment, valid for seven consecutive days, is collected at the park's entrance stations and at the visitor center at Furnace Creek. (If you enter the park on Route 190, there is no entrance station; remember to stop by the visitor center to pay the fee.) Annual park passes, valid only at Death Valley, are $20.

Getting Around: Distances can be deceiving in Death Valley: what seems close can be very far away. Some sights appear in clusters, but others require extensive travel. The trip from Death Valley Junction to Scotty's Castle, for example, can take three hours or more. Such distances between the major attractions in Death Valley make it necessary to travel by vehicle. Much of the park can be toured on regularly scheduled bus tours, but these often don't allow time for hikes to sites not seen from the road, such as Salt Creek, Golden Canyon, and Natural Bridge. The best option is to drive to a number of the sites, get out of the car, and walk.

When driving in Death Valley reliable maps are a must, as signage is often limited or, in some places, nonexistent. Other important accessories include a compass, a mobile phone (though these don't always work in remote areas), and extra food and water (3 gallons per person per day is recommended, plus additional radiator water). If you're able to take a four-wheel drive, bring it: many of Death Valley's most spectacular canyons are only reachable in a 4X4. Be aware of possible winter closures or driving restrictions due to snow.

California State Department of Transportation Hotline. This agency has updates on Death Valley road conditions. | 916/445–7623 or 800/427–7623 | www.dot.ca.gov.

Permits: Though a permit is not required for groups of fewer than 15 people, if you're planning an overnight visit to the backcountry, complete a registration form at the Furnace Creek visitor center. Backcountry camping is allowed in areas that are at least 2 mi from maintained campgrounds and the main paved or unpaved roads, and 0.25 mi from water sources. Most abandoned mining areas are restricted to day use.

Public Telephones: You'll find public telephones at Furnace Creek visitor center and Stovepipe Wells ranger station, as well as at the park's gas stations and lodgings.

Rest Rooms: Flush toilets are available at many of the campgrounds throughout the park and at Scotty's Castle. There are public rest rooms at Furnace Creek visitor center and Stovepipe Wells ranger station.

Accessibility: All of Death Valley's visitor centers, contact stations, and museums are accessible to all visitors. The campgrounds at Furnace Creek, Sunset, and Stovepipe Wells have wheelchair-accessible sites. The grounds at Scotty's Castle are accessible to the mobility-impaired and the guided tour of the main house has provisions for a wheel chair lift to the upper floors. Route 190, Badwater Road, Scotty's Castle Road, and paved roads to Dante's View and Wildrose provide access to the major scenic viewpoints and historic points of interest.

Emergencies: For all emergencies, call 911. Note that cell phones don't work in many parts of the park.

Lost and Found: The park's lost-and-found is at the Furnace Creek visitor center.

Good Tours

DEATH VALLEY IN ONE DAY

What you can see and do in one day at Death Valley depends a lot on where you plan to enter and exit the park. If you begin the day in Furnace Creek, you can see many different sights without doing much driving. Make sure you bring plenty of water with you, and some food in case you get hungry in a remote location. Get up early and drive the 20 mi on Badwater Road to **Badwater,** which looks out on the lowest point in the Western Hemisphere and is a dramatic place to watch the sunrise. Returning north, stop at Natural Bridge, a medium-size conglomerate rock formation that has been hollowed at its base to form a span across the canyon, and then at the **Devil's Golf Course,** so named because of the large pinnacles of salt present here. Detour to the right onto Artists Drive, a 9-mi one-way, northbound route that passes **Artists Palette.** The reds, yellows, oranges, and greens come from minerals in the rocks and the earth. Four miles north of Artists Drive you will come to the **Golden Canyon Interpretive Trail,** a 2-mi round-trip that winds through a canyon with colorful rock walls. Just before Furnace Creek, take Route 190 east 3 mi to **Zabriskie Point** (another great place to watch the sunrise) and the **Twenty Mule Team Canyon.** By this time you'll be ready to return to Furnace Creek, where you can have lunch and visit the Death Valley Museum at the Furnace Creek visitor center. Here you'll find photographs and artifacts that outline the valley's past. Heading north from Furnace Creek, pull off the highway and take a look at the **Harmony Borax Works.** Twenty miles up the road are the **Sand Dunes,** a good place to be at sunset.

DEATH VALLEY IN TWO DAYS

On your first day in the park follow the itinerary above. On the second day, make the one-hour drive to the park's north end for a tour of **Scotty's Castle,** with its unique construction and living-history program. Then drive to nearby **Ubehebe Crater,** a volcanic crater that's well worth a visit. Return to Route 190 and drive about 20 mi south, toward Furnace Creek. Turn left onto the Titus Canyon access road, and drive to the parking area. **Fall Canyon** is a 3.5-mi one-way hike. From the Titus Canyon parking area, walk 0.5 mi north along the base of the mountains to a large wash. Go 2.5 mi up the canyon to a 35-foot dry fall.

DEATH VALLEY
NATIONAL PARK

EXPLORING
ATTRACTIONS NEARBY
DINING
LODGING
CAMPING AND RV
FACILITIES
SHOPPING
ESSENTIAL
INFORMATION

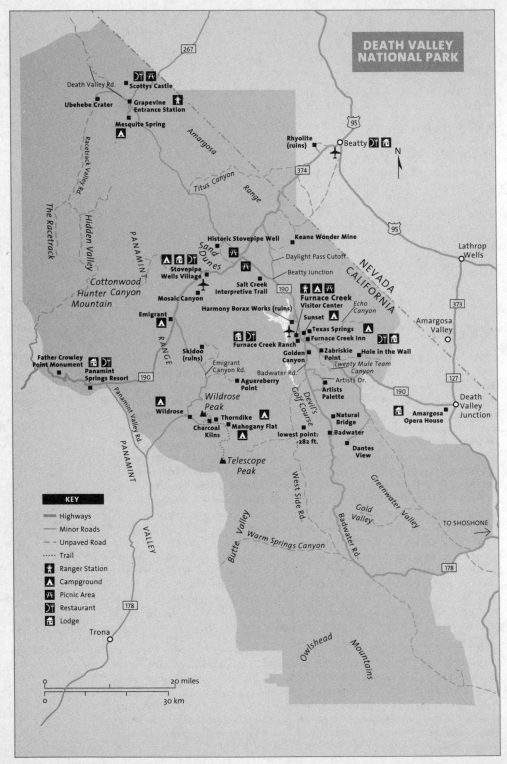

DEATH VALLEY
NATIONAL PARK

267

Death Valley Rd.
Scottys Castle

Ubehebe Crater   Grapevine
                        Entrance Station

Mesquite Spring

Rhyolite
(ruins)   Beatty   N

95

374

Racetrack Valley Rd.

The Racetrack

Hidden Valley

Amargosa

Titus Canyon   Range

NEVADA
CALIFORNIA

Lathrop
Wells

PANAMINT

Cottonwood
Hunter Canyon
Mountain

Historic Stovepipe Well   Keane Wonder Mine

Sand
Dunes

Stovepipe
Wells Village   Daylight Pass Cutoff

Beatty Junction

Mosaic Canyon   Salt Creek
                       Interpretive Trail   Furnace Creek
                                                   Visitor Center   Echo
                                                                           Canyon

Emigrant   Harmony Borax Works (ruins)   Sunset

                                                   Texas Springs

Furnace Creek Ranch   Furnace Creek Inn

Skidoo   Golden   Zabriskie
(ruins)   Canyon   Point   Hole in the Wall

Emigrant
Canyon Rd.   Badwater Rd.   Twenty Mule Team
                                          Canyon

Father Crowley
Point Monument   Aguereberry
                        Point   Artists
Panamint   Palette
Springs Resort

190   Wildrose
Peak   Artists Dr.

Wildrose   Thorndike   Natural
                                     Bridge
          Charcoal   Mahogany Flat   Badwater
          Kilns
                          lowest point: Dantes
                          -282 ft.   View

Telescope
Peak

West Side Rd.

Devil's
Golf Course

Greenwater Valley

Gold
Valley

TO SHOSHONE

373

Amargosa
Valley

127

Death
Valley
Junction

Amargosa
Opera House

PANAMINT

VALLEY

Panamint Valley Rd.

178

Trona

RANGE

KEY

━━━ Highways
─── Minor Roads
─ ─ ─ Unpaved Road
········ Trail
Ranger Station
Campground
Picnic Area
Restaurant
Lodge

Butte Valley   Warm Springs Canyon

Badwater Rd.

Owlshead   Mountains

178

0   20 miles

0   30 km

You can continue by climbing around to the falls on the south side. If you want, follow the canyon another couple of miles or return to the parking area. To see the **Titus Canyon Narrows** follow the gravel road up the wash. Return the way you came, or continue another 4 mi to Klare Springs, where you can see petroglyphs.

Attractions

PROGRAMS AND TOURS

Evening Programs. The visitor center presents talks on such topics as birds of the park, characters of Death Valley during the 1800s, desert bighorn sheep, the area's geology, and the mining of borax. These high-quality, informative presentations are led by park rangers. | Furnace Creek visitor center, Rte. 190, 30 mi northwest of Death Valley Junction | 760/786–2331 | Free | Oct.–May, daily 7 PM.

Gadabout Tours. This company offers multiday trips through Death Valley to see Harmony Borax Works, Ubehebe Crater, the Rhyolite Bottle House, and Zabriskie Point. Tours, which start from Ontario, CA, also stop at the Amargosa Opera House and Scotty's Castle. | 700 E. Tahquitz Canyon Way, Palm Springs, CA 92262 | 760/325–5556 or 800/952–5068 | www.gadabouttours.com.

Orientation. Furnace Creek visitor center offers orientation programs every half hour. | Furnace Creek visitor center, Rte. 190, 30 mi northwest of Death Valley Junction | 760/786–2331 | Free | Daily 8–6.

SCENIC DRIVES

★ **Artists Drive.** This 9-mi route skirts the foothills of the Black Mountains and provides colorful views of the changing landscape. Once inside the palette, the huge expanses of the valley are replaced by the intimate, small-scale natural beauty of pigments created by volcanic deposits. It's a quiet, lonely drive. You can reach this one-way road by heading north off Badwater Road.

Titus Canyon. Named for a young mining engineer who perished there, this is a box canyon where limestone walls tower several hundred feet above the floor. Thirty-five miles from Furnace Creek, a steep, occasionally rough gravel road makes the 26-mi one-way descent through the canyon (4x4s and vehicles with high clearance are recommended). The lighting is best at midday, when the sunshine creeps down the steep canyon walls. The road is subject to closures due to flash flooding; be aware when driving on dry river beds. You'll exit the canyon onto Scotty's Castle Road, which you can take southeast for 33 mi to return to Furnace Creek. Allow six hours for the trip. The road is closed in summer.

SIGHTS TO SEE

Charcoal Kilns. In 1877 George Hearst's Modock Consolidated Mining Company completed construction of the kilns to make charcoal for fueling nearby silver-lead smelters. The kilns closed in 1878 after the mines shut down, but their ruins remain. | Wildrose Canyon Rd., 37 mi south of Stovepipe Wells.

Dante's View. Part of the Black Mountains, Dante's View marks the eastern boundary of the park. Here, 5,475 ft up, you can see nearly 100 mi in the dry desert air. A short walk from the parking area can provide astounding views of the highest and lowest points in the contiguous United States. The tiny blackish patch far below is Badwater, at 282 ft below sea level; on the western horizon is Mount Whitney, which rises to 14,494 ft. | Dante's View Rd. off Rte. 190, 30 mi south of Furnace Creek.

★ **Devil's Golf Course.** This wildly varied terrain includes thousands of miniature salt pinnacles, carved into surreal shapes by the desert wind. In places, perfectly round holes descend into the ground through the minerals. The salt was pushed up to the surface by pressure created as underground salt- and water-bearing gravel crystallized. Nothing grows on this barren landscape. | Badwater Rd., 13 mi south of Furnace Creek.

DEATH VALLEY
NATIONAL PARK

EXPLORING
ATTRACTIONS NEARBY
DINING
LODGING
CAMPING AND RV
FACILITIES
SHOPPING
ESSENTIAL
INFORMATION

To avoid crowds in national parks, avoid in-season holidays that create three-day weekends. Also find out ahead of time if the park you are interested in is a destination for college students on spring break. Ask park personnel for the dates of college breaks in their state.

Furnace Creek Visitor Center. The center's exhibits and artifacts provide a broad overview of how Death Valley formed. A bookstore run by the Death Valley Natural History Association is also inside. | Rte. 190, 30 mi northwest of Death Valley Junction | 760/786–2331 | www.nps.gov/deva | Daily 8–6.

Harmony Borax Works. Built in 1882 by W. T. Coleman, the Harmony Borax Mill was the first successful borax mining operation in Death Valley. Long fallen into ruins, the factory now consists of crumbling adobe walls, the old boiler, and some of the vats. The Borax Museum, 2 mi south of the borax works, houses original mining machinery and historical displays in a building that once served as a miner boardinghouse. | Harmony Borax Works Rd., west of Rte. 190, 2 mi north of Furnace Creek.

Sand Dunes at Mesquite Flat. These ever-changing products of the Earth and wind have steep rippled sides, sharp curving crests, and a beautiful, sun-bleached hue. There are no trails here; you can roam where you please. Watch for animal tracks and interesting formations. Bring lots of water, and remember where you parked your car: it's easy to become disoriented in this ocean of sand. If you lose your bearings, simply climb to the top of a dune and scan the horizon for the parking lot. | Rte. 190, 21 mi north of Furnace Creek.

★ **Scotty's Castle.** Construction on this Moorish mansion, begun in 1924, was never completed. Death Valley Scotty (whose real name was Walter Scott) told many that he built the house with gold from his secret mine. In fact, his friend, Chicago millionaire Albert Johnson, paid for its construction. Johnson was happy to play along with Scotty's tall tale. Once a hotel, the Castle hosted such luminaries as Bette Davis and Norman Rockwell. Today you can take a walk on the grounds or join costumed park rangers on a 1939 living history tour of the mansion, which contains handmade furniture and an enormous pipe organ. The in-season wait at Scotty's can be from one to two hours, but you can time it so that you take your lunch break while you wait. | Rte. 190, 53 mi northwest of Furnace Creek | 760/786–2395 or 760/786–2226 | $8 | Grounds: daily 7:30–6; tours: daily 9–5.

Twenty Mule Team Canyon. This canyon was named after the animal that helped the famous 49er travelers cross the harsh landscape of the Valley. As you drive along the loop road off Route 190, the soft rock walls reach high up on both sides, as if you were on an amusement-park ride. Remains of prospectors' tunnels are visible here, along with some brilliant rock formations. The road is subject to closures due to flash flooding; be aware when driving on dry river beds. Trailers are not permitted. | Twenty Mule Team Rd. off Rte. 190, 1.5 mi south of Zabriskie Point.

Ubehebe Crater. Five hundred feet deep and 0.5 mi across, this windy crater resulted from violent underground steam and gas explosions about 3,000 years ago; its volcanic ash spread out over most of the area, and the cinders are as thick as 150 ft near the crater's rim. You'll get some superb views of the valley from here, and you can take a fairly easy hike around the west side of the rim to Little Hebe Crater, one of a smaller cluster of craters to the south and west. | North Death Valley Hwy., 8 mi northwest of Scotty's Castle.

★ **Zabriskie Point.** Although only about 710 ft in elevation, this is one of Death Valley National Park's most scenic spots, overlooking a striking panorama of wrinkled, multicolor hills. | Rte. 190, 5 mi south of Furnace Creek.

Sports and Outdoor Activities

BICYCLING

There are no bike rentals in the park, but mountain biking is permitted on any of the back roads open to the public. These roads receive very little traffic. A free flier with suggested bike routes is at the visitor center. On-road bicycling is becoming increasingly popular along the paved roads of Death Valley, particularly in the cooler months from late fall through early spring, but be aware that there are no shoulders on these roads and that drivers are often distracted by the surrounding scenery.

BIRD-WATCHING

Approximately 250 bird species have been identified in Death Valley. The best spot is along Salt Creek Interpretive Trail, where you might see ravens, common snipes, spotted sandpipers, killdeer, and great blue herons. Along the fairways at Furnace Creek Golf Club (stay off the grass) look for kingfishers, peregrine falcons, hawks, Canada geese, yellow warblers, and the occasional golden eagle. Scotty's Castle is another good place.

FOUR-WHEELING

With 650 mi of dirt roads within 3 million acres of backcountry, Death Valley is a popular destination among four-wheel-drive enthusiasts. Driving off established roads is strictly prohibited in the park.

Butte Valley. This 21-mi road in the southwest of the park climbs from 200 ft below sea level to an elevation of 4,000 ft. The geological formations along this drive reveal the development of Death Valley. | Trailhead on Warm Spring Canyon Road, 50 mi south of Furnace Creek visitor center.

Hunter Mountain. From Teakettle Junction to the park boundary, this 20-mi road climbs from 4,100 ft to 7,200 ft, winding through a piñon-and-juniper forest. This route may be closed or muddy in winter and spring. | Trailhead 28 mi southwest of Scotty's Castle.

GOLF

Furnace Creek Golf Club. Here you can opt to play 9 or 18 holes. The club rents clubs and carts, and greens fees are reduced if you're a guest of the Furnace Creek Ranch or the Furnace Creek Inn. Special rates for 2 to 20 weeks of play are available. In winter reservations are essential. | Rte. 190, Furnace Creek | 760/786–2301 | $28–$55, $18–$30 after 1 PM | Tee off 6 AM–3:30 PM; pro shop 6 AM–5 PM.

HIKING

Hiking trails and routes abound throughout the park, though few of them are maintained by the park service. They can bring you to sights you would miss from the road. You should generally plan your walks for before or after the noonday sun. However, paths through canyons are sometimes partially shielded from the sun and not as hot, so you can hike these at midday. Bring lots of water, wear protective clothing, and be wary of tarantulas, black widows, scorpions, snakes, and other potentially dangerous creatures. Pick up brochures on hiking at the visitor center. Some of the best trails are unmarked; ask locals for directions.

★**Keane Wonder Mine.** Allow two hours for the 2-mi round-trip trail that follows an out-of-service aerial tramway to this mine. The way is steep, but the views of the valley are spectacular. Do not enter the tunnels or hike beyond the top of the tramway—it's dangerous. The trailhead is 2 mi down an unpaved and bumpy access road. | Access road off Beatty Cutoff Rd., 17.5 mi north of Furnace Creek.

Mosaic Canyon. A gradual uphill trail (4 mi round-trip) winds through the smoothly polished walls of this narrow canyon. There are dry falls to climb at the upper end of the canyon. The 2-mi access road is rough in places but accessible to most vehicles. | Access road off Rte. 190, 0.5 mi west of Stovepipe Wells Village.

★**Natural Bridge Canyon.** Although the 2-mi access road can be rough, this 0.5-mi round-trip walk has interesting geological features in addition to the bridge itself. | Access road off Badwater Road, 15 mi south of Furnace Creek.

Salt Creek Interpretive Trail. Take a close look at Salt Creek, with its vegetation, birds, and desert pupfish, on this 0.5-mi boardwalk circuit that loops through a spring-fed wash. The floor of the creek's wash is alive with aquatic plants such as pickerelweed and salt grass. Look closely and you may find the tracks of nocturnal visitors such as bobcats, coyotes, and snakes. The tiny pupfish is the only native fish species living in Death Valley. Stand still

DEATH VALLEY
NATIONAL PARK

EXPLORING
ATTRACTIONS NEARBY
DINING
LODGING
CAMPING AND RV
FACILITIES
SHOPPING
ESSENTIAL
INFORMATION

and you may see one of these shy, inch-long fish moving in the shadows of overhanging vegetation. | 1 mi down a gravel road off Rte. 190, 14 mi north of Furnace Creek.

Telescope Peak Trail. The 14-mi round-trip begins at Mahogany Flat Campground. The steep trail winds through piñon, juniper, and bristlecone pines, with excellent views of Death Valley and Panamint Valley. Ice axes and crampons may be necessary in winter—check at the visitor center. It takes a minimum of eight hours to hike to the top of the 11,049-foot peak and then return. Getting to the peak is a strenuous endeavor; take plenty of water and only attempt it in fall or summer unless you're an experienced hiker. | Off Wildrose Rd., south of Charcoal Kilns.

★ **Titus Canyon.** The narrow floor of Titus Canyon is made of hard-packed gravel and dirt, and it's a constant, moderate uphill walk. Klare Spring and some petroglyphs (rock carvings) are 5.5 mi from the mouth of the canyon, but you can get a feeling for the area on a shorter walk. The views here are vertical: canyon walls rising 40–60 ft and the rugged, rocky ridges above them. The canyon's steep walls and deep shadows make the trip eerie and desolate. | Access road off Scotty's Castle Rd., 33 mi northwest of Furnace Creek.

HORSEBACK AND CARRIAGE RIDES

Furnace Creek Ranch. Here you can set off on a one- or two-hour guided horseback or carriage ride. Morning wagon rides depart from the general store. The rides traverse trails with views of the surrounding mountains, where multicolor volcanic rock and alluvial fans form a background for date palms and other vegetation. Evening carriage rides take passengers around the golf course and Furnace Creek Ranch. Cocktail rides, with champagne, Margaritas, and hot spiced wine, are available. | Rte. 190, Furnace Creek | 760/786–2345 Ext. 339 | $20–$35 | Reservations essential | Oct.–May.

Attractions Nearby

★ **Johannesburg.** Founded in 1896 as a slightly upmarket suburb of the rough gold-mining town of Randsburg, Johannesburg is very ghostly these days. Spirits are said to dwell in the stunning Old West cemetery in the hills above town. The ghost town is one of the region's great hidden treasures. | U.S. 395, 1 mi south of Randsburg, CA.

Marta Becket's Amargosa Opera House. Marta Becket, an artist and dancer from New York, first visited the former railway town of Amargosa while on tour in 1964. Three years later she returned and bought a boarded-up theater. To compensate for the sparse crowds in the early days, Becket painted a Renaissance-era Spanish audience on the walls and ceiling, turning the theater into a trompe l'oeil masterpiece. Becket now performs her blend of ballet, mime, and 19th-century melodrama to sell-out crowds (call ahead to reserve a seat). | Rte. 127, Death Valley Junction, CA | 760/852–4441 | $15 | Oct.–May (through Mother's Day weekend).

Randsburg, CA. The Rand Mining District first boomed when gold was discovered in the Rand Mountains in 1895. Along with neighboring settlements, it grew further due to the success of the Yellow Aster Mine, which yielded $3 million worth of gold before 1900. Rich tungsten ore, used in World War I to make steel alloy, was discovered in 1907, and silver was found in 1919. Randsburg is one of the few gold-rush communities not to have become a ghost town; the tiny city jail is among the original buildings still standing in this town with a population under 100. | U.S. Rte. 395, near the junction with Rte. 14, CA.

Shoshone Museum. The museum chronicles the local history of Death Valley and houses a unique collection of period items, and minerals and rocks from the area. The building also houses the Death Valley Chamber of Commerce and functions as the visitor center for the southeastern entrance to Death Valley. | Rte. 127, Shoshone, CA | 760/852–4414 | www.shoshonevillage.com | Free | Daily 8–4.

Dining

In Death Valley

19th Hole. American/Casual. Overlooking the world's lowest golf course (214 ft below sea level), this open-air spot serves hamburgers, hot dogs, chicken, and sandwiches. There is drive-through service for golfers in carts. | Furnace Creek Golf Club, Rte. 190, Furnace Creek | 760/786–2345 | $6–$10 | AE, D, DC, MC, V | Closed June–Sept. No dinner.

★ **Inn Dining Room.** Contemporary. Fireplaces, beam ceilings, and spectacular views provide a visual feast to match the inn's ambitious menu. Dishes may include such desert-theme items as rattlesnake empanadas and crispy cactus, as well as such simpler fare as cumin-lime shrimp, lamb, and New York strip steak. An evening dress code (no jeans, T-shirts, or shorts) is enforced. Lunch is served October–May only, but you can always have afternoon tea, an inn tradition since 1927. Breakfast and Sunday brunch are also served. | Furnace Creek Inn Resort, Rte. 190, Furnace Creek | 760/786–2345 | www.furnacecreekresort.com | Reservations essential | $25–$28 | AE, D, DC, MC, V.

Panamint Springs Resort Restaurant. American. This is a great place for steak and a beer, or pasta and a salad. In summer, evening meals are served outdoors on the porch, which has spectacular views of Panamint Valley. They also serve breakfast and lunch. | Rte. 190, 31 mi west of Stovepipe Wells | 775/482–7680 | Reservations essential | $15–$25 | AE, D, MC, V.

Toll Road Restaurant. American. There are wagon wheels in the yard and Old West artifacts on the interior walls at this restaurant in the Stovepipe Wells Village hotel. A stone fireplace heats the dining room. A full menu, with steaks, chicken, fish, and pasta, is served October through mid-May; breakfast and dinner buffets are laid out during summer. | Rte. 190, Stovepipe Wells | 760/786–2604 | $14–$25 | AE, D, DC, MC, V | No lunch mid-May–Oct.

Wrangler Steak House and 49er Coffee Shop. Steak. There are two casual, family-style restaurants at the Furnace Creek Resort. Both serve good food in simple surroundings. The coffee shop serves typical American fare for breakfast, lunch, and dinner. The Wrangler offers buffet breakfast and lunch, and dinner favorites such as filet mignon, lobster tails, and barbecue pork ribs. It's slightly more formal than the coffee shop, and patrons pay higher prices for more attentive service. | Furnace Creek Ranch, Rte. 190, Furnace Creek | 760/786–2345 | www.furnacecreekresort.com | $7–$18 Coffee Shop; $24–$29 Steak House | AE, D, DC, MC, V.

Near the Park

There are fast-food and chain establishments, as well as some ethnic eateries, in the California communities of Ridgecrest, Victorville, and Barstow.

Burro Inn. American. Breakfast, lunch, and dinner is served here around the clock, with such American basics as eggs, pancakes, hamburgers, and hot and cold sandwiches. There are daily dinner specials after 11 AM; there's a prime rib dinner on Friday and Saturday nights. | U.S. 95 and 3rd St., Beatty, NV | 775/553–2445 | $3–$13 | AE, MC, V.

★ **Crowbar Café and Saloon.** American/Casual. Housed in an old wooden building with antique photos adorning the walls and mining equipment standing in the corners, the Crowbar serves surprisingly good food in enormous helpings. Fare ranges from steaks to taco salads. Home-baked fruit pies make fine desserts in the desert. | Rte. 127, Shoshone | 760/852–9908 | $6–$13 | AE, D, MC, V.

Randsburg Opera House Café. American. A very small diner in a very small town, this old wooden café is the meeting place for locals. Standard breakfast fare and a skimpy selection of burgers and sandwiches are all there is, but the staff is friendly. The only other options in town are the saloon and the general store. | 26741 Butte Ave., Randsburg | 760/374–1037 | Closed weekdays. No dinner. | $3–$6 | No credit cards.

Rita's Cafe. American. Inside the Stagecoach Hotel's casino, the brick-walled, 100-seat diner serves 24 hours a day. Breakfast standards are eggs, pancakes, and waffles; sandwiches and burgers are served for lunch. Pizza, meat loaf, and chicken-fried steak are among the dinner specials; calorie counters can order a dieter's plate or a chef's salad. | U.S. 95, Beatty, NV | 775/553–2419 | $6–$20 | AE, D, MC, V.

Lodging

In Death Valley

During the busy season (November–March) you should make reservations for lodgings within the park at least one month in advance.

★**Furnace Creek Inn.** Built in 1927, this adobe-brick-and–stone lodge nestles in one of the greenest oases in the park. A warm mineral stream gurgles throughout the property, and the pool is fed by a warm spring with waters at a constant 85°F. Some rooms have superb views of the valley, while others overlook the lush garden. Rooms have Spanish-tile floors, antique ceiling fans, and pedestal sinks; some have balconies and spa bathtubs. Reservations for spring weekends should be made one to two months in advance. Rooms are substantially discounted from mid-May to mid-October (the inn may close entirely in summer, depending on business). Certain amenities, such as room service and massage, are only available during peak season. Restaurant, room service. In-room data ports, some in-room hot tubs. Cable TV with video games. 4 tennis courts. Pool. Massage, sauna. Bar. Shop. | Near intersection of Rte. 190 and Badwater Rd. | 760/786–2345 | fax 760/786–2423 | www.furnacecreekresort.com | 68 rooms | $245–$360 | AE, D, DC, MC, V.

Furnace Creek Ranch. What was once crew headquarters for the Pacific Coast Borax Company is now the family-oriented, less expensive sister motel to the Furnace Creek Inn. Though it exudes a sense of the rustic life, facilities are thoroughly modern. The rooms all have views of an 18-hole golf course, and some have balconies. 3 restaurants. Some refrigerators. 18-hole golf course, 4 tennis courts. Pool. Horseback riding. Bar. Shop. Playground. Laundry facilities. | Rte. 190, Furnace Creek | 760/786–2345 or 800/528–6367 | fax 760/786–2423 | www.furnacecreekresort.com | 224 rooms | $137–$159 | AE, D, DC, MC, V.

Panamint Springs Resort. Ten miles inside the west entrance of the park, this low-key resort overlooks the sand dunes and peculiar geological formations of the Panamint Valley. It's a modest mom-and-pop-style operation with a wraparound porch and rustic furnishings. One room has a king-size bed, and two of the rooms accommodate up to six people. A pay phone, a gas pump, and a grocery store are on the premises. Because the resort uses satellite telephones to link to the outside world, it is sometime difficult to reach the property. Keep trying—it may take a day or two, but you'll eventually get through. Restaurant. Bar. Shops. Some pets allowed (fee). No room phones. No room TVs. No smoking. | Rte. 190, 28 mi west of Stovepipe Wells | 775/482–7680 | www.deathvalley.com | fax 775/482–7682 | 14 rooms, 1 cabin | $65–$79 | AE, D, MC, V.

Stovepipe Wells Village. If you prefer quiet nights and an unfettered view of the night sky and nearby sand dunes, this property will no doubt suit you. No telephones break the silence here, and only the deluxe rooms have televisions. Rooms are simple yet comfortable and offer views of the wide-open desert. Tapwater in the rooms is unsuitable for drinking, but there is plenty of purified water available. There are also 15 full RV hookups on the grounds. Restaurant. Some refrigerators. Pool. Bar. Shop. Some pets allowed (fee). No room phones. No TV in some rooms. No smoking. | Rte. 190, Stovepipe Wells | 760/786–2387 | fax 760/786–2389 | www.stovepipewells.com | 83 rooms | $64–$83 | AE, D, MC, V.

Near the Park

Amargosa Hotel. The Pacific Coast Borax Company built the Amargosa in 1923 to serve railroad passengers stopping in Death Valley Junction, then a borax-mining town. This adobe building, neighbor to the Amargosa Opera House, was renovated and reopened in 1991. The spartan rooms have one or two double beds. Reservations should be made at least one to two months in advance in winter. No room phones. No room TVs. No smoking. | Rte. 127, Death Valley Junction, CA | 760/852–4441 | 14 rooms | $45 | AE, MC, V.

Burro Inn. In this two-story wood motel, each room has queen-size beds. There's one suite with a queen-size Murphy bed, couches, and kitchenette. RV drivers will find 42 pull-through spots with hookups. Restaurant. Some kitchenettes. Cable TV. Some pets allowed (fee). | U.S. 95 and 3rd St., Beatty, NV | 775/553–2225 | 62 rooms | $39–$59 | AE, MC, V.

The Cottage Hotel. An unexpectedly genteel lodging in rough-and-tumble Randsburg, this B&B resulted from a painstaking makeover of the boom-era hotel. The wallpapered rooms are done in Victorian style but have modern bathrooms. Two have private balconies. A back garden and a cedar-lined room with a hot tub are bonuses. The cottage next door has a kitchen, but its occupants don't get the free breakfast that guests of the hotel do. Some kitchenettes. Cable TV. Hot tub. No room phones. No smoking. | 130 Butte Ave., Randsburg | 760/374–2285 or 888/268–4622 | fax 760/374–2132 | www.randsburg.com | 4 rooms, 1 cottage | $85 | AE, D, MC, V | CP.

Exchange Club Motel. This modern casino-motel is clean and quiet. Some rooms have king- or queen-size beds, and one is equipped with a Jacuzzi. Two rooms are accessible to people using wheelchairs. Restaurant. Refrigerators. Cable TV. Bar. Laundry facilities. | 614 Main St., Beatty, NV | 775/553–2333 | 44 rooms | $48 | AE, D, MC, V.

Shoshone Inn. Built in 1956, the rustic Shoshone Inn is the only motel in town. Rooms are simple and cozy, but the big draw here is the warm spring-fed swimming pool built into the foothills. A market, café, gas station, and museum are all within walking distance. Restaurant. Some kitchenettes. Cable TV. Pool. Laundry facilities. Some pets allowed. No smoking. | Rte. 127, Shoshone, CA | 760/852–4335 | www.shoshonevillage.com | 16 rooms | $50–$66 | AE, D, MC, V.

Camping and RV Facilities

In Death Valley

Not all campsites in Death Valley National Park are open year-round. Holidays October–March are busy times, but the only time it may be difficult to find a site is during the 49er Encampment Days, which are held in early November.

When camping in the park, bring equipment that can handle extreme temperatures. The low-elevation campgrounds (Furnace Creek, Mesquite Springs, and Texas Spring) all have a few mesquite trees and creosote bushes, but not enough to provide shade; for the most part, the campsites sit among dry, dusty, rock-strewn terrain. In summer, you may prefer the higher-elevation campsites of Mahogany Flat, Thorndike, and Wildrose. Although there's much more vegetation at these three campgrounds than at any of those in the valley, you still won't be camping under the shade of a large tree; the harsh climate here tends to produce dwarfed vegetation. The temperature is generally 15 to 20 degrees cooler than it is on the valley floor. Backcountry camping is allowed in areas that are at least 2 mi from maintained campgrounds and the main paved or unpaved roads, and 0.25 mi from water sources. You will need a high-clearance or a 4X4 vehicle to reach these locations. For your own safety, fill out a voluntary backcountry registration form so the rangers will know where to find you.

You may build fires in the fire grates that are available at all campgrounds except Sunset and Emigrant. Fires may be restricted during summer at Thorndike, Mahogany Flat, and Wildrose (check with rangers about current conditions). At Stovepipe Wells, there are fire rings only at the tent-camping sites, not at the RV sites. Wood-gathering is prohibited at all campgrounds. A limited supply of firewood is available at general stores in Furnace Creek and Stovepipe Wells, but since prices are high and supplies limited, you're better off bringing your own if you intend to camp.

Furnace Creek. This campground, 196 ft below sea level, has some shaded tent sites. Pay showers, a laundry, and a swimming pool are at nearby Furnace Creek Ranch. Reservations are accepted for stays between mid-October and mid-April; at other times sites are available on a first-come, first-served basis. There are also two group campsites that can accommodate 40 people each. Flush toilets. Dump station. Drinking water. Fire grates, picnic tables. Public telephone. Ranger station. | 136 tent/RV sites | Rte. 190, Furnace Creek | 301/722–1257 or 800/365–2267 for reservations | http://reservations.nps.gov | $16 | Reservations payable with AE, D, MC, V; otherwise, no credit cards.

★ **Mahogany Flat.** If you have a four-wheel-drive vehicle and want to scale Telescope Peak, the park's highest mountain, you might want to sleep at one of the few shaded spots in Death Valley, located at a cool 8,133 ft. It's the most scenic campground, set among piñon pines and junipers, with a view of the valley. Pit toilets. Fire grates, picnic tables. | 10 tent sites | Off Wildrose Rd., south of Charcoal Kilns | No phone | Free | Reservations not accepted | Closed Dec.–Feb.

Mesquite Springs. There are tent and RV spaces here, some of them shaded, but no RV hookups. No generators are allowed. Since Mesquite Springs is the only campground on the north end of the park, it attracts younger campers intent on getting away from the crowds. Pit toilets. Dump station. Drinking water. Fire grates, picnic tables. | 30 tent/RV sites | Access road 2 mi south of Scotty's Castle | No phone | $10 | Reservations not accepted | No credit cards.

Panamint Springs Resort. Part of a complex that includes a motel and cabin, this campground is surrounded by cottonwoods. The daily fee includes use of the showers and rest rooms. Flush toilets. Full hookups, partial hookups (water), dump station. Drinking water, showers. Fire grates, picnic tables. Public telephone. General store, service station (gas only). | 26 tent sites, 42 RV sites | Rte. 190, 28 mi west of Stovepipe Wells | 775/482–7680 | fax 775/482–7682 | $12–$25 | AE, D, MC, V.

Stovepipe Wells Village. This is the second-largest campground in the park. Like Sunset, this area is little more than a giant parking lot, but pay showers and laundry facilities are available at the adjacent motel. Flush toilets. Dump station. Drinking water. Public telephone. General store. Swimming (pool). | 191 tent/RV sites | Rte. 190, Stovepipe Wells | 760/786–2387 | $10 | Reservations not accepted | No credit cards | Closed mid-Apr.—mid-Oct.

Sunset Campground. This huge campground is a gravel-and-asphalt RV mecca. It also serves as an overflow site for tents. hookups are not available, but you can walk across the street for pay showers, laundry facilities, and a swimming pool at the Furnace Creek Ranch. Many of the campers here are senior citizens who migrate to Death Valley each winter to play golf and tennis or just to enjoy the mild, dry climate. No fires are allowed. Flush toilets. Dump station. Drinking water. Public telephone. Ranger station. Play area. | 1,000 tent/RV sites | Sunset Campground Rd., 1 mi north of Furnace Creek | No phone | $10 | Reservations not accepted | No credit cards | Closed mid-Apr.—mid-Oct.

★ **Texas Spring.** This campsite south of the visitor center has good facilities and is a few dollars cheaper than Furnace Creek. No generators are allowed. In spring, not all sites may be available for RV use. Flush toilets. Dump station. Drinking water. Fire grates, picnic tables. | 92 tent/RV sites | Off Badwater Rd., south of the Furnace Creek | 800/365–2267 | $12 | Reservations not accepted | No credit cards | Closed mid-Apr.—mid-Oct.

Wildrose. Since it's on a paved road at a lower elevation (4,100 ft) than nearby Mahogany Flat, Wildrose is less likely to be closed because of snow in winter. The view here is not as spectacular as that from Mahogany Flat, but it does overlook the northern end of the valley. Pit toilets. Drinking water (Apr.—Nov. only). Fire grates, picnic tables. | 23 tent/RV sites | Wildrose Canyon Road, 37 mi south of Stovepipe Wells | No phone | Free | Reservations not accepted.

DEATH VALLEY CAMPGROUNDS

	Total # of sites	# of RV sites	# of hook-ups	Drive-to sites	Hike-to sites	Flush toilets	Pit toilets	Drinking water	Showers	Fire grates/pits	Swimming	Boat access	Playground	Dump station	Ranger station	Public telephone	Reservation possible	Daily fee per site	Dates open
Furnace Creek	136	136	0	•	•	•		•		•				•	•	•	•**	$16	Y/R
Mahogany Flat	10	10	0	•			•		•								Free	Mar.–Nov.
Mesquite Spring	30	30	0	•		•		•						•				$10	Y/R
Panamint Springs Resort	68	42	42	•		•		•	•	•				•			•	$12–25	Y/R
Stovepipe Wells Village	191	191	0	•		•		•						•		•		$10	Oct. 15–Apr. 15
Sunset	1000	1000	0	•		•		•					•	•	•	•		$10	Oct. 15–Apr. 15
Texas Spring	92	92	0	•		•		•		•				•				$12	Oct. 15–Apr. 15
Wildrose	23	23	0	•			•		•									Free	Oct. 15–Apr. 15

* In summer only   ** Reservation fee charged   Y/R=Year-round
UL=Unlimited   ULP=Unlimited primitive   LD=Labor Day   MD=Memorial Day

DEATH VALLEY NATIONAL PARK | 131

Shopping

Experienced desert travelers carry an ice chest stocked with food and beverages. You're best off replenishing your food stash in Ridgecrest, Barstow, or Pahrump, larger towns that have a better selection and nontourist prices.

Furnace Creek Store. This convenience store carries groceries, souvenirs, camping supplies, film, and other basics. | Rte. 190, Furnace Creek | 760/786–2345.

The Randsburg General Store. The town's informal visitor center sells maps and rockhounding guides and has a terrific selection of books on the gold rush and the Californian desert. With a century-old soda fountain, it's also a good place to stop to quench your thirst. It's open daily, unlike most of the town's dozen antiques shops, which tend to be shuttered during the week (though sometimes they open in the afternoon). | 35 Butte Ave., Randsburg, CA | 760/374–2418.

Stovepipe Wells Village General Store. You can buy gifts, sundries, food, and camping supplies at this combination grocery–souvenir shop. | Rte. 190, Stovepipe Wells | 760/786–2387.

Essential Information

ATMS (24-HOUR): Furnace Creek Ranch Registration Office | Rte. 190, north of the Furnace Creek visitor center. **Stovepipe Wells Village** | Rte. 190, 23 mi northwest of Furnace Creek.

AUTOMOBILE SERVICE STATIONS: Furnace Creek Gas Station | Rte. 190, Furnace Creek | 760/786–2232. **Stovepipe Wells Gas Station** | Rte. 190, Stovepipe Wells | 760/786–2578. **Scotty's Castle Gas Station** | Scotty's Castle, Rte. 190, 53 mi northwest of Furnace Creek | 760/786–2325.

POST OFFICES: Death Valley Post Office | Rte. 190, 0.5 mi south of the Furnace Creek visitor center, Death Valley, 92328 | 706/786–2223.

LASSEN VOLCANIC NATIONAL PARK

NORTHWESTERN CALIFORNIA

Route 89, 8 mi north of Route 36 and 51 mi east of I–5; Route 89, 1 mi south of Route 44 and 48 mi east of I–5.

A dormant plug dome, Lassen Peak is the focus of Lassen Volcanic National Park's 165.6 square mi of distinctive landscape. The peak began erupting in May 1914, sending pumice, rock, and snow thundering down the mountain and gas and hot ash billowing into the atmosphere. Lassen's most spectacular outburst occurred in 1915 when it blew a cloud of ash some 7 mi into the stratosphere. The resulting mudflow destroyed vegetation for miles in some directions; the evidence is still visible today, especially in Devastated Area. The volcano finally came to rest in 1921. Now fumaroles, mudpots, lakes, and bubbling hot springs create a fascinating but dangerous landscape that is surprisingly easy to explore.

When to Visit

The park is open year-round, though most roads are closed from late October through mid-June.

SCENERY AND WILDLIFE

Because of its varying elevations, Lassen has several different ecological habitats. Below 6,500 ft you can find ponderosa pine, Jeffrey pine, sugar pine, white fir, and several species of manzanita, gooseberry, and ceanothus. Wildflowers—wild iris, spotted coral-root, pyrola, violets, and lupine—surround the hiking trails in spring and early summer. The Manzanita Lake area has the best bird-watching opportunities, with pygmy and great horned owls, white-headed and downy woodpeckers, golden-crowned kinglets, and Steller's jays. The lake area also is home to rubber boas, garter snakes, brush rabbits, Sierra Nevada red foxes, black-tailed deer, coyotes, and the occasional mountain lion.

At elevations of 6,500–8,000 ft are red fir forests populated by many of the same wildlife as the lower regions, with the addition of black-backed three-toed woodpeckers, blue grouse, snowshoe hare, pine martens, and the hermit thrush. Above 8,000 ft the environment is harsher, with bare patches of land between subalpine forest. You'll find whitebark pine, groves of mountain hemlock, and the occasional wolverine. Bird watchers should look for gray-crowned rosy finches, rock wrens, pikas, golden eagles, falcons, and hawks. California tortoise-shell butterflies can be found on the highest peaks. If you can visit in winter, you'll see one of the park's most magnificent seasonal sights: massive snowdrifts reaching 30–40 ft high.

HIGH AND LOW SEASON

Snow covers the ground from late October to mid-June and most roads are closed from October until June. Winters can be severe, but hikers and snow lovers visit the park even in the dead of winter. As soon as the heavy snow melts, usually by mid-June, visitors begin trickling into the park. Peak season is mid-July to mid-September, when days are sunny, warm, and mostly dry and nights are cool. August is the most popular month in the park and February is the least popular.

Average High/Low Temperature (°F) and Monthly Precipitation (in inches)

	JAN	FEB.	MAR.	APR.	MAY	JUNE
LASSEN	41/21	43/23	46/25	52/27	62/33	71/39
VOLCANIC	9.2	7.3	7.6	3.9	2.1	1.3
	JULY	AUG.	SEPT.	OCT.	NOV.	DEC.
	80/42	80/41	72/37	62/32	47/27	41/22
	0.3	0.7	1.5	4.3	8.3	8.4

FESTIVALS AND SEASONAL EVENTS

SUMMER
....

Aug.: **Almanor Arts Show.** Chester's local artists show and sell handmade crafts on the first weekend of the month. | 530/283–3402.

FALL
....

Sept.: **Street Rod Extravaganza.** The weekend after Labor Day, Chester turns the streets over to 1950s nostalgia. | 800/350–4838.

Nearby Towns

The tiny logging town of **Chester,** 17 mi from the park, serves as the commercial center for the entire Lake Almanor area. Because of its proximity to the park, it is one of the best kicking-off points—but the accommodations and services are limited. **Susanville,** 35 mi east of Chester, is a high-desert town named after a pioneer's daughter. The county seat, it is the area's primary population and commercial center. Named for its vibrant cliffs and sand, **Red Bluff** maintains a mix of Old West toughness and late 1800s gentility: restored Victorians line the streets west of Main Street, while the downtown looks like a stage set for a spaghetti western. This small working-class city is a good place to stock up before heading into the park; it sits 50 mi from Lassen's south entrance via Route 36. With a population of 80,000, **Redding** is the largest city in the extreme northern portion of California. It sits 32 mi north of Red Bluff via I–5 and 50 mi west of the park's north entrance via

LASSEN VOLCANIC
NATIONAL PARK

EXPLORING
ATTRACTIONS NEARBY
DINING
LODGING
CAMPING AND RV
FACILITIES
SHOPPING
ESSENTIAL
INFORMATION

Route 44. Both Red Bluff and Redding offer the most accommodations and services in the area; each is an hour's drive from the park.

INFORMATION

Chester Chamber of Commerce | Box 1198 | 529 Main St., Chester, 96020 | 800/350–4838 | www.chester-lakealmanor.com. **Lassen County Chamber of Commerce** | Box 338 | 84 N. Lassen St., Susanville, 96130-0338 | 530/257–4323 | www.lassencountychamber.org. **Red Bluff Chamber of Commerce** | Box 850 | 100 Main St., Red Bluff, 96080 | 530/527–6220 | www.redbluffchamberofcommerce.com. **Redding Convention and Visitors Bureau** | 777 Auditorium Dr., Redding, 96001 | 800/874–7562 or 530/225–4100 | www.visitredding.org.

Exploring Lassen

PARK BASICS

Contacts and Resources: Lassen Volcanic National Park Headquarters | Box 100 | 38050 Rte. 36 E, Mineral, CA 96063–0100 | 530/595–4444 | www.nps.gov/lavo.

Hours: The park is open 24 hours a day, year-round, though during the winter, many of the park's attractions are covered by snow and are inaccessible by car and foot.

Fees: The vehicle admission fee is $10 and is valid for seven days. Those who enter by bus, on foot, bicycle, motorcycle, or horse pay $5 for a seven-day pass. Senior citizens who are U.S. residents over the age of 62 pay $10 for a lifetime pass, and permanently disabled U.S. residents are admitted free. You can also purchase an annual pass for unlimited visits to Lassen Volcanic National Park and Whiskeytown National Recreation area (in the Shasta-Trinity National Forest) for $25.

Getting Around: The 30-mi main park road, known as both Lassen Park Road and Route 89, starts at the park's southwest entrance, broadly loops around three sides of Lassen Peak, and exits the park on the northwest side; this road is closed to through traffic from late October to June or July due to snowfall. The speed limit within the park is 35 mph, unless otherwise noted. You'll find numerous turnouts along the route, most of which have roadside markers and interpretive exhibits. There is no public transportation within the park.

Permits: You need a wilderness permit for backcountry camping; permits are available free at the Loomis Museum, north and south entrance stations, and the park's headquarters in Mineral. You can also complete an on-line application in advance and either fax or e-mail your request; visit the park's Web site for complete details (www.nps.gov/lavo).

Public Telephones and Rest Rooms: There are public telephones and rest rooms at Lassen Chalet, Southwest Campground, the Manzanita Camper Store, and the Loomis Plaza (between Ranger Station and the museum). There are flush toilets, but no telephones at Summit Lake North campground and Manzanita Lake campground. There are vault toilets at all picnic areas and at various locations throughout the park.

Accessibility: Park headquarters and the Loomis Museum are both fully accessible to those with limited mobility. There are accessible public rest rooms—most of them open in summer only—at the Loomis Museum, and the Camper Store at Manzanita Lake, the picnic area and campground site at Summit Lake, and at the Lassen Chalet and the campground in the southwest entrance area. The vault toilets at Kings Creek and Lake Helen picnic areas are completely accessible, but the vault toilets at the Bumpass Hell and Lassen Peak parking areas and those at the Manzanita Lake campground may require assistance. The Devastated Area interpretive trail and the Sulphur Works boardwalk are accessible, as are certain naturalist programs; check at park headquarters. Park headquarters offers a TDD information line for the hearing impaired at 530/595–3480.

Emergencies: In case of a fire or medical emergency, dial 911. To reach the Park Protection Rangers contact the park headquarters (530/595–4444 Ext. 5151) or the Loomis Ranger Station (530/595–4444 Ext. 5187). During the camping season, the ranger stations at Summit Lake and Warner Valley are also staffed, though neither of these stations have phones.

Lost and Found: The park's main lost-and-found areas are at the Loomis Museum and the park headquarters. Alternatively, you can go to the nearest ranger station if you lose an object or want to turn one in.

Good Tours

LASSEN VOLCANIC IN ONE DAY

Start your day early at the northwest entrance to the park, accessible via Route 44 from Redding. Stop at the **Loomis Museum.** From the museum parking lot, you can take the easy, 1-mi round-trip **Lily Pond Nature Trail.** Once you're back at the museum, drive down to **Manzanita Lake**; take a mid-morning break and pick up supplies for a picnic lunch at the **Camper Store.** Take the main road, toward **Lassen Peak.** As you circle the peak on its northern flank, you'll come upon **Devastated Area,** testimony to the damage done by the 1915 eruptions. Continue to **Summit Lake** where you can picnic and swim, or to **Kings Creek,** an area of lush meadows where you can picnic and hike to **Kings Creek Falls**; allow about 2½ hours to make the 3-mi hike, which ends in a 700-ft descent to the falls. If time allows, continue to the **Sulphur Works,** where a boardwalk leads out over the boiling springs. Exit the park via the southwest entrance, or return back to the northwest entrance, stopping at overlooks along the way to see views of the setting sun.

LASSEN VOLCANIC IN TWO DAYS

For a two-day tour, approach the park from the southeast, driving 17 mi from Chester to Warner Valley along Warner Valley Road, which parallels Hot Springs Creek. Drakesbad Guest Ranch is at the end of the road (park at the designated trailhead just before the ranch); from here, you can take one of two hikes, either to **Devils Kitchen** or **Boiling Springs Lake.** You can also make the trip to Boiling Springs on horseback, but you'll need to make reservations with the ranch. Return to Chester for lunch at one of the restaurants in town. Head north from Route 36 on Route 89 to enter the park via the southwest entrance. You'll shortly reach **Lassen Chalet,** where you can pick up camping supplies for an overnight in the park. North of the chalet is **Sulphur Works.** Continue to Kings Creek by car and stop for a breather at the picnic area. From here, it's a 3-mi hike to **Kings Creek Falls.** In the late afternoon, continue about 4.5 mi to the campgrounds at **Summit Lake.** (If you're visiting at peak periods in summer, secure your site at the campground as early as possible and return to the sights you missed along the way.) Check the bulletin board to see if there are any ranger programs that evening. Alternatively, if you don't wish to camp, you can return to Chester for the night.

On day two, drive north to the **Devastated Area** parking lot. Here a short, barrier-free paved trail takes about 20 minutes to walk round-trip; examples of various types of volcanic rock are visible on both sides of the trail. After making the loop, head north to **Manzanita Lake** and the **Camper Store,** where you can have a light lunch. Nearby is the **Loomis Museum.** End your day with an easy 1-mi **nature walk** starting from the museum's parking lot.

Attractions

PROGRAMS AND TOURS

All park programs are free. Due to extreme budget cuts by the federal government, the park offers few, if any, ranger-led hikes or programs, depending on when you visit. For current information on what is available, check the park bulletin boards or information centers, or call 530/595–4444.

Junior Ranger Program. Children 7–12 can spend two hours with rangers learning about the park through games, activities, and observation. You can pick up Junior Ranger cards

LASSEN VOLCANIC
NATIONAL PARK

EXPLORING
ATTRACTIONS NEARBY
DINING
LODGING
CAMPING AND RV
FACILITIES
SHOPPING
ESSENTIAL
INFORMATION

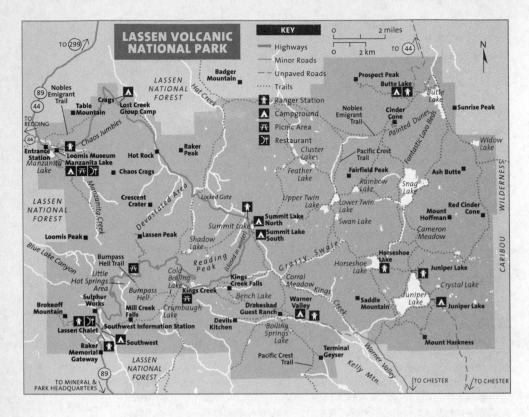

at the Loomis Museum or park headquarters in Mineral. | Manzanita Lake Amphitheater, near the Loomis ranger station at Manzanita Lake and at Summit Lake Amphitheater | Check at park headquarters, Loomis Museum, or park bulletin boards for dates and times.

Manzanita Lake Evening Programs. Check the campground for specific topics covered in regular 45-minute ranger-led programs. | Loomis Museum | 530/595–4444 Ext. 5133 | Check bulletin boards for times and dates.

Starry Nights. Rangers discuss myths and contemporary theories about galaxies, stars, and planets, beneath the night sky in a 45-minute program. | Devastated Area parking lot, Lassen Park Rd., 2.5 mi north of Summit Lake | Check park bulletin boards or park headquarters for times and dates.

SCENIC DRIVES

Lassen Park Road (Route 89). The paved road through Lassen Volcanic National Park is only 30 mi long; there are no side roads. Lassen Peak is visible from many parts of the road; the most scenic portion of the drive is between Kings Creek picnic area and the information center near the southwest entrance station. This portion passes near most of the boiling springs and a majority of the park's trail heads.

SIGHTS TO SEE

Boiling Springs Lake. A worthwhile, if occasionally muddy, 1-mi hike from the Drakesbad Guest Ranch, Boiling Springs Lake is surrounded by trees, and usually shrouded in mist. Constant bubbles release sulfuric steam into the air. | At the end of Warner Valley Rd.

★**Bumpass Hell.** This site's quirky name came about when a man with the last name of Bumpass was badly burned after falling into the boiling springs. A scenic 3-mi round-trip hike brings you up close to springs, steam vents, and mud pots. There's a gradual climb of 500 ft during the first mile of the hike before a 250-ft descent to the basin. Stay on trails and boardwalks near the thermal areas: what appears to be firm ground may be only a thin crust over scalding mud. | Lassen Park Rd., 6 mi north of the southwest entrance station.

Chaos Jumbles. More than 300 years ago, an avalanche from the Chaos Crags lava domes scattered hundreds of thousands of rocks—many of them 2–3 ft in diameter—over a couple of square miles. | Lassen Park Rd., 2 mi north of the northwest entrance station.

Devastated Area. True to its name, Devastated Area offers a bleak vista. The 1915 eruptions of Lassen Peak cleared the area of all vegetation, though there are a few signs of life after all these years. | Lassen Park Rd., 2.5 mi north of Summit Lake.

Devil's Kitchen. One of the three main geothermal areas of the park, Devil's Kitchen is a great place to view mudpots, steam vents, and boiling waters, as well as a variety of wildlife. It's much less frequented than Bumpass Hell, so you can expect more solitude during your hike. | Off Warner Valley Rd., at Drakesbad Guest Ranch.

Hot Rock. This 400-ton boulder tumbled down from the summit during the volcano's active period and was still hot to the touch when locals discovered it nearly two days later. Although it's cool now, it's still an impressive sight. | Lassen Park Rd., 7 mi south of northwest entrance station.

★ **Lassen Peak.** When this now-dormant plug dome volcano erupted in 1915, it spewed a huge mushroom cloud with debris 7 mi into the air. For a fabulous panoramic view of the area, hike the 2.5 mi to the 10,457-ft summit. | Lassen Park Rd., 7 mi from the southwest entrance station.

Loomis Museum. This museum displays artifacts of the park's 1914–1915 eruptions, including some of the original photographs taken by Benjamin Loomis, who was instrumental in the park's establishment. There are also excellent exhibits on the area's Native American history and culture, including a number of woven baskets. In the auditorium, the museum presents two 15-minute films on the park's history. | Lassen Park Rd. at Manzanita Lake | 530/595–4444 Ext. 5180 | Free | Memorial Day–mid-June and early Sept.–late Sept., Fri.–Sun. 9–5; mid-June–Labor Day, daily 9–5.

Manzanita Lake. Lassen Peak is reflected in the waters of Manzanita Lake, which has good catch-and-release trout fishing, as well as a pleasant trail from which to view the area's abundant wildlife. | Lassen Park Rd. at northwest entrance station.

Park Headquarters Information Station. Pick up maps, books, permits, trail and road guides, and inquire about children's activities and ranger-led programs here. You'll also find a rest room and a first-aid station here. | 38050 Rte. 36 E, 9 mi south of the southwest entrance station in Mineral | 530/595–4444 | Early Sept.–late May, weekdays 8–4:30; late May–mid-June, Thurs.–Mon. 8–4:30; mid-June–early Sept., daily 8–4:30.

Sulphur Works Thermal Area. Proof of the Lassen Peak's volatility becomes evident shortly after you enter the park at the southwest entrance. Boardwalks take you over bubbling mud and boiling springs and through sulfur-emitting steam vents. | Lassen Park Rd., 1 mi from the southwest entrance station.

Summit Lake. The midpoint between the northern and southern entrances, Summit Lake is a good place to take a midday swim. A trail leads around the lake shore and several other trails head off toward a cluster of smaller lakes in the more remote eastern section of the park. | Lassen Park Rd., 17.5 mi from southwest entrance station.

Sports and Outdoor Activities

BICYCLING

Biking is not allowed on any of the park trails, but is allowed on Lassen Park, Warner Valley, Juniper Lake, and Butte Lake roads.

LASSEN VOLCANIC
NATIONAL PARK

EXPLORING
ATTRACTIONS NEARBY
DINING
LODGING
CAMPING AND RV
FACILITIES
SHOPPING
ESSENTIAL
INFORMATION

Bodfish Bicycles. You can rent 24-gear dirt bikes at $8 per hour—with a two-hour minimum—or for $28 a day. | 149 Main, Chester | 530/258–2338 | Tues.–Sat. 10–5.

FISHING

The best place to fish is in Manzanita Lake or at Hat Creek, though fishing is also allowed at Butte Lake, 35 mi northwest of Susanville via Route 44. Make sure that you stop at Loomis Museum or park headquarters for a brochure on the in-park fishing regulations. A California freshwater fishing license is required to fish within Lassen National Park. You can pick up an application at most sporting goods stores (call 530/225–2300 for the nearest location) or download it from the California Department of Fish and Game's Web site (www.dfg.ca.gov).

HIKING

There are 150 mi of hiking trails within the park, 17 mi of which are part of the Pacific Crest Trail. The trails vary greatly, some winding through coniferous forest, and others across alpine tundra or along waterways.

Bumpass Hell Trail. Boiling springs, steam vents, and mudpots are featured on this 3 mi round-trip hike. There's an overall descent of 700 ft from the parking lot to the base of the area. Expect to spend about three hours to do the loop. | Lassen Park Rd., 6 mi from the southwest entrance station.

Chaos Crags Hike. This 3.6-mi round-trip hike includes a 700-ft climb to the base of the crags—protruding tubes of lava—for views of the area. | Trailhead 0.5 mi from Loomis Museum on the road to Manzanita Lake campground.

Cinder Cone Trail. Though it's a little out of the way, this is one of Lassen's most fascinating trails. The 4-mi round-trip hike to the cone summit includes a steep 800-ft climb over ground that's very loose in parts, so this is one for more experienced hikers. Pick up the self-guided trail brochure for 50¢ at Loomis Museum, park headquarters, or the trailhead. | West end of Butte Lake Campground, on Rte. 44, 35 mi northwest of Susanville.

Crumbaugh Lake Hike. A 3-mi round-trip hike that goes through meadows and forests to Cold Boiling Lake and Crumbaugh Lake, this excursion is an excellent way to view spring wildflowers. | Kings Creek picnic area, Lassen Park Rd., 13 mi north of the southwest entrance station.

Kings Creek Falls Hike. This is a good hike for nature photographers, as it takes you past forests dotted with wildflowers and, of course, past Kings Creek Falls. The 3-mi round-trip trail takes about 2½ hours to complete. | Lassen Park Rd., 12 mi from the southwest entrance station.

Lassen Peak Hike. This trail winds 2.5 mi to the mountaintop. It's a tough climb—2,000 ft uphill on a steady, steep grade—but the reward is a spectacular view. At the peak you can see into the rim and view the entire park (and much of the Far North). Bring sunscreen and water. | Lassen Park Rd., 7 mi north of the southwest entrance station.

Mill Creek Falls. Start at the Southwest Campground for a 2½-hour (4.6-mi) hike through forests and wildflowers to an important watershed where waters from two thermal areas join to create the park's highest waterfall. | Southwest Campground, near the southwest entrance station.

HORSEBACK RIDING

Drakesbad Guest Ranch. This in-park property offers guided horseback rides to nonguests who make reservations in advance. You can take a 45-minute trip to Boiling Springs or a half-day ride to Willow Lake or an all-day, five-lake loop tour. | End of Warner Valley Rd. | 530/529–1512 Ext. 120 | $21–$175 | Mid-June–mid-Oct.

SNOWSHOEING

On your own, you can try snowshoeing anywhere in the park. The gentlest places are in the northern district of the park; the more challenging terrain is in the south. There are no snowshoe rentals for independent hikers, so you must bring your own. You can rent snowshoes outside the park at Lassen Mineral Lodge (Route 36, Mineral | 530/595–4422) for $12 a day.

Snowshoe Walks. On Saturdays from early January through early April, park rangers lead 1–2 mi (two-hour round-trip) snowshoe hikes exploring the park's geology and winter ecology. The hikes require moderate exertion at an elevation of 7,000 ft; children under 8 are not allowed. You can rent the shoes for $1 per person. Walks are first-come, first-served; meet by the snowshoe sign outside the Lassen Chalet. | Lassen Park Rd. near the southwest entrance station | 530/595–4444 | Free | Early Jan.–early Apr., Sat. at 1:30.

Attractions Nearby

Scenic Drives

Lassen Scenic Byway. Beginning in Chester, this 185-mi scenic drive loops through the forests, volcanic peaks, geothermal springs, and lava fields of Lassen National Forest and Lassen National Park. It's an all-day excursion into dramatic wilderness; the road goes through the park and Lassen National Forest, veers southeast towards Susanville, then cuts west to make a loop around Lake Almanor before ending in Chester. The road is partially inaccessible in winter; call the Almanor Ranger District headquarters or Caltrans for current road conditions. From Chester, take Route 36 west to Route 89 north through the park (subject to closures due to snow), then Route 44 east to Route 36 west. Optionally, at Route 147, cut south to loop around Lake Almanor, and return to Route 89 north; at Route 36, turn east to return to Chester. | Almanor Ranger District 530/258–2141; Caltrans 800/427–7623.

Sights to See

Bizz Johnson Trail. From its starting point at the Susanville Depot Trailhead visitor center and museum, this 25-mi trail follows a defunct line of the Southern Pacific railroad through canyons and upland forests along the Susan River. You can hike the trail, ride a mountain bike, or go on horseback. | 601 Richmond Rd., Susanville | 530/257–0456 | www.ca.blm.gov/eaglelake/bizztrail.html | Free.

★ **Eagle Lake.** Ringed by high desert in the north and alpine forests in the south, this 22,000-acre natural lake is one of the largest in the state. It's a popular destination for picnicking, hiking, boating, and above all fishing—the native Eagle Lake trout is highly prized. | 20 mi northwest of Susanville on Eagle Lake Rd. (Rte. A1) | www.shastacascade.org/blm/eagle/lake.htm | Free.

Kelly-Griggs House Museum. This Victorian-era home, built in 1880, is filled with period artifacts and local antiques. Photos and costumes are on display in several of the rooms. | 311 Washington St., Red Bluff | 530/527–1129 | Donation requested | Thurs.–Sun. 1–4, or by appointment.

Lake Almanor. This 52-square-mi lake in the shadow of Mount Lassen was created in 1914 by the Pacific Gas and Electric Company for hydroelectric power, but it's also a popular draw for campers, swimmers, boaters, water-skiers, and fishermen. Despite its altitude (4,500 ft), the lake warms to above 70°F in summer. | Almanor Ranger district headquarters, 900 W. Rte. 36, Chester | 530/258–2141 | Free.

Lake Shasta Caverns. You'll get an eyeful of geological formations on the one-hour guided tour of these caverns. The journey begins with a catamaran ride across Lake Shasta. Take I–5 19 mi north of Redding to the Shasta Caverns Road exit. | Shasta Caverns Rd., 2 mi off I–5 | 530/238–2341 or 800/795–2283 | www.lakeshastacaverns.com | $18 | June–Aug., tours on the half hour, daily 9–4; Apr., May, and Sept., tours on the hour, daily 9–3; Oct.–Mar., tours at 10, noon, and 2.

Shasta State Historic Park. This park, 3 mi west of Redding, is on the site of a town that once was home to 2,500 people during the Gold Rush. The old courthouse is now a museum, while other buildings in the town have been restored to their original look. | 15312 Rte. 299 W, Old Shasta | 530/243–8194 | $2 | Courthouse Museum, Wed.–Sun. 10–5; park grounds, daily dawn–dusk.

★ **Shasta-Trinity National Forests.** With more than 2 million acres of richly wooded mountains in north-central California, Shasta-Trinity is the home of Mount Shasta, Castle Crags, the Trinity Alps, and Whiskeytown-Shasta-Trinity National Recreation Area. The area is full of hiking trails, camping, backpacking, and other outdoor activities. | 204 W. Alma, Mount Shasta | 530/926–4511 | www.r5.fs.fed.us/shastatrinity | Free | Daily dawn–dusk.

Turtle Bay Exploration Park and Museum. At this great place for families, you'll find everything from fine art to live animals on display. Contemporary art exhibits, historical county artifacts, and ethnic arts and crafts fill the galleries. Outside there are miles of walking trails through a 220-acre arboretum and wetlands. You'll also find live animals and an aquarium featuring fish from the Sacramento River. Paul Bunyan's Forest Camp shows logging and ecology exhibits and a very popular butterfly house (summer only). | 800 Auditorium Dr., Redding | 530/243–8850 | www.turtlebay.org | $5 | Oct.–May, Tues.–Sun. 9–5; June–Sept. daily 9–5.

Waterworks Park. This amusement park near I–5 has rides and activities including the Flash Flood, three flumes, and a kids' pool with slides. | 151 N. Boulder Dr., Redding | 530/246–9550 | www.waterworkspark.com | $17 | Memorial Day–Labor Day, call for hours.

Dining

In Lassen Volcanic

Lassen Chalet. American. A café and snack bar complement the grocery and camping supplies stores here. You can buy beer and wine, and even get an espresso. | Lassen Park Rd., at the southwest entrance station | 530/595–3376 or 530/529–1512 | May–late June, daily 9–4; late June–early Sept., daily 9–6; early Sept.–Oct., daily 9–4 | MC, V.

Picnic Areas.

Kings Creek. The picnic tables are beside a creek in a shady area. There are vault toilets, but no other amenities at this area. | Off Lassen Park Rd., 11.8 mi from the southwest entrance station.

Lake Helen. This site has views of several peaks, including Lassen Peak. It has picnic tables and vault toilets, but no other amenities. | Lassen Park Rd., 6 mi north of southwest entrance station near the Bumpass Hell trailhead.

Manzanita Lake. In addition to the Camper Store, you'll find picnic tables and potable water at Manzanita Lake; rest rooms are nearby. | Lassen Park Rd., near the northwest entrance ranger station.

Summit Lake Campgrounds. These two campgrounds are equipped with picnic tables, fire grates, drinking water, and toilets. | Lassen Park Rd., 12 mi south of Manzanita Lake and 17.5 mi north of southwest entrance station.

Near the Park

★ **Benassi's.** Italian. For dinner, the area's most popular northern Italian eatery offers steaks and seafood in addition to homemade pasta specials. Quick lunches are also available, including carry-out delicatessen sandwiches. | 159 Main St., Chester | 530/258–2600 | $9–$16 | MC, V | Closed Mon., Oct. –Apr. No dinner Sun.

Grand Cafe. American. This downtown coffee shop, under continuous family ownership since the 1920s, serves reliable, traditional breakfasts and lunches. The decor is all original, including the individual jukeboxes at every booth. Breakfast is also available. | 730 Main St., Susanville | 530/257–4713 | $4–$10 | No credit cards | Closed Sun. No dinner.

Hatch Cover. Seafood. Dark-wood paneling and views of the adjacent Sacramento River create the illusion of dining aboard a ship, especially on the outside deck, which has views of Mount Shasta. The menu emphasizes seafood, but you can also get steaks, chicken, pasta, and combination plates. There is also an extensive menu of appetizers. | 202 Hemsted Dr. (from Cypress Ave. exit off I–5, turn left, then right onto Hemsted Dr.), Redding | 530/223–5606 | $9–$26 | AE, D, MC, V | No lunch weekends.

Josephina's. Mexican. A loyal clientele comes to this traditional Mexican restaurant for tacos, enchiladas, and chiles rellenos. It's open late on weekends. They also serve breakfast. | 1960 Main St., Susanville | 530/257–9262 | $5–$12 | MC, V.

★ **Peter Chu's Mandarin Cuisine.** Chinese. Though it sits on the second floor of the passenger terminal of Redding Airport, you'll find delicious traditional Mandarin and Hunan dishes at this upscale Asian restaurant. The dining room has views beyond the tarmac to Mount Shasta and Lassen peak. | 6751 Airport Rd., Redding | 530/222–1364 | $8–$16 | AE, MC, V.

St. Francis Champion Steakhouse. Steak. Inside the historic St. Francis Hotel, this steak house is decorated in an Old West theme and is all about meat. Those who succeed in finishing the "grand champion" 64-ounce-steak dinner get their meal on the house; otherwise, it'll cost you $54.95. | 830 Main St., Susanville | 530/257–4820 | $15–$30 | AE, MC, V | Closed Sun.–Mon.

Snack Box. American. Unabashedly corny pictures and knickknacks decorate the renovated Victorian cottage that holds the family-owned Snack Box. But it's the soups, omelets, burgers, and hearty sandwiches that keep folks coming back for more. You can also eat breakfast here. | 257 Main St., Red Bluff | 530/529–0227 | $4–$8 | AE, MC, V | No dinner.

Lodging

In Lassen Volcanic
★ **Drakesbad Guest Ranch.** This late-19th-century cabin at 5,700 ft provides the only lodging within the park itself. Kerosene lamps light most of the rustic rooms; quilts, propane heating, and the natural hot springs–fed pool help keep you warm on brisk evenings. All meals are included in the price of your stay and are served family- or buffet-style in the main dining room. Dining room. Pool. Fishing. Hiking, horseback riding, volleyball. Some pets allowed. No a/c, no room phones. No room TVs. | End of Warner Valley Rd. | 530/529–1512 | www.drakesbad.com | 6 lodge rooms (3 with shared bath), 8 bungalows, 4 cabins, 1 duplex (shared shower) | $121–$143 per person | D, MC, V | Closed early Oct.–early June | FAP.

Near the Park
★ **Bidwell House.** This two-story 1901 wooden farm house sits on 2 acres of aspen-studded lawns and gardens. You can gaze at Lake Almanor from the front porch. A separate cottage is available. The full breakfast features the inn's specialties—omelets and blueberry-walnut pancakes. The dining room is open for dinner Thursday–Saturday. Cable TV. No a/c, no room phones. No smoking. | 1 Main St., Chester | 530/258–3338 | www.bidwellhouse.com | 14 rooms | $80–$155 | MC, V | BP.

Chester Manor Motel. This very clean, remodeled 1950s-era one-story motel is within easy walking distance of restaurants and offers picnic tables among the pine groves on its 2.5 acre lot. Six of their 18 rooms are two-bedroom suites; all rooms have hair dryers and coffee pots. Picnic area. Refrigerators, microwaves. Cable TV. Exercise equipment. Some pets

LASSEN VOLCANIC
NATIONAL PARK

EXPLORING
ATTRACTIONS NEARBY
DINING
LODGING
CAMPING AND RV
FACILITIES
SHOPPING
ESSENTIAL
INFORMATION

allowed. No a/c. No smoking. | 306 Main St., Chester | 530/258–2441 or 888/571–4885 | fax 530/258–3523 | www.chestermanor.com | 18 rooms | $60–$94 | AE, MC, V.

Lamplighter Lodge. With inexpensive clean rooms and an outdoor swimming pool, this motel is a good place for families and budget travelers to spend the night in Red Bluff. | 210 S. Main St., Red Bluff | 530/527–1150 | 50 rooms, 2 suites Microwaves, refrigerators. Pool. | AE, D, MC, V | CP.

Lassen Mineral Lodge. Because of its location 9 mi from the southwest entrance to the park (the closest of any property in the area), this motel books up its rooms well in advance. Reserve as far ahead as possible. You can rent cross-country skis, snowshoes, and snowboards at the lodge's ski shop; there's also a general store. Restaurant. Bar. Shops. No a/c, no room phones. No room TVs. No smoking. | Rte. 36 E, Mineral | 530/595–4422 | www. lassenminerallodge.com | 20 rooms | $69–$80 | AE, D, MC, V.

★ **River Inn.** This hotel is across from Redding Convention Center and 0.5 mi west of the I–5 and Route 299 junction. Rooms are comfortable and come with amenities like 25" TVs and small outdoor patios. You can borrow a fishing pole from the hotel to fish in the nearby lake. Restaurant, picnic area. Some in-room hot tubs, refrigerators. Cable TV with movies. Pool. Hot tub, sauna. Bar. Business services. Some pets allowed (fee). | 1835 Park Marina Dr., Redding | 530/241–9500 or 800/995–4341 | fax 530/241–5345 | www.reddingriverinn.com | 79 rooms | $64–$100 | AE, D, DC, MC, V.

St. Francis Hotel. Susanville's oldest continuously operated guest house was built of brick in 1914. The simple, clean rooms are furnished with wooden antiques, and public spaces include a sitting parlor and a rear courtyard patio. Restaurant. Cable TV. Bar. No a/c, no room phones. No room TVs. No smoking. | 830 Main St., Susanville | 530/257–4820 | fax 530/257–4195 | 28 rooms (16 with private bath) | $40–$65 | AE, D, MC, V.

Camping and RV Facilities

In Lassen Volcanic

Sites at Lassen's eight campgrounds are on a first-come, first-served basis; for groups of more than 10 adults reservations are required at one of the park's group campsites at Lost Creek, Juniper Lake, and Butte Lake (call 530/335–7029). Campfires are restricted to fire rings. Lassen has black bears, so be sure to secure your food and garbage properly by using the bear boxes provided at the park's campsites.

Juniper Lake. On the east shore of the park's largest lake at an altitude of 6,792 ft, campsites are close to shore in a wooded area. This site is not a good choice for trailers or for people who need the comforts of home. To reach it, you have to take a rough dirt road that leads 13 mi north of Chester and enters at the southeast corner of the park. Pit toilets. Bear boxes, fire pits, picnic tables. Swimming (lake). | 18 tent sites | $12 | Late June–early Oct.

Manzanita Lake Campground. The largest of Lassen Volcanic National Park's eight campgrounds is near the northwest entrance. A trail near the campground leads to Crags Lake. There's plenty of fish in Manzanita Lake, and the campground has a boat launch. You can find food and a gift shop at the nearby Camper Store. This campground is the only one in the park with a dump station ($5 fee) and coin-operated showers. Flush toilets. Dump station. Drinking water, guest laundry, showers. Bear boxes, fire pits, picnic tables. Public telephone. General store. Swimming (lake). | 179 tent sites | Lassen Park Rd. at northwest entrance | 530/595–4444 | $16 | Mid-May–late Sept.; then until snow closure, but without running water.

Southwest Walk-In. This relatively small campground is at 6,700 ft near Lassen Chalet, and lies within a red fir forest with views of Brokeoff Peak. Drinking water is only available from late May until late September; the rest of the year water and toilets are available at nearby

Lassen Chalet. RVs can park overnight in the Lassen Chalet parking area for $10; register at the campground. Flush toilets. Drinking water. Bear boxes, fire grates, picnic tables. | 21 tent sites | Adjacent to southwest entrance station | $14.

Summit Lake North. This is the higher and drier of the two campgrounds at Summit Lake. It's completely forested and has easy access to backcountry trails. You'll have better luck observing the deer that graze here than you will fishing in the lake. RVs up to 30 ft long can park here. Flush toilets. Drinking water. Bear boxes, fire pits, picnic tables. Swimming (lake). | 46 tent/RV sites | Lassen Park Rd., 12 mi south of Manzanita Lake and 17.5 mi north of southwest entrance | $16 | Late June–early Sept.

Summit Lake South. Less crowded than its neighbor to the north, this campground has wet meadows where wild flowers grow in the spring. RVs up to 30 ft long can park here. Pit toilets. Drinking water. Bear boxes, fire pits, picnic tables. Swimming (lake). | 48 tent/RV sites | Lassen Park Rd., 12 mi south of Manzanita Lake and 17.5 mi north of southwest entrance | $14 | Late June–late Sept.

Warner Valley. Accessible via a dirt road 17 mi north of Chester, this campground is close to Drakesbad Guest Ranch and Boiling Springs Lake. The quiet, woodsy setting makes it feel more remote than it is. The campground is not recommended for RVs trailers. Pit toilets. Drinking water. Bear boxes, fire grates, picnic tables. Swimming (river). | 18 tent sites | Warner Valley Rd., 1 mi west of Warner Valley ranger station | $14 | Early June–early Oct.

Near the Park

Hat Creek. In Lassen National Forest north of Lassen Volcanic National Park, this very nice campsite is alongside Hat Creek, known as an excellent trout stream. Nearby are a grocery store, a gas station, and a Laundromat with showers. The campground may close periodically due to fire danger. Flush toilets. Dump station. Drinking water. Fire grates, picnic tables. | 75 tent/RV sites | 1 mi south of Old Station on Rte. 89/44 | 530/336–5521 | $15 | Reservations not accepted.

Shopping

Manzanita Lake Camper Store. You can pick up food (including beer and wine), souvenirs, camping supplies, wood, and gasoline here. There are also showers and a Laundromat. | Lassen Park Rd., near Manzanita Lake | 530/335–7557 or 530/529–1512 | Closed Nov.–Apr.

Lassen Chalet. In-season, the store here sells food and camping supplies as well as gifts, apparel, espresso, beer, and wine. | Lassen Park Rd., near the southwest entrance station | 530/595–3376 or 530/529–1512 | Closed Nov.–Apr.

Essential Information

ATMS (24-HOUR): Bank of America | 955 Main St., Red Bluff | 800/346–7693. **Plumas Bank** | 255 Main St., Chester | 530/258–4161. **Bank of America** | 1300 Hilltop Dr. (Near the junction of I–5, Rte. 299, and Rte. 44), Chester | 530/246–3992.

AUTOMOBILE SERVICE STATIONS: Antelope Beacon | 615 Antelope Blvd., Redding | 530/527–5436. **Main Street Chevron** | 1055 S. Main St., Redding | 530/527–4243.

POST OFFICES: Red Bluff Post Office | 447 Walnut St., Red Bluff, 96080 | 530/527–1455 or 800/275–8777.

SEQUOIA AND KINGS CANYON NATIONAL PARKS

CENTRAL CALIFORNIA

Sequoia: 36 mi east of Visalia on Route 198. Kings Canyon: 53 mi east of Fresno on Route 180. There is no automobile entrance on the eastern side of the Sierra.

As early as the 1850s greedy promoters were looking for ways to make money off the natural wonders of the American West. In 1853 large sections of bark were stripped from California's Sequoias and shipped to London to be exhibited for a fee. At that time most Europeans did not believe that trees could be that big and dismissed the exhibition as a fraud. The venture was a financial failure.

The silent giants of Sequoia and Kings Canyon, surrounded by vast granite canyons and towering snowcapped peaks, strike awe in most everyone who sees them. No less than famed naturalist John Muir proclaimed the sequoia tree "the most beautiful and majestic on earth." Though often overshadowed by Yosemite National Park to the north, the two parks that protect the mighty conifer are spectacular in their own right. Sequoia and Kings Canyon share a boundary and are administered together. They encompass 1,353 square mi, rivaled only by Yosemite in rugged Sierra beauty. The topography ranges from foothill chaparral at an elevation of 1,500 ft in the west, to the giant sequoia belt at 5,000 to 7,000 ft, to the towering peaks of the Great Western Divide and the Sierra Crest. Mount Whitney, the highest point in the contiguous United States at 14,494 ft, is the crown jewel of the eastern side.

There was a time, beginning in the 1860s, when people came to these timberlands to cut trees. By 1890, however, the area's beauty was officially recognized, as was its value as a watershed, and the destruction was checked by the establishment of a 50,000-acre Sequoia National Park, the country's second national park. A week later, tiny 2,560-acre General Grant National Park was designated and additional acreage was granted to Sequoia. Years of prodding by environmentalists resulted in further growth of the park. In 1940 the General Grant Park was expanded to include the high country around the South Fork Kings River, and was renamed Kings Canyon National Park. In 1965, Cedar Grove and Tehipite Valley were protected within the Kings Canyon domain. Today, 1.5 million people visit the parks annually.

PUBLICATIONS

The Sequoia and Kings Canyon National Parks Visitors Guide is a free newspaper that gives essential information about visiting Sequoia and Kings Canyon. It's available at park entrance gates or in advance by contacting the parks directly. Contact Sequoia Natural History Association for the *Sequoia and Kings Canyon Official National Park Handbook*, which covers topics such as local climate, plant and animal adaptations, sequoias, and man's impact on the park. For detailed information on planning a backcountry hiking trip, contact the parks for *Backcountry Basics*, a free newsletter.

When to Visit

SCENERY AND WILDLIFE

The two parks comprise 865,952 acres on the western flank of the Sierra and can be divided into three distinct zones cut by stream and river canyons. In the west, from about 1,500 to 4,500 ft, are the lower elevation foothills—rolling hills covered with shrubby chaparral vegetation or golden grasslands dotted with oaks. At middle elevation, from about 5,000 ft to 9,000 ft, there are rock formations mixed with meadows and huge stands of conifers. The giant sequoia belt is here, which you can explore by foot in summer and by cross-country ski or snowshoe in winter. The high alpine section of the parks is extremely rugged, a land of harsh rock formations in a string of peaks reaching above 13,000 ft and crowned by Mount Whitney at 14,494 ft. To the north, the Kings River cuts a swath through the backcountry and over the years has formed a granite canyon that, in places, towers nearly 4,000 ft above the canyon floor. From Junction Overlook, on the drive to

Cedar Grove, you can see the 8,200-ft drop from Spanish Mountain to the Kings River, as well as the confluence of the Middle and South forks of the Kings River.

Wildlife and plants change with the elevation. The gently rolling foothills are primarily oak woodland and chaparral. Chamise and red-barked manzanita grow here, as does the occasional yucca plant. The amount of groundwater determines the density of the oak groves, which, in early spring, are carpeted with knee-high grass. Fields of white popcorn flower cover the hillsides in spring, and the yellow fiddleneck flourishes. In summer, intense heat and absence of rain cause the hills to turn golden-brown. Small creatures stalk these lands, including the bushy-tailed California ground squirrel. Black bears, coyotes, skunks, and gray fox are also present, as is the scrub jay, a noisy blue and gray bird that scolds anyone who crosses its path.

The parks' mid-zone forests, home to the sequoias, are what draw the crowds. But there are also evergreens—red and white fir, incense cedar, and ponderosa pines to name a few. Wildflowers, including yellow blazing star and red Indian paintbrush, bloom from spring to late summer. Golden-mantled ground squirrels, Steller's jays, mule deer, and, of course, black bears inhabit the area. Black bears are most active in the fall, when they binge before winter hibernation. One of the most obvious inhabitants is the Douglas squirrel, or chickaree, who spends most of his days loudly policing his territory, and clipping cones from the tops of the trees. In the high country, with its fierce weather and scarcity of soil, vegetation is sparse. Foxtail and whitebark pines have gnarled and twisted trunks, the result of years of high wind, heavy snowfall, and freezing temperatures. Life is smaller here than at lower elevations, and in summer you can see yellow-bellied marmots, pikas, weasels, mountain chickadees, and Clark's nutcrackers. Leopard lilies and shooting stars grow near streams and meadows.

Many high-elevation areas of the parks cannot be traversed in winter, and some roads are closed from early November to late April. The climbing season is June to October. Spring through fall is the best time to view Mount Whitney, since the best vantage point— Whitney Portal Road, off U.S. 395 just south of Lone Pine—is closed in winter.

HIGH AND LOW SEASON

The best times to visit the parks are late spring and early fall, when the temperatures are moderate and the crowds thin. Summertime can draw hoards of tourists to see the giant sequoias, and the few, narrow roads mean congestion at peak holiday times. If you must visit in summer, try to go during the week, when crowds and traffic are lighter and the beauty and majesty of the parks is less disturbed by human activity. By contrast, there are few visitors in wintertime, and you may feel as though you have the parks all to yourself. Because of heavy snows, sections of the main road through the parks can be closed without warning, and low-hanging clouds can move in and obscure mountains and valleys for days. Should you visit at this time, be sure to check road and weather conditions before venturing out.

Temperatures and precipitation in the chart below are for the mid-level elevations, generally between 4,000 and 7,000 ft. At higher elevations, average temperatures drop and average precipitation rises; at lower elevations, temperatures rise—by as much as 20°F in summer—and annual precipitation drops.

Average High/Low Temperature (°F) and Monthly Precipitation (in inches)

	JAN.	FEB.	MAR.	APR.	MAY	JUNE
SEQUOIA AND KINGS CANYON	42/24	44/25	46/26	51/30	58/36	68/44
	4.7	4.3	4.4	2.6	0.8	0.2
	JULY	AUG.	SEPT.	OCT.	NOV.	DEC.
	76/51	76/50	71/45	61/38	50/31	44/27
	0.1	0.2	0.7	1.2	3.3	3.7

FESTIVALS AND SEASONAL EVENTS

WINTER

Dec.: **Annual Trek to the Tree.** Christmas carolers gather at the base of General Grant Tree, the nation's official Christmas tree. | 559/565–4307.

SPRING

Mar.: **Diaz Lake Trout Derby.** The first Saturday of the month, you can take a shot at the "big one" in this fully stocked lake 3,700 ft above sea level and 3 mi south of Lone Pine on the eastern side of the Sierra. Prizes are awarded for all age groups. | 760/876–4444 or 877/253–8981 | www.lonepinechamber.org.

Apr.: **Jazzaffair.** Held just south of the parks in the town of Three Rivers, a festival of mostly swing jazz takes place at several locations, with shuttle buses between sites. The festival is usually the second weekend of the month. | 559/561–4549 | www.highsierrajazzband.com.

May: **Mule Days.** About 700 mules compete in more than 155 events during the Nation's Premier Mule Show each Memorial Day weekend in downtown Bishop. The Mule Days began in 1969 and today crowds exceed 30,000. Country-singing stars appear on Thursday night. The nation's largest nonmotorized parade takes place Saturday at 10 AM. | 760/872–4263 | www.muledays.org.

Redbud Festival. This two-day arts-and-crafts festival in Three Rivers highlights work by local artists. It usually takes place in the middle or at the end of the month. | 559/561–3160.

Woodlake Rodeo. A weekend-long event thrown by the Woodlake Lions, this rodeo draws large crowds to Woodlake (near Three Rivers) on Mother's Day weekend. | 559/564–8555.

SUMMER

Aug.–Sept.: **Tri-County Fair, Wild West Rodeo.** Live entertainment, rodeo shows, and livestock displays contribute to this Labor Day weekend fair at Sierra Street and Fair Drive in Bishop. | 760/873–3588 | www.tricountyfair.com.

FALL

Sept.: **Celebrate Sequoias Festival.** On the second Saturday of the month, rangers guide field trips to the lesser known groves of Sequoia National Park. Call Grant Grove visitor center for details. | 559/565–4307.

Nearby Towns

In the foothills of the Sierra along the Kaweah River, **Three Rivers** is a leafy hamlet whose livelihood depends largely on tourism from Sequoia and Kings Canyon. Close to Sequoia's Ash Mountain entrance, this is a good spot to find a room when park lodgings are full. **Bishop** is very close to the northeastern side of Kings Canyon, but the absence of roads across the mountains puts the town far away from the park's automobile entrances. If you have time, consider traveling on the eastern side of the Sierra. The range is marked by a gentle slope on the western side and a sharp, dramatic drop-off on the eastern side that gives way to the Great Basin and its high-mountain desert and giant volcanic calderas that extend well into Nevada. Craggy mountaintops are snowy throughout summer and make the drive on U.S. 395 spectacular. Bishop is not picturesque, but it's the biggest town along this route and has many services for weary travelers.

Mount Whitney looms high above the tiny, high-mountain-desert community of **Lone Pine,** another town in the eastern Sierra, where numerous Hollywood westerns have been filmed. As you approach from the south, note the gigantic lake bed that was once Owens Lake, before Los Angelinos drained the water to fill their swimming pools. Shut the windows if the wind is blowing as you drive past: high concentrations of airborne minerals, once diluted by the lake's water, can cause respiratory distress. Nonetheless, the high peaks, arid landscape, and scrubby brush are beautiful in their vastness and austerity.

INFORMATION

Bishop Area Chamber of Commerce | 690 N. Main St., Bishop, 93514 | 760/873–8405 | www.bishopvisitor.com. **Lone Pine Chamber of Commerce** | 126 S. Main St., Box 749, Lone Pine, 93545 | 760/876–4444 or 877/253–8981 | www.lonepinechamber.org. **Visalia Chamber of Commerce and Visitors Bureau** | 720 W. Mineral King Ave., Visalia, 93291 | 559/734–5876 or 877/847–2542 | www.visaliachamber.org.

Exploring Sequoia

PARK BASICS

Contacts and Resources: Delaware North Park Services | Box 89, Sequoia National Park, CA 93262 | 559/565–4070 or 888/252–5757 | www.visitsequoia.com. **Sequoia and Kings Canyon National Parks** | 47050 Generals Hwy. (Rte. 198), Three Rivers, CA 93271–9651 | 559/565–3341 or 559/565–3134 | www.nps.gov/seki. **Sequoia Natural History Association (SNHA).** The SNHA operates Crystal Cave and the Pear Lake Ski Hut, and provides educational materials and programs. | HCR 89 Box 10, Three Rivers, CA 93271 | 559/565–3759 | www.sequoiahistory.org. **U.S. Forest Service, Sequoia National Forest** | 900 W. Grand Ave., Porterville, CA 93527 | 559/784–1500 | www.fs.fed.us/r5/sequoia.

Hours: The park is open daily 24 hours.

Fees: The vehicle admission fee is $10 and valid for seven days. Those who enter by bus, on foot, bicycle, motorcycle, or horse pay $5 for a seven-day pass. Senior citizens who are U.S. residents over the age of 62 pay $10 for a lifetime pass, and permanently disabled U.S. residents are admitted free. There's one fee for both parks.

Getting Around: Private vehicles are necessary for travel to the major sites within the parks. Ongoing improvements to Generals Highway can cause delays up to an hour at peak times. Routes 180 and 198 are connected by Generals Highway, a paved two-lane road that's open year-round, though portions between Lodgepole and Grant Grove may be closed following heavy snowstorms. From Route 198 to Giant Forest, Generals Highway is extremely narrow and climbs 5,000 ft in 20 mi steep grades (5%–8%) and heavy traffic may cause vehicles to overheat. To avoid overheated brakes, use low gears on downgrades.

If you are traveling in an RV or with a trailer, study a map of the parks and the restrictions on these vehicles. RVs longer than 22 ft and autos pulling trailers should not travel beyond Potwisha campground on Route 198. Route 180 is a straighter, easier route than Route 198. Maximum vehicle length is 40 ft, or 50 ft combined length for vehicles with trailers. Drivers of RVs over 22 ft long and those who are not comfortable negotiating mountain roads should avoid the twisting, narrow, 16-mi southern stretch between the Potwisha Campground and Giant Forest.

Snowstorms are common from late October through April. Unless you have four-wheel drive with snow tires, always carry chains and know how to apply them to the tires on the drive axle. Generals Highway between Lodgepole and Grant Grove is sometimes closed by snow. The Mineral King Road from Route 198 into southern Sequoia National Park is closed 2 mi below Atwell Mill either on November 1 or with the first heavy snow. The Buckeye Flat–Middle Fork Trailhead Road is closed from mid-October to mid-April when the Buckeye Flat Campground closes. The lower Crystal Cave Road is closed when the cave closes in November. Its upper 2 mi, as well as the Panoramic Point and Moro Rock-Crescent Meadow roads are closed with the first heavy snow. Spring opening dates depend on the weather. For current conditions, call the park at 559/565–3341 Ext. 4.

SEQUOIA AND
KINGS CANYON
NATIONAL PARKS

EXPLORING
ATTRACTIONS NEARBY
DINING
LODGING
CAMPING AND RV
FACILITIES
SHOPPING
ESSENTIAL
INFORMATION

Though many of the major attractions in both parks can be reached by automobile, most of the acreage is without roads. Simply driving through the parks can be disappointing. To access the panoramic views and striking geological features, you have to hike; and you have more than 800 mi of trails from which to choose.

Permits: If you plan to camp in the backcountry, your group must have a backcountry camping permit, which costs $15 for hikers or $30 for stock users (horseback riders, etc.). One permit covers the entire group, regardless of the group's size. Availability of permits depends upon trailhead quotas. Advance reservations are accepted by mail, fax, or e-mail for a $15 processing fee, beginning March 1, and must be made at least three weeks in advance. Without a reservation, you may still get a permit on a first-come, first-served basis starting at 1 PM the day before you plan to hike. For more information on backcountry camping or travel with pack animals (horses, mules, burros, or llamas), call the Wilderness Permit Office (530/565–3761), or visit the parks' Web site (www.nps.gov/seki/resform.htm), where you can find permit applications.

Reservations for climbing Mount Whitney are difficult to obtain. Overnight and day permits are available through the U.S. Forest Service by lottery each February. A few permits are available in May if other hikers have canceled. For more information, contact the Inyo National Forest Office.

Inyo National Forest Office | 873 N. Main St., Bishop, CA 93514 | 760/873–2400 | www.fs.fed.us/r5/inyo. **Wilderness Permit Reservations** | HCR 89 Box 60, Three Rivers, CA 93271 | 559/575–3766 | fax 559/565–4239.

Public Telephones: Public telephones may be found at the park entrance station, visitor centers, ranger stations, some trailheads, and at all restaurants and lodging facilities in the park.

Rest Rooms: Public rest rooms may be found at all visitor centers and campgrounds. Additional locations include Hospital Rock, Wolverton, Crescent Meadow, Giant Forest Museum, and Crystal Cave.

Accessibility: All of the visitor centers, the Giant Forest Museum, and Big Trees Trail are wheelchair-accessible, as are some short ranger-led walks and talks. General Sherman Tree can be reached via a paved, level trail near a parking area. None of the caves is accessible and wilderness areas must be reached by horseback or on foot. Some picnic tables are extended to accommodate wheelchairs. Many of the major sites are in the 6,000 ft range and thin air at high elevations can cause respiratory distress for people with breathing difficulties. Carry oxygen if necessary. Contact the park's main number for more information.

Emergencies: Call 911 from any telephone within the park in an emergency. Rangers at the Foothills and Lodgepole visitor centers and the Mineral King Ranger Station are trained in first aid. National Park rangers have legal jurisdiction within park boundaries: contact a ranger station or visitor center for police matters. For non-emergencies, call the parks' main number, 559/565–3341.

Lost and Found: Report lost items or turn in found items at any visitor center or ranger station. Items are held at a central location and are handled by park rangers. For more information, call park headquarters at 559/565–3181.

Good Tours

SEQUOIA IN ONE DAY

From late spring through early fall, you can see most of the major sights in Sequoia in less than a day. Start out on Route 198 and enter Sequoia National Park in early morning. Head for **Foothills visitor center**; a half-hour here gives you a good overview of the area and an idea of what you want to see in the parks. If you are visiting in summer, pick up tickets for the tour of Crystal Cave; tickets are not available at the cave itself.

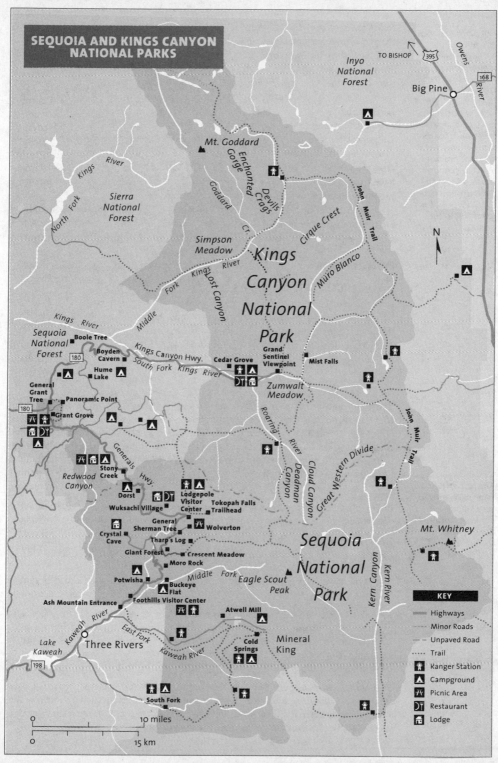

SEQUOIA AND KINGS CANYON NATIONAL PARKS

Inyo National Forest

TO BISHOP 395

Big Pine

Owens River

168

Mt. Goddard

Enchanted Gorge

Devils Crags

Goddard Cr.

Cirque Crest

John Muir Trail

Simpson Meadow

Kings River

Lost Canyon

Muro Blanco

Kings Canyon National Park

North Fork Kings River

Sierra National Forest

Middle Fork

Kings River

Sequoia National Forest

Boole Tree

Boyden Cavern

180

Hume Lake

Kings Canyon Hwy.

Cedar Grove

South Fork Kings River

Grand Sentinel Viewpoint

Mist Falls

General Grant Tree

Panoramic Point

Grant Grove

180

Zumwalt Meadow

Roaring River

Deadman Canyon

Cloud Canyon

Great Western Divide

John Muir Trail

Generals Hwy.

Stony Creek

Redwood Canyon

Dorst

Lodgepole Visitor Center

Tokopah Falls Trailhead

Wuksachi Village

General Sherman Tree

Wolverton

Crystal Cave

Tharp's Log

Giant Forest

Crescent Meadow

Moro Rock

Potwisha

Middle Fork

Eagle Scout Peak

Sequoia National Park

Mt. Whitney

Kern Canyon

Kern River

Buckeye Flat

Ash Mountain Entrance

Foothills Visitor Center

Atwell Mill

Lake Kaweah

Kaweah River

Three Rivers

198

East Fork

Kaweah River

Cold Springs

Mineral King

South Fork

N

0 ____ 10 miles

0 ____ 15 km

KEY

— Highways

--- Minor Roads

– – Unpaved Road

···· Trail

Ranger Station

Campground

Picnic Area

Restaurant

Lodge

HEATING UP

Fire plays a crucial role in the propagation of sequoia trees. Unlike other tree species in the area, the sequoia's cones remain closed on the tree and retain their seeds for more than 20 years. Hot air from fire dries out older cones, causing them to open up, and in one to two weeks, the seeds fall to the ground.

Follow Generals Highway north to the **Crystal Cave** turnoff and take the 50-minute tour. Next, head north and turn onto Moro Rock-Crescent Meadow Road. If you are able, climb the steep 0.25-mi staircase leading to the summit of **Moro Rock,** a large granite dome from which you can gaze out over the western end of Sequoia National Park. Even from a short distance up, you can get a wonderful view. From there, check out the midsummer wildflower show at **Crescent Meadow.** A 2-mi round-trip hike from the meadow leads to **Tharp's Log,** the summer home of Hale Tharp, built inside a fallen sequoia.

Return to Generals Highway, bypass Giant Forest, and drive north to **Lodgepole Village** for lunch. Afterward, tour the **Lodgepole visitor center,** which has excellent park history exhibits. Backtrack on Generals Highway and continue south to reach **General Sherman Tree,** the world's largest living tree, which is a short walk from the parking area. If you have time to spare, stroll down **Congress Trail,** a 2-mi loop through the heart of the sequoia forest that takes one to two hours to complete.

Return to your car, and drive south for about 2 mi to reach **Giant Forest.** After walking the 0.7-mi **Big Trees Trail,** which passes through forest and meadow in an easy loop, stop at the **Giant Forest Museum** to learn about the giant sequoia.

Attractions

PROGRAMS AND TOURS

Sequoia Sightseeing Tours offers daily guided tours through Sequoia. Visitor centers have maps for self-guided tours of the park. Ranger-led walks and programs take place throughout the year in Lodgepole Village. Forest Service campgrounds have activities from Memorial Day to Labor Day. Schedules for activities are posted on bulletin boards and at visitor centers.

★ **Crystal Cave Tour.** Crystal Cave has relatively undisturbed marble formations, produced from limestone that has metamorphosed under tremendous heat and pressure. The standard tour is 50 minutes in length. In summer, the park offers a four- to six-hour "wild cave" tour (reservations required) and a 90-minute discovery tour, a less-structured excursion with fewer people. Tickets are available only at Lodgepole or Foothills visitor centers and must be purchased by 4 PM and at least 90 minutes in advance. | Crystal Cave Rd., off Generals Hwy., 12 mi north of Ash Mountain entrance | 559/565–3759 | www.sequoiahistory.org | $9 | Mid-May–Oct., daily 10–4.

Evening Programs. In summer, the park shows documentary films and slide shows, and has evening lectures. Locations and times vary; pick up a schedule at any visitor center or check bulletin boards near ranger stations. | 559/565–3341.

The last grizzly bear in California was killed near Sequoia National Park in 1922.

Junior Ranger Program. This self-guided program is offered year-round for children over five. Pick up a Junior Ranger booklet at any of the visitor centers. When your child finishes an activity, a ranger signs the booklet. Kids earn a patch upon completion, which is given at an awards ceremony. It isn't necessary to complete all activities to be awarded a patch. | 559/565–3341.

★ **Seminars.** Expert naturalists lead seminars on a range of topics, including birds, wildflowers, geology, botany, photography, park history, backpacking, and pathfinding. Some courses offer transferable credits. Reserve in advance. For information and prices, pick up a course catalogue at any visitor center or from Sequoia Natural History Association. | 559/565–3759 | www.sequoiahistory.org.

Sequoia Sightseeing Tours. The only licensed tour operator in either park offers daily interpretive sightseeing tours in a 10-passenger van with a friendly, knowledgeable guide. Reservations are essential. They also offer private tours of Kings Canyon. | 559/561–4489 | www.sequoiatours.com | Box 1086 Three Rivers 93271.

SCENIC DRIVES

★ **Generals Highway.** Connecting the two parks from Grant Grove to Giant Forest and the foothills to the south, this narrow, twisting road runs past Stony Creek, Lost Grove, Little Baldy, General Sherman Tree, Amphitheater Point, and Foothills visitor center. Stop to see the Giant Forest Museum, which focuses entirely on the ecology of the sequoia. Also stop at the Lodgepole visitor center, which has excellent exhibits and audiovisual programs describing the Sierra Nevada and the natural history of the area. Under normal conditions it takes two hours to complete the drive one way, but when parks are crowded in summer, traffic can slow to a crawl in some areas.

Mineral King Road. Accessible from Memorial Day weekend through October (weather permitting), this small, winding, rough, steep road begins outside the park south of the Ash Mountain entrance, off Route 198. Trailers and RVs are prohibited. The exciting 25-mi drive ascends approximately 6,000 ft to a subalpine valley, where there are a ranger station and limited facilities. Bring a picnic lunch. Many backpackers use this as a trailhead, and you can take a fine day hike from here as well. Allow 90 minutes for the one-way drive.

SIGHTS TO SEE

Auto Log. At one time, cars drove right on top of this giant fallen sequoia. Now it's a great place to pose for pictures. | Moro Rock–Crescent Meadow Rd., 1 mi south of Giant Forest.

Crescent Meadow. Walk on fallen logs and trails through spectacular fields of summertime wildflowers. | End of Moro Rock–Crescent Meadow Rd., 2.6 mi east off Generals Hwy.

★ **Crystal Cave.** Ten-thousand feet of passageways in this marble cave were created by acidic groundwater that seeped in. Formations are relatively undisturbed. Tickets are not available at the cave; purchase them by 2:30 PM from Lodgepole or Foothills visitor center. | Crystal Cave Rd., 6 mi west off Generals Hwy. | 559/565–3759 | www.sequoiahistory.org | $9 | Mid-May—mid-Oct., daily 10–4.

Foothills Visitor Center. Exhibits focusing on the foothills and resource issues facing the parks are on display here. You can also pick up books, maps, and a list of ranger-led walks, and get wilderness permits. | Generals Hwy. (Rte. 198), 1 mi north of the Ash Mountain entrance | 559/565–3135 | Oct.–mid-May, daily 8–4:30; mid-May–Sept., daily 8–5.

★ **General Sherman Tree.** This, the world's largest living tree, is estimated to be about 2,100 years old. | Generals Hwy. (Rte. 198), 2 mi south of Lodgepole visitor center.

★ **Giant Forest Museum.** You'll find outstanding exhibits on the ecology of the giant sequoia at the park's premier museum. Though housed in a historic building, it is entirely wheelchair accessible. | Generals Hwy., 4 mi south of Lodgepole visitor center | 559/565–4480 | Memorial Day–mid-June, daily 8–5; mid-June–early Sept., daily 8–6; early Sept.–late May, daily 9–4:30 | Free.

Lodgepole Visitor Center. The center has exhibits on the early years of the park and a slide program on geology and forest life. They also sell books and maps. | Generals Hwy. (Rte. 198), 21 mi north of Ash Mountain entrance | 559/565–4436 | Mid-Apr.–mid-June, daily 8–5; mid-June–Sept., daily 8–6; Oct.–mid-Apr., hrs. vary (call for times).

Mineral King. This subalpine valley sits at 7,800 ft at the end of a steep, winding road. The trip from the park's entrance can take up to two hours. This is the highest point to which you can drive in the park. | End of Mineral King Rd., 25 mi east of Generals Hwy. (Rte. 198), east of Three Rivers.

Mineral King Ranger Station. The small visitor center here houses a few exhibits on the history of the area; wilderness permits and some books and maps are available. | End of Mineral King Rd., 25 mi east of East Fork entrance | 559/565–3768 | Early June–mid-Sept., daily 7–4:30.

★ **Moro Rock.** Climb the steep 400-step staircase 300 ft to the top of this granite dome for spectacular views of the Great Western Divide and the western regions of the park. To the

SEQUOIA AND
KINGS CANYON
NATIONAL PARKS

EXPLORING
ATTRACTIONS NEARBY
DINING
LODGING
CAMPING AND RV
FACILITIES
SHOPPING
ESSENTIAL
INFORMATION

BLOOMING BEAUTIES

Wildflowers bloom most of the summer in the parks. If you visit in spring, look for them in the foothills. As summer wears on and temperatures rise, you'll have to climb to ever-higher locations to see them. Unusual, magnificent species occur at the highest elevations in August in the moraine and alpine meadows.

southwest you look down the Kaweah River to Three Rivers, Lake Kaweah, and—on clear days—the Central Valley and the Coast Range. To the northeast are views of the High Sierra. Thousands of feet below lies the middle fork of the Kaweah River. | Moro Rock–Crescent Meadow Rd., 2 mi east off Generals Hwy. (Rte. 198) to parking area.

Tunnel Log. You can drive your car through this tunnel carved in a fallen sequoia. There's a bypass for larger vehicles. (There is no upright drive-through sequoia tree in the park. There used to be one in Yosemite, but it fell in 1969.) | Moro Rock–Crescent Meadow Rd., 2 mi east of Generals Hwy. (Rte. 198).

Walter Fry Nature Center. The hands-on nature exhibits here are designed primarily for children. The center is closed most of the year. | Lodgepole Campground, 0.5 mi east of Lodgepole visitor center | 559/565–4436 | July–Labor Day, weekends noon–5.

Sports and Outdoor Activities

No off-road driving is allowed in the parks. Boating, rafting, and snowmobiling are also prohibited.

BICYCLING

If you would rather travel by bicycle than by car, you may be disappointed. Bicycles are allowed only on the paved roads, and the steep highways have such narrow shoulders that cyclists should be extremely cautious.

BIRD-WATCHING

Not seen in most parts of the United States, the white-headed woodpecker and the pileated woodpecker are common in most mid-elevation areas here. There are also many hawks and owls, including the renowned spotted owl. Species are diverse in the parks due to the changes in elevation, and range from warblers, kingbirds, thrushes, and sparrows in the foothills to goshawk, blue grouse, red-breasted nuthatch, and brown creeper at the highest elevations. Ranger-led bird-watching tours are held on a sporadic basis. Call the parks at 559/565–3341 for more information.

CROSS-COUNTRY SKIING

For a one-of-a-kind experience, cut through the groves of mammoth sequoias in Giant Forest. Some of the Crescent Meadow Trails (*see* Hiking, *below*) are suitable for skiing as well. None of the trails is groomed. You can park at Giant Forest. Note that roads can be precarious in bad weather. Some advanced trails begin at Wolverton.

Wuksachi Village Lodge. Rent skis here. Depending on snowfall amounts, there may also be instruction available. Reservations are recommended. Marked trails cut through Giant Forest, which sits 5 mi south of the lodge. | Off Generals Hwy. (Rte. 198), 2 mi north of Lodgepole | 559/565–4070 | $15–$20 ski rental | Daily 9–4.

Pear Lake Ski Hut. Primitive lodging is available at this backcountry hut, reached by a steep and extremely difficult 7-mi trail from Wolverton. Only expert skiers should attempt this trek. Space is limited; make reservations well in advance. | Trailhead at end of Wolverton Rd., 1.5 mi northeast off Generals Hwy. (Rte. 198) | 559/565–3759 | $20 | Mid-Dec.–mid-Apr.

FISHING

There's limited trout fishing in the creeks and rivers from late April to mid-November. The Kaweah River is a popular spot. Some of the park's secluded backcountry lakes have good fishing. A California fishing license is $11.05 for two days, $30.70 for 10 days (discounts are available for state residents) and is required for persons 16 and older. For park regulations, closures, and restrictions, call the parks at 559/565–3341 or stop at a park visitors center. Licenses and fishing tackle are usually available in Lodgepole.

California Department of Fish and Game | 916/653–7661 | www.dfg.ca.gov.

HIKING

The best way to see the parks is to hike them. The grandeur and majesty of the Sierra is best seen up close. Carry a hiking map—available at any visitor center—and plenty of water. Check with rangers for current trail conditions, and be aware of rapidly changing weather. As a rule of thumb, plan on trekking 1 mph. For books about hikes in Sequoia National Park, contact the **Sequoia Natural History Association.** | HCR 89 Box 10, Three Rivers | 559/565-3759 | www.sequoiahistory.org.

Big Trees Trail. The Giant Forest is known for its trails through sequoia groves. You can get the best views of the big trees from the meadows, where flowers are in full bloom by June or July. The 0.7-mi wheelchair-accessible trail circles Round Meadow. | Off Generals Hwy. (Rte. 198), near the Giant Forest Museum.

★ **Congress Trail.** This easy 2-mi trail is a paved loop that begins near General Sherman Tree and winds through the heart of the sequoia forest. Watch for the groups of trees known as the House and Senate, and the individual trees called the President and McKinley. | Off Generals Hwy. (Rte. 198), 2 mi north of Giant Forest.

★ **Crescent Meadow Trails.** John Muir reportedly called Crescent Meadow the "gem of the Sierra." Brilliant wildflowers bloom here by midsummer, and a 1.8-mi trail loops around the meadow. A 1.6-mi trail begins at Crescent Meadow and leads to Tharp's Log, a cabin built from a fire-hollowed sequoia. | End of Moro Rock–Crescent Meadow Rd., 2.6 mi east off Generals Hwy. (Rte. 198).

Little Baldy Trail. Climbing 700 vertical feet in 1.75 mi of switchbacking, this trail ends at a granite dome with a great view of the peaks of the Mineral King area and the Great Western Divide. The walk to the summit and back takes about four hours. | Little Baldy Saddle, Generals Hwy. (Rte. 198), 11 mi north of Giant Forest.

Marble Falls Trail. The 3.7-mi, moderately strenuous hike to Marble Falls crosses through the rugged foothills before reaching the cascading water. Plan on three to four hours one-way. | Off the dirt road across from the concrete ditch near site 17 at Potwisha Campground, off Generals Hwy. (Rte. 198).

Mineral King Trails. Many trails to the high country begin at Mineral King. At 7,800 ft, this is the highest point to which one can drive in either of the parks, and the Great Western Divide runs right above this area. Get a map and provisions, and check with rangers about conditions. | Trailhead at end of Mineral King Rd., 25 mi east of Generals Hwy. (Rte. 198).

Tokopah Falls Trail. This moderate trail follows the Marble Fork of the Kaweah River for 1.75 mi one way and dead-ends below the impressive granite cliffs and cascading waterfall of Tokopah Canyon. It takes 2½ to 4 hours to make the 3.5-mi round-trip journey. The trail passes through a mixed-conifer forest. | Off Generals Hwy. (Rte. 198), 0.25 mi north of Lodgepole Campground.

HORSEBACK RIDING

Scheduled trips take you through redwood forests, flowering meadows, across the Sierra, or even up to Mount Whitney. Costs per person range from $20 for a one-hour guided ride to around $200 per day for fully guided trips for which the packers do all the cooking and camp chores.

Horse Corral Pack Station. Hourly, half-day, full-day, or overnight trips through Sequoia are available for beginning and advanced riders. | Off Big Meadows Rd., 12 mi east of Generals Hwy. (Rte. 198) between Sequoia and Kings Canyon national parks | 559/565-3404 in summer, 559/564-6429 in winter | www.horsecorralpackers.com | $25–$95 day trips | May–Sept.

Mineral King Pack Station. Day and overnight tours in the high-mountain area around Mineral King are available here. | End of Mineral King Rd., 25 mi east of East Fork entrance

SEQUOIA AND KINGS CANYON NATIONAL PARKS

EXPLORING

ATTRACTIONS NEARBY

DINING

LODGING

CAMPING AND RV FACILITIES

SHOPPING

ESSENTIAL INFORMATION

WATER POWER

The heavy snow that falls in the Sierra Nevada between October and May provides California with its water and electricity. Nearly all the rivers out of the mountains end in reservoirs in the foothills and are funneled to the rest of the state through a vast series of aqueducts. Look for them as you approach the mountains or drive through the Central Valley.

| 559/561–3039 in summer, 520/855–5885 in winter | mineralking.tripod.com | $25–$75 day trips | July–late Sept. or early Oct.

SLEDDING

The Wolverton area, on Route 198 near Giant Forest, is a popular sledding spot, where sleds, inner tubes, and platters are allowed. You can buy sleds and saucers, starting at $8, at the Wuksachi Village Lodge (559/565–4070), 2 mi north of Lodgepole.

SNOWSHOEING

Snowshoers may stay at the Pear Lake Ski Hut (*see* Cross-Country Skiing, *above*). You can rent snowshoes for $15–$20 at the Wuksachi Village Lodge (559/565–4070), 2 mi north of Lodgepole.

Giant Forest area. There may be naturalist-guided snowshoe walks as conditions permit (weekends only). Make reservations and check schedules at Giant Forest Museum. Snowshoes are provided for a $1 donation. | Giant Forest Museum, Generals Hwy. (Rte. 198) | 559/565–4480 or 559/565–4481 | Mid-Dec.–mid-Mar.

SWIMMING

Drowning is the number one cause of death in both Sequoia and Kings Canyon parks. Though it is sometimes safe to swim in the parks' rivers in the late summer and early fall, it is extremely dangerous to do so in the spring and early summer, when the snowmelt from the high country causes swift currents and icy temperatures. Stand clear of the water when the rivers are running, and stay off wet rocks to avoid falling in. Check with rangers if you're unsure about conditions or to learn the safest locations to wade in the water.

Exploring Kings Canyon

PARK BASICS

Contacts and Resources: Kings Canyon Park Services. Some park services, including lodging, are operated by this company. | Box 909, Kings Canyon National Park, CA 93633 | 559/335–5500 or 866/522–6966 | www.sequoia-kingscanyon.com. **Sequoia and Kings Canyon National Parks** | 47050 Generals Hwy. (Rte. 198), Three Rivers, CA 93271–9651 | 559/565–3341 | www.nps.gov/seki. **U.S. Forest Service** | 900 W. Grand Ave., Porterville, CA 93527 | 559/784–1500 | www.r5.fs.fed.us/sequoia.

Hours: The park is open 24 hours a day, seven days a week.

Fees: There is one fee for both Sequoia and Kings Canyon parks. For details, *see* Park Basics *in* Exploring Sequoia, *above*.

Getting Around: Route 180 into Cedar Grove is closed at the Hume Lake junction from early November to late April. For information on traveling between parks, *see* Park Basics *in* Exploring Sequoia.

Permits: *See* Park Basics *in* Exploring Sequoia.

Public Telephones: Public telephones can be found at the park entrance station, visitor centers, ranger stations, some trailheads, and at all restaurants and lodging facilities in the park.

Rest Rooms: Public rest rooms can be found at all visitor centers and campgrounds. Additional locations include Roads End, Grizzly Falls, Big Stump, and Columbine.

Accessibility: All of the visitor centers are wheelchair accessible. Some tours and programs should be feasible for people with mobility problems. Caves are not accessible and there are no roads through wilderness areas. Some picnic tables in developed areas of the parks are extended to accommodate wheelchairs. Note that many of the major sites are in the 6,000 ft range and thin air at high elevations may cause respiratory distress for people with breathing difficulties. Carry oxygen if necessary. Contact the park's main number for more information.

Emergencies: Call 911 from any telephone within the park in an emergency. Rangers at the Cedar Grove and Grant Grove visitor centers are trained in first aid. National Park rangers have legal jurisdiction within park boundaries. Contact a ranger station or visitor center for police matters. For nonemergencies, call the park's main number, 559/565–3341.

Lost and Found: *See* Park Basics *in* Exploring Sequoia.

A Good Tour

KINGS CANYON IN ONE DAY

You can see the major sights of Kings Canyon in less than a day. Enter the park from Route 180 east, or from Sequoia National Park via Generals Highway north. Your first stop is **Grant Grove Village.** Tour the visitor center to pick up maps and learn about the geological history of Kings Canyon. Leave your car here, or drive the 0.75 mi to the parking lot for **General Grant Tree,** which has been standing for about 2,000 years. Reach the tree, which President Calvin Coolidge ordained as the Nation's Christmas Tree in 1926, via a half-mile loop trail. Nearby, a 2.3-mi (one-way) spur road—not recommended for trailers or RVs—leads to **Panoramic Point,** from which you can see the jagged escarpment of granite peaks looming some 20 mi in the distance. While in the village, you can also pick up supplies for a picnic lunch.

Return to Route 180 east and drive through the **Sequoia National Forest.** The road leads along the scenic **Kings River Canyon,** which in places is deeper than the Grand Canyon. Stop along the way at any of the overlooks to see the dramatic and changing view. About 30 mi east of Grant Grove (allow one hour for the drive on this winding road), the road descends to **Cedar Grove,** which occupies the upper end of a glacial U-shape valley. While this valley lacks the towering waterfalls of Yosemite National Park, it's full of huge granite cliffs and monoliths similar to those at the more northern park. Cedar Grove is a good place to sit on a rock next to the Kings River and enjoy a picnic. If you arrive in late afternoon, watch the sinking sun cover the granite in a golden wash.

Attractions

PROGRAMS AND TOURS

There are no regularly scheduled tours of Kings Canyon. Grant Grove visitor center has maps of self-guided park tours. Ranger-led programs take place throughout the year in Grant Grove. Cedar Grove and Forest Service campgrounds have activities from Memorial Day to Labor Day. Check bulletin boards or visitor centers for schedules. For information on programs and activities, *see* Attractions *in* Exploring Sequoia.

SCENIC DRIVES

Generals Highway. *See* Scenic Drives *in* Exploring Sequoia.

★ **Kings Canyon Highway.** Winding alongside the powerful Kings River, drive below the towering granite cliffs and past two tumbling waterfalls in Kings Canyon. One mile past the Cedar Grove Village turnoff, the U-shape canyon becomes broader, and you can see evidence of its glacial past and the effects of wind and water on the granite. Four miles farther is Grand Sentinel Viewpoint, where you can see the 3,500-ft tall granite monolith and some of the most interesting rock formations in the canyon. The drive takes about one hour each way. Follow Route 180 east from Grant Grove.

SIGHTS TO SEE

Canyon View. The glacial history of Kings Canyon is evident from this viewpoint. Note the canyon's giant "U" shape, which sparked John Muir to compare it to Yosemite to the north. | Kings Canyon Hwy.–Rte. 180, 1 mi east of the Cedar Grove turnoff.

SEQUOIA AND KINGS CANYON NATIONAL PARKS

EXPLORING
ATTRACTIONS NEARBY
DINING
LODGING
CAMPING AND RV FACILITIES
SHOPPING
ESSENTIAL INFORMATION

ALL WET?

If you plan to take a hike, carry lots of water and a bring an extra layer of clothes, including a pocket-size rain poncho. Summer thunderstorms appear seemingly out of nowhere, and if your clothes get wet, you risk developing hypothermia, a serious condition that can be deadly. Be prepared and stay dry.

Cedar Grove Visitor Center. This historic log ranger station provides information services and sells books and maps. | Kings Canyon Hwy., 30 mi east of park entrance | 559/565–3793 | Spring–fall, daily 9–4.

★ **Fallen Monarch.** No matter how tall you are, you can walk through the entire 100-ft length of this burned-out, fallen sequoia near the General Grant Tree. Early explorers, cattle ranchers, and Native Americans used the log for shelter, and soldiers who began patrolling the area in the late 1880s used it to stable their horses. | Trailhead 1 mi north of Grant Grove visitor center.

Gamlin Cabin. Built as a summer cabin in 1867, this building was used primarily for storage. Listed on the National Register of Historic Places, the cabin was returned to an area close to its original site in 1931 and was rehabilitated in 1981. The roof and lower timber are giant sequoia. | Trailhead 1 mi north of Grant Grove visitor center.

General Grant Tree. The nation's Christmas tree, this is also the world's third-largest living tree. | Trailhead 1 mi north of Grant Grove visitor center.

Grant Grove Visitor Center. A slide show, map sections, and other sequoia and human history exhibits trace the history of Grant Grove, which is the original portion of General Grant National Park. Books, maps, and wilderness permits are available for sale. | Generals Hwy. (Rte. 198), 3 mi northeast of Rte. 180, Big Stump entrance | 559/565–4307 | Summer, daily 8–6; spring and fall, daily 9–4:30; winter, daily 9:30–4:30.

Knapp's Cabin. During the Roaring '20s wealthy Santa Barbara businessman George Knapp commissioned extravagant fishing expeditions into Kings Canyon. To store quantities of gear, he built a small cabin, which still stands. | Kings Canyon Hwy., 2 mi east of Cedar Grove Village turnoff.

★ **Redwood Mountain Grove.** This is the largest grove of giant sequoias in the world. As you head south through Kings Canyon toward Sequoia on Generals Highway, several paved turnouts allow you to look out over the treetops. The grove itself is accessible only on foot or by horseback. | Drive 5 mi south of Grant Grove on Generals Hwy. (Rte. 198), then turn right at Quail Flat; follow it 1.5 mi to the Redwood Canyon trailhead.

Road's End Permit Station. If you're planning to hike the backcountry, you can pick up a permit and information on the backcountry here. You can also rent or buy bear canisters, a must for campers. When the station is closed, you can still complete a self-service permit form. | 5 mi east of Cedar Grove Visitor Center, at the end of Kings Canyon Hwy. | Late May–late Sept., daily 7–3:30 | No phone.

Sports and Outdoor Activities

No off-road driving or bicycling is allowed in the park. Boating, rafting, and snowmobiling are also prohibited.

BICYCLING

Bicycles are allowed only on the paved roads in Kings Canyon, and cyclists should be extremely cautious along the steep highways and narrow shoulders.

BIRD-WATCHING

For information on bird-watching in Sequoia and Kings Canyon national parks, *see* Sports and Outdoor Activities *in* Sequoia National Park, *above*.

CROSS-COUNTRY SKIING

Roads to Grant Grove are easily accessible during heavy snowfall, making the trails here a good choice over Giant Forest when harsh weather hits.

Grant Grove Ski Touring Center. The Grant Grove Market doubles as the ski-touring center, where you can rent cross-country skis in winter. This is a good starting point for a number of marked trails, including the Panoramic Point Trail and the General Grant Tree Trail (see Hiking, below). | Grant Grove Market, Generals Hwy. (Rte. 198), 3 mi northeast of Rte. 180, Big Stump entrance | 559/335–2665 | $6–$11 | Summer, daily 8 AM–9 PM; fall–spring, daily 9–6.

FISHING

There is limited trout fishing in the park from late April to mid-November. Kings River is a popular spot. Some of the park's secluded backcountry lakes have good fishing. Licenses ($10.75 for two days, $29.40 for 10 days, less for state residents) are required for those over 16, and are available, along with fishing tackle, in Grant Grove and Cedar Grove. Only Grant Grove is open year-round.

California Department of Fish and Game | 916/653–7661 | www.dfg.ca.gov.

HIKING

You can enjoy many of Kings Canyon's sights from your car, but you'll miss out on the more visceral experiences of hearing the birds in the trees and your footsteps crunching on pine needles as you pass through the forest. The giant gorges of Kings Canyon and the sweeping vistas of some of the highest mountains in the United States are best seen on foot. Carry a hiking map—available at any visitor center—and plenty of water. Check with rangers for current trail conditions, and be aware of rapidly changing weather.

★ **Big Baldy.** This hike climbs 600 ft and 2 mi up to the 8,209-ft summit of Big Baldy. Your reward is the view of Redwood Canyon. The round-trip hike is 4 mi. | Trailhead 8 mi south of Grant Grove on Generals Hwy. (Rte. 198).

Big Stump Trail. A walk along this 1-mi trail graphically demonstrates the toll heavy logging takes on the wilderness. | Trailhead near Rte. 180, Big Stump Entrance.

Buena Vista Peak. For a 360-degree view of Redwood Canyon and the High Sierra, make the 2-mi ascent to Buena Vista. | Trailhead off Generals Hwy. (Rte. 198), south of Kings Canyon Overlook, 7 mi southeast of Grant Grove.

Don Cecil Trail. This trail climbs the cool north-facing slope of Kings Canyon, passes Sheep Creek Cascade and provides several good views of the canyon and the 11,000-ft Monarch Divide. The trail leads to Lookout Peak, which affords an incredible panorama of the park's backcountry. It's a strenuous, all-day hike—13 mi round-trip—and climbs 4,000 ft. | Trailhead off Kings Canyon Hwy., across from parking lot, 0.2-mi west of Cedar Grove Village.

General Grant Tree Trail. One of the shortest trails in the parks is the one that leads to General Grant Tree, the third-largest living tree in the world. The trail is only 0.3 mi, but it passes Gamlin Cabin and Fallen Monarch. It's paved and fairly level. | Trailhead off Generals Hwy. (Rte. 198), 1 mi northwest of Grant Grove visitor center.

★ **Hotel Creek Trail.** For gorgeous canyon views, take this trail from the canyon floor at Cedar Grove up a series of switchbacks until it splits. Follow the route left through chaparral to the forested ridge and rocky outcrop known as Cedar Grove Overlook, where you can see Kings Canyon stretching below. This strenuous 5-mi round-trip hike gains 1,200 ft and takes three to four hours to complete. For a longer hike, return via Lewis Creek Trail for an 8-mi loop. | Trailhead at Cedar Grove pack station, 1 mi east of Cedar Grove Village.

Mist Falls Trail. This sandy trail follows the glaciated South Fork Canyon through forest and chaparral, past several rapids and cascades, to one of the largest waterfalls in the two parks. Nine miles round-trip, the hike is relatively flat, but climbs 600 ft in the last mile. It takes four to five hours to complete. | Trailhead at end of Kings Canyon Hwy., 5.5 mi east of Cedar Grove Village.

Panoramic Point Trail. While in Grant Grove take the time to walk out to Panoramic Point. Trailers and RVs are not permitted on the steep and narrow road. A 0.25-mi walk from the parking lot leads to a viewpoint where you can see the High Sierra from Mount Goddard

SEQUOIA AND KINGS CANYON NATIONAL PARKS

EXPLORING
ATTRACTIONS NEARBY
DINING
LODGING
CAMPING AND RV FACILITIES
SHOPPING
ESSENTIAL INFORMATION

HORSE SENSE

Don't be surprised to see mules and horses on the parks' many trails. If you're hiking and a pack animal approaches, the animal has the right of way. Step to the downhill side of the trail, if possible, and stay still and quiet while the animal passes.

in northern Kings Canyon National Park to Eagle Scout Peak in Sequoia. Mount Whitney can't be seen from the west side of the park because of the height of the Great Western Divide. | End of Panoramic Point Rd., 2.3 mi from Grant Grove Village.

★ **Redwood Canyon Trail.** Depending on whether you hike the perimeter of two adjoining loops or take only one of them, this 6- or 10- mi trek in Redwood Canyon leads through the world's largest grove of sequoias. Take in the cascades, the quiet pools of Redwood Creek, and the mixed conifer forest on a short walk, day hike, or overnight backpacking trip. | Drive 5 mi south of Grant Grove on Generals Hwy. (Rte. 198), then turn right at Quail Flat; follow it 1.5 mi to the Redwood Canyon trailhead.

Roaring River Falls Walk. Take a shady five-minute walk to this forceful waterfall that rushes through a narrow granite chute. The trail is paved and fully accessible. | Trailhead 3 mi east of Cedar Grove Village turnoff from Kings Canyon Hwy.

Zumwalt Meadow Trail. Walk past high granite walls and the meandering Kings River, en route to the lush Zumwalt Meadow. The trail is 1.5 mi long. | Trailhead 4.5 mi east of Cedar Grove Village turnoff from Kings Canyon Hwy.

HORSEBACK RIDING

One-day destinations by horseback out of Cedar Grove include Mist Falls and Upper Bubb's Creek. In the backcountry, many equestrians head for Volcanic Lakes or Granite Basin, ascending trails that reach elevations of 10,000 ft. Costs per person range from $20 for a one-hour guided ride to around $200 per day for fully guided trips for which the packers do all the cooking and camp chores.

Cedar Grove Pack Station. Take a day or overnight trip along the Kings River Canyon. Popular routes include the Rae Lakes Loop and Monarch Divide. | Kings Canyon Hwy., 1 mi east of Cedar Grove Village | 559/565–3464 in summer, 559/337–2314 off-season | Call for prices | May–Oct.

Grant Grove Stables. A one- or two-hour trip through Grant Grove is a good way to get a taste of horseback riding in Kings Canyon. | Rte. 180, 0.5-mi north of Grant Grove visitor center, Three Rivers | 559/335–9292 in summer, 559/337–2314 off-season | $25–$40 | June–Labor Day, daily 8–6.

SLEDDING

In winter, Kings Canyon has a few great places to play in the snow. Sleds, inner tubes, and platters are allowed at both the Azalea Campground area on Grant Tree Rd., 0.25-mi north of Grant Grove visitor center, and at the Big Stump picnic area, 2 mi north of the lower Rte. 180 entrance to the park.

SNOWSHOEING

Snowshoeing is good around Grant Grove, where you can take naturalist-guided snowshoe walks mid-December through mid-March as conditions permit. You can rent snowshoes for a $1 donation at the Grant Grove visitor center for ranger-led walks; make reservations at the Grant Grove visitor center for the guided weekend snowshoe walks. Alternatively, if you prefer to take a self-guided walk, you can rent snowshoes at the Grant Grove Market (559/335–2665).

SWIMMING

Drowning is the number-one cause of death in both Sequoia and Kings Canyon parks. Though it is sometimes safe to swim in the parks' rivers in the late summer and early fall, it is extremely dangerous to do so in the spring and early summer, when the snowmelt from the high county causes swift currents and icy temperatures. Stand clear of the water when the rivers are running, and stay off wet rocks to avoid falling in. Check with rangers if you're unsure about conditions or to learn the safest locations to wade in the water.

Attractions Nearby

Scenic Drives

★ **Whitney Portal.** At 14,494 ft, Mount Whitney is the highest mountain in the continental United States. Though there's no road that ascends the peak, you can catch a glimpse of the mountain on the eastern side of Sequoia. From U.S. 395, head west out of Lone Pine on Whitney Portal Road. After 13 mi of winding road, the pavement ends at the trailhead to the top of the mountain. You must have a permit to hike the trail. Permits are available from the Mt. Whitney Ranger District of Inyo National Forest. | Box 8, Lone Pine, 93545 | 760/876–6200.

Sights to See

★ **Ancient Bristlecone Pine Forest.** This unusual park makes up 28,000 acres in Inyo National Forest. Some of the gnarled and majestic trees are more than 4,000 years old, a millennium older than the oldest redwoods. There are self-guided trails through the forest. | Rte. 168, off U.S. 395, 12 mi south of Bishop | 760/873–2400, 760/873–2500 for recorded information | Free | Memorial Day–Oct. or early Nov., daily dawn–dusk weather permitting.

Boyden Cavern. The Kern River runs through a canyon that's deeper than the Grand Canyon. The seepage of its waters has created many caves in this area, well below the surface of the ground. If you can't make it to Crystal Cave in Sequoia, Boyden is a reasonable substitute, but the operations here aren't on par with those at the former. Tours depart on the hour. | Kings Canyon Hwy.–Rte. 180, between Grant Grove and Cedar Grove, Sequoia National Forest | 209/736–2708 | www.caverntours.com/boydenrt.htm | $10 | Apr.–May and Oct.–Nov., daily 10–4; June–Sept., daily 10–5.

Lake Kaweah. The Kaweah River rushes out of the Sierra from high above Mineral King in Sequoia National Park. When it reaches the hills above Central Valley the water collects in Lake Kaweah, a reservoir operated by the Army Corps of Engineers. You can fish, swim, hike, camp, or picnic on its shores. | 34443 Sierra Dr., about 25 mi east of Visalia on Generals Hwy. (Rte. 198), Lemon Cove | 559/597–2301 or 559/561–3155; 877/444–6777 (campground reservations) | www.reserveusa.com | Free; camping $16, boat launch $3.

Laws Railroad Museum and Historical Site. Built around the original railroad depot and Locomotive No. 9, this museum is dedicated to the history of a once-active railroad community. Exhibit buildings, including a carriage house and a doctor's office, surround the site. | Silver Canyon Rd. exit off U.S. 6, 6 mi northeast of Bishop | 760/873–5950 | www.thesierraweb.com/bishop/laws | Donations | Daily 10–4, weather permitting.

★ **Sequoia National Forest.** Covering 1,139,500 acres in central California, this forest runs from the San Joaquin Valley foothills to the crest of the Sierra Nevada, and abuts Sequoia and Kings Canyon National Parks on the south and east. Of the world's sequoia groves, more than half are here. Three National Recreation Trails and a section of the Pacific Crest Trail wind through the landscape. Four streams are designated National Wild and Scenic Rivers; some of the nation's liveliest whitewater is found on the Forks section of the Kern. Lake Isabella (11,000 acres) is one of the area's largest reservoirs. There's cross-country skiing and snowmobiling in winter, 900 mi of trail for hiking, camping, and picnicking. | 900 W. Grand Ave., Porterville | 559/784–1500 | www.fs.fed.us/r5/sequoia | Free.

Anglers go for 10- to 12-inch trout on **Hume Lake,** in Sequoia National Forest, also ideal for swimming and boating. Built as a mill pond, the lake supplied water for a flume that floated rough-cut sequoia lumber to the planing mill at Sanger, 54 mi below in the San Joaquin Valley. | Hume Lake Rd., 3 mi. southeast off Rte. 180.

At the **Hume Lake Forest Service District Office,** pick up maps and books on the Hume Lake area. | 35860 Kings Canyon Hwy.–Rte. 180 | 559/338–2251 | Weekdays 8–4:30; open Sat. in summer.

Dining

In Sequoia

Lodgepole Market and Snack Bar. Fast Food. Visit the market for sandwiches and salads to go. In summer, there is a deli for sandwiches and a snack bar for breakfast, pizza, and hamburgers. | Next to Lodgepole visitor center | 559/565–3301 | $4–$6 | AE, D, DC, MC, V | Closed early Sept.–mid-Apr.

Picnic Areas. You can find many lovely spots in which to enjoy an alfresco meal in the park.

Crescent Meadow. This area near Moro Rock has vistas over the meadows. Tables are under the giant sequoia, off the parking area. There are rest rooms and drinking water. Fires are not allowed. | End of Moro Rock–Crescent Rd., 2.6 mi east off Generals Hwy. (Rte. 198).

Foothills Picnic Area. Near the parking lot at the southern entrance of the park, this small area has tables on grass. Drinking water and rest rooms are available. | Near Foothills visitor center.

Halstead Meadow. Tables are at the edge of the meadow at this area off the main road and a short walk from parking. Grills and rest rooms are provided, but there's no drinking water. The Dorst campground is nearby. | Generals Hwy. (Rte. 198), 4 mi north of Lodgepole junction.

Hospital Rock. Native Americans once ground acorns into meal at this site; outdoor exhibits tell the story. Tables are on grass a short distance from the parking lot. Grills, drinking water, and rest rooms are available. The Buckeye Flat campground is nearby. | Generals Hwy. (Rte. 198), 6 mi north of Ash Mountain entrance.

Pinewood Picnic Area. Picnic in Giant Forest, among the giant sequoia trees. Drinking water, rest rooms, and grills are provided. | Generals Hwy. (Rte. 198), 2 mi north of Giant Forest Museum, half way between Giant Forest Museum and General Sherman Tree.

Wolverton Meadow. At a major trailhead to the backcountry, this is a great place to stop for lunch before a hike. The area sits in a mixed-conifer forest adjacent to parking. Drinking water, grills, and rest rooms are available. | Wolverton Rd., 1.5 mi northeast off Generals Hwy. (Rte. 198).

★ **Wuksachi Village Dining Room.** Contemporary. Huge windows that look out on the trees run the length of the high-ceiling dining room at Sequoia's only upscale restaurant. The contemporary California menu borrows elements from European cooking. This is the best place to eat in either park. Reservations are essential for dinner. They also serve lunch, and there's a buffet at breakfast. | Generals Hwy. (Rte. 198), 2 mi east of Lodgepole visitor center | 559/565–4070 | $12–$22 | AE, D, DC, MC, V.

In Kings Canyon

Cedar Grove Market. Fast Food. You can pick up sandwiches and salads to go at this market. | Cedar Grove Village | 559/565–0100 | $3–$10 | AE, D, MC, V | Mid-Apr.–late Oct., daily 8–8.

Cedar Grove Restaurant. American/Casual. This cafeteria-style restaurant serves eggs at breakfast, sandwiches and hamburgers at lunch and dinner, and in the evening also offers several specials like chicken-fried steak. | Cedar Grove Village | 559/565–0100 | $5–$10 | AE, D, MC, V | Closed Oct.–May.

Grant Grove Restaurant. American/Casual. Come here year-round for simple family-style dining. The restaurant serves full breakfasts, and hot entrées and sandwiches for lunch and dinner. Counter service is available. | Grant Grove Village | 559/335–5500 | $5–$18 | AE, D, MC, V.

Picnic Areas. Kings Canyon has three developed picnic sites.

Big Stump. At the edge of a logged sequoia grove, some trees still stand at this site. Near the park's entrance, the area is paved and next to the road. It's the only picnic area in either park that is plowed in the winter time. Rest rooms, grills, and drinking water are available, and the area is entirely accessible. | Just inside Rte. 180, Big Stump entrance.

Columbine. This grassy picnic area near the sequoias is relatively level. Tables, rest rooms, drinking water, and grills are available. | Grant Tree Rd., just off Generals Hwy. (Rte. 198), 0.5-mi northwest of Grant Grove visitor center.

Grizzly Falls. A short walk from the parking area leads to a grassy picnic spot near the bottom of a canyon. The area is not level. Tables and rest rooms are available, grills and water are not. | Off Rte. 180, 2.5 mi west of Cedar Grove entrance.

Near the Parks

Firehouse Grill. American. This simple country restaurant serves hearty meals like steaks, teriyaki chicken, and fettuccine Alfredo. A selection of seafood is also available. | 635 N. Main St. (U.S. 395), Bishop | 760/873–4888 | $10–$19 | AE, D, MC, V.

Gateway Restaurant and Lodge. American. The patio of this local favorite overlooks the Kaweah River. Dishes include baby-back ribs and a large portion of eggplant parmigiana. There are also a cocktail lounge and guest rooms for overnight visitors. Reservations are essential on weekends. | 45978 Sierra Dr., Three Rivers | 559/561–4133 | $14–$29 | AE, D, MC, V.

Mount Whitney Restaurant. American/Casual. Pictures from old movies shot in the area adorn the walls of this family-style restaurant. In addition to standard diner fare, you can choose from burgers made of buffalo, ostrich, and venison. | U.S. 395 and Whitney Portal Rd., Lone Pine | 760/876–5751 | $7–$13 | D, MC, V.

★ **Noisy Water.** American. The name of this restaurant comes from the Kaweah River, which flows within view of the many windows. All-American fare—eggs, pancakes, burgers, and steaks—are served for breakfast, lunch, and dinner. Vegetarian and healthy options are available. Stunning views of the river can be had from the glass-enclosed patio. | 41775 Sierra Dr., Three Rivers | 559/561–4917 | $11–$20 | AE, D, MC, V | Closed Wed.

Stony Creek Restaurant. American/Casual. This family-style restaurant in Sequoia National Forest serves soups, sandwiches, and burgers at lunch and pasta, salads, fish, and steaks in the evening. | Generals Hwy. (Rte. 198), between Sequoia and Kings Canyon parks, 12 mi south of Grant Grove, Sequoia National Forest | 559/565–3909 | $6–$15 | AE, D, MC, V | Closed mid-Oct.–May.

Lodging

In Sequoia

Silver City Resort. High on Mineral King Road, this resort offers an excellent alternative to staying at one of the more crowded properties at lower elevations of the park. Lodgings range from modern Swiss-style chalets to rustic traditional alpine cabins. There's a small convenience store and restaurant on-site; the restaurant serves breakfast and lunch every day and dinner on Friday and Saturday nights. Some cabins share a central shower and bath. The creek has a beach area. Restaurant. In-room data ports, some kitchenettes. Beach. Hiking. No a/c, no phones in some rooms. No room TVs. | Mineral King Rd., 3 mi west of Mineral King ranger station | 559/561–3223, 805/528–2730 off-season | fax 805/528–8039 | www.silvercityresort.com | 14 cabins | $70–$250 | MC, V | Closed late Oct.–May.

★ **Wuksachi Village and Lodge.** Three cedar-and-stone lodge buildings house comfortable rooms with modern amenities. Set at 7,200 ft above sea level, many of them have spectacular views of the surrounding mountains. Of all the lodgings in the two parks, this is the nicest. Restaurant. In-room data ports. Hiking. Cross-country skiing. Bar. No a/c. No room TVs. | Generals Hwy. (Rte. 198), 2 mi east of Lodgepole visitor center, 21 mi south of Grant Grove | 559/253–2199 or 888/252–5757 | fax 559/456–0542 | www.visitsequoia.com | 102 rooms | $160–$229 | AE, D, DC, MC, V.

SEQUOIA AND
KINGS CANYON
NATIONAL PARKS

EXPLORING
ATTRACTIONS NEARBY
DINING
LODGING
CAMPING AND RV
FACILITIES
SHOPPING
ESSENTIAL
INFORMATION

In Kings Canyon

Cedar Grove Lodge. Accommodations are close to the road, but Cedar Grove retains a quiet atmosphere with motel-style rooms. Book far in advance. Most rooms have two queen-size beds. Some kitchenettes. No room TVs. | Cedar Grove Village | 559/335–5500 | fax 559/335–5507 | www.sequoia-kingscanyon.com | 21 rooms | $99–$110 | AE, D, DC, MC, V | Closed Nov.–Apr.

Grant Grove Cabins. Some of the wood-paneled cabins here have heaters, electric lights, and private baths, but most have woodstoves, battery lamps, and shared baths. If you like to rough it, you can opt for the rustic cabins, but note that there's no insulation, except in the "deluxe rustic" cabins. All cabins have heat. You can also book a tent cabin, which is a cabin with a canvas roof; the tent cabins are not available in winter. No a/c, no room phones. No room TVs. | Grant Grove Village | 559/335–5500 | fax 559/335–5507 | www.sequoia-kingscanyon.com | 9 cabins with bath, 27 cabins with shared baths; 18 tent cabins with shared bath | $45–$60 | AE, D, DC, MC, V.

John Muir Lodge. Built in 1999, this modern timber-sided lodge is nestled in a wooded area near Grant Grove Village. The 30 rooms all have queen beds and private baths. There's a comfortable lobby with a stone fireplace, but no restaurant. No a/c. No room TVs. | 24 rooms, 6 suites | Grant Grove Village | 559/335–5500 | fax 559/335–5507 | www.sequoia-kingscanyon.com | $140 | AE, D, DC, MC, V.

Near the Parks

The only lodging immediately outside the parks is in Three Rivers. As a last resort you can get a room in Visalia or Fresno, about an hour from the south and north entrances, respectively. Bishop, Lone Pine, and Independence, on the eastern side of the parks on U.S. 395, are a long day's drive from the parks' automobile entrances.

Three Rivers Reservation Center. If none of the properties listed here suits your needs, check with this agency. | 559/561–0410.

Best Western Bishop Holiday Spa Lodge. Anglers and nature enthusiasts often make this two-story motel-style lodge their home base while taking advantage of the area; the hotel even offers fish-cleaning services. Microwaves, refrigerators. Cable TV. Pool. Hot tub. Some pets allowed. | 1025 N. Main St., Bishop | 760/873–3543 or 800/576–3543 | fax 760/872–4777 | www.bestwestern.com | 89 rooms, 1 suite | $75–$99 | AE, D, DC, MC, V.

Best Western Holiday Lodge. This two-story stucco lodge is 8 mi from Sequoia National Park and 4 mi from Lake Kaweah. The lobby has a stone fireplace and Navajo-print fabrics. Refrigerators. Cable TV. Pool. Hot tub. Playground. Some pets allowed (fee). | 40105 Sierra Dr., Three Rivers | 559/561–4119 or 888/523–9909 | fax 559/561–3427 | www.bestwesterncalifornia.com | 54 rooms | $89–$111 | AE, D, DC, MC, V | CP.

Cinnamon Creek Ranch. Rooms have mountain views at this remote 10-acre ranch with resident donkeys. One room has a private terrace overlooking the river. Reservations are required. Some kitchens. In-room VCRs. Hot tub. Hiking. | Box 584, Three Rivers, 93271 | 559/561–1107 | www.cinnamoncreek.com | 2 rooms, 2 cabins | $110–$180 | AE, D, MC, V | CP.

Comfort Inn. Surrounded by the High Sierra, this Swiss-facade motel is central to many hiking and fishing areas, and the backside of Mount Whitney is an hour's drive away. Picnic area. Microwaves, refrigerators. Cable TV. Pool. Hot tub. Laundry facilities. Some pets allowed. | 805 N. Main St., 0.5-mi south of U.S. 6 and U.S. 395, Bishop | 760/873–4284 | fax 760/873–8563 | www.comfortinn.com | 54 rooms | $90 | AE, D, MC, V | CP.

Dow Villa Motel and Hotel. Movie stars stayed here years ago while shooting westerns in the nearby Alabama Hills. A modern building has been added to the original portion of the hotel, and though it lacks the charm of the older part, its motel-style units are comfortable. Many of the rooms in the older hotel share bathrooms. Some refrigerators. Some in-room VCRs. Pool. Hot tub. | 310 S. Main St., Lone Pine | 760/876–5521 or 800/824–

9317 | fax 760/876–5643 | www.dowvillamotel.com | 91 rooms, 50 with bath | $40–$125 | AE, D, DC, MC, V.

Lazy J Ranch Motel. In the foothills of the Sierra Nevada alongside the Kaweah River lies this single-story motel. Some rooms have fireplaces, and the cabins are fully equipped, some with fireplaces. Picnic area. Refrigerators. Cable TV, in-room VCRs. Pool. Fishing. Playground. Laundry facilities. Some pets allowed (fee). | 39625 Sierra Dr., Three Rivers | 559/561–4449 or 800/341–8000 | fax 559/561–4889 | www.bestvalueinn.com | 12 rooms, 6 cottages | $95–$210 | AE, D, DC, MC, V | CP.

Montecito-Sequoia Lodge. In Sequoia National Forest, this family-oriented resort has packages that include all meals and activities. It offers everything from skiing and snowboarding in winter to sailing and horseback riding in summer. Lodge rooms have private baths; cabins share a central bath. From mid-June to Labor Day, there's a six-night minimum, but you can book a one-night stay on Saturday nights in summer. Tennis court. Pool, lake. Spa. Boating. Fishing. Bicycles. Hiking, horseback riding, volleyball. Cross-country skiing, tobogganing. Children's programs (seasonal, ages 2–18). No a/c, no room TVs. | 8000 Generals Hwy. (Rte. 198), 11 mi south of Grant Grove, between Sequoia and Kings Canyon parks | 559/565–3388 or 800/227–9900 | fax 559/565–3223 | www.montecitosequoia.com | 13 cabins, 36 lodge rooms | $89–$150 | AE, D, MC, V | MAP.

Sierra Lodge. Hundred-year-old oak trees surround this '50s-modern property, which is near Lake Kaweah and the entrance to Sequoia National Park. There are several different room styles; some have wood-burning fireplaces. The lodge has mountain views and a small library. Picnic area. Refrigerators. Cable TV, some in-room VCRs. Pool. | 43175 Sierra Dr. (Rte. 198), Three Rivers | 559/561–3681 or 800/367–8879 | fax 559/561–3264 | www.sierra-lodge.com | 17 rooms, 5 suites | $50–$80 | AE, D, DC, MC, V.

Stony Creek Lodge. Sitting at 6,800 ft among peaceful pines, Stony Creek is on national forest land between Grant Grove and Giant Forest. Rooms are plain, but are carpeted and have private showers. There's also a restaurant and a market in the lodge. Restaurant. Cable TV with movies. Shops. No a/c, no room phones. | Generals Hwy. (Rte. 198), between Sequoia and Kings Canyon parks, 12 mi south of Grant Grove, Sequoia National Forest | 559/565–3909 | fax 559/565–3913 | www.sequoia-kingscanyon.com | 11 rooms | $125 | AE, D, DC, MC, V | Closed mid-Sept.–mid-June | CP.

Winnedumah Hotel. Built in 1927, this B&B with mahogany woodwork once hosted the stars and film crews that shot early Westerns. Today you can still enjoy the old-fashioned lobby, wisteria-covered patio, and the vintage furniture. Inexpensive hostel-style lodgings are available. Independence is about 30 mi from Bishop or Lone Pine. Fishing. Hiking. No phones in some rooms. No room TVs. No smoking. | 211 N. Edwards, Independence 93526 | 760/878–2040 | fax 760/878–2833 | www.winnedumah.com | 24 rooms, 18 with bath | $55–$65 | AE, D, DC, MC, V | CP.

Camping and RV Facilities

In Sequoia

Atwell Mill Campground. At the end of Mineral King Road at 6,650 ft, this tents-only campground is surrounded by meadows and pines. No RVs are permitted up the rough road. Phones, a general store, and showers are nearby. There are accessible sites here. Pit toilets. Drinking water. Bear boxes, fire grates, picnic tables. | 21 sites | Mineral King Rd., 7 mi west of Mineral King ranger station | No phone | $12 | Reservations not accepted | No credit cards | Late May–late Oct.

★ **Buckeye Flat Campground.** Adjacent to Paradise Creek, this small, tents-only campground is on the Kaweah River at 2,800 ft. There are accessible sites here. Flush toilets. Drinking water. Bear boxes, fire grates, picnic tables. | 28 sites | Off Generals Hwy. (Rte. 198), 6 mi north of Ash Mountain entrance | No phone | $18 | Reservations not accepted | No credit cards | Late May–Oct. 1.

Cold Springs Campground. At the crest of Mineral King Road at 7,500 ft, this mid-size campground is for tents only. There are no accessible sites here. Pit toilets. Drinking water. Bear boxes, picnic tables. Public telephone. General store (nearby), ranger station. | 40 sites | Mineral King Rd., 0.25 mi west of Mineral King ranger station | 559/565–3768 | $12 | Reservations not accepted | No credit cards | Late May–late Oct.

Dorst Creek Campground. This large campground is at 6,700 ft. Use the bear boxes: this is a popular area for the furry creatures to raid. Reservations, made by mail or through the Web site, are essential in summer. There are accessible sites here. Flush toilets. Dump station. Drinking water. Bear boxes, fire grates, picnic tables. Public telephone. | 204 sites for tents or RVs | Generals Hwy. (Rte. 198), 8 mi north of Lodgepole visitor center, near Kings Canyon border | 301/722–1257 or 800/365–2267 | fax 301/722–1174 | http://reservations.nps.gov | $20 | D, MC, V | Memorial Day–Labor Day.

Lodgepole Campground. This large campground gets crowded in high season and is open year-round. It's set at 6,700 ft. Reservations are essential in summer. There are accessible sites here. Flush toilets. Dump station. Drinking water, guest laundry, showers. Bear boxes, fire grates, picnic tables, food service. Public telephone. Ranger station. | 214 sites for tents or RVs | Off Generals Hwy. (Rte. 198), 0.5 mi east of Lodgepole visitor center | 301/722–1257 or 800/365–2267 | fax 301/722–1174 | http://reservations.nps.gov | $20 | D, MC, V.

★**Potwisha Campground.** On the Marble Fork of the Kaweah River, this mid-size campground with attractive surroundings is at 2,100 ft. Some sites are wheelchair accessible. The grounds are open for camping year-round. Flush toilets. Dump station. Drinking water. Bear boxes, fire grates, picnic tables. Public telephone. | 42 sites for tents or RVs up to 30 ft | Generals Hwy. (Rte. 198), 4 mi north of Ash Mountain entrance | No phone | www.nps.gov/seki | $18 | Reservations not accepted | No credit cards.

South Fork Campground. Set at 3,600 ft, this tiny campground is at the southernmost corner of Sequoia. At the end of a dirt road, it best accommodates tent campers. It's open year-round. Pit toilets. Running water (nonpotable). Bear boxes, fire grates, picnic tables. | 10 sites for tents only | End of South Fork Rd., 12 mi east of Generals Hwy. (Rte. 198) | No phone | $12, May–Labor Day; free rest of the year | Reservations not accepted | No credit cards.

In Kings Canyon

Azalea Campground. In the western section of Kings Canyon, this camp is set at 6,500 ft near the big trees. It's open year-round. There are accessible sites here. Flush toilets. Drinking water. Bear boxes, fire grates, picnic tables. Public telephone. General store, ranger station (nearby). | 110 sites for tents or RVs | Grant Tree Rd., 0.25 mi north of Grant Grove visitor center | No phone | $18 | Reservations not accepted | No credit cards.

Canyon View Campground. One of three sites near Cedar Grove, this campground is near the start of the Don Cecil Trail, which leads to Lookout Point. The elevation of the camp is 4,600 ft along the Kings River. There are no accessible sites. Flush toilets. Drinking water. Bear boxes, fire grates, picnic tables. Public telephone. | 37 sites for tents only | Off Kings Canyon Hwy., 0.5-mi east of Cedar Grove Village | No phone | $18 | Reservations not accepted | No credit cards | Late May–late Sept., as needed.

Crystal Springs Campground. Near the Grant Grove Village and the towering sequoias, this camp is set at 6,500 ft. There are accessible sites here. Flush toilets. Drinking water. Bear boxes, fire grates, picnic tables. Public telephone. | 62 sites for tents or RVs | Off Generals Hwy. (Rte. 198), 0.25-mi north of Grant Grove visitor center | No phone | $18 | Reservations not accepted | No credit cards | Memorial Day–Labor Day.

Moraine Campground. Close to the Kings River and a short walk from Cedar Grove Village, this camp is set at 4,600 ft along the Kings River. There are no accessible sites. Flush toilets. Drinking water. Bear boxes, fire grates, picnic tables. Public telephone. Swimming (river). | 120 sites for tents or RVs | Off Kings Canyon Hwy., 0.75 mi west of Cedar Grove Village | No phone | $18 | Reservations not accepted | No credit cards | Late May–late Sept., as needed.

Sentinel Campground. Cedar Grove Village is an easy walk from this busy campground, set at 4,600 ft along the Kings River. Flush toilets. Drinking water. Bear boxes, fire grates, picnic tables. Public telephone. | 82 sites for tents or RVs | Off Kings Canyon Hwy., 0.25-mi west of Cedar Grove Village | No phone | $18 | Reservations not accepted | No credit cards | Mid-Apr.–mid–Nov.

★ **Sheep Creek Campground.** Of the overflow campgrounds, this is one of the prettiest. The camp, like the adjacent Cedar Grove, is set at 4,600 ft along the Kings River. Flush toilets. Drinking water. Bear boxes, fire grates, picnic tables. Public telephone. | 111 sites for tents or RVs | Off Kings Canyon Hwy., 1 mi west of Cedar Grove Village | No phone | $18 | Reservations not accepted | No credit cards | Late May–late Sept., as needed.

Sunset Campground. Many of the easiest trails through Grant Grove are adjacent to this large camp, set near the giant sequoias at 6,500 ft. Flush toilets. Drinking water. Bear boxes, fire grates, picnic tables. Public telephone. | 200 sites for tents or RVs | Off Generals Hwy. (Rte. 198), near Grant Grove visitor center | No phone | $18 | Reservations not accepted | No credit cards | Memorial Day–late Sept.

Near the Parks

Big Meadows Campsites. Sites at this 7,600-ft-high camp are scattered along Big Meadows Creek. Though the area is pretty, there are limited facilities. There is no drinking water. Pit toilets. Fire grates, picnic tables. | 30 sites for tents or RVs up to 22 ft | Forest Rd. 14S11, 5 mi east off Generals Hwy. (Rte. 198), 7 mi southeast of Grant Grove | 559/338–2251 | Free | Reservations not accepted | Late May–Oct.

Hume Lake Campground. Hume Lake is small and lovely, but gets busy in summer. The campground has many more sites for tents than RVs. It's set at 5,200 ft. Flush toilets. Drinking water. Bear boxes, fire grates, picnic tables. Public telephone. Swimming (lake). | 60 sites for tents, 14 sites for RVs to 22 ft | Hume Lake Rd., 3 mi south of Kings Canyon Hwy. (Rte. 180) | 877/444–6777 | www.reserveusa.com | $16 (reservation fee $9) | Reservations essential | AE, D, MC, V | Late May–Oct.

Landslide Campground. On a creek that feeds nearby Hume Lake, this quiet camp is set at 5,800 ft. Pit toilets. Drinking water. Fire grates, picnic tables. General store nearby. | 9 sites for tents only | Tenmile Rd., 12 mi northeast of Grant Grove off Hume Lake Rd. from Rte. 180 | 559/338–2251 | $12 | Reservations not accepted | Late May–Oct.

Princess Campground. Good for small RVs and tents, this camp is at 5,900 ft in Sequoia National Forest, near Hume Lake. There's a fee to use the dump station, which is the only one in the area. Pit toilets. Dump station. Drinking water. Fire grates, picnic tables. | 50 sites for tents, 40 sites for RVs to 22 ft | Rte. 180, 6 mi north of Grant Grove entrance | 877/444–6777 | www.reserveusa.com | $14 (reservation fee $9) | Reservations essential | AE, D, MC, V | Late May–Oct.

Stony Creek Campground. Along a creek at 6,400 ft, this campground is between Sequoia and Kings Canyon parks. Flush toilets. Drinking water. Fire grates, picnic tables. Public telephone. | 49 sites for tents or RVs | Generals Hwy. (Rte. 198), 13 mi south of Grant Grove | 877/444–6777 | www.reserveusa.com | $16 (reservation fee $9) | Reservations essential | AE, D, MC, V | Late May–Oct.

Tenmile Campground. Above Hume Lake at 5,800 ft, this tiny camp is rustic for its lack of facilities. There is no drinking water. Pit toilets. Fire grates, picnic tables. | 13 sites for tents or RVs | Tenmile Rd., 5 mi northeast of Grant Grove, off Hume Lake Rd. from Rte. 180 | 559/338–2251 | Free | Reservations not accepted | Late May–Oct.

SEQUOIA AND
KINGS CANYON
NATIONAL PARKS

EXPLORING
ATTRACTIONS NEARBY
DINING
LODGING
**CAMPING AND RV
FACILITIES**
SHOPPING
ESSENTIAL
INFORMATION

SEQUOIA/KINGS CANYON CAMPGROUNDS

	Total # of sites	# of RV sites	# of hook-ups	Drive-to sites	Hike-to sites	Flush toilets	Pit toilets	Drinking water	Showers	Fire grates/pits	Swimming	Boat access	Playground	Dump station	Ranger station	Public telephone	Reservation possible	Daily fee per site	Dates open
INSIDE SEQUOIA																			
Atwell Mill	21	0	0	•			•	•	•	•						•		$12	MD–Nov.
Buckeye Flat	28	0	0	•		•		•		•						•		$18	Apr.–Oct.
Cold Springs	40	0	0	•		•		•	•	•					•	•		$12	MD–Nov.
Dorst Creek	218	200	0	•		•		•		•				•*		•	•*	$20	MD–LD
Lodgepole	250	149	0	•		•		•		•				•*	•	•	•*	$20	Y/R
Potwisha	44	44	0	•		•		•		•				•	•	•		$18	Y/R
South Fork	10	0	0	•			•			•								$12*	Y/R
INSIDE KINGS CANYON																			
Azalea	110	88	0	•		•		•	•	•					•	•		$18	Y/R
Canyon View	37	0	0		•	•		•		•					•	•		$18	MD–Oct.
Crystal Springs	67	41	0	•		•		•	•	•					•	•		$18	MD–Oct.
Moraine	120	120	0	•		•		•	•	•					•	•		$18	May–Oct.
Princess	90	50	0	•			•	•		•			•					$14	May–Oct.
Sentinel	82	83	0	•		•		•	•	•					•	•		$18	May–Oct.
Sheep Creek	111	111	0	•		•		•	•	•					•	•		$18	May–Oct.
Sunset	179	179	0	•		•		•	•	•					•	•		$18	MD–Oct.

* In summer only   ** Reservation fee charged   Y/R=Year-round
UL=Unlimited   ULP=Unlimited primitive   LD=Labor Day   MD=Memorial Day

Shopping

Cedar Grove Gift Shop and Market. Pick up supplies, food, bear canisters, and souvenirs here. | Cedar Grove Village, Kings Canyon National Park | 559/565–0100 | Closed late Oct.–mid-May.

Grant Grove Gift Shop. This shop sells handicrafts, film, and souvenirs. | Grant Grove Village, Kings Canyon National Park | 559/335–5500 Ext. 1615.

Grant Grove Market. The only market in Grant Grove, you can get supplies, emergency gasoline, and bear canisters here. You can rent cross-country skis and snowshoes in winter. | Grant Grove Village, Kings Canyon National Park | 559/335–2665.

Lodgepole Market and Gift Shop. Find supplies, emergency gasoline, outdoor equipment, bear canisters, gifts, and sandwiches at the park's main store. | Next to Lodgepole visitor center, Sequoia National Park | 559/565–3301.

Silver City Resort. Ice and a limited selection of supplies are available at this privately owned resort. | Mineral King Rd., 21 mi east of Three Rivers, Sequoia National Park | 559/561–3223 | Closed Nov.–late May.

Stony Creek Market. You can pick up snacks and basic foodstuffs at the market on Generals Highway in the Sequoia National Forest. | Generals Hwy. (Rte. 198), Stony Creek Village, 13 mi south of Grant Grove. | 559/565–3909 | Closed early Sept.–mid-June.

Wuksachi Gift Shop. You can buy candy and souvenirs here. | Wuksachi Village, Sequoia | 559/565–4070.

Essential Information

ATMS (24-HOUR): Lodgepole Market | Next to Lodgepole visitor center, Sequoia National Park. **Grant Grove Village Gift Shop** | Grant Grove Village, Kings Canyon National Park.

AUTOMOBILE SERVICE STATIONS: There is no gasoline in either park. If you're traveling in Kings Canyon, you can find gas at Hume Lake; traveling in Sequoia, fuel up in Three Rivers. Cans of emergency gasoline are available at Lodgepole Market and Grant Grove Market for $6 a gallon. For emergency repairs, towing, lock-outs, or jump-starts, your best bet is to call AAA or a service station in a neighboring town. **Three Rivers Chevron** | 41907 Sierra Dr., Three Rivers | 559/561–3835. **Hume Lake Christian Camps Gas Station** | Hume Lake Rd., off Rte. 180, 11 mi east of Grant Grove | 559/335–2000 Ext. 279. **DKR Automobile Service Center** | 515 S. Main St., Bishop | 760/873–7041.

POST OFFICES: Kings Canyon National Park Branch | 86724 Rte. 180, Grant Grove Village, Kings Canyon National Park, 93633 | 559/335–2499. **Sequoia National Park Branch.** | Lodgepole Village, Sequoia National Park, 93262 | 559/565–3468. **Three Rivers Main Post Office** | 40857 Sierra Dr., Three Rivers, 93271 | 559/561–4261.

YOSEMITE NATIONAL PARK

EAST-CENTRAL CALIFORNIA

Route 120 east to the Big Oak Flat entrance or west to the Tioga Pass entrance (summer only); Route 140 east to the Arch Rock entrance; Route 41 to the South entrance. Yosemite Valley is 180 mi from Kings Canyon National Park and 340 mi from Lassen Volcanic National Park.

You can lose your perspective in Yosemite. This is a land where everything is big. Really big. There are big rocks, big trees, and big waterfalls. The park has been so extravagantly praised and so beautifully photographed that some people wonder if the reality can possibly measure up. For almost everyone it does. With 1,189 square mi of parkland, 94.5% of it undeveloped wilderness accessible only to the backpacker and horseback rider, Yosemite is a nature lover's wonderland. The western boundary dips as low as 2,000 ft in the chaparral-covered foothills; the eastern boundary rises to 13,000 ft at points along the Sierra crest. Yosemite Valley has many of the park's most famous sites and is easy to reach, but take the time to explore the high country above the Valley and you'll see a different side of Yosemite; the fragile and unique alpine terrain is arresting. Wander through this world of wind-warped trees, scurrying animals, and bighorn sheep, and you'll come away with a distinct sense of peace and solitude.

Abraham Lincoln established Yosemite Valley and the Mariposa Grove of Giant Sequoias as public land in 1864, when he deeded the land to the state of California. This grant was the first of its kind in America, and it laid the foundation for the establishment of national and state parks. The high country above the Valley, however, was not protected. John Muir, concerned about the destructive effects of over-grazing on subalpine meadows, rallied together a team of dedicated supporters and lobbied for expanded protection of lands surrounding Yosemite Valley. As a result of their efforts, Yosemite National Park was established by Congress on October 1, 1890.

PUBLICATIONS

Write or call the park to obtain the park's newspaper, the *Yosemite Guide*, an indispensable resource, which lists everything from trip planning to seasonal activities. It's also available on-line at www.nps.gov/yose/trip/guide and in person upon your arrival. For a detailed calendar of activities, including operating hours of all facilities, also send for *Yosemite Today* or pick up a copy when you arrive; it's on-line at www.nps.gov/yose/now. Additionally, The Yosemite Association sells the 77-page *Yosemite Road Guide*, which tells the story behind each road marker in the park. They also sell a visitor kit ($20), which you can order in advance of your trip. **Yosemite Association** | Box 230, El Portal, 95318 | 209/ 379–1906 | www.yosemite.org.

When to Visit

HIGH AND LOW SEASON

With summer come the crowds. During extremely busy periods, like the 4th of July, you may experience delays at the entrance gates. If you can only make it here in the warmest months, try to visit mid-week. In winter, heavy snows occasionally cause road closures, and tire chains or four-wheel drive may be required on roads that remain open. Tioga Road is closed from late October through the end of May or middle of June, depending on snow melt. The road to Glacier Point beyond the turnoff for Badger Pass is closed after the first major snowfall, usually in late October through May. Mariposa Grove Road is typically closed for a shorter period in winter. The ideal time to visit is from mid-April through Memorial Day and from mid-September through October, when the park is only moderately busy and the days are usually sunny and clear.

SCENERY AND WILDLIFE

Dense stands of incense cedar, Douglas fir—as well as ponderosa, Jeffrey, lodgepole, and sugar pines—cover much of the park, but the stellar stand out, quite literally, is the *Sequoia sempervirens*, the giant sequoia. Sequoias grow only along the west slope of the Sierra Nevada between 4,500 and 7,000 ft in elevation. Starting from a seed the size of a rolled oat flake, each of these ancient monuments assumed remarkable proportions in adulthood; you can see them in the Mariposa Grove. In late May the Valley's dogwood trees bloom with white, starlike flowers. Wildflowers, such as black-eyed Susan, bull thistle, cow parsnip, lupine, and meadow goldenrod, peak in June in the Valley and in July at higher elevations. Yosemite's waterfalls are at their most spectacular in May and June. By summer's end, some falls will have dried up. They begin flowing again in late fall, and in winter they may be hung dramatically with ice. Visit the park during the period of the full moon, and you can stroll in the evening without a flashlight and still make out the silhouettes of the giant granite monoliths and ribbons of falling water. Regardless of the season, sunset casts a brilliant orange light onto Half Dome, a stunning sight.

The most visible animals are the mule deer, the only kind of deer in Yosemite. Though sightings of bighorn sheep are infrequent in the park itself, you can sometimes see them on the eastern side of the Sierra Crest, just off Route 120 in Lee Vining Canyon. The American black bear, which often has a brown, cinnamon, or blond coat, is the only species of bear in Yosemite (the California grizzlies were hunted to extinction in the 1920s), though few people ever see them. Watch for the blue Steller's jay along trails, in campgrounds, and around public buildings. The golden eagle is sometimes seen soaring above the Valley.

Average High/Low Temperature (°F) and Monthly Precipitation (in inches) in Yosemite Valley. In the high country, temperatures are cooler—by as much as 10–20°F in Tuolumne Meadows—and precipitation greater.

	JAN.	FEB.	MAR.	APR.	MAY	JUNE
YOSEMITE	48/29	53/30	55/32	61/36	69/43	78/49
	5.7	5.5	5.2	3.4	1.4	0.8

	JULY	AUG.	SEPT.	OCT.	NOV.	DEC.
	85/55	84/55	79/49	70/42	56/34	47/29
	0.2	0.4	0.9	2.0	5.2	5.0

FESTIVALS AND SEASONAL EVENTS
WINTER

Nov.–Dec.: **Vintners' Holidays.** Free two- and three-day seminars by California's most prestigious vintners are held midweek in the Great Room of the Ahwahnee Hotel in Yosemite Valley and culminate in an elegant, albeit pricey, banquet dinner. Arrive early for seats in the free seminars; book early for lodging and dining packages. | 559/253–5641 | www.yosemitepark.com.

Dec.: **The Bracebridge Dinner.** Held at the Ahwahnee Hotel in Yosemite Valley every Christmas since 1928, this 17th-century-themed madrigal dinner is so popular, that to secure a seat, you must book in mid-May. | 559/252–4848 | www.yosemitepark.com.

Jan.–Feb.: **Chefs' Holidays.** Celebrated chefs present cooking demonstrations and five-course meals at the Ahwahnee Hotel in Yosemite Valley on weekends from early January through early February. Special lodging packages are available; space is limited. | 559/253–5641 | www.yosemitepark.com.

SPRING

May: **Fireman's Muster.** North of Sonora in the old mining town of Columbia, history springs to life at this festival of antique fire engines, with hose-spraying contests and a parade of the old pumpers the major highlights. | 209/536–1672.

Mother Lode Roundup Parade and Rodeo. On Mother's Day weekend the town of Sonora celebrates its gold-mining, agricultural, and lumbering history with a parade, rodeo, entertainment, and food. | 209/532–7428 or 800/446–1333.

SUMMER

July: **Mammoth Lakes Jazz Jubilee.** This festival, founded in 1989, is hosted by the local group Temple of Folly Jazz Band and takes place in 10 venues,

YOSEMITE
NATIONAL PARK

EXPLORING
ATTRACTIONS NEARBY
DINING
LODGING
CAMPING AND RV
FACILITIES
SHOPPING
ESSENTIAL
INFORMATION

most with dance floors. | 760/934–2478 or 800/367–6572 | www.
mammothjazz.org.

Mother Lode Fair. Sonora was settled by miners from Mexico and has
never forgotten its gold-mining roots. The Mother Lode Fair held at
Mother Lode Fairgrounds celebrates this unique time in California his-
tory. | 209/532–7428 or 800/446–1333.

Aug.:   **Bluesapalooza.** For one long weekend every summer, Mammoth Lakes
hosts a blues and beer festival—with emphasis on the beer tasting. |
760/934–0606 or 800/367–6572 | www.mammothconcert.com.

Nearby Towns

Marking the southern end of the Sierra's gold-bearing Mother Lode, **Mariposa** is the last
moderate-sized town before you enter Yosemite from the southwest. In addition to a mining
museum, Mariposa has numerous shops, restaurants, and service stations. Motels and
restaurants dot both sides of Route 41 as it cuts through the town of **Oakhurst,** once a
boomtown during the Gold Rush. Oakhurst has a population of about 13,000 and sits
just south of Yosemite National Park. The gracious city of **Sonora** retains evidence of its
own vibrant, Gold Rush history. Stroll Washington Street and see Old West storefronts,
with their second-story porches, and 19th-century hotels. Sonora is the seat of Tuolumne
County, 70 mi west of Yosemite Village. The tiny town of **Lee Vining** is home to eerily beautiful, salty Mono Lake, where millions of migratory birds nest. You'll pass through Lee Vining
if you're coming to Yosemite through the eastern entrance (which is closed in winter).
Visit **Mammoth Lakes,** about 40 mi southeast of Yosemite's Tioga Pass entrance, for
excellent skiing and snowboarding in winter, with fishing, mountain biking, hiking, and
horseback riding in summer. Nine deep-blue lakes form the Mammoth Lakes Basin, and
another hundred dot the surrounding countryside. At the base of Mammoth Mountain
sits Devils Postpile National Monument, smooth, vertical, basaltic columns formed by
volcanic and glacial forces.

INFORMATION

Lee Vining Office and Information Center | Box 29, Lee Vining, CA 93541 | 760/647–6595 |
www.leevining.com. **Mammoth Lakes Visitors Bureau** | Along Rte. 203 (Main St.), near Sawmill
Cutoff Rd., Box 48, Mammoth Lakes, CA 93546 | 760/934–2712 or 888/466–2666 | www.
visitmammoth.com. **Mariposa County Visitors Bureau** | 5158 Rte. 140, Box 967, Mariposa,
CA 95338 | 209/966–7082 or 888/554–9013 | www.homeofyosemite.com. **Tuolumne County
Visitors Bureau** | Box 4020, Sonora, CA 95370 | 209/533–4420 or 800/446–1333 | www.
thegreatunfenced.com. **Yosemite Sierra Visitors Bureau** | 41969 Rte. 41, Oakhurst, CA 93644
| 559/683–4636 | www.go2yosemite.net.

Exploring Yosemite

PARK BASICS

Contacts and Resources: Yosemite National Park | Information Office, Box 577, Yosemite
National Park, 95389 | 209/372–0200 | www.nps.gov/yose. **Yosemite Concession Services**
| 5410 E. Home Ave., Fresno, 93727 | 559/252–4848 lodging, 209/372–1240 tours |
www.yosemitepark.com.

Fees: The vehicle admission fee is $20 per car and valid for seven days. Individuals arriv-
ing by bus, or on foot, bicycle, motorcycle, or horseback pay $10 for a seven-day pass.

Hours: The park is open 24 hours a day, every day, year-round.

Getting Around: Although you can visit the Yosemite Valley sites in your car, doing so is
discouraged in summer, since traffic congestion and exhaust are serious problems in the

park. When it's especially crowded, some roads are closed to private vehicles. You can avoid traffic jams by leaving your car at any of the designated lots and taking the free shuttle bus, which serves eastern Yosemite Valley year-round, every day. From May to September, shuttles run from 7 AM to 10 PM; the rest of the year, shuttles run from 9 AM to 10 PM. For more information on shuttles within the park, visit www.nps.gov/yose/trip/shuttle.htm or call 209/372–1240.

Note that there are few gas stations within Yosemite, so fuel up before you reach the park. From late fall until early spring, the weather is unpredictable and driving can be treacherous. You should carry chains no matter what route you take. They are often mandatory on Sierra roads in snowstorms. If you have to buy chains in the Valley, you'll pay twice the normal price. For information about road conditions, call 800/427–7623 or 209/372–0200 from within California or go to | www.dot.ca.gov.

Permits: Wilderness permits are required to overnight in Yosemite's backcountry. Permits are free if obtained in person at wilderness permit offices at Big Oak Flat, Hetch Hetchy, Tuolumne, Wawona, the Wilderness Center, and Yosemite Valley in summer; fall through spring, visit the Valley visitor center. Overnight hiking is restricted to limit human impact on natural areas. It's a good idea to make reservations for wilderness permits especially for a visit in May through September. (Note that making a request for a reservation does not guarantee you'll get one.) You can reserve two days to 24 weeks in advance, by calling 209/372–0740, logging on to www.nps.gov/yose, or by writing to Wilderness Permits, Box 545, Yosemite, 95389. Include your name, address, daytime phone, number of people in your party, trip date, alternative dates, starting and ending trailheads, and a brief itinerary. There's a $5 per person processing fee.

Fishing licenses are required and cost $11.05 for two days or $30.70 for 10 days. Full season licenses cost $30.70 for state residents, and a whopping $82.45 for nonresidents. Fishing season runs from late April to November 15.

Public Telephones: Public telephones are at park entrance stations, visitor centers, all restaurants and lodging facilities in the park, gas stations, and in Yosemite Village.

Rest Rooms: Public rest rooms are at the Valley Visitor Center, Village Store, and Nature Center at Happy Isles; at the Vernal Falls footbridge, Yosemite Falls, Tuolumne Meadows, and Glacier Point; and at the Swinging Bridge, Cathedral Beach, Sentinel Beach, Church Bowl, and El Capitan picnic areas.

Accessibility: Many of the Valley floor trails—particularly at Lower Yosemite Falls, Bridalveil Falls, and Mirror Lake—are accessible to wheelchairs, though some assistance may be required. The Valley visitor center is fully accessible. Many of Yosemite's facilities are being upgraded to make them more accessible. For complete details, pick up the park's accessibility brochure at any visitor center. People with respiratory difficulties should take note of the park's high elevations. The Valley floor is approximately 4,000 ft above sea level, but Tuolumne Meadows and parts of the high country hover around 10,000 ft.

Emergencies: In an emergency, call 911, or 9–911 from hotel rooms. You can also call the Yosemite Medical Clinic in Yosemite Village at 209/372–4637. The clinic provides 24-hour emergency care. Drop-in and urgent care is available. For non-urgent medical matters, schedule an appointment.

Lost and Found: To inquire about items lost or found in Yosemite's restaurants, hotels, lounges, shuttles, or tour buses, call Yosemite Concession Services at 209/372–4357. For items lost or found in other areas of the park, contact the National Park Service at 209/379–1001.

Good Tours

YOSEMITE IN ONE DAY

One day is enough for a whirlwind tour of the highlights, but it leaves little time for lingering or enjoying the many trails and activities. If one day is all you have, you'll want to

YOSEMITE
NATIONAL PARK

EXPLORING
ATTRACTIONS NEARBY
DINING
LODGING
CAMPING AND RV
FACILITIES
SHOPPING
ESSENTIAL
INFORMATION

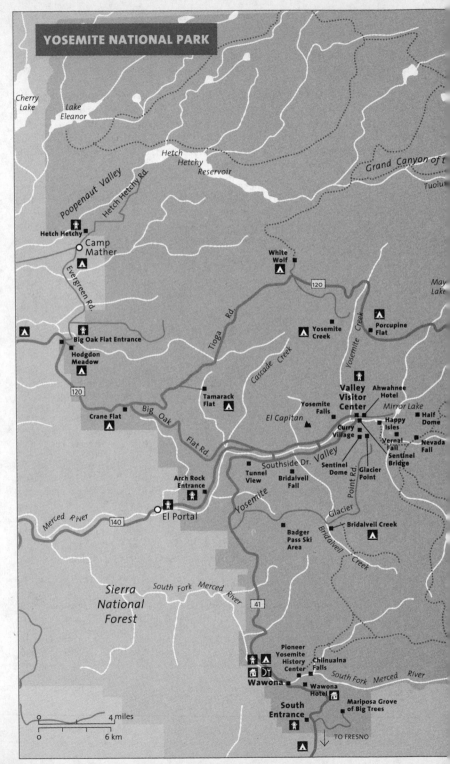

YOSEMITE NATIONAL PARK

Cherry Lake

Lake Eleanor

Hetch Hetchy Reservoir

Grand Canyon of t

Tuolu

Poopenaut Valley

Hetch Hetchy Rd.

Hetch Hetchy

Camp Mather

White Wolf

120

May Lake

Evergreen Rd.

Tioga Rd.

Yosemite Creek

Porcupine Flat

Yosemite Creek

Big Oak Flat Entrance

Hodgdon Meadow

Cascade Creek

120

Valley Visitor Center

Ahwahnee Hotel

Mirror Lake

Crane Flat

Big Oak Flat Rd.

Tamarack Flat

Yosemite Falls

Happy Isles

Half Dome

El Capitan

Curry Village

Vernal Fall

Nevada Fall

Sentinel Dome

Sentinel Bridge

Southside Dr.

Valley

Glacier Point Rd.

Tunnel View

Bridalveil Fall

Glacier Point

Arch Rock Entrance

Yosemite

Glacier

El Portal

140

Bridalveil Creek

Merced River

Badger Pass Ski Area

Bridalveil Creek

Sierra National Forest

South Fork Merced River

41

Pioneer Yosemite History Center

Chilnualna Falls

South Fork Merced River

Wawona

Wawona Hotel

Mariposa Grove of Big Trees

South Entrance

4 miles

6 km

TO FRESNO

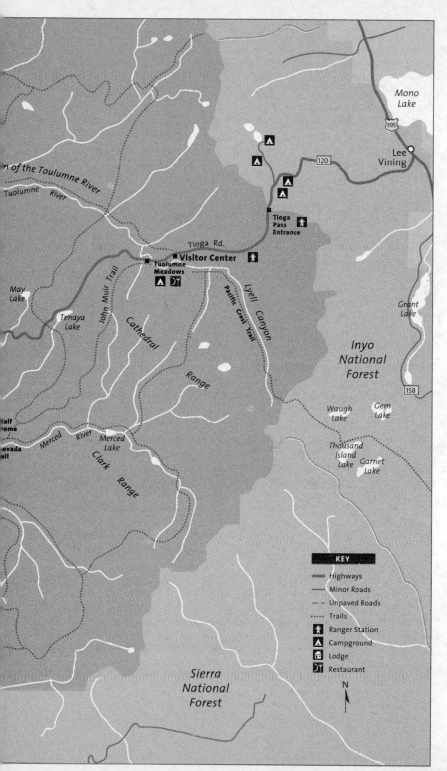

Mono
Lake

395

Lee
Vining

120

Tioga
Pass
Entrance

Tuolumne River

Tuolumne River

n of the Toulumne River

Tioga Rd.

■ Visitor Center
Tuolumne
Meadows

May
Lake

Tenaya
Lake

John Muir Trail

Cathedral

Range

Lyell Canyon

Pacific Crest Trail

Grant
Lake

Inyo
National
Forest

158

Waugh
Lake

Gem
Lake

Half
ome

evada
all

Merced   River

Merced
Lake

Clark

Range

Thousand
Island
Lake

Garnet
Lake

KEY

Highways
Minor Roads
Unpaved Roads
Trails
Ranger Station
Campground
Lodge
Restaurant

N

Sierra
National
Forest

YOSEMITE
NATIONAL PARK

EXPLORING
ATTRACTIONS NEARBY
DINING
LODGING
CAMPING AND RV
FACILITIES
SHOPPING
ESSENTIAL
INFORMATION

YOSEMITE'S FIRST RESIDENTS

Native Americans have been present in Yosemite for over 8,000 years. When the first non-native explorers entered Yosemite Valley in 1849, they met the Southern Sierra Miwoks. The Miwoks hunted, fished, and harvested acorns, which were ground into meal on stones, to eat and trade with other tribes.

spend it in Yosemite Valley. As you travel on the 10-mi one-way loop drive to the visitor center, make stops at vista points and pull-outs as you come to them.

Your first stop as you enter the Valley from the west is the graceful 620-ft cascade of **Bridalveil Fall.** As you continue east, you'll spot 3,593-ft **El Capitan,** the world's largest granite monolith, across the Valley. Follow signs to **Yosemite Village** and stop in at the **Valley visitor center** to pick up maps and brochures. Behind the center, walk through a small, re-created **Ahwahneechee village.** For more Native American lore, take a quick peek at the **Yosemite Museum** next door, where there's an impressive collection of baskets. If you're a photography buff, the nearby **Ansel Adams Gallery** is a must-see. Next, amble over to **Sentinel Bridge,** walk to its center, and take in the best view of **Half Dome,** with its reflection in the Merced River. Before you leave the Village, stop at the Village Store or a snack bar to pick up provisions for a picnic lunch. (If the park is particularly crowded, leave your car in the day-use lot and ride the free shuttle bus to the remaining Valley sights.)

Return to your car, drive over Sentinel Bridge, turn left, and continue on Southside Drive toward **Curry Village.** Hardy hikers may want to go straight to the day-use lot, walk to the end of the shuttle-bus road, and climb the moderately steep trail to the footbridge overlooking 317-ft **Vernal Fall** (1.5 mi round-trip; allow 1½ hours). Looping back toward Yosemite Village, follow signs to the **Ahwahnee Hotel.** Even if you aren't staying in this elegant lodge, it's worth a visit.

Back on the main road heading west, drive to **Yosemite Falls,** the highest waterfall in North America. This is a great spot to fit in a short hike by following the mile-long loop trail through the forest back to the parking lot. If you have time at the end of the day, drive up to **Glacier Point** for a sunset view of the Valley and surrounding peaks.

YOSEMITE IN THREE DAYS

If you have three days, start at the **Valley Visitor Center** to gather maps and orient yourself on the geology and history of the park. Head west for a short hike to **Yosemite Falls.** Afterward, continue driving west for a valley view of giant, granite **El Capitan.** Continue west on Northside Drive, and follow signs for **Route 41 (Wawona Road),** heading south. At the Chinquapin junction make a left turn onto Glacier Point Road (summer only). From **Glacier Point** you'll get a phenomenal bird's-eye view of the entire valley, including **Half Dome, Vernal Fall,** and **Nevada Fall.** If you want to avoid the busloads of tourists at Glacier Point, stop at **Sentinel Dome** instead. After a 1-mi hike, you get a view similar to the one from Glacier Point.

YOSEMITE'S LANTERN

When the full moon illuminates Yosemite's canyon walls just a few evenings a month, the glow from the shimmering granite is so bright that you can see clearly enough to night-hike with your flashlight off. However, you should never hike at night without a flashlight and extra batteries.

On day two, head south on Route 41 and visit the **Mariposa Grove of Big Trees** and the **Pioneer Yosemite History Center.** Stop at the historic **Wawona Hotel** and have lunch. Return to Yosemite Valley on Route 41, stopping at the **Tunnel View** pull-out to take in the breathtaking panorama of the Valley, with the afternoon sun lighting up the peaks. Back in the Valley, stop at **Bridalveil Falls** on the right side of the road. Head to the **Ahwahnee Hotel** for an afternoon drink, and view the paintings of Native American tribal leaders hanging in the hotel's lobby.

On the third day have breakfast near the Valley visitor center in **Yosemite Village.** See the **Ansel Adams Gallery,** the re-created **Ahwahneechee Village,** and the **Yosemite Museum.** Pick up light provisions before hiking to **Vernal Fall** or **Nevada Fall.** Picnic on the trail or in the Valley, then after lunch, visit **Tuolumne Meadows,** 55 mi east of the Valley on **Tioga Road (Route 120)** (summer only). This is the most extensive meadow system in the Sierra Nevada. Picnickers and day hikers enjoy the crystalline lakes, rolling fields, and rounded granite domes. Many backpackers begin their journeys from here, but you'll need to get acclimated to the 8,575-ft altitude.

Attractions

PROGRAMS AND TOURS

Most of the guided tours in the park are conducted by Yosemite Concession Services Corporation. Call two days to a week in advance to verify schedules and to make reservations, if they're required.

Art Classes. Professional artists conduct workshops in watercolor, etching, drawing, and other subjects. Subject to availability of funding, classes are held outdoors 10 AM–2 PM at inspiring spots, depending on the weather. Bring your own materials or purchase the basics at the Art Activity Center, next to the Village Store. Call to verify scheduling. | Art Activity Center, Yosemite Village | 209/372–1442 | www.yosemitepark.com | Free | early Apr.–early Oct., 9:30–4:30.

Big Trees Tram Tour. This open-air tram tour of the Mariposa Grove of Big Trees takes one hour. The trip does not include transportation from the Valley to the Grove, so plan to drive or take the shuttle. | 209/372–1240 | $11 | Usually June–Oct., depending on snowfall.

★ **Camera Walks.** Photography enthusiasts shouldn't miss the two-hour guided camera walks offered by professional photographers. Some walks are hosted by the Ansel Adams Gallery, some by Yosemite Concession Services, and the meeting points vary. All are free. Participation is limited, so call up to 10 days in advance, or visit the gallery. | 209/372–4413 or 800/568–7398 | www.yosemitepark.com or www.anseladams.com | Free | Reservations essential.

Glacier Point Tour. This four-hour trip takes you from Yosemite Valley (you're picked up from your hotel) to the Glacier Point vista, 3,214 ft above the Valley floor. | 209/372–1240 | $29.50 | Reservations essential | June–Oct.

Grand Tour. For a full-day tour of the Mariposa Grove and Glacier Point, try the Grand Tour. Though the tour stops for lunch at the historic Wawona Hotel, the meal is not included. | 209/372–1240 | $55 ($7 additional for lunch) | Reservations essential | June–Thanksgiving.

Junior Ranger Program. Children 3–13 can participate in the informal, self-guided Little Cub and Junior Ranger programs. Stop at the Valley visitor center or Happy Isles to pick up a handbook ($5), which children take with them around the park to complete activities. Once done, rangers perform a small ceremony, presenting kids with certification and a badge. | Valley visitor center | 209/372–0299.

Moonlight Tour. A late-evening version of the Valley Floor Tour takes place on moonlit nights, depending on weather conditions. | 209/372–1240 | $20.50 | Apr.–Sept.

Ranger-Led Programs. In the evenings, lectures by rangers, slide shows, and documentary films present unique perspectives on Yosemite. On summer weekends, Camp Curry hosts a sing-along campfire program. Programs vary according to season, but there's usually at least one ranger-led activity per night in the Valley; schedules and locations are published in *Yosemite Guide*. | 209/372–0299 | Free.

The Nature Center at Happy Isles hosts a one-hour **children's program** (ages 5–7) in summer, usually a few days a week, when a ranger is available.

Tuolumne Meadows Tour. If you want a full day's outing to the high country, opt for this ride up Tioga Road to Tuolumne Meadows. You stop at several overlooks, and you can connect with another shuttle at Tuolumne Lodge. This is mostly for hikers and backpackers who want to reach high-country trailheads, but anyone can ride. | 209/372–1240 | $23 | Reservations essential | July–Labor Day.

Valley Floor Tour. Take a 26-mi, two-hour tour of the Valley's highlights, with narration on area history, geology, and plant and animal life. It operates with either trams or enclosed motor coaches, depending on weather conditions. | 209/372–1240 | $20.50 | Year-round.

To reach Yosemite Valley in the 1860s, visitors had to take a boat from San Francisco to Stockton, followed by a 16-hour stagecoach ride and a 57-mi, 37-hour horseback ride into the valley.

Yosemite Theater. Theatrical and musical presentations are offered at various times throughout the year. One of the best-loved is Lee Stetson's portrayal of John Muir in *Conversation with a Tramp, John Muir's Stickeen and Other Fellow Mortals*, and *The Spirit of John Muir*. Tickets should be purchased in advance at the Valley visitor center. Unsold seats are available at the door at performance time, 8 PM. | Valley visitor center auditorium; Yosemite Lodge Theater | 209/372–0299 | $7–$10.

SCENIC DRIVES

Route 41. Curvy Route 41 from the South entrance station provides great views and stopover points en route to the Valley. Just past the gate, an offshoot to the right leads to the Mariposa Grove of Big Trees (it's closed once there's snow on the ground). A few miles farther north on Route 41 is Wawona, where you can stop for lunch. Drive another 15 mi, and you come to the turn-off for Glacier Point. Farther along on Route 41, you pass through a tunnel, where you can pull off the road and park. "Tunnel View" is one of the most famous views of Yosemite Valley, with El Capitan on the left, Bridalveil Fall on the right, and Half Dome as a backdrop. Continue another 5 mi on Route 41, and you reach Yosemite Valley.

Tioga Road. In summer, a drive up Tioga Road (Route 120) to the high country will reward you with gorgeous alpine scenery, including crystal-blue lakes, grassy meadows dotted with wildflowers, and high-alpine peaks. Keep a sharp eye out for the neon colors of rock climbers, who seem to defy gravity on the cliffs. Wildflowers peak in July and August. The one-way trip to Tioga Pass takes approximately 1½ hours.

SIGHTS TO SEE

ARRANGING YOUR COMPOSITION

Photographing Yosemite can be tricky. To capture the size and scope of the mountains, place something in the foreground and middle-ground of your shot, like a tree branch and a field of flowers. The light is best in the early morning and late afternoon, when shadows are long and colors most saturated.

★ **Ahwahnee Hotel.** Built in 1927, this stately lodge of granite and concrete beams, stained to look like redwood, is a perfect man-made complement to Yosemite's natural majesty. Even if you aren't a guest, take time to visit the immense parlors with their walk-in hearths and priceless, antique Native American rugs and baskets. The dining room, its high ceiling interlaced with massive sugar-pine beams, is extraordinary. Dinner is formal, breakfast and lunch more casual. | Yosemite Valley | 209/372–1489.

Ahwahneechee Village. Tucked behind the Valley visitor center, a short loop trail of about 100 yards circles through a re-creation of an Ahwahneechee Native American village as it might have appeared in 1872, 21 years after the Native Americans' first contact with Europeans. Markers explain the lifestyle of Yosemite's first residents. Allow 30 minutes to see it all. | Yosemite Village | Free | Daily sunrise–sunset.

Ansel Adams Gallery. See the works of the master Yosemite photographer. Some of Adams' original prints are for sale. An elegant photography shop sells more prints and camera supplies. You can also sign up for photography workshops; see the gallery's Web site or call for details. There are also private showings of fine prints on Saturdays. | Yosemite Village | 209/372–4413 or 800/568–7398 | www.anseladams.com | Free | Apr.–Oct., daily 9–6; Nov.–Mar. 9–5.

Curry Village. Opened in 1899 by David and Jenny Curry, Curry Village offers tented lodgings for a modest price. This is where you should come to rent rafts or bicycles. There are several stores, an evening campfire program in summer, and an ice-skating rink in winter. | Yosemite Valley.

★ **El Capitan.** Rising 3,593 ft—more than 350 stories—above the Valley, El Capitan is the largest exposed-granite monolith in the world. It's almost twice the height of the Rock of Gibraltar. Look for climbers scaling the vertical face. | Off Northside Dr., about 4 mi west of the Valley visitor center.

★ **Glacier Point.** A Yosemite hotspot for its sweeping, bird's-eye views, Glacier Point looms 3,214 ft above the Valley. From the parking area, walk a few hundred yards and you'll see waterfalls, Half Dome, and other mountain peaks. Glacier Point is a popular hiking destination. You can hike up, or take a bus ($15) to the top and hike down. The bus runs June through October, weather permitting; call 209/372–1240 for schedule. | Glacier Point Rd., 16 mi northeast of Rte. 41.

★ **Half Dome.** Though you may have seen it on countless postcards and calendars, it's still arresting to see Half Dome, the Valley's most recognizable formation, which tops out at an elevation of 8,842 ft. The afternoon sun lights its face with orange and yellow shades that are reflected in the Merced River. Stand on the Sentinel Bridge at sunset for the best view.

Hetch Hetchy Reservoir. The Hetch Hetchy Reservoir, which supplies water and hydro-electric power to San Francisco, is about 40 mi from Yosemite Valley. Some say John Muir died of heartbreak when this grand valley was dammed and flooded beneath 300 ft of water in 1913. | Hetch Hetchy Rd., about 15 mi north of the Big Oak Flat entrance station.

High Country. The above–tree line, high-alpine region east of the Valley—land of alpen-glow and top-of-the-world vistas—is often missed by those only focusing on the Valley's more publicized splendors. If you've never seen Sierra high country, go. If you've already been there, you know why it's not to be missed. Summer wildflowers, which usually spring up mid-July through August, carpet the meadows and mountainsides with pink, purple, blue, red, yellow, and orange. On foot or on horseback are the best ways to get there. For information on trails and backcountry permits, check with the visitor center.

Le Conte Memorial Lodge. The Valley's first visitor center is now operated by the Sierra Club, featuring a small children's library, environmental exhibits, and evening programs. It's across from Housekeeping Camp. | Southside Dr. | Memorial Day–Labor Day, Wed.–Sun. 10–4.

★ **Mariposa Grove of Big Trees.** Mariposa is Yosemite's largest grove of giant sequoias. The Grizzly Giant, the oldest tree here, is estimated to be 2,700 years old. You can visit the trees on foot or, in summer, on a one-hour tram tour. If the road to the grove is closed in sum-mer, which happens when Yosemite is crowded, park in Wawona and take the free shut-tle (9 AM to 4:30 PM) to the parking lot. The access road to the grove may also be closed by snow for extended periods from November to mid-May. You can still usually walk, snow-shoe, or ski in. | Rte. 41, 2 mi north of the South entrance station.

Nature Center at Happy Isles. Named after the pair of little islands where the Merced River enters Yosemite Valley, this family-oriented center has books, dioramas, and interactive exhibits on the park, with special attention paid to recent natural phenomena, such as recurring rockslides. | Off Southside Dr. | Free | Mid-May–Oct., 10–noon, 12:30–4.

Pioneer Yosemite History Center. Yosemite's first log buildings, relocated here from around the park, make up this historic collection near the Wawona Hotel. Enter on the covered bridge that welcomed the park's first tourists. There's also a homesteader's cabin, a black-smith's shop, a bakery, and a U.S. Cavalry headquarters, all from the late-19th or early 20th centuries. Wednesday through Sunday in summer, costumed docents play the roles of the pioneers. Ask about ranger-led walks and horse-drawn stage rides, which happen sporadically. | Rte. 41, Wawona | 209/375–9531 or 209/379–2646 | Free | Building interiors are open mid-June–Labor Day, Wed. 2–5, Thurs.–Sun. 10–1 and 2–5.

Sentinel Dome. The view from here is similar to that from Glacier Point, except you can't see the Valley floor. A 1.1-mi path climbs to the viewpoint from the parking lot. The trail is long and steep enough to keep the crowds away, but it's not overly rugged. | Glacier Point Rd., off Rte. 41.

★ **Tuolumne Meadows.** The largest subalpine meadow in the Sierra, at 8,600 ft, is a popu-lar way station for backpack trips along the Sierra-scribing Pacific Crest and John Muir trails. The colorful wildflowers peak in mid-July and August. Tioga Road provides easy access to the high country, but the highway closes when snow starts to fall, usually in mid-Octo-ber. | Tioga Rd. (Rte. 120), about 8 mi west of the Tioga Pass entrance station.

YOSEMITE
NATIONAL PARK

EXPLORING
ATTRACTIONS NEARBY
DINING
LODGING
CAMPING AND RV
FACILITIES
SHOPPING
ESSENTIAL
INFORMATION

SHADES OF FALL

Visit Yosemite Valley in autumn and you may miss the waterfalls, but instead you will get to see extraordinary colors. Dogwood leaves turn pink and white, oak leaves red and yellow, and the grasses in the meadows every shade of gold. Fallen leaves dot the ground like paint on an artist's palette.

Valley Visitor Center. For maps, guides, and information from park rangers, be sure to stop here. There's a Sierra visitor bureau and exhibits on the history of Yosemite Valley. | Yosemite Village | 209/372–0299 | www.yosemitepark.com | Free | Memorial Day–Labor Day, daily 8–6; Labor Day–Memorial Day, daily 9–5.

★ **Waterfalls.** When the snow starts to melt (usually peaking in May), almost every rocky lip or narrow gorge becomes a spillway for streaming snowmelt churning down to meet the Merced River. But even in drier months, the waterfalls can be breathtaking. If you choose to hike any of the trails to or up the falls, be sure to wear shoes with good, no-slip soles; rocks can be extremely slippery. Stay on trails at all times.

Bridalveil Fall, a filmy fall of 620 ft that is often diverted as much as 20 ft one way or the other by the breeze, is the first marvelous view of Yosemite Valley you will see if you come in via Route 41.

Climb Mist Trail from Happy Isles for an up-close view of 594-ft **Nevada Fall,** the first major fall as the Merced River plunges out of the high country toward the eastern end of Yosemite Valley. If you don't want to hike, you can see it from Glacier Point.

At 1,612 ft, **Ribbon Fall** is the highest single fall in North America. It's also the first valley waterfall to dry up in summer; the rainwater and melted snow that create the slender fall evaporate quickly at this height. Look just west of El Capitan from the Valley floor; you can best see the fall from the base of Bridalveil Fall.

Fern-covered black rocks frame 317-ft **Vernal Fall,** and rainbows play in the spray at its base. Take Mist Trail from Happy Isles to see it, or if you'd rather not hike, go to Glacier Point for a good view.

Yosemite Falls—which form the highest waterfall in North America and the fifth-highest in the world—are actually three falls, one on top of another. The water from the top descends all of 2,425 ft, and when the falls run hard, you can hear them thunder all across the Valley. To view them up close, head to their base on the trail from Camp 4.

★ **Wawona Hotel.** In the southern tip of Yosemite, this was the park's first lodge, built in 1879. With a whitewashed exterior and wraparound verandas, this is a fine example of Victorian resort architecture—a blend of rusticity and elegance—and is now a National Historic Landmark. All the hotel annexes on this estate were built by 1918. The Wawona is an excellent place to stay or stop for lunch when making the drive from the South Entrance to the Valley; the dining room is open weekends only from January through March. | Rte. 41, Wawona | 209/375–1425.

Wilderness Center. The staff at the Wilderness Center in Yosemite Village provides free wilderness permits for overnight camping, maps, and advice to hikers heading into the backcountry. When the center is closed, go to the Valley visitor center next door. | Yosemite Village | Memorial Day–Labor Day, daily 7:30–6.

Yosemite Museum. With demonstrations in beadwork, basket-weaving, and other traditional activities, the museum elucidates the cultural history of Yosemite's Miwok and Paiute people. | Yosemite Village | 209/372–0299 | Free | Daily 9–noon and 1–4:30.

Sports and Outdoor Activities

BICYCLING

The eastern valley has 12 mi of paved bike paths, or you can ride on 196 mi of paved park roads. Kids under 18 must wear a helmet. Bikes are not allowed on hiking trails or in the backcountry. Stick to the Valley floor for the safest, easiest terrain.

Yosemite Bike Rentals. You can rent bikes by the hour ($5.50) or by day ($21) from either Yosemite Lodge or Curry Village bike stands. Helmets are always included. Bikes with child trailers, baby-jogger strollers, and wheelchairs are also available. | Yosemite Lodge or Curry Village | 209/372–1208 | www.yosemitepark.com | $5.50, $21 | Apr.–Oct.

BIRD-WATCHING

More than 200 bird species have been spotted in the park, including the sage sparrow, pygmy owl, blue grouse, and mountain bluebird. Park rangers lead free bird-watching walks in Yosemite Valley in summer, one day each week, when staff members are available. Binoculars are sometimes available for loan.

Birding Seminars. The Yosemite Association sponsors two- to four-day seminars for beginning and intermediate birders. Meeting points vary. | 209/379–1906 or 209/379–2321 | www.yosemite.org | $80–$225 | Apr.–Aug.

FISHING

The waters in Yosemite are not stocked. Trout, mostly brown and rainbow, live here but are not plentiful. Yosemite's fishing season begins on the last Saturday in April and ends on November 15. Some waterways are off-limits at certain times; be sure to inquire at the visitor center about regulations. You will need a license to fish; *see* Permits *under* Exploring Yosemite, *above.* Buy your license in season at Yosemite Village Sport Shop (209/372–1286), between the Village Store and the Old Bank Building, or at the Wawona Store (209/375–6574). Or buy it any time of year by writing the **Department of Fish and Game.** | 3211 S St., Sacramento, 95814 | 916/227–2245 | www.dfg.ca.gov.

GOLF

Wawona Golf Course. There's a 9-hole, par-35 course at Wawona. Different tee positions per side provide an 18-hole, par-70 format. | Rte. 41 | 209/375–6572 Wawona Golf Shop | www.yosemitepark.com | $14.50–$23.60 | Mid-Apr.–Oct., daily.

HIKING AND BACKPACKING

From paved rambles to multiday scrambles, Yosemite's 840 mi of trails have a hike for you. Be sure to purchase a detailed guide and topographic map, on sale in park stores and visitor centers. Overnight stays in the backcountry require a wilderness permit (*see* Permits *under* Exploring Yosemite, *above*). If you prefer a guided hike, the Yosemite Mountaineering School can take you on an organized full- or half-day trek; call 209/372–8344 or log onto www.yosemiteparktours.com.

"A Changing Yosemite" Interpretive Trail. This self-guided, wheelchair- and stroller-accessible walk begins about 75 yards in front of the Valley visitor center. It follows the road, then circles through Cook's Meadow on a paved path. An informative pamphlet explains the continually changing geology of the Valley. Allow 45 minutes for the 1-mi loop. | Across from the Valley visitor center.

Chilnualna Falls Trail. This Wawona-area trail runs 4 mi one-way to the top of the falls, then leads into the backcountry, connecting with miles of other trails. This is one of the park's most inspiring and secluded trails—albeit strenuous. Past the tumbling cascade, and up through forests, you'll emerge before a panoramic vista at the top. | Chilnualna Falls Rd., off Rte. 41.

Four-Mile Trail. You can take the hiker bus up to Glacier Point ($15), and then descend from there, zigzagging through the forest to the Valley floor, where you can catch a free shuttle back to your starting hiker-bus stop. If you decide to hike up Four-Mile Trail and back down again, allow about six hours for the 9.5-mi round-trip (the trail was lengthened to make it less steep). The elevation change is 3,220 ft. | Glacier Point.

★**John Muir Trail to Half Dome.** Ardent and courageous trekkers can continue on from the top of Nevada Fall, off Mist Trail, to the top of Half Dome. Some hikers attempt this entire 10- to 12-hour, 16.75-mi round-trip trek from Happy Isles in one day. If you're planning to do this, remember that the 4,800-ft elevation gain and the altitude of 8,842 ft will cause shortness of breath. Backpackers can hike to a campground in Little Yosemite Valley near the top of Nevada Fall the first day, then climb to the top of Half Dome and hike out the next day; it's highly recommended that you get your wilderness permit reservations at

YOSEMITE
NATIONAL PARK

EXPLORING
ATTRACTIONS NEARBY
DINING
LODGING
CAMPING AND RV
FACILITIES
SHOPPING
ESSENTIAL
INFORMATION

least a month in advance. Wear hiking boots and bring gloves. The last pitch up the back of Half Dome is very steep. The only way to climb this sheer rock face is to pull yourself up using the steel cable handrails, which are in place only from late spring to early fall. Those who brave the ascent will be rewarded with an unbeatable view of Yosemite Valley below and the high country beyond. Before heading out, check conditions with rangers; don't attempt the final ascent if there are any storm clouds overhead. | Happy Isles.

★ **Mist Trail.** You'll walk through rainbows when you visit 317-ft Vernal Fall. The hike to the bridge at the base of the fall is only moderately strenuous and less than 1 mi long. It's another steep (and often wet) 0.75-mi grind up to the top. From there, you can continue 2 more mi to the top of Nevada Fall, a 594-ft cascade as the Merced River plunges out of the high country. The trail is open late spring to early fall, depending on snowmelt. | Happy Isles.

★ **Panorama Trail.** Starting at Glacier Point, the trail circles 8.5 mi down through forest, past the secluded Illilouette Falls, and to the top of Nevada Fall. There the trail connects with Mist Trail and the John Muir Trail. You pass Nevada then Vernal Fall on your way down to the Valley floor for a total elevation loss of 3,200 ft. Arrange for an early morning bus ride to Glacier Point, and allow a full day for this hike. | Glacier Point.

★ **Yosemite Falls Trail.** This is the highest waterfall in North America. The upper fall (1,430 ft), the middle cascades (675 ft), and the lower fall (320 ft) combine for a total of 2,425 ft and, when viewed from the valley, appear as a single waterfall. The 0.25-mi trail leads from the parking lot to the base of the falls. Upper Yosemite Fall Trail, a strenuous 3.5-mi climb rising 2,700 ft, takes you above the top of the falls. | Northside Dr. at Camp 4.

HORSEBACK RIDING

Reservations must be made in advance at the hotel tour desks or by phone. For any of the overnight saddle trips, which use mules, phone on or after September 15 to request a lottery application for the following year (559/253–5673). Scenic trail rides range from two hours to full days; rates listed below are for two-hour to full-day rides. Six-day High Sierra saddle trips are also available.

Tuolumne Meadow Stables | Tioga Rd. | 209/372–8427 | www.yosemitepark.com | $40–$80 | Memorial Day–Labor Day | Reservations essential.

Valley Stables | Yosemite Valley | 209/372–8348 | www.yosemitepark.com | $40–$80 | Memorial Day–Labor Day | Reservations essential.

Wawona Stables | Rte. 41 | 209/375–6502 | www.yosemitepark.com | $40–$80 | Memorial Day–Labor Day | Reservations essential.

ICE-SKATING

Curry Village Ice Skating Rink. The admission fee is $6.50, and the skate rental fee is $3.25. | Curry Village | 209/372–8341 | www.yosemitepark.com | Mid-Nov.–mid-Mar.

RAFTING

Rafting is permitted only on designated areas of the Middle and South Forks of the Merced River. Check with the visitor center for closures and other restrictions.

Curry Village Raft Stand. The rental fee is per person and covers the raft, paddles, and life-jackets, plus a shuttle to the launch point on Sentinel Beach. You raft 3 mi down the Merced River, and a tram takes you back to Curry Village. | 209/372–8319 | www.yosemitepark.com | $13.50 | Late May–July.

ROCK CLIMBING

The granite canyon walls of Yosemite Valley are world-renowned for rock climbing. El Capitan, with its 3,593-ft vertical face, is the most famous and difficult of all, but there are many other options for all skill levels.

Yosemite Mountaineering School and Guide Service. The one-day basic lesson includes some bouldering and rappelling, and three or four 60-ft climbs. Climbers must be at least 10 (kids under 12 must be accompanied by a parent or guardian) and in reasonably good physical condition. Intermediate and advanced classes include instruction in belays, self-rescue, summer snow climbing, and free climbing. If you're already an experienced climber, ask at the mountain shop what areas are best for your skill level. | Curry Village Mountain Shop | 209/372–8344 | www.yosemitepark.com | $70–$170 | Apr.–Nov.

SKIING AND SNOWSHOEING

Badger Pass. A free, 40-minute shuttle ride takes you from Yosemite Valley to Badger Pass, where you can ski downhill and cross-country. Badger Pass opened in 1934 and is the oldest operating ski area in California (and the only one in the park). It's a compact area with gentle terrain, ideal for families and beginners. Four chairlifts and one surface lift access nine runs. If you're staying in one of Yosemite's hotels, you ski free Sunday through Thursday between January and March. Ski and snowshoe lessons and rentals are available. There is also a wide variety of organized cross-country ski tours available, including overnight snow-camping trips. | Glacier Point Rd. | 209/372–8444 or 209/372–1000 | www.yosemitepark.com | Downhill lift ticket $31, equipment rental $22.50; cross-country rentals $17–$21; snowshoe rentals $15 | Mid-Dec.–early Apr.

SWIMMING

Several swimming holes with small sandy beaches can be found in midsummer along the Merced River at the eastern end of Yosemite Valley. Find gentle waters to swim; currents are often stronger than they appear and temperatures are chilling. To conserve riparian habitats, step into the river at sandy beaches and other obvious entry points. Do not attempt to swim above or near waterfalls or rapids; fatalities have occurred. There are outdoor swimming pools at Curry Village (209/372–8324) and Yosemite Lodge (209/372–1250). Nonguests pay a $2 fee.

Attractions Nearby

Sights to See

★ **Bodie Ghost Town.** Old shacks and shops, abandoned mine shafts, a Methodist church, the mining village of Rattlesnake Gulch, and the remains of a small Chinatown are among the sights at this fascinating ghost town. At an elevation of 8,200 ft, the town boomed from about 1878 to 1881, but by the late 1940s, all its residents had departed. A state park was established in 1962, with a mandate to preserve the town in a state of "arrested decay," but not to restore it. Evidence of Bodie's wild past survives at an excellent museum, and you can tour an old stamp mill (where ore was stamped into fine powder to extract gold and silver) and a ridge that contains many mine sites. No food, drink, or lodging is available in Bodie; the nearest picnic area is a half-mile away. The town is 23 mi from Lee Vining, north on U.S. 395, east on Route 270. The last 3 mi are unpaved. Snow may close Route 270 late fall through early spring, but you can ski the 13 mi from the highway to the park. | Main and Green Sts., Bodie | 760/647–6445 | Park $2; museum free | Park: Memorial Day–Labor Day, daily 8–7; Sept.–May, daily 8–4. Museum: Memorial Day–Labor Day, daily 9–6; Sept.–May, hrs vary.

★ **Devils Postpile National Monument.** East of Mammoth Lakes lies a rock formation of smooth, vertical basalt columns sculpted by volcanic and glacial forces. A short, steep trail winds to the top of the 60-ft cliff for a bird's-eye view of the columns. Follow Route 203 west from Mammoth Lakes to the ski area, where you must board a shuttle to the monument. | Minaret Rd., Mammoth Lakes | 760/934–2289, 760/934–0606 shuttle | www.nps.gov/depo | Free, shuttle bus $7 | Late June–late Oct., daily.

A 2-mi hike past the Postpile leads to the monument's second scenic wonder, **Rainbow Falls,** where a branch of the San Joaquin River plunges more than 100 ft over a lava

YOSEMITE
NATIONAL PARK

EXPLORING
ATTRACTIONS
NEARBY
DINING
LODGING
CAMPING AND RV
FACILITIES
SHOPPING
ESSENTIAL
INFORMATION

ledge. When the water hits the pool below, sunlight turns the resulting mist into a spray of color. In summer, the area is accessible only by shuttle bus from the Mammoth Mountain ski area. Scenic picnic spots dot the banks of the river. | 760/934–0606 | $7 | June–Nov., daily.

Hot Creek Geologic Site. Forged by an ancient volcanic eruption, the Hot Creek Geologic Site is a landscape of boiling hot springs, fumaroles, and occasional geysers about 10 mi southeast of the town of Mammoth Lakes. You can soak (at your own risk) in hot springs or walk along boardwalks through the canyon to view the steaming volcanic features. Fly-fishing for trout is popular upstream from the springs. | Hot Creek Hatchery Rd. east of U.S. 395, Mammoth Lakes | 760/924–5500 | Free | Daily sunrise–sunset.

En route to Hot Creek Geologic Site is the **Hot Creek Fish Hatchery,** the breeding ponds for most of the fish (3–5 million annually) with which the state stocks eastern Sierra lakes and rivers. | Hot Creek Hatchery Rd. east of U.S. 395, Mammoth Lakes | 760/934–2664 | Free | June–Oct., daily 8–4, depending on snowfall.

★**Mono Lake.** Since the 1940s the city of Los Angeles has diverted water from the streams that feed the lake, lowering its water level and exposing striking towers of tufa, or calcium carbonate. Court victories by environmentalists have forced a reduction of the diversions, and the lake is again rising. Millions of migratory birds nest in and around Mono Lake. | South of Lee Vining on U.S. 395.

If you join the naturalist-guided **South Tufa Walk,** bring your binoculars for close-up views of Mono Lake's wildlife and calcified tufa towers. Tours depart the South Tufa parking lot 5 mi east of U.S. 395 on Route 120 and last about 1½ hours. | 760/647–3044 | www.monolake.org | $3 | Weekends 1 pm.

Yosemite Mountain–Sugar Pine Railroad. This 4-mi, narrow-gauge, steam-powered railroad excursion takes you along the rails near Yosemite's south gate. Travel back to a time when powerful locomotives once hauled massive log trains through the Sierra. There's also a moonlight special, with dinner and entertainment. Take Route 41 south from Yosemite about 8 mi. | 56001 Rte. 41, Fish Camp | 559/683–7273 | www.ymsprr.com | $13–$36.50 | Mar.–Oct., daily.

Dining

In Yosemite

In addition to the dining options listed here, you'll find fast-food grills and cafeterias, plus temporary snack bars, hamburger stands, and pizza joints lining park roads in summer. Many dining facilities in the park are open summer only.

★**Ahwahnee Hotel Dining Room.** Continental. This is the most dramatic dining room in Yosemite, if not California. The massive room has a 34-ft ceiling supported by immense sugar-pine beams, and floor-to-ceiling windows. In the evening, everything glows with candlelight. Specialties on the often-changing menu include salmon, duckling, and prime rib. | Yosemite Valley, about 0.75 mi east of the visitor center | 209/372–1489 | Reservations essential | $23–$36 | AE, D, DC, MC, V | Jacket required at dinner.

Food Court at Yosemite Lodge. American/Casual. Fast and convenient, the food court serves simple fare, ranging from hamburgers and pizzas to pastas, carved roasted meats, and salads at lunch and dinner. There's also a selection of beer and wine. At breakfast, there are pancakes and eggs made any way you like. | Yosemite Valley, about 0.75 mi west of the visitor center | 209/372–1265 | $3–$12 | AE, D, DC, MC, V.

Mountain Room Restaurant. American. The food becomes secondary when you see Yosemite Falls through the wall of windows in the Yosemite Lodge dining room. Grilled trout and salmon, steak, and pasta are a few of the menu choices. Kids' menu. | Yosemite

Valley, about 0.75 mi west of the visitor center | 209/372–1281 | $17–$25 | AE, D, DC, MC, V | No lunch. Closed weekdays Thanksgiving–Easter.

Pavillion Buffet. American/Casual. For a hot meal, cafeteria-style, come to this Curry Village restaurant. Bring your tray outside to the deck, and take in the views of the Valley's granite walls. | Curry Village | 209/372–8303 | $5–$12 | AE, D, DC, MC, V | No lunch. Closed mid-Oct.–mid-Apr.

Picnic Areas. Ready-made picnic lunches are available through Yosemite hotels with advance notice. Otherwise, stop at the grocery stores in the Village to pick up supplies. Many picnickers prefer to hike along one of the many scenic trails and choose an impromptu spot or vista point to enjoy their meal. Otherwise, there are 13 designated picnic areas around the park. Rest rooms and grills or fire grates are available at those in the Valley only.

Cathedral Beach is on Southside Drive underneath spire-like Cathedral Rocks. There are usually fewer people here than at the eastern end of the Valley. No drinking water.

Tucked behind the Ahwahnee Hotel, **Church Bowl** nearly abuts the granite walls below the Royal Arches. If you're walking from the Village with your supplies, this is the shortest trek to a picnic area. No drinking water.

At the western end of the Valley on Northside Drive, the **El Capitan** picnic area has great views straight up the giant granite wall above. No drinking water.

On Southside Drive, **Sentinel Beach** is right alongside a running creek and the Merced River. Because it has the most amenities, it's usually the most crowded. No drinking water.

Just east of Sentinel Beach on Southside Drive, **Swinging Bridge** is the name of a little wooden footbridge that crosses the Merced River, past the picnic area. No drinking water.

Right next to Sentinel Beach on Southside Drive, **Yellow Pine** is named for the towering trees that cluster on the banks of the Merced River. No drinking water. No rest room.

Outside the valley, there are picnic areas at the Cascades Falls, Glacier Point, Lembert Dome, Mariposa Grove, Wawona, Tenaya Lake, and Yosemite Creek.

Tuolumne Meadows Grill. Fast Food. Serving continuously throughout the day, this fast-food grill cooks up breakfast, lunch, and dinner. Stop in for a quick meal before exploring the Meadows. | Tioga Rd. (Rte. 120) | 209/372–8426 | $3–$7 | AE, D, DC, MC, V | Closed Oct.–Memorial Day.

Tuolumne Meadows Lodge. American. Adjacent to the Tuolumne River under a giant tent canopy, you can have hearty American fare at breakfast or dinner. The meals are the best you'll find in the Meadows. | Tioga Rd. (Rte. 120) | 209/372–8413 | Reservations essential | $13–$22 | AE, D, DC, MC, V | No lunch. Closed Oct.–Memorial Day.

The Village Grill. Fast Food. For a simple hamburger or grilled sandwich, this family-friendly eatery in Yosemite Village will satisfy. | 209/372–1207 | $5–$7 | AE, D, DC, MC, V | No breakfast, no dinner after 5:00 PM. Closed Oct.–May.

★ **Wawona Hotel.** American. Watch deer graze on the meadow while you dine in the romantic, candlelit dining room of the whitewashed Wawona Hotel, which dates from the late 1800s. The American style cuisine favors fresh California ingredients and flavors. Trout is a menu staple. There's also a Sunday brunch. | Rte. 41, Wawona | 209/375–1425 | Jacket required at dinner | $17–$27 | Reservations essential | AE, D, DC, MC, V | Closed weekdays Thanksgiving–Easter.

White Wolf Lodge. American. The casual, rustic dining room at this high-country historic lodge fills up at breakfast and dinner. The short menu offers good, basic meat-and-potato meals. | Tioga Rd. (Rte. 120), 45 minutes west of Tuolumne Meadows | 209/372–8416 | Reservations essential | $12–$17 | AE, D, DC, MC, V | No lunch. Closed Oct.–June.

Near the Park

Banny's Café. Contemporary. A calm, pleasant environment and hearty yet refined dishes make Banny's an attractive alternative to Sonora's noisier eateries. Try the grilled salmon fillet with scallion rice and ginger-wasabi aioli. | 83 S. Stewart St., Sonora | 209/533–4709 | $12–$15 | D, MC, V | No lunch Sun.

★ **Erna's Elderberry House.** Continental. The restaurant, operated by Vienna-born Erna Kubin, owner of Château du Sureau, is an expression of her passion for beauty, charm, and impeccable service. Red walls and dark beams accent the dining room's high ceilings, and arched windows reflect the glow of many candles. A seasonal six-course prix-fixe dinner is accompanied by superb wines. The moment the waitstaff places all the plates on the table in perfect synchronicity, you know this will be a meal to remember. Erna's also serves a champagne Sunday brunch. | 48688 Victoria La., Oakhurst | 559/683–6800 | Reservations essential | $82 | AE, MC, V | No lunch. Closed 3 weeks in Jan.

Iron Door Grill. American/Casual. If you're coming into Yosemite via Route 120, you'll pass by the Iron Door, one of the oldest operating saloons in California. Stop in for a drink, then head next door to the grill, which serves simple, straightforward American fare at lunch; at dinner, there are pastas, seafood, and sauté dishes, as well as grilled steaks. | 18751 Main St. (Rte. 120), Groveland | 209/962–6244 | $4–$7 lunch; $8–$19 dinner | MC, V.

The Mogul. Steak. This longtime steak house serves great prime rib, charbroiled shrimp, grilled beef, and fresh fish. There are no surprises here, just hearty, straightforward American food. Dinners come with soup or salad, and you won't leave hungry. There's also a kids' menu. | Mammoth Tavern Rd., off Old Mammoth Rd., Mammoth Lakes | 760/934–3039 | $12–$22 | AE, D, MC, V | No lunch.

Nevados. Contemporary. You can't go wrong at Nevados. The top choice of many locals, you'll find contemporary California cuisine that draws from European and Asian cooking. The menu presents imaginative—though accessible—preparations of seafood, duck, veal, beef, and game. Everything is made in-house, and there's an excellent three-course prix-fixe menu. The atmosphere is convivial and welcoming, and the bar is always bustling. | Main St. at Minaret Rd., Mammoth Lakes | 760/934–4466 | Reservations essential | $19–$26 | AE, D, DC, MC, V | Closed early June and late Oct.–early Nov. No lunch.

Nicely's. American. Pictures of local attractions decorate this eatery, which has been around since 1965. Try the blueberry pancakes and homemade sausages at breakfast. For lunch or dinner, try the chicken-fried steak or the fiesta salad. Kids' menu. | U.S. 395 and 4th St., Lee Vining | 760/647–6477 | $9–$15 | MC, V | Closed Wed. in winter.

Ocean Sierra Restaurant. Contemporary. Deep in the woods about 14 mi southeast of Mariposa, this comfortable spot serves seafood, meat, pasta, and vegetarian dishes. The owner-chef uses produce from her own garden, including the delicate crystallized rose petals that top desserts, among them five different flavors of crème brûlée. From Route 49 south, take Triangle Road 2.5 mi northeast. | 3292 E. Westfall Rd., Mariposa | 209/742–7050 | $19–$26 | D, MC, V | Closed Mon.–Thurs. No lunch.

Lodging

In Yosemite

Reserve your room or cabin in Yosemite as far in advance as possible. You can make a reservation up to a year before your arrival. The Ahwahnee, Yosemite Lodge, and Wawona Hotel are often sold out on weekends, holiday periods, and all days between May and September within minutes after the reservation office opens. All reservations for lodging in Yosemite are made through **Yosemite Concession Services Corporation.** | 5410 E. Home Ave., Fresno, CA | 559/252–4848 | fax 559/456–0542 | www.yosemitepark.com.

★ **Ahwahnee Hotel.** This *grande dame* of the National Park system, one of a handful of great lodges built in the 1920s, is all granite boulders and exposed timbers. The main common area has a pair of massive stone fireplaces, an irresistible place to settle into enormous chairs. Now a National Historic Landmark, the hotel is decorated with Native American rugs and baskets, and graced with views of Yosemite through towering windows. In the Ahwahnee's comfortable rooms you'll enjoy some of the amenities found in a luxury hotel, including turn-down service and guest bathrobes. Wine seminars and cooking demonstrations by celebrated chefs are held in winter. Restaurant, room service. In-room data ports, refrigerators. Tennis court. Pool. Bar. Shops. No a/c in some rooms. | Yosemite Valley, 0.75 mi east of the visitor center | 559/252–4848 (reservations); 209/372–1407 (front desk) | 123 rooms | $359 | AE, D, DC, MC, V.

Curry Village. This is a large community of cabins, tent cabins, and basic hotel rooms in a wooded area on the eastern end of Yosemite Valley, in the shadow of Glacier Point. The one-room cabins, spartan but adequately furnished, are less expensive than Yosemite's hotels, but not all have bathrooms. Tent cabins have wood frames and a roof and walls of canvas; they share central bath and shower facilities. Linen service is provided, but cooking is not allowed. Pool. Bicycles. Ice-skating. No a/c, no room phones. No room TVs. | Yosemite Valley | 559/252–4848 reservations; 209/372–8333 (front desk) | 19 rooms; 182 cabins, 102 with bath; 427 tent cabins | $59–$112 | AE, D, DC, MC, V.

Redwoods Guest Cottages. The only lodging in the park not operated by Yosemite Concession Services Corporation, this collection of private cabins and homes in the Wawona area is a great alternative to the overcrowded Valley. Fully furnished cabins range from small, romantic one-bedroom units to bright, resort-like, six-bedroom houses with decks overlooking the river. Most have fireplaces. The property rarely fills up, even in summer, so it's a good choice for last-minute lodging; there's a two-night minimum in the off-season and a three-night minimum in summer. In-room data ports, kitchenettes. In-room VCRs. Some pets allowed (fee). No a/c in some rooms. | 8038 Chilnualna Falls Rd., off Rte. 41, Wawona | 209/375–6666 | fax 209/375–6400 | www.redwoodsinyosemite.com | 120 units | $193–$583 | AE, D, MC, V.

Wawona Hotel. An old-fashioned Victorian estate of whitewashed buildings with wrap-around verandas, this circa-1879 National Historic Landmark is in the southern end of the national park, near the Mariposa Grove of Big Trees. Most rooms are small and do not have a private bath. The cozy Victorian parlor in the main hotel is pleasant and romantic, with a fireplace, board games, and a pianist who plays ragtime tunes most evenings. There's a 9-hole golf course adjacent to the property. Restaurant. 9-hole golf course, putting green, tennis court. Pool. Horseback riding. Bar. No a/c, no room phones. No room TVs. No smoking. | Rte. 41, Wawona | 559/252–4848 | 104 rooms (54 with shared bath) | $113–$168.

White Wolf Lodge. Set in the high country in a subalpine meadow, this tiny lodge offers rustic accommodations in tent cabins without baths or in cabins with baths. If you want to hike the backcountry, this is an excellent base camp. Restaurant. No a/c, no room phones. No room TVs. | Off Tioga Rd. (Rte. 120), 45 minutes west of Tuolumne Meadows | 24 tent cabins, 4 cabins | $59–$88 | Mid-June–early Sept.

Yosemite Lodge. This 1915 lodge in Yosemite Valley is so near Yosemite Falls that you can hear the water roar. Though it once housed the U.S. Army Cavalry, today it looks like a discrete 1950s motel-resort complex, with several satellite buildings painted brown and white to blend in with the landscape. Rooms have two double beds, while the larger "lodge rooms" also have dressing areas and balconies. Restaurant. In-room data ports. Pool. Bicycles. Bar. No a/c. No room TVs. No-smoking rooms. | Yosemite Valley, about 0.75 mi west of the visitor center | 239 rooms | $112–$143.

Near the Park

If you can't find a room at one of the lodgings listed here, you can turn to several agencies for assistance.

YOSEMITE
NATIONAL PARK

EXPLORING
ATTRACTIONS NEARBY
DINING
LODGING
CAMPING AND RV
FACILITIES
SHOPPING
ESSENTIAL
INFORMATION

Mariposa Visitors Center. The center has brochures filled with listings of hotels, motels, and bed-and-breakfasts in the county. | 209/966–2456 | www.homeofyosemite.com.

Tuolumne County Visitor Bureau. Brochures distributed by this office provide information on individual lodgings in the county. | 209/533–4420 or 800/446–1333 | www.thegreatunfenced.com.

Yosemite Sierra Visitors Bureau. The bureau prints a lodging guide for the region south of the national park, including Fish Camp and Oakhurst. | 559/683–4636 | www.go2yosemite.net.

Best Western Sonora Oaks. The standard-issue motel rooms at this East Sonora establishment are roomy with some outside sitting areas. Some rooms have fireplaces, whirlpool tubs, and hillside views. Because the motel is right on Route 108, the front rooms can be noisy. Restaurant. Pool. Hot tub. Bar. | 19551 Hess Ave., Sonora | 209/533–4400 or 800/532–1944 | fax 209/532–1964 | 96 rooms, 4 suites | $88–$96 | AE, D, DC, MC, V.

★ **Château du Sureau.** This romantic inn, adjacent to Erna's Elderberry House, is out of a children's book. From the moment you drive through the wrought-iron gates and up to the fairy-tale castle, you will be pampered. You'll fall asleep in the glow of a crackling fire amid goose-down pillows and a fluffy comforter. After a hearty full breakfast in the morning, relax in the piano room, which has an exquisite ceiling mural. Room TVs are available by request only. Restaurant, dining room. In-room data ports. Pool. No room TVs. No smoking. | 48688 Victoria La., Box 577, Oakhurst | 559/683–6860 | fax 559/683–0800 | www.chateausureau.com | 10 rooms, 1 villa | $350–$550 | AE, MC, V | BP.

Comfort Inn of Mariposa. This white three-story building with a broad veranda sits on a hill above Mariposa. Some of the comfortable rooms have sitting areas. It's about an hour from Yosemite's western gate on Route 140, but a good bet if other properties in the area are booked. Pool. Outdoor hot tub. | 4994 Bullion St., Mariposa | 209/966–4344 or 800/321–5261 | www.comfortinn.com | fax 209/966–4655 | 59 rooms, 2 suites | $80–$90 | AE, D, DC, MC, V | CP.

The Homestead. Five cottages on 160 secluded acres of land sit just south of Yosemite in Ahwahnee. Quiet and peaceful, each is very comfortably furnished, with fireplaces and full kitchens. One of the cottages is wheelchair accessible. The Homestead is about 3 mi west of Oakhurst and 15 mi south of the park. Kitchens. Cable TV. No room phones. | 41110 Rd. 600, Ahwahnee | 559/683–0495 | fax 559/683–8165 | www.homesteadcottages.com | 5 cottages | $134–$194 | AE, D, MC, V | CP.

Lavender Hill. This 1900 Victorian house has views of downtown from the porch swings on the wraparound veranda. There's also a peaceful garden. The rooms are sunny and filled with period antiques. The gourmet country breakfast often includes fresh fruit from the property. Library. No room phones. No room TVs. No smoking. | 683 Barretta St., Sonora | 209/532–9024 or 800/446–1333 Ext. 290 | www.lavenderhill.com | 4 rooms | $95–$125 | AE, D, MC, V | BP.

Little Valley Inn. Pine paneling, historical photos, and old mining tools recall Mariposa's heritage at this modern B&B with three comfortable guest bungalows. All rooms have private entrances, baths, and decks. One suite sleeps five people and includes a kitchen. Refrigerators. Cable TV. No room phones. | 3483 Brooks Rd., off Rte. 49, Mariposa | 209/742–6204 or 800/889–5444 | fax 209/742–5099 | www.littlevalley.com | 4 rooms, 1 suite, 1 cabin | $104–$130 | MC, V | CP.

Snowcreek Resort. In a valley surrounded by mountain peaks, this 355-acre modern condominium community on the outskirts of Mammoth Lakes contains one- to four-bedroom units. All have kitchens, living and dining rooms, and fireplaces; some have washers and dryers. You are welcome to free use of the well-supplied athletic club. Kitchens. Cable TV.

9-hole golf course, 9 tennis courts. 2 pools. Health club, hot tub, sauna. Racquetball. No a/c. No smoking. | 1254 Old Mammoth Rd., Mammoth Lakes | 760/934–3333 or 800/544–6007 | fax 760/934–1619 | www.snowcreek.com | 180 condos | $145–$480 | AE, D, MC, V.

Swiss Chalet. One of the most reasonably priced motels in town, the Swiss Chalet has great views of the mountains and simple comfortable rooms. There's a fish-cleaning area and a freezer to keep your summer catch fresh. Kitchenettes. Cable TV. Hot tub, sauna. Some pets allowed (fee). No a/c. No smoking. | 3776 Viewpoint Rd., Mammoth Lakes | 760/934–2403 or 800/937–9477 | fax 760/934–2403 | www.mammoth-swisschalet.com | 21 rooms | $65–$95 | AE, D, MC, V.

★**Tamarack Lodge Resort.** Tucked away on the edge of the John Muir Wilderness Area, this original 1924 log lodge has the most rustic and charming of all accommodations in the Mammoth Lakes area. Rooms in the main lodge can be fairly spartan, and some share a bathroom. If you prefer more privacy, you can opt for one of the cabins, which range from simple to luxurious and come in a variety of sizes. The main building is surrounded by quiet woods, and cross-country ski trails loop past the cabins. In warm months fishing, canoeing, hiking, and mountain biking are close by. The cozy cabins are modern, neat, and clean, with knotty-pine kitchens and private baths; some have fireplaces or wood-burning stoves. The romantic Lakefront Restaurant serves outstanding contemporary French-inspired cuisine, with an emphasis on game. Restaurant. Some kitchenettes. Cross-country skiing. No a/c. No room TVs. No smoking. | Lake Mary Rd., off Rte. 203, Mammoth Lakes | 760/934–2442 or 800/237–6879 | fax 760/934–2281 | www.tamaracklodge.com | 11 rooms, 25 cabins | $84–$350 | AE, MC, V.

Tenaya Lodge. One of the region's largest hotels, the Tenaya Lodge is for people who enjoy wilderness treks by day but prefer lots of comfort at night. The deluxe rooms have mini-bars and other extras, and the suites have balconies. Fish Camp is 4 mi south of Yosemite's south entrance. 2 restaurants, room service. In-room data ports, some minibars. Cable TV with movies and video games. Pool, indoor pool. Health club, hot tub. Hiking. Bicycles. Cross-country skiing. Bar. Baby-sitting, children's programs (ages 5–12), playground. Laundry service. Business services. No smoking. | 1122 Rte. 41, Fish Camp | 559/683–6555 or 888/514–2167 | fax 559/683–0249 | www.tenayalodge.com | 244 rooms, 6 suites | $215–$309 | AE, D, DC, MC, V.

Tioga Lodge. Just 2.5 mi north of Yosemite's eastern gateway, this 19th-century building has been by turns a store, a saloon, a tollbooth, and a boarding house. Now restored and expanded, it's a popular lodge that's close to local ski areas and fishing spots. Ask about the summer boat tours of Mono Lake. Restaurant. No a/c, no room phones. No room TVs. No smoking. | U.S. 395, Lee Vining | 760/647–6423 or 888/647–6423 | fax 760/647–6074 | www.tiogalodge.com | 13 rooms | $95–$105 | AE, D, MC, V | Closed Nov.–Mar.

Camping and RV Facilities

In Yosemite

There are lots of camping sites in Yosemite (nearly 2,000 in summer, 400 year-round), and though none of them have RV hookups, they fill up quickly, especially in the Valley. Reservations are required at most of Yosemite's campgrounds, especially in summer. You can reserve a site up to five months in advance; bookings made more than 21 days in advance require pre-payment. Unless otherwise noted, book your site through the central NPS reservations office. **National Park Reservation Service** | Box 1600, Cumberland, MD 21502 | 800/436–7275 | http://reservations.nps.gov | D, MC, V | Daily 7–7.

Bridalveil Creek Campground. This wooded spot on Glacier Point Road above the Valley Set is at an elevation of 7,200 ft. You can hike to Glacier Point's magnificent Valley views.

YOSEMITE
NATIONAL PARK

EXPLORING
ATTRACTIONS NEARBY
DINING
LODGING
CAMPING AND RV
FACILITIES
SHOPPING
ESSENTIAL
INFORMATION

Flush toilets. Drinking water. Bear boxes, grills, picnic tables. Public telephone. | 74 sites | Glacier Point Rd. off Rte. 41 | $12 | June–Sept.

Camp 4. Formerly known as Sunnyside Walk-In, this is the only Valley campground available on a first-come, first-served basis and the only one west of Yosemite Lodge. It is a favorite for rock climbers and solo campers, so it fills quickly and is typically sold out by 9 AM every day spring through fall. Flush toilets. Drinking water, showers (nearby). Bear boxes, fire grates, picnic tables. Public telephone. Ranger station. | 35 sites | Off Northside Dr. | $5.

Crane Flat Campground. On the western boundary, south of Hodgdon Meadow, the camp is 17 mi from the Valley but far from the Valley's bustle. A small grove of sequoias is nearby. Flush toilets. Drinking water. Bear boxes, fire pits, picnic tables. General store, ranger station. | 166 sites | Rte. 120, 10 mi east of the Big Oak Flat entrance | $18 | Reservations essential | June–Oct.

Hodgdon Meadow Campground. This campground is in an isolated spot at the park's western boundary. Reservations are required May through September. Flush toilets. Drinking water. Bear boxes, grills, picnic tables. Ranger station. | Rte. 120, at the Big Oak Flat entrance | 105 sites | $18.

Housekeeping Camp. These rustic three-wall cabins with canvas roofs, set on a beach along the Merced River, are difficult to come by; reserving a year in advance is advised. They are not the prettiest sites in the valley, but they're good for travelers with RVs or those without a tent who want to camp. You can cook on gas stoves rented from the front desk. Toilets and showers are in a central building, and there's a camp store for provisions. Flush toilets. Drinking water, guest laundry, showers. Bear boxes, fire pits, grills, picnic tables. Electricity. General store. Swimming (river). | 226 units | Southside Dr., 0.5 mi west of Curry Village | 559/252–4848 | www.yosemitepark.com | $58 | AE, D, MC, V | Reservations essential | May–Oct.

Lower Pines Campground. This campground on the Merced River is a short walk away from the Mirror Lake and Mist trails. Flush toilets. Drinking water. Bear boxes, fire grates, picnic tables. Public telephone. Ranger station. Swimming (river). | 60 sites | East Yosemite Valley | $18 | Reservations essential | Apr.–Oct.

North Pines Campground. It's on the Merced River, near plenty of trailheads. Like other campgrounds in the Valley, sites are close together and there is little privacy. Flush toilets. Drinking water, showers. Bear boxes, fire grates, picnic tables. Public telephone. Ranger station. Swimming (river). | 80 sites | East Yosemite Valley | $18 | Reservations essential.

Porcupine Flat Campground. In the high country, 16 mi west of Tuolumne Meadows, this campground is at 8,100 ft. If Tuolumne Meadows is full, this is a good bet. There is no water. Pit toilets. Fire grates, bear boxes, picnic tables. | 52 sites | Tioga Rd. (Rte. 120), 16 mi west of Tuolumne Meadows | $8 | Reservations not accepted | June–Sept.

Tamarack Flat Campground. In an isolated, forested area at 6,300 ft, this primitive campground has no water and accommodates only small RVs. From the Big Oak Flat entrance station, take Route 120 for 3 mi down a winding access road. Pit toilets. Bear boxes, fire grates, picnic tables. | 52 sites | Off Rte. 120 | $8 | Reservations not accepted | June–Sept.

★**Tuolumne Meadows Campground.** This large, high-country campground affords easy access to high peaks with spectacular views. You can use the hot showers at the Tuolumne Meadows Lodge at certain times of the day. Half the sites are first-come, first-serve, but arrive very early if you hope to get one. The beautiful scenery makes this one of the most sought-after campgrounds in Yosemite. Flush toilets. Dump station. Drinking water. Bear boxes, fire grates, picnic tables. Public telephone. General store, ranger station. | 304 sites | Tioga Rd. (Rte. 120), 46 mi east of the Big Oak Flat entrance station | $18 | June–Sept.

Upper Pines Campground. This is the Valley's largest campground. Like the others at this end of the Valley, it's near the river. Flush toilets. Dump station. Drinking water, showers.

YOSEMITE CAMPGROUNDS

	Total # of sites	# of RV sites	# of hook-ups	Drive-to sites	Hike-to sites	Flush toilets	Pit toilets	Drinking water	Showers	Fire grates/pits	Swimming	Boat access	Playground	Dump station	Ranger station	Public telephone	Reservation possible	Daily fee per site	Dates open
INSIDE THE PARK																			
Bridalveil Creek	74	74	0	•		•		•		•					•	•	•	$12	Jun.–Sep.
Camp 4	35	0	0	•	•	•		•		•					•	•		$5	Y/R
Crane Flat	166	166	0	•		•		•		•						•	•	$18	Apr.–Oct.
Housekeeping Camp	226	0	0	•		•		•	•	•	•						•	$58	May–Oct.
Lower Pines	60	60	0	•		•		•		•					•	•	•	$18	Apr.–Oct.
North Pines	80	80	0	•		•				•					•	•	•	$18	Y/R
Tuolumne Meadows	314	314	0	•		•		•	•	•				•	•	•	•	$18	Jun.–Sep.
Upper Pines	238	238	0	•		•		•		•	•			•	•	•	•	$18	Y/R
Wawona	93	93	0	•		•		•		•				•	•	•	•	$18	Y/R
White Wolf	87	87	0	•		•		•		•						•		$12	Jun.–Sep.
NEAR THE PARK																			
Dimond O	38	38	0	•			•	•		•							•	$14	Apr.–Oct.
Ellery Lake	12	12	0	•			•	•		•								$15	Jun.–Sep.
Minaret Falls	27	27	0	•			•	•		•								$15	Jun.–Sep.
Summerdale	39	39	0	•			•	•		•	•							$16	May–Sep.

* In summer only
UL=Unlimited
** Reservation fee charged
ULP=Unlimited primitive
Y/R=Year-round
LD=Labor Day MD=Memorial Day

Bear boxes, fire grates, picnic tables. Public telephone. Ranger station. Swimming (river). | 238 sites | East Yosemite Valley | $18 | Reservations essential.

Wawona Campground. Near the Mariposa Grove, sites here are less closely packed than those in the Valley, but it's an hour's drive to the Valley's major attractions. Reservations are essential May through September. Flush toilets. Drinking water. Bear boxes, fire grates, picnic tables. Ranger station. Swimming (river). | 93 sites | Rte. 41, 1 mi north of Wawona | $18.

White Wolf Campground. Set in the beautiful high country at 8,000 ft, this is a prime spot for hikers. RVs up to 30 ft long are permitted. Flush toilets. Drinking water. Bear boxes, fire grates, picnic tables. Public telephone. Ranger station. | 75 sites | Tioga Rd. (Rte. 120), 15 mi east of the Big Oak Flat entrance | $12 | Reservations not accepted | June–Sept.

Yosemite Creek Campground. This secluded campground is a good starting point for spectacular hikes to the rim of the Valley and the top of Yosemite Falls. There's no water available. The dirt access road is not suitable for RVs. Pit toilets. Bear boxes, fire grates, picnic tables. Public telephone. | 40 sites | Off Tioga Rd. (Rte. 120), about 35 mi east of the Big Oak Flat entrance | $8 | Reservations not accepted | June–Sept.

Near the Park
Dimond O Campground. Set at 4,400 ft, the camp is 2 mi from Yosemite's western border, the closest to the park. When the park's campgrounds are sold out and you want to be within an hour's drive of the Valley, this is a good bet. From Route 120, take Evergreen Road (2 mi west of the Big Oak Flat entrance station) north and continue 6 mi. Pit toilets. Drinking water. Bear boxes, grills, picnic tables. | 38 sites for tents or RVs. | Evergreen Rd. | 209/962–7825 (information), 877/444–6777 (reservations) | www.reserveusa.com | $14 | Reservations essential | No credit cards | Apr.–Oct.

Ellery Lake Campground. High in the Inyo National Forest at 9,600 ft, you'll find fishing and camping near a high country lake. There are several other campgrounds in the immediate vicinity if this one is full. Flush toilets. Drinking water. Bear boxes, grills, picnic tables. | 12 sites | Off Rte. 120, 4 mi before Yosemite's Tioga Pass entrance | 760/873–2408 or 760/647–3044 | $11 | Reservations not accepted | No credit cards | June–Oct.

Minaret Falls Campground. At 7,700 ft, this is one of several campgrounds near Devils Postpile National Monument. It's close to many trails in the high country above Mammoth Lakes, including the Pacific Crest Trail. Pit toilets. Drinking water. Bear boxes, grills, picnic tables. | 27 sites | Off Minaret Rd. (Rte. 203), 6 mi past the Devils Postpile entrance, Mammoth Lakes | 760/924–5500 | $15 per night, plus additional one-time road access fee ($7–$20) | Reservations not accepted | No credit cards | June–Sept.

Summerdale Campground. A fine alternative when Yosemite's campgrounds near Wawona are full, this camp is set at 5,800 ft just outside Yosemite's south gate. Pit toilets. Drinking water. Bear boxes, grills, picnic tables. Swimming (river). | 39 sites | Off Rte. 41, 1 mi past Fish Camp | 559/877–2218 | $16 | Reservations not accepted | No credit cards | May–Sept.

Tioga Lake Campground. When campgrounds at Tuolumne Meadows are full, this is a great backup. Like adjacent Ellery Lake, this is a camp in the high country at 9,600 ft. Take a left off Route 120 1 mi before the park entrance. Pit toilets. Drinking water. Grills, picnic tables. | 13 sites | Rte. 120, before the Tioga Pass entrance | 760/873–2408 or 760/647–3044 | $11 | Reservations not accepted | No credit cards | June–Sept.

Shopping
The Ahwahnee Gift Shop. Featuring signature Ahwahnee china, jewelry, and Native American Crafts, this is the only gift shop in the hotel. | Ahwahnee Hotel | 209/372–1409 | AE, D, DC, MC, V.

Ansel Adams Gallery. At the Valley's most elegant gift shop, you'll find original prints, Native American crafts, photography supplies, and camera rentals. | Yosemite Village | 209/372–4413 or 800/568–7398 | AE, D, MC, V.

Art Activity Center. Satisfy your artistic needs at the only art supply store in the Valley. | Yosemite Village | 209/372–1442 | AE, D, DC, MC, V | Closed Nov.–Mar.

Crane Flat Store. This small store is easily overlooked, but if you're coming in from the west on Route 120, it's a convenient spot to get gas and pick up snacks and camping supplies. | Rte. 120 | 209/379–2742 | AE, D, DC, MC, V.

Tuolumne Meadows Store and Mountain Shop. The Tuolumne store is the only spot in the high country where you can buy backpacking and camping supplies and food. | Rte. 120 | 209/372–8428 | AE, D, DC, MC, V | Closed Nov.–May.

Village Sport Shop. Open all year, this shop carries an extensive selection of outdoor gear, including fishing and camping supplies. | Yosemite Village | 209/372–1286 | AE, D, DC, MC, V.

Village Store. This is the Valley's largest grocery store, with a gift shop in the front. | Yosemite Village | 209/372–1253 | AE, D, DC, MC, V.

Wawona Grocery Store and Gift Shop. This is the Wawona area's only market; it carries essential supplies, ice cream, snacks, gifts, reproduction handicrafts, and books. | Rte. 41 | 209/375–6574 | AE, D, MC, V.

Yosemite Bookstore. An extensive selection of maps and books is available at this store in the Valley visitor center. | Yosemite Village | 209/372–0299 | AE, D, DC, MC, V.

Yosemite Lodge Nature Shop. Here you'll find sculpture, music, videos, and apparel. | Yosemite Village | 209/372–1438 | AE, D, DC, MC, V.

Yosemite Museum Book Shop. In addition to books, the museum shop sells traditional Native American arts and crafts. | Yosemite Village | 209/372–0295 | AE, D, MC, V.

YOSEMITE
NATIONAL PARK

EXPLORING
ATTRACTIONS NEARBY
DINING
LODGING
CAMPING AND RV
FACILITIES
SHOPPING
**ESSENTIAL
INFORMATION**

Essential Information

ATMS (24-HOUR): There are ATMs in the Village Store, the Curry Village Store, and Yosemite Lodge.

AUTOMOBILE SERVICE STATIONS: There are gas stations at Crane Flat, Tuolumne Meadows, and Wawona. There's one **full service garage** in Yosemite Village, but no gas is available there. | Yosemite Village | 209/372–8390.

POST OFFICES: Curry Village Post Office | Curry Village, 95389 | 209/372–4475 | Closed Labor Day–Memorial Day. **El Portal Post Office** | 5508 Foresta Rd., El Portal, 95318 | 209/379–2311. **Main Post Office** | Yosemite Village, 95389 | 209/372–4475. **Wawona Post Office** | Rte. 41, Wawona, 95389 | 209/375–6574. **Yosemite Lodge Post Office** | 95389 | 209/372–4853.

FIELD GUIDE: CALIFORNIA

Ecological Communities

Alpine meadows. Above the tree line (10,000–11,000 ft) of the Sierra, these meadows are fragile landscapes. At this elevation plant growth is limited by little available soil, frigid temperatures, and scarce water. Because of the deep snowpack and severe climate, the growing season is short and the ecosystem less diverse. Wildflowers make the most of the brief summers—snowplants, lupine, buttercups, aster, and goldenrod burst into color, providing a feast for hummingbirds, while shorthair grasses feed deer and bighorn sheep. The marmot, pike, porcupine, and Yosemite toad also populate alpine meadows.

Deserts. In the Great Basin, beyond the craggy, saw-toothed eastern slope of the Sierra Nevada, little rain falls. The deserts in this area, including the Mojave and Death Valley, support only highly adapted species, such as the desert tortoise, jack rabbit, and tarantula. The animals are mostly nocturnal, and plants have unusually wide or deep root systems—some as long as 60 ft—to help them gather the maximum amount of moisture available in the arid landscape.

Forests. California's climate supports evergreen, mixed-conifer, and deciduous forests. Cool, wet ocean air nurtures redwoods along the coast from Monterey to the Oregon border. Abundant water on the western slope of the Sierra supports montane forests of many tree and plant species, including the white fir, sugar pine, incense cedar, and giant sequoia. Because of its dry air, the eastern Sierra has only sparse forests. The coastal forests support the river otter, beaver, black bear, salmon, and trout; the montane forests of the western and eastern slopes of the Sierra support the black bear, badger, bighorn sheep, gray fox, and coyote. Salamanders, frogs, chipmunks, squirrels, deer, hawks, and eagles live throughout the region.

Foothills woodland and chaparral. On the western slope of the Sierra, between 500 and 5,000 ft, grasslands dotted with oak and thick scrubby chaparral forests, with drought-resistant plants 3–8 ft tall, thrive in the warm climate. Manzanita berries and acorns feed bears, deer, rodents, and birds. Development and grazing by livestock are encroaching on these lands, threatening an important part of the ecosystem.

Marine. The Pacific Ocean, unlike the Atlantic, has a high phosphorous content, making it rich with sea life. It's not uncommon to sight whales migrating off the coast and dolphins playing around the bows of moving boats. At low tide along the coast and on the Channel Islands, creatures that cling to the rocky shoreline—sea urchins, hermit crabs, sea stars, anemones, and the like—appear briefly above the waterline in tide pools. To see them, wear rubber-soled, closed-toe shoes or waders, and tread as lightly as possible while you explore.

Montane meadows. Lower in elevation than alpine meadows, these landscapes of dense sedge, perennial herbs, and, in summer, wildflowers, are found amid the mixed conifer forests of the High Sierra. Because of their comparatively longer growing season, they tend to be more diverse and productive than alpine meadows, but just as fragile.

Perennial grasslands. Much of California's Central Valley and the low-elevation land west of the foothills chaparal zone was grassland before extensive development took place. As you drive through remote, unfarmed areas of the valley, look for the hills of remaining golden grass for which the Golden State is named. Oak groves dot the landscape; insects, reptiles, and small mammals forage through the grass; and woodpeckers, sparrows, jays, and sapsuckers fly overhead.

Riparian. West of the Sierra, stands of willow, alder, and cottonwood grow along the borders of streams and lakes. California's richest terrestrial habitats for breeding and wintering land-birds, these riparian zones have been overrun by development at a faster rate than any other habitat, with the possible exception of perennial grasslands. Only 5–10% of the original riparian habitat of California exists today, and much of what remains continues to be developed. These habitats support more endangered land-bird species than any other type in the state, and of the 36 species that rely heavily upon them, 21 have seen substantial population decline and are either legally protected by the state or federal governments, or appear on species-of-concern lists. Some restoration efforts are being made along the Sacramento River and elsewhere in the state.

Sequoia Zone. Between 5,000 and 7,000 ft on the western slope of the Sierra south of Lake Tahoe, the giant sequoia thrives in about 75 groves. Dependent on moisture-laden air from the Pacific, the sequoias are part of the larger mixed-conifer forest.

Fauna

BIRDS

Acorn woodpecker. Look in the Sierra foothills for this bird's red head, white face and belly, and black wings. It forages primarily in the canopy of pine and oak woodlands, but it will occasionally drop to the ground to pick up fallen acorns.

Brown pelican. On the Channel Islands, look for this rare bird standing on its eggs to incubate them. In flight, the huge dark bird soars high above the water and plunges from great heights to catch fish.

Golden eagle. Similar in appearance to a turkey vulture, this eagle is recognizable by its golden-brown body, feathered head, pale flight feathers, and the white patches at the tips of its tail. The wings, when fully extended, span 6 ft. The eagle soars mostly over rugged terrain, where updrafts are strong.

Great horned owl. This owl gets its name from the tufts of feathers on its head, which look like horns. Its plumage may be brown, red, or white. Highly adaptable, the owl can roost in areas of dense foliage, on cliff ledges, or in the abandoned nests of other birds.

Peregrine falcon. Although it was removed from the endangered species list in 1999, the peregrine falcon remains very rare. Its plumage is grey, the head is capped with black, the underwings are barred black and white, and the tail is long and thin with gray and white bands. The peregrine falcon feeds mostly on other birds, sometimes diving from great heights to hit prey in mid-air.

Steller's jay. This bird's mostly blue plumage yields to streaks of black by the tail. Look for this loud and aggressive creature perched on tree branches in the mountains, waiting for an opportunity to swoop down for stray morsels of food. If you picnic, you may spot one watching you.

Turkey vulture. Often mistaken for a hawk due to its broad wingspan, the vulture soars high above grasslands looking for rodents. The head is red and featherless, the body and wings are dark gray, and in flight, the wingtips appear white.

Western tanager. The tanager lives mostly in the Sierra and on California's north coast in summer, migrating to Central America in winter. The male has a distinctive red face, yellow belly, and black wings with white bars; the female has a yellow face and is often mistaken for an oriole, but she can be distinguished by her white wing bars.

FISH

Salmon. The Pacific salmon is a strong, silvery fish that can jump over 6 ft into the air on its journey upriver to spawn. The damming of many California rivers has blocked large numbers of salmon from spawning upstream in their birthplaces, but restoration efforts are underway, including the partial destruction of some of the state's dams.

Trout. Look for trout in cold waters, particularly in the Sierra Nevada. The Department of Fish and Game regularly stocks lakes and rivers to keep up with the demands of fishermen.

INSECTS

Monarch butterfly. Bright orange wings with black lines and two rows of spots mark this common butterfly. The monarch flies farther than any other moth or butterfly in the world, and always makes a return trip. From November through March, large numbers of monarchs cluster along the central and north coasts, as well as on the Channel Islands. The greatest numbers can be found in the town of Pacific Grove and south of San Luis Obispo in Montaña de Oro State Park and Pismo State Beach.

Ticks. The tiny, brown arachnid can be as small as the head of a pin and as large as 1.5 inches. Though only a small percentage carry Lyme disease, watch out for ticks in the grasslands of the Sierra foothills. After hiking, check all areas of exposed skin. If you find a tick stuck to you, remove it entirely with tweezers. Don't leave any portion of the body or legs embedded in your skin.

MAMMALS

Bighorn sheep. Famous for its huge, spiraling horns, which it uses to compete for mating rights, the bighorn ram weighs 150–300 lbs. The ewe grows straight horns up to 10 inches long and weighs 100–200 lbs. The wool of this sheep ranges in coloring from dark brown to buff to white. Bighorns native to the eastern California mountains faced near-extinction after the introduction of domestic sheep brought disease and competition for food. Since the 1970s, efforts to restore its habitat have fostered the growth of the species, and though they are rarely seen by humans, you might find one grazing in the eastern section of Yosemite or in Owens Valley, east of Sequoia and Kings Canyon. Listen for the rams butting their horns in fall. The crashing sound can be heard up to a half mile away.

Black bear. The grizzly has been extinct in California since 1922, but the black bear continues to thrive. Its colors range from light brown to black. An omnivore, the bear is an opportunistic feeder, so make every effort to keep human food away from it. Quickly habituated to human food and to the presence of people, the bear can become aggressive and destructive. Information on safe food storage is available at all parks, and it should be followed diligently.

Coyote. The coyote roams most of the mountain and desert areas of California, preying primarily on deer. It's smaller than a wolf and not very afraid of humans. You'll hear it howl at night in desolate areas.

Deer. The mule deer, the most common in the western United States, has long ears and is larger than the white-tailed deer. You'll see both species throughout the mountains.

Fox. The gray fox, common throughout California, has coarse gray fur and white underparts. The Channel Islands gray fox, a relative of the mainland gray, is about the size of a housecat and is found nowhere else. Both species feed on insects, fruit, grains, and small rodents.

Marmot. Resembling a woodchuck, the marmot is a 1.5- to 2-ft-long, furry, burrowing rodent that feeds mostly on plants. It has a stout body, short legs, and, in the Sierra, a yellow belly.

Mountain lion. Also called a cougar, and once common throughout much of the state, the mountain lion remains important for its role in keeping the deer population in check. Although deer is its primary food source, the mountain lion also eats rodents and other small mammals and birds. Born with a spotted coat, the lion matures into an adult of a solid tan color with white underparts. The male grows up to 8 ft, including the tail, and 190 lbs. If you encounter one, do not crouch down or run. Give the animal an escape route and make yourself appear as tall as possible. Lift small children off the ground. If the animal is aggressive, shout, wave your arms, throw stones, and fight back if attacked.

Seals and sea lions. In the Channel Islands, huge numbers and several species of sea lion congregate on the shore. The sea lion has small ear flaps and long front flippers. The seal, also present on the islands, has thicker fur and a smaller body than the sea lion. Sea lions also congregate by the hundreds off San Francisco's Pier 39. Seals and sea lions eat fish, squid, and even birds.

Whale. Several species of whale, notably the gray whale, migrate along the California coast in fall and winter. Born almost black, the gray whale turns gray with white splotches in adulthood, when it can grow up to 50 ft long. It has no dorsal fin and is prey to the killer whale, which you might spot around the Channel Islands. The humpback, which is black with a black-and-white underside, is up to 40 ft long, while the blue whale, which is blue-gray with a yellow underside caused by clinging microorganisms, is up to 80 ft long. Both can be spotted off the California coast in summer.

REPTILES

Desert banded gecko. This nocturnal gecko is pale-yellow or light-gray with reddish-brown spots and bands along the length of its body. You might spot one below 3,500 ft in Death Valley in springtime.

Desert tortoise. You might see California's state reptile moving slowly across the deserts east of the Sierra. Look for the sandy brown pentagons that make up its hard, domed shell. Check for it in the shade under your car when leaving the desert.

Rattlesnake. Watch where you walk as you hike around the foothills. The rattlesnake only bites when it is teased or handled; stay away from it. It will give you ample warning of its presence by rattling its tail. The snake's colorings are brown, gray, or green with lighter spots on its topside, and it grows 3–4 ft long. For food, the rattlesnake kills lizards, rabbits, mice, squirrels, and other small animals by biting its prey and injecting venom through its fangs. The snake is protected in the national parks.

Zebra-tailed lizard. One of the fastest lizards in the desert, the zebra-tailed lizard has gray-and-black horizontal stripes on its tail, which it sometimes curls over its back and waves from side-to-side.

Flora

AQUATIC PLANTS

Eelgrass. A relative of terrestrial grasses, slender, green eelgrass grows up to 12 inches tall in salt water and is one of the few flowering plants in the ocean. In estuaries and the sea, it provides breeding area and habitat for crabs, fish, snails, and many other animals.

Kelp. Giant forests of waving, slimy, green kelp grow beneath the Pacific Ocean's surface, providing food and shelter to thousands of plants and sea animals. In spring, the unfurling plant can grow as much as 18 inches per day, and in winter, strong waves yank it from the rocks, littering the beach with its huge stalks.

SUCCULENTS

Barrel cactus. Standing 4–8 ft at maturity, this cylindrical cactus with well-defined vertical ribs is one of the largest in North America. Its heavy spines are bright-red or yellow in color and hide the trunk of the plant, where large quantities of water are stored. In spring the cactus produces flowers on the top of its barrel. Look for this cactus in desert washes and under canyon walls in the Mojave Desert.

Buckhorn cholla. Widely distributed in the Mojave Desert, this cactus stands 3–15 ft. Like a dense bush, its many branches are covered with sharp, gray or purplish spines that overlap in different directions. Unlike the barrel cactus, the spines are not sheathed and do not hide the trunks of the plant.

FLOWERS

California poppy. The California state flower grows ubiquitously from the coast to the Sierra foothills. The flowers are bright orange and range in height from a few inches to a foot tall. Picking one could earn you a fine of $100.

Chamise. The most abundant wildflower in the Sierra foothills has whitish-yellow blooms that grow along the ends of long stalks that, in turn, fan out from the plant's main stem.

Coreopsis. Commonly called the tree sunflower, these big bushes of yellow flowers found on the Channel Islands are so bright and numerous that they are sometimes visible from the mainland. You can also find them along the coastline.

GRASSES AND GROUND COVER

Ice plant. Though found all along the Pacific coast, ice plant is native to South Africa and was imported to stabilize sandy banks and dunes. Also called sea fig, its fleshy leaves grow low to the ground and yield purple flowers. Though an attractive plant, it competes with native species that depend on dune movement for survival. If its growth is left unchecked the ice plant can quickly cover entire beaches.

Purple needlegrass. In grasslands and in the Sierra foothills chaparal zones, particularly on the western slope, needlegrass grows in bunches up to 2 ft tall and has a slightly purple hue. Because its roots extend downward as much as 20 ft, it is highly drought-resistant.

SHRUBS

Manzanita. You can spot this shrub, with its distinct red-brown branches and smooth bark, throughout central and northern California on open, dry, sunny sites that extend to the edges of oak and conifer forests. It most often stands 6–12 ft.

Sagebrush. Found in the deserts of the eastern Sierra and in the Great Basin, pungently fragrant sagebrush has a woody stem and thin, small silver-green leaves. Native Americans burned it in ceremonies to purify the heart and spirit.

TREES

Aspen. Known for its smooth greenish-white bark and vibrantly colored fall foliage, aspens grow in groves in moist, high-elevation habitats in the Sierra. The largest stands in California are near Monitor Pass, off Route 89 above its intersection with U.S. 395.

Dogwood. Common in Yosemite, Sequoia, and Kings Canyon national parks around 3,000–4,000 ft, the dogwood blooms white flowers in spring. In autumn, the deep-green leaves turn pink, then white before falling off the tree.

Oak. Fourteen varieties of oak tree grow in California, the most common of which is the canyon live oak. All of them are hardwood and acorn-bearing. Some, like the black oak, are deciduous, while the live oak varieties are evergreen. Look for oaks at elevations up to 6,000 ft.

Pines. Several common pines grow in the Sierra, with each species occurring only within specific elevation zones. In order, from lowest to highest, you'll find the ponderosa, sugar, Jeffrey, lodgepole, and foxtail pines; the last grows above 9,500 ft and has gnarled branches at the top of its short, stout trunk. In the upper elevations of the deserts, look for juniper, piñon, and bristlecone pines, the oldest living trees on the planet. On the Channel Islands, look for the rare torrey pine.

Redwood. These giant trees, the tallest in the world, can grow to 360 ft and live as long as 2,000 years. Once common along the entire North Coast, the tree has been devastated by human activity. Ninety-six percent of the old-growth stands have been logged, but you can still see old-growth forests in Muir Woods north of San Francisco, and Big Basin State Park north of Santa Cruz.

Sequoia. The world's largest living tree (in volume) and one of the fastest growing, the giant sequoia, grows up to 30 ft in diameter and 300 ft high. Sequoia groves are only on the western slope of the Sierra Nevada, generally at 5,000–7,000 ft.

Geology and Terrain

Alluvial fans. Cloudbursts in the desert cause water to rush down the faces of barren mountains and hills. Since it cannot be easily absorbed into the dry, packed soil, the water fans out into rivulets and streams, leaving behind indelible grooves. Look for these distinctive features in Death Valley and the Mojave Desert.

Canyons. As glaciers moved over and through parts of the Sierra 1–3 million years ago, they carved canyons in the land. The most obvious remnants of their movement, which left smooth, almost polished granite, can be seen in Yosemite Valley and Kings Canyon, the latter of which is at points deeper than even the Grand Canyon.

Caves. Numerous caves and caverns exist throughout the Sierra Nevada. Though they differ somewhat in their geology, they give you an opportunity to descend below the earth's surface and learn about the forces of heat and water upon rocks and minerals. Crystal Cave in Sequoia National park has excellent examples of stalactites and stalagmites.

Granite. The Sierra Nevada has been nicknamed the Range of Light for the reflection of the sun off granite. During the Mesozoic (about 240–65 million years ago) intense heat percolated upward from the earth's crust as the oceanic plate collided with the continental plate. The heat pushed igneous granite to the surface. Because of its high quartz content, it sparkles in bright light.

Hot Springs. Past the eastern escarpment of the Sierra, evidence of the region's volcanic history remains in the giant caldera of the high-mountain desert. Hot springs issue from the earth and form small- to medium-size pools in the ground, some of which are suitable for bathing. If you should stumble upon one, never jump in without first testing the water's temperature. The locals keep many of the springs secret, but in some places people have piped the hot waters into developed pools. While driving on U.S. 395, look for road signs pointing the way to numerous hot springs.

Lakes and reservoirs. In winter, parts of the Sierra receive some of the deepest snow-pack found anywhere on the North American continent. Most of the spring and summer run-off from the melting snows is caught in reservoirs in the foothills and routed to farmlands and cities throughout the state via a complex system of levees and aqueducts, which you'll no doubt see in the foothills and Central Valley. But much of the water remains in the mountains, forming lakes, most notably giant Lake Tahoe. The lakes are an essential part of the ecosystem, providing water for birds, fish, and plant life. Their appearance is a relatively new feature of the landscape, likely occurring 3–4 million years ago at the time of the formation of the Sierra crest.

Sierra Nevada. The Sierra Nevada mountain range is marked by a gentle rise on the west side and a sharp drop-off on the east side. The land east of the crest sank dramatically by several thousand feet some 3–4 million years ago, thus the eastern escarpment has no foothills. Moisture from the Pacific cools as the air rises up the mountains, eventually condensing and falling as rain or snow. So little water is left in the air by the time it crosses the range that the giant valleys and deserts to the east remain dry much of the year. Gaps in the crest, like Donner Pass on I–80 near Lake Tahoe, give evidence of large rivers that once flowed westward to the ocean. The Pacific Crest Trail, which travels from Mexico to Canada, follows the line of the Sierra crest.

Volcanoes. Until about 33 million years ago, the Sierra was a much lower mountain range, with peaks of only about 3,000 ft. When volcanic activity began, the bulk of it occurring 10–5 million years ago, the flow of lava thrust the mountains upward from below and spilled out over the surface, hardening into new top layers of rock. Evidence of the region's volcanic history is most visible in the area around Mount Lassen, where you can see recent manifestations of the geological forces of volcanism.

VACATION COUNTDOWN Your checklist for a perfect journey

Way Ahead

- ❏ Devise a trip budget.
- ❏ Write down the five things you want most from this trip. Keep this list handy before and during your trip.
- ❏ Book lodging and transportation.
- ❏ Arrange for pet care.
- ❏ Photocopy any important documentation (passport, driver's license, vehicle registration, and so on) you'll carry with you on your trip. Store the copies in a safe place at home.
- ❏ Review health and home-owners insurance policies to find out what they cover when you're away from home.

A Month Before

- ❏ Make restaurant reservations and buy theater and concert tickets. Visit fodors.com for links to local events and news.
- ❏ Familiarize yourself with the local language or lingo.
- ❏ Schedule a tune-up for your car.

Two Weeks Before

- ❏ Create your itinerary.
- ❏ Enjoy a book or movie set in your destination to get you in the mood.
- ❏ Prepare a packing list.
- ❏ Shop for missing essentials.
- ❏ Repair, launder, or dry-clean the clothes you will take with you.
- ❏ Replenish your supply of prescription drugs and contact lenses if necessary.

A Week Before

- ❏ Stop newspaper and mail deliveries.
- ❏ Pay bills.
- ❏ Stock up on film and batteries.
- ❏ Label your luggage.
- ❏ Finalize your packing list—always take less than you think you need.
- ❏ Pack a toiletries kit filled with travel-size essentials.
- ❏ Check tire treads.
- ❏ Write down your insurance agent's number and any other emergency numbers and take them with you.
- ❏ Get lots of sleep. You want to be well-rested and healthy for your impending trip.

A Day Before

- ❏ Collect passport, driver's license, insurance card, vehicle registration, and other documents.
- ❏ Check travel documents.
- ❏ Give a copy of your itinerary to a family member or friend.
- ❏ Check your car's fluids, lights, tire inflation, and wiper blades.
- ❏ Get packing!

During Your Trip

- ❏ Keep a journal/scrapbook as a personal souvenir.
- ❏ Spend time with locals.
- ❏ Take time to explore. Don't plan too much. Let yourself get lost and use your Fodor's guide to get back on track.

The Mountains and the Plains

Travel through America's heartland today, and it's easy to see why early proponents of the national park system were enamored of the natural beauty of America. They felt grandeur of the Rocky Mountains, the Dakota badlands, and the wide-open prairie matched the magnificence of the historic cathedrals and castles of Europe. Their legacy lives on in the parks of Colorado, Wyoming, Montana, and the Dakotas. You can sail across a vast sea of prairie land in the Great Plains, encounter an emerald oasis in the Black Hills, explore stark badlands in North and South Dakota, and greet rugged ridgelines and glacier-carved valleys in the fabled Rocky Mountains.

This is a land of almost too much sky—you can see farther than 100 mi from certain viewpoints. The mountains and the plains beckon you with irresistible hiking trails tough enough to keep your heart pumping fast, equally challenging climbs, plenty of cross-country skiing, snowshoeing, horseback riding, spelunking, wildlife viewing, fishing, and of course the unbeatable views. As you walk in the timeless footsteps of Native Americans, frontier explorers, trappers, traders, miners, muleskinners, and madams you'll gain a sense of the history that shaped the West, a history that continues to shape America today.

Rules of the Road

In spring and early summer thunderstorms may appear without warning, and they sometimes carry hail. In winter and late spring, snowstorms close many roads and highways. Be prepared for what each season offers and equip your vehicle accordingly. Winter survival kits should include snow tires or chains; a shovel; a window scraper; flares or a reflector; a blanket or sleeping bag; a first-aid kit; sand, gravel, or traction mats. At any time of year you should carry a flashlight with extra batteries; matches, a lighter, and candles; paper; nonperishable foods; a tow chain or rope; and plenty of water. Check on weather and road conditions before you travel.

In This Chapter

Badlands National Park • Glacier National Park • Grand Teton National Park • Rocky Mountain National Park • Theodore Roosevelt National Park • Wind Cave National Park • Yellowstone National Park

License Requirements: To drive in South Dakota, you must be at least 14 years old and have a valid United States, Canadian, or international driver's license. To drive in Colorado, Montana, North Dakota, and Wyoming, you must be at least 16 with a valid driver's license.

Right Turn on Red: In Colorado, Montana, North Dakota, South Dakota, and Wyoming, you may turn right at a red light after stopping, when the intersection is clear of both pedestrians and vehicles, unless otherwise posted.

Seatbelt and Helmet Laws: In Montana, drivers and passengers must wear seatbelts. In Colorado, the Dakotas, and Wyoming, all front-seat passengers under 18 years of age and all drivers must wear seatbelts. In all five states, children under age 5 must ride in a federally approved child safety seat. If they exceed 40 pounds, the child may be secured with a seatbelt. Motorcyclists 17 and under are required to wear a helmet in all five states. Eye protection is recommended for all motorcyclists, and is required in South Dakota.

Speed Limits: In Colorado, Montana, South Dakota, and Wyoming the speed limit is 75 mph on interstates, except as posted near metro areas; in North Dakota, the speed limit is 70 mph. Colorado state highways have a speed limit of 65–75 mph except in urban areas. The posted limit is 55–65 mph on state and secondary highways in South Dakota and Wyoming. In Montana, state highway limits are 70 mph during the day and 65 mph at night. In North Dakota, the state highway limit is 65 mph.

For More Information: Colorado Highway Patrol | 303/239–4500. **Montana Highway Patrol** | 406/444–3780. **North Dakota Department of Transportation** | 701/328–2500. **South Dakota Highway Patrol** | 605/773–3105. **Wyoming Department of Transportation** | 307/777–4484.

Dakota Badlands to the Rocky Peaks Driving Tour
FROM THEODORE ROOSEVELT TO ROCKY MOUNTAIN

Distance: 750–900 mi   Time: 7 days
Breaks: Overnight in Medora, ND; Deadwood, Rapid City, Custer, and Hot Springs, SD; and Estes Park, CO

This tour begins in North Dakota, but you can start in Colorado and work your way north, taking the tour backward. If you only have four days, skip either North Dakota or the Colorado–Wyoming segment. Avoid the tour at the height of winter, when heavy snowfall can make roads impassable.

① You'll enter North Dakota's badlands on I-94. You know you're there when the grassy plains you've been following forever give way to tall ridges of fire-colored rock. Take exit 32 and proceed to Painted Canyon scenic overlook for your first tremendous view of **Theodore Roosevelt National Park.** Spend your first day in the South Unit; if you have the time, Chateau de Mores State Historic Site is worth a stop. Overnight in the historic frontier town of **Medora.**

② On day two, head south on a 186-mi trek along U.S. 85 through vast plains, finally seeing the dark recesses of the Black Hills grow in your windshield. After a stop in **Spearfish,** one of South Dakota's most attractive communities, travel the **Spearfish Canyon National Scenic Byway,** which welcomes you with 1,000-ft-high limestone palisades that tower over U.S. 14A. As you wind through the 19-mi-long gorge, notice Spearfish Creek splashing along the canyon floor and the scent of Black Hills spruce in the air.

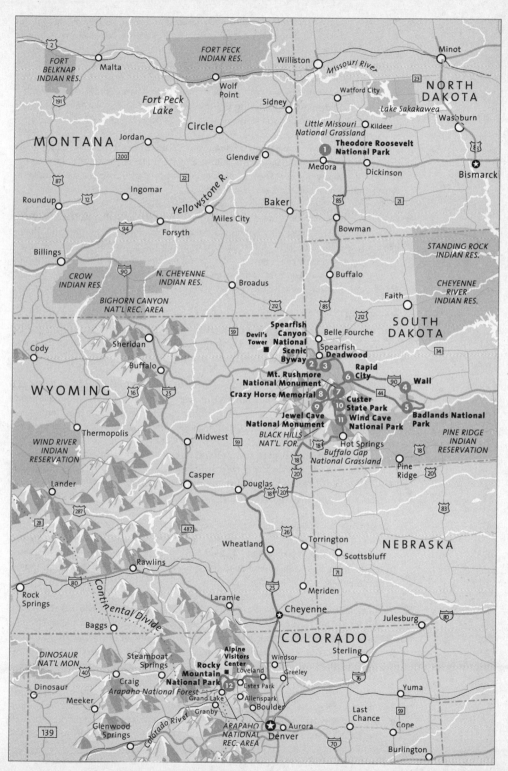

FORT
BELKNAP
INDIAN RES.

Malta

FORT PECK
INDIAN RES.

Williston

Missouri River

Minot

NORTH
DAKOTA

Watford City

Lake Sakakawea

Washburn

Wolf
Point

Sidney

Fort Peck
Lake

MONTANA

Jordan

Circle

Glendive

Little Missouri
National Grassland

Kildeer

Medora

**Theodore Roosevelt
National Park**

Dickinson

Bismarck

Roundup

Ingomar

Yellowstone R.

Miles City

Baker

Bowman

Billings

Forsyth

Broadus

CROW
INDIAN RES.

N. CHEYENNE
INDIAN RES.

BIGHORN CANYON
NAT'L REC. AREA

Buffalo

Faith

STANDING ROCK
INDIAN RES.

CHEYENNE
RIVER
INDIAN RES.

Belle Fourche

SOUTH
DAKOTA

Cody

Sheridan

Devil's
Tower

**Spearfish
Canyon
National
Scenic
Byway**

Spearfish
Deadwood

Buffalo

**Mt. Rushmore
National Monument**

Crazy Horse Memorial

Rapid
City

Wall

WYOMING

Thermopolis

WIND RIVER
INDIAN
RESERVATION

Lander

Midwest

BLACK HILLS
NAT'L. FOR.

**Jewel Cave
National Monument**

**Custer
State Park**
**Wind Cave
National Park**

Hot Springs

Buffalo Gap
National Grassland

**Badlands National
Park**

PINE RIDGE
INDIAN
RESERVATION

Pine
Ridge

Casper

Douglas

Rawlins

Rock
Springs

Baggs

DINOSAUR
NAT'L MON

Dinosaur

Meeker

Steamboat
Springs

Craig

Arapaho National Forest

Wheatland

Torrington

Scottsbluff

NEBRASKA

Meriden

Continental Divide

Laramie

Cheyenne

Julesburg

COLORADO

Sterling

**Alpine
Visitors
Center**

**Rocky
Mountain
National Park**

Windsor

Greeley

Loveland

Estes Park

Grand Lake
Granby

Allenspark

Boulder

Colorado River

**ARAPAHO
NATIONAL
REC. AREA**

Aurora

Denver

Last
Chance

Yuma

Cope

Glenwood
Springs

Burlington

❸ Eventually you'll reach the twin towns of **Deadwood** and **Lead,** where you can get out of the car and stretch your legs. Visit Deadwood's **Adams Memorial Museum** to see rare artifacts from the town's colorful past. The Old Style Saloon No. 10 bills itself as "the only museum in the world with a bar" and offers music, blackjack, poker, and slots. Upstairs, at the Deadwood Social Club, you'll discover outstanding food at reasonable prices and the best wine selection in the state. Check into one of Deadwood's 19th-century hotels, and spend the evening ducking into the doorways of the town's 80 gaming halls or dancing to live music at Saloon No. 10.

❹ In the morning, drive 12 mi east on U.S. 14A to I–90, then turn east and drive 84 mi to the town of **Wall,** home to **Wall Drug Store.** Founded on the premise that free ice water would attract road-weary travelers, the internationally known emporium carries all manner of Westernalia, and 6,000 pairs of cowboy boots.

❺ After a stop at Wall Drug Store, head south on Route 240 into **Badlands National Park,** a 380-square-mi geologic wonderland. Badlands Loop Road wiggles through this moon-like landscape for 32 mi. Don't forget to breathe deeply in this land of wonder. The park's air quality ranks with the cleanest spots in the nation. When you've had enough of barren landscapes and endless horizons, head for the hills. Either get back on I–90 or take scenic Route 44 from Cedar Pass northwest 55 mi to Rapid City, where you'll stay the night.

❻ **Rapid City** is western South Dakota's largest city and the gateway to the Black Hills. From here you can visit several national parks, memorials, and monuments on day trips. The city also has countless museums, shops, and fun parks. You can choose to add a day to your tour to explore the attractions in and around Rapid City.

❼ Leave Rapid City on U.S. 16. Go south 21 mi to Keystone, then go northwest on Route 244 (the Gutzon Borglum Memorial Highway) for 3 mi to **Mount Rushmore National Memorial,** where you can view the huge, carved renderings of four American presidents. Next continue west on Route 244 to **Hill City,** another mining town turned tourism mecca.

❽ The **Crazy Horse Memorial,** the colossal mountain carving of the legendary Lakota leader, is just south of Hill City on U.S. 16/385. The memorial's complex includes the Indian Museum of North America, which displays beautiful bead and quillwork representing many of the continent's Native nations.

❾ **Custer,** 5 mi south of Crazy Horse Memorial on U.S. 385, is a friendly community surrounded by some of the most incredible scenery in the Black Hills, including **Needles Highway, Cathedral Spires,** and **Harney Peak.** Squeeze in a visit to **Jewel Cave National Monument** to see the beautiful nailhead and dogtooth spar crystals that line its more than 100 mi of passageways.

❿ Next head over to **Custer State Park,** 5 mi east of Custer on U.S. 16A. The incredible park has 115 square mi of scenic beauty, with exceptional drives, lots of wildlife, and finger-like granite spires rising from the forest floor. Stay in one of four enchanting mountain lodges, relax on a hayride and at a chuck-wagon supper, or take a Jeep tour into the buffalo herds.

⓫ Begin day five of your trip with a visit to **Wind Cave National Park,** south of Custer State Park via Route 87 and U.S. 385. The park has 28,000 acres of wildlife habitat above ground and the world's sixth-longest cave below. Take a morning cave tour and a short drive through the park, then head 6 mi south on U.S. 385 to **Hot Springs** for lunch. Here you can see still more historic sandstone buildings, the amazing **Mammoth Site,** and take a dip into **Evans Plunge.**

Day six of your trek is a 300-mi, five- or six-hour drive, which begins as you travel 40 mi south-southwest on U.S. 18, across the border to Wyoming and the junction with U.S. 85. Proceed south on U.S. 85 for 47 mi to Lusk and turn west on U.S. 18/20 for 41 mi to I–25. Continue south for 115 mi to **Cheyenne** for a lunch stop, then 9 mi to the Colorado line. Drive 42 mi south on I–25, passing Fort Collins, to Loveland, where you'll exit the interstate and continue west on U.S. 34. As you drive, notice the **Front Range** growing in your windshield to the southwest. Stretching from the Wyoming border down the eastern slope of the Rocky Mountains to just north of Denver, the Front Range region is home to several medium-size cities, including Fort Collins (population, 120,000), Boulder (94,000), Greeley (76,500), Longmont (71,000), and Loveland (54,000). There's a lot to see along the Front Range, from the historic fur post at **Fort Vasquez** to the oldest operating hotel in Colorado at **Empire,** which has hosted the likes of P. T. Barnum and General Ulysses S. Grant and his cohort, William T. Sherman (whom Grant later made a general).

⑫ Once you reach **Rocky Mountain National Park,** the last stop on your tour, take Trail Ridge Road across the Continental Divide to Grand Lake. Along the route, you'll encounter numerous switchbacks and view avalanche areas, flower-filled meadows, cascading waterfalls, and alpine tundra. If you want to enter the park at Grand Lake, count on a two-hour drive from Denver: I–70 west to U.S. 40 north to U.S. 34 north.

Glacier Lakes to the Tetons Driving Tour
FROM GLACIER TO GRAND TETON

Distance: 850–1,000 mi   Time: 7 days
Breaks: Overnight in East Glacier, Lake McDonald, and Missoula, MT; Yellowstone National Park and Jackson, WY

❶ Start your tour in **Glacier National Park,** with its 1,500 square mi of exquisite ice-carved terrain. A drive on the cliff-hugging Going-to-the-Sun Road over the Continental Divide is a must. Overnight at **Lake McDonald Lodge.** Opened in 1914, Lake McDonald is one of the great lodges of the West. Spend a second day in Glacier to go river rafting, horseback riding, or hiking.

❷ On day three of your tour, drive southwest on U.S. 2 to Kalispell, then south on U.S. 93, where you'll hug the western shoreline of **Flathead Lake** for about 43 mi to the town of Polson. Flathead is the largest natural freshwater lake in the western United States— take time to breathe it all in.

❸ It's only 123 mi from Kalispell to Missoula, but the shear beauty of the scenery amid the **Flathead Indian Reservation,** looking to the east at the vast Mission Range, makes the trip seem somewhat longer. Stop by the **National Bison Range** near Ravali. The range is a 30-square-mi preserve of natural grasslands established in 1908 to protect one of the few surviving herds of American bison.

❹ Overnight in **Missoula,** at the intersection of five valleys and the junction of three great rivers. This is Montana's hippest town, with excellent galleries, gift shops, and restaurants, as well at the University of Montana and the Missoula Children's Theatre.

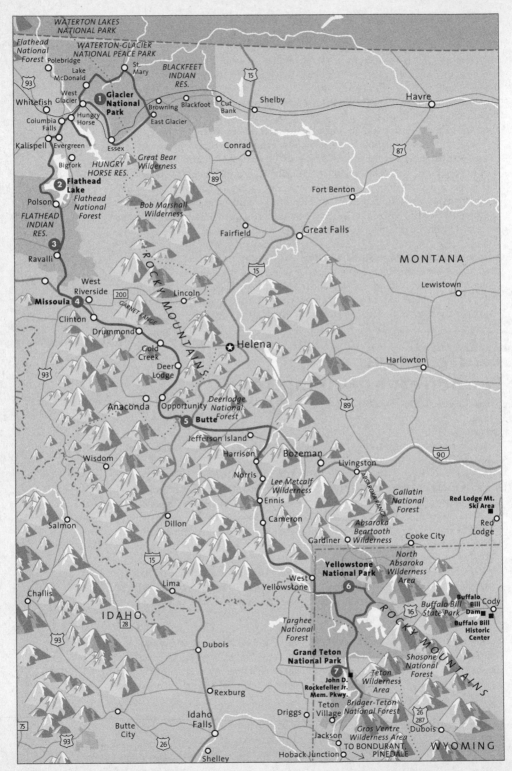

⑤ Day four of your trek takes you 119 mi southeast on I–90 to the century-old mining town of **Butte,** where the lavish Copper King Mansion reveals what you could buy with an unlimited household budget. To get to West Yellowstone from Butte, follow I–90 east 28 mi to U.S. 287, then turn south and drive 106 mi. Overnight in one of Yellowstone's old hotels, or if you don't want to drive the whole way, spend the night in Butte or **Bozeman.**

⑥ Devote day five to a comprehensive tour of **Yellowstone National Park.** The 142-mi Grand Loop Road passes nearly every major attraction in the park, and you'll discover interpretive displays, overlooks and short trails along the way. Most motorists easily spend a day on the Loop. You really can't go wrong with a stay at the **Old Faithful Inn,** where lodgepole walls and ceiling beams, an immense volcanic rock fireplace, and green-tinted, etched windows provide the ideal example of what national park lodgings were originally meant to be. Spend a second day in Yellowstone to explore the park's hiking trails or to go fishing.

⑦ On day seven, the final day of your tour, get an early start in an easterly direction on the Grand Loop Road, turning south at Grant Village onto U.S. 89/287. Proceed 43 mi south to **Grand Teton National Park,** whose northern boundary is 7 mi from Yellowstone's south entrance. The sheer ruggedness of the Tetons makes them seem imposing and unapproachable, but a drive on Teton Park Road, with frequent stops at scenic turnouts, will get you up close and personal with the peaks. Overnight in one of the park lodges.

When to Visit

Peak tourist season in the mountains and plains region falls between Memorial Day and Labor Day, when daytime temperatures are warm and evenings are cool. Summer traffic in the parks—particularly in Yellowstone—can be a bear, but, if you absolutely love camping, ranger talks, and the low murmur of a few thousand fellow Americans as you visit the parks, stick to the summer season. Fall weather is usually sunny and warm, although by October the thermometer may fall below freezing and there may be some snow. Winter is generally frigid, with lots of snow, but if you love to ski or snowshoe, it's the perfect season to visit this region. Spring is often wet, cold, and unpredictable, with surprise snowstorms as late as April and flurries into May. Spring welcomes life back to the parks—trees show tiny green buds, the first wildflowers bloom, and baby bison, elk, and deer are born.

CLIMATE

Summer in the Rockies is short, beginning in late June and ending in September. At its height in late July and August temperatures can climb into the 90s, but the frequent afternoon thunderstorms always cool things down a little. By late October, and through the winter into May, days are blustery, averaging in the 30s and 40s (even colder in Montana), and nights freezing. Temperatures can dip as low as -40°F in winter (primarily east of the Continental Divide). On the plains winter is equally cold, but summer lasts longer and gets hotter. With few shade trees, the badlands can broil under the sun in 100°F-plus heat. Spring and fall on the plains bring cool, pleasant temperatures in the 60s. But if there is one constant, it is that the weather at any time of year is unpredictable: it can vary considerably, even within a single day.

What to Pack

Hikers and campers should be prepared for abrupt changes in weather at any time of the year in the Dakotas, Wyoming, Colorado, and Montana. In fact, in all but the Dakotas, snow is not unheard of at higher elevations any month of the year. In winter, stay home unless you thrive on unpredictable weather and the chance of icy roadways. In spring, summer, and fall, bring rain gear. Even in summer, wearing several layers is your best safeguard against fickle weather. Insect repellent, sunscreen, sunglasses, and a hat also are worth carrying. Your packing checklist for any mountain trek also should include a bandanna, water-resistant camera, day pack, fleece gloves, fleece pullover, fleece vest, hiking boots, extra laces, liner socks, long johns, thick socks, trousers or shorts, a T-shirt, turtleneck, and lots of water.

BADLANDS NATIONAL PARK

SOUTHWESTERN SOUTH DAKOTA

Exit 110 or 131 off I–90, or Rte. 44 east to Rte. 377. Badlands National Park is 70 mi east of Rapid City and 73 mi northeast of Wind Cave National Park.

So stark and isolated are the chiseled spires, ragged ridgelines, and deep ravines of South Dakota's badlands, that Lt. Col. George Custer once described the area as "hell with the fires burned out." While a bit more accessible and host to considerably more life than the depths of the underworld, the landscape of the badlands is easily the strangest in the state. Ruthlessly ravaged over ages by wind and rain, the 380 square mi of wild terrain continues to erode and evolve, sometimes visibly changing shape in a few days. Despite harsh conditions, a community of prairie creatures, from bison and bald eagles to rattlesnakes and pronghorn antelope, thrive on the untamed territory. Fossil evidence shows that mammals have roamed the area for over 35 million years. In fact, there are more Oligocene fossil deposits in the badlands than anywhere else in the world. Within the ancient rock formations, paleontologists have detected the evolution of such mammals as horses, cats, sheep, rhinoceroses, and pigs, plus traces of various birds and reptiles.

The park, first established as a national monument in 1939, then designated a national park in 1978, is divided into three units: the North Unit, which includes the Badlands Wilderness Area, and the Stronghold and Palmer units, which are within Pine Ridge Indian Reservation. The National Park Service and the Oglala Sioux Tribe manage the southern units together. The northern unit is far more user-friendly and attracts the majority of visitors. Much of the southern units is accessible only on foot or by four-wheel drive or high-clearance recreational vehicle.

PUBLICATIONS

A free newspaper, *The Prairie Preamble,* is published annually and is available at the park's visitor centers. Several park brochures on such topics as geology, photography, and horseback riding in the park are free at the visitor centers and from www.nps.gov/badl.

When to Visit

SCENERY AND WILDLIFE

The sharply defined lines and edges of the park's cliffs, canyons, and mesas are all the more impressive when viewed in the morning or late afternoon, when the low-hanging sun catches the rock forms and casts them in deep shadow, highlighting their depth and providing definition to their ethereal structure. The morning is probably the better choice, since the mid- to late-afternoon sun turns the rock walls into an oven. However, those who brave the high temperatures are more than aptly rewarded—a sunset and subsequent moonrise over the badlands are two of the most beautiful experiences the park has to offer.

If you stick around for a badlands sunset, you are rewarded with a display of animal life few daytime visitors see. Many of the park's creatures are nocturnal and begin their day's activity around sunset, about the same time that the daytime animals start to settle down for the night. For a few brief moments, both the day and night creatures can be seen roving around the park—a rare occurrence that is repeated only at sunrise, when the animal roles are reversed. At these two times of the day, it's not unusual to see herds of pronghorn antelope and mule deer dart across the flat plateaus, coyotes slinking around canyon walls, prairie dogs barking warnings from the safety of their burrows, and sharptail grouse running through the tall grass, as golden eagles, turkey vultures, and hawks soar on the rocky region's updrafts.

HIGH AND LOW SEASON

The vast majority of visitors descend on the park between Memorial Day and Labor Day. Fortunately, the park's vast size and isolation prevents it from ever being too packed. A possible exception is the first week in August when hundreds of thousands of motorcycle enthusiasts flock to the Black Hills for the annual Sturgis Motorcycle Rally, and many mark Badlands National Park as one of their stops. On the flipside, it's possible to drive Badlands Loop Road in winter without seeing more than one or two other vehicles. In summer, temperatures typically hover around 90°F, and sudden mid-afternoon thunderstorms are not unusual. Although storms put on a spectacular show of thunder and lightning, they rarely rain for more than 10 or 15 minutes. Autumn weather is generally sunny and warm. Snow usually appears by late October. Early spring is often wet, cold, and unpredictable, and freak snowstorms appear as late as April. By May the weather usually stabilizes, once again bringing pleasant 70°F days.

Average High/Low Temperatures (°F) and Monthly Precipitation (in inches)

	JAN.	FEB.	MAR.	APR.	MAY	JUNE
BADLANDS	40/8	43/10	51/22	62/33	72/44	82/60
	.30	.40	1.0	1.90	2.60	2.80
	JULY	AUG.	SEPT.	OCT.	NOV.	DEC.
	90/57	92/55	78/46	65/34	48/21	35/10
	2.0	1.60	1.20	1.20	.50	.40

FESTIVALS AND SEASONAL EVENTS

WINTER

Jan.–Feb.: **Black Hills Stock Show and Rodeo.** Watch world-champion wild horse races, bucking horses, timed sheepdog trials, draft horse competitions, and steer wrestling during this two-week-long professional rodeo at the Rushmore Plaza Civic Center in Rapid City. The stockman's banquet and ball are not to be missed. | 605/355–3861 or 605/258–2863.

SPRING

Mar.: **Badlands Quilt Show.** A three-day display of the region's finest hand- and machine-made quilts, plus quilting classes, demonstrations, and sales, are held in Wall's community center. | 605/279–2945.

SUMMER

June–Aug.: **Red Cloud Indian Art Show.** Native American artists' paintings and sculptures are the focus of this 11-week-long exhibition, beginning on the second Sunday in June, at the Red Cloud Indian School in Pine Ridge. | 605/867–5491.

Aug.: **Central States Fair.** Top-name grandstand entertainment, professional rodeos, cattle shows, 4-H days, a carnival, a petting zoo, and a German tent make up this classic regional fair, held at Central States Fairgrounds in Rapid City. | 605/355–3861.

BADLANDS
NATIONAL PARK

EXPLORING
ATTRACTIONS NEARBY
DINING
LODGING
CAMPING AND RV
FACILITIES
SHOPPING
ESSENTIAL
INFORMATION

Aug.:	**Fee Free Day.** Each year on August 25th, the park opens its doors to all for free. Special programs are held all day at the Ben Reifel visitor center.	605/433–5361.
	Oglala Nation Powwow and Rodeo. This traditional powwow and rodeo is hosted by the Oglala Sioux tribe at the Powwow Grounds on the west side of Pine Ridge.	605/867–5821.

Nearby Towns

Built against a steep ridge of badland rock, **Wall** was founded in 1907 as a railroad station, and is today the town nearest to Badlands National Park, 8 mi from the Pinnacles entrance to the North Unit. Wall is home to about 850 residents and the world-famous Wall Drug Store, best known for its fabled jackalopes and free ice water. **Pine Ridge,** about 35 mi south of the Stronghold Unit, is on the cusp of Pine Ridge Indian Reservation. The town was established in 1877 as an Indian agency for Chief Red Cloud and his band of followers. With 2,800 square mi, the reservation, home and headquarters of the Oglala Sioux, is second in size only to Arizona's Navajo Reservation. **Rapid City,** in the eastern buttes of the Black Hills, is South Dakota's second-largest city and a good base from which to explore the treasures of the state's southwestern corner, including the badlands 70 mi to the east, Mount Rushmore and Wind Cave National Park 25 mi and 50 mi to the south respectively, and neighboring Black Hills National Forest.

INFORMATION

Oglala Sioux Tribe | Box 570, Kyle, SD 57764 | 605/455–2584. **Rapid City Chamber of Commerce, and Convention and Visitors Bureau** | 444 Mount Rushmore Rd. N, Rapid City, SD 57701 | 605/343–1744 or 800/487–3223 | www.rapidcitycvb.com. **Wall–Badlands Area Chamber of Commerce** | 501 Main St., Wall, SD 57790 | 605/279–2665 or 888/852–9255 | www.wall-badlands.com.

Exploring Badlands

PARK BASICS

Contacts and Resources: Badlands National Park | Box 6, Interior, SD 57750 | 605/433–5361 | www.nps.gov/badl. **Badlands Natural History Association** | Box 47, Interior, SD 57750 | 605/433–5489 | fax 605/433–5248 | www.nps.gov/badl/exp/bnha.htm. **Ben Reifel Visitor Center** | Rte. 240, Cedar Pass, SD 57750 | 605/433–5361.

Hours: The park is open 24 hours, seven days a week, year-round.

Fees: Park fees, collected year-round and good for seven days, are $10 per car or $5 per person on a motorcycle or on foot. Bus rates are $25–$100, depending on the number of passengers aboard.

Getting Around: Badlands National Park is one of the least developed places on Earth, and few roads, paved or otherwise, pass within park boundaries. Badlands Loop Road (Route 240) is the most traveled road through the park, and the only one that intersects I–90. It's well-maintained and rarely crowded. Portions of Route 44 and Route 27 run at the fringes of the badlands, connecting the visitor centers and Rapid City. Keep an eye on your speed— bison roam the flat, grassy plains these roads cut through, and it's common to come up over the crest of a hill and find one standing on the road. Some roads through the park are unpaved, and should be traveled with care when wet. Sheep Mountain Table Road, a 7 mi road carved out by homesteaders in the early 20th century, is the only public road into the Stronghold Unit of the park. It is impassable when wet, with deep ruts—sometimes only high-clearance vehicles can get through. Off-road driving is prohibited. There's plenty of free parking at the visitor centers, scenic overlooks, and trailheads. Some of the trailhead lots may get full in peak season, but never do all the lots fill up at one time.

Permits: A backcountry permit isn't required for hiking or camping in Badlands National Park, but it's a good idea to check in at park headquarters before setting out on a back-country journey. Backpackers may set up camps anywhere except within a half mile of roads or trails. Open fires are prohibited.

Public Telephones: You'll find pay phones at the Ben Reifel visitor center, Cedar Pass Lodge, and Cedar Pass Campground.

Rest Rooms: There are public rest rooms at picnic areas, campgrounds, the Ben Reifel vis-itor center, Cedar Pass Lodge, Cedar Pass Campground, the Door/Window/Notch trail-head, the Fossil Exhibit trailhead, and the White River visitor center.

Accessibility: The Ben Reifel and White River visitor centers and Cedar Pass Lodge are all fully wheelchair accessible. Two trails—the Fossil Exhibit Trail and the Window Trail—have reserved parking and are accessible by ramp, although they are quite steep in places. The Door, Cliff Shelf, and Prairie Wind trails are accessible by boardwalk. Cedar Pass campground has two fully accessible sites, plus many other sites that are sculpted and easily negoti-ated by wheelchair users. The campground's office and amphitheater also are accessible. The Bigfoot Picnic Area has reserved parking, ramps, and an accessible pit toilet. Other areas of the park are very rugged and can be difficult or impossible to navigate by those with limited mobility. Visit the park's Web site at www.nps.gov/badl/pphtml/basics.html or call 605/433-5361.

Emergencies: In case of a fire or medical emergency, call 911. There are no fire call boxes in the park. Rangers can provide basic first aid. For assistance, call 605/433-5361, or go to either visitor center or the Pinnacles entrance ranger station.

Lost and Found: The park's lost-and-found is at the Ben Reifel visitor center (605/433-5361).

Good Tours

BADLANDS IN ONE DAY

Start your day with breakfast in **Wall** (the doughnuts at **Wall Drug Store** even lure locals off I-90). Be sure to pack a picnic lunch and plenty of water, then enter the park via the northeast entrance (exit 131 off I-90), and follow Route 240 into the Cedar Pass area toward the **Ben Reifel visitor center,** where you should stop to pick up maps and information about the park.

Stop at the **Big Badlands Overlook** along the way to get a good feel for the landscape. Hike any one of several trails you'll pass, or if you prefer guided walks, arrive at the visi-tor center in time to join the **Fossil Talk** and brief walk at 11:00 AM on the **Fossil Exhibit Trail.** Even if you miss the talk, you should come back and hike this 0.25-mi trail before your morning is over. The badlands are one of the richest fossil fields in the world, and along the trail are examples of six extinct creatures, now protected under clear plastic domes. After your morning walk, continue along the highway until you reach the **Jour-ney Overlook Picnic Area,** a couple miles up on the right. Here you can enjoy a packed lunch amidst grassy prairies, with the sharp, rocky badland formations all around you.

In the afternoon continue along **Badlands Loop Road** stopping at the various over-looks and taking a break for a hike or two. When you reach the junction with **Sage Creek Rim Road,** turn left and follow it along the northern border of the **Badlands Wilderness Area.** This is bison country. Be sure to stop at the **Roberts Prairie Dog Town Overlook,** espe-cially if you haven't encountered the little hyperactive animals previously. The park is less developed the farther you travel on Sage Creek Rim Road, allowing you the opportunity to admire the sheer isolation and untouched beauty of badlands country. Hold out for a glorious sunset over the shadows of the nearby Black Hills, and keep your eyes open for animals stirring about. Continue forward until you reach Route 44 near the town of Scenic, at which point you can head west back to Rapid City or east to Interior and I-90.

BADLANDS
NATIONAL PARK

EXPLORING
ATTRACTIONS NEARBY
DINING
LODGING
CAMPING AND RV
FACILITIES
SHOPPING
ESSENTIAL
INFORMATION

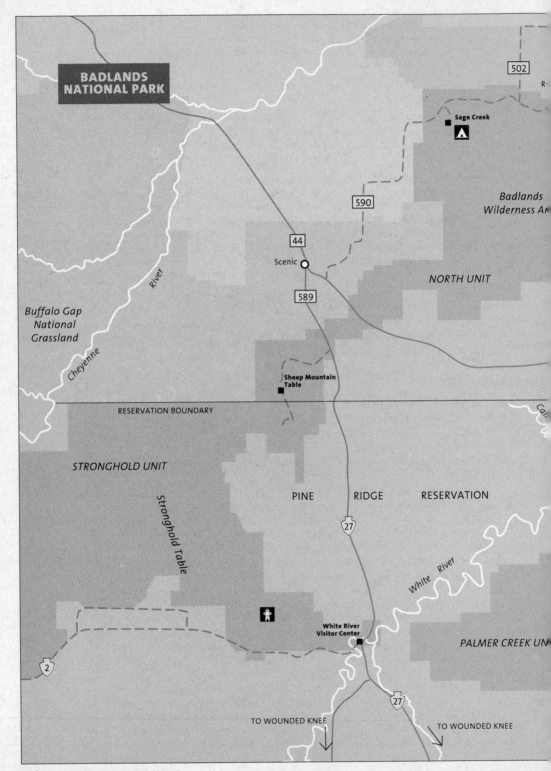

BADLANDS
NATIONAL PARK

502

R

Sage Creek

590

Badlands
Wilderness Ar

44

Scenic

589

NORTH UNIT

Buffalo Gap
National
Grassland

River

Cheyenne

Sheep Mountain
Table

RESERVATION BOUNDARY

Cah

STRONGHOLD UNIT

Stronghold Table

PINE   RIDGE   RESERVATION

27

White River

2

White River
Visitor Center

PALMER CREEK UN

27

TO WOUNDED KNEE

TO WOUNDED KNEE

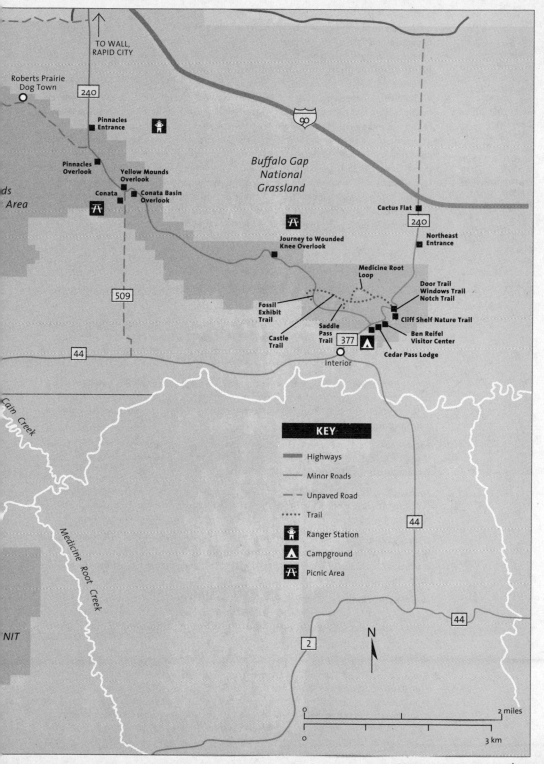

TO WALL,
RAPID CITY

Roberts Prairie
Dog Town

240

Pinnacles
Entrance

Buffalo Gap
National
Grassland

Pinnacles
Overlook

Yellow Mounds
Overlook

Conata

Conata Basin
Overlook

ds
Area

Cactus Flat

240

Journey to Wounded
Knee Overlook

Northeast
Entrance

509

Medicine Root
Loop

Door Trail
Windows Trail
Notch Trail

Fossil
Exhibit
Trail

Cliff Shelf Nature Trail

Saddle
Pass
Trail

377

Ben Reifel
Visitor Center

Castle
Trail

Cedar Pass Lodge

44

Interior

NIT

Medicine Root Creek

ain Creek

KEY

Highways

Minor Roads

Unpaved Road

Trail

Ranger Station

Campground

Picnic Area

44

44

2

N

0   2 miles

0   3 km

BADLANDS IN TWO DAYS

Before you begin a multiday visit to the badlands, be sure to stock up on enough drinking water and food, as both resources are hard to come by in the park. Water found in the backcountry is so laden with silt and minerals that it's impossible to purify. Also be sure to bring along a compass, topographical map, and rain gear.

On your first day follow the one-day itinerary above. On your second day, drive to the **White River visitor center** inside the Pine Ridge Indian Reservation. Pause to view exhibits on the history and culture of the Lakota people. You can abandon your car at the visitor center and hike east into the **Stronghold Unit.** If your car is equipped with four-wheel drive, and if conditions are dry, you can take the 7-mi, unpaved **Sheep Mountain Table Road** into the Stronghold Unit as far as you'd like before you decide to stop and hike east into this vast undeveloped wilderness. Take care when walking and camping in the Stronghold Unit. This area was used as a gunnery range for the United States Air Force and the South Dakota National Guard from 1942 until around 1968. Discarded remnants and unexploded ordnance make this area potentially dangerous. If you do find fragments of this era, do not handle them. Report the location to a ranger.

Attractions

PROGRAMS AND TOURS

All park programs and activities are free. Contact the Ben Reifel visitor center at 605/433–5361 to confirm daily schedules.

Affordable Adventures Badlands Tour. Take a seven-hour narrated tour through the park and surrounding badlands with this Rapid City–based company for a flat fee of $85 per person. The small size of each van means tours can easily be customized. | Box 546, Rapid City, 57709-0546 | 605/342–7691 | www.enetis.net/~carol.

Evening Program. Watch a 40-minute outdoor slide presentation on the wildlife, natural history, paleontology, or another aspect of the badlands. The shows typically begin around 9 PM. Check with the rangers for exact times and topics. | Cedar Pass campground amphitheater | Mid-June–mid-Aug., daily.

Focus Weeks. Focus on fire, ferrets, flora or fauna; each week in summer an important park resource is featured in special ranger-led walks and talks. Meeting points vary; check schedules at the visitor centers. | July 4–mid-Aug., daily.

Fossil Talk. What were the South Dakota badlands like millions of years ago? This tour of protected fossil exhibits will inspire and answer all your questions. | Fossil Exhibit Trail, 5 mi west of the Ben Reifel visitor center | Mid-June–mid-Aug., daily 11 AM, 2 PM.

Geology Walk. Learn the geologic story of the White River badlands in a 45-minute walk. The terrain can be rough in places, so be sure to wear hiking boots or sneakers. A hat is a good idea, too. | Door/Window Trail parking, 2 mi east of the Ben Reifel visitor center | Mid-June–mid-Aug., daily 9 AM.

Junior Ranger Program. Children ages 7–12 may participate in this 45-minute adventure, typically a short hike, game, or other hands-on activity focused on badlands wildlife, geology, or fossils. Parents are welcome. | Cedar Pass Campground Amphitheater | 605/433–5361 | June–Aug., daily 12:30.

SCENIC DRIVES

★ **Badlands Loop Road.** The simplest and most popular drive through the badlands is on two-lane Badlands Loop Road (Route 240 outside the park). The drive circles from exit 110 off I–90 through the park and back to the interstate at exit 131. Start from either end and make your way around to the various overlooks along the way. Pinnacles Overlook and Yellow Mounds Overlook are outstanding places to examine the sandy pink- and brown-toned ridges and spires distinctive to the badlands. At a certain point the landscape flattens out slightly to the north, revealing spectacular views of mixed grass prairies. In the rugged Cedar Pass area, the drive takes you past some of the park's best trails.

Sage Creek Rim Drive. This drive follows the road less traveled, and covers rougher terrain than Badlands Loop Road. Enter the park via the Pinnacles entrance, then turn west onto unpaved Sage Creek Rim Road. The road is completely negotiable by most vehicles, but should be avoided during a thunderstorm when the sudden rush of water may cause flooding. The road follows the northern border of the park for several miles, passing several overlooks. Only a third of this area is composed of the eroded rocky spires and sharp ridges distinctive to the park. A vast mixed grass prairie covers the rest. Keep an eye out for free-roaming bison along this route. The road continues out of the park and junctions with Route 44 near the town of Scenic. A quick 30-mi drive east will take you through a portion of Buffalo Gap National Grassland and into the Cedar Pass area, while a 50 mi drive west will take you to Rapid City.

SIGHTS TO SEE

Ancient Hunters Overlook. Perched above a dense fossil bed, this overhang is where prehistoric bison hunters drove herds of buffalo over the edge. | 22 mi northwest of the Ben Reifel visitor center.

★ **Badlands Wilderness Area.** This 100-square mi area is part of the largest prairie wilderness in the United States and takes up about 25% of the park. About two-thirds of the Sage Creek region is mixed-grass prairie, making it the ideal grazing grounds for bison, pronghorn, and many of the park's other native animals. Feel free to hike your own route into the untamed prairie, but remember that any water in this region is unfit for drinking—be sure to pack your own.

Ben Reifel Visitor Center. Although the visitor center is at the extreme eastern edge of the park, in the developed Cedar Pass area, it's a good idea to stop here to pick up park brochures and maps. The lodge, campground, amphitheater, and six trails are less than 2 mi away. | Badlands Loop Rd. (Rte. 240), Interior | 605/433–5361 | Early June–mid-Aug., daily 7–7; mid-Aug.–mid-Oct., daily 8–5; mid-Oct.–early Apr., daily 9–4; early Apr. 6–early June, daily 8–5.

Big Badlands Overlook. From this overlook, 90% of the park's one million annual visitors get their first views of the White River Badlands. | 5 mi northeast of the Ben Reifel visitor center.

The Big Pig Dig. In a depression by the Conata Basin picnic area, paleontologists dig for fossils and field questions from curious visitors. This site was named for a large fossil originally thought to be the remainder of a prehistoric pig, though it actually turned out to be from a small, hornless rhinoceros. The dig is open and staffed from June through August. | 17 mi northwest of the Ben Reifel visitor center | Early June–late Aug., hrs vary.

Journey Overlook. See Bigfoot Pass, where Sioux chief Big Foot and his band traveled through the badlands on their way to that fateful day at Wounded Knee, December 29, 1890. | 7 mi northwest of the Ben Reifel visitor center.

Palmer Creek Unit. If you're feeling especially adventurous, you may attempt to hike into the Palmer Creek Unit 2 mi east of the White River visitor center. This is the most isolated section of the park—no recognized roads pass through its borders. You must obtain permission from private landowners to pass through their property. If you plan on exploring here, count on spending two days—one day in and one day out. | 3–10 mi east of the White River visitor center.

Roberts Prairie Dog Town and Overlook. Once a homestead, today this site is owned by a large colony of black-tailed prairie dogs. | 5 mi west of Badlands Loop Rd. on Sage Creek Rim Rd.

Stronghold Unit. With few paved roads and no campgrounds, the park's southern unit is difficult to access without a four-wheel drive or high clearance vehicle. However, if you're

BADLANDS
NATIONAL PARK

EXPLORING
ATTRACTIONS NEARBY
DINING
LODGING
CAMPING AND RV
FACILITIES
SHOPPING
ESSENTIAL
INFORMATION

willing to trek, the unit's isolation provides a rare opportunity to explore badlands rock formations and prairies completely undisturbed. Much of the Badlands' Stronghold District was used from 1942 to 1968 as a gunnery range for the U.S. Air Force and South Dakota National Guard. Bomber pilots would frequently target the large fossil remains of an elephant-size titanothere, which gleamed bright white from the air. Hundreds of fossils were destroyed during this time. Beware of such remnants as old automobiles-turned-targets, unexploded bombs, shells, rockets, and other hazardous materials. If you see unexploded ordnance (UXO) while hiking in the Stronghold Unit, be sure to note the location so you can report it to a ranger later, steer clear of it, and find another route.

The 3-mi-long **Stronghold Table** can be reached only by crossing a narrow land bridge just wide enough to let a wagon pass. It is here in 1890, just prior to the Massacre at Wounded Knee, that some 600 Sioux gathered to perform one of the last known Ghost Dances, a ritual in which the Sioux wore white shirts that they believed would protect them from bullets. Permission from private landowners is required to gain access to the table. Go to the White River visitor center for instructions. | 7 mi west of the White River visitor center.

White River Visitor Center. Any visit to the Stronghold or Palmer units should be preceded by a stop at this information center for maps and information about road and trail conditions. You can also see fossils and Lakota artifacts and learn about Sioux culture then and now. | 25 mi south of Rte. 44 via Rte. 27 | June–Aug., daily 10–4.

Yellow Mounds Overlook. Contrasting sharply with the badlands pinnacles, these mounds greet you with soft yet vivid yellows, reds, and purples. | 16 mi northwest of the Ben Reifel visitor center.

Sports and Outdoor Activities

BICYCLING

Bicycles are permitted only on designated roads, which may be paved or unpaved. They are prohibited from closed roads, trails, and the backcountry. Flat-resistant tires are recommended.

Rushmore Bicycles. Based in the central Black Hills, this local outfitter has nearly 50 mountain bikes available to rent by the day or half-day, including comfort cruisers, standard mountain bikes, and high-end demo bikes. Inquire about guided bike tours of park. Reservations are essential. | 107 Elm St., Hill City, 57745 | 605/574-3930 | www.rushmorebicycles.com.

Sheep Mountain Table Road. In the south unit on the Pine Ridge Indian Reservation, this 7-mi dirt road, ideal for mountain biking, climbs Sheep Mountain for unique views from a high, flat mesa. The road should only be taken when dry. The terrain is level for the first 3 mi, then it climbs the table and levels out again. At the top you can see a great view of the entire Stronghold Unit. | About 14 mi north of the White River visitor center on Rte. 27.

Two Wheeler Dealer Cycle and Fitness. This family owned-and-operated outfitter, founded in 1972, stocks more than 1,000 new bikes for sale or rent. Service is exceptional here, and you can get trail and route information for Badlands National Park and the Black Hills at the counter. | 100 East Blvd. N, Rapid City | 605/343-0524 | www.twowheelerdealer.com.

BIRD-WATCHING AND WILDLIFE VIEWING

Bring along a pair of binoculars, and, especially around sunset, get set to watch the badlands come to life. Jackrabbits, bats, prairie dogs, gophers, porcupines, fox, coyote, skunks, bobcats, horned lizards, prairie rattlers, deer, pronghorn, bighorn sheep, and bison all call the badlands home. Although very rare, weasels, mountain lions, and the endangered black-footed ferret can also be spotted roaming the park. Also, more than 215 bird species have been recorded in the area, including herons, pelicans, cormorants, egrets, swans, geese, hawks, eagles (both golden and bald), falcons, vultures, cranes, doves, and cuckoos.

Scheels All Sport. In Rapid City's Rushmore Mall, Scheels is one of the few places in the area to carry a wide selection of all-weather hiking clothes and binoculars suitable for wildlife viewing. | 2200 N. Maple Ave., Rapid City | 605/342–9033.

HIKING

The isolation and otherworldliness of the badlands are best appreciated with a walk through them. Take time to examine the dusty rock beneath your feet, look for fossils and animals, and remember, bring at least one liter of water per person.

Castle Trail. This easy hike stretches for 5.5 mi one-way from the Fossil Exhibit trailhead on Badlands Loop Road to the parking area for the Door and Windows trails; if you choose to use the Medicine Root Loop, which detours off the Castle Trail, you'll add a half mile to the trek. | 5 mi north of the Ben Reifel visitor center.

Cliff Shelf Nature Trail. This 0.5-mi loop winds through a wooded prairie oasis in the middle of dry, rocky ridges and climbs 200 ft to a peak above White River Valley for an incomparable view. Look for chipmunks, squirrels, and red-wing blackbirds in the wet wood, and eagles, hawks, and vultures at hilltop. | 1 mi east of the Ben Reifel visitor center.

Door Trail. A 0.75-mi round-trip trail leads through a natural opening, or door, in a badlands rock wall. The eerie sandstone formations and passageways beckon, but it's recommended that you stay on the trail. The first 100 yards of the trail are on a boardwalk. | 2 mi east of the Ben Reifel visitor center.

★**Fossil Exhibit Trail.** Fossils of early mammals are displayed under glass along this 0.25-mi, wheelchair-accessible loop. | 5 mi west of the Ben Reifel visitor center.

Notch Trail. One of the park's more interesting hikes, this 1.5-mi round-trip trail takes you over moderately difficult terrain and up a ladder. Winds at the notch can be fierce, but it's worth lingering for the view of the White River Valley and the Pine Ridge Indian Reservation. | 2 mi north of the Ben Reifel visitor center.

Saddle Pass Trail. This hike, which connects with Castle Trail and Medicine Root Loop, is a steep, 0.25-mi climb up the side of "The Wall," an impressive rock formation. | 2 mi west of the Ben Reifel visitor center.

Window Trail. This 200-yard trail ends at a natural hole, or window, formation in a rock wall. Looking though, you'll see more of the distinctive badlands pinnacles and spires. | 2 mi north of the Ben Reifel visitor center.

HORSEBACK RIDING

The park has one of the largest and most beautiful territories in the state in which to ride a horse. Horses are prohibited only on marked trails, roads, and developed areas. The mixed-grass prairie land of the Badlands Wilderness Area is especially popular with riders.

★**Gunsel Horse Adventures.** A local outfitter since 1968, Gunsel provides multiday pack trips into the badlands, Black Hills National Forest, and Buffalo Gap National Grassland. The four-, seven-, or ten-day trips are all-inclusive, with the exception of sleeping bags and personal effects. Reservations are essential. | Box 1575, Rapid City 57709 | 605/343–7608 | www.gunselhorseadventures.com | $200 per day.

Attractions Nearby

Sights to See

Bear Country U.S.A. Bears, wolves, elk, bighorns, and other North American wildlife roam free on 250 privately owned acres. Bear cubs, wolf pups, and other park offspring are housed in a walk-through area. Allow at least 1½ hours for your visit. | U.S. 16, Rapid City | 605/343–2290 | www.bearcountryusa.com | $9.50 | May–Oct., daily 8–6:30.

BADLANDS
NATIONAL PARK

EXPLORING
**ATTRACTIONS
NEARBY**
DINING
LODGING
CAMPING AND RV
FACILITIES
SHOPPING
ESSENTIAL
INFORMATION

Black Hills Caverns. Frost crystal, amethyst, logomites, calcite crystals, and other specimens fill this cave, first discovered by pioneers in the late 1800s. Half-hour and hour tours are available. | 2600 Cavern Rd., Rapid City | 605/343–0542 | www.blackhillscaverns.com | $8 per hour, $7 per half-hour | May–mid-June and mid-Aug.–Sept., daily 8:30–5:30; mid-June– mid-Aug., daily 8–8.

Black Hills National Forest. Hundreds of miles of hiking, mountain biking, and horseback riding trails crisscross this million-acre forest on the western edge of the state. Entry points include Custer, Deadwood, Hill City, Hot Springs, Lead, Rapid City, Spearfish, and Sturgis. | Visitor center: 803 Soo San Dr., Rapid City | 605/343–8755 | www.fs.fed.us/bhnf | Free | Visitor center: mid-May–Sept., daily 8–6.

Black Hills Petrified Forest. An audio-visual presentation and a guided nature walk teach you the geologic evolution of western South Dakota. Allow about an hour for your visit. | 8228 Elk Creek Rd., Rapid City | 605/787–4884 | www.elkcreek.org | $6.50 | Memorial Day– Labor Day, daily 8–7; May and Sept., daily 9–5.

Children's Science Center. A great rainy-day alternative if you have young children, the Center offers interactive learning programs about wild animals, the universe, and the planet. Programs change with the season. Call ahead for information. | 515 West Blvd., Rapid City | 605/394–6996 | www.hpcnet.org/sdsmt/csc | $3 | Tues.–Sat. 10–4.

Dahl Fine Arts Center. A 180-ft panorama, enhanced by a sound-and-light presentation, brings 200 years of American history to life. The Dahl also has a gallery of original work by regional artists for sale. | 713 7th St., Rapid City | 605/394–4101 | Free | Tues.–Sat. 10–5, Sun. 1–5.

Dinosaur Park. Constructed by the Civilian Conservation Corps in the 1930s, these seven life-size replicas of colossal prehistoric reptiles guard the crest of Skyline Drive where you have a view of the entire city. | 940 Skyline Dr., , Rapid City | Free | Daily 6 AM–10 PM.

Journey Museum. Interactive exhibits explore the history of the Black Hills from the age of the dinosaurs to the days of the pioneers. | 222 New York St., Rapid City | 605/394–6923 | www.journeymuseum.org | $6 | Memorial Day–Labor Day, daily 9–5; Labor Day–Memorial Day, Mon.–Sat. 10–5, Sun. 1–5.

★ **Mount Rushmore National Memorial.** One of the nation's most popular attractions, the giant likenesses of Washington, Jefferson, Lincoln, and Theodore Roosevelt lie just 65 mi west of Badlands. An excellent visitor center and viewing station makes the trip even more pleasurable. For more on Mount Rushmore, *see* Wind Cave National Park. | Rte. 244, Keystone | 605/574–2523 | www.nps.gov/moru | Parking $8.

Museum of Geology. This South Dakota School of Mines and Technology museum hosts a fine collection of fossilized bones from giant dinosaurs, marine reptiles, and prehistoric mammals. It also contains extensive collections of agates, fossilized cycads, rocks, gems, and minerals. | 501 E. St. Joseph St., O'Harra Memorial Building, Rapid City | 605/394–2467 or 800/544–8162 | Free | Memorial Day–Labor Day, Mon.–Sat. 8–6, Sun. noon–6; Labor Day–Memorial Day, weekdays 8–5, Sat. 9–4, Sun. 1–4.

Red Cloud Indian School Heritage Art Museum. Exquisite star quilts and works by artists representing 30 tribes fill the galleries. | 100 Mission Dr., Pine Ridge | 605/867–5491 | Free | June–Aug., daily 8–5; Sept.–May, Mon.–Sat. 8–5.

★ **Reptile Gardens.** The world's largest reptile collection and one of the Black Hills' premier family attractions has snakes, gators, crocs, and four entertaining shows. Don't miss the stunning botanical gardens. | 8955 U.S. 16, Rapid City | 605/342–5873 or 800/335–0275 | $10 | Apr.–late May and early Sept.–Oct., daily 9–5; Memorial Day–Labor Day, daily 8–7.

Sitting Bull Crystal Caverns. Crystalline chambers, reflecting pools, and limestone fill these underground caverns, named in honor of Sioux holy man Sitting Bull. Check out mirrorlike Diamond Lake and the abundant dogtooth spar crystals. | 13745 U.S. 16, Rapid City | 605/342–2777 | $7 | June–Aug., daily 7–7; May and Sept.–Oct., daily 8–5.

★ **Storybook Island.** Nursery rhymes come to life in animated and real-life scenes at this children's fantasy theme park, which also has children's summer theater. | 1301 Sheridan Lake Rd., Rapid City | 605/342–6357 | Donations accepted | Memorial Day–Labor Day, daily 8–8.

★ **Wall Drug Store.** This South Dakota original got its start by offering free ice-water to road-weary travelers. Today its four dining rooms seat 520 visitors. The walls are covered with art for sale. A life-size mechanical Cowboy Orchestra and Chuckwagon Quartet greet you in the store, and in the Wall Drug backyard you'll see an animated T-rex and replicas of Mount Rushmore and a native village. The attached Western Mall has 14 shops selling all kinds of souvenirs, from T-shirts to fudge. | 510 Main St., Wall | 605/279–2175 | www.walldrug.com | Free | Memorial Day–Labor Day, daily 6 AM–10 PM; Labor Day–Memorial Day, daily 6:30–6.

Wounded Knee Historical Site. A solitary stone obelisk commemorates the site of the December 29, 1890 massacre at Wounded Knee, the last major conflict of between the United States military and American Indians. Nearly 300 Indians and 30 soldiers were killed in the massacre. | 12 mi northwest of Pine Ridge, along U.S. 18 | Free.

Tours
★ **Mysterious Badlands Tour.** Golden Circle Tours schedules eight-hour narrated trips to the badlands, Custer State Park, and to Mount Rushmore and Crazy Horse memorials in bright yellow and white passenger vans. Prices average around $65 per person, depending on how many people are in your group. | 605/673–4349 or 877/811–4349 | www.goldencircletours.com.

Dining

In Badlands
Cedar Pass Lodge Restaurant. American. Cool off within dark, knotty pine walls under an exposed-beam ceiling, and enjoy a hearty meal of steak, trout, or the restaurant's specialty, Indian tacos made with fry bread. | 1 Cedar St. (Rte. 240), Interior | 605/433–5460 | $8–$18 | AE, D, MC, V | Closed Nov.–Mar.

Picnic Areas. You may picnic wherever your heart desires, but the National Park Service does provide several structured picnic areas. The wind may blow hard enough to make picnicking a challenge, but the views are unrivaled.

A dozen or so covered picnic tables are scattered over the **Conata picnic area,** which rests against a badlands wall a half-mile south of Badlands Loop Road. There's no potable water, but there are bathroom facilities and you can enjoy your lunch in peaceful isolation at the threshold of the Badlands Wilderness Area. The Conata Basin area is to the east, and Sage Creek area is to the west. | 15 mi northwest of the Ben Reifel visitor center on Conata Rd.

There are only a handful of tables at **Journey overlook,** and no water, but the incredible view makes it a lovely spot to have lunch. Rest rooms are available. | 7 mi northwest of the Ben Reifel visitor center on Badlands Loop Rd.

Directly behind the **White River visitor center** are four covered tables where you can picnic simply and stay protected from the wind. | 25 mi south of Rte. 44 on Rte. 27.

Near the Park
For restaurants in Custer, Hill City, Hot Springs, Keystone, and Deadwood *see* Wind Cave National Park.

★ **Botticelli Ristorante Italiano.** Italian. Statues and columns give this northern Italian eatery a classic European appearance. Daily specials, seafood and otherwise, complement the main menu's chicken, veal, and creamy pasta dishes. | 523 Main St., Rapid City | 605/348–0089 | $8–$25 | AE, MC, V.

Cactus Family Restaurant and Lounge. American. Delicious hotcakes and pies await you at this full-menu restaurant in downtown Wall. In summer you'll find a roast-beef buffet large enough for any appetite. | 519 Main St., Wall | 605/279–2561 | $7–$15 | D, MC, V.

Elkton House Restaurant. American. For a terrific hot roast-beef sandwich served on white bread with gravy and mashed potatoes, make your way to this comfortable, family-friendly restaurant. The dining room is sunlit and the service is fast. | 203 South Blvd., Wall | 605/279–2152 | $7–$15 | D, MC, V.

Firehouse Brewing Co. American. Occupying a historic 1915 firehouse, the state's first brew pub is ornamented throughout with brass fixtures and fire-fighting equipment. The six house beers are the highlight of the menu, which also includes pastas, salads, and gumbo. There's usually outdoor entertainment on summer weekends. | 610 Main St., Rapid City | 605/348–1915 | $6–$18 | AE, D, DC, MC, V.

★ **Fireside Inn Restaurant and Lounge.** Steak. With a warm fireplace and some of the best beef in the Dakotas, your evening can't go wrong here. The spacious patio is ideal for cocktails before dinner. Try the bean soup, New York steak, or the 20-ounce prime rib. The inn is west of Rapid City on Route 44. | 23021 Hisega Rd., Rapid City | 605/342–3900 | $14–$40 | AE, D, DC, MC, V.

Landmark Restaurant and Lounge. American. This frilly restaurant in Rapid City's grandest historic hotel, the 1928 Hotel Alex Johnson, is popular for its lunch buffet and dinner specialties, which include prime rib, beef Wellington, Cajun dishes, and wild game. | 523 6th St., Rapid City | 605/342–1210 | $15–$34 | AE, D, DC, MC, V.

Western Art Gallery Restaurant. American. This large restaurant in the Wall Drug store displays more than 200 original oil paintings, all with a Western theme. Try a hot beef sandwich or a buffalo burger. The old-fashioned soda fountain has milkshakes and homemade ice cream. | 510 Main St., Wall | 605/279–2175 | $4–$11 | AE, D, MC, V.

Lodging

In Badlands

Badlands Inn. At this inn where every room faces Badlands National Park, awaken to a panoramic view of sunrise over Vampire Peak and the other rugged peaks of the badlands. Picnic area. Hiking. Some pets allowed (fee). No smoking. | Rte. 377, Interior 57750 | 605/433–5401 | 22 rooms | $53–$67 | AE, D, MC, V | Closed Nov.–Mar.

★ **Cedar Pass Lodge.** Each small, stucco cabin has two beds and views of the badlands peaks. The lodge's gallery displays the work of local artists, and the gift shop is well-stocked with local crafts, including quill and beadwork. There are hiking trails on the premises. Restaurant, picnic area. Hiking. Some pets allowed (fee). No room phones. No room TVs. | 1 Cedar St. (Rte. 240), Interior 57750 | 605/433–5460 | fax 605/433–5560 | 22 cabins | $55 | AE, D, MC, V | Closed mid-Oct.–mid-Apr.

Near the Park

For lodging in Custer, Hill City, Hot Springs, Keystone, and Deadwood *see* Wind Cave National Park.

Ann's Motel. This motel, one block from Wall Drug, has small but clean rooms, each equipped with a coffeemaker and full-size bathtubs. Microwaves, refrigerators. Cable TV. | 114 4th Ave., Wall 57790 | 605/279–2501 | 20 rooms | $60–$65 | AE, D, MC, V.

★ **Audrie's Bed and Breakfast.** Victorian antiques and an air of romance greet you at this out-of-the-way inn, 7 mi west of Rapid City on Route 44 in the heart of the Black Hills. You can stay in comfortable suites and creekside cabins, most with fireplaces and private baths. In-room hot tubs. Cable TV. No smoking. | 23029 Thunderhead Falls Rd., Rapid City 57702 | 605/342–7788 | 2 suites, 7 cabins | $115–$175 | No credit cards | BP.

Badlands Budget Host Motel and Campground. Every room in this motel has views of the Buffalo Gap National Grasslands, one mile away. You can have breakfast and dinner on the premises or walk to a nearby restaurant. Restaurant, room service. Pool, wading pool. Playground. Laundry facilities. Some pets allowed. | Rte. 377, Interior 57750 | 605/433–5335 or 800/388–4643 | 21 rooms | $50–$58 | D, MC, V.

Badlands Ranch and Resort. This 2,000-acre ranch is just outside the national park. The ranch house and cabins have spectacular views of the park. The grounds and 16-bed lodge are ideal for summer family vacations and reunions. Hunting guides are provided in season. Picnic area. Pool. Fishing. Hiking, horseback riding. Playground. | Rte. 44, Interior 57750 | 605/433–5599 or 877/433–5599 | fax 605/433–5598 | www.badlandsranchandresort.com | 4 rooms, 7 cabins, 1 lodge, 35 hookups | $48–$90 | AE, D, MC, V.

Best Western Plains. This pleasant motel is 7 mi from Badlands National Park and 4 blocks from downtown Wall. Each room has a coffeemaker, and there's a restaurant 1½ blocks away. Two-bedroom family suites for up to 7 people are available. Cable TV. Pool. Business services. Some pets allowed (fee). | 712 Glenn St., Wall 57790 | 605/279–2145 or 800/528–1234 | fax 605/279–2977 | 74 rooms, 8 suites | $69–$105, $125–$150 suites | AE, D, DC, MC, V | CP.

Circle View Guest Ranch. This B&B has spectacular views of the badlands, and is 30 mi from downtown Wall. Except for the fireplaces, the guest rooms lack the usual charm of a bed-and-breakfast and look more like hotel rooms. Picnic area. Kitchenettes. Cable TV. Hiking. | 20055 Rte. 44 E, Scenic, 57780 | 605/433–5582 | www.circleviewranch.com | 7 rooms | $50–$125 | MC, V.

Coyote Blues Village B&B. This European-style lodge on 30 Black Hills acres (12 mi north of Hill City) displays an unusual mix of antique furnishings and contemporary art. Hearty Swiss-American breakfasts include homemade bread. Some rooms have a private deck with a hot tub. A creek runs through the property. Refrigerators. Cable TV. Exercise equipment. Hiking. No smoking. | Off U.S. 385, Hill City 57745 | 605/574–4477 or 888/253–4477 | fax 605/574–2101 | www.coyotebluesvillage.com | 7 rooms | $75–$139 | D, MC, V.

Holiday Inn Rushmore Plaza. Within the eight-story atrium of this hotel, glass elevators ascend and descend beside a waterfall and lush trees. The hotel is next to the civic center. Restaurant, room service. In-room data ports, in-room safes, some refrigerators. Cable TV. Indoor pool. Exercise equipment, hot tub, sauna. Bar. Laundry facilities. Business services. Airport shuttle. | 505 N. 5th St., Rapid City 57701 | 605/348–4000 | fax 605/348–9777 | 205 rooms, 48 suites | $114, $139 suites | AE, D, DC, MC, V.

Hotel Alex Johnson. Period furnishings re-create the Jazz Age in this nine-floor 1928 hotel in downtown Rapid City. The lobby's wood-beam ceiling, gigantic chandelier, and leather, button-back wing chairs will entrance you. Some rooms are more state-of-the-art, while others retain antique decorations. Restaurant. Some in-room hot tubs, some refrigerators. Cable TV. Bar (with entertainment). Airport shuttle. | 523 6th St., Rapid City 57701 | 605/342–1210 or 800/888–2539 | fax 605/342–7436 | www.alexjohnson.com | 141 rooms, 2 suites | $98–$145 | AE, D, DC, MC, V.

Radisson Hotel Rapid City/Mount Rushmore. Murals and a large Mount Rushmore rendering in the marble floor distinguish the lobby of this nine-floor hotel in the heart of Rapid City. Rooms are spacious and contemporary, and there are several shops on the hotel's main floor. Restaurant, room service. In-room data ports, some in-room hot tubs. Cable TV. Indoor pool. Bar. Business services. Airport shuttle. | 445 Mount Rushmore Rd., Rapid City

57701 | 605/348–8300 | fax 605/348–3833 | www.radissonrapidcity.com | 176 rooms, 5 suites | $114–$189, $229–$289 suites | AE, D, DC, MC, V.

Camping and RV Facilities

In Badlands

There are no designated campgrounds in Stronghold Unit, but you may pitch a tent anywhere that's 0.5 mi from a road or trail. Be careful of the remains of military gunning. Despite these historical reminders of civilization, your camping experience in Stronghold Unit will only emphasize the sheer isolation of the badlands. Fires are not allowed anywhere in the park.

Cedar Pass Campground. This campground is the most developed in the park. It's right next door to the Ben Reifel visitor center, Cedar Pass Lodge, and a half-dozen hiking trails. You can buy $1 or $2 bags of ice at the lodge. Flush toilets, pit toilets. Dump station. Drinking water. Public telephone. Ranger station. | 96 sites | Rte. 377, 0.25 mi south of Badlands Loop Rd. | 605/433–5361 | $10 | Mid-Apr.–mid-Oct.

Sage Creek Primitive Campground. The word to remember here is primitive. If you want to get away from it all, this lovely, isolated spot surrounded by nothing but fields and crickets is the right camp for you. There are no designated campsites, and the only facilities are pit toilets and horse hitches. Pit toilets. | 25 mi west of Badlands Loop Rd. on Sage Creek Rim Rd. | Free.

Near the Park

Arrow Campground. Since this campground is managed together with a small motel, good facilities are easily accessible. From I–90, take exit 109 or 110 into Wall. The grounds are two blocks from downtown Wall. Flush toilets. Full hookups, partial hookups (electric and water), dump station. Drinking water, showers. Fire grates. Electricity, public telephone. Play area, swimming (pool). | 100 sites (36 with full hookups, 36 with partial hookups) | 515 Crown St., Wall | 605/279–2112 or 800/888–1361 | $14–$22 | May–Oct. 15.

Badlands/White River KOA. Southeast of Interior, this campground's green, shady sites spread over 31 acres are pleasant and cool after a day among the dry rocks of the national park. White River and a small creek border the property on two sides. Cabins and cottages are also available. Flush toilets. Full hookups, partial hookups (electric and water), dump station. Drinking water, showers. Fire grates, picnic tables. Public telephone. General store. Play area, swimming (pool). | 144 sites (44 with full hookups, 38 with partial hookups) | 4 mi south of Interior on Rte. 44, Interior | 605/433–5337 | www.koa.com | $18–$25 | Mid-Apr.– early Oct.

Berry Patch Campground. This well-developed, grassy campground is especially convenient for RVs. Bus tours to area sights depart from the campground daily. Take exit 60 off I–90. Flush toilets. Full hookups, partial hookups, dump station. Drinking water, showers. Fire grates, picnic tables. Electricity, public telephone. General store. Play area, swimming (pool). | 150 sites (123 with full hookups, 27 with partial hookups) | 1860 E. North St., Rapid City | 605/341–5588 | $18–$34.

Happy Holiday RV Resort. Outside of Rapid City on U.S. 16, this campground has the advantage of easy access to Mount Rushmore and beautiful forest surroundings. There are also onsite cabins and motel rooms. You get 10% off on gas when you stay here. Flush toilets. Full hookups, partial hookups (electric and water), dump station. Drinking water, guest laundry, showers. Fire grates, picnic tables. Electricity, public telephone. General store, service station. Play area, swimming (pool). | 258 sites (170 with full hookups, 88 with partial hookups) | 8990 U.S. 16 S, Rapid City | 605/342–7365 | fax 605/342–1122 | www. happyholidayrvresort.com | $33–$36, $24 tent site.

	Total # of sites	# of RV sites	# of hook-ups	Drive-to sites	Hike-to sites	Flush toilets	Pit/chemical toilets	Drinking water	Showers	Fire grates	Swimming	Boat access	Playground	Dump station	Ranger station	Public telephone	Reservation possible	Daily fee per site	Dates open
INSIDE THE PARK																			
Cedar Pass Campground	96	96	0	•		•	•	•						•	•	•		$10	Apr.–Oct.
Sage Creek Primitive	ULP	ULP	0	•	•		•											Free	Y/R
NEAR THE PARK																			
Arrow Campground	100	100	72	•		•		•	•	•	•		•	•			•	$14–22	May–Oct.
Badlands/ White River KOA	144	144	82	•		•		•	•	•	•		•	•			•	$18–25	Apr.–Oct.
Berry Patch Campground	150	150	150	•		•		•	•				•	•			•	$18–34	Y/R
Happy Holiday	258	258	258	•		•		•	•	•	•		•	•			•	$24–36	Y/R

* In summer only ** Reservation Fee Charged Y/R=Year Round
UL=Unlimited ULP=Unlimited Primitive LD=Labor Day MD=Memorial Day

Shopping

Badlands Grocery. This small, friendly grocer, 2 mi south of the Ben Reifel visitor center, has meats, dairy products, bakery items, and camping supplies. | 10 Main St., Interior | 605/433–5445.

Cedar Pass Lodge Gift Store. The shop's extensive collection includes locally made bead and quillwork, Black Hills gold, and silver and turquoise jewelry, as well as postcards, pottery, books, and films. The convenience store has refreshing drinks and snacks. | 1 Cedar St. (Rte. 240), Interior | 605/433–5460 | Closed Nov.–mid-Mar.

Wall Drug Store. More of an amusement park than a store, you can still get your basic necessities here (except groceries), along with clothes, gifts, art, and the strangest souvenirs you'll ever be tempted to spend money on. | 510 Main St., Wall | 605/279–2175.

Essential Information

ATMS: Cedar Pass Lodge | 1 Cedar St. (Rte. 240), Interior | 605/433–5460. **Black Hills Federal Credit Union** | 605 Main St., Wall | 605/279–2350. **First Western Bank** | 418 Main St., Wall | 605/279–2141.

AUTOMOBILE SERVICE STATIONS: Badlands Automotive | 216 4th Ave., Wall | 605/279–2827. **DE's Tire & Muffler** | 216 W. 7th Ave., Wall | 605/279–2168. **Harvey's Cowboy Corner** | Rte. 44 at Rte. 377, Interior | 605/433-5333. **Wall Auto Livery Amoco** | 311 S. Blvd., Wall | 605/279–2325.

POST OFFICES: Interior Post Office | 1 Main St., Interior, 57750 | 605/433–5345. **Wall Post Office** | 529 Main St., Wall, 57790 | 605/279–2466.

GLACIER NATIONAL PARK

NORTHWESTERN MONTANA

East entrances: U.S. 89 to Many Glacier or St. Mary; Rte. 49 to Two Medicine. West entrances: U.S. 2 to West Glacier; North Fork Rd. to Polebridge.

The massive peaks of the Continental Divide are the backbone of Glacier National Park and its sister park, Canada's Waterton Lakes National Park. From their slopes, melting snow and alpine glaciers yield streaming ribbons of clear, frigid water, the headwaters of rivers that flow west to the Pacific Ocean, north to the Arctic Ocean, and southeast to the Atlantic Ocean via the Gulf of Mexico. The parks embody the essence of the Rocky Mountains, where raw nature dominates. Coniferous forests, thickly vegetated stream bottoms, and green-carpeted meadows and basins provide homes and sustenance for all kinds of wildlife. In the backcountry you can see some of the Rockies' oldest geological formations and numerous rare species of mammals, plants, and birds. The Going-to-the-Sun Road, which snakes through the precipitous center of Glacier, is one of the most dizzying rides on the continent.

In the rocky northwest corner of America's fourth largest state, Glacier encompasses over one million acres (1,563 square mi) of untrammeled wilds. There are 37 named glaciers within the park, 200 lakes, and 1,000 mi of streams. Neighboring Waterton Lakes National Park, across the border in Alberta, Canada, covers another 130,000 acres. In 1932, the parks were unified to form the Waterton-Glacier International Peace Park—the first international peace park in the world—in recognition of the two nations' friendship and dedication to peace.

PUBLICATIONS

Pick up *Glacier Explorer* and, for kids, the *Junior Ranger* newspaper, as well as other information pamphlets, maps, and safety leaflets at park headquarters and visitor centers.

The *Waterton/Glacier Guide*, produced jointly by the two parks, contains articles on activities, special events, wildlife-interpretive programs, and religious services within the parks. It provides suggested excursions, camping information, and warnings about park hazards. The newspaper is at park entrances, visitor centers, and on-line at www.nps.gov/glac. You can get the *Glacier National Park Vacation Planner* by mail from park headquarters or on-line. For more in-depth data, the Glacier Natural History Association sells a wide array of books, maps, and videos. You can order a free brochure from the association. **Glacier Natural History Association** | Box 310, West Glacier, 59936 | 406/888–5756 | www.glacierassociation.org.

When to Visit

SCENERY AND WILDLIFE
In summer, a profusion of new flowers, grasses, and budding trees covers the landscape high and low. Spring attracts countless birds, from golden eagles riding thermals north to Canada and Alaska, to rare harlequin ducks dipping in creeks. Snow-white mountain goats, with their wispy white beards and curious stares, are seen in alpine areas, and sure-footed bighorn sheep graze the high meadows in the short summers. The largest population of grizzly bears in the lower 48 states live in the wild country in and around the park. Winter visits to Glacier offer easy tracking of many large animals like moose, elk, deer, the mountain lion, wolf, lynx, and their smaller neighbors the snowshoe hare, pine marten, beaver, and muskrat. Feeding animals is illegal and a hazard to people, who may become the victims of aggressive animals.

To minimize the risk of contact with bears and mountain lions, hike only during the day, hike in groups, and make lots of noise by singing, talking loudly, and clapping hands, especially near blind corners and streams. If you camp in the backcountry, wash your utensils after every meal, and hang food and cooking gear in a tree, well away from your sleeping area. At campgrounds, store your food and cooking gear in a closed, hard-side vehicle.

Never approach a bear or any other park animal, no matter how cute, cuddly, and harmless it may appear. If you encounter a bear, don't run. Back away slowly and assume a nonthreatening posture. If the bear charges, drop into the fetal position, protect your head and neck, and do not move. It's the opposite if you encounter a mountain lion: act aggressively, throw rocks or sticks, and try to look large by holding up a pack or branches. Always keep children very close to you.

HIGH AND LOW SEASON
Of the 2 million annual visitors to Glacier, the vast majority drive through the gates between July 1 and September 15, when the streams are flowing, wildlife is roaming, and the pavement is dry. More and more people, however, take advantage of the park in the shoulder seasons and winter. Glacier's park headquarters and Apgar visitor center are open limited hours throughout the cold season, serving skiers and snowshoers. Snow removal on the alpine portion of Going-to-the-Sun Road is usually completed by mid-June, but you should call ahead, and the opening of Logan Pass at the road's summit opens the Glacier National Park to summer activities. By July 1 all naturalist programs are fully underway. Canada's Victoria Day, celebrated with a long weekend in late May, marks the beginning of the season in Waterton. Come October, snow forces the closing of most roads in the park. Temperatures reach into the 90s in summer and drop as low as -40°F in winter. Be prepared for weather extremes any time of year: it can snow even in August.

GLACIER
NATIONAL PARK

EXPLORING
ATTRACTIONS NEARBY
DINING
LODGING
CAMPING AND RV
FACILITIES
SHOPPING
ESSENTIAL
INFORMATION

Naturalists estimate that only 850 grizzly bears live in the lower 48 states, in areas that include Glacier, North Cascades, and Yellowstone national parks.

Average High/Low Temperatures (°F) and Monthly Precipitation (in inches)

	JAN.	FEB.	MAR.	APR.	MAY	JUNE
GLACIER	31/16	35/16	42/22	54/31	65/37	70/44
	3.25	1.86	2.06	2.07	2.97	3.35
	JULY	AUG.	SEPT.	OCT.	NOV.	DEC.
	78/48	78/45	62/39	52/31	34/24	28/16
	1.95	1.45	1.83	2.93	3.76	3.09

FESTIVALS AND SEASONAL EVENTS
WINTER

Dec.: **Root Beer Classic.** A 60-mi sled-dog race begins in the community of Pole-bridge on Glacier's western border and challenges teams of dogs in two 30-mi heats. Skijoring, skiers behind dogs, and sprint races run on shorter trails. The races take place on the last weekend of the year. | 406/881–2909.

Jan.: **Annual Ski Fest.** This worldwide cross-country ski celebration introduces newcomers to kick-and-glide skiing. Pageantry, equipment demonstrations, games, and family activities are scheduled at the Izaak Walton Inn in Essex. | 406/888–5700 | www.izaakwaltoninn.com.

Feb.: **Whitefish Winter Carnival.** For more than 40 years, Whitefish has been the scene of outstanding winter fun, including a parade, a night-time torchlight parade on skis, and activities for young and old. | 406/862–3501 or 877/862–3548.

SPRING

Apr.: **The Taste of Bigfork.** Start with samplings of fresh Chilean sea bass in Thai red curry sauce or Terrine de Caille with apricots, and you've tasted a portion of what's wonderful about the village by the bay. The last Sunday in April is reserved for this Bigfork fundraiser for local charities and the chamber. | 406/837–5888.

Apr.–May: **Show Me Day.** One of Glacier's biggest events is the plowing of the Going-to-the-Sun Road. Shuttles take viewers to watch road crews plow tons of packed snow from the mountaintop road, creating man-made avalanches in the process. National Park Service employees provide spotting scopes and information for the roadside show. | 406/888–7800.

SUMMER

July: **Days of Peace and Friendship.** Held between July 1 (Canadian Independence Day) and July 4 (American Independence Day), this event filled with special programs, including hikes with rangers and historical presentations, celebrates the International Peace Park theme. | 403/859–5133 or 406/888–7800.

North American Indian Days. This four-day, Blackfeet tribal event brings Native Americans from every region of the United States and Canada. You can watch traditional drumming and dancing contests and the crowning of Miss Blackfeet in Browning. | 406/338–7521 or 406/338–7276.

Aug.: **Huckleberry Days.** Celebrating the purple delicacy's ripening, the three-day event presents huckleberry goodies from daiquiris to desserts. Downtown Whitefish is lined with sidewalk sales, street dances, and a huckleberry cook-off. | 406/862–3501 or 877/862–3548 | www.whitefishchamber.com.

Sept.: **Columbia Falls Threshing Bee.** Steam threshing machines, steam plows, antique tractors, and engines flex muscles in the Parade of Power, organized by the Northwest Montana Antique Power Association in Columbia Falls. Participants challenge friends and neighbors to tractor barrel races and shingle-making events. | 406/892–2072 or 406/892–3142.

Oct.: **Glacier Jazz Stampede.** During this four-day festival at various venues around Flathead Valley, you can hear ragtime, Dixieland swing, modern, and big-band jazz. Workshops for students, gospel services on Sunday, and costume contests complete the offerings. | 406/758–2800.

Nearby Towns

Early tourists to Glacier National Park first stopped in **East Glacier,** where the Great Northern Railway had established a station. Although most people coming from the east now enter by car through St. Mary, East Glacier, population about 400, attracts visitors with its quiet, secluded surroundings and lovely Glacier Park Lodge. **West Glacier** is the park's gateway town on the opposite border. The green waters of the Flathead River's Middle Fork and several top-notch outfitters make West Glacier an ideal base for river sports. Quaint and cozy, **Waterton Townsite** is a tidy community of tourist and government services in the center of Waterton Lakes National Park, Glacier's sister park north of the Canadian border. On Flathead Lake's pristine northeast shore, **Bigfork** twinkles with decorative lights that adorn its shops, galleries, and restaurants. By summer, flowering baskets dangle from every fence, deck, and walk, surrounding outdoor diners with color and lining the brick walkway to the Bigfork Playhouse's nightly musical productions. **Whitefish** makes an excellent base from which to visit Glacier, plus Whitefish Lake State Park, the Big Mountain ski area, and Whitefish Lake Golf Course, the state's only 36-hole championship golf course. With a population of 6,000, the town has a well-developed nightlife scene, and good restaurants, galleries, and shops.

INFORMATION

Bigfork Area Chamber of Commerce | Box 237, Bigfork, MT 59911 | 406/837–5888 | www. bigfork.org. **East Glacier Chamber of Commerce** | Box 260, East Glacier, MT 59434 | 406/ 226–4403. **Glacier Country Regional Tourism Office** | Box 1035, Big Fork, MT 59911-1035 | 406/ 837–6211 or 800/338–5072 | www.glacier.visitmt.com. **Waterton Chamber of Commerce and Visitors Association** | Box 50, Waterton Lakes National Park, AB, Canada ToK 2Mo | 403/859– 2224 or 403/859–2203 | www.watertonchamber.com. **Whitefish Chamber of Commerce** | Box 1120, Whitefish, MT 59937 | 406/862–3501 or 877/862–3548 | www.whitefishchamber.org.

Exploring Glacier

PARK BASICS

Contacts and Resources: Glacier National Park | Box 128, West Glacier, MT 59936 | 406/888– 7800 | www.nps.gov/glac. **Glacier-Waterton Visitors Association** | Box 96, West Glacier, MT 59936 | 406/387–4053 | fax 406/387–4982 | www.glacierwaterton.com. **Waterton Lakes National Park** | Waterton Park, AB, Canada TOK 2MO | 403/859–2224 or 800/748–7275 | fax 403/859–2650 | www.parkscanada.gc.ca/waterton.

Hours: Glacier and Waterton are open year-round; however, most roads and facilities close October through May due to snow. Park headquarters are open year-round, weekdays 8–4:30.

Fees: Entrance fees for Glacier National Park are $10 per vehicle, or $5 for one person on foot or bike, good for seven days; $20 for a one-year pass. A day pass to Waterton Lakes National Park costs C$5 (C$2.50 per child), and a four-day pass costs C$20. The annual pass is C$55. Passes to Glacier and Waterton must be paid for separately at their respective park entrances.

In 2000, visitors made 285,891,275 recreational trips to America's national parks. By comparison, the U.S. population is approximately 280 million.

Getting Around: The roads in both Waterton and Glacier are two-lane paved, two-lane gravel or one-lane gravel roads that deteriorate from moisture freezing and thawing. Drive slowly, watch for changing road conditions and anticipate that rocks and wildlife may be around the corner. Road reconstruction is part of the park experience as there are only a few warm months in which road crews can complete projects. The speed limit is 45 mph or less where posted. Scenic pullouts are frequent; watch for other vehicles pulling in or out and watch for children in and around parking areas. Prepare for winter storms with survival kits that include snow tires or chains, a shovel and window scraper, flares or a reflector, a blanket or sleeping bag, a first-aid kit, sand, gravel or traction mats, a flashlight with extra batteries, matches, a lighter and candles, paper, nonperishable foods, drinking water, and a tow chain or rope. Call 406/888–7800 or visit www.nps.gov/glac to check road conditions before traveling.

Glacier Park, Inc. operates a shuttle along the Going-to-the-Sun Road July 1 to Labor Day. Buses make stops at major trailheads, campgrounds, and other developed areas between Lake McDonald Lodge and Rising Sun Motor Inn. Rates vary according to the length of the ride. For schedules and fares call 406/226–5666 or see www.glacierparkinc.com.

Proof of citizenship, such as a passport or birth certificate, is required to cross the Canadian/United States border in either direction. You may have to wait in line at the Customs station. *Landed residents of Canada and non-U.S. and non-Canadian citizens from a visa waiver country or with a valid visitor visa entering the U.S. from Canada must pay $6 (cash only) at the border for a required I94 form, available at the Port of Entry.* Customs officers will ask you a series of questions about where you are going, where you are from, and the like. You and your vehicle are subject to a random search. Firearms are prohibited except hunting rifles, for which you need advance permission. For more information about United States Customs, call 406/335–2611; for Canadian Customs, 403/344–3767.

Permits: Glacier requires you to have a permit to camp in the backcountry. The permit is $4 per person per day and you can get it from the Apgar Backcountry Permit Center (406/888–7800) after mid-April for the upcoming summer. Advance reservations cost $20. Mail a request and a check after mid-April to Backcountry Reservations, Glacier National Park Headquarters, West Glacier, 59936. No fishing license is required in Glacier, but there are regulations for the May to November fishing season. Pick up a pamphlet at the visitor centers.

Waterton requires backcountry camping permits for use of its 13 backcountry camp spots, with reservations available up to 90 days in advance. Buy the permit for C$6 per adult per night—reserve for an additional C$10—at the visitor reception centre (403/858–5133). A Waterton fishing permit costs C$7 per week and C$13 per year.

Public Telephones: Public telephones may be found at Avalanche Campground, Glacier Highland Motel and Store, Apgar, St. Mary visitor center, Two Medicine Campstore and all park lodges except Granite Park Chalet and Sperry Chalet.

Rest Rooms: Portable toilets are located along several roadside pullouts on Going-to-the-Sun Road. Additionally, public rest rooms may be found at the Apgar visitor center, Logan Pass visitor center, St. Mary visitor center, as well as at Many Glacier, Avalanche Creek, Goat Haunt, Two Medicine, Walton, and the Waterton Townsite campgrounds.

Accessibility: All park visitor centers are wheelchair accessible, and most of the campgrounds and picnic areas are paved, with extended-length picnic tables and accessible rest rooms. Three of Glacier's nature trails are wheelchair accessible: the Trail of Cedars, one of the busiest, is a lovely boardwalk loop through an ancient western red cedar forest; the 0.6-mi, round-trip, paved Running Eagle Falls Trail offers some climbing and descending; and the Oberlin Bend Trail, just west of Logan Pass, brings you to a view of the Garden Wall. In Waterton, the Linnet Lake Trail, Waterton Townsite Trail, Cameron Lake day-use area, and the International Peace Park Pavilion are wheelchair accessible.

Emergencies: In case of a fire or medical emergency, call 911. You should also contact park rangers at 406/888–7800 in Glacier (406/888–9005 when you're outside the park) or 403/859–2113 in Waterton. Note that cell phones do not work in most of the park, and there are no fire call boxes. Park rangers can administer first-aid. In summer, the West Glacier Urgent Care Clinic (406/888-9005), behind the fire house, is open.

For Glacier National Park security, call 406/888–7800. In Waterton, call the park warden at 403/859–2224. The Royal Canadian Mounted Police office is located at the corner of Waterton Avenue and Cameron Falls Drive in Waterton Townsite and can be reached at 403/859–2244.

Lost and Found: Glacier's lost-and-found is at park headquarters in West Glacier (406/888–7800).

Good Tours

GLACIER IN ONE DAY

It's hard to beat the **Going-to-the-Sun Road** for a one-day trip in Glacier National Park. This itinerary takes you from west to east—if you're starting from St. Mary, take the tour backwards. First call Glacier Park Boat Tours (406/257–2426) to make a reservation for the **St. Mary Lake or Lake McDonald boat tour,** depending on which direction you take. Then, drive up Going-to-the-Sun Road to **Avalanche Creek Campground,** and take a 30-minute stroll along the fragrant **Trail of the Cedars.** Afterward, continue driving up—you can see views of waterfalls and wildlife to the left and an awe-inspiring, precipitous drop to the right. At the summit, **Logan Pass,** your arduous climb is rewarded with a gorgeous view of immense peaks, sometimes complemented by a herd of mountain goats. Stop in at the **visitor center** for park information, ask about any grizzly bear, bighorn sheep, or even wolverine sightings in the area, then take the 1.5-mi **Hidden Lake Trail** up to several prime wildlife-viewing spots. Picnic at the overlook above Hidden Lake. In the afternoon, continue driving east over the mountains. Stop at the **Jackson Glacier Overlook** to view one of the park's largest glaciers. Continue down; eventually the forest thins, the vistas grow broader, and a gradual transition to the high plains begins. When you reach **Rising Sun Campground,** take the one-hour St. Mary Lake boat tour to St. Mary Falls. If you'd rather hike, the 1.2-mi **Sun Point Nature Trail** also leads to the falls. Take the Lake McDonald boat tour if you're driving from east to west.

GLACIER IN THREE DAYS

Three days allow you to fully experience both the east and west sides of Glacier, as well as visit **Waterton Lakes National Park** in Canada. On your first day, follow the one-day itinerary, then join the ranger-hosted **Evening Campfire Program** at the Rising Sun campground amphitheater, or the **Evening Slide Program** inside the St. Mary visitor center. Both programs run almost every summer night at 8 PM; topics are posted at visitor centers and campgrounds.

Spend your second day on Glacier's east side among aspens, wildflower meadows and breezy lakes. Take the **Iceberg Lake Hike** with rangers, most mornings at 8:30 AM, or if you're not up for a long hike, take the **Many Glacier boat trip** over Swiftcurrent and Josephine Lakes. Picnic at the lake and return on the boat or hike the shore trail back.

On your third day, take Chief Mountain Highway to Waterton Lakes National Park. Visit **Waterton Townsite** for an early lunch—Zum's Eatery and Mercantile is a good bet. After lunch, walk the easy 2-mi **Townsite Loop,** then take the scenic, two-hour, **Waterton International Shoreline Cruise** across the boundary to **Goat Haunt Ranger Station** and back. A ranger-led Dock Talk offers a glimpse into the natural and human history of the Waterton Valley.

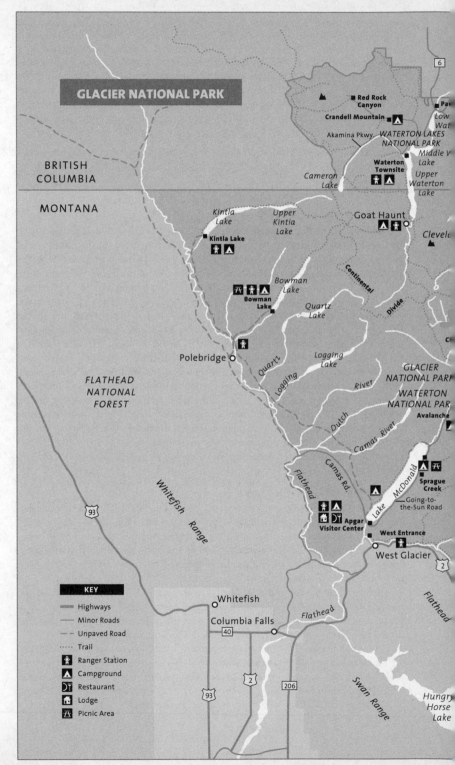

GLACIER NATIONAL PARK

Red Rock
Canyon

Crandell Mountain

Akamina Pkwy.

WATERTON LAKES
NATIONAL PARK

Pa
Low
Wat

Middle V
Lake

BRITISH
COLUMBIA

Cameron
Lake

Waterton
Townsite

Upper
Waterton
Lake

MONTANA

Kintla
Lake

Upper
Kintla
Lake

Goat Haunt

Clevela

Kintla Lake

Continental

Bowman
Lake

Quartz
Lake

Divide

Bowman
Lake

Logging
Lake

Polebridge

Quartz

Logging

GLACIER
NATIONAL PAR

River

WATERTON
NATIONAL PAR

FLATHEAD
NATIONAL
FOREST

Dutch

Camas River

Avalanche

Camas Rd.

Flathead

Sprague
Creek

Whitefish
Range

Lake McDonald

Going-to-
the-Sun Road

Apgar
Visitor Center

West Entrance

West Glacier

93

Whitefish

Flathead

Flathead

Columbia Falls

40

Swan Range

Flathead

Hungr
Horse
Lake

KEY

— Highways
— Minor Roads
- - Unpaved Road
··· Trail
Ranger Station
Campground
Restaurant
Lodge
Picnic Area

93

2

206

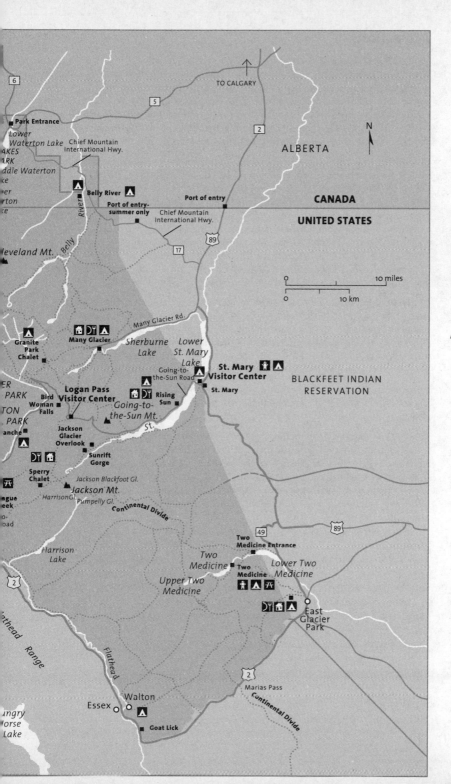

6

5

TO CALGARY

2

N

■ Park Entrance

*Lower
Waterton Lake*

ALBERTA

Chief Mountain
International Hwy.

*AKES
ARK
ddle Waterton
ke*

*er
rton
e*

▲ Belly River ▲

Port of entry ■

CANADA

Port of entry–
summer only

Chief Mountain
International Hwy.

*Belly
River*

89

UNITED STATES

eveland Mt.

17

0 _____ 10 miles

0 _____ 10 km

Many Glacier Rd.

St. Mary
Visitor Center

St. Mary ■

BLACKFEET INDIAN
RESERVATION

▲ Granite
Park
Chalet

🏠🍴▲
Many Glacier

*Sherburne
Lake*

*Lower
St. Mary
Lake*

Going-to-
the-Sun Road

R
PARK
TON
PARK

Logan Pass
Visitor Center

Bird
Woman
Falls

🏠🍴
Rising
Sun

*Going-to-
the-Sun Mt.*

St.

anche

Jackson
Glacier
Overlook

▲

🍴🏠

Sunrift
Gorge

Sperry
Chalet

🏕

Jackson Blackfoot Gl.

Jackson Mt.

*ague
eek*

HarrisonGl. *Pumpelly Gl.*

Continental Divide

*o-
oad*

*Harrison
Lake*

49

89

Two
Medicine Entrance

2

*Flathead
Range*

*Two
Medicine*

*Upper Two
Medicine*

Two
Medicine

🏃🏠🏕

*Lower Two
Medicine*

🍴🏠▲

○ East
Glacier
Park

Flathead

2

Marias Pass

Essex ○ ○ Walton

▲

*ungry
orse
ake*

■ Goat Lick

Continental Divide

GLACIER
NATIONAL PARK

EXPLORING
ATTRACTIONS NEARBY
DINING
LODGING
CAMPING AND RV
FACILITIES
SHOPPING
ESSENTIAL
INFORMATION

Since 1968, the National Park Service has successfully set nearly 3,800 prescribed fires. These are used to reduce hazardous fuel loads of undergrowth, grasses, and shrubs.

Attractions

PROGRAMS AND TOURS

Adventure Camps. One-day naturalist courses for kids 6–8 and week-long hiking and rafting trips for kids 11–13 are offered through this program. Some camps involve backcountry camping while others are based out of the Big Creek or Glacier Park field camps. Some programs are designed for adult-child teams. Subjects range from ecology and birding to wildflowers, predators and prey, and backcountry medicine. | 137 Main St., Box 7457, Kalispell 59904 | 406/755–1211 | www.glacierinstitute.org | $20–$300.

★ **Glacier Park Boat Tours.** The Glacier Park Boat Company offers guided tours of the park by boat on five of the park's major lakes. A Lake McDonald cruise takes you from the dock at Lake McDonald Lodge to the middle of the lake for an unparalleled view of the Continental Divide's Garden Wall. Cruises on Swiftcurrent Lake and Lake Josephine depart from Many Glacier Lodge and offer views of the Continental Divide. Two Medicine Lake cruises leave from the dock near the ranger station, and cross to the head of the lake and several trailheads. St. Mary Lake cruises leave from the launch near Rising Sun Campground and head to sights like Red Eagle Mountain. The tours last 45 minutes to 1½ hours. You can also rent rowboats ($10 per hour) and small motor boats ($19 per hour). | Box 5262, Kalispell 59903 | 406/257–2426 | www.glacierparkboats.com | $9.50–$12 | June–Sept.

Glacier Park, Inc. Van Tours. Glacier Park, Inc. schedules driver-narrated tours that cover most of the park accessible by road. The tour of Going-to-the-Sun Road is a favorite, with plenty of photo opportunities at roadside pullouts. Some of the tours are conducted in "Jammers," vintage 1936 red buses with roll-back tops. Short trips and full-day trips are available. Reservations are essential. | 106 Cooperative Way, Suite 104, Kalispell, 59901 | 406/756–2444 | fax 406/257–0384 | www.glacierparkinc.com | $11–$65 | June–Sept.

Junior Ranger Program. Children ages 6–12 can become a Junior Ranger by completing the activities detailed in the *Junior Ranger* newspaper, available at park visitor centers. | 406/888–7800 | Free.

THE GARDEN WALL

An abrupt and jagged wall of rock juts above Going-to-the-Sun Road and is visible from the road as it follows Logan Creek from just past Avalanche Creek Campground for about 10 mi to Logan Pass. The knife-edge wall, called an arête, was created by massive glaciers moving down the valleys on either side of it.

Ranger-Led Programs. Park rangers conduct various naturalist activities at St. Mary, Apgar, Logan Pass, Many Glacier, Goat Haunt, and Two Medicine. A complete schedule of programs is listed in *Glacier Explorer* The activities include evening slide programs, guided hikes, and boat tours. | Apgar campground, Avalanche Creek campground, Fish Creek campground, Glacier Park Lodge, Lake McDonald Lodge, Many Glacier campground and hotel, St. Mary visitor center, and Two Medicine campground | 406/888–7800 | Free | July–Labor Day, daily.

Many campgrounds at Glacier, including Fish Creek, Swiftcurrent, Rising Sun, and Two Medicine campgrounds, host **Evening Campfire Programs** at 8 or 9 PM with park rangers who lead discussions about any of the park's unique features, including wildlife, geology, and cultural history. Topics and dates are posted at each campground, and at Glacier Park Lodge, McDonald Lake Lodge, and the St. Mary visitor center.

The many **Children's Programs** at Glacier vary from year to year, but typically involve ranger-led, hands-on activities, such as role-playing skits and short hikes. Kids learn about bears, wolves, geology, and much more. Check the park newspaper or at the Apgar Education Cabin for schedules and locations.

The 7.8-mi **International Peace Park Hike** along Upper Waterton Lake is jointly led by Canadian and American park interpreters. Enjoy lunch at the International Border, before continuing on to Goat Haunt in Glacier National Park, Montana. Return to Waterton via boat ($22). | Waterton Townsite | 403/859–5133 | July–Aug., Sat. 10 AM.

★ **Sun Tours.** Tour the park and learn the Blackfeet perspective at the same time. Native guides concentrate on Glacier's features as relevant to the Blackfeet Nation, past and present. In summer, tours depart daily from East Glacier (8 AM) and St. Mary (9:15 AM) in 24-passenger, air-conditioned coaches. | 29 Glacier Ave., East Glacier | 406/226–9220 or 800/786–9220 | www.glacierinfo.com | $35–$45 | June–Sept., daily.

Waterton Inter-Nation Shoreline Cruise. This two-hour boat tour departs Waterton Townsite and cruises down Upper Waterton Lake across the border into Goat Haunt, Montana. The narrated tour passes scenic bays, sheer cliffs, and snow-clad peaks. | Waterton Townsite Marina | 403/859–2362 | fax 403/938–5019 | www.watertoninfo.ab.ca/m/cruise | $24 | May–early Oct.

SCENIC DRIVES

Chief Mountain International Highway (Rte. 17–Canada Rte. 6). Off U.S. 89, north of Saint Mary and Babb, Route 17 begins the climb northwestward toward Waterton Townsite. You pass east of Chief Mountain, and eventually deciduous trees give way to mixed conifers, mostly lodgepole pine and spruce. As Route 17 crosses the border, and you go through the Customs station, the road becomes Canada Route 6. You won't encounter a park entrance station until about 6 mi south of Waterton Townsite. From there drive down Canada Route 5 and the Red Rock Parkway toward Waterton Lakes and the Lewis Overthrust geological formation. Finally Waterton Townsite unfolds before you in one of the most comprehensive views of the park. The Red Rock Parkway closes for the winter at the end of October, and Chief Mountain Highway closes near the end of December. The customs station closes September 30, and reopens in May.

★ **Going-to-the-Sun Road.** This magnificent, 50-mi, east–west highway crosses the crest of the Continental Divide at Logan Pass and traverses the towering Garden Wall. Driving on Going-to-the-Sun Road is very slow-going and not for the faint of heart, but it's also arguably the most beautiful drive in the country. It connects Lake McDonald on the west side of Glacier with St. Mary Lake on the east side. On the way to the summit, ample turnoffs provide views of the high country and glacier-carved valleys. The drive is susceptible to frequent delays in summer for road maintenance and high-season crowds. To avoid traffic jams and parking problems, take the road early in the morning or late in the evening (when the lighting is awesome ideal for photos and the wildlife is most likely to appear). On the return trip, take scenic U.S. 2 for 90 mi around the southern end of the park. From late October to late May or June, deep snows close most of Going-to-the-Sun Road. Vehicle size is restricted to under 21 ft long, 10 ft high, and 8 ft wide, including mirrors, between Avalanche Creek campground and Sun Point. If you don't want to drive, take a tour with Glacier Park, Inc. (406/226–5666).

Many Glacier Road. This 12-mi drive enters Glacier on the northeast side of the park, west of Babb, and travels along Sherburne Lake for almost 5 mi, penetrating a glacially carved valley surrounded by mountains. As the road moves toward the mountains, it passes through meadows and a scrubby forest of lodgepole pines, aspen, and cottonwood. The farther you travel up the valley, the more clearly you'll be able to see Grinnell and Salamander glaciers. The road passes the magnificent Many Glacier Hotel and ends at the Swift Current Campground. It's usually closed from October to May.

Waterton Drives. Waterton is a much smaller park than Glacier, so a one-day excursion allows time for more than one driving route. Aside from Chief Mountain International Highway is Akamina Parkway, which goes to Cameron Lake, at the base of the Continental Divide. The Red Rock Parkway takes you from the prairie up the Blakiston Valley to Red Rock Canyon, where water has cut through the earth, exposing red sedimentary rock. Wildlife viewing is very good on this drive. You can easily cover all three routes in one day. There are numerous picnic areas, pullouts, exhibits, and trailheads along these roads and at Cameron Lake and Red Rock Canyon.

SIGHTS TO SEE

Apgar. Entering Glacier National Park at the west entrance, you come to a stop sign about a mile inside the park. If you turn left, you will reach Apgar, on the southwest end of Lake McDonald. Apgar is a tiny hamlet with a few shops, motels, ranger buildings, a campground,

GLACIER
NATIONAL PARK

EXPLORING
ATTRACTIONS NEARBY
DINING
LODGING
CAMPING AND RV
FACILITIES
SHOPPING
ESSENTIAL
INFORMATION

THE LAST GLACIERS

The last of the giant glaciers melted about 10,000 years ago, leaving valleys carved in their wake and over 650 glacial lakes. Today about 37 small glaciers around 6,000 years old are scattered among the mountains. They reveal how glaciation scrubs and carves away at the Rocky Mountains. The largest, Blackfoot Glacier, measures less than 1.5 square mi.

a historic school house, and lake access for swimming, fishing, and boating. In summer, Apgar is the hub of activity for the west side of the park. From November to early May, no services remain open, except the weekend-only visitor center. | 2 mi north of the west entrance.

The small **Apgar Visitor Center** is a great first stop if you're entering the park from the west. You can get all kinds of park information, maps, permits, and books here. The large relief map inside is a replica of the park; you can use it to plan your route and get a glimpse of where you're going. | 406/888–7800 or 406/888–7939 | www.nps.gov/glac | Mid-May–Sept., daily 8–8; Oct. daily 8–4:30; Nov.–mid-May, weekends 8–4:30.

The **Apgar Education Cabin,** next to the visitor center, is filled with animal posters, kids' activities, and maps. | 406/888–7939 | Mid-June–Labor Day, daily 2:30–4.

Baring Falls. An easy 1.3-mi hike from the Sun Point parking area leads to a spruce and Douglas fir wood. Cross a log bridge over Baring Creek and you arrive at the base of gushing Baring Falls. | 11 mi east of Logan Pass on Going-to-the-Sun Rd.

Belly River Country. Trailing through both parks is the Belly River Valley, with lovely low meadows and large alpine lakes. Waters from Belly River eventually drain into Hudson Bay. Backcountry camp spots see few human footprints and lots of bear tracks. One trailhead is south of the Chief Mountain Customs Station on Route 17. Another trailhead lies 2 mi north of the station on Canada Route 6, at the Belly River campground. The trails from the campground provide the only access to Cracker (12 mi round-trip), Cosley (15 mi round-trip), Glenns (18 mi round-trip), Helen (25 mi round-trip), and Elizabeth (16 mi round-trip) backcountry lakes. | Rte. 17 to Canada Rte. 6 | 406/888–7800.

The Garden Wall. An abrupt and jagged wall of rock juts above Going-to-the-Sun Road and is visible from the road as it follows Logan Creek from just past Avalanche Creek Campground at about 10 mi to Logan Pass. The knife-edge wall, called an arête, was created by massive glaciers moving down the valleys on either side of it. | Going-to-the-Sun Rd.

Goat Haunt. Reached only by foot trail or tour boat from Waterton Townsite, Goat Haunt, on the U.S. end of Waterton Lake, is stomping grounds to mountain goats, moose, grizzlies, black bears, and the ranger posted at this remote station. The ranger gives thrice-daily Dock Talks, free 10-minute overviews of natural and human history in Waterton Valley. You can see exhibits in the ranger station, camp, and picnic. Customs restrictions apply. | South end of Waterton Lake | 406/888–7800 or 403/859–2362 | tour boat $22 | Mid-May–Oct., daily.

Goat Lick Overlook. From this highway pullout, you may see more than a dozen mountain goats at a natural salt lick on a cliff above the Middle Fork of the Flathead River. Take a short, paved trail from the parking lot to the observation point. | 2.5 mi east of Walton Ranger Station on U.S. 2.

Grinnell and Salamander Glaciers. Formed only about 4,000 years ago, these two glaciers were one ice mass until 1926, and they continue to shrink. Icebergs often float in Grinnell Lake across from the glaciers. The best viewpoint is reached by the 5.5-mi Grinnell Glacier Trail from Many Glacier. | 5.5 mi from Swift Current campground on Grinnell Glacier trail.

Jackson Glacier. As you descend Going-to-the-Sun Road on the east side of the Continental Divide, you come into view of Jackson Glacier looming in a rocky pass across the upper St. Mary River valley. If it isn't covered with snow, you'll see sharp peaks of ice. The glacier is shrinking and may disappear in another 100 years. | 5 mi east of Logan Pass.

Lake McDonald. From one end to the other, beautiful Lake McDonald is 10 mi long and accessible year-round on Going-to-the-Sun Road. Take a boat ride to the middle for a unique view of the surrounding glacier-clad mountains. You can go fishing and horseback riding at either end of the lake. Three drive-in campgrounds are beside the shore at Apgar, Fish Creek, and Sprague Creek. | 2 mi from the West entrance at Apgar.

★ **Logan Pass.** At 6,660 ft, Logan Pass, the highest point in the park accessible by motor vehicle, presents unparalleled views of both sides of the Continental Divide. It's the apex of

Going-to-the-Sun Road, and a must-see. The pass is frequented by mountain goats, bighorn sheep, and grizzly bears—trailheads spread out from the visitor center to wildlife-viewing points. There's no phone and no food services here, so be sure to bring along enough water and provisions for the round-trip. The road and the pass are both extremely crowded in July and August. | 34 mi from West Glacier, 18 mi from St. Mary.

Built of stone, the **Logan Pass Visitor Center** stands sturdy against the severe weather that forces it to close in winter. Snow often dapples the high alpine terrain around the visitor center late into spring, providing moisture for the summer wildflowers. Park information, books, and maps are stocked inside. Rangers staff the center and give 10-minute talks on the alpine environment. | 406/888–7800 | Mid-June–Oct., daily 9–4:30.

★ **Many Glacier.** On the shore of Swiftcurrent Lake, the historic, Swiss-style Many Glacier Lodge has a restaurant, bar, gift shop, and a lovely foyer. You can enjoy the quiet deck overlooking Swiftcurrent Lake. The view of jagged peaks over the lake is worth packing a camera. You can book boat rentals and cruises. There's also a campground, camp store, ranger station, horseback riding outfitter, and several trailheads in the area. | 12 mi west of Babb on Many Glacier Rd. | 406/888–7800 or 406/732–7741 | Late June–late Sept., daily.

Running Eagle Falls. Sometimes called "Trick Falls," this cascade near Two Medicine is actually two different waterfalls from two different sources. In spring, when the water level is high, the upper falls join the lower falls for a 40-ft drop into Two Medicine River; in summer, the upper falls dry up, revealing the lower, 20-ft falls that start midway down the precipice. | 2 mi east of the Two Medicine Entrance.

St. Mary Lake. Catch one of Glacier's most popular views here—when the breezes calm, the lake acts as a reflecting pool mirroring the snowcapped granite peaks that line the St. Mary Valley. The Sun Point Nature Trail follows the lake's shore 1 mi each way. You can buy interpretive brochures for 50¢ at the trailhead on the north side of the lake, about halfway between the Logan Pass and the St. Mary visitor center. Use it and drop it at the box at the other end of the trail so that it may be recycled. | 1 mi from St. Mary on Going-to-the-Sun Rd.

St. Mary Visitor Center. This visitor center, the largest in the park, has a huge relief map of the park's peaks and valleys. Rangers can answer your questions, and they host a 45-minute slide show program each evening at 7:30. Traditional Blackfeet dancing and drumming performances are held weekly. The center has books and maps for sale, and there are large viewing windows facing 10-mi-long St. Mary Lake. | Going-to-the-Sun Rd., off U.S. 89 | 406/732–7750 | Mid-May–mid-Oct., daily 8 AM–4:30 PM and 8 PM–9 PM.

Two Medicine Valley. Rugged, often windy and always beautiful, this remote valley, 9 mi from Route 49, is surrounded by some of the park's most stark, rocky peaks. Rent a canoe, take a narrated boat tour, camp, or hike. Be aware that bears frequent the area. You'll find a camp store, a gift shop, and a picnic area here, but no lodging. The road is closed from late October through late May. | Two Medicine entrance, 9 mi east of Rte. 49 | 406/888–7800, 406/257–2426 boat tours.

Waterton Information Centre. Come to this visitor center, on the eastern edge of Waterton Townsite, to orient yourself in Canada's Waterton Lakes National Park. You can pick up brochures and buy maps and books. Rangers are on hand to answer questions and give directions. | Waterton Rd. | 403/859–5133 or 403/859–2224 | fax 403/859–2650 | www.parkscanada.gc.ca/waterton | Mid-May–mid-June, daily 8–6; mid-June–early Sept., daily 8–8; early Sept.–early Oct., daily 9–6.

Sports and Outdoor Activities

BICYCLING

Pedaling is as good a way as any to see either Glacier or Waterton. Cyclists in Glacier must stay on roads or bike routes and are not permitted on hiking trails or in the backcoun-

GLACIER
NATIONAL PARK

EXPLORING
ATTRACTIONS NEARBY
DINING
LODGING
CAMPING AND RV
FACILITIES
SHOPPING
ESSENTIAL
INFORMATION

try. Many Glacier Road and the roads around Lake McDonald have milder slopes than else-where in the park. The one-lane, unpaved Inside North Fork Road from Apgar to Polebridge is well-suited to mountain bikers. Two Medicine Road is an intermediate paved route, with a mild grade at the beginning, becoming steeper as you approach Two Medicine Campground. Much of the western half of Going-to-the-Sun Road is closed to bikes from 11 to 4. Other restrictions apply during peak traffic periods and road construction, so inquire at park entrances or visitor centers before you go.

Waterton Lakes National Park allows bikes on some designated trails such as the 2-mi Townsite Loop Trail. A ride on mildly sloping Red Rock Canyon Road isn't too difficult. Cameron Lake Road is an intermediate route. Contact the Waterton Information Centre for information about closures or for other suggested routes.

Austin-Lehman Adventures. An early morning ride through Glacier with this outfitter is unforgettable. You'll ride in the early morning when the dew makes the prairies gleam and wildlife is often visible. You can also tour landmark lodges on an inn-to-inn bicycle tour. The Mountain Wilderness Adventure is a combination bike-and-hike tour. | Box 81025, Billings, 59108 | 800/575–1540 or 406/655–4591 | fax 406/651–9236 | www.austinlehman.com | July–Aug.

BOATING

Glacier Park Boat Company. You can rent small row and motorized boats, or take one of the popular summer cruises this company offers on Lake McDonald, Two Medicine, St. Mary, Josephine, and Swiftcurrent lakes. Cruises last 45 minutes to 1½ hours. Direct your inquiries to their offices at each lake's dock. | 406/257–2426 | Tours $9.50–$12; rentals $10 per hour | www.glacierparkboats.com | Mid-June–Aug.

FISHING

Both Glacier and Waterton have a number of lakes and rivers where the fishing is good. The sportfishing species include burbot (ling), northern pike, whitefish, grayling, cutthroat, rainbow, and lake (Mackinaw), kokanee salmon, and brook trout. In both parks, the fishing season runs from the third Saturday in May to November 30. In Glacier, a fishing license is not required. In Waterton, a license, available at the information center, costs C$7 per week and C$13 annually, and a bait ban is in effect throughout all Waterton park waters. A catch-and-release policy is enforced in both parks and is required in several popular spots, such as Lower McDonald Creek, Hidden Lake outlet, and for all cutthroat trout caught on the North Fork of the Flathead River. You should stop at a visitor center for a copy of the regulations and a list of waters closed to fishing. Note that fishing on both the North Fork and the Middle Fork of the Flathead River requires a Montana conservation license for $7 plus a Montana fishing license, which costs $15 for two consecutive days or $60 for a season, and are available at most convenience stores, sports shops, and from the Montana Department of Fish, Wildlife, and Parks (406/752–5501).

HIKING

With 730 mi of marked hiking trails in Glacier and another 120 mi in Waterton, the Peace Park is a hiker's paradise. Hiking maps for both park's trails are available at all visitor centers, entrance stations, and on-line. Ask about trail closures due to bear or mountain lion activity before hiking. For backcountry hiking, pick up a permit from park headquarters or the Apgar backcountry office, or mail in a reservation request to the Backcountry Office. **Backcountry Reservations** | Glacier National Park, West Glacier, 59936 | 406/888–7939 | www.nps.gov/glac/maps.htm.

Avalanche Lake Trail. From Avalanche Creek Campground, take this 3-mi trail leading up to one of many mountain-ringed lakes in the park: Avalanche Lake. The walk is relatively easy (it ascends 500 ft), making this one of the most accessible backcountry lakes in the park. Crowds fill the parking area and trail during July and August, and on sunny weekends in May and June. | 15 mi north of Apgar on Going-to-the-Sun Rd.

Grinnell Glacier Trail. The strenuous 5.5-mi hike to Grinnell Glacier, the park's largest and most accessible glacier, is marked by several spectacular viewpoints. You start at Swiftcurrent Lake's picnic area, climb a moraine to Lake Josephine, then climb to the Grinnell Glacier overlook. Halfway up, turn around to see the prairie land to the northeast. You can short-cut the trail by 2 mi each way by taking two scenic boat rides across Swiftcurrent and Josephine lakes. From July to mid-September, a ranger-led hike departs from the Many Glacier Hotel boat dock most mornings at 8:30. Check with the ranger station to make sure the hike is scheduled for the morning you want to go. | Josephine boat dock.

★ **Hidden Lake Nature Trail.** This uphill, 1.5-mi, self-guided trail runs from Logan Pass southwest to Hidden Lake Overlook, from which you get a beautiful view of the lake and McDonald Valley. In spring, ribbons of water pour off the rocks surrounding the lake. A boardwalk protects the abundant wildflowers and spongy tundra on the way. | Logan Pass visitor center.

Highline Trail. From the Logan Pass parking lot, hike north along the Garden Wall and just below the craggy Continental Divide. Wildflowers dominate the 7.6 mi to Granite Park Chalet where hikers with reservations can overnight. Return to Logan Pass along the same trail or hike down 4.5 mi (a 2,500-ft descent) on the Loop Trail to the Going-to-the-Sun Road. | Logan Pass visitor center.

Iceberg Lake Trail. This moderately strenuous 9-mi round-trip hike passes the gushing Ptarmigan Falls, then climbs to its namesake, where icebergs bob in the chilly mountain loch. Mountain goats hang out on sheer cliffs above, bighorn sheep graze in the high mountain meadows, and grizzly bears dig for glacier lily bulbs, grubs, and other delicacies. Rangers lead hikes here almost daily in summer, leaving at 8:30 AM. | Swiftcurrent Inn parking lot off Many Glacier Rd.

Snowshoe and Blakiston Valley Trails. These two trails form a 15-mi loop around the north and south sides of Anderson Peak in the northwest part of Waterton Lakes National Park. Both are major access routes for several backcountry destinations. | Red Rock Canyon Trailhead, at the end of Red Rock Pkwy.

★ **Trail of the Cedars.** This wheelchair-accessible, 0.5-mi boardwalk loop through an ancient cedar and hemlock forest is a favorite of families with small children and people with disabilities. Interpretive signs describe the habitat and natural history of the rain forest, and explain the importance of wild fires. Note that the boardwalk can be slick if wet. | Avalanche Creek campground, 15 mi north of Apgar on Going-to-the-Sun Rd.

Two Medicine Valley Trails. One of the least-developed and least-visited parts of Glacier, the lovely southeast corner of the park is a good place for a quiet day hike, although you should look out for sign of bears. At the northeast end of the campground, you'll find the trailhead to Oldman Lake and Pitamakan Pass. The trailhead to Upper Two Medicine Lake and Cobalt Lake begins west of the boat dock and camp supply store, where you can make arrangements for a boat pick-up or drop-off across the lake. | Two Medicine campground, 9 mi west of Rte. 49.

HORSEBACK RIDING

Horses are permitted on many trails within the parks; check with the visitor center about seasonal exceptions. Horseback riding is prohibited on paved roads. You can pick up a brochure about suggested routes and outfitters from any visitor center or entrance station. The Sperry Chalet trail to the view of Sperry Glacier above Lake McDonald is a tough 7-mi climb.

Glacier Gateway Outfitters. Take a full- or half-day ride in the Two Medicine area with Blackfeet cowboy guides. Rides begin at Glacier Park Lodge in East Glacier and climb through aspen groves to high-country views of Dancing Lady and Bison mountains. Reservations are suggested. | Box 411, East Glacier, 59434 | 406/226–4408; 406/338–5560 in winter | $25–$48 | May–Sept.

GLACIER
NATIONAL PARK

EXPLORING
ATTRACTIONS NEARBY
DINING
LODGING
CAMPING AND RV
FACILITIES
SHOPPING
ESSENTIAL
INFORMATION

Mule Shoe Outfitters. Weather permitting you can saddle up at stables at Apgar, Lake McDonald, and Many Glacier. Trips range from an hour long to all day. | Box 322, West Glacier, 59936 | 406/888–5121 or 406/732–4203; 928/684–2328 in winter | www.mule-shoe.com | $25–$120 | Reservations essential | Early June–Sept. 15.

RAFTING

Sign up for a guided whitewater rafting trip in the pristine waters of the Flathead River drainages. If you bring your own raft, be sure to check with the local raft companies for advisories on water temperature, flow, and hazards. Start at Ousel Creek and float to West Glacier on the Middle Fork of the Flathead.

Wild River Adventures. These zany whitewater boaters will paddle you over the Middle Fork of the Flathead, and peddle you tall tales all the while. | 11900 U.S. 2 E, West Glacier | 406/387–9453 or 800/700–7056 | fax 413/403–5035 | www.riverwild.com | $40–$73 | Mid-May.–Sept.

SKIING AND SNOWSHOEING

Cross-country skiing and snowshoeing are increasingly popular in the Peace Park, especially on the U.S. side. Glacier National Park distributes a free pamphlet entitled *Ski Trails of Glacier National Park,* which describes 16 ski trails that have been identified by the park. You can start at Lake McDonald Lodge and ski cross-country up Going-to-the-Sun Road. The 2.5-mi Apgar Natural Trail, which begins at the Apgar visitor center, is popular with snowshoers. No restaurants or stores are open in winter in Glacier so you must bring your own food and equipment. For maps and more information, contact park headquarters.

Skiing in Waterton Lakes National Park is concentrated along the Akamina Parkway, especially near Cameron Lake. Pick up the free pamphlet *Winter Activities* from Waterton Information Centre.

Cameron Ski Trail. The Cameron Ski Trail is an easy, 3-mi round-trip trail beginning at the Little Prairie picnic site. | 3 mi from the visitor information centre on Akamina Pkwy.

★ **The Dipper Ski Trail.** Along the upper Akamina Parkway, the moderately difficult, 4-mi round-trip trail begins at the Rowe trailhead. | 5 mi from the visitor center on Akamina Pkwy., Waterton Townsite | 403/859–5140 | Dec.–Mar.

Glacier Park Ski Tours. Take a one-day or multiday guided ski or snowshoe trip on the park's winter trails. On overnight trips, you stay in snow huts. Full-moon ski tours are offered for small groups. Guides and skiers meet at the trailheads. | Box 4833, Whitefish, 59937 | 800/646–6043 Ext. 3724 | $30–$150 | Mid-Nov.–May.

Outback Ski Shack. You can rent skis from this store on the golf course in Whitefish. | 1200 U.S. 93 N, Whitefish | 406/862–9498 | $14–$18 | Dec.–Mar.

Outfitters

Glacier Raft Company and Outdoor Center. In addition to running whitewater, scenic, and fishing trips, this outfitter will set you up with camping, backpacking, and fishing gear. There's a full-service fly fishing shop and outdoor store. You can stay in one of nine cabins that sleep from 6 to 14 people. | #6 Going-to-the-Sun Rd., West Glacier, 59936 | 406/888–5454 or 800/235–6781 | fax 406/888–5541 | www.glacierraftco.com | Year-round; rafting mid-May–Sept.

Glacier Wilderness Guides and Montana Raft Company. Whitewater rafting, backcountry hiking, and fishing trips can be combined on the adventure trips conducted by these talented guides. You take their fly-fishing course, and get your Montana fishing license, before a half-day, full-day, or overnight fishing trip. One popular three-day hiking trip begins at Logan Pass and travels 7.6 mi below the Garden Wall on the Highline Trail. You spend the night in the rustic Granite Park Chalet, and the next day you choose your hike, perhaps the 3.2-mi climb to a knife-edge arête to look over the Continental Divide at Grinnell Glacier. | 11970 U.S. 2 E, West Glacier | 406/387–5555 or 800/521–7238 | fax 406/387–5656 | www.glacierguides.com | Mid-May–late Sept.

Great Northern Whitewater. River outfitters since 1977, they offer trips of three hours to three days, guided fly-fishing, kayak and canoe trips. You can also rent canoes for a ride around the lake. In winter enjoy snowmobiling or cross-country and downhill skiing on miles of trails or in the backcountry. | 12127 U.S. 2 E., 1 mi west of West Glacier, West Glacier | 406/387–5340 or 800/735–7897 | fax 406/387–9007 | www.gnwhitewater.com | $41–$67 | Year-round; rafting May–Sept.

Attractions Nearby

Scenic Drive

North Fork Road. From Camas Road 11 mi northwest of Apgar, make a right onto the 43-mi, mostly gravel Outside North Fork Road, which follows the west boundary of the national park and parallels the North Fork of the Flathead River. The river-bottom terrain is marked by lodgepole-pine flats and frequented by Glacier's wolf packs. To the west, you can see Whitefish Range, where the Moose Fire began in August 2001, burning over 110 square mi, 44 of which are inside the park. Fire-scarred Huckleberry Mountain is to the south. The road runs through areas terribly burnt, such as Big Creek Campground, and continues north to the Canadian border. About 22 mi south of the border, turn east into Polebridge, where you can stop for snacks at the Polebridge Mercantile. North of Polebridge, the fires of 1988 scoured out the forest, leaving standing ghost trees. Some of the new growth is 20 ft tall. The road continues north across a bridge over the North Fork River and into the park once again. Keep an eye out for wolves, moose, grizzlies, and black bears. Just after the entrance station, turn left and go north over Bowman Creek, where a spur road leads east to Bowman Lake. The rough, one-lane route straight ahead dead-ends at Kintla Lake. You can see a few old private homesteads in the Big Meadow area, which are not open to the public. Allow three hours to drive from Apgar to Kintla Lake.

Sights to See

★ **Lewis and Clark National Historic Trail Interpretive Center.** Follow the trail that the Corps of Discovery traveled 200 years ago (1803–06) in search of an overland route to the Pacific Ocean and experience their struggles and successes. The center shows what it was like for travelers and Native Americans of the era through films, exhibits, and live programs. Take the self-guided tour, and watch the costumed interpreters conduct demonstrations. | 4201 Giant Springs Rd., Great Falls | 406/727–8733 | www.fs.fed.us/r1/lewisclark/lcic.htm | $5 | Memorial Day–Sept., daily 9–6; Oct.–Memorial Day, Tues.–Sat. 9–5, Sun. noon–5.

Museum of the Plains Indian. On the north end of town, this museum has been in operation since the 1930s. Now run by the Blackfeet, the museum houses a stunning collection of ancient artifacts from the Blackfeet and other Plains peoples. | U.S. 2 at U.S. 89, Browning | 406/338–2230 | $4 | June–Sept., daily 9–5; Oct.–May, weekdays 10–4:30.

Polebridge. On the banks of the North Fork of the Flathead River, this tiny community has just one store, one restaurant and saloon, one camp store and one hostel, yet it is a gem in the wilderness. You can see where a massive wildfire burned up to some of the buildings in 1988 and how quickly new growth has advanced. The entrance station (staffed in summer only) is the gateway to Bowman and Kintla lakes, as well as Logging and Quartz lakes, which are in the backcountry and accessible only by hiking trails. | 26 mi northwest of West Glacier on Inside North Fork Rd. | 406/888–7800 | Entrance station: June–Sept., daily.

Stumptown Museum. Railroad history, local gags like the fur-covered trout, and fine black-and-white photo displays complete this eclectic collection housed track-side at the Amtrak station in the Whitefish Railroad Depot. While looking over the gift shop, ask for a free historical walking tour map of Stumptown, Whitefish's nickname. Call to confirm hours before stopping by. | 500 Depot St., Suite 101, Whitefish | 406/862–0067 | www.whitefishmt.com/stumphis/index.html | Donation suggested | June–Sept., daily 10–4; Oct.–May, daily 11–3.

Dining

In Glacier

Lake McDonald Lodge Dining Room. American. Pasta, steak, and salmon are standards on the menu here. Don't miss the apple bread pudding with caramel-cinnamon sauce for dessert. The adjoining coffee shop, a cheaper alternative, serves an enormous Indian taco—layers of chili, cheese, onions, tomatoes, sour cream, guacamole, and olives on *bannik*, a flat, fried Native American bread. | 10 mi north of Apgar on Going-to-the-Sun Rd. | 406/888–5431 or 406/892–2525 | $12–$28 | AE, D, MC, V | Closed late Sept.–early June.

Many Glacier Dining Room. American. Sophisticated cuisine is served in this early 20th-century chalet. Each night there's a chef's special. For a true Montana creation, have a huckleberry daiquiri. | Many Glacier Rd. | 406/732–4411 or 406/892–2525 | $15–$29 | AE, D, MC, V | Closed late Sept.–early June.

Picnic Areas. There are picnic spots at each campground and visitor center. Each one has tables, grills, and drinking water in summer.

    Sun Point, on the north side of St. Mary Lake, is one of the most beautiful places in the park for a picnic, yet it remains quiet and remote. | Sun Point trailhead.

    With all of the activity going on at **Many Glacier,** not to mention the provisions to be had there, it's no wonder so many people love to picnic in this lively spot. | End of Many Glacier Rd.

Prince of Wales Hotel Dining Room. Canadian. Enjoy upmarket cuisine before a dazzling view of Waterton Lake in this century-old chalet high on a hill overlooking the lake. Choose from a fine selection of wines to accompany your meal. Every afternoon a British high tea is served in Valerie's Tea Room (with the same great view); true to form, tea includes finger sandwiches, scones and other pastries, and chocolate-dipped fruits. | Waterton Townsite | 403/859–2231 | C$19–C$39 | AE, MC, V | Closed Oct.–May.

Near the Park

Cafe Max. American/Casual. The menu changes frequently in this cozy Main Street café where appetizers are likely to have a French flair; try Camembert fritters with brandied apricots. Entrées, which have Montana twists, include buffalo osso buco, or fresh wild salmon coated with black and white sesame seeds, broiled and topped with huckleberry chutney. | 121 Main St., Kalispell | 406/755–7687 | Reservations essential | $18–$26 | AE, MC, V | Closed Mon. No lunch.

Glacier Park Lodge Dining Room American. Here you'll enjoy fine dining in a natural megalog structure with all the amenities of a first-class dining room that was originally a steak place. Though the restaurant now serves pasta, seafood and chicken as well, ribs and steaks are still the house specialties. | Rte. 49, next to railroad station, East Glacier | 406/226–5600 | fax 406/226–9152 | D, MC, V | Closed Oct.–May.

★**La Provence.** French. Like a Paris café, the outdoor seating offers garden dining and a flower-studded view down Bigfork's main street. A changing gallery of local artists' work decorates the inside walls. The owner/chef presents works of dining art with dishes like French onion soup with Gruyère cheese served inside a large onion, and venison tenderloin with figs and Bordeaux sauce from his native Avignon, France. An international wine list and traditional chocolate soufflé polish the Mediterranean meals. The outdoor dining may get cool, so bring a sweater. | 408 Bridge St., Bigfork | 406/837–2923 | Reservations essential | $14–$19 | AE, MC, V | Closed Sun.

Serrano's. Mexican. After a day on the dusty trail, fresh Mexican dinner is quite a treat whether dining inside the small cabin or outside in the lush back patio. Make reservations during July, August, and early September. | 29 Dawson Ave., East Glacier | 406/226–9392 | $7–$15 | AE, D, DC, MC, V | Closed Oct.–Apr.

Showthyme! American/Casual. The town's former bank building was erected in 1908 using hand-made bricks that still show the brick makers' fingerprints. The old bank has become a restaurant, where in summer you can dine outdoors, either street-side or bay-side. Signature dishes include fresh ahi tuna with sweet soy-ginger and wasabi aioli over Jasmine rice. | 548 Electric Ave., Bigfork | 406/837–0707 | Reservations essential | $13–$22 | AE, D, MC, V | No lunch.

Tupelo Grille. Southern. Fresh fish tops the daily specials and eclectic samplings include Cajun spices and pasta dishes. This cozy café is best known for its bread pudding dessert. | 17 Central Ave., Whitefish | 406/862–6136 | $11–$22 | AE, MC, V | Closed 2 wks in Nov.

Lodging

In Glacier

Apgar Village Lodge. The cabins and motel units here have views of the lake, and most of the cabins have kitchens. The furnishings are Western-style, and you can also go Western with a picnic prepared at the barbecue pits on the grounds. Restaurant. Cable TV. Boating. Hiking. Shops. | Apgar | 406/888–5484 | fax 406/888–5273 | www.westglacier.com | 20 rooms, 28 cabins | $67–$233 | AE, D, MC, V | Closed mid-Oct.–Apr.

Bayshore Inn. The L-shape Bayshore Inn wraps around the shoreline of Upper Waterton Lake and parallels a gravel beach. The motel is the most modern in the Peace Park, with an ice cream parlor on the premises. Restaurant, room service. Bar. Laundry facilities. | 111 Waterton Ave., Waterton Townsite | 403/859–2211 or 888/527–9555 | fax 403/859–2291 | www.bayshoreinn.com | 70 rooms | $139–$149 | AE, MC, V.

★ **Granite Park Chalet.** Early tourists used to ride horses through the park 7 to 9 mi each day and stay at a different chalet each night. The Granite Park is one of two chalets still standing (the other one is the Sperry Chalet). You can reach it only by hiking trails. A combination of public and private funds is being used to transform the chalet back into a full-service hotel, but for now it's still used by hikers overnighting in the backcountry. You must bring sleeping bags and your own food, and you need a reservation. You can park at Logan Pass visitor center and hike 7.6 mi or at the Loop trailhead and hike uphill 4 mi. | 7.6 mi south of Logan Pass | 406/387–5555 or 800/521–7238 | fax 406/387–5656 | 12 rooms | $72 | AE, D, MC, V | Closed mid-Sept.–early July.

Kilmorey Lodge. The only hotel in Waterton Townsite open year-round, the old-style Kilmorey Lodge faces the lake and is surrounded by trees. Many rooms have antique furniture and feather quilt-covered beds. Restaurant, room service. Bar. | 117 Evergreen Ave., Waterton Townsite | 403/859–2334 or 888/859–8669 | fax 403/859–2342 | www.watertonpark.com | 23 rooms | $108–$213 | AE, D, DC, MC, V.

Lake McDonald Lodge. Opened in 1914 and meticulously maintained ever since, Lake McDonald is one of the great historic lodges of the West. A Swiss chalet in design, it has open stairways with burled newels, and massive timbers surrounding stone fireplaces. The lobby is filled with stuffed and mounted wild animals. The lodge is 10 mi east of West Glacier on Going-to-the-Sun Road. Restaurant. Boating. Hiking. Bar. No a/c. No smoking. | Going-to-the Sun Rd. | 406/892–2525 | www.glacierparkinc.com | fax 406/888–5681 | 100 rooms | $92–$142 | AE, D, MC, V | Closed late Sept.–late May.

★ **Many Glacier Hotel.** This grand old Western lodge has a great hall pillared with massive peeled timbers. Enjoy the spectacular views from the vast veranda above the lake. Built in 1915 by Great Northern Railway president Louis Hill, this is the largest lodging in the

GLACIER
NATIONAL PARK

EXPLORING
ATTRACTIONS NEARBY
DINING
LODGING
CAMPING AND RV
FACILITIES
SHOPPING
ESSENTIAL
INFORMATION

park. Restaurant. Bar. No a/c. | 12 mi west of Babb on Many Glacier Rd. | 406/892–2525 | fax 406/892–1375 | www.glacierparkinc.com | 214 rooms | $111–$142, $219 suites | AE, D, MC, V | Closed late Sept.–mid-May.

Prince of Wales Hotel. Over the border in Waterton National Park, Canada, this historic, Swiss chalet–style hotel built in the 1920s overlooks Waterton Lake. The large windows in the lobby give grand mountain views. High tea is served daily. Restaurant. Bar. Shop. | 3 mi from Waterton Park entrance, Waterton Townsite | 403/859–2231 or 406/892–2525 | www.glacierparkinc.com | 86 rooms | C$179–C$799 | AE, MC, V | Closed late Sept.–early June.

Sperry Chalet. One of the two surviving Great Northern chalets, Sperry Chalet is a full-service backcountry hotel that is only accessible on foot or horseback. A steep 6-mi trail from Lake McDonald Lodge leads to the chalet, yielding commanding views along the way. Mule Shoe Outfitters will pack in you and your gear for a fee. You can park at Lake McDonald Lodge. Restaurant. | Trailhead across from Lake McDonald Lodge on Going-to-the-Sun Rd. | 406/387–5654 or 888/345–2649 | www.sperrychalet.com | 17 rooms | $255 | AE, MC, V | Closed early Sept.–early July.

Swiftcurrent Motor Inn. These plain but practical motel and cabin units at the end of Many Glacier Road have spectacular views of the mountains. Restaurant. Laundry facilities. Shops. | 12 mi west of Babb on Many Glacier Rd. | 406/892–2525 | www.glacierparkinc.com | 62 rooms, 26 cabins | $41–$100 | AE, D, MC, V | Closed late Sept.–early June.

Village Inn at Apgar. You cannot beat the view from this two-story motel-style wood structure on the shore of Lake McDonald. Some rooms have balconies, and all overlook the lake and mountains. Some kitchenettes. Fishing. | West end of Lake McDonald, in Apgar | 406/892–2525 | www.glacierparkinc.com | 36 rooms | $104–$169 | AE, D, MC, V | Closed late Sept.–June.

Near the Park

Belton Chalet and Lodge. This elegant lodge across from the Amtrak station (previously a Great Northern Railway stop) was built in 1910, the same year Glacier National Park was dedicated. Guests used to step off the train and head directly for the winningly decorated rooms, fine dining room, great stone fireplace, and crisp view of Glacier's mountain peaks. Restaurant. Shops. No smoking. | 12575 U.S. 2 E, West Glacier | 406/888–5000 or 888/235–8665 | www.beltonchalet.com | 25 rooms, 2 cabins | $120–$260 | AE, MC, V | Late May–mid-Oct. | CP.

★ **The Garden Wall Inn Bed and Breakfast.** This lovely restored B&B in Whitefish, near the Amtrak station and historic downtown, provides luxurious guest rooms, serves a three-course breakfast, and is staffed by knowledgeable park hikers, skiers, and explorers who will gladly share with you their favorite recreation spots. No smoking. | 504 Spokane Ave., Whitefish | 406/862–3440 or 888/530–1700 | www.gardenwallinn.com | 5 rooms | $95–$155 | AE, D, MC, V | BP.

Glacier Park Lodge. Originally built in 1913 by the Great Northern Railway, this full-service lodge is across from the Amtrak station. The lodge's walls are supported by 500–800-year-old fir logs and 3-ft-thick cedar logs, and they're decorated with antique rail-travel posters advertising Glacier National Park. Rooms are sparse with a simple elegance. The common areas draw you with massive fireplaces, card tables, and friendly conversation with other guests and staff from around the globe. Restaurant. 9-hole golf course. Pool. Horseback riding. Bar. Shop. | U.S. 2 at Rte. 49, East Glacier | 406/892–2525 | 160 rooms, 1 house | $135–$299 | AE, D, MC, V | Closed late Sept.–early June.

Grouse Mountain Lodge. The spacious rooms and sun porch of this lodge have views of the Whitefish Mountain Range, the Big Mountain Ski Resort, and manicured Whitefish Lake Golf Course. Shopping and fine dining are downtown. Each room is stylishly and individually decorated, with state-of-the-art baths. Deluxe and family suites are available. Dining room, room service. Some in-room hot tubs, some kitchenettes, some refrigerators. Cable

TV. 36-hole golf course, tennis court. Indoor pool. Hot tubs, sauna. Downhill skiing. Bar. Business services. Airport shuttle. | 2 Fairway Dr., Whitefish | 406/862–3000, 800/321–8822, or 877/862–1505 | fax 406/863–2901 | www.montanasfinest.com | 145 rooms | $179–$239 | AE, D, DC, MC, V.

★ **Hidden Moose Lodge.** Built into the side of a hill, this lodge evokes the rugged history of the state with rustic, wood furniture, wide porches and verandas, and thick log beams. You'll find tall French doors and warm quilts on the bed. Nature trails lead through gardens and forest to Whitefish Lake. You can arrange for a rafting or horseback riding trip from the lodge. Cable TV. Hot tub. Fishing. Bicycles. Hiking, horseback riding. No smoking. | 1735 East Lakeshore Dr., Whitefish | 406/862–6516 or 888/733–6667 | fax 406/862–6514 | www.hiddenmooselodge.com | 13 rooms | $99–$135 | AE, D, MC, V | BP.

Kandahar Lodge. The entrance to this three-story lodge has window arches and side panels of etched glass that display mountain and forest scenes by local Whitefish artist Myni Fergeson. Inside, the sunken lobby contains more original art, an impressive rock fireplace, and period antiques. Three floors house spacious, modern rooms, and ski trails abound outside. Restaurant. Some kitchenettes. Cable TV. Hot tub, massage, sauna. Bar. Laundry facilities. Business services. | Big Mountain Rd., Whitefish | 406/862–6098 or 800/862–6094 | fax 406/862–6095 | www.kandaharlodge.com | 50 rooms | $179–$219 | AE, D, MC, V | BP.

The Resort at Glacier, St. Mary Lodge. Your choices are many at this resort. There are rooms and suites at Great Bear Lodge, luxurious Pinnacles cottages, and special cabins for large families. All the lodge rooms have pine furniture and some have air-conditioning units (the only ones in Glacier). You have access to shops, pizza, a coffee bar, and a formal dining room. Restaurant. Horseback riding. Bar. Shops. Laundry facilities. Some pets allowed (fee). No smoking. | U.S. 89 and Going-to-the-Sun Rd., St. Mary | 406/732–4431, 800/368–3689, 208/726–6279 winter | fax 406/732–9265, 208/726–6282 winter | www.glcpark.com | 93 rooms, 12 suites, 20 cabins | $89–$325 | AE, D, MC, V | Closed Oct.–Apr.

Camping and RV Facilities

In Glacier

Apgar Campground. This large, busy campground on Lake McDonald is popular for the many activities and services available in the Apgar area. You can boat, fish, or swim in the lake; sign up for horseback rides; or hike. Apgar's stores and visitor center are a short walk away. About 25 sites are suitable for RVs. Flush toilets. Dump station. Drinking water. Bear boxes, fire grates. Public telephone. Ranger station. | 192 sites | Apgar Rd. | 406/888–7800 | $15 | Reservations not accepted | No credit cards | May–Sept.

Avalanche Creek Campground. This peaceful campground is shaded by huge red cedars and bordered by Avalanche Creek. Avalanche Lake trail and the Trail of the Cedars begin here. Some campsites and the comfort stations are wheelchair accessible. There are 50 sites for RVs up to 26 ft. Flush toilets. Dump station. Drinking water. Bear boxes, fire grates, picnic tables, food service. Public telephone. Swimming (lake). | 87 sites | 15 mi north of Apgar on Going-to-the-Sun Rd. | 406/888–7800 | $15 | Reservations not accepted | No credit cards | June–Sept.

Bowman Lake Campground. A quiet spot near Polebridge, this campground has several trailheads and a pebble beach. It's accessible by a one-lane dirt road only, so campers and RVs are not recommended. Pit toilets. Bear boxes, fire grates, picnic tables. Ranger station. | 48 sites | Bowman Lake Rd., 6.5 mi from Polebridge Ranger Station | 406/888–7800 | $12 | Reservations not accepted | No credit cards | Mid-May–mid-Sept.

Fish Creek Campground. The quietest campground on Lake McDonald is surrounded by thick evergreen forest, but you can still see a beautiful sunrise reflected off the lake and Snyder Ridge. There are 80 sites suitable for RVs up to 26 ft. Flush toilets. Dump station.

GLACIER CAMPGROUNDS

	Total # of sites	# of RV sites	# of hook-ups	Drive-to sites	Hike-to sites	Flush toilets	Pit/chemical toilets	Drinking water	Showers	Fire grates	Swimming	Boat access	Playground	Dump station	Ranger station	Public telephone	Reservation possible	Daily fee per site	Dates open
INSIDE THE PARK																			
Apgar	192	25	0	•	•	•		•		•	•	•		•	•	•		$15	May–Sept.
Avalanche Creek	87	50	0	•		•		•		•	•			•		•		$15	June–Sept.
Bowman Lake	48	0	0	•	•		•			•	•	•			•			$12	May–Sept.
Fish Creek	180	80	0	•		•		•						•				$17	June–Oct.
Kintla Lake	13	0	0	•	•		•			•	•			•				$12	May–Sept.
Many Glacier	110	13	0	•		•	•	•		•	•			•	•	•		$14	May–Sept.
Rising Sun	83	10	0	•		•		•		•				•				$15	May–Sept.
Sprague Creek	25	25	0	•		•		•		•	•							$15	May–Sept.
St. Mary	148	25	0	•		•		•						•	•	•	•	$17	May–Sept.
Two Medicine	99	13	0	•		•		•		•		•		•	•	•		$15	May–Sept.
Waterton Townsite	238	207	98	•	•	•	•	•	•	•	•	•	•	•	•	•		$15–23	Apr.–Oct.
NEAR THE PARK																			
St. Mary/ Glacier KOA	169	169	169	•		•		•	•	•	•	•		•	•	•	•	$22–37	May–Oct.
Sundance	31	31	31	•		•		•	•	•				•	•			$13–19	May–Oct.

* In summer only   ** Reservation Fee Charged   Y/R=Year-round
UL=Unlimited   ULP=Unlimited Primitive   LD=Labor Day   MD=Memorial Day

Drinking water. | 180 sites | 2 mi north of Apgar visitor center on Glacier Rte. 7 | 406/888–7800 or 800/365–2267 | $17 | MC, V | June–late Oct.

Kintla Lake Campground. Beautiful and remote, this small campground is a trout fisherman's favorite. Trails lead from the campground into the backcountry. The one-lane dirt access road is rough, so RVs are not recommended. Pit toilets. Dump station. Bear boxes, fire grates, picnic tables. | 13 sites | 14 mi north of Polebridge Ranger Station on Inside North Fork Rd. | $12 | Reservations not accepted | No credit cards | Mid-May–mid-Sept.

★ **Many Glacier Campground.** This campground is adjacent to the Many Glacier Hotel and the shops and activities based there. Several hiking trails begin at Many Glacier. This campground can accommodate 35-ft RVs. You can use a credit card to pay when you reserve by phone; it's cash-only at the campground. Flush toilets, pit toilets. Dump station. Drinking water, guest laundry, showers. Bear boxes, fire grates, picnic tables, food service. Public telephone. Ranger station. | 110 sites | Many Glacier Rd. | 406/888–7800 | $14 | No credit cards | Late May–late Sept.

Rising Sun Campground. On the north side of St. Mary Lake, this campground can be windy and cool, but is ideal if you want to go boating and fishing first thing in the morning. Towed units are not allowed. Flush toilets. Dump station. Drinking water. Bear boxes, fire grates, picnic tables, food service. | 83 sites | 5 mi west of St. Mary visitor center on Going-to-the-Sun Rd. | 406/888–7800 | $15 | Reservations not accepted | No credit cards | Late May–mid-Sept.

St. Mary Campground. On the east end of St. Mary lake, near the park entrance, this spot is good for fishing, and the restaurants and shops of St. Mary are just a couple of miles away. Flush toilets. Dump station. Drinking water. Bear boxes, fire grates, picnic tables. Public telephone. Ranger station. | 148 sites | 1 mi west of the St. Mary visitor center | 406/888–7800, 800/365–2267 reservations | $17 | MC, V | Mid-May–late Sept.

Sprague Creek Campground. Along the eastern side of Lake McDonald, this campground is for tents, RVs, and campers only; no towed units are allowed. This sometimes noisy, roadside camp spot offers spectacular views of the lake and sunsets, fishing from shore, and great rock skipping on the beach. Lake McDonald Lodge, restaurants, gift shops, and grocery store are 1 mi north on Going-to-the-Sun Rd. Flush toilets. Drinking water. Bear boxes, fire grates, picnic tables. | 25 sites | Going-to-the-Sun Rd., 1 mi S of Lake McDonald Lodge | 406/888–7800 | $15 | Reservations not accepted | No credit cards | Mid-May–mid-Sept.

★ **Two Medicine Campground.** In the remote, southeastern side of the park, this is often the last campground to fill during the height of summer. Though it's not near a town or any facilities, the area around the campground is scenic, and there's boat access at nearby Two Medicine Lake. Off-road primitive camping is permitted. Flush toilets. Dump station. Drinking water. Bear boxes, fire grates, picnic tables, food service. Public telephone. General store, ranger station. | 99 sites | Two Medicine Rd., 9 mi from Rte. 49 | 406/888–7800 | $14 | Reservations not accepted | No credit cards | Late May–late Sept.

Waterton Townsite Campground. In town and near the lake shore, the campground can be busy, noisy, and windy, but it does offer grassy, flat camping, kitchen shelters, and a view down the lake into the U.S. part of the peace park. The town's restaurants and shops are within walking distance. Flush toilets. Full hookups, dump station. Drinking water, guest laundry, showers. Fire grates, picnic tables. Public telephone. | Waterton Ave. and Vimy Ave. | 238 sites | $16–$24 | Reservations not accepted | No credit cards | Late Apr.–early Oct.

Near the Park

★ **St. Mary/Glacier Park KOA Kampground.** This full-service campground 1 mi west of town has everything from hot tubs to canoe rentals, a playground, game room, and, of course, lake access. The camp store sells groceries and souvenirs. There are barbecue dinners nightly. Besides the tent and RV sites, there are two cottages, four double cabins, and 21 single cabins. Flush toilets. Full hookups, partial hookups (electric and water), dump station. Drinking water, guest laundry, showers. Fire grates, picnic tables. Public telephone.

GLACIER
NATIONAL PARK

EXPLORING
ATTRACTIONS NEARBY
DINING
LODGING
CAMPING AND RV
FACILITIES
SHOPPING
ESSENTIAL
INFORMATION

THE "CROWN OF THE CONTINENT"

The history of Glacier National Park started long before Congress named the spectacular wilderness a national park. Native Americans, including the Blackfeet, Kootenai, and Salish, regularly traversed the area's valleys for centuries before white immigrants arrived. For the most part, these migratory people crossed the Rocky Mountains in search of sustenance in the form of roots, grasses, berries, and game. Many tribes felt that the mountains—with their unusual glacier-carved horns, cirques, and arêtes—were spiritually charged. Later, white people would be similarly inspired by Glacier's beauty and would nickname the area atop the Continental Divide the "Crown of the Continent."

The first white trappers arrived in the area as early as the 1780s. Then, in 1805, Lewis and Clark passed south of what is now Glacier National Park. Attracted by the expedition's quickly disseminated reports of abundant beaver, many more trappers, primarily British, French, and Spanish, began migrating to the region from the north, south, and east. For most of the early to mid-1800s, human activity in the area was limited to lone trappers and migrating Native Americans.

On their journey west, Lewis and Clark sought but did not find the elusive pass over the Rockies, now known as Marias Pass on the southern edge of Glacier National Park. Whether their scouts were unaware of the relatively low elevation—5,200 ft—in the pass, or whether they feared the Blackfeet that controlled the region, is unknown. The pass was not discovered, in fact, until 1889, when surveyors for the Great Northern Railway finally found it in the dead of winter. By 1891 the Great Northern Railway's tracks had crossed Marias Pass, and by 1895 the railroad had completed its westward expansion, thus ensuring continued settlement of the West.

As homesteaders, miners, and trappers poured into the Glacier area in the late 1800s, the Native American population seriously declined. The Blackfeet were devastated by smallpox epidemics—a disease previously unknown in North America—from the mid-1800s until the early 1900s. The disease, and a reduced food supply due the overhunting of buffalo, stripped the Blackfeet of their power and, eventually, their land. In 1895, the tribe sold the area now within the national park to the U.S. government, who opened it to miners. Returns on the mines were never very substantial, and most were abandoned by the 1905.

Between the late 1880s and 1900, *Forest and Stream* magazine editor George Grinnel made several trips to the mountains of northwestern Montana. He was awed by the beauty of the area, and he urged the U.S. government to give it park status, thereby protecting it from mining interests and homesteaders. At the same time, the Great Northern Railway company, eager to bring customers out from the east, also was spreading the word about the area's recreational opportunities. The company built seven backcountry chalets to house guests, and promised tourists from the east a back-to-nature experience with daylong hikes and horseback rides between the strategically placed chalets. Visitors arrived by train at West Glacier, took a stagecoach to Lake McDonald, a boat to the lakeside Snyder Hotel, and began their nature adventures from there. Between Grinnel's political influence and the Great Northern's financial interests, Congress found reason enough to establish Glacier National Park; the bill was signed by president William Howard Taft in 1910.

General store. | 169 sites (60 with full hookups; 72 with partial hookups), 27 cabins | 106 West Shore Rd., St. Mary | 406/732–4122, 800/562–1504 for reservations | fax 406/732–4327 | www.goglacier.com | $22–$37, $50–$150 cabins | D, MC, V | May 15–Sept.

Sundance RV Park and Campground. This older campground, 6 mi south of West Glacier, was built with families in mind. It's close to numerous roadside attractions, including a water park, as well as Glacier. Bicyclists and hikers drop in for $3 showers. Flush toilets. Partial hookups (electric and water), dump station. Drinking water, guest laundry, showers. Fire grates, picnic tables. Play area. | 10545 U.S. 2 E, Coram | 406/387–5016 | 31 sites with partial hookups, 1 cabin | $13–$19, $35 cabin | MC, V | May 15–Oct. 15.

Shopping

In Glacier and Waterton, general stores are small and have limited inventories. Most stores sell fishing and camping supplies as well as snacks and drinks. You'll find them in commercial areas of the park, such as Apgar, Rising Sun, Swiftcurrent, and Two Medicine, open in summer only.

The Cedar Tree. You can buy artwork such as paintings, photography, and sculpture here. | Apgar Rd., Apgar | 406/888–5232 | Closed mid-Sept.–May.

Montana House of Gifts. Weaving and other works of art are for sale here. | Apgar Rd., Apgar | 406/888–5393 | Closed mid-Sept.–May.

Prince of Wales Gift Shop. Since the lodge is a "must see," so is a stop in the gift shop for curios, post cards and other tourist goods. The shop also has an incredible view of the park and lake. | Prince of Wales Hotel, Waterton Townsite | 403/859–2231 | Closed Oct.–May.

St. Mary Lodge Gift Shop. This fully stocked outdoor store also has a country market and probably the park's largest selection of t-shirts and souvenirs. | Going-to-the-Sun Rd. at U.S. 89 | 406/732–4431 or 800/368–3689 | Closed Oct.–late May.

Schoolhouse Gifts. Come here for clothing and quality artists' work. | Apgar Rd., Apgar | 406/888–5235 | Closed Nov.–mid-May.

Essential Information

ATMS: You'll find cash machines at Lake McDonald Lodge, Many Glacier Lodge, St. Mary Lodge, Glacier Park Lodge, and, in Waterton Townsite, at Tamarack Village Square.

AUTOMOBILE SERVICE STATIONS: Glacier Highland Store | 12555 U.S. 2 E, West Glacier | 406/888–5427 | Closed mid-Oct.–Apr. **Lodge at St. Mary Exxon** | Going-to-the-Sun Rd. at U.S. 2, St. Mary | 406/732–4431 | Closed mid-Oct.–Apr. **Pat's** | 224 Mountain View Rd., Waterton Townsite | 403/859–2266.

POST OFFICES: West Glacier | 110 Going-to-the-Sun Rd., 59936 | 406/888–5591. **East Glacier** | U.S. 2, north of town, 59434 | 406/226–5534. **Waterton Townsite** | 102a Windflower Ave., ToK 2Mo | 403/859–2294.

GRAND TETON NATIONAL PARK

NORTHWESTERN WYOMING

12 mi north of Jackson, WY on U.S 26/89/191 and 7 mi south of Yellowstone National Park on U.S. 89/191/287.

Your jaw will probably drop the first time you see the Teton Range jutting up from the Jackson Hole valley floor. With no foothills to get in the way, you will have a close-up view of magnificent, jagged peaks capped with snow—even before you step out of your car. This massif is long on natural beauty. Before your eyes, mountain glaciers creep imperceptibly down 12,605-ft Mount Moran. Large and small lakes are strung along the range's base, multicolor wildflowers cover the valley floor, and Wyoming's great abundance of wildlife scampers about the meadows and mountains. In Grand Teton National Park, short trails lead through willow flats near Jackson Lake connecting with longer trails that lead into the canyons of the Teton Range. Boats skim the waters of Jackson and Jenny lakes, depositing visitors on the wild western shore of Jenny, while guided float trips meander down a calm stretch of the tortuous Snake River. A trip to the backcountry—which has more than 200 mi of trails, from the novice-accessible Cascade Canyon to the expert's Teton Crest—reveals the majesty of what the Shoshone tribes called *Teewinot* (Many Pinnacles).

PUBLICATIONS

The *Grand Teton Official Map and Guide* and the seasonal park newspaper, *Teewinot*, are distributed free at park entrances. You can purchase excellent park-related books at Grand Teton visitor center book stores. The shops are run by the Grand Teton Natural History Association, a nonprofit cooperating organization that also distributes videos and children's books about the park and its environs. **Grand Teton Natural History Association** | Box 170, Moose, WY 83012 | 307/739–3403 | www.grandtetonpark.org.

When to Visit

The park is open year-around, though many services are curtailed in winter. All interior park roads are generally open from early May through late October. Before Memorial Day and after late September services in the park are limited, but Moose visitor center stays open all winter, except on Christmas Day.

SCENERY AND WILDLIFE

Your best chance to see wildlife is in the early morning or late evening (think dawn and dusk), along forest edges. Elk are the region's most common large mammals. The best place to view elk in summer is on Teton Park Road; find elk in winter south of the park on the National Elk Refuge, where some 7,500 of the animals spend the colder months. Oxbow Bend and Willow Flats are good places to look for moose, beaver, and otter any time of year. Pronghorn and bison appear in summer along Jackson Hole Highway and Antelope Flats Road, and black bear inhabit the forests along lake shores and the backcountry, although sightings are not common. Birds include bald eagles and ospreys, which can be spotted along the Snake River throughout the year. In addition, there are killdeer in marshy areas and trumpeter swans, mallards, and Canada geese on the river and nearby ponds.

HIGH AND LOW SEASON

Summer is definitely high season in Grand Teton National Park. Nearly 4 million visitors travel through the region; July and August are the park's most crowded months. In Jackson dining and lodging rates are generally highest in summer. The lowest rates and smallest crowds can be found in spring and fall, both in the park and throughout the surrounding area, but note that some services won't be available. In April most of Teton Park Road is open to bicyclists, in-line skaters, and hikers only, an off-season treat for observers of wildlife. When park lodgings and visitor services are closed for winter the crowds in the park are genuinely sparse. Most of Teton Park Road is closed late October through early May, but Jackson Hole Highway remains open, providing access to cross-country ski trails and frozen Jackson Lake. However, because of the popularity of the excellent downhill skiing in the area, winter is a very busy time around Teton Village and in Jackson. Winter dining and lodging rates at Teton Village are often higher than in summer.

Average High/Low Temperatures (°F) and monthly Precipitation (in inches)

	JAN.	FEB.	MAR.	APR.	MAY	JUNE
GRAND TETON	26/1	31/4	39/12	49/22	60/31	70/38
	2.61	2.0	1.60	1.45	1.90	2.20
	JULY	AUG.	SEPT.	OCT.	NOV.	DEC.
	80/42	78/41	68/34	56/26	38/14	26/2
	1.20	1.40	1.30	1.0	2.14	2.47

FESTIVALS AND SEASONAL EVENTS

More information on most of the following events can be obtained from the Jackson Hole Chamber of Commerce and the park visitor centers.

WINTER

Dec.: Skiers celebrate Christmas and New Year's Eve with **torchlight parades** at Snow King Mountain in Jackson and at Jackson Hole Mountain Resort. | 307/739–2770 or 307/733–5200.

Dec–Mar.: At Walk Festival Hall in Teton Village, **Grand Teton Music Festival** presents monthly concerts featuring solo performers as well as duos and groups. | 307/733–1128.

SPRING

Apr.: The **Pole-Pedal-Paddle** is a ski-cycle-canoe relay race starting at Jackson Hole Ski Resort and finishing down the Snake River. | 307/733–6433.

May: Jackson's **Old West Days** include a rodeo, Native American dancers, a Western swing dance contest, and cowboy poetry readings. | 307/733–3316.

SUMMER

May–Aug.: Each spring and summer the **Teton County Historical Society** sponsors monthly field trips to regional sites such as pioneer ranches. | 307/733–9605.

May–Sept.: Between Memorial Day and Labor Day, gunslingers stage **The Shootout** daily except Sunday in the Jackson town square. Don't worry, the bullets aren't real. | 307/733–3316.

July–Aug.: During the **Grand Teton Music Festival** a schedule of symphony orchestra performances is presented at Walk Festival Hall in Teton Village and outdoors near Jackson Hole Resort. There's also a winter concert schedule. | 307/733–1128.

FALL

Sept.–Oct.: Each year, artists in various media show and sell their work in Jackson at the **Jackson Hole Fall Arts Festival.** Special events include poetry readings and dance performances. Jackson's many art galleries have special exhibits and programs. | 307/733–3316.

Nearby Towns

The major gateway to Grand Teton National Park is **Jackson,** often referred to by visitors as Jackson Hole. Actually, Jackson Hole is the mountain-ringed valley that houses Jackson and much of Grand Teton National Park. The community of roughly 7,000 permanent residents hosts more than 3 million visitors annually. Expensive homes and fashionable shops have sprung up all over, but Jackson manages to maintain at least part of its true Western character. With its raised wooden sidewalks and old-fashioned store-fronts (some now being replaced with more modern styles), the town center still looks a bit like a Western movie set. There's a lot to do here, both downtown (museums, art galleries, fine dining, western dancing) and in the surrounding countryside (hiking, climbing, floating down the Snake River). If it's skiing you're after, **Teton Village** is the place for you. It's not an incorporated city or town; rather, Teton Village is a cluster of businesses that centers around the facilities of the Jackson Hole Ski Resort—a tramway, gondola, and various other lifts. The community resounds to the clomp of ski boots in winter and to the strains of the Grand Teton Music Festival in summer. There's ample lodging, dining, and shopping here.

On the "backside of the Tetons," as eastern Idaho is known, **Driggs** is a western gateway to Yellowstone Country and Grand Teton National Park. Easygoing and rural, Driggs resembles the Jackson of a few decades ago. From here you have to cross a major mountain pass to reach the park; note that the pass is sometimes closed in winter by avalanches. If you prefer an easier drive into the park but want to avoid the hubbub of Jackson and Teton Village, you can stay in **Dubois,** about 55 mi east of Jackson. The least known of the gateway communities to Grand Teton and Yellowstone, this town of 1,000 has all the services of the bigger towns. In Dubois you can still get a room for the night during the peak summer travel period without making a reservation weeks or months in advance (though it's a good idea to call a week or so before you intend to arrive). Dubois's other treasure is its vast amount of nearby public land, where you can camp and hike in summer and snowmobile and race dogsleds in winter.

INFORMATION

Dubois Chamber of Commerce | Box 632, Dubois, WY 82513 | 307/455–2556 | fax 307/455–3168 | www.duboiswyoming.org. **Eastern Idaho Visitor Information Center** | 630 W. Broadway, Box 50498, Idaho Falls, ID 83405 | 208/523–1010 or 866/365–6943 | fax 208/523–2255 | www.idahofallschamber.com. **Jackson Chamber of Commerce** | Box 550, Jackson, WY 83001 | 307/733–3316 | fax 307/733–5585 | www.jacksonholechamber.com. **Teton Valley Chamber of Commerce** | 81 N. Main St. #C, Box 250, Driggs, ID 83422 | 208/354–2500 | fax 208/354–2517 | www.tetonvalleychamber.com.

Exploring Grand Teton

PARK BASICS

Contacts and Resources: For general information about the park, contact **Grand Teton National Park** | Box 170, Moose, 83012 | 307/739–3300, 307/739–3400 TTY | www.nps.gov/grte. For information on activities at Jackson Lake, contact **Colter Bay Visitor Center** | 2 mi off U.S. 89/191/287, 5 mi north of Jackson Lake Junction | 307/739–3594. For information on lodging, dining, and tours in the park contact the park's largest concessionaire, **Grand Teton Lodge Company** | Box 250, Moran, 83013 | 307/543–2811, 307/543–3100, or 800/628–9988 | fax 307/543–3143 | www.gtlc.com.

Hours: The park is open 24 hours a day, seven days a week, year-round.

Fees: Park entrance fees, payable at the Moose, Granite Canyon, and Moran entrances, are $20 per car, truck, or RV, $15 per motorcycle or snowmobile, and $10 per person entering on foot or bicycle. Annual park passes are $40. You can also buy a $20 pass that's good for seven days in both Grand Teton and Yellowstone parks.

Getting Around: The best way to see Grand Teton National Park is by car. Unlike Yellowstone's Grand Loop, Grand Teton's road system doesn't allow for easy tour-bus access to all the major sights. Only a car will get you close to Jenny Lake, into the remote east Jackson Hole hills, and to the top of Signal Mountain. You can stop at many points along the roads within the park for a hike or a view. Be extremely cautious in winter when whiteouts and ice are not uncommon. Jackson Hole Highway (U.S. 89/191) runs the entire length of the park, from Jackson to Yellowstone National Park's south entrance (it's also Route 26 south of Moran Junction and U.S. 287 north of Moran Junction). This road is open all year from Jackson to Moran Junction and north to Flagg Ranch, 2 mi south of Yellowstone. Depending on traffic, the southern (Moose) entrance to Grand Teton is about 15 minutes from downtown Jackson via Jackson Hole Highway. Coming from the opposite direction on the same road, the northern boundary of the park is about 15 minutes south of Yellowstone National Park. Also open year-round, U.S. 26/287 runs east from Dubois over Togwotee Pass to the Moran entrance station, a drive of about one hour.

Two back-road entrances to Grand Teton require high-clearance vehicles. Both are closed by snow from November through mid-May and are heavily rutted through June. The Moose–Wilson Road (Route 390) starts at Route 22 in Wilson (west of Jackson) and travels 12 mi north past Teton Village, then turns into an unpaved road for 3 mi leading to the Moose entrance. It's closed to large trucks, trailers, and RVs. Even rougher is 60-mi Grassy Lake Road, which heads east from Route 32 in Ashton, Idaho, through Targhee National Forest. It connects with U.S. 89/287 in the John D. Rockefeller Jr. Memorial Parkway, which is actually a park, not a road, sandwiched between Grand Teton and Yellowstone.

Permits: Backcountry permits, which must be obtained in person at Moose or Colter Bay visitor centers or Jenny Lake ranger station, are free and required for all overnight stays outside designated campgrounds. Seven-day boat permits, available year-round at Moose visitor center and in summer at Colter Bay and Signal Mountain ranger stations, cost $10 for motorized craft and $5 for nonmotorized craft and are good for 7 days.

Public Telephones: Public telephones may be found at park visitor centers and at Colter Bay Store, Dornan's, Jackson Lake Lodge, Leek's Marina, and Signal Mountain Lodge.

Rest Rooms: Public rest rooms may be found at all park visitor centers, campgrounds, and ranger stations (at Colter Bay, Moose, Jenny Lake, and Buffalo near the Moran entrance). There are rest rooms at the picnic area north of Moose on Teton Park Road, at String Lake picnic area, and at Colter Bay picnic area.

Accessibility: The frontcountry portions of Grand Teton are largely accessible to people in wheelchairs. There's designated parking at most sites, and some interpretive trails are easily accessible. You will find accessible trails and facilities at Cottonwood Creek Picnic Area, Leek's Marina, Menor's Ferry, Moose Village, South Jenny Lake, and String Lake. Additionally, the Chapel of the Transfiguration, Colter Bay Village, and Lizard Creek Campground have partially accessible routes. A number of the park's picnic areas (Cottonwood Creek, South Jenny Lake trailhead, and String Lake) are fully accessible and some (Colter Bay Village campground, Moose visitor center) are partially accessible. TDD telephones are available at Colter Bay visitor center (307/739–3544) and at Moose visitor center (307/739–3400). For an Easy Access guide to the park, stop by one of the visitor centers or contact the park at 307/739–3600, 307/739–3400 (TTY), or www.nps.gov/grte.

Many Grand Teton bus tours, float trips, fishing trips, lake cruises, and wagon rides are fully or partially accessible; ask the independent operators for details. One company, **Access Tours,** caters specifically to people with physical disabilities. The company can also give you general information about places that are easily accessible in Teton, Glacier, and Yellowstone. | Box 499, Victor, ID 83455 | 208/787–2338 or 800/929–4811 | fax 208/787–2332 | www.accesstours.org.

Emergencies: In case of a fire, medical, or police emergency in the park, dial 911. For medical or police emergencies you can also call 307/739–3300. Park law enforcement rangers are located at ranger stations (at Colter Bay, Jenny Lake, and Moose). In the park, you can receive medical attention at **Grand Teton Medical Clinic** near the Chevron station next to Jackson Lake Lodge. | 0.5 mi north of Jackson Lake Junction | 307/543–2514 or 307/733–8002 | Mid-May–mid-Oct., daily 10–6. **St. John's Hospital** in Jackson is the hospital closest to the park. | 625 E. Broadway Ave., Jackson | 307/733–3636 or 800/877–7078.

Lost and Found: The park's lost-and-found is at Moose visitor center.

Good Tours

GRAND TETON IN ONE DAY

Begin the day by packing a picnic lunch or picking one up at a Jackson eatery. Arrive at Moose visitor center in time for a 9 AM, two-hour, guided **Snake River float trip** (make reservations in advance with one of the dozen or so outfitters that offer the trip). When you're back on dry ground, drive north on **Teton Park Road,** stopping at scenic turnouts—don't miss Teton Glacier—until you reach Jenny Lake Road, which is one-way headed south. After a brief stop at **Cathedral Group Turnout,** park at the Jenny Lake ranger station and take the 20-minute boat ride to **Cascade Canyon Trailhead** for a short hike. You can take your lunch with you to enjoy along the trail; be sure to carry out all your trash. Return to your car by early afternoon, drive back to Teton Park Road, and head north to **Signal Mountain Road** to catch a top-of-the-park view of the Tetons. In late afternoon descend the mountain and continue north on Teton Park Road. At Jackson Lake Junction you can go east to **Oxbow Bend** or north to **Willow Flats,** both excellent spots for wildlife viewing. At **Jackson Lake Lodge** an early dinner accompanied by a vista of the Tetons will rejuvenate you for the trip north to Colter Bay Marina, where you can board a 1½-hour sunset cruise across Jackson Lake to **Waterfalls Canyon.** Spend the night in cabins at Colter Bay or a room at Jackson Lake Lodge. You can reverse this route if you're heading south from Yellowstone: start the day with a 7:30 breakfast cruise from Colter Bay and end it with a sunset float down the Snake River.

GRAND TETON IN TWO DAYS

Spend one day as suggested above, then choose among the many ways to explore the park more fully. Take an all-day hike, a white-water raft trip, a horseback trail ride, or a gentle meander around **Jenny Lake.** Explore some of Grand Teton's human history by visiting the **Indian Arts Museum** at Colter Bay visitor center, **Menor's Ferry, Chapel of the Transfiguration, Cunningham Cabin,** and **Mormon Row.** Cap off the day with dinner in the elegant dining room of **Jenny Lake Lodge,** or take advantage of the excellent wine cellar and the chuck-wagon dinner at **Dornan's.** If you still have energy to spare, you can spend the night whooping it up at a cowboy bar in **Jackson.**

Attractions

PROGRAMS AND TOURS

Campfire Programs. Park rangers lead free nightly slide shows from June through September at the Colter Bay, Flagg Ranch Resort, Gros Ventre, and Signal Mountain amphitheaters. Topics include Teton wildlife, history, and geology. For schedules of topics check the park newspaper, *Teewinot,* or at visitor centers. | Colter Bay: 2 mi off U.S. 89/191/287, 5 mi north of Jackson Lake Junction | Flagg Ranch Resort: John D. Rockefeller Jr. Memorial Pkwy., 4 mi north of the national park boundary | Gros Ventre: 4 mi off U.S. 26/89/191 and 1.5 mi west of Kelly on Gros Ventre River Rd., 7 mi south of Moose Junction | Signal Mountain: Teton Park Rd., 4 mi south of Jackson Lake Junction | 307/739–3399 or 307/739–3594 | June–July, nightly at 9:30; Aug.–Sept., nightly at 9.

Flagg Ranch Resort Campfire Program. Park rangers give talks about park history, wildlife, and geology at this campground north of the park. | John D. Rockefeller Jr. Memorial Pkwy., 4 mi north of Grand Teton National Park boundary | 307/543–2861 | Free | June–July, nightly at 8; Aug.–Sept., nightly at 7:30.

Grand Teton Lodge Company Bus Tours. Half-day tours depart from Colter Bay Village or Jackson Lake Lodge and include visits to scenic viewpoints, visitor centers, and other park sites. Buy tickets in advance at Colter Bay Marina or Jackson Lake Lodge activities desks. | Colter Bay Village or Jackson Lake Lodge | 307/543–2811 or 800/628–9988 | $30–$50 | Mid-May–early Oct., daily.

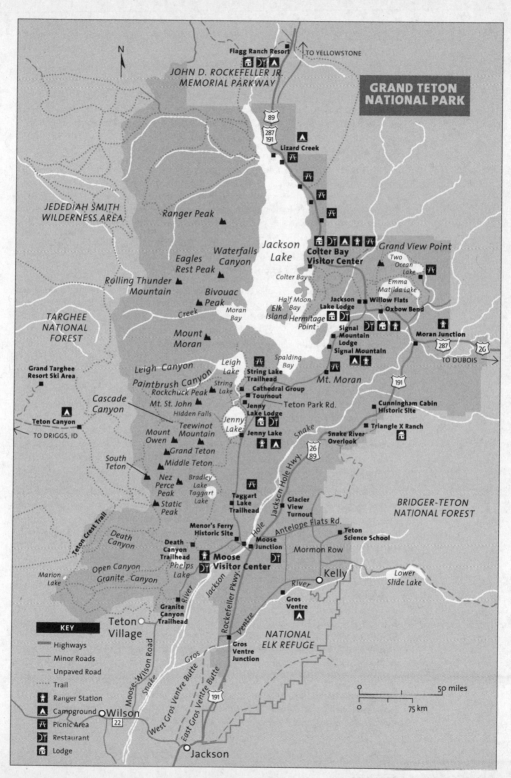

N

Flagg Ranch Resort
JOHN D. ROCKEFELLER JR. MEMORIAL PARKWAY
TO YELLOWSTONE

89
287
191

Lizard Creek

JEDEDIAH SMITH WILDERNESS AREA

Ranger Peak

Waterfalls Canyon

Jackson Lake

Colter Bay
Colter Bay Visitor Center

Grand View Point

Two Ocean Lake

Eagles Rest Peak

Rolling Thunder Mountain

Bivouac Peak

Emma Matilda Lake

Willow Flats

Half Moon Bay
Elk Island

Jackson Lake Lodge

Oxbow Bend

TARGHEE NATIONAL FOREST

Creek

Moran Bay

Hermitage Point

Signal Mountain Lodge
Signal Mountain

Moran Junction

287

26
TO DUBOIS

Mount Moran

Spalding Bay

Leigh Canyon

Leigh Lake

String Lake Trailhead

Mt. Moran

191

Grand Targhee Resort Ski Area

Paintbrush Canyon
Rockchuck Peak

String Lake

Cathedral Group Tournout

Cunningham Cabin Historic Site

Cascade Canyon

Mt. St. John
Hidden Falls

Jenny Lake Lodge

Teton Park Rd.

Triangle X Ranch

Teton Canyon
TO DRIGGS, ID

Mount Owen

Teewinot Mountain

Jenny Lake

Jenny Lake

Snake

Snake River Overlook

South Teton

Grand Teton

Middle Teton

Nez Perce Peak

Bradley Lake

Taggart Lake

26
89

Static Peak

Taggart Lake Trailhead

Glacier View Turnout

BRIDGER-TETON NATIONAL FOREST

Death Canyon

Menor's Ferry Historic Site

Hole

Antelope Flats Rd.

Teton Science School

Marion Lake

Death Canyon Trailhead

Phelps Lake

Open Canyon

Granite Canyon

Moose Visitor Center

Moose Junction

Mormon Row

Kelly

Lower Slide Lake

River

Jackson

Granite Canyon Trailhead

Gros Ventre

River

Gros Ventre

KEY

Teton Village

Rockefeller Pkwy.

Ventre

NATIONAL ELK REFUGE

Highways
Minor Roads
Unpaved Road
Trail
Ranger Station
Campground
Picnic Area
Restaurant
Lodge

Moose-Wilson Road

Snake

Gros Ventre Junction

Gros

West Gros Ventre Butte

East Gros Ventre Butte

50 miles

75 km

Wilson

22

191

Jackson

GRAND TETON NATIONAL PARK | 253

Gray Line Bus Tours. Full-day bus tours provide an overview of Grand Teton National Park. They depart from Jackson. | 16 W. Martin La., Jackson | 307/733–4325 or 800/443–6133 | fax 307/733–2689 | $65 plus park entrance fee | Memorial Day–Sept.

Jackson Lake Cruises. Grand Teton Lodge Company runs 1½-hour Jackson Lake scenic cruises from Colter Bay Marina throughout the day as well as breakfast cruises, and sunset steak-fry cruises. One cruise, known as Fire and Ice, shows how forest fires and glaciers have shaped the Grand Teton landscape. | 2 mi off U.S. 89/191/287, 5 mi north of Jackson Lake Junction | 307/543–3100, 307/543–2811, or 800/628–9988 | www.gtlc.com | Scenic cruise $16; breakfast cruise $28; steak-fry cruise $46 | Late May–mid-Sept.

Jackson Lake Lodge Ranger Talks. Visit the Wapiti Room to hear a slide-illustrated ranger presentation on topics such as area plants and animals, geology, and natural history. For a more informal atmosphere, chat with the ranger who is available on the back deck of the lodge 6:30–8 PM daily, early June through early September. | U.S. 89/191/287, 0.5 mi north of Jackson Lake Junction | 307/739–3300 | Late June–mid-Aug., nightly at 8:30.

Ranger Walks. Rangers lead free walks throughout the park in summer, from a one-hour lakeside stroll at Colter Bay to a three-hour hike from Jenny Lake. Call for itineraries, times, and reservations. | 307/739–3300, 307/739–3400 TTY | Early June–early Sept.

Teton Aviation Center. These folks can give you a bird's-eye view of the Tetons from a glider or small airplane. Flights leave from Driggs-Reade Memorial Airport. Glider flights are not available when the temperature drops below freezing. | 675 Airport Rd., Driggs, ID | 208/354–3100 or 800/472–6382 | fax 208/354–3200 | www.tetonaviation.com | Glider flights $199 per hour; airplane flightseeing $165 per hour | Year-round.

Teton Science School. Adults can join one of the school's single- or multiday wildlife expeditions in Grand Teton, Yellowstone, and surrounding forests to see and learn about wolves, bears, mountain sheep, and other animals. Junior high and high school students can take multiweek field ecology courses while living at the school, backpacking and camping out. Weekdays, kids in grades 1–6 can join Young Naturalists programs that don't involve sleepovers. In previous years program topics have included "Water World," "Insectopia," and "A Place Called Dirt." | Box 68, Kelly, 83011 | 307/733–4765 | fax 307/739–9388 | www.tetonscience.org | Adult programs $55–$1,950; youth programs $195–$2,950 | Year-round.

Young Naturalist Program. Children ages 8–12 learn about the natural world of the park as they take an easy 2 mi hike with a ranger. Kids should wear old clothes and bring water, rain gear, and insect repellent. The hike, which takes place at Jenny Lake or Colter Bay, is 1½ hours long and is limited to 12 children. Parents must pick up children promptly at 3 PM. | Jenny Lake: meet at the flag pole at the visitor center; Colter Bay: meet at the visitor center | 307/739–3399 or 307/739–3594 | Mid-June–mid-Aug., daily 1:30.

SCENIC DRIVES

Antelope Flats Road. Off Jackson Hole Highway 1 mi north of Moose Junction, this road wanders eastward over rolling plains and sagebrush flats that are home to pronghorn, bison, and moose. The road intersects Mormon Row, where you can see abandoned homesteaders' barns and houses from the turn of the 20th century. Less than 1 mi past Mormon Row is a four-way intersection where you can turn right to loop around past the town of Kelly and Gros Ventre campground and rejoin Jackson Hole Highway at Gros Ventre Junction.

Jackson Hole Highway (U.S. 89/191). Slicing through the middle of Jackson Hole, this highway passes views of the Teton Range along most of its distance, with a turnout at the Snake River Overlook and another good one with a view of the Snake River at Oxbow Bend.

★ **Jenny Lake Scenic Drive.** Providing the park's best roadside close-ups of the Tetons, this road winds south through groves of lodgepole pine and open meadows. Roughly 2 mi down the one-way road, the Cathedral Group Turnout faces 13,770-ft Grand Teton (the range's highest peak), flanked by 12,928-ft Mount Owen and 12,325-ft Mount Teewinot.

Signal Mountain Road. This exciting drive climbs 700 ft along a 5-mi stretch of switchbacks. As you travel through forest you can catch glimpses of Jackson Lake and Mount Moran. The trip ends with a sweeping view of Jackson Hole and the entire 40-mi Teton Range. Sunset is the most scenic time to make the climb up Signal Mountain.

Teton Park Road. Linking Moose Junction with Jackson Lake Junction, this 20-mi drive is the closest to the Teton Range. It skirts Jackson Lake, with Signal Mountain looming to the east. Farther south, turnouts give you excellent views of Mount Moran and the Cathedral Group (the three highest peaks in the Teton Range).

SIGHTS TO SEE

Chapel of the Sacred Heart. This small log chapel sits in the pine forest with a view of Jackson Lake. | 0.25 mi east of Signal Mountain Lodge, off Teton Park Rd., 4 mi south of Jackson Lake Junction | Services June–Sept., Sat. 5:30 PM and Sun. 8 AM and 10 AM.

★ **Chapel of the Transfiguration.** This tiny chapel built in 1925 is still a functioning Episcopal church. Couples come here to exchange vows with the Tetons as a backdrop, and tourists come to take photos of the small church with its awe-inspiring view. | 0.5 mi off Teton Park Rd., 2 mi north of Moose Junction | Late May–late Sept., Sunday: Eucharist 8 AM, service 10 AM.

Colter Bay Visitor Center. The auditorium hosts several free daily programs about Indian culture and natural history. Daily at 11 and 3, a 30-minute "Teton Highlights" ranger lecture provides tips on park activities. | 2 mi off U.S. 89/191/287, 5 mi north of Jackson Lake Junction | 307/739–3594 | Mid-May–mid-June and Sept., daily 8–5; mid-June–Labor Day 8–8.

Spend an hour or two at the **Indian Arts Museum,** which has examples of Plains Indian weapons and clothing. From June through early September, you can see crafts demonstrations by tribal members, take ranger-led tours of the museum, and listen to a daily 45-minute ranger program on Indian culture.

Cunningham Cabin Historic Site. At the end of a gravel spur road, an easy 0.75-mi trail runs through sagebrush around Pierce Cunningham's 1890 log cabin homestead. Cunningham, an early Jackson Hole homesteader and civic leader, built his cabin in Appalachian dogtrot style, joining two halves with a roofed veranda. Watch for badgers, coyotes, and Uinta ground squirrels in the area. The site is open year-round, and a pamphlet is available at the trailhead. | 0.5 mi off Jackson Hole Hwy., 6 mi south of Moran Junction | Year-round.

★ **Jackson Lake.** The biggest of Grand Teton's glacier-scooped lakes, this body of water in the northern reaches of the park was enlarged by construction of the Jackson Lake Dam in 1906. You can fish, sail, and windsurf on the lake, or hike trails near the shoreline. Three marinas (Colter Bay, Leeks, and Signal Mountain) provide access for boaters, and several picnic areas, campgrounds, and lodges overlook the lake. | U.S. 89/191/287 from Lizard Creek to Jackson Lake Junction, and Teton Park Rd. from Jackson Lake Junction to Signal Mountain Lodge.

Jenny Lake. Named for the Native American wife of mountain man Beaver Dick Leigh, this alpine lake south of Jackson Lake draws boaters to its pristine waters and hikers to its tree-shaded trails. | Jenny Lake Rd., 2 mi off Teton Park Rd. 12 mi north of Moose Junction.

Jenny Lake Visitor Center. Geology exhibits, including a relief model of the Teton Range, are on display at the Jenny Lake Visitor Center. | South Jenny Lake Junction, 0.5 mi off Teton Park Rd., 8 mi north of Moose Junction | Early June–early Sept., daily 8–7; early Sept.–late Sept., daily 8–5.

★ **Menor's Ferry Historic Area.** The ferry on display is not the original, but it's an accurate re-creation of the craft built by Bill Menor in the 1890s, and it demonstrates how people

GRAND TETON
NATIONAL PARK

EXPLORING
ATTRACTIONS NEARBY
DINING
LODGING
CAMPING AND RV
FACILITIES
SHOPPING
ESSENTIAL
INFORMATION

crossed the Snake River before bridges were built. The original buildings used by Menor house historical displays, including a photo collection; one building has been turned into a small general store. You can pick up a pamphlet for a self-guided tour. | 0.5 mi off Teton Park Rd., 2 mi north of Moose Junction | Year-round.

Moose Visitor Center. The center has exhibits of rare and endangered species and the geology and natural history of the Greater Yellowstone area. In the auditorium you can see a video called *The Nature of Grand Teton* and other videos on topics that range from geology to wolves. | Teton Park Rd., 0.5 mi north of Moose Junction | 307/739–3399 | June–Aug., daily 8–7; Sept.–May, daily 8–5.

★ **Oxbow Bend.** This spot overlooks a quiet backwater left by the Snake River when it cut a new southern channel. White pelicans stop here on their spring migration (many stay on through summer), trumpeter swans visit frequently, and great blue herons nest amid the cottonwoods along the river. Use binoculars to search for bald eagles, ospreys, moose, beaver, and otter. The Oxbow is known for the reflection of Mount Moran that marks its calm waters in early morning. | U.S. 26/89/191/287, 2 mi east of Jackson Lake Junction.

Willow Flats. You will almost always see moose grazing in the marshy area of Willow Flats, in part because it has a good growth of willow trees, which moose both eat and hide in. | U.S. 89/191/287, 1 mi north of Jackson Lake Junction.

Sports and Outdoor Activities

BICYCLING

Jackson Hole's long, flat profile and mountain scenery attract 10-speed and mountain bikers of all skill levels. Teton Park Road and Jackson Hole Highway are generally flat with long, gradual inclines, and have well-marked shoulders. Grand Teton has few designated bike paths, so cyclists should be very careful when sharing the road with vehicles, especially RVs and trailers. A bike lane allows for northbound bike traffic along the one-way Jenny Lake Loop Road, a one-hour ride. The River Road, 4 mi north of Moose, is an easy four-hour mountain-bike ride along a ridge above the Snake River. Bicycles are not allowed on trails or in the backcountry.

Teton Cycle Works. The oldest shop in town offers mountain- and road-bike rentals, sales, accessories, and repairs. | 175 N. Glenwood St., Jackson | 307/733–4386 | Mar.–Oct.

Teton Mountain Bike Tours. If you're a mountain biker you can take guided half-, full-, or multiday tours with this company. They are the only company to go into both Grand Teton and Yellowstone national parks, as well as to the Bridger-Teton and Targhee national forests. Tours available for all skill levels include some specially designed for families. Their Teton tours are all half- or full-day outings. | Box 7027, Jackson 83002 | 307/733–0712 or 800/733–0788 | www.wybike.com | $45–$100 for half- to full-day trips | May–Sept.

BIRD-WATCHING

Teton-country birds include bald eagles and osprey, which nest near Oxbow Bend throughout summer. White pelicans also stop at the Oxbow on their northerly migration in spring. Nearby Willow Flats is host to similar bird life plus sandhill cranes. You can see trumpeter swans at Oxbow Bend and Two Ocean Lake. Look for songbirds, such as pine and evening grosbeaks and Cassin's finches, in surrounding open pine and aspen forests. Similar songbirds inhabit Grandview Point, as do blue and ruffed grouse. Keep binoculars handy while traveling along Antelope Flats Road: you may spot red-tailed hawks and prairie falcons. At Taggart Lake you'll see woodpeckers, bluebirds, and hummingbirds. In all over 300 species of birds inhabit the park.

Phelps Lake. This valley lake is a great spot for bird-watching. The moderate 1.8-mi round-trip Phelps Lake Overlook Trail takes you up conifer- and aspen-lined glacial moraine to a view that's accessible only by trail. Expect abundant bird life: Western tanagers, northern flickers, and ruby-crowned kinglets thrive in the bordering woods, and hummingbirds feed on scarlet gilia beneath the overlook. | Moose-Wilson Rd., about 3 mi off Teton Park Rd., 1 mi north of Moose Junction.

BOATING

Motorboats are allowed on Jenny, Jackson, and Phelps lakes. On Jenny Lake, there's an engine limit of 10 horsepower. You can launch your boat at Colter Bay, Leek's Marina, Signal Mountain, and Spalding Bay.

Colter Bay Marina. All types of services are available to boaters, including free parking for boat trailers and vehicles, free mooring, boat rentals, guided fishing trips, and fuel. The marina, on Jackson Lake, is operated by the Grand Teton Lodge Company. | 2 mi off U.S. 89/191/287, 5 mi north of Jackson Lake Junction | 307/543–2811 | Mid-May–mid-Oct.

At Colter Bay Marina you can rent motorboats, row boats, and canoes from **Grand Teton Lodge Company.** Reservations are not accepted. | 307/543–3100, 307/543–2811, or 800/628–9988 | www.gtlc.com | Motor boats $22 per hour, row boats and canoes $10 per hour | Early June–late Sept.

Leek's Marina. Both day and short-term parking for boat trailers and vehicles is available for up to three nights maximum. There are no boat rentals, but you can get fuel, and there's free short-term docking plus a pizza restaurant. This marina is operated by park concessionaire Signal Mountain Lodge. | U.S. 89/191/287, 6 mi north of Jackson Lake Junction | 307/543–2831 | Mid-May–mid-Sept.

Signal Mountain Lodge Marina. The marina rents pontoon boats, deck cruisers, motorboats, kayaks, and canoes by the hour or for full-day cruising. You can also obtain fuel, oil, and overnight mooring. | Teton Park Rd., 3 mi south of Jackson Lake Junction | 307/543–2831 | Canoes $10 per hour, motorboats $21 per hour, runabouts $38 per hour, pontoon boats $56 per hour. Mooring $20 per night | Mid-May–mid-Sept.

Spalding Bay. You can launch your boat here and park your trailer and vehicle for the day. There's no docking or mooring available. | 2 mi off Teton Park Rd., 7 mi south of Jackson Lake Junction.

FISHING

Rainbow, brook, lake, and native cutthroat trout inhabit the park's waters. The Snake's 75 mi of river and tributary are world-renowned for their fishing. To fish in Grand Teton National Park you need a Wyoming fishing license. A day permit for nonresidents is $10 and an annual permit is $65 plus a $10 conservation stamp; for state residents a license costs $15 per season plus $10 for a conservation stamp. You can buy a fishing license at Colter Bay Marina, Moose Village Store, Signal Mountain Lodge, and at area sporting-goods stores. Or you can get one direct from **Wyoming Game and Fish Department.** | 420 N. Cache St., Box 67, Jackson, 83001 | 307/733–2321.

Grand Teton Lodge Company. The park's major concessionaire operates guided Jackson Lake fishing trips that include boat, guide, and tackle. The company also offers guided fly-fishing trips on the Snake River. Make reservations at the activities desks at Colter Bay Village or Jackson Lake Lodge, where trips originate. | Colter Bay Marina or Jackson Lake Lodge | 307/543–2811, 307/543–3100, or 800/628–9988 | fax 307/543–3143 | www.gtlc.com | $104–$350 and up | June–Sept.

Signal Mountain Lodge. You can take a guided two-hour, full- or half-day fishing trip on Jackson Lake, leaving from the marina here. | Teton Park Rd., 3 mi south of Jackson Lake Junction | 307/543–2831 | fax 307/543–2569 | www.signalmountainlodge.com | $60 per hour | Mid-May–mid-Sept.

HIKING

Much of the spectacular mountain scenery of Grand Teton is best seen by hiking. You can get trail maps and information about hiking conditions from rangers at the park visitor

GRAND TETON
NATIONAL PARK

EXPLORING
ATTRACTIONS NEARBY
DINING
LODGING
CAMPING AND RV
FACILITIES
SHOPPING
ESSENTIAL
INFORMATION

centers at Moose, Jenny Lake, or Colter Bay. Popular trails are those around Jenny Lake, the Leigh and String lakes area, and Taggart Lake Trail, with views of Avalanche Canyon. Other trails let you experience the Grand Teton backcountry on longer hikes lasting from a few hours to several days. You can also do some off-trail hiking in the park. Pick up backcountry trail information from any ranger station or visitor center. Frontcountry or backcountry, you may see moose and bears, but keep your distance. Pets are not permitted on trails or in the backcountry, but you can take them on paved frontcountry trails so long as they are on a leash no more than 6 ft long.

Cascade Canyon Trail. Take the 20-minute boat ride from the Jenny Lake dock to the start of a gentle, 0.5-mi climb to 200-ft Hidden Falls, the park's most popular and crowded trail destination. Listen here for the distinctive bleating of the rabbitlike pikas among the glacial boulders and pines. To reach the Cascade Canyon trailhead, go to the Jenny Lake visitor center to catch a ride across Jenny Lake with **Jenny Lake Boating** (Jenny Lake Rd., 2 mi off Teton Park Rd., 12 mi south of Jackson Lake Junction | 307/734–9227 | $5–$7 | June–early Sept.).

Colter Bay Nature Trail Loop. This very easy, 1.75-mi round-trip excursion treats you to views of Jackson Lake and the Tetons. As you follow the level trail from Colter Bay visitor center and along the forest's edge, you may see moose and bald eagles. Allow yourself two hours to complete the walk. | 2 mi off U.S. 89/191/287, 5 mi north of Jackson Lake Junction.

Death Canyon Trail. This 7.6-mi trail is a strenuous hike with lots of hills to traverse, ending with a climb up into Death Canyon. | Off Moose–Wilson Rd., 4 mi south of Moose Junction.

★ **Jenny Lake Trail.** You can walk to Hidden Falls from Jenny Lake ranger station by following the mostly level trail around the south shore of the lake to Cascade Canyon Trail. Jenny Lake Trail continues around the lake for 6.5 mi. It's an easy trail that will take you two to three hours depending on how fast you walk. | South Jenny Lake Junction, 0.5 mi off Teton Park Rd., 8 mi north of Moose Junction.

Leigh Lake Trail. The flat trail follows String Lake's northeastern shore to Leigh Lake's south shore, covering 2 mi in a round-trip of about an hour. You can extend your hike into an easy 7.5-mi, four-hour round-trip by following the forested east shore of Leigh Lake to Bearpaw Lake. Along the way you'll have views of Mount Moran across the lake, and you may be lucky enough to spot a moose. | String Lake Trailhead, 0.5 mi west of Jenny Lake Rd., 14 mi north of Moose Junction.

Lunchtree Hill Trail. One of the park's easiest trails begins at Jackson Lake Lodge and leads 0.5 mi to the top of a hill above Willow Flats. The area's willow thickets, beaver ponds, and wet, grassy meadows make it a birder's paradise. Look for sandhill cranes, hummingbirds, and the many types of songbirds described in the free bird guide available at visitor centers. You might also see moose. The round-trip walk takes no more than half an hour. | U.S. 89/191/287, 0.5 mi north of Jackson Lake Junction.

String Lake Trail. This easy 3.5-mi, three-hour loop around String Lake lies in the shadows of 11,144-ft Rockchuck Peak and 11,430-ft Mount Saint John. | 0.5 mi west of Jenny Lake Rd., 14 mi north of Moose.

HORSEBACK RIDING
Colter Bay Village Corral. Grand Teton Lodge Company offers one- and two-hour rides from Colter Bay Village to a variety of destinations. Half-day trips, for advanced riders only, go to Hermitage Point. Some rides include breakfast or dinner eaten along the trail. | 2 mi off U.S. 89/191/287, 5 mi north of Jackson Lake Junction | 307/543–2811, 307/543–3100, or 800/628–9988 | fax 307/543–3143 | www.gtlc.com | Short rides $25–$39, breakfast rides $40, dinner rides $47 | June–Aug.

Jackson Lake Lodge Corral. Several trail rides depart daily, operated by Grand Teton Lodge Company. One-hour rides give an overview of the Jackson Lake Lodge area; two-hour rides go to Emma Matilda Lake, Oxbow Bend, and Christian Pond. Experienced riders can take a half-day ride to Two Ocean Lake. Some rides include breakfast or dinner eaten along the trail. | U.S. 89/191/287, 0.5 mi north of Jackson Lake Junction | 307/543–2811, 307/543–3100, or 800/628–9988 | fax 307/543–3143 | www.gtlc.com | Short rides $25–$39, breakfast rides $40, dinner rides $47 | June–Aug.

MOUNTAIN CLIMBING

Exum Mountain Guides. Started by climbing pioneers Paul Petzoldt and Glen Exum, this company offers a variety of climbing experiences and instruction, ranging from one-day mountain climbs to ice climbing and backcountry adventures on skis and snowboards. Though most of their climbing centers on the Teton Range, they also lead trips to other sites in Wyoming and the region, and they have an international climbing program as well. | Box 56, Moose, 83012 | 307/733–2297 | One-day climbs $200–$340, climbing schools $105–$170 | Year-round.

Jackson Hole Mountain Guides. Mountain climbers get a leg up in the Tetons from this outfit. They offer schools for beginning to advanced climbers, teaching both rock and ice climbing. Guided trips concentrate on the Tetons and other Wyoming locations. | 165 N. Glenwood St., Box 7477, Jackson, 83002 | 307/733–4979 or 800/239–7642 | One-day guided climbs $210–$300, climbing classes $90–$150 | Year-round.

RIVER EXPEDITIONS

If you're floating the Snake River on your own, you are required to purchase a permit that costs $10 per raft and is valid for the entire season, or one for $5 per raft for seven days. Permits are available year-round at Moose visitor center and at Colter Bay, Signal Mountain, and Buffalo (near Moran entrance) ranger stations in summer. Before you set out, check with park rangers for current conditions.

You may prefer to take one of the many guided float trips through calm-water sections of the Snake; outfitters pick you up at the float trip parking area near Moose visitor center for a 10- to 20-minute drive to upriver launch sites. All concessionaires provide ponchos and life preservers. Early morning and evening floats are your best bets for wildlife viewing, but be sure to carry a jacket or sweater. Float season runs mid-April to December.

Barker-Ewing Scenic Float Trips. If you'd like to sit back and be a passenger, travel the peaceful parts of the Snake looking for wildlife with this company, which operates exclusively on the scenic Snake in Grand Teton National Park. | Box 100–J, Moose, 83012 | 307/733–1800 or 800/365–1800 | www.barkerewingscenic.com | $40 | May–Sept.

Grand Teton Lodge Company Snake River Float Trips. This company operates exclusively within Grand Teton National Park. Chose from a scenic float trip, one that also includes lunch, or an evening trip that includes a steak-fry dinner. Make reservations at the activities desk at Colter Bay Village or Jackson Lake Lodge. | 307/543–2811, 307/543–3100, or 800/628–9988 | fax 307/543–3143 | www.gtlc.com | Scenic float $41, lunch float $46, steak-fry float $52 | June–Aug.

Lewis and Clark River Expeditions. To experience some wet and wild stretches of river, get in touch with these folks who put you in rubber rafts for an exhilarating ride. You can also take a more leisurely scenic float or have a steak-fry along with your river trip. | 335 N. Cache St., Box 720, Jackson, 83001 | 307/733–4022 or 800/824–5375 | www.lewisandclarkexpeds.com | $29–$65 | Mid-May–mid-Sept.

Mad River Boat Trips. This company leads a variety of white-water and scenic float trips, some combined with lunch or dinner. Start or end your trip with a visit to their river museum, which has photos and information. There are even old boats from expeditions on Wyoming waters, dating back to John Wesley Powell's first expedition on the Green River in the 1870s. | 1255 S. U.S. 89, Box 10940, Jackson, 83002 | 307/733–6203 or 800/458–7238 | www.mad-river.com | $31–$51 | Mid-May–Sept.

Snake River Kayak and Canoe. Get some instruction in the fine art of paddling and test yourself on the river. | Box 4311, Jackson, 83001 | 307/733–9999 or 800/529–2501 | www.snakeriverkayak.com | One-day clinics $85–$250, multiday instruction $445–$995 | Apr.–Oct.

Triangle X Float Trips. This company offers subdued river trips in Grand Teton National Park, including shorter 5 mi floats and a sunset supper float. | 2 Triangle X Ranch Rd., Moose, 83012 | 307/733–5500 or 888/860–0005 | www.trianglex.com | $25–$50 | Mid-May–late Sept.

SKIING

Grand Teton National Park has some of North America's finest and most varied cross-country skiing. Ski the gentle 3-mi Swan Lake–Heron Pond Loop near Colter Bay visitor center, the mostly level 9-mi Jenny Lake Trail, or the moderate 4-mi Taggart Lake–Beaver Creek Loop and 5-mi Phelps Lake Overlook trail, which have some steep descents. Advanced skiers should head for the Teton Crest Trail. In winter all overnight backcountry travelers must register at park headquarters in Moose to obtain a free permit.

Jack Dennis Outdoor Shop. This place stocks skis and snowboards for sale and rent, and outdoor gear for any season. | 50 E. Broadway Ave., Jackson | 307/733–3270 | www.jackdennis. com | Ski rental $18–$30, snowboard and boot rental $25 | Year-round.

Pepi Stegler Sports Shop. You can buy or rent skis or snowboards at this shop in Teton Village. Owned by Jack Dennis Outdoor Shop, the store is conveniently located at the base of the Jackson Hole ski mountain. | Teton Village | 307/733–3270 | www.jackdennis.com | Ski rental $18–$30, snowboard and boot rental $25 | Nov.–Apr.

SNOWMOBILING

You can snowmobile on the Continental Divide snowmobile trail as well as on Jackson Lake. You must first purchase an annual $15 permit at a park entrance station. The speed limit within the park is 35 mph.

Cowboy Village Resort at Togwotee. You can rent a snowmobile here and then ride it on an extensive trail network along the Continental Divide. | U.S. 26/287, Box 91, Moran | 307/543–2847 or 800/543–2847 | www.cowboyvillage.com | Snowmobile rentals $129–$189 per day | Nov.–Apr.

Attractions Nearby

For more attractions near Grand Teton, *see* Yellowstone National Park.

Scenic Drives

Gros Ventre Road. Along this road about 0.5 mi north of Kelly you can see the scar formed in 1925, when Sheep Mountain slid into the Gros Ventre River. The landslide created a natural dam that formed Slide Lake. Two years later, in 1927, heavy rain caused the dam to fail, resulting in a flood that nearly wiped out the small town of Kelly. The dam was subsequently strengthened. It's about 6 mi (20 minutes) from Kelly to Slide Lake, where you can climb on the massive boulders that form the dam and follow an interpretive trail. The road also provides access to forest campgrounds.

Togwotee Pass. Named for Sheepeater Indian Chief Togwotee, this mountain pass linking Moran and Dubois is open year-round. In summer you can see high mountain meadow, lots of willow groves where moose like to munch, and possibly even a grizzly. In winter those same meadows are covered by snow and used by people on snowmobiles. The 55-mi route on U.S. 26/287 takes a little over an hour to drive in summer and possibly longer in winter, when it can become snow-packed or icy. There's an interpretive area midway that provides information about early logging operations.

Sights to See

Bridger-Teton National Forest. This 3.4-million-acre forest has something for everyone: history, hiking, camping, and wildlife. It encompasses the Teton Wilderness east of Grand Teton National Park and John D. Rockefeller Memorial Parkway, and south of Yellowstone National Park, the Gros Ventre Wilderness southeast of Jackson, and the Bridger Wilderness farther south and east. No motor vehicles are allowed in the wildernesses, but there are many scenic drives, natural springs, and cultural sights like abandoned lumber camps in the national forest between the wildernesses. Get information about the forest at Jackson Hole and Greater Yellowstone visitor center in Jackson. | 340 N. Cache St. | 307/739–5500 | www.fs.fed.us/btnf | Free, some picnic sites $5.

Caribou–Targhee National Forest. The Targhee division of this forest includes the region primarily on the west side of the Teton Range, mainly in Idaho. Recreation includes camping, hiking, and wildlife watching. | Rte. 22 and U.S. 26 west of Jackson | 208/354–2312 | www.fs.fed.us/r4/caribou-targhee | Free.

Jackson Hole and Greater Yellowstone Visitor Center. Stop here to get information about area attractions and events and to see wildlife displays that include bronze elk sculptures outside and a stuffed herd of elk in the lobby. The center is jointly operated by several organizations and governmental agencies—State of Wyoming, Jackson Hole Chamber of Commerce, U.S. Forest Service, U.S. Fish and Wildlife Service, U.S. Department of the Interior, and Wyoming Game and Fish Department—so you can get information related to all public lands in the region. | 532 N. Cache St., Jackson | 307/733–3316 | www.fs.fed.us/jhgyvc | Memorial Day–Sept., daily 8–7; Oct.–Memorial Day, daily 9–5.

Museum of the Mountain Man. Tucked away in Pinedale an hour's drive south of Jackson, this museum preserves the history of the mountain man. The basement gallery is devoted to Sublette County pioneer and ranch history. | 700 E. Hennick St., Pinedale | 307/367–4101 | www.museumofthemountainman.com | $4 | May–Sept., daily 10–5.

National Bighorn Sheep Interpretive Center. The local variety is known as the Rocky Mountain bighorn, but you can learn about all kinds of bighorn sheep here. The center has mounted specimens and hands-on exhibits that illustrate a bighorn's body language, habitat, and characteristics. Wildlife-viewing tours are conducted in winter. | 907 W. Ramshorn Ave., Dubois | 307/455–3429 or 888/209–2795 | $2 | Memorial Day–Labor Day, daily 9–8; Labor Day–Memorial Day, daily 9–5; wildlife viewing tours mid-Nov.–Mar.

★ **National Elk Refuge.** More than 7,000 elk spend winter in the National Elk Refuge, which was established in 1912 to rescue starving herds. The animals migrate to the refuge grounds in late fall and remain until early spring. Trumpeter swans live here, too, as do bald eagles, coyotes, and wolves. In winter you can take a wagon or sleigh ride through the herd. In summer, migration means that there are fewer big game animals here, but you likely will see waterfowl and you can also fish on the refuge. | 2820 Rungius Rd., Jackson | 307/733–9212 | www.fws.gov | Sleigh rides $13 | Year-round; sleigh rides mid-Dec.–Mar.

National Wildlife Art Museum. An impressive collection of wildlife art—most of it devoted to North American species—is displayed in the 13 galleries displaying the work of artists Karl Bodmer, Albert Bierstadt, Charles Russell, John Clymer, Robert Bateman, Carl Rungius, and others. You can also use one of the spotting scopes set up in areas overlooking the National Elk Refuge to watch wildlife in its native habitat. | 2820 Rungius Rd., Jackson | 307/733–5771 | www.wildlifeart.org | $8 | June–Sept. and Dec.–Mar., daily 9–5; Apr.–May and Oct.–Nov., Mon.–Sat. 9–5, Sun. 1–5

Teton Village Aerial Tram. Take a 20-minute ride up 10,450-ft Rendezvous Mountain, accompanied by an informal conductor's narrative. At the top is a platform with a view of Jackson Hole, a snack bar, and a trailhead. The trailhead provides access to Marion Lake and Granite Canyon trails, both of them moderate to strenuous mostly downhill hikes (11.8 mi and 12.4 mi, respectively) that take about seven hours to complete. | Teton Village | 307/733–2292 | $15 | Late May–late June and Sept., daily 9–5; late June–Aug., daily 9–6.

GRAND TETON
NATIONAL PARK

EXPLORING

**ATTRACTIONS
NEARBY**

DINING

LODGING

CAMPING AND RV
FACILITIES

SHOPPING

ESSENTIAL
INFORMATION

Wind River Historical Center. Displays here cover local geology, the archaeology of the Mountain Shoshone (Sheepeater Indians), and the story of the men and women—tie hacks—who cut railroad ties from lodgepole pine in the Wind River valley. | 909 W. Ramshorn Ave., Dubois | 307/455–2284 | $1 | June–Sept., daily 9–5; Oct.–May, daily 10–4.

Tours

Teton Wagon Train and Horse Adventures. Multiday covered wagon rides and horseback trips follow Grassy Lake Road on the "back side" of the Tetons. You can combine the trip with a river trip and a tour of Yellowstone and Grand Teton. | Box 10307, Jackson, 83001 | 307/734–6101 or 888/734–6101 | fax 208/787–3098 | www.tetonwagontrain.com | Wagon trip $745; combination trip $1,595 | June–Aug.

Dining

In Grand Teton

Chuckwagon Steak and Pasta House. American. The extremely popular Chuckwagon serves both steak and pasta. Across from Colter Bay Marina in a sprawling, pine-shaded building, the restaurant draws families staying at Colter Bay as well as sightseers from Jackson Lake boat tours. | 2 mi off U.S. 89/191/287, 5 mi north of Jackson Lake Junction | 307/543–2811 | $8–$16 | AE, MC, V | Closed late Sept.–late May.

Dornan's. Barbecue. Hearty portions of beef, beans, potatoes, stew, and lemonade or hot coffee are the standbys at Dornan's, which is easily identified by its tepees. Locals know this spot for the barbecue cooked over wood fires. You can eat your chuck-wagon meal inside the tepees if it happens to be raining or windy; otherwise, sit at outdoor picnic tables with views of the Snake River and the Tetons. There is also a pizza parlor where lunch is served year-round, but the chuckwagon operates September–May only. | 10 Moose Rd., off Teton Park Rd. at Moose Junction | 307/733–2415 | $14–$18 | MC, V.

★**Jackson Lake Lodge Mural Room.** American. The ultimate park dining experience is found in this large room that gets its name from a 700-square-ft mural painted by western artist Carl Roters. The mural details an 1837 Wyoming mountain-man rendezvous and covers two walls of the dining room. Select from a menu that includes trout, elk, beef, and pasta. The tables face tall windows affording a panoramic view of Willow Flats and Jackson Lake to the northern Tetons. | U.S. 89/191/287, 0.5 mi north of Jackson Lake Junction | 307/733–3100 or 800/628–9988 | $18–$27 | AE, MC, V | Closed mid-Oct.–late May.

Jackson Lake Lodge Pioneer Grill. American/Casual. With an old-fashioned soda fountain, friendly service, and seats along a winding counter, this eatery recalls a 1950s-era luncheonette. It's favored by families and senior citizens. | U.S. 89/191/287, 0.5 mi north of Jackson Lake Junction | 307/543–2811 Ext. 1911 | $4–$12 | AE, MC, V | Closed early Oct.–late May.

★**Jenny Lake Lodge Dining Room.** American. Elegant yet rustic, this is Grand Teton National Park's finest dining establishment. The menu offers fish, pasta, chicken, and beef; the wine list is extensive. Dinner is prix-fixe; lunch is à la carte. | Jenny Lake Rd., 2 mi off Teton Park Rd., 12 mi north of Moose Junction | 307/733–4647 or 800/628–9988 | fax 307/543–3143 | $49 | AE, MC, V | Jacket required | Reservations essential | Closed early Oct.–late May.

John Colter Cafe Court. American/Casual. At this Colter Bay Village spot you can buy hamburgers, hot and cold New York–style deli sandwiches, and ice cream à la carte or by the meal. | 5 mi north of Jackson Lake Lodge | 307/543–2811 | $4–$8 | AE, MC, V | Closed early Sept.–early June.

The Peaks. American. Part of Signal Mountain Lodge, this casual room has exposed ceiling beams and big square windows overlooking southern Jackson Lake and the Tetons. The emphasis here is on fish: Rocky Mountain trout is marinated, lightly floured, and grilled, or simply grilled and topped with lemon-parsley butter. | Teton Park Rd., 4 mi south of Jackson Lake Junction | 307/543–2831 | fax 307/543–2569 | $10–$20 | AE, D, MC, V | Closed mid-Oct.–mid-May.

Picnic Areas. The park has 11 designated picnic areas, each with tables and grills, and most have pit toilets and water pumps or faucets. In addition to those listed here you can find picnic areas at Colter Bay Village campground, Colter Bay visitor center, Cottonwood Creek, the east shore of Jackson Lake, Moose visitor center, and South Jenny Lake trailhead and String Lake trailhead.

From the intimate lakeside picnic area near **Chapel of the Sacred Heart** you can look across southern Jackson Lake to Mount Moran. | 0.25 mi east of Signal Mountain Lodge, off Teton Park Rd., 4 mi south of Jackson Lake Junction.

The big **Colter Bay visitor center** picnic area, spectacularly located right on the beach at Jackson Lake, gets crowded in July and August, but it's close to flush toilets and stores. | 2 mi off U.S. 89/191/287, 5 mi north of Jackson Lake Junction.

North of Colter Bay, four scenic roadside picnic spots dot the **east shore of Jackson Lake.** | U.S. 89/191/287, 6 mi, 8 mi, 9 mi, and 12 mi north of Jackson Lake Junction.

Adjacent to the Jenny Lake shuttle boat dock is the shaded, pine-scented **Hidden Falls** picnic site. An easy 0.5-mi hike takes you to to the falls. Take the shuttle boat across Jenny Lake to reach the Cascade Canyon trailhead. | At the Cascade Canyon trailhead.

Slightly less crowded than the picnic area at Colter Bay visitor center, the lakeside **Signal Mountain Lodge** picnic area can accommodate a big group. Flush toilets and stores are nearby. | Teton Park Rd., 4 mi south of Jackson Lake Junction.

Scenic but crowded, the picnic area at **String Lake Trailhead** lies in pine forest at the base of the Teton Range. | Jenny Lake Rd., 2 mi off Teton Park Rd., 12 mi north of Moose Junction.

One of the park's most isolated and uncrowded picnic sites is about 6 mi northwest of the Moran entrance station at the east end of **Two Ocean Lake.** A mile north of the entrance station turn east onto Pacific Creek Road, and about 2 mi in from U.S. 26/89/181 take a left (turning north) on the first dirt road. Two Ocean Lake is about 2 mi down the dirt road. | Off Pacific Creek Rd., 2 mi east of U.S. 26/89/191.

Near the Park

Though the park itself has some excellent restaurants, don't miss dining in Jackson, the hub of the Rocky Mountain culinary world. Several restaurants combine game, fowl, and fish with Old World preparations and New-Age health consciousness. Steaks are usually cut from grass-fed Wyoming beef. Poultry and pasta dishes are heavily influenced by Alpine tradition, but other styles of preparation are catching on.

★ **Bar J Chuckwagon.** American/Casual. This may be the best value in Jackson Hole. You get a full ranch-style meal plus a complete Western show featuring singing, stories, and even cowboy poetry. The dinner and show take place inside if necessary, so don't let the weather keep you away. Reservations recommended. | Rte. 390, 6 mi north of Jackson | 307/733–3370 | $24 | D, MC, V | Closed Oct.–Memorial Day.

Billy's Giant Hamburgers. American/Casual. Sharing an entrance with Cadillac Grille, Billy's is 1950s-style, with a few booths and a bunch of tall tables with high stools. Though you can choose from a variety of sandwiches, Billy's specialty is big—really big—burgers that are really good. | 55 N. Cache Dr., Jackson | 307/733–3279 | $8–$26 | AE, MC, V.

The Bunnery. Café. Tucked into a tiny spot in the Hole-in-the-Wall Mall, this is where locals go for breakfast, though you can get a great lunch or dinner as well. It's usually busy so there may be a short wait, but the food's worth it. Breads are home-baked, mostly of a combined grain known as OSM (oats, sunflower, millet), and they've been known to sell and ship the bread to customers throughout the world. | 130 N. Cache St., Jackson | 307/733–5474 | $7–$15 | MC, V.

Cadillac Grille. American/Casual. Sharing an entrance with Billy's Giant Hamburgers, this contemporary spot serves beef, pasta, fish, and chicken. | 55 N. Cache Dr., Jackson | 307/733–3279 | $9–$26 | AE, MC, V.

Calico. American. On the road between Jackson and Teton Village, this former pizza place now also serves pastas and rotisserie chicken, prime rib, and Italian sausage. The bar occupies what used to be the Mormon Church on Mormon Row at Grovont (now a ghost town)—the building was moved to its present site many years ago. There's open-air dining and a playground outside. | 2650 Teton Village Rd., 2.5 mi west of Teton Village | 307/733–2460 | $11–$20 | AE, MC, V | No lunch.

Cowboy Cafe. American. This small downtown restaurant serves homemade food, including sandwiches and steaks, buffalo burgers, chicken, pork and fish. | 115 Ramshorn Ave., Dubois | 307/455–2595 | $7–$13 | D, MC, V.

Jedediah's House of Sourdough. American/Casual. Friendly, noisy, and elbow-knocking, this restaurant a block east of the town square in a historic home caters to the big appetite. Try the sourdough pancakes, called sourjacks, or Teton taters and eggs. There's a kids' menu and outdoor deck dining. Breakfast also served. | 135 E. Broadway Ave., Jackson | 307/733–5671 | $10–$18 | AE, D, DC, MC, V.

Mangy Moose. American. Folks pour in off the ski slopes for a lot of food and talk at this two-level restaurant-plus-bar with an outdoor deck. Antiques and oddities, including a full-size stuffed caribou (complete with sleigh) suspended from the ceiling, decorate the space. The noise level is high, but you get decent fare at fair prices and a chance to try the house Moose Brew beer. Beef dominates the menu, though you can also get buffalo meat loaf. | Teton Village | 307/733–4913 | $10–$17 | AE, MC, V.

★**Nani's Genuine Pasta House.** Italian. The ever-changing menu at this cozy, almost cramped, restaurant may include braised veal shanks with saffron risotto or other regional Italian cooking. The place is almost hidden behind a motel and is designed to attract gourmets, not tourists. The menu changes nightly. | 242 N. Glenwood St., Jackson | 307/733–3888 | $12–$23 | MC, V.

Rustic Pine Steakhouse. Steak. The bar here is one of Wyoming's more memorable spots, where locals and visitors congregate to share news about hunting or hiking. The steak house serves mouth-watering steak and seafood in a quiet atmosphere. | 123 Ramshorn Ave., Dubois | 307/455–2772 | $10–$20 | MC, V | No lunch.

★**Snake River Grill.** Contemporary. One of Jackson's best dining options, this sophisticated dining room offers creatively prepared free-range veal chops, grilled venison, and grilled Idaho red-rainbow trout. There's an extensive wine list. | 84 E. Broadway Ave., Jackson | 307/733–0557 | $18–$48 | AE, MC, V | Closed Apr. and Nov. No lunch.

Sweetwater Restaurant. Mediterranean. The log cabin atmosphere might not seem to match the menu, but the combination works. Start with smoked buffalo carpaccio or eggplant rouille; then go on to lamb dishes, mesquite chicken, or shrimp *spetses* (simmered in tomato and garlic with feta cheese). | 85 S. King St., Jackson | 307/733–3553 | $13–$26 | AE, D, MC, V.

Lodging

In Grand Teton

Colter Bay Village. Near Jackson Lake, this complex of western-style cabins—some with one room, others with two or more rooms—are within walking distance of the lake. The property has splendid views and an excellent marina and beach for the windsurfing crowd (you'll need a wet suit). The tent cabins aren't fancy and they share communal baths, but they do keep the wind and rain off. There's also a 116-space RV park. 2 restaurants. Lake.

Boating. Fishing. Hiking. Bar. Shops. Laundry facilities. Some pets allowed. | 2 mi off U.S. 89/191/287, 5 mi north of Jackson Lake Junction | 307/733–3100 or 800/628–9988 | fax 307/543–3143 | 166 cabins, 66 tent cabins | $36 tent cabins, $70–$134 1-3 bedroom cabins | AE, MC, V | Closed late Sept.–late May (shorter season for tent cabins).

Dornan's Spur Ranch Cabins. Near Moose visitor center in Dornan's all-in-one shopping–dining–recreation development, these one- and two-bedroom cabins have great views of the Tetons and the Snake River. Each of the log cabins has a full kitchen as well as a generously sized living-dining room and a furnished porch with a Weber grill in summer. Restaurant. Boating. Hiking. Bar. Shops. | 10 Moose Rd., off Teton Park Rd. at Moose Junction | 307/733–2522 | fax 307/733–3544 | www.dornans.com | 12 cabins | $140–$210 | D, MC, V.

Jackson Lake Lodge. This large full service resort stands on a bluff with spectacular views across Jackson Lake to the Tetons. The upper lobby has 60-ft picture windows and a collection of Native American artifacts and Western art. Many of the guest rooms have spectacular lake and mountain views, while others have little or no view. There are in-house religious services; the bar has live entertainment. 2 restaurants. Some refrigerators. Pool. Hiking, horseback riding. Bar. Business services. Airport shuttle. Some pets allowed. | U.S. 89/191/287, 0.5 mi north of Jackson Lake Junction | 307/543–3100 or 800/628–9988 | fax 307/543–3143 | www.gtlc.com | 385 rooms | $135–$235 | AE, MC, V | Closed early Oct.–mid-May.

★ **Jenny Lake Lodge.** Nestled well off Jenny Lake Road, the lodge borders a wildflower meadow, and its guest cabins are well spaced in lodgepole-pine groves. Cabin interiors, with sturdy pine beds and handmade quilts and electric blankets, live up to the elegant rustic theme, and cabin suites have fireplaces. Breakfast, bicycle and horseback riding, and dinner are included in the price. Restaurant. Boating. Bicycles. Hiking, horseback riding. Lounge. | Jenny Lake Rd., 2 mi off Teton Park Rd., 12 mi north of Moose Junction | 307/733–4647, 307/733–3100, or 800/628–9988 | fax 307/543–3143 | www.gtlc.com | 37 cabins | $444 | AE, DC, MC, V | Closed early Oct.–late May | MAP.

★ **Moulton Ranch Cabins.** Along Mormon Row, these cabins stand a few dozen yards south of the famous Moulton Barn, which you see on brochures, jigsaw puzzles, and photographs of the park. The land was once part of the T. A. Moulton homestead, and the cabins are still owned by the Moulton family. The quiet property has views of both the Teton Range and the Gros Ventre Range and the owners can regale you with stories about the early homesteaders. There's a dance hall in the barn, making this an ideal place for family and small group reunions. Picnic area. Hiking. No pets. No smoking. | Off Antelope Flats Rd., U.S. 26/89/191, 2 mi north of Moose Junction | 307/733–3749 or 208/529–2354 | www.moultonranchcabins.com | 4 units | $85–$135 | MC, V | Closed Oct.–May.

Signal Mountain Lodge. Relaxed lodging amid the pines is available here, on Jackson Lake's southern shoreline. The main building has a cozy lounge and a grand pine deck overlooking the lake. Cabins are equipped with sleek kitchens and pine tables. The smaller log cabins are in shaded areas, and eight of them have a fireplace. Rooms 151–178 have lake views. 2 restaurants. Kitchenettes, some refrigerators. Lake. Dock. Boating. Fishing. Hiking. Bar. Shops. | Teton Park Rd., 4 mi south of Jackson Lake Junction | 307/543–2831 | fax 307/543–2569 | www.signalmountainlodge.com | 47 rooms, 32 log cabins | $95–$235 | AE, D, MC, V | Closed mid-Oct.–mid-May.

Near the Park

Reservation Services. You can reserve rooms near the park through two agencies.

Jackson Hole Central Reservations handles hotels as well as B&Bs. | Box 2618, Jackson, 83001 | 307/733–4005 or 800/443–6931 | www.jacksonholeresort.com.

You can make reservations for most motels in Jackson through **Resort Reservations.** | 85 Perry St. Jackson, 83002 | 307/733–6331 or 800/329–9205 | www.jacksonhole.net.

★ **Amangani.** You need truly deep pockets to stay here, but the exquisite architecture and flawless design make this "peaceful home" on a cliff edge on Gros Ventre Butte pure luxury. Huge two-story windows in the simple yet magnificent lobby overlook the Teton valley, and a generous use of redwood, sandstone, and cedar complements the natural setting. Rooms have gas fireplaces and balconies overlooking the valley, and the bathtubs offer great sunset views. You won't find more amenities, better service, or more understated elegance anywhere in the valley. Restaurant, room service. In-room data ports, in-room safes, refrigerators. In-room VCRs. 2 tennis courts. Pool. Health club, hot tub, massage, steam room, spa. Bar. Library. Laundry service. Business services. Airport shuttle. | 1535 N.E. Butte Rd., Jackson | 307/734–7333 or 877/734–7333 | fax 307/734–7332 | www.amangani.com | 40 suites | $700–$1,100 | AE, D, DC, MC, V.

Antler Inn. Like real estate agents say, location, location, and location are the three things that matter, and few motels in Jackson are as convenient to the town square as this one, just a block south. The motel rooms are standard, but some have fireplaces. In-room data ports. Hot tub. Some pets allowed. | 43 W. Pearl St., Jackson | 307/733–2535 or 800/522–2406 | fax 307/733–4158 | 110 rooms | $94–$110 | AE, D, DC, MC, V.

Black Bear Country Inn. The Wind River runs behind this redwood cabin-style motel, which has basic rooms with outdoor patios and tables. The large, five-person apartment with a full kitchen is ideal for groups and families. Picnic area. Microwaves, refrigerators. | 505 W. Ramshorn Ave., Dubois | 307/455–2344 or 800/873–2327 | fax 307/455–2626 | www.blackbearcountryinn.com | 16 rooms, 1 apartment | $99 rooms, $219 apartment | AE, D, DC, MC, V.

Flagg Ranch Resort. A sprawling property 4 mi north of the park, Flagg Ranch puts up guests in cabins spread out in the pine forest. The big, attractive cabins have pine furnishings. With its Western-style restaurant, plus float trips and snow coach tours that leave from the premises, this resort is particularly popular with families. There's a grocery store and gas station on the grounds. Restaurant. Hiking. Snowmobiling. Bar. Shops. Laundry facilities. Some pets allowed (fee). | John D. Rockefeller Jr. Memorial Pkwy., 4 mi north of Grand Teton National Park boundary | 307/543–2861 or 800/443–2311 | fax 307/543–2356 | www.flaggranch.com | 92 cabins | $140–$155 | AE, D, MC, V | Closed mid-Oct.–mid-Dec. and mid-Mar.–mid-May.

Grand Targhee Ski and Summer Resort. Perched on the west side of the Tetons, this small but modern facility has the uncrowded, stroll-around atmosphere of a small village in the Alps. The motel-style rooms have lodgepole furniture; condominiums have an adobe fireplace and a semi-private balcony. 5 restaurants. Pool. Spa, outdoor hot tub. Cross-country skiing. Airport shuttle. | 3300 Ski Hill Rd., Box SKI, Alta, 83414 | 307/353–2300 or 800/827–4433 | fax 307/353–8148 | www.grandtarghee.com | 65 rooms, 32 condos | $111–$350 | AE, D, MC, V.

Intermountain Lodge. Modern, small, log cabins nestled amongst cottonwood trees have basic, comfortable furnishings. Each cabin houses two units; the rooms have showers but no bathtubs. Picnic area. Kitchenettes. Outdoor hot tub. Volleyball. Laundry facilities. No smoking. | 34 Ski Hill Rd., Driggs, ID 83422 | 208/354–8153 | fax 208/354–2998 | 20 rooms | $49–$74 | CP | AE, D, MC, V.

Lost Creek Ranch. Upscale, Old World, and luxurious, this dude ranch 8 mi north of Moose and right on the edge of Grand Teton Park has large, well-furnished rooms and cabins with unsurpassed views. You get entertainment in the evening, a horse to ride, a scenic Snake River float trip, a ticket to the Jackson Hole Rodeo, hiking in Grand Teton National Park, and full spa services, including the steam, weight, sauna, and aerobics rooms. For additional fees you can participate in fishing trips, white-water rafting trips, skeet shooting, and spa treatments. Restaurant, picnic area. Some kitchenettes, refrigerators. Tennis court. Pool. Health club, hot tub, massage, sauna, spa, steam room. Hiking, horseback riding. Shops. Children's programs (ages 6–12). Laundry service. Airport shuttle. | Box 95, Old Ranch Rd.,

Moose, 83012 | 307/733–3435 | fax 307/733–1954 | www.lostcreek.com | 10 cabins | $5,550–$13,000 per week for 2–4 guests | AE, D, DC, MC, V | Closed Oct.–May | FAP.

Parkway Inn. Each room has a distinctive look in oak or wicker, and all are filled with antiques, from 19th-century pieces onward. The overall effect is homey and delightful—especially appealing if you plan to stay several days or longer. Pool. Hot tub. Business services. | 125 N. Jackson St., Jackson | 307/733–3143 or 800/247–8390 | fax 307/733–0955 | www.parkwayinn. com | 37 rooms, 12 suites | $179–$219 | AE, D, DC, MC, V | CP.

Snake River Lodge and Spa. From goose-down comforters and plush robes in every room to facials, salt glows, manicures, and hydrotherapy at the spa, this ski-in resort adjacent to Jackson Hole Ski Area pampers you. The indoor-outdoor pool area, where waterfalls cascade over large boulders and rocks, has a fire pit and views of the Jackson Hole ski area. The five-story Spa and Health Club has separate men's and women's floors with steam rooms and soaking tubs. Restaurant, room service. In-room data ports, refrigerators. Pool. Gym, hot tub, massage, sauna, spa, steam room. Bar. Shops. Business services. | 7710 Granite Loop Rd., Teton Village | 307/732–6000 or 800/445–4655 | fax 307/732–6009 | www.snakeriverlodge.com | 80 rooms, 40 condominiums | $325–$450 rooms, $550–$1,275 condominiums | AE, DC, MC, V.

Stagecoach Motor Inn. This downtown motel has a large backyard and play area, including a replica stagecoach for kids to climb on, but the play area is bordered by Pretty Horse Creek so young children require some supervision. Some rooms have full kitchens and many have refrigerators. Picnic area. Refrigerators. Pool. Hot tub. Playground. Laundry facilities. Airport shuttle. Some pets allowed (fee). | 103 E. Ramshorn Ave., Dubois | 307/455–2303 or 800/455–5090 | fax 307/455–3903 | 42 rooms, 6 suites | $60–$98 | AE, D, MC, V.

Wort Hotel. The locals have been gathering at this Jackson landmark half a block from the town square since the early 1940s, and you can view the history of Jackson in the photos and clippings posted in the lobby. The spacious rooms have lodgepole furniture and comfortable armchairs. Junior suites have large sitting areas. Restaurant, room service. Hot tubs. Exercise equipment. Bar. Business services. | 50 N. Glenwood St., Jackson | 307/733–2190 or 800/322–2727 | fax 307/733–2067 | www.worthotel.com | 60 rooms | $275–$375 rooms, $375–$550 suites | AE, D, MC, V.

Wyoming Inn. When you enter the lobby of this inn and see the carving of two large bighorn sheep facing off, you know you're in the West. The rooms, done in soft blues and greens, have comfortable sitting areas and desks; some have gas fireplaces and Jacuzzis. There are two computers with Internet access in the lobby, and guests have complimentary membership at Jackson Hole Athletic Club. In-room data ports, some kitchenettes, some refrigerators. Some in-room hot tubs. Business services. Airport shuttle. Some pets allowed. | 930 W. Broadway, Jackson | 307/734–0035 or 800/844–0035 | fax 307/734–0037 | www.wyoming-inn.com | 73 rooms | $249–$329 | AE, D, MC, V | CP.

Camping and RV Facilities

In Grand Teton

Check in at National Park Service campsites as early as possible—sites are assigned on a first-come, first-served basis. You can camp in the park's backcountry year-round, provided you have the requisite permit and are able to gain access to your site. Between June 1 and September 15, backcountry campers in the park are limited to one stay of up to 10 days. You can reserve a backcountry site for a $15 nonrefundable fee by faxing a request to the backcountry permit office at 307/739–3438 or by writing to the office at Box 170, Moose, 83012. You can also take a chance that the site you want will be open when you show up, in which case you pay no fee. Campfires are prohibited in the backcountry except at designated lakeshore campsites.

GRAND TETON CAMPGROUNDS

	Total # of sites	# of RV sites	# of hook-ups	Drive-to sites	Hike-to sites	Flush toilets	Pit/chemical toilets	Drinking water	Showers	Fire grates	Swimming	Boat access	Playground	Dump station	Ranger station	Public telephone	Reservation possible	Daily fee per site	Dates open
INSIDE THE PARK																			
Colter Bay	350	238	0	•	•	•		•	•	•		•		•	•	•		$12	May–Sept.
Colter Bay Trailer Village	116	116	116	•		•		•	•			•		•	•	•	•	$39	May–Sept.
Gros Ventre	360	360	0	•		•		•		•				•	•	•		$12	Apr.–Oct.
Jenny Lake	49	0	0	•		•		•		•					•	•		$12	May–Sept.
Lizard Creek	60	60	0	•		•				•								$12	June–Sept.
Signal Mountain	86	86	0	•		•		•		•		•		•	•	•		$12	May–Oct.
NEAR THE PARK																			
Bridger-Teton National Forest	616	613	0	•		•	•	•		•							•**	$0–15	June–Nov.
Flagg Ranch Village	150	75	75	•		•		•	•	•				•	•		•	$22–45	May–Sept.
Caribou-Targhee National Forest	845	802	0	•			•	•	•							•	•**	$8–24	June–Sept.

* In summer only   ** Reservation Fee Charged   Y/R=Year Round
UL=Unlimited   ULP=Unlimited Primitive   LD=Labor Day   MD=Memorial Day

★ **Colter Bay Campground.** Busy, noisy, and filled by noon, this campground has both tent and trailer or RV sites—and one great advantage: it's centrally located. Try to get a site as far from the nearby cabin road as possible. This is the only national parks-operated campground in the park that has hot showers. The maximum stay is 14 days. Flush toilets. Dump station. Drinking water, guest laundry, showers. Bear boxes, fire grates, picnic tables. | 350 tent or RV-trailer sites | 2 mi off U.S. 89/191/287, 5 mi north of Jackson Lake Junction | 307/739–3603 | $12 | Reservations not accepted | AE, D, MC, V | Mid-May–late Sept.

Colter Bay RV Park. Adjacent to the National Park Service–operated Colter Bay Campground, this concessionaire-operated campground is the only RV park in Grand Teton where you can get full hookups. Flush toilets. Full hookups, dump station. Drinking water, guest laundry, showers. Bear boxes, fire grates, picnic tables. | 116 RV sites with full hookups | 2 mi off U.S. 89/191/287, 5 mi north of Jackson Lake Junction | 307/543–2811 | $39 | Reservations not accepted | AE, MC, V | Late May–late Sept.

Gros Ventre. The park's biggest campground is set in an open, grassy area on the bank of the Gros Ventre River, away from the mountains and 2 mi southwest of Kelly. Try to get a site close to the river. The campground usually doesn't fill until nightfall, if at all. There's a maximum stay of 14 days. Flush toilets. Dump station. Drinking water. Bear boxes, fire grates, picnic tables. | 360 tent or RV sites | 4 mi off U.S. 26/89/191, 1.5 mi west of Kelly on Gros Ventre River Road, 6 mi south of Moose Junction | 307/739–3603 | $12 | Reservations not accepted | AE, D, MC, V | Late Apr.–early Oct.

★ **Jenny Lake.** Wooded sites and Teton views make this the most desirable campground in the park, and it fills early. The small, quiet facility allows tents only, and limits stays to a maximum of seven days. Flush toilets. Drinking water. Bear boxes, fire grates, picnic tables. | 49 sites | Jenny Lake Rd., 0.5 mi off Teton Park Rd., 8 mi north of Moose Junction | No phone | $12 | Reservations not accepted | No credit cards | Late May–late Sept.

Lizard Creek. Views of Jackson Lake, wooded sites, and the relative isolation of this campground make it a relaxing choice. You can stay here no more than 14 days. No vehicles over 30 ft are allowed. Flush toilets. Drinking water. Bear boxes, fire grates. | 60 tent/trailer sites | U.S. 89/191/287, 12 mi north of Jackson Lake Junction | 307/739–3603 | $12 | Reservations not accepted | No credit cards | Early June–early Sept.

Signal Mountain. This campground in a hilly setting on Jackson Lake has boat access to the lake. No vehicles or trailers over 30 ft are allowed. There's a maximum stay of 14 days. Flush toilets. Dump station. Drinking water. Fire grates, picnic tables. | 86 tent/trailer sites | Teton Park Rd., 3 mi south of Jackson Lake Junction | No phone | $12 | Reservations not accepted | AE, D, MC, V | Early May–mid-Oct.

Near the Park
When the campgrounds in the park are full you can usually find a campsite in one of several commercial Jackson Hole campgrounds or in nearby Bridger-Teton and Targhee national forests. Outside the park there are RV-and-tent campgrounds as well as roadside campgrounds and backcountry sites.

Bridger-Teton National Forest. There are 45 developed campgrounds in the forest, though none have hookups or showers. A few campgrounds have corrals and most have drinking water. You can reserve in advance for some of the campsites. Pit toilets. Fire pits, picnic tables. | U.S. 26/287 east of Moran Junction; U.S. 89 and U.S. 189 south of Jackson; U.S. Forest Service Reservations, 340 N. Cache St., Box 1888, Jackson, 83001 | 307/739–5500 or 800/280–2267 | fax 307/739–5010 | www.fs.fed.us/btnf | Free–$15 | No credit cards | June–Nov., depending on area.

Caribou–Targhee National Forest. There are about 30 campgrounds here. Drinking water. Fire pits, picnic tables. | Rte. 22 and U.S. 26 west of Jackson; 1405 Hollipark Dr., Idaho Falls,

GRAND TETON
NATIONAL PARK

EXPLORING
ATTRACTIONS NEARBY
DINING
LODGING
**CAMPING AND RV
FACILITIES**
SHOPPING
ESSENTIAL
INFORMATION

ID 83403 | 208/624–3151; campground reservations 877/444–6777 | www.fs.fed.us/r4/caribou | $8–$24 | AE, D, MC, V | June–Sept.

Flagg Ranch Resort Campground. Turn off the highway 4 mi north of the park and just north of the main Flagg Ranch entrance to reach this campground. Set in a wooded area near the north bank of Snake River, the facility has sites that vary in size. There are public telephones nearby. Flush toilets. Full hookups. Drinking water, guest laundry, showers. Fire pits, food service. General store, service station. | 75 RV sites (all with full hookups), 75 tent sites | John D. Rockefeller Jr. Memorial Pkwy. 4 mi north of Grand Teton National Park boundary Moran, WY 83013 | 307/543–2861 or 800/443–2311 | fax 307/543–2356 | www.flaggranch.com | $22–$45 | AE, D, MC, V | Mid-May–late Sept.

Shopping

Inside the park you can buy basic items, from food to souvenirs. Outside the park, particularly in Jackson, shopping opportunities abound. Bustling Town Square is surrounded by storefronts that house a mixture of galleries, specialty shops, and outlets (most of them small-scale) with moderate to expensive prices.

Colter Bay Village. The park's northern hub has a grocery store, tackle and gift shop, and a bookstore in the visitor center. | 2 mi off U.S. 89/191/287, 5 mi north of Jackson Lake Junction | 800/628–9988 | Closed Oct.–mid-May.

Dornan's Grocery. You can buy clothing, groceries, gifts and souvenirs here. They also have a startlingly good wine shop. | 10 Moose Rd., off Teton Park Rd. at Moose Junction | 307/733–2415 | Closed Dec.–Mar.

Flagg Ranch Resort. Groceries, gifts, souvenirs, and clothing are available here. | U.S. 89/191/287, 4 mi north of Grand Teton National Park boundary, Moran | 307/543–2861 or 800/443–2311.

Jack Dennis Sports. Jackson's premier sports shop—an internationally known fishing and sporting headquarters—is well stocked with the best in outdoor equipment for winter and summer. You can get everything from a canoe or backpack to skis and kayaks, plus clothing and other supplies. | 50 E. Broadway Ave., Jackson | 307/733–3270.

Jackson Lake Lodge. You can get your shopping fix at the shops on the second floor of the lodge's main building. There are a western and adventure wear store, a gift shop and a T-shirt shop. | U.S. 89/191/287, 0.5 mi north of Jackson Lake Junction | Closed late Oct.–mid-May.

Jenny Lake Lodge. This gift shop has good selection of quality souvenirs and gift items. | Jenny Lake Rd., 2 mi off Teton Park Rd., 12 mi north of Moose Junction | 307/733–4647 | Closed Nov.–May.

Moose Village Store. You can find fishing licenses, groceries, gifts, and souvenirs, along with a good selection of books related to local history, nature, and geology, at this shop located across from the visitor center. | Teton Park Rd., 1 mi north of Moose Junction | 307/733–3471 or 307/543–3360.

Signal Mountain Lodge. A variety of gifts, groceries, and clothing can be purchased here. They usually have a good selection of western-style women's clothing. | Teton Park Rd., 4 mi south of Jackson Lake Junction | 307/543–2831 | Closed mid-Oct.–mid-May.

Essential Information

ATMS: In the park, ATMs are at Colter Bay Grocery and General Store, Dornan's, Jackson Lake Lodge and Signal Mountain Lodge. You can also find ATMs at Flagg Ranch Resort and at banks in Jackson.

AUTOMOBILE SERVICE STATIONS: Automobile service stations are located in the park at Colter Bay Village, Dornan's, Jackson Lake Lodge, and Signal Mountain Lodge. Auto and RV repair is available at Colter Bay Village.

POST OFFICES: The Moose, Moran, and Kelly post offices are in the park. **Driggs Post Office** | 70 S. Main St., Driggs, ID 83422 | 800/275-8777. **Dubois Post Office** | 804 W. Ramshorn, Dubois, 82513 | 307/455-2735. **Jackson Downtown Station Post Office** | 220 W. Pearl St., Jackson, 83001 | 307/739-1740. **Jackson Main Post Office** | 1070 Maple Way, Jackson, 83002 | 307/733-3650. **Kelly Post Office** | Kelly Rd., Kelly, 83011 | 307/733-8884. **Moose Post Office** | Visitor Center Moose Village, 83012 | 307/733-3336. **Moran Post Office** | Moran Junction, Moran, 83013 | 307/543-2527.

ROCKY MOUNTAIN NATIONAL PARK

NORTH CENTRAL COLORADO

U.S. 34 or U.S. 36 west to Estes Park; U.S. 34 east to Grand Lake; Route 7 north to Allenspark (Wild Basin entrance).

One of the best-loved national parks, Rocky Mountain receives almost 3½ million visitors annually, and it's no wonder why: the park's more than 415 square mi are crossed by only three roads, but 350 mi of hiking trails. The sweeping vistas take in snow-dusted peaks, high-country lakes, meadows flushed with wildflowers, rushing mountain streams, and cool dense forests of lodgepole pine and Engelmann spruce. And the views from the park's namesake mountains are incomparable. More than 114 named mountains measure higher than 10,000 ft in elevation. The high, wind-whipped ecosystem of alpine tundra is seldom found outside the Arctic, yet it makes up one-third of the park's terrain. Up or down, you'll have ample opportunity to see wildlife, including elk, moose, and bighorn sheep.

Rocky Mountain National Park comprises lands that were part of the Louisiana Purchase, acquired by the U.S. government in 1803. Fifty-seven years later, the first white settler, Joel Estes, moved his family into a cabin in what would become Estes Park, and by 1909 a naturalist named Enos Mills had moved here and begun a campaign to save the area. In 1915 President Woodrow Wilson set aside 358.5 square mi of this land, near the heart of Colorado, to be preserved and protected as a national park (an additional 46.5 square mi were added 75 years later); since then Rocky Mountain has been welcoming people from around the globe.

PUBLICATIONS

Pick up the park newspaper, *High Country Headlines*, at any entrance station or visitor center for information about the park and a schedule of park programs and events. *The Trail Ridge Road Guide* will inform you about sights to see along the drive.

When to Visit

SCENERY AND WILDLIFE

The views around each bend of Trail Ridge Road—of moraines and glaciers, and craggy hills framing emerald meadows carpeted with blue columbine and Indian paintbrush— are truly spectacular: nature's workshop on an epic scale. Three distinct ecosystems define the landscape. The montane ecosystem is in the park's lower regions; the dense, moist subalpine ecosystem is between 9,000 and 11,500 ft.; and the high alpine tundra ecosystem is above 11,500 ft, where only small, low-growing plants and the toughest of animals can survive the severe climate and harsh winds.

ELEVATION ILLS

If you aren't used to it, the high altitude of Rocky Mountain National Park can catch you off guard. Drink plenty of water to help stave off the effects of altitude sickness—dizziness, headache, shortness of breath, or nausea. And slather on the sunscreen—it's easy to get sunburned at high altitude.

The park has such an abundance of wildlife that you can usually engage in prime viewing from the seat of your car. A group of cars pulled over at a seemingly random section of road, passengers intently staring at something in the distance, is a good bet that an animal is within sight. May through mid-October is the best time to see the bighorn sheep that congregate in the Horseshoe Park–Sheep Lakes area, just past the Fall River entrance. Elk can be seen year-round in the park and the surrounding area. Kawuneeche Valley, on the park's western side, is the most likely location to glimpse a moose. At night, listen for the eerie vocalizing of coyotes.

Fall is an excellent time to spot wildlife, when many animals begin moving down from the higher elevations. This is also when you'll hear the male elk bugle mating calls to their female counterparts, which draws large crowds to popular "listening" spots in the early evening: Horseshoe Park, Moraine Park, and Upper Beaver Meadows. Feeding any wildlife in the park is forbidden.

HIGH AND LOW SEASON

More than two-thirds of visitors to Rocky Mountain come in summer, when the climate is welcoming and Trail Ridge Road is open. But even though the park is far more crowded than it once was, you can access places in the backcountry that look and feel as wild as they did when Native Americans roamed these woods and peaks. In early fall, after most of the crowds have left, you can enjoy brilliant autumn foliage. In winter, the backcountry snow can be 4 ft deep and the wind brutal at high elevations, but skiing, snowshoeing and ice fishing still draw the cold-weather adventurer.

Average High/Low Temperatures (°F) and Monthly Precipitation (in inches)

	JAN.	FEB.	MAR.	APR.	MAY	JUNE
ROCKY MOUNTAIN	38/16 .40	40/17 .50	45/20 .90	53/25 1.20	62/34 2.0	72/41 1.70

	JULY	AUG.	SEPT.	OCT.	NOV.	DEC.
	78/46 2.30	76/44 2.0	69/37 1.40	59/30 .90	46/22 .60	39/16 .50

FESTIVALS AND SEASONAL EVENTS

WINTER

Feb.: **Discovery Snowshoe Festival.** A 5K snowshoe race, snowshoe demos, a kids' obstacle course, and guided hikes in the national park are some of the events organized by the Estes Park Chamber Resort Association in early February. | 970/586–4431 or 800/443–7837.

SUMMER

June: **Chili Cook-off.** Sponsored by the Grand Lake Fire Department, this competition draws entrants from all over Colorado and even New Mexico. Look for the heat at Town Park. | 970/627–8428.

The Wool Market. The country's largest exhibition of natural fibers is held in Estes Park. Watch shearing and spinning contests, and see animal shows where goats, sheep, llamas, and alpacas are judged for their wool. | 970/586–6104.

July: **Rooftop Rodeo.** An Estes Park tradition for more than 75 years, the six days of events include a parade, nightly rodeos, and an arts-and-crafts fair. | 970/586–6104.

Western Weekend. Part of a 50-plus-year tradition, the festivities include a 5K run and walk, a pancake breakfast, musical entertainment, a parade, and a buffalo barbecue in Grand Lake in mid-July. The Grand Lake Yacht

Club simultaneously puts on a wooden boat show. | 970/627–3402 or 800/531–1019.

FALL

Sept.: **Longs Peak Scottish Irish Festival.** Classic highland dancing, athletic competitions, arts and crafts, a parade, and Celtic music are all part of the fun the weekend after Labor Day in Estes Park. The festival, running for close to three decades, is the largest of its kind in the U.S. | 970/586–6308 or 800/903–7837.

Oct.: **Elk Fest.** This Estes Park event includes seminars on photographing and tracking wildlife, archery demonstrations, bugling contests, and a wildlife art exhibit. | 970/586–6104.

Nearby Towns

As the most popular gateway to Rocky Mountain National Park, **Estes Park** bustles with visitors all summer long. The town is at an altitude of more than 7,500 ft before a stunning backdrop of 14,255-ft Longs Peak and surrounding mountains. In winter, the locals catch their breath, and businesses take a hiatus. **Grand Lake,** just outside the west entrance to Rocky Mountain, is Estes Park's quieter cousin. While busy in summer, the lakeside town has a low-key, Western graciousness. Grand Lake is on the northern shore of Colorado's largest natural lake in full view of the Continental Divide's rugged peaks. At the southwestern entrance to Rocky Mountain National Park, Arapaho National Forest, and Arapaho National Recreational Area, the small town of **Granby** is a good base for year-round recreation, including big-game hunting, skiing at nearby SolVista resort, and water sports on the large Lake Granby reservoir.

INFORMATION

Estes Park Chamber Resort Association | 500 Big Thompson Ave., Estes Park, CO 80517 | 970/586–4431 or 800/443–7837 | www.estesparkresort.com. **Grand Lake Area Chamber of Commerce** | 14700 U.S. 34, Box 57 Grand Lake, 80447 | 970/627–3402 or 800/531–1019 | www.grandlakechamber.com. **Greater Granby Area Chamber of Commerce** | 81 W. Jasper, Box 35, Granby, 80446 | 970/887–2311 or 800/325–1661 | www.granbychamber.com.

Exploring Rocky Mountain

PARK BASICS

Contacts and Resources: Rocky Mountain National Park | 1000 U.S. 36, Estes Park, CO 80517-8397 | 970/586–1206 | www.nps.gov/romo.

Hours: The park is open 24 hours a day. Beaver Meadows visitor center, the main information resource on the park's eastern side, is open daily 8–5 (until 9 PM in summer). The Kawuneeche visitor center, on the park's west side, is open daily 8–4:30, until 6 PM in summer.

Fees: Entrance fees are $15 per week per private passenger vehicle. If you enter on bicycle, motorcycle, horseback, or on foot, you pay $5 for a weekly pass. An annual pass costs $30.

Getting Around: Trail Ridge Road, the main thoroughfare, is usually open from Memorial Day to mid-October. In winter, the road is plowed up to Many Parks Curve on the east side and the Colorado River trailhead on the west side.

Gravel-surfaced, extremely curvy Old Fall River Road is open from July to September, weather permitting, and traffic goes one-way only (uphill). Pulled trailers and vehicles longer than 25 ft are prohibited.

Nine-mile Bear Lake Road was completed in 1928. Although the road from Sprague Lake to Bear Lake will be reconstructed during the 2004 summer season, the road itself and all facilities will be open to the public via the park's free shuttle bus, which runs daily

ROCKY MOUNTAIN
NATIONAL PARK

EXPLORING
ATTRACTIONS NEARBY
DINING
LODGING
CAMPING AND RV
FACILITIES
SHOPPING
ESSENTIAL
INFORMATION

from mid-June to mid-September (and weekends into October). Private vehicles are allowed on Bear Lake Road as far as Sprague Lake. Parking is only allowed in designated areas, and you'll need a permit to park overnight.

Permits: If you are planning an overnight trek into the backcountry, you must buy a permit for a specific backcountry campsite. From May 1 through October 31 the cost is $15 per party (it's free the rest of the year, but you'll still need the permit). You can pick up the permit at the backcountry office, east of Beaver Meadows visitor center, or at Kawuneeche visitor center on the west side of the park. Phone reservations for backcountry campsites can be made between March 1 and May 15 and after October 1 by calling the backcountry office at 970/586–1242.

To fish in the park, you must have a valid Colorado fishing license if you're more than 16 years old. Licenses are available from sporting goods stores and cost $5.25–$40, depending on how long you plan to fish and whether you're an in-state or out-of-state resident. See www.wildlife.state.co.us/fishing for more information.

Public Telephones: Public telephones may be found at the Beaver Meadows, Kawuneeche, and Fall River visitor centers and at most park campgrounds.

Rest Rooms: Public rest rooms may be found at all visitor centers and campgrounds, at several picnic areas, and at Bear Lake, Sprague Lake, Lawn Lake Trailhead, Timber Lake Trailhead, and Milner Pass.

Accessibility: All visitor centers are fully accessible to mobility-impaired people. The Sprague Lake, Bear Lake, Coyote Valley, and Lily Lake trails are all hard-packed gravel, 0.5- to 1-mi, accessible loops. An accessible backcountry campsite at Sprague Lake can accommodate up to 12 campers, including six wheelchair users. Many of the park's ranger-led programs are appropriate for people with disabilities; check the park newspaper for details. Bear Lake shuttle buses are also wheelchair accessible.

Emergencies: In an emergency, call 911. You can also call 970/586–1203, the park's dispatch office. There are no fire-call boxes within the park, but there are emergency phones at Cow Creek, Lawn Lake, Longs Peak, and Wild Basin trailheads. Medical assistance is available at any visitor center, as well as at the ranger stations at Longs Peak and Wild Basin (staffed daily in summer and weekends only in winter).

Lost and Found: The park's lost-and-found is at the backcountry office next to Beaver Meadows visitor center (970/586–1242). On the west side of the park, lost-and-found items can be retrieved at Kawuneeche visitor center (970/586–1206).

Good Tours

ROCKY MOUNTAIN IN ONE DAY

Starting your day in Estes Park, drive west on U.S. 36 into the national park, and stop for an hour at **Beaver Meadows visitor center.** Watch the 20-minute film or tour the exhibits to get acquainted with the park. Pick up a map, a copy of the park newspaper, and some of the various informative leaflets.

Drive through the Beaver Meadows entrance station and continue northwest on U.S. 36 past Deer Ridge junction. Turn left toward Endovalley, and drive straight through to **Old Fall River Road,** which begins where the paved road ends. The 9-mi gravel route runs one-way uphill to **Alpine visitor center.** After about 1.4 mi, pull over and walk the short path to view chasm falls, a plume of white cascading through a narrow granite slot. If you're driving a vehicle longer than 25 ft or a pulled trailer, or if Fall River Road is closed, head up **Trail Ridge Road** instead. Pick up lunch at the Trail Ridge Store snack bar, or you can picnic at any one of the pullouts you pass on your way back down. You may have to eat in your car to avoid the wind.

Take Trail Ridge Road back toward Estes Park, stopping at the overlooks along the way. When you get back to U.S. 36, go south 4 mi to **Bear Lake Road.** Follow the road south to

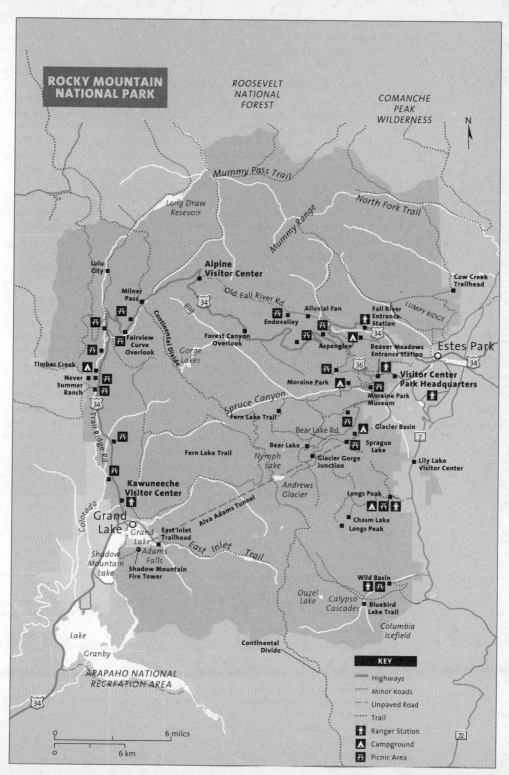

ROCKY MOUNTAIN NATIONAL PARK

ROOSEVELT NATIONAL FOREST

COMANCHE PEAK WILDERNESS

N

Mummy Pass Trail

Long Draw Reservoir

North Fork Trail

Mummy Range

Lulu City

Alpine Visitor Center

Cow Creek Trailhead

Milner Pass

Old Fall River Rd

34

Alluvial Fan

Fall River Entrance Station

LUMPY RIDGE

34

Endovalley

Big

Continental Divide

Forest Canyon Overlook

Aspenglen

Beaver Meadows Entrance Station

Estes Park

Fairview Curve Overlook

Gorge Lakes

36

34

Timber Creek

Moraine Park

Visitor Center Park Headquarters

Never Summer Ranch

Spruce Canyon

Moraine Park Museum

34

Fern Lake Trail

Bear Lake Rd.

Glacier Basin

7

Fern Lake Trail

Bear Lake

Sprague Lake

Trail Ridge Rd.

Nymph Lake

Glacier Gorge Junction

Lily Lake Visitor Center

Kawuneeche Visitor Center

Andrews Glacier

Longs Peak

Colorado

Alva Adams Tunnel

Chasm Lake

Grand Lake

Grand Lake

East Inlet Trailhead

Longs Peak

Shadow Mountain Lake

Adams Falls

East Inlet Trail

Shadow Mountain Fire Tower

Wild Basin

Ouzel Lake

Calypso Cascades

Bluebird Lake Trail

Lake Granby

Columbia Icefield

Continental Divide

KEY

ARAPAHO NATIONAL RECREATION AREA

34

Highways

Minor Roads

Unpaved Road

Trail

6 miles

Ranger Station

6 km

Campground

72

Picnic Area

Sprague Lake, and walk the 0.5-mi trail around it. Or to visit **Bear Lake** itself, take the park's free shuttle from the parking lot at the start of Bear Lake Road. Stretch your legs on a stroll to nearby Nymph Lake (1 mi round-trip), or relax quietly by the water before heading back to your camp or hotel.

ROCKY MOUNTAIN IN THREE DAYS

With a few days to explore the park, you can see both the east and west sides, and some of the park's less-frequented areas as well. Set out early from Estes Park on your first day, stopping at Beaver Meadows visitor center to get maps and brochures. After the entrance station, turn south onto Bear Lake Road. Drive 4 mi to the shuttle bus parking area across from **Glacier Basin Campground** and leave your car there. The free shuttle will take you to Bear Lake. If you're feeling acclimated to the altitude, venture out on the 5-mi round-trip hike to Mills Lake. Otherwise, stroll the 0.5-mi nature trail around Bear Lake or the moderate 0.5- to 1-mi trail up to Nymph and Dream lakes.

In the early afternoon, join a ranger-led talk to learn about some of the park's wildlife. Half-hour programs at **Fall River visitor center** focus on bears or cougars. A talk at the Sheep Lakes parking lot off U.S. 34 describes the wildlife of the Horseshoe Park area. Or visit **Moraine Park Museum** on Bear Lake Road to view the exhibits on park geology. In the evening, either drive across Trail Ridge Road to spend the night in or around Grand Lake, or stay in Estes Park, and cross to the west side of the park the next morning. The advantage of taking Trail Ridge Road in the evening is that you'll encounter fewer people on the road. Plus the glow of late-afternoon light on rugged peaks is a memorable sight.

Spend your second day on the park's west side. Take a morning **Wildflower Walk** from **Kawuneeche visitor center,** hike to the meadows past Adam's Falls, about 2 mi one-way on **East Inlet Trail,** or hike to **Lulu City,** 3.6 mi down **Colorado River Trail.** In the afternoon, visit historic **Never Summer Ranch.** Head back to Estes Park to spend the night in town, or stay at one of the park campgrounds and enjoy an **evening campfire program.**

On your third day drive south of Estes Park on Route 7 to the **Wild Basin area,** in the southeastern section of the park. Though still popular, this region attracts fewer people than busy Bear Lake. If you're feeling comfortable with the altitude, go for a long day hike (it's 5 mi each way) to Ouzel Lake, or for a shorter hike, stop at one of the waterfalls along the way. If you'd prefer to let someone else do the walking, a couple of stables in Allenspark offer horseback rides in Wild Basin. On your way back to Estes Park later in the day, stop at **Lily Lake** off Route 7. A 1-mi loop trail encircles the lake, and the visitor center has displays on the local flora and fauna. An easy, 1½-hour, ranger-led walk that focuses on the history of Longs Peak leaves from the Lily Lake parking lot several afternoons a week.

Attractions

PROGRAMS AND TOURS

Junior Ranger Program. Pick up a Junior Ranger activity book (in English or Spanish) at any visitor center. Program content has been developed for children ages 6–12 and focuses on environmental education, identifying birds and wildlife within the park and outdoor safety skills. Once a child has completed all of the activities, a ranger will look over the book and award a Junior Ranger badge. | 970/586–1206 | Free.

Ranger-Led Programs. A visit to Rocky Mountain isn't complete until you've joined one of the free hikes, talks, or activities conducted by those who know the park best. More than 150 programs for all ages and interests are scheduled each summer, on both the east and west sides of the park. Topics may include the wildlife, geology, vegetation, or history of the park. Kodak-sponsored photography seminars are also offered. In winter, rangers lead snowshoeing and cross-country ski tours. At night, storytelling, slide shows, and talks may be part of the evening campfire program, held in summer at park campgrounds and at Beaver Meadows visitor center. There are also evening hikes and star-gazing sessions. On Friday, stories, songs, and marshmallow roasts take place at Never Summer Ranch. Kids

KODAK'S TIPS FOR PHOTOGRAPHING LANDSCAPES AND SCENERY

Landscape
- Tell a story
- Isolate the essence of a place
- Exploit mood, weather, and lighting

Panoramas
- Use panoramic cameras for sweeping vistas
- Don't restrict yourself to horizontal shots
- Keep the horizon level

Panorama Assemblage
- Use a wide-angle or normal lens
- Let edges of pictures overlap
- Keep exposure even
- Use a tripod

Placing the Horizon
- Use low horizon placement to accent sky or clouds
- Use high placement to emphasize distance and accent foreground elements
- Try eliminating the horizon

Mountain Scenery: Scale
- Include objects of known size
- Frame distant peaks with nearby objects
- Compress space with long lenses

Mountain Scenery: Lighting
- Shoot early or late; avoid midday
- Watch for dramatic color changes
- Use exposure compensation

Tropical Beaches
- Capture expansive views
- Don't let bright sand fool your meter
- Include people

Rocky Shorelines
- Vary shutter speeds to freeze or blur wave action
- Don't overlook sea life in tidal pools
- Protect your gear from sand and sea

In the Desert
- Look for shapes and textures
- Try visiting during peak bloom periods
- Don't forget safety

Canyons
- Research the natural and social history of a locale
- Focus on a theme or geologic feature
- Budget your shooting time

Rain Forests and the Tropics
- Go for mystique with close-ups and detail shots
- Battle low light with fast films and camera supports
- Protect cameras and film from moisture and humidity

Rivers and Waterfalls
- Use slow film and long shutter speeds to blur water
- When needed, use a neutral-density filter over the lens
- Shoot from water level to heighten drama

Autumn Colors
- Plan trips for peak foliage periods
- Mix wide and close views for visual variety
- Use lighting that accents colors or creates moods

Moonlit Landscapes
- Include the moon or use only its illumination
- Exaggerate the moon's relative size with long telephoto lenses
- Expose landscapes several seconds or longer

Close-Ups
- Look for interesting details
- Use macro lenses or close-up filters
- Minimize camera shake with fast films and high shutter speeds

Caves and Caverns
- Shoot with ISO 1000+ films
- Use existing light in tourist caves
- Paint with flash in wilderness caves

From *Kodak Guide to Shooting Great Travel Pictures* © 2000 by Fodor's Travel Publications

usually have a blast on programs like "Ranger for a Day," "Skins and Skulls," "The Importance of Being a Beaver/Rocky Mountain's Engineers," and "Tales for Tots" (for preschool-age kids with an accompanying adult). Look for the extensive program schedule in *High Country Headlines* | 970/586–1206 | Free.

Rocky Mountain Field Seminars. The Rocky Mountain Nature Association, a nonprofit organization that promotes education about the park, offers some 100 different, hands-on seminars for kids and adults on topics such as natural history, geology, bird-watching, wildflower identification, wildlife biology, writing, photography, sketching, and Native American leather and beads. The three-hour classes are taught by expert instructors, and students can usually receive academic credit for the classes. | 1895 Fall River Rd., Estes Park | 970/586–3262 or 800/748–7002 | www.rmna.org | $15–$65 per day | Jan.–Oct.

SCENIC DRIVES

Bear Lake Road. Paved 9-mi Bear Lake Road branches off U.S. 36 shortly after the Beaver Meadows entrance station and dead-ends at Bear Lake. Due to major reconstruction on the road during the 2004 summer season, you must take a free shuttle to see the lake. The ride allows you to view some of the park's signature peaks, including Hallett, Flattop, and the 14,255-ft Longs.

Old Fall River Road. This 9-mi, one-way, narrow gravel road is made up of a series of switchbacks and is much less traveled than Trail Ridge Road, despite the gorgeous views each switchback reveals. Under construction from 1913 to 1920, Old Fall River was the first road leading into the high country of Rocky Mountain National Park. It starts at Endovalley picnic area and roughly follows a path along Fall River used by Native Americans to cross the mountains. Your upward journey will take you through a subalpine ecosystem to the harsh environment of the alpine tundra. The road ends at 11,796-ft Fall River Pass, near Alpine visitor center. Take Trail Ridge Road back down (25 mi to Estes Park, 24 mi to Grand Lake). Old Fall River Road is generally open from early July to late September.

★ **Trail Ridge Road.** Designated a National Scenic Byway and an All-American Road, 48-mi-long Trail Ridge Road, opened in 1933, is Rocky Mountain National Park's star attraction. It's also the world's highest continuous paved highway, topping out at 12,183 ft. You'll cross the Continental Divide at Milner Pass, elevation 10,758 ft. In normal summer traffic, it's a two-hour drive from the east side of the park to the west side, or vice versa, but it's best to give yourself three to four hours to allow for leisurely breaks at the numerous overlooks. Twelve pullouts have interpretive signs that highlight the various climatic zones, glacial formations, plant life, and rugged peaks visible from Trail Ridge. You can purchase the inexpensive *Trail Ridge Road Guide* at any visitor center.

Plowing the road for its traditional Memorial Day weekend opening can be a two-month project. A particularly interesting time to drive the road is shortly after it opens—the snowbanks that the plows tunneled through can easily reach 20 ft high. The middle part of the road closes down again by mid-October, though you can still drive up about 10 mi from the west and 8 mi from the east.

SIGHTS TO SEE

Alluvial Fan. On July 15, 1982, the 79-year-old dam at Lawn Lake (in the north of the park) burst, and the "escaped" water roared into Estes Park, killing three people and causing major flooding. Another result of the flood was the creation of the alluvial fan, a pile of glacial and streambed debris up to 44 ft deep, which the violent waters deposited on the north side of Horseshoe Park. A 0.5-mi trail allows you to explore the fan up close. You can also get a good view of it from the Rainbow Curve lookout on Trail Ridge Road. | Fall River Rd., about 3 mi from the Fall River entrance station.

Alpine Visitor Center. At the top of Trail Ridge Road, you'll find this state-of-the-art visitor center, with excellent exhibits, and Trail Ridge Store. The center is open only when Trail Ridge Road is navigable. | Trail Ridge Rd., 22 mi from the Beaver Meadows entrance station | 970/586–1206 | Memorial Day–mid-Oct., daily 9–5.

★ **Bear Lake.** This small alpine lake below Flattop Mountain and Hallett Peak is one of the most popular destinations in the park, thanks to its picturesque location, easy accessibility, and the good surrounding hiking trails. A shuttle to the lake is the only option during the summer of 2004, when construction is due to close part of Bear Lake Road to private vehicles. | Bear Lake Rd., 10 mi southwest of Beaver Meadows visitor center.

Beaver Meadows Visitor Center. The visitor center, which houses park headquarters, was designed by the Frank Lloyd Wright School of Architecture at Taliesen West, whose trademark is integrating buildings into their natural surroundings. Completed in 1966, it is now on the National Register of Historic Places. The surrounding utility buildings, also on the National Register, are noteworthy examples of the Rocky Mountain Rustic–style buildings that the Civilian Conservation Corps constructed during the Depression. In addition to an orientation film, the center has a large relief map of the park. | U.S. 36, before the Beaver Meadows entrance station | 970/586–1206 | Mid-June–Labor Day, daily 8–9; early Sept.–mid-June, daily 8–5.

Fall River Visitor Center. The center has a comprehensive wildlife education display, including exhibits on animals typical to the eastern side of the park and tips on how best to view wildlife. The center's Discovery Room, which houses everything from old ranger outfits to elk antlers, coyote pelts, and big horn sheep skulls for hands-on exploration, is a favorite with kids (and adults). | U.S. 34, at the Fall River entrance station | 970/586–1206 | Mid-June–Labor Day, daily 9–6; winter hrs vary.

Farview Curve Overlook. At an elevation of 10,120 ft, this lookout affords a panoramic view of the Colorado River near its origin and the Grand Ditch, a water diversion project dating from 1890 that's still in use today. You can also see the once-volcanic peaks of Never Summer Range along the park's western boundary. | Trail Ridge Rd., about 18 mi west of Alpine visitor center.

Forest Canyon Overlook. This is one of the most awe-inspiring and easily accessible viewpoints in the park. Beyond the classic U-shape glacial valley of Forest Canyon lies a high-alpine cirque of ice-blue pools (the Gorge Lakes) framed by ragged peaks. You truly get a sense of nature's forces at work. | Trail Ridge Rd., about 14 mi east of Alpine visitor center.

Kawuneeche Visitor Center. The park's only west-side source of visitor information has exhibits on the plant and animal life of the area, as well as a large three-dimensional map of the park. | U.S. 34, before the Grand Lake entrance station | 970/586–1206 | Mid-June–mid-Aug., daily 8–6; mid-Aug.–mid-June, daily 8–4:30.

Lily Lake Visitor Center. This small information center has displays on the birds, other animals and plants that call the lake's riparian habitat home. | Rte. 7, about 6 mi south of Estes Park | 970/586–1206 | Memorial Day–Labor Day, daily 9–4:30.

Longs Peak. At 14,255 ft above sea level, mighty Longs Peak, adjacent to Mount Meeker in the park's southeast quadrant, is one of 54 mountains in Colorado that reach above the 14,000-ft mark. It's also the northernmost fourteener in the Rocky Mountains. You can see its distinctive flat-top, rectangular-shape summit from many spots on the park's east side and Trail Ridge Road. The mountain was named in honor of Major Stephen H. Long, who led an expedition in 1820 up the Platte River to the base of the Rockies. The first recorded climb of the peak was August 1868. | Rte. 7 to the Longs Peak Trailhead, 9 mi south of Estes Park.

Lulu City. A few remnants of cabins and mining equipment are all that remain of this one-time silver mining town, established in 1880. Mining in the area never proved profitable, however, and by 1884 the town was largely abandoned. You can reach Lulu City by hiking the 3.6-mi Colorado River Trail. As you hike, look for wagon ruts from the old Stewart Toll Road and the ruins of cabins in Shipler Park. The Colorado River is a mere stream at this point, flowing south from its headwaters at nearby La Poudre Pass. | Off Trail Ridge Rd., 10.5 mi north of Grand Lake.

Moraine Park Museum. Housed in one of the buildings of the historic former Moraine Lodge, the museum also serves as a visitor information center. Exhibits coordinated by the Denver Museum of Nature and Science emphasize the geology of the park, including information on the glaciers that formed Moraine Park. Additional displays give insight into the park's different ecosystems and some of the characteristic wildlife. | Bear Lake Rd., 1.4 mi from Beaver Meadows entrance station | 970/586–1206 | Late May–mid-Oct., daily 9–4:30; shorter hours in spring and fall; closed in winter.

Never Summer Ranch. On the site of the original Holzwarth homestead and a rustic 1920s resort and dude ranch—Holzwarth's Trout Lodge—buildings have been restored to serve as an interpretive center. You can take a free guided or self-guided tour to view the original lodge, workshops, icehouse, and taxidermy building. Reaching the ranch involves an easy 0.5-mi hike off Trail Ridge Road. | Off Trail Ridge Rd., 9 mi north of Grand Lake | Mid-June to Labor Day, daily 10–4.

Shadow Mountain Fire Lookout. The lookout, which gives you a 360-degree view of the surrounding peaks and lakes, was built in 1933 and used for spotting fires until the early 1990s. It was restored in the mid-1990s and is now listed in the National Register of Historic Places. To access the lookout, start at the East Shore Trailhead, between Grand and Shadow Mountain lakes, and hike 4.8 mi along the East Shore and Shadow Mountain trails. An elevation gain of about 1,500 ft makes this a steep trip. | Jericho Rd., 0.5 mi south of downtown Grand Lake.

Wild Basin Area. The Wild Basin area, in the southeast region of the park, consists of lovely expanses of subalpine forest punctuated by streams and lakes. The area's high peaks, along the Continental Divide, are not as easily accessible as those in the vicinity of Bear Lake; hiking to the base of the Divide and back constitutes a long day. Nonetheless, a visit here is well worth the drive south from Estes Park, and because the Wild Basin trailhead is set apart from the park hub, crowding isn't a problem. | Off Rte. 7, 12.7 mi south of Estes Park.

Sports and Outdoor Activities

BICYCLING

There are no bike paths in the park, and bikes are not allowed on trails. Trail Ridge Road is too strenuous for most people. Remember, although the grade of this road doesn't exceed 7%, it *begins* at an altitude most people will have trouble with, and going from east to west there's a 15-mi uphill stretch (the climb from west to east is shorter but steeper). Those who have an extra lung or two to spare, however, might tackle a ride up the gravel, 9-mi Old Fall River Road, then ride down Trail Ridge (Old Fall River is one way uphill).

Colorado Bicycling Adventures. The company will ferry you by van to the top of Trail Ridge Road, then let you loose to coast down the road by bicycle. The store also rents and sells bikes. | 184. E. Elkhorn Ave., Estes Park | 970/586–4241 | www.coloradobicycling.com | $70 for shuttle, $15–$25 daily for rentals | Tues.–Sun. 9–5.

Rocky Mountain Sports. Bicycle rentals are available hourly and by the day. | 830 Grand Ave., Grand Lake | 970/627–8124 | $8–$22 | May–Sept., daily 9–6; Oct.–Apr. hrs vary.

BIRD-WATCHING

Spring and summer are the best times for bird-watching in Rocky Mountain. Go early in the morning, before the crowds arrive. Lumpy Ridge is the nesting ground of raptors such as golden eagles, red-tailed hawks, and peregrine. You can see migratory songbirds from South America in their summer breeding grounds near the Endovalley Picnic Area. The alpine tundra is habitat for white-tailed ptarmigan. The alluvial fan, along the Roaring River, is an excellent place for viewing broad-tailed hummingbirds, hairy woodpeckers, robins, ouzels, and the occasional raptor. Some of the ranger-led programs focus on bird-watching.

FISHING

Rocky Mountain is a wonderful place to fish—German brown, brook, rainbow, cutthroat, and greenback cutthroat trout live here—but it's not the best place for a catch. Check with a visitor center about regulations and information on specific closures, catch-and-release areas, and limits on size and possession. No fishing is allowed at Bear Lake. Rangers recommend the more remote backcountry lakes, since they are less crowded. Anyone older than 16 needs a Colorado fishing license, which you can obtain at local sporting-goods stores. See www.wildlife.state.co.us/fishing for more information.

Estes Angler. In addition to selling and renting fishing gear, the shop offers guided fly-fishing trips into the park year-round. Outings range from four to eight hours, and there's one guide for every three people. | 338 W. Riverside Dr., Estes Park | 970/586–2110 | $125–$225 | May–Sept., daily 8–6; Oct.–Apr., Wed.–Sat. 9–5.

Scot's Sporting Goods. Scot's gives half-day and full-day fishing instruction from May through September. Clinics, geared toward first-timers, focus on casting, reading the water, identifying insects for flies, and properly presenting natural and artificial flies to the fish. Half-day excursions into the park are available for three or more people. You can also rent and buy gear. | 2325 Spruce Ave., Estes Park | 970/586–2877 | $100–$190 | May–Sept., daily 8–8; Oct.–Apr. daily 9–5.

HIKING

The park contains 350 mi of hiking trails, meaning you could theoretically wander for weeks. The majority of visitors, however, explore just a small portion of these trails, so some of the park's most accessible, and scenic, paths can resemble a backcountry highway on busy summer days. The high-alpine terrain around Bear Lake is the park's most popular hiking area, and while it's well worth exploring (in the early morning or late afternoon if you wish to avoid the high-season crowds), you would do well to venture onto some of the park's less-trodden byways. For a truly remote experience, hike one of the trails in the far northern end of the park or in the Wild Basin area to the south. Pick up a topographic map at a visitor center before hitting the trails. Keep in mind that trails at higher elevations may have some snow on them even in July. And because of afternoon thunderstorms on most summer afternoons, an early morning start is highly recommended; the last place you want to be when a storm approaches is on a peak or elsewhere above treeline.

Bluebird Lake Trail. The 4.8-mi climb from the Wild Basin trailhead to Ouzel Lake (1,510-ft elevation gain) is especially scenic. You'll pass Copeland Falls, Calypso Cascades, and Ouzel Falls, plus an area that was burned in a lightning-instigated fire in 1978, today a mix of bright pink fireweed and charred tree trunks. | Off Rte. 7, 12.7 mi south of Estes Park.

Chasm Lake Trail. It would be hard to find a lake in Colorado with a more impressive backdrop than Chasm Lake, situated in the shadow of Longs Peak and Mount Meeker. As the Chasm Lake Trail (4.2 mi, 2,360-ft elevation gain) is reached via the Longs Peak Trail, expect to encounter plenty of other hikers. Just before the lake, you'll have to climb a small rock ledge, which can be a bit of a challenge for the less surefooted; follow the cairns for the most straightforward route. Once atop the ledge, you'll catch your first memorable view of the lake. | Off Rte. 7, 9 mi south of Estes Park.

Deer Mountain Trail. This 6-mi round-trip trek to the top of 10,083-ft-high Deer Mountain is a great way for hikers who don't mind a bit of a climb to enjoy the views from the summit of a lesser peak. You'll gain about 1,000 ft of elevation as you follow the switchbacking trail through ponderosa pine, aspen, and fir trees. The reward at the top is a panorama of the park's east side mountains. | Deer Ridge Junction, U.S. 34 at U.S. 36, 3 mi north of the Beaver Meadows entrance station.

East Inlet Trail. For a short hike to a lovely picnic spot, take this trail to Adams Falls starting from the east shore of Grand Lake. It's less than 0.5 mi to the Falls, and you climb about 79 ft in elevation. If you wish to hike farther, follow the trail another 1.5 mi past two moun-

ROCKY MOUNTAIN
NATIONAL PARK

EXPLORING
ATTRACTIONS NEARBY
DINING
LODGING
CAMPING AND RV
FACILITIES
SHOPPING
ESSENTIAL
INFORMATION

tainside meadows, or all the way to Lone Pine Lake, 5.5 mi from your starting point. | W. Portal Rd., about 2 mi south of Grand Lake.

Fern Lake Trail. Heading to Odessa Lake from the north involves a steeper hike, but you'll encounter fewer fellow hikers than if you begin at Bear Lake. Along the way, you'll come to the Arch Rocks; The Pool, an eroded formation in the Big Thompson River; two water-falls—Fern and Marguerite; and Fern Lake (4 mi from your starting point). Odessa Lake itself lies at the foot of Tourmaline Gorge, below the craggy summits of Gabletop Mountain, Little Matterhorn, Knobtop Mountain, and Notchtop Mountain. For a full day of spectacular scenery, continue past Odessa to Bear Lake (8.5 mi total), where you can pick up the shuttle back to the Fern Lake Trailhead. To get to the trailhead, turn west off Bear Lake Rd., just past the Moraine Park Museum. | Off Bear Lake Rd., about 1.5 mi south of the Beaver Meadows entrance station.

Glacier Gorge Trail. The 5-mi round-trip hike to Mills Lake can be crowded, but the reward is one the park's prettiest lakes, set against the breathtaking backdrop of Longs Peak, Pagoda Mountain, and the Keyboard of the Winds. There's a modest elevation gain of 700 ft. About 0.5 mi in, you pass Alberta Falls, a popular destination in and of itself. The hike travels along Glacier Creek, under the shade of subalpine forest. Just 0.5 mi past Mills Lake is the petite Jewel Lake. Black Lake, at the head of Glacier Gorge 4 mi from the trailhead, is also a dramatic destination. | Off Bear Lake Rd., 9 mi south of the Beaver Meadows entrance station.

★**Longs Peak Trail.** Climbing this 14,255-ft mountain (one of 54 "fourteeners" in Colorado) is an ambitious goal for many people. Only those who are very fit and acclimated to the altitude should attempt it. The 16-mi round-trip hike up Longs requires a predawn start (3 AM is ideal) so that you're off the summit before the typical summer afternoon thunderstorm hits. Also, the last 2 mi or so of the trail are very exposed—you have to traverse narrow ledges with vertigo-inducing drop-offs. All that said, summiting Longs can be one of the most rewarding hikes you'll ever attempt. The Keyhole route is the traditional means of ascent, and the number of people going up it on a summer day can be astounding given the rigors of the hike. The Loft route, which ascends between Longs and Mount Meeker from Chasm Lake, is just as scenic, however it is not clearly marked and is therefore difficult to navigate and much less frequented. | Off Rte. 7, 9 mi south of Estes Park.

HORSEBACK RIDING

Horses and riders can access 260 mi of trails in Rocky Mountain. Two liveries within the park offer trail rides mid-May through late September. Several stables in Estes Park and Grand Lake also give guided rides in the park.

Allenspark Livery. The stable offers rides into the Wild Basin area in the park's southeast corner, from shorter (three-hour-plus) tours that head for Calypso Cascades or Ouzel Falls to all-day outings to Thunder or Pear Lakes. | 211 Main St., Allenspark | 303/747–2551 | $45–$85 | June–mid Sept.

Sombrero Ranches, Inc. Sombrero operates several stables in the national park and in Estes Park, Allenspark, and Grand Lake. The guided rides last two to eight hours. Destinations from the Grand Lake stables include Tonahutu Creek, Cascade Falls, Granite Falls, and Lake Nokoni. | 304 W. Portal Rd., Grand Lake | 970/627–3514 | www.sombrero.com | $35–$80 | Mid-May–late Sept.

Trips from **Glacier Creek Stables** may head for Emerald Mountain, the Wind River, Alberta Falls, and Storm Pass. | Off Bear Lake Rd., near Sprague Lake | 970/586–3244.

Trips from **Moraine Park Stables** head north or west to Beaver Meadows, Beaver Mountain, and Fern and Odessa Lakes. To get to the stables, take Bear Lake Road. When you pass Moraine Park Museum, turn west toward the Fern Lake Trailhead. | Off Bear Lake Rd. | 970/586–2327.

National Park Gateway Stables and Cowpoke Corner Corrals. Guided trips into the national park range from two-hour rides to Little Horseshoe Park to full-day rides along the Roaring River to Lawn or Ypsilon Lake. | 46000 Fall River Rd. | 970/586–5269 or 970/586–5890 | www.nationalparkgatewaystables.com | $25–$80 | D, MC, V | mid May–early Oct.

ROCK AND ICE CLIMBING

There are hundreds of classic climbs here for novice to expert rock climbers. The burgeoning sport of ice climbing, which requires ropes, special "ice tools," plastic boots, crampons, and an imperviousness to cold, also thrives in Rocky Mountain. Well-known spots include Hidden Falls in the Wild Basin area, Loch Vale, and Emerald and Black Lakes.

The Diamond. Named for its distinctive shape, this sheer cliff on the east face of Longs Peak is the site of more than 30 routes. The "easiest," the Casual Route, is rated 5.10. | Rte. 7, 9 mi south of Estes Park.

Lumpy Ridge. These granite crags 1 mi north of Estes Park draw climbers from along Colorado's Front Range. Some of the routes are closed from March to July, due to nesting raptors. Its rock outcroppings, including the distinctive Twin Owls, rise behind the Stanley Hotel and can be seen from town. Mainliner, a 5.9-rated, six-pitch route on Lumpy's Sundance Buttress, is one of the classics. | MacGregor Ave., off Rte. 34.

Petit Grepon. If you're interested in a spectacular setting, try this internationally famous spire, southwest of Bear Lake, above Sky Pond. It attracts rock climbers from all over the world. Hike south from the Glacier Gorge Trailhead. | End of Bear Lake Rd.

Colorado Mountain School. This climbing concessionaire is the oldest continuously operating U.S. guide service and an invaluable resource. Guides lead introductory courses, daylong climbs, and even international expeditions. Equipment rentals for ice or rock climbing are available. Make reservations as far as six weeks in advance for climbs in summer. | 351 Moraine Ave., Estes Park | 970/586–5758 or 888/267–7783 | www.cmschool.com | $35–$80.

SKIING

Backcountry skiing within the park ranges from gentle cross-country outings to full-on telemarking down steep chutes and glaciers. Come spring, when avalanche danger decreases, the park has some classic ski descents for those on telemark or alpine touring equipment. If you plan on venturing off-trail, take a shovel, probe pole, and avalanche transceiver. Check the park newspaper, *High Country Headlines,* for ranger-guided cross-country tours throughout the winter and spring.

Bear Lake Area Trails. The Bear Lake and Glacier Gorge Junction trailheads are good starting points for a skinny ski tour on any number of trails. | End of Bear Lake Rd.

A 4-mi round-trip ski on the **Dream Lake Trail** to Dream and Emerald lakes involves only moderate climbing and provides breathtaking views of the high peaks.

The half-day, novice-to-intermediate trek from Glacier Gorge Junction to Sprague Lake follows the **Glacier Creek Trail** along the south side of the creek.

The snowfields on Flattop Mountain are easily accessible from the **Flattop Mountain Trail** and can be handled by intermediates.

The 8-mi round-trip tour from Bear Lake to Hollowell Park, via the **Mill Creek Trail,** generally has good snow.

Tonahutu Creek Trail. This gently sloping route on the park's west side traverses broad expanses of meadowland. | Kawuneeche visitor center.

Colorado River Trail. For a full-day tour on easy terrain, ski this trail to Lulu City. | Timber Creek Campground.

Hidden Valley Snow Play Area. Throughout the winter, local telemark skiers and children on sleds and dishes flock to this old ski area, off the eastern section of Trail Ridge Road. Though it's no longer operational, the area's runs are pretty much intact (though stumps

ROCKY MOUNTAIN
NATIONAL PARK

EXPLORING
ATTRACTIONS NEARBY
DINING
LODGING
CAMPING AND RV
FACILITIES
SHOPPING
ESSENTIAL
INFORMATION

and branches are not cleared away), and you can spend a satisfying day skinning up and schussing down. | Trail Ridge Rd., 2.5 mi west of the U.S. 36 junction.

SNOWMOBILING

Only on the west side of the park are you permitted to think snowmobile. Snowmobilers must register at Kawuneeche visitor center and can travel the unplowed section of Trail Ridge Road up to Milner Pass, at the Continental Divide. Access to snowmobile trails in Arapahoe National Forest is by Country Road 491, off U.S. 34 north of Grand Lake in the national park.

Grand Lake Snowmobile Rental. Located at Elk Creek campground, this snowmobile rental company has been doing it longer than anyone else in Grand Lake. Rentals are available for two, four, or eight hours. | 143 County Rd. 48, Grand Lake | 970/627–8502 | $65–$160 | Late Nov.–mid-Apr.

Spirit Lake Polaris & Rentals. Snowmobile rentals are available for two, four, or eight hours. | 347 Portal Rd., Grand Lake | 970/627–9288 or 800/894–3336 | www.spiritlakerentals. com | $60–$180 | Mid-Nov.–Mar.

SNOWSHOEING

Each winter for the past several years, the popularity of snowshoeing in the park has increased by leaps and bounds. It's a wonderful way to experience Rocky Mountain's majestic winter side, when the jagged peaks are softened with a blanket of snow, the summer hordes are nonexistent, and the landscape takes on a pristine character. You can snowshoe virtually any of the summer hiking trails that are still accessible by road in winter, many of which become popular cross-country ski trails. You could also head out on the unpaved roads through Beaver Meadows for an easy 3-mi loop trip. For a ranger-guided snowshoe tour, refer to the park newspaper, *High Country Headlines*.

Outdoor World. Daily snowshoe rentals, which include poles, are available. | 156 E. Elkhorn Ave., Estes Park | 970/586–2114 | $8.

Outfitters

Estes Park Mountain Shop. This outfitter will cater to all your outdoor needs. Group and private, half-day and full-day, guided fly-fishing trips into the park are given year-round for all levels. The store stocks fishing, hiking, skiing, snowshoeing, and climbing equipment for sale or rental. | 358. E. Elkhorn Ave., Estes Park | 970/586–6548 or 800/504–6642 | www. estesparkmountainshop.com.

Never Summer Mountain Sports. The shop rents cross-country skis, boots, and poles, and sells hiking and climbing gear as well. | 919 Grand Ave., Grand Lake | 970/627–3642.

Warming House. The owners have extensive backpacking experience in Rocky Mountain and abroad, so you can trust them to outfit your expedition with anything you need. They have camping and snowshoe rentals, including poles, and they're ready with tips and pointers to start you on your way. | 790 Moraine Ave., Estes Park | 970/586–2995 | www. warminghouse.com.

Attractions Nearby

Aerial Tramway. This suspended tramway moves at 1,000 ft per minute, and the enclosed passenger cars offer spectacular views of the Continental Divide from the top of Prospect Mountain in Estes Park. | 420 E. Riverside Dr., Estes Park | 970/586–3675 | $8 | Mid-May–mid-Sept., daily 9–6:30.

Arapaho–Roosevelt National Forest. Nearly 1,250 square mi of mountain vistas, forests, and lovely scenery await the hiker, camper, picnicker, and angler, including the Indian Peaks Wilderness Area, which straddles the Continental Divide. The national forest surrounds

Estes Park on the north, east, and south. For more information, check in at the ranger office in Estes Park or in Granby (970/887–4100). | 161 2nd St., Estes Park | 970/586–3440 | Free | Office: Thurs.–Sun. 9–5.

Arapaho National Recreation Area. The U.S. Forest Service has set aside 56 square mi of the Arapaho National Forest, including Lake Granby and Shadow Mountain Lake, which are especially suitable for water-based recreation; the entrance is 6 mi northeast of Granby. You can boat, fish, hunt, and camp. Call the Sulphur Ranger District office in Granby for information. | 9 Ten Mile Dr., Granby | 970/887–4100 | Free | Office: Memorial Day–Labor Day, weekdays 8–4:30, Sat. 8–noon; early Sept.–late May, weekdays 8–4:30.

Enos Mills Original Cabin. Enos Mills, the "father" of Rocky Mountain National Park, once lived in this cabin 8 mi south of Estes Park. Built in 1885, it's on 200 undeveloped acres in the shadow of Long's Peak. A nature guide and self-guided nature trails are also available. | 6760 Rte. 7, Estes Park | 970/586–4706 | Free | Memorial Day–Labor Day, Tues.–Sat. 11–5; Sept.–May, Sat. 11–4.

Nederland. Once a mining hub for gold, silver, and tungsten, Nederland is on the edge of the Indian Peaks Wilderness of the Arapaho National Forest. The one-time hippie community has become increasingly sophisticated, as former residents of nearby Boulder seek a more rural lifestyle in the mountains, but retains its offbeat character. | Rte. 72, 25 mi south of Allenspark | www.nederlandchamber.org.

Dining

In Rocky Mountain

Picnic Areas. Though windy, Rocky Mountain's picnic spots are clean and beautiful. There are pit toilets at each one.

Hollowell Park, in a meadow near Mill Creek, is a lovely spot for picnic. The Mill Creek Basin trailhead is at your disposal. You can reach Hollowell via the Bear Lake Road shuttle in summer. There are 10 tables, no running water, and no fire grates. | Off Bear Lake Rd., between the Moraine Park Museum and Glacier Basin campground.

With 27 tables and fire grates, the **Endovalley** picnic area is the largest in the park. The views here are of aspen groves, Fall River Pass, and a beautiful lake by the alluvial fan. | U.S. 34, at the beginning of Old Fall River Rd.

Lovely **Lake Irene** is on the park's west side near the Continental Divide and has six picnic tables. | Trail Ridge Rd., about 0.5 mi west of Milner Pass.

The four tables at **Tuxedo Park** are near lively Glacier Creek. | Bear Lake Rd., 2.8 mi south of U.S. 36.

Trail Ridge Store Snack Bar. Fast Food. The park's lone eatery, near the the top of Trail Ridge Road, serves up light meals like chili, burgers, soup, and sandwiches. | Trail Ridge Rd., adjacent to Alpine visitor center | $1–$5 | AE, D, MC, V | Closed mid-Oct.–Memorial Day.

Near the Park

★**Dunraven Inn.** Italian. A favorite of both locals and out-of-towners, the Dunraven offers home-style Italian cooking, a long wine list, pictures of Mona Lisa, and a bar with walls and ceiling decorated with approximately $14,000-worth of signed dollar bills from playful clientele. Popular dishes include lasagna, shrimp scampi, veal parmigiana, and fresh fish. The newer Dunraven Downtown (101 W. Elkhorn Ave.) has a similar menu and also serves lunch. | 2470 Rte. 66, Estes Park | 970/586–6409 | Reservations essential | $8–$28 | AE, D, MC, V | No lunch.

Fawn Brook Inn. Continental. Cozy, warm, and slightly rustic in an alpine way, the inn was built in 1927 and operated first as a general store, then as a small hunting lodge. Now lauded as one of the most romantic settings in the area, the restaurant (owned by a Dutch-Austrian couple) serves classic European-style specialties such as roast duckling, venison,

LONG GONE HOTEL

The park was the site of many hotels and inns that no longer exist. One of the most unusual was the "Boulderfield Hotel," a primitive lodging at 13,000 ft along the Longs Peak trail. It was run from 1927 to 1935 by Bob and Dorothy Collier, who provided meals and shelter to guides and their clients on the ascent of Longs Peak.

and veal medallions. | Rte. 7, 2.8 mi from U.S. 36, Allenspark | 303/747–2556 | Reservations essential | $29–$48 | AE, MC, V | No lunch. Closed Jan.-Feb. 13.

Grand Lake Lodge Restaurant. Contemporary. Built in 1920, the restaurant at this historic lodge has high, timber-vaulted ceilings and a spectacular view of Grand and Shadow Mountain Lakes. A breakfast buffet is served daily (on Sunday it becomes a decadent champagne brunch), and lunch specialties include grilled rainbow trout. For dinner choose from such mouth-watering fare as grilled filet mignon with shiitake mushrooms, sesame-seared salmon, pistachio-accented elk medallions, or oven-roasted leg of lamb in a mint and hazelnut rub. Kid's menu. | Off U.S. 34, 0.25 mi north of Grand Lake, Grand Lake | 970/627–3185 | www.grandlakelodge.com | Reservations essential | $15–$21 | AE, D, MC, V | Closed mid-Sept.–early June.

Longbranch Restaurant. German. This stylish Western coffee shop offers German, Mexican, Continental, and American dishes. Stick to what the German owners do best—goulash, schnitzel, and sauerbraten with homemade spaetzle. Schatzi's, next door and under the same ownership, specializes in pizza and pasta. | 185 E. Agate, U.S. 40, Granby | 970/887–2209 | $8–$19 | D, MC, V | Closed in Nov. and Apr.

Mama Rose's. Italian. The Victorian decorations and large fireplace make this local favorite especially inviting. Favorite dishes include veal or chicken parmigiana, and fettuccine Alfredo. There's also open-air dining on a patio overlooking the Big Thompson River. Kid's menu. | 338 E. Elkhorn Ave., Estes Park | 970/586–3330 | $7–$18 | AE, D, MC, V | Closed Dec.–Mar. No lunch Mon.–Sat.

Mountain Inn. American/Casual. This log-cabin, country-style restaurant is casual, and the service is friendly. Specialties include fried chicken, prime rib, and a giant chicken potpie. Vegetables and potatoes are served family-style in big bowls. A kids' menu is available. | 612 Grand Ave., Grand Lake | 970/627–3385 | $11–$20 | D, MC, V.

Nicky's Resort. Greek. Elegant wood beams, oak paneling, and a huge picture window framing mountain and river views make this a sophisticated dining spot. In addition to steaks (they age and cut their own meat here), Nicky's is known for sirloin with onions, peppers, and feta; gyros; moussaka; and spanakopita. Kid's menu. | 1350 Fall River Rd., Estes Park | 970/586–5376 | $9–$20 | AE, D, DC, MC, V.

★**Notchtop Bakery and Café.** Café. This natural foods restaurant provides a tasty alternative to the usual tourist fare. Breakfasts include delicious pastries, organic granola or muesli, and burritos. Inventive soups, salads, and sandwiches are served at lunch, while the dinner menu includes tuna with wasabi sauce and veggie entrées like fire-roasted green chiles stuffed with herb mashed potatoes. Coffee drinks, microbrews, and live entertainment on Sunday make the Notchtop a good place to stop by. | Upper Stanley Village, Estes Park | 970/586–0272 | $5–$10 | D, MC, V.

Pancho and Lefty's. Mexican. Housed in a round building that dates back to 1915, this family-oriented Mexican spot is known for fajitas, rellenos, and other traditional fare. Everything is made from scratch, and Margaritas are always on tap. | 1120 Grand Ave., Grand Lake | 970/627–8773 | $7–$20 | D, MC, V.

The Rapids Restaurant. Continental. One of the most picturesque settings for dining in Grand Lake is at this aptly named gourmet restaurant at the historic Rapids Lodge; get a window-side table and drink in the view of rushing Tonahutu Creek. For dinner, you can choose from among Italian dishes, such as lasagna and veal marsala; prime rib or filet mignon; or rack of lamb, pan-seared elk medallions, and seafood. | 209 Rapids La., Grand Lake | 970/627–3707 | $14–$35 | AE, MC, V | Closed Nov. and Apr. No lunch.

Terrace Inn. Contemporary. This small, intimate bistro-style restaurant adds a touch of sophistication to the local dining scene. Try the eggs Benedict with smoked salmon for breakfast. Dinner specialties include cedar-plank salmon (grilled and served on a plank of cedar), mesquite-grilled tenderloin of beef, or chicken piccata. | 813 Grand Ave., Grand Lake

| 970/627–3000 | www.grandlaketerraceinn.com | $4–$22 | MC, V | Closed early Nov.–Thanksgiving and in early May.

Wild Basin Lodge Restaurant. Contemporary. Along the banks of the St. Vrain River, with a huge deck facing Rocky Mountain, this is a wonderful outdoor (and indoor) dining experience. Try the cherry-and-apple–stuffed pork chop, almond-and-macadamia–crusted halibut, or for some of everything, the "Taste of Colorado" dinner buffet on Monday and Tuesday nights. A Sunday brunch buffet is also offered weekly. | 1130 County Rd. 84 W, Allenspark | 303/747–2274 | $10–$25 | MC, V | No lunch.

Lodging

Near the Park

Allenspark Lodge. This sprawling, three-story lodge is made entirely of pine timbers, with unique rooms of every imaginable shape and configuration scattered throughout. Two of the units can connect to sleep up to five; a couple seeking a little more privacy might choose the "hideaway room" with a cozy gas fireplace. An apartment with full kitchen is also available. Hot tub. No a/c, no room phones. No room TVs. No kids under 14. No smoking. | 184 Main St., Allenspark | 303/747–2552 | 14 rooms | $70–$140 | AE, D, MC, V | CP.

Aspen Lodge Ranch Resort and Conference Center. This ultimate family resort is set on 82 wooded acres 8 mi south of Estes Park. The log-and-stone lobby, with vast fireplace, is the largest log structure in Colorado. Rooms (all with balconies) and cabins are simply furnished but comfortable. Meals and activities are part of the guest ranch packages. Nightly entertainment might include Western dance lessons and campfire BBQs. There's a three-night minimum stay from Memorial Day to Labor Day. Restaurant, picnic area. Tennis court. Pool. Exercise equipment, hot tub, massage, sauna. Boating. Fishing. Bicycles. Hiking, horseback riding, racquetball, volleyball. Cross-country skiing, ice-skating. Bar. Baby-sitting, children's programs (ages 3–17). Business services. No a/c. No smoking. | 6120 Rte. 7, Estes Park | 970/586–8133 or 800/332–6867 | fax 970/586–8133 | www.aspenlodge.net | 36 rooms, 23 cabins | $109–$179 per room for bed-and-breakfast, $160–$195 per person for guest ranch | AE, D, DC, MC, V | Nov.–Apr. groups only.

★ **Appenzell Inn.** Though the Appenzell is set amid "motel row" in Estes Park, the bright, cozy suites are among the most attractive in town. They range in size from studio to two-bedroom, and all are furnished with knotty-pine furniture in a warm, Swiss-inspired style. The pub is a cheery little place to relax with a cold drink after a day in the park. Gas grills are available on the decks and patios. The inn takes its no-smoking policy seriously; tobacco is not even allowed on the premises, and smoking outdoors is also verboten. In-room hot tubs, some kitchenettes. Cable TV, in-room VCRs. Pool. Bar. Laundry facilities. No smoking. | 1100 Big Thompson Ave., Estes Park | 970/586–2023 or 800/475–1125 | www.appenzellinn.com | $95–$280 | 28 suites | AE, D, MC, V.

Braeside Bed and Breakfast. The Braeside house has been in owner Patty Gillette's family since it was built in 1918. Rooms have knotty-pine wood paneling, and a claw-foot tub graces the upstairs bath. Fluffy robes are provided during your stay. A small private cabin behind the house sleeps up to four and has a full kitchen and wood-burning fireplace. Some rooms share a bath. Outdoor hot tub. Some pets allowed. No a/c, no room phones. No smoking. | 2175 Hwy. 66, Estes Park | 970/586–6845 | www.braesidecabin.com | 3 rooms | $105–$120 | MC, V | BP.

Estes Park Center/YMCA of the Rockies. One look at the elk who consider it home, and you'll know this is not your typical Y. The 860-acre resort is ideal if you're traveling with children. You'd be challenged to think of an activity that isn't offered here, from games to sports to craft workshops to nature studies. The resort has a roller- and ice-skating rink, a museum, a general store, and its own post office. As for accommodations, you can choose from motel-style lodge rooms or two- to four-bedroom mountain-style cabins, all with full

ROCKY MOUNTAIN
NATIONAL PARK

EXPLORING
ATTRACTIONS NEARBY
DINING
LODGING
CAMPING AND RV
FACILITIES
SHOPPING
ESSENTIAL
INFORMATION

kitchens (many have fireplaces, too). 3 restaurants, picnic area. Some kitchenettes. Miniature golf, tennis court. Pool. Exercise equipment. Fishing. Bicycles. Basketball, horseback riding, volleyball. Library. Shops. Playground. Some pets allowed. No a/c, no phones in some rooms. | 2515 Tunnel Rd., Estes Park | 970/586–3341 | www.ymcarockies.org | 475 rooms, 204 cabins | $72–$102 rooms, $74–$278 cabins | MC, V.

★ **Gateway Inn.** With mountain-lodge style and a full slate of amenities, this inn is one of Grand Lake's newest and most popular hotels. A large deck outside the bar offers a prime view of Shadow Mountain Lake. The spacious rooms are comfortably outfitted with hand-built log furniture; some also have gas fireplaces and balconies. Though the lodge is on a somewhat grand (for Grand Lake) scale, it's owned by a couple, so you can still receive more personalized attention. In-room data ports. Cable TV. Exercise equipment, outdoor hot tub, massage, sauna. Bar. Shops. Business services. No a/c. No smoking. | U.S. 34, at the entrance to Grand Lake, Grand Lake | 970/627–2400 or 877/627–1352 | www.gatewayinn.com | 31 rooms | $99–$150 | AE, D, MC, V.

Grand Lake Lodge. Built of lodgepole pine in 1920, the lodge has been run by the same family since 1954, and the main building is a National Historic Landmark. The large deck with its lovely view of Grand and Shadow Mountain Lakes is billed as "Colorado's favorite front porch," and, indeed, this is where you'd want to spend most of your down time, as the rustic guest cabins are exceedingly simple (though they book up months in advance). The popular restaurant is another big draw. There's a two-night minimum stay most of the time. Restaurant, picnic area. Some kitchenettes. Pool. Outdoor hot tub. Basketball, horseback riding, volleyball. Bar. Shops. Playground. Laundry facilities. Business services. No a/c, no room phones. No room TVs. No smoking. | 15500 U.S. 34, Grand Lake | 970/627–3967 | fax 970/627–9495 | www.grandlakelodge.com | $79–$165 | 56 cabins | AE, D, DC, MC, V | Closed mid-Sept.–early June.

★ **Mountain Lakes Lodge.** The cabins at this small, folksy resort are individually decorated, with whimsical details like stuffed animals peeking out of unexpected places, horseshoe drawer pulls, and hand-sewn blue-jean curtains. Much of the rustic wood furniture has been crafted by lodge owner Dave Mawhorter. Some cabins have gas log stoves and private decks. You can fish right out your back door on the waterway that connects Shadow Mountain Lake and Lake Granby. There's a two-night minimum stay. Kitchenettes. Cable TV. Fishing. Volleyball. Playground. Some pets allowed. No a/c, no room phones. No smoking. | 10480 U.S. 34, Grand Lake | 970/627–8448 | www.mountainlakeslodge.com | 10 cabins, 1 house | $65–$135 | MC, V.

Rapids Lodge. This handsome lodgepole-pine structure, built in the early 1900s next to the rapids of Tonahatu Creek, is one of the oldest hotels in the area. Stay in one of the lodge rooms, which have antique furnishings, quilts, and floral wallpaper. Some have claw-foot tubs, too. The three cabins are fairly spartan. The modern condominiums, most with kitchens and fireplaces, and Hill Top House are good options for a large group. Restaurant. Some kitchenettes. Cable TV, some in-room VCRs. Bar. No a/c. | 209 Rapids La., Grand Lake | 970/627–3707 | fax 970/627–8573 | www.rapidslodge.com | 7 rooms, 19 condos, 1 house | $75–$185 | AE, MC, V | Closed Apr. and Nov.

Stanley Hotel. F. O. Stanley, who invented the Stanley Steamer automobile, built this hotel in 1909 from wood milled at the old Hidden Valley sawmill. This is the place that inspired Stephen King to pen *The Shining*, though the film version was shot elsewhere. The Stanley has a white-painted wood exterior and a classic grand-hotel style that's not often found in Colorado. Each room is furnished with antiques and has a modern bathroom. Guided tours of the hotel relate ghost stories and history. Restaurant. Cable TV. Tennis court. Pool. Volleyball. Bar. Shops. Playground. Business services. No a/c. | 333 Wonderview Ave., Estes Park | 970/586–3371 or 800/976–1377 | fax 970/586–4964 | www.stanleyhotel.com | 138 rooms | $179–$299 | AE, D, DC, MC, V.

Taharaa Mountain Lodge. On a plateau overlooking the Continental Divide, this luxury mountain lodge, built in 1997, commands sweeping views from its wraparound decks, which are accessible from every room. (Taharaa is the French Polynesian word for "beautiful view.") Each room has a fireplace and a unique theme, from the Ute room with a carved, Native American bed, to the Southwestern-style Taharaa suite, with a Taos drum coffee table. After a day of exploring the park, enjoy a complimentary happy hour by the huge fireplace in the great room or relax in the hot tub gazebo. In-room data ports, some in-room hot tubs. Some in-room VCRs. Pool. Exercise equipment, hot tub, sauna. Business services. No TV in some rooms. No kids under 13. No smoking. | 3110 South St. Vrain, Estes Park | 970/577–0098 or 800/597–0098 | fax 970/577–0819 | www.taharaa.com | 11 rooms, 1 suite | $135–$285 | AE, D, MC, V | BP.

★ **Western Riviera Motel.** This small, friendly motel books up far in advance, thanks to the basic but spotless accommodations, affable owners, and prime lakeside location. Even the cheapest units, though small, are pleasant. A deck with tables lets you enjoy a view onto the lake, and a lakeshore trail winds right in front of the motel. Picnic area. Refrigerators. Cable TV. Outdoor hot tub. No a/c. No smoking. | 419 Garfield Ave., Grand Lake | 970/627–3580 | fax 970/627–3320 | www.westernriv.com | 15 rooms | $90–$150 | MC, V.

★ **Woodlands on Fall River.** One of many condo lodges that have sprung up along Fall River, these comfortably furnished, one- and two-bedroom units are well-kept yet not so high on the price scale. All have wood-burning fireplaces and private patios or decks facing the river. The free video library is a nice touch. In-room data ports, some in-room hot tubs, kitchenettes. Cable TV, in-room VCRs. No a/c. | 1888 Fall River Rd., Estes Park | 970/586–0404 or 800/721–2279 | fax 970/586–3297 | www.woodlandsestes.com | 16 rooms | $79–$137 | AE, D, MC, V.

Camping and RV Facilities

In Rocky Mountain

Aspenglen Campground. Set in open pine woodland along Fall River, this campground doesn't have the views of Moraine Park or Glacier Basin, but it is small and peaceful. There are a few excellent walk-in sites for those who want to pitch a tent away from the crowds but still close to the car. Flush toilets. Drinking water. Fire grates. Public telephone. | 54 sites | Off U.S. 34, 0.5 mi south of the Fall River entrance station | No phone | $18 | No credit cards | Mid-May–Oct.

Glacier Basin Campground. Nestled among lodgepole pines near Glacier Creek, this campground has views of the Continental Divide. It's a convenient base for a hike, as several trails begin in the vicinity. The group sites are for tents only and accommodate 10–50 campers, depending on which site you reserve. Flush toilets. Dump station. Drinking water. Fire grates. Public telephone. | 150 sites, 15 group sites | Bear Lake Rd., 4 mi south of the Beaver Meadows entrance station | 800/365–2267 | www.reservations.nps.gov | $18, $35–$65 group sites | Reservations essential | D, MC, V | Late May–mid-Sept.

Longs Peak Campground. This small campground, quieter and more isolated than the others in the park, is for tents only. If you're planning a hike to Longs Peak, it's a good place to be for the requisite predawn start. Flush toilets, pit toilets. Drinking water. Fire grates. | 26 sites | Off Rte. 7, about 9 mi south of Estes Park | No phone | $12 | No credit cards.

Moraine Park Campground. This campground is in a ponderosa pine forest on a plateau overlooking the Big Thompson River and the meadows of Moraine Park. Of the campground's five loops of sites, only two remain open in winter, when the ranger station closes and the water is shut off. Flush toilets, pit toilets. Dump station. Drinking water. Fire grates. Public telephone. | 247 sites | Off U.S. 36, 1.5 mi south of the Beaver Meadows entrance station | 800/365–2267 | www.reservations.nps.gov | $12–$18, $25–$50 group sites | Reservations essential | D, MC, V.

Timber Creek Campground. Angler's love this riverside campground. Views of the Never Summer Mountains can be had from the camp's west side. Flush toilets, pit toilets. Dump

ROCKY MOUNTAIN
NATIONAL PARK

EXPLORING
ATTRACTIONS NEARBY
DINING
LODGING
CAMPING AND RV
FACILITIES
SHOPPING
ESSENTIAL
INFORMATION

ROCKY MOUNTAIN CAMPGROUNDS

	Total # of sites	# of RV sites	# of hook-ups	Drive-to sites	Hike-to sites	Flush toilets	Pit/chemical toilets	Drinking water	Showers	Fire grates	Swimming	Boat access	Playground	Dump station	Ranger station	Public telephone	Reservation possible	Daily fee per site	Dates open
INSIDE THE PARK																			
Aspenglen	54	49	0	•	•	•		•		•						•		$18	May–Oct.
Glacier Basin	150	85	0	•		•		•		•				•*	•	•	•	$18	May–Sept.
Longs Peak	26	0	0	•		•*	•	•*		•					•			$12	Y/R
Moraine Park	247	63	0	•		•*	•	•*		•				•*	•*	•	•	$10–16	Y/R
Timber Creek	100	70	0	•		•*	•	•*		•				•*	•	•		$12–18	Y/R
NEAR THE PARK																			
Arapaho National Recreation Area	324	296	21	•		•	•	•		•	•	•		•	•	•	•	$12–20	May–Sept.
Mary's Lake Campground & RV Park	150	150	100	•		•		•	•	•			•	•		•	•	$24–36	May–Sept.
National Park Resort	100	100	100	•		•		•	•	•				•		•	•	$25–33	Y/R
Winding River Resort	151	105	105	•		•	•	•	•	•				•	•	•	•	$20–25	May–Sept.

* In summer only   ** Reservation Fee Charged   Y/R=Year Round
UL=Unlimited   ULP=Unlimited Primitive   LD=Labor Day   MD=Memorial Day

station. Drinking water. Fire grates. Public telephone. | 100 sites | Trail Ridge Rd., 10 mi north of Grand Lake entrance | No phone | $12–$18 | No credit cards.

Near the Park

Arapaho National Recreation Area. There are five campgrounds, operated by a private management company, on Shadow Mountain Lake and Lake Granby, with access to boat ramps. Flush toilets, pit toilets. Partial hookups (electric and water). Drinking water. Fire grates, picnic tables. Public telephone. Ranger station. | 296 sites (21 with hookups) | U.S. 34, about 3 mi south of Grand Lake | 970/887–0056 or 877/444–6777 | www.reserveusa.com | Reservations essential | $12–$20 | AE, D, MC, V | Mid-May–Sept.

Mary's Lake Campground and RV Park. The campground is across the road from Mary's Lake; no swimming is allowed in the lake, but you can fish for trout. There's also a pool, basketball court, horseshoe pits, and rec room with pool tables, air hockey, and video games. Prices are based on two people per site; each additional person is $3 extra. Flush toilets. Full hookups, partial hookups (electric and water), dump station. Drinking water, guest laundry, showers. Fire pits, picnic tables. Public telephone. General store. | 150 sites (60 with full hookups, 40 with partial hookups) | 2120 Mary's Lake Rd., Estes Park | 970/586–4411 or 800/445–6279 | fax 970/586–4493 | www.maryslakecampground.com | $24–$36 | Reservations essential | D, MC, V | May–mid-Sept.

National Park Resort. The campsites, cabins, and motel rooms of this resort are just outside Rocky Mountain's Fall River entrance station. You can walk to the restaurant and snack bar next to Fall River visitor center. Despite the name, the resort is privately owned. The RV sites with full hookups are in a separate location from those for tents and pop-up campers. Flush toilets. Full hookups, partial hookups (electric and water), dump station. Drinking water, showers. Fire pits, picnic tables. | 100 sites (25 with full hookups, 75 with partial hookups) | 3501 Fall River Rd., Estes Park | 970/586–4563 | www.natlparkresort.com | $25–$33 | Reservations essential | AE, D, MC, V | Year-round.

Winding River Resort Village. Not to be confused with Winding River Ranch, this family resort is just outside of the national park boundary and has tent and RV sites in addition to a few cabins and lodge rooms. Relax with a game of volleyball, softball, Frisbee golf, basketball, or horseshoes. Flush toilets, portable toilets. Full hookups, partial hookups (electric and water), dump station. Drinking water, guest laundry, showers. Fire pits, picnic tables. Public telephone. General store. | 151 sites (38 with full hookups, 67 with partial hookups) | 1447 County Rd. 491, Grand Lake | 970/627–3215 | www.windingriverresort.com | $20–$25 | Reservations essential | AE, D, MC, V | May 15–Sept.

Shopping

The visitor centers sell a limited selection of books and souvenirs.

Trail Ridge Store. This is the park's only store per se (though you'll find a small selection of park souvenirs and books at the visitor centers). Trail Ridge stocks sweatshirts and jackets, postcards, and assorted craft items. | Trail Ridge Rd., adjacent to Alpine visitor center | Closed mid-Oct.–late May.

Essential Information

ATMS: Country Supermarket | 900 Moraine Ave., U.S. 36, next to the Conoco, Estes Park | 970/586–2702. **Lariat Saloon** | 1121 Grand Ave., Grand Lake | 970/627–9965. **Lone Eagle gas station** | 720 Grand Ave., Grand Lake | 970/627–3281. **WestStar Bank** | 363 E. Elkhorn Ave., Estes Park | 970/586–4412.

AUTOMOBILE SERVICE STATIONS: Amoco-Granby Minimart | 516 E. Agate Ave., Granby | 970/887–2411. **Conoco-National Park Village** | 900 Moraine Ave., U.S. 36, Estes Park | 970/586–2139. **Lakeview General Store** | 14626 U.S. 34, Grand Lake | 970/627–3479. **Schrader's Country Store** | 561 Big Thompson Ave., Estes Park | 970/586–0235.

ROCKY MOUNTAIN
NATIONAL PARK

EXPLORING
ATTRACTIONS NEARBY
DINING
LODGING
CAMPING AND RV
FACILITIES
SHOPPING
**ESSENTIAL
INFORMATION**

POST OFFICES: **Estes Park Post Office** | 215. W. Riverside Dr., Estes Park, 80517 | 970/586–0170.
Grand Lake Post Office | 520 Center Dr., Grand Lake, 80447 | 970/627–3340.

THEODORE ROOSEVELT NATIONAL PARK

WESTERN NORTH DAKOTA

South Unit: Off I–94, exits 24 and 27 or exit 32 (Painted Canyon Overlook). North Unit: Off U.S. 85.

An experiment in solitude is how you might describe a drive west across the open plains of North Dakota on Interstate 94. This is a part of the country where you can travel for 30 mi without seeing a house or business. Then you spy craggy ravines, tablelands, and gorges and know at once you're in the badlands. The terrain has remained virtually unchanged since Theodore Roosevelt stepped off the train here in the fall of 1883. He was then 24 and eager to shoot his first bison. Within two weeks, Roosevelt had purchased the Maltese Cross open-range cattle ranch, and the following year he returned to buy the Elkhorn ranch; both are now a part of the 110 square mi national park that bears his name. The 26th president became dedicated to the preservation of the animals and land he saw devastated by hunting and overgrazing. Roosevelt established the U.S. Forest Service and over time signed into law five national parks, 150 national forests, 51 bird reserves, and four game preserves totaling about 360,000 square mi. Theodore Roosevelt National Park was established in 1947 to commemorate his efforts. The park is divided into three units: North, South, and the Elkhorn Ranch. The Little Missouri River winds through all three, and plenty of bison, deer, antelope, coyote, prairie dogs, and bald eagles inhabit the land. Climb the peaks and you will get exceptional views of the canyons, caprocks, petrified forest, and other bizarre geological formations that make up the badlands.

PUBLICATIONS

The National Park Service and the Theodore Roosevelt Nature and History Association publish or order an extensive collection of books, posters, videos, and audio recordings on Theodore Roosevelt and the park named after him. These are on sale in park visitor centers and by mail. For a full catalog, visit www.nps.gov/thro/tr_shop.htm.

When to Visit

SCENERY AND WILDLIFE

The park's landscape is one of prairies marked by cliffs and rock chasms made of alternating layers of sandstone, siltstone, mudstone, and bentonite clay. In spring the prairies are awash with tall grasses, wildflowers. and shrubs including sage, blue harebell, and poison ivy. Box elders, elms, junipers, cottonwood trees, and ash trees fill the forests.

The optimum time to see and photograph wildlife is in the early morning hours and just before dusk, when it's cool enough for the animals to emerge from shelter to drink from streams and rivers and graze in the pastures. A herd of 300–400 elk live only in the South Unit, where they seem to favor the Buck Hill area. Wild horses are also in the South Unit only, usually in the eastern section. The North Unit has a herd of longhorns that are often found in the bison corral area about 2.5 mi west of the visitor center along the scenic drive. More than 500 bison live throughout the park.

HIGH AND LOW SEASON

Fewer than 500,000 people visit the park each year, so it's rarely crowded. July and August tend to be the busiest months, and the South Unit receives the greater number of visitors. The best times of year to see wildlife and hike comfortably in western North Dakota are May through October. December through February the park is all but desolate, but it's a beautiful time to see the wildlife as they cope with the snow and ice.

Average High/Low Temperature (°F) and and Monthly Precipitation (in inches)

	JAN.	FEB.	MAR.	APR.	MAY	JUNE
THEODORE	27/1	34/8	43/18	58/30	71/40	79/50
ROOSEVELT	.39	.36	.62	1.43	2.27	3.36

	JULY	AUG.	SEPT.	OCT.	NOV.	DEC.
	87/55	87/52	75/41	62/30	43/17	32/7
	2.05	1.42	1.4	0.86	0.48	0.45

FESTIVALS AND SEASONAL EVENTS
WINTER

Dec.: **Old-Fashioned Cowboy Christmas.** Held the first full weekend in December in downtown Medora, the festivities begin with a wreath-hanging ceremony at the community center, followed by Christmas poetry readings, a holiday doll show, sleigh rides, and a dance. | 701/623–4910.

Jan.: **Christmas Tree Bonfire.** A local potter fires specially designed pottery by placing it in a pit beneath this bonfire, which is kept burning for four days in a field between Medora and Beach. Proceeds from the sale of the pottery benefit local charities. Local businesses provide brats and hot chocolate at this event. | 701/872–3855.

SPRING

May: **Roughrider International Art Show.** More than 75 artists hailing from all over the west enter this juried art show hosted by Williston's Airport International Inn. | 701/774–9041 or 800/615–9041.

May: **Dakota Cowboy Poetry Gathering.** In Medora, locally and nationally known cowboy poets read their works on a weekend that includes a Western art show and crafts display. | 701/623–4444 or 800/633–6721.

SUMMER

June: **Fort Union Trading Post Rendezvous.** This annual event at the Fort Union Trading Post National Historic Site in Williston is held the third full weekend in June to demonstrate the historic role of fur traders on the Missouri River as well as the crafts and music of the early 1800s. | 701/572–9083 | www.nps.gov/fous.

July: **Taylor Horsefest.** Horse lovers can watch a parade of horse-drawn rigs, horseback riders, and breed displays on the last Saturday in July in Dickinson. There are also cowboy movies, poetry, and arts and crafts in Taylor (17 mi east of Dickinson, 1 mi north of I–94). | 701/483–4988, 701/974–2355, or 800/279–7391.

Killdeer Mountain Roundup Rodeo. Begun in 1923, this is North Dakota's oldest PRCA (Professional Rodeo Cowboys Association)–sanctioned rodeo. The community goes all out, hosting a Native American and frontier encampment, classic car show, parade, fireworks display, and street dance on July 4th at the Killdeer rodeo grounds. | 701/764–5777.

Aug.: **Slope County Farmers Fair.** This old-fashioned, three-day country fair in Amidon has watermelon-eating contests, egg tosses, and three-legged races. On Saturday there's a livestock show, demolition derby, and horseshoe tournament. Sunday has religious services at the fairgrounds, a quilt show, a rodeo, and a black powder fun shoot. The fair ends with a pig roast, a sweet corn supper, and a rally for charitable donations. | 701/879–6270.

Aug.: **Founder's Day.** You can enter Theodore Roosevelt National Park for free on August 25 to commemorate the establishment of the National Park Service on that date in 1916. The visitor centers host lectures and slide shows and serve cookies and lemonade. | 701/623–4466.

FALL

Oct.: **Rummage in the Badlands.** A holiday crafts show at the Medora Community Center accompanied by numerous garage sales around town make the last weekend of October a time for treasure hunting. | 701/623–4910.

Nov.: **Wildlife Show and Feed.** On the opening night of deer hunting season, locals bring mounted trophy animals to the Medora Community Center and everyone enjoys a meal of game meats prepared in different ways. | 701/623–4910.

Nearby Towns

Medora, gateway to the park's South Unit, is a walkable town with several museums, tiny shops and plenty of restaurants and places to stay. Its Wild West history is reenacted in a madcap musical production each night in summer. To the east is **Dickinson** (pop. 17,700), the largest town near the national park. Dickinson became an agricultural trade center soon after it was founded in 1880. Oil was discovered in the area in the 1950s, and ever since the Queen of the Prairies—as Dickinson is fondly called—has enjoyed a balanced economy of manufacturing, agriculture, and oil production. North of Dickinson and about 35 mi east of the park's North Unit, **Killdeer** (pop. about 700) is known for its Roundup Rodeo—North Dakota's oldest—and its gorgeous scenery. Killdeer is the place to fill your tank, since there isn't another gas station around for 40 mi. **Williston** (pop. about 13,000) is 60 mi north of the North Unit, just over the Missouri River. The town was founded in 1887 when the Great Northern Railway Company built a station where the rails met the river. James J. Hill, the company president, named the developing town in honor of his friend and backer, D. Willis James. The Amtrak stop nearest to the national park is in Williston.

INFORMATION

Dickinson Convention and Visitors Bureau | Box 181, 58601 | 701/483–4988 or 800/279–7391 | www.dickinsonnd.com. **Killdeer City Hall** | 214 Railroad St., 58640 | 701/764–5295 | www.killdeer.com. **Medora Chamber of Commerce** | 272 Pacific Ave., Box 186, 58645 | 701/623–4910 | www.medorand.com. **McKenzie County Tourism Bureau** | 201 5th St. NW, Watford City, 58854 | 701/842–2804 or 800/701–2804. **Theodore Roosevelt Medora Foundation** | 500 Pacific Ave., Box 198, 58645 | 701/623–4444 or 800/633–6721 | www.medora.com. **Williston Convention and Visitors Bureau** | 10 Main St., 58801 | 701/774–9041 or 800/615–9041 | www.willistonnd.com.

Exploring Theodore Roosevelt

PARK BASICS

Contacts and Resources: Theodore Roosevelt National Park | Box 7, Medora, 58645-0007 | 701/623–4466 South Unit, 701/842–2333 North Unit, 701/575–4020 Painted Canyon | www.nps.gov/thro.

Fees: The entrance pass is $5 per person or $10 maximum per vehicle and is good for seven days. A $20 annual pass allows admission to the park for an entire year.

Hours: The park is open year-round. *Note that the North Unit is in the Central Time Zone. The South Unit and the Painted Canyon visitor center are in the Mountain Time Zone.*

Getting Around: There are no size restrictions on vehicles entering the park. The speed limit ranges from 25–35 mph, but be careful of buffalo and other wildlife on the roadway, particularly in the early evening hours. Do not get out of your vehicle when buffalo or other animals are in the vicinity. Parking is free and there's ample parking space at all trail heads. No public transportation is available. Roads are in good condition with wide shoulders and good visibility. Some roads are closed in winter due to snow and ice pack.

Permits: A backcountry permit, free from the visitor centers, is required for overnight camping away from campgrounds.

Public Telephones: Public telephones can be found at the South Unit's Cottonwood Campground, at the Painted Canyon visitor center, and at the North Unit visitor center.

Rest Rooms: You can find public rest rooms at each of the visitor centers and campgrounds in the park.

Accessibility: The flat terrain of this park allows for relatively easy access for people with mobility impairments. The visitor centers, campgrounds, and historic sites such as Roosevelt's cabin, are all wheelchair accessible, and films at the visitor centers are close-captioned. The first part of the Little Mo Nature Trail in the North Unit and the 0.25-mi Skyline Vista Trail in the South Unit are both paved.

Emergencies: There are no fire call boxes in the park. In case of a fire or medical emergency dial 911 or the Billings County Sheriff's Office at 701/623–4323. You should also phone the rangers in each unit: 701/623–4379, 701/623–4466 or 701/623–4562 (after-hours) in the South Unit; 701/842–2580, 701/842–2333 or 701/842–4266 (after-hours) in the North Unit. Park rangers are equipped to provide emergency first-aid.

Lost and Found: There's a lost-and-found in each visitor center.

Good Tours

THEODORE ROOSEVELT IN ONE DAY

If you only have one day to spend in the park, focus on the South Unit. Pack a picnic lunch to eat in the park at midday, then arrive early at the **Painted Canyon Scenic Overlook** for a sweeping and colorful vista of the canyon's rock formations. Stay awhile to watch the effect of the sun's progress across the sky, or come back in the evening to witness the deepening colors and silhouettes in the fading sunlight. Continue to the **South Unit Visitor Center** in Medora, spending about an hour here touring the Theodore Roosevelt exhibit and the **Maltese Cross Cabin.** Plan to circle the 36-mi **Scenic Loop Drive** at least twice: once to stop and walk a few trails and visit the overlooks, and once in the evening hours to watch the wildlife. On your first time around, go counterclockwise. Stop first at **Scoria Point Overlook** and again to hike the 0.6-mi **Ridgeline Nature Trail.** Continue around the loop, stopping at the North Dakota Badlands and Boicourt overlooks to gaze at the strange, ever-changing terrain of the badlands. When you pass through Peaceful Valley, take time to look for prairie dog towns. Have lunch at the **Cottonwood picnic area,** then use a couple of hours in the afternoon to hike either Jones Creek Trail or the Coal Vein Nature Trail, or sign up for a horseback ride at **Peaceful Valley Ranch.**

Return to your car at least an hour before sunset, and drive slowly around Scenic Loop Drive once more, clockwise this time, to view the wildlife. Be prepared to get caught in a buffalo traffic jam, as the huge creatures sometimes block the road and aren't in any hurry to move. Don't honk at them—they don't like it—and don't get out of your car. Above

THEODORE
ROOSEVELT
NATIONAL PARK

EXPLORING
ATTRACTIONS NEARBY
DINING
LODGING
CAMPING AND RV
FACILITIES
SHOPPING
ESSENTIAL
INFORMATION

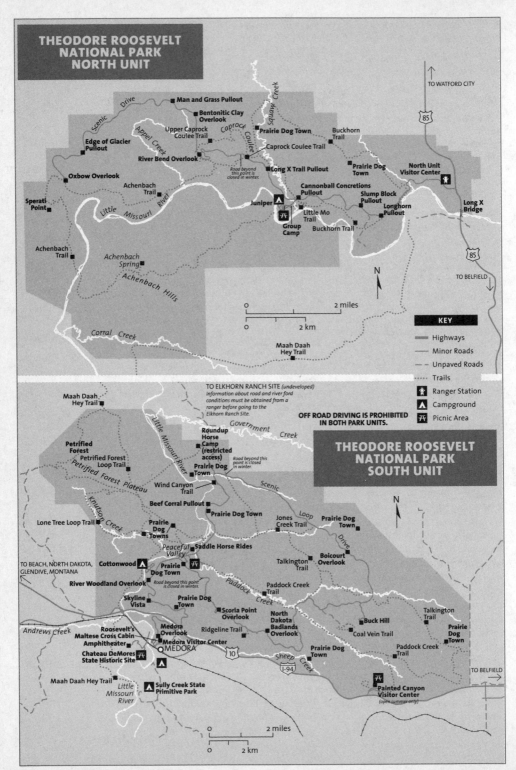

THEODORE ROOSEVELT NATIONAL PARK NORTH UNIT

TO WATFORD CITY

85

Man and Grass Pullout

Bentonitic Clay Overlook

Upper Caprock Coulee Trail

Scenic Drive

Appel Creek

Caprock Coulee

Squaw Creek

Prairie Dog Town

Buckhorn Trail

Caprock Coulee Trail

Edge of Glacier Pullout

River Bend Overlook

Road beyond this point is closed in winter.

Long X Trail Pullout

Prairie Dog Town

North Unit Visitor Center

Oxbow Overlook

Achenbach Trail

Little Missouri River

Cannonball Concretions Pullout

Juniper

Little Mo Trail

Group Camp

Buckhorn Trail

Slump Block Pullout

Longhorn Pullout

Long X Bridge

Sperati Point

Achenbach Trail

Achenbach Spring

Achenbach Hills

85

TO BELFIELD

N

0 — 2 miles
0 — 2 km

Corral Creek

Maah Daah Hey Trail

KEY

Highways
Minor Roads
Unpaved Roads
Trails
Ranger Station
Campground
Picnic Area

Maah Daah Hey Trail

TO ELKHORN RANCH SITE (undeveloped)
Information about road and river ford conditions must be obtained from a ranger before going to the Elkhorn Ranch Site.

Government Creek

OFF ROAD DRIVING IS PROHIBITED IN BOTH PARK UNITS.

Petrified Forest

Petrified Forest Loop Trail

Petrified Forest Plateau

Little Missouri River

Roundup Horse Camp (restricted access)

Road beyond this point is closed in winter.

Prairie Dog Town

Wind Canyon Trail

Scenic

THEODORE ROOSEVELT NATIONAL PARK SOUTH UNIT

Beef Corral Pullout

Knutson Creek

Lone Tree Loop Trail

Prairie Dog Towns

Prairie Dog Town

Jones Creek Trail

Loop

Prairie Dog Town

Drive

Peaceful Valley

Saddle Horse Rides

Talkington Trail

Boicourt Overlook

TO BEACH, NORTH DAKOTA, GLENDIVE, MONTANA

Cottonwood

Prairie Dog Town

Road beyond this point is closed in winter.

Paddock Creek

Paddock Creek Trail

River Woodland Overlook

Skyline Vista

Prairie Dog Town

Scoria Point Overlook

Ridgeline Trail

North Dakota Badlands Overlook

Buck Hill

Coal Vein Trail

Talkington Trail

Prairie Dog Town

Andrews Creek

Roosevelt's Maltese Cross Cabin Amphitheater

Medora Overlook

Medora Visitor Center

MEDORA

Chateau DeMores State Historic Site

10

Prairie Dog Town

Sheep Creek

Paddock Creek Trail

I-94

N

Maah Daah Hey Trail

Little Missouri River

Sully Creek State Primitive Park

Painted Canyon Visitor Center
(open summer only)

TO BELFIELD

0 — 2 miles
0 — 2 km

all, plan to be at **Buck Hill** for one of the most spectacular sunsets you'll ever see. Bring a jacket, because it's a bit windy and it gets chilly as the sun sets. After dark, drive carefully out of the park—elk and other animals may still be on the road.

THEODORE ROOSEVELT IN THREE DAYS

Enjoy the South Unit on your first day, as described above. On the second day, visit the North Unit, beginning with a stop at the **North Unit Visitor Center** and a conversation with the rangers about where wildlife is currently active. Also check with the rangers to see if they will be leading a half-day hike in the afternoon. Along the 14-mi **Scenic Drive,** you can stop to take two self-guided trails: the short **Little Mo Nature Trail** and **Caprock Coulee Nature Trail,** an easy 5-mi loop through dry water gulches. Eat lunch at one of several overlooks or at the **Juniper Campground picnic area.**

Be back at the campground by 2 PM for the ranger-led **Naturalist's Choice Hike** (remember that the North Unit is on Central Time). Have an early dinner in Watford City before returning to Scenic Drive an hour or so before sunset for close encounters with longhorns, bison, and other creatures. Make sure to watch the sunset from **Oxbow Overlook.** Don't hurry away once the sun is down, for this is one of the park's best spots for stargazing. It gets chilly at night here even in summer, so bring a jacket.

Dedicate your third day in the park to an outdoor adventure. Make arrangements for a **guided day-hike** or **horseback ride,** or **rent bikes** to ride along the Maah Daah Hey Trail. If you are visiting in May or June, consider a **one-day float trip** on the Little Mo.

Attractions

PROGRAMS AND TOURS

For more information on park programs, contact the visitors centers: 701/623–4466 South Unit; 701/842–2333 North Unit.

Evening Campfires. Rangers host hour-long slide presentations and discussions on such subjects as park history, archaeology, forest and brush fires, and wildlife, following the Evening Ranger Hike. Look for times and subjects posted at the campgrounds in each unit. | Cottonwood Campground, South Unit; Juniper Campground, North Unit | Free | June–mid-Sept., daily.

Ranger-Led Walks. Rangers lead one-hour walks and full- and half-day hikes on the trails of both units and through the backcountry and Elkhorn Ranch, discussing such subjects as geology, paleontology, and wildlife. Check at the entrances of the campgrounds or at the visitor centers for times, topics, departure points, and destinations. | Free | June–mid-Sept., daily.

The **Evening Ranger Hike** is a one-hour hike to any point within the park, depending on the interests of the ranger, who also leads a discussion on a park topic, such as geology or natural history. Times and meeting places vary; check with the visitor center. | June–mid-Sept., daily.

Plant life is the focus of the **Naturalist's Choice Hike,** a one-hour walk in the North Unit. | June–mid-Sept., daily 2 PM.

Stargazing Party. The air at Theodore Roosevelt National Park has been officially certified to be at least 80 percent pure, making the park ideal for astronomical observation. On an early August weekend, the Northern Sky Astronomical Society sets up telescopes on Buck Hill or another high point in the park for an all-night star-watching party. Check at a visitor center for dates. | No phone | www.und.edu/org/nsas | Free.

TR Country. This 13-minute film (shown every half-hour) takes you on a visual tour of the wildlife, scenery, and history of western North Dakota and is narrated with Roosevelt's own words. | South Unit, North Unit, and Painted Canyon visitor centers | Free | Daily.

LITTLE MO'S CURVE

During the Ice Age, the Little Missouri River became blocked by ice and had to leave its old bed and form a new channel. You can see the sharp turn at Sperati Point in the North Unit. Before its change of course, the river drained into Hudson Bay; now it drains into the Gulf of Mexico.

Visitor Center Ranger Presentations. Rangers conduct oral presentations at the South Unit visitor center on subjects such as cowboy clothing, seasonal changes in the park and the history of cattle ranching. Presentation times vary. | Free | June–mid-Sept., daily.

SCENIC DRIVES

South Unit Scenic Loop Drive. A 36-mi, two-way scenic loop takes you past prairie dog towns, coal veins, trailheads, and panoramic views of the badlands. Information on the park's natural history is posted at the various overlooks. Some of the best views in the park can be seen from Scoria Point Overlook, Boicourt Overlook, North Dakota Badlands Overlook, Skyline Vista, and Buck Hill.

North Unit Scenic Drive. The 14-mi, two-way North Unit drive follows rugged terrain above spectacular views of the canyons, and is flanked by more than a dozen turn-outs with interpretive signs. Notice the slump blocks, massive segments of rock that have slipped down the cliff walls over time. Farther along you'll pass through badlands coulees, deep-water clefts that are now dry. There's always a good chance of meeting bison, mule deer, and longhorns along the way.

SIGHTS TO SEE

★ **Buck Hill.** At 2,855 ft, this is one of the highest points in the park and provides a spectacular 360-degree view of the badlands. This is the most popular place in the South Unit from which to view the sunset. | 17 mi counterclockwise from the visitor center.

Elkhorn Ranch. The third unit of the park is composed of the 218 acres (0.34 square mi) of ranch land Theodore Roosevelt first purchased in 1884. Today there are no buildings here, although foundation blocks outline the original house and outbuildings. You do not need a permit to trek through the land, but you should check with one of the visitor centers about river fording and road conditions before you go. | 35 mi north of the South Unit visitor center.

★ **Maltese Cross Ranch Cabin.** Next door to the South Unit visitor center (7 mi from its original site in the river bottoms) sits the cabin Theodore Roosevelt commissioned to be built on his Dakota Territory property. The sturdy ponderosa pine logs that make up the cabin had to be floated down the Little Missouri River. Inside the cabin are Roosevelt's original writing table and rocking chair, as well as other traditional period furnishings. You can tour the cabin year-round. Interpretive tours are held on the half hour every day June–September. | South Unit entrance, exits 24 and 27 off I–94.

North Unit Visitor Center. A bookstore and a gift shop, as well a small auditorium where you can watch park films, help you get to know the park. | North Unit entrance, off U.S. 85 | 701/842–2333 | www.nps.gov/thro | Daily 9–5:30.

Oxbow Overlook. The view from this spot at the end of the North Unit drive looks over the unit's westerly badlands and the Little Missouri River, where it takes a sharp turn south.

For an even better view of the river's 90-degree angle, take the short, 1.5-mi round-trip trail to **Sperati Point,** 430 ft above the riverbed. | 14 mi west of the visitor center.

★ **Painted Canyon Scenic Overlook.** Catch your first glimpse of badlands majesty here—the South Unit canyon's colors change dramatically with the movement of the sun across the sky. | Exit 32 off I–94.

Painted Canyon Visitor Center. Easily reached off of Interstate 94, this visitor center has a gift shop and bookstore, a hands-on exhibit for kids about wildlife in the park and a large display on the topography of the badlands. | Exit 32 off I–94 | 701/575–4020 | www.nps.gov/thro | Mid-June–Labor Day, daily 8–6; Apr.–mid-June, daily 8:30–4:30; early Sept.–mid-Nov., daily 8:30–4:30.

Peaceful Valley Ranch. Once the home of a successful horse-ranching family, this 1885 house and valley is now the base for trail rides in the South Unit. | 7 mi north of the visitor center.

Petrified Forest. Although bits of petrified wood have been found all over the park, the densest collection is in the South Unit's west end, accessible on foot or horseback via the Petrified Forest Loop Trail from Peaceful Valley Ranch (10 mi round-trip) or from the park's west boundary (3 mi round-trip). | Trailheads: Peaceful Valley Ranch (7 mi north of the South Unit visitor center); west boundary (10 mi north of exit 23 off I-94/U.S. 10, via an unpaved road).

Scoria Point Overlook. See where coal seams in the South Unit's hills have, over time, caught fire and baked the surrounding sand and earth. | 9.5 mi counterclockwise from the visitor center.

★ **South Unit Visitor Center.** Sometimes called the Medora visitor center, this building houses a large auditorium for films about the park, plus an excellent exhibit on Theodore Roosevelt's life. On display are artifacts such as the clothing Roosevelt wore while ranching in the Dakota Territory, his firearms, and several writings in his own hand reflecting his thoughts on the nation's environmental resources. A bookstore and public rest rooms are available. | South Unit entrance, exits 24 and 27 off I-94 | 701/623-4466 | www.nps.gov/thro | June–Sept., daily 8–8; Oct.–May, daily 8–4:30.

Sports and Outdoor Activities

BICYCLING

Bicycling is North Dakota's number-one participant sport, and the roads in the North and South Units of Theodore Roosevelt National Park are challenging and scenic. There are no bike lanes, so cyclists should be careful of the traffic. Bikes are not allowed off-road. Cyclists on the multi-use Maah Daah Hey Trail, which connects the North and South units of the park and crosses through them, must take alternate routes around the park itself.

Dakota Cyclery Adventures. You can rent bikes and equipment from this company that provides shuttle service to both units of the park and guided tours of the Maah Daah Hey Trail outside the park. Rides are available for different endurance and skill levels. | 275 3rd Ave., Medora | 701/623-4808 or 888/321-1218 | www.dakotacyclery.com | Memorial Day–Labor Day.

CANOEING

A float trip down the Little Missouri River, a designated State Scenic River, is an ideal way to experience the beauty and solitude of the North Dakota Badlands and Theodore Roosevelt National Park. It takes three or four days to canoe the 110 mi from the North Unit to the South Unit. The river ice generally breaks up by early April. May and June are the best months for float trips.

Wayne's Sport Center. Gear and boats of all sizes are available for rent here. Wayne or a member of his staff will give you a ride to the river. | Rte. 23 E, Watford City | 701/842-3294.

FISHING

Catfish, little suckers, northern pikes, and goldeneyes are among the underwater inhabitants of the Little Missouri River. If you wish to fish in the park or elsewhere in the state and are over age 16, you must obtain a North Dakota fishing license. For out-of-state residents, a three-day permit is $11, a seven-day permit is $15 and a one-year permit is $25. For in-state residents, a one-year permit is $11. You can obtain a license from the **North Dakota Fish and Game Commission** (100 N. Bismarck Expressway, Bismarck, 58501 | 701/328-6300 | www.state.nd.us/gnf). In Medora, the **Medora Convenience Store** (200 Pacific Ave., at the entrance to the South Unit | 701/623-4479) sells fishing licenses.

Greg Simonson Fishing Services. A champion of several regional and state fishing tournaments, the owner of this outfitter leads individuals or groups on expeditions through the park and the outlying grasslands. | 13892 U.S. 85 N, Alexander | 701/828-3425.

THEODORE
ROOSEVELT
NATIONAL PARK

EXPLORING
ATTRACTIONS NEARBY
DINING
LODGING
CAMPING AND RV
FACILITIES
SHOPPING
ESSENTIAL
INFORMATION

HIKING

There are excellent trails throughout the national park and the Little Missouri National Grasslands. Backcountry hiking is allowed, but you'll need a permit (free from any visitor center) to camp in the wild. You should inquire about river conditions before setting out on a hike. For hiking guides, *see* Outfitters, *below.*

Achenbach Trail. This 16-mi round-trip, moderate-to-difficult trail begins at the North Unit's Juniper Campground, climbs through the Achenbach Hills, descends to the river and ends at Oxbow Overlook. Check with rangers about river-fording conditions. For a shorter (6-mi) hike to Oxbow, begin at the River Bend Overlook.

Buckhorn Trail. A thriving prairie dog town is just 1 mi from the trailhead of this 11-mi North Unit trail. It travels over level grasslands, then it loops back along the banks of Squaw Creek.

Caprock Coulee Trail. This trail begins on the scenic drive about 8 mi west of the North Unit visitor center and follows a 4.3-mi loop around the pockmarked lower-badlands coulees (dry water gulches). There's a slow incline that takes you up 300 ft. Portions of the trail are slippery.

Little Mo Nature Trail. Flat and only 1.1-mi long, this trail starts at the Juniper Campground and passes through woodlands to the river's edge. The first 0.7 mi is wheelchair accessible.

★ **Maah Daah Hey Trail.** Hike, bike, or ride horseback on the 96-mi Maah Daah Hey Trail, the most popular and well-maintained trail in western North Dakota. Its name means "grandfather" or "been here long" in the Mandan language. The trail starts at Sully Creek State Primitive Park (3 mi south of the South Unit visitor center) and traverses all three park units and the Little Missouri National Grasslands. Note that you cannot bike the portions of the trail that are within Theodore Roosevelt National Park. Maps are available at the park visitor centers and from the U.S. Forest Service (701/225–5151).

For maps and information on the trail you can write to the **Maah Daah Hey Trail Association.** | Box 156, Bismarck, 58501 | 701/628–2747 | www.maahdaahhey.com.

Ridgeline Nature Trail. This tiny (0.6 mi) loop is dotted with informative signs about the ecology of the badlands. The first few yards are steep and difficult, and there's a steep descent at the end, but otherwise the trail is even.

HORSEBACK RIDING

The best way to see many of the park's sights is on horseback. Horses are only allowed on the 80 mi of marked horse trails or cross-country. Riders taking multiday trips through the park must camp in the Round-Up Group Horse Camp or in the backcountry, and must have a permit.

Peaceful Valley Ranch Horse Rides. Experienced guides help you to see the park the way the trappers, ranchers, and pioneers did a century ago. Rides are 90 minutes to five hours long. | Scenic Loop Dr., South Unit | 701/623–4568 | $20–$75.

Little Knife Outfitters. Take a guided one-day, two-day, or weeklong horseback trip on the Maah Daah Hey Trail. Knowledgeable guides will tell you all you want to know about the ecology and cultural history of the area. Beginners are welcome. | Box 82, Watford City, 58584 | 701/842–2631 | www.littleknifeoutfitters.com | May–Sept.

OUTFITTERS

Badlands Adventures. This outfit can take you on a guided hike or canoe trip through the Little Missouri National Grasslands. A trek on the Maah Daah Hey Trail is a good choice. Your guide, a North Dakota native, will explain the area's history and plant life, and teach you survival techniques. The trips can last several hours to several days. | 19 S. Main St., Dickinson | 701/227–4317 | www.badlandsadventures.com.

Attractions Nearby

Scenic Drive

Enchanted Highway. This self-guided 30-mi driving tour on Route 21 south of Dickinson takes you past metal sculptures, designed by a local artist, of a pheasant family, a grasshopper family, a 150-ft-long gaggle of geese, a 51-ft Teddy Roosevelt, and a tin family with a 45-ft father, 44-ft mother, and 23-ft son. | Exit 72 off I–94, Rte. 21 between Lefor and Regent | 701/483–4988 or 800/279–7391 | Free.

Sights to See

Burning Hills Amphitheater. Built into a badlands bluff in 1958, this seven-story amphitheater 1 mi west of Medora is the area's most beloved performance space. Concerts and performances of all kinds take place here. If you sit near the top, you can enjoy a panoramic view of the badlands, with an occasional elk grazing in the distance. | 3422 Chateau Rd., Medora | 701/623–4444 or 800/633–6721 | fax 701/623–4494 | www.medora.com | Early June–Labor Day.

★ Well worth your while in summer is a performance of the **Medora Musical**, a theatrical tribute to the Old West, its history, and its personalities. | 701/623–4444 or 800/633–6721 | $21–$23 | Early June–Labor Day, daily 8:30 PM.

Chateau de Mores State Historic Site. The French nobleman for whom the chateau is named erected this 26-room mansion in 1883 with his wife, Medora, for whom the town was named. He also built a meat-packing plant and encouraged other cattle ranchers to settle in the area. The couple hosted extravagant hunting parties and even entertained Theodore Roosevelt during his Dakota ranching days, but never realized their cattle empire. When their business ventures failed, the De Mores's returned to France. The chateau has been restored and interpretive tours are offered in summer. About 1 mi from the chateau is De Mores Memorial Park, in which stands a lone brick chimney, all that remains of the meat-packing plant. | 1 Chateau La., Medora | 701/623–4355 | fax 701/623–4921 | $6 | Mid-May–mid-Sept., daily 8:30–6, mid-Sept.–mid-May, by appointment only.

★ **Dakota Dinosaur Museum.** A huge triceratops casting greets you at the entrance of this museum, which houses dozens of dinosaur bones, fossilized plants and seashells, and local rocks and minerals. | 200 Museum Dr., Dickinson | 701/225–3466 | www.dakotadino.com | $6 | Memorial Day–Labor Day, daily 9–6; Labor Day–mid-Oct. and mid-Apr.–Memorial Day, Mon.–Sat. 9–4, Sun. 11–4; mid-Oct.–Dec. and Mar.–mid-Apr., Fri.–Sun. 11–4.

Fort Buford State Historic Site. Built in 1866 near the confluence of the Missouri and Yellowstone rivers, this military post was the site of Sitting Bull's surrender in 1881. See the restored officers' quarters and the unusual, sometimes humorous, tombstones in the soldiers' cemetery. | 15349 39th La. NW, Williston | 701/572–9034 | Free | Mid-May–mid-Aug., daily 9–6; mid-Aug.–mid-May, by appointment only.

Fort Union Trading Post National Historic Site. Built by John Jacob Astor's American Fur Company, the fort was the most important fur and bison hide trading center on the upper Missouri River, 1828–67. Walk around the reconstructed grounds, which include tepees and the original palisade and three-story bastions of Fort Union. | 15550 Rte. 1804, Williston | 701/572–9083 | www.nps.gov/fous | Free | Memorial Day–Labor Day, daily 8–8; Sept.–May, daily 9–5:30.

Little Missouri National Grasslands. This is the largest (1,600 square mi) and most diverse of 19 national grasslands in the western United States. It takes three hours to complete a self-guided driving tour, beginning and ending in Medora, and covering 58 mi. The best time to see the wildlife is in early morning or late afternoon. Don't forget a camera and binoculars. There are no hiking trails, but off-road hiking is permitted. For a copy of the driving tour, contact the Forest Service in Dickinson or the South Unit visitor center. | Forest Service, 161 21st St. W, Dickinson, 58601 | 701/225–5151 | www.fs.fed.us/r1/dakotaprairie.

★ **Little Missouri State Park.** Called "Mako Shika" or "where the land breaks" by the Sioux, the unusual land formations here create the state's most awe-inspiring scenery. The bee-hive-shape rock formations resulted from the erosion of sedimentary rock deposited millions of years ago by streams flowing from the Rocky Mountains. Undeveloped and rugged, this wilderness area has primitive camping and 75 mi of horse trails. | Off Rte. 22, 15 mi north of Killdeer | 701/764–5256 summer, 701/794–3731 winter | www.state.nd.us/ndparks | $4 per vehicle | Daily.

Take a two- to six-hour guided horseback ride through the wilds of the Little Missouri State Park. The expert riders who run **Badlands Trail Rides** will match you with a horse that is right for you. | 10460 Ken St. NW, Killdeer | 701/764–5219 | www.badlandstrailrides.com | $25 (2 hrs)–$75 (6 hrs) per person | Year-round.

Medora Doll House. Antique dolls and toys fill almost every inch of this small house, built by the Marquis de Mores in 1884. Also known as the von Hoffman House, it's listed on the National Register of Historic Places. | 485 Broadway, Medora | 701/623–4444 or 800/633–6721 | fax 701/623–4494 | www.medora.com | $4 | Memorial Day–Labor Day, daily 10–6.

Pioneer Trails Museum. This museum in Bowman, on U.S. 12 south of the national park's South Unit, has a working fossil lab and exhibits on local culture and history. You can join museum staff at local archaeological digs in summer. | 12 1st Ave. NE, Bowman | 701/523–3600 | $2 | June–Aug., Mon.–Sat. 9–5, Sun. 1:30–5; Sept.–May, Mon.–Sat. 10–4, Sun. 1:30–4.

White Butte and Black Butte. At 3,506 ft, White Butte is North Dakota's highest point. Directly opposite is Black Butte, which is equally striking. Both are on private land, but you can easily view them from the highway. Hiking is permitted at White Butte with permission of the landowner. | 6 mi south of Amidon on U.S. 85 | 701/523–5880 or 701/879–6236 | Free | Daily.

Dining

In Theodore Roosevelt

Picnic Areas. Whether you choose to picnic on the shores of the Little Missouri River or before a view of the badlands, you'll find all of the park's picnic sites clean and well-maintained.

The South Unit's **Cottonwood picnic area** is in a lovely valley near the river. There are has fire pits, drinking water, rest rooms, eight open tables, and eight covered tables. | 5.5 mi north of the visitor center.

The **Juniper picnic area** is the only picnic site in the North Unit. It has eight sheltered tables and 20 open tables with grills, plus drinking water and rest rooms. | 5 mi west of the visitor center.

You'll find eight covered tables, drinking water, rest rooms, and a spectacular view at the **Painted Canyon Visitor Center.** | Exit 32 off I–94.

Near the Park

★ **Buckskin Bar and Grill.** Steak. This steak house, saloon, and dance hall seats 350 in several dining rooms. Built in 1915, the building has rough wood walls, original wood floors, and tin ceilings. Stuffed critters are mounted on the walls in one room; the other rooms have photographs of local cowboy celebrities who dine here. Steak and seafood is the kitchen's focus, with prime rib a specialty. For dessert, the homemade apple cobbler is a must. Kids' menu. | 416 Central Ave., Killdeer | 701/764–5321 | $7–$20 | MC, V.

★ **Cowboy Cafe.** American. This cozy, locally owned and operated café specializes in home-made soups, caramel rolls, and delicious roast beef specials. Be prepared for a short wait since the restaurant is popular with both locals and visitors. | 215 4th St., Medora | 701/623–4343 | $4–$7 | No credit cards.

Dakota Farms Family Restaurant. American/Casual. The Dakota Farms serves breakfast all day and has a local reputation for fair prices and good service. Come in for all-you-can-eat fish on Fridays. Kids' menu. No alcohol. | 1906 2nd Ave. W, Williston | 701/572–4480 | $6–$10 | AE, D, MC, V.

Georgia's and the Owl. American. The family's pet owl, which once reigned in this restaurant, is deceased, but stuffed owls and other owl paraphernalia makes Georgia's a fun place to visit. Try the prime rib dinner or the steak. | U.S. 85 at Main St., Amidon | 701/879–6289 | $12–$20 | No credit cards | Closed Sun. and Oct.–May.

Gramma Sharon's Cafe. American/Casual. For home-cooked, inexpensive meals try Gramma's, but don't come for the atmosphere: it's attached to a gas station. The café is known for great omelets and biscuits. Kids' menu. No alcohol. | U.S. 2 and U.S. 85 W, Williston | 701/572–1412 | $6–$13 | D, MC, V.

★ **Iron Horse Restaurant.** American/Casual. Great breakfasts, burgers, and tenderloin sandwiches draw locals to this independently owned restaurant with rough-hewn benches and barn-wood walls. A spiral staircase leads to an upstairs dining room. | 201 Main St., Medora | 701/623–9894 | $8–$15 | AE, D, MC, V.

Knights of Columbus Club. American. The K of C Club is great for lunch: there's a noon buffet with soup, salad, caramel rolls, and homemade filled breads (apple and poppy are the best). Prime rib is another special. | 1531 W. Villard St., Dickinson | 701/483–0186 | $6–$27 | AE, MC, V | Closed Sun.

Long Pines Steak House. Steak. Great rib-eyes and fillets are what this restaurant is known for. Check out the big wreath in the center of the dining room—it's decorated according to the whims of the staff. The restaurant is in Bowman, on U.S. 12 south of the national park's South Unit. | 13 1st Ave. NW, Bowman | 701/523–5201 | $12–$15 | AE, MC, V | Closed Sun.

Pitchfork Steak Fondue. American/Casual. Rib-eye steaks are prepared on the tines of pitchforks in classic western style. A full buffet accompanies the meat, all of it served with a view of the badlands and live musical entertainment. | Tjaden Terrace, Medora | 701/623–4444 or 800/633–6721 | $20 | AE, D, MC, V | Closed early Sept.–May.

Rattlesnake Creek Brewery and Grill. American. If the remarkable beer doesn't strike you, the Killdeer Mountain potatoes will: these scalloped potatoes in cream are cooked with secret spices for fiery flavor. The chili is a close second on the inventive meat-and-potatoes menu and the homemade dill bread is irresistible. | 2 W. Villard St., Dickinson | 701/483–9518 | $10–$16 | AE, D, DC, MC, V | Closed Sun.

Trapper's Kettle Restaurant. American/Casual. Be prepared for reminders of the fur trade at this restaurant's two locations—traps, furs, stuffed and mounted animals and a canoe that holds the salad bar. The chili topped with melted cheese and the fried scones are sure to please. | 3901 2nd Ave. W, Williston | 701/774–2831 | $5–$9 | AE, D, MC, V.

Lodging

Near the Park

AmericInn Motel and Suites. Glowing wood, mounted animals, and western themes dominate this motel. The two-story building is three blocks from downtown; restaurants and stores are nearby. Cable TV. Indoor pool. Hot tub, sauna. Laundry facilities. Business services. Some pets allowed. | 75 E. River Rd. S, Medora | 701/623–4800 or 800/634–3444 | fax 701/623–4890 | www.americinn.com | 56 rooms, 8 suites | $63, $99–$190 suites | AE, D, DC, MC, V | CP.

★ **Dahkotah Lodge and Guest Ranch.** A real working cattle ranch, the Dahkotah offers tenderfeet a major life-style change, if only for a few days. You'll have no phone and no TV at this single-story, cedar-sided lodge 19 mi outside Medora. What you will have are three meals a day and the opportunity to join a cattle drive or pack trip. Horseback riding. No room phones. No room TVs. | 4456 W. River Rd., Medora | 701/623–4897 or 800/508–4897 in ND | www.dahkotahlodge.com | 4 cabins | $60 | AE, D, MC, V | BP.

Hartfiel Inn Bed-and-Breakfast. Rooms here have hardwood floors with area rugs, iron four-poster or brass beds, and wood desks; there's a working fireplace in the common living room. Breakfast, chosen from a menu, is served in the formal dining room or on the tile terrace overlooking the lavish gardens, which have a waterfall, a cottage with a hot tub and stereo, and a statue of the goddess Hebe. Some in-room VCRs. Hot tub. Library. Some pets allowed. No smoking. | 509 3rd Ave. W, Dickinson | 701/225–6710 | fax 701/225–1184 | 3 rooms (2 with shower only), 1 suite | $69–$79, $99 suite | MC, V | BP.

Hospitality Inn. This three-story motel across from the Prairie Hills Mall has a huge lobby where you can relax on couches before the fireplace. A mezzanine overlooks the pool. Restaurant, room service. Some refrigerators. Cable TV. Indoor pool. Hot tub, sauna. Bar. Laundry facilities. Business services. Airport shuttle. Some pets allowed. | 532 15th St. W, Dickinson | 701/483–5600 or 800/422–0949 | fax 701/483–0090 | 149 rooms | $68–$81 | AE, D, DC, MC, V.

Logging Camp Ranch. Run by the same family for four generations, this 10,000-acre working cattle and buffalo ranch lies about 20 mi northwest of Amidon. Rooms in the main house and in four hand-built log cabins have modern facilities, handmade furnishings, and cowboy art-decked walls. You can arrange to go trapshooting and horseback riding. Some kitchenettes, some microwaves, some refrigerators. Fishing. Hiking, horseback riding. No a/c in some rooms, no room phones. No room TVs. | HCR3 Box 26A, Bowman | 701/279–5501 | fax 701/279–6663 | www.loggingcampranch.com | 8 rooms, 4 cabins | $50 cabins, $65 rooms | MC, V.

Mountain View Motel. Small-town hospitality and clean rooms welcome you to this traditional one-story brick motel that's festively decorated for every holiday. Cable TV. No a/c in some rooms. | 300 Mountain View, Killdeer | 701/764–5843 | 19 rooms | $35–$40 | AE, D, MC, V.

Naard Creek Ranch. This secluded log cabin is set on a 340-acre plot in the badlands about 21 mi northwest of Killdeer. It accommodates up to 10 people. Microwaves, refrigerators. Hiking. No room phones. No smoking. | 11580 6th St. NW, Killdeer | 701/863–6911 | www.naardcreek.com | 1 cabin | $75–$100 | No credit cards.

★ **Rough Riders Hotel.** Built in 1883, this downtown hotel is operated by the Theodore Roosevelt Medora Foundation, a nonprofit organization that restores historic buildings in Medora. Rooms on the second floor have country-style, western antiques, brass beds, patchwork quilts, and red velvet drapes. You'll have pool privileges at the Badlands Motel, four blocks away. Restaurant. Cable TV. No smoking. | 301 3rd Ave., Medora | 701/623–4444 or 800/633–6721 | fax 701/623–4494 | www.medora.com | 9 rooms (7 with shower only) | $84–$98 | AE, D, MC, V.

Camping and RV Facilities

In Theodore Roosevelt

Cottonwood Campground. Nestled under juniper and cottonwood trees on the bank of the Little Missouri River, the only campground in the South Unit is a wonderful place to watch buffalo, elk, and other wildlife drink from the river at sunrise and just before sunset. Cottonwood is open year-round, but flush toilets are only available May–September. Pit toilets are available the remainder of the year. Flush toilets. Drinking water. Grills, picnic tables. | 78 sites | 5.5 mi north of the South Unit visitor center | 701/623–4466 | $10 | Reservations not accepted | No credit cards.

THEODORE ROOSEVELT CAMPGROUNDS

	Total # of sites	# of RV sites	# of hook-ups	Drive-to sites	Hike-to sites	Flush toilets	Pit/chemical toilets	Drinking water	Showers	Fire grates	Swimming	Boat access	Playground	Dump station	Ranger station	Public telephone	Reservation possible	Daily fee per site	Dates open
INSIDE THE PARK																			
Cottonwood	78	30	0	•	•	•*	•	•		•								$10	Y/R
Juniper	50	25	0	•		•*	•	•*		•				•				$10	Y/R
Round-Up Group Horse Camp	10	0	0		•		•	•		•							•	$20	May–Sept.
NEAR THE PARK																			
Bar X Ranch	15	15	15	•		•	•	•	•	•							•	$7–13	Y/R
Burning Coal Vein	5	5	0	•	•		•			•								Free	Y/R
East View	15	10	10	•				•	•									$15–20	Y/R
Medora	200	105	105	•		•		•	•	•	•			•			•	$21–25	May–Sept.
Red Trail	104	104	100	•	•			•	•	•				•		•	•	$14–26	May–Sept.
Sully Creek State	45	45	0	•	•		•		•	•								$9	Y/R

* In summer only
UL=Unlimited
** Reservation Fee Charged
ULP=Unlimited Primitive
Y/R=Year Round
LD=Labor Day   MD=Memorial Day

Juniper Campground. The sites here are surrounded by the trees that give the campground its name. Don't be surprised if you see a bison herd wander through on its way to the Little Missouri River. Drinking water and flush toilets are only available May–September; there are pit toilets the remainder of the year. There are no RV hookups. Flush toilets. Drinking water. Grills, picnic tables. | 50 sites | 5 mi west of the North Unit visitor center | 701/842–2333 | $10 | Reservations not accepted | No credit cards.

Near the Park

Bar X Ranch. Catering to horseback riding, mountain biking, and hiking enthusiasts, this guest ranch and campground is 2 mi south of Medora and adjacent to the Maah Daah Hey trail. Flush toilets. Partial hookups. Drinking water, showers. Fire pits, picnic tables. | 2 cabins, 15 sites with partial hookups | 9 mi south of Medora via East River Rd. | Box 103, Medora | 701/623–4300 | $7–$13 tents or campers, $75 cabins | No credit cards.

Burning Coal Vein Campground. An underground coal vein has been burning for more than a century on this National Grasslands site managed by the U.S. Forest Service. The fumes and collapsing earth have resulted in some very unusual terrain and trees. You'll find no running water or electricity in this primitive campground. Pit toilets. Fire pits. | U.S. 85, 15 mi north of Amidon | 5 sites | 701/225–5151 | Free | Reservations not accepted.

East View Campground. Deer and wild turkey are your neighbors in this extremely secluded campground with incredible views of buttes and badlands. The owners will bring you drinking water in coolers. Killdeer is an hour's drive northwest of Medora. Flush toilets. Showers. Grills, picnic tables. Electricity. | 15 sites (10 with partial hookups) | 10460 Ken St., NW, Killdeer | 701/764–5219 | $15–$20 | Reservations not accepted | No credit cards.

Medora Campground. This shaded campground is on the west side of Medora within walking distance of downtown. Basketball and volleyball courts are nearby. Flush toilets. Full hookups, dump station. Drinking water, guest laundry, showers. Grills, picnic tables. Electricity, public telephone. General store. Swimming (pool). | 200 sites (105 with hookups) | 195 3rd Ave., off Pacific Ave., Medora | 701/623–4444 or 800/633–6721 | fax 701/223–3347 | $15 tents, $21–$25 RVs | AE, D, MC, V | May–Sept.

Red Trail Campground. Live country music is performed every night from June through Labor Day in front of the store at this campground six blocks from downtown Medora. Red Trail was built especially to accommodate RVs. Flush toilets. Full hookups, dump station. Drinking water, guest laundry, showers. Grills, picnic tables. Electricity, public telephone. General store. Play area. | 104 sites (100 with hookups) | 250 E. River Rd. S, off Pacific Ave., Medora | 701/623–4317 or 800/621–4317 | $14 tents, $20–$26 RVs | MC, V | May–Sept.

Sully Creek State Campground. On an 80-acre park at the head of the Maah Daah Hey Trail, this campground complete with horse corrals is perfect if you're planning a bike or horseback trip on the trail, or a canoe trip on the Little Missouri River. You'll find squeaky clean pit toilets and solar-powered showers. Pit toilets. Showers. Fire pits, picnic tables. Swimming (river). | 45 sites | East River Rd., 3 mi south of Medora | 701/623–4496 | $5 per horse, $9 per site | Reservations not accepted | No credit cards.

Shopping

Visitor Centers. All three of the park's visitor centers sell books, including a nice selection of children's books, plus posters, postcards, T-shirts, and videos. The South Unit shop is the largest. Proceeds benefit the park.

Book Corral. For books on western regional history and other topics stop by this bookstore in downtown Medora. | 425 Broadway, Medora | 701/623–4345.

Chateau Nuts. Nuts of every imaginable variety are stocked in huge quantities in this little downtown shop. | 350 Main St., Medora | 701/623–4825.

Medora Convenience Store. In addition to purchasing your fishing license, gassing up the car, or renting a canoe, you can buy snacks and camping supplies at this store outside the South Unit's entrance. | 200 Pacific Ave., Medora | 701/623–4479.

★ **Prairie Fire Pottery.** Handmade stoneware and terra-cotta tiles are displayed and sold in this studio and showroom. The studio supplies 27 different animal-track tiles to zoos and parks worldwide. | 127 Main St. E, Beach | 701/872–3855.

Sacajawea Trading Post. The post specializes in Lewis and Clark merchandise, artwork, gifts, and Montana silver. | 245 Broadway, Medora | 701/623–5050.

Essential Information

ATMS: First International Bank and Trust | 100 N. Main St., Watford City | 701/842–2381. **First State Bank** | 365 3rd Ave., Medora | 701/623–5000. **Medora Convenience Store** | 200 Pacific Ave., at the South Unit entrance, Medora | 701/623–4479.

AUTOMOBILE SERVICE STATIONS: Medora Convenience Store. You can get gas at the entrance to the South Unit of the park, but the nearest full-service station is 17 mi away in Belfield. | 300 Pacific Ave., Medora | 701/623–4479.

POST OFFICES: Medora Post Office | 311 3rd Ave., 58645 | 701/623–4385.

WIND CAVE NATIONAL PARK

SOUTHWESTERN SOUTH DAKOTA

Route 87, 50 mi south of Rapid City; U.S. 385, 7 mi north of Hot Springs. Badlands National Park is 73 mi to the northeast.

Here is your chance to go spelunking, discover curious underground speleothems (cave formations), and emerge to hike or watch wildlife all in one day. There are more than 100 mi of mapped passageways in Wind Cave, and more than 44 square mi of wilderness preserve above and around it. As you crawl through the cave, hundreds of bison, elk, deer, and pronghorn roam prairies, granite-walled canyons, and ponderosa forests on the surface. But take your time. The cave has a world of wonders to show you: perfect examples of mineral box work, gypsum beard that sways from the heat of a lamp, and delicate helicite balloons that would burst at the touch of a finger. And to think 95% of Wind Cave has yet to be navigated. Theodore Roosevelt made Wind Cave the country's seventh national park, and the first dedicated to preserving a cave, on January 3, 1903.

PUBLICATIONS

Wind Cave publishes a newspaper called *Passages*. Pick it up at the visitor center or at the Hot Springs, Custer, Keystone, and Rapid City Chambers of Commerce. Call 605/745–4600 to have a copy mailed to you.

When to Visit

SCENERY AND WILDLIFE

The hills and prairies of the park are the greenest in late spring and early summer, when the thawed snow and spring rains have saturated the Black Hills with moisture. Much of the park's wildlife can be seen at this time, out scouring the prairies for young vegetation and soaking up the sun's rays before the heat grows too extreme. American bison, elk, pronghorn antelope and mule deer all graze within the park's boundaries. By late August the grasslands have reached their driest stage and turned into a gold-brown, contrasted by the dark green ponderosa pine forests. Within a month, the aspen and elm groves within the forest begin to change, adding bright red and yellow hues to the land-

WAYWARD WIND

Homesteaders Jesse and Tom Bingham first discovered Wind Cave when they heard air whistling through the rocky opening. Legend goes that the airflow was so strong that day that it knocked Tom's hat clean off his head. Jesse came back a few days later to show the trick to some friends, but it didn't happen quite as he planned. The wind, now flowing in the opposite direction, stole Jesse's hat and vacuumed it into the murky depths of the cave.

scape. Wild turkey and prairie dogs are usually busy during these months, preparing for mating season and the coming winter cold. When the parklands finally become covered with snow, the dark evergreen forests and the untouched whiteness of the prairies are a beautiful, utterly peaceful sight to behold. The roving herds of bison and packs of coyotes that move along the fringes of the forest are an added bonus to the watchful winter visitor.

HIGH AND LOW SEASON

The heaviest crowds pour into Wind Cave National Park in summer. However, the park and the surrounding Black Hills are large enough to diffuse the masses, so neither the cave nor the prairie above are ever too packed, except the first week in August when the Black Hills are host to one of the world's largest biker gatherings. Weather in the Black Hills is highly unpredictable. Summer afternoon thunderstorms occur quickly, frequently, and with little warning. While they may cool things down a bit and put on a big show of thunder and lightning, they rarely last long. Fall weather is typically sunny and mild, with temperatures around 60°F. Overnight temperatures can drop below freezing as early as September, and snow may start to fly in October. Spring is cold, wet, and unpredictable, with freak snowstorms showing up as late as April. The mountain temperatures usually begin to stabilize in May, when 60°F and 70°F days return to the area.

Average High/Low Temperature (°F) and and Monthly Precipitation (in inches)

	JAN.	FEB.	MAR.	APR.	MAY	JUNE
WIND CAVE	40/8	43/10	51/22	62/33	72/44	82/60
	.30	.40	1.0	1.90	2.60	2.80
	JULY	AUG.	SEPT.	OCT.	NOV.	DEC.
	90/57	92/55	78/46	65/34	48/21	35/10
	2.0	1.60	1.20	1.20	.50	.40

FESTIVALS AND SEASONAL EVENTS
SUMMER

June: **Mammoth Days.** See artifacts displays, and picnic on the lawn at the Mammoth Site in Hot Springs. Kids can join in the mammoth games. | 605/745–6017.

Crazy Horse Volksmarch. This 10-km (6.2-mi) hike up the mountain where the giant Crazy Horse Memorial is still being carved is the largest event of its kind. It takes place on the first full weekend in June. | 605/673–4681.

Victorian Days. Celebrate the glory days of turn-of-the-20th-century Hot Springs. A guided walking tour of the historic district and Victorian tea at the Pioneer Museum are followed by a dance and silent auction. You can browse through local arts-and-crafts booths, see an old time picture studio, and take a carriage ride. | 605/745–4140 or 800/325–6991.

July: **Gold Discovery Days.** A parade, carnival, balloon rally, arts-and-crafts fair, firemen's ball, and more, are all part of the fun one weekend in late July in downtown Custer. | 800/992–9818.

Days of '76. This Deadwood festival has earned PRCA honors as Best Small Outdoor Rodeo numerous times. Rodeo performances, two parades with vintage carriages and coaches, street dances, and western arts-and-crafts, all with a beautiful Black Hills backdrop, make this one of the best events in South Dakota. | 800/999–1876.

Sept.: **Deadwood Jam.** The Black Hills' premier music event, held in downtown Deadwood, showcases the top in country, rock, and blues music. | 800/ 999–1876 or 605/578–1876.

Oct.: **Custer State Park Buffalo Roundup.** The nation's largest buffalo roundup is also one of South Dakota's most exciting events. Watch as cowboys and park crews saddle up and corral the park's 1,400 head of bison so that they may later be vaccinated. Check out the Buffalo Roundup Arts Festival and Buffalo Wallow Chili Cook-off. | 605/255–4515.

Nearby Towns

Hot Springs is the gateway to Wind Cave National Park, 7 mi north of town, and scores of other natural and historical sites, including Evans Plunge, a large naturally heated indoor-outdoor pool; the Mammoth Site, where nearly 50 woolly and Columbian mammoths have been unearthed to date; and the Black Hills Wild Horse Sanctuary. **Custer** is where George Armstrong Custer and his expedition first discovered gold in 1874, leading to the gold rush of 1875–76. Minutes away from Wind Cave, Mount Rushmore, Crazy Horse Memorial, and Custer State Park, Custer is an excellent base for a Black Hills vacation. **Keystone** is the closes town to Mount Rushmore and, therefore, has an abundance of motels, restaurants, and gift shops. A visit to the Borglum Historical Center will enlighten you about Mount Rushmore's sculptor. If you would rather stay in a small, quiet mountain town, **Hill City,** founded by gold miners in 1876, is one of the most charming communities in the Black Hills. Surrounded by heavy pine forests and imbued with a full logging, mining, and railroad history, the town embodies the essence of the region and attracts many visitors. A decade after legalized gambling was restored in the community of **Deadwood,** $150 million has gone into restoring this once infamous gold camp, turning the entire town into a National Historic Landmark. Brick streets, old-fashioned trolleys, period lampposts, and original Victorian architecture make Deadwood irresistible.

INFORMATION

Custer County Chamber of Commerce | 615 Washington St., Custer, SD 57730 | 605/673–2244 or 800/992–9818 | www.custersd.com. **Deadwood Chamber of Commerce** | 735 Main St., Deadwood, SD 57732 | 605/578–1876 or 800/999–1876 | www.deadwood.org. **Hill City Area Chamber of Commerce** | Box 253, Hill City, SD 57745 | 605/574–2368 or 800/888–1798 | www.hillcitysd.com. **Hot Springs Area Chamber of Commerce** | 801 S. 6th St., Hot Springs, SD 57747-2962 | 605/745–4140 or 800/325–6991 | www.hotsprings-sd.com. **Keystone Chamber of Commerce** | 110 Swanzey St., Keystone, SD 57751-0653 | 605/666–4896 or 800/456–3345 | www.keystonechamber.com.

Exploring Wind Cave

PARK BASICS

Contacts and Resources: Wind Cave National Park | U.S. 385 (Box 190), Hot Springs, SD 57747 | 605/745–4600 | fax 605/745–4207 | www.nps.gov/wica.

Hours: The park is open year-round. The visitor center is open daily 8–6 in May and September, 8–7 June through August, and 8–4:30 the rest of the year (October through April).

Fees: There's no fee to enter the park; cave tours cost $3–$20.

Getting Around: U.S. 385 and Route 87 travel the length of Wind Cave National Park on the west side. Additionally, two unpaved roads, Forest Service Roads 5 and 6, traverse the northeastern part of the park vertically, intersecting in the middle of it. Forest Service Road 5 joins Route 87 at the north border of the park. Speed limits are posted most commonly

CURIOUS CRYSTALS

Thin, spidery box work and other Wind Cave formations are created when water moves through the cave, dissolving the limestone, then evaporating, leaving behind deposits of crystallized gypsum (calcium sulfate).

at 45 and 35 mph. Wildlife—including bison, which can weigh around a ton—frequent the areas around the highways, making a faster speed dangerous for both drivers and animals. No off-road driving is permitted. There's ample free parking at the visitor center, although it can get full in mid-summer, the peak of the tourist season. There are multiple unpaved pullouts and small parking lots along Route 87 and U.S. 385, especially near trailheads.

Permits: The requisite backcountry camping and horseback riding permits are both free from the visitor center.

Public Telephones: Public telephones may be found at the visitor center and Elk Mountain Campground.

Rest Rooms: Public rest rooms may be found at the visitor center and Elk Mountain Campground.

Accessibility: The visitor center is entirely wheelchair accessible, but only a few areas of the cave itself are navigable by those with limited mobility. Arrangements can be made in advance for a special ranger-assisted tour for a small fee.

Emergencies: Dial 911 for emergencies, then call the visitor center at 605/745–4600. Rangers can provide basic first aid. Further medical attention is available at Custer Community Hospital in Custer, Southern Hills Hospital in Hot Springs, or Rapid City Regional Hospital. There are no fire call boxes in the park. Report a fire at the visitor center. Rangers and the Elk Mountain Campground host can also assist you with any security-related issues.

Lost and Found: The park's lost-and-found is at the visitor center; the phone number is 605/745–4600.

Good Tours

WIND CAVE IN ONE DAY

Pack a picnic lunch, then head to the **visitor center** to purchase tickets for a morning tour of **Wind Cave.** Visit the exhibit rooms in the visitor center while waiting for your tour to begin, or just after the tour. By the time you complete your tour, you will probably be ready for lunch. Drive or walk the quarter mile to the picnic area north of the visitor center. The refreshing air and deep emerald color of the picnic area's pine woodlands will flavor your meal. Or travel south 7 mi on U.S. 385 to Hot Springs for a hearty meal in one of several good (and air-conditioned) eateries.

In the afternoon, take a leisurely drive through the parklands south of the visitor center, passing through **Gobbler Pass** and **Bison Flats** for an archetypal view of the park and to look for wildlife. On your way back up north, follow U.S. 385 east toward **Wind Cave Canyon.** If you enjoy bird-watching, park your car at a turnout and hike the 1.8-mi trail into the canyon, where you can spot swallows and great horned owls in the cliffs and woodpeckers in the dead trees at the bottom. Next, get back on the highway going north, take a right on Route 87, and continue a half-mile to the turnout for **Centennial Trail.** Hike the trail about 2 mi to the junction with **Lookout Point Trail,** turn right and return to Route 87. The whole loop is about 4.75 mi. If you're tired or short on time, however, skip the Centennial/Lookout Point trails and continue driving north to the top of Rankin Ridge. A pullout to the right serves as the starting point for 1.25-mi **Rankin Ridge Trail.** It loops around the ridge, past **Lookout Tower**—the park's highest point and a great place to view the whole park—and ends up back at the pullout. This trail is an excellent opportunity to enjoy the fresh air, open spaces, and diversity of wildlife that the park offers, even if you're not a keen outdoors person. Conclude your day by exiting the park on Route 87 and driving through **Custer State Park.** Have dinner in any one of several Black Hills restaurants in Custer, Hill City, or Rapid City.

WIND CAVE IN TWO DAYS

Follow the one-day itinerary on your first day in the park. Split your second day between a drive through the wild northeastern section of the park and another cave tour. Head to the visitor center to purchase your tickets as early as possible, especially if you're visiting in summer.

To get to the northeastern section of the park, catch the unpaved Forest Service Road 5 at the northern park border. You are more than likely to see grazing buffalo and pronghorn from this little-traveled road through the backcountry. When you reach the junction with Forest Road 6, take a left and head north until you reach 2.7-mi **Boland Ridge Trail,** which cuts right through the park's vast eastern wilderness. You should make it back to the visitor center before 1 for your second cave tour.

If you haven't eaten outside yet, dinner provides the perfect opportunity. A barbecue among the towering pines and light breezes of the Black Hills is a truly serene experience. You can pick up food and charcoal at grocery stores in Hot Springs, Custer, or Hill City, and then cook using the fire pits at **Elk Mountain Campground.** At 9, head for the campground's amphitheater for the 45-minute, ranger-led outdoor campfire talk.

Attractions

PROGRAMS AND TOURS

Campfire Program. A park ranger lectures for about 45 minutes on topics from wildlife to park management to cave history. Information is posted at the visitor center, Elk Mountain campground, and on-line. | Elk Mountain Campground amphitheater | June–Labor Day, nightly 8 or 9 PM; Sept. Tues., Thurs., Sat. 7 PM.

★ **Cave Tours.** You can choose between five different ranger-led tours of Wind Cave if you visit from June through August; the rest of the year, only one or two are available. All tours depart from the visitor center, and on each you pass incredibly beautiful cave formations, including extremely well-developed box work. The least-crowded times to visit in summer are mornings and weekends. The cave is 53°F year-round, so bring a sweater, and always wear comfortable, closed-toe shoes. There are reduced prices for adults over 62 and children. Tour schedules, program times, and meeting points are subject to change, so double check this information with the visitor center. | U.S. 385 to Wind Cave visitor center | 605/745–4600 | $6–$9, $20.

The **Candlelight Cave Tour** lets you explore a section of the cave where there is no sidewalk or lighting. Everyone carries a lantern similar to those used in expeditions in the 1890s. The tour lasts two hours and covers one mile of the cave. Children under 8 are not admitted. Reservations essential. | Early June–Labor Day, twice daily.

On the **Fairgrounds Cave Tour,** you visit some of the largest rooms in the cave, including the Fairgrounds room, with nearly every example of calcite formation found in the cave. There are some 450 steps, leading up and down, on this 1½-hour tour. | Early June–Labor Day, five times daily.

You don't need to go far to see box work, popcorn, and flowstone formations. Just take the relatively easy, one-hour **Garden of Eden Cave Tour,** which only covers about a quarter mile and 150 stairs. | Oct.–Apr., three times daily.

The popular, 1¼-hour **Natural Entrance Cave Tour** takes you a half mile into the cave, over 300 stairs (most heading down), and out an elevator exit. | Early June–Labor Day, nine times daily; Labor Day–late Sept., seven times daily.

For a serious caving experience, sign up for the challenging, four-hour **Wild Caving Tour.** You get basic training in spelunking, and then you crawl and climb through fissures and corridors, most lined with gypsum needles, frostwork, and box work. You'll also see artifacts left by early explorers. Expect to get dirty. Wear shoes with good traction, long pants, and a long-sleeve shirt. The park provides kneepads, gloves, and hardhats with headlamps. You must be at least 16 to take this tour; 16- and 17-year-olds must show signed consent from a parent or guardian. | $20 | Reservations essential | Early June–mid-Aug., daily 1 PM; mid-Aug.–Labor Day, weekends 1 PM.

Discovery Activity. Park rangers lead a discussion on local wildlife, plants, geology, area history, cave surveying, and other topics. Talks are often accompanied by demonstrations. Check with the visitor center for topics, times, and meeting points. | June–Labor Day.

Junior Ranger Program. Kids 12 and younger can earn a junior ranger badge by completing activities that teach them about the park's ecosystems, the cave, the animals, and protecting the environment. Pick up the junior ranger guidebook for $1.50 at the visitor center. | Wind Cave visitor center.

Prairie Hike. This two-hour exploration of parkland habitats begins with a short ranger talk at the visitor center, but then moves to a nearby trailhead. Your own supply of water and hiking boots or comfortable shoes are advised. | Early June–mid-Aug., daily 9 AM.

SCENIC DRIVES

Rankin Ridge Drive (North Entrance). Entering the park across the north border via Route 87 is probably the most beautiful drive into the park. As you leave behind the grasslands and granite spires of Custer State Park and enter Wind Cave National Park, you'll see the prairie, forest, and wetland habitats of the backcountry and some of the oldest rock in the Black Hills. The silvery twinkle of mica, quartz, and feldspar crystals dot Rankin Ridge east of Route 87, and gradually give way to limestone and sandstone formations, which have eroded more quickly than the hard crystals found farther north.

Bison Flats Drive (South Entrance). Entering the park from the south on U.S. 385 will take you past Gobbler Ridge and into the hills commonly found in the southern Black Hills region.

After a couple of miles, the landscape gently levels onto the Bison Flats, one of the mixed grass prairies on which the park prides itself. You might see a herd of grazing buffalo between here and the visitor center. You'll also catch panoramic views of the parklands and surrounding hills. The rocks in this part of the park—mostly brown and light-gray sandstone—are some of the Black Hills' youngest, having been formed a mere 200 million years ago. Farther north on U.S. 385, the terrain once again becomes more chiseled. Hills and limestone bluffs make up the park's western border.

SIGHTS TO SEE

Rankin Ridge Lookout Tower. Some of the best panoramic views of the park and surrounding hills can be seen from this tower, which at 5,013 ft, is the highest point in the park. Hike Rankin Ridge loop to get there. | 4 mi north of the visitor center.

★ **Wind Cave.** Discovered by the Bingham brothers in 1881, Wind Cave was named for the strong currents of air that blow in or out of the entrance. This is related to the difference in atmospheric pressure between the cave and the surface. When the atmospheric pressure is higher outside than inside the cave, the air blows in, and vice versa. With more than 100 mi of known passageway divided into three different levels, Wind Cave ranks the sixth longest worldwide. It is host to an incredibly diverse and complete collection of geologic formations, including more box work than any other known cave, plus a series of underground lakes. The cave tours sponsored by the National Park Service allow you to see examples of unusual and beautiful formations with such names as button popcorn, starburst, Christmas trees, frostwork, nail quartz, helicite bushes, and gypsum flowers. | U.S. 385 to Wind Cave visitor center.

Wind Cave Canyon. Here's one of the best birding areas in the park. As you hike down the trail, the steep-sided canyon widens to a panoramic view east across the prairies. | About 0.5 mi east of the visitor center.

Wind Cave Visitor Center. The visitor center sits on top of the cave. Besides being the primary place to get general park information, it has three exhibit rooms with displays on cave exploration, cave history, cave formations, the Civilian Conservation Corps, park wildlife, and resource management. | 3 mi north of the park's southern border off U.S. 385 | 605/745–4600 | www.nps.gov/wica | May, daily 8–6; June–Aug., daily 8–7:30; Sept., daily 8–6; Oct.–Apr., daily 8–4:30.

Sports and Outdoor Activities

BICYCLING

Bikes are prohibited on all of the park's trails and in the backcountry. Cyclists may ride on designated roads, and on 111-mi Centennial Trail, once it passes the park's northern border.

Rushmore Bicycles. This local outfitter has nearly 50 mountain bikes for rent by the day or half-day, including comfort cruisers and high-end demo bikes. Kids' bikes are also available. Once you have your rentals, you can tow them with a bike trailer or simply have them dropped at your hotel for an additional fee. Reservations are essential. | 107 Elm St., Hill City | 605/574–3930 | www.rushmorebicycles.com.

Two Wheeler Dealer Cycle and Fitness. A full-service bicycle outfitter based in Rapid City, Two Wheeler Dealer carries more than 1,000 different bikes for sale or rent. Service is top-notch, and trail maps are available. | 100 E. Blvd. N, Rapid City | 605/343–0524 | www.twowheelerdealer.com.

BIRD-WATCHING

Many bird species are attracted to the protected habitats of Wind Cave National Park, making it a prime location to watch for some of the area's beautiful birds. The limestone walls of Wind Cave Canyon are ideal nesting grounds for cliff swallows and great horned owls, while the standing dead trees on the canyon floor attract red-headed and Lewis

WIND CAVE
NATIONAL PARK

EXPLORING
ATTRACTIONS NEARBY
DINING
LODGING
CAMPING AND RV
FACILITIES
SHOPPING
ESSENTIAL
INFORMATION

woodpeckers. Early morning or late afternoon are the best times to spot them. The ponderosa forests of Rankin Ridge are where you can see larger birds-of-prey, including turkey vultures, hawks, and golden eagles, which are commonly seen soaring above the hills on mid-afternoon updrafts. Wind Cave's parklands are typically more arid than the forests and plains of the northern Black Hills, where waterfowl such as ducks, geese, swans, and herons are more common.

HIKING

There are more than 30 mi of hiking trails within the park boundaries. If you prefer to find your own way, hiking into the wild, untouched backcountry is perfectly safe, provided you have a map (available from the visitor center) and a good sense of direction. Remember that wild animals are roaming the same territory that you are, including coyotes and bison. While bison may appear to be nothing more than big hairy cows, they are really very wild. They can easily weigh a ton, and if threatened can outrun a horse. Buffalo are especially unpredictable during the rut, or mating season, in late July and August. Admire their majestic power and typically peaceful nature from a distance.

Boland Ridge Trail. If you want to get away from the crowds, this is your trail. It's a strenuous, 2.7-mi hike up to Boland Ridge, but the panorama from the top is well worth it—sunset from this remote point is absolutely spectacular. The trailhead is off Forest Service Road 6, 1 mi north of the junction with Forest Service Road 5.

Centennial Trail. Constructed to celebrate South Dakota's centennial, this trail bisects the Black Hills from north to south, covering 111 mi of territory. Designed for bikers, hikers, and horses, this trail is rugged but accommodating. Bike-riding is not allowed within park boundaries. Pick the trail up off Route 87, 2 mi north of the visitor center.

Cold Brook Canyon Trail. Starting on the west side of U.S. 385 2 mi south of the visitor center, this 1.4-mi mildly strenuous trail traverses a former prairie dog town, the edge of an area burned by a controlled fire in 1986, and through Cold Brook Canyon to the park boundary fence.

Highland Creek Trail. This difficult 8.6-mi trail is the longest and most diverse in the park. The southern trailhead stems from Wind Cave Canyon trail 1 mi east of U.S. 385. The northern trailhead is on Forest Service Road 5. The trail traverses mixed-grass prairies, ponderosa pine forests, and the riparian habitats of Highland Creek, Beaver Creek, and Wind Cave Canyon.

Lookout Point Trail. From the Centennial trailhead on Route 87, the 2.2-mi Lookout Point Trail follows the prairie, traverses Lookout Point, and ends at Beaver Creek. Cross over to the Centennial Trail to make a 4.8-mi loop.

Sanctuary Trail. Beginning on the east side of Route 87 about 1 mi north of the Rankin Ridge fire tower road, this 3.6-mi, fairly tough trail travels over hills, passes a large prairie dog town, and ends at Highland Creek Trail. You can see the Rankin Ridge fire tower at the intersection of Centennial Trail.

Wind Cave Canyon Trail. This easy 1.8-mi trail follows Wind Cave Canyon to the park boundary fence. The canyon provides the best opportunity in the park for bird-watching.

SPELUNKING

You may not explore Wind Cave on your own, but the Wild Caving Tour will not disappoint. It's a genuine caving trip in an undeveloped, untamed, underground labyrinth. The park provides hard hats, kneepads, and gloves, and all cavers are required to have long pants, a long-sleeved shirt, and hiking books or shoes with nonslip soles. If you prefer lighted passages and stairways to dark crawlspaces, any of the cave's other four guided tours might appeal to you. No matter how you choose to explore the cave, keep in mind that the uneven passages are often wet and slippery and that the cave's air temperature is 53°F year-round.

Outfitters

Granite Sports. Come here for all of your camping, climbing, and hiking gear needs. | 301 Main St., Hill City | 605/574–2121.

Scheels All Sport. In Rapid City's Rushmore Mall, Scheels is one of the few places in the area to carry a wide selection of all-weather hiking clothes and binoculars suitable for bird-watchers. | 2200 N. Maple Ave., Rapid City | 605/342–9033.

Attractions Nearby

For more sights and tours in the Black Hills region, *see* Badlands National Park.

Scenic Drive

Iron Mountain Road. Laid out by Senator Peter Norbeck, this 17-mi scenic drive leads from Custer State Park to Keystone and is best known for its three pigtail bridges—consecutive loops over rustic timber trestles, replacements for the standard switchbacks commonly used in mountain road construction. As you drive through three narrow tunnels on the roadway, you'll find perfectly framed views of the four Presidential faces on Mount Rushmore. | Rte. 16A.

Sights to See

★ **Adams Memorial Museum.** The oldest history museum in the Black Hills is an exceptional repository of historic memorabilia from the region's past, including the first locomotive used in the area, photos of the town's early days, and the largest gold nugget ever discovered in the Black Hills. | 54 Sherman St., Deadwood | 605/578–1714 | www.adamsmuseumandhouse.org | Free | May–Sept., Mon.–Sat. 9–6, Sun. noon–5; Oct.–Apr., Mon.–Sat. 10–5.

Angostura Reservoir State Recreation Area. Water-based recreation is the main draw at this park 10 mi south of Hot Springs. Besides the marina, you'll find a floating convenience store, a beach-side restaurant, four campgrounds and modern cabins. Boat and Wave-Runner rentals are available. | U.S. 385, off Rte. 79, Hot Springs | 605/745–6996 | $5 | Daily dawn–dusk.

Beautiful Rushmore Cave. Stalagmites, stalactites, flowstone, ribbons, columns, helicites, and the "Big Room" are all part of the worthwhile tour into this cave. In 1876, miners found the opening to the cave while digging a flume into the mountainside to carry water to the gold mines below. The cave was opened to the public in 1927, just before the carving of Mount Rushmore began. | Rte. 40, Keystone | 605/255–4384 or 605/255–4634 | www.beautifulrushmorecave.com | $7 | May 1–Memorial Day, daily 9–5; Memorial Day–Labor Day, daily 8–8; Labor Day–Oct., daily 9–5.

Big Thunder Gold Mine. You can take a guided tour through an underground gold mine, get some free gold ore samples, and do a little gold panning yourself. | Rte. 40, Keystone | 605/666–4847 or 800/314–3917 | www.bigthundergoldmine.com | $6.95 | May–mid-Oct., daily 9–5.

Black Hills Wild Horse Sanctuary. Hundreds of wild mustangs inhabit this 11,000-acre preserve of rugged canyons, forests, and grasslands along the Cheyenne River. Take a guided tour or hike, and sign up for a chuck-wagon dinner. Drive 14 mi south of Hot Springs until you see signs off Route 71. | Rte. 71, Hot Springs | 605/745–5955 or 800/252–6652 | www.gwtc.net/~iram | $15 | Memorial Day–Labor Day, Mon.–Sat. 9:30–5; tours at 10, 1, and 3.

★ **Crazy Horse Memorial.** This colossal mountain carving still in progress depicts Lakota leader Crazy Horse atop his steed. At the memorial's base are a restaurant, gift shop, and legendary work by Crazy Horse sculptor Korczak Ziolkowski. From Custer, go 5 mi north on U.S. 385. | U.S. 385, Custer | 605/673–4681 | www.crazyhorse.org | $8 per person, $19 per vehicle | June–Aug., daily 7–8:30; Sept.–May, daily 8–5.

WIND CAVE
NATIONAL PARK

EXPLORING
ATTRACTIONS
NEARBY
DINING
LODGING
CAMPING AND RV
FACILITIES
SHOPPING
ESSENTIAL
INFORMATION

At the base of the memorial, the **Indian Museum of North America** houses one of the most impressive collections of Plains Indian artifacts in the country.

★ **Custer State Park.** Considered the crown jewel of South Dakota's state park system, visitors flock to these 115 square mi of scenic grandeur, granite spires, and pristine mountain lakes to view wildlife and explore outstanding hiking trails. Take the 18-mi Wildlife Loop Road to see prairies teeming with animals. Here, a buffalo jam is much more likely than a traffic jam. The park's several lodges provide comfortable retreats for road-weary travelers. The 14-mi Needles Highway between the State Game Lodge and Sylvan Lake Resort takes you past immense granite spires towering over the forest floor. | U.S. 16A, Custer | 605/255–4515 | www.state.sd.us/sdparks | $5 Nov.–Apr.; $10 May–Oct. | Daily.

Flintstones Bedrock City. Step into Bedrock at this Stone Age fun park with rides on the Flintmobile and the Iron Horse train. Play areas, a theater, camping, gifts, and brontoburgers and dinodogs at the drive-in round out the Flintstone experience. The park is on the western edge of Custer. | U.S 385 at U.S. 16, Custer | 605/673–4079 | www.flintstonesbedrockcity.com | $6 | Mid-May–mid-Sept., daily 8:30–8.

★ **Jewel Cave National Monument.** Even though its 125 mi of surveyed passages make this cave the world's third largest, it isn't the size of Jewel Cave that draws visitors. It's the rare crystalline formations that abound in the cave's vast passages. Some of them are so beautiful and uncommon that they were unknown until they were discovered in Jewel Cave. | 27 mi west of Custer on Rte. 16, Custer | 605/673–2288 | www.nps.gov/jeca | Tours: $8–$20 | June–Aug., daily 8–7:30; Sept.–May, 8–4:30.

★ **Mammoth Site of Hot Springs.** Nearly 50 giant mammoths have already been unearthed from a prehistoric sinkhole in Hot Springs, where the creatures came to drink 26,000 years ago. You can watch the excavation in progress and take guided tours. | 1800 Rte. 18, Hot Springs | 605/745–6017 or 800/325–6991 | www.mammothsite.com | $5 | Daily, call for hrs.

★ **Mount Rushmore National Memorial.** One of the nation's most famous attractions, the carving of Mount Rushmore was begun by sculptor Gutzon Borglum in 1927 and finished in 1941. Borglum died in March of that year, leaving his son, Lincoln, to continue the work for a few months longer. The giant, 60-ft-high likenesses of Presidents Washington, Jefferson, Lincoln, and Theodore Roosevelt grace a massive granite cliff, which, at an elevation of 5,725 ft, towers over the surrounding countryside and faces the sun most of the day. The memorial is equally spectacular at night, when a special lighting ceremony (June–mid-September) dramatically illuminates the carving. From Keystone, take Route 244 (Gutzon Borglum Memorial Highway) west 3 mi. | Rte. 244, Keystone | 605/574–2523 | www.nps.gov/moru | Free | Daily.

Old Style Saloon #10. Come here to have a drink, listen to music, and socialize. Thousands of artifacts, vintage photos, and even a two-headed calf set the scene. There's live entertainment nightly, gaming, and excellent food upstairs at the Deadwood Social Club. A reenactment of "The Shooting of Wild Bill Hickok" is featured four times a day in summer. | 657 Main St., Deadwood | 605/578–3346 | www.saloon10.com | Memorial Day–Labor Day, Sun.–Mon. 8 AM–2 AM, Tues.–Sat. 8 AM–3 AM; early Sept.–late May, daily 8 AM–2 AM.

Dining

In Wind Cave

Elk Mountain Campground Picnic Area. You don't have to be a camper to use this well-developed picnic spot, which has more than 70 tables, fire pits, and rest rooms with running water. Some of the tables are on the prairie, others are amidst the pines. | 0.5 mi north of the visitor center.

Wind Cave Picnic Area. Wind Cave's picnic area is small and simple, equipped with nothing but a dozen tables and a potable-water pump. On the edge of a prairie and a grove of ponderosa, it's a peaceful, pretty place to enjoy a meal. | 0.25 mi north of the visitor center.

Near the Park

For dining in Rapid City, *see* Badlands National Park.

★**Alpine Inn.** American. Here you'll find a bit of European charm in the Old West. The lunchtime menu changes daily but always has healthy selections of sandwiches and salads (no fried food). There's only one item on the dinner menu: filet mignon. Lunch is offered on the veranda overlooking Main Street. Beer and wine are the only alcoholic beverages served. | 225 Main St., Hill City | 605/574–2749 | $5–$10 | No credit cards | Closed Sun.

Blue Bell Lodge and Resort. American. Feast on fresh trout or buffalo, which you can have as a steak or a stew, in this rustic log building within the boundaries of Custer State Park. Kids' menu. | About 6 mi south of U.S. 16A junction on Rte. 87, Custer | 605/255–4531 or 800/658–3530 | $19–$20 | AE, D, MC, V | Closed mid-Oct.–mid-May.

Buffalo Dining Room. American. With stunning views of Mount Rushmore before you, you won't mind waiting for your meal in this glass-enclosed cafeteria. The menu lists many choices for breakfast, lunch, and dinner, including standard fare like burgers and pasta, plus a very popular buffalo stew. You can end your meal with a "monumental bowl of ice cream" or fresh-made fudge. | Rte. 244, Keystone | 605/574–2515 | $6–$11 | AE, D, MC, V | No dinner mid-Oct.–early Mar.

★**Deadwood Social Club.** American. Come here for a homey, relaxing dining experience with light jazz and blues in the background, historic photos on the walls, and one of South Dakota's best wine selections in the cellar. The restaurant is known for Black Angus beef and chicken, seafood, and pasta dishes. | 657 Main St., Deadwood | 605/578–3346 or 800/952–9398 | $8–$18 | AE, MC, V | Closed Mon.

★**Jake's.** Contemporary. Owned by actor Kevin Costner, this is undoubtedly one of South Dakota's premier dining experiences. Cherry wood, fireplaces, special lighting, and live piano music create an elegant and romantic scene. Good dinner choices are the fresh fish, buffalo roulade, Cajun seafood tortellini, or filet mignon. | 677 Main St., Deadwood | 605/578–3656 | Reservations essential | $19–$29 | AE, D, DC, MC, V | Closed Sun.

Seven Sisters Steakhouse and Lounge. Contemporary. Elegant fireplaces and babbling fountains complement this restaurant's unique menu. There's plenty to choose from, but the locals come mainly for the sizzling steak. | U.S. 18, near the Mammoth Site, Hot Springs | 605/745–6666 | $9–$18 | DC, MC, V.

State Game Lodge and Resort. American. President Calvin Coolidge once frequented the historic Pheasant Dining Room for tasty meals of meticulously prepared buffalo or pheasant. There's a salad bar and a buffet at lunch. Take Route 16A 13 mi east of Custer. Kids' menu. | Rte. 16A, Custer | 605/255–4541 or 800/658–3530 | Reservations essential | $15–$28 | AE, D, MC, V | Closed mid-Oct.–mid-May.

Sylvan Lake Resort. American/Casual. The Lakota Dining Room has an exceptional view of Sylvan Lake and Harney Peak, the highest point between the Rockies and the Swiss Alps. On the menu are buffalo selections, including steaks. A fine alternative to meat is the rainbow trout. You can enjoy your cocktail or tea out on the veranda. Kids' menu. From Hill City, drive south on U.S. 385 past Mount Rushmore to Route 87. The resort is 9 mi south of Hill City. | Rte. 87, Hill City | 605/574–2561 | $10–$20 | AE, D, MC, V | Closed Oct.–mid-May.

WIND CAVE
NATIONAL PARK

EXPLORING
ATTRACTIONS NEARBY
DINING
LODGING
CAMPING AND RV
FACILITIES
SHOPPING
ESSENTIAL
INFORMATION

Lodging

Near the Park

Good deals for lodging in mountain surroundings can be found in the smaller Black Hills towns of Hill City, Custer, and Hot Springs, and in the outlying areas. To find the best value, choose a hotel far from I–90. For lodging in Rapid City, *see* Badlands National Park.

American President's Resort. This resort specializes in family reunions. The individual cabins come complete with kitchens. Camping with full hookups is available. Picnic areas. Some kitchenettes. Miniature golf. Pool. Spa. Horseback riding. Playground. Laundry facilities. | U.S. 16A, Custer | 605/673–3373 | 45 cabins, 70 campsites | $19–$27 campsites, $70–$269 cabins | D, MC, V.

Best Western Inn by the River. This two-story inn is three blocks from downtown and 10 mi south of Wind Cave. Rooms are spacious and done in pleasant tones of blue and peach. Cable TV. Pool. | 602 W. River St., Hot Springs | 605/745–4292 or 888/605–4292 | fax 605/745–3584 | 31 rooms | $50–$110 | AE, D, DC, MC, V | CP.

Blue Bell Lodge and Resort. This hideaway retreat in Custer State Park is made up of hand-crafted log cabins with modern interiors and fireplaces, a lodge, a conference center, and a campground. Hayrides and cookouts are part of the entertainment, and you can sign up for trail rides and overnight pack trips on old Indian trails with the nearby stable. From Custer, take Route 16A east in the state park, then take Route 87 south about 6 mi. Restaurant, picnic area. Some kitchenettes, some refrigerators. Cable TV. Hiking, horseback riding. Bar. Playground. Laundry facilities. Some pets allowed. No a/c, no phones in some rooms. | Rte. 87, Custer | 605/255–4531 or 800/658–3530 | fax 605/255–4706 | 29 cabins | $87–$170 | AE, D, MC, V.

Buffalo Rock Lodge B & B. A large, native rock fireplace surrounded by hefty logs is at the heart of this rustic lodge decorated with Western artifacts. You can view Mount Rushmore from the large deck and take walks through the surrounding pine forest filled with wildflowers. In-room hot tubs. Fishing. Hiking. Some pets allowed. | Playhouse Rd., off Rte. 16A, Keystone | 605/666–4781 or 888/564–5634 | 3 rooms | $125–$150 | DC, MC, V | CP.

Bullock Hotel. A casino occupies the main floor of this meticulously restored hotel, which was built by Deadwood's first sheriff, Seth Bullock, in 1895. You'll spot the hotel's pink granite facade right away. Rooms are furnished in Victorian style with reproductions of the original furniture. Restaurant, room service. Some in-room hot tubs. Cable TV. Bar. Business services. | 633 Main St., Deadwood | 605/578–1745 or 800/336–1876 | fax 605/578–1382 | 36 rooms | $75–$250 | AE, D, MC, V.

Comfort Inn Hot Springs. Near U.S. 385, and three blocks from downtown, this hotel offers easy access to the Mueller Civic Center. Family suites are available, and some rooms have views of a little river. Some in-room hot tubs, microwaves, refrigerators. Cable TV. Pool. Exercise equipment, hot tub. Laundry facilities. Business services. Some pets allowed. | 737 S. 6th St., Hot Springs | 605/745–7378 or 800/228–5150 | fax 605/745–3240 | 51 rooms, 9 suites | $109, $159 suites | AE, D, MC, V | CP.

Custer Mansion. This delightful B&B is in a Victorian Gothic mansion on 1.25 acres of gardens and aspen trees where you can wander. One of the six guest rooms has a TV and VCR. Picnic area. Some in-room hot tubs. Outdoor hot tub. No room phones. No smoking. | 35 Centennial Dr., Custer | 605/673–3333 | fax 605/673–6696 | 6 rooms | $75–$105 | MC, V | BP.

Dakota Prairie Ranch B & B. On this fourth-generation cattle ranch you can tag along and help with the chores, go on wagon and trail rides, and visit a prairie dog town. The ranch house, with country and antique furnishings, is 20 minutes southeast of Hot Springs, and 15 minutes from the Black Hills, Pine Ridge Indian Reservation, and the Wild Horse Sanctuary. A hearty breakfast awaits in the morning, and you can arrange for lunch and dinner, too. Hunting is allowed in season. Some rooms share a bath. Hot tub.

Fishing. | U.S. 385, Hot Springs | 605/535–2001 or 888/535–2001 | 3 rooms, 2 suites | $60–$100 | D, MC, V | BP.

Deadwood Gulch Resort. Pine-clad hills, a little creek, and a deck from which to view the mountains are at your disposal at this resort 1 mi from town. A trolley stops in front of the hotel to take you to various sites in Deadwood. There's also a casino on the premises. Restaurant. Cable TV. Pool. Hot tub. Bicycles. Hiking. Bar. Some pets allowed (fee). | Rte. 85 S, Deadwood | 605/578–1294 or 800/695–1876 | fax 605/578–2505 | www.deadwoodgulch.com | 96 rooms | $109 | AE, D, DC, MC, V.

French Creek Guest Ranch B & B. Soak up views of the Needles formation while you sit on the porch of this luxurious B&B. On a 25-acre working horse ranch, French Creek is designed to meet the needs of the traveling horse owner: the stable has eight wooden box stalls each with its own run. Horses may be boarded for an additional fee. Facilities are also available for a horse trailer or camper hookup. The ranch is 1.5 mi from Custer State Park. Restaurant. Refrigerators. Tennis court. Sauna. Fishing. Basketball, hiking, horseback riding, volleyball. No kids under 13. | Rte. 16A, Custer | 605/673–4790 or 877/673–4790 | fax 605/673–4767 | 3 rooms | $65–145 | D, MC, V | BP.

Lodge at Palmer Gulch. In an idyllic valley near Mount Rushmore, the lodge is shadowed by the massive granite ramparts of Harney Peak. With its pools, waterslide, outdoor activities, and kids' programs, this is a great place for families. A free shuttle takes you to Mount Rushmore and Crazy Horse. Camping is allowed on the premises. Restaurant, picnic area. Some kitchenettes. Cable TV. Miniature golf. 2 pools. Hot tub, sauna. Basketball, horseback riding, volleyball. Playground. Some pets allowed. No a/c in some rooms, no phones in some rooms. | 12620 Rte. 244, Hill City | 605/574–2525 or 800/562–8503 | fax 605/574–2574 | 62 rooms, 30 cabins | $113–$182 | D, MC, V.

Powder House Lodge. Amid the pines off U.S. 16A, this rustic lodge has comfy cabins and a friendly staff. The lodge caters to family vacations with its outdoor heated pool, access to hiking trails, nearby stables, playground, and proximity to Mount Rushmore. Restaurant. Cable TV. Outdoor pool. Playground. | 24127 U.S. 16A, Keystone | 605/666–4646 or 800/321–0692 | 37 rooms, 12 cabins | $80–$165 | AE, D, MC, V.

Raspberry and Lace B & B. This turn-of-the-20th-century homestead is 8 mi north of Custer, 6 mi south of Hill City, and 4 mi from the Crazy Horse monument. The Mickelson Trail passes nearby, and there's a trout stream on the property. Refrigerators. Hot tub. Fishing. Hiking. | 12175 White Horse Rd., Custer | 605/574–4920 | 4 rooms | $80–$100 | AE, D, MC, V.

Roosevelt Inn. This mid-size inn, less than 1 mi from the east entrance of the Mount Rushmore memorial, is one of the closest hotels to the "Faces" (though you cannot see them from the inn). Mountain view rooms are especially inviting in autumn. Some suites have balconies. Cable TV. Pool. | 206 Old Cemetery Rd., Keystone | 605/666–4599 or 800/257–8923 | fax 605/666–4535 | 23 rooms | $45–$195 | AE, MC, V.

State Game Lodge and Resort. Once the Summer White House for President Coolidge, and host to President Eisenhower as well, this stately stone-and-wood lodge has well-appointed rooms and pine-shaded cabins. You can arrange for Jeep rides into the buffalo area. Restaurant, picnic area. Cable TV. Hiking. Bar. Some pets allowed. No a/c in some rooms, no phones in some rooms. | Rte. 16A, Custer | 605/255–4541 or 800/658–3530 | fax 605/255–4706 | 7 lodge rooms, 40 motel rooms, 33 cabins | $75–$225 lodge rooms, $80–$350 cabins, $99–$140 motel rooms | AE, D, MC, V.

★ **Strutton Inn B & B.** This luxurious three-story Victorian home sits on four lovely acres. Enjoy the view from the 140 ft veranda, with a gazebo on each corner. Inside this well-furnished retreat are enormous, stately rooms, the owners' antique doll and crystal collection, and a 46-inch big screen TV. Microwaves, refrigerators. Airport shuttle. No smoking. | 12042 W. U.S. 16, Custer | 605/673–2395 or 800/226–2611 | 9 rooms | $85–$139 | MC, V | BP.

WIND CAVE NATIONAL PARK

EXPLORING
ATTRACTIONS NEARBY
DINING
LODGING
CAMPING AND RV FACILITIES
SHOPPING
/ ESSENTIAL INFORMATION

Super 8 Motel Hot Springs. This motel is next to the Mammoth Site and about 1 mi from the restaurants downtown. Many rooms have a view of the hills, and several large family-size rooms are available. Some microwaves, some refrigerators. Cable TV. Laundry facilities. Some pets allowed. | 800 Mammoth St., Hot Springs | 605/745–3888 | fax 605/745–3385 | 48 rooms | $92 | AE, D, MC, V | CP.

★ **Sylvan Lake Resort.** The spacious stone-and-wood lodge overlooks pristine Sylvan Lake. Rustic cabins, some with fireplaces, are scattered along the cliff and in the forest. Numerous hiking trails make this a great choice for active families. Restaurant, dining room, picnic area. Lake. Beach. Boating. Hiking. Bar. | Custer State Park, Hill City | 605/574-2561 or 800/658-3530 | fax 605/574-4943 | 35 rooms in lodge, 31 cabins | $95–$235 cabins, $100–$145 | AE, D, MC, V.

Camping and RV Facilities

In Wind Cave

Camping in the parkland's backcountry means you can explore the thick pine forests and wild prairies during the most exciting times—sundown and sunrise. The powerful blend of golden-pink hues on the horizon, the utter stillness, and the increased chance of seeing roaming animals are more than ample reason to "rough it" for a night.

Elk Mountain Campground. If you prefer a sculpted campsite and relative proximity to civilization, Elk Mountain campground is an excellent choice. You can experience the peaceful pine forests and wild creatures of the park without straying too far from the safety of the beaten path. Sites 24 and 69 are reserved for campers with disabilities. There are no RV hookups. Flush toilets. Running water (non-potable). Fire grates. Public telephone. | 0.5 mi north of the visitor center | 75 sites | 605/745–4600 | $6–$12 | Apr.–late Oct.

Near the Park

Custer Crossing Campground and Store. In a pass 15 mi south of Deadwood where George A. Custer led his expedition through the Black Hills in 1874, Custer Crossing Campground offers a great way to enjoy the pristine beauty of the surrounding hills without leaving civilization entirely—the owners also run a service station and restaurant, which serves a full breakfast to campers. Flush toilets. Partial hookups (electric), dump station. Drinking water, showers. Fire grates, picnic tables, food service. Electricity, public telephone. General store, service station. Play area. | 20 sites (all with partial hookups), 11 cabins | U.S. 385, Deadwood | 605/584–1009 | fax 605/584–1009 | $15–$18, $25 cabins.

Mount Rushmore KOA–Palmer Gulch Lodge. This huge commercial campground on Route 244 west of Mount Rushmore offers shuttles to the mountain, bus tours, and car rentals. You can use any of three hot tubs and two pools. There are also furnished cabins and primitive camping cabins. Flush toilets. Full hookups, partial hookups (electric and water), dump station. Drinking water, guest laundry, showers. Fire grates, picnic tables, food service. Electricity, public telephone. Service station. Play area, swimming (2 pools). | 500 sites (130 with full hookups, 192 with partial hookups), 85 cabins | 12620 Rte. 244, Hill City | 605/574–2525 | fax 605/574–2574 | $22–$30 | May–Sept.

★ **Whistler Gulch Campground.** In a forested canyon overlooking the town of Deadwood, this well-developed campground—and its modern log lounge—has a spectacular view. Flush toilets. Full hookups. Drinking water, guest laundry, showers. Fire grates, picnic tables. Electricity, public telephone. General store. Play area, swimming (pool). | 126 sites (97 with full hookups) | U.S. 85 S, Deadwood | 605/578–2092 or 800/704–7139 | fax 605/578–2094 | $20–$30 | May–Sept.

WIND CAVE CAMPGROUNDS

	Total # of sites	# of RV sites	# of hook-ups	Drive-to sites	Hike-to sites	Flush toilets	Pit/chemical toilets	Drinking water	Showers	Fire grates	Swimming	Boat access	Playground	Dump station	Ranger station	Public telephone	Reservation possible	Daily fee per site	Dates open
INSIDE THE PARK																			
Elk Mountain Campground	75	75	0	•						•						•	•	$6–12	Apr.–Oct.
NEAR THE PARK																			
Custer Crossing Campground	20	20	20	•	•			•	•	•					•	•	•	$15–18	Y/R
Mt. Rushmore KOA	500	500	322	•		•		•	•	•	•		•	•		•	•	$22–30	May–Sept.

Shopping

Wind Cave National Park Bookstore. The only retail establishment on park grounds, this bookstore sells trail maps, guides to the Black Hills, and books on the geology and history of Wind Cave and neighboring Jewel Cave. | Wind Cave Visitor Center, U.S. 385 | 605/745-4600 | Closed Nov.–Mar.

Essential Information

ATMS: Wells Fargo Bank | 101 S. Chicago St., Hot Springs | 605/745-4120.

AUTOMOBILE SERVICE STATIONS: Big D Oil Company | 381 U.S. 16, Custer | 605/673-2262.
Norton's Sinclair | 1845 University Ave., Hot Springs | 605/745-3219.

POST OFFICES: Custer Post Office | 643 Mount Rushmore Rd., Custer, 57730 | 605/673-4248.
Hot Springs Post Office | 146 N. Chicago St., Hot Springs, 57747 | 605/745-4117.

YELLOWSTONE NATIONAL PARK
NORTHWESTERN WYOMING

East Entrance: 52 mi west of Cody, WY on U.S. 14/16/20. South entrance: 53 mi north of Jackson, WY on U.S. 89/191/287. West Entrance: U.S. 20 at West Yellowstone, MT. North Entrance: U.S. 89 at Gardiner, MT. Northeast Entrance: 2 mi west of Cooke City, MT on U.S. 212.

A "window on the earth's interior" is how one geophysicist described Yellowstone National Park, and it's true that few places in the world can match Yellowstone National Park's collection of accessible wonders, from rainbow-color hot springs to thundering geysers. As you visit the park's hydrothermal areas, you'll be walking on top of the Yellowstone Caldera—a 28-by-47-mi collapsed volcanic cone, which last erupted about 600,000 years ago. The park's geyser basins, hot mud pots, fumaroles (steam vents), and hot springs are kept bubbling by an underground pressure cooker filled with magma.

Yellowstone's appeal is as strong today as it was in 1872, when the region became the country's first national park. The lure for the more than 3 million people who visit annually is the park's diversity of wildlife. Long known for its elk and buffalo herds, Yellowstone is once again home to North American wolves thanks to an experimental repopulation program.

PUBLICATIONS

One of the best historical references is Lee Whittlesey's *Yellowstone Place Names*, a detailed narrative about the park's many sights and sites. A much more critical history is Alston Chase's controversial *Playing God in Yellowstone*, which chronicles a century of government mismanagement. The classic geological, ecological, and human history of the park is *The Yellowstone Story*, two volumes by Aubrey L. Haines. For more information on geology, read William R. Keefer's *The Geologic Story of Yellowstone National Park*. Three other excellent titles are *Roadside History of Yellowstone Park*, by Winfred Blevins; *Yellowstone Ecology: A Road Guide*, by Sharon Eversman and Mary Carr; and *Roadside Geology of the Yellowstone Country*, by William J. Fritz.

When to Visit

SCENERY AND WILDLIFE

Yellowstone's scenery is astonishing any time of day, though the play of light and shadow makes the park most appealing in early morning and late afternoon. That is exactly when you should be out looking for wildlife, as most are active around dawn and dusk. May and June are the best months for seeing baby bison, moose, and other young arrivals.

Spring and early summer find the park covered with wildflowers, while autumn is a great time to visit because of the vivid reds and golds of the changing foliage. Winters visitors are the ones who see the park at its most magical, with steam billowing from geyser basins to wreath trees in ice, and elk foraging close to roads transformed into ski trails.

HIGH AND LOW SEASON

Most people visit Yellowstone in summer, when warm days give way to brisk evenings. You'll find the biggest crowds—*really big* crowds—from mid-July to mid-August. There are fewer people in the park the month or two before and after this peak season, but there are also fewer dining and lodging facilities open. There's also a bit more rain, especially at the lower elevations. Except for holiday weekends, there are few visitors in winter. You must plan ahead if you want to visit during this time, as snowy conditions mean most roads are closed to most vehicles from early November to early May. Remember that snow is possible the entire year at high elevations such as Mount Washburn.

Average High/Low Temperature (°F) and Monthly Precipitation (in inches)

	JAN.	FEB.	MAR.	APR.	MAY	JUNE
YELLOWSTONE	29/10	34/13	40/17	49/26	60/34	70/41
	1.10	.75	1.10	1.20	2.0	2.0
	JULY	AUG.	SEPT.	OCT.	NOV.	DEC.
	80/47	78/45	67/37	56/29	38/19	30/12
	1.50	1.40	1.30	1.0	1.0	1.0

FESTIVALS AND SEASONAL EVENTS

WINTER

Feb.: **Buffalo Bill Birthday Ball.** Hundreds of folks don their turn-of-the-20th-century attire and dance in Cody until the wee hours in this celebration of William F. Cody's birthday. | 307/587–2297.

SPRING

Mar.: **Winter Carnival.** A traditional parade downtown kicks off this snowy celebration in Red Lodge. Other events include a costume contest, a firehose race, and a treasure hunt for the kids. | 406/446–1718.

World Snowmobile Expo. Top-notch racing is combined with a sneak peek at next year's hot models. The SnowWest SnoCross attracts racers to West Yellowstone from throughout the snowbelt. | 406/646–7701.

SUMMER

June–Aug.: **Cody Nite Rodeo.** Some western towns host a rodeo now and then, but come summer Cody has one every night. The action includes bronco busting and bull riding. | 307/587–5155.

Aug.: **Burnt Hole Rendezvous.** At a primitive camp near West Yellowstone you can learn about pre-1840s crafts, try your hand at tomahawk and knife throwing, and enjoy Native American dancers. | 406/646–7110.

FALL

Sept.: **Old Settler's Days.** Celebrating Livingston's pioneer history, this event in Clyde Park includes an art show, a quilt display, and entertainment. | 406/686–4796.

Nearby Towns

Wyoming has three gateways into Yellowstone: Cody to the east and Jackson and Dubois on the south. Named for William F. "Buffalo Bill" Cody, the town of **Cody** sits near the park's

Nineteenth-century souvenir hunters prowled around Yellowstone with shovels and axes, hacking up and prying out pieces of ornamental rock and mineral deposits.

East Entrance. Situated at the mouth of the Shoshone Canyon (where the north and south forks of the Shoshone River join), Cody is a good base for hiking trips, horseback riding excursions, and white-water rafting on the North Fork of the Shoshone or the Clarks Fork of the Yellowstone. Cody is also home to one of the region's finest museums—the Buffalo Bill Historical Center, sometimes called the "Smithsonian of the West." Because of its proximity to two national parks, Grand Teton and Yellowstone, **Jackson** is the busiest community in the region in summer. It has the widest selection of dining and lodging options. The least well known gateway to the national parks, the little town of **Dubois** is a great base if you want to stay far from the madding crowds. Both lead to the park's South Entrance. For more on Jackson and Dubois, *see* Grand Teton National Park.

The most popular gateway from Montana—particularly in winter—is **West Yellowstone,** near the park's West Entrance. This is where the open plains of southwestern Montana and northeastern Idaho come together along the Madison River Valley. Affectionately known among winter recreationists as the "snowmobile capital of the world," this town of 1,000 is also a good place to go for fishing, horseback riding, and downhill skiing. There's also plenty of culture, as this is where you'll find the Museum of the Yellowstone. As the only entrance to Yellowstone that's open the entire year, **Gardiner** is always bustling. The town's Roosevelt Arch has marked the park's North Entrance since 1903, when President Theodore Roosevelt dedicated it. The Yellowstone River slices through town, beckoning fishermen and rafters. The town of 800 has quaint shops and good restaurants. To the north of Gardiner is **Livingston,** a town of 7,500 known for its charming historic district.

With both Yellowstone and the Absaroka-Beartooth Wilderness at its back door, the village of **Cooke City** is a good place for hiking, horseback riding, mountain climbing, and other outdoor activities. Some 50 mi to the east, **Red Lodge** provides a lot more options for dining and lodging. At the base of the Beartooth Mountains, the town is one of Montana's premier ski destinations. These communities guard the Northeast Entrance, least used of all entry points to the park. But it's by far the most spectacular entrance. Driving along the Beartooth Scenic Byway between Red Lodge and Cooke City you'll cross the southern tip of the Beartooth range, literally in the ramparts of the Rockies.

INFORMATION

Cody Country Chamber of Commerce | 836 Sheridan Ave., WY 82414 | 307/587–2297 | fax 307/527–6228 | www.codychamber.org. **Cooke City Chamber of Commerce** | Box 1071, Cooke City, MT 59020 | 406/838–2495 | www.lewisclark.org. **Dubois Chamber of Commerce** | 616 West Ramshorn, Dubois, WY 82513 | 307/455–2556 | www.duboiswyoming.org. **Gardiner Chamber of Commerce** | 222 Park St., Box 81, Gardiner, MT 59030 | 406/848–7971 | www.gardinerchamber.com. **Jackson Chamber of Commerce** | 990 W. Broadway, Jackson, WY 83001 | 307/733–3316 | fax 307/733–5585 | www.jacksonholeinfo.com. **Livingston Chamber of Commerce** | 208 W. Park St., MT 59047 | 406/222–0850 | www.livingston.avicom.net. **Park County Travel Council (Cody)** | 836 Sheridan Ave., Box 2777, Cody, WY 82414 | 307/587–2297 | www.pctc.org. **Red Lodge Chamber of Commerce** | 601 N. Broadway, Red Lodge, MT 59068 | 406/446–1718 | www.redlodge.com. **West Yellowstone Chamber of Commerce** | 30 Yellowstone Ave., West Yellowstone, MT 59758 | 406/646–7701 | www.westyellowstonechamber.com.

LAKE LORE

Yellowstone Lake has 110 mi of shoreline. In winter you can sometimes spot a coyote attempting to outsmart an otter as it surfaces through a spot in a lake that has not frozen over.

Exploring Yellowstone

PARK BASICS

Contacts and Resources: Yellowstone Association | Box 117, Yellowstone National Park, WY 82190 | 307/344–2293. **Yellowstone National Park** | Box 168, Mammoth, WY 82190 | 307/344–7381, 307/344–2386 TDD | fax 307/344–2005 | www.nps.gov/yell.

Hours: Depending on the weather, Yellowstone is generally open late April to October and mid-December to early March. From mid-October to late April only one road—from the Northeast entrance at Cooke City to the North entrance at Gardiner—is open to wheeled vehicles; other roads are used by over-snow vehicles.

Fees: Entrance fees of $20 per car and $15 per visitor arriving on a bus, motorcycle, or snow-mobile entitle visitors to seven days in both Yellowstone and Grand Teton. An annual pass to the two parks costs $40.

Getting Around: The best way to keep your bearings in Yellowstone is to remember that the major roads form a figure-eight. It doesn't matter at which point you begin, as you can hit most of the major sights if you follow the entire route. The 370 mi of public roads in the park are both a blessing and a curse. They provide easy access to extraordinary sights, but that means you'll encounter many motor homes pulled over on narrow shoulders so that the occupants can photograph grazing elk or buffalo cows with their calves. The roads are often poorly maintained and riddled with potholes. Work on the roads may mean you'll encounter periodic closures; check with park rangers for information on road repairs.

All roads except those between Mammoth Hot Springs and the North Entrance and Cooke City and the Northeast Entrance are closed to wheeled vehicles from mid-October to early late April; they are only open to over-snow vehicles from mid-December to mid-March. Remember that roads don't open at the same time. The road from Mammoth Hot Springs to Norris generally opens mid-April. The West Entrance opens in mid-April, while the East and South entrances open early May. The last to open is the road from Tower Falls to Canyon Village, which sees its first traffic at the end of May.

Permits: Fishing permits are required if you want to take advantage of Yellowstone's abundant lakes and streams. Live bait is not allowed, and for all native species of fish, a catch and release policy stands. Anglers 16 and older must purchase a 10-day permit for $10 or a season permit for $20; Those 12 to 15 need a free permit, and those 11 and under do not need a permit but must be supervised by an adult. All camping outside of designated campgrounds requires a free backcountry permit. Horseback riding also requires a free permit. All permits are available at all ranger stations and visitor centers.

Public Telephones: Public telephones are near visitor centers and major park attractions.

Rest Rooms: Public rest rooms may be found at all visitor centers. They are also located at Old Faithful Village beside the Hamilton Store and at Snow Lodge and the Old Faithful Inn, in Tower-Roosevelt beside the Hamilton Store, and in Madison and West Thumb near the information station and winter warming hut.

Accessibility: Yellowstone has long been a Park Service leader in providing for people with disabilities. Rest rooms with sinks and flush toilets designed for those in wheel-chairs are in all developed areas except Norris and West Thumb, where more rustic facilities are available. Accessible campsites and rest rooms are at Bridge Bay, Canyon Village, Madison, and Grant Village campgrounds, while accessible campsites are found at both Lewis Lake and Slough Creek campgrounds. Ice Lake has an accessible backcountry campsite. An accessible fishing platform is about 3.5 mi west of Madison at Mount Haynes Overlook. For details, contact the accessibility coordinator at 307/344–2018 or 307/344–2386 (TDD).

Emergencies: In case of emergency, dial 911 or 307/344–7381. There are ranger stations in Canyon Village, Fishing Bridge, Grant Village, Lake Village, Mammoth Hot Springs, and Old Faithful Village. There are also three clinics in Yellowstone. Lake Clinic, behind the Lake Hotel, is open mid-May to mid-October 8:30–8:30. Mammoth Clinic, next to the post office in Mammoth Hot Springs, is open weekdays 8:30–1 and 2–5. Old Faithful Clinic, in the rear of the parking lot behind Old Faithful Inn, is open mid-May to mid-October 8:30–5.

Lost and Found: You can turn in any found item or search for a lost object at any ranger station or visitor center.

Good Tours

YELLOWSTONE IN ONE DAY

If you have just one day in Yellowstone, there's no way you can see everything. Concentrate on a single area of the park. If you're entering through the North or Northeast entrance, begin at dawn looking for wolves and other animals in Lamar Valley, then head to **Tower-Roosevelt** and take a horseback ride into the surrounding forest. After your ride, continue west to **Mammoth Hot Springs,** where you can hike the **Lower Terrace Interpretive Trail** past Liberty Cap and other strange, brightly colored limestone formations. If you drive 1.5 mi south of the visitor center you will reach the **Upper Terrace Drive,** where you'll be treated to close-ups of hot springs. In the late afternoon, drive south, keeping an eye out for wildlife as you go—you're almost certain to see elks, buffalos, and possibly even a bear. When you reach **Old Faithful,** you can place the famous geyser into context by walking the 1.5-mi **Geyser Hill Loop** or a variety of other trails. Since you've come all this way, you will probably want to join the throngs waiting for the next eruption. Do it from the deck of the **Old Faithful Inn,** a building that certainly deserves a bit of your exploring time.

If you enter the park from the south or west, it makes sense to focus on the geyser basins around Old Faithful, Norris Geyser, and the Grand Canyon of the Yellowstone. Start with an early morning trip to **Old Faithful,** as the trails here are frequently visited by elk before the crowds arrive. After exploring the area head north, taking a detour onto the Firehole Lake Drive to see Great Fountain Geyser. When you reach **Norris Geyser Basin,** walk 0.25 mi out to Steamboat Geyser, the world's tallest of its kind (it seldom erupts; the last time was in 2000). You can easily spend all afternoon at Norris enjoying the sights and poking through the geyseriana at Norris Museum, or you can head east to **Canyon Village** to hike the trails in the late afternoon.

If you're arriving from the east, start with sunrise at **Lake Butte,** then spend the early morning viewing wildlife such as buffalo, elk, deer, coyotes, and trumpeter swans in Hayden Valley. Drive counterclockwise around Grand Loop Road to morning sightseeing at **Canyon Village,** viewing the spectacular **Grand Canyon of the Yellowstone.** In early afternoon stop at **Old Faithful,** then head southeast to **Yellowstone Lake** for a late afternoon boat ride at Bridge Bay and an elegant dinner at the **Lake Yellowstone Hotel.**

YELLOWSTONE IN TWO DAYS

On your first day enter the park through the East Gate, heading over Sylvan Pass. Take a break at **Fishing Bridge** (the ice cream at the Hamilton Store is great on a hot day) and watch for the grizzly bears that like to fish in this area. Stop for lunch at the **Lake Yellowstone Hotel** before turning north through Hayden Valley to **Canyon Village.** There you can view the **Grand Canyon of the Yellowstone** from Inspiration Point or Artist Point, then take a hike along the canyon rim. Spend the night at Canyon Village in either the Dunraven or Cascade Lodges.

On your second day travel west from Canyon Village to Madison. If this is your last day in the park turn south at Madison toward Old Faithful Village, spending the morning exploring **Norris Geyser Basin.** Then continue on south to **Old Faithful** and have lunch at the **Old Faithful Inn** or the **Old Faithful Snow Lodge.** Plan to spend the afternoon exploring the Old Faithful Geyser Basin and spend the night in either the Inn or the Snow Lodge before you head south and then east over Craig Pass to **Grant Village** before heading east back to your starting point.

Attractions

PROGRAMS AND TOURS

Yellowstone offers a busy schedule of guided hikes, evening talks, and campfire programs. Check *Discover Yellowstone,* the newsletter available at all entrances and visitor centers, for dates and times.

Campfire Programs. Gather around to hear tales about Yellowstone's fascinating history, with hour-long programs on topics ranging from the return of the bison to 19th-century photographers. Events are held at campgrounds in Bridge Bay, Canyon, Madison, and Mammoth Hot Springs. | June–Aug., nightly 9 and 9:30.

Grub Steak Expeditions and Tours. These tours, ranging from half a day to several days in length, focus on photography, geology, history, wildlife, and other topics. They're led by a former Yellowstone park ranger, professional photographer, and retired teacher. | Box 1013, Cody, WY 82414 | 307/527–6316 or 800/527–6316 | www.grubsteaktours.com | $200–$300.

Xanterra Parks and Resorts. The company that runs most of the concessions in the park offers bus, boat, horseback and stagecoach tours of Yellowstone in summer and skiing, snowmobiling, and snowshoeing treks in winter. | Box 165, Mammoth Hot Springs, Yellowstone, WY 82190 | 307/344–7901 | www.travelyellowstone.com.

Yellowstone Alpen Guides. You can choose from six one-day tours of Yellowstone, Grand Teton, and the surrounding area. Tours are conducted in comfortable motor coaches that pick you up at your hotel or campground. | 555 Yellowstone Ave., West Yellowstone, MT | 406/646–9374 | www.yellowstoneguides.com | $40–$50 | Apr.–mid-Oct.

Yellowstone Institute. This nonprofit organization, housed in log cabins in Lamar Valley, offers a wide range of summer and winter courses about the ecology, history, and wildlife of Yellowstone. Search with a historian for the trail the Nez Perce Indians took in their flee from the U.S. Army a century ago, or get tips from professional photographers on how to get the perfect shot of a trumpeter swan. Facilities are fairly primitive—guests do their own cooking and camp during some of the courses—but prices are reasonable. Some programs are specifically designed for young people and families. | North Park Rd., between Tower-Roosevelt and Northeast Entrance | 307/344–2294 | www.yellowstoneassociation.org/institute | Year-round, programs vary with season.

SCENIC DRIVES

Blacktail Deer Plateau Drive. Keep an eye out for coyotes on this dirt road that traverses sagebrush-covered hills and forests of lodgepole pines. The entrance is east of Mammoth Hot Springs.

East Entrance Road. Crossing the Absaroka Range, this 16-mi drive meanders through the park's most beautiful alpine setting. As you reach the top of Sylvan Pass you'll have spectacular views of Yellowstone Lake.

Firehole Lake Drive. About 8 mi north of Old Faithful Village, the 3-mi road takes you past Great Fountain Geyser, which shoots out jets of water that occasionally reach as high as 200 ft. If you're touring the park in winter, watch for bison along this one-way road.

Northeastern Grand Loop. A 19-mi segment of Grand Loop Road running between Canyon Village and Roosevelt Falls, this byway passes some of the park's finest scenery, twisting beneath a series of leaning basalt towers 40–50 ft high. That behemoth to the east is 10,243-ft Mount Washburn.

South Entrance Road. The sheer black lava walls of the Lewis River Canyon make this a memorable drive. Turn into the parking area at the highway bridge for a close-up view of the spectacular Lewis River Falls, one of the park's most-photographed sights.

Upper Terrace Loop Drive. Limber pines as old as 500 years line this 1.5-mi loop near Mammoth Hot Springs. You'll also spot a variety of mosses growing through white travertine, composed of lime deposited here by the area's hot springs.

West Entrance Road. An especially good choice for a sunset drive, this road follows the Madison River for 14 mi. In winter you'll see lots of bison and elk, and occasionally even swans.

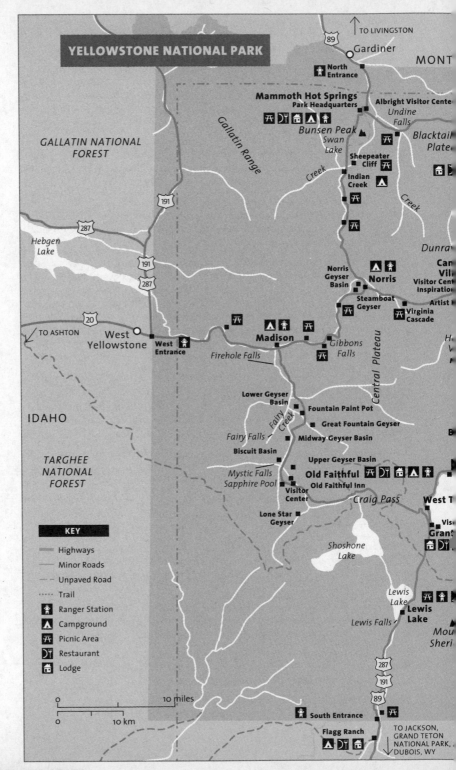

YELLOWSTONE NATIONAL PARK

TO LIVINGSTON

89

Gardiner

MONT

North
Entrance

Mammoth Hot Springs
Park Headquarters

Albright Visitor Cente

Undine
Falls

Bunsen Peak

Blacktai
Plate

Swan
Lake

Sheepeater
Cliff

Indian
Creek

GALLATIN NATIONAL
FOREST

Gallatin Range

Creek

Creek

Dunra

191

287

Norris
Geyser
Basin

Norris

Can
Vil

Visitor Cent
Inspiratio

Hebgen
Lake

191

287

Steamboat
Geyser

Artist

Virginia
Cascade

20

TO ASHTON

West
Yellowstone

West
Entrance

Madison

Gibbons
Falls

Central Plateau

H
V

Firehole Falls

IDAHO

Lower Geyser
Basin

Fairy Creek

Fountain Paint Pot

Great Fountain Geyser

Fairy Falls

Midway Geyser Basin

Biscuit Basin

Upper Geyser Basin

B

Old Faithful

Craig Pass

West T

Vis

Grant

TARGHEE
NATIONAL
FOREST

Mystic Falls
Sapphire Pool

Visitor
Center

Old Faithful Inn

Lone Star
Geyser

Shoshone
Lake

KEY

Highways

Minor Roads

Unpaved Road

Trail

Ranger Station

Campground

Picnic Area

Restaurant

Lodge

Lewis
Lake

Lewis
Lake

Lewis Falls

Mou
Sheri

287

191

89

0   10 miles

0   10 km

South Entrance

Flagg Ranch

TO JACKSON,
GRAND TETON
NATIONAL PARK,
DUBOIS, WY

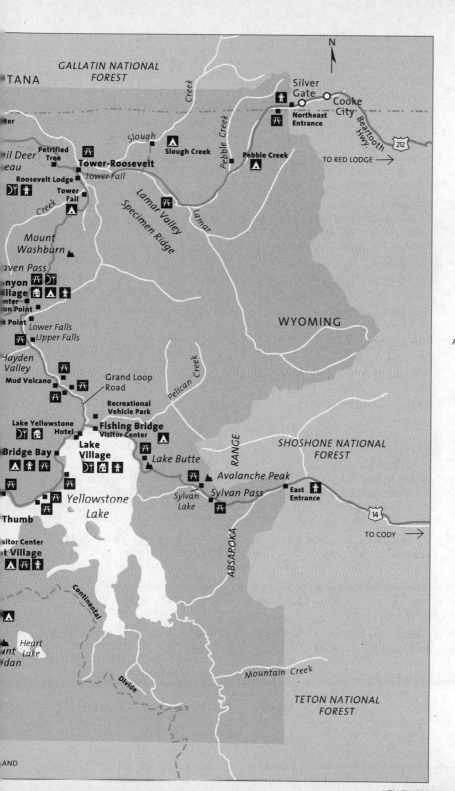

YELLOWSTONE
NATIONAL PARK

EXPLORING
ATTRACTIONS NEARBY
DINING
LODGING
CAMPING AND RV
FACILITIES
SHOPPING
ESSENTIAL
INFORMATION

SIGHTS TO SEE

Albright Visitor Center. Serving as bachelor quarters for cavalry officers from 1886 to 1918, this red-roof building now holds a museum with exhibits on the early inhabitants of the region and a theater showing films about the history of the park. | Mammoth Hot Springs | 307/344–2263 | June–Aug., daily 8–7; Sept., daily 9–6; Oct.–May, daily 9–5.

Back Basin. There are several geysers in this area, the most famous being the Steamboat Geyser. Although it performs only periodically, when it does it shoots a stream of water nearly 400 ft. Echinus Geyser erupts roughly every hour. | Grand Loop Rd. at Norris.

Canyon Visitor Center. Located in Canyon Village, the center has an exhibit about bison dealing with the history of the animals and their current status in Yellowstone. | Canyon Village | 307/242–2550 | June–Sept., daily 8–7.

Fishing Bridge Visitor Center. With a distinctive stone-and-log design, this building, dating from 1931, has been designated a National Historic Landmark. It has exhibits on birds and other wildlife found in Yellowstone. | East Entrance Road, 1 mi from Grand Loop Rd. | 307/242–2450 | June–Aug., daily 8–7; Sept., daily 9–6.

★ **Grand Canyon of the Yellowstone.** A cascading waterfall and rushing river carved this 24-mi-long canyon. The red and ochre canyon walls are topped with emerald-green forest. The best view of the falls is from Artist Point. | Great Loop Rd. at Canyon Village.

Grant Village Visitor Center. This visitor center on the shores of Lake Yellowstone is closest to the park's South Entrance. Here you can see a video on the role of fire in Yellowstone. | Grant Village | 307/242–2650 | June–Aug., daily 8–7; Sept., daily 9–6.

Lake Butte. Reached by a spur road heading east from Fishing Bridge, this wooded promontory rising 615 ft above Yellowstone Lake is a prime spot for watching the sunset. | 2 mi east of Fishing Bridge on East Entrance Rd.

Lake Yellowstone Hotel. Completed in 1891, this historic structure is the oldest lodging in any national park. It got its columned entrance in 1903, when the original bland facade was reworked by the architect of the Old Faithful Inn. It's now on the National Register of Historic Places. | At the far end of Lake Village Rd. | 307/344–7901 | Closed late Sept.–mid-May.

Lower Geyser Basin. Shooting more than 150 ft, the Great Fountain Geyser is the most spectacular sight at this basin. Less impressive but more regular is White Dome Geyser, which shoots from a 20-ft-tall cone. You'll also find pink mud pots and blue pools at Fountain Paint Pots. | Midway between Madison and Old Faithful Village on Grand Loop Rd.

Madison Information Center. This information center is in a National Historical Landmark. It provides general park information. | Grand Loop Rd. at West Entrance Rd. | 307/344–2821 | June–Aug., daily 8–7; Sept.–early Oct., daily 9–5.

Mammoth Hot Springs. Multicolored travertine terraces formed by slowly escaping hot water mark this unusual geological formation. Elk are frequent visitors, as they graze nearby. | Mammoth Hot Springs.

Midway Geyser Basin. Called "Hell's Half Acre" by writer Rudyard Kipling, Midway Geyser Basin is actually an extension of the Lower Geyser Basin. Here you'll find the richly colored pools of Grand Prismatic Spring and Excelsior Geyser, two of the largest hot springs in the world. | Midway between Madison and Old Faithful Village on Grand Loop Rd.

Museum of the National Park Ranger. Called the Norris Soldier Station when it housed soldiers who guarded the park from 1886 to 1916, this historic building screens a movie that tells the story of the National Park Service. | Grand Loop Rd. at Norris | June–Oct. daily 10–5.

★ **Norris Geyser Basin.** The oldest such basin in Yellowstone, Norris is constantly changing. Some geysers might suddenly stop flowing, but others soon blow and hiss to life. Here

THE WORLD'S FIRST NATIONAL PARK

The remote region now encompassed by Yellowstone National Park was inhabited by humans as long as 10,000 years ago. By the time Euro-Americans arrived on the scene, the Shoshone were the predominant people of the area, though the harshness of the climate and landscape kept their numbers few. John Colter, formerly of the Lewis and Clark expedition, was the first white visitor to Yellowstone, in 1807–08. Trappers such as Jim Bridger followed, and reports of northwestern Wyoming's wonders began to make their way into print. Many of these were dismissed as being too fantastic to be true. Prospectors had a go at Yellowstone starting in the 1870s, but it proved far richer in scenic wonders than in precious metals.

In 1871 and 1872, Ferdinand V. Hayden of the U.S. Geological Survey led an official expedition of scientists, along with painter Thomas Moran and photographer William H. Jackson, into the area. The beauty depicted in Moran's watercolors and Jackson's photographs, and the findings detailed in Hayden's report to Congress, were so impressive that they inspired a movement to protect the wilderness of northwestern Wyoming. Yellowstone became the world's first national park in 1872.

The federal government learned its earliest lessons in national park management here. In 1886, following 14 years of poor civilian management of Yellowstone National Park, the Cavalry was called in to take over. Thinking they would be there only a short time, the troops initially established Camp Sheridan, near the base of the Mammoth Terraces. Later they built Fort Yellowstone in the Mammoth area. You can still visit the original red-roofed buildings, which now serve as park offices and a visitor center.

Some of the first people to visit the American West as tourists were attracted by Yellowstone, and the park accommodated them in grand style. When it opened in 1891, Lake Yellowstone Hotel was typical of the luxurious hotels built by railroad companies for their passengers. Backed by the Northern Pacific Railroad, the hotel stood on the north end of Yellowstone Lake, where Indians and mountain men were known to have gathered for many years. In the lobby of the pale yellow hotel, afternoon chamber music still provides a refreshing reminder of old-style tourism in the wilderness. So popular was the park that Lake Yellowstone Hotel was soon joined by other lodgings. Built on the former site of an earlier lodging called "The Shack," the Old Faithful Inn was designed to reflect its natural surroundings. Around 40 workers, most of them railroad trestle builders, raised the hotel in the winter of 1903–1904. The rhyolite stone and tall, straight lodgepole pines used to construct the hotel were taken from the surrounding land, and trees twisted by disease became the ornamental railings and details of the interior. When completed, the 140-room inn became the standard by which future national parks lodges would be judged. Rough-paneled, equipped with sinks but not private baths, rooms in the original portion of the hotel are much as they were back then. The inn was expanded to its present size in 1915 and 1927.

you'll discover colorfully named features such as Whirligig Geyser, Whale's Mouth, Emerald Spring, and Arch Steam Vent. | Grand Loop Rd. at Norris.

★ **Old Faithful.** The mysterious plumbing of Yellowstone has lengthened Old Faithful's cycle over the years, but the geyser still spouts the same amount of water—in a plume that sometimes reaches to 180 ft—every 92 minutes or so. Sometimes it doesn't shoot so high, but in those cases the eruption usually lasts longer. To find out when Old Faithful is next expected to erupt, check at any of the visitor centers. Marked hiking trails and cross-country ski trails in the Upper Geyser Basin converge at Old Faithful. | Old Faithful Bypass Rd.

Old Faithful Inn. It's hard to imagine that any work could be accomplished when snow and ice blanket the region, but this historic hotel was constructed in winter 1903. The inn is as massively rustic as the Lake Yellowstone Hotel is elegant. Other than two flat-roof wings added in 1913 and 1927, it looks much as it did when it opened in 1904. | Old Faithful Bypass Rd. | 307/344–7311 | Closed late Oct.–early May.

Old Faithful Visitor Center. Located 600 ft from Old Faithful, this A-frame building has one of the best views in the park. A 100-seat theater shows a movie about geysers. The backcountry office and a clinic are located nearby. | Old Faithful Bypass Rd. | 307/545–2750 | June–Aug., daily 8–7; Sept., daily 8–6; Oct., daily 9–5.

Petrified Tree. This ancient redwood is reached by a short walk from a parking area. | Grand Loop Rd., 1 mi west of Tower-Roosevelt.

Porcelain Basin. The ground bulges and belches from the underground pressure at this geothermal field. Here you'll find bubbling pools, some milky white and others ringed in orange because of the minerals in the water. The area is reached by a mile-long boardwalk. | Midway between Madison and Old Faithful Village on Grand Loop Rd.

Specimen Ridge. The world's largest concentration of petrified trees can be found in this ridge in the park's northeast corner. There are also plenty of unusual fossils, such as impressions of leaves left behind on rocks. | East of Tower-Roosevelt on Northeast Entrance Rd.

West Thumb. The unusual name of this small geyser is derived from its location along a digit-like projection of Yellowstone Lake. This area, full of geysers and hot springs, is reached by a short boardwalk loop. | Grand Loop Rd., 22 mi from South Entrance.

West Thumb Information Station. This little log cabin houses a bookstore run by the nonprofit Yellowstone Association. In winter it serves as a warming hut. | West Thumb | Late May–Sept., daily 9–5.

Yellowstone Lake. North America's largest mountain lake, Yellowstone Lake was formed when glaciers that once covered the region receded. Many visitors head here for the excellent fishing, but others simply like to sit along the shore. In winter you can sometimes see otters and coyotes stepping gingerly on the ice at the lake's edge. | Grand Loop Rd. between Fishing Bridge and Grant Village.

Sports and Outdoor Activities

BICYCLING

More and more visitors tour Yellowstone by bicycle every year, despite the heavy traffic, large vehicles, and rough, narrow, shoulderless roads that make it somewhat hazardous. To be on the safe side, ride single-file and wear a helmet and reflective clothing. Remember that some routes, such as those over Craig Pass, Sylvan Pass, and Dunraven Pass, are especially challenging because of their steep climbs. Bikes are prohibited on most hiking trails and in the backcountry.

Blacktail Plateau Drive. Running parallel to Grand Loop Road, this gravel road is one-way for cars traveling east, but bicycles are allowed in both directions. The west entrance to the road is 9 mi east of Mammoth Hot Springs, while the east entrance is 2 mi west of Tower-Roosevelt. Mountain bikes are recommended.

Fountain Freight Road. Fountain Flats Drive departs the Grand Loop Road south of the Nez Perce picnic area and follows the Firehole River to a trailhead 1.5 mi away. From there, the Fountain Freight Road continues along the old roadbed, giving bikers access to the Sentinel Meadows Trail and the Fairy Falls Trail. The total length of the route is 5.5 mi. Mountain bikes are recommended; you'll share Fountain Flats Drive with one-way automobile traffic and the Freight Road with hikers.

Natural Bridge Road. Leading off Grand Loop Road at Bridge Bay, this easy 1-mi bike loop leads to Natural Bridge, formed when Bridge Creek cut through a 50-ft cliff.

Old Faithful to Morning Glory Pool. This paved 2-mi trail starts at the Hamilton Store at Old Faithful Village, loops near Old Faithful Geyser, and ends at Morning Glory Pool. The entire route is through a geyser basin, so stay on the trail. Watch for elk and buffalo.

Old Gardiner Road. Automobiles and bicycles share this gravel road running parallel to U.S. 89 between Mammoth Hot Springs and the nearby town of Gardiner; cars can only travel north, but bikes are allowed in both directions. The 5-mi route has views of the Gardiner River. Mountain bikes are recommended.

BOATING

Yellowstone Lake attracts the most attention, but the park is filled with pristine waters waiting to be explored. Most of its 175 lakes, except for Sylvan Lake, Eleanor Lake, and Twin Lakes, are open for boating. You must purchase a $5 permit for nonmotorized boats and floatables or a $10 permit for motorized boats at Bridge Bay Marina, Grant Village visitor center, Lewis Lake Campground, or Mammoth Hot Springs visitor center.

Xanterra Parks and Resorts. Watercraft from rowboats to powerboats are available at Bridge Bay Marina by the hour or by the day for trips on Yellowstone Lake. You can even rent 22- and 34-ft cabin cruisers. | Grand Loop Rd., 2 mi south of Lake Village | 307/344–7311 | Mid-June–mid-Sept., 8 AM–9:30 PM | $5.50–$25.

FISHING

Anglers flock to Yellowstone on Memorial Day weekend, when fishing season begins. By the time the season ends in November, thousands have found a favorite spot along the park's rivers and streams. Many varieties of trout—cutthroat, brook, lake, and rainbow—along with grayling and mountain whitefish inhabit Yellowstone's waters. Popular sport fishing opportunities include the Gardner and Yellowstone Rivers as well as Soda Butte Creek, but the top fishing area in the region is Madison River, known to fly fishermen throughout the country. Catch and release is the general policy. Get a copy of the fishing regulations at any visitor center. Fishing supplies are at all Hamilton stores; the biggest selection is at Bridge Bay.

HIKING

There are 1,210 mi of trails and 85 trailheads in Yellowstone. Trails are occasionally closed due to weather conditions or bear activity.

Avalanche Peak Trail. Starting across from a parking area, the difficult 4-mi, four-hour round-trip climbs 2,150 ft to the peak's 10,566-ft summit, from which you'll see the rugged Absaroka Mountains running north and south. Some of these peaks have patches of snow year-round. Look around the talus and tundra near the top of Avalanche Peak for alpine wildflowers and butterflies. Don't try this trail before late June or after early September—it may be covered in snow. At any time of year, carry a jacket: the winds at the top are strong. | 19 mi east of Lake Junction on the north side of East Entrance Rd.

Back Basin Trail. A 1.5-mi loop passes Emerald Spring, Steamboat Geyser, Cistern Spring (which drains when Steamboat erupts), and Echinus Geyser. The latter erupts 50–100

YELLOWSTONE
NATIONAL PARK

EXPLORING
ATTRACTIONS NEARBY
DINING
LODGING
CAMPING AND RV
FACILITIES
SHOPPING
ESSENTIAL
INFORMATION

ft every 35–75 minutes, making it Norris's most dependable big geyser. | Grand Loop Rd. at Norris.

Beaver Ponds Loop Trail. This 2½-hour, 5-mi round-trip starts at Liberty Cap, climbing 400 ft through 0.5 mi of spruce, fir, and open meadows, past beaver ponds (look for their dams) and spectacular views of Mammoth Terraces on the way down. Moose, antelope, and occasional bears may be sighted. | Grand Loop Rd. at Old Gardiner Rd.

Biscuit Basin Trail. This 2.5-mi round-trip trail goes via a boardwalk across the Firehole River to colorful Sapphire Pool. | 3 mi north of Old Faithful Village off Grand Loop Rd.

Brink of the Lower Falls Trail. To hear and feel the Yellowstone River's power, follow the steep side trails into the Grand Canyon of the Yellowstone. This trail switchbacks 0.5 mi one way from the parking area, 600 ft down to the brink of Lower Falls. | 1.75 mi south of Inspiration Point on North Rim Trail.

Bunsen Peak Trail. Past the entrance to Bunsen Peak Road, the moderately difficult 4-mi, three-hour round-trip climbs 1,300 ft to Bunsen Peak for a panoramic view of Blacktail Plateau, Swan Lake Flats, the Gallatin Mountains, and the Yellowstone River valley (use a topographical map to locate these landmarks). | Grand Loop Rd., 1.5 mi south of Mammoth Hot Springs.

Fountain Paint Pot Nature Trail. This easy 0.5-mi loop boardwalk passes hot springs, colorful mud pots, and dry fumaroles at its highest point. | Grand Loop Rd. at Firehole Lake Dr.

Geyser Hill Loop. Head counterclockwise around the Old Faithful boardwalk 0.7 mi from the visitor center, crossing the Firehole River to reach this 1.3-mi loop. On your left is violent, but infrequent, Giantess Geyser. Normally active only a few times each year, Giantess spouts 100–250 ft high for five to eight minutes once or twice hourly for 12 to 43 hours. A bit farther on your left is Doublet Pool, two adjacent springs whose complex ledges and deep blue waters are highly photogenic. Near the loop's end on your right, Anemone Geyser starts as a gentle pool, overflows, bubbles, and finally erupts, 10 ft or more, repeating the cycle every three to eight minutes. | Old Faithful Village.

Heart Lake–Mount Sheridan Trail. The very difficult 24-mi, 13-hour round-trip provides one of the park's top overnight backcountry experiences. After traversing 5.5 mi of partly burned lodgepole pine forest, the trail descends into Heart Lake Geyser Basin, reaching Heart Lake at the 8-mi mark. This is one of Yellowstone's most active thermal areas—the biggest geyser here is Rustic Geyser, which erupts 25–30 ft about every 15 minutes. Circle around the northern tip of Heart Lake and camp at one of five designated backcountry sites on the western shore (remember to get your permit beforehand). Leave all but the essentials here as you take on the 3-mi, 2,700-ft climb to the top of 10,308-ft Mount Sheridan. To the south, if you look very carefully, are the Tetons. | 1 mi north of Lewis Lake on the east side of South Entrance Rd.

Lower Terrace Interpretive Trail. This trail leads past the most outstanding features of the multicolor, steaming Mammoth Hot Springs. Start at Liberty Cap, at the area's north end, named for its resemblance to Revolutionary War patriots' caps. Head uphill on the boardwalks past bright and ornately terraced Minerva Spring. Alternatively, drive up to the Lower Terrace Overlook on Upper Terrace Drive and take the boardwalks down past New Blue Springs (which, inexplicably, is no longer blue) to the Lower Terrace. This route works especially well if you can park a second vehicle at the foot of Lower Terrace. Either route should take about an hour. | Grand Loop Rd., 0.7 mi west of Mammoth Hot Springs.

Morning Glory Pool Trail. An easy 1.5-mi (one-way) boardwalk trek from Old Faithful visitor center passes stately Castle Geyser, which possesses the biggest cone in Yellowstone. It currently erupts every 10 to 12 hours, to heights of 90 ft for up to an hour. Morning Glory Pool, named for its resemblance in shape and color to the flower, is a testament to human ignorance: tons of coins and trash tossed into it over the years clogged its vent, causing brown and green bacteria to spread across the surface. | Old Faithful Village.

Mud Volcano Interpretive Trail. This 0.75-mi round-trip trail loops gently around seething, sulfuric mud pots with such names as Sizzling Basin and Black Dragon's Cauldron and around Mud Volcano itself. | 10 mi south of Canyon Village on Grand Loop Rd.

Mystic Falls Trail. From the Biscuit Basin boardwalk's west end, a trail gently climbs 1 mi (3.5 mi round-trip from Biscuit Basin parking area) through heavily burned forest to the lava-rock base of 70-ft Mystic Falls. It then switchbacks up Madison Plateau to a lookout with the park's least-crowded view of Old Faithful and Upper Geyser Basin. | 3 mi north of Old Faithful Village off Grand Loop Rd.

★ **North and South Rim Trails.** Offering great views of the Grand Canyon of the Yellowstone, the 1.75-mi North Rim Trail runs from Inspiration Point to Chittenden Bridge, while the 2-mi South Rim Trail starts at Chittenden Bridge and makes its way to Artist Point. You can wander along small sections of these trails, or combine them into a three-hour trek through on of the park's most breathtaking areas. Especially scenic is the 0.5-mi section of the North Rim Trail from the Brink of the Upper Falls parking area to Chittenden Bridge that hugs the rushing Yellowstone River as it approaches the canyon. Both trails are partly paved and fairly level. | 1 mi south of Canyon Village.

Observation Point Loop. A 2-mi round-trip from the Old Faithful visitor center, this trail leaves Geyser Hill Loop boardwalk and becomes a trail shortly after the boardwalk crosses the Firehole River; it circles a picturesque overview of Geyser Hill with Old Faithful Inn as a backdrop. | Old Faithful Village.

Old Faithful Geyser Loop. Old Faithful and its environs in the Upper Geyser Basin are rich in short-walk options, starting with three connected loops that depart from Old Faithful visitor center. The 0.75-mi loop simply circles the benches around Old Faithful, filled nearly all day long in summer with tourists. Currently erupting approximately every 92 minutes, Yellowstone's most frequently erupting big geyser—although not its largest or most regular—reaches heights of 100 to 180 ft, averaging 130 ft. | Old Faithful Village.

Osprey Falls Trail. The 4-mi, two-hour round-trip starts near the entrance of Bunsen Peak Road. A series of switchbacks drops 800 ft to the bottom of Sheepeater Canyon and the base of the Gardner River's 151-ft Osprey Falls. As at Tower Fall, the canyon walls are basalt columns formed by ancient lava flow. | Bunsen Peak Rd. 3 mi south of Mammoth Hot Springs.

Porcelain Basin Trail. At Norris Geyser Basin, this 0.75-mi, partial-boardwalk loop leads from the north end of Norris Museum through whitish geyserite stone and past extremely active Whirligig and other small geysers. | Grand Loop Rd. at Norris.

Shoshone Lake–Shoshone Geyser Basin Trail. This 22-mi, 11-hour moderately difficult overnight trip combines several shorter trails. The trail starts at DeLacy Creek Trail, gently descending 3 mi to the north shore of Shoshone Lake. On the way, look for sandhill cranes and browsing moose. At the lake turn right and follow the North Shore Trail 8 mi, first along the beach and then through lodgepole forest. Make sure you've reserved one of the several good backcountry campsites. Take time to explore the Shoshone Geyser Basin, reached by turning left at the fork at the end of the trail and walking about 0.25 mi. The next morning turn right at the fork, follow Shoshone Creek for 2 mi, and make the gradual climb over Grant's Pass. At the 17-mi mark the trail crosses the Firehole River and divides; take a right onto Lone Star Geyser Trail and continue past this fine coned geyser through Upper Geyser Basin backcountry to Lone Star Geyser Trailhead. | 8 mi east of Old Faithful Village on north side of Grand Loop Rd.

Skyline Trail. In the park's northwest corner, the extremely difficult 16.5-mi, 10-hour trail is another combination trail that climbs up and over numerous peaks whose ridgelines mark the park's northwest boundary before looping sharply back down via Black Butte Creek. | U.S. 191, 25 mi north of West Yellowstone.

Slough Creek Trail. Starting at Slough Creek Campground, this trail climbs steeply for the first 1.5 mi before reaching expansive meadows and prime fishing spots, where moose are

YELLOWSTONE
NATIONAL PARK

EXPLORING
ATTRACTIONS NEARBY
DINING
LODGING
CAMPING AND RV
FACILITIES
SHOPPING
ESSENTIAL
INFORMATION

common and grizzlies occasionally wander. From this point the trail, now mostly level, meanders another 9.5 mi to the park's northern boundary. | 7 mi east of Tower-Roosevelt off Northeast Entrance Rd.

Specimen Creek Trail. Starting at Specimen Creek Trailhead, follow this trail 2.5 mi and turn left at the junction, passing petrified trees to your left past the junction. At the 6.5-mi mark, turn left again at the fork and start climbing 1,400 ft for 2 mi up to Shelf Lake, one of the park's highest bodies of water at 9,200 ft. Stay at one of the pair of designated backcountry campsites. Just past the lake is the beginning of Skyline Trail, which follows the ridge with steep drop-offs on either side. Watch for bighorn sheep as you approach Bighorn Peak's summit. The trail's most treacherous section is just past the summit, where it drops 2,300 ft in the first 2.5 mi of descent; make sure you take a left where the trail forks at the big meadow just past the summit to reach Black Butte Creek Trail. Moose and elk can be seen along this last 2.5-mi stretch. | U.S. 191, 27 mi north of West Yellowstone.

★ **Storm Point Trail.** Well-marked and mostly flat, this 1.5-mi loop leaves the south side of the road for a perfect beginner's hike out to Yellowstone Lake. The trail rounds the western edge of Indian Pond, then passes moose habitat on its way to Yellowstone Lake's Storm Point, named for its frequent afternoon wind storms and crashing waves. Heading west along the shore, you're likely to hear the shrill chirping of yellow-bellied marmots, rodents that grow as long as 2 ft. Also look for ducks, pelicans, and trumpeter swans. | 3 mi east of Lake Junction on East Entrance Rd.

Tower Fall Trail. From the lookout point at Tower Fall, this 0.5-mi (round-trip) trail switchbacks down through pine trees matted with luminous green wolf lichen to the base of the waterfall. There, you will find yourself at the northern end of the Grand Canyon of the Yellowstone. | Grand Loop Rd., 3 mi south of Tower-Roosevelt.

Uncle Tom's Trail. Spectacular and very strenuous, this 700-step trail descends 500 ft from the parking area to the roaring base of the Lower Falls of the Yellowstone. Much of this walk is on steel sheeting, which can have a film of ice in early morning or in spring and fall. | Artist Point Dr., about 0.5 mi east of Chittenden Bridge.

HORSEBACK RIDING

About 50 area outfitters lead horse-packing trips and trail rides into Yellowstone. Expect to pay about $1,000 for a four-night backcountry trip, including meals, accommodations, and guides. A guide must accompany all horseback riding trips.

★ **Gunsel Horse Adventures.** Sign up with Gunsel for a 4-, 7-, or 10-day pack trip into the backcountry. The trips are a great way to see moose, bear, deer, elk, and wolves in Yellowstone's forests. You need bring only your sleeping bag and personal effects. | Box 1575, Rapid City, SD 57709 | 605/343–7608 | www.gunselhorseadventures.com | $200 per day | June–Sept.

Rimrock Dude Ranch. Outfitter Gary Fales has been leading multiday pack trips into Yellowstone for decades, operating out of his dude ranch west of Cody. His favorite trip heads into the Southeast corner of Yellowstone by leaving from near the East Entrance, riding up Eagle Creek and into Thorofare country before following the South Fork of the Shoshone River out of the park area. Rimrock also does trips into the northeast area of Yellowstone, visiting Frost Lake and the Lamar Valley. Trips last a week and include backcountry camping, fishing, hiking, and horseback activities. | 2728 Northfork Route, Cody, WY 82414 | 307/587–3970 | fax 307/527–5014 | www.rimrockranch.com | $1,350 per week MAP | May–Sept.

Ron Dube's Wilderness Adventures. Ron and Carol Dube take 3-, 5-, 7-, and 10-day trips into Yellowstone. | Box 167, Wapiti, WY 82450 | 307/527–7815 | fax 307/527–6084 | www.huntinfo.com | $1000 3-day trip; $5,280 8-day trip. MAP | June–Aug.

Wilderness Pack Trips. You can take a one-day ride, or participate in a multiday pack trip in the northeast region of the park, primarily the Lamar Valley. | Box 1146, Livingston, MT 59047 | 406/222–5128 | www.wildernesspacktrips.com | $175 per day up to $2,150 for multiday trips | July–Sept.

Xanterra Parks and Resorts. One- and two-hour horseback trail rides leave from three sites in the park: Mammoth Hot Springs, Roosevelt Lodge, and Canyon Village. Children must be at least 8 years old and 48 inches tall; kids 8–11 must be accompanied by someone age 16 or older. | Box 165, Mammoth Hot Springs, Yellowstone, WY 82190 | 307/344–7901 | www.travelyellowstone.com | $26–$40 | May–Sept.

SKIING AND SNOWSHOEING

Even those who have visited Yellowstone many times in summer would never recognize it after the first snow. Rocky outcroppings are smoothed over by snow. Waterfalls that tumbled over the sides of canyons have been transformed into jagged sheets of ice. Canyon Village, West Thumb, and Madison have warming huts that are intermittently staffed; huts at Indian Creek, Fishing Bridge, and Old Faithful Village are unstaffed. All are open 24 hours.

Lone Star Geyser Trail. This easy trail, which leads 2.3 mi to the Lone Star Geyser, starts south of Keppler Cascades. You can ski back to the Old Faithful area. | Shuttle at Old Faithful Snow Lodge; trailhead 3.5 mi west of Old Faithful Village.

Madison River Bridge Trails. Five ski trails begin at the Madison River Bridge trailhead. The shortest is 4 mi and the longest is 14 mi. | West Entrance Rd., 6 mi west of Madison.

Xanterra Parks and Resorts. At Mammoth Hot Springs Hotel and Old Faithful Snow Lodge you can rent skis and snowshoes. Skier shuttles run from Mammoth Hotel to Mammoth Terraces and to Tower and from Old Faithful Snow Lodge to Fairy Falls. | Mammoth Hot Springs Hotel or Old Faithful Snow Lodge | 307/344–7901 | www.travelyellowstone.com | $11–$28 | Dec.–Mar.

SNOWMOBILING

Snowmobiling is one of the most exhilarating ways to experience Yellowstone, but you'll have to abide by the following regulations. You must have a reservation, a guide and a four-stroke snowmobile. There are daily limits to the number of riders in the park.

Flagg Ranch Resort. The resort south Yellowstone rents snowmobiles that you can ride directly into the park. They also provide transportation to the Jackson area snowmobile trails. | John D. Rockefeller Jr. Memorial Pkwy., 2 mi south of Yellowstone National Park boundary | www.flaggranch.com | 307/543–2861 | Snowmobile rentals $140–$155 per day | Dec.–Mar.

Pahaska Teepee. Just outside the East Entrance, this full-service resort rents four-stroke snowmobiles and leads guided treks into Yellowstone. | 183 Yellowstone Hwy., Cody, WY | 307/527–7701 or 800/628–7791 | www.pahaska.com | $155 for snowmobile rentals, $250 per day for guide service | Year-round, ski equipment Dec.–Mar.

Rendezvous Snowmobile Rentals. You can rent a two-stroke or a four-stroke machine at this West Yellowstone business. | 415 Yellowstone Ave., West Yellowstone, MT | 406/646–9564 or 800/426–7669 | $99–$129 | Dec.–Apr.

Xanterra Parks and Resorts. This outfitter rents snowmobiles from Mammoth Hotel and Old Faithful Snow Lodge. | Mammoth Hot Springs Hotel or Old Faithful Snow Lodge | 307/344–7311 | www.travelyellowstone.com | $115 per day | mid-Dec.–early Mar.

Attractions Nearby

For additional attractions nearby, *see* Grand Teton National Park.

Beartooth Nature Center. See eye-to-eye with mountain lions and pumas at this nonprofit center sheltering injured animals that cannot be released in the wild. There are year-round educational programs and a summer camp for children. | 2nd Ave. East, Red Lodge, MT | 406/446–1133 | www.beartoothnaturecenter.org | $6 | June–Sept., daily 10–5:30; Oct.–May, daily 10–2.

YELLOWSTONE
NATIONAL PARK

EXPLORING
**ATTRACTIONS
NEARBY**
DINING
LODGING
CAMPING AND RV
FACILITIES
SHOPPING
ESSENTIAL
INFORMATION

★**Buffalo Bill Historical Center.** Five museums rolled into one, this sprawling complex includes the Whitney Gallery of Western Art, the Plains Indian Museum, the Cody Firearms Museum, the Draper Museum of Natural History, and the Harold McCracken Research Library. Plan to spend at least four hours, or even more if you're really interested in the Old West. | 720 Sheridan Ave., Cody, WY | 307/587–4771 | www.bbhc.org | $15 | May, daily 8–8; June–Sept., daily 7 AM–8 PM; Oct., daily 8–5; Nov.–Mar., Thurs.–Mon. 10–2; Apr., daily 10–5.

Grizzly Discovery Center. This nonprofit center is devoted to protecting the natural habitat of grizzlies and other endangered species. Get up close to the bears and grey wolves that live here. | 201 S. Canyon, West Yellowstone, MT | 406/646–7001 or 800/257–2570 | $8.50 | Oct.–Apr., daily 8–dusk; May–Sept., daily 8 AM–8:30 PM.

Peaks to Plains Museum. Artifacts from the early days of fur trading and mining are on display at this small museum. | 224 S. Broadway, Red Lodge, MT | 406/446–3667 | $3 | Weekdays 8–5, weekends 1–5.

Dining

In Yellowstone

Canyon Lodge Cafeteria. American/Casual. The park's busiest lunch spot, it serves such traditional American fare as meat loaf and hot turkey sandwiches. For early risers, it also has a full breakfast menu. | Canyon Village | 307/344–7311 | $6–$12 | AE, D, DC, MC, V | Closed mid-Sept.–early June.

Grant Village Restaurant. American. The floor-to-ceiling windows of this lakeshore restaurant provide views of Yellowstone Lake through the thick stand of pines. The most contemporary of the park's restaurants, it makes you feel at home with pine-beam ceilings and cedar-shake walls. Try the fettuccine primavera. | Grant Village | 307/344–7311 | Reservations essential | $14–$22 | AE, D, DC, MC, V | Closed late Sept.–late May.

Lake Lodge Cafeteria. American. This casual eatery, popular with families, serves up hearty lunches and dinners. It also has a full breakfast menu. | Lake Village Rd. | 307/344–7311 | $6–$12 | AE, D, DC, MC, V | Closed mid-Sept.–early June.

Lake Yellowstone Hotel Dining Room. American. This double-colonnaded dining room off the hotel lobby will have you gazing through the big square windows overlooking the lake. As this is one of the park's most elegant restaurants, it tends to attract a clientele that tends to be older and more sedate. Try the prime rib prepared in a dry marinade of thyme, rosemary, and garlic. Reservations are required for dinner. | Lake Village Rd. | 307/344–7311 | $12–$30 | AE, D, DC, MC, V | Closed early Oct.–mid-May.

Mammoth Hot Springs Dining Room. American. A wall of windows overlooks an expanse of green that was once a military parade and drill field at Mammoth Hot Springs. The art deco–style restaurant, decorated in shades of gray, green, and burgundy, has an airy feel with its bentwood chairs. One entrée is pan-fried trout topped with pecans and lemon butter. | Mammoth Hot Springs | 307/344–7311 | Reservations essential | $15–$28 | AE, D, DC, MC, V | Closed mid-Oct.–mid-Dec. and mid-Mar.–mid-May.

Old Faithful Inn Dining Room. American. Lodgepole walls and ceiling beams, a giant volcanic rock fireplace graced with a painting of Old Faithful, and green-tinted windows etched with scenes from the 1920s set the mood here. Soaked in history, the restaurant has always been a friendly place where servers find time amid the bustle to chat with diners. Don't pass up the grilled chicken breast glazed with honey-lemon butter. | Old Faithful Village | 307/344–7311 | Reservations essential | $15–$28 | AE, D, DC, MC, V | Closed late Oct.–early May.

Old Faithful Lodge Cafeteria. American/Casual. Serving family-friendly fare like lasagna and pizza, this outdoor eatery has some of the best views of Old Faithful. | South end of Old Faithful Bypass Rd. | 307/344–7311 | Closed mid-Sept.–mid-May | $5–$10 | AE, D, DC, MC, V.

★ **Old Faithful Snow Lodge.** American. From the wood and leather chairs with etched figures of park animals to the intricate lighting fixtures that resemble snow-capped trees, you'll appreciate the atmosphere of Old Faithful Snow Lodge. The huge windows give you a view of the Old Faithful area, and you can sometimes see the famous geyser as it erupts. Aside from Mammoth Hot Springs Dining Room, this is the only place in the park where you can enjoy a relaxing lunch or dinner in winter. The French onion soup will warm you up on a chilly afternoon. | Old Faithful Village | 307/344–7311 | $12–$28 | AE, D, DC, MC, V | Closed mid-Oct.–mid-Dec., mid-Mar.–mid-May.

Picnic Areas. There are 49 picnic areas in the park, ranging from secluded spots with a couple of tables to more popular stops with a dozen or more tables and more amenities. Only nine—Snake River, Grant Village, Spring Creek, Nez Perce, Old Faithful East, Bridge Bay, Cascade Lake Trail, Norris Meadows, and Yellowstone River—have fire grates. Only gas stoves may be used in the other areas. None has running water; all but a few have pit toilets.

Firehole River. The Firehole River rolls past and you might see elk grazing along its banks. This picnic area has 12 tables and one pit toilet. | Grand Loop Rd., 3 mi south of Madison.

Fishing Bridge. This picnic area has 11 tables within the busy Fishing Bridge area. It's walking distance to the amphitheater, store, and visitor center. | East Entrance Road, 1 mi from Grand Loop Rd.

Gibbon Meadows. You are likely to see elk or buffalo along the Gibbon River from one of nine tables at this area, which has a handicapped accessible pit toilet. | Grand Loop Rd., 3 mi south of Norris.

Pony Express Snack Shop. American/Casual. When the kids are hungry, stop by this spot off the lobby of Old Faithful Inn for burgers, sandwiches, and french fries any time of day. | Old Faithful Village | 307/344–7311 | $5–$10 | AE, D, DC, MC, V | Closed early Oct.–late May.

Roosevelt Lodge Dining Room. American. At this rustic log cabin set in a pine forest, the menu ranges from barbecued ribs and Roosevelt beans to hamburgers and french fries. For a real western adventure, call ahead to join a chuck-wagon cookout that includes an hour-long trail ride or a stagecoach ride. | Tower-Roosevelt | 307/344–7311 | $12–$30 | AE, D, DC, MC, V | Closed early Sept.–early June.

Terrace Grill. American/Casual. Although the exterior looks rather elegant, this restaurant in Mammoth Hot Springs only serves fast food. | Mammoth Hot Springs | 307/344–7311 | $5–$10 | AE, D, DC, MC, V | Closed late Sept.–mid-May.

Near the Park

For more dining options (in Jackson and Dubois), *see* Grand Teton National Park.

Cassie's Supper Club. Steak. Steaks and prime rib are the mainstays at this Cody institution. The hometown favorite is the stuffed mushrooms. Early in the evening the atmosphere is low-key, but at about 9 the band warms up and the dancing begins. | 214 Yellowstone Ave., Cody, WY | 307/527–5500 | $15–$30 | AE, D, MC, V.

Old Piney Dell. Steak. A favorite among locals, this small restaurant on the banks of Rock Creek has good steak and Wiener schnitzel as well as daily pasta specials. It's part of the Rock Creek Resort. | Rock Creek Rd., Red Lodge, MT | 406/446–1196 | $16–$23 | AE, D, DC, MC, V | No lunch Mon.–Sat.

Proud Cut Saloon. Steak. Some of the best prime rib in northwest Wyoming is served in this cowboy-style restaurant and bar decorated with historic photographs of cowboys working at the huge TA Ranch near Meeteetse. Owner Del Nose says he serves "kick-ass cowboy cuisine," which means steak, shrimp, crab legs, and ½-pound cheeseburgers. | 1227 Sheridan Ave., Cody, WY | 307/527–6905 | $13–$22 | D, MC, V.

Stephan's. Contemporary. This intimate restaurant adorned with burlap tablecloths is a Cody favorite. Good bets are seafood like shrimp, halibut, and tuna, as well as specialties like filet mignon stuffed with Gorgonzola, sun-dried tomatoes, and Portobello mushrooms. | 1367 Sheridan Ave., Cody, WY | 307/587–8511 | $12–$20 | AE, D, MC, V.

Trapper's Inn. American. This popular restaurant recalls the days of the mountain men with massive breakfasts featuring sourdough pancakes, biscuits, and rolls. Trout with eggs will fortify you for a day exploring Yellowstone. Lunch standouts include buffalo burgers on sourdough bread, while there are plenty of hearty steaks for dinner. | 315 Madison Ave., West Yellowstone, MT | 406/646–9375 | $12–$18 | AE, D, MC, V.

Yellowstone Mine. American. Decorated with mining equipment such as picks and shovels, this is a place for casual family-style dining. Town residents come in for the steaks and seafood. | U.S. 89, Gardiner, MT | 406/848–7336 | $10–$20 | AE, D, MC, V | No lunch.

Lodging

In Yellowstone

Park lodgings range from two of the national park system's magnificent old hotels to simple cabins to bland modern motels. Make reservations at least two months in advance for July and August for all park lodgings. Old Faithful Snow Lodge and Mammoth Hot Springs Hotel are the only accommodations open in winter; rates are the same as in summer.

Canyon Lodge & Cabins. The clusters of plain pine-frame cabins and two motel-style lodges here are among Yellowstone's more mundane lodgings. The cabins, all duplex or fourplex units, have beds but no other amenities to speak of. Most have no bath and share a bathhouse. In the much newer lodges, pine wainscoting and brown carpets set the tone. The lodges stand among the trees above the Grand Canyon of the Yellowstone at the farthest edge of Canyon Village. 3 restaurants. Horseback riding. Bar. Shop. | North Rim Dr. at Grand Loop Rd. | 307/344–7901 | fax 307/344–7456 | www.travelyellowstone.com | 81 lodge rooms, 532 cabins | $63–$148 | AE, D, DC, MC, V | Closed Sept.–May.

Grant Village Lodge. The six lodge buildings that make up this facility have rough pine exteriors painted gray and rust that remind you of a big-city motel. These rooms are basic with few features beyond a bed and night stand. 2 restaurants. Bar. Shops. | Grant Village | 307/344–7901 | fax 307/344–7456 | www.travelyellowstone.com | 300 rooms | $101–$115 | AE, D, DC, MC, V | Closed mid-Sept.–late May.

Lake Lodge. Among the pines not far from Lake Yellowstone Hotel, this lodge was built in 1920 but has been modernized so that the accommodations resemble those of a fairly standard motel. There are views of the lake from the lodge, but not the rooms. Bar. Shops. | At the far end of Lake Village Rd. | 307/344–7901 | fax 307/344–7456 | www.travelyellowstone.com | 186 rooms | $60–$122 | AE, D, DC, MC, V | Closed mid-Sept.–mid-June.

★ **Lake Yellowstone Hotel.** This distinguished hotel, dating from 1891, attracts mainly older visitors who gather in the sun room each afternoon to gaze at the lake. Others browse behind the etched green windows of the expensive Crystal Palace gift shop or warm themselves on chilly days before the tile-mantel fireplace in the colonnaded lobby. Rooms have brass beds and solid pine furniture. Set unobtrusively in the trees behind the Lake Yellowstone Hotel are pine-paneled cabins that provide more basic accommodations. Restaurant. Bar. Shops. | At the far end of Lake Village Rd. | 307/344–7901 | fax 307/344–7456 | www.travelyellowstone.com | 158 rooms, 102 cabins | $89–$191 | AE, D, DC, MC, V | Closed late Sept.–mid-May.

Mammoth Hot Springs Hotel and Cabins. Built in 1937, this hotel has a spacious art deco lobby. The rooms are smaller and less elegant than those at the park's other two historic hotels, but the hotel is less expensive and usually less crowded. In summer these rooms can get awfully hot, but you can open the window. The cabins, set amid lush lawns, are the nicest inside the park. This is one of only two lodging facilities open in winter. Some rooms have hot tubs, a nice amenity after a day of cross-country skiing. 2 restaurants. Horseback riding. Bar. Shops. | Mammoth Hot Springs | 307/344–7901 | fax 307/344–7456 | www.travelyellowstone.com | 97 rooms, 67 with bath; 2 suites; 115 cabins, 76 with bath | $66–$300 | AE, D, DC, MC, V | Closed mid-Sept.–mid-Dec. and mid-Mar.–late May.

★ **Old Faithful Inn.** When you breeze through the iron-latched front door, you enter a log-pillared lobby of one of the most distinctive national park lodgings. From the main building, where many gables dot the wood-shingled roof, you can watch Old Faithful erupt. Rooms in the 1904 "Old House" have brass beds, and some have deep claw-foot tubs. Rooms in the 1927 west wing contain antique cherry-wood furniture, while those in the 1913 east wing have Stickley furniture and tremendous four-poster beds. First-floor rooms in the Old House are the hotel's noisiest, so ask for a rear-facing room if you are seeking some quiet. 2 restaurants. Bar. Shops. No phones in some rooms. | Old Faithful Village | 307/344–7901 | fax 307/344–7456 | www.travelyellowstone.com | 327 rooms, 6 suites | $79–$371 | AE, D, DC, MC, V | Closed late Oct.–early May.

Old Faithful Lodge Cabins. Not to be confused with the Old Faithful Snow Lodge, these small, plain cabins are a good budget option. Restaurant. Shop. | At far end of Old Faithful Bypass Rd. | 307/344–7901 | fax 307/344–7456 | www.travelyellowstone.com | 97 cabins | $56–$80 | Closed mid-Sept.–mid-May | AE, D, DC, MC, V.

★ **Old Faithful Snow Lodge.** Built in 1998, this massive structure brings back the grand tradition of park lodges by making good use of heavy timber beams and wrought-iron accents in the distinctive facade. Inside you'll find soaring ceilings, natural lighting, and a stone fireplace in the spacious lobby. Nearby is a long sitting room where writing desks and overstuffed chairs invite you to linger. Rooms combine traditional style with modern amenities. This is one of only two lodging facilities open in winter, when the only way to get here is over-snow vehicles. Restaurant. Cross-country skiing, snowmobiling. Bar. No a/c. | At far end of Old Faithful Bypass Rd. | 307/344–7901 | fax 307/344–7456 | www.travelyellowstone.com | 95 rooms, 33 cabins | $80–$160 | AE, D, DC, MC, V | Closed mid-Oct.–mid-Dec. and mid-Mar.–May.

Roosevelt Lodge. Near the beautiful Lamar Valley in the park's northeast corner, this simple lodge dating from the 1920s surpasses some of the more expensive options. The rustic accommodations, in nearby cabins set around a pine forest, mean you need to bring your own bedding. You can arrange for horseback or stagecoach rides. Restaurant. Horseback riding. Bar. Shops. | Tower–Roosevelt Junction on Grand Loop Rd. | 307/344–7901 | fax 307/344–7456 | www.travelyellowstone.com | 80 cabins, 12 with bath | $56–$96 | AE, D, DC, MC, V | Closed early Sept.–early June.

Near the Park

For more lodging options (in Jackson and Dubois), *see* Grand Teton National Park.

Cody Guest Houses. These cottages make a great base from which to explore the area. Lovingly restored and elegantly decorated, the Victorian has lace curtains and antique furniture. The Western Lodge, with four bedrooms, has a fireplace and a yard with a barbecue pit. The Annie Oakley and Buffalo Bill cottages both come with a full kitchen. The Garden and Executive Suite apartments have a full kitchen, laundry facilities, and yard with gazebo. Some kitchenettes. Laundry facilities. | 1525 Beck Ave., Cody, WY | 307/587–6000 or 800/587–6560 | fax 307/587–8048 | www.codyguesthouses.com | 30 houses and cottages | $95–$450 | AE, D, MC, V.

Pahaska Teepee Resort. Buffalo Bill's original hideaway in the mountains is 2 mi east of Yellowstone. Most of the small, basic cabins are scattered through a pine forest. For big groups there's a seven-room house complete with a hot tub and a deck with a great view. One of a half dozen lodges along the road to the East Entrance, this one is closest to the park. In winter, the lodge grooms a network of cross-country ski trails and rents skis and

YELLOWSTONE
NATIONAL PARK

EXPLORING
ATTRACTIONS NEARBY
DINING
LODGING
CAMPING AND RV
FACILITIES
SHOPPING
ESSENTIAL
INFORMATION

snowmobiles. Restaurant. Horseback riding. Cross-country skiing, snowmobiling. Bar. No a/c, no room phones. | 183 Yellowstone Hwy., Cody, WY | 307/527–7701 or 800/628–7791 | fax 307/527–4019 | www.pahaska.com | 52 cabins | $90–$140 | D, MC, V.

Pollard Hotel. Buffalo Bill, Calamity Jane, and other legends have stayed at this 1893 landmark in the heart of Red Lodge's historic district. Lovingly restored, it has a balcony that overlooks the gallery and fireplace. Some of the comfortable rooms have mountain views. Restaurant. Some in-room hot tubs. Cable TV. Health club, hot tub. Business services. No smoking. | 2 N. Broadway, Red Lodge, MT | 406/446–0001 or 800/765–5273 | fax 406/446–0002 | www.pollardhotel.com | 35 rooms, 4 suites | $125–$265 | AE, D, MC, V | CP.

Rimrock Dude Ranch. One of the oldest ranches on the North Fork of the Shoshone River, Rimrock is open year-round, offering both snowmobile trips and horseback riding adventures into the surrounding mountains. Lodging is in small cabins with good views of the North Fork Valley. Restaurant. Refrigerators. Pool. Airport shuttle. No a/c | 2728 North Fork Hwy., Cody, WY | 307/587–3970 or 800/208–7468 | fax 307/527–5014 | www.rimrockranch.com | 9 cabins | $1,250 for 7-day minimum | MC, V.

Camping and RV Facilities

In Yellowstone

Yellowstone has a dozen campgrounds scattered around the park. Most campgrounds have flush toilets, and some campgrounds have coin-operated showers and guest laundry. Most campgrounds are operated by the National Park Service and are available on a first come, first served basis. Those campgrounds run by Xanterra—Bridge Bay, Canyon, Fishing Bridge, Grant Village, and Madison—accept bookings in advance. To reserve, call 307/344–7311. Larger groups can reserve space in Bridge Bay, Grant, and Madison from late May through September.

Camping outside designated areas is strictly prohibited, but there are about 300 backcountry sites available all over the park. Permits are free and reservations are $20, regardless of the length of time spent in the park or the number of people in the group. These sites may be reserved in advance by visiting any ranger station or by mail at Backcountry Office, Box 168, Yellowstone National Park, WY 82190.

Bridge Bay. The park's largest campground, Bridge Bay rests in a wooded grove. You can rent boats at the nearby marina, take guided walks, or listen to rangers lecture about the history of the park. Don't expect solitude, as there are more than 400 campsites. Hot showers and laundry are 4 mi north at Fishing Bridge. Flush toilets. Dump station. Drinking water, showers. Fire pits. Public telephone. Ranger station. | 430 tent/RV sites | 3 mi southwest of Lake Village on Grand Loop Rd. | 307/344–7311 | fax 307/344–7456 | www.travelyellowstone.com | $16 | AE, D, DC, MC, V | Late May–mid-Sept.

Canyon. The campground is accessible to Canyon's many short trails, which makes it a hit with families. Near a Laundromat and visitor center. Flush toilets. Drinking water, guest laundry, showers. Fire pits. Public telephone. Ranger station. | 272 tent/RV sites | North Rim Dr., 0.25 mi east of Grand Loop Rd. | 307/344–7311 | fax 307/344–7456 | www.travelyellowstone.com | $16 | AE, D, DC, MC, V | Early June–early Sept.

Fishing Bridge RV Park. Although Fishing Bridge is on Yellowstone Lake, there's no boat access here. Near Bridge Bay Marina, this is the only facility in the park that caters exclusively to recreational vehicles. Because of bear activity in the area, only hard-sided campers are allowed. Liquid propane is available. Flush toilets. Full hookups, dump station. Drinking water, guest laundry, showers. Public telephone. Ranger station. | 340 RV sites | East Entrance Rd. at Grand Loop Rd. | 307/344–7311 | fax 307/344–7456 | www.travelyellowstone.com | $29 | AE, D, DC, MC, V | Mid-May to mid-Sept.

Grant Village. The park's second-largest campground, Grant Village has some sites with great views of Yellowstone Lake. Some of the sites are handicapped accessible. The campground has a boat launch but no dock. Guest laundry. Flush toilets. Dump station. Drinking water, showers. Public telephone. Ranger station. | 425 tent/RV sites | South Entrance Rd., 2 mi south of West Thumb | 307/344–7311 | fax 307/344–7456 | www.travelyellowstone. com | $15 | AE, D, DC, MC, V | Late June–late Sept.

Indian Creek. In a picturesque setting next to a creek, this campground is in the middle of a prime wild-life viewing area. There are some combination sites that can accommodate trailers of up to 45 ft. Pit toilets. Fire pits. | 75 tent/RV sites | 8 mi south of Mammoth Hot Springs on Grand Loop Rd. | 307/344–2017 | $10 | No credit cards | Early June–mid-Sept.

Lewis Lake. It's a bit off the beaten track, which means this campground south of Grant Village is quieter than most. Also, it's a good choice for boaters who don't want to fight the crowds, because it's the only campground besides Bridge Bay and Grant Village that has a boat launch. Pit toilets. Drinking water. Fire pits. Ranger station. | 85 tent/RV sites | 6 mi south of Grant Village on South Entrance Rd. | 307/344–2017 | $10 | No credit cards | Late June–Oct.

Madison. Although it's as large as Canyon, Lewis Lake tends to be a little quieter. Right on the Madison River, there are plenty of hiking trails nearby. The campground can accommodate trailers up to 45 ft. Flush toilets. Dump station. Drinking water. Public telephone. Ranger station. | 280 tent/RV sites | Grand Loop Rd. at Madison | 307/344–7311 | fax 307/344–7456 | www.travelyellowstone.com | $15 | AE, D, DC, MC, V | Early May–mid-Oct.

Mammoth Hot Springs. The sagebrush-covered hillside where Mammoth Hot Springs is located often attracts elk and mule deer. There are plenty of things to do at the nearby visitor center, including evening talks by park rangers. The campground is more exposed than most, so it gets hot on summer days. Flush toilets. Drinking water. Fire pits. Public telephone. Ranger station. | 85 tent/RV sites | North Entrance Rd. at Mammoth Hot Springs | 307/344–2017 | $12 | AE, D, DC, MC, V.

Norris. Because it adjoins the Gibbon River, this campground is a favorite among anglers. Brook trout and grayling are the prizes caught here. The campground can accommodate trailers up to 45 ft. Flush toilets. Drinking water. Ranger station. | 116 tent/RV sites | Grand Loop Rd. at Norris | 307/344–2177 | $12 | No credit cards | Mid-May–late Sept.

Pebble Creek. Near a 10,554-ft peak called the Thunderer, this campground offers some unforgettable views. It's also smaller than most, which means it tends to be a little quieter. It allows trailers up to 45 ft. Pit toilets. Fire pits. | 32 tent/RV sites | Northeast Entrance Rd., 22 mi east of Tower Roosevelt Junction | 307/344–2017 | $10 | No credit cards | June–late Sept.

Slough Creek. Reached by a little-used spur road, this creekside campground is about as far from the beaten path as you can get without actually camping in the backcountry. It's popular among fishing aficionados, who come here for the trout. Pit toilets. Fire pits. | 29 tent/RV sites | Northeast Entrance Rd., 10 mi east of Tower Roosevelt Junction | 307/344–2017 | $10 | No credit cards | Late May–late Oct.

Tower Fall. It's within hiking distance of the roaring waterfall, so this campground gets a lot of foot traffic. It can accommodate shorter trailers. Hot water and flush toilets are at Tower Store rest rooms nearby. Pit toilets. Fire pits. | 32 tent/RV sites | 3 mi southeast of Tower-Roosevelt on Grand Loop Rd. | 307/344–2017 | $10 | No credit cards | Mid-May–Sept.

Near the Park

For additional camping near Yellowstone, *see* Grand Teton National Park.

Flagg Ranch Village. In a wooded area near the Snake River, this sprawling complex is 2 mi from the south entrance of Yellowstone. It has a main lodge with dining room, bar, con-

YELLOWSTONE
NATIONAL PARK

EXPLORING
ATTRACTIONS NEARBY
DINING
LODGING
**CAMPING AND RV
FACILITIES**
SHOPPING
ESSENTIAL
INFORMATION

YELLOWSTONE CAMPGROUNDS

	Total # of sites	# of RV sites	# of hook-ups	Drive-to sites	Hike-to sites	Flush toilets	Pit/chemical toilets	Drinking water	Showers	Fire grates	Swimming	Boat access	Playground	Dump station	Ranger station	Public telephone	Reservation possible	Daily fee per site	Dates open
INSIDE THE PARK																			
Bridge Bay	430	430	0	•		•		•		•		•		•	•	•	•*	$16	May–Sept.
Canyon	272	272	0	•		•		•	•	•					•	•	•	$16	June–Sept.
Fishing Bridge RV Park	340	340	340	•		•		•	•					•	•	•	•	$29	May–Sept.
Grant Village	425	425	0	•		•		•	•	•		•		•	•	•	•	$16	June–Sept.
Indian Creek	75	75	0	•			•			•								$10	June–Sept.
Lewis Lake	85	85	0	•			•	•		•		•			•			$10	June–Oct.
Madison	280	280	0	•		•		•						•	•	•	•	$15	May–Oct.
Mammoth Hot Springs	85	85	0	•		•		•							•	•		$12	Y/R
Norris	116	116	0	•		•		•							•	•		$12	May–Sept.
Pebble Creek	32	32	0	•			•			•								$10	June–Sept.
Slough Creek	29	29	0	•			•			•								$10	May–Oct.
Tower Fall	32	32	0	•			•			•								$10	May–Sept.
NEAR THE PARK																			
Ponderosa	140	140	140	•		•		•	•					•	•		•	$18–30	May–Oct.
Flagg Ranch Village	150	75	75	•		•		•	•	•						•	•	$22–48	May–Sept.
Wagon Wheel	48	40	40	•		•		•	•							•	•	$26–34	MD–Sept.

* In summer only   ** Reservation Fee Charged   Y/R=Year Round
UL=Unlimited   ULP=Unlimited Primitive   LD=Labor Day   MD=Memorial Day

venience store and gas station. Flush toilets. Full hookups. Drinking water, guest laundry, showers. Fire pits, food service. Public telephone. | 150 tent/RV sites | Moran, WY 83013 | 307/733–8761 or 800/443–2311 | $22–$45 | D, MC, V | Mid-May–Sept.

Ponderosa Campground. This campground and RV park has shaded sites. Camp in one of the tepees for a change of pace. Flush toilets. Partial hookups, dump station. Drinking water, guest laundry, showers. Public telephone. General store. Play area. | 140 tent/RV sites, 9 tepees | 1815 8th St., Cody, WY 82414 | 307/587–9203 | $18–$30, $21 tipis | No credit cards | May–Oct.

Wagon Wheel Campground and Cabins. A few blocks west of Yellowstone, this campground has tent and RV sites along with cozy one-, two-, and three-bedroom cabins. Flush toilets. Full hookups. Drinking water, guest laundry, showers. Public telephone. | 408 Gibbon Ave., West Yellowstone, MT 59758 | 406/646–7872 | www.wagonwheelrv.com | 40 RV sites, 8 tent sites, 9 cabins | $26–$34 | No credit cards | Memorial Day–Sept. 15.

Shopping

The oldest national park concessionaire, Hamilton Stores has been serving Yellowstone since 1915. Today the company runs 15 park stores, some of which are interesting destinations themselves. The Old Faithful Lower Store, for example, has a knotty pine porch with benches that beckon tired hikers, as well as an inexpensive and very busy lunch counter. All stores sell souvenirs ranging from the tacky (cowboy kitsch and rubber tom-toms) to the authentic ($60 buffalo-hide moccasins and $200 cowboy coats). From May to September, most stores are open 7:45 AM to 9:45 PM; Mammoth Hot Springs is open year-round. All the stores accept credit cards.

Bridge Bay Marina Store | Bridge Bay Marina | 307/242–7326. **Canyon General Store** | Canyon Village | 307/242–7377. **Fishing Bridge General Store** | Fishing Bridge | 307/242–7200. **Grant Village General Store** | Grant Village | 307/242–7266. **Grant Village Mini Store** | Grant Village | 307/242–7390. **Lake General Store** | Lake Village | 307/242–7563. **Mammoth General Store** | Mammoth Hot Springs | 307/344–7702. **Roosevelt Store** | Tower-Roosevelt | 307/344–7779. **Yellowstone General Store #300** | Old Faithful Village | 307/545–7282. **Yellowstone General Store #301** | Old Faithful Village | 307/545–7237. **Tower Fall Store** | Tower Fall | 307/344–7786. **Yellowstone Nature Store** | Old Faithful Village | 307/344–7757.

Essential Information

ATMS (24-HOUR): Automatic teller machines are at Fishing Bridge General Store, Grant Village General Store, Lake Yellowstone Hotel, Mammoth General Store, Old Faithful Inn, Old Faithful Snow Lodge, Old Faithful Upper Store, Canyon General Store, and Canyon Lodge.

AUTOMOBILE SERVICE STATIONS: Canyon Village Repair Service | Canyon | 406/848–7333 | Closed early Nov.–May. **Fishing Bridge Service Station** | Fishing Bridge | 406/848–7333 | Closed mid-Sept.–mid-May. **Grant Village Service Station** | Grant Village | 406/848–7333 | Closed late Sept.–mid-May. **Mammoth Hot Springs Service Station** | Mammoth Hot Springs | 406/848–7333 | Closed mid-Oct.–early May. **Old Faithful Lower Station** | Old Faithful Village | 406/848–7333 | Closed early Nov.–late Apr. **Old Faithful Upper Station** | Old Faithful Village | 406/848–7333 | Closed late Aug.–late May. **Tower Junction Service Station** | Tower Junction | 406/848–7333 | Closed early Sept.–early June.

POST OFFICES: Canyon Village Post Office | Canyon Village 82190 | 307/242–7323 | Closed early Sept.–mid-May. **Grant Village Post Office** | Grant Village 82190 | 307/242–7338 | Closed early Sept.–mid-May. **Lake Post Office** | Lake Village 82190 | 307/242–7383 | Closed early Sept.–mid-May. **Mammoth Hot Springs Post Office** | Mammoth Hot Springs 82190 | 307/344–7764. **Old Faithful Post Office** | Old Faithful 82190 | 307/545–7252 | Closed early Sept.–mid-May.

YELLOWSTONE
NATIONAL PARK

EXPLORING
ATTRACTIONS NEARBY
DINING
LODGING
CAMPING AND RV
FACILITIES
SHOPPING
ESSENTIAL
INFORMATION

FIELD GUIDE: THE MOUNTAINS AND THE PLAINS

Ecological Communities

Alpine. At elevations over 11,500 ft, the alpine tundra has arctic temperatures, strong winds, and barren stretches. Trees vanish and a meadowland of flowering grasses, mosses, and lichens appears briefly in summer, only to change color with the onset of autumn. The few plants that can survive at these elevations generally resemble mossy clumps with long roots, although many startlingly beautiful wildflowers such as alpine avens, dwarf clover, and the alpine forget-me-not bloom briefly in late June or early July.

Cliffs. Though you may not usually think of them as habitats, cliffs actually support an amazing array of wildlife, including rock wrens, rock squirrels, falcons, swifts, and bighorn sheep. Cliffs are found throughout the mountains and plains.

Forests. Many of the forests found in the mountains and plains region are mixes of pine, spruce, and aspen. Among the trees of the northernmost park—Glacier—conifers are most prevalent, with 15 species at various elevations, including lodgepole pine, ponderosa pine, Douglas fir, western red cedar, Pacific yew, and western hemlock. Lodgepole pine grows in old burns at all elevations. Cedar, yew, and hemlock form dense thickets in low, dark, wet areas on the western side of the Continental Divide. At least 10 broadleaf species are also present in the region's parks, most found at lower elevations. Examples are black cottonwood, quaking aspen, willow, paper birch, alder, and maple. Forests support small mammals like the squirrel, plus deer, elk, moose, the black bear, and the wolverine. Grouses, jays, sparrows, robins, and warblers also thrive in the forest.

Grasslands. Found on plains and plateaus, and in valleys and canyons, grasslands have often suffered from over-grazing of livestock, which has allowed sagebrush, snakeweed and other shrubby species to invade. The best example of unaltered grassland habitat may be found at Badlands National Park. The grasses feed bison, mule deer, pronghorn, bighorn sheep, prairie dogs, and sharptail grouse, some of which in turn feed coyotes, snakes, golden eagles, hawks, and turkey vultures.

Montane. This ecosystem, from 7,000 to 9,000 ft above sea level, is full of slopes, valleys, stands of ponderosa pine, Western wallflowers, and Easter daisies. It supports numerous species of bats, chipmunks, marmots, squirrels, deer, jays, and smaller populations of the rarely seen black bear, mountain lion, and elk.

Riparian. Characterized by an abundance of water, riparian habitat is plentiful throughout the region in all but the Dakota badlands. In the canyons and coulees, stream banks may be lined with cottonwoods where birds build nests. In mountainous areas and grasslands, riparian zones support such wildlife as migrating waterfowl and beaver. Excellent examples of riparian zones are Jackson Lake in Grand Teton, Yellowstone Lake and River in Yellowstone, and Lake McDonald in Glacier.

Subalpine. The subalpine ecosystem, found at elevations of 9,000 to 11,500 ft, straddles the tree line and supports forests of Engelmann spruce, lodgepole pine, aspen, fir, huckleberry, and a plethora of wildflowers. Some of the trees have been stunted and sculpted into bizarre shapes by the wind. They are known as *krummholz* (German for "crooked wood") and often survive for several centuries. The mountain goat, bighorn sheep, elk, grizzly, snowshoe hare, hawk, and eagle live or migrate through the subalpine Rockies.

Fauna

Bald Eagle. There is nothing quite like watching a mature bald eagle ride the thermal updrafts of a mountain range. It doesn't develop its white head and tail until it's at least four years old.

Golden Eagle. With a wingspan measuring as much as 6 ft, the golden eagle is perfection in flight. Jackrabbits, cottontails and carrion make up the diet of this bird, federally protected since 1962.

Mountain Bluebird. This pretty little bird lives a fast-paced life in the forest above 5,000 ft. The male is characterized by its brilliant blue color, while the female is brownish gray with blue tinges on the wings.

Rock Wren. A small gray-black bird with a white chest, the rock wren lives in cliff crevices, nooks, and crannies and paves its nest with small rocks. The bird nests high on cliff faces and sends its melodious song out to hikers.

Western Tanager. Common in coniferous forests, a breeding western tanager is a sight to behold. The male has a bright red head, yellow body and black wings, the color of which tones down in winter, when he loses the distinctive red-colored head. The female is yellow with brown wings.

FISH

Trout. Montana, Wyoming, and Colorado still hold claim to some of America's best blue-ribbon trout streams. Anglers may pursue brook, cutthroat, German brown, lake, or rainbow trout in virtually every state in the region. Black Hills streams are ideal for beginning fisherman, where anglers can fill their creel with German browns.

Walleye. The "Great Lakes" of the Dakotas, created by the giant earth-rolled dams on the Missouri River, support outstanding walleye fishing. The walleye is related to the perch, though it looks more like a pike.

INSECTS

Wasp. This smooth-bodied insect lives throughout the region. It will generally not attack unless the hive is approached or touched. If you are allergic to wasp or bee stings, be sure to talk to your doctor before your trip.

Mosquito. Especially ferocious in Montana, the biting mosquito is female, with a needlelike organ adapted to puncture the skin of animals to suck their blood. Carry plenty of repellent, and bring nets if you plan to camp in the backcountry.

MAMMALS

American Bison. Virtually exterminated by over-hunting in the 19th century, the bison has made a resurgence in the mountains and plains region. Seemingly docile and slow, this unpredictable mammal is, in fact, amazingly agile. Even a one-ton bull can outrun a horse, and in much of the wild West, bison encounters account for more deaths than bear attacks.

Bighorn Sheep. Once on the verge of extinction, this magnificent animal is now relatively commonplace in western parks. Both sexes grow horns, but only the males' curl back around on themselves. The bigger the horns, the older the animal.

Black Bear. Actually black, brown or cinnamon, this bear is the most common in the West. It's about 3 ft tall at the shoulders when on all fours. You won't find one in the Dakotas, unless it's housed at a private tourist attraction.

Grizzly Bear. Yellowstone is home to some 200 of the approximately 850 grizzly bears surviving in the lower 48 states. It is bigger (3.5 ft tall at the shoulders) than the black bear and has a flat-face profile and a pronounced hump between the shoulders. Grizzly fur has a range of colors, from almost-black to light cream.

Elk. The region's most common large mammal, the elk is among its most elusive. You are most likely to see these majestic animals at dawn and dusk in Yellowstone National Park, near Jackson Hole, in Rocky Mountain National Park, and in South Dakota's Custer State Park. In autumn, the mating bugle of a bull elk—who can weigh as much as 700 pounds—can be heard for miles in the wildlands of the West.

Mountain Lion. The mountain lion (also known as the cougar, panther, or puma) is a tawny feline with black-tipped ears and tail. Although smaller than the jaguar, it's one of North America's largest cats. The adult male may be more than 8 ft long and generally weighs 130–150 pounds. The adult female grows to about 7 ft long and weighs 65–90 pounds. These beautiful cats have made a resurgence in the West and can be found throughout the region.

Prairie Dog. Named by a member of the Lewis and Clark expedition for its shrill warning cry like a dog's bark, the prairie dog is prevalent throughout the West. The black-tailed prairie dog is cinnamon in color, inhabits grasslands, and is known to build large underground towns. The white-tailed prairie dog is the largest of the species, has a short white tail, and is yellow in color.

Pronghorn. North America's fastest land mammal, the pronghorn is most often found in large, wide-open spaces. It has been known to run for several miles at 30–35 mph and to hit top speeds of 65 mph. It is often incorrectly called an antelope.

Rocky Mountain Goat. This blunt, square-looking animal has a narrow head with slender, black, shiny horns rising in a backward curve to a length of 10–12 inches. Its coat is white, and it grows a double beard of long hair. With cushioned, skid-proof pads on its hooves, the mountain goat is an extremely sure-footed and agile animal. You'll see these goats above the timberline throughout the Rockies.

Rocky Mountain Wolf. An endangered species re-introduced to Yellowstone in 1995 through a controversial recovery program, the wolf is now thriving.

REPTILES

Rattlesnake. You can't mistake a rattlesnake for much else. When spooked, it will warn you of its presence with a distinctive rattle of its tail. Be aware of your surroundings and give it plenty of room.

Flora

FLOWERS

Lupine. This bright bluish-purple flower blooms throughout the cooler summer months, but it detests the heat. Its leaves are easy to identify, as they spread like fingers from a central point.

Purple Coneflower. This perennial wildflower has a showy, cone-shaped center ringed with a single row of purple petals. The plant grows tall and blooms summer through fall even under adverse conditions. It thrives on sandy soil and full sun or partial shade.

Purple Larkspur. Purple-and-white, this wildflower grows in sandy soil and rises above nearby plants on 2-ft-tall stalks.

Scarlet Gilia. Commonly mistaken for Eaton's penstemon, this red flower has leaves of a narrow, fernlike structure. Flowers point up and have five symmetrical blossoms.

Shooting Star. This delicate "inside-out" flower is one of the first spring flowers to bloom, as early as the end of February. Look for the pink, light purple, or white blossoms in light, dry soil on or near rocky bluffs and especially around limestone.

Wild Rose. This pink flower blooms singly or up to four in a cluster May through July. You'll see it growing up to 6 ft high in moist sites. Rose-hips, the fruit of the wild rose, contain more vitamin C, calcium, phosphorus, and iron than oranges, and can be dried for tea or used for jelly or sauce. The hips are eaten by birds; deer and elk browse the foliage.

GRASSES AND GROUND COVER

Bluestem grass. Before development and climatic changes caused a decline in its growth this tall, bluish grass was among the most widespread of the native plains grasses, sustaining great herds of buffalo, deer, elk, and other animals.

Buffalo grass. This is the only indigenous warm-season turf grass in the area from the Great Plains to Mexico, including most of Texas. Buffalo grass is so named because it was a primary food source of the American buffalo. As a native grass, it survives the harshest climates and is drought-resistant. Low-growing, curly, and fine in texture, it was used by early farmers to build sod homes.

SHRUBS

Rocky Mountain Juniper. This common Rocky Mountain shrub is found from British Columbia to Texas. It prefers cooler, moist sites, and in Colorado it grows above elevations of 5,000 ft. Juniper foliage has a fine texture and appears somewhat lacy and gray. The young juniper has a regular conical form with a pointed top, but the shrub becomes broad and irregular with age. Its cones are bluish when they mature.

Sagebrush. With fragrant, gray-green leaves and edible blue, red, or scarlet flowers, this plant is a kitchen essential, often used to flavor meat. You'll notice it on vast tracts of alkaline flats throughout the west.

TREES

Douglas Fir. Distinguished by long, shiny, pointed needles, this tree lives up to 1,000 years. Young firs have gray, smooth bark, while the older trees are dark and scaly. The roots of the Douglas fir were used by Native Americans for basket weaving and the twigs were used for arrow shafts.

Ponderosa Pine. One of the most heavily harvested trees in the U.S., these trees grow in spacious stands and can reach heights of 100 ft. The bark on older trees is orange or reddish and exudes a distinctive fragrance similar to vanilla.

Quaking Aspen. Found in damp places between 6,000 and 11,000 ft, this tree derives its name from the "shimmering" or quaking action of its leaves in a brisk wind. Aspen grow in groves and explode in a riot of yellow and gold each fall.

Willow. Less common than pine, willows often grow streamside with cottonwoods. Native Americans used the inner bark of the willow to make a tea that reduced fever and relieved pain. The bark and stems contain salicin, which, when ingested, breaks down into salicylic acid, the active ingredient in aspirin.

Geology and Terrain

Badlands. The Dakota badlands are the result of 60 million years of geologic activity. Much of the sedimentary rock that eroded from the Black Hills was deposited in the Badlands, along with ash from the volcanoes in the Yellowstone area. Water flowed over the landscape and carved out huge buttes and cliffs in a process that continues to this day. In the relatively soft, half-hardened rocks the elements carved drainage channels with a distinctive V shape, creating a network of ravines and ridgelines. These formations are devoid of vegetation because erosion carries off seeds and roots.

The Black Hills. South Dakota's Black Hills began as a mountainous landscape covered with limestone and shale sedimentary rock, but this covering gradually eroded away, exposing a granite face. Much of the sedimentary rock that eroded from the Black Hills was deposited in the Badlands.

Canyons. Fractures in the rock of the Earth's surface turn into canyons when softer layers of rock erode. The shape of a canyon will depend on the hardness of the rock that eroded and on the configuration of the hard and soft layers. A narrow, slotlike canyon generally results when the composition of the rock is the same all the way down.

Caves. As travelers to the region soon surmise, the mountains are spotted with caves of varying lengths and complexity, formed by water seeping through the rock over the ages. Jewel Cave and Wind Cave, each with more than 100 mi of mapped passageway, rank as fourth and seventh longest in the world, respectively, and each is home to incredibly rare specimens.

The Continental Divide. The Continental Divide of North America is a ridge that crosses the continent from north to south, separating water flowing east and water flowing west. The divide follows the crest of the Rockies through Glacier, Yellowstone, and Rocky Mountain national parks.

Geothermal Features. Hissing geysers, burbling mud pots, and boiling cauldrons have fascinated travelers ever since mountain man John Coulter described them to an unbelieving public in 1810. Today, these "freaks of a fiery nature," as Rudyard Kipling described them, are still clearly visible in Yellowstone National Park. Geysers, hot springs, and fumaroles are created when superheated water rises to the earth's surface from a magma chamber below. In the case of geysers, the water is trapped under the surface until the pressure is so great that it bursts through. Mud pots are a combination of hot water, hydrogen sulfide gas, and dissolved volcanic rock. The mixture looks like a hot, smelly, burping pudding.

Glaciers. A glacier is formed when more snow falls in winter than is melted in summer. Gradually, the snow accumulates and turns into a glacier—solid ice that flows and slides down a mountain, gouging out a valley and oftentimes eventually melting into a lake.

Lakes. Prairie potholes, reservoirs, and natural lakes water the region and provide sustenance for animals and waterfowl. Replenished in a seasonal cycle older than man, these catch-basins capture the runoff from high mountain snows that trickle down through alpine streams to the areas below.

Plains. After the retreat of Wisconsin glaciation, a period of dry warmth allowed for the expansion of grasslands across the Great Plains. Once home to vast herds of bison that blackened the prairie for miles, the plains today serve as America's breadbasket, supplying much of the nation and parts of the world with dairy products, grain, seeds, cattle, poultry, and pork.

The Rocky Mountains. The Rocky Mountain chain reaches from northwestern Canada down through Washington, Idaho, Montana, Wyoming, Colorado, Utah, and into New Mexico. The huge mountains were raised 70–130 million years ago during the last of three great uplifts, when massive tectonic plates collided, pushing the Earth's crust upwards. The soft rocks eroded and were split by deep fault zones, exposing the harder granite for which the mountains are known. Later, during several ice ages about 1.6– 2 million years ago, glaciers carved sheer walls and sharp peaks into the mountains, which are what you see now in Glacier, Yellowstone, Grand Teton, and Rocky Mountain national parks.

Canyon Country

Hoodoos, needles, balanced rocks, and canyons a mile deep are around every corner.
Sunsets turn rocks to gold, platinum, and copper every evening. Wild Western rivers
wind through the desert in ribbons of blue and green, between great walls of rock that
rise out of the earth-like ships. This is canyon country, where the rocks are red, the
canyons deep, and the fragrance of sagebrush lingers in the air. If you're lucky as you cruise
along the highway, you'll see coyote zipping past in search of food and pronghorn grazing on the sage flats. You'll see more stars in one night than you've seen in the city for a
dozen years. You'll discover canyon country.

At Zion National Park, in Utah, you are humbled as you stand beneath elegantly hued
rock walls. Suddenly a thunderstorm breaks out and you are witness to the Virgin River in
violent flood stage, running red with sand and silt from the high backcountry. The next day,
Bryce Canyon gives you a break from the hot desert as you climb to nearly 9,000 ft. The pink
and white hoodoos are the strangest things you've ever seen. By June, the snow has melted
in Nevada's Great Basin National Park and you can drive the mountain roads to see the oldest
living things on earth, the bristlecone pine. The air is clear and a sense of well-being washes
over you. Back in Utah at Capitol Reef, you'll understand why Native Americans called the
dramatic region "land of sleeping rainbow," when you see the palate of colors. There are
places here to be absolutely alone, save for the mule deer or bighorn sheep.

Walk beneath Delicate Arch, the fiery red, freestanding arch that's the most famous
feature of Arches National Park. At Canyonlands, stand before Native American rock art
2,000 years old and hike past an old cowboy camp tucked back in a cave, and know that
you are, indeed, in the wild American West. Crossing into Colorado, stop at Mesa Verde
National Park to visit ancestral Puebloan villages that were mysteriously abandoned in
AD 1250. The Black Canyon of the Gunnison gives your eye a break from so much red rock
as you gaze into the very basement of the earth, at Precambrian rock nearly two billion
years old. Then it's on to Arizona, where you cross Monument Valley and the Navajo

In This Chapter

Indian Reservation on your way to the Grand Canyon. As you approach there's no sign that there's a mile-deep hole in the earth just beyond that ridge. Then you stop, get out of your car, and look over the rim. For a few seconds, you cannot speak. The colors, the breadth, the depth of this canyon are beyond words. You are standing at the lip of one of the world's great wonders, gazing upon the quintessence of canyon country.

RULES OF THE ROAD

While driving throughout canyon country you will see yellow road signs with black cows on them. These signs signify that you are driving in territory designated as "open range." This means cattle are grazing outside of fences and may be loitering on the highway or crossing the road. Please be on the alert for cattle on the highway in canyon country and when you see them alongside the road slow down, for they may suddenly decide to walk in front of you. Hitting a cow can result in serious injury to you, damage to your vehicle, and death or injury for the cow. Plus, you may be have to pay the owner for the cow in the event of an accident. Exercise caution in open range.

License Requirements: To drive in Arizona, Colorado, Nevada, and Utah you must be at least 16 years old and have a valid driver's license.

Right Turn on Red: Unless there is a sign prohibiting it, you may make a right turn on red after a full stop in Arizona, Colorado, Nevada, and Utah.

Seat Belt and Helmet Laws: If you are sitting in the front seat of any vehicle in Arizona, Colorado, Nevada, or Utah, the law requires you wear a seat belt. In Nevada and Utah children under the age of 10 must wear a seat belt, no matter where in the car they are riding. Arizona and Colorado mandate that children up to 4 years old or 40 pounds ride in an approved safety seat; Utah sets the age limit at 2. All motorcyclists (drivers and passengers) in Nevada are required to wear helmets; in Arizona and Utah only those under 18 must do so.

Speed Limits: Wherever you drive in canyon country be sure to check speed limit signs carefully and often. On interstates in Arizona, Colorado, Nevada, and Utah speed limits can be as high as 75 mph. Arizona limits motor vehicles to 55 mph in heavily traveled areas, and in Colorado individual speed limits are posted along all major thoroughfares and in all municipalities. Colorado Highway Patrol are ubiquitous. On U.S. highways in Nevada the speed limit is 70—even in the heart of Las Vegas and Reno you can do 65 mph on the interstates. Not surprisingly, Nevada isn't known for speed traps. The story is different in Utah, where the speed limit is 55 mph on most highways, particularly in urban areas. Where posted, you are allowed to drive 65 mph. Transition zones from one speed limit to another are indicated with pavement markings and additional signs. Utah Highway Patrol are unforgiving if you're stopped, so don't speed.

For More Information: Arizona Department of Public Safety or Arizona Highway Patrol | 602/223–2000. **Colorado Highway Patrol |** 303/239–4500. **Nevada Department of Motor Vehicles |** 702/486–4368. **Nevada Highway Patrol |** 775/687–5300. **Utah Department of Motor Vehicles |** 801/965–4518. **Utah Highway Patrol |** 801/297–7780.

Canyon Country Driving Tour
FROM ZION TO GRAND CANYON

Distance: 1,000–1,200 mi   Time: 10–14 days
Breaks: Overnight in Springdale, Bryce, Torrey or Teasdale, and Moab, UT; Cortez, CO; Bluff, UT or Kayenta or Tuba City, AZ; Tusayan and North Rim, AZ

The wonderful thing about touring canyon country is that you can begin from one of many points. If you are arriving in the area from Colorado, you can easily start the tour from I–70. If you are approaching from Las Vegas, I–15 is a natural highway to begin your expedition. Likewise, I–40 and U.S. 89 get you started on this loop if you are coming from the south. For purposes of this narrative, the journey begins from I–15. No matter which direction you drive, you can make a complete loop without retracing any major routes.

1 Arrive at **Zion National Park** via I–15. If you are traveling north on I–15, take the Route 9 exit. If you are southward bound, exit at the Route 17 exit. Both state highways are very well marked as routes into the park. Spend your afternoon in the park and overnight in **Springdale.**

2 After another morning or a full day in Zion depart the area via Route 9, the **Zion–Mount Carmel Highway.** You'll pass through a 1.1-mi-long tunnel that is so narrow, RVs and towed vehicles are required to pay to be escorted through. When you emerge you are in slickrock country, where huge, petrified sandstone dunes are etched by ancient waters. Stay on Route 9 for 23 mi and then turn north onto U.S. 89. After 42 mi you will reach Route 12, where you should turn east and drive 14 mi.

3 Approaching the entrance of **Bryce Canyon National Park,** you'll notice that the air is a little cooler here than it was at Zion, so get out and enjoy it. Spend an afternoon or a full day here, then overnight in the park or at Ruby's Inn.

4 You have little choice other than to drive spectacular **Utah Scenic Byway–Route 12,** one of only a dozen All American Roads nationwide, to get to your next destination. If the views don't take your breath away, the narrow, winding road with little margin for error will.

5 Route 12 winds over and through **Grand Staircase-Escalante National Monument.** The views from the narrow "hogback" are nothing short of incredible. About 14 mi past the town of Escalante on Rte. 12 stop at **Calf Creek Recreation Area** to stretch your legs on a 5.5-mi round-trip hike to a gorgeous backcountry waterfall. Or for a less athletic break, **Anasazi Indian Village State Park** in Boulder is a good place to stop. Past Boulder Rte. 12 continues to gain elevation as you pass over Boulder Mountain.

6 At the intersection of Rtes. 12 and 24, turn east onto Rte. 24. You have traveled 112 mi from Bryce Canyon to reach **Capitol Reef National Park.** Plan on spending the night either in the park at the Fruita campground or in **Torrey** or **Teasdale.** There are many, many lodging options here depending on your taste.

7 When you leave Capitol Reef you will travel east and north for 75 mi on Rte. 24 through some wide open country. If you want a break after about an hour, stop at **Goblin Valley State Park** 12 mi off Rte. 24. Kids love to run around the red rock "goblins" that populate this small park. Continuing on Rte. 24 to I–70 at Green River, turn onto the interstate and continue your journey.

8 Thirty-one mi from Green River you'll see an exit for Moab and Arches and Canyonlands national parks. Take this exit south onto U.S. 191 and travel about 27 mi to **Arches National Park.** Spend the rest of the day in Arches, which holds the world's largest concentration of natural rock windows or arches.

9 At the end of your day head into **Moab,** the best home base while you visit Arches and Canyonlands. There are dozens of places to stay here and as many places to eat. Plan on spending at least three nights in Moab while you explore the area. Get an early start in the morning for another day in Arches, perhaps including a hike in the Fiery Furnace.

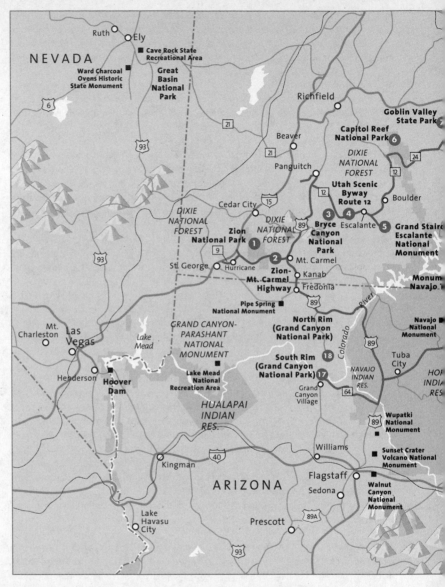

10 Launch your **Canyonlands National Park** experience the following day. On your way to
the Island in the Sky District U.S. 191 crosses the **Colorado River.** If you can squeeze in a
raft trip on this legendary Western artery, do it. Ten mi north of Moab you'll reach Rte.
313, which leads to Island in the Sky. Take a detour en route to visit the mesa top of **Dead
Horse Point State Park:** After 15 mi on Rte. 313 turn right onto the unnamed road and continue
for 6 mi to reach the Dead Horse fee station. From the park you will have magnificent
views of the Colorado River as it "goosenecks" through the canyons below.

11 Return to Rte. 313 and drive another 7 mi past the Dead Horse turnoff to reach the visitor center for **Island in the Sky District.** Once you drive the 12 mi to Grand View Point,
you'll understand how this district of Canyonlands got its name: The mesa top is like a
magic carpet floating above all of canyon country.

UTAH

Green River

Arches National Park

Grand Junction

Colorado R. Scenic Byway

Dead Horse Point State Park

Moab

Needles District (Canyonlands National Park)

Paonia

Delta

Hotchkiss

GUNNISON NATIONAL FOREST

Montrose

Black Canyon of the Gunnison National Park

Island in the Sky District (Canyonlands National Park)

Wilson Arch

Newspaper Rock State Historic Monument

Telluride

COLORADO

Monticello

Edge of the Cedars State Park

Blandings

Hovenweep National Monument

Dolores

Natural Bridges National Monument

Bluff

Cortez

Durango

SOUTHERN UTE INDIAN RESERVATION

Mesa Verde National Park

Valley al Park

Four Corners National Monument

NAVAJO NATION RES.

Kayenta

Farmington

Bloomfield

Taos

Chaco

Window Rock

NEW MEXICO

Los Alamos

Santa Fe

Jemez

Pecos

Second Mesa

Gallup

San Ysidro

Bernalillo

Petroglyph

Albuquerque

Holbrook

Acoma

12 On your way back to Moab take time to follow **Colorado River Scenic Byway–Route 128** for a few miles upriver. Also off U.S. 191 between Rte. 313 and Moab, **Rte. 279 (Potash Road)** travels along the Colorado River as well, but the highlight on this route is ancient Native American rock art. You'll reach the first rock art panels after about 4.8 mi.

13 In the morning it's time to make some choices. Today you leave Moab, traveling south on U.S. 191. Forty-two mi south of Moab you can turn onto Rte. 211 and drive 34 mi to Canyonlands' **Needles District,** which is distinctly different from Island in the Sky. Or you can save yourself 48 mi by skipping this part of the park and driving straight to Monticello. Moab to Monticello is 46 mi.

⑭ If you want to include **Mesa Verde National Park** on your tour, take U.S. 491 from Monticello to Cortez, CO, and follow U.S. 160 into the park. From Monticello to Mesa Verde is a trip of about 90 not particularly impressive miles. The park, however, is more than worth the drive. If you do make the extra drive to Colorado, consider spending two days (overnight in Cortez) so you can also see **Wetherill Mesa.** Then you can head for Monument Valley and the Navajo Nation, via U.S. 160 to Kayenta, AZ. Along the way, stop for a fun photo-op at **Four Corners National Monument.**

⑮ A less crowded alternative to Mesa Verde is the more remote **Hovenweep National Monument,** which you can reach by driving 36 mi south of Monticello on U.S. 191, past Blanding to Rte. 262. After about 15 mi on a mostly paved road (the unpaved section is very brief) you will truly feel like you are in the middle of nowhere. At this unusual ancestral Puebloan site you can take a short but fascinating walk into the canyon to see the square tower buildings. Return to U.S. 191 (or skip Hovenweep and Mesa Verde altogether) and continue south to the small town of **Bluff.** If you've hit Needles and Hovenweep today, Bluff will be a great, quiet place to stay the night.

⑯ Just a few miles past Bluff you'll see Rte. 163, which is your route to Arizona. At Mexican Hat you'll cross the San Juan River, the boundary for the Navajo Nation. Take a couple of hours to do the 17-mi self-guided drive into the spectacular, deep-red desert of **Monument Valley Navajo Tribal Park,** whose buttes and spires you will recognize from countless movie westerns and television commercials. If it's late in the day you might stay at **Gouldings Lodge** in Monument Valley (even if you don't overnight there, stop at the famous historic trading post) or in **Kayenta.** Otherwise, drive on through Navajo lands toward the Grand Canyon. Unless you are lucky enough to have reservations at El Tovar or another in-park property, it's a good idea to overnight in **Tuba City** and start fresh the next day to drive to the Grand Canyon.

⑰ At Tuba City U.S. 89 heads south toward Rte. 64 and north toward Alt. 89. Depending on the direction you choose you will end up at the South or North rim of **Grand Canyon National Park.** To see the canyon from both directions, start with the **South Rim.** You can overnight just outside the park in **Tusayan.**

⑱ After a day or two at the South Rim, backtrack to U.S. 89 to head north. Mid-May through mid-October you can visit the more serene **North Rim** by heading south from Alt. 89 on Rte. 67. You'll have quite a different experience of the canyon at the two rims, so it's worth visiting both. At the North Rim, reserve in advance so you can stay at Grand Canyon Lodge.

To reach Zion National Park from the Grand Canyon, take Alt. 89 north through the mountains. The road is winding and steep, but oh-so-beautiful. You'll pass Fredonia, AZ and Kanab, UT before picking up equally beautiful Rte. 9 (the Zion-Mount Carmel Highway) westward to Zion. If you're heading back to Las Vegas from the North Rim take U.S. 89 south to Flagstaff, and if you're coming from the South Rim take U.S. 180 south to Williams. In both towns you can pick up I–40 west.

When to Visit

If you can plan your canyon country vacation for spring or fall you will be mightily rewarded. Arches, Canyonlands, Capitol Reef, the South Rim of the Grand Canyon, and Zion are exceptional at these times of year. The parks at higher elevations—Bryce Canyon, Black Canyon of the Gunnison, the North Rim of the Grand Canyon, Great Basin, and Mesa Verde—experience erratic winter-like conditions into spring, and inclement weather and road conditions begin earlier in the fall. In heavy snowfall years these parks might have snow on the ground until May or even June. Still, the cooler times of year can be the best in the parks if you are seeking a more private experience of natural beauty. Even the dead of winter is an excellent time to visit those parks that are open. Zion, Arches, and Canyonlands, for instance, receive little snow and often have daytime temperatures in the mid-30s to 40s, making for perfect hiking and biking.

July and August temperatures in much of canyon country can exceed 100°F, which puts a cramp in hiking, picnicking and other outdoor activities. But the parks are fully staffed, campgrounds are up and running, the junior ranger program is in full swing, and tour operators inside and outside the parks are open for business. You've got to come in summer if you want to go river rafting, or if you want to take guided horseback rides and 4X4 excursions into the backcountry. All the restaurants and hotels will be open, and there'll be lots of opportunities for fun nearby. For the greatest range of options in activities, dining, and lodging, high season is the time to come to canyon country.

CLIMATE

Canyon country is a dry region, with monthly rainfall seldom exceeding 2 inches. Average temperatures range from January lows in the teens to August highs into the low 100s. At any given time, though, temperatures vary widely because of significant differences in elevation. At Grand Canyon, for example, temperatures on the rim will differ vastly from those on the canyon floor. The same is true for Great Basin, which climbs to 12,000 ft.

What to Pack

Layering is the key to packing for a trip to canyon country at any time of the year. Temperatures vary wildly whether you are in the sun or shade and you may find yourself peeling off jackets and then putting them back on again. Likewise, when the sun sets at night, temperatures drop rapidly and you'll want to have a jacket with you. You'll also be changing elevation a great deal as you tour the area, and temperatures can get 10 to 30 degrees cooler as you gain elevation. During spring and fall it's a good idea to bring along a fleece jacket to wear over long sleeved shirts. In winter, add a down or insulated coat of some kind to your bag as well as a warm hat and gloves. Spring and fall weather can also call for headgear to protect your ears from cooler temperatures.

A word about summer: canyon country can be extremely hot and you will be tempted to hike in shorts and tank tops, but you should wear a broad brimmed hat and a light colored, long-sleeved cotton shirt to protect yourself from the violent rays of the sun. In fact, during the summer you can leave all your dark-color clothing at home. The desert calls for light colors that reflect the sun.

Be sure to pack hiking boots or at least sturdy athletic shoes so you don't miss out on hiking some of the more beautiful trails in the parks. If you plan on a river raft trip throw in a bathing suit and some kind of shoe that can get wet. During spring runoff you'll need rain gear or waterproof clothing plus fleece to keep you warm and dry on the river.

Essential items also include sunscreen, water bottles, and some kind of a day pack to carry extra clothing, camera, film, and snacks while you're touring the parks. Many of the parks, or large areas within, are undeveloped and have nowhere to purchase food, water, or other supplies. Especially at Zion, the South Rim of the Grand Canyon, and (possibly) Bryce Canyon, you'll need to pack lunch and other supplies for the day since you'll be leaving your car behind. Throw in a couple of plastic zipper bags to store your trash and food scraps until you reach a garbage can. Go the extra mile and pick up trash left by thoughtless visitors before you.

ARCHES AND CANYONLANDS NATIONAL PARKS

SOUTHEASTERN UTAH

Arches: U.S. 191, 5 mi north of Moab. Canyonlands: Island in the Sky District, 32 mi northwest of Moab on Route 313 west of U.S. 191; Needles District, Route 211 west of U.S. 191. Arches is 21 mi from Island in the Sky, the nearest Canyonlands district.

"This is the most beautiful place on earth" must have been the thought that ran through the mind of Edward Abbey on his first morning as a seasonal park ranger at Arches National Park. Inspired by the region's grandeur, he wrote the classic *Desert Solitaire* during his stay at Arches in the 1950s. Today, visitors are still awed by the park, which holds the world's greatest concentration of natural stone arches—more than 2,000 of them. The red rock landscape of Arches awakens and challenges the imagination: balanced rocks teeter unthinkably on pedestals; Three Penguins greet you at the park entrance; the Fiery Furnace appears to burn like a wildfire at sunset. It's easy to spot many of the arches from your car, but getting out to hike beneath the spans and giant walls of orange rock gives you a much better idea of their proportion. No doubt, you will feel that you're walking in the most beautiful place on earth, even if it does look more like Mars.

If Arches National Park looks like Mars, Canyonlands resembles the moon. In this part of Utah, thousands of miles of canyons have been cut into the Earth by the Green and Colorado rivers and mushroomlike rock formations rise randomly out of the ground. Divided into three distinct land districts and the river district, Canyonlands can be a little daunting to visit. Unless you have several days, you will likely have to choose between the Island in the Sky District or the Needles District—and they are distinctly different in character. From any of the park overlooks at the Island in the Sky District, you can see for miles and look down thousands of feet to canyon floors. Chocolate-brown canyons are capped by white rock and deep red monuments rise nearby. In the Needles District pink, orange, and red rock is layered with white rock and stands in spires and pinnacles around grassy meadows. Extravagantly red mesas and buttes interrupt the horizon, as in a picture postcard of the old West. Beyond the well-traveled Island in the Sky and Needles districts, only the wildest visitors walk in the footsteps of Butch Cassidy in the Maze District, for it is accessible only by four-wheel-drive vehicles. Other adventurers tackle the rivers of Canyonlands, which are as untamed and undammed as when John Wesley Powell explored them in the mid-1800s.

PUBLICATIONS

In addition to the park visitor centers, the Moab Information Center at Center and Main streets is a good place to find books to enhance your visit to the parks. A small book, *Hiking Guide to Arches National Park,* by Damian Fagan, gives you detailed information on all the hiking trails. You can also pick up *Road Guide to Arches National Park,* by Peter Anderson, which has basic information about the geology and natural history you'll see as you pass through the park. If it's wildflower season, a guidebook to the colorful blossoms you'll see, *Canyon Country Wildflowers* by Damian Fagan, is a good choice. If you're interested in ancient Native American rock art, you might want to pick up *Into the Mystery: A Driving Tour of Moab Area Rock,* by Janet Lowe. An excellent, compact field guide for both Arches and Canyonlands is *A Naturalist's Guide to Canyon Country,* by David Williams and Gloria Brown. You can find comprehensive advice on hiking trails, backcountry roads, and trip planning in *Exploring Canyonlands and Arches National Parks* by Bill Schneider. A pocket-size trail guide, *Best Easy Day Hikes: Arches and Canyonlands* by Bill Schneider, lets you hit the trails with confidence. And every visitor to this area should read the classic by Edward Abbey, *Desert Solitaire.* You can order these and other books from **Canyonlands Natural History Association** | 3031 S. U.S. 191, Moab 84532 | 800/840–8978 | www.cnha.org.

When to Visit

SCENERY AND WILDLIFE

As in any desert environment, the best time to see wildlife in Arches and Canyonlands is in the early morning or late evening. Summer temperatures keep most animals tucked away in cool places. In Arches lizards crawl around all day even in summer, and if you're very lucky you'll spot one of the beautiful, turquoise-necklace collared lizards. It's more likely you'll see the western whiptail. Ravens populate the park throughout the day. Your chances of seeing wildlife are fairly good in Canyonlands because there are fewer people and less traffic to scare the animals away. Mule deer, jackrabbits, and small rodents such as packrats are usually active in cool morning hours or near dusk. You may spot a lone coyote foraging day or night. Both parks protect small herds of desert bighorns, and some of their tribe are often seen early in the morning grazing beside U.S. 191 south of Arches. Canyonlands' Island in the Sky District is home to some 250 bighorns and the Maze shelters about 100. If you're lucky enough to spot one of these regal animals, do not approach it even if it is alone, as bighorn sheep are skittish by nature and easily stressed. Also report your sighting to the park visitor center so rangers can keep track of the herd.

At sunset, the rock formations in Arches glow like fire and you'll often find photographers behind their tripods waiting for the sweet light to descend upon Delicate Arch or other formations. Sunsets over the vast network of canyons that stretch out below Canyonlands' Island in Sky are all but guaranteed to leave you amazed and elated. Likewise, late afternoon color in the spires and towers at the Needles District is a humbling, awe-inspiring scene.

HIGH AND LOW SEASON

The busiest times of year for both parks are spring and fall. In Arches, blooming wildflowers and temperatures in the 70s bring the year's largest crowds. Compared to most national parks, Canyonlands is seldom crowded, but in spring backpackers and four-wheelers populate the trails and roads. During Easter Week, some of the four-wheel-drive trails in the park are used for Jeep Safari, so if you are a wilderness purist, avoid that week. The crowds thin out in summer as the thermostat approaches 100°F in July and then soars beyond that for about four weeks. But it's a great time to get out on the Green or Colorado rivers as they wind through Canyonlands. High water is usually in June, depending on snowmelt in the Rockies. In August, sudden, dramatic cloudbursts create rainfalls over red rock walls.

Fall brings everybody back to the parks, and with good reason: the weather is perfect, with clear, warm days and crisp, cool nights. October is the only autumn month that gets much rain, but when you consider how little rain falls in the desert (average annual rainfall is only 8 inches), it shouldn't stop you from coming.

The parks almost clear out in winter, and you can hike any of the trails in nearly perfect solitude from December through February. Though few realize it, winter can be the best time to visit this part of the country. Snow seldom falls in the valley beneath the La Sal Mountains and when it does, Arches is a photographer's paradise as snow drapes slickrock mounds and natural rock windows. Winter at Canyonlands is one of nature's most memorable shows, with red rock dusted white and low-floating clouds partially obscuring canyons and towers.

ARCHES AND CANYONLANDS NATIONAL PARKS

EXPLORING
ATTRACTIONS NEARBY
DINING
LODGING
CAMPING AND RV FACILITIES
SHOPPING
ESSENTIAL INFORMATION

Average High/Low Temperatures (°F) and Monthly Precipitation (in inches)

	JAN.	FEB.	MAR.	APR.	MAY	JUNE
ARCHES	44/19	53/25	64/33	76/39	84/49	98/58
	.50	.50	.90	1.2	1.1	.10

	JULY	AUG.	SEPT.	OCT.	NOV.	DEC.
	100/62	99/61	86/50	77/40	58/32	48/21
	1.2	.80	.80	1.6	1.2	.50

Note: Extreme highs at Arches often exceed 100 degrees during July and August.

CANYONLANDS	JAN.	Feb.	Mar.	Apr.	May	Jun.
	39/19	46/23	55/30	64/34	73/46	87/58
	.63	.29	1.07	.76	.71	.50
	JUL.	Aug.	Sep.	Oct.	Nov.	Dec.
	92/62	90/60	82/51	68/40	51/29	38/22
	1.15	.92	.69	1.0	.86	.60

FESTIVALS AND SEASONAL EVENTS

WINTER

Dec.: **Electric Light Parade.** If you visit Arches or Canyonlands in early December, you will avoid the crowds and also be in Moab for this fun, and often silly, local event. Merchants, clubs, and other organizations build whimsical floats with Christmas lights for a nighttime parade down Main Street. | 435/259–7814.

Jan.: **Bluff International Balloon Festival.** Colorful balloons congregate in Bluff and take to the skies over the San Juan River and all of Utah's canyonlands. | 435/672–2303.

Feb.: **Canyonlands Half Marathon and 5-Mile Run.** No doubt because of the spectacular scenery and great weather, Moab's half-marathon is fast becoming one of America's favorite running events. | 435/259–4525.

SPRING

Apr.: **Jeep Safari.** Every year during Easter week thousands of four-wheel-drive vehicles descend on Moab to tackle some of the toughest backcountry roads in America. | 435/259–7625.

May: **Moab Arts Festival.** Artists from all around the Four Corners area come to Moab to display and sell their work. The festival is small enough to be fun and prices are affordable. | 435/259–2742.

SUMMER

June: **Butch Cassidy Days.** Honoring the western outlaw tradition of southeastern Utah, this Moab event features a PRCA rodeo, parade, shoot-outs, and other cowboy activities. | 435/259–6226.

July: **Pioneer Days.** Each July 24, the state of Utah closes down to celebrate its Mormon heritage. From Salt Lake City to the most remote corners of the state, towns throw parades and parties honoring the men and women who crossed the country to find the right place to live. Your best bets for finding festivities near Arches and Canyonlands are in Blanding, Monticello, and Moab. | 435/587–2992.

FALL

Sept.: **Green River Melon Days.** All the watermelon you can eat, an old-fashioned parade, and other small-town-America activities await you. The melons are always ripe and scrumptious. | 435/564–3526.

Moab Music Festival. Listen to classical music under the dome in the red rocks near Arches, or attend a special river concert 30 mi downstream on the Colorado River, outside Canyonlands. This is one event truly worth driving great distances to attend. | 435/259–7003.

Oct.: **Canyonlands Fat Tire Festival.** The first Fat Tire Festival took place in 1985, and the rest, as they say, is history. The event more or less put Moab and Utah's canyonlands region on the map as the mountain biking capital of the world. It's a melting pot of mountain bikers who ride, race, play, and party around canyon country and the Moab area. | 801/375–3231.

Four Corners Indian Art Market. Edge of the Cedars State Park in Blanding hosts this juried art show and sale each year. Native American artists from around the Four Corners region display their work. | 435/687–2238.

Nov.: **Canyonlands Film Festival.** In the tradition of Sundance and Telluride film festivals, Moab's film society screens eclectic films by independent filmmakers from all over the world. | 435/259–0046.

Nearby Towns

Near the Colorado River in a beautiful valley between red rock cliffs, with the La Sal Mountains rising to 12,000 ft 20 mi away, **Moab** is the major gateway to Arches and Canyonlands national parks. Here you'll find the area's greatest number of sports outfitters to help you enjoy the parks. The town itself is an interesting, eclectic place to visit, especially if you're looking for fine restaurants with good wine lists, abundant shopping, and varied lodging. Roughly 55 mi south of Moab is **Monticello.** Convenient to the Needles District of Canyonlands, this town lies at an elevation of 7,000 ft, making it a cool refuge from the desert in summer. In winter, it gets downright cold and sees deep snow; the Abajo Mountains, whose highest point is 11,360 ft, rise to the west of town. Motels serve the steady stream of tourists who venture south of Moab, but Monticello still offers very few dining or shopping opportunities.

Blanding, 21 mi south of Monticello, prides itself on old-fashioned conservative values. By popular vote there's a ban on the sale of liquor, beer, and wine, so the town has no state liquor store and its restaurants do not serve alcoholic beverages. Blanding is a good resting point if you're traveling south from Canyonlands to Natural Bridges Natural Monument, Grand Gulch, Lake Powell, or the Navajo Nation. About 108 mi south of Arches and 21 mi south of Monticello, tiny **Bluff** is doing its best to stay that way. It's a great place to stop if you aren't looking for many amenities but value beautiful scenery, silence, and starry nights. Bluff is the most common starting point for trips on the San Juan River, which serves as the northern boundary for the Navajo Reservation. The town is also a wonderful place to overnight if you're planning a visit to Hovenweep National Monument, about 30 mi away on Route 262.

INFORMATION

Blanding Chamber of Commerce | Box 792, Blanding, 84511 | 435/678–2791 or 800/574–4386 | www.blandingutah.org.**Blanding Visitor Center** | N. U.S. 191, Blanding 84511 | 435/678–3662. **Business Owners of Bluff** | www.bluffutah.org. **Grand County Travel Council (Moab)** | 125 E. Center St., Moab, 84532 | 435/259–1370, 435/259–8825, or 800/635–6622 | www.discovermoab.com. **Moab Information Center** | Center and Main Sts., Moab, 84532 | 435/259–8825. **San Juan County Community Development and Visitor Services (Bluff and Monticello)** | 117 S. Main St., Box 490, Monticello, 84535 | 435/587–3235 or 800/574–4386 | www.canyonlands-utah.com.

Exploring Arches

PARK BASICS

Contacts and Resources: Arches National Park | N. U.S. 191, Moab, 84532 | 435/719–2299, 435/719–2200, 435/719–2391 for the hearing-impaired | www.nps.gov/arch.

Hours: Arches National Park is open year-round, seven days a week, around the clock.

Fees: Admission to the park is $10 per vehicle and $5 per person on foot, motorcycle, or bicycle, good for seven days. You must pay admission to Canyonlands separately. A $25 local park pass grants you admission to both the Arches and Canyonlands parks for one year.

ARCHES AND
CANYONLANDS
NATIONAL PARKS

EXPLORING
ATTRACTIONS NEARBY
DINING
LODGING
CAMPING AND RV
FACILITIES
SHOPPING
ESSENTIAL
INFORMATION

Getting Around: The park road runs 18 mi from the entrance to Devils Garden. Branching off the main road are two spurs, one (2.5 mi) that takes you to The Windows section and the other (1.6 mi) that leads to the Delicate Arch trailhead and viewpoint. There are several four-wheel-drive roads in the park; always check at the visitor center for conditions before attempting to drive them. Note that the road leading to the park (U.S. 191) may be backed up mid-morning through early afternoon. There's likely to be less traffic if you hit the park roads by 8 or wait until lunch time or sunset.

Permits: Permits are required for backcountry camping and for hiking without a park ranger in the Fiery Furnace. You can purchase a Fiery Furnace permit ($2 per person for adults, $1 for kids 7–12) at the visitor center.

Public Telephones: You can find a public telephone only at the park's visitor center.

Rest Rooms: You can find public rest rooms at the visitor center, Devils Garden Campground, and Balanced Rock picnic area, as well as at the following trailheads: Delicate Arch trailhead, Delicate Arch Viewpoint, Devils Garden, Fiery Furnace, and Windows section. The only flush toilets are at the visitor and campground; the rest are vault or pit toilets.

Accessibility: Not all park facilities meet federally mandated ADA standards, but as visitation to Arches climbs, the park is making efforts to increase accessibility. Visitors with mobility impairments can access the visitor center, all rest rooms throughout the park, and one campsite (#37) at the Devils Garden Campground. The Park Avenue Viewpoint is a paved path with a slight decline near the end, and both Delicate Arch and Balanced Rock viewpoints are partially hard surfaced.

Emergencies: In the event of a fire or a medical emergency, dial 911 or contact a park ranger. There are no first aid stations in the parks; report to the visitor center for assistance. Park rangers are at the visitor center. To reach law enforcement, dial 911 or contact a park ranger.

Lost and Found: For lost-and-found, stop by the park's visitor center.

Good Tours

ARCHES IN ONE DAY

Rise early for your day in Arches National Park. You'll need to pack snacks, lunch, and plenty of water as there's no food service in the park. Start by taking the 3-mi round-trip hike from the **Delicate Arch** trailhead while the day is still cool. The hike is strenuous but richly rewarding. Pause for a healthful snack before heading for **Landscape Arch,** the second of the park's two must-see arches. To get there you must hike through **Devils Garden,** a great spot for morning photography. If you're accustomed to hiking you might next hike out to **Double O,** a trip that is well worth the effort but that can be tough after the hike to Delicate Arch—especially in July or August. If you do hike to Double O, take your lunch with you and have a picnic in the shade of a juniper or in a rock alcove. Don't forget to pack out every scrap of paper and food. You might substitute the hike into Devils Garden with the ranger-guided **Fiery Furnace** walk if you manage to get a spot on the popular hike. Whichever hike you take, by the time you return you'll be ready to see the rest of the park by car, with some short strolls on easy paths. Drive to **Balanced Rock** for photos, then on to **The Windows.** Wander around on the easy gravel paths for more great photo-ops. Depending on what time the sun is due to set, go into town for dinner before or after you drive out to Delicate Arch or the Fiery Furnace—or to the **La Sal Mountain Viewpoint** if you don't want to go that far—and watch the sun set the rocks on fire.

ARCHES IN TWO OR THREE DAYS

Pack lunch, snacks, and water each day before you head into the park. On the first day, stop at the **visitor center** and sign up for a ranger-guided Fiery Furnace walk for day two or three. Now make a beeline for the **Devils Garden** trailhead so it's still as cool as possi-

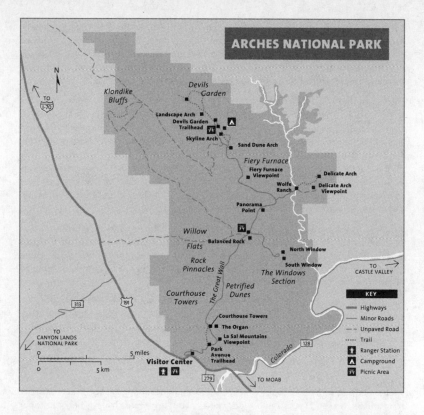

ARCHES AND
CANYONLANDS
NATIONAL PARKS

EXPLORING
ATTRACTIONS NEARBY
DINING
LODGING
CAMPING AND RV
FACILITIES
SHOPPING
ESSENTIAL
INFORMATION

ble when you begin your hike. Stop at all the arches and walk all the way to **Dark Angel,** and return to the trailhead and your car via the primitive loop. Along the way, be sure to take the short hike off the loop to **Private Arch.** All told, the Devils Garden hike will take about four or five hours and is very strenuous. You'll be best prepared for the hike out if you have lunch somewhere along the trail. This is a primitive area of the park where people can easily become lost, so watch carefully for the rock cairns that mark the trail. After the hike, drive toward the park exit, stopping for a walk to **Sand Dune and Broken arches.** These are easy strolls across flat areas and will stretch out those tired muscles. Stop at the viewpoints along the way to take photos and breathe in the amazing desert air. In **The Windows,** stroll the gravel path that winds around the arches, visiting as many arches as you have energy for. Make sure you are in the park at sunset, either before or after having dinner in Moab.

The day of your **Fiery Furnace** walk you can also plan to hike to **Delicate Arch.** If you take a morning hike to Delicate Arch you can be in the shade of the fins inside the Fiery Furnace during the hottest part of the day. If you take a morning walk in the Fiery Furnace, plan on a sunset hike to Delicate Arch. It's a good idea to take a flashlight along in case the sun moves at a faster pace than you do. Fill in your spare time with a walk on the **Park Avenue** trail. If you have one more day, take a rafting trip on the **Colorado River** as it runs along the boundary of the park.

Attractions

PROGRAMS AND TOURS

For more information on current schedules and locations of park programs, contact the visitor center (435/719–2299) or check the bulletin boards located throughout the park.

ARCH OR BRIDGE?

To be defined as an arch, a rock opening must be in a continuous wall of rock and have a minimum opening of 3 ft in any one direction. A natural bridge differs from an arch in that it is formed by water flowing beneath it.

Campfire Program. Every evening mid-March through October, a park ranger presents a program around the campfire at Devils Garden Campground. It's a great way to learn about subjects such as mountain lions, the Colorado River, human history in Arches National Park, or the night life of animals. | Devils Garden Campground Amphitheater, 17.7 mi from the park entrance, 0.5 mi off the main road | Free | Mid-Mar.–Oct., nightly at 9.

★ **Fiery Furnace Walk.** Join a park ranger on a two or three hour walk through a mazelike labyrinth of rock fins and narrow sandstone canyons. You'll see arches that can't be viewed from the park road and spend time listening to the desert. You should be relatively fit and not afraid of heights if you plan to take this moderately strenuous walk. Wear sturdy hiking shoes, sunscreen, and a hat, and bring at least a quart of water. Walks into the Fiery Furnace are usually offered twice a day (hours vary) and leave from Fiery Furnace viewpoint. Tickets may be purchased for this popular activity up to seven days in advance at the visitor center. | Fiery Furnace Trailhead, about 15 mi from the visitor center off the main park road | $8 adults, children 7–12 $4 | Mid-Mar.–Oct., daily.

Junior Ranger Program. Kids 6–12 can pick up a Junior Ranger booklet at the visitor center. It's full of activities, word games, drawings, and educational material about the park and the wildlife. To earn your Junior Ranger badge you must complete the booklet, attend a ranger program or watch the park slide program, and gather a bag of litter or bring 20 aluminum cans to be recycled. | 435/719–2299 | Free.

Nature Walks. You can really get to know Arches National Park by joining these walks with park rangers. Many of the walks explore The Windows section of the park, but they also visit other areas of the park. Topics include geology, desert plants, and the survival tactics of animals. Check at the visitor center or on park bulletin boards for times, topics, and locations. | Free.

SCENIC DRIVE

Arches Main Park Road. Although they are not formally designated as such, the main park road and its two short spurs are scenic drives, and you can see much of the park from your car. The main road takes you through Courthouse Towers, where you can see Sheep Rock and the Three Gossips, then alongside the Great Wall and the Petrified Dunes. A drive to The Windows section takes you to Double Arch, North and South windows, and Turret Arch; you can see Skyline Arch along the roadside as you approach the campground. The road to Delicate Arch is not particularly scenic, but allows you hiking access to one of the park's main features. Allow about two hours to drive the 36-mi round-trip, more if you explore the spurs and their features and stop at viewpoints along the way.

SIGHTS TO SEE

Balanced Rock. One of the park's favorite sights, this rock has remained mysteriously balanced on its pedestal for who knows how long. The formation's total height is 128 ft, with the huge balanced rock rising 55 ft above the pedestal. A short loop (0.3 mi) around the base gives you an opportunity to stretch your legs and take photographs. | 9.2 mi from the park entrance on the main road.

★ **Delicate Arch.** The familiar symbol of Arches National Park, if not for the entire state of Utah, Delicate Arch is tall enough to shelter a four-story building. The arch is a remnant of an Entrada sandstone fin; the rest of the rock has eroded and now frames the La Sal Mountains in the background. You can drive a couple of miles off the main road to view the arch from a distance, or you can hike right up to it. The trail is a moderately strenuous 3-mile round-trip hike. | 13 mi from the park entrance, 2.2 mi off the main road.

Desert Nature Trail. Outside the visitor center is this 0.2-mi loop that only takes a few minutes to walk. Before you begin you can pick up a Desert Nature Trail Guide, which will help you identify various desert plants you'll see throughout the park. | At the park entrance.

Double Arch. In The Windows section of the park, Double Arch has appeared in several Hollywood movies. Less than 0.25 mi from the parking lot, the spectacular rock formation can be reached in about 10 minutes. | 11.7 mi from the park entrance on the main road.

Fiery Furnace. This forbiddingly named area is so labeled because its orange spires of rock look much like tongues of flame, especially in the late afternoon sun. You can view it from the Fiery Furnace Viewpoint or take a challenging ranger-guided hike right into its midst. | About 15 mi from the park entrance on the main road.

★ **Landscape Arch.** This natural rock opening competes with Kolob Arch at Zion National Park for the title of largest geologic span in the world. Measuring 306 ft from base to base, it appears as a delicate ribbon of rock bending over the horizon. In 1991, a slab of rock about 60 ft long, 11 ft wide, and 4 ft thick fell from the underside, leaving it even thinner. You can reach the arch by walking a rolling, gravel 1.6-mi-long trail. | Devils Garden, 18 mi from the park entrance on the main road.

Sand Dune Arch Trail. Kids love this trail because erosion has created a giant sandbox beneath the namesake arch. While it's an easy trail, remember that sand is difficult to walk in. A cautionary note: do not climb or jump off the arch; rangers have dealt with several accidents involving people who have done so. Allow about 15 minutes to walk the 0.3 mi to the arch and back to your car. The trail intersects with the Broken Arch Trail, so if you visit both arches, it's a 1.5 mi round-trip. | 16 mi from the park entrance on the main road.

Skyline Arch. An easy walk from the parking lot gives you closer views and better photos of the arch. The short trail is 0.4 mi round-trip and only takes a few minutes to travel. | 16.5 mi from the park entrance on the main road.

Visitor Center. A stop at the visitor center before you drive the switchbacks into the park will do much to make your sightseeing more meaningful. Take time to view the park video, and shop the bookstore for trail guides, books, and maps to enhance to your visit. Exhibits inform you about geology, natural history, and ancestral Puebloan presence in the Arches area. Construction on a new visitor center began in late 2003; it is slated for completion in early 2005. | At the park entrance | 435/719-2299 | Daily; closed Christmas Day.

The Windows. Many people with limited time to spend in the park drive to this area. Here you can see a large concentration of natural windows and walk a path that winds beneath them. | 11.7 mi from the park entrance, 2.5 mi off the main road.

Wolfe Ranch. Built in 1906 out of Fremont cottonwoods, this rustic one-room cabin housed the Wolfe family after their first cabin was lost to a flash flood. The family lived in what is now Arches National Park from 1898 to 1910. In addition to the cabin you'll also see remains of a root cellar and a corral. Even older than these structures is the Ute rock art panel that's near the Delicate Arch trailhead. About 150 ft past the footbridge and before the trail starts to climb, you can see images of bighorn sheep as well as some smaller images believed to be dogs. To reach the panel, follow the narrow dirt trail along the rock escarpment until you see the interpretive sign. | 12.9 mi from the park entrance, 1.2 mi off the main road.

Sports and Outdoor Activities

BICYCLING

There's outstanding mountain biking all around Arches National Park, but the park proper is not the best place to explore on two wheels. Bicycles are only allowed on established roads and since there are no shoulders, cyclists share the roadway with drivers and pedestrians gawking at the scenery. If you do want to take a spin in the park, try Willow Flats Road, the old entrance to the park. The road is about 6.5 mi long one way and starts directly across from the Balanced Rock parking lot. It's a pretty ride on dirt and sand through slickrock, pinyon, and juniper country. You must stay on the road with your bicycle or you

ARCHES AND
CANYONLANDS
NATIONAL PARKS

EXPLORING
ATTRACTIONS NEARBY
DINING
LODGING
CAMPING AND RV
FACILITIES
SHOPPING
ESSENTIAL
INFORMATION

chance steep fines. *See* Sports and Outdoor Activities: Canyonlands, *below* and Outfitters, *below* for more information on biking in the area.

HIKING

Getting out on any one of the park trails will surely cause you to fall in love with this Martian landscape. But remember: you are hiking in a desert environment. Many people succumb to heat and dehydration because they do not drink enough water. Park rangers recommend a gallon of water per day per person.

Broken Arch Trail. An easy walk across open grassland, this loop trail passes Broken Arch, which is also visible from the road. The arch gets its name because it appears to be cracked in the middle, but it's not really broken. The trail is 2 mi round-trip, and you should allow about an hour for the walk. | End of Sand Dune Arch trail, 0.3 mi off the main park road 11 mi from the park entrance.

Delicate Arch Trail. To see the park's most famous freestanding arch up close takes some effort. The 3-mi round-trip trail ascends a steep slickrock slope that offers no shade—it's very hot in summer. What you find at the end of the trail is, however, worth the hard work. You can walk under the arch and take advantage of abundant photo-ops, especially at sunset. In spite of its difficulty, this is a very popular trail. Allow anywhere from one to three hours for this hike, depending on your fitness level and how long you plan to linger at the arch. The trail starts at Wolf Ranch. | 13 mi from the park entrance, 2.2 mi off the main road.

★ **Devils Garden Trail.** If you want to take a longer hike in the park, head out on this network of trails, where you can see a number of arches. You will reach Tunnel and Pine Tree arches after only 0.4 mi on the gravel trail, and Landscape Arch is 0.8 mi from the trailhead. Past Landscape Arch the trail changes dramatically, increasing in difficulty with many short, steep climbs. You will encounter some heights as you inch your way across a long rock fin. The trail is marked with rock cairns, and it's always a good idea to locate the next one before moving on. Along the way to Double O Arch, 2 mi from the trailhead, you can take short detours to Navajo and Partition arches. A round-trip hike to Double O takes from two to three hours. For a longer hike, include Dark Angel and/or return to the trailhead on the primitive loop. This is a difficult route through fins with a short side trip to Private Arch. If you hike all the way to Dark Angel and return on the primitive loop, the trail is 7.2 mi round-trip. Allow about five hours for this adventure, take plenty of water, and watch your route carefully. | 18 mi from the park entrance on the main road.

Fiery Furnace Hiking. Rangers strongly suggest taking the guided hike through this area before you set out on your own, as there is no marked trail. A hike here is a a challenging but fascinating trip through rugged terrain into the heart of Arches. The trail occasionally requires the use of hands and feet to scramble up and through narrow cracks and along narrow ledges above drop-offs. To hike this area on your own you must get a permit at the visitor center ($2). If you are not familiar with the Furnace you can get easily lost and cause resource damage, so watch your step and use great caution. | About 15 mi from the visitor center off the main park road.

Park Avenue Trail. Walk under the gaze of Queen Nefertiti, a giant rock formation that some observers think has Egyptian-looking features. The nearby rock walls resemble a New York City skyline—hence the name, Park Avenue. The trail is fairly easy, with only a short hill to navigate. It's 2 mi round-trip, or, if you are traveling with companions you can have one of them pick you up at the Courthouse Towers Viewpoint, making it a 1 mi trek downhill. Allow about 45 minutes for the one-way journey. | 2 mi from the park entrance on the main road.

Tower Arch Trail. In a remote, seldom visited area of the park, this trail takes you to a giant rock opening. If you look beneath the arch you will see a 1922 inscription left by Alex Ringhoffer, who "discovered" this section of the park. Reach the trail by driving to the Klondike Bluffs parking area via a dirt road that starts at the main park road across from Broken

Arch. Check with park rangers for road conditions before attempting the drive. Allow from two to three hours for this hike. | 24.5 mi from the park entrance, 7.7 mi off the main road.

ROCK CLIMBING

Rock climbers travel from across the country to scale the sheer red rock walls of Arches National Park and surrounding areas. Most climbing routes in the park require advanced techniques. Permits are not required, but you are responsible for knowing park regulations and restricted routes. One popular route in the park is Owl Rock in the Garden of Eden (about 10 mi from the visitor center), which ranges in difficulty from 5.8 to 5.11 on a scale that goes up to 5.13+. Many climbing routes are available in the Park Avenue area, about 2.2 mi from the visitor center. These routes are also extremely difficult climbs. Before climbing, it's a good idea to stop at the visitor center and talk with a ranger.

Exploring Canyonlands

PARK BASICS

Contacts and Resources: Canyonlands National Park. | 2282 W. Resource Blvd., Moab, 84532 | 435/719–2313, Backcountry Reservation Office 435/259–4351 | www.nps.gov/cany.

Hours: Canyonlands National Park is open 24 hours a day, seven days a week, year-round.

Fees: Admission is $10 per vehicle and $5 per person on foot, motorcycle, or bicycle, good for seven days. Your Canyonlands pass is good for all the park's districts. There's no entrance fee to the Maze District of Canyonlands. A $25 local park pass grants you admission to both Arches and Canyonlands for one year.

Getting Around: Before starting a journey to any of Canyonlands' three districts, make sure your gas tank is topped off, as there are no services inside the large park. Island in the Sky is 32 mi from Moab, Needles District is 80 mi from Moab, and the Maze is more than 100 mi from Moab. The Island in the Sky road from the district entrance to Grand View Point is 12 mi, with one 5-mi spur to Upheaval Dome. The Needles scenic drive is 10 mi with two spurs about 3 mi each. Roads in the Maze, suitable only for rugged, high-clearance, four-wheel-drive vehicles, wind for hundreds of miles through the canyons. Within the parks, safety and courtesy mandate that you always park only in designated pull-outs or parking areas.

Permits: In Canyonlands, you need a permit for overnight backpacking, four-wheel-drive camping, mountain-bike camping, four-wheel-drive day use in Horse and Lavender canyons (Needles District), and river trips. You can get information on the Canyonlands reservation and permit system by visiting the park's Web site at www.nps.gov/cany or by calling the reservations office at 435/259–4351.

Public Telephones: You can find public telephones at the park's visitor centers, as well as at Hans Flat Ranger Station in the Maze District.

Rest Rooms: In Island in the Sky, public rest rooms are at the visitor center, Willow Flat Campground, Grand View Point, and Upheaval Dome Trailhead. In the Needles, you can find facilities at the visitor center, Squaw Flat Campground, and Big Spring Canyon Overlook Trail. In the Maze, the Hans Flat Ranger Station has rest rooms, and at Horseshoe Canyon you can find relief at the trailhead. The only flush toilet is at the Needles visitor center; the rest are vault toilets.

Accessibility: There are currently no trails in Canyonlands that are accessible to people in wheelchairs, but Grand View Point and Buck Canyon Overlook at Island in the Sky are wheelchair accessible. The visitor centers at the Island in the Sky and Needles districts are also accessible, and the park's pit toilets are accessible with some assistance.

Emergencies: In the event of a fire or a medical emergency, dial 911 or contact a park ranger. There are no first aid stations in the parks; report to the visitor center for assis-

ARCHES AND
CANYONLANDS
NATIONAL PARKS

EXPLORING
ATTRACTIONS NEARBY
DINING
LODGING
CAMPING AND RV
FACILITIES
SHOPPING
ESSENTIAL
INFORMATION

tance. Park rangers are located at the visitor center. To reach law enforcement, dial 911 or contact a park ranger.

Lost and Found: For lost-and-found, stop by a visitor center.

Good Tours

CANYONLANDS IN ONE DAY

If you only have one day to visit Canyonlands National Park, you'll have to choose between the Island in the Sky and the Needles districts, because you can't do both. The two districts are distinctly different. At the Island you are on a giant mesa top enjoying expansive vistas into and across the canyonlands region, including the Needles and Maze districts of the park. In the Needles District, you are driving and walking among the needles and buttes, rather than looking out over them.

If you're making your trip to Canyonlands in conjunction with a visit to Arches and you're headed back to the interstate afterward, your best choice is **Island in the Sky.** Before leaving town, top off your gas tank, pack a picnic lunch, and stock up on plenty of water. Make sure you have extra film for your camera, too. Stop at the **visitor center,** watch the 15-minute orientation film, and browse the books, maps and postcards. Afterwards, head out into the Island. Make your first stop along the main park road at **Shafer Canyon Overlook.** A short walk takes you out on a finger of land and gives you views over both sides into the canyon. From here you can see Shafer Trail as it hugs the canyon wall. Drive next to **Mesa Arch.** Grab your camera and a bottle of water for the short hike out to the arch perched on the edge of a cliff. After your hike, continue on the main park road to **Buck Canyon Overlook.** From here you get great views of White Rim as it spreads out beneath you, the La Sal Mountains, and sheer red rock walls. Drive next to **Grand View Point,** stroll along the edge of the rim for awhile, and see how many landmarks you can find in the distance. Have your picnic lunch at the Grand View Point picnic area. Afterward, head back toward the visitor center but turn left on **Upheaval Dome Road.** Take it to **Island in the Sky Campground** so you can see the Green River from the nearby overlook. Head next to the Upheaval Dome parking lot. Hike up to the first **Upheaval Dome viewpoint,** and if you have more energy and a little sense of adventure, continue to the second overlook before returning to your car. If you're still up for some walking, stop at **Aztec Butte** and walk across the level, grassy meadow before making a climb up the slickrock in search of the ancient Native American ruins. If you have four-wheel drive and aren't afraid of heights, you might consider returning to Moab via **Shafer Trail and Potash Road.** While on this four-wheel-drive road, take a quick drive over to **Musselman Arch** before you leave the park.

If you're more interested in a day of hiking, hike **Syncline Loop Trail** at Island in the Sky, or travel to the Needles District via U.S. 191 and Route 211, and hike **Chesler Park Trail** until it connects with Joint Trail.

CANYONLANDS IN TWO OR THREE DAYS

Spend the first day as above, getting acquainted with the Island in the Sky District. The next morning, drive the 80 mi from Moab to the **Needles District** and set up for an overnight at one of the wonderful campsites there. Hit the **Joint Trail** or any of the trails that begin from Squaw Flat campground and spend the day hiking in the backcountry of the park. Attend the **campfire program** that evening and sleep under more stars than you've seen in a long, long time. The next morning before you leave the Needles, take the brief but terrific little hike to **Cave Springs.** If you have four-wheel drive, you might drive to the **Colorado River overlook** before heading on to your next destination.

If you can squeeze in one more day, contract with an outfitter to take you on a **4X4 adventure,** either into the backcountry of the Needles or on the White Rim of the Island in the Sky, or see Canyonlands from the Colorado River on a **jet boat/jeep trip.**

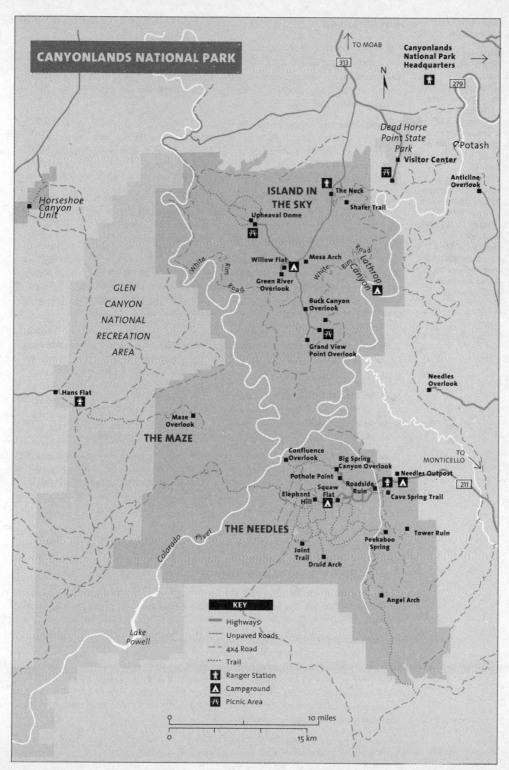

CANYONLANDS NATIONAL PARK

TO MOAB

313

N

Canyonlands
National Park
Headquarters

279

Dead Horse
Point State
Park

Potash

Visitor Center

Anticline
Overlook

Horseshoe
Canyon
Unit

ISLAND IN
THE SKY

The Neck

Shafer Trail

Upheaval Dome

White

Rim

Road

Willow Flat

Mesa Arch

White

Rim

Road

Lathrop

Canyon

GLEN
CANYON
NATIONAL
RECREATION
AREA

Green River
Overlook

Buck Canyon
Overlook

Grand View
Point Overlook

Needles
Overlook

Hans Flat

Maze
Overlook

THE MAZE

Confluence
Overlook

Big Spring
Canyon Overlook

TO
MONTICELLO

Pothole Point

Needles Outpost

211

Elephant
Hill

Squaw
Flat

Roadside
Ruin

Cave Spring Trail

THE NEEDLES

Peekaboo
Spring

Tower Ruin

Colorado

River

Joint
Trail

Druid Arch

Angel Arch

Lake
Powell

KEY

Highways

Unpaved Roads

4x4 Road

Trail

Ranger Station

Campground

Picnic Area

0   10 miles

0   15 km

MYSTERIOUS MARKINGS

The most common type of rock inscription in southeastern Utah, petroglyphs are images cut into rock. You'll find them pecked into the dark brown or black "desert varnish," a combination of iron or manganese oxides and minute clay particles bonded to the rock surface. Pictographs are painted onto rock and are usually found on light-colored walls.

Attractions

PROGRAMS AND TOURS

For more information on current schedules and locations of park programs, contact the **visitor centers** or check the bulletin boards throughout the park. Note that programs change periodically and may sometimes be cancelled because of limited staffing. | 435/259–4712 Island in the Sky, 435/259–4711 Needles.

Campfire Program. You can enrich your visit to Canyonlands by attending a campfire program. Topics include wildlife, cultural and natural history of the park, Native American legends, cowboy history, and geology. Scheduling of programs depends on staffing. Check with the visitor center or on park bulletin boards for more information. | Willow Flat Campground, Island in the Sky; Squaw Flat Campground, Needles | Free | ½ hour after sunset.

Grand View Point Geology Talk. By attending this session you can learn something about the geology that created Canyonlands. The talks are generally offered twice daily between April and October; check at the visitor centers for times and locations. | Grand View Point, 12 mi from the park entrance on the main park road, Island in the Sky | Apr.–Oct., daily.

Horseshoe Canyon Guided Hike. April through October, join a park ranger for a guided hike into Horseshoe Canyon. The hike is 6.5 mi round-trip, with a steep drop into the canyon and a corresponding climb out at the end of the four- to five-hour hike. Walks depart from the west rim parking lot, which is on a dirt road that may be impassable to two-wheel-drive vehicles in bad weather. | Horseshoe Canyon Trailhead, 32 mi off Rte. 24, Maze | 435/259–2652 | Apr.–Oct., weekends 9 AM.

Junior Ranger Program. This program is the same as the Junior Ranger Program at Arches (*above*). | 435/259–4712 Island in the Sky, 435/259–4711 Needles | Free.

SCENIC DRIVES

Island in the Sky Park Road. The park road in this Canyonlands district is 12 mi long and connects to a 5-mi side road to the Upheaval Dome area. You can enjoy many of the park's vistas by stopping at the overlooks, but you'll need to get out of your car for the best views. Once you get to the park, allow about two hours to explore this route by car.

Needles District Park Road. You'll feel certain that you've driven into a picture postcard as you roll along the park road in the Needles District. Red mesas and buttes rise against the horizon, blue mountain ranges interrupt the rangelands, and the colorful red and white needles stand like soldiers on the far side of grassy meadows. The drive is about 10 mi one-way. This short drive takes only about half an hour.

SIGHTS TO SEE

★ **Grand View Point.** At the end of the main road of Island in the Sky, don't miss this 360-degree view that extends all the way to the San Juan Mountains in Colorado on a clear day. | 12 mi from the park entrance on the main road, Island in the Sky.

Green River Overlook. Near Island in the Sky Campground you can get a good look at the Green River as it flows through the park. | 7 mi from the park entrance, about 1 mi off Upheaval Dome Road, Island in the Sky.

Hans Flat Ranger Station. This remote spot is nothing more than a stopping point for permits, books, and maps before you strike out into the Maze District of Canyonlands. To get here, you must drive 46 mi on a dirt road that is sometimes impassable to two-wheel-drive vehicles. There's a pit toilet, but no water, food, or services of any kind. Past Hans Flat, you'll need a high-clearance, four-wheel-drive vehicle to access the Maze. | 46 mi east of Rte. 24; 21 mi south and east of the Y-junction and Horseshoe Canyon kiosk on the dirt road, Maze | 435/259–2652 | Daily 8–4:30.

Island in the Sky Visitor Center. Stop and watch the orientation film and then browse the book store for information about the Canyonlands region. Exhibits help explain animal adaptations as well as some of the history of the park. | Past the park entrance on the main park road, Island in the Sky.

★ **Mesa Arch.** Even though it can be crowded, you simply can't visit Island in the Sky without taking the quick 0.5-mi walk to Mesa Arch. The arch is above a cliff that drops nearly 1,000 ft to the canyon bottom. Views through the arch of Washerwoman Arch and surrounding buttes, spires, and canyons make this a favorite photo opportunity. | 6 mi from the park entrance on the main road, Island in the Sky.

Needles District Visitor Center. This gorgeous building that blends into the landscape is worth seeing, even if you don't need the books, trail maps, or other information available inside. | Less than 1 mi from the park entrance on the main park road, Needles.

Pothole Point Trail. This is an especially good stop after a rainstorm, which fills the potholes with water. Stop to study the communities of tiny creatures, including fairy shrimp, that thrive in the slickrock hollows. You'll discover dramatic views of the Needles and Six Shooter Peak, too. The easy 0.6-mi round-trip walk takes about 45 minutes. There's no shade, so wear a hat. | About 9 mi from the park entrance on the main road, Needles.

Roadside Ruin. For a look at an ancestral Puebloan granary, hop out of your car and take this 20-minute walk in the desert. There's only one short little climb up over some slickrock. The views of the deep red mesas that surround the park are another reason to make this stop. | Less than 1 mi from the park entrance on the main road, Needles.

Shafer Trail. This road was probably first established by ancient Native Americans, but in the early 1900s ranchers used it to drive cattle into the canyon. Originally narrow and rugged, it was upgraded during the uranium boom, when miners hauled ore by truck from the canyon floor. You can see the road's winding route down canyon walls from Shafer Canyon Overlook. Today Shafer Trail is used by daring four-wheelers and energetic mountain bikers. It descends 1,400 ft to the White Rim and another 700 ft to the Colorado River. | Less than 1 mi from the park entrance on the main road, Island in the Sky.

Upheaval Dome. This colorful, mysterious crater is one of the many wonders of Island in the Sky. Some geologists believe it to be an eroded salt dome, but others have theorized that it is an eroded meteorite impact dome. To see it, you'll have to walk a short distance to the overlook. | 11 mi from the park entrance on Upheaval Dome Road, Island in the Sky.

Wooden Shoe Arch. See if you can find the tiny window in the rock that looks very much like a wooden shoe with a turned up toe. You won't have to find it on your own; there's a marker on the park road. | About 5 mi from the park entrance on the main road, Needles.

ARCHES AND
CANYONLANDS
NATIONAL PARKS

EXPLORING
ATTRACTIONS NEARBY
DINING
LODGING
CAMPING AND RV
FACILITIES
SHOPPING
ESSENTIAL
INFORMATION

Sports and Outdoor Activities

BICYCLING

The only cycling in Canyonlands National Park is on existing roads. There is little enough vehicle traffic that you might enjoy a tour along the Needles District main road, which is fairly flat. More traffic and lots of hills and curves make the Island in the Sky road a little more hazardous. Opt instead for the unpaved roads in either district, but understand that you are sharing the road with four-wheel-drive vehicles and you may have to eat some dust from time to time. *See* Four-Wheeling, *below* for more Canyonlands routes, and Outfitters, *below,* for more information on biking in the area.

White Rim Road. Mountain bikers all over the world like to brag that they've ridden this 112-mi road around Island in the Sky. The trail's fame is well-deserved: it traverses steep roads, broken rock, and ledges as well as long stretches that wind through the canyons and look down onto others. There's always a good chance you'll see bighorn sheep here, too. Permits are not required for day use, but if you're biking White Rim without an outfitter you'll need careful planning and backcountry reservations (make them as far in advance as possible through the reservation office, 435/259–4351). Information about permits can be found at www.nps.gov/cany. There's no water on this route. White Rim Road starts at the end of Shafer Trail near Musselman Arch. | Off the main park road about 1 mi from the entrance, then about 11 mi on Shafer Trail; or off Potash Rd. (Rte. 279) at the Jug Handle Arch turnoff about 18 mi from U.S. 191, then about 5 mi on Shafer Trail, Island in the Sky.

RIVER EXPEDITIONS

Seeing Canyonlands National Park from the river is a great and rare pleasure. Long stretches of calm water on the Green River are perfect for lazy canoe trips. In Labyrinth Canyon north of the park boundary and in Stillwater Canyon in the Island in the Sky District, the river is quiet and calm and there's plenty of shoreside camping. The Island in the Sky leg of the Colorado River, from Moab to its confluence with the Green River and downstream a few more miles to Spanish Bottom, is ideal for both canoeing and for rides with an outfitter in a large, stable jet boat. If you want to take a self-guided flat water float trip in the park you must obtain a $20 permit, which you have to request by mail or fax. Make your upstream travel arrangements with a shuttle company before you request a permit. For permits, contact the reservation office at park headquarters (435/259–4351).

Below Spanish Bottom, about 64 mi downstream from Moab, 49 mi from the Potash Road ramp, and 4 mi south of the confluence, the Colorado churns into the first rapids of legendary Cataract Canyon. Home of some of the best white water in the United States, this piece of river between the Maze and the Needles District rivals the Grand Canyon stretch of the Colorado River for adventure. During spring melt-off these rapids can rise to staggering heights and deliver heart-stopping excitement. The canyon cuts through the very heart of Canyonlands, where you can see this amazing wilderness area in its most pristine form. The water calms down a bit in summer but still offers enough thrills for most people. Outfitters will take you for the ride of your life in this wild canyon, where the river drops more steeply than anywhere else on the Colorado River (in 0.75 mi, the river drops 39 ft). You can join an expedition lasting anywhere from one to six days, or you can purchase a $30 permit for a self-guided trip from park headquarters. For information about river expedition outfitters, see Outfitters, below.

FOUR-WHEELING

Nearly 200 mi of challenging backcountry roads lead to campsites, trailheads, and natural and cultural features in Canyonlands. All of the roads require high-clearance, four-wheel-drive vehicles, and many are inappropriate for inexperienced drivers. Especially before you tackle the Maze, be sure that your four-wheel-drive skills are well honed and that you are capable of making basic road and vehicle repairs. Carry at least one full-size spare tire, extra gas, extra water, a shovel, a high-lift jack, and—October through April—chains for all four tires. Double-check to see that your vehicle is in top-notch condition, for you definitely don't want to break down in the interior of the park: towing expenses can exceed $1,000. For overnight four-wheeling trips you must purchase a $30 permit, which you can reserve in advance by contacting the Backcountry Reservations Office (435/259–4351). Cyclists share all roads, so be aware and cautious of their presence. Vehicular traffic traveling uphill has the right-of-way. It's best to check at the visitor center for current road conditions before taking off into the backcountry. You must carry a washable, reusable toilet with you in the Maze district and carry out all waste.

Colorado River Overlook. The first half of this road is fairly easy. The second half, however, deteriorates rapidly with a few large rocks and stair-step drops in the last 1.5 mi. Many people prefer to walk the last part of the road to the overlook. The overlook, which has no guard rails, gives you wonderful views of the Colorado River. The road is about 11 mi round-trip and takes about five hours to drive. | Visitor center, Needles.

Elephant Hill. So intimidating is this Needles route that many people get out and walk while the experienced drivers tackle the steep grades, loose rock, and stair-step drops. The road is so difficult that you can walk it faster than you can drive it: to negotiate some of the tight turns you have to back up on steep cliffs. Beyond the elephant's hump the road remains equally challenging. From Elephant Hill trailhead to Devil's Kitchen it's 3.5 mi; from the trailhead to the Confluence Overlook, a popular destination, it's a 16-mi round-trip and requires at least eight hours. | 7 mi from the park entrance off the main park road, Needles.

Flint Trail. This remote, rugged road is the most used road in the Maze District, but don't let that fool you into thinking it's smooth sailing. It is very technical with 2 mi of switch-backs that drop down the side of a cliff face. You reach Flint Trail from the Hans Flat Ranger Station, which is 46 mi from the closest paved road (Rte. 24 off I–70). From Hans Flat to the end of the road at the Doll House it's 41 mi, a drive that takes about seven hours one-way. From Hans Flat to the Maze Overlook it's 34 mi. The Maze is not generally a des-tination for a day trip, so you'll have to purchase an overnight backcountry permit for $30. | Hans Flat Ranger Station 46 mi east of Rte. 24, Maze.

Horse Canyon/Peekaboo Trails. Know what you're doing if you choose to take this route, which traverses a protected canyon up Salt Creek Wash to ancient Native American rock art and ruin sites. The two roads travel along the canyon bottom, where deep sand, deep water, and quicksand are common. The first stretch, Peekaboo Trail, leads to Peekaboo Spring, where vehicle campsites are near some great rock art. Beyond that, Horse Canyon Trail passes several arches and Tower Ruin, one of the park's best preserved pieces of ancient archi-tecture. Take binoculars to get a good view of it. It is 5.5 mi from the trailhead to Tower Ruin. Past Tower Ruin you can travel only about 3 mi more before you encounter a boul-der that has to be driven over, causing your vehicle to tip and leave its paint on the oppo-site wall. You must purchase a $5 permit to make the Horse Canyon/Peekaboo drive; only 10 private vehicles are allowed into the area each day. | Through the gate at the end of Cave Springs Rd., 1 mi from the park entrance, Needles.

Lavender Canyon. You'll be able to see many arches and archaeological sites from this rarely used road, which follows a canyon bottom where you may encounter deep sand, deep water, and quicksand in addition to two major creek crossings with steep banks. Allow all day for the 40-mi round trip. The park requires drivers to obtain a $5 permit for day use; there's no vehicle camping allowed in this canyon. Only eight private vehicles are allowed into the area each day. Do not enter if it has been raining or if rain threatens. | Off Rte. 211 outside the park entrance, Needles.

White Rim Road. Winding around and below the Island in the Sky mesa top, the dramatic 112-mi White Rim Road offers a once-in-a-lifetime driving experience. As you tackle Mur-phy's Hogback, Hardscrabble Hill, and more formidable obstacles, you will get some fan-tastic views of the park. A trip around the loop takes two to three days and you must make reservations almost a year in advance for an overnight campsite—unless you're lucky enough to snap up a no-show or cancellation. For reservation information call the Backcountry Reservation Office (435/259–4351). White Rim Road starts at the end of Shafer Trail near Musselman Arch. | Off the main park road about 1 mi from the entrance, then about 11 mi on Shafer Trail; or off Potash Rd. (Rte. 279) at the Jug Handle Arch turnoff about 18 mi from U.S. 191, then about 5 mi on Shafer Trail, Island in the Sky.

HIKING

Canyonlands National Park is a good place to saturate yourself in the intoxicating colors, smells, and textures of the desert. Many of the trails are long, rolling routes over slick-rock and sand in landscapes dotted with juniper, pinyon, and sagebrush. Interconnect-ing trails in the Needles District provide excellent opportunities for week-long backpacking excursions. The Maze trails are primarily accessed via four-wheel-drive vehicle. In the sepa-rate Horseshoe Canyon area Horseshoe Canyon Trail takes a considerable amount of effort to reach, as it is more than 100 mi from Moab, 32 mi of which are a bumpy, and often sandy, dirt road.

ARCHES AND
CANYONLANDS
NATIONAL PARKS

EXPLORING
ATTRACTIONS NEARBY
DINING
LODGING
CAMPING AND RV
FACILITIES
SHOPPING
ESSENTIAL
INFORMATION

Aztec Butte Trail. Chances are good you'll enjoy this hike in solitude. It begins level, then climbs up a steep slope of slickrock. The highlight of the 2-mi round-trip hike is the chance to see ancestral Puebloan granaries. | About 6 mi from the park entrance on Upheaval Dome Rd., Island in the Sky.

★ **Cave Spring Trail.** One of the best, most diverse trails in the park takes you past a historic cowboy camp, prehistoric Native American petroglyphs, and great views along the way. About half of the trail is in shade, as it meanders under overhangs. Slanted, bumpy slickrock make this hike more difficult than others, and two ladders make the 0.6-mi round-trip walk even more of an adventure. Allow about 45 minutes. | 2.6 mi from the park entrance off the main park road on Cave Springs Rd., Needles.

Chesler Park Loop. Chesler Park is a grassy meadow dotted with spires and enclosed by a circular wall of colorful "needles." One of Canyonlands' more popular trails leads through the area to the famous Joint Trail. The trail is 6 mi round-trip to the viewpoint. | Elephant Hill Trailhead, about 7 mi from the park entrance off the main park road, Needles.

Grand View Point Trail. If you're looking for a level walk with some of the grandest views in the world, stop at Grand View Point and wander the 2-mi trail along the cliff edge. Most people just stop at the overlook and drive on, so the trail is not as crowded as you might think. On a clear day you can see up to 100 mi to the Maze and Needles districts of the park, the confluence of the Green and Colorado rivers, and each of Utah's major laccolithic mountain ranges: the Henrys, Abajos, and La Sals. | 12 mi from the park entrance on the main park road, Island in the Sky.

Horseshoe Canyon Trail. You arrive at this detached unit of Canyonlands National Park via a washboarded, two-wheel-drive dirt road. Park at the lip of the canyon and hike 6.5 mi round-trip to the Great Gallery, considered by some to be the most significant rock art panel in North America. Ghostly life-size figures in the Barrier Canyon style populate the amazing panel. The hike is moderately strenuous, with a 750 ft descent. Allow at least six hours for the trip and take a gallon of water per person. There's no camping allowed in the canyon, although you can camp on top near the parking lot. | 32 mi east of Rte. 24, Maze.

Joint Trail. Part of the Chesler Park Loop, this well-loved trail follows a series of deep, narrow fractures in the rock. A shady spot in summer, it will give you good views of the Needles formations for which the district is named. The loop travels briefly along a four-wheel-drive road and is 11 mi round-trip; allow at least five hours to complete the hike. | Elephant Hill Trailhead, 7 mi from the park entrance off the main park road, Needles.

Slickrock Trail. If you're on this trail in summer make sure you're wearing a hat, because you won't find any shade along the 2.4-mi round-trip trek across slickrock. This is one of the few frontcountry sites where you might see bighorn sheep. | About 10 mi from the park entrance on the main road, Needles.

Syncline Loop Trail. Are you up for a long, full day of hiking? Try this 8-mi trail that circles Upheaval Dome. You not only get great views of the dome, you actually make a complete loop around its base. Stretches of the trail are rocky, rugged, and steep. | 11 mi from the park entrance on Upheaval Dome Rd., Island in the Sky.

Upheaval Dome Trail. It's worth the steep hike to see this formation, which is either an eroded salt dome or a meteorite crash site. You reach the main overlook after just 0.5 mi, but you can double your pleasure by going on to a second overlook for a better view. The trail becomes steep and rough after the first overlook. Round-trip to the second overlook is 2 mi. | 11 mi from the park entrance on Upheaval Dome Rd., Island in the Sky.

★ **Whale Rock Trail.** If you've been hankering to walk across some of that pavement-smooth stuff they call slickrock, the hike to Whale Rock will make your feet happy. This 1-mi round-trip adventure, complete with handrails to help you make the tough 100-ft climb, takes you to the very top of the whale's back. Once you get there, you are rewarded with great views of Upheaval Dome and Trail Canyon. | 11 mi from the park entrance on Upheaval Dome Rd., Island in the Sky.

ROCK CLIMBING

Canyonlands and many of the surrounding areas draw climbers from all over the world. Permits are not required, but because of the sensitive archaeological nature of the park, it's imperative that you stop at the visitor center to pick up regulations pertaining to the park's cultural resources. Popular climbing routes include Moses and Zeus Towers in Taylor Canyon, and Monster Tower and Washerwoman Tower on the White Rim Road. Like most routes in Canyonlands, these climbs are for experienced climbers only.

Outfitters

BICYCLING

Chile Pepper Bikes. For bicycle rentals, repairs, and espresso, stop here before you hit the trails. | 550½ N. Main St., Moab | 435/259–4688 or 888/677–4688 | www.chilebikes.com.

Nichols Expeditions. These professional outfitters take about a dozen multiday bike trips a year into the backcountry of Canyonlands National Park. Departure dates and routes are predetermined, so contact them for a schedule. | 497 N. Main St., Moab | 435/259–3999 or 800/648–8488 | fax 435/259–2312 | www.nicholsexpeditions.com.

Poison Spider Bicycles. This is a fully loaded shop staffed by young, friendly bike experts. | 497 N. Main St., Moab | 435/259–7882 or 800/635–1792.

Rim Cyclery. For full-suspension bike rentals and sales, solid advice on trails, and parts, equipment and gear, this is the oldest bike shop in town. | 94 W. 100 South, Moab | 435/259–5333 or 888/304–8219 | www.rimcyclery.com.

Rim Tours. Reliable, friendly and professional, this outfit can take you on a great guided mountain bike tour. Trips include Gemini Bridges, the Slickrock Trail, Klondike Bluffs, and many other locations—including the White Rim Trail in Canyonlands. | 1233 S. U.S. 191, Moab | 435/259–5223 or 800/626–7335 | fax 435/259–3349 | www.rimtours.com.

Western Spirit Cycling. This place offers fully supported, go-at-your-own-pace multiday bike tours throughout the region, including trips to the 140-mi Kokopelli Trail, which runs from Grand Junction, Colorado, to Moab. Guides versed in the geologic wonders of the area cook up meals worthy of the scenery each night. There's also the option to combine a Green River kayak trip with the three-night bike route. | 478 Mill Creek Dr., Moab | 435/259–8732 or 800/845–2453 | fax 435/259–2736 | www.westernspirit.com.

FOUR-WHEELING

Coyote Land Tours. For a big adventure in a big vehicle, try a half-day tour with this company. They'll take you into the backcountry in a Mercedes Unimog. | 731 Mulberry La., Moab | 435/259–6649 | www.coyoteshuttle.com.

Highpoint Hummer Tours. If you'd rather let someone else do the driving for your off-road experience, try these folks who run around in open-air Hummer vehicles. They offer two- and four-hour "high" adventure trips as well as "low" adventure tours for the more timid backcountry traveler. You can also rent ATV's here. | 281 N. Main St., Moab | 435/259–2972 or 877/486–6833 | fax 435-259-9336 | www.highpointhummer.com.

MULTISPORT

Adrift Adventures. This outfitter can get you out on the Colorado or Green rivers for either daylong or multiday raft trips. Adrift also offers a unique combination horseback ride and river trip, as well as motor-coach tours into Arches, rock art tours, and 4X4 excursions into Canyonlands. | 378 N. Main, Moab | 435/259–8594 or 800/874–4483 | fax 435-259-7628 | www.adrift.net.

Coyote Shuttle. If you need a ride to or from your bicycle trailhead or river trip, call the Coyote. These folks also do shuttles to and from Green River for the train and bus service there. | 55 W. 300 South, Moab | 435/259–8656 | www.coyoteshuttle.com.

NAVTEC. A fast little boat engineered by this outfit gets you down the Colorado River and through Cataract Canyon in one day. They also offer trips lasting up to six days, as well as 4X4 trips into the backcountry of Canyonlands. Raft rentals are also available here. | 321 N. Main St., Moab | 435/259–7983 or 800/833–1278 | fax 435/259–5823 | www.navtec.com.

Oars. This company can take you rafting on the Colorado River and four-wheeling in the parks. For those not into white water they also offer a calm water ride on the Colorado. | 543 N. Main St., Moab | 435/259–5865 or 800/342–5938 | www.oarsutah.com.

Roadrunner Shuttle. Call this company for ride to the airport or for a river or bike shuttle. They'll even take you to Salt Lake City or Grand Junction, CO. | 435/259–9402 | www.roadrunnershuttle.com.

RIVER EXPEDITIONS

Canyon Voyages Adventure Co. An excellent choice for a day trip on the Colorado River is this friendly, professional company. It's also the only company that operates a kayak school for those who want to learn how to run the rapids on their own, and you can rent rafts and kayaks here. Inside the booking office is a great shop that sells river gear, outdoor clothes, hats, sandals, and backpacks. | 211 N. Main St., Moab | 435/259–6007 or 800/733–6007 | fax 435/259–9391 | www.canyonvoyages.com.

Holiday River Expeditions. You can rent a canoe or book a raft trip on the Green and Colorado rivers at this reliable company with decades of river experience. | 1055 E. Main St., Green River | 800/624–6323 | fax 801/266–1448 | www.bikeraft.com.

Sheri Griffith Expeditions. Purchased by travel giant Abercrombie & Kent in 2000, this long-time Moab outfitter offers trips through the whitewater of Cataract, Westwater, and Desolation canyons, on the Green River. Specialty expeditions include river trips for women, writers, or families. You might also enjoy one of their more luxurious expeditions, which make roughing it a little more comfortable. | 2231 S. U.S. 191, Moab | 435/259–8229 or 800/332–2439 | fax 435/259–2226 | www.griffithexp.com.

Tag-A-Long Expeditions. This company holds more permits with the National Park Service and has been taking people into the whitewater of Cataract Canyon and Canyonlands longer than any other outfitter in Moab. They also run four-wheel-drive expeditions into the backcountry of the park as well as calm water excursions on the Colorado River. They are the only outfitter allowed to take you into the park via both water and 4X4. Trips run from half-day to six days in length. | 452 N. Main St., Moab | 435/259–8946 or 800/453–3292 | www.tagalong.com.

Tex's Riverways. The folks at Tex's will take very good care of you when you rent a canoe for a self-guided trip, and will shuttle you to and from the Green or Colorado rivers. | 691 N. 500 West, Moab | 435/259–5101 | www.texsriverways.com.

Western River Expeditions. For a day trip on the Colorado River or to rent a "ducky" (inflatable kayak), try this reputable company. | 225 S. Main St., Moab | 435/259–7019 or 800/453–7450 | fax 801/942–8514 | www.westernriver.com.

Attractions Nearby

Scenic Drives

Colorado River Scenic Byway—Route 128. One of the most scenic drives in the country is Route 128, which intersects U.S. 191 3 mi south of Arches. The 37-mi highway runs along the Colorado River northeast to I–70. The drive from Moab to I–70 takes about an hour.

Colorado Riverway Scenic Byway—Route 279. If you're interested in Native American rock art, this scenic drive along the Colorado River is a perfect place to spend a couple of hours. If you start late in the afternoon, the cliffs will be glowing orange as the sun sets. Along the first part of the route you'll see signs reading "Indian Writings." Park only in designated areas to view the petroglyphs on the cliff. At the 18-mi marker you'll see Jug Handle Arch on the cliff side of the road. Continue a few miles more to reach the end of the pavement. Here the road turns into a four-wheel-drive road that takes you into the Island in the Sky District of Canyonlands. Do not continue on this road unless you are in a high-clearance four-wheel-drive vehicle with a full gas tank and plenty of water. Allow about two hours round-trip for this Scenic Byway drive.

La Sal Mountain Loop. Although the Arches and Canyonlands area is best known for its slickrock desert, it's also the gateway to the 12,000-ft La Sal Mountains, the second-highest mountain range in Utah. Beginning 8 mi south of Moab on Old Airport Road (a left turnoff from U.S. 191), the 62-mi drive climbs over the western flank of the range before entering red rock country and connecting to Route 128 to the north. You'll drive about 20 mi of scenic Route 128 before hitting U.S. 191 just north of Moab. Once snow flies, portions of the La Sal Mountain Loop are impassable. Allow about three hours for this drive in good weather.

Sights to See

Courthouse Wash. Although this rock art panel fell victim to a sad and unusual case of vandalism in 1980, when someone scoured the petroglyphs and pictographs that had been left by four cultures, you can still see ancient images if you take a short walk from the parking area on the left-hand side of the road. | U.S. 191, about 2 mi south of the entrance to Arches National Park.

Dan O'Laurie Museum. Ancient and historical Native Americans are remembered in exhibits of sandals, baskets, pottery, and other artifacts. Other displays chronicle early Spanish expeditions into the area, and the history of uranium discovery and exploration. | 118 E. Center St., Moab | 435/259–7985 | $2 per person; $5 per family | Apr.–Oct., Mon.–Sat. 1–8; Nov.–Mar., Mon.–Thurs. 3–7, Fri. and Sat. 1–7.

Dead Horse Point State Park. One of the finest state parks in Utah overlooks a sweeping oxbow of the Colorado River, some 2,000 ft below, and the upside-down landscapes of Canyonlands National Park. Dead Horse Point itself is a small peninsula connected to the main mesa by a narrow neck of land. As the story goes, cowboys used to drive wild horses onto the point and pen them there with a brush fence. Some were accidentally forgotten and left to perish. Facilities at the park include a modern visitor center and museum, a 21-site campground with drinking water, and an overlook. | 34 mi from Moab at the end of Rte. 313 | 435/259–2614, 800/322–3770 for campground reservations | http://parks.state.ut.us | $7 per vehicle | Daily 8–6.

Dinosaur Museum. The kids will no doubt enjoy a break from all that driving at this small museum. Skeletons, fossil logs, footprints, and reconstructed dinosaur skin are all on display. Hallways hold a collection of movie posters featuring Godzilla and other dinosaur-like monsters dating back to the 1930s. | 754 S. 200 West, Blanding | 435/678–3454 | $2 | Apr.–Oct., Mon.–Sat. 9–5; extended hours in summer.

★ **Edge of the Cedars State Park.** Tucked away on a back street in Blanding is one of the nation's foremost museums dedicated to the ancestral Puebloan Indians. The museum displays a variety of pots, baskets, spear points, and such. Interestingly, many of these artifacts were donated by pot hunters—archaeological looters. Behind the museum, you can visit an actual Anasazi ruin. | 660 W. 400 North St., Blanding | 435/678–2238 | http://parks.state.ut.us | $5 per vehicle | May–Sept., daily 8–8; Oct.–Apr., daily 9–5.

Fisher Towers. On the Colorado River northeast of Arches and very near Moab, you can take one of America's most scenic—yet unintimidating—river raft rides. This is the perfect place

ARCHES AND
CANYONLANDS
NATIONAL PARKS

EXPLORING
ATTRACTIONS
NEARBY
DINING
LODGING
CAMPING AND RV
FACILITIES
SHOPPING
ESSENTIAL
INFORMATION

to take the family or to learn to kayak with the help of an outfitter. The river rolls by the red Fisher Towers as they rise into the sky in front of the La Sal Mountains. A day trip on this stretch of the river will take you about 15 mi. Outfitters offer full- or half-day adventures here. | 17 mi upriver from Rte. 128 near Moab.

Gray–Desolation Canyon. Desolation is not really a fair name for this beautiful, lush canyon along the Green River. It's a favorite destination of canoe paddlers, kayakers, and beginning rafters. There are lots of rapids on this stretch of the Green, but they are on the small side and deliver lots of laughs. Families with children of almost any age can share this adventure and even paddle on their own under the watchful eyes of a guide. This trip requires four or five days to complete. | On the Green River.

Hovenweep National Monument. If you're headed south from Canyonlands and have an interest in ancestral Puebloan culture, a visit to this monument is a must. It's a little out of the way along a remote stretch of the Utah-Colorado border southeast of Blanding, but seeing the unusual tower structures (which may have been used for astronomical observation) is worth the effort. A 0.5-mi walking tour, or a more rigorous 1.5-mi hike into the canyon, takes you to the ancient dwellings. A 32-site campground is available for overnighters in tents or small vehicles. | Rte. 262, 28 mi east of U.S. 191 | 970/562–4282 | www.nps.gov/hove | $6 | Daily 8 AM–sunset.

John Wesley Powell River History Museum. Here you can see what it was like to travel down the Green and Colorado rivers in the 1800s. A series of interactive displays tracks the Powell Party's arduous, dangerous 1869 journey. The center also houses the River Runner's Hall of Fame, a tribute to those have followed in Powell's wake. An art gallery reserved for works thematically linked to river exploration is also on site. | 885 E. Main St., Green River | 435/564–3427 | $2 per person, $5 per family | Apr.–Sept., daily 8–8; Oct.–Mar., daily 9–5.

La Sal Mountains. If you want a break from the desert heat, wander up to this laccolithic mountain range about 30 mi from Arches National Park. You can picnic in a meadow or take one of many alpine hikes in this largely undiscovered area. There's also a scenic drive that gives you some great vistas of the valley. The roads can be impassable in winter, but the cross-country skiing is great. | U.S. 191, 12 mi southeast of Moab, Moab | 435/259–7155.

Moab Information Center. This downtown visitor center is the place to find information on Arches and Canyonlands national parks, as well as other destinations in the Four Corners region. It has a wonderful book store operated by Canyonlands Natural History Association. The hours vary, but from March through October the center opens daily at 8 AM and closes sometime between 7 and 9 PM. November through February, the center is open a few hours each morning and afternoon. | Center and Main Sts., Moab | 435/259–8825 | Call for hrs.

Moab Rim Adventure Park. If you'd love to see Moab from a higher vantage point but don't want to huff and puff up a mountain to do it, jump on the chairlift that takes you to the top of the Moab Rim. The views are spectacular, and hiking and biking trails start here (your bike can hitch a ride with you on the chairlift). If you want to play "shoots and ladders" with your bicycle, head for the hair-raising 12-mi challenge trail at the top. A mile off Main Street at the south end of town, it's a little tough to find. | 985 W. Kane Creek Blvd., Moab | 435/259–7799 | $10; no extra charge for bicycles | Mar.–Oct., daily 9 AM–dark.

Natural Bridges National Monument. When Elliot McClure visited Natural Bridges National Monument in 1931, his car slowly disintegrated. First his headlights fell off. Next, his doors dropped off. Finally, his bumpers worked loose, and the radiator broke away. Today a drive to the three stone bridges is far less hazardous. All roads are paved and a scenic 9-mi route takes you to stops that overlook Sipapu, Owachomo, and Kachina bridges. There's also a 13-site primitive campground. Natural Bridges is a drive of about 100 mi from the Needles District of Canyonlands National Park. | Rte. 275 off Rte. 95 | 435/692–1234 | www.nps.gov/nabr | $6 per vehicle | Daily 7 am–sunset.

★ **Newspaper Rock Recreation Site.** One of the West's most famous rock art sites, this large panel contains Native American etchings that accumulated on the rock over the course of 2,000 years. Apparently, early pioneers and explorers to the region named the site Newspaper Rock because they believed the rock, crowded with drawings, constituted a written language with which early people communicated. Archaeologists now agree the petroglyphs do not represent language. This is one of many "newspaper rocks" throughout the southwest. | Rte. 211, about 15 mi west of U.S. 191.

Scott M. Matheson Wetlands Preserve. The best place around for bird-watching, this desert oasis is home to hundreds of species of birds, including such treasures as the Pied-billed Grebe, the Cinnamon Teal, and the Northern Flicker. It's also a great place to spot beaver and muskrat playing in the water. The preserve is home to three bat species: the Western pipistrel, the pallid bat, and the hoary bat. A boardwalk winds through the preserve to a viewing shelter. | Near the intersection of 500 West and Kane Creek Blvd. | 435/259–4629.

Sego Canyon. About 39 mi from Moab, this is one of the most dramatic and mystifying rock art sights in the area. On the canyon walls you can see large, ghostlike rock art figures etched by Native Americans approximately 4,000 years ago. There's also art left by the Ute Indians 400–700 years ago. This canyon is a little out of the way, but well worth the drive. | About 4 mi off I–70 exit 185, Thompson Springs.

Westwater Canyon. In this narrow, winding canyon near the Utah-Colorado border, the Colorado River cuts through the oldest exposed geologic layer on earth. The result is craggy black granite jutting out of the water with red sandstone walls towering above. This section of the river is rocky and considered highly technical for rafters and kayakers, but it dishes out a great whitewater experience in a short period of time. Most outfitters offer this trip as a one-day getaway, but you may also linger in the canyon as long as three days to complete the journey. | About 51 mi northeast of Moab on the Colorado River.

Wilson Arch. Between Arches and the Needles District of Canyonlands, this giant roadside arch makes a great photo stop. In Moab, you can still find historical photos of an airplane flying through this arch. No one has tried the stunt lately, probably because it's now illegal. | U.S. 191, 23 mi south of Moab.

Tours

Canyonlands by Night. Certainly one of the more unusual ways to spend an evening around here, this night-time ride takes you upstream from Moab on the Colorado River. A narrator relates regional history and legends as you float along the river and giant spotlights illuminate the canyon walls. Despite the name, the company does not take you into the park. | 1861 N. U.S. 191, Moab | 435/259–5261 or 800/394–9978 | fax 435/259–2788 | www.canyonlandsbynight.com | $38 adults, $22 ages 6–12, $8.50 ages 2–5.

Dining

In Arches

Picnic Areas. Arches has a couple of nice places where you can enjoy a picnic lunch.

The view is the best part of the picnic spot at **Balanced Rock.** There are no cooking facilities or water, but there are picnic tables. If you sit just right you might find some shade under a small juniper; otherwise, this is an exposed picnic site. Pit toilets are nearby. | Opposite the Balanced Rock parking area, 9.2 mi from the park entrance on the main road.

At the end of the park road you can have your picnic lunch at **Devils Garden** before or after you go hiking. You will find grills, water, picnic tables, rest rooms, and depending on the time of day, some shade from large junipers and rock walls. | 18 mi from the park entrance on the main road.

ARCHES AND CANYONLANDS NATIONAL PARKS

EXPLORING
ATTRACTIONS NEARBY
DINING
LODGING
CAMPING AND RV FACILITIES
SHOPPING
ESSENTIAL INFORMATION

In Canyonlands

Picnic Areas. Have a picnic in a lovely setting and enjoy the quiet of the park.

Stopping at **Grand View Point** for a picnic lunch might be one of your more memorable vacation events. It's a gorgeous spot in which to recharge your energy and stretch your legs. There are picnic tables, grills, rest rooms, and a little shade if you sit near a juniper or pinyon. | 12 mi from park entrance on the main road, Island in the Sky.

Charming is a word that comes to mind to describe the picnic area nestled among the pinyon and juniper trees at the **Upheaval Dome** trailhead. There are no real vistas here, but the location is convenient to the Syncline Loop and Upheaval Dome trails. You'll find picnic tables, grills, and rest rooms, but no running water. | 11 mi from the park entrance on Upheaval Dome Road, Island in the Sky.

Near the Parks

★ **Buck's Grill House.** Southwestern. For a taste of the American West, try the buffalo meat loaf or elk stew served at this popular dinner spot. The steaks are thick and tender and the gravies will have you licking your fingers. A selection of southwestern entrées including duck tamales and buffalo chorizo tacos round out the menu. Vegetarian diners don't despair; there are some tasty choices for you, too. A surprisingly good wine list will complement your meal. Outdoor patio dining accompanied by the trickle of a waterfall will end your day perfectly. | 1393 N. U.S. 191, Moab | 435/259–5201 | $5–$20 | D, MC, V | Closed Sat. after Thanksgiving–mid-February. No lunch.

★ **Center Café.** Contemporary. This little jewel in the desert has a courtyard for outdoor dining. The mood inside is Spanish Mediterranean, made even more lovely by the fireplace. From grilled black Angus beef tenderloin with caramelized onion and Gorgonzola, or roasted eggplant lasagna with feta cheese and Moroccan olive marinara, there is always something here to make your taste buds go "ah." This treasure has been named "Best Restaurant in Southern Utah" more than once. Be sure to ask for the impressive wine list. | 60 N. 100 West, Moab | 435/259–4295 | $16–$28 | D, MC, V | Closed Dec.–Jan. No lunch.

Cow Canyon Trading Post. American. Tiny but absolutely charming, this restaurant next to a classic trading post serves three dinner entrées daily. Meals are creative and diverse, with a touch of ethnic flair. There's usually a grilled meat with plenty of fresh vegetables, and you can enjoy beer or wine with your meal. | U.S. 191 and Rte. 163, Bluff | 435/672–2208 | $12–$17 | AE, MC, V | Closed Nov.–Mar. No lunch.

Eddie McStiff's. American/Casual. This casual restaurant and microbrewery serves up pizzas and zesty Italian specialties to go with 13 freshly brewed concoctions such as raspberry and blueberry wheat beer and a smooth cream ale. | 57 S. Main St., Moab | 435/259–2337 | $6–$17 | MC, V | Closed mid-Dec.–mid-Feb. No lunch Mon.–Thurs.

Eklecticafe. Eclectic. This small place is easy to miss but worth searching out for one of the more creative menus in Moab. Breakfast and lunch items include a variety of burritos and wraps, scrambled tofu, Polish sausage, Indonesian satay kebabs, and many fresh, organic salads. On nice days, you can take your meal outside to the large covered patio. In winter you'll want to stay inside by the wood-burning stove. | 352 N. Main St., Moab | 435/259–6896 | $6–$8 | MC, V | No dinner weekdays; no lunch weekends.

Fat City Smokehouse. American/Casual. This is a meat lover's paradise. The sandwiches are piled high with turkey, beef, pork, ham, or sausage, and the barbecued ribs, chicken, and garlic sausage are memorable. Flame-grilled steaks will make you think you're eating at the best cowboy camp. Don't be discouraged if you aren't a meat-eater. The vegetarian-friendly menu includes a Portobello mushroom sandwich and a garden burger. You can also have cold beer with your meal. | 2 S. 100 West, Moab | 435/259–4302 | $7–$17 | MC, V | Closed Dec.–Jan.

Homestead Steak House. American/Casual. The folks here specialize in authentic Navajo fry bread and Navajo tacos. The sheepherder's sandwich, with your choice of beef, turkey, or ham and all the trimmings, is also made with fry bread and is quite popular—and big! You can have breakfast (except on weekends), lunch, or dinner here. No alcohol is served. | 121 E. Center St., Monticello | 435/678–3456 | $6–$18 | AE, D, MC, V | No breakfast weekends.

Isabella's Pizzeria. Pizza. The best pizza in Moab is served at this family-owned and -operated restaurant. Microbrew on tap tastes good after a day in the desert. | 471 S. Main St., Moab | 435/259–6446 | $6–$17 | MC, V.

La Hacienda. Mexican. This family-run local favorite serves good south-of-the-border meals at an equally good price. The helpings are generous and the service is friendly—and yes, you can order a margarita. You can also get breakfast here, but they don't open until 11 AM. | 574 N. Main St., Moab | 435/259–6319 | $6–$14 | AE, D, MC, V.

Miguel's Baja Grill. Mexican. Miguel Valdes brought his traditional recipes to Moab from Baja California Sur. His specialty is fish tacos, but the molé is the best in the West and this is the only place for hundreds of miles to get ceviche. Authentic Mexican specials that change daily diversify the menu even more. The narrow corridor space is colorful, lively, and as authentic as the food. | 51 N. Main St., Moab | 435/259–6546 | $6–$13 | AE, D, MC, V | Closed mid-Nov.–Feb.

Moab Diner. American/Casual. For breakfast, lunch, and dinner this is the place where the locals go. A mixture of good old-fashioned American food and southwestern entrées gives you plenty to choose from. | 189 S. Main St., Moab | 435/259–4006 | $7–$14 | D, MC, V.

Poplar Place. American/Casual. This local landmark for fun and lively dining is known for its appetizers, pizzas, and sandwiches. Roof-top dining is perfect for warm summer evenings in the desert. | 11 E. 100 N. Main St., Moab | 435/259–6018 | $7–$18 | MC, V | Closed Dec.–Jan.

Ray's Tavern. American/Casual. Ray's is something of a western legend and a favorite hangout for river runners. Stop here for great tales about working on the river as well as for the best all-beef hamburger in two counties. | 25 S. Broadway, Green River | 435/564–3511 | $6–$8 | AE, D, MC, V.

★ **Sorrel River Grill.** American. The most scenic dining experience in the area is 17 mi down the road from Moab at the Sorrel River Ranch. Outdoor dining makes the most of views over the Colorado River, the La Sal Mountains, and the red rock spires and towers that surround the ranch. The seasonal menu changes regularly for the freshest ingredients. A full spa menu is available. Plenty of veggie entrées round out the menu. | Mile Marker 17.5, Rte. 128, Moab | 435/259–4642 | $15–$27 | AE, MC, V | No lunch.

Sunset Grill. American. Housed in the cliffside home of former uranium kingpin Charlie Steen, this restaurant is a Moab landmark. The views into the valley and of the Colorado River are magnificent, especially at sunset. The salmon is always reliable and the steaks are generously cut and juicy. | 900 N. Main St., Moab | 435/259–7146 | $12–$24 | AE, D, MC, V | Closed Sun. No lunch.

Lodging

Near the Parks

Cedar Breaks Some of the best nightly lodging values near Arches and Canyonlands are rental condominiums, such as this in-town condo complex convenient to everything. Each unit has two bedrooms and its own balcony or patio that overlooks a grassy lawn. Moab Lodging, which takes your reservations for these units, also handles cozy little neighborhood apartments that are available for one night or many. Kitchenettes. In-room VCRs. Outdoor hot tub. Laundry facilities. Some pets allowed (fee). No smoking. | 50 E. Center St., Moab, 84532 | 435/259–5125 or 888/272–8181 | fax 435/259–6079 | www.moabutahlodging.com | 6 units | $95–$135 | AE, MC, V.

ARCHES AND
CANYONLANDS
NATIONAL PARKS

EXPLORING
ATTRACTIONS NEARBY
DINING
LODGING
CAMPING AND RV
FACILITIES
SHOPPING
ESSENTIAL
INFORMATION

Days Inn. One of the largest properties in Monticello, this is also one of the nicest, with a heated indoor pool and a hot tub for soaking adventure-weary bodies. Some microwaves, some refrigerators. Cable TV. Indoor pool. Hot tub. | 549 N. Main St., Box 759, Monticello, 84535 | 435/587–2458 | fax 435/587–2191 | 43 rooms | $64–$82 | AE, D, DC, MC, V.

★ **Dreamkeeper Inn.** Serenity is just a wish away at this bed and breakfast in a quiet Moab neighborhood, on large, shady grounds filled with flower and vegetable gardens. The rooms line a hallway in the ranch-style home, and each opens onto the pool, patio, and courtyard area, where you may want to have your morning coffee. Or, you may prefer to have breakfast in the sunny indoor dining area. The owner/innkeepers are warm and generous. Refrigerators. Some in-room VCRs. Pool. Outdoor hot tub. No kids under 15. No smoking. | 191 S. 200 East, Moab, 84532 | 435/259–5998 or 888/230–3247 | fax 435/259–3912 | www.dreamkeeperinn.com | 6 rooms | $90–$135 | AE, D, MC, V.

Four Corners Inn. This family-owned motel offers large rooms and a bite to eat in the morning. If you're lucky you'll run into the owner, who tells stories of historical Blanding. The gift shop sells handmade quilts and trading post items. Kitchenette, some microwaves, some refrigerators. Cable TV. Some pets allowed. | 131 E. Center St. (U.S. 191), Blanding, 84535 | 435/678–3257 or 800/574–3150 | fax 435/678–3186 | 32 rooms | $50–$76 | AE, D, MC, V.

★ **Fry Canyon Lodge.** If Natural Bridges National Monument or any destination south of Canyonlands is on your agenda, make it a point to stay here. Built in 1955, the lodge was lovingly renovated in the mid-1990s. It's not fancy, but it's certainly unique. A sturdy porch is handy for gazing at the sunset or reading, which is just about all there is to do here when you're not hiking. Perhaps the biggest surprise is an on-site restaurant with gourmet-quality breakfast and dinner. A stay here is more a memorable experience than a night's sleep. Restaurant. | Mile Post 71, Rte. 95, Blanding 84533 | 254/381–7060 | www.frycanyon.com | 10 rooms | $74–$99 | AE, D, MC, V.

★ **Gonzo Inn.** When creating this eclectic inn the owners gave careful attention to design, color, and art. The furnishings are all decidedly contemporary, using much metal and steel, and some rooms have fireplaces. The pool, hot tub, and courtyard overlook a shady, pretty pathway that winds for 2 mi along Mill Creek. Some in-room hot tubs, some kitchenettes. Pool. Outdoor hot tub. Some pets allowed (fee). No smoking. | 100 W. 200 South, Moab, 84532 | 435/259–2515 or 800/791–4044 | fax 435/259–6992 | www.gonzoinn.com | 21 rooms, 22 suites | $129–$299 | AE, D, MC, V.

Landmark Inn. One of Moab's older deluxe motels delivers a little bit of character at a great price. Murals hand-painted by a local artist grace the walls of each room and, true to the aesthetic of the 1960s, there are still avocado-green bath fixtures in some of the rooms. The motel is convenient to many downtown restaurants and shops. The kids will love it because of the 52 ft water slide. Some kitchenettes, microwaves, refrigerators. Cable TV. Pool. Outdoor hot tub. Laundry facilities. | 168 N. Main St., Moab, 84532 | 435/259–6147 or 800/441–6147 | fax 435/259–5556 | 36 rooms | $50–$90 | AE, D, MC, V.

★ **Pack Creek Ranch.** A legend in the area, this guest ranch sits beneath the snowcapped summits of the La Sal Mountains. Horses graze in the pastures and mule deer frequent the grounds. Cabins have one to four bedrooms with bent-willow furnishings and full kitchens; most have stone fireplaces. There are no TVs or phones to disturb the peace and quiet. The main feature here is solitude in a spectacular setting—you can swim or soak within earshot of the creek. Kitchenettes. Pool. Hot tub, massage, sauna. Horseback riding. Some pets allowed (fee). No room phones. No smoking. | 20 mi from Moab on the La Sal Mountain Loop Rd. off Old Airport Rd. and Ken's Lake turnoff | Box 1270, Moab, 84532 | 435/259–5505 | fax 435/259–8879 | www.packcreekranch.com | 11 cabins, 1 ranch house | $95–$225 | AE, D, MC, V.

Recapture Lodge. Known for its friendliness, this popular and regionally famous inn runs guided tours into the surrounding canyon country and presents nightly slide shows about local geology, art, and history. The plain motel rooms offered at good prices book up fast, so be sure to call ahead for reservations. Pool. Outdoor hot tub. | U.S. 191, Box 309, Bluff, 84512 | 435/672–2281 | fax 435/672–2284 | 28 rooms | $48–$56 | AE, D, MC, V.

Red Cliffs Adventure Lodge. You can have it all at this gorgeous, classically western property. The Colorado River rolls by right outside your door, canyon walls reach for the sky in all their red, red glory, and you can gaze at it all from your private river-front patio. Rooms are decidedly western in flavor, with log furniture, lots of wood and saltillo tile. Added attractions include an on-site winery, a movie memorabilia museum, and guided rafting, hiking, biking, and horseback riding adventures into the desert. You can hook up to high-speed Internet in your room. Restaurant, room service. In-room data ports, kitchenettes. Cable TV, in-room VCRs. Pool. Gym, outdoor hot tub. Volleyball. Shops. Laundry facilities. | Milepost 14, Rte. 128, Moab, 84532 | 435/259–2002 or 800/325–6171 | www.redcliffslodge.com | 69 rooms, 1 suite | $169, $269 suite | AE, D, MC, V.

Red Rock Lodge and Suites. Great prices on lodging are available at this eclectic motel. The Cisco building is half of an old motel that was floated down the Colorado River on a barge before it found its home near downtown Moab. It has been gorgeously renovated with oak stairs, railings, and lots of amenities. The Painted Lady buildings are bright and fun, with front porches and an old West appeal. The 12 suites are big enough for families or groups traveling together. The Red Rock building has basic motel rooms but is quiet, safe, and comfortable. All are within walking distance of downtown restaurants and shops. In-room data ports, some kitchenettes. Cable TV, some in-room VCRs. Pool. Hot tub. Some pets allowed. No smoking. | 51 N. 100 West, Moab, 84532 | 435/259–5431 or 877/207–9708 | fax 435/259–3823 | www.red-rocklodge.com | 47 rooms, 4 suites | $55–$125 | AE, D, MC, V.

Red Stone Inn. Truly one of the best bargains near the parks, this motel offers small but adequate rooms in a location convenient to restaurants and shops. Knotty pine walls and western furnishings give it a little more flair than most motels in this price range. Pool. Laundry facilities. Some pets allowed. | 535 S. Main St., Moab, 84532 | 435/259–3500 or 800/722–1972 | fax 435/259–2717 | www.moabredstone.com | 52 rooms | $60–$75 | AE, D, MC, V.

★**Sorrel River Ranch.** This luxury ranch about 24 mi from Arches National Park is the ultimate getaway. On the banks of the Colorado River, all rooms offer either a river view or mountain view. No matter which way you look in a landscape studded with towering red cliffs, buttes and spires, the vista is spectacular. Rooms are furnished with hefty log beds, tables, and chairs, along with western art and Native American rugs. Some of the bath tubs even have views of the river and sandstone cliffs. You can choose to relax in the spa and have aromatherapy and a pedicure, go river rafting or mountain biking, or take an ATV out for a spin. Restaurant. Kitchenettes. Some in-room VCRs. Pool. Exercise equipment, outdoor hot tub, massage. Basketball, horseback riding. Baby-sitting, playground. Laundry facilities. No smoking. | Mile Marker 17.5, Rte. 128, Box K, Moab, 84532 | 435/259–4642 or 877/359–2715 | fax 435/259–3016 | www.sorrelriver.com | 27 suites, 32 rooms | $209–$379 | AE, MC, V.

Sunflower Hill Bed and Breakfast. Tucked away on a quiet neighborhood street, this turn-of-the-20th-century dwelling is operated by a family who make their guests feel truly welcome. Antiques and farmhouse treasures, well-tended gardens, and pathways make you feel like you're in the country. The full breakfast is buffet-style and features a vegetable frittata, side meats, and home-baked pastries. Outdoor hot tub. No room phones. No smoking. | 185 N. 300 E, Moab, 84532 | 435/259–2974 or 800/662–2786 | www.sunflowerhill.com | 9 rooms, 3 suites | $90–$195 | AE, D, MC, V.

Triangle H. Quiet and well-maintained, this motel would be a bargain anywhere. It is convenient to the Needles District and destinations south. Microwaves, refrigerators. Cable TV. | 164 E. U.S. 491, Monticello | 435/587–2274 or 800/657–6622 | fax 435/587–2175 | 26 rooms | $32–$52 | AE, D, MC, V.

ARCHES AND
CANYONLANDS
NATIONAL PARKS

EXPLORING
ATTRACTIONS NEARBY
DINING
LODGING
CAMPING AND RV
FACILITIES
SHOPPING
ESSENTIAL
INFORMATION

Camping and RV Facilities

In Arches

★ **Devils Garden Campground.** One of the most unusual campgrounds in the national park system, this small campground makes the most of its natural setting. March through October, when the campground is always full, you are required to pre-register for your site at the visitor center between 7:30 and 8 AM or at the entrance station after 8 AM. Off-season, sites are available on a first-come, first-served basis. Flush toilets. Drinking water. Fire grates, picnic tables. | 52 sites | 18 mi from the park entrance on the main park road | 435/719–2299, 435/259–4351 group reservations | fax 435/259–4285 | $10.

In Canyonlands

Needles Outpost. You may need to stop here for gas, supplies, or an icy drink and good meal after hiking, and you can also camp here. This privately run campground isn't as pretty or private as others in and near Needles, but a chat with the owners will be a guaranteed hoot. Flush toilets. Dump station. Drinking water, showers. Fire grates, food service. Service station. | 23 sites | Rte. 211 about 1.5 mi inside the park entrance, Needles | 435/979–4007 | www.needlesoutpost.com | $15 | AE, D, MC, V | Mid-Mar.–Oct.

★ **Squaw Flat Campground.** Squaw Flat may well be the best campground in the national park system. The sites are spread out in two different areas, giving each site almost unparalleled privacy. Each site has a rock wall at its back, and shade trees. The sites are filled on a first come, first served basis. Flush toilets. Drinking water. Fire pits, picnic tables. | 25 sites | About 5 mi from the park entrance off the main road, Needles | 435/259–7164 | $10.

Willow Flat Campground. From this little campground on a mesa top, you can walk to spectacular views of the Green River. Most sites have a bit of shade from juniper trees. To get to Willow Flat you have to travel down a rough, washboarded road with tight and tricky turns. Since the drive is so difficult and only two sites are really suitable for RVs, RVers might prefer another campground. Filled on a first-come, first-served basis only. Pit toilets. Drinking water. Fire pits, picnic tables. | 12 sites | About 9 mi from the park entrance off the main park road, Island in the Sky | 435/259–4712 | $5.

Near the Parks

Arch View Campground and Resort. For a "room with a view," pitch your tent or park your RV at this hilltop campground. Shady tent sites are available as well as RV sites and 14 cabins. Flush toilets. Full hook-ups, dump station. Drinking water, guest laundry. Fire pits, grills, picnic tables, food service. Public telephone. General store, service station. Play area, swimming (pool). | 57 sites with hook-ups, 20 tent sites, 9 cabins | N. U.S. 191 at Rte. 313, Moab, 84532 | 435/259–7854 or 800/813–6622 | fax 435/259–1562 | www.archviewresort.com | $15–$22; $29–$79 cabins | AE, D, MC, V.

Bureau of Land Management Campgrounds. There are 342 sites at 18 different BLM campgrounds near Arches and Canyonlands national parks. Most of these are in the Moab area near Arches and Canyonlands Island in the Sky District, along the Route 128 Colorado River corridor, on Kane Creek Road, and on Sand Flats Road. All sites are primitive and, except for Wind Whistle and Hatch Point, have no water. Campsites go on a first-come, first-served basis. For a complete listing of BLM sites in the area, call 435/259–6111 or go to www.blm.gov/utah/moab.

Canyonlands Campground. Although this camping park is in downtown Moab, you get the feeling you are in a shady retreat. Because it's downtown, all local amenities are convenient. Flush toilets. Full hook-ups, partial hook-ups (electric and water), dump station. Drinking water, guest laundry, showers. Grills, picnic tables. Electricity, public telephone. General store, service station. Swimming (pool). | 111 sites with hook-ups; 31 tent sites; 8 cabins | 555 S. Main St., Moab | 435/259–6848 or 888/522–6848 | www.canyonlandsrv.com | $17–$32 | AE, D, MC, V.

ARCHES/CANYONLANDS CAMPGROUNDS

	Total # of sites	# of RV sites	# of hook-ups	Drive-to sites	Hike-to sites	Flush toilets	Pit toilets	Drinking water	Showers	Fire grates/pits	Swimming	Boat access	Playground	Dump station	Ranger station	Public telephone	Reservation possible	Daily fee per site	Dates open
INSIDE ARCHES																			
Devils Garden	52	52	0	•		•	•	•		•								$10	Y/R
INSIDE CANYONLANDS																			
Squaw Flat	25	25	0	•		•	•	•		•								$10	Y/R
Willow Flat	12	2	0	•			•	•		•								$5	Y/R
NEAR THE PARKS																			
Arch View	77	57	57	•		•		•	•	•	•		•	•		•	•	$14.50–21.95	Feb.–Nov.
Canyonlands	160	129	129	•		•		•	•	•				•		•	•	$17–32	Y/R
Dead Horse Point State Park	21	21	0	•		•		•		•				•	•	•	•**	$9	Mar.–Oct.
Moab Valley	142	62	62	•		•		•	•					•		•	•	$17–27	Y/R
Slickrock	198	131	115	•		•		•	•	•	•			•		•	•	$17–29	Y/R
Up the Creek	20	0	0	•	•			•	•	•							•	$10	Mar.–Oct.

* In summer only   ** Reservation fee charged   Y/R=Year-round
UL=Unlimited   ULP=Unlimited primitive   LD=Labor Day   MD=Memorial Day

ARCHES AND CANYONLANDS NATIONAL PARKS | **387**

Dead Horse Point State Park. A favorite of almost everyone who has ever camped here, either in RVs or tents, this mesa-top campground fills up a little later in the day than the national park campgrounds. It is impressively set near the edge of a 2,000-ft cliff above the Colorado River. If you want to pay for your stay with a credit card you must do so during business hours (8–6 daily); otherwise you must pay in cash. Flush toilets. Dump station. Drinking water. Picnic tables. Public telephone. Ranger station. | 21 sites | Rte. 313, 18 mi off U.S. Hwy. 191 | 435/259–2614, 800/322–3770 reservations | http://parks.state.ut.us | $7 | MC, V.

Moab Valley RV and Campark. Near the Colorado River, with a 360-degree view, this campground seems to get bigger and better every year. Just 2 mi from Arches National Park, it's convenient for sightseeing, river rafting, and other area attractions. On-site you can pitch some horse shoes, perfect your putting, or soak in the hot tub. The campground is spotlessly clean, with everything from tent sites to cottages. Flush toilets. Full hook-ups, dump station. Drinking water, guest laundry, showers. Grills, picnic tables. Public telephone. Electricity. General store. Play area, swimming (pool). | 130 sites with hook-ups; 33 cabins | 1773 N. U.S. 191, Moab, 84532 | 435/259–4469 | www.moabvalleyrv.com | $17–$26 camping sites; $34–$65 cabins | MC, V.

Slickrock Campground. At one of Moab's older campgrounds you'll find lots of mature shade trees and all of the basic amenities, plus three hot tubs where adults have the priority. About 3 mi from Arches National Park and next to Buck's Grill House, this can make a comfortable home base. Flush toilets. 94 full hook-ups, 21 partial hook-ups (electric and water), dump station. Drinking water, guest laundry, showers. Grills, picnic tables, food service. Electricity, public telephone. General store. Swimming (pool). | 198 sites (115 with hook-ups), 14 cabins | 1301½ N. U.S. 191, Moab, 84532 | 435/259–7660 or 800/448–8873 | fax 435/259–7776 | www.slickrockcampground.com | $17–$29 | MC, V.

★ **Up the Creek Campground.** This neighborhood campground lies under big cottonwoods on the banks of Mill Creek. Even though you are near downtown, you'll feel like you're in the woods—the campground has walk-in tent sites only. Flush toilets. Drinking water, showers. Grills, picnic tables. | 20 sites | 210 E. 300 South, Moab, 84532 | 435/259–6995 | $10 per person | Mid-Mar.–Oct.

Shopping

Arches Book Company. You can't beat the warm ambience or friendly service at this popular bookstore. Every title you'd want, from the top bestsellers to local authors, is here, along with your favorite coffee drink. Sit in the window, read a book, chat with locals, and watch people pass by as you sip an espresso. | 78 N. Main St., Moab | 435/259–0782 | www.archesbookcompany.com.

Arches Visitor Center Bookstore. Operated by Canyonlands Natural History Association, this is the place to buy maps, guidebooks, and material about the natural and cultural history of Arches National Park. | At the park entrance | 435/259–8161, 435/259–6003, 800/840–8978 to order books.

Back of Beyond Books. A decidedly "green" bookstore, this one features an excellent selection of books on environmental studies, Native American cultures, western water issues, and western history. | 83 N. Main St., Moab | 435/259–5154 or 800/700–2859.

Dave's Corner Market. You can skip the long lines at the supermarket and shop at one of Moab's favorite convenience stores. You can get most anything you might need, including some of the best cappuccino and Colombian coffee in town. The store is also the heartbeat of the local community and the place where everyone discusses local politics. | 401 Mill Creek Dr., Moab | 435/259–6999.

Family Drug. Right near the post office and all the downtown shops, you can pick up toothpaste, sodas, candy, and other road necessities that you may have left at home, as well as prescription medicines. | 90 N. Main St., Moab | 435/259–7771.

Gearheads. If you forgot anything for your camping, climbing, hiking, or other outdoor adventure, you can get it here. This store is packed not only with essentials, but with hard-to-find things like booties and packs for your dog. | 471 S. Main St., Moab | 435/259–4327.

Lema Kokopelli Gallery. These folks have built a reputation for fair prices on a giant selection of Native American jewelry and other art by First Nations people. Everything you buy here will be authentic. | 70 N. Main St., Moab | 435/259–5055.

Needles Outpost. Truly an outpost of civilization, this store stocks civilized things such as gifts, sundries, and ice. | Rte. 211 about 1.5 mi inside the Canyonlands park entrance off the main park road, Needles | 435/979–4007.

Needles Visitor Center and Bookstore. You can shop for high-quality books, maps, posters, postcards, videos, and all sorts of guidebooks to Canyonlands at this great little store operated by Canyonlands Natural History Association. | About 2 mi from the park entrance on the main park road, Needles | 435/259–4711, 435/259–6003 to order books.

San Juan Pharmacy. Offering one-stop shopping for film, pharmacy items, and gifts, this store is convenient to the Needles District of Canyonlands. | 148 S. Main, Monticello | 435/587–2302.

Thin Bear Indian Arts. This tiny little trading post has operated in the same location for 29 years. Authentic jewelry, rugs, baskets and pottery are for sale at this friendly spot. | 1944 S. Main St., Blanding | 435/678–2940.

Tom Till Gallery. After you visit Arches and Canyonlands, stop here to buy stunning original photographs of the parks by one of the nation's best-loved landscape photographers. | 61 N. Main St., Moab | 435/259–9808.

Walker Drug Co. A Moab landmark since the 1950s, this is as close as you'll get to a department store for more than 100 mi. The pharmacy and drugstore satisfy your health and beauty needs, but you can also buy forgotten camping supplies, swimsuits, hats, sunglasses, souvenirs, and almost anything else. | 290 S. Main St., Moab | 435/259–5959.

Essential Information

ATMS: Wells Fargo Bank | 4 N. Main St., Moab | 16 S. Main St., Monticello. **Zions Bank** | 300 S. Main St., Moab.

AUTOMOBILE SERVICE STATIONS: American Car Care Center/Chip's Grand Tire | 312 N. Main St., Moab | 435/259–7909. **Canyonlands Amoco** | 555 S. Main St., Moab | 435/259–7212. **Certified Ford Domestic Repair Service** | 500 S. Main St., Moab | 435/259–6107. **Northside Texaco** | 220 N. Main St., Moab | 435/259–2587. **Parkway Texaco** | 17 N. Main St., Monticello | 435/587–2555. **Walker Phillips 66** | 299 S. Main St., Moab | 435/259–6030.

POST OFFICES: Moab Branch Post Office | 50 E. 100 North, Moab, 84532 | 435/259–7427. **Monticello Branch Post Office** | 197 S. Main St., Monticello, 84535 | 435/587–2294.

BLACK CANYON OF THE GUNNISON NATIONAL PARK

WESTERN COLORADO

South Rim: 15 mi east of Montrose, via U.S. 50 and Route 347. North Rim: 11 mi south of Crawford, via Route 92 and the North Rim Road.

Approximately two million years in the making, Black Canyon of the Gunnison River is one of the West's most awe-inspiring sights. The park contains the deepest 14 mi of the 48-mi-long canyon. A vivid testament to the powers of erosion, this gash in the Earth's

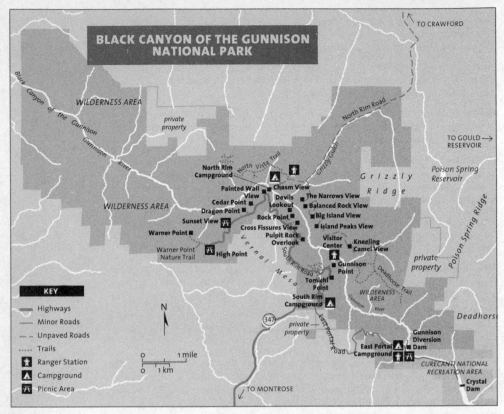

crust reaches depths of 2,700 ft and at its narrowest is a mere 40 ft wide. The rock exposed by the river's persistent carving is more than 1.7 billion years old. The canyon's name comes from the fact that so little sunlight can penetrate; it's eternal shadows keep plant growth inside the canyon scarce.

When to Visit

SCENERY AND WILDLIFE

Spring and early summer are the best times for bird-watching: you may spot peregrine falcons nesting in May and June, especially in the vicinity of Painted Wall, or other birds of prey such as red-tailed hawks, Cooper's hawks, and golden eagles circling overhead at any time of year. In summer, turkey vultures join the flying corps, and in winter, bald eagles. Also keep an eye out for blue grouse, which frequent the trails and roadsides.

Mule deer, elk (most commonly seen in winter), and bobcat (occasionally glimpsed in fall, winter, and spring) also call the park home. In spring and fall, you may see a porcupine among pinyon trees on the rims. Listen for the distinctive, high-pitched chirp of the yellow-bellied marmot, which hangs out on sunny, rocky outcrops near South Rim visitor center, Oak Flat Trail, and Chasm View lookout. From the campgrounds at night, you're likely to hear the spine-tingling yips of coyotes, as they gather on the rim. Mountain lions also live in the park (though they're rarely seen), as do black bears, which are sometimes spotted in dry years, when they have to forage more widely for food.

HIGH AND LOW SEASON

Summer is the busiest season, with July being the busiest month. A spring or fall visit gives you two advantages: fewer people and cooler temperatures—in summer, especially in years with little rainfall, daytime temperatures often reach into the 90s. A winter visit to the park brings even more solitude, as campgrounds are shut down and only about 2 mi of South Rim Road are plowed.

Average High/Low Temperature (°F) and Monthly Snowfall/Rainfall (in inches)

	JAN.	FEB.	MAR.	APR.	MAY	JUNE
BLACK CANYON	36.6/14.0	42.3/15.8	49.9/17.8	46.9/23.7	67.0/37.1	75.3/43.6
	24/1.8	19.6/1.5	8.9/1.2	11.6/2.2	4.2/1.8	1.0

	JULY	AUG.	SEPT.	OCT.	NOV.	DEC.
	83.9/51.3	81.2/49.6	71.5/42.4	61.6/30.6	48.3/23.3	36.7/11.9
	1.9	2.5	.3/2.4	3.5/2.3	16.2/1.7	18/1.5

Nearby Towns

The primary gateway to Black Canyon is **Montrose,** 15 mi northeast of the park. The legendary Ute Chief, Ouray, and his wife, Chipeta, lived near here in the mid-19th century. Today, Montrose straddles the important agricultural and mining regions along the Uncompahgre River, and its traditional downtown is a shopping hub. Montrose may be the official gateway to the park, but the closest town (11 mi) to Black Canyon's North Rim is **Crawford,** a small hillside enclave amid the sheep and cattle ranches of the North Fork Valley with a small downtown area. If you continue northeast on Route 92 (20 mi), you'll hit **Paonia,** a unique and charming blend of the old and new West. Career environmentalists and hippie-types who have escaped the mainstream mix with long-time ranchers, miners, and fruit growers. Eleven miles northwest of Crawford on Route 92 is the small ranching and mining community of **Hotchkiss.** You'll still find the trappings and sensibilities of the Old West here, from cowboy bars to fields of livestock to the annual summertime rodeo.

INFORMATION

Montrose Visitors and Convention Bureau | 433 S. 1st, Montrose, CO 81402 | 970/240–1414 or 800/873–0244 | www.visitmontrose.net. **Crawford Area Chamber of Commerce** | Box 22, Crawford, CO 81415 | 970/921–4000 | www.crawfordcountry.org. **Hotchkiss Chamber of Commerce** | Box 158, Hotchkiss, CO 81419 | 970/872–3226. **Paonia Chamber of Commerce** | Box 366, Paonia, CO 81428 | 970/527–3886 | www.paoniachamber.com.

Exploring Black Canyon of the Gunnison

PARK BASICS

Contacts and Resources: Black Canyon of the Gunnison National Park. | 102 Elk Creek, Gunnison, CO 81230 | 970/641–2337 | www.nps.gov/blca.

Hours: The park is open year-round, 24 hours a day.

Fees: Entrance fees are $7 per week per vehicle. Visitors entering on bicycle, motorcycle, or on foot pay $4 for a weekly pass.

Getting Around: The park has three roads: South Rim, North Rim, and East Portal. South Rim Road, reached by Route 347, is the primary thoroughfare and, as its name implies, winds along the canyon's South Rim. From about late November to early April, depending on the amount of snowfall, the road is not plowed past the visitor center at Gunnison Point. North Rim Road, reached by Route 92, is usually open from May through Thanksgiving; in winter the road is unplowed. The serpentine East Portal Road descends abruptly to the Gunnison River on the park's south side. The road is usually open from the beginning of May through the end of November, though these dates may vary depending on snowfall. Because of the grade, vehicles or vehicle–trailer combinations longer than 22 ft are not permitted.

THE LONG WAY 'ROUND

A bridge that would span the canyon's two rims was proposed in the 1930s, but was never built. Thus it takes a couple of hours—through unforgettable scenery—to drive from one rim around to the other.

The park has no public transportation. Parking along South Rim Road for more than a few minutes is strongly discouraged. For a hike into the canyon, you'll be asked to park at one of the overlooks.

Permits: To access the inner canyon, whether for hiking, climbing, camping, or kayaking, you must pick up a backcountry permit (no fee) at South Rim visitor center, North Rim ranger station, or East Portal ranger station, in adjoining Curecanti National Recreation Area.

To fish in the park, you must have a valid Colorado fishing license if you're more than 16 years old, available through the Department of Wildlife Web site www.wildlife.state.co.us/fishing.

Public Telephones: Public telephones may be found at South Rim visitor center and South Rim campground.

Rest Rooms: Public rest rooms may be found at South Rim visitor center and South Rim campground; Tomichi Point, Pulpit Rock, Sunset View, and High Point overlooks; North Rim ranger station and North Rim Campground; and Kneeling Camel viewpoint.

Accessibility: South Rim visitor center is accessible to people with mobility impairments, as are most of the sites at South Rim campground. Accessible (i.e., drive-to) overlooks on the South Rim include Tomichi Point, the alternate gravel viewpoint at Pulpit Rock (the main one is not accessible), Chasm View (gravel), Sunset View, and High Point. Balanced Rock (gravel) is the only accessible viewpoint on the North Rim. None of the park's hiking trails is accessible.

Emergencies: In the event of a medical or police emergency, dial 911. Medical assistance is available at South Rim visitor center and, in summer, at North Rim ranger station. Report fires to South Rim visitor center or North Rim ranger station.

Lost and Found: The park's lost-and-found is at South Rim visitor center and North Rim ranger station (summer only).

Good Tours

BLACK CANYON IN ONE DAY

Pack a lunch and head to the canyon's South Rim, beginning with a stop at the **visitor center.** Before getting back into the car, take in your first view of Black Canyon from **Gunnison Point,** adjacent to the visitor center. Then set out on a driving tour of the 7-mi **South Rim Road,** allowing the rest of the morning to stop at the various viewpoints that overlook the canyon. Don't miss **Chasm View** and **Painted Wall View,** and be sure to stretch your legs along the short (0.7-mi round-trip) **Cedar Point Nature Trail.** If your timing is good, you'll reach **High Point,** the end of the road, around lunchtime. After lunch, head out on **Warner Point Nature Trail** for a hike of about an hour (1.5 mi round-trip). Then retrace your drive along South Rim Road back to the visitor center. If you're up for more hiking, head out on the 2-mi **Oak Flat Loop Trail,** which will bring you 300 ft below the canyon rim. Otherwise—or afterward—drive down the steep and windy **East Portal Road** to the edge of the Gunnison River.

BLACK CANYON IN TWO DAYS

On day one, follow the South Rim itinerary. Head out early on the second day and follow **North Rim Road** to its end, stopping at the overlooks along the way. Be sure to pause at **Narrows View,** the first overlook, to see how restricting the canyon becomes below. To wrap up to your visit, head back along the road to **North Rim Campground** and hike along **North Vista Trail** (3 mi round-trip) to Exclamation Point. If it's being offered, the ranger-led sunset stroll along **Chasm View Nature Trail** is the perfect way to end your visit.

Attractions

SCENIC DRIVES

South Rim Road. This paved 7-mi-long stretch from Tomichi Point to High Point is the park's main road. The drive follows the canyon's level South Rim; 12 overlooks are accessible from the road, most via short gravel trails. Several short hikes onto the rim also begin roadside. Allow between two and three hours round-trip.

North Rim Road. Black Canyon's North Rim is much less frequented, but no less spectacular—the walls here are near vertical. To reach the 15.5-mi North Rim Road, take the signed turnoff from Route 92 in Crawford. The road is paved for about the first 4 mi; the rest is gravel. After 11 mi, turn left at the intersection (North Rim Campground is to the right). There are six overlooks as the road snakes along the rim's edge. Kneeling Camel, 4.5 mi out at road's end, provides the broadest view of the canyon. Set aside about two hours for a tour of the North Rim.

East Portal Road. The only way to access the Gunnison River from the park by car is via this paved route, which drops approximately 2,000 ft down to the water in only 5 mi, giving it a steep, 16% grade. (Vehicles longer than 22 ft are not allowed on the road; if you're towing a trailer, you can unhitch it at a parking area near the entrance to South Rim campground.) The bottom is actually in the adjacent Curecanti National Recreation Area. A tour of East Portal Road, with a brief stop at the bottom, takes about 45 minutes.

SIGHTS TO SEE

★**Chasm View.** From this heart-in-your-throat viewpoint, the canyon walls plummet 1,820 ft to the river, but are only 1,100 ft apart at the top. As you peer down into the depths, keep in mind that this section of canyon encompasses the Gunnison's greatest rate of descent, crashing down 240 ft within a mile. | 3.5 mi from the visitor center on South Rim Rd.

Crystal Dam/Gunnison Tunnel. Crystal Dam, in Curecanti National Recreation Area bordering the park, is the origination point for the 6-mi-long Gunnison Tunnel, which diverts water for farming in the Uncompahgre Valley to the southwest. The feasibility of a tunnel was determined by William Torrence and Abraham Lincoln Fellows, who made a brave and unprecedented raft trip through the canyon in 1901. | At the end of E. Portal Rd.

Narrows View. Look upriver from this North Rim overlook and you'll be able to see into the canyon's narrowest section, just a slot really, with only 40 ft between the walls. The canyon is also steeper (1,725 ft) here than it is wide at the rim (1,150 ft). | North Rim Rd., first overlook past the ranger station.

North Rim ranger station. This small facility on the park's North Rim provides information and assistance when North Rim Road is open. | North Rim Rd., 11 mi from Rte. 92 turnoff | Memorial Day to Labor Day, daily 8–6.

★**Painted Wall.** Best seen from Painted Wall View along South Rim Road, this is Colorado's tallest cliff, 2,250 ft high. Pinkish swathes of pegmatite (a crystalline, granitelike rock) give the cliff a colorful, marbled appearance. | 3.7 mi from the visitor center off South Rim Rd.

South Rim Visitor Center. The park's only visitor center offers interactive exhibits as well as two orientation videos: one details the geology and history of the canyon, the other includes the history of the Gunnison water diversion tunnel and flora and fauna in the park. | 1.5 mi from the entrance station on South Rim Rd. | 970/641–2337 | Memorial Day to Labor Day, daily 8–6; Labor Day to Memorial Day, daily 8:30–4.

Sports and Outdoor Activities

BICYCLING

Bikes are not permitted on any of the trails, but cycling along South Rim Road or mountain biking on the unpaved North Rim Road is a great way to view the park. You'll need to bring your own bike, as there are no shops that rent in the immediate vicinity.

BOATING

The stretch of the Gunnison River that goes through the park is one of the premier kayak challenges in North America, with Class IV and Class V rapids, and portages required around bigger drops. Early visitors to the canyon declared this section unnavigable, and the fact that a few intrepid kayakers make the journey today is somewhat amazing.

FISHING

The three dams built upriver in Curecanti National Recreation Area have created prime trout fishing. In fact, the section of Gunnison River that goes through the park has been designated a Gold Medal water, with abundant rainbows and browns. Certain restrictions apply: only artificial flies and lures are permitted, and a Colorado fishing license is required for people aged 16 and older. Rainbow trout are catch-and-release only, and there are size and possession limits on brown trout (check at the visitor center). Most anglers access the river from the bottom of East Portal Road; an undeveloped trail goes along the riverbank for about 0.75 mi.

HIKING

All trails can be hot in summer and most don't receive much shade, so bring water and wear a hat. Dogs are permitted, on leash, on Rim Rock, Cedar Point Nature, and Chasm View Nature trails.

Hiking into the inner canyon, while doable, is not for the faint of heart—or step. Six named routes lead down to the river, but they are not maintained or marked. In fact, the park staff won't even call them trails; they refer to them as "controlled slides." These super-steep, rocky routes vary in one-way distance from 1 to 2.75 mi, and the descent can be anywhere from 1,800 to 2,702 ft. Your reward, of course, is a rare look at the bottom of the canyon and the fast-flowing Gunnison. Don't attempt an inner-canyon hike without plenty of water (the park's recommendation is four quarts per person). For descriptions of the routes, and the necessary permit to hike them, stop at the visitor center or North Rim ranger station. Dogs are not permitted in the inner canyon.

Cedar Point Nature Trail. This short (0.7 mi round-trip) interpretive trail leads out from South Rim Road to two overlooks. It's an easy stroll, and signs along the way detail the surrounding plants. | South Rim Rd., 4.2 mi from South Rim visitor center.

Chasm View Nature Trail. The park's shortest trail (0.3 mi round-trip), starts at North Rim Campground and offers an impressive 50-yard walk right along the canyon rim as well as an eye-popping view downstream of Painted Wall and Chasm View, 1,100 ft across on the South Rim. | North Rim Campground, 11.25 mi from Rte. 92.

Deadhorse Trail. Despite its somewhat sinister name, Deadhorse Trail (5- to 6-mi round-trip) is actually an easy-to-moderate hike, starting on an old service road from the Kneeling Camel View. The trail's farthest point provides the park's easternmost viewpoint. From this overlook, the canyon is much more open, with pinnacles and spires rising along its sides. If you want to give yourself a bit of a scare, take the mile-long loop detour, about halfway through the hike. (The detour isn't marked—just look for the only other visible trail). At the two informal overlooks, you'll be perched—without guardrails—atop the highest cliff in this part of the canyon. | At the end of North Rim Rd.

North Vista Trail. The trail begins at North Rim ranger station. The moderate round-trip hike to and from Exclamation Point is 3 mi; a more difficult foray to the top of 8,563-ft Green

Mountain (a mesa, really), with about 800 ft of elevation gain, is 7 mi round-trip. You'll hike along the North Rim; keep an eye out for especially gnarled pinyon trees—the North Rim is the site of some of the oldest groves of pinyons in North America, between 400 and 700 years old. | North Rim Rd., 11 mi from Rte. 92 turnoff.

Oak Flat Trail. This 2-mi loop trail, which begins and ends just west of the visitor center, is the most demanding of the South Rim hikes, as it brings you about 300 ft below the canyon rim. In places, the trail is narrow and crosses some steep slopes, but you won't have to navigate any steep drop-offs. Oak Flat is the shadiest of all the South Rim trails; small groves of aspen and thick stands of Douglas fir along the loop offer some respite from the sun. | Adjacent to the visitor center, 1.5 mi from the entrance station on South Rim Rd.

Rim Rock Trail. Begin hiking this 1-mi round-trip nature trail at either the Tomichi Point overlook or at the trailhead near Loop C in South Rim campground. The terrain is primarily flat and exposed to the sun, with a bird's-eye view into the canyon. An interpretative pamphlet, which corresponds to markers along the route, is available at the visitor center and the campground trailhead.

Warner Point Nature Trail. The 1.5-mi round-trip hike starts from High Point. You'll enjoy fabulous vistas of the San Juan and West Elk Mountains and Uncompahgre Valley. Warner Point, at trail's end, has the steepest dropoff from rim to river: a dizzying 2,702 ft. | At the end of South Rim Rd.

HORSEBACK RIDING
Horses are permitted only on Deadhorse Trail (don't take the name literally!) along the North Rim. No outfitters run trips into the park, so you'll have to bring your own horse by trailer to the end of North Rim Road.

ROCK CLIMBING
Climbing Black Canyon's sheer cliffs is one of Colorado's premier big-wall challenges for advanced rock climbers, and some routes can take several days to complete, with climbers sleeping on narrow ledges or "portaledges." Closures due to nesting birds of prey apply at certain times of the year. Though there's no official guide to climbing in the park, reports from other climbers are kept on file at the visitor center.

If you want to get in some easier climbing, head for the Marmot Rocks bouldering area, about 100 ft south of South Rim Road between Painted Wall and Cedar Point overlooks (park at Painted Wall). Four boulder groupings offer a variety of routes rated from easy to very difficult; a pamphlet with a diagrammed map of the area is available at the visitor center.

SKIING AND SNOWSHOEING
From late November to early April, South Rim Road is not plowed past the visitor center, offering park visitors a unique opportunity to cross-country ski or snowshoe on the road. It's possible to ski or snowshoe on the unplowed North Rim Road, too, but it's about 4 mi from where the road closes, through sagebrush flats to the canyon rim.

The park offers ranger-led snowshoe walks in winter, usually once a day on weekends. Tours leave from the visitor center and go along the rim for about 2 mi, often on Rim Rock Trail. A limited supply of snowshoe gear is available for use at no charge; call 970/249–1914 Ext. 23, to reserve equipment and a space on a tour.

Attractions Nearby
Crawford State Park. The focus of this 337-acre park is Crawford Reservoir, created in 1963 when a dam was built to increase the supply of irrigated water to the surrounding ranches and farms. Boating and water-skiing are permitted on the reservoir, as are swimming and fishing (the lake is stocked with rainbow trout). The park has a 1-mi-long handicapped-accessible hiking trail along with the "primitive" 0.5-mi Indian Fire Nature Trail by the reser-

BLACK CANYON OF THE GUNNISON NATIONAL PARK

EXPLORING
ATTRACTIONS NEARBY
DINING
LODGING
CAMPING AND RV FACILITIES
SHOPPING
ESSENTIAL INFORMATION

voir on the park's west side. | 1 mi south of Crawford, off Hwy. 92 | 970/921–5721 | www.parks.state.co.us/crawford | $4.

★ **Curecanti National Recreation Area.** Curecanti, named in honor of a Ute Indian chief, encompasses 40 mi of striking eroded volcanic landscape along U.S. 50. Three reservoirs were created by dams constructed in the 1960s: Blue Mesa, Colorado's largest man-made lake at almost 20 mi long; Morrow Point, and Crystal Dam. You can go boating (paid permit required), windsurfing, fishing, and swimming in all three. Camping, horseback riding, and hiking (pets are allowed on all trails but must be leashed) are also available. Check in at one of the three visitor centers along U.S. 50 for additional information. | 20 mi east of Montrose off U.S. 50 | 970/641–2337 | www.nps.gov/cure.

At the western entrance to the recreation area, about 15 mi from Black Canyon, the **Cimarron Visitor Center** displays vintage railroad cars, an 1882 trestle listed on the National Register of Historic Places, and a reconstruction of a railroad stockyard. | 970/249–4074 | Memorial Day–Labor Day, daily 9–4.

Morrow Point Boat Tour. Hour-and-a-half tours take you out and back on Morrow Point Reservoir, which lies within Curecanti National Recreation Area in upper Black Canyon. A park ranger comes along on the 40-ft pontoon boat to provide details of the natural and cultural history of the area. To reach the boat dock, you'll have to descend 232 steps and hike for 0.75 mi, so allow about 45 minutes to get there. | Tours leave from the end of Pine Creek Trail, 1 mi west of the junction of U.S. 50 and Rte. 92 | 970/641–0402 | $9 | Memorial Day–Labor Day, daily 10 and 12:30.

Ute Indian Museum and Ouray Memorial Park. The museum commemorates the life of the famed Ute Indian chief Ouray and his wife, Chipeta, and depicts the history of the Ute tribe with artifacts and dioramas. Chipeta's grave is also here, 2 mi south of Montrose. | 17253 Chipeta Rd., Montrose | 970/249–3098 | $3 | May–Sept., Mon.–Sat. 9–4:30, Sun. 11–4:30; Oct.–Apr., Mon.–Sat. 9–4:30.

Dining

In Black Canyon

Picnic Areas. There are picnic areas at High Point, Pulpit Rock, and Sunset View overlooks, and at the bottom of East Portal Road. Pit toilets are available at all sites; High Point and East Portal offer the most shade. All picnic sites are closed when it snows.

Rim House. American/Casual. This lunch-only snack bar sells burgers, sandwiches, light snacks, and ice cream. | South Rim Rd., at Pulpit Rock Overlook | $5–$7 | MC, V | Late Sept.–mid-May. No dinner.

Near the Park

★ **Camp Robber Cafe.** Eclectic. This small, bistro-style restaurant serves Montrose's most creative cuisine. Try such entrées as tortilla-crusted fresh red snapper, green-chile pistachio-crusted pork medallions, and spicy shrimp pasta. At lunch, salads, sandwiches (mesquite-grilled chicken cordon bleu), or blue-corn enchiladas fuel hungry hikers. | 228 E. Main, Montrose | 970/240–1590 | $6–$16 | AE, MC, V | Closed Mon.

The Casa. Eclectic. The Casa, in an 1896 Victorian, receives many locals' vote as the best place to eat in Paonia. The menu provides a welcome variety to the basic steak and chicken emphasis of the area's restaurants, with such entrées such as prime rib fajitas and the casa cioppino (shellfish and other seafood in a spicy lemon tomato broth over angel hair pasta). | 312 Grand Ave., Paonia | 970/527–4343 | $8–$15 | MC, V | No lunch Sat.

Sicily's Italian Restaurant. Italian. This is the place to come for pizza and calzones, as well as traditional Italian favorites such as manicotti, chicken marsala, and shrimp scampi. Homemade desserts include cheesecake, key lime pie, and German chocolate cake. | 1135 E. Main St., Montrose | 970/240–9199 | $7–$16 | AE, D, DC, MC, V | No breakfast.

Zack's. Barbecue. On Saturday nights, the local ranching families flock to Zack's for the tastiest barbecue around; choose from ham, beef, chicken, or ribs. Steak and catfish dinners are also available on Friday through Sunday nights. This informal eatery serves up breakfast and lunch (burgers, sandwiches), too. | 721 E. Bridge St., Hotchkiss | 970/872–3199 | $3–$16 | D, MC, V.

Lodging

Near the Park

Black Canyon Motel. One of Montrose's better values, this motel has rooms that are large, clean, and modern and provides a good selection of amenities. Some in-room hot tubs, some microwaves, some refrigerators. Cable TV. Pool. Outdoor hot tub. Playground. Laundry facilities. Business services. | 1605 E. Main St. (U.S. 50), Montrose | 970/249–3495 or 800/348–3495 | fax 970/249–0990 | www.innfinders.com/blackcyn | 49 rooms, 5 suites | $55–$75, $65–$95 suites | AE, D, DC, MC, V.

★**Bross Hotel.** The brick Bross Hotel, on a quiet, shady street in downtown Paonia, was opened in 1906 by the local deputy sheriff. Rooms are furnished with turn-of-the-20th-century antiques and handmade quilts. Common areas include a parlor and a spacious lounge with board games. In-room data ports. Outdoor hot tub. Library. Business services. No a/c. No smoking. | 312 Onarga St., Paonia | 970/527–6776 | fax 970/527–7737 | www.paonia-inn.com | 10 rooms | $80–$100 | DC, MC, V.

Country Lodge. This family-friendly motel has a homey touch, thanks to knotty-pine walls, a garden courtyard with pool and hot tub, and two separate play areas, for older and younger kids. A newer three-bedroom log house, with full kitchen and washer-dryer, is available for nightly rentals in summer. Some kitchenettes, some microwaves, some refrigerators. Cable TV. Pool. Outdoor hot tub. Playground. | 1624 E. Main St. (U.S. 50), Montrose | 970/249–4567 | fax 970/249–3082 | www.countryldg.com | 22 rooms | $56–$85, $125 house | AE, D, DC, MC, V.

★**Lathrop House Bed and Breakfast.** A more personable alternative to the motels, this B&B is in a home from 1902. The five guest rooms have antique furnishings and some unusual color schemes; the lightest and airiest is the third-floor Roman room, with a slope-ceiling private bath. Cable TV. Laundry facilities. No kids under 14. No smoking. | 718 E. Main St., Montrose | phone/fax 970/240–6075 | www.lathrophouse.com | 5 rooms, 2 with shared bath, 1 with private half bath | $65–$85 | D, DC, MC, V.

★**Leroux Creek Inn.** This sophisticated B&B has five southwestern-style guest rooms—each with private tiled bath—within an adobe house, which keeps them blessedly cool during summer. A gorgeous deck overlooks the inn's 46 acres, which include a vineyard. Dinner prepared by one of the owners, who is French, is available by advance request. Outdoor hot tub. No a/c, no room phones. No kids under 16. No smoking. | 1220 3100 Rd., Hotchkiss | 970/872–4746 | www.lerouxcreekinn.com | 5 rooms | $135–$155 | MC, V.

Camping and RV Facilities

In Black Canyon

At both of the park's drive-to campgrounds there's a limit of eight people per site, and camping is limited to 14 days; reservations are not accepted. Water has to be trucked up to the campgrounds, so use it in moderation; it's shut off in mid- to late September. Generators are not allowed at South Rim and are highly discouraged on the North Rim. RVs are permitted at North Rim Campground, but keep in mind that you won't be able to squeeze in a rig that's much longer than 30 ft.

North Rim Campground. This small campground, nestled amid pinyon and juniper, offers the basics along the quiet North Rim. Pit toilets. Drinking water. Fire grates, picnic tables. Ranger station. | 13 sites | North Rim Rd., 11.25 mi from Rte. 92 | $10, $5 when water is shut off | May–Oct.

South Rim Campground. The campground is right inside the park entrance, on the canyon rim, and about a mile from the visitor center. The RV hook-ups are in Loop B, and those sites are priced higher. It's possible to camp here year-round, but the loops are not plowed, so you'll have to hike in with your tent. Pit toilets. Partial hook-ups (electric). Drinking water. Fire grates, picnic tables. Public telephone. | 66 tent sites, 23 camper sites | South Rim Rd., 1 mi from the visitor center | $10, $15 for Loop B, $5 in winter.

Near the Park

Cedar Creek RV Park. This close-to-town park in Montrose has an 18-hole miniature golf course and a gift shop that sells RV supplies. You can pitch a tent along Cedar Creek, but individual sites are not designated. Flush toilets. Full hook-ups, partial hook-ups (electric and water), dump station. Drinking water, guest laundry, showers. Fire pits, picnic tables. Public telephone. Play area. | 8 tent sites, 47 camper sites with full hook-ups, 16 with partial hook-ups | 126 Rose La., Montrose | 970/249–3884 or 877/426–3884 | www.cedarcreekrv.com | $17–$24.

Crawford State Park. The park has two campgrounds, Iron Creek and Clear Fork. Both are alongside Crawford Reservoir. You'll have to pay the $4 park admission fee in addition to the camping fee. You can reserve a campsite, for $7 extra, by calling 800/678–2267 or through the park's Web site. | 1 mi south of Crawford off Hwy. 92 | 970/921–5721 | www.parks.state.co.us/crawford | $7–$20.

Clear Fork. Clear Fork stays open year-round, but the water is shut off from about mid-November to April. Flush toilets. Drinking water, showers. Fire grates, picnic tables. | 5 tent sites, 16 tent-RV sites.

Iron Creek. There's a wildlife kiosk and boat ramp at the campground. Flush toilets. Partial hook-ups (electric and water), dump station. Drinking water, showers. Fire grates, picnic tables. Public telephone. | 44 tent-RV sites | Apr.–mid-Nov.

East Portal. Though technically in Curecanti National Recreation Area, this shady riverside campground is close enough to be in Black Canyon. Pit toilets. Drinking water. Fire grates, picnic tables. Ranger station. | 15 sites | Bottom of East Portal Rd. | $10, $5 when water is shut off | Early May–late Nov.

Shopping

Rim House. The park's only store is open from mid-May to late September and has a small gift shop as well as food. | South Rim Rd., at Pulpit Rock Overlook | No phone.

Essential Information

ATMS (24-HOUR): Community First National Bank | 401 E. Main St., Montrose | 970/249–1111.

AUTOMOBILE SERVICE STATION: Supermart | 938 S. Townsend Ave., Montrose | 970/240–4612.

POST OFFICE: Montrose Post Office | 321 S. 1st St., Montrose, 81401 | 970/249–6654.

BRYCE CANYON NATIONAL PARK

SOUTHERN UTAH

Route 63, 3 mi south of junction with Route 12.

A land that captures the imagination and the heart, Bryce is a favorite among Utah's national parks. Even in a region rich with extraordinary landscapes and brilliant colors, Bryce Canyon's star shines especially bright. Once you catch a glimpse of the fanciful "hoodoos" that populate the park, it's easy to understand why. Looking at Bryce Canyon is much like gazing at the clouds: in the colorful rock formations you will find the shapes of animals, ships, castles, or carriages. Surrounded by such wonders, you cannot help but contemplate a universe that contains such an amazing, awe-inspiring place.

This astonishing landscape was named for Ebenezer Bryce, a pioneer cattleman and the first permanent settler in the area. His description of the landscape, oft repeated today, was succinct: "It's a hell of a place to lose a cow." The rock formations you see at Bryce Canyon began forming about 60 million years ago. At that time, fresh water lakes filled the shallow basins in southern Utah. When they receded, about 2,000 ft of lime-rich sediment was deposited, and the lack of fossils in that layer suggests that the lakes were inhospitable environments. Some 16 million years ago, the earth in the Colorado Plateau—of which Bryce is a part—broke up and tilted, creating great blocks of rock-faulted uplands, which were then attacked by weathering and erosion. Water seeped into cracks in the rock, froze, expanded, and shattered the surrounding rock. Runoff from rain or melting snow created gullies that carried away soft layers of rock. In the process, Bryce Canyon was formed. Because of its origins and shape Bryce is actually an amphitheater, not a canyon, in geological terms. The hoodoos that populate the amphitheater took on their unusual shapes because the top layer of rock—"cap rock"—is harder than the layers below it. If erosion undercuts the soft rock beneath the cap too much, the hoodoo will tumble. But Bryce will never be without hoodoos, because as the amphitheater's rim recedes, new hoodoos are formed.

PUBLICATIONS

Useful maps and publications can be purchased from the bookstore at the park's visitor center. *Bryce Canyon National Park*, by Fred Hirschmann, is the best of the color photo books. Tully Stoud's 44-page *Bryce Canyon Auto and Hiking Guide* includes information on the geology and history of the area. The *Bryce Canyon Hiking Guide*, with an amphitheater hiking map and aerial photo, supplements the free map given to you at the entrance. To prepare your children for their trip to the park, consider ordering the 32-page *Kid's Guide to Bryce Canyon* for children 5–10. Books about Bryce Canyon National Park are available at the visitor center bookstore, which is operated by **Bryce Canyon Natural History Association.** | Bryce Canyon, 84717 | 435/834–4602 or 888/362–2642.

When to Visit

Bryce Canyon National Park is open year-round. Campgrounds may close seasonally because of lack of services (one loop of North Campground remains open throughout winter), and roads may occasionally close in winter while heavy snow is cleared.

SCENERY AND WILDLIFE

Because of its high elevation, Bryce experiences wildflower season in late summer. Fall color is also a sight to behold as the aspen, bigtooth maple, and other hardwoods turn golden. In winter, snow provides a good canvas on which to look for the footprints of mountain lion, mule deer, elk, and coyote, and the snow offers a brilliant contrast to the pink rock of the amphitheater. Whenever you come, by all means be outdoors in the park at sunrise or sunset. A walk along the Rim Trail will give you goose bumps as the light plays with the craggy, pink, white, and red rocks. These hours are the best time to discover the

MEN OF STONE

Paiute Indians called the Bryce Canyon area Unka timpe-wa-wince-pock-ich, which means "red rocks standing like men in a bowl-shape canyon." According to the legend, the animals and humanlike creatures who inhabited the amphitheater angered the deity Coyote because they worked too long beautifying their home. Coyote threw their paints on them and turned them to stone where they still stand today.

park's true personality. Wildlife also roams about at these times of day; look for mule deer or elk in roadside meadows. Marmot might be out any time of day at the south end of the park, although they hibernate in winter. You can visit a prairie dog colony at the large meadow south of the visitor center, although these playful little critters do hibernate in winter. The park's 160 species of birds can be spotted almost any time during the day— see if a Steller's jay doesn't follow you on a hike along the rim.

HIGH AND LOW SEASON

If you choose July, August, or September to see Bryce Canyon, you'll be visiting with the rest of the world. During these months, traffic on the main road can test the most patient driver, and lodging may be difficult to find inside and outside the park. If it's solitude you're looking for, come to Bryce any time between October and March. The snow may be flying, but imagine the multi-hued rocks under an icing of white.

Average High/Low Temperatures (°F) and Monthly Precipitation (in inches)

	JAN.	FEB.	MAR.	APR.	MAY	JUNE
BRYCE CANYON	39/8	41/13	48/17	56/25	68/31	75/38
	1.7	1.4	1.4	1.2	0.8	0.6
	JULY	AUG.	SEP.	OCT.	NOV.	DEC.
	83/47	80/45	74/37	63/29	51/19	42/11
	1.4	2.2	1.4	1.4	1.2	1.6

FESTIVALS AND SEASONAL EVENTS

WINTER

Feb.: **Bryce Canyon Winter Fest.** Cross-country ski races, snow sculpting contests, and ski archery will keep you warm in the brisk temperatures. This event takes place at Ruby's Best Western Inn outside the park entrance. | 435/834–5341 or 800/468–8660.

SUMMER

June: **Chariots in the Sky Balloon Festival.** Watch colorful balloons rise into the air at Panguitch and drift above canyon country. Each year there are 30 or more balloons. | 866/590–4134.

Utah Summer Games. More than 7,000 Utahans compete in everything from archery to horseshoes, arm wrestling, basketball, and gymnastics at Southern Utah University in Cedar City. | 435/865–8421 or 800/354–4849.

Quilt Walk Festival. In their initial attempt to settle Panguitch in 1864, the starving and winter-weary settlers had to lay quilts over snow pits to complete a trip to gather provisions. Each year Panguitch commemorates its forebears with quilting classes, a quilt walk dinner theater, a pioneer home tour, craft shows, and a cowboy action shoot. | 866/590–4134.

Utah Shakespearean Festival. This world-class festival in Cedar City features several stage productions of works by Shakespeare and others. The Greenshow, with jugglers, puppet shows, and folks dressed in Elizabethan period costume, adds to the festivities. The Royal Feaste, a popular dinner event, requires reservations. | 435/586–7880 or 800/752–9849.

July: **Old Time Fiddlers and Bears Festival.** This Cannonville event is an old-fashioned fiddling contest with a twist. In 1987 they barbecued up a marauding bear that had been feasting on the residents' chickens and apricots. Now they serve bear burgers and homemade root beer during the festival. | 800/444–6686.

Escalante Pioneer Day Celebration. An annual daylong celebration commemorates the original settlers of the area and includes a parade, a rodeo, and a dance in downtown Escalante. | 435/826–4205.

Panguitch Pioneer Day Celebration. At one of the biggest Pioneer Day celebrations in the state, Panguitch does it right with an invitational rodeo, parade, historical program, barbecue, children's races, and dance. | 435/676–8585 or 800/444–6689.

Nearby Towns

Only 24 mi northwest of Bryce Canyon on U.S. 89, **Panguitch** is a good jumping-off point for exploring the area. All visitor services are available here. The town is noted for the distinctive brick architecture of its early homes and outbuildings, and for the original facades of some of its late 19th-century Main Street commercial structures. About 50 mi northeast of Bryce, **Escalante,** the western gateway to Grand Staircase-Escalante National Monument, is another base for visitors. Escalante has modern amenities and is home to one of Utah's unique state parks, Escalante Petrified Forest State Park. If you're traveling through southwestern Utah on I–15, **Cedar City** will be your exit to Bryce. The largest city you'll encounter in this part of Utah, it is 78 mi from Bryce Canyon. Cedar City is steeped in Mormon pioneer heritage. Today the city's claims to fame are its popular Utah Shakespearean Festival and a major state university.

INFORMATION

Color Country Travel Region (Cedar City, Escalante, Panguitch) | 906 N. 1400 West, Box 1550, St. George, 84770 | 800/233–8824. **Garfield County Travel Council (Escalante, Panguitch)** | 55 S. Main St., Panguitch, 84759 | 435/676–8826 or 800-444-6689 | www.brycecanyoncountry. com. **Iron County Travel Council (Cedar City)** | 581 N. Main, Box 1007, Cedar City, 84720 | 435/ 586–5124 or 800/354–4849.

Exploring Bryce Canyon

PARK BASICS

Contacts and Resources: Bryce Canyon National Park | Box 170001, Bryce Canyon, 84717 | 435/834–5322 | fax 435/834–4102 | www.nps.gov/brca.

Hours: The park is open 24 hours a day.

Fees: The entrance fee is $20 per vehicle for a seven-day pass and $5 for pedestrians or bicyclists. An annual Bryce Canyon park pass, good for one year from the date of purchase, costs $30. This pass can also be used on the park shuttle. If you leave your private vehicle outside the park, the one-time entrance fee, including transportation on the shuttle, is $15.

Getting Around: You can see the highlights of the park via the well-maintained road that runs the length of main scenic area, but in high season you may encounter heavy traffic and parking areas filled to capacity. Additionally, Bryce Canyon's roads are undergoing major reconstruction through 2004. The shuttle bus system, which operates mid-May through the end of September, is a good alternative to fighting traffic and delays caused by construction. Park your car at the staging area on the left side of Route 12, about 3 mi north of the park entrance, and hop the shuttle that departs about every 10–15 minutes. The first stop is Ruby's Inn, followed by the park visitor center. The shuttle makes stops at all the major overlooks and facilities in the north portion of the park. It does not go beyond Bryce Point. The shuttle is free with admission to the park. For information on the Bryce Canyon National Park shuttle, contact park personnel at 435/834–5322 or www.nps.gov/brca.

Permits: A $5 backcountry permit, available from the visitor center, is required for camping in the park's interior. Camping is allowed only on Under-the-Rim Trail and Rigg's

BRYCE CANYON
NATIONAL PARK

EXPLORING
ATTRACTIONS NEARBY
DINING
LODGING
CAMPING AND RV
FACILITIES
SHOPPING
ESSENTIAL
INFORMATION

Spring Loop, both south of Bryce Point. Campfires are not permitted and camping is only allowed at designated sites.

Public Telephones: Inside the park, public telephones are located at Bryce Canyon Lodge, Bryce Canyon Pines General Store, Sunset Campground, and the visitor center. Outside the park, Ruby's Inn has public telephones.

Rest Rooms: Rest rooms inside the park are at Bryce Canyon Lodge, Bryce Canyon Pines General Store, the south end of North Campground, Sunset Campground, Sunset Point, the visitor center, and Yovimpa Point. Outside the park, there are public rest rooms at Ruby's Inn and the attached Ruby's General Store.

Accessibility: Most park facilities were constructed between 1930 and 1960. Some have been upgraded for handicap accessibility, while others can be used with some assistance. Because of the park's natural terrain, only a 0.5-mi section of the Rim Trail between Sunset and Sunrise Points is wheelchair accessible. The 1-mi bristlecone Loop Trail at Rainbow Point has a hard surface and could be used with assistance, but several grades do not meet standards. Handicapped parking is marked at all overlooks and public facilities. Accessible campsites are available at Sunset Campground.

Emergencies: In an emergency, dial 911. To contact park police, go to the visitor center or find a park ranger.

Lost and Found: The park's lost-and-found is at the visitor center.

Good Tours

BRYCE CANYON IN ONE DAY

Bryce Canyon can easily be experienced in one day. Begin your day with a stop at the **visitor center** to get an overview of the park and to purchase books and maps to enhance your visit. Watch the video presentation on the park and peruse exhibits about the natural and cultural history of Bryce Canyon. Thus informed, drive to **Bryce Canyon Lodge** to see the historic property. From the lodge, you can walk out to the **Rim Trail** and stroll for as long as you like. After your walk, drive the 18-mi **main park road,** stopping at the overlooks along the way. Allowing for traffic, and if you stop at all 13 overlooks, this drive will take you between two and three hours.

If you have the time and energy for a hike, the easiest route into the amphitheater is the **Queen's Garden Trail** at Sunrise Point. Although this is the least strenuous route into the amphitheater, it still involves a steep descent and climb out. Alternatively, a short, rolling hike along the **Bristlecone Loop Trail** at Rainbow Point rewards you with spectacular views and a cool walk through a forest of bristlecone pines. If you don't have time to drive the 18 mi to the end of the park, skip Bryce Canyon Lodge and drive the 2-mi stretch of road from the visitor center to **Inspiration Point** and the next 2 mi to **Bryce Point.** This short jaunt will introduce you to the spectacular landscape that you'll surely want to return to when you have more time.

End your day with sunset at Inspiration Point. Make sure you have your camera ready to catch the dramatic play of light on the colorful hoodoos. If you have still have time, dine at Bryce Canyon Lodge, but be sure to make reservations in the morning. As you leave the park, stop at famous **Ruby's Inn** for a piece of Native American jewelry, souvenirs for the kids, and snacks for the road.

BRYCE CANYON IN TWO OR THREE DAYS

Starting at the **visitor center** early on your first day, talk with rangers about trail and weather conditions and pick up maps and books. Drive the 18-mi **scenic road,** stopping at the overlooks along the way. At Rainbow Point, walk the 1-mi round-trip **Bristlecone Pine Trail.** Picnic at **Sunrise Point** to energize for a hike to Tower Bridge via the **Fairyland Loop Trail.** Take time to rest in the shady area near the bridge before making the strenuous hike

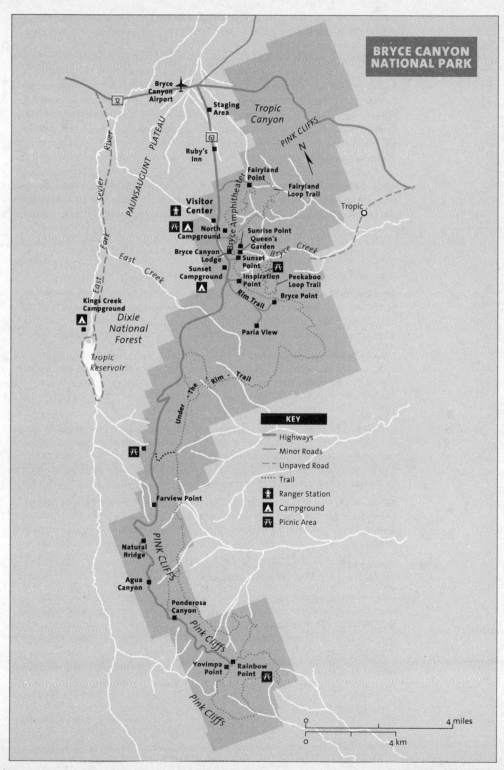

BRYCE CANYON
NATIONAL PARK

Bryce
Canyon
Airport

12

Staging
Area

*Tropic
Canyon*

63

PINK CLIFFS

Ruby's
Inn

N

Fairyland
Point

Fairyland
Loop Trail

Tropic

**Visitor
Center**

North
Campground

Bryce Amphitheater

Sunrise Point
Queen's
Garden

Bryce Creek

Bryce Canyon
Lodge

Sunset
Point

Sunset
Campground

Inspiration
Point

Peekaboo
Loop Trail

Bryce Point

Sevier River

East Fork

East Creek

Kings Creek
Campground

*Dixie
National
Forest*

Rim Trail

Paria View

*Tropic
Reservoir*

Under · The · Rim · Trail

KEY

Highways
Minor Roads
Unpaved Road
Trail
Ranger Station
Campground
Picnic Area

Farview Point

Natural
Bridge

PINK CLIFFS

Agua
Canyon

Ponderosa
Canyon

Pink Cliffs

Yovimpa
Point

Rainbow
Point

Pink Cliffs

0   4 miles

0   4 km

out. Either before or after sunset at **Inspiration Point,** dine at **Bryce Canyon Lodge** (you need to make reservations in the morning). While at the lodge, make reservations for a horseback ride for tomorrow.

A **ride into the amphitheater** via horse or mule is a memorable way to see Bryce Canyon. Even the two-hour journey is worth taking, but you'll see much more of the park on the half-day expedition. Upon returning to the rim, stop at **Ruby's Inn** for lunch and some fun shopping. When the sun begins to slant low in the sky, head out to the **Rim Trail** near Sunset Point. Later, attend a **ranger program** at the campfire circle at North or Sunset campground, or the Bryce Canyon Lodge Auditorium. Check to see if an astronomer from Hansen Planetarium is giving a **star party** while you're in the park. Schedules and topics of all park programs are posted at the visitor center, campgrounds, and Bryce Canyon Lodge.

If you have one more day to spend in the park, and tons of stamina, take one more, longer hike into the depths of the amphitheater. Hike the uncrowded **Fairyland Loop Trail** for a full immersion in the beauty of Bryce Canyon. A shorter option is the **Trail to the Hat Shop.** Both trails are strenuous, descending 900 ft into the amphitheater, but they allow you to truly experience this magnificent park.

Attractions

PROGRAMS AND TOURS

Bryce Canyon Scenic Tours. Enjoy a scenic two-hour tour of Bryce Canyon with knowledgeable guides who describe the area's history, geology, and flora and fauna. Choose from a sunrise tour, sunset tour, or general tour of the park. Specialized or private tours can also be arranged. | 435/834–5200 or 800/432–5383 | www.brycetours.com | $29 and up.

Bryce Canyon Airlines/Helicopters. For a once-in-a-lifetime view of Bryce Canyon National Park, join professional pilots and guides for a helicopter ride over the park. Flights depart from Ruby's Inn Heliport. You can swoop over the amphitheater for as long as 15 minutes to more than an hour. Small airplane tours and charter services are also available. | 435/834–5341 or 800/528–1234 | www.brycecanyonairlines.com | $55–$225.

Campfire and Auditorium Programs. Bryce Canyon's natural diversity comes alive during talks held at the campfire circles in the park's two campgrounds or at Bryce Canyon Lodge. Lectures, slide programs, and audience participation introduce you to geology, astronomy, wildlife adaptations to the climate, wildfires, social and cultural history, and many other topics related to Bryce Canyon and the West.

Canyon Hike. Take an early morning walk among the hoodoos of Queen's Garden or Navajo Loop Trail. A ranger points out the formations and explains some of the amphitheater's features as you go. The hike is 2–3 mi long mi and takes two–three hours to complete.

Geology Talk. Rangers relate the geologic story of Bryce Canyon in short sessions held at various times and locations around the park.

Junior Ranger Program. This program runs from Memorial Day to Labor Day; children ages 6 to 12 can sign up at the park visitor center. Activities vary depending on the park ranger, but a session might involve learning about geology and wildlife using arts and crafts and games. Schedules of events and topics are posted at the visitor center, Bryce Canyon Lodge, and on North and Sunset campground bulletin boards.

Moonlight Hike. Imagine how the hoodoos look by the light of a full moon. Three times each month, at or near full moon, you can take this two-hour hike with a park ranger. You must make reservations in person on the day of the hike. Check at the visitor center if you're in the park during a full moon.

Rim Walk. Stroll along the gorgeous rim of Bryce Canyon with a park ranger on a 1-mi, 1½-hour outing.

Star Party. Once a month, an astronomer from Hansen Planetarium leads an evening with telescopes. You will see more stars in the clear, clean night sky than you ever imagined were up there.

SCENIC DRIVES

Main Park Road. One of the delights of Bryce Canyon National Park is that much of the park can be viewed from scenic overlooks on the main road that travels 18 mi from the park entrance south to Rainbow Point. Allow two to three hours to travel the entire 36-mi round-trip. The park road is open year-round, but may be closed temporarily after heavy snowfalls to allow for clearing. The 18-mi main park road provides outstanding views of the park and southern Utah scenery. Major overlooks are rarely more than a few minutes' walk from the parking areas. From many overlooks you can see more than 100 mi on clear days. On crisp winter days, views from Rainbow or Yovimpa points are restricted only by the curvature of the Earth. On the drive from the visitor center to Rainbow Point, you climb 1,100 ft in elevation. As you ascend, the forest changes from ponderosa pine to spruce, fir, and aspen. All overlooks lie east of the road. To make your drive easy, proceed to the southern end of the park and stop at the overlooks on your northbound return. Trailers are not allowed beyond Sunset Campground. Day users may park trailers at the visitor center or other designated sites; check with park staff for parking options. RVs can drive throughout the park, but vehicles longer than 25 ft are not allowed at Paria View.

SIGHTS TO SEE

Unless otherwise noted, all sights are located along the park's 18-mi main road.
Agua Canyon. This is a good spot to see the play of light on the colorful hoodoos. | About 12 mi south of the park entrance.

Bryce Canyon Lodge. Designed by Gilbert Stanley Underwood for the Union Pacific Railroad, the park's lodge was built in 1924. A National Historic Landmark, the lodge has been faithfully restored, right down to the lobby's huge limestone fireplace and log and wrought-iron chandelier, plus bark-covered hickory furniture made by the same company that created the originals. Inside the historic building are a restaurant, a gift shop, and information on park activities; guests of the lodge stay in the numerous log cabins on the wooded grounds. | About 2 mi south of the park entrance | 435/834–5361 or 303/297–2757.

Bryce Point. You'll find the trailhead to the Under-the-Rim-Trail here, as well as views of the Black Mountains and Navajo Mountain. | About 5.5 mi south of the park entrance on Inspiration Point Rd.

★ **Fairyland Point.** At the scenic overlook closest to the park entrance (look for the sign marking the road off the main park road), you'll see views of Fairyland Amphitheater and its delicate, fanciful forms. The Sinking Ship and other formations stand before the grand backdrop of the Aquarius Plateau and distant Navajo Mountain. Because it's not on the main park road, many people miss this spectacular view. | 1 mi off the main park road, 1 mi north of the visitor center.

Natural Bridge. This arch was carved in the rock by rain and frost erosion. | About 11 mi south of the park entrance.

Queen Victoria. Looking every bit like a queen, this rock formation sports a crown and glorious full skirt. It can only be viewed by hiking a popular, moderately strenuous trail. | Queen's Garden Trail.

★ **Sunrise Point.** Named for its stunning views at dawn, this is a popular stop for everyone who comes to Bryce Canyon and is the starting point for the Queen's Garden Trail and the Fairyland Loop Trail. | About 2 mi south of the park entrance near Bryce Canyon Lodge.

Sunset Point. Bring your camera and plenty of film to this favorite overlook to watch the late-day sun paint its magic on the hoodoos. | About 2 mi south of the park entrance near Bryce Canyon Lodge.

A HELLUVA PLACE
TO LOSE A PIPE

T.C. Bailey, the U.S. Deputy Surveyor who explored the park in 1876, spent two days searching the area for his large meerschaum pipe, which, though usually chained to him, had been lost. His hunt was unsuccessful, but the pipe was found several years later.

★ **Rainbow Point.** On a clear day at this overlook, you can see as far as 90 mi to Arizona. | 18 mi south of the park entrance.

Thor's Hammer. You can only see Thor's Hammer, a delicate formation similar to a balanced rock, if you hike 521 ft down into the amphitheater. | Navajo Loop Trail.

Visitor Center. You can visit with park rangers, watch a video about Bryce Canyon, study exhibits, or shop for informative books, maps, and other materials here. You can also obtain backcountry permits here or receive first aid, emergency, or lost-and-found services. | About 1 mi south of the park entrance | 435/834–5322 | www.nps.gov/brca | Oct.–June, daily 8–4:30; July–Sept., daily 8–8.

Wall of Windows. Openings carved into a wall of rock illustrate the drama of erosion that formed Bryce Canyon. The only way to visit this spot is to hike, or ride horseback, down the Peekaboo Trail. | Peekaboo Loop Trail.

Sports and Outdoor Activities

BIRD-WATCHING

More than 170 bird species have been identified in Bryce. Violet green swallows and White-throated swifts are common, as are Steller's jays. American coots, Rufous hummingbirds, and mountain bluebirds frequent Bryce as well. Lucky bird-watchers will see Golden eagles floating across the skies above the pink rocks of the amphitheater. The best time to spot birds is May through July, during the migration season. A birder's checklist is available at the visitor center.

HIKING

To get up close and personal with the park's hoodoos, hike into the amphitheater. Because of steep descents and ascents, most of the hikes are moderately strenuous. Always remember that you are hiking at elevations of up to 9,100 ft, where you can fall victim to altitude sickness—headaches, light-headedness, nausea, and stomach cramps—if you're not used to exercising at elevation. Uneven terrain calls for sturdy hiking boots and summer heat demands a hat and sunscreen. Don't descend into the amphitheater without water. For trail maps and information, stop at the visitor center.

Bristlecone Loop Trail. Hike through dense spruce and fir forest to exposed cliffs where ancient bristlecone pines survive. Some of the trees here are more than 1,700 years old. You might see yellow-bellied marmots and blue grouse on this trail. These critters are not found at lower elevations in the park. The popular 1-mi trail takes about an hour to hike. | Rainbow Point, on the main park road 18 mi south of the park entrance.

★ **Fairyland Loop Trail.** Hike into whimsical Fairyland Canyon on this strenuous but uncrowded 8-mi trail. The trail winds around hoodoos, across trickles of running water, and finally to a natural window in the rock. Allow about four to five hours for your trip. The trailheads are at Fairyland Point and north of Sunrise Point. | Fairyland Point: 1 mi off the main park road 1 mi south of the park entrance; Sunrise Point: about 2 mi south of the park entrance.

Navajo Loop Trail. A steep descent via a series of switchbacks leads to Wall Street, a narrow canyon with high rock walls and towering fir trees. The northern end of the trail brings Thor's Hammer into close view. Allow about one to two hours on this 1.5-mi trail. | Sunset Point, about 2 mi south of the park entrance.

★ **Navajo/Queen's Combination Loop.** By walking a combination of the Queen's Garden and Navajo Loop trails, you can see some of the best of Bryce on a 3-mi hike that takes two to three hours. The trail takes you past fantastic formations and through an open forest of pine and juniper on the amphitheater floor. Descend into the amphitheater via Navajo and ascend via the less demanding Queen's Garden, then return to your starting point via the Rim Trail. | Navajo Loop: Sunset Point, 2 mi south of the park entrance; Queens Garden: near Sunrise Point, about 2 mi south of the park entrance.

Peekaboo Loop. If you want a good workout, hike this steep trail past the Wall of Windows and the Three Wisemen. The trail is used by horses in spring, summer and fall, and they have the right-of-way. Start at Bryce, Sunrise, or Sunset Point and allow from three to four hours to hike either 5 or 7 mi. | Bryce Point: 2 mi off the main park road about 5.5 mi south of the park entrance; Sunrise Point, about 2 mi south of the park entrance; Sunset Point, about 2 mi south of the park entrance.

Queen's Garden. This is the easiest hike into the amphitheater and also the most crowded. Allow from two to three hours to hike 2 mi. | Sunrise Point, about 2 mi south of the park entrance.

Riggs Spring Loop Trail. One of the park's more rigorous day hikes, or a relaxed overnighter (pick up a backcountry permit at the visitor center if you'll be camping), this 9-mi trail between Yovimpa and Rainbow points takes about four to five hours to hike. | Yovimpa and Rainbow points, 18 mi south of the park entrance.

★ **Rim Trail.** If you prefer your exercise in short, slow doses, you'll find any stretch of this 11-mi trail suitable for strolling, especially the paved area between Sunrise and Sunset points. Hike any part of the trail (which stretches from Bryce Point to Fairyland Point) for outstanding views of hoodoos from above, as well as vistas that stretch over 100 mi. Allow five to six hours if you hike the entire 11 mi. | Access at Fairyland, Sunrise, Sunset, Inspiration, and Bryce points.

BRYCE CANYON
NATIONAL PARK

EXPLORING
ATTRACTIONS NEARBY
DINING
LODGING
CAMPING AND RV
FACILITIES
SHOPPING
ESSENTIAL
INFORMATION

Tower Bridge. This short, uncrowded hike on the Fairyland Loop Trail takes you to a natural bridge deep in the amphitheater. Walk through pink and white "badlands" with hoodoos all around on this 3-mi trip (not a loop) that takes two to three hours. | Sunrise Point, 1 mi off the main park road, south of the park entrance.

Trail to the Hat Shop. Once you get to the "hat shop" you'll understand why this trail has such a fanciful name. Hard gray caps balance precariously atop narrow pedestals of softer, rust-colored rock. Allow three to four hours to travel this strenuous 4-mi trail. | Bryce Point, 2 mi off the main park road about 5.5 mi south of the park entrance.

Under-the-Rim Trail. Serious backpackers can fully immerse themselves in the mystical landscape of Bryce on this 22.5-mi trail. Starting at Bryce Point, the trail travels to Rainbow Point, passing through the Pink Cliffs, traversing Agua Canyon and Pondersoa Canyon, and taking you to several springs. As the name suggests, most of the hike is on the amphitheater floor; the elevation change is about 1,500 ft. You'll be hiking across up-and-down terrain among ponderosa pine. Four trails accessible from the main park road allow you to walk Under-the-Rim as a series of day hikes. To hike the entire trail in one go, allow at least two days. You must obtain a backcountry permit at the visitor center if you intend to stay in the amphitheater overnight. Also inquire there about the availability of water. | Access from Bryce Point, Swamp Canyon, Ponderosa Canyon, and Rainbow Point.

HORSEBACK RIDING

Make the most of your visit to the West by saddling up a horse or mule and descending to the floor of the Bryce Canyon amphitheater. Most of the folks who take this exciting expedition have no riding experience, so don't hesitate to join in. Mules will give you the smoothest, most sure-footed ride. A two-hour ride ambles along the amphitheater floor to the Fairy Castle before returning to Sunrise Point. The half-day expedition follows Peekaboo Trail, winds past the Fairy Castle and the Alligator, and passes the Wall of Windows before returning to Sunrise Point.

Canyon Trail Rides. To arrange for a trail ride (reservations are suggested), call or stop by the Canyon Trail Rides desk in Bryce Canyon Lodge. These friendly folks have been around for years and are the only trail-ride outfitters inside the park. | Bryce Canyon Lodge, off the main park road about 2 mi south of the park entrance | 435/679–8665 or 435/834–5500 | www.canyonrides.com | $30–$45.

SKIING

Unlike Utah's four other national parks, Bryce Canyon usually receives plenty of snow, making it an ideal and increasingly popular cross-country ski area. The park's 2.5-mi Fairyland ski loop is marked but ungroomed, as is the 5-mi Paria loop, which runs through ponderosa forests into long, open meadows.

Ruby's Inn. You can rent skis from Ruby's, which grooms a 31-mi private trail that connects to an ungroomed trail in the park. | Rte. 63, 1 mi north of the park entrance | 435/834–5341 | www.rubysinn.com.

SNOWSHOEING

The National Park Service lends out snowshoes free of charge at the visitor center; just leave your driver's license or a major credit card with a ranger. You can snowshoe on the rim trails, but the Park Service discourages their use below the rim.

Attractions Nearby

SIGHTS TO SEE

★ **Cedar Breaks National Monument.** From the rim of Cedar Breaks, a natural amphitheater similar to Bryce Canyon plunges 2,000 ft into the Markagunt Plateau. Short alpine hiking trails along the rim make this a wonderful summer stop. Although its roads may be closed in winter due to heavy snow, the monument stays open for cross-country skiing and snowmobiling. | Rte. 14, 23 mi east of Cedar City, Brian Head | 435/586–9451 | www.nps.gov/cebr | $3 per person | Visitor center open late-May–mid-Oct., daily 8–6.

Dixie National Forest. This expansive forest stretches for 170 mi across Utah, with elevations from only 2,800 ft at St. George to over 11,000 ft on Boulder Mountain. Recreational opportunities include hiking, camping, picnicking, and horseback riding, plus fishing, canoeing, sailing, swimming, and waterskiing at one of the several lakes, streams, and reservoirs. There are 26 campgrounds within the forest: some are free, others require fees. For information contact Dixie National Forest Headquarters. | 82 N. 100 East, Cedar City | 435/865–3700, 800/280–2267 for campground information | www.fs.fed.us/dxnf | Free | Daily.

Escalante Petrified Forest State Park. This park 48 mi east of Bryce Canyon off Route 12 was created to protect a huge repository of fossilized wood and dinosaur bones. Learn all about petrified wood, which is easily spotted along two short interpretive trails. There's an attractive swimming beach at the park's Wide Hollow Reservoir, which is also good for boating, fishing, and birding. | 710 N. Reservoir Rd., Escalante | 435/826–4466 | http://parks.state.ut.us | $5 | Daily.

★ **Grand Staircase–Escalante National Monument.** Larger than most national parks, this formidable monument is popular with backpackers and hard-core mountain-bike enthusiasts. You can explore the rocky landscape, which represents some of America's last wilderness, via dirt roads with a four-wheel-drive vehicle. Views into the monument are most impressive from Route 12 between Escalante and Boulder. Calf Creek Falls is an easy 6-mi round-trip hike from the trailhead at Calf Creek Recreation Area (on Route 12 north of Escalante). At the end of your walk, a large waterfall explodes over a cliff hundreds of ft above. It costs nothing to visit the park, but fees apply for camping and backcountry permits. | 318 N. 100 East, Kanab | 435/644–6400 | www.ut.blm.gov/monument | Free | Daily.

Kodachrome Basin State Park. As soon as you see it, you'll understand why the park earned this name from the National Geographic Society. The sand pipes seen here are found no other place in the world. You can hike any of the trails to spot some of the 67 pipes in or around the park. The short Angels Palace Trail takes you quickly into the park's interior, up, over, and around some of the badlands. | 7 mi south of Cannonville, off Rte. 12 | 435/679-8562 | http://parks.state.ut.us | $5 | Daily.

Otter Creek State Park. You can enjoy year-round recreation, including fishing, boating, and camping, at this large state park. Otter Creek Reservoir is the centerpiece of this favorite RV haunt. | 4 mi northwest of Antimony on Rte. 22, Antimony | 435/624–3268 | www.utah.com/stateparks/otter creek.htm | $4 | Daily.

Dining

In Bryce Canyon

Bryce Canyon Lodge. American. Set among towering pines, this rustic old lodge is the only place to dine within the park. Many menu items change each year. Try anything with their tomatillo sauce, and stick with the simpler dishes. | About 2 mi south of the park entrance | 435/834–5361 | Reservations essential | $12–$20 | AE, DC, MC, V | Closed late Nov.–Mar.

Bryce Canyon Pines General Store. You can pick up snacks, drinks, juices, and quick meals at this multipurpose facility at Sunrise Point. Picnic tables under pine trees offer a shady break. | About 0.5 mi off the main park road 2 mi south of the park entrance | 435/834–5441 or 800/892–7923 | AE, D, MC, V | Closed mid-Nov.–Mar.

Picnic Areas. There are three picnic areas inside the park.

The area near **North Campground** has picnic tables and grills. It's a shady, alpine setting among ponderosa pine. | About 0.25 mi south of the visitor center.

A small (and undeveloped) picnic area lies north of Far View Point near a place locals call **Piracy Point.** This area offers little else than a picnic table slightly off the main road. | About 8 mi south of the park entrance on the main park road.

The more scenic of the park's two developed picnic areas is **Yovimpa Point** at the southern end of the park. The picnic area is shady and quiet, and looks out onto the 100-mi vistas from the rim. There are tables and rest rooms. | 18 mi south of the park entrance.

Near the Park

Bryce Canyon Pines Restaurant. American. Known for homemade soups like tomato-broccoli and corn chowder, and for fresh berry and cream pies, this homey, antiques-filled restaurant 6 mi northwest of the park entrance dishes up quality comfort food. | Rte. 12, about 15 mi from Tropic | 435/834–5441 | $5–$16 | AE, D, DC, MC, V.

Doug's Place. American. In the tiny hamlet of Tropic, east of Bryce Canyon, Doug's specializes in steak dishes such as *Milanesa* (breaded, with tomato sauce), and *Milanesa à la Neopolitonia* (with ham and Swiss cheese). Also on the menu are inexpensive taco salads, hamburgers, soft flour tacos, Texas-style barbecue, and homemade pies and sweet rolls. On Friday and Saturday nights Doug's serves a great prime-rib dinner. The restaurant has live entertainment every night but Sunday. | 141 N. Main St., Tropic | 435/679–8633 or 800/993–6847 | $4–$21 | AE, D, DC, MC, V.

Fosters Family Steakhouse. Steak. With a stone fireplace and picture windows, Fosters is a clean, relatively quiet, modern steak house, and one of the most pleasant restaurants in the area. The menu features prime rib, steaks, and basic chicken and seafood dishes. Beer is the only alcohol served. | Rte. 12, 2 mi west of the junction with Rte. 63 | 435/834–5227 | $6–$17 | AE, D, MC, V | Closed Mon.–Thurs. in Jan.

Harold's Place. American. About 15 mi west of Bryce Canyon, on Route 12 at the entrance to Red Canyon, stands this establishment designed to resemble a log cabin. The large menu includes a variety of steaks, lamb, seafood, pastas, and salads. Try Harold's Favorite for breakfast and get eggs anyway you like, potatoes, your choice of meat, and a bottomless cup of coffee all for five bucks. | 3066 Rte. 12, 7 mi from Panguitch | 435/676–2350 | $8–$14 | MC, V | Closed Nov.–Mar. No lunch.

BRYCE CANYON
NATIONAL PARK

EXPLORING
ATTRACTIONS NEARBY
DINING
LODGING
CAMPING AND RV
FACILITIES
SHOPPING
ESSENTIAL
INFORMATION

★ **Milt's Stage Stop.** American. Locals and an increasing number of tourists have discovered the terrific food at this dinner spot in beautiful Cedar Canyon, about 78 mi from Bryce Canyon. It's known for its 12-ounce rib-eye steak, its prime rib, and its fresh crab, lobster, and shrimp dishes. In winter, deer feed in front of the restaurant as a fireplace blazes away inside. A number of hunting trophies decorate the rustic building's interior, and splendid views of the surrounding mountains delight patrons year-round. | UT 14, 5 mi east of town in Cedar Canyon, Cedar City | 435/586–9344 | $13–$42 | AE, D, DC, MC, V | No lunch.

Lodging

In Bryce Canyon

★ **Bryce Canyon Lodge.** A few feet from the amphitheater's rim and trailheads is this rugged stone and wood lodge. You have your choice of suites on the lodge's second level, motel-style rooms in separate buildings (with the unexpected touch of balconies or porches), and cozy lodgepole-pine cabins, some with cathedral ceilings and gas fireplaces. Reservations are hard to come by, so call several months ahead. Or if you're feeling lucky, call the day before your arrival—cancellations occasionally make last-minute bookings possible. Horseback rides into the park's interior can be arranged in the lobby. Restaurant. No a/c, no room TVs. No smoking. No pets. | 2 mi south of the park entrance, 84717 | 435/834–5361 or 303/297–2757 | fax 435/834–5464 | www.brycecanyonlodge.com | 114 rooms, 3 suites | $110–$130 | AE, D, DC, MC, V | Closed Nov.–Mar.

Near the Park

Bard's Inn Bed and Breakfast. Rooms in this restored turn-of-the-20th-century house 78 mi from Bryce Canyon are named after heroines in Shakespeare's plays. There are wonderful antiques throughout and handcrafted quilts grace the beds. Enjoy a full breakfast that includes fresh home-baked breads such as nutmeg blueberry muffins, plus fruit, juices, and oven-shirred eggs. No room phones. No smoking. | 150 S. 100 West St., Cedar City, 84720 | 435/586–6612 | 7 rooms | $80–95 | AE, MC, V.

Best Western Ruby's Inn. North of the park entrance and housing a large restaurant and gift shop, this is "Grand Central Station" for visitors to Bryce. Rooms vary in age, with sprawling wings added as the park gained popularity. All of the guest rooms are consistently comfortable and attractive, however. Centered between the gift shop and restaurant, the lobby of rough-hewn log beams and poles sets a southwestern mood. There's a liquor store on site. Memorial Day to Labor Day Ruby's hosts a rodeo every night but Sunday. It takes place across the road at the rodeo grounds. 2 restaurants. Indoor pool, outdoor pool. Laundry facilities. | Rte. 63, 1 mi off Rte. 12, Bryce, 84764 | 435/834–5341 or 800/468–8660 | fax 435/834–5265 | www.rubysinn.com | 368 rooms | $95–$130 | AE, D, DC, MC, V.

Bryce Canyon Pines. This quiet, no-surprises motel complex is tucked into the woods 6 mi from the park entrance. Most of the rooms have excellent mountain views. There are also a campground and horseback riding on the premises. Restaurant. Cable TV. Indoor pool. | Rte. 12, Bryce, 84764 | 435/834–5441 or 800/892–7923 | fax 435/834–5330 | www.brycecanyonpines.com | 51 rooms | $75 | AE, D, DC, MC, V.

Bryce Canyon Resort. This rustic lodge stands across from the local airport and 3 mi from the park entrance. Cabins and cottages are also available for those seeking a tad more privacy. Restaurant. In-room data ports. Cable TV. Indoor pool. Laundry facilities. Some pets allowed (fee). | 13500 E. Rte. 12, Bryce, 84764 | 435/834–5351 or 800/834–0043 | fax 435/834–5256 | 57 rooms, 2 suites | $85, $95 suites, $60–$95 cabins/cottages | MC, V.

Bryce Valley Inn. Rest your head in the tiny town of Tropic, where this down-to-earth motel offers simple accommodations. A small gift shop sells Native American crafts. Restaurant. Laundry facilities. Some pets allowed (fee). | 199 N. Main (Rte. 12), Tropic, 84776

| 435/679–8811 or 800/442–1890 | fax 435/679–8846 | www.brycevalleyinn.com | 63 rooms | $55–$75 | AE, D, MC, V.

Bryce View Lodge. Next to the park entrance, this motel has reasonable rates. It's operated by Ruby's Inn, so you can use the pool and other amenities at Ruby's next door. 2 restaurants. Cable TV. Laundry facilities. Some pets allowed. | Rte. 63, 1 mi off Rte. 12, Bryce, 84764 | 435/834–5180 or 888/279–2304 | fax 435/834–5181 | www.bryceviewlodge.com | 160 rooms | $35–$66 | AE, D, DC, MC, V.

Doug's Country Inn. With rustic, wood-beam rooms and homemade quilts on the beds, this inn is small and intimate. If you stay in Tropic, this is one of the better choices of lodging. Restaurant. Some pets allowed (fee). | 141 N. Main St., Tropic, 84776 | 435/679–8633 or 800/993–6847 | www.dougsplace.net | 28 rooms | $55 | AE, D, DC, MC, V.

Camping and RV Facilities

In Bryce Canyon

North Campground. A cool, shady retreat in a forest of ponderosa pines, this is a great home base for your exploration of Bryce Canyon. You are near the general store, Bryce Canyon Lodge, trailheads, and the visitor center. Sites are available on a first-come, first-served basis and the campground usually fills by early afternoon in July, August, and September. One loop of the campground remains open throughout winter. Flush toilets. Dump station. Drinking water. Fire grates, picnic tables. Public telephone. General store. | 107 sites, 47 for RVs | About 0.5 mi south of the visitor center off the main park road | 435/834–5322 | www.nps.gov/brca | $10 | Reservations not accepted | No credit cards | May–Oct.

Sunset Campground. This serene alpine campground is within walking distance of Bryce Canyon Lodge and many trailheads. All sites are filled on a first-come, first-served basis. The campground fills by early afternoon in July, August, and September, so get your campsite before you sightsee. Flush toilets. Dump station. Drinking water. Fire grates, picnic tables. Public telephone. General store. | 111 sites, 49 for RVs | 2 mi south of the visitor center off the main park road | 435/834–5322 | www.nps/gov/brca | $10 per night | Reservations not accepted | No credit cards | May–Oct.

Near the Park

Bryce Canyon Pines. This campground 6 mi from the park entrance is shady and quiet. It's on the grounds of Bryce Canyon Pines motel. Flush toilets. Full hook-ups. Drinking water, showers. Fire grates. Electricity, public telephone. Play area, swimming (pool). | 40 sites, 25 with hook-ups | Rte. 12, Bryce | 435/834–5441 or 800/892–7623 | fax 435/834–5330 | www.color-country.net/~bcpines | $16–$22 | D, DC, MC, V | Apr.–Nov.

Bryce Valley KOA. On the quiet side of Bryce, this campground has the lowest (and warmest) elevation of any camping spot near Bryce Canyon. Everything you need for a quiet night of sleep and comfort is right here, near the slot canyons of the Paria River. There's a cooking pavilion for group get-togethers. Flush toilets, full hook-ups, dump station. Drinking water, guest laundry, showers. Fire grates, grills, picnic tables. Electricity, public telephone. General store. Play area, swimming (pool). | Rte. 12 at the Kodachrome Basin turnoff, Cannonville | 65 RV sites, 20 tent sites, 5 cabins | 435/679–8988 or 888/562–4710 | www.koa.com | $18–$28 | AE, D, MC, V | Mar.–Nov.

★ **Calf Creek Recreation Area.** Near a creek and surrounded by shade trees, this campground is a treasure in Grand Staircase–Escalante National Monument. Make camp early; the first-come, first-served campground fills by noon in busy summer months. The campground is designed for tents and few of the sites are appropriate for RVs. Flush toilets. Drinking water. Fire grates. | Rte. 12, 15 mi east of Escalante and 8 mi west of Boulder | 13 sites | 435/826–5499 | www.publiclands.org | $7 | Reservations not accepted | No credit cards.

BRYCE CAMPGROUNDS

	Total # of sites	# of RV sites	# of hook-ups	Drive-to sites	Hike-to sites	Flush toilets	Pit toilets	Drinking water	Showers	Fire grates/pits	Swimming	Boat access	Playground	Dump station	Ranger station	Public telephone	Reservation possible	Daily fee per site	Dates open
INSIDE THE PARK																			
North	107	47	0	•		•		•		•				•	•	•		$10	Y/R
Sunset	111	49	0	•		•		•	•	•				•*		•		$10	May–Oct.
NEAR THE PARK																			
Bryce Canyon Pines	40	25	25	•		•		•		•			•			•	•	$16–22	Apr.–Nov.
Bryce Valley KOA	90	65	65			•		•	•	•	•		•			•	•	$18–28	Mar.–Nov.
Calf Creek Recreation Area	13	0	0	•		•		•										$7	Y/R
Escalante Petrified Forest (SP)	22	22	0	•		•		•	•	•	•			•		•	•**	$14	Y/R
Kings Creek (NF)	37	37	0	•		•		•		•	•	•		•				$9	May–Sep.
Kodachrome Basin State Park	27	27	0	•		•		•	•	•				•	•	•	•**	$14	Y/R
Red Canyon (NF)	37	37	0	•		•		•		•				•	•			$10	Apr.–Oct.
Red Canyon RV Park	35	35	35	•		•		•	•	•				•		•	•	$10–18	Apr.–Oct.
Riverside	300	65	65	•		•		•	•	•		•	•	•		•	•	$15–22	May–Oct.
Ruby's Inn	110	127	127	•		•		•	•	•				•		•	•	$16–25	Apr.–Oct.
White Bridge (NF)	29	29	0	•		•	•	•									•	$10	May–Oct.

* In summer only
UL=Unlimited
** Reservation fee charged
ULP=Unlimited primitive
Y/R=Year-round
LD=Labor Day
MD=Memorial Day

★ **Escalante Petrified Forest State Park.** This is an especially dandy place to pitch your tent or park your RV (all the sites accommodate either). The 130-acre Wide Hollow Reservoir adds boating and swimming to the recreation here. Flush toilets. Dump station. Drinking water, showers. Fire grates. Swimming (lake). | 22 sites | Rte. 12, about 45 mi east of Bryce Canyon National Park, Escalante | 435/538–7221, 800/322–3770 reservations | http://parks.state.ut.us/ | $14 | No credit cards.

Kings Creek Campground. Tenters will be right at home in this remote, pretty campground in Dixie National Forest, although all the sites can also take RVs. The campground is on a dirt road about 11 mi from the entrance to Bryce Canyon National Park, west of the park boundary and near Tropic Reservoir. Flush toilets. Dump station. Drinking water. Fire grates. | 37 sites, 1 group site | 7 mi south of Rte. 12, west of the junction with Rte. 163 | 435/676–8815 | www.fs.fed.us/dxnf/campground/kingcreek.html | $9 | No credit cards | Mid-May–mid-Sept.

★ **Kodachrome Basin State Park.** If a well-developed, scenic campground is where you want to rest your weary head, you will find that this is one of the best. All of the sites are appropriate for either tents or RVs. The campground is about 23 mi east of Bryce Canyon and 9 mi southeast of Cannonville. Flush toilets. Dump station. Drinking water, showers. Grills, picnic tables. | 27 sites | 9 mi south of Rte. 12 near Cannonville | 435/679–8562, 800/322–3770 reservations | http://parks.state.ut.us | $14 | No credit cards.

Red Canyon. This primitive campground in Dixie National Forest is surrounded by pine trees in a brilliant red rock canyon. All the sites work for either tents or RVs. Flush toilets. Dump station. Drinking water, showers. Fire grates. Ranger station. | 37 sites | Rte. 12, about 8 mi from the entrance to Bryce Canyon National Park | 435/676–8815 | www.fs.fed.us/dxnf/campground/redcanyon | $10 | No credit cards | May or June (weather permitting)–Oct.

Red Canyon RV Park. In red rock country very similar to that of Bryce Canyon, this desert campground is 16 mi from the national park. Besides RV sites, primitive and full service cabins are available. Flush toilets. Full hook-ups, dump station. Drinking water, showers. Fire grates. Electricity, public telephone. | 35 sites | Rte. 12, 1 mi east of U.S. 89 | 435/676–2690 | www.redcanyon.net | $10–$18 | AE, D, MC, V | Apr.–Oct.

Riverside Resort. As its name suggests, many of the sites here are on the banks of the Sevier River (where you can play or fish), making this a great spot to call home for a few days. A large meadow accommodates overflow tent camping, and a small motel is also on site. Flush toilets. Dump station. Drinking water, showers. Grills. Electricity, public telephone. General store. Play area, swimming (river). | 65 RV sites; unlimited tent camping | U.S. 89, Hatch | 435/735–4223 or 800/824–5651 | www.riversideresort-utah.com | $15–$22 | D, MC, V.

Ruby's Inn Campground and RV Park. North of the entrance to Bryce Canyon National Park, this campground sits amid pine and fir trees. It's part of the Ruby's Inn complex. Flush toilets. Full hook-ups, dump station. Drinking water, guest laundry, showers. Grills, picnic tables. Electricity, public telephone. General store. Swimming (pool). | 110 RV and tent sites, 5 cabins, 8 tepees | Rte. 63, 1 mi off Rte. 12, Bryce | 435/834–5341 | www.rubysinn.com | $16–$40 | AE, D, DC, MC, V | Apr.–Oct.

White Bridge. About 30 mi from Bryce Canyon on the way to Cedar Breaks National Monument, this alpine meadow campground is primitive but it will satisfy those seeking a quiet camping experience. Panguitch Creek trickles nearby and Panguitch Lake is 4 mi away. All of the sites are suitable for tents or RVs. Drinking water. Fire grates. | 29 sites | 12 mi southwest of Panguitch on Rte. 143 | 435/865–3700 | www.fs.fed.us/dxnf/campground/whitebridge.html | $10 | No credit cards | May or June (weather permitting)–Oct.

Shopping

Bryce Canyon Lodge Gift Shop. The lodge's small gift shop carries Native American and southwestern crafts, T-shirts, dolls, books, souvenirs, and sundries. | Bryce Canyon Lodge, off the main park road about 2 mi south of the park entrance | 435/834–5361.

Bryce Canyon Pines General Store. Here you can buy groceries, T-shirts, hats, books, film, postcards, and camping items that you might have left behind. | About 0.5 mi off the main park road 2 mi south of the park entrance | 800/892–7923 or 435/834–5441.

Ruby's General Store. Shopping at Ruby's souvenir heaven is an integral part of the Bryce Canyon experience. This large, lively store is packed with everything imaginable emblazoned with the park's name, from thimbles to sweatshirts. Native American arts and crafts, western wear, camping gear, groceries, and sundries are plentiful. There is a large selection of children's toys and trinkets. | Rte. 63, north of the park | 435/834–5341.

Visitor Center. The Bryce Canyon National History Association runs a bookstore inside the park visitor center, where you can find maps, trail guides, videos, and postcards. | About 1 mi south of the park entrance | 435/834–4102 or 888/362–2642.

Essential Information

ATMS: Ruby's Inn | Rte. 63, 1 mi north of the park entrance.

AUTOMOBILE SERVICE STATIONS: American Car Care Center | 1 mi outside the park on Rte. 63 | 435/834–5232. **Tesoro at Ruby's Inn** | Rte. 63, 1 mi north of the park entrance | 435/834–5341.

POST OFFICES: Bryce Canyon Lodge. | About 2 mi south of the park entrance off the main park road, Bryce Canyon, 84717 | 435/834–5123 | Closed Nov.–Mar. **Ruby's Inn.** | Rte. 63, 1 mi north of the park entrance, Bryce, 84764 | 435/834–8088.

CAPITOL REEF NATIONAL PARK
SOUTH-CENTRAL UTAH

Route 24, 75 mi south of I–70 via Loa and Torrey, or 91 mi south of I–70 via Hanksville.

Your senses will be delighted by a visit to Capitol Reef National Park. Here, you are saturated in colors that are almost indescribable—nowhere else in the West are the colors so dramatic. The dominant Moenkopi rock formation is a rich, red-chocolate hue. Deep blue-green juniper and pinyon stand out against it. Other sandstone layers are gold, ivory, and lavender. Sunset brings out the colors in an explosion of copper, platinum, and orange, then dusk turns the cliffs purple and blue. The texture of rock deposited in ancient inland seas and worn by subsequent erosion is pure art. The park preserves the Waterpocket Fold, a giant wrinkle in the earth that extends 100 miles between Thousand Lake Mountain and Lake Powell. When you climb high onto the rocks or into the mountains, you can see this remarkable geologic wonder and the jumble of colorful cliffs, massive domes, soaring spires and twisting canyons that surround it. It's no wonder Native Americans called this part of the country the "land of sleeping rainbow."

But your eyes will not be alone in their joy: the fragrance of pine and sage rises from the earth, and canyon wrens sing to you as you sit by the water. Flowing across the heart of Capitol Reef is the Fremont River, a narrow little creek that can turn into a swollen, raging torrent during desert flash floods. The river sustains cottonwoods, wildlife, and verdant valleys rich with fruit. During fruit harvest, your sensory experience is complete when you bite into a perfect ripe peach or apple from the park's orchards. Your soul, too, will be gratified here. You can walk the trails in relative solitude and enjoy the beauty without confronting crowds on the roads or paths. All around you are signs of those who came before: ancient Native Americans of the Fremont culture, Mormon pioneers who settled the land, and other courageous explorers who traveled the canyons. It is a rare thrill to feel the past overtake the present.

PUBLICATIONS

Capitol Reef: Canyon Country Eden by Rose Houk is an award-winning collection of photographs and lyrical essays on the park. The story of historic Fruita, its settlements and orchards is told in *Red Rock Eden* by George Davidson. *Explore Capitol Reef Trails* by Marjorie Miller and John Foster is a comprehensive hiking guide to the park. A brief background of the Fremont culture in Capitol Reef appears in *Dwellers of the Rainbow, Fremont Culture in Capitol Reef National Park* by Rose Houk. You can learn about the basic geology of the park in *Geology of Capitol Reef National Park* by Michael Collier. If you are exploring the backcountry of Cathedral Valley you'll want the park's newspaper-style publication, which serves as a road guide. These and other publications about Capitol Reef National Park are available at the gift shop or by mail from **Capitol Reef Natural History Association** | HC 70, Box 15, Torrey, 84775 | 435/425–3791 Ext. 113 | fax 435/425–3098 | www.nps.gov/care/nha/.

When to Visit

SCENERY AND WILDLIFE

The golden rock and rainbow cliffs are at their finest at sunset, when it seems as if they are lit from within. That's also when mule deer wander through the orchards near the campground. Many of the park's animals move about only at night to escape the heat of the day, but pinyon blue jays flit around the park all day. Of course, the best place to see wildlife is near the Fremont River, where animals are drawn to drink. Ducks and small mammals such as the yellow-bellied marmot live nearby. Desert bighorn sheep also live in Capitol Reef, but they are elusive. Your best chance of spotting the sheep is during a long hike deep within the park. If you should encounter a sheep, do not approach it: they've been known to charge human beings.

HIGH AND LOW SEASON

Capitol Reef is still a quiet treasure among America's national parks. Spring and early summer bring the most visitors to the park; folks clear out in the height of summer as temperatures reach the mid-90s, and then early fall brings people back to the park for the apple harvest and crisp autumn temperatures. The park could seldom be called crowded, although the campground does fill daily throughout spring, summer, and fall. Trails remain fairly unpopulated year-round, perhaps because of the difficult nature of many of them. You're not bound to get wet, since annual rainfall is only about 7 inches. Peak season for rain is in late summer, when thunderstorms move in briefly. When it does rain, however, devastating flash floods can wipe out park roads and leave you stranded. Snowfall is usually light, especially at lower elevations.

Average High/Low Temperatures (°F) and Monthly Precipitation (in inches)

	JAN.	FEB.	MAR.	APR.	MAY	JUN.
CAPITOL REEF	43/22	46/28	57/34	62/38	74/48	85/57
	.69	.29	.37	.91	.37	.37

	JUL.	AUG.	SEPT.	OCT.	NOV.	DEC.
	92/64	89/64	78/55	64/42	50/28	41/22
	.96	1.03	1.50	.55	.48	.30

CAPITOL REEF
NATIONAL PARK

EXPLORING
ATTRACTIONS NEARBY
DINING
LODGING
CAMPING AND RV
FACILITIES
SHOPPING
ESSENTIAL
INFORMATION

FESTIVALS AND SEASONAL EVENTS
SUMMER

June: **Wayne County Horse Races.** Riders from all over the state bring their horses to Loa to try to claim the prize money in this annual event. | 435/836–2632.

July: **July 4th Celebration.** Torrey has taken the celebration of Independence Day to new levels of fun. They start the celebration each year with a parade. There's a flea market on the town streets, and later that night, a barbecue or lamb fry. The evening events include a dance at the Big Apple Pavilion. | 435/425–3335.

Bicknell International Film Festival. Don't get out your best black beret to attend this event—it's a spoof on the serious film festivals that you read about, and for which you can't get tickets unless you live in Hollywood. This festival begins with the world's fastest parade, a 60-mph procession that starts in Torrey and ends in Bicknell. Included in the crazy events is a swap meet and mutton fry. | 435/836–2632.

Aug.: **Wayne County Fair.** The great American county fair tradition is at its finest in Loa. Look at hand-made quilts and other crafts, see agricultural exhibits, play games, and eat plenty of good food while you spend a day at the fair. | 435/836–2662.

FALL

Sept.: **Art from the Land Workshop.** The Entrada Institute, a nonprofit organization committed to educating people about the Capitol Reef region, sponsors this annual event. Art exhibits, readings, and writing workshops are the highlight of this three-day celebration of creativity and culture. | 435/425–3265.

Nearby Towns

Probably the best home base for exploring the park, **Torrey,** just outside the park, is a pretty little town with lots of personality. Giant old cottonwood trees make it a shady, cool place to stay, and you'll find the townsfolk friendly and accommodating. A little farther west on Route 24, **Teasdale** is a tiny, charming settlement cradled in a cove of the Aquarius Plateau. The first time anyone sees Teasdale, they try to figure out a way to live in the bucolic town. The homes—many of which are well-preserved older structures—look out onto brilliantly colored cliffs and green fields. **Bicknell** lies another few miles west of Capitol Reef. Small and quiet, the town sits on a bench at the base of Thousand Lake Mountain and painted cliffs. There's not much happening here, which in and of itself makes it a wonderfully quiet place to rest your head. The Wayne County seat of **Loa** is 10 mi west of Torrey. Pioneers settled this little town in the 1870s. A former Mormon missionary who had served in Hawaii named the town, and a rock from Mauna Loa rests at a historic marker. The Loa Ranger District office can give you all the information you might need on camping, fishing, and hiking in the Fish Lake National Forest, which lies to the north and east of town.

If you head south from Torrey instead of west, you can take a spectacular 32-mi drive along Route 12 to **Boulder,** a town so remote that its mail was carried on horseback until 1940. Today, ranching is the primary occupation of folks who live here. You can stop to visit Anasazi State Park or take a detour on the partially unpaved Burr Trail. One of southern Utah's nicest inns—with an impressive restaurant—is in Boulder. In the opposite direction from Torrey, 51 mi east on Route 24, **Hanksville** is more a crossroads than anything else. You can fill your stomach and your gas tank here and pick up souvenirs at the convenience stores.

Garfield County Travel Council (Boulder) | 55 S. Main St., Panguitch, 84759 | 435/676–8826 | www.brycecanyoncountry.com. **Wayne County Travel Council (Bicknell, Hanksville, Loa, Teasdale, Torrey)** | Box 7, Teasdale, 84773 | 435/425–3365 or 800/858–7951 | www.capitolreef.org.

Exploring Capitol Reef

PARK BASICS

Contacts and Resources: Capitol Reef National Park | Torrey, 84775 | 435/425–3791 | www.nps.gov/care.

Hours: The park is open all year, every day, around the clock. The visitor center opens at 8 AM daily and closes between 4:30 and 6 depending on the season.

Fees: There is no fee to enter Capitol Reef except to travel the Scenic Drive, a fee of $4 payable on the honor system at the beginning of the road.

Getting Around: Route 24 runs across the middle of Capitol Reef National Park, so even folks traveling between points west and east of the park with no intention of touring the park get a scenic treat on their way. This state road is paved all 15 mi of its way through the park. The park's Scenic Drive, which is 9 mi long, is a spur off Route 24 and is paved until you enter Capitol Gorge. From November through February, and sometimes even into March, you might have to contend with winter driving conditions to reach the park via Route 24. There are many four-wheel-drive roads in and near the park; if you intend to travel these remote roads, go only with a 4X4 and be prepared for the unexpected.

Permits: Permits are required for backcountry camping. You can pick up a free permit at the visitor center.

Public Telephones: Public telephones are at the visitor center and at Fruita Campground.

Rest Rooms: Public rest rooms are available at the visitor center and Fruita Campground, as well as at Chimney Rock and Hickman Bridge trailheads.

Accessibility: Like many of the undeveloped western national parks, Capitol Reef doesn't have many trails that are accessible to people in wheelchairs. The visitor center, museum, slide show, and rest rooms are all accessible, as is the campground amphitheater where evening programs are held. The Fruita Campground Loop C rest room is accessible, as is the boardwalk to the petroglyph panel on Route 24, 1.2 mi east of the visitor center.

Emergencies: In the event of an emergency, dial 911, contact a park ranger, or report to the visitor center. To contact park police dial 435/425–3791.

Lost and Found: The park's lost-and-found is at the visitor center.

Good Tours

CAPITOL REEF IN ONE DAY

Pack a picnic lunch, snacks, and cold drinks to take with you, because there are no restaurants in the park. Start your journey at the **visitor center,** where you can study a three-dimensional map of the area, watch the short slide show, and browse the many books and maps related to the park. Then head for **Scenic Drive,** stopping at the **Historic Gifford Farmhouse** for a tour and a visit to the gift shop. Next, drive to the **Grand Wash Trail** and walk as far as you like. Upon returning to your car, continue to the end of Scenic Drive. Road conditions permitting, drive into **Capitol Gorge** to the Capitol Gorge Trailhead and take the easy walk to see the **Pioneer Register** and, if you don't mind a very brief climb, the **deep water-pockets.** Returning on Scenic Drive, stop at the shady picnic area just past the Historic Gifford Farmhouse to eat lunch. After your meal, drive to the intersection of Route 24 and turn east. Along this stretch of Route 24 stop to see the old **Fruita School**

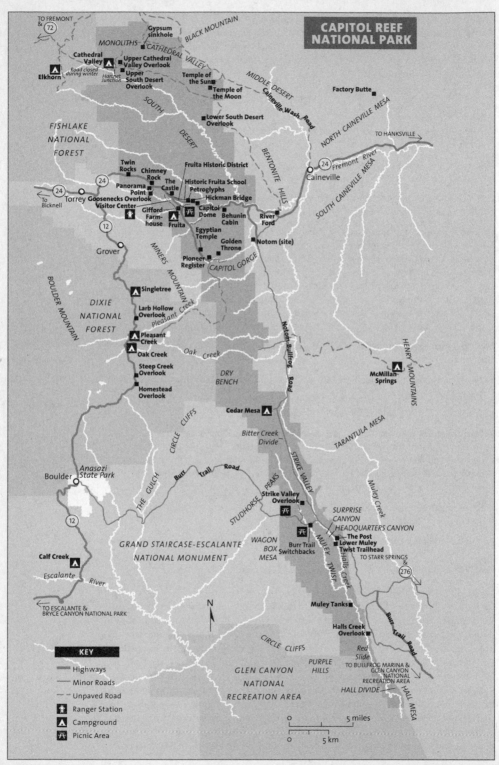

CAPITOL REEF
NATIONAL PARK

TO FREMONT
& 72

Gypsum
sinkhole

MONOLITHS

BLACK MOUNTAIN

CATHEDRAL VALLEY

Cathedral
Valley

Upper Cathedral
Valley Overlook

Elkhorn

Road closed
during winter

Hartnet
Junction

Upper
South Desert
Overlook

Temple of
the Sun

Temple of
the Moon

MIDDLE DESERT

Caineville Wash Road

Factory Butte

NORTH CAINEVILLE MESA

TO HANKSVILLE

FISHLAKE
NATIONAL
FOREST

SOUTH

DESERT

Lower South Desert
Overlook

BENTONITE HILLS

24

Fremont River

Caineville

SOUTH CAINEVILLE MESA

Twin
Rocks

Chimney
Rock

Fruita Historic District

Historic Fruita School

To
Bicknell

24

Torrey

Panorama
Point

Goosenecks Overlook

The
Castle

Petroglyphs

Hickman Bridge

Visitor Center

Gifford
Farm-
house

Capitol
Dome

Behunin
Cabin

River
Ford

12

Grover

Fruita

Egyptian
Temple

Golden
Throne

Notom (site)

MINERS

MOUNTAIN

Pioneer
Register

CAPITOL GORGE

BOULDER MOUNTAIN

DIXIE
NATIONAL
FOREST

Singletree

Pleasant Creek

Larb Hollow
Overlook

Oak Creek

Pleasant
Creek

Oak Creek

Steep Creek
Overlook

DRY
BENCH

Notom-Bullfrog Road

McMillan
Springs

HENRY MOUNTAINS

Homestead
Overlook

Cedar Mesa

Bitter Creek
Divide

TARANTULA MESA

CIRCLE CLIFFS

STRIKE VALLEY

STUDHORSE PEAKS

Anasazi
State Park

Boulder

THE GULCH

Burr   Trail   Road

Strike Valley
Overlook

SURPRISE
CANYON

HEADQUARTERS CANYON

Muley Creek

12

GRAND STAIRCASE-ESCALANTE

NATIONAL MONUMENT

WAGON
BOX
MESA

Burr Trail
Switchbacks

The Post
Lower Muley
Twist Trailhead

MULEY   TWIST

Halls Creek

TO STARR SPRINGS &

276

Calf Creek

Escalante   River

TO ESCALANTE &
BRYCE CANYON NATIONAL PARK

N

Muley Tanks

CIRCLE   CLIFFS

Halls Creek
Overlook

PURPLE
HILLS

Red
Slide

Burr   Trail   Road

GLEN CANYON

NATIONAL

RECREATION AREA

TO BULLFROG MARINA &
GLEN CANYON
NATIONAL
RECREATION AREA

HALL DIVIDE

HALL MESA

KEY

Highways

Minor Roads

Unpaved Road

Ranger Station

Campground

Picnic Area

0   5 miles

0   5 km

house and the **petroglyphs,** and take the moderate hike to **Hickman Bridge.** After your hike, continue on Route 24 to visit the **Behunin Cabin.** Next you'll have to backtrack a few miles on Route 24 to find the Goosenecks and Sunset Point trailheads. Walk to the **Goosenecks** overlook first, and then take the **Sunset Point Trail** in time to watch the setting sun hit the colorful cliffs.

CAPITOL REEF IN TWO OR THREE DAYS

If you're camping, the first thing to do is to get a campsite in **Fruita Campground.** Spend the first day as above, then spend the night where 19th-century pioneers must have laid their heads. Start your second morning by walking along the **Fremont River Trail;** when you get to the top you'll have views of the Fruita area from 800 ft above. Return to the campground and pack a lunch and plenty of water for a good day of hiking. From the campground you can pick up the **Cohab Canyon Trail,** which takes you 1.7 mi to the Hickman Bridge parking lot. While in Cohab Canyon you can also take a short side trail to the **Fruita Orchard Overlook.** Return to the campground via the same route. This evening, walk over toward the orchards and watch the mule deer graze. If you have one more day, explore either the **Waterpocket Fold** area or **Cathedral Valley,** checking first at the visitor center for road conditions and recommendations. Visits to both areas require a substantial amount of driving on unpaved roads. Most of the hikes in the Waterpocket Fold area are strenuous; Cathedral Valley hikes are easier.

Attractions

PROGRAMS AND TOURS

You can obtain current information about ranger talks and other park events at the visitor center or by checking bulletin boards at the campground.

Evening Program. In the amphitheater at the campground, you can attend a lecture, slide show, or other ranger-led activity to learn about Capitol Reef's geology, Native American cultures, wildlife, or other features. A schedule of topics and times is posted at the visitor center. | Amphitheater, Loop C, Fruita Campground, about 1 mi from the visitor center on Scenic Dr. | 435/425–3791 | Free | May–Sept., nightly 0.5 hour after sunset.

Hondoo Rivers and Trails. Fast gaining a reputation for high-quality, educational trips into the backcountry of Capitol Reef National Park, these folks pride themselves on delivering a unique, private experience. Trips are designed to explore the geologic landforms in the area, seek out wildflowers in season, and to encounter free roaming mustangs, bison, and bighorn sheep when possible. Single- or multiday trips can be arranged. | 90 E. Main St., Torrey | 435/425–3519 or 800/332–2696 | www.hondoo.com.

Junior Ranger Program. To become a Junior Ranger, each child who participates in this self-guided program completes a combination of activities in the Junior Ranger booklet, attends a ranger program, interviews a park ranger, and/or picks up litter. When you finish the program you receive a patch to sew onto your favorite jacket. Allow about two hours for the ranger talk. | At the visitor center | 435/425–3791 | $1.50.

Ranger Talks. Each day at the visitor center rangers give brief talks on park geology. Times change, so check at the center for a current schedule. | At the visitor center | 435/425–3791 | Free | May–Oct. daily.

SCENIC DRIVE

Capitol Reef Scenic Drive. This paved road starts at the visitor center and winds its way through colorful sandstone cliffs into Capitol Gorge. There the road becomes unpaved, and road conditions may vary because of weather and amount of use. Check with the visitor center before entering Capitol Gorge. Scenic Drive is 9 mi long, with about the last quarter of it unpaved.

BUFFALO COMEBACK

In 1941, the Utah Division of Wildlife Resources introduced 18 buffalo into the western foothills of the Henry Mountains near Capitol Reef. Today, their descendants make up one of the few wild, free-roaming buffalo herds in the country.

SIGHTS TO SEE

Behunin Cabin. Elijah Cutler Behunin used blocks of sandstone to build this cabin in 1882. Floods in the lowlands made life too difficult, and he moved on before the turn of the 20th century. The house is empty, but you can peep through a window. | Rte. 24, 6.2 mi east of the visitor center.

Capitol Dome. One of the rock formations that gave the park its name, this giant, golden dome is visible in the vicinity of the Hickman Bridge trailhead. | Rte. 24, about 2 mi east of the visitor center.

★ **Capitol Gorge.** At the entrance to this gorge Scenic Drive becomes unpaved. The narrow, twisting road on the floor of the gorge was a route for pioneer wagons traversing this part of Utah starting in the 1860s. After every flash flood, pioneers would laboriously clear the route so wagons could continue to go through. The gorge became the main automobile route in the area until 1962, when Route 24 was built. The short drive to the end of the road is an adventure in itself and leads to some interesting hiking trails. | Scenic Dr., 9 mi south of the visitor center.

Travelers passing through Capitol Gorge in the 19th and early 20th centuries etched the canyon wall with their names and the date they passed. Directly across the canyon from this **Pioneer Register.** and about 50 ft up are signatures etched into the canyon wall by an early USGS survey crew. It is illegal to write or scratch on the canyon walls today; violations are taken very seriously. You can reach the register via an easy 1-mi hike from the end of the road. | Off Scenic Dr., 9 mi south of the visitor center.

The Castle. This prominent geological landmark towers over the visitor center. | Rte. 24 at the visitor center.

Chimney Rock. Even in a landscape of spires, cliffs, and knobs, this deep-red landform is unmistakable. | Rte. 24, about 3 mi west of the visitor center.

Fremont Indian Petroglyphs. Nearly 1,000 years ago the Capitol Reef area was occupied by the Fremont Indians, whose culture was tied very closely to the ancestral Puebloan (Anasazi) culture. Fremont rock art can be identified by the large trapezoidal figures often depicted wearing headdresses and ear baubles. Capitol Reef's petroglyphs are on a north-facing cliff wall. You can see more petroglyphs by walking along the cliff face, but stay on the boardwalk and do not climb the slope. | Rte. 24, 1.2 mi east of the visitor center.

★ **Fruita Historic District.** In 1880 Nels Johnson became the first homesteader in the Fremont River valley, building his home near the confluence of Sulphur Creek and the Fremont River. Other Mormon settlers followed and established small farms and orchards near the confluence, creating the village of Junction. The orchards thrived, and in 1902 the settlement's name was changed to Fruita. The orchards are preserved and protected as a Rural Historic Landscape.

An old **Blacksmith Shop.** exhibits tools, farm machinery, and harnesses dating from the late 1800s, and Fruita's first tractor (which didn't arrive here until 1940). You can hear a recording in which a rancher talks about living and working in Fruita during the 1940s–60s. | Scenic Dr., about 1 mi south of the visitor center.

Planted by Mormon pioneer settlers and their descendants, **Fruit Orchards** are still lovingly maintained by the park service. You can often see mule deer wandering here at dusk, making for great photographs. During harvest season, you can pick cherries, apricots, peaches, pears and apples (the park charges for fruit harvested). A two-person crew maintains the orchards, which contain about 3,000 trees, with pruning and irrigation. | Scenic Dr., less than 1 mi from the visitor center.

Mormon settlers built one-room log **Historic Fruita School** in 1896. In addition to classes, Mormon church meetings, dances, town meetings, and other community functions also took place in this building. The school closed in 1941 because there were no longer enough students to attend. You can peek inside the windows and listen to a recording of a former teacher recalling what it was like to teach here in the 1930s. | Rte. 24, 1 mi from the visitor center.

Mormon polygamist Calvin Pendleton built this primitive abode in 1908 and lived here with his family for eight years, followed by the Jorgen Jorgenson family, who resided here from 1916 to 1928. In 1928 Jorgenson's son-in-law, Dewey Gifford, bought the homestead and settled in with his family for 41 years. The last residents of Fruita, the Giffords sold their home to the National Park Service in 1969. The **Historic Gifford Farmhouse** has been faithfully restored, with several of the rooms furnished in period furniture and housewares. The former kitchen of the house has been converted to a gift shop. | Scenic Dr., 1 mi from the visitor center | 435/425–3791 | www.nps.gov/care | Free | Daily 11–5.

Goosenecks Trail. This nice little walk gives you a good introduction to the land surrounding Capitol Reef. You'll no doubt enjoy the dizzying views from the overlook. It's only 0.2 mi round-trip to the overlook, and a very easy walk. Sunset Point Trail starts from the same parking lot. | Rte. 24, about 3 mi west of the visitor center.

★ **Grand Wash Road.** A dirt road follows this twisting route down a canyon for about a mile. The unpaved, sometimes sandy, bumpy road winds between steep canyon walls. Allow a little more than half an hour for your adventure. Before taking this drive, check at the visitor center for flash flood warnings. | Off Scenic Dr. about 5 mi from the visitor center.

Sunset Point Trail. Benches along this easy, 0.7-mi round-trip trail invite you to sit and meditate surrounded by the colorful desert. At the trail's end, you will be rewarded with broad vistas into the park; it's an even better treat if you do it at sunset. The trail starts in the same spot as the Goosenecks Trail, so you might as well walk both routes. You'll be glad you did. | Rte. 24 about 3 mi west of the visitor center.

Visitor Center. Stop at the visitor center for an introduction to the park. Watch a film, talk with rangers, or peruse the many books, maps, and materials offered for sale in the bookstore. | Rte. 24, 11 mi east of Torrey and 19 mi west of Caineville | 435/425–3791 | Mid-May–Sept., daily 8–6; Oct. and mid-Apr.–mid-May daily 8–5; Nov.–mid-Apr., daily 8–4:30.

Waterpocket Fold. While all of Capitol Reef is part of the 100-mi wrinkle in the earth known as the Waterpocket Fold, you can really only see the fold from the air or a higher elevation. The Notom-Bullfrog Road takes you right into the narrow fold. The road starts opposite the Orientation Pullout on Route 24 at the East Entrance to the park and is about 34 mi long, mostly unpaved and bumpy. To really see the "fold" in the earth, you can drive Route 12 west of the park onto Boulder Mountain. From an elevation of 9,400 ft, you can better understand the geology of the area. | Rte. 24, 10 mi west of the visitor center.

Sports and Outdoor Activities

Remember: whenever you venture into the desert—that is, wherever you go in Capitol Reef—take plenty of water. Experts recommend that active people drink a gallon of water per person per day in summer.

BICYCLING

Bicycles are only allowed on established roads in the park. Since Route 24 is a state highway and receives a substantial amount of through traffic, it's not the best place to peddle. Scenic Drive is better, but the road is narrow and you have to contend with drivers dazed by the beautiful surroundings. Four-wheel-drive roads are certainly less traveled, but they are often sandy, rocky, and steep. You cannot ride your bicycle in washes or on hiking trails. Wild Hare Expeditions (*see* Outfitter, *below*) offers guided bike tours in the park, and also rents out bicycles.

Cathedral Valley. In this very remote part of the park you can enjoy solitude and a true backcountry ride on one of Utah's famous scenic backways (Cathedral Valley Scenic Backway). You'll be riding on surfaces that include dirt, sand, bentonite clay, and rock, and you will also ford the Fremont River. There are steep hills and switchbacks, wash crossings, and

CAPITOL REEF
NATIONAL PARK

EXPLORING
ATTRACTIONS NEARBY
DINING
LODGING
CAMPING AND RV
FACILITIES
SHOPPING
ESSENTIAL
INFORMATION

stretches of deep sand. Summer is not a good time to try this ride, as water is very diffi-cult to find and temperatures may exceed 100°F. The entire route is about 60 mi long; dur-ing a multiday trip you can camp at the primitive campground with five sites, located about midway through the loop. | Off Rte. 24 at Caineville or at River Ford Rd. 5 mi west of Caineville on Rte. 24.

South Draw Road. This is a very strenuous ride that traverses dirt, sand, and rocky surfaces and crosses several creeks that may be muddy. It's not recommended in winter or spring because of deep snow at higher elevations. If you like fast downhill rides, however, this trip is for you—it will make you feel like you have wings. The route starts at an elevation of 8,500 ft on Boulder Mountain and ends 15 mi later at 5,500 ft in the Pleasant Creek park-ing area at the end of Scenic Drive. | At the junction of Bowns Reservoir Rd. and Rte. 12, 13 mi south of Torrey.

FOUR-WHEELING

You can explore Capitol Reef by 4X4 on a number of exciting backcountry routes. Driv-ers without high-clearance, four-wheel-drive vehicles should not attempt to make these drives. Road conditions can vary greatly depending on recent weather patterns. Spring and summer rains can leave the roads muddy, washed out, and impassable even to four-wheel-drive vehicles. Always check at the Capitol Reef visitor center for current condi-tions before you set out. Carry water, supplies, and preferably a cell phone on your trip. Wild Hare Expeditions (*see* Outfitter, *below*) offers guided 4X4 tours in the park.

Cathedral Valley Scenic Backway. The north end of Capitol Reef, known as Cathedral Val-ley, is filled with towering monoliths, panoramic vistas, and a stark desert landscape. The drive through the valley is a 58-mi loop that you can begin at River Ford on Route 24. From there the loop travels northwest, giving you access to Glass Mountain, South Desert, and Gypsum Sinkhole. Turning southeast at the sinkhole, the loop takes you past the side road that accesses the Temples of the Moon and Sun, then becomes Caineville Wash Road before ending at Route 24, 7 mi east of your starting point. Caineville Wash Road has two water crossings. Including stops, allow a half-day for the drive on the unpaved road. If your time is limited, you may want to tour only the Caineville Wash Road. Starting from Route 24, the driving time on this route to lower Cathedral Valley is only about two hours. When you check at the visitor center for road conditions, you can pick up a self-guided auto tour brochure for $1. | River Ford Rd. 11.7 mi east of the visitor center on Rte. 24, or at Caineville, about 18 mi east of the visitor center on Rte. 24.

HIKING

Most of the trails in the park include steep climbs, but there are a few easy-to-moder-ate hikes. A short drive from the visitor center takes you to a dozen trails, and a park ranger can advise you on combining trails or locating additional routes. Wild Hare Expeditions (*see* Outfitter, *below*) offers guided hikes in the park.

★ **Capitol Gorge Trail and the Tanks.** Starting at the Pioneer Register, about a mile from the Capitol Gorge parking lot, is a trail that climbs to the Tanks (deep waterpockets). After a scramble up about 0.2 mi of steep trail with cliff drop-offs you can look down into the Tanks and can also see a natural bridge below the lower tank. Including the walk to the Pioneer Register, allow an hour or two for this interesting little hike. | At the end of Scenic Dr., 9 mi south of the visitor center.

Chimney Rock Trail. You're almost sure to see ravens drifting on thermal winds around the deep red Mummy Cliff that rings the base of the Chimney Rock Trail. This loop trail begins with a steep climb to a rim above Chimney Rock. The trail is 3.5 mi round-trip, with a 600-ft elevation change. You should allow three to four hours. | Rte. 24, about 3 mi west of the visitor center.

★ **Cohab Canyon Trail.** Children particularly love this hike for the geological features and native creatures, such as rock wrens and western pipistrels (canyon bats), that you see along the way. One end of the trail is directly across from the Fruita Campground on Scenic Drive, and the other is across from the Hickman Bridge parking lot. The first quarter mile from Fruita is pretty strenuous, but then the walk becomes easy except for turnoffs to the overlooks, which are strenuous but short. Along the way you'll find miniature arches, skinny side canyons, and honeycombed patterns on canyon walls where the wrens make nests. The trail is 3.2 mi round-trip to the Hickman Bridge parking lot. The Overlook Trail adds 2 mi to the journey. Allow one to two hours to overlooks and back; allow two to three hours to Hickman Bridge parking lot and back. | About 1 mi south of the visitor center on Scenic Dr., or about 2 mi east of the visitor center on Rte. 24.

Fremont River Trail. What starts as a quiet little stroll beside the river turns into an adventure. The first half mile of the trail is wheelchair accessible as you wander past the orchards next to the Fremont River. After you pass through a narrow gate, the trail changes personality and you're in for a steep climb on an exposed ledge with drop-offs. The views at the top of the 770-ft ascent are worth it as you look down into the Fruita Historic District. The trail is 2.5 mi round-trip; allow two hours. | Near the amphitheater off Loop C of the Fruita Campground, about 1 mi from the visitor center.

★ **Golden Throne Trail.** As you hike to the base of the Golden Throne you may be fortunate enough to see one of the park's elusive desert bighorn sheep. You're more likely, however, to spot their small, split-hoof tracks in the sand. The trail itself is 2 mi of gradual elevation gain with some steps and drop-offs. The Golden Throne is hidden until you near the end of the trail, then suddenly you find yourself looking at a huge sandstone monolith. If you hike near sundown the throne burns gold, salmon, and platinum. The round-trip hike is 4 mi, and you should allow two to three hours. | At the end of Capitol Gorge Rd., at the Capitol Gorge trailhead, 9 mi south of the visitor center.

Grand Wash. At the end of unpaved Grand Wash Road you can continue on foot through the canyon to its end at the Fremont River. The long, flat hike takes you through a wide wash between canyon walls. It's an excellent place to study the geology up close. The round-trip hike is 4.5 mi, and you should allow two to three hours for your walk. It's a good idea to check at the ranger station for flash flood warnings before entering the wash. | Rte. 24 east of the Hickman Bridge parking lot (about 4 mi east of the visitor center), or at the end of Grand Wash Rd., off Scenic Dr. about 5 mi from the visitor center.

Hickman Bridge Trail. This trail is a perfect introduction to the park. It leads to a natural bridge of Kayenta sandstone, which has a 135-ft opening carved by intermittent flash floods. Early on, the route climbs a set of steps along the Fremont River, and as the trail tops out onto a bench, you'll find a slight depression in the earth. This is what remains of an ancient Fremont pit house, a kind of home that was dug into the ground and covered with brush. The trail splits, leading along the right-hand branch to a strenuous uphill climb to the Rim Overlook and Navajo Knobs. Stay to your left to see the bridge, and you'll encounter a moderate up-and-down trail. As you continue up the wash on your way to the bridge, you'll notice a Fremont granary on the right side of the small canyon. Allow about an hour and a half to walk the 2-mi round-trip. The walk to the bridge is one of the most popular trails in the park, so expect lots of company along the way. | Rte. 24, 2 mi east of the visitor center.

HORSEBACK RIDING

Many areas in the park are closed to horses and pack animals, so it's a good idea to check with the visitor center before you set out with your animals. Day use does not require a permit, but you need to get one for overnight camping with horses and pack animals. Unless you ride with a park-licensed outfitter, you have to bring your own horse, as no rentals are available.

Old Wagon Trail. For spectacular views of Waterpocket Fold, try this trail. It gradually climbs along the long rampart of Miners Mountain, merging for a short distance with an

CAPITOL REEF
NATIONAL PARK

EXPLORING
ATTRACTIONS NEARBY
DINING
LODGING
CAMPING AND RV
FACILITIES
SHOPPING
ESSENTIAL
INFORMATION

old route that goes beyond into Boulder Mountain. There's very little shade on this trail. Allow two to three hours. | About 6 mi south of the visitor center on Scenic Dr.

South Draw. This route gives you access to Tantalus Flats and Boulder Mountain or a return via Pleasant Creek. | At the end of Scenic Dr., 9 mi south of the visitor center.

Outfitter

Wild Hare Expeditions. For a real taste of the backcountry of Capitol Reef National Park, take a hiking, biking, or 4X4 expedition with this enthusiastic outfitter. Guides will teach you more in one fun day about geology, wildlife, and land ethics than you thought possible. | 2600 E. Rte. 24, Torrey | 435/425–3999 | www.color-country.net/~thehare.

Attractions Nearby

Scenic Drives

★ **Burr Trail Scenic Backway.** Branching east off Route 12 in Boulder, Burr Trail travels through the Circle Cliffs area of Grand Staircase/Escalante National Monument into Capitol Reef. The views are of backcountry canyons and gulches. The road is paved between Boulder and the eastern boundary of Capitol Reef, then unpaved but well maintained inside the park. It leads into a hair-raising set of switchbacks that ascends 800 ft in 0.5 mi. The switchbacks are not suitable for RVs or vehicles towing trailers. Before attempting to drive this route from Boulder, check with the Capitol Reef visitor center for road conditions. From Boulder to its intersection with Notom-Bullfrog Road the route is 36 mi long.

Notom-Bullfrog Road. You can access the Waterpocket Fold and some spectacular, virtually unexplored territories via this road. The road starts opposite the Orientation Pullout on Route 24 near the park's East Entrance. From Route 24, the Notom-Bullfrog Road is 34 mi one-way, connecting with the Burr Trail.

★ **Utah Scenic Byway Route 12.** Named as one of only 20 All-American Roads in the United States by the National Scenic Byways Program, Route 12 is not to be missed. The 32-mi stretch between Torrey and Boulder winds through alpine forests and passes vistas of some of America's most remote and wild landscape. It is not for the faint of heart or those afraid of narrow, winding mountain roads, but it is worth all the heart palpitations.

Utah Scenic Byway Route 24. This state road runs 72 mi between Hanksville and Loa, right through Capitol Reef. Colorful rock formations in all their hues of red, cream, pink, gold, and deep purple extend from one end of the route to the other. The closer you get to the park the more colorful the landscape becomes. The vibrant rock finally gives way to lush green hills and the mountains west of Loa.

SIGHTS TO SEE

Anasazi State Park. Anasazi is a Navajo word interpreted to mean "ancient enemies." What the Anasazi called themselves we will never know, but today their descendants, the Hopi people, prefer the term ancestral Puebloan. This state park is dedicated to the study of that mysterious culture, with a largely unexcavated dwelling site, a museum with interactive exhibits, and a reproduction of a six-room pueblo. | 460 N. Rte. 12, Boulder | 435/335–7308 | http://parks.state.ut.us | $5 per vehicle | Memorial Day–Labor Day, daily 8–6; Labor Day–Memorial Day, daily 9–5.

Fish Lake. Not surprisingly, Fish Lake is known for its fishing, but you needn't have tackle box in hand to enjoy this spot: mountain scenery and a quiet setting are the real draws. In fact, the lake is so beautiful that the 1.4 million-acre Fish Lake National Forest was named after it. Some great hikes explore the higher reaches of the area (one trail leads to the 11,633-ft summit of Fish Lake Hightop Plateau). Cyclists can take fall and summer rides on Forest Service roads or along Route 12, which circles the east and north ends of the lake. If you come to engage in the namesake activity, Fish Lake is stocked annually with lake trout, rainbow trout, and splake; a large population of brown trout is native to the lake. | 138 S. Main, Loa | 435/836–2811, 435/638–1033, or 435/896–9233 | Free.

Goblin Valley State Park. All of the landscape in this part of the country is strange and surreal, but Goblin Valley takes the cake as the weirdest of all. It's full of hundreds of gnome-like rock formations colored in a dramatic orange hue. Short, easy trails wind through the goblins, which delight children. | Rte. 24, 12 mi north of Hanksville | 435/564–3633 | http://parks.state.ut.us | $5 per vehicle | Daily 8 AM–sunset.

San Rafael Swell. A massive fold and uplift in the Earth's crust is some of the most visually stunning landscape in southeastern Utah. About 80 mi long north-to-south and 30 mi wide east-to-west, this giant formation rises 2,100 ft above the desert. The Swell, as it is known locally, is northeast of Capitol Reef, between I–70 and Route 24. It's easily seen from I–70, 19 mi west of Green River. You can stop and take photos from several viewpoints along I–70. | BLM San Rafael Resource Area, 900 North and 700 East, Price | 435/637–4584.

Dining

In Capitol Reef
Picnic Areas. There are no restaurants inside Capitol Reef National Park, but there are some nice shady spots for a picnic.

In a grassy meadow near the Historic Gifford Farmhouse, with the Fremont River flowing by, is the idyllic **Gifford Farm picnic area.** Picnic tables, drinking water, grills and a convenient rest room make it perfect.

Near the Park
★ **Café Diablo.** Southwestern. This popular Torrey restaurant keeps getting better and better. Innovative southwestern entrées include buffalo tenderloin, quail and rabbit sausage, black-bean falafel, and local trout crusted with pumpkin seeds and served with a cilantro lime sauce. If you're really adventurous, try the rattlesnake cakes, made with free range desert rattler and served with ancho-rosemary aioli. | 599 W. Main St. (Rte. 24), Torrey | 435/425–3070 | $15–$29 | MC, V | Closed Nov.–Apr. No lunch.

Capitol Reef Café. American/Casual. For standard fare that will please everyone in the family, visit this unpretentious restaurant. Favorites include the 10-vegetable salad and the flaky fillet of locally caught rainbow trout. | 360 W. Main St. (Rte. 24), Torrey | 435/425–3271 | $9–$24 | AE, D, MC, V | Closed Nov.–Apr.

★ **Hell's Backbone Grill.** Contemporary. One of the best restaurants in southern Utah, this remote spot is worth the drive from any distance. The menu is inspired by Native American, Western Range, southwestern, and Mormon pioneer recipes. The owners, who are also the chefs, use only fresh, organic foods that have a historical connection to the area. Because they insist on fresh foods, the menu changes weekly. Outdoor dining overlooking a tiny pond on the grounds of Boulder Mountain Lodge is a treat. A respectable list of wine and draft beer rounds out the meal. | 20 N. Rte. 12, Boulder | 435/335–7464 | $10–$24 | AE, D, MC, V | Closed Nov.–Mar.

Rim Rock Restaurant. American/Casual. Attached to a motel, this restaurant serves large portions of steak, chicken, and fish. Kids will enjoy the varieties of spaghetti, while adults will marvel at the 50-ingredient molé sauce. | 2523 E. Rte. 24, Torrey | 435/425–3388 | $10–$24 | AE, MC, V.

Stan's Burger Shack. American/Casual. This is the traditional pit stop along the route between Lake Powell and Capitol Reef. Great burgers, fries, and shakes—and the only homemade onion rings you'll find for miles and miles—can fill your belly. | 140 S. Rte. 95, Hanksville | 435/542–3330 | $5–$7 | AE, D, MC, V.

CAPITOL REEF
NATIONAL PARK

EXPLORING
ATTRACTIONS NEARBY
DINING
LODGING
CAMPING AND RV
FACILITIES
SHOPPING
ESSENTIAL
INFORMATION

Lodging

Near the Park

Best Western Capitol Reef Resort. If you're looking for a good home base with great views of the colorful cliffs, you will appreciate this hilltop resort—and you're just minutes from the park. Restaurant. In-room data ports, some in-room hot tubs, some minibars, some microwaves, some refrigerators. In-room VCRs. Tennis court. Outdoor pool. Outdoor hot tub. Horseback riding. Laundry facilities. | 2600 E. Rte. 24, Torrey, 84775 | 435/425–3761 or 888/610–9600 | fax 435/425–3300 | www.bestwestern.com/capitolreefresort | 80 rooms, 20 suites | $99–$159 | AE, D, DC, MC, V | Closed mid-Dec.–early Jan.

★ **Boulder Mountain Lodge.** If you're traveling between Capitol Reef and Bryce Canyon national parks, don't miss this wonderful lodge along scenic Route 12. A 5-acre pond on the pastoral grounds is a sanctuary for ducks, coots, and other waterfowl, and horses graze in a meadow opposite. Large, modern rooms with balconies or patios offer gorgeous views of the wetlands. The main lodge contains a great room with fireplace, and there's a fine art gallery and remarkably good restaurant on the premises. The service and care given guests here is impeccable. Outdoor hot tub. Some pets allowed (fee). No smoking. | Rte. 12 at Burr Trail, Boulder, 84716 | 435/335–7460 or 800/556–3446 | fax 435/335–7461 | www.boulder-utah.com | 20 rooms | $85–$153 | D, MC, V.

Capitol Reef Inn. Travelers on a tight budget can't beat the simple, well-lit rooms here. The walls are thin, but the rooms are big. Restaurant. Microwaves, refrigerators. Cable TV. Outdoor hot tub. Some pets allowed. | 360 W. Main St., Torrey, 84775 | 435/425–3271 | 10 rooms | $40–$52 | AE, D, MC, V | Closed Nov.–Mar.

Chuck Wagon Lodge. Foremost at this lodge are friendly service and immaculate rooms. The owner has taken great care to create comfortable accommodations where once there was nothing but an RV park. The especially nice outdoor pool is one of the larger ones in the southern half of the state. There are standard rooms, cabins, and some real economy rooms above the old general store. Pool. Hot tub. Shops. | 12 W. Main St., Torrey, 84773 | 435/425–3335 or 800/863–3288 | fax 435/425–3434 | www.austinschuckwagonmotel.com | 25 rooms, 3 cabins | $45–$100 | AE, DC, MC, V | Closed Nov.–Mar.

★ **Muley Twist Inn.** This gorgeous B&B sits on 30 acres of land, with expansive views of the colorful landscape that surrounds it. A wrap-around porch, contemporary furnishings, and classical music drifting through the air add to a stay here. In-room data ports. Library. No a/c. No room TVs. No smoking. | 125 S. 250 West, Teasdale, 84773 | 435/425–3641 or 800/530–1038 | fax 435/425–3640 | www.go-utah.com/muleytwist | 5 rooms | $99–$109 | AE, MC, V.

★ **Pine Shadows.** If you're looking to hide out in the rocks, this is the place to stay. Full housekeeping cabins are tucked against the pink-and-white cliffs and surrounded by pine trees. The cabins are large, clean, and fully equipped with a kitchen, VCR, one or two beds, and a futon. | 125 S. 195 West, Teasdale 84773 | 435/425–3939 or 800/708–1223 | fax 435/425–3651 | www.pineshadowcabins.net | 6 cabins | $75 | MC, V.

Rim Rock Inn. Situated on a bluff with outstanding views into the desert, this motel was the first one built to accommodate visitors to Capitol Reef. Under energetic management it has been completely renovated, so rooms are clean and ample—and a good bargain, to boot. The on-site restaurant is a local favorite. Restaurant. Cable TV. | 2523 E. Rte. 24, Torrey, 84775 | 435/259–3398 or 888/447–4676 | www.therimrock.com | 19 rooms | $49–$69 | AE, MC, V | Closed Jan.–Feb.

SkyRidge Bed and Breakfast. Each of the inn's windows offers an exceptional year-round view of the desert and mountains surrounding Capitol Reef National Park. The walls are hung with the works of local artists, and unusual furniture—each piece chosen for its look and feel—makes the guest rooms and common areas both stimulating and comfortable. Meals here are excellent, including afternoon hors d'oeuvres and sangria. Breakfast might see you feasting on apple-stuffed croissants or homemade cinnamon rolls. Dining room. Hot tub. | 950 E. Rte. 24, Box 750220, Torrey, 84775 | 435/425–3222 | fax 435/425–3222 | www. skyridgeinn.com | 6 rooms | $115–$172 | AE, MC, V.

Camping and RV Facilities

In Capitol Reef

Cathedral Valley Campground. You'll find this primitive campground, about 30 mi from Route 24, in the park's remote northern district. The only way here is via a high-clearance road that should not be attempted when wet. Pit toilets. Grills, picnic tables. | 5 tent sites | Hartnet Jct., on Caineville Wash Rd. | 435/425–3791 | Free | Reservations not accepted.

Cedar Mesa Campground. Wonderful views of the Waterpocket Fold and Henry Mountains surround this primitive campground in the park's southern district. The road to the campground does not require a high-clearance vehicle, but it's not paved and you should not attempt to drive it if the road is wet. Pit toilets. Grills, picnic tables. | 5 tent sites | Notom-Bullfrog Rd., 22 mi south of Rte. 24 | 435/425–3791 | Free | Reservations not accepted.

★ **Fruita Campground.** Near the orchards and the Fremont River, this shady campground is a great place to call home for a few days. The sites nearest the river or the orchards are the very best. Loop C is most appropriate for RVs, although the campground has no hookups. Flush toilets. Drinking water. Grills, picnic tables. | 71 sites, 7 tent-only | Scenic Dr., about 1 mi south of the visitor center | 435/425–3791 | $10 | Reservations not accepted.

Near the Park

Sunglow Campground. Managed by the U.S. Forest Service, this secluded little campground is next to red cliffs in a pinyon forest. All of the sites are suitable for moderately sized RVs or tents, but RVers should know that the campground's roads are narrow and winding with some tight turns. The water is turned off September–April. Pit toilets. Drinking water. | 10 sites | Rte. 24, 1 mi east of Bicknell | 435/836–2800 | $5 | Reservations not accepted.

Thousand Lakes RV Park and Campground. This is understandably one of the area's most popular RV parks. There's lots of grass and shade, and the level 22-acre site provides good views of the surrounding red cliffs. Western-style cookouts each weeknight can fill your belly after a day of hiking or driving. Flush toilets. Full hook-ups, dump station. Drinking water, guest laundry, showers. Fire pits, grills, picnic tables. Public telephone. General store. Play area, swimming (pool). | 58 RV sites, 9 tent sites, 7 cabins | 1050 W. Rte 24, Torrey | 435/425–3500 or 800/355–8995 | $13–$19, $29 –$55 for cabins | D, MC, V | Apr.–Oct.

Shopping

Chuck Wagon General Store. You can find just about anything you need at this country store. Groceries, camping gear, cold drinks, and fresh baked goods are all available. | 12 W. Main St., Torrey | 435/425–3288.

Historic Gifford Farmhouse Gift Shop. The Capitol Reef Natural History Association runs a gift shop inside the park's historic farm home, selling jellies, soaps, looped rugs, and Roseville pottery. You can also pick up a cold soda and candy for the kids. | Scenic Dr., about 1 mi from the visitor center | 435/425–3621.

Red D Market. This small hometown market can meet most of your grocery needs. | 378 S. 300 East, Bicknell | 435/425–3521.

Robber's Roost Books and Beverages. At this quiet little store you can find books by regional authors along with guidebooks, maps, T-shirts, and unique art items. You can get a caffeine buzz here, too. The shop is only open from Easter to Halloween. | 185 W. Main St., Torrey | 435/425–3265.

Royal's Foodtown. Restock your cooler or RV refrigerator at this local grocery store. There's also a bakery on site. | 135 S. Main, Loa | 435/836–2841.

Visitor Center Bookstore. The Capitol Reef National Park visitor center stocks a wide variety of books, maps, trail guides, posters, and postcards to help you make the most of your visit. | Rte. 24, 11 mi east of Torrey and 19 mi west of Caineville | 435/425–3791.

Essential Information

ATMS: Far West Bank | 115 S. Main St., Loa | 435/836–2394.

AUTOMOBILE SERVICE STATIONS: Blackburn Sinclair and Towing | 178 E. Main St., Bicknell | 435/425–3432. **Brian Auto Parts and Service** | 233 S. Main, Loa | 435/836–2343 or 435/836–2455. **Hollow Mountain Service Station** | 200 N. Rte. 95, Hanksville | 435/542–3298. **Hidden Falls Resort Capitol Reef Sinclair Fuel Station** | 2424 E. Rte. 24, Torrey | 435/425–3956. **Stan's Chevron** | 350 S. Rte. 95, Hanksville | 435/542–2017. **Wonderland Texaco** | Rtes. 12 and 24, Torrey | 435/425–3345.

POST OFFICES: Bicknell Post Office | 70 E. Main St., Bicknell, 84715 | 435/425–3478. **Loa Post Office** | 12 N. Main St., Loa, 84747 | 435/836–2879. **Torrey Contract Post Office** | 75 W. Main (inside the Torrey Trading Post), Torrey, 84775 | 435/425–3716.

GRAND CANYON NATIONAL PARK

NORTH-CENTRAL ARIZONA

South Entrance: 58 mi north of Williams on Rte. 64, 80 mi northwest of Flagstaff on U.S. 180. East Entrance (South Rim): 50 mi west of Tuba City on Rte. 64. North Entrance: 76 mi south of Fredonia on Rte. 67.

The world's most beautiful scar, according to many, the Grand Canyon is a sight that everyone should see at least once in a lifetime. At 277 mi long, 18 mi across at its widest spot, and more than a mile below the rim at its deepest point, the canyon is painted in hues that range from muted pastels to deep purples, vibrant yellows, fiery reds, and soft blues, depending on the ever-changing light. The canyon got its start more than 65 million years ago, when a series of violent geological upheavals created a domed tableland now called the Colorado Plateau. The Colorado River continues to sculpt the canyon's walls into otherworldly stone monuments, cliffs, and buttes. Indeed, the Grand Canyon is famous for its vertigo-inspiring cliffs, but it offers countless other pleasures that are less obvious. The best way to experience them is to hike into the canyon. "What one finds," wrote author and naturalist Joseph Wood Krutch, "will be what one takes the trouble to look for—the brilliant little flower springing improbably out of the bare, packed sand, the lizard scuttling with incredible speed from cactus clump to spiny bush, the sudden flash of a bright-colored bird. This dry world, all of which seems so strange to you, is normal to them. It is their paradise, their universe as it ought to be."

Of the 5 million people who visit the park annually, 90% enter it at the South Rim, which is busy year-round. The North Rim draws only about 10% of the Grand Canyon's visitors but is, many believe, even more gorgeous than the South Rim. There's also plenty to see on the five-hour drive from Grand Canyon Village on the South Rim to Grand Canyon Lodge on the North Rim, which is only about 10 mi away as the crow flies, but 210 mi by car, passing through Kaibab National Forest.

PUBLICATIONS

Before you go, request the complimentary *Trip Planner*, updated regularly by the National Park Service, by writing to: Trip Planner, Grand Canyon National Park, Box 129, Grand Canyon, AZ, 86023. You can also get the trip planner on-line, by visiting www.nps.gov/grca/

grandcanyon/trip_planner. As you enter the park, you should get *The Guide,* a free newspaper with a detailed area map and a complete schedule of free programs. The *Grand Canyon Accessibility Guide* is free from the visitor centers and at park entrances. Books on various aspects of the canyon—geology, history, and scenery—are for sale in the visitor centers, various gift shops, and museums at both rims, as well as through the Grand Canyon Association. The association developed *A Guide to Grand Canyon National Park and Vicinity,* by Sandra Scott, in conjunction with the parks service, and also sells numerous videos and trail guides. **Grand Canyon Association** | Box 399, Grand Canyon, 86023 | 928/638–2481 | fax 928/638–2484 | www.grandcanyon.org/bookstore.

When to Visit

SCENERY AND WILDLIFE

It's no wonder the Grand Canyon is popular with geologists. Almost two billion years worth of the Earth's history is written between the colored layers of sedimentary rock that are stacked from the river bottom to the top of the plateau. The South Rim's Coconino Plateau is fairly flat, at an elevation of about 7,000 ft, and covered with stands of pinyon and ponderosa pine, juniper, and Gambel's oak. On the Kaibab Plateau on the North Rim, Douglas fir, spruce, quaking aspen, and more ponderosa pine trees prevail. In spring, you're likely to see asters, sunflowers, and lupine in bloom at both rims.

Eighty-eight mammal species inhabit the park, as well as 300 species of birds, 24 kinds of lizards, and 24 kinds of snakes. The rare Kaibab squirrel is found only on the North Rim, and the pink Grand Canyon rattlesnake lives at lower elevations within the canyon. Both are unique to the Grand Canyon. Hawks and ravens are visible year-round, usually coasting on the wind above the canyon. In spring, summer, and fall, mule deer are abundant at the South Rim, even aggressive. Don't be tempted to feed them; it's illegal, and it will disrupt their natural habits and increase your risk of being bitten.

Both sunrise and sunset in the park are spectacular when skies are clear. In any season, some of the best spots to enjoy or photograph them are along Hermit Road west of Grand Canyon Village and Yaki and Lipan points between the Village and Desert View, and Cape Royal on the North Rim.

HIGH AND LOW SEASON

High season is from mid-May to October. If you can arrange it, try to visit in fall to avoid the huge crowds that fill the park every summer and during spring break. You might encounter cold weather, but chances are good that most days will be clear and pleasantly cool or even warm. And with fewer crowds, reservations are much easier to come by and prices may drop. Also consider a winter visit to the South Rim (the North Rim is closed in winter). Snow on the ground only enhances the site's sublime beauty.

Average High/Low Temperatures (°F) and Monthly Precipitation (in inches)

	JAN.	FEB.	MAR.	APR.	MAY	JUNE
SOUTH RIM	41/18	45/21	51/25	60/32	70/39	81/47
	1.3	1.5	1.3	.93	.66	1.8
	JULY	AUG.	SEP.	OCT.	NOV.	DEC.
	84/54	82/53	76/47	65/36	52/27	43/20
	1.8	2.2	1.5	1.1	.94	1.6
	JAN.	FEB.	MAR.	APR.	MAY	JUN.
NORTH RIM	37/16	39/18	44/21	53/29	62/34	73/40
	3.1	3.2	2.6	1.7	1.1	1.9
	JUL.	AUG.	SEP.	OCT.	NOV.	DEC.
	77/46	75/45	69/40	59/31	46/24	14/2
	1.9	2.8	1.7	1.3	1.4	2.8

GRAND CANYON
NATIONAL PARK

EXPLORING
ATTRACTIONS NEARBY
DINING
LODGING
CAMPING AND RV
FACILITIES
SHOPPING
ESSENTIAL
INFORMATION

After an early expedition into the Grand Canyon, Lieutenant Joseph Ives said, "The region is, of course, altogether valueless. Ours has been the first, and will doubtless be the last, party of whites to visit this profitless locality."

	JAN.	FEB.	MAR.	APR.	MAY	JUNE
INNER CANYON	56/36	62/42	71/48	82/56	92/63	101/72
	.68	.75	.79	.47	.03	.84
	JUL.	AUG.	SEP.	OCT.	NOV.	DEC.
	106/78	103/75	97/69	84/58	68/46	57/37
	.84	1.4	.97	.65	.43	.87

FESTIVALS AND SEASONAL EVENTS

WINTER

Nov.–Dec.: **Annual Holiday Lights Festival.** More than 2 million lights are set ablaze each night in Flagstaff starting on the evening after Thanksgiving—the lighting ceremony is held at the Little America Hotel—through the New Year. | 928/779–7979 or 800/435–2493.

Dec.: **Mountain Village Holidays.** Crafts sales and art exhibits showcasing Native American jewelry take place the entire month of December in Williams. There's also a Parade of Lights on the first Saturday of the month. | 928/635–4061.

Feb.: **Winterfest.** More than 100 events celebrate Flagstaff's winter landscape, including sled-dog races, Nordic and alpine skiing competitions, sleigh rides, historic walking tours, and special children's activities. | 928/774–4505 or 800/842–7293.

SPRING

May: **Bill Williams Rendezvous Days.** A black-powder shooting competition, a carnival, street dances, and pioneer arts-and-crafts sales take place on Memorial Day weekend in honor of Williams' namesake mountain man. | 928/635–4061.

SUMMER

May–Sept.: **Celebration of Native American Art.** Exhibits of work by Zuni, Hopi, and Navajo artists are displayed all summer long at the Museum of Northern Arizona and at the Coconino Center for the Arts, both in Flagstaff. | 928/774–5211 or 928/779–6921.

Aug.: **Summerfest in Flagstaff.** Artists and musicians from around the United States gather at the Fort Tuthill County Fairgrounds to show their work and listen to music. | 928/774–9541.

FALL

Sept.: **Coconino County Fair.** Rides, games, livestock exhibits, and concerts are the draw at this old-fashioned Labor Day weekend fair. It's held at the Coconino County Fairgrounds in Flagstaff. | 928/774–5139.

Grand Canyon Music Festival. Chamber music is performed in the Shrine of Ages at Grand Canyon Village three weekends in September. | www.grandcanyonmusicfest.org.

Labor Day Rodeo. A rodeo and an Old West celebration, with roping and riding competitions, take place each Labor Day weekend in Williams. | 928/635–4061.

Northern Arizona Fair. Agricultural displays and contests (including livestock and produce), a talent show, and a beauty contest are among the highlights of this Fredonia event. | 928/643–7241.

Sedona Jazz on the Rocks. Live ensembles perform in the red-rock terrain at the Sedona Cultural Park, a 30-minute drive southwest of Flagstaff on U.S. 89A. | 928/282–1985.

Oct.: **Western Navajo Fair.** Performances of traditional Navajo songs and dances, a powwow, parades, concerts, arts-and-crafts displays, rodeos, a carnival, and a free barbecue are the events scheduled during this week-long fair in Tuba City. | 928/283–4716.

Nearby Towns

Tusayan, the gateway to the park's South Entrance, was developed to accommodate Grand Canyon visitors, and is ideal if you want to get up and be at the South Rim by early morning. Cheaper, bigger, and with more cultural sights to see, **Flagstaff** and **Williams** are popular second choices, though they're both more than an hour away from the Grand Canyon by car (Williams is closer by 20 mi). Flagstaff, just 15 mi southwest of the beautiful San Francisco Peaks, has two observatories, a good symphony, and Northern Arizona University. Williams, named for Bill Williams, a trapper in the 1820s and '30s, was founded when the railroad passed through it in 1882. Now Williams' Main Street is historic Route 66. From here you can catch the Grand Canyon Railway, a slow, narrated ride to the canyon.

Tuba City, headquarters of the western portion of the Navajo Nation, is 50 mi east of the Grand Canyon's East Entrance in a fairly isolated, though beautiful, region of the Painted Desert. To the north lies **Marble Canyon,** which marks the geographical beginning of the Grand Canyon at its northeastern tip. It's a good stopping point if you are driving U.S. 89 to the North Rim. Also nearby is Lees Ferry, where most Colorado River rafting trips through the Canyon begin. **Fredonia,** a small community of about 1,200, approximately an hour's drive north of the Grand Canyon, is often referred to as the gateway to the North Rim; it's also relatively close to Zion and Bryce Canyon national parks.

INFORMATION

Flagstaff Chamber of Commerce | 101 W. Rte. 66, Flagstaff, 86001 | 928/774–4505 | www.flagstaff.az.us. **Flagstaff Visitor Center** | 1 E. Rte. 66, Flagstaff, 86001-5588 | 928/774–9541 or 800/842–7293 | www.flatstaffarizona.org. **Fredonia Town Office** | 130 N. Main St., Fredonia, 86022 | 928/643–7241. **Grand Canyon Chamber of Commerce** | Box 3007, Grand Canyon, 86023 | 928/527–0359 | www.grandcanyonchamber.com. **Navajoland Tourism Dept. (Tuba City)** | Box 663, Window Rock, 86515 | 928/871–7371 or 928/871–6436. **Page/Lake Powell Chamber of Commerce (Marble Canyon)** | Box 727, 644 N. Navajo, Tower Plaza, Grand Canyon National Park, 86040 | 928/645–2741 or 888/261–7243 | www.page-lakepowell. com. **Williams and National Forest Service Visitors Center and Chamber of Commerce** | 200 W. Railroad Ave., Williams, 86046 | 928/635–4061 | www.thegrandcanyon.com.

Exploring Grand Canyon

PARK BASICS

Contacts and Resources: Grand Canyon National Park | Box 129, Grand Canyon 86023 | 928/638–7888 | fax 928/638–7797 | www.nps.gov/grca.

Hours: The South Rim is open year-round. Canyon View Information Plaza is open daily 8 to 6 from late-May through early September, and daily 8 to 5 from early September through late-May. The North Rim is open mid-May through mid-October, and the visitor center is open daily 8–6.

Fees: It costs $20 per motorized vehicle to enter the park. Individuals arriving by bicycle or foot pay $10. Backcountry permits are $10 plus $5 per person per night.

Getting Around: In summer, South Rim roads are congested, and it's often easier, and sometimes required, to park your car and take the free shuttle, which operates year-round (weather permitting) on three routes: Hermit Road (formerly West Rim Drive), the Village Route, and Kaibab Trail Route. From March 1 to November 30, only the shuttle is allowed on the 8-mi Hermit Road. The ride is free, and bus stops are clearly marked throughout the park.

If you decide to use your own vehicle on the South Rim, be aware that while parking is free once you pay the $20 park entrance fee, it can be difficult to find a spot, especially during peak hours of the busiest summer weeks. Try the large lot in front of the general store near Yavapai Lodge or the Maswik Transportation Center lot, which is served by the shuttle bus. The North Rim is not affected by the shuttle system. From mid-October to mid-May, roads to the North Rim close. Weather information and road conditions for both rims, updated at 7 AM daily, can be obtained by calling 928/638–7888.

Permits: Hikers descending into the canyon for an overnight stay need a backcountry permit, which can be obtained in person or by contacting the Backcountry Office (928/638–7888). The office's free *Backcountry Trip Planner* can help answer your hiking questions. Permits are limited, so make your reservation as far in advance as you can (reservations are not taken more than four months ahead of arrival). A visit to the park's Web site will go far in preparing you for the permit process. Day hikes into the canyon or anywhere else in the national park do not require a permit; overnight stays at Phantom Ranch require reservations but no permits. Overnight camping in the national park is restricted to designated campgrounds.

Public Telephones: There are public telephones at all visitor centers and lodgings.

Rest Rooms: There are public rest rooms at all visitor centers, lodgings, and restaurants.

Accessibility: Rim Trail and all the viewpoints along the South Rim are accessible to wheelchairs. For detailed information, see the *Grand Canyon Accessibility Guide,* free from Canyon View Information Plaza, Yavapai Information Station, Tusayan Museum, Desert View Information Center, and all entrance stations. There are free wheelchairs for use inside the park; inquire at one of the information centers. Temporary handicapped-parking permits are available at Canyon View Information Plaza, Yavapai Observation Center, and all entrance stations. Wheelchair-accessible tours are offered by prior arrangement through Grand Canyon National Park Lodges (928/638–2631). TDD phones are available as well.

Emergencies: In case of a fire or medical emergency, dial 911; from in-park lodgings dial 9-911. To report a security problem contact the Park Police (928/638–7805), stationed at all visitor centers.

The **Grand Canyon Walk-in Clinic** at 1 Clinic Road is staffed by physicians weekdays 8–5 and Sat. 9–noon. Emergency medical services are available 24 hours a day. Call 928/638–2551 or 928/638–2469.

For minor health problems, a nurse practitioner at **North Rim Clinic** accepts appointments or walk-ins. The Clinic, in Cabin 1, Grand Canyon Lodge, is open Friday–Monday 9–noon and 3–6, and Tuesday 9–noon. Call 928/638–2611 Ext. 222.

Lost and Found: Report lost or stolen items or turn in found items at Canyon View Information Plaza or Yavapai Observation Station at 928/638–7798 from Tuesday to Friday, 8–5. For items lost or found at a dining or lodging establishment, call 928/638–2631.

Good Tours

GRAND CANYON IN ONE DAY

Although Grand Canyon National Park covers more than 1,900 square mi, you can see all of the primary sights at the South Rim in one full day. Start early, pack a picnic lunch, then take the shuttle to **Canyon View Information Plaza** just north of the South Entrance, where you can pick up information about the Canyon and see your first incredible view at **Mather Point.** Continue east along **Desert View Drive** for about 2 mi to get to **Yaki Point,** your first stop. Next, continue 7 mi east to **Grandview Point,** where you'll get a good view of Krishna Shrine and Vishnu Temple, among other buttes. Go another 4 mi east and you'll come to another good spot for a view, **Moran Point.** Then, take the shuttle 3 mi farther to the **Tusayan Ruin and Museum,** a good place to get out and stretch your legs. The small display area is devoted to preserving the history of the Ancestral Puebloans who inhabited the region 800 years ago. After the museum, continue another mile east to **Lipan Point,** where you'll be treated to one of the best angles in the park from which to view the Colorado River and some of its whitewater rapids. **Navajo Point,** the highest elevation on the South Rim, is less than a mile farther. **Desert View and Watchtower** are the final stops along the shuttle route, again less than a mile beyond Navajo Point. Climb the stairs to the third-floor roof of the stone-and-mortar Watchtower for views of the Painted Desert to the east, the Vermilion Cliffs to the north, and the Colorado River below. Have your lunch at one of the picnic tables listed in the "Dining" section below.

After lunch, return to Grand Canyon Village and take a walk on the paved **Rim Trail** to **Maricopa Point.** Along the way, stop in at the historic **El Tovar Hotel,** where you can make reservations for dinner. Before your walk or afterward, you can go souvenir shopping in the village.

If you have time in the late afternoon before dinner, take the shuttle on **Hermit Road** to **Hermit's Rest,** 8 mi one-way. Stop at **Powell Memorial,** a tribute to the explorer who measured, charted, and named many of the creeks and small canyons in the park; **Hopi Point,** where you can see Shiva Temple and the thin line of the Colorado River below; **the Abyss,** perhaps the most awesome stop on the route, which reveals a sheer drop of 3,000 ft to the Tonto Plateau; and Hermits Rest, the westernmost viewpoint on the South Rim and a good place to watch the sunset.

GRAND CANYON IN THREE DAYS

A visit of three days will allow you to experience the Grand Canyon more fully. On your first day, follow the one-day itinerary above, but spend more time exploring the sights on Desert View Drive, and take a leisurely picnic or luncheon in Grand Canyon Village. Leave Hermit Road for your second morning, riding the shuttle as described in the one-day itinerary, or drive to Grand Canyon Airport for a small-plane or helicopter tour of the area. Have lunch in Tusayan, and cool off in the **IMAX theater** while you watch a short but big film on the Grand Canyon that may reenact your flightseeing trip. Return to Grand Canyon Village, and join one of the free educational programs led by park rangers, such as **Lure of the Canyon** or the **Fossil Walk.**

On your third day, hike on **Bright Angel Trail,** or plan a longer hike into the canyon. Remember, it will take twice as long to hike back up as it does to hike down, so plan your trip accordingly. Pick up trail maps at Canyon View Information Plaza and bring plenty of water.

GRAND CANYON IN SIX DAYS

Stay six days between May and October and you can visit the North Rim as well as the South. First follow the three-day South Rim itinerary. On the morning of your fourth day, start out on the long but rewarding drive to the North Rim. From Grand Canyon Village, take Route 64 east out of the park for 55 mi. Turn left onto U.S. 89, and head north over the Painted Desert. You'll see thousands of square miles of mesas and windswept plains. At Bitter Springs, bear left onto U.S. 89A, and drive 14 mi west to the **Navajo Bridge,** hanging 500 ft above the Colorado River. Once used for car traffic, the narrow steel bridge is now pedestrian-only, and it's extremely photogenic. A newer bridge beside it carries cars across the river. About a mile east of Navajo Bridge is **Marble Canyon Lodge,** a good place to stop for lunch. At Jacob Lake, 55 mi past Marble Canyon, turn left and drive south on Route 67. The remaining 45 mi to the North Rim of the Grand Canyon lie ahead.

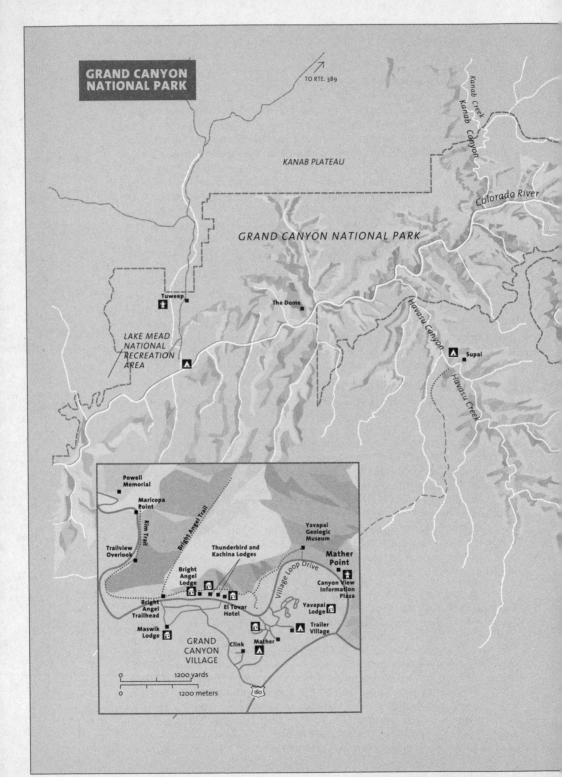

GRAND CANYON
NATIONAL PARK

TO RTE. 389

KANAB PLATEAU

Kanab Creek

Kanab Canyon

Colorado River

GRAND CANYON NATIONAL PARK

Tuweep

The Dome

Havasu Canyon

Supai

LAKE MEAD
NATIONAL
RECREATION
AREA

Havasu Creek

Powell
Memorial

Maricopa
Point

Rim Trail

Bright Angel Trail

Trailview
Overlook

Thunderbird and
Kachina Lodges

Yavapai
Geologic
Museum

Mather
Point

Village Loop Drive

Bright
Angel Lodge

Canyon View
Information
Plaza

Bright
Angel
Trailhead

El Tovar
Hotel

Yavapai
Lodge

Maswik
Lodge

GRAND
CANYON
VILLAGE

Clink

Mather

Trailer
Village

1200 yards

1200 meters

180

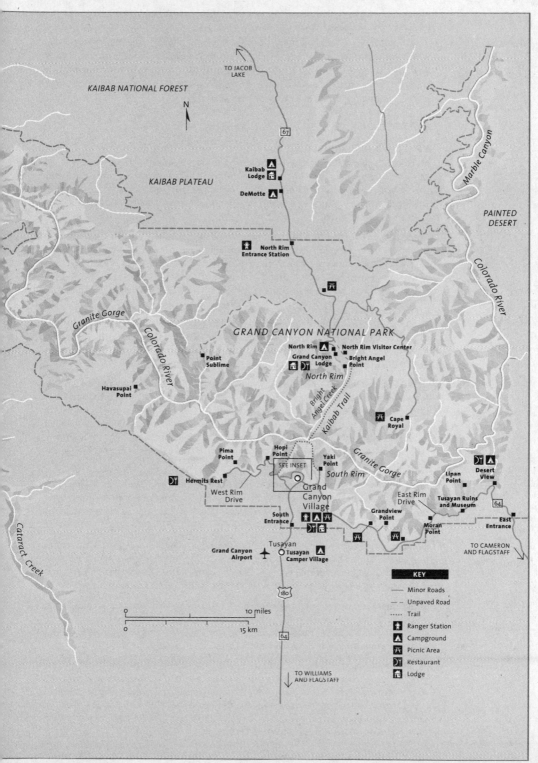

TO JACOB
LAKE

KAIBAB NATIONAL FOREST

N

KAIBAB PLATEAU

67

Kaibab
Lodge

DeMotte

North Rim
Entrance Station

PAINTED
DESERT

Marble Canyon

Colorado River

Granite Gorge

Colorado River

GRAND CANYON NATIONAL PARK

Point
Sublime

North Rim   North Rim Visitor Center
Grand Canyon
Lodge   Bright Angel
                Point

Havasupai
Point

North Rim

Bright
Angel Creek

Kaibab Trail

Cape
Royal

Pima
Point

Hopi
Point   Yaki
SEE INSET   Point
            South Rim

Granite Gorge

Lipan   Desert
Point   View

Hermits Rest

West Rim
Drive

Grand
Canyon
Village

East Rim
Drive

Tusayan Ruins
and Museum

64

South
Entrance

Grandview
Point

East
Entrance

Moran
Point

Cataract Creek

TO CAMERON
AND FLAGSTAFF

Grand Canyon
Airport

Tusayan

Tusayan
Camper Village

180

0   10 miles

0   15 km

KEY

Minor Roads

Unpaved Road

Trail

Ranger Station

Campground

Picnic Area

Restaurant

Lodge

64

TO WILLIAMS
AND FLAGSTAFF

Along Route 67, you'll drive over the summit of the 9,000-ft Kaibab Plateau. Spend the night at **Grand Canyon Lodge** on the North Rim.

Spend the next day hiking around the area. The most popular trails are **Transept Trail,** which starts near the Grand Canyon Lodge, and **Cliff Springs Trail,** which starts near **Cape Royal.** If you're not too car-weary, drive out Cape Royal Road 11 mi to **Point Imperial.** At 8,803 ft, it's the highest vista on either rim. Spend a second night at Grand Canyon Lodge before beginning the long drive back on your sixth day.

Attractions

PROGRAMS AND TOURS

Air Grand Canyon. Choose from three different 30–100-minute small-plane tours of the canyon, or a three-hour tour that includes Monument Valley. You can custom design your trip as well. | Box 3399, Grand Canyon, 86023 | 928/638–2686 or 800/247–4726 | fax 928/638–9598 | www.airgrandcanyon.com | $74–$174; Monument Valley $260 | AE, D, DC, MC, V | Reservations essential.

Grand Canyon Field Institute. Instructors lead guided educational tours, hikes around the canyon, and weekend programs at the South Rim. Tour topics include everything from archaeology and backcountry medicine to photography and natural history. Contact GCFI for a schedule and price list. | Box 399, Grand Canyon, 86023 | 928/638–2485 | fax 928/638–2484 | www.grandcanyon.org/fieldinstitute | $75–$1,200 | DC, MC, V | Reservations essential.

Grand Canyon National Park Lodges Van Tours. An inexpensive three-hour van tour of Cape Royal, Angels Window, and other scenic viewpoints on the North Rim departs daily from the Grand Canyon Lodge, where you can make reservations. | 14001 E. Iliff, Suite 600, Aurora, CO 80013 | 303/338–6000 | fax 303/338–2045 | www.grandcanyonlodges.com | $20 | AE, D, MC, V | Reservations essential | May–Sept.

Grand Canyon Outback Jeep Tours. If you'd like to get off the pavement and see parts of the park that are accessible only by dirt road, a jeep tour can be just the ticket. From March through October, Grand Canyon Outback leads daily, 1$\frac{1}{2}$- to 4$\frac{1}{2}$-hour, off-road tours within the park, as well as in Kaibab National Forest. The rides are bumpy and not recommended for people with back injuries. | Box 1772, Grand Canyon, 86023 | 928/638–5337 or 800/320–5337 | fax 928/638–5337 | www.grandcanyonjeeptours.com | $35–$54 | AE, MC, V | Reservations essential.

Junior Ranger Discovery Pack Program. Children ages 7–11 use field guides, binoculars, magnifying glasses, and other exploration tools on this one-hour ranger-led program. Meet the rangers at Canyon View Information Plaza on Tuesday, Thursday, Saturday, or Sunday at 9 AM. | 928/638–7888 | Free.

Kenai Helicopters. From May through September, Kenai conducts two popular helicopter tours of the canyon daily: the 30-minute Central Corridor tour and the 45-minute Majestic Grand Canyon tour. | Box 1429, Grand Canyon, 86023 | 928/638–2412 or 800/541–4537 | fax 928/638–9588 | www.flykenai.com | $105–$164 | AE, D, MC, V | Reservations essential.

Marvelous Marv. For a personalized experience, take this private tour of the Grand Canyon and surrounding sights any time of year. Rides can be rough; if you have had back injuries, check with your doctor before taking a jeep tour. | Box 544, Williams, 86046 | 928/635–4948 | www.marvelousmarv.com | $70 | No credit cards | Reservations essential.

Papillon Helicopters. The world's largest helicopter sightseeing company, Papillon offers three different tours of the area. All start from the South Rim's Grand Canyon airport: the 30-minute North Canyon tour, the 45-minute Imperial tour, and the day-long or overnight Havasupai excursion. Special charters and flights from Las Vegas are also available. | Box 455, Grand Canyon, 86023 | 928/638–2419 or 800/528–2418 | fax 928/638–3235 | www.papillon.com | $115–$175 | AE, D, MC, V | Reservations essential.

Ranger Programs. The National Park Service sponsors all sorts of orientation activities, such as daily guided hikes and talks, at both the North and South rims. The focus may be on any aspect of the canyon—from geology, flora and fauna to history and early inhabitants. For schedules, go to Canyon View Information Plaza on the South Rim or the Grand Canyon Lodge on the North Rim. | Box 129, Grand Canyon, 86023 | 928/638–7888 | www.nps.gov/grca | Free.

Lure of the Canyon, a 30-minute talk on the history and geology of the park, is held in the lobby of Canyon View Information Plaza. | Daily 10:30 AM and 3:30 PM.

Take the **Remnant Impressions Fossil Walk,** on the patio of Bright Angel Lodge, and you'll see the remains of brachiopods, sponges, and other marine creatures that lived 260 million years ago. | Daily 4 PM.

Explore the ever-changing colors of the canyon at sunset on the 0.5-mi **Spirit of Sunset Walk.** Meet at Desert View and Watchtower, and allow 40 minutes. | 928/638–7888 | Daily, one hour before sunset.

Way Cool for Kids. Rangers coordinate these free, hour-long introductions to the park for children ages 7–11, daily at 9 AM. Kids and rangers walk around the Village Rim area and talk about local plants and animals, history, or archaeology. | South Rim Park Headquarters, Parking Lot A | 928/638–7888 | Free.

SCENIC DRIVES

Cape Royal Road. On the North Rim, a drive to a pair of the area's best-loved canyon vistas awaits you. Starting at Grand Canyon Lodge, drive north on the road for a couple of miles, and bear left at the fork. Continue north 11 mi to Point Imperial—at 8,803 ft, it's the highest vista on either rim, with views of the much of the canyon plus thousands of square miles of the surrounding countryside. After stopping here, backtrack the 11 mi to the fork and, instead of going back to the lodge, head southeast on the road to Cape Royal, about a 15 mi drive. Just beyond the trailhead for Cliff Springs Trail is the site of Angels Window, a giant, erosion-formed hole through which you can see across the canyon to the South Rim. The drive back to Grand Canyon Lodge is 23 mi.

Desert View Drive. This 25-mi road, formerly called East Rim Drive, leads to several of the South Rim's most spectacular turnouts. To get to the drive, turn right about 3 mi north of the South Entrance station. Two miles east is the left turn for the short, well-marked road leading to Yaki Point (except for December–January, when you can drive to Yaki Point, you must take the shuttle). Next, travel about 7 more mi east to Grandview Point, which reveals a group of buttes, including Krishna Shrine and Vishnu Temple, as well as a short stretch of the Colorado River below. Other stops along the route include Moran Point, Tusayan Ruin and Museum, Lipan Point, and Desert View and Watchtower.

Hermit Road. Formerly known as West Rim Drive, this 8-mi drive is the most popular on the South Rim and because of heavy congestion, it's closed to cars from March 1 through November 30. A free shuttle bus will transport you to the eight scenic stops along the way. First you'll come to Trailview Overlook, from which you can see the San Francisco Peaks, Red Butte, and Bill Williams Mountain all to the southeast. Subsequent stops are the Powell Memorial, Hopi Point, Mojave Point, the Abyss, Pima Point, and Hermits Rest.

SIGHTS TO SEE

The Abyss. At an elevation of 6,720 ft, the Abyss is one of the most awesome stops on Hermit Road, revealing a sheer drop of 3,000 ft to the Tonto Platform, a wide terrace of Tapeats sandstone layers about two-thirds of the way down the canyon. From the Abyss you'll also see several isolated sandstone columns, the largest of which is called the Monument. | About 5 mi west of Hermit Road Junction on Hermit Rd.

Canyon View Information Plaza. The orientation center near Mather Point provides pamphlets and resources to help you plan your sightseeing. Park rangers are on hand to answer questions and aid in planning Grand Canyon excursions. A bookstore is stocked

Wearing a wet bandana around your neck while hiking is a good way to keep cool in hot weather.

with books covering all topics on the Grand Canyon. A daily schedule for ranger-led hikes and evening lectures is posted on a bulletin board inside. A shuttle bus will get you there. | East side of Grand Canyon Village | 928/638–7888 | Late May–early Sept., daily 8–7; early Sept.–late May, daily 8–5; hours may vary.

Desert View and Watchtower. From the top of the 70-ft stone-and-mortar watchtower, even the muted hues of the distant Painted Desert to the east and the Vermilion Cliffs rising from a high plateau near the Utah border are visible. In the chasm below, angling to the north toward Marble Canyon, an imposing stretch of the Colorado River reveals itself. Up several flights of stairs, the Watchtower houses a glass-enclosed observatory with powerful telescopes. | About 23 mi east of Grand Canyon Village on Desert View Dr. | 928/638–2736 | 25¢ to climb the Watchtower | Daily 8–7 or 8–8 in summer, daily 9–5 in winter.

Grandview Point. At an elevation of 7,496 ft, the view from here is one of the finest in the canyon. To the northeast is a group of dominant buttes, including Krishna Shrine, Vishnu Temple, Rama Shrine, and Shiva Temple. A short stretch of the Colorado River is also visible. Directly below the point, and accessible by the steep and rugged Grandview Trail is Horseshoe Mesa, where you can see the ruins of Last Chance Copper Mine. | About 12 mi east of Grand Canyon Village on Desert View Dr.

★**Hermits Rest.** This westernmost viewpoint and Hermit Trail, which descends from it, were named for the "hermit" Louis Boucher, a 19th-century French-Canadian prospector who had a number of mining claims and a roughly built home down in the canyon. Canyon views from here include Hermit Rapids and the towering cliffs of the Supai and Redwall formations. The stone building at Hermits Rest sells curios and refreshments. | About 8 mi west of Hermit Road Junction on Hermit Rd.

Hopi Point. From here (elevation 7,071 ft) you can see a large section of the Colorado River; although it appears as a thin line, the river is nearly 350 ft wide below this overlook. Across the canyon to the north is Shiva Temple, which remained an isolated section of the Kaibab Plateau until 1937. In that year, Harold Anthony of the American Museum of Natural History led an expedition to the rock formation in the belief that it supported life that had been cut off from the rest of the canyon. Imagine the expedition members' surprise when they found an empty Kodak film box on top of the temple. Directly below Hopi Point lies Dana Butte, named for a prominent 19th-century geologist. In 1919, an entrepreneur proposed connecting Hopi Point, Dana Butte, and the Tower of Set across the river with an aerial tramway, a technically feasible plan that fortunately has not been realized. | About 4 mi west of Hermit Road Junction on Hermit Rd.

Kolb Studio. Built in 1904 by the Kolb brothers as a photographic workshop and residence, this building provides a view of Indian Gardens, where, in the days before a pipeline was installed, Emery Kolb descended 3,000 ft each day to get the water he needed to develop his prints. Kolb was doing something right; he operated the studio until he died in 1976 at age 95. The gallery here has changing exhibitions of paintings, photography, and crafts. There's also a bookstore. | About 0.25 mi west of Hermit Road Junction on Hermit Rd. | 928/638–7888.

A few feet away is the **Bright Angel Trailhead,** the starting point for perhaps the best-known trail to the bottom of the canyon.

Lipan Point. Here at the canyon's widest point, you can get an astonishing visual profile of the gorge's geologic history, with a view of every eroded layer of the canyon. You can also see Unkar Delta, where a creek joins the Colorado to form powerful rapids and a broad beach. Ancestral Puebloan farmers worked the Unkar Delta for hundreds of years, growing corn, beans, and melons. | About 25 mi east of Grand Canyon Village on Desert View Dr.

Lookout Studio. Built in 1914 to compete with the Kolbs' photographic studio, the building was designed by architect Mary Jane Colter. The combination lookout point and gift shop has a collection of fossils and geologic samples from around the world. An upstairs loft provides another excellent overlook into the mighty gorge below. | About 0.25 mi west of Hermit Road Junction on Hermit Rd.

Maricopa Point. This site merits a stop not only for the arresting scenery, which includes the Colorado River below, but also for its view of a defunct mine. On your left as you face the canyon are the Orphan Mine and a mine shaft and cable lines leading up to the rim. The mine, which started operations in 1893, was worked first for copper and then for uranium until the venture came to a halt in 1969. The Battleship, the red butte directly ahead of you in the canyon, was named during the Spanish-American War, when battleships were in the news. | About 2 mi west of Hermit Road Junction on Hermit Rd.

Mather Point. You'll likely get your first glimpse of the canyon from this viewpoint, one of the most impressive and accessible on the South Rim. Named for the National Park Service's first director, Stephen Mather, this spot yields extraordinary views of the Grand Canyon, including deep into the Inner Gorge and numerous buttes: Wotan's Throne, Brahma Temple, and Zoroaster Temple, among others. The Grand Canyon Lodge, on the North Rim, is almost directly north from Mather Point and only 10 mi away—yet you have to drive nearly 210 mi to get from one spot to the other. | Near Canyon View Information Plaza.

Mohave Point. From here you can view 5,401-ft Cheops Pyramid, the grayish rock formation behind Dana Butte, plus some of the strongest rapids on the Colorado River. The Granite and Salt Creek rapids are navigable, but not, you can imagine, without plenty of effort. | About 5 mi west of Hermit Road Junction on Hermit Rd.

Moran Point. This point was named for American landscape artist Thomas Moran, who painted Grand Canyon scenes from many points on the rim but was especially fond of the play of light and shadows from this location. He first visited the Canyon with John Wesley Powell in 1873. "Thomas Moran's name, more than any other, with the possible exception of Major Powell's, is to be associated with the Grand Canyon," wrote the noted canyon photographer Ellsworth Kolb. It's fitting that Moran Point is a favorite spot for photographers and painters. | About 17 mi east of Grand Canyon Village on Desert View Dr.

Navajo Point. A possible site of the first Spanish view into the Canyon in 1540, this peak is also at the highest elevation (7,498 ft) on the South Rim. | About 21 mi east of Grand Canyon Village on Desert View Dr.

★ **North Rim.** The Grand Canyon's more remote rim overlooks vistas as dramatic as those you can see from the South Rim. Higher in elevation and less visited than the southern part of the national park, the North Rim has a distinctly different feel, with taller forests and crisper weather. The North Rim is open from mid-May through mid-October.

The walk to **Bright Angel Point** is only 1 mi round-trip, but it's an exciting trek, accented by sheer drops on each side of the trail. In a few spots where the route is extremely narrow, metal railings ensure visitors' safety. Resist the temptation to clamber out to precarious perches to have your picture taken. Every year several people die from falls at the Grand Canyon. | At the North Rim visitor center.

From **Cape Royal,** the southernmost viewpoint on the North Rim, you'll see a large slice of the Grand Canyon. The 1-mi (round-trip) Cliff Springs trail starts here. Half a mile to the north is Angels Window, a giant erosion-formed natural bridge. | 23 mi southeast of the North Rim visitor center.

The highest vista point (elevation 8,803 ft) at either rim, **Point Imperial** offers magnificent views of the canyon, the Painted Desert to the east, the Little Colorado River to the southeast, the distant Vermilion Cliffs to the north, and the 10,000-ft Navajo Mountain to the northeast in Utah. | About 11 mi northeast of North Rim visitor center.

The trip to **Point Sublime** is an excellent option for those who want to get off the beaten path, but it's intended for high-clearance vehicles only. Check with a park ranger or at the information desk at Grand Canyon Lodge before taking this journey. The road winds for 17 mi through gorgeous high country to the point, which lives up to its name. You may

GRAND CANYON
NATIONAL PARK

EXPLORING
ATTRACTIONS NEARBY
DINING
LODGING
CAMPING AND RV
FACILITIES
SHOPPING
ESSENTIAL
INFORMATION

camp here only with a permit from the Backcountry Office at the park ranger station. | About 20 mi west of the North Rim visitor center.

Pima Point. Enjoy a bird's-eye view of Tonto Platform and Tonto Trail, which winds its way through the canyon for more than 70 mi. Also to the west, two dark, cone-shape mountains—Mount Trumbull and Mount Logan—are visible on the North Rim on clear days. They rise in stark contrast to the surrounding flat-top mesas and buttes. | About 7 mi west of Hermit Road Junction on Hermit Rd.

Powell Memorial. Here you'll find a granite statue honoring the memory of John Wesley Powell, who measured, charted, and named many of the canyons and creeks of the Colorado River. It was here that the dedication ceremony for Grand Canyon National Park took place on April 3, 1920. | About 3 mi west of Hermit Road Junction on Hermit Rd.

Trailview Overlook. Look down on a dramatic view of the Bright Angel and Plateau Point trails as they zigzag down the canyon. In the deep gorge to the north flows Bright Angel Creek, one of the few permanent tributary streams of the Colorado River in the region. Toward the south is an unobstructed view of the distant San Francisco Peaks, as well as of Bill Williams Mountain (on the horizon) and Red Butte (about 15 mi south of the canyon rim). | About 2 mi west of Hermit Road Junction on Hermit Rd.

Tusayan Ruin and Museum. The museum contains evidence of early human habitation in the Grand Canyon and information about Ancestral Puebloan people. *Tusayan* comes from a Hopi phrase meaning "country of isolated buttes," which certainly describes the scenery. The partially intact rock dwellings here were occupied for roughly 20 years around AD 1200 by 30 or so Native American hunters, farmers, and gatherers. They eventually moved on, like so many others, perhaps pressured by drought and depletion of natural resources. A museum and a bookstore display artifacts, models of the dwellings, and exhibits on modern tribes of the region. Free 30-minute guided tours—as many as five a day in summer, fewer in winter—are given daily. | About 20 mi east of Grand Canyon Village on Desert View Dr. | 928/638–2305 | Free | Daily 9–5.

Yaki Point. Stop here for an exceptional view of Wotan's Throne, a majestic flat-top butte named by François Matthes, a U.S. Geological Survey scientist who developed the first topographical map of the Grand Canyon. Due north is Buddha Temple, capped by limestone. Newton Butte, with its flat top of red sandstone, lies to the east. | About 2 mi east of Grand Canyon Village on Desert View Dr.

Yavapai Observation Station. A panorama of the canyon is visible through the building's large windows. The station has temporary exhibits of the canyon's fossil record. | Adjacent to Grand Canyon Village | Free | Daily 8–8.

Sports and Outdoor Activities

HIKING

Bright Angel and South Kaibab are the two most popular trails on the South Rim, but rangers can help you design a trip that best suits your abilities. Under no circumstances attempt a day hike from the rim to the river and back. Remember that when it's 80°F on the South Rim, it's 110°F on the canyon floor. Overnight hikes in the Grand Canyon require a permit ($10 plus $5 per person per night) that can be obtained only in person or by written or faxed request to the **Backcountry Information Center** (Box 129, Grand Canyon, 86023 | 928/638–7875 | fax 928/638–2125 | www.nps.gov/grca) in Grand Canyon Village. The office has hiking maps, and the free *Backcountry Trip Planner* can answer your hiking questions.

★ **Bright Angel Trail.** This well-maintained trail is one of the most popular and scenic hiking paths from the South Rim to the bottom of the canyon (9 mi). Originally a bighorn sheep path and later used by the Havasupai, it was widened late in the 19th century for prospectors and has since become an avenue for mule and foot traffic. Rest houses are equipped with water at the 1.5- and 3-mi points from May through September and at Indian

Gardens year-round. Plateau Point, about 1.5 mi from Indian Gardens, is as far as you should go on a day hike. Bright Angel Trail is the least intimidating footpath into the canyon, but because the climb out from the bottom is an ascent of 5,510 ft, the trip should be attempted only by those in good physical condition and should be avoided in midsummer due to extreme heat. The top of the trail, a tight set of switchbacks, can be icy in winter. Note that you will be sharing the trail with mule trains, which have the right-of-way and sometimes leave unpleasant surprises in your path.

Clear Creek Trail. Only make this 9-mi hike if you are prepared for an overnight trip. The trail departs from Phantom Ranch at the bottom of the canyon and leads across the Tonto Platform to Clear Creek, where drinking water is usually available, but should be treated.

Cliff Springs Trail. An easy 1-mi North Rim walk near Cape Royal, Cliff Springs Trail leads you through a forested ravine to another excellent view of the canyon. Narrow and precarious in spots, the trail passes ancient dwellings, winds beneath a limestone overhang, and terminates at Cliff Springs.

Hermit Trail. Beginning on the South Rim beyond Hermits Rest, this 9-mi (one-way) trail drops more than 5,000 ft to Hermit Creek, which usually flows year-round. It's a strenuous hike back up and only for serious hikers. There's an abundance of lush growth and wildlife, including desert bighorn sheep, along this trail.

North Kaibab Trail. On the North Rim, the trailhead to North Kaibab Trail is about 2 mi north of the Grand Canyon Lodge and is open only from May through October. This is a long, steep hike that drops 5,840 ft over a distance of 14.5 mi and is recommended for experienced hikers only. After about 7 mi, you might stop at the Cottonwood Campground, which has drinking water in summer, rest rooms, shade trees, and a ranger. Like Bright Angel and South Kaibab trails, this one also leads to Phantom Ranch.

Ribbon Falls. Moderately strenuous, but shaded, this trail is a 6.1-mi hike from Phantom Ranch and Bright Angel Campground. The first part of the hike follows the stream between narrow canyon walls.

Rim Trail. The most popular walking path at the South Rim is 12-mi (one-way) Rim Trail, which runs along the edge of the canyon from the first overlook on Desert View Drive to Hermits Rest. This walk, which is paved to Maricopa Point, allows visits to several of the South Rim's historic landmarks.

★**South Kaibab Trail.** This trail starts at Yaki Point, 4 mi east of Grand Canyon Village. Because the trail is so steep and has no water, many hikers return via the less-demanding Bright Angel Trail. During this 7-mi trek to the Colorado River, you're likely to encounter mule trains and riders. At the river, the trail crosses a suspension bridge and runs on to Phantom Ranch.

Tonto Trail. A very strenuous 13.8-mi loop, Tonto Trail should only be attempted in cool weather; summer temperatures on the trail often reach 100 degrees. It runs from South Kaibab Trailhead to Bright Angel Trailhead, and there's little shade.

Transept Trail. A popular walk on the North Rim, this 1.5-mi trail starts near Grand Canyon Lodge, ducks through dense forests, and emerges on the rim to a dramatic view of a large stream through Bright Angel Canyon. This is the best trail for viewing fall foliage.

Widforss Trail. Round-trip, Widforss Trail is 9.8 mi with an elevation change of 200 ft, unusual for a rim hike. On the North Rim west of Grand Canyon Lodge, the trail leads to Widforss Point. It passes through shady forests of pine, spruce, fir, and aspen, and you are likely to see wildflowers in summer.

HORSEBACK RIDING AND MULE RIDES

Mule rides provide an intimate glimpse into the canyon for those who have the time, but not the stamina, to see the canyon on foot. Reservations are essential for all of the rides listed.

GRAND CANYON NATIONAL PARK

EXPLORING
ATTRACTIONS NEARBY
DINING
LODGING
CAMPING AND RV FACILITIES
SHOPPING
ESSENTIAL INFORMATION

EL RIO COLORADO

The Spanish named the Colorado River for the red-hued sediments that ran through it. The "Red River," however, has rarely flowed red since the Glen Canyon Dam was built in 1963, keeping most of the sediment backed up behind it. Without the sediment, the river flows through the canyon a deep blue-green, remains very cold year-round, and seldom floods.

Apache Stables. There's nothing like a horseback ride to immerse you in the western experience. From stables behind the Moqui Lodge near Tusayan, these folks offer gentle horses and a ride that will meet most budgets. | U.S. 180 | 928/638–2891 | $12.50–$100 | www.apachestables.com | Mar.–Nov., daily.

Canyon Trail Rides. Reserve far in advance for a mule trip with this very popular outfitter. You pick up your mule at the Grand Canyon Lodge. A trusty mule rents for about $15 per hour, $35 for a half day, and $85 for a full day. | 435/679–8665 | www.canyonrides.com.

Grand Canyon National Park Lodges Mule Rides. This trip delves into the canyon from the South Rim. Riders must be at least 4' 7" tall, weigh less than 200 pounds, and understand English. Children under 15 must be accompanied by an adult. Riders must be in fairly good physical condition, and pregnant women are advised not to take these trips. | 14001 E. Iliff, Suite 600, Aurora, CO 80013 | 303/338–6000 | fax 303/338–2045 | www.grandcanyonlodges.com | $130–$494 | May–Sept., daily.

RAFTING

White-water trips down the Colorado River and through the Grand Canyon are said by most rafting aficionados to be the adventure of a lifetime. Trips range 3–14 days in length. Reservations are essential for all of the trips listed below.

Arizona Raft Adventures. This well-established company organizes 6–14-day combination paddle-and-motor trips for all skill levels. Credit cards are not accepted. | 4050 E. Huntington Rd., Flagstaff, 86004 | 928/526–8200 or 800/786–7238 | fax 928/526–8246 | www.azraft.com | $1,510–$3,040 | May–Oct.

Canyoneers. With a reputation for high quality and a roster of 3–13-day trips, this outfitter is popular with those who want to include some hiking as well. The five-day "Best of the Grand" includes a hike down to Phantom Ranch. | Box 2997, Flagstaff, 86003 | 928/526–0924 or 800/525–0924 | fax 928/527–9398 | www.canyoneers.com | $695–$2,700 | Apr.–Sept.

Diamond River Adventures. Owned and operated by a mother-and-daughters team, Diamond River offers both oar-powered and motorized river trips from 4 to 14 days. | Box 1300, Page, 86040 | 928/645–8866 or 800/343–3121 | fax 928/645–9536 | www.diamondriver.com | $800–$2,500 | May–Sept.

Grand Canyon Expeditions. This expert, long-established outfitter has guided the likes of the Smithsonian Institution along the Colorado River. You can count on them to take you down the river safely and in style: They limit the number of people on each boat to 14, and evening meals might include filet mignon, pork chops, or shrimp. | Box O, Kanab, UT 84741 | 435/644–2691 or 800/544–2691 | fax 435/644–2699 | www.gcex.com | $2,095–$2,995 for 8 to 14 days | Apr.–Sept.

SKIING

Although you can't schuss down into the Grand Canyon, you can cross-country ski in the woods near the rim, and in the Kaibab National Forest, when there's enough snow.

Canyon Village Marketplace. This shop in the South Rim's Grand Canyon Village rents equipment and can guide you to the best trails. | 928/638–2234 or 928/638–2262.

Attractions Nearby

SIGHTS TO SEE

Glen Canyon National Recreation Area. This huge preserve covers more than 1,500 square mi in northeastern Arizona and southern Utah, including Lake Powell, which has more than 1,900 mi of shoreline. You can swim, water-ski, fish, boat, hike, and camp. South of Lake Powell, the landscape gives way to the Echo Cliffs, orange sandstone formations rising up to 1,000 ft above the surrounding desert. At Bitter Springs, U.S. 89 ascends the cliffs and provides a spectacular view of the Kaibab Plateau and Vermilion Cliffs. The Carl Hayden Visitor Center at Glen Canyon Dam, 2 mi west of Page, has a three-dimensional map of the area. | Visitor center: U.S. 89 and Scenic View Dr., 86040 | www.nps.gov/glca | 928/608–6404 | $10 per vehicle | Visitor center: Memorial Day–Labor Day, daily 7–7; Labor Day–Memorial Day, daily 8–5.

Grand Canyon Railway. First established in 1901, the railway still transports passengers in railcars that date from the 1920s. The scenic train route runs from the Williams Depot to the South Rim of the Grand Canyon (2½ hours each way). There are several classes of service; some tickets include food and beverages. Take time to visit the small railroad museum and vintage railcar at the depot in Williams. | N. Grand Canyon and Fray Marcos Blvds., Williams | 800/843–8724 | $58–$147; depot free | Departs daily at 10 AM; arrives at the canyon at 12:15, returning to Williams at 5:45.

IMAX Theater. For an altogether different sort of view of the Grand Canyon, head to the IMAX Theater in nearby Tusayan. *Grand Canyon: The Hidden Secrets* is shown here on a six-story high, 82-ft wide screen. It will make you feel like you're floating over the chasm. | On Rte. 64, 2 mi south of the South Entrance | 928/638–2468 | fax 928/638–2807 | www.grandcanyonimaxtheater.com | $10 | Mar.–Oct. 8:30–8:30; Nov.–Feb. 10:30–6:30.

Lees Ferry. Most Colorado River rafting trips begin at this site, which is at a sharp bend in the river about 5 mi northeast of the town of Marble Canyon. Named for John D. Lee, who constructed the first ferry to cross the Colorado here in 1872, the spot was a ferry crossing until 1928, when Navajo Bridge was built over Marble Canyon. You can fish for the huge trout in this stretch of the river. | Off U.S. 89A, 86036 | Free | Daily.

Pipe Spring National Monument. One of the few reliable sources of water in this part of Arizona is in this park 90 mi from the North Rim and 14 mi from Fredonia. In summer there are living-history demonstrations on ranching operations or weaving, for example, at the rock fort and ranch. The fort was built to fend off Indian attacks (which never came because a peace treaty was signed before it was finished). It eventually became the headquarters for a dairy operation and in 1871 became the first telegraph station in the Arizona territory. About 0.5 mi north of the monument is a campground, and a picnic area. | HC 65, Box 5, Fredonia, 86022 | 928/643–7105 | www.nps.gov/pisp | $3 | Historic structures daily 8–4:30; visitor center/museum daily 8–5.

Dining

In Grand Canyon

Arizona Room. Steak. This casual, southwestern-style steak house has wrought-iron wall sconces, Native American–inspired prints, and superb canyon views. For dinner, there's good prime rib as well as salmon and vegetarian offerings. | Bright Angel Lodge, Grand Canyon Village | 928/638–2631 | Reservations not accepted | $15–$22 | AE, D, DC, MC, V.

Bright Angel Restaurant and Fountain. American/Casual. The specialty here is casual, affordable dining. No-surprises dishes can fill your belly at breakfast, lunch, or dinner. | Bright Angel Lodge, Grand Canyon Village | 928/638–2631 | Reservations not accepted | $5–$10 | AE, D, DC, MC, V.

Canyon Cafe at Yavapai Lodge. American/Casual. Stop at this refueling spot after a day of touring, or to have a bite before heading out for some sightseeing. | Yavapai Lodge, Grand Canyon Village | 928/638–2360 | Reservations not accepted | $5–$8 | AE, D, DC, MC, V.

★ **El Tovar Dining Room.** Continental. El Tovar Hotel has the best restaurant for miles, but don't expect quality to be commensurate with prices. The classic 19th-century room of hand-hewn logs and beamed ceilings is worth seeing, but the food is hit or miss. The Continental menu changes seasonally. | El Tovar Hotel, Grand Canyon Village | 928/638–2631 | Reservations essential | $12–$32 | AE, D, DC, MC, V.

★ **Grand Canyon Lodge Dining Room.** American. The historic lodge houses a huge, high-ceiling dining room with spectacular views and very good food; you might find pork medallions, red snapper, and spinach linguine with red clam sauce on the dinner menu. | Grand Canyon Lodge, Bright Angel Point | 928/638–2611 | Reservations essential | $12–$28 | AE, D, DC, MC, V | Closed winter.

Grand Canyon Lodge Snack Bar. American/Casual. Dining choices are very limited on the North Rim, so this is your best bet for a meal on a budget. The selections—hot dogs, burgers, sandwiches, yogurt—are standard but sufficient. | Grand Canyon Lodge, Bright Angel Point | 928/638–2611 | Reservations not accepted | $3–$7 | AE, D, DC, MC, V | Closed winter.

Maswik Cafeteria. American/Casual. You can pick up a burger or an affordable Mexican dish at this food court. | Maswik Lodge, Grand Canyon Village | 928/638–2360 | Reservations not accepted | $5–$8 | AE, D, DC, MC, V.

Picnic Areas There are several large picnic facilities within the park.

Buggeln, about 15 mi east of Grand Canyon Village on Desert View Drive, has some secluded, shady spots, and is wheelchair accessible.

Cape Royal, approximately 23 mi south of North Rim Visitor Center, is the most popular designated picnic area on the North Rim because of its panoramic views.

Desert View, on Desert View Drive, approximately 23 mi east of Grand Canyon Village, is a large, popular picnic spot that offers little shade in summer, but is wheelchair accessible.

Grandview Point, on Desert View Drive, approximately 12 mi east of Grand Canyon Village, has wonderful views and nicely spaced tables.

North Rim Visitor Center, at the end of Route 67, approximately 10 mi south of North Entrance, is adjacent to the visitor center and is often crowded with tourists who have just arrived in the park.

Point Imperial, approximately 11 mi northeast of the North Rim visitor center, has shade and offers some privacy.

South Kaibab Trailhead on Desert View Drive, approximately 1 mi east of Grand Canyon Village, is the closest picnic area to Grand Canyon Village, but is often filled with hikers' cars.

Near the Park

Café Espress. American/Casual. This lively natural foods restaurant offers a predominately vegetarian menu. It's known for tempeh burgers, pita pizzas, and salads, but there are usually daily chicken and fish specials. Breakfast is also available. | 16 N. San Francisco St., Flagstaff | 928/774–0541 | $6–$9 | AE, MC, V.

★ **Cottage Place.** Continental. This small, intimate restaurant in a 1901 cottage is known for traditional dishes such as chateaubriand, charbroiled lamb chops, and rack of lamb, plus an extensive wine list. Kids' menu. | 126 W. Cottage Ave., Flagstaff | 928/774–8431 | $21–$40 | AE, MC, V | Closed Mon. No lunch.

Cruisers Café 66. American/Casual. Route 66 icons fill this renovated gas station, formerly Tiffany's Lube Lounge. The menu and the spirit of the place remain lively—be sure to check out the old gasoline logos and the couple of old gas pumps. Standard American dishes are your best bet; stay away from the pasta. | 233 W. Rte. 66, Williams | 928/635–2445 | $7–$10 | AE, DC, MC, V.

Grand Canyon Coffee Café. Café. You'll find the best espresso drinks in Williams here, plus wonderful sandwiches on homemade focaccia. Try an egg-cream soda with Ghirardelli chocolate if you're feeling nostalgic. Harley-Davidson artifacts, some of which are for sale, fill the space. | 125 W. Rte. 66, Williams | 928/635–1255 | $2–$6 | MC, V | Closed Sun.

Hogan Restaurant. Southwestern. This nondescript little restaurant next to the Quality Inn Tuba City cooks up mostly southwestern and Mexican dishes. Both the enchiladas and tamales are quite good. Breakfast is also available. | Main St. (Rte. 264), Tuba City | 928/283–5260 | $7–$10 | AE, D, DC, MC, V.

Lees Ferry Lodge Restaurant. American. Paintings and photographs of fish and fishermen adorn the walls of this restaurant in rustic Lees Ferry Lodge. The filet mignon and the barbecue pork ribs are winners, as is the house specialty, trout. Breakfast is also available. | U.S. 89A, mile marker 54.5, Marble Canyon | 928/355–2231 | $7–$18 | MC, V.

Marble Canyon Lodge Dining Room. American. This multilevel dining room set in the historic 1929 Marble Canyon Lodge, 0.25 mi west of Navajo Bridge, is known for fresh seafood and great steaks. Kids' menu. | U.S. 89A, Marble Canyon | 928/355–2225 or 800/726–1789 | $15–$27 | MC, V.

Pancho McGillicuddy's. Mexican. Originally the Cabinet Saloon, this restaurant is on the National Register of Historic Places. Gone are the spittoons and pipes—the smoke-free dining area is now done in Mexican style, which sets the scene for such specialties as armadillo eggs, the local name for deep-fried jalapeños stuffed with cheese. | 141 Railroad Ave., Williams | 928/635–4150 | $8–$17 | MC, V.

Rod's Steak House. Steak. You can't miss this steak house with the plastic Angus cow out front. Obviously the emphasis here is on meat—sizzling mesquite-broiled steaks, prime rib, and the like. Steaks are often overcooked, so order yours a bit rarer than you actually want it. A children's menu is available. | 301 E. Rte. 66, Williams | 928/635–2671 or 800/562–5545 | $8–$17 | D, MC, V.

Lodging

In Grand Canyon

Grand Canyon National Park Lodges, the parks concessionaire, also known as, handles all bookings for the lodges within the national park. | 14001 E. Iliff, Suite 600, Aurora, CO 80014 | 303/297–2757 | fax 303/338–2045 | www.grandcanyonlodges.com | $69–$290 | AE, D, MC, V.

Bright Angel Lodge. This rustic hostelry built by the Fred Harvey Company in 1935 sits just a few yards back from the canyon rim. It has rooms in the main lodge plus in quaint cabins to the side. Restaurant. Hair salon. | Grand Canyon Village | 303/297–2757 reservations, 928/638–2631 switchboard | fax 303/297–3175 | 30 rooms, 42 cabins | $50–$125 | AE, D, DC, MC, V.

★ **El Tovar Hotel.** Built in 1905 of native stone and heavy pine logs, El Tovar reflects the style of old European hunting lodges and is regarded as one of the finest of the national park hotels. Restaurant. Hair salon. | Grand Canyon Village | 303/297–2757 reservations, 928/638–2631 switchboard | fax 303/297–3175 | 70 rooms, 10 suites | $124–$286 | AE, D, DC, MC, V.

★ **Grand Canyon Lodge.** This historic property, constructed in the 1920s and '30s, is the premier lodging facility in the North Rim area. The main building has limestone walls and timber ceilings. Additional lodging options include small, rustic cabins, larger cabins (some with a canyon view and some with two bedrooms), and traditional motel rooms in newer units. Restaurant. | Adjacent to the North Rim Visitor Center | 303/297–2757 reservations, 928/638–2611 switchboard | fax 303/297–3175 | Closed mid-Oct.–mid-May | 44 rooms | $87–$112 | AE, D, MC, V.

Phantom Ranch. Mule riders and hikers frequent this no-frills lodging at the bottom of the Grand Canyon. There's a dormitory ($26 per person) accessible only to hikers; cabins are exclusively for mule riders. Restaurant. | On the canyon floor | 303/297–2757 reservations, 928/638–2631 switchboard | fax 303/297–3175 | 4 dormitories, 9 cabins | $26–$72 | AE, D, MC, V.

Near the Park

Best Western. This motel is in a pine forest on the edge of the Kaibab National Forest, west of Williams. In-room data ports. Cable TV. Pool. Hot tub. Bar (seasonal). Laundry facilities, laundry service. Business services. | 2600 W. Bill Williams Ave. (Rte. 66), Williams, 86046 | 928/635–4400 | fax 928/635–4488 | www.bestwestern.com | 79 rooms, 10 suites | $89–$135, $125–$181 suites | AE, D, DC, MC, V.

Best Western Grand Canyon Squire. Lacking some of the charm of the older lodges, this upscale motel compensates with cheerful southwestern-style rooms and a long list of amenities. Restaurant. Pool. Hair salon, hot tub. Bowling. | 1.5 mi south of South Rim entrance on U.S. 180/Rte. 64, Tusayan, 86023 | 928/638–2681 or 800/528–1234 | 250 rooms | $129–$189 | AE, D, MC, V.

Cameron Trading Post. Southwestern-style rooms at this modern two-story complex have carved-oak furniture, tile baths, and balconies overlooking the Colorado River. The original native-stone landscaping—including fossilized dinosaur tracks—of the 1930s inn previously on this site has been retained, as has the small, well-kept garden with lilacs, roses, and crab-apple trees. Restaurant. | On U.S. 89, 1 mi north of Rte. 64, Cameron, 86020 | 928/679–2231 or 800/338–7385 Ext. 414 | fax 928/679–2350 | www.camerontradingpost.com | 62 rooms, 4 suites | $89–$135, $125–$181 suites | AE, D, DC, MC, V.

Cliff Dwellers Lodge. Built in 1949, this dining and lodging complex sits at the foot of the Vermilion Cliffs. Rooms in the modern motel building are attractive and clean. Restaurant. | U.S. 89A, 9 mi west of Navajo Bridge, Marble Canyon, 86036 | 928/355–2228 or 800/433–2543 | fax 928/355–2229 | www.cliffdwellerslodge.com | 21 rooms | $65–$86 | AE, D, MC, V.

Fray Marcos Hotel. Western art by a local artist decorates the grand lobby of this hotel, which has a huge flagstone fireplace. Southwestern-style rooms have large bathrooms. Restaurant. Cable TV. Pool. Gym, hot tub. Bar. Business services. | 235 N. Grand Canyon Blvd., Williams, 86046 | 928/635–4010 or 800/843–8724 | fax 928/635–2180 | 196 rooms | $79–$129 | AE, D, MC, V.

★ **The Grand Hotel.** A stone-and-timber structure in the heart of the Tusayan strip, the Grand has clean, generic motel rooms, each with one king or two twin beds. You can see live country-western music or Native American dancing each evening at the on-premises steak house. Restaurant. In-room data ports. Pool. Hot tub. Bar. Shop. Some pets allowed. | $99–$159 | Rte. 64, Tusayan, 86023 | 928/638–3333 | fax 928/638–3131 | 120 rooms | AE, MC, V.

Holiday Inn. This family-friendly motel is three blocks from the Grand Canyon Railway Depot and a mile from Cataract Lake, which offers good fishing. Restaurant, room service. Some refrigerators. Pool. Hot tub. Bar. Laundry facilities, laundry service. Business services. Some pets allowed. | 950 N. Grand Canyon Blvd., Williams, 86046 | 928/635–4114 | fax 928/635–2700 | 120 rooms, 12 suites | $79–$99, $99–$119 suites | AE, D, DC, MC, V.

Holiday Inn Express Hotel and Suites. In this western-theme all-suite property you can wake up surrounded by mug shots of John Wayne or by chairs upholstered with Route 66 fabric. Each suite has a king bedroom and a living room with a double sofa bed, as well as coffeemaker and a wet bar. Restaurant. Microwaves, refrigerators. Cable TV, in-room VCRs. | U.S. 180, Tusayan, 86023 | 928/638–3100 or 800/465–4329 | fax 928/638–0123 | www.gcanyon.com/index.cfm?fuseaction=azrooms | 132 suites | $99–$159 | AE, MC, V.

Inn at 410. Built in 1894, this craftsman-style home is within walking distance of historic downtown Flagstaff, in a quiet but convenient area. It's an inviting, upscale alternative to the usual Flagstaff chain motels. Picnic area. Some in-room hot tubs, refrigerators. No room phones. No room TVs. No smoking. | 410 N. Leroux St., Flagstaff, 86001 | 928/774–0088 or 800/774–2008 | fax 928/774–6354 | www.inn410.com | 6 rooms, 3 suites | $135–$145, $160–$190 suites | MC, V.

Jacob Lake Inn. Basic cabins and standard motel units—without phones or TVs—are available at this 5-acre complex in Kaibab National Forest. All rooms overlook the highway. The bustling lodge center, a popular stop for those heading to the North Rim, has a grocery, a coffee shop, a restaurant, and a large gift shop. | U.S. 89A, Jacob Lake, 86022 | 928/643–7232 | www.jacoblake.com | 14 rooms, 22 cabins | $69–$122 | AE, D, DC, MC, V.

Jeanette's. If you prefer the clean lines of 1920s design to Victorian froufrou, consider staying at this art deco bed-and-breakfast. One room has a private porch, another a fireplace. Jeanette is famous for her baked compotes, banana cream pancakes, and smoothies. All room have private baths; relax in your huge claw-foot tub. No room phones. No room TVs. No children. No smoking. | 3380 E. Lockett Rd., Flagstaff, 86004 | 928/527–1912 or 800/752–1912 | www.jeanettesbb.com | 4 rooms | $115–$145 | D, MC, V.

Kaibab Lodge. This 1920s property has cabins with plain, motel-style furnishings. The lodge is in the woods 5 mi north of the North Rim entrance. Dining room. | Rte. 67, 86022 | Mid-May–late Oct. 928/638–2389; Jan.–Apr. 928/526–0924 (in AZ) or 800/525–0924 (outside AZ) | 30 rooms | $80–$150 | D, MC, V | Closed Oct 15–May 15.

Lees Ferry Lodge. All the simple rooms in this lodge have a different theme; you'll find the bear room, the fish room, and the cowboy room, among others. The services here are geared toward trout-fishing groups. Restaurant. No room phones. No room TVs. | U.S. 89A (mile marker 54.5), Marble Canyon, 86036 | 928/355–2231 | 10 rooms | $53 | AE, MC, V.

Little America Hotel of Flagstaff. The biggest hotel in Flagstaff is surrounded by a 500-acre evergreen forest on the east side of town. Rooms are plush, with such extras as bathroom phones. Take exit 198 off I–40. 3 restaurants, room service. Refrigerators. Cable TV. Pool. Gym, hot tub. Hiking, volleyball. Bar. Playground. Laundry facilities, laundry service. Business services. Airport shuttle. | 2515 E. Butler Ave., Flagstaff, 86004 | 928/779–2741 or 800/352–4386 | fax 928/779–7983 | www.flagstaff.littleamerica.com | 241 rooms, 7 suites | $119–$129, $150–$250 suites | AE, D, DC, MC, V.

Marble Canyon Lodge. This lodge opened in 1929 on the same day the Navajo Bridge was dedicated. Three types of accommodations are available: rooms with lace curtains, brass beds, and hardwood floors in the original building; standard motel rooms in the newer building across the street; and two-bedroom apartments, each containing a queen and a single bed. You can sit on the porch swing and look out on the Vermilion Cliffs or play the piano that was brought over from Lees Ferry in the 1920s. Restaurant. Bar. Shop. Laundry facilities. Pets allowed. No room phones. | U.S. 89A, 0.25 mi west of Navajo Bridge, Marble Canyon, 86036 | 928/355–2225 or 800/726–1789 | fax 928/355–2227 | 52 rooms | $60–$71 | AE, D, MC, V.

Ramada Inn Grand Canyon This motel on 27 acres is one of the better maintained in town. There's a good steak house on the premises and country-and-western bands in summer. Hiking trails crisscross the property. Restaurant, picnic area, room service. Some microwaves, some refrigerators. Cable TV. Pool. Hot tub. Hiking. Bar. Pets allowed. | 642 E. Bill Williams Ave., Williams | 928/635–4431 | fax 928/635–2292 | www.ramadainngrandcanyon.com | 96 rooms | $86–$125 | AE, D, MC, V.

Quality Inn. The attractive atrium here is a good place for drinks. Rooms are well designed, clean, and comfortable. In addition to standard guest rooms, there are 56 one-bedroom suites, each with two TVs, a refrigerator, and microwave. Restaurant. Pool. Hot tub. Airport shuttle. | 6 mi south of rim on U.S. 180, Tusayan, 86023 | 928/638–2673 or 800/221–2222 | fax 928/638–9537 | 232 rooms | $99–$188 | AE, D, DC, MC, V.

Quality Inn Tuba City. The standard rooms at this motel are spacious and well maintained. The Tuba City Trading Post is also here. It's fine for an overnight stop before or after a visit to the Hopi Mesas between Tuba City and Kayenta. Restaurant. Some in-room data ports. Cable TV. Laundry facilities. Some pets allowed. | Main St. and Moenabe Rd., Tuba City, 86045 | 928/283–4545 or 800/644–8383 | fax 928/283–4144 | www.qualityinn.com | 80 rooms | $102 | AE, D, DC, MC, V.

Red Garter. Built in 1897, this former bordello is now a bed-and-breakfast with an old-fashioned feel. It's near railroad tracks, but trains run infrequently. Rooms have 12-ft ceilings

GRAND CANYON
NATIONAL PARK

EXPLORING
ATTRACTIONS NEARBY
DINING
LODGING
CAMPING AND RV
FACILITIES
SHOPPING
ESSENTIAL
INFORMATION

with skylights and antiques. The goodies at the on-site bakery are popular with everyone. Ask for the "Best Gal" room; it's the hands-down favorite. Cable TV. No room phones. No kids under 8. No smoking. | 137 W. Railroad Ave., Williams, 86046 | 928/635–1484 or 800/328–1484 | 4 rooms | $85–$120 | D, MC, V | Closed Dec.–Jan.

Sheridan House Inn. This bed-and-breakfast, among pine trees a few blocks off Route 66, provides a soothing alternative to crowded park lodgings. Hors d'oeuvres are served every afternoon, and the rates include breakfast and dinner. Cable TV, in-room VCRs. Gym, hot tub. Business services. | 460 E. Sheridan Ave., Tusayan | 928/635–9441 or 888/635–9345 | www.grandcanyonbedandbreakfast.com | 6 rooms, 2 suites | $145–$210, $185–$250 suites | AE, D, MC, V.

Camping and RV Facilities

In Grand Canyon

Desert View Campground. Popular for the spectacular view of the canyon at nearby Watchtower, this campground gets booked up fast in summer. Flush toilets. Drinking water. Fire grates. Service station, ranger station. | 50 sites | 23 mi east of Grand Canyon Village off Rte. 64 | No phone. | $10 | Reservations not accepted | May–Oct.

Mather Campground. Because of its central location and modern comfort stations, this campground is always busy. Flush toilets. Drinking water, guest laundry, showers. Fire grates. Ranger station, service station. | 319 sites | Grand Canyon Village | 301/722–1257 or 800/365–2267 reservations | $15 | Reservations essential.

North Rim Campground. This is the only designated campground at the park's North Rim. Flush toilets. Dump station. Drinking water, showers. Fire grates. Ranger station. | 83 sites | 3 mi north of the North Rim entrance | 800/365–2267 | $15 | May–Oct.

Trailer Village. This campground is just a five-minute walk from the general store in Grand Canyon Village. Because of their proximity to the Village, the sites, though wooded, are not very private. Flush toilets. Full hook-ups. Drinking water. Dump station. Fire grates. Public telephone. | 78 sites with full hook-ups | Grand Canyon Village | 928/638–2887, 888/297–2757 reservations | $25 | Reservations essential.

Near the Park

DeMotte Campground. Open mid-May to mid-October, this campground is owned by the U.S. Forest Service but managed by a concessionaire. It's in a beautiful area surrounded by tall pines, 20 mi north of the rim on Route 67. Pit toilets. Drinking water. Fire grates. | 23 sites | Rte. 67, 20 mi north of the North Rim, Fredonia, 86022 | 928/643–7395 | $12 | Mid-May–mid-Oct.

Flintstones Bedrock City. With a gift shop full of Flintstones memorabilia, a diner, and a game room, this mini-city is a favorite with kids. You can pick up camping supplies and groceries here. Flush toilets. Full hook-ups. Drinking water, guest laundry, showers. Fire grates. | 60 sites (32 with full hook-ups) | U.S. 180 at Rte. 64, 30 mi south of the South Entrance, Valle, 86046 | 928/635–2600 | $12 | Apr.–Oct.

Grand Canyon Camper Village. More of a city than a village, this huge campground almost always has availability, but the sites aren't very private, and the place can get noisy. Flush toilets. Full hook-ups, partial hook-ups (electric and water), dump station. Drinking water, showers. Fire grates. Public telephone. | 285 sites (85 with full hook-ups, 200 with partial hook-ups) | Rte. 64, 2 mi south of the South Rim entrance, 86023 | 928/638–2887 | $26–$30.

Jacob Lake Campground. Tucked in among the pine trees is this idyllic campground 45 mi from the north entrance to Grand Canyon National Park. Sites can accommodate tents, trailers and small RVs. Flush toilets, pit toilets. Drinking water. Fire grates. | U.S. 89A at Rte. 67, Jacob Lake, 86022 | 53 sites | 928/643–7395 | $12 | Mid-May–mid-Oct.

GRAND CANYON CAMPGROUNDS

	Total # of sites	# of RV sites	# of hook-ups	Drive-to sites	Hike-to sites	Flush toilets	Pit toilets	Drinking water	Showers	Fire grates/pits	Swimming	Boat access	Playground	Dump station	Ranger station	Public telephone	Reservation possible	Daily fee per site	Dates open
INSIDE THE PARK																			
Bright Angel	33	0	0	•	•			•									•	Free	Y/R
Desert View	50	50	0	•		•		•		•					•	•		$10	Apr.–Nov.
Indian Garden	15	0	0	•			•	•									•	Free	Y/R
Mather	319	319	0	•		•		•		•				•	•	•	•	$15	Y/R
North Rim	83	83	0	•		•		•	•	•				•	•	•	•	$15	May–Oct.
Trailer Village	78	78	78	•		•		•		•				•		•	•	$25	Y/R
NEAR THE PARK																			
Demotte (NF)	23	23	0	•		•		•		•					•			$12	May–Oct.
Flintstones Bedrock City	60	32	32	•		•		•	•	•							•	$12	Y/R
Grand Canyon Camper Village	260	260	260	•		•		•	•	•				•		•	•	$26–30	Y/R
Jacob Lake Campground	53					•		•		•								$12	May–Oct.
Kaibab Camper Village	130	80	70	•			•	•		•				•		•		$12–22	May–Nov.
Ten X Campground	70	0	0	•			•	•										$10	May–Sep.

* In summer only   ** Reservation fee charged   Y/R=Year-round
UL=Unlimited   ULP=Unlimited primitive   LD=Labor Day   MD=Memorial Day

Kaibab Camper Village. In a wooded area popular with cross-country skiers, this is the closest campground with full hook-ups to the North Rim. Flush toilets. Full hook-ups, partial hook-ups (electric and water). Drinking water, showers. Fire grates, picnic tables. Public telephone. | 130 sites (70 with full hook-ups; 10 with partial hook-ups, 50 tent only) | Rte. 67, 0.25 mi south of U.S. 89A | 928/643–7804, 928/526–0924, or 800/525–0924 | fax 928/527–9398 | $12–$22 | Mid-May–mid-Oct.

Ten X Campground. This campground is in the Kaibab National Forest. No reservations are accepted, except for groups of six or more. Pit toilets. Drinking water. | Rte. 64, 9 mi south of South Rim entrance, 86023 | 70 sites | 928/638–2443 | $10 | May–Sept.

Shopping

Canyon Village Marketplace. The main store in Grand Canyon Village sells a full line of camping, hiking, and backpacking supplies in addition to groceries. There is another location at Desert View (928/638–2393). There is also a small shop at Tusayan. | 928/638–2262.

Desert View Trading Post. At the end of the Desert View Drive, the trading post sells Native American handcrafts, including jewelry and pottery. | About 23 mi west of Grand Canyon Village on Desert View Dr. | 928/638–2360.

Hopi House. This beautiful shop, housed in an adobe structure, sells high-quality jewelry, pottery, rugs, and katsinas. | Adjacent to El Tovar Hotel in Grand Canyon Village | 928/638–2631.

North Rim General Store. This is a good place to shop for camping and hiking supplies, as well as snacks. | Rte. 67, 2 mi north of Grand Canyon Lodge | 928/638–2611 Ext. 370.

Tusayan General Store. This popular shop sells everything from inexpensive trinkets to high-quality Native American rugs. | Tusayan, 5 mi south of Grand Canyon Village on Rte. 64 | 928/638–2854.

Verkamp's. This shop, adjacent to El Tovar Hotel, is the best place on the South Rim to buy inexpensive souvenirs like T-shirts, postcard books, and videos of the canyon. The store also has Native American jewelry. | Grand Canyon Village | 928/638–2242.

Essential Information

ATMS: There are no banking facilities on the North Rim of the park; the closest ATM is in Jacob Lake, about 40 mi to the north. **Bank One** | Adjacent to Canyon Village Marketplace in Grand Canyon Village.

AUTOMOBILE SERVICE STATIONS: Desert View Chevron | About 23 mi west of Grand Canyon Village on Desert View Dr. | 928/638–2365. **North Rim Chevron** | 1 mi north of Grand Canyon Lodge | 928/638–2611 Ext. 290. **Xanterra Public Garage.** Emergency service (no gas) is available 24 hours. | Grand Canyon Village | 928/638–2631.

POST OFFICES: Grand Canyon Post Office | Grand Canyon Village, 86023 | 928/638–2512. **North Rim Post Office** | Grand Canyon Lodge, 86023 | 928/638–2611.

GREAT BASIN NATIONAL PARK
EASTERN NEVADA

Route 488, 5 mi west of its junction with Route 487. From Ely or the Nevada/Utah border, take U.S. 6/50 to Route 487.

Beautiful in a stark and wild way, the Great Basin is a stretch of approximately 200,000 square mi. Great Basin National Park, one of the smallest national parks in the country

(77,180 acres), occupies only a minute fraction of that area, yet it exemplifies the land-scape and ecology of the region. This high desert (4,500 ft–6,200 ft in elevation) occupies the wide northern part of Nevada, the equivalent of 75% of the state. The western edge of the Wasatch Front meets the Great Basin and Range Province. Small mountain ranges parade across farmland on the north and a huge desert stretches south to central Utah. There are a few rivers, and their waters evaporate in the dry air or eventually sink into the soil. Surface water in the Great Basin has no outlet to the sea, so it pools in more than 200 small basins throughout the steep mountain ranges. Along with these alpine lakes, the dramatic mountains shelter lush meadows, limestone caves, and bristlecone pines. Within the park itself is the southernmost permanent glacier on the continent and, at 13,063 ft, the second-highest mountain peak in Nevada.

PUBLICATIONS

To get off on the right foot, read *Hiking Great Basin National Park* by Bruce Grubbs. Rose Houk writes about hiking in the park in *Trails to Explore in Great Basin National Park*. For a geological tour of the Great Basin, select *Geology of the Great Basin* by Bill Fiero or *Basin and Range* by John McPhee. You can order books from the **Great Basin Natural History Association** (775/234–7270 | www.nps.gov/grba/gbnha/gba.htm), which operates the bookstore at the park visitor center.

When to Visit

SCENERY AND WILDLIFE

Despite the cold, dry conditions in Great Basin National Park, 411 different plant species thrive; 13 are considered sensitive species. The plants have developed some ingenious methods of dealing with the desert's harshness. Many of the flowering plants will only grow and produce seeds in a year when there is enough water. The park's plants provide a variety of habitats for animals. In the sagebrush desert you'll find jackrabbits, ground squirrels, chipmunks, and mice. You might see pronghorns on the open sagebrush and grass plains near the park entrance. The park is home to coyotes, kit fox, and badgers, but sightings are rare. Mule deer and striped skunks abound in the pygmy forest of pinyon pine and juniper trees. Shrews, ringtail cats, and weasels make their homes around the springs and running streams. Mountain lions, bobcats, marmots, and mountain sheep live on the rugged slopes and in valleys. Seasonal changes in food supply and habitat quality, or overcrowding, can sometimes force animals to relocate. Often a species may be found in one mountain range but not another similar one, simply because there's no way for the animal to cross the desert of the valley floors.

HIGH AND LOW SEASON

As one of the least-visited national parks in the country, attracting fewer than 100,000 people each year, Great Basin National Park is never crowded. The high desert weather here is typically mild in summer (average high temperature is 85°F) and harsh in winter (temperatures hover in the low teens), so most park visitors come in summer and very few visit in January and February. The campgrounds at Baker Creek Road and the area above Upper Lehman Creek are usually closed November–June, depending on weather conditions. In summer you'll be comfortable in shorts and T-shirts during the day, but temperatures drop at night so bring light jackets and pants. If you plan to hike around Wheeler Peak, bring a jacket, pants, and appropriate shoes. In winter, heavy coats, jeans, and sweaters are recommended.

Average High/Low Temperature (°F) and monthly precipitation (in inches)

	JAN.	FEB.	MAR.	APR.	MAY	JUNE
GREAT BASIN	41/18	44/21	48/24	56/31	66/40	76/48
	1.0	1.0	1.5	1.1	1.3	0.9

	JULY	AUG.	SEPT.	OCT.	NOV.	DEC.
	86/57	83/56	75/47	62/47	49/26	42/20
	0.9	1.2	1.1	1.2	1.0	0.9

FESTIVALS AND SEASONAL EVENTS
SUMMER

May–Sept.: **Silver State Classic Challenge.** The country's largest (and longest) open-road race for amateur fast-car enthusiasts shows off street-legal muscle cars that reach a top speed of 200 mph. The race runs from Preston to Hiko. To get there head south from Ely on Route 318. | 775/289–8877.

Aug.: **White Pine County Fair.** A hay contest (kids try to find an object hidden in the hay); livestock, flower, and vegetable judging; carnival rides and a midway; and a buckaroo breakfast make this fair, held Labor Day weekend at the County Fairgrounds, the real thing. | 775/289–8877.

Nearby Towns

An hour's drive west of the park entrance at the intersection of three U.S. highways, **Ely** (population 4,830) is the biggest town in the area. It grew up in the second wave of the early Nevada mining boom, right at the optimistic turn of the 20th century. For 70 years copper kept the town in business, but when it ran out in the early 1980s Ely declined fast. Then, in 1986, the National Park Service designated Great Basin National Park 68 mi to the east and the town got a boost. Ely has since been rebuilt and revitalized and is now home to a railroad museum, the county seat, and a great old hotel-casino (Hotel Nevada), as well as the basic tourist amenities. If you want to get closer to the park you can stay in tiny **Baker** (population 50), which sits at the main park entrance. Really just a cluster of small businesses a few miles south of U.S. 6/50 on Route 487, the hamlet is 5 mi from the visitor center.

INFORMATION

Ely Bristlecone Convention Center | 150 6th St., Ely, 89301 | 775/289–3720 or 800/496–9350 | www.elynevada.net/bristlecone_convention_center.htm. **Great Basin Business and Tourism Council** | 10 Main St., Baker, 89311 | No phone | www.greatbasinpark.com. **White Pine Chamber of Commerce** | 636 Aultman St., Ely, 89301 | 775/289–8877 | www.whitepinechamber.com.

Exploring Great Basin

PARK BASICS

Contacts and Resources: Great Basin National Park | Rte. 488, Baker, 89311 | 775/234–7331 | fax 775/234–7269 | www.nps.gov/grba.

Hours: The park is open every day year-round. May–August, visitor center hours are 8–4:30; hours may vary from year to year due to staffing and budget constraints.

Fees: Admission to the park is free, but there's a $2–$8 fee to tour Lehman Caves.

Getting Around: Baker Creek Road and portions of Wheeler Peak Scenic Drive, above Upper Lehman Creek, are closed from November to June. The road to the visitor center and the roads to the developed campgrounds are paved, but the going is tough in winter and two-wheel-drive cars don't do well. RVs and trailers aren't allowed above Lower Lehman Creek.

With an 8% grade, the road to Wheeler Peak is steep and curvy, but not dangerous. The roads to primitive campsites are gravel and dirt.

Permits: Everyone ages 12 and older needs a Nevada state fishing license to fish in Great Basin National Park. The resident license costs $5 for kids 12–15 and $21 for those 16 and older; the short-term nonresident license is $12. For information on fishing licenses contact the Nevada Division of Wildlife at http://ndow.org. Backcountry hikers do not have to obtain permits, but for your own safety you should fill out a form at the visitor center before you set out.

Public Telephones: The only public phone in the park is at the visitor center.

Rest Rooms: The visitor center has public rest rooms, as does the nearby picnic area. Vault toilets are available at all the developed campgrounds: Baker Creek, Lower Lehman Creek, Upper Lehman Creek, and Wheeler Peak.

Accessibility: Designated handicap parking spaces are available at the visitor center, where there is a ramp over the curb. The center itself is fully accessible to those with impaired mobility, all on one level. The Great Basin National Park slide show is captioned. At the front desk you can borrow wheelchairs to use in the center and in the first room of Lehman Caves. A cut curb provides access to a table and fire grate at the picnic area near the visitor center, which also has accessible rest rooms. Three campgrounds within the park are accessible: Upper Lehman Creek Campground, Wheeler Peak Campground, and Baker Creek Campground. Note that the Upper Lehman Creek Campground rest room access ramp is steep.

Emergencies: In case of fire or in a medical or police emergency, dial 911 or report to the ranger station at the visitor center.

Lost and Found: The park's lost-and-found is at the visitor center.

A Good Tour

GREAT BASIN IN ONE DAY

Start your visit with a tour of **Lehman Caves.** If you have time before or after the tour, hike the short **Mountain View Nature Trail** near the visitor center. Stop for lunch at the Lehman Caves Cafe or have a picnic near the visitor center, then take a leisurely drive up to **Wheeler Peak.** You can stop about halfway along your drive to hike the short **Osceola Ditch Trail,** otherwise just enjoy the fantastic mountain views from the two overlooks. If you're feeling energetic when you reach Wheeler Peak, hike some of the trails there, then savor the drive back to the visitor center and browse the gift shop.

Attractions

PROGRAMS AND TOURS

Campfire Programs. On summer evenings the park offers campfire programs at Upper Lehman Creek Campground and Wheeler Peak Campground. The 40–60-minute programs cover a range of subjects related to the Great Basin's cultural and natural history and resources. Dress warmly and bring a flashlight. Program times vary, so call for information. | Wheeler Peak Scenic Dr., 4 mi (Upper Lehman Creek) and 12 mi (Wheeler Peak) from the visitor center | 775/234-7331 | Free | June–Aug., at Upper Lehman Creek Campground and Fri.–Sat. at Wheeler Peak Campground. Check at visitor center for schedule.

SCENIC DRIVE

Wheeler Peak Scenic Drive. Less than a mile from the visitor center off Route 488, turn onto this paved road that winds its way up to elevations of 10,000 ft. The road takes you through pygmy forest in lower elevations; as you climb, the air cools. Along the way, two overlooks offer awe-inspiring views of the Snake Range mountains and a short hiking trail leads to views of an old mining site. Turn off at Mather Overlook, elevation 9,000 ft, for the best photo ops. At Wheeler Peak, the end of the road, you can stretch your legs on self-guided hiking trails. The drive is 12 mi one way; allow 1¼ hours for the round-trip, not including hikes.

GREAT BASIN
NATIONAL PARK

EXPLORING
ATTRACTIONS NEARBY
DINING
LODGING
CAMPING AND RV
FACILITIES
SHOPPING
ESSENTIAL
INFORMATION

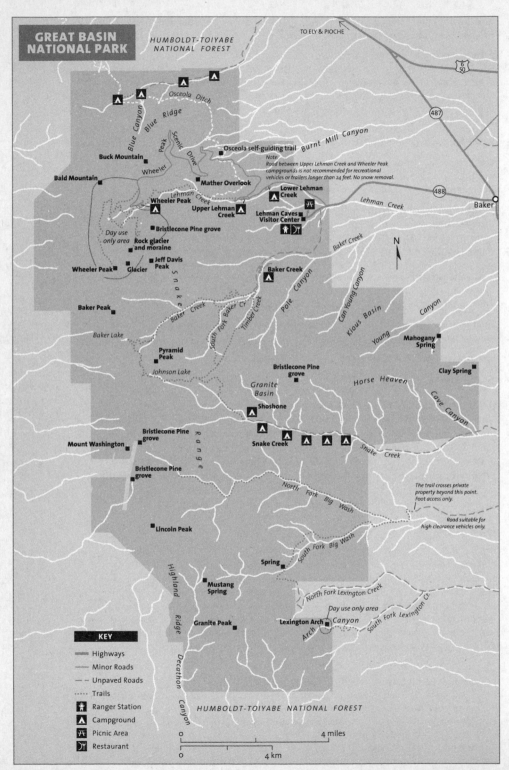

GREAT BASIN
NATIONAL PARK

HUMBOLDT-TOIYABE
NATIONAL FOREST

TO ELY & PIOCHE

6
50

487

Osceola Ditch

Blue Canyon

Blue Ridge

Peak

Scenic Drive

Burnt Mill Canyon

Osceola self-guiding trail

Note:
Road between Upper Lehman Creek and Wheeler Peak
campgrounds is not recommended for recreational
vehicles or trailers longer than 24 feet. No snow removal.

Buck Mountain

Wheeler

Bald Mountain

Mather Overlook

Lehman Creek

488

Lehman Creek

Baker

Wheeler Peak

Upper Lehman
Creek

Lower Lehman
Creek

Lehman Caves
Visitor Center

Bristlecone Pine grove

Day use
only area

Rock glacier
and moraine

Baker Creek

N

Wheeler Peak

Jeff Davis
Peak

Glacier

Snake

Baker Creek

Pole Canyon

Baker Creek

Can Young Canyon

Baker Peak

South Fork Baker Cr.

Timber Creek

Kious Basin

Young

Canyon

Mahogany
Spring

Baker Lake

Pyramid
Peak

Johnson Lake

Bristlecone Pine
grove

Granite
Basin

Horse Heaven

Clay Spring

Cave Canyon

Range

Shoshone

Mount Washington

Bristlecone Pine
grove

Snake Creek

Snake Creek

Bristlecone Pine
grove

The trail crosses private
property beyond this point.
Foot access only.

North Fork Big Wash

Road suitable for
high clearance vehicles only.

Lincoln Peak

South Fork Big Wash

Spring

Highland

North Fork Lexington Creek

Mustang
Spring

Ridge

Day use only area

South Fork Lexington Cr.

Granite Peak

Lexington Arch

Arch

Canyon

Decathon

Canyon

HUMBOLDT-TOIYABE NATIONAL FOREST

KEY

Highways

Minor Roads

Unpaved Roads

Trails

Ranger Station

Campground

Picnic Area

Restaurant

0   4 miles

0   4 km

SIGHTS TO SEE

★ **Lehman Caves.** In 1885, rancher and miner Absalom Lehman discovered the underground wonder that's now named after him. Although the name suggests that there's more than one cave here, Lehman is a single limestone and marble cavern 0.25 mi long. Inside, stalactites, stalagmites, helictites, flowstone, popcorn, and other bizarre mineral formations cover almost every surface. Lehman Caves is one of the best places to see rare shield formations, created when calcite-rich water is forced from tiny cracks in a cave wall, ceiling or floor. Year-round the cave maintains a constant, damp temperature of 50°F, so wear a light jacket and nonskid shoes when you take the tour. Guided tours conducted by the park service run 30–90 minutes; the full 90-minute tour route is 0.54 mi round-trip. Children under age 5 are not allowed on the 90-minute tours, and those under 16 must be accompanied by an adult. Tours run four times a day between 9 and 4. | Visitor Center, Rte. 488, 1 mi from the park entrance | 775/234–7331 | www.nps.gov/grba/lehmancaves.htm | $2–$8 | May–Sept. 9–4:30.

Visitor Center. Here you can see exhibits on the flora, fauna, and geology of the park, or join a tour to Lehman Caves. Books, videos, and souvenirs are for sale; a coffee shop is attached. | Rte. 488, 1 mi from the park entrance | 775/234–7331 | May–Sept. 8–4:30.

Next door to the visitor center, peek into **Rhodes Cabin,** a tiny building with walls lined with black-and-white photographs of the park's earlier days.

Sports and Outdoor Activities

Great Basin National Park is a great place for experienced outdoor enthusiasts. There are no outfitters to guide you through the park, and there are no nearby shops that rent or sell sporting equipment, so you should bring everything you might need and be prepared to go it alone—always with a companion, of course.

CROSS-COUNTRY SKIING

Lehman Creek Trail is the most popular cross-country skiing trail in the park. It's marked with orange flags, making it easy to find. The lower part of the trail is usually free of snow, but you may need snowshoes to reach the skiable upper section.

HIKING

When hiking, always carry water and remember that the trails are at high elevations, so pace yourself accordingly. For your own protection do not enter abandoned mineshafts or tunnels. In the backcountry few of the trails are maintained; stop at the visitor center for maps and information on trail conditions. Park rangers strongly recommend backcountry registration.

Mountain View Nature Trail. Just past the Rhodes cabin on the right side of the visitor center, this short and easy trail is marked with signs describing the plants. The path passes the original entrance to Lehman Caves and loops back to the visitor center. It's a great way to spend your time while you wait for your cave tour to start. | Visitor Center, Rte. 488, 1 mi from the park entrance.

Osceola Ditch Trail. In 1890, at a cost of $108,223, the Osceola Gravel Mining Company constructed an 18-mi-long trench known as the Osceola Ditch. The ditch was part of an attempt to glean gold from the South Snake Range, but water shortages and the company's failure to find much gold forced the mining operation to shut down in 1905. You can reach portions of the eastern section of the ditch on foot via the Osceola Ditch Trail. This is an easy 0.3 mi round-trip hike, or you can go all the way to Strawberry Creek. Allow yourself a couple of hours to complete the longer round-trip hike at an altitude of about 8,400 ft. | Wheeler Peak Scenic Dr.

GREAT BASIN
NATIONAL PARK

EXPLORING
ATTRACTIONS NEARBY
DINING
LODGING
CAMPING AND RV
FACILITIES
SHOPPING
ESSENTIAL
INFORMATION

EARLY
INHABITANTS

The Great Basin
region has been
home to humans
for more than
10,000 years. The
Fremont culture
irrigated corn,
beans, and squash
in the valleys and
hunted in the
mountains around
present-day Baker,
Nevada, and
Garrison, Utah, in
1100–1300. Starting
about 1300, the
Shoshone and
Paiute peoples
lived in the area;
the pinyon nut was
the mainstay of
their diet.

★ **Wheeler Peak Trails.** From the parking area at the end of Wheeler Peak Scenic Drive, you can embark on a hike over several connecting trails. These trails are for day use only. | Wheeler Peak Scenic Dr., 12 mi from the visitor center.

Though the park has several bristlecone pine groves, the only way to see the ancient trees up close is to hike the **Bristlecone Pine Trail.** From the parking area to the grove, it's a moderate 1.4-mi hike that takes about an hour one-way.

bristlecone Pine Trail leads to two other trails. To the right as you head past the grove is the **Alpine Lakes Loop Trail,** a moderate 2.7-mi trek that loops past Stella and Teresa Lakes and returns you to bristlecone Pine Trail in about two hours.

Turn left off bristlecone Pine Trail past the grove to connect with **Glacier Trail.** The trail skirts the southernmost permanent ice field on the continent and ends with a view of a small alpine glacier. From there it's less than 5 mi back to the parking lot. Allow 2½ hours for the moderate hike.

Attractions Nearby

Scenic Drive

U.S. 93 Scenic Byway. The 68 mi between the park and Ely make a beautiful drive with diverse views of Nevada's paradoxical geography: desert vegetation and lush mountains. You'll catch an occasional glimpse of a snake slithering on the road's shoulder or a lizard sunning on a rock. A straight drive to Ely takes a little more than an hour; if you have the time to take a dirt-road adventure, don't miss the Ward Charcoal Ovens or a peek at Cave Lake.

Sights to See

Cave Lake State Recreation Area. High in the pine and juniper forest of the big Schell Creek Range that borders Ely on the east, this is an idyllic spot. You can spend a day fishing for rainbow and brown trout in the reservoir and a night sleeping under the stars. Arrive early; it gets crowded. Access may be restricted in winter. | 15 mi southeast of Ely via U.S. 6/50/93 | 775/728–4467 | www.state.nv.us/stparks | $3 | Daily.

ALL DRIED UP

During the last ice
age, vast Lake
Bonneville covered
the northwestern
part of Utah and
extended into
Nevada. About
15,000 years ago
the lake's edge was
a mere 10 mi from
the current
boundary of Great
Basin National
Park. When the
climate warmed
about 10,000 years
ago the lake
evaporated,
eventually leaving
only the Great Salt
Lake near Salt Lake
City, Utah, more
than 150 mi away.

Nevada Northern Railway Museum. During the mining boom the Nevada Northern Railroad connected East Ely, Ruth, and McGill to the transcontinental rail line in the northeast corner of Nevada. The whole operation is now a museum. You can tour the depot, offices, warehouses, yard, roundhouses, and repair shops and catch a ride on one of the trains in the summer. | 1100 Ave. A, Ely | 775/289–2085 | http://nevadanorthernrailway.net | $3 | Memorial Day–Labor Day, daily 9:30–4.

Ward Charcoal Ovens Historic State Monument. In the desert south of Ely is this row of ovens. The ovens turned pinyon, juniper, and mountain mahogany into charcoal, which was used for refining local silver and copper ore. It's worth the drive from Ely to take in this well-preserved piece of Nevada mining history. | 7 mi south of Ely on U.S. 6/50, and 11 mi southwest on Cave Valley Rd. | 775/728–4460 | www.state.nv.us/stparks | $3 | Daily.

Dining

In Great Basin

Lehman Caves Cafe and Gift Shop. American/Casual. The menu here includes light breakfast, soup-and-sandwich lunches, hot drinks, soft drinks, and home-baked desserts. They hand-make large ice cream sandwiches. | Next to the visitor center | 775/234–7221 | $4–$6 | AE, D, MC, V | Closed Nov.–Mar. No dinner.

Near the Park

The Border Inn. American. This part of Nevada is ranch country, so it's no surprise that meat-and-potatoes dominates the menu at the Border Inn. You'll find hearty fare like hamburgers, chicken-fried steak, pork chops, and, of course, steaks. Breakfast is also served. | U.S. 6/50, 13 mi east of Great Basin National Park, Baker | 775/234–7300 | $5–$11 | AE, D, MC, V.

Red Apple Family Restaurant. American. This restaurant defines "down home." The meals are home-cooked fare, ranging from three-egg omelets (your choice of ingredients) to chicken-fried steak. The most expensive item on the menu, a 12-ounce T-bone steak with all the fixings, costs $12.95. The waitstaff is ready with smiles and carafes of coffee. You can also get breakfast. | 2160 Aultman St., Ely | 775/289–8585 | $8–$18 | AE, D, MC, V.

T and D's Country Store, Restaurant, and Lounge. American/Casual. The bright and cheerful restaurant in this large white-brick building occupies a sunroom where windows line the walls. Salads, hot and cold sandwiches, ribs, and chicken are the core of the menu; you can order pizza and Mexican food as well. | 1 Main St., Baker | 775/234–7264 | $7–$20 | AE, D, DC, MC, V.

Lodging

Near the Park

The Border Inn. Located on the Utah-Nevada border, this motel has air-conditioned rooms with twin, double, and queen beds. The only gas station in the area is right here. Restaurant. Some kitchenettes. | U.S. 6/50, 13 mi east of Great Basin National Park, Baker | 775/234–7300 | 26 rooms | $31–$39 | AE, D, MC, V.

Holiday Inn and Prospector Casino of Ely. For no-surprises rooms and on-site gambling, this is a good bet. Restaurant. Cable TV. Pool. Gym. | 1501 Ave. F, Ely | 775/289–8900 or 800/465–4329 | fax 775/289–4607 | www.holidayinn.com | 61 rooms | $95 | AE, D, DC, MC, V.

Hotel Nevada. One of the oldest hotel buildings in the state, this landmark in the middle of town is nonetheless in excellent shape. Built in 1908, it's a big square brick building in downtown Ely. The luxury rooms are especially nice. The hotel has a casino. Restaurant. Cable TV. Bars. Business services. Some pets allowed. | 501 Aultman St., Ely | 775/289–6665 or 800/406–3055 | fax 775/289–4715 | www.hotelnevada.com | 65 rooms | $20–$69 | AE, D, DC, MC, V.

Jailhouse Motel and Casino. This modern motel at the main downtown intersection has a curious jailhouse theme—the rooms are referred to as "cells." Restaurant. Cable TV. Some pets allowed. | 211 5th St., Ely | 775/289–3033 or 800/841–5430 | fax 775/289–8709 | 47 rooms | $40–$49 | AE, D, DC, MC, V.

Motel 6. The largest lodging in Ely has no-surprises contemporary-style rooms with modern furnishings. In-room data ports. Cable TV. Pool. Laundry facilities. Some pets allowed. | 770 Ave. O, Ely | 775/289–6671 or 800/466–8356 | fax 775/289–4803 | 99 rooms | $35–$49 | AE, D, MC, V.

Ramada Inn Copper Queen and Casino. In the casino, which encircles the pool, you can feed the slots to the aroma of chlorine. The rooms have king or queen-size beds, and every one has a coffee pot. The staff will drive you to the Ely airport. Restaurant. Microwaves, refrigerators. In-room data ports. Cable TV. Indoor pool. Hot tub. Bar. Business services. | 701 Ave. I, Ely | 775/289–4884 or 800/851–9526 | fax 775/289–1492 | 65 rooms | $50–$120 | AE, D, DC, MC, V.

Silver Jack Motel. This motel surrounds a lawn with trees and a patio—a nice place to relax in the early evening. The motel also rents out the Getaway Cabin, which sleeps up to seven people two blocks away, and a rustic hideaway for two adults—a converted bunkhouse on the Baker Ranch, a working outfit. Some pets allowed. No room phones. | 10 Main St., Baker | 775/234–7323 | 7 rooms | $39–$85 | D, MC, V.

Camping and RV Facilities

In Great Basin

Great Basin National Park has four developed campgrounds, but the Lower Lehman Creek area is the only one open year-round. Primitive campsites around Snake and Strawberry creeks are open year-round and are free; however, snow and rain can make access to the sites difficult. Water is only provided in summer; if you're camping in winter, bring your own. None of the campgrounds have RV hook-ups.

Baker Creek Campground. The turnoff is just past the park entrance, on the left as you approach the visitor center. Pit toilets. Drinking water. Fire grates, picnic tables. | 32 sites | 2.5 mi south of Rte. 488, 3 mi from the visitor center | No phone | $10 | Reservations not accepted | May–Oct., depending on weather conditions.

Lower Lehman Creek Campground. It's the first turnoff past the visitor center. Pit toilets. Drinking water. Fire grates, picnic tables. | 11 sites | 2.5 mi from the visitor center on Wheeler Peak Scenic Dr. | No phone | $10 | Reservations not accepted.

Upper Lehman Creek Campground. The entrance is about a mile past the Lower Lehman Creek turnoff. Pit toilets. Drinking water. Fire grates, picnic tables. | 24 sites | 4 mi from the visitor center on Wheeler Peak Scenic Dr. | No phone | $10 | Reservations not accepted | May–Oct., depending on weather conditions.

Wheeler Peak Campground. This scenic, cool campground is at the end of Wheeler Peak Scenic Drive, at an elevation of 10,000 ft. RVs cannot camp here because they cannot negotiate the twisting road past Upper Lehman Creek. In fact, nothing over 24 ft long is allowed beyond this point. The campground is closed for most of the year because of snow. Pit toilets. Drinking water. Fire grates, picnic tables. | 37 sites | 12 mi from the visitor center on Wheeler Peak Scenic Dr. | No phone | $10 | Reservations not accepted | May–Sept., depending on weather conditions.

Shopping

Great Basin Natural History Association Book Store. Everything you need to enrich your experience touring the park and traveling in the region is available here. There is an excellent selection of books, maps, and trail guides. | Visitor center, Rte. 488, 1 mi from the park entrance | 775–234–7270.

Lehman Caves Cafe and Gift Shop. The park's shop sells souvenirs, T-shirts, books, toys, Native American jewelry, Great Basin pottery, and travel items. | Next to the visitor center | 775/234–7221 | Closed mid-Oct.–mid-Apr.

Silver Jack Gift Shop. This store attached to a motel is one of just two places to shop in Baker. You can buy artworks such as paintings, sculptures in various mediums, and antler art. | 10 Main St., Baker | 775/234–7323 | Closed Nov.–Mar.

T and D's Grocery Store. The large white-brick building also houses a restaurant and a bar. The store is small and offers basic food items. It's not a place to stock up on supplies, but it's good for replenishing the basics. | 1 Main St., Baker | 775/234–7264 | Closed Nov.–Mar.

Essential Information

ATMS: The Border Inn | U.S. 6/50, 13 mi east of Great Basin National Park, Baker | 775/234–7300.

AUTOMOBILE SERVICE STATIONS: Baker Ranch Sinclair | Rte. 487 and Pioche St., Baker. **The Border Inn** | U.S. 6/50, 13 mi east of Great Basin National Park, Baker | 775/234–7300. **POST OFFICES: Baker Post Office** | 101 Carson St., Baker, 89311 | 775/234–7231. **Ely Downtown**

Post Office | 415 5th St., Ely, 89301 | 775/289–4537. **Ely Nevada Post Office** | 2600 bristlecone Ave., Ely, 89301 | 775/289–9276.

MESA VERDE NATIONAL PARK
SOUTHWESTERN COLORADO

U.S. 160, 10 mi east of Cortez and 35 mi west of Durango.

Ancient dwellings of the Ancestral Puebloan people are the centerpiece of Mesa Verde National Park. The inhabitants of Mesa Verde lived peacefully in the area from about AD 500 to 1300, leaving behind more than 3,500 archaeological sites spread out over 80 square mi of Federal land. The park was created in 1906, due in large part to the tireless efforts of Virginia McClurg and Lucy Peabody to protect the cliff dwellings. In 1978 the park became one of the first eight places to be designated a World Cultural Heritage Site by the United Nation's UNESCO.

But Mesa Verde, "Green Table" in Spanish, is much more than an archaeologist's dreamland. Rising dramatically from the San Juan Basin, the jutting cliffs are cut by a series of complex canyons and covered with green, from pines in the higher elevations down to mountain brush. As you wind your way up along the park's twisting roads, sudden sweeping vistas of the Mancos and Montezuma valleys unfold. From the tops of the smaller mesas, you can look across to the cliff dwellings in the rock faces of other mesas. Dwarfed by the towering cliffs, the sand-color dwellings look almost like a natural occurrence in the midst of the desert's harsh beauty.

When to Visit

The best times to visit the park are late May, early June, and most of September, when the weather is fine but the summer crowds have thinned. Winter is an interesting time for day trips from surrounding areas; the sight of the sandstone dwellings sheltered from the snow in their cliff coves is spectacular.

SCENERY AND WILDLIFE

Since 2000, wildfires have claimed thousands upon thousands of acres inside Mesa Verde National Park. Visitors will see the scars for a long time, as it can take as long as 300 years for an evergreen woodland to restore itself. In spring and summer, however, you'll still see brightly colored blossoms, sage, yucca, mountain mahogany, and the persistent rebirth of plantlife along the roadsides and in the canyons. The yellow Perky Sue blooms in May and June. Sand-loving blue lupines are seen along the roadways in the higher elevations, and bright-red Indian paintbrushes are scattered throughout the rocky, arid cliffs.

Mule deer are the most frequently sighted of the park's larger animals. Coyotes often run alongside or across the road. In August and September you may spot elk or black bears at the canyon bottoms. About 200 species of birds, including red-tailed hawks and golden eagles, live in Mesa Verde, as does the poisonous prairie rattler. The animals of Mesa Verde seek shelter from the extreme heat of the day in trees and under brush. The best time to spot them is in the early morning hours or just before dusk. You'll find them near sources of water. Ask park rangers about the most likely places to view animals.

HIGH AND LOW SEASON

Mid-June through August are Mesa Verde's most crowded months. In July and August, lines at the museum and visitor center may last half an hour.

The mesa gets as many as 100 inches of snow in winter. Snow may fall as late as May and as early as October, but there's rarely enough to hamper travel. Afternoon thunder showers are common in July and August.

Average High/Low Temperatures (°F) and Monthly Precipitation (in inches)

	JAN.	FEB.	MAR.	APR.	MAY	JUNE
MESA VERDE	38/16	42/21	48/26	57/32	68/41	80/41
	1.6	1.4	1.9	1.1	1.1	.60

	JULY	AUG.	SEP.	OCT.	NOV.	DEC.
	85/57	82/55	74/48	63/38	48/27	39/19
	.60	1.9	1.5	1.7	1.8	1.7

FESTIVALS AND SEASONAL EVENTS

SPRING

Late May/ **Mountain Ute Bear Dance.** This traditional dance, held on the Ute
early June: reservation south of Cortez, celebrates spring and the legacy of the bear who taught the Ute people its secrets. | 970/565–3751.

May: **Iron Horse Bicycle Classic.** This annual Memorial Day bicycle race begins at the train station in Durango and pits cyclists against the Durango and Silverton Narrow-Gauge Railroad train. The racers bike the 47 mi of the train route to Silverton. | 970/259–4621.

SUMMER

May–Sept.: **Native American Dances.** The Cortez Cultural Center invites performers from the Ute, Navajo, and Hopi tribes to perform traditional dances from their respective cultures each evening at 7:30. | 970/565–1151.

June: **Ute Mountain Round Up Rodeo.** Since 1928, this parade and rodeo has drawn people to the American Legion Arena in Cortez the second weekend in June to see roping and riding as it is actually performed on local ranches. | 970/565–4485.

July: **Durango Fiesta Days.** This annual festival brings a parade, rodeo, barbecue, street dance, and pie auction to the La Plata County Fair Grounds in Durango on the last weekend of the month. | 970/247–8835.

Aug.: **Montezuma County Fair.** Farm animals are exhibited and judged, and arts and crafts are sold at this fair held the first week in August in Cortez's Montezuma County Fairgrounds. | 970/565–1000.

Escalante Days. A parade down Main Street in Dolores kicks off this full day of fun. Other activities include a pancake breakfast, a bike race, a car show, a fireman's barbecue, arts-and-crafts booths, and live music in Flanders Park. | 970/882–4018.

FALL

Sept.–Oct.: **Rocky Mountain Colorfest.** Durango celebrates the change of seasons with on-going driving tours, Victorian home tours, train rides, and pow-wows for six weeks each fall. | 970/247–8230 or 800/525–8855.

Oct.: **Indian Summer Run.** On Columbus Day weekend, runners from throughout the country participate in this half-marathon from the entrance of Mesa Verde National Park to Centennial Park in Cortez. | 970/565–3414.

Durango Cowboy Gathering. A rodeo, western art exhibitions, cowboy poetry readings, storytelling, and a dance draw cowboys and cowgirls to Durango the first weekend in October. | 970/259–2165.

Nearby Towns

A onetime market center for sheep and cattle ranchers, **Cortez** is now the largest gateway town to Mesa Verde National Park and a base for tourists visiting the Four Corners region of Colorado. You can still see a rodeo and cattle drive here at least once a year. **Dolores,** steeped in a rich railroad history, is set on the Dolores River, 20 mi north of Mesa Verde. Neighboring both the San Juan National Forest and McPhee Reservoir, the second largest lake in the state, Dolores is a favorite of outdoor enthusiasts. East of Mesa Verde, **Durango** became a town in 1881 when the Denver and Rio Grande Railroad pushed its tracks across the neighboring San Juan Mountains. Within 10 years, Durango had become the region's main municipality and a gateway to the American Southwest.

INFORMATION

Cortez/Mesa Verde Visitor Information Bureau | 928 E. Main St., Cortez, 81321 | 970/565–8227 or 800/253–1616 | www.swcolo.org. **Dolores Chamber of Commerce** | 201 Railroad Ave., Dolores, 81323 | 970/882–4018 or 800/807–4712 | www.doloreschamber.com. **Durango Area Tourism Office** | 111 S. Camino Del Rio, Durango, 81301 | 970/247–0312 or 800/525–8855 | www.durango.org.

Exploring Mesa Verde

PARK BASICS

Contacts and Resources: Mesa Verde National Park | Box 8, Mesa Verde, CO 81330–0008 | 970/529–4465 | www.nps.gov/meve.

Hours: The facilities at Mesa Verde National Park open each day at 8 AM and close at sunset from Memorial Day through Labor Day. The rest of the year, the facilities close at 5. Wetherill Mesa, all the major cliff dwellings, and Morefield ranger station are open only from Memorial Day through Labor Day. Far View visitor center, Far View Lodge, and Morefield Campground are open mid-April through mid-October.

Fees: Admission is $10 per vehicle for a seven-day permit. An annual permit is $20. Ranger-led tours of Cliff Palace, Long House, and Balcony House are $2.50 per person.

Getting Around: Public transportation is not available and off-road vehicles are prohibited in the park. Most of the scenic drives at Mesa Verde involve steep grades and hairpin turns, particularly on Wetherill Mesa. Vehicles over 8,000 pounds or 25 ft are prohibited on this road. Towed vehicles are prohibited past Morefield Campground. Check the condition of your vehicle's brakes before driving the road to Wetherill Mesa. Roads may be closed due to fire or weather conditions. For the latest information, tune your radio to the Traveler's Information Station at 1610 AM, or call the ranger station at 970/529–4461.

Permits: Backcountry hiking and fishing are not permitted at Mesa Verde.

Public Telephones: Public telephones can be found at Morefield Campground and Morefield Village, Far View visitor center, Far View Lodge, Far View Terrace, Spruce Tree Terrace, park headquarters, and the Wetherill Mesa snack bar.

Rest Rooms: Public rest rooms may be found at Morefield Campground and Morefield Village, Far View visitor center, Far View Lodge, Far View Terrace, Spruce Tree Terrace, park headquarters, the Wetherill Mesa snack bar, Montezuma Valley Overlook, Cliff Palace, and Balcony House.

Accessibility: Steep cliffs, deep canyons, narrow trails, and hard-to-reach archeological sites mean accessibility is limited within Mesa Verde. Service dogs cannot be taken into Balcony House, Cliff Palace, or Long House because of ladders in those sites. None of these sites is accessible to those with mobility impairments. If you have heart or respiratory ailments, you may have trouble breathing in the thin air at 7,000 to 8,000 ft. Wheelchairs with wide rim wheels are recommended on trails, some of which do not meet legal grade requirements. For the hearing impaired, park videos are open captioned and TDD services are available (970/529–4633). Mesa Top Loop Road provides the most comprehensive and accessible view of all the archaeological sites.

Emergencies: To report a fire or call for aid, dial 911 or 970/529–4461. First-aid stations are located at Morefield Campground, Far View visitor center, and Wetherill Mesa.

MESA VERDE NATIONAL PARK

EXPLORING
ATTRACTIONS NEARBY
DINING
LODGING
CAMPING AND RV FACILITIES
SHOPPING
ESSENTIAL INFORMATION

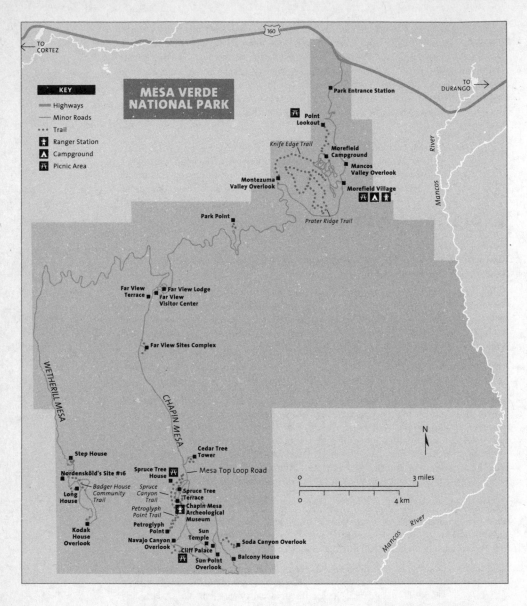

KEY

— Highways
— Minor Roads
••• Trail
🛉 Ranger Station
⛺ Campground
🎑 Picnic Area

MESA VERDE NATIONAL PARK

The security office is at park headquarters on Chapin Mesa, 5 mi south of the visitor center on Mesa Top Loop Road; the phone number is 970/529–4461, or call 911.

Lost and Found: The park's lost-and-found is at the **Chief Ranger's office** at park headquarters. | 5 mi south of visitor's center on Mesa Top Loop Rd. | 970/529–4469.

Good Tours

MESA VERDE IN ONE DAY

For a full experience of Mesa Verde, take at least one ranger-led tour of a major cliff dwelling site, as well as a few self-guided walks. Arrive early; it takes about 45 minutes to reach Far View visitor center from the park entrance.

Start your day at Far View visitor center, where you can pick up park information and purchase tickets for Cliff Palace or Balcony House tours on Chapin Mesa. If it's going to be a hot day, you might want to take an early morning or late-afternoon tour. Drive to the **Chapin Mesa Museum** to learn about the area and its history. Just behind the museum, 0.5-mi-long **Spruce Tree House trail** leads to the best preserved cliff dwelling in the park. Then drive to Balcony House for a ranger-led tour.

Have lunch at the Spruce Tree House cafeteria or the Cliff Palace picnic area. After lunch, take the ranger-led tour of **Cliff Palace.** Use the rest of the day to explore the overlooks and trails off the two 6-mi loops of **Mesa Top Loop Road.** Take **Petroglyph Point Trail** to see Mesa Verde's well-preserved collection of rock carvings. A leisurely walk along the mesa top's **Point Lookout Trail** will give provide you with beautiful bird's-eye views of the canyon below. Be sure to stop and see the view from **Park Point** on the drive back to the entrance.

If possible, stay in the area for at least one night. The view of the sunrise, sunset, and starry night sky here are rarely matched from any other point on Earth.

MESA VERDE IN TWO DAYS

With two days to spend at Mesa Verde, your second day should be devoted to **Wetherill Mesa,** weather permitting. Start early, pack a picnic lunch, then drive to Far View visitor center (45 minutes from the entrance) to purchase tickets for the ranger-led tour of Long House. The 12-mi drive from the visitor center to Wetherill Mesa is steep and filled with hairpin curves. Take your time and enjoy the view from any of the five turnouts. Once on the Wetherill Mesa, take the hour-long, ranger-led tour of **Long House,** then try the self-guided tour of **Step House.**

Around noon, eat your lunch at the Wetherill picnic area before a view of Wild Horse Canyon. After lunch, drive to the parking area for the **Badger House Community Trail.** Plan to take about two hours to wander through the Badger House community, which consists of several stops along a level, pleasant trail through the woods. You should head out around 3:30 and be prepared to exit Wetherill Mesa when the road closes at 4:30. If you haven't already seen it, stop at **Park Point,** off the main park road, for an incredible view of the Four Corners area.

Attractions

PROGRAMS AND TOURS

ARAMARK. The park concessionaire provides all-day and half-day guided tours of the Mesa Top Loop Road sites from mid-April through mid-October. The tours depart in vans or buses from Morefield Campground and Far View Lodge. Guides lead discussions about the history, geology, and excavation process in Mesa Verde. At the major cliff dwellings, rangers take over the tour. | ARAMARK Mesa Verde, Box 277, Mancos, CO 81328 | 970/533–1944 or 800/449–2288 | fax 970/533–7831 | www.visitmesaverde.com | $35–$60 | mid-Apr.–mid-Oct., daily.

The **Balcony House Half-Day Tour** focuses on the last 100 years that the Ancestral Puebloans lived in the park. Guides talk about how the pueblos were built. You can stop at Sun Point Pueblo, Sun Temple, Square House Tower, and the Twin Trees site. Rangers take over the tour in Balcony House. The tour costs $36 and includes admission to the dwellings. Depart Far View Lodge at 1 PM and return at 4 PM.

Take the **Cliff Palace All-Day Tour** for a guided visit of the archaeological museum, the Puebloan structures along Mesa Top Loop Road, and Spruce Tree House, ending at the museum. At Cliff Palace the tour is ranger-led. Depart Morefield Campground at 9 and Far View Lodge at 9:30, and return around 5 PM. The $55 ticket includes lunch and admission into dwellings.

Learn about the first 600 years the Ancestral Puebloans lived in the park during the **Spruce Tree Half-Day Tour,** which takes you to the Mesa Top Loop Road sites and through

MESA VERDE
NATIONAL PARK

EXPLORING
ATTRACTIONS NEARBY
DINING
LODGING
CAMPING AND RV
FACILITIES
SHOPPING
ESSENTIAL
INFORMATION

If you've got kids, don't miss a tour of Balcony House. Youngsters especially love climbing the ladders, crawling through the tunnels, and clambering around the nooks and crannies of this cliff dwelling.

Spruce Tree House. The tour costs $34. Depart from Morefield Campground at 8:30 and Far View Lodge at 9, and return at noon.

Cliff Palace/Sun Temple Talks. Interpretive talks on park-related subjects are held twice daily at Cliff Palace Overlook near the Sun Temple parking area. | Cliff Palace Overlook, Mesa Top Loop Rd. | 970/529–4465 | Memorial Day–Labor Day, daily 10–10:30, 4–4:30.

Evening Ranger Campfire Program. A park ranger presents a different 45-minute program or slide presentation each night of the week. | Morefield Campground Amphitheatre, 4 mi south of the park entrance | 970/529–4465 | Memorial Day–Labor Day, daily 9–9:45.

Far View Sites Walk. A free, one-hour, ranger-led walk through the Far View sites and pueblo dwellings takes place every afternoon at 4 PM from Memorial Day through Labor Day. | Far View Complex, 1.5 mi south of the visitor center | 970/529–4465.

Junior Ranger Program. Children ages 4–12 can earn a certificate and badge for successfully completing a two-page questionnaire about the park. | Far View visitor center or Chapin Mesa Museum | 970/529–4465.

★ **"Mesa Verde—Legacy of Stone and Spirit."** This 25-minute film is shown daily every half hour in the museum's auditorium. | Chapin Mesa Museum | 970/529–4465.

Ranger-Led Tours. Balcony House, Cliff Palace, and Long House can only be explored on a ranger-led tour, each of which lasts about an hour. Buy tickets for these at Far View visitor center on the day of the tour, or at the Morefield Campground Ranger Station on the evening before the tour, between 5 PM and 8:30 PM. Tours take place from mid-April through mid-October. | 970/529–4465 | $2.50 per tour.

SCENIC DRIVES

Park Entrance Road. The main park road leads you from the entrance to Far View visitor center, on 15 mi of switchbacks, which reveal far-ranging vistas of the surrounding areas. You can stop at a couple of pretty overlooks along the way, but hold out for Park Point, which, at the mesa's highest elevation (8,572 ft), affords unobstructed 360-degree views.

Mesa Top Loop Road. This 12-mi drive skirts the scenic rim of Chapin Mesa, reaching several of Mesa Verde's most important archaeological sites, including Square Tower House and Sun Temple. Two of the parks' most impressive viewpoints are also on this road: Navajo Canyon Overlook and Sun Point Overlook, from which you can see Cliff Palace, Sunset House, and other dwellings built into the rock face opposite. The road is open daily 8 AM to sunset.

Wetherill Mesa Road. The 12-mi mountain road has sharp curves and steep grades. Roadside pull-outs offer unobstructed views of the Four Corners region. The two cliff dwellings open to the public here are Step House and Long House. The Basketmaker pithouses open to the public are in the Badger House community. The road is open from Memorial Day through Labor Day, daily 8–4:30.

SIGHTS TO SEE

Badger House Community. A self-guided walk takes you through a group of subterranean dwellings, called pithouses, and above-ground storage rooms. The community dates back to AD 650, the Basketmaker Period, and covers seven acres of land. Most of the pithouses and kivas—religious or ceremonial rooms—were connected by an intricate system of tunnels, some up to 41 ft long. Allow about an hour to see all the sites. | 12 mi from the visitor center on Wetherill Mesa Rd. | Memorial Day–Labor Day, 8–4:30.

★ **Balcony House.** The stonework of this 40-room cliff dwelling, which housed about 40 or 50 people, is impressive, but you're likely to be even more awed by the skill it took to reach this place. Perched in a sandstone cove 600 ft above the floor of Soda Canyon, Balcony House seems almost suspended in space. Even with the aid of modern steps and a partially paved trail, today's visitors must climb two wooden ladders (the first one 32 ft high) to enter. Surrounding the house are a courtyard with a parapet wall and the intact balcony for which the house is named. The site is only accessible on a ranger-led tour. Purchase your ticket at the visitor center. | 8.5 mi southeast of the visitor center on Cliff Palace Loop Rd. | $2.50 | Late-May–mid-Oct, daily 9–5.

Cedar Tree Tower. A self-guided tour takes you to, but not through, a tower and kiva built between 1100 and 1300 and connected by a tunnel. There are a few other tower-and-kiva combinations in the park—they are thought to have been either religious structures or signal towers. | 4 mi south of the visitor center on the park entrance road. | Daily 8 AM–sunset.

★**Chapin Mesa Archeological Museum.** The museum tells the entire story of the cliff-dwelling people and gives as complete an understanding as possible of the Basketmaker and Ancestral Puebloan cultures through detailed dioramas and exhibits, including original textiles, sandals, and kiva jars. A separate hands-on room is for children. | 5 mi south of the visitor center on the park entrance road. | 970/529–4465 | Free | Apr.–mid-Oct., daily 8–6:30; mid-Oct.–Mar., daily 8–5.

★**Cliff Palace.** This was the first major Mesa Verde dwelling seen by cowboys Charlie Mason and Richard Wetherill in 1888. It is also the largest, containing about 150 rooms and 23 kivas on three levels. Getting there involves a steep downhill hike and four ladders. Purchase tickets at the visitor center for the one-hour, ranger-led tour through this dwelling. | 7 mi south of the visitor center on Cliff Palace Loop Rd. | $2.50 | Mid-May–mid-Oct., daily 9–5.

Far View Sites Complex. This is believed to have been one of the most densely populated areas in Mesa Verde, comprising as many as 50 villages in a 0.5-square-mi area at the top of Chapin Mesa. Most of the sites here were built between AD 900 and 1300, though occupation is thought to have gone back even earlier. Begin the self-guided tour at the interpretive panels in the parking lot, then proceed down a 0.5-mi, level trail. The ranger-led Far View Sites Walk takes place daily at 4. | 1.5 mi south of the visitor center on the park entrance road | Mid-May–mid-Oct., daily 8–6:30.

★**Far View Visitor Center.** Buy tickets for the Cliff Palace, Balcony House, and Long House ranger-led tours here. An extensive selection of books and videos on the history of the park are also for sale. Rangers are on hand to answer questions and explain the history of the ancestral Puebloans. | 15 mi south of the park entrance | 970/529–5036 | Mid-May–mid-Oct., daily 8–6:30; mid-Oct.–mid-May, daily 9–5.

Kodak House Overlook. Get a very impressive view into Kodak House and its several small kivas at this viewpoint. The house was so named when Swedish researcher absentmindedly left his Kodak cameras behind here in 1891. This is the closest you'll get to Kodak House, which is closed to the public. | 12 mi from the visitor center on Wetherill Mesa Rd.

Long House. Excavated in 1959 through 1961, this Wetherill Mesa cliff dwelling is the second largest in Mesa Verde. It is believed that about 150 people lived in Long House, so named because of the size of its cliff alcove. The spring at the back of the cave is still active today. The ranger-led tour begins a short distance from the parking lot and takes about 45 minutes. | 12 mi from the visitor center on Wetherill Mesa Rd. | $2.50 | Memorial Day–Labor Day, daily 10–4.

Morefield Campground Ranger Station. Tickets for the ranger-led tours of Cliff Palace, Balcony House, and Long House may be purchased here Memorial Day through Labor Day, daily from 5 PM to 8:30 PM. You can also stop here for information about the park and to buy books in the small bookstore. | 4 mi south of the park entrance | Memorial Day–Labor Day, 5 8:30 PM.

Navajo Canyon Overlook. Interpretive panels at this viewpoint explain how the geology and terrain of the canyons and cliffs of Mesa Verde made possible the construction of the cliff dwellings. | 12 mi south of the visitor center on Mesa Top Loop Rd.

MESA VERDE
NATIONAL PARK

EXPLORING
ATTRACTIONS NEARBY
DINING
LODGING
CAMPING AND RV
FACILITIES
SHOPPING
ESSENTIAL
INFORMATION

Anthills contribute an important ingredient in the pottery that vastly improved the Basketmaker standard of living. Pueblo potters, as did their ancestors, collect the small pebbles from the ants' nests to grind up and use as temper, the material added to clay to prevent the vessels from cracking as they dry.

Nordensköld's Site #16. This site, named after the Swedish scientist who discovered it in 1891, is easily accessible on foot and continues to reveal pottery and other artifacts. | 15 mi from the visitor center on Wetherill Mesa Rd.

Park Point Fire Lookout. This viewpoint, the highest in the park, presents spectacular views of the mesas and the Fours Corners region. Shiprock, New Mexico, lies 32 mi to the south, and Colorado's Ute Mountain is 13 mi west to the west. On the clearest days, you can see Utah's Manti-LaSal Mountains 110 mi to the northwest. | 10 mi south of the park entrance | Daily 8 AM–sunset.

Soda Canyon Overlook. This is the place to get the best view of Balcony House. Interpretive panels explain details of the house and the geology of the canyon below. | 9 mi south of the visitor center on Mesa Top Loop Rd.

Spruce Tree House. The best-preserved site in the park, this dwelling contains 114 living rooms and eight kivas. It's the only dwelling where you can actually enter a kiva, via a short ladder, just as the original inhabitants did. Although the tour through it is self-guided, there's always a park ranger on site to answer questions. The trail starts behind the museum and descends 170 ft—you'll find yourself puffing on the way back up, but it's worth the effort. | 5 mi south of the visitor center on the park entrance road. | Mar.–Nov., daily 9–5.

Step House. So-named because of a crumbling prehistoric stairway leading up from the dwelling, Step House is reached via a paved, though steep, trail. The house is one of the least visited dwellings in the park. | 12 mi from the visitor center on Wetherill Mesa Rd. | Memorial Day–Labor Day, daily 8–4:30.

Sun Point Overlook. You can see 12 different dwellings from this overlook on the edge of Chapin Mesa. Interpretive panels explain the details of the canyon and various dwellings. | 12 mi south of the visitor center on Mesa Top Loop Rd.

Sun Temple. Although researchers assume it was probably a ceremonial structure, they are unsure of the purpose of this complex with no doors or windows in most of its chambers. Because the building was not quite half finished when it was left in 1276, some researchers surmise it might have been constructed to stave off whatever disaster caused its builders to leave. | 8 mi south of the visitor center on Cliff Palace Loop Rd. | Daily 8 AM–sunset.

Triple Village Pueblo Sites. Three dwellings built atop each other from AD 750 to 1150 at first look like a mass of jumbled walls, but an interpretive panel helps identify the dwellings. The 325-ft trail from the walking area is paved and wheelchair accessible. | 8 mi south of the visitor center on Mesa Top Loop Rd.

Sports and Outdoor Activities

BIRD-WATCHING

You can see turkey vultures between April and October, large flocks of ravens hang around all summer, and ducks and waterfowl fly through from mid-September through mid-October. Among the park's other large birds, mostly found on the northern escarpments of each mesa, are red-tailed hawks, great-horned owls, and a few golden eagles. The dark-blue Steller's jay frequently pierces the pinyon-juniper forest with its cries, and hummingbirds dart from flower to flower. Ask for a checklist of the park's birds, including about 200 species, at the museum desk.

HIKING

No backcountry hiking is permitted in Mesa Verde due to the fragile nature of the ancient dwellings and artifacts. However, several trails lead beyond the park's most-visited sites.

Knife Edge Trail. Take this trail for an easy 2-mi (round-trip) walk around the north rim of the park. If you stop at all the flora identification points that the trail guide pamphlet suggests, the hike should take about 1½ to 2 hours. The patches of asphalt you're likely to spot along the way are leftovers from Knife Edge Road, built in 1914 as the main entryway into the park.

★ **Petroglyph Point Trail.** The highlight of this 2.8-mi loop is the largest and best-known group of petroglyphs in Mesa Verde. Since the trail offshoots from Spruce Tree House Trail, it is only accessible when Spruce Tree House is open, March through November, daily 9–5.

Point Lookout Trail. This curvy, 2.3-mi trail meanders along the top of Chapin Mesa and brings you to beautiful vistas of the Mancos and Montezuma valleys.

Prater Ridge Trail. This loop, which starts and finishes at Morefield Campground, is the longest hike (7.8 mi round-trip) you can take inside the park and affords fine views of Morefield Canyon to the south and the San Juan Mountains to the north.

Soda Canyon Overlook Trail. One of the easiest and most rewarding strolls in the park, this little trail travels 1.5 mi round-trip through the forest on almost completely level ground. The overlook is an excellent point from which to photograph the cliff dwellings. The trailhead is about 0.25 mi past the Balcony House parking area.

Spruce Canyon Trail. If you want to venture down into the canyon, this is your trail. It's only 2 mi long, but you can go down about 600 ft in elevation.

SKIING

The Cliff Palace Loop Road is closed to automobile traffic in winter, but it's open for ski-touring when there's enough snow. Along this easy 6-mi loop through pinyon pine and juniper forest are several overlooks of the cliff dwellings. There are also 3 mi of beginner's trails starting in Morefield Campground. Contact the park ranger's office at 970/529–4461 for permission and conditions.

STARGAZING

Since there are no large cities in the Four Corners region, there is very little artificial light to detract from the stars in the night sky. Some of the best locations in the park for stargazing are Far View Lodge, Morefield Campground, and the Montezuma, Park Point, and Mancos Scenic Overlooks.

Attractions Nearby

★ **Anasazi Heritage Center.** More than 3 million Native American artifacts, including beautiful pottery, ornaments, and tools, were excavated from sites all over the Four Corners region and are preserved and exhibited in this state-of-the-art museum. A hands-on tour gives you the chance to grind corn, weave on a loom, and wander through a replica of an ancestral Puebloan dwelling. | 27501 Rte. 184, Dolores, 81323 | 970/882–4811 | www.co.blm.gov/ahc | $3; free Nov.–Feb. | Mar.–Oct., daily 9–5; Nov.–Feb., daily 9–4.

★ **Cortez Cultural Center.** Exhibits focus on regional artists and artisans, the Ute Mountain branch of the Ute tribe, and various periods of ancestral Puebloan culture. Summer evening programs include Native American dances, sandpainting, rug weaving, pottery-making demonstrations, and storytelling events. The adjacent park contains an authentic Navajo hogan and Ute tepee. | 25 N. Market St., Cortez, 81321 | 970/565–1151 | www.cortezculturalcenter.org | Free | June–Aug., weekdays 10–9, Sat. 1–9; May and Sept., Mon.–Sat. 10–6; Oct.–Apr., weekdays 10–5.

Crow Canyon Archaeological Center. A one-day archaeology program explains the excavation process and the ancestral Puebloan culture through a hands-on laboratory tour and a visit to a current excavation site, with lunch included. The week-long excavation program requires reservations. | 23390 Rd. K, Cortez, 81321 | 970/565–8975 or 800/422–8975 | www.crowcanyon.org | $50 per day, $900 per week | Mar.–Oct.

MESA VERDE
NATIONAL PARK

EXPLORING
ATTRACTIONS
NEARBY
DINING
LODGING
CAMPING AND RV
FACILITIES
SHOPPING
ESSENTIAL
INFORMATION

★ **Durango and Silverton Narrow Gauge Railroad.** In service since 1882, this train still makes its daily 3½-hour runs between Silverton and Durango along a spectacularly scenic mountain route. Travel in comfort in restored 1882 parlor cars, or ride in the open-air gondolas. Listen to the train's shrill whistle as the locomotive chugs along the Animas River Valley and, at times, clings precariously to the hillside. Advance reservations required. | 479 Main Ave., Durango | 970/247–2733 | www.durangotrain.com | $60–$100 round-trip | Mid-May–Oct. several trips daily; late Nov.–early May 1 trip daily; closed other times.

Four Corners Monument. A stone slab marks the only spot where four states—Colorado, Arizona, Utah, and New Mexico—meet. This is photo-op country. Snacks and souvenirs, as well as American Indian arts and crafts, are sold on site, but otherwise there is nothing but desert for miles around. To get here, travel south from Cortez on U.S. 160 for about 40 mi. You can't miss the signs. | U.S. 160 | $3 per vehicle | Daily 8–6.

McPhee Reservoir. The second-largest lake in Colorado provides some of the state's best boating, waterskiing, and fishing—minus the crowds. To date, McPhee Reservoir has been stocked with 4½ million fish. The marina is 8 mi north of Dolores. | Rte. 184, Dolores | 970/882–7296 | Free | Daily 7–9; closed in winter.

★ **Trimble Hot Springs.** This is a great place to soak achy muscles, especially if you've been doing some hiking. In addition to an Olympic-size pool and two therapy pools, there's a spa and a picnic area. Don't worry if you've forgotten your towel or swimsuit—both are for rent here. | Rte. 203, off U.S. 550, 7 mi north of Durango | 970/247–0111 | www.trimblehotsprings.com | $9 | Mid-May–mid-Oct., daily 8 AM–11 PM, mid-Oct.–mid-May, Tues.–Fri. 9 AM–8:30 PM.

Ute Mountain Tribal Park. Part of the Ute Mountain Indian Reservation, this large archaeological site has been set aside to preserve ancestral Puebloan dwellings, including many cliff dwellings marked by wall paintings and petroglyphs. Entry is by reservation only, and primitive camping trips are also available. Tours begin at the Ute Mountain Tribal Complex. | U.S. 160 at U.S. 491, Towaoc | 970/565–9653 or 800/847–5485 | www.utemountainute.com | $18 for ½-day tour, $30 for full-day tour | Apr.–Oct.

Dining

In Mesa Verde

Far View Terrace. American/Casual. This full-service cafeteria offers great views, plentiful choices, and reasonable prices. Fluffy blueberry pancakes are often on the breakfast menu. Dinner options might include a Navajo taco piled high with all the fixings. Daily specials are offered. Don't miss the creamy malts and homemade fudge, and stop at the espresso bar for a shot that will keep you going while you sightsee. | Across from the visitor center on Mesa Top Loop Rd. | 970/529–4444 | $4–$8 | D, MC, V | Closed late Oct.–early Apr.

Knife's Edge Cafe. Café. Though it's in the Morefield Campground, the café is open to all visitors. An all-you-can-eat pancake breakfast is served every morning from 7:30 to 10, and at night there's an all-you-can-eat barbecue dinner from 5 to 8. | 4 mi south of the park entrance | 970/565–2133 | $4–$7 | AE, D, MC, V | Closed Labor Day–Memorial Day. No lunch.

★ **Metate Room.** American. Tables in this southwestern-style dining room are candlelit and cloth-covered, but the atmosphere remains casual. A wall of windows affords wonderful Mesa Verde vistas. The menu includes American staples like steak and seafood, but game meats such as quail, venison, and rabbit occasionally appear as well. For appetizers, try Anasazi beans and Mesa bread. | Far View Lodge, across from the visitor center | 970/529–4421 | $17–$20 | AE, D, DC, MC, V | Closed late-Oct.–early Apr. No lunch.

Picnic Areas. There are four picnic areas in the park.

The **Cliff Palace Picnic Area** has four wooden tables under shade trees and rest rooms, but no running water. | 7 mi south of the visitor center.

★   The **Park Headquarters Loop Picnic Area** is the nicest and largest in the park. It has 40 tables under shade trees and a great view into Spruce Canyon, as well as flush toilets and running water. | 6 mi south of the visitor center.

There are only two tables in the tiny **Montezuma Valley Overlook Picnic Area,** 5 mi west of the park entrance.

Ten tables placed under lush shade trees, along with drinking water and rest rooms, make the **Wetherill Mesa Picnic Area** a very pleasant spot for lunch. | 12 mi southwest of the visitor center.

Spruce Tree Terrace. American/Casual. A limited selection of hot food and sandwiches is all you'll find at this cafeteria, but the patio is pleasant, and since it's across the street from the museum, it's convenient. The Terrace is also the only food concession open year-round. | 5 mi south of the visitor center on the park entrance road. | 970/529–4521 | $3–$8 | AE, D, DC, MC, V | No dinner Dec.–Feb.

Wetherill Mesa Snack Bar. American/Casual. There isn't much of an offering here, just chips, soft drinks, and pre-packaged sandwiches served on picnic tables under an awning, but it's the only choice on Wetherill Mesa. | 12 mi southwest of the park entrance | $4–$6 | No credit cards | Closed Labor Day–Memorial Day.

Near the Park

★ **Bar-D Chuckwagon and Dinner Show.** Barbecue. Take in barbecued beef, beans, and biscuits along with an earful of the Bar-D Wranglers western singing group, which performs every night at 7:30, rain or shine. | 8080 County Rd. 250, Durango | 970/247–5753 or 888/800–5753 | www.bardchuckwagon.com | $16–$19 | MC, V | Closed Labor Day–Memorial Day.

Carver's Brewing Company. Southwestern. This local microbrewery has a coffeehouse and bakery up front, and a hopping sports bar and patio in the back. There are about eight original beers on tap at any given time. Try the fajitas or the homemade bread bowls filled with soup or salad. There's open-air dining with live music on Thursday and Saturday. Breakfast is also served and a kids' menu is available. | 1022 Main Ave., Durango | 970/259–2545 | $11–$25 | AE, D, MC, V.

German Stone Oven Restaurant Bakery. German. This restaurant and bakery serves authentic German fare, as well as a few American and vegetarian dishes. Favorite menu items include Wiener schnitzel, sauerbraten, sirloin steak, pork chops, and imported beer. The dining room is filled with antiques and collectibles from Germany, France, and Italy; you can also eat on the garden patio. Not recommended for children. | 811 Railroad Ave., Dolores | 970/882–7033 | $11–$16 | MC, V | Closed Tues., Wed. and Jan.–Apr.

★ **Millwood Junction.** American. This rambling restaurant, made out of wood from seven local barns, has everything you'd want for a fun night out: good drinks, good food, and, on summer weekends, top-notch entertainment. An excellent Friday-night seafood buffet (all you can eat for $13.95) draws folks from four states. | U.S. 160 at Main, Mancos | 970/533–7338 | $15–$19 | AE, DC, MC, V | No lunch Sept.–Apr.

Olde Tymer's Café. American/Casual. Locals flock to this former drugstore for the hamburgers, and to bask in the feel of days gone by. The tin ceiling, artifacts, and photos that cover the walls combine to give it the appearance of a 1920s dance hall. | 1000 Main Ave., Durango | 970/259–2990 | $6–$9 | AE, MC, V.

Red Snapper. Seafood. It takes more than 200 gallons of saltwater to fill the aquariums in this lively restaurant housed in one of the town's older buildings. On the menu: oysters Durango, with jack cheese and salsa. They also have a salad bar and kids' menu. No smoking. | 144 E. 9th St., Durango | 970/259–3417 | $12–$28 | AE, D, MC, V | No lunch.

Lodging

In Mesa Verde

Far View Lodge. All rooms in the park lodge have a private balcony with terrific views of Arizona, Utah, and New Mexico in the distance. Otherwise, quarters are motel-style and basic, with a southwestern touch. Talks with guest speakers on various park topics, and multimedia shows on the ancestral Puebloans, are held nightly. Restaurant. Some refrigerators. Bar. Shop. Laundry facilities. Some pets allowed. No smoking. | Across from the visitor center, 15 mi southwest of the park entrance. Reservations: ARAMARK Mesa Verde, Box 277, Mancos, 81328 | 970/529–4421 or 800/449–2288 | fax 970/529–4411 | 150 rooms | $96–$106 | AE, D, DC, MC, V | Closed mid-Oct.–mid-Apr.

Near the Park

Anasazi Motor Inn. This is definitely the nicest hotel in downtown Cortez, mostly because its air-conditioned rooms are spacious, carpeted, and pleasantly decorated with furniture in southwestern colors. Outside, you'll find horseshoe and volleyball pits. Restaurant. In-room data ports. Cable TV, some in-room VCRs. Pool. Hot tub. Bar. Shop. Business services. Airport shuttle. Some pets allowed. | 640 S. Broadway, Cortez, 81321 | 970/565–3773, 800/972–6232 outside CO | fax 970/565–1027 | 87 rooms | $57–$71 | AE, D, DC, MC, V.

Apple Orchard Inn. This farmhouse is in a 4.5-acre apple orchard tucked into the lush Animas Valley 8 mi north of Durango. Six cottages surround a flower-bedecked pond, complete with friendly geese. Cherry-wood antiques, feather beds, and handcrafted armoires furnish the handsome rooms. Dining room, picnic area. Refrigerators. Some in-room VCRs. No smoking. | 7758 Rte. 203, Durango, 81302 | 970/247–0751 or 800/426–0751 | www.appleorchardinn.com | 4 rooms, 6 cottages | $135–$150, $160–$195 cottages | AE, D, MC, V.

Gable House. This 1892 Queen Anne bed-and-breakfast is on the state and national registers of historic places. Each room is furnished with antiques and has a separate entrance. The neighborhood is quiet and green, and downtown Durango is five blocks away. Laundry facilities. No kids under 10. | 805 E. 5th Ave., Durango, 81320 | 970/247–4982 | www.durangobedandbreakfast.com | 3 rooms | $85–$185 | MC, V.

★ **General Palmer Hotel.** This bed-and-breakfast is in a restored Victorian building next door to the Durango and Silverton Narrow Gauge Depot. Each room is meticulously decorated with antiques and comes with a teddy bear on the bed. In-room data ports, some in-room hot tubs, some minibars, some refrigerators. Cable TV. Laundry service. No smoking. | 567 Main Ave., Durango, 81320 | 970/247–4747 or 800/523–3358 | fax 970/247–1332 | www.generalpalmerhotel.com | 39 rooms | $98–$275 | AE, D, DC, MC, V.

Jarvis Suite Hotel. This former theater in the center of downtown Durango became a hotel in 1984, about a century after its curtain first went up. It's loaded with western relics like antique furniture and wagon-wheel light fixtures. In-room data ports, kitchens, microwaves. Cable TV, some in-room VCRs. Laundry facilities. Business services. | 125 W. 10th St., Durango, 81320 | 970/259–6190 or 800/824–1024 | fax 970/259–6190 | www.durangohotel.com | 21 suites | $94–$174 suites | AE, D, DC, MC, V.

Lightner Creek Inn. An elk preserve and a bird sanctuary flank this 1903 homestead, 3 mi west of Durango. Each room or suite is cheerfully and differently decorated with flowered wallpaper, wood furniture, and down duvets or quilts. In-room data ports, some in-room hot tubs. Business services. No a/c. No room TVs. No smoking. | 999 Rte. 207, Durango, 81320 | 970/259–1226 or 800/268–9804 | fax 970/259–9526 | www.lightnercreekinn.com | 10 rooms | $85–$205 | AE, D, DC, MC, V.

★ **Logwood Bed-and-Breakfast.** This large, cedar-log building on the Animas River is 12 mi north of Durango. Each room has a hand-made, log bed and beautiful views of the Needle Mountains and the Animas River Valley. No TV in some rooms. No smoking. | 35060

U.S. 550 N, Durango, 81320 | 970/259–4396 or 800/369–4082 | fax 970/259–9670 | www.durango-logwoodinn.com | 7 rooms | $100–$150 | AE, MC, V.

National 9 Inn–Sand Canyon. The true gem in this basic, locally owned motel with simple rooms is its adjacent casual-Italian restaurant. Downtown Cortez is three blocks away. Restaurant. In-room data ports, some microwaves. Cable TV. Outdoor pool. Bar. Laundry facilities. | 301 W. Main St., Cortez, 81321 | 970/565–8562 or 800/524–9999 | fax 970/565–0125 | www.sandcanyon.com | 28 rooms | $40–$69 | AE, D, MC, V.

★ **New Rochester Hotel.** The rooms in this small, 19th-century hotel are decorated in an Old West style and named after some of the many Hollywood films that were made in Durango. Framed movie posters, mismatched furniture, wagon-wheel chandeliers, and restored, original features make for a chic but funky interior. Some kitchenettes, refrigerators. Cable TV, some in-room VCRs. Business services. Some pets allowed (fee). No smoking. | 726 E. 2nd Ave., Durango, 81301 | 970/385–1920 or 800/664–1920 | fax 970/385–1967 | www.rochesterhotel.com | 11 rooms, 1 suite | $139–$209 | AE, D, DC, MC, V.

Strater Hotel. This Victorian beauty opened in 1887 and has been lovingly restored with crystal chandeliers, beveled windows, original oak beams, flocked wallpaper, and plush velour curtains. Restaurant. In-room data ports. Cable TV. Hot tub. Bar. Business services. | 699 Main Ave., Durango, 81301 | 970/247–4431 or 800/247–4431 | fax 970/259–2208 | www.strater.com | 93 rooms | $139–$209 | AE, D, DC, MC, V.

Camping and RV Facilities

In Mesa Verde

★ **Morefield Campground.** With more than 400 shaded campsites, access to trailheads, and plenty of amenities, the only campground in the park is an appealing mini-city for campers. Reservations are accepted only for tent and group sites. Flush toilets. Partial hook-ups, dump station. Drinking water, guest laundry, showers. Fire grates, grills, picnic tables, food service. Electricity, public telephone. General store, service station, ranger station. | 435 sites, 15 with hook-ups | 4 mi south of the park entrance, Box 8, Mesa Verde, 81330–0008 | 970/533–1944 or 800/449–2288 | fax 970/533–7831 | www.visitmesaverde.com | $19–$25 | AE, D, DC, MC, V | Late-Apr.–mid-Oct.

Near the Park

A-and-A Mesa Verde RV Park and Campground. This 30-acre lot, directly across the highway from Mesa Verde National Park, has all the facilities of a hotel. There's a modern bath house, recreation room, miniature golf course, sports field, a pool and hot tub, and a kennel. You can even camp in a log cabin. Flush toilets. Full hook-ups, dump station. Drinking water, guest laundry, showers. Fire grates, grills, picnic tables. Electricity, public telephone. General store. Play area, swimming (pool). | 72 sites, 45 with hook-ups; 4 cabins | 34979 U.S. 160, Mancos, 81328 | 800/972–6620 or 970/565–3517 | fax 970/565–7141 | www.mesaverdecamping.com | $21–$35 | D, MC, V.

Mesa Verde RV Resort. For a full-service campground geared toward accommodating RVs, stop about a half-mile east of the national park's entrance. The resort has several pull-through shaded sites, a gift shop with southwestern art, and indoor and outdoor hot tubs. Flush toilets. Full hook-ups, dump station. Drinking water, guest laundry, showers. Picnic tables. Electricity. General store. Swimming (pool). | 43 sites, 21 with hook-ups | 970/533–7421 or 800/776–7421 | 35303 U.S. 160, Mancos, 81328 | www.mesaverdervresort.com | $20–$28 | MC, V.

San Juan National Forest Campgrounds. More than 1,000 sites in three dozen campgrounds are scattered across the 2 million acres of this national forest. | Forest Service, 15 Burnett Court, Durango, 81301 | 970/882–2346 or 970/247–4874 | www.fs.fed.us/r2/sanjuan.

The largest and best-equipped campground in the forest is **McPhee Campground,** which is surrounded by paved roads and has several wheelchair-accessible sites. It's at an

MESA VERDE
NATIONAL PARK

EXPLORING
ATTRACTIONS NEARBY
DINING
LODGING
**CAMPING AND RV
FACILITIES**
SHOPPING
ESSENTIAL
INFORMATION

altitude of about 7,400 ft, and many of the sites overlook McPhee Reservoir below. Take Route 184 south 7 mi from Dolores to Country Road 25, then turn north to onto Forest Road 271. Flush toilets. Partial hook-ups (electric and water), dump station. Drinking water, showers. Fire pits, grills, picnic tables. Electricity, public telephone. | 76 sites, 16 with hook-ups | Forest Rd. 271 | 970/882–2346 or 970/247–4874 | $12–$14 | Reservations essential | May–mid-Oct.

Shopping

Chapin Mesa Archeological Museum Shop. Books and videos are the primary offering here with more than 400 titles on ancestral Puebloan and southwestern topics. | 21 mi southwest the park entrance on Mesa Top Loop Rd. | 970/529–4465.

Far View Lodge Shop. This small shop provides a good selection of jewelry and upscale gifts reflecting the Native American culture of the area. | 15 mi south of the park entrance on the Mesa Top Loop Rd. | 970/529–4421 or 800/449–2288.

Far View Terrace Store. This is the largest gift shop in the park and has a wide selection gifts and toys for children, Native American art, a Christmas section, and T-shirts galore. | 15 mi south of the park entrance on Mesa Top Loop Rd. | 970/529–4421 or 800/449–2288.

Spruce Tree Terrace Shop. At this typical park gift shop, you'll find calendars, T-shirts, bumper stickers, and magnets as well as food and sundries. | 21 mi south of the park entrance on Mesa Top Loop Rd. | 970/529–4521.

Essential Information

ATMS: First National Bank | 178 E. Frontage Rd., Mancos | 970/533–7798.

AUTOMOBILE SERVICE STATION: Sinclair Service Station | Morefield Campground, 4 mi from the park entrance | 970/565–2407.

POST OFFICES: Mancos Post Office | 291 N. Walnut St., 81328 | 970/533–7754. **Mesa Verde National Park Post Office** | Park headquarters, Chapin Mesa, 81330 | 970/529–4554.

ZION NATIONAL PARK

SOUTHWESTERN UTAH

Route 9, 21 mi east of I–15 and 24 mi west of U.S. 89

Colored by platinum sunrises and magenta sunsets, towering 2,000-ft sandstone walls embrace you in Zion National Park. Here, rocks resemble cathedrals, temples, and courthouses. Trails through the sheltering canyon reveal delicate hanging gardens, serene hidden pools, and quiet, shady spots of solitude. So diverse is this place that 85% of Utah's flora and fauna species are found here. Some, like the tiny Zion snail, appear nowhere else in the world. There's truly no other place like Zion Canyon.

At the heart of Zion National Park is the Virgin River, a tributary of the Colorado River. This muddy little stream is responsible for carving the great canyon you see. It's hard to believe that such a small river made the great canyon of Zion—until you see it become a rumbling red torrent in spring runoff or during summer thunderstorms, when the noisy waters become thick with debris being carried away from the canyon toward the sea. If you're lucky, you'll be in Zion Canyon during such a moment. Waterfalls pour from the cliffs, clouds float through the canyon, and then the sun comes out and you know you are walking in one of the West's most loved and sacred places.

Most visitors to Zion experience only the main canyon, but there is much more to the park. The Kolob Canyons area, in the extreme northwestern section of the park, is considered by some to be the most beautiful part of Zion National Park. There's little evidence of this beauty from the entrance point off I–15, but once you negotiate the first switchback on the park road, you are hit with a vision of red rock cliffs shooting out of the earth. As you climb in elevation you are treated first to a journey through these canyons, then with a view into the chasm.

PUBLICATIONS

Towers of Stone by J.L. Crawford summarizes the essence of Zion National Park, its land-scape, plants, animals, and human history. *Zion National Park: Sanctuary In The Desert* by Nicky Leach gives you a photographic overview and a narrative journey through the park. Learn more about the geology of Zion in a small booklet, *An Introduction to the Geology of Zion*, by Al Warneke. The fascinating story of the construction of the mile-long Zion Tunnel in the 1920s is told in *The Zion Tunnel, From Slickrock to Switchback*, by Donald T. Garate. In wildflower season be sure to pick up a copy of *Wildflowers of Zion National Park*, by Dr. Stanley L. Welsh. Contact the Zion Natural History Association for all of these books and more. **Zion Natural History Association** | Zion National Park, Springdale, 84767 | 435/772–3264 | www.zionpark.org.

When to Visit

SCENERY AND WILDLIFE

The elegance of Zion Canyon is most apparent as the morning sun starts to light the canyon walls, or when the sunset brings out the brilliant colors of the rock. In the rainy months of March and September, you're likely to see waterfalls and fog, or low floating clouds that create a quiet, mysterious mood. In fall, the park explodes in autumn color as the leaves turn shocking yellow and orange. Winter can also be dramatic, with a dusting of snow and in-canyon clouds hugging the peaks. You are more likely to see wildlife in off-seasons because there's less human and vehicular traffic. But the introduction of the park shuttle has allowed some animals to return to the park's interior, so even in high season you can spot mule deer wandering in shady glens as you ride through the park, espe-cially in early morning and near dusk. The best opportunity for viewing wildlife is on the hiking trails. You'll see a large variety of lizards and you may be be surprised by a Gambel's quail. Mountain lion and ringtail cats prowl the park, but you're more likely to spot their tracks than the elusive animals themselves.

HIGH AND LOW SEASON

Zion is the most heavily visited national park in Utah, receiving nearly 2.5 million visi-tors each year. The lion's share of visitors come to the park between April and October, when upper Zion Canyon is accessed only by free shuttle bus to reduce traffic conges-tion. Summer in the park is hot and dry except for sudden cloudbursts, which can create flash flooding and spectacular waterfalls. You can expect afternoon thunderstorms between July and September. It never gets bitterly cold in this part of the state, so consider planning your visit for some time other than peak season. You can expect to encounter winter driving conditions November through March, and although most park programs are suspended, winter is truly a delicious time to see the canyons. During these months the shuttle does not operate. Zion Canyon Scenic Drive is open to private vehicles and the colorful rock may be dusted with a light snow.

Average High/Low Temperatures (°F) and Monthly Precipitation (in inches)

	JAN.	FEB.	MAR.	APR.	MAY	JUNE
ZION	52/29	57/31	63/36	73/43	83/52	93/60
	1.6	1.6	1.7	1.3	0.8	0.6

	JULY	AUG.	SEP.	OCT.	NOV.	DEC.
	100/68	97/66	91/60	78/49	63/37	53/30
	0.8	1.6	0.8	1.0	1.2	1.5

Note: Extreme highs in Zion can often exceed 100°F in July and August.

FESTIVALS AND SEASONAL EVENTS

S.P.R.I.N.G.

Mar.: **Hurricane Easter Car Show.** Classic cars from all over the West descend on Hurricane for this event, which attracts about 7,000 people each year. On Easter Sunday there's a slow Rod Run through Zion National Park. | 435/635–5720.

Apr.: **Dixie Downs Horse Races.** For more than 25 years, St. George Lions Club has hosted two spring weekends of horse racing to prepare horses for the larger tracks in summer. | 435/652–9067.

May: **Washington Cotton Festival.** Honoring southern Utah's cotton-growing heritage, St. George hosts beauty pageants, dutch oven cook-offs, and a firefighter competition. You'll have a cotton-pickin' good time. | 435/634–9850.

May–Sept.: **High Country Drag Races.** The High Country Raceway Association stages drag races at a derelict airport 10 mi south of St. George off River Rd. Afternoon races on Memorial Day weekend kick off the drag racing season. Every Saturday night in summer, street cars, dragsters, and other vehicles race under the lights. | 435/652–9560.

F.A.L.L.

Aug.: **Western Legends Roundup.** This nostalgic festival is for anyone with a love of cowboys, pioneer life, or Native American culture. For three days the small town of Kanab fills with cowboy poets and storytellers, musicians, western arts and crafts vendors, and Native American dancers and weavers. Wagonmaking, quilt shows, and a parade are all part of the fun. | 435/644–5033 or 800/733–5263.

Sept.: **Dixie Roundup.** Sponsored by the St. George Lions Club, the Dixie Roundup rodeo has been a tradition for decades. The real novelty of the professional event is that it's held on the green grass of Sun Bowl stadium. | 435/628–1658.

Nearby Towns

It's hard not to love **Springdale** when everywhere you look the views leave you breathless. In spite of growth, the town on the southern boundary of Zion National Park has kept much of its charm and beauty. There are a surprising number of wonderful places to stay and eat, and if you take the time to stroll the main drag, or make use of frequent shuttle stops, you'll find some great shops and galleries. On your way to Springdale, if you arrive in southwestern Utah via plane or are driving from Las Vegas, you'll probably pass through **St. George.** This city was founded in 1861, when Mormon leaders sent 300 families here to grow cotton. As a source of cotton, the area became known as "Utah's Dixie." The largest town in the area, St. George is known for its golf courses and its increasing popularity as a retirement community. It's about 43 mi west of Zion.

On Route 9 between St. George and Zion stands the small town of **Hurricane.** Pronounced "HUR-aken," this community on the Virgin River has experienced enormous growth, probably owing to the boom in nearby St. George. Hurricane is home to one of Utah's most scenic 18-hole golf courses. Continue past Hurricane and Zion along a stunning stretch of Route 9 to reach picturesque **Kanab,** which has played cameo roles in more than 100 movies and television shows. Today it's the gateway community for Grand Staircase-Escalante National Monument and is a great strategic base for exploring Zion, Bryce, and the Grand Canyon's North Rim.

Color Country Travel Region (Hurricane) | 906 N. 1400 West, Box 1550, St. George, 84770 | 800/233–8824 | www.colorcountry.org. **Kane County Travel Council (Kanab)** | 89 S. 100 East, Kanab, 84741 | 435/644–5033 or 800/733–5263 | www.visitsouthernutah.com. **St. George Chamber of Commerce** | 97 E. St. George Blvd., 84771 | 435/628–1658 | www.stgeorgechamber.com. **Washington County Travel and Convention Bureau (St. George)** | 1835 Convention Center Dr., St. George, 84770 | 800/869–6635. **Zion Canyon Visitors Bureau** | Box 331, Springdale, 84767 | 888/518–7070 | www.zionpark.com.

Exploring Zion

PARK BASICS

Contacts and Resources: Zion National Park | Springdale, 84767-1099 | 435/772–3256 | www.nps.gov/zion. **Kolob Canyons Visitor Center** | Exit 40 off I–15 | 435/586–9548.

Hours: The park is open daily year-round, 24 hours a day.

Fees: Entrance to Zion National Park is $20 per vehicle for a seven-day pass. People entering on foot or by bicycle or motorcycle pay $10 per person (not to exceed $20 per family) for a seven-day pass. Entrance to the Kolob Canyons section of the park costs only $10, and you receive credit for this entrance fee when you pay to enter Zion Canyon.

Getting Around: Zion's main park road, Zion Canyon Scenic Drive, is closed to private vehicles from April through October. However, the park's easy-to-use **shuttle system** makes visiting Zion Canyon a pleasure, and it's been remarkably successful. The park shuttle route starts at the visitor center, where the parking lot is typically full between 10 and 3 daily from May through September. To avoid parking hassles, leave your car in the town of Springdale and ride the free town shuttle to the park entrance. Town shuttle stops are at Eagles Nest, Driftwood Motel, Bit and Spur Restaurant, Zion Park Inn, Bumbleberry Inn, Pizza and Noodle Co., Watchman Cafe, Flanigan's Inn, and Zion Giant Screen Theater. From the theater you can walk across a small foot bridge to the visitor center and transfer to the park shuttle. The town and park shuttles are free, but you must pay the park entrance fee. Mid-May–mid-September the shuttles operate 5:30 AM–11:15 PM daily; April–mid-May and early September–October, they run 6:30 AM–10:15 PM daily. For more information on the shuttle system, call the park (435/772–3256) or visit the park Web site (www.nps.gov/zion). From November through March, private vehicles are allowed on Zion Canyon Scenic Drive.

If you enter or exit Zion via the East Entrance you will have the privilege of driving a gorgeous, twisting 24-mi stretch of the Zion–Mount Carmel Highway (Route 9). Two tunnels, including the highway's famous 1.1-mi tunnel, lie between the east park entrance and Zion Canyon. The tunnels are so narrow that vehicles more than 7'10" wide or 11'4" high require traffic control while passing through. Rangers, stationed at the tunnels 8–8 daily, April–October, stop oncoming traffic so you can drive down the middle of the tunnels. Large vehicles must pay an escort fee of $10 at either park entrance. West of the tunnels the highway meets Zion Canyon Scenic Drive at Canyon Junction, about 1 mi north of the visitor center.

Permits: Permits are required for backcountry camping and overnight climbs. The maximum size of a group hiking into the backcountry is 12 people. The cost for permits for 1–2 people is $10 per person; 3–6 people, $15 per person; 7–12 people, $20 per person. Permits and hiking information are available at the visitor center.

Public Telephones: Public telephones may be found at South Campground, Watchman Campground, Zion Canyon visitor center, Zion Lodge, and Zion Museum.

Rest Rooms: Public rest rooms are located at The Grotto, Kolob Canyons visitor center, Temple of Sinawava, Weeping Rock Trailhead, Zion Canyon visitor center, Zion Human History Museum, and Zion Lodge.

Accessibility: Both visitor centers, all shuttle buses, and Zion Lodge are fully accessible to wheelchairs. Several campsites (sites A24 and A25 at Watchman Campground and sites 103, 114, and 115 at South Campground) are reserved for people with disabilities, and two trails—Riverside Walk and Pa'rus Trail—are accessible with some assistance.

Emergencies: In the event of an emergency, dial 911, report to a visitor center, or contact a park ranger at 435/772–3322.

The nearest hospitals are in St. George, Cedar City, and Kanab. In summer the **Zion Canyon Medical Clinic** is open and accepts walk-in patients. | 120 Lion Blvd., Springdale | 435/772–3226 | Memorial Day–Sept., Mon.–Sat. 9–5.

Lost and Found: The park's lost-and-found is at the Zion Canyon visitor center.

Good Tours

ZION IN ONE DAY

A one-day visit to the park restricts you to Zion Canyon, but there's more than enough to enjoy here. Begin your day early with a stop at the **visitor center,** where outdoor exhibits inform you about the park's geology, wildlife, and history, and how to best enjoy the park. Catch the **shuttle** to head up into Zion Canyon. Make the **Zion Human History Museum** your first stop. You can watch a 22-minute orientation program on the park and visit the exhibits highlighting human occupation of the area. After reboarding the shuttle, travel to the **Court of the Patriarchs** viewpoint to take photos and walk the short path. Then pick up the next bus headed into the canyon. Stop at Zion Lodge and cross the road to the **Emerald Pools** trailhead, and take a hike.

Before reboarding the shuttle, stop at **Zion Lodge** for lunch in the snack shop or dining room and a browse through the gift shop. Take the shuttle to the **Weeping Rock** trailhead for a short, cool walk up to the curious dripping waterfall. Ride the next shuttle to the end of the road, where you can walk to the gateway of the canyon narrows on the paved, accessible **Riverside Walk.**

Reboard the shuttle to return to Zion Lodge for a **horseback ride** into the canyon, or you can ride the shuttle back to the visitor center to pick up your car. Head out onto the beautiful **Zion–Mount Carmel Highway** with its long, curving tunnels, making sure your camera is loaded and ready for stops at viewpoints along the road. Once you reach the park's East Entrance, turn around, and on your return trip stop to take the short hike up to **Canyon Overlook.** Now you're ready to rest your feet at a screening of "Zion Canyon—Treasure of the Gods" at the **Zion Giant Screen Theater.** In the evening, you might want to attend a **ranger program** at one of the campground amphitheaters or at Zion Lodge. Or you can follow a relaxing dinner in **Springdale** with a stroll to the downtown galleries and shops.

ZION IN TWO DAYS

On your first day follow the one-day itinerary. Start your second day with an excursion to the **Kolob Canyons** area of the park via **Kolob Terrace Rd.** This steep road is not recommended for long vehicles, but you will be rewarded with a glimpse of the brilliant red, towering canyons of this seldom-visited part of the park. Turn around at Kolob Reservoir to backtrack to Route 9 and return to **Zion Canyon.** Enjoy a leisurely stroll along the Virgin River via the **Pa'rus Trail.** Stop at **Zion Lodge** for lunch, then head for **Angels Landing Trail.** Without going on an extended backpack trip, there's no better way to get to know Zion Canyon than to hike this rigorous trail. If you prefer to take it easy, try the shorter, less strenuous hikes on the **Hidden Canyon and Watchman trails,** which give you an intimate experience of the canyon.

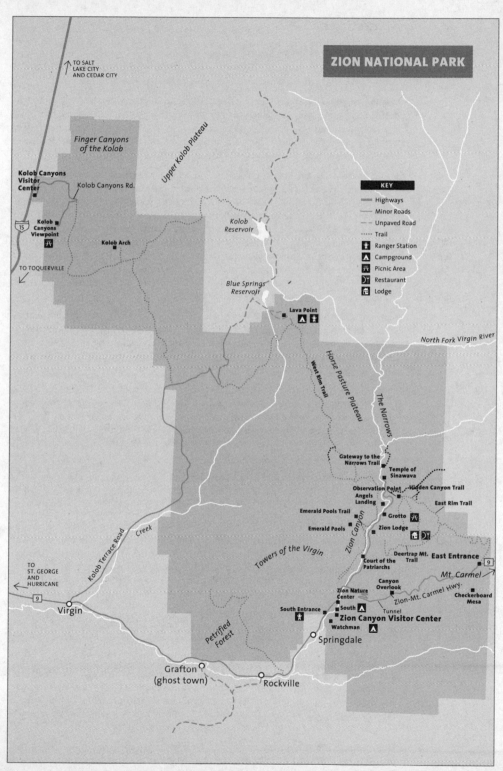

ZION NATIONAL PARK

TO SALT
LAKE CITY
AND CEDAR CITY

Finger Canyons
of the Kolob

Upper Kolob Plateau

Kolob Canyons
Visitor
Center

Kolob Canyons Rd.

Kolob
Reservoir

KEY

Highways
Minor Roads
Unpaved Road
Trail
Ranger Station
Campground
Picnic Area
Restaurant
Lodge

15

Kolob
Canyons
Viewpoint

Kolob Arch

TO TOQUERVILLE

Blue Springs
Reservoir

Lava Point

North Fork Virgin River

West Rim Trail

Horse Pasture Plateau

The Narrows

Gateway to the
Narrows Trail

Temple of
Sinawava

Hidden Canyon Trail

Observation Point

Angels
Landing

East Rim Trail

Emerald Pools Trail

Grotto

Emerald Pools

Zion Lodge

Zion Canyon

Deertrap Mt.
Trail

East Entrance

9

TO
ST. GEORGE
AND
HURRICANE

Kolob Terrace Road

Creek

Towers of the Virgin

Court of the
Patriarchs

Mt. Carmel

Canyon
Overlook

Checkerboard
Mesa

9

Virgin

Zion Nature
Center

South Entrance

South

Tunnel

Zion-Mt. Carmel Hwy.

Zion Canyon Visitor Center

Watchman

Petrified
Forest

Springdale

Grafton
(ghost town)

Rockville

Attractions

PROGRAMS AND TOURS

Check at Zion Canyon and Kolob Canyons visitor centers and bulletin boards throughout the park for locations, schedules, and topics of ranger-led activities.

Evening Programs. Held each evening in campground amphitheaters and in Zion Lodge, these entertaining 45-minute ranger-led programs inform you on subjects such as geology and history. You may learn about the bats that swoop through the canyons at night, the silent ways of the mountain lion, or how plants and animals adapt to life in the desert. Programs may include a slide show or audience participation.

Junior Ranger Program. Kids 6–12 can have fun learning about plants, animals, geology, and archaeology through hands-on activities, games, and hikes. You can earn a certificate, pin, and patch by attending one session of the Junior Ranger Program at the Zion Nature Center and one other ranger-led activity in the park. Children 5 or younger can earn a Junior Ranger decal by completing an activity sheet available at the Zion Canyon visitor center. Kids can earn a Junior Ranger badge by completing an activity booklet (available at the Zion Canyon and Kolob Canyons visitor centers) during their visit to Zion. Sign up for Junior Ranger programs at the Zion Nature Center half an hour before they begin. | Zion Nature Center, near the entrance to South Campground 0.5 mi north of the South Entrance | 435/772–3256 | One-time $2 fee | Daily 9–11:30 and 1:30–4.

Morning and Afternoon Hikes. These 1- to 2-mi ranger-led walks can greatly enhance your understanding of the geology, wildlife, and history of Zion National Park. Each park ranger selects a favorite destination, which may change daily. Inquire at the visitor center or check park bulletin boards for locations and times. Wear sturdy footgear and bring a hat, sunglasses, sunscreen, and water.

Shuttle Tours. To learn about the geology, ecology, and history of Zion Canyon, join a park ranger for a two-hour narrated tour on a park shuttle bus. You'll make several stops along the way to take photographs and hear park interpretation from the ranger. The tour departs from the Zion Canyon visitor center and travels to the Temple of Sinawava. Free tickets are available at the visitor center, where a schedule of tour times is also posted. | Zion Canyon Visitor Center | 435/772–3256 | Free | May–Sept., daily.

Zion Canyon Field Institute. Take a class on edible plants, geology, photography, adobe brick-making, or many other topics. Classes, held outdoors throughout the park, are limited to small groups. | 435/772–3246 or 800/635–3959 | www.zionpark.org | $25–$200 | Year-round.

SCENIC DRIVES

★ **Kolob Canyons Road.** You reach this scenic drive in the extreme northwestern section of the park via Exit 40 off I–15, 38.6 mi and less than an hour's drive from Springdale. The road climbs through a pinyon–juniper forest dotted with ponderosa pine, fir, and quaking aspen to an overlook that affords views of the Finger Canyons of the Kolob. A printed interpretive guide to the 10-mi round-trip park drive is for sale at the visitor center.

Kolob Terrace Road. A 44-mi round-trip drive takes you from Route 9 in Virgin to Lava Point for another perspective on the park. The winding drive overlooks the cliffs of the Left and Right Forks of North Creek. It ends at the blue waters of Kolob Reservoir outside the park boundaries.

Zion Canyon Scenic Drive. Sheer, vividly colored cliffs tower 2,000 ft above the road that meanders along the floor of Zion Canyon. As you roll through the narrow, steep canyon you'll pass the Court of the Patriarchs, the Sentinel, and the Great White Throne, among other imposing rock formations. Zion Canyon Scenic Drive is accessed only by park shuttle April through October, but you can drive it yourself the rest of the year.

★ **Zion–Mount Carmel Highway.** Under no circumstances should you miss driving this stretch of road on the east side of the park. Built in 1927–1930, the highway was built over rough terrain and right through thick walls of rock. It's hard to say what is more outstanding about this drive: the views of colorful slickrock etched by time, the road's hairpin curves and challenging grades, or the two narrow tunnels blasted through the cliffs. From Zion Canyon Scenic Drive, it's 24 mi to the town of Mount Carmel Junction, with many scenic turnouts along the way. Vehicles more than 7'10" wide or 11'4" high require ranger assistance and a $10 fee (payable an either park entrance station) to pass through the tunnels.

SIGHTS TO SEE

★ **Checkerboard Mesa.** The distinctive pattern on this huge, white mound of sandstone was created by a combination of vertical fractures and the exposure of horizontal bedding planes by erosion. | Zion–Mount Carmel Hwy., 1 mi west of the East Entrance.

Court of the Patriarchs. This trio of colorful peaks overlooking Birch Creek bears the names of, from left to right, Abraham, Isaac, and Jacob. Mount Moroni is the reddish peak on the far right, which partially blocks your view of Jacob. You can see the Patriarchs better by hiking a half mile up Sand Bench Trail. | Zion Canyon Scenic Dr., 1.5 mi north of Canyon Junction.

Great White Throne. Towering over the Grotto picnic area near Zion Lodge is this massive 6,744-ft rock peak. | Zion Canyon Scenic Dr., about 3 mi north of Canyon Junction.

★ **Kolob Canyons.** From I–15 you get no hint of the beauty that awaits you after you ascend the first switchback on 5-mi-long Kolob Canyons Road. Most visitors audibly gasp when they get their first glimpse of the red canyons that rise suddenly and spectacularly out of the earth. The scenic drive winds amid these towers as it rises in elevation, until finally you reach a viewpoint that overlooks the hidden treasure of Zion National Park. The shortest hike in this section of the park is the Middle Fork of Taylor Creek Trail, which is 2.7 mi one way to Double Arch Alcove, and gets pretty rugged toward the end. The visitor center is open year-round but during heavy snowfall Kolob Canyons Road may be closed. | Kolob Canyons Rd. east of I–15, Exit 40.

  Kolob Canyons Visitor Center. Here there's a small bookstore, exhibits on park geology, and rangers to answer questions about the park. | Exit 40 off I–15 | 435/586–9548 | Oct.–Apr., daily 8–4:30; May–Sept., daily 7–7.

Weeping Rock. Once you take the short, paved walk up to the weeps, you'll understand why this is one of the most popular stops in the park. Wildflowers and delicate ferns thrive near a spring-fed waterfall that seeps out of a cliff. The light "rain" that constantly falls from Weeping Rock feels great on a hot day, and you can walk behind the trickle of water. In fall, this area bursts with color. The 0.2-mi trail to the west alcove takes about 25 minutes round-trip. It is paved, but it is too steep for wheelchairs. | Zion Canyon Scenic Dr., about 4 mi north of Canyon Junction.

Zion Canyon Visitor Center. Unlike most national park visitor centers, which are filled with indoor displays, the center at Zion presents almost all of its visitor information in an appealing outdoor exhibit area. Beneath shade trees beside a gurgling brook, displays help you plan your stay in the park and introduce you to the geology, flora, and fauna of the area. Inside the visitor center, a large bookstore operated by Zion Natural History Association sells field guides and other publications. The state-of-the-art building is a fascinating sight in its own right because of its energy conserving design. | At the South Entrance to the park | 435/772–3256 | www.nps.gov/zion | Apr.–Oct., daily 8–7; Nov.–Mar., daily 8–5.

Zion Human History Museum. For a complete overview of the park with special attention to human history, stop at the museum. Exhibits explain how humans interacted with the geology, wildlife, plants, and unpredictable weather in Zion Canyon from prehistory to the present. A 22-minute film that plays throughout the day provides a good introduction to the park. | Zion Canyon Scenic Dr., about 1 mi north of the South Entrance | 435/772–3256 | www.nps.gov/zion | May–Sept., daily 8–5.

Zion Lodge. The Union Pacific Railroad constructed the first Zion Lodge in 1925, with buildings designed by architect Stanley Gilbert Underwood. A fire destroyed the original building but it was rebuilt so as to recapture some of the look and feel of the first building. The original western-style cabins are still in use today. Among giant cottonwoods across the road from the Emerald Pools trailhead, the lodge houses a restaurant, snack bar, and gift shop. | Zion Canyon Scenic Dr., about 3 mi north of Canyon Junction | 435/772–3213 | www.zionlodge.com.

★ **Zion–Mount Carmel Tunnels.** A highlight of the drive along the Zion–Mount Carmel Highway are the narrow tunnels that transport you through solid rock. As you travel from one end of the longest (1.1 mi) tunnel to the other, portals along one side provide a few glimpses of cliffs and canyons, and when you emerge on the other side you find that the landscape has changed dramatically. Vehicles more than 7′10″ wide or 11′4″ high require a ranger escort through the tunnels. For a fee of $10 (payable at either entrance station) a ranger will stop oncoming traffic so you can drive down the middle of the tunnels. | Zion–Mount Carmel Hwy., about 5 mi and 7.5 mi east of Canyon Junction.

Sports and Outdoor Activities

BICYCLING

The introduction of the park shuttle has improved bicycling conditions in Zion National Park, for cyclists no longer share Zion Canyon Scenic Drive with thousands of cars. Be advised, though, that there are several large buses plying the park road at any given time. Bicycles are only allowed on established park roads and on the Pa'rus Trail, a level 2-mi ride that runs along the Virgin River. You cannot ride your bicycle through the Zion–Mount Carmel tunnel and must transport your bike by motor vehicle along this stretch of the highway.

Bicycles Unlimited. These folks are a treasure trove of information on mountain biking in southern Utah. They rent bikes and sell parts, accessories, and guidebooks. | 90 S. 100 East, St. George | 435/673–4492 or 888/673–4492 | www.bicyclesunlimited.com.

Springdale Cycles. These folks rent bikes, car racks, and trailers, and can give you tips on the local trails. | 932 Zion Park Blvd., Springdale | 435/772–0575 | www.thundertours.com.

FISHING

Sitting at over 8,000 ft elevation, Kolob Reservoir offers good trout angling. Look for the dirt road at the end of Kolob Terrace Road, about 5 mi north of Lava Point. If you do decide to fish in the park, you need to purchase a Utah State Fishing License.

HIKING

The best way to experience Zion Canyon is to walk beneath and between its towering cliffs. You can buy a detailed guide to the trails of Zion at the visitor center bookstore. Whether you're heading out for a day of rock-hopping or an hour of strolling, you should carry—and drink—plenty of water to counteract the effects of southern Utah's arid climate. Wear a hat and sunscreen, and wear sturdy shoes or boots.

★ **Angels Landing Trail.** Truly one of the most spectacular hikes in the park, this trail is an adventure for those not afraid of heights. On your ascent you must negotiate Walter's Wiggles, a series of 21 switchbacks built out of sandstone blocks, and traverse sheer cliffs with chains bolted into the rock face to serve as handrails. In spite of its hair-raising nature, this is a popular trail that attracts many people. Small children should skip this trail, and all other children should be carefully supervised while on this route. Allow 2½ hours round-trip if you stop at Scout's Lookout, and four hours if you keep going to where the angels play. | Zion Canyon Scenic Drive, about 4.5 mi north of Canyon Junction.

Canyon Overlook Trail. It's a little tough to locate this trailhead, but you'll find it if you watch for the parking area just east of Zion–Mount Carmel tunnel. The trail is moderately steep but only 1 mi round-trip; allow an hour to hike it. The trail's-end overlook gives you views of the West and East Temples, Towers of the Virgin, the Streaked Wall, and other Zion Canyon cliffs and peaks. | Rte. 9, east of Zion–Mount Carmel Tunnel.

East Rim Trail. This trail is an excellent moderate one-way hike from the East Entrance of the park to Weeping Rock. It takes about seven hours. The view of Checkerboard Mesa, Jolley Gulch and the entire White Cliffs area of Zion's eastern edge are visible from this trail, as are views of Angels Landing and Cathedral Mountain. | Rte. 9 about 4 mi east of Canyon Junction.

Emerald Pools Trail. The Emerald Pools are formed by a year-round creek coming out of Heaps Canyon. Two small waterfalls with pools below are the main attractions here. The popular trail to the pools is paved up to the lower pool and is suitable for baby strollers and for wheelchairs with assistance. Beyond the lower pool, the trail becomes rocky and steep as you progress toward the middle and upper pools. A less crowded and exceptionally enjoyable return route is along the Kayenta Trail, which connects to the Grotto Trail. Allow 50 minutes round-trip to the lower pool and 2½ hours round-trip to the middle and upper pools. | Zion Canyon Scenic Dr., about 3 mi north of Canyon Junction.

Grotto Trail. This flat and very easy trail takes you from Zion Lodge to the Grotto picnic area, traveling for the most part along the park road. Allow 20 minutes or less for the walk. If you are up for a longer hike, connect with the Kayenta Trail after you cross the footbridge, and head for the Emerald Pools. You will begin gaining elevation, and it's a steady, steep climb to the pools. Give yourself two to three hours if you're going to hike to the Emerald Pools and back. | Zion Canyon Scenic Dr., about 3 mi north of Canyon Junction.

Hidden Canyon Trail. This steep, 2-mi round-trip hike takes you up 1,000 ft in elevation. Not too crowded, the trail is paved all the way to Hidden Canyon. Allow about three hours for the round-trip hike. | Zion Canyon Scenic Dr., 3.2 mi north of Canyon Junction.

★ **Narrows Trail.** On a hot, clear day there are few things more enjoyable than a walk in the river. This route does not follow a trail or path; rather, you are walking on the riverbed, no matter how much water is in it. The gateway of the Narrows admits adventurous souls deeper into Zion Canyon than most visitors go. As beautiful as it is, this hike is not for everyone. To see the Narrows you must wade upstream through chilly water and over uneven, slippery rocks. Just to cross the river, you must walk deliberately and slowly using a walking stick. Be prepared to swim, as chest-deep holes may occur even when water levels are low. Like any narrow desert canyon, this one is famous for sudden flash flooding even when skies are clear. Before attempting to hike into the Narrows always check with park rangers about the likelihood of flash floods. A day trip up the lower section of the Narrows is 6 mi one-way to the turnaround point. Allow at least five hours round-trip. | At the end of Riverside Walk.

Pa'rus Trail. This trail parallels and sometimes crosses the Virgin River. The 2-mi hiking and biking trail begins at South Campground and proceeds north along the river to the beginning of Zion Canyon Scenic Drive. It's paved and gives you great views of the Watchman, the Sentinel, and Temple and Towers of the Virgin. Dogs are allowed on this trail as long as they are on a leash. Cyclists must follow traffic rules on this heavily used trail. | Rte. 9 (main park road), 5 mi north of South Entrance.

Riverside Walk. Beginning at the Temple of Sinawava shuttle stop at the end of Zion Canyon Scenic Drive, this trail is a delightful 1-mi round-trip stroll along the Virgin River. The river gurgles by on one side of the trail; on the other side, wildflowers bloom out of the canyon wall in fascinating hanging gardens. This is the park's most popular trail; it is paved and suitable for baby strollers and for wheelchairs with assistance. A round-trip walk takes about an hour and a half. At the end of the trail is the beginning of the Narrows Trail. | Zion Canyon Scenic Dr., about 5 mi north of Canyon Junction.

Sand Bench Trail. A loop trip on this sandy bench gives you a different perspective on the views you see from the Court of the Patriarchs overlook. The route is 1.9 mi long, with a

ZION NATIONAL PARK

EXPLORING
ATTRACTIONS NEARBY
DINING
LODGING
CAMPING AND RV FACILITIES
SHOPPING
ESSENTIAL INFORMATION

steep climb onto the pinyon–juniper covered plateau. The trail can be used all year, but it's dusty in summer. Spring through fall, the trail is heavily used by horseback riders. Allow three hours round-trip to hike the trail. | Court of the Patriarchs overlook, 1.5 mi north of Canyon Junction.

Taylor Creek Trail. In the Kolob Canyons area of the park, this trail immediately descends to parallel Taylor Creek, sometimes crossing it, sometimes shortcutting benches beside it. You'll pass the historic Larsen Cabin before you enter the canyon of the Middle Fork, where the trail becomes rougher. After passing the old Fife Cabin, the canyon bends to the right and delivers you to Double Arch Alcove, a large, colorful grotto with a high arch towering above. The distance one-way to Double Arch is 2.7 mi. Allow about four hours round-trip for this hike. | Kolob Canyons Rd., about 1.5 mi from Kolob Canyons visitor center.

Watchman Trail. For a view of the town of Springdale and a look at lower Zion Creek Canyon and the Towers of the Virgin, take this moderately strenuous hike that begins on a service road east of Watchman Campground. Some spring-fed seeps create hanging gardens and attract wildlife here. Allow two hours for this 3-mi hike. There are some moderate cliff edges on this route, so children should be supervised carefully. | East of Rte. 9 (main park road), on the access road inside the South Entrance.

HORSEBACK RIDING

Grab your hat and boots and see Zion Canyon the way the pioneers did—on the back of a horse or mule. This is a sure way to make your trip to Zion National Park memorable.

Canyon Trail Rides. These friendly folks have been around for years, and they are the only outfitter for trail rides inside the park. Anyone over age 5 can participate in guided rides along the Sand Bench Trail. The horses work from late March through October; you may want to make reservations ahead of time. | Across the road from Zion Lodge | 435/679–8665 | www.canyonrides.com | $20–$45.

Attractions Nearby

SIGHTS TO SEE

Best Friends Animal Sanctuary. Formerly homeless dogs, cats, burros, horses, and other animals occupy one of the most scenic homes in America. White cliffs stand watch over the once neglected and abused critters, and a pretty little creek trickles by. Truly one of Utah's most unusual destinations, Best Friends is the largest no-kill animal shelter in the United States, with no fewer than 1,800 animals living here at any time. The 350-acre sanctuary gives unwanted pets, farm animals, and other creatures a permanent home or makes them available for adoption. Tours are available by reservation. | 5001 Angel Canyon Rd., Kanab | 435/644–2001 | www.bestfriends.org | Donations accepted | Daily.

Coral Pink Sand Dunes State Park. This sweeping expanse of pink sand seems to come from nowhere, but in fact it comes from eroding sandstone. Funneled through a notch in the rock, wind picks up speed and carries grains of sand into the area. Once the wind slows down, the sand is deposited, creating this giant playground for dune buggies, ATVs, and dirt motorcycles. A small area is fenced off for walking, but the sound of wheeled toys is always with you. Children love to play in the sand, but before you let them loose check the surface temperature; it can become very hot. | Yellowjacket and Hancock Rds., 12 mi off U.S. 89, near Kanab | 435/648–2800 | www.stateparks.utah.gov | $5 | Daily.

St. George Tabernacle. When Brigham Young visited the pioneers he had sent to grow cotton around St. George, he found them demoralized and plagued by difficulties after only a year in the area. To help raise their spirits he ordered the construction of a tabernacle. The edifice, financed with tithes and built with local sandstone, took 13 years to complete. | Main and Tabernacle Sts., St. George | 435/628–4072 | Free | Daily.

St. George Temple. Completed in 1877, this gleaming white landmark was among the first temples built as pioneers settled Utah, and is still in use today. The temple is quite a sight at night, when it's lit up against the dark, starry sky. You can stop in at the visitor center to join a tour of the grounds. | 250 E. 400 South, St. George | 435/673–5181 | Free | Daily 9–9.

★ **Snow Canyon State Park.** Red Navajo sandstone mesas and formations are crowned with black lava rock, creating high-contrast vistas from either end of the canyon. From the campground you can scramble up huge sandstone mounds and overlook the entire valley. | 1002 Snow Canyon Dr., Ivins | 435/628–2255 | www.stateparks.utah.gov | $5 | Daily.

Zion Giant Screen Theater. Escape to the cool confines of a movie theater featuring a screen that's six stories high. The 40-minute film *Zion Canyon–Treasure of the Gods* takes you on an adventure through Zion and other points in canyon country. Other films, including Hollywood features, are shown in the theater. | 145 Zion Park Blvd., Springdale | 435/772–2400 or 888/256–3456 | www.zioncanyontheatre.com | $8 | Nov.–Mar. noon–7; Apr.–Oct. 10–8.

Dining

In Zion

ZION NATIONAL PARK

EXPLORING
ATTRACTIONS NEARBY
DINING
LODGING
CAMPING AND RV
FACILITIES
SHOPPING
ESSENTIAL
INFORMATION

Castle Dome Snack Bar. American/Casual. Right next to the Zion Lodge shuttle stop and adjoining the gift shop, this small fast-food restaurant defines convenience. Hikers on the go can grab a banana or a sandwich here, or you can while away an hour with ice cream on the sunny patio. | Zion Canyon Scenic Dr., 3.2 mi north of Canyon Junction | 435/772–3213 | www.zionlodge.com | $3–$8 | AE, D, DC, MC, V.

Picnic Areas. Whether in the cool of Zion Canyon or on a point overlooking the drama of Kolob Canyons, a Zion picnic can be a relaxing break in a busy day of exploring.

A shady lunch retreat, **The Grotto,** has drinking water, fire grates, picnic tables, and rest rooms. The amenities make the Grotto ideal for families. A short walk takes you to Zion Lodge, where you can pick up fast-food. | Zion Canyon Scenic Dr., 3.5 mi north of Canyon Junction.

You can enjoy the views while you have your lunch at the **Kolob Canyons Viewpoint** picnic table. Rest rooms and drinking water are available at the Kolob Canyons visitor center. | Kolob Canyons Rd., 5 mi from Kolob Canyons visitor center.

On your way to or from the Junior Ranger Program feed your kids at the **Zion Nature Center** picnic area. When the Nature Center is closed, you can use the rest rooms in South Campground. | Near the entrance to South Campground 0.5 mi north of South Entrance | 435/772–3256.

Zion Lodge Dining Room. American. This is the only full-service restaurant inside the park. A rustic reproduction of the original lodge dining room, the restaurant is hung with historic photos. Patio dining overlooking the front lawn of the lodge is also available. A good selection of steak, fish, and poultry is offered for dinner, and lunch includes a variety of sandwiches and salads. The restaurant is also open for breakfast. | Zion Canyon Scenic Dr., 3.2 mi north of Canyon Junction | 435/772–3213 | www.zionlodge.com | Reservations essential | $12–$22 | AE, D, DC, MC, V.

Near the Park

★ **Bit and Spur Restaurant and Saloon.** Mexican. This restaurant has been a legend in Utah for decades. A seasonal menu offers a variety of familiar Mexican entrées, including burritos, tacos, and tostadas, but the kitchen also gets creative. Try the sweet potato tamale with tomatillo salsa, or the *puerco relleno,* grilled pork tenderloin filled with walnuts, apples, Gorgonzola, and raisins. Get here early so you can eat outside and enjoy the lovely grounds and great views. | 1212 Zion Park Blvd., Springdale | 435/772–3498 | Reservations essential | $17–$26 | D, MC, V | No lunch.

When visiting parks or communities populated by Native Americans, always *ask permission* before taking photographs of people or their homes.

Scaldoni's Grill. Italian. At this local favorite you can't go wrong if you're hankering for Italian food. Not in the mood for Italian? Don't despair: they also serve a variety of steaks and seafood, all in delightful surroundings with good views of St. George. | 929 Sunset Blvd., St. George | 435/674–1300 | $9–$23 | AE, D, MC, V | Closed Sun.

Sol Foods. American/Casual. For a quick, healthful meal any time of day, stop at this convenient restaurant outside the park's South Entrance. Daily specials include spanakopita, quiche, lasagna, and a variety of salads. They'll also prepare picnic baskets or box lunches for your day in the park. Nearby is Sol's ice cream parlor, with hand-dipped ice cream cones, banana splits, and espresso. There's plentiful patio seating near the Virgin River, with views into the park. | 95 Zion Park Blvd., Springdale | 435/772–0277 | $5–$15 | MC, V | Closed Jan.

★ **Spotted Dog Cafe at Flanigan's Inn.** Contemporary. Named in honor of the family dog of Springdale's original settlers, this restaurant is worthy of any special occasion. Entrées include lamb, chicken, steak, and, of course, locally grown trout, which is encrusted in pumpkin seed and pan-seared. The restaurant really struts its stuff in the pork tenderloin with apple-almond sauce and mango chutney. Through the wall of windows you can gaze at the rich colors of the Zion landscape. Breakfast is available. | 428 Zion Park Blvd., Springdale | 435/772–3244 | $12–$23 | AE, DC, MC, V | No lunch.

Sullivan's Rococo. American. Specializing in beef and seafood, this St. George restaurant is known for its prime rib. Because it sits atop a hill overlooking town, you can enjoy spectacular views from your table. | 511 Airport Rd., St. George | 435/628–3671 | $13–$51 | AE, D, DC, MC, V.

Zion Pizza and Noodle Co. Pizza. Everyone in Springdale loves this place, and it's easy to understand why. Creative pizzas such as Thai chicken or hot-and-spicy burrito pizza put some punch into the menu, as do the linguine with peanuts and the spaghetti with homemade marinara sauce. The restaurant is housed in a former church, where you can dine indoors or in the beer garden, which specializes in microbrews. No wine or cocktails are served. | 868 Zion Park Blvd., Springdale | 435/772–3815 | $8–$13 | No credit cards | Closed Dec.–Feb.

Lodging

In Zion

Zion Lodge. Although the original lodge burned down in 1966, the rebuilt structure convincingly re-creates the classic look of the old inn. Knotty pine woodwork and log and wicker furnishings accent the lobby. Lodge rooms are modern but not fancy, and the historic western-style cabins (which date from the 1930s) have gas-log fireplaces. This is a place of quiet retreat, so there are no televisions—kids can amuse themselves outdoors on the abundant grassy lawns. The lodge is within walking distance of trailheads, horseback riding, and, of course, the shuttle stop. This popular spot requires reservations at least six months in advance. Restaurant. No room TVs. | Zion Canyon Scenic Dr., 3.2 mi north of Canyon Junction | 435/772–3213, 303/297–2757, or 888/297–2757 | fax 435/772–2001 | www.zionlodge.com | 121 rooms | $120–$143 | AE, D, DC, MC, V.

Near the Park

Best Western Abbey Inn. The rooms are large and decorated with Victorian flair, using rich cherry wood and deep colors. There's an arcade for the kids. All rooms have coffee makers, and a full, hot breakfast is included. Microwaves, refrigerators. Pool. Gym, outdoor hot tub. Laundry facilities. | 1129 S. Bluff St., St. George, 84770 | 435/652–1234 or 888/222–3946 | fax 435/652–5950 | www.bwabbeyinn.com | 130 rooms | $75–$115 | AE, D, DC, MC, V | BP.

Best Western Zion Park Inn. This spacious and modern facility has large rooms. The Switchback Grille will get you going in the morning with a hearty breakfast. The inn is a stop on the park shuttle route, so one step out the door and you're on your way to Zion National Park. Restaurant. Pool. Outdoor hot tub. Shops. Playground. Laundry facilities. Some pets allowed (fee). | 1215 Zion Park Blvd., Springdale, 84767 | 435/772–3200 or 800/934–7275 | fax 435/772–2449 | www.zionparkinn.com | 114 rooms, 6 suites | $95–$109 | AE, D, DC, MC, V.

★ **Cliffrose Lodge and Gardens.** Flowers decorate the 5-acre grounds of this friendly, charming lodge. Comfy rooms will keep you happy after a long hike, and from your balcony you can continue to enjoy views of the towering, colorful cliffs. The Virgin River is just outside your door; you can have a picnic or barbecue there. The Cliffrose is within walking distance of the Zion Canyon visitor center and shuttle stop. Restaurants, shops, and the giant-screen movie theater are nearby. Cable TV. Pool. Outdoor hot tub. Beach. | 281 Zion Park Blvd., Box 510, Springdale, 84767 | 435/772–3234 or 800/243–8824 | fax 435/772–3900 | www.cliffroselodge.com | 36 rooms | $119–$165 | AE, D, MC, V.

★ **Desert Pearl Inn.** By all means stay here when you visit Zion National Park, but be forewarned: you won't want to leave. Every room is a suite, with vaulted ceilings and thick carpets, plus cushy throw pillows, Roman shades, oversize windows, bidets, sleeper sofas, and tile showers with deep tubs. The pool area is exceptionally beautiful, with a large, free-form pool, a double-size hot tub, and showers and rest rooms at poolside. Large balconies or patios adjoin each room and overlook either the Virgin River or the pool. In-room data ports, in-room safes, kitchenettes, refrigerators. Cable TV, in-room VCRs. Pool. Outdoor hot tub. Shops. | 707 Zion Park Blvd., Springdale, 84767 | 435/772–8888 or 888/828–0898 | fax 435/772–8889 | www.desertpearl.com | 60 suites | $103–$123 | AE, D, MC, V.

Green Gate Village Historic Bed and Breakfast Inn. This collection of eight vintage homes offers elegantly comfortable accommodations in downtown St. George, complete with eclectic touches such as massive antique beds and historic photographs mingled with the modern convenience of jetted tubs and fax machines. Pool. Hot tub. No smoking. | 76 W. Tabernacle St., St. George, 84770 | 435/628–6999 or 800/350–6999 | fax 435/628–6989 | www.greengatevillage.com | 16 rooms | $79–$189 | AE, D, DC, MC, V.

Parry Lodge. Back in the 1930s movie stars stayed here, and the names of those who slept in each room are listed above the doors of the older units. Hollywood-theme photos decorate the lobby. Despite the age of the hotel, rooms are well-maintained and comfortable. Restaurant. Pool. | 89 E. Center St., Kanab, 84741 | 435/644–2601 or 800/748–4104 | fax 435/644–2605 | www.parrylodge.com | 89 rooms | $51–$86 | AE, D, DC, MC, V.

Seven Wives Inn. Two historic homes and a cottage constitute this B&B. It is said that Brigham Young slept here and that one of the buildings may have been a hiding place for polygamists after the practice was outlawed in the 1880s. In fact, the inn is named for an ancestor of the owner who indeed had seven wives. Not surprisingly, the rooms are named after those wives. Antiques are liberally used in the decor, and guest rooms are elaborately and carefully decorated. You'll see lots of flowers and pastels. One room has a jetted tub installed in a Model T Ford. Dining room. Pool. Some pets allowed (fee). No smoking. | 217 N. 100 West, St. George, 84770 | 435/628–3737 or 800/600–3737 | fax 435/628–5646 | www.sevenwivesinn.com | 13 rooms | $85–$250 | AE, D, DC, MC, V.

Camping and RV Facilities

In Zion

South Campground. All the sites here are under big cottonwood trees, granting campers some relief from the summer sun. The best sites are near the Virgin River. The campground operates on a first come-first, first-served basis, and sites are usually taken before noon each day during high season. Many of the sites are suitable for either tents or RVs, although there are no hook-ups. Flush toilets. Dump station. Drinking water. Fire grates, picnic tables. | 126 sites | Rte. 9 (main park road) 0.5 mi north of South Entrance | 435/772–3256 | $16 | Reservations not accepted | No credit cards | Mid-Apr.–mid-Sept.

ZION CAMPGROUNDS

	Total # of sites	# of RV sites	# of hook-ups	Drive-to sites	Hike-to sites	Flush toilets	Pit toilets	Drinking water	Showers	Fire grates/pits	Swimming	Boat access	Playground	Dump station	Ranger station	Public telephone	Reservation possible	Daily fee per site	Dates open
INSIDE THE PARK																			
South	126	126	0	•		•		•		•				•		•		$16	Apr.–Sep.
Watchman	160	91	91	•		•		•		•				•		•	•	$16–20	Y/R
NEAR THE PARK																			
Coral Pink Sand Dunes State Park	22	22	0	•		•		•	•	•				•	•		•**	$14	Y/R
Mukuntuweep	230	30	30	•		•		•	•	•				•		•	•	$15–19	Y/R
Zion Canyon	200	100	100	•		•		•	•	•	•		•	•			•	$18–22	Y/R
Zion River Resort	133	112	112	•		•		•	•	•	•		•	•		•	•	$27–41	Y/R

* In summer only	** Reservation fee charged	Y/R=Year-round
UL=Unlimited	ULP=Unlimited primitive	LD=Labor Day MD=Memorial Day

Watchman Campground. This large campground on the Virgin River operates on a reservation system between April and October but you do not get to choose your own site. Sometimes you can get same-day reservations, but don't count on it. Flush toilets. Partial hook-ups (electric), dump station. Drinking water. Fire grates, picnic tables. | 160 sites, 91 with hook-ups | Access road off Zion Canyon visitor center parking lot | 435/772–3256, 800/365–2267 reservations | $16 without electricity, $18 with electricity; prime river sites $20 | D, MC, V.

Near the Park
Coral Pink Sand Dunes State Park. Roughly 25 mi from Zion, this small and pretty campground tends to be less crowded than those at the national park. Be warned, however, that most of Coral Pink's campers are here to ride their ATVs, dune buggies, and motorcycles across the sand dunes. The campground is open all year, but there's no water October–Easter. Flush toilets. Dump station. Drinking water, showers. Fire grates, picnic tables. Ranger station. | 22 sites | 10 mi south of Mount Carmel Junction on U.S. 89 | 435/648–2800, 800/322–3770 reservations | $14.

Mukuntuweep. This shady campsite lies at the East Entrance to Zion. At 6,300 ft, it's slightly cooler than the campgrounds on the other side of the park, but unlike those, Mukuntuweep has no river flowing by. Flush toilets. Full hook-ups, dump station. Drinking water. Public telephone. | 230 sites, 30 with hookups | 12120 W. Rte. 9 | 435/648–2154 | fax 435/648–2829 | www.xpressweb.com/zionpark | $15 for tents, $19 for RVs | AE, D, MC, V.

Zion Canyon Campground. In Springdale about a half mile from the South Entrance to the park, this campground is surrounded on three sides by the canyon's rock formations. Many of the sites are on the river. Flush toilets. Full hook-ups, dump station. Drinking water, guest laundry, showers. Fire grates, picnic tables, food service. Electricity, public telephone. General store. Play area, swimming (river). | 110 RV sites, 110 tent sites | 479 Zion Park Blvd., Springdale | 435/772–3237 | fax 435/772–3844 | www.zioncanyoncampground.com | $18–$22 | D, MC, V.

Zion River Resort RV Park Campground. This resort has everything an RV camper could want, with the possible exception of shade. Most of the trees haven't grown up yet, but there are some premium sites along the river where the cottonwoods are mature. You can also rent a cabin or teepee. Flush toilets. Full hook-ups. Drinking water, guest laundry, showers. Grills, picnic tables. Electricity, public telephone. General store. Play area, swimming (pool). | 133 sites, 112 with hook-up | 12 mi west of park on Rte. 9 | 435/635–8594 or 800/838–8594 | www.zionriverresort.com | $27–$41 | AE, D, MC, V.

ZION NATIONAL PARK

EXPLORING
ATTRACTIONS NEARBY
DINING
LODGING
CAMPING AND RV
FACILITIES

SHOPPING
ESSENTIAL
INFORMATION

Shopping
Canyon Offerings. Come to this shop for some of Zion's snazziest and most fun souvenirs. It's packed with gifts for mom, grandma, and the kids, and has one of the best selections of handcrafted jewelry in the region. | 933 Zion Park Blvd., Springdale | 435/772–3456 or 800/788–2443.

Fred Harvey Trading Company Gift Shop. Discover many local treasures, including Native American jewelry, handmade gifts, books, and other souvenirs here. | Zion Lodge, Zion Canyon Scenic Dr., 3.2 mi north of Canyon Junction | 435/772–3213.

Happy Camper Market. This store is handily located next to the park's South Entrance. If you can't find your groceries, camping supplies, or forgotten items here, you probably don't need 'em. | 95 Zion Park Blvd., Springdale | 435/772–3402.

Ranch Road Fine Art. For some amazing images of Zion National Park and the surrounding area, stop by this exquisite little gallery outside the South Entrance. | 205 Zion Park Blvd., Springdale | 435/772-0465.

Zion Canyon Visitor Center Bookstore. Books, maps, puzzles, posters, postcards, videos, and even water bottles are available at this comprehensive shop. | Zion Canyon Visitor Center, at the South Entrance to the park | 435/772–3264.

Zion Park Market. This small grocery store carries fresh produce, ice, firewood, and camping supplies. | 855 Zion Park Blvd., Springdale | 435/772–3251.

Essential Information

ATMS: Zion Giant Screen Theater | 145 Zion Park Blvd., Springdale. **Zions Bank** | 921 Zion Park Blvd., Springdale.

AUTOMOBILE SERVICE STATIONS: Kanab Tire Center and Kwik Lube | 265 E. 300 S, Kanab | 435/644–2557. **Springdale Chevron** | 1593 Zion Park Blvd., Springdale | 435/772–3922. **Tony's Auto Care and Towing Service** | 861 Red Rock Rd. #9, St. George | 435/674–3515. **Zion's Sinclair** | Rte. 9, at the East Entrance to Zion National Park, Orderville | 435/638–2828.

POST OFFICE: Springdale Branch | 624 Zion Park Blvd., Springdale, 84767 | 435/772–3950.

FIELD GUIDE: CANYON COUNTRY

Ecological Communities

Cliffs. At first glance it might not seem that cliffs are a significant habitat. After all, what can live on a cliff? The answer is canyon wrens, rock wrens, rock squirrels, falcons, swifts, and bighorn sheep. Cliffs are ubiquitous throughout canyon country.

Forests. Many of the forested areas in canyon country are mixed conifer forests that include Douglas firs, white firs, and other evergreens. They share the earth with Gambel's oak and Quaking aspen. At higher elevations (approximately 8,000–11,000 ft) you will come across dense forests of Blue spruce and subalpine fir, and in isolated highlands and in canyons throughout the region you can find ponderosa pine. The North Rim of the Grand Canyon is an excellent example of spruce-fir forest and ponderosa pine forest. Lodgepole pine thrives in Colorado Plateau forest ecosystems where snow lingers into late spring and precipitation, usually in the form of heavy winter snows, exceeds 40 inches a year.

Great Basin Desert. The only true desert ecosystem in the Colorado Plateau is the Great Basin desert, a high, cold desert that includes all of Nevada, western, southern, and southeastern Utah, and northern Arizona. All of the parks in canyon country, except those in Colorado, fall within this general desert ecosystem. Large areas receive most of their annual precipitation (usually between 2 and 9 inches of rain) in the form of snow. The Great Basin Desert is dominated by a few shrubs, including Shadscale and sagebrush.

Great Basin Grassland. These lands exist in valleys, canyons, and plateaus throughout canyon country. In almost every case, livestock grazing has depleted the grasses and allowed Big sagebrush, snakeweed, and other shrubby species to dominate. The best places to see this habitat unaltered are at Wupatki National Monument in Arizona and in Canyonlands National Park.

Pinyon-Juniper Woodlands. These "forests" comprised primarily of pinyon pine and juniper trees thrive between 4,800 and 7,500 ft in elevation. You will see them at mid-elevation on slopes and plateaus throughout northern Arizona, southern Utah, and

Nevada, and at lower elevations in Colorado. Big sagebrush and cliffrose are common, as are Pinyon jays, Clark's nutcrackers, and many rodents.

Potholes. When bowl-like indentions in rock fill up with water after a rainfall or snowmelt, tiny brine shrimp, fairy shrimp, tadpoles, snails, and the larvae of many insects live in these important life-supporting systems. Because potholes dry up quickly the creatures who live there have developed highly specialized adaptations. For example, most have an accelerated reproductive cycle. Some lay eggs that hatch at staggered intervals and some of the eggs will hatch after the next rainfall, even if the pothole has been dry. You will see this habitat throughout canyon country, most especially at Arches, Canyonlands, and Capitol Reef national parks.

Riparian. Canyon country is defined by its aridity, but there are areas with abundant water. Where there is water you will find quite different species than in dryer areas. In the canyons, riparian areas support the great blue heron and stream banks are lined with Fremont cottonwood where many birds will nest. Willows and tamarisk also grow abundantly here. In the mountains, there may be beaver, and lush trees such as spruce, Douglas fir, and other conifers. Excellent examples of riparian areas in the region's parks are the Fremont River at Capitol Reef, the Virgin River in Zion, the Colorado and Green rivers in Canyonlands, and, of course, the Colorado River in Grand Canyon.

Seeps, Springs, and other Wetlands. Underground springs surprise the casual hiker in canyon country. Water seeps out of cliff faces, supporting delicate hanging gardens of ferns and mosses and wildflowers that wouldn't grow anywhere else. If you are attentive, you will find this fascinating habitat at just about every park you visit.

Subapline Meadows. Intermingled with spruce-fir forests, these meadows can take the form of small glades or extensive grasslands. They occur at elevations between 8,000 and 11,000 ft. Elk, mule deer, and black bear may wander the meadows searching for food, and hummingbirds feast on wildflower nectar. The La Sal Mountains near Arches and Canyonlands National parks have some good examples of subalpine meadow.

Timberline and Montane Pine Woodlands. At timberline, generally between 9,000 and 11,000 ft, conditions are too windy, dry, and cold for most trees. Only subalpine fir, bristlecone, and Limber pine survive here. Yellow-bellied marmots live here, as do Clark's nutcrackers. You will find this habitat in Great Basin National Park.

Fauna

BIRDS

Bald Eagle. America's national bird, with its 70–90-inch wingspan, is a delight to behold as you travel through the West. Those with the trademark white head and tail are at least 4 or 5 years old; immature balds are brown with mottled white underwings and tail. A young bald eagle looks much like a golden eagle, but it has a shorter tail and longer head than a golden.

Black-billed Magpie. Noisy magpies seem to be everywhere in canyon country. This easily identifiable 19-inch bird has a long tail, white wing bars, and a black-and-white body. It's not found east of the Rockies.

Black-chinned Hummingbirds. The most commonly seen hummingbird in canyon country is this one, identified by the metallic green on the upper part of the wings and back. If you get a close look in the right light, you will see there is a purple patch just below its black chin. This tiny bird beats its wings approximately 50 times per second.

Broad-tailed Hummingbird. This hummer lives in cool, mountainous areas. It has a red throat and broad tail along with a metallic green back like the black-chinned hummingbird.

Clark's Nutcracker. This chunky, 12-inch gray bird with black wings and tail feathers is a bold scavenger at campgrounds. They are common in high coniferous forests, but can also drift into desert and lowland areas of the West.

Gambel's Quail. Common in desert scrublands and thickets where there is a permanent water source nearby, this gregarious 11-inch bird is easily identified by the black plume that rises off its head and patches of chestnut on its sides. The male has a black face. You are likely to see this distinctive bird at Capitol Reef National Park.

Golden Eagle. Federally protected since 1962, the golden eagle has a light golden head and a 6-ft wingspan, with well defined white patches near the tips of the outer wings.

Great Blue Heron. It's hard to miss a great blue heron when it rises from a body of water. The tallest bird in the region, with a 6-ft wingspan, it has a long, thin neck and pointed yellow beak. The blue-gray bird stands in shallow water to fish for its meals.

Hawks. In addition to the Red-tailed hawk, three species of hawks inhabit the Colorado Plateau, all of them with gray-and-white striped underwings, a gray back, and a dark head. The Cooper's hawk is most common; it lives near streams and other water sources. The smallest of the area's hawks, the Sharp-shinned hawk has a wingspan of only about 25 inches. It lives in mountainous regions and moves to lower elevations in the winter. Also found at higher elevations is the Goshawk. Hawks can have a wingspan of up to 50 inches.

Mountain Bluebird. Flitting to and fro in the forest above 5,000 ft, this pretty little bird is brilliant blue if male and brownish gray with blue tinges on the wings if female. In both sexes it has a chestnut color breast. Sadly, bluebird habitat is shrinking as people continue to remove dead trees and cut off dead limbs where the bluebirds nest.

Peregrine Falcon. Only two pairs of these birds were known to exist in 1975, and the species was on the endangered and threatened wildlife list until 1999. At present approximately 160 pairs nest in Utah. Its long, pointed wings span 36–44 inches; its wings are slate-blue, as is its back, and dark bars cover a white chest. Its black head and neck give the appearance of a hood, and dark markings look like sideburns on the face.

Raven. There is no mistaking the large, jet-black bird that seems always playful and curious. Ravens resemble crows but are larger and have a more stately bill. Crows more often nest near riparian areas, while ravens are often found cruising in the mountains or high above canyons. Do not feed ravens or drop food for them.

Red-tailed Hawk. The most widespread large bird of prey in the United States generally lives near riparian areas. You will commonly see this cinnamon-color bird sitting on telephone poles or fence posts. Its relatively short, reddish tail is a distinguishing characteristic.

Rock Wren. Closely related is the canyon wren, this small gray-black bird with a white chest lives in cliff crevices, nooks, and crannies.

Steller's Jay. This big blue bird with a black crest, throat, and upper breast has a distinctive crown as well. It is aggressive and often haunts campgrounds and balconies searching for food. You'll definitely see these birds at Great Basin and Bryce Canyon.

Western Tanager. If you happen to see western tanager in breeding season, you'll think that an exotic bird has escaped from its owner. The male has a bright red head, yellow body and black wings. The color tones down in the winter and he loses his distinctive red head. The female is yellow with brown wings. These 7–8-inch birds are common in coniferous forests.

MAMMALS

Each park in canyon country is home to dozens of species of mammals, including a variety of mice and other rodents, mule deer, ringtail cats, mountain lion, bobcats, and, at the very highest elevations in each region, black bear. The list below is far from comprehensive, but represents those animals you are most likely to see during your visit to the parks. Many animals are nocturnal and tend to hibernate during the heat of the day, so unless you are yourself a night owl, you aren't likely to see them. Other animals, such as mountain lion, are so good at hiding from humans that few people ever see them. If you do encounter animals in the parks, do not approach them. While they may seem like they are used to people, they are still wild and may attack. Never feed animals or drop food for them: They may become ill or may become so accustomed to human food that they can starve to death when they can no longer get it during the winter. Human food also causes wild animals to frequent campgrounds and other frontcountry park locations, which is dangerous not only for visitors but for the animals themselves.

Bighorn Sheep. This magnificent animal was once on the verge of extinction as a result of hunting, disease, and competition from domestic sheep. On the rocky slopes that it inhabits it climbs over seemingly impossible terrain. Both sexes grow horns, but only the male's curl back around on themselves. The bigger the horns, the older the animal.

Coyote. The clever and resourceful coyote lives throughout the United States, but you're more likely to see one out West, traveling solo across highways, through the desert, or near rivers. Looking like a small, yellow-brown dog, it has a distinctive bark; you may hear it yap, whine, or howl in the middle of the night.

Desert Cottontail. Loved by everyone (including coyotes, mountain lions, and other predators), this furry little creature is widespread throughout canyon country. The Nuttall's cottontail looks similar, but it lives at higher elevations and has short, black-tipped ears.

Hopi Chipmunk. This tiny fellow, identifiable by its striped face and back, is one of the most commonly seen animals in canyon country—and everyone's favorite. Unlike the squirrel, the Hopi chipmunk does not carry its tail over its head when it runs. Smaller and lighter, the closely related Least chipmunk also occurs in this region.

Jackrabbit. This big hare prefers open areas that have grasses to eat and shrubs to hide under. Recognizable by its very long ears and black tail, the long-legged animal can sprint up to 35 mph, alternating with 20-ft leaps.

Marmot. You are likely to encounter the largest member of the squirrel family in the higher plateaus of the region. It inhabits rocky places on mountain slopes or in meadows. The curious animal has a long, bushy tail and a yellow belly.

Mule Deer. This ungulate is the most commonly seen animal in the national parks of canyon country, typically wandering near campgrounds at dusk and dawn. When startled it moves in a sort of springing motion, and all four legs leave the ground at once. No other North American deer moves in this manner, which is known as "stotting."

Pallid Bat. You're more likely to see this canyon country bat walking on the ground than flying. That's where it finds its food, such as lizards, scorpions, and small mice. As the name would imply, this bat is pale in color; it also has a strong odor and a 14-inch wingspan.

Pinyon Mouse. The most abundant and conspicuous mouse in the region, the pinyon mouse can be identified by its large ears, though you might have to stay up at night to see it. As its name suggests, the mouse lives primarily in pinyon-juniper forests.

Prairie Dog. So named for its vocalizations that sound like a dog barking, this sociable rodent inhabits grasslands. Two varieties live north and west of the Colorado River: The cinnamon-color Black-tailed prairie dog, known for building large towns, and the yellow-coated White-tailed prairie dog, the largest of the species. South and east of the Colorado River, the Gunnison's prairie dog does not build large towns but separate colonies that are close together, sometimes giving the impression of a "town." Another variety, the Utah prairie dog, is found only in the far western part of Utah. Most prairie dogs stand 12–14 inches tall on their hind legs.

Pronghorn. When you come across large, wide open spaces look for this ungulate with a white rump and black markings around its face and neck. Its horns are dark in color and rise nearly vertically from its head. Ranging in height from 48 to 56 inches and in weight from 90 to 125 pounds, the pronghorn regularly runs for several miles at a speed of 30–35 mph. It has few predators because no animal can outrun its top speed of 65 miles per hour. Although often called an antelope, it is not of that species.

Western Pipistrelle. As the sun sets over canyon country during summer months, you are bound to see this bat flying near lights to scoop up small insects. The tiny creature weighs less than a nickel and hides in rocky crevices during the day, although it is one of the few bats that you might see in daytime.

REPTILES

Collared Lizard. This bright-green and yellow creature stands out like a lost piece of jewelry in the desert. A large lizard ranging 8–14 inches in length, it commonly poses on tops of boulders to scan the area for food. It has a black ring around its neck.

Great Basin Gopher Snake. Because of its close resemblance to the rattlesnake, this harmless reptile is often killed by frightened humans. Light brown to yellow, with darker blotches, the 30–72-inch snake is the most common snake in canyon country.

Northern Whiptail. The whiptail species takes its name from the motion of its long tail, which can be up to 2.5 times the length of its body. The lizard's body is only 2–4 inches in length, but its total length from snout to tail can be as long as 12 inches. As it runs, the pale gray-brown reptile with black markings whips its tail from side to side. Predators sometimes nip off part of the wriggling tail.

Plateau Lizard. A rather plain brown fellow with a not particularly long tail, this lizard has a blue marking on its underside. It is anywhere from 4 to 7 inches long and has long claws that it uses for climbing. You'll find it scampering among the rocks and shrubs throughout the day.

Plateau Striped Whiptail. One of 12 varieties of whiptail in the southwestern United States, this is a long, narrow, striped lizard. Whiptails of this particular variety are all female. They reproduce by laying unfertilized but viable eggs that yield clones of the mother.

Rattlesnakes. When you hear its distinctive rattling warning you of its presence you can't mistake a rattlesnake for anything else. During the day this snake likes to stay cool by lying in the shade, and at night it hunts for food. The Grand Canyon is home to the unique pink rattlesnake, while the only rattlesnake in the Arches and Canyonlands area is the midget-faced, a shy reptile that is the smallest (at only 20 to 30 inches)— and one of the most lethal—of its species.

Striped Whipsnake. One of the fastest moving snakes in the region, this snake lives in pinyon-juniper forests and sage flats. During the day it hunts for lizards, mice, and small snakes. It is black or brown, with four narrow stripes running the length of its 36–60-inch body.

Wandering Garter Snake. Unlike many of its numerous garter snake cousins this particular variety does not need to live near a permanent water source and is happy in arid canyon country. It got the "garter" part of its name because its striped pattern resembles the designs once found on garters that hold up men's socks. These snakes range between 18 and 43 inches in length.

Flora

FLOWERS

Common Paintbrush. The brilliant red of this early bloomer is not really a blossom but the bracts from a narrow tube that protrudes from the leaf. Found in clumps of up to a foot in diameter, usually close to the ground, it has narrow, hairy leaves. At least three varieties grow in canyon country.

Evening Primrose. Usually found in sandy desert areas, this white flower most often appears in April. Blossoms open in early evening and close in the morning to prevent water loss during extreme heat. You'll often find both pink and white blossoms on the same plant.

Groundsel. This bright yellow flower appears on clusters of stalks about 10 inches tall. A member of the sunflower family, it grows throughout the region in sandy, gravelly, or clay soils. Its dark-green leaves have many lobes.

Larkspur. Rising out of sandy soil on 2-ft-tall stalks, this blossom is quite unusual: The two lower petals are short, wide, and purple, and the two upper petals are white and narrow.

Lupine. A bright bluish-purple, this flower blooms throughout the cooler summer months but can't stand the heat. Its leaves are easy to identify as they spread like fingers from a central point. Commonly seen at higher elevations and in cooler months, this member of the pea family is about 9 inches tall.

Mules Ears. Named for the long, narrow leaves that look like mules ears (and are very rough and scratchy), this flower grows close to the ground in dramatic, bright-yellow clumps. The clumps may grow to be several feet wide and are often seen in sand dunes.

Narrowleaf Yucca. A member of the agave family, this plant has sharp, narrow spikes for leaves. If weather conditions and the water supply are amenable, it will bloom in spring, producing a cream-color flower on a stalk up to 5 ft tall.

Penstemon. There are over 250 species of penstemon, but one of the most common in this area is the Eaton's penstemon. It has shiny, spearpoint leaves that clasp the flower stalk, and blossoms that are often red and droop downward from a 2-ft-tall stem.

Prince's Plume. True to its regal name, this showy, yellow flower grows up to 4 ft tall. It has large leaves at the base, and smaller, more narrow leaves higher up on the stem. The blossoms resemble large plumes or wands.

Scarlet Gilia. Often mistaken for Eaton's penstemon, this red flower is common throughout the region. The leaves are narrow, fern-like structures and the flowers point up with five symmetrical blossoms.

SHRUBS

Big Sagebrush. That wonderful fragrance you smell on the canyon country breeze is no doubt sagebrush, which grows from Nebraska to California and from New Mexico to Montana—the widest distribution of any North American shrub. It is a dusty pale green bush with petal-like leaves that grow together in bundles. If you have any doubt you're looking at sagebrush, put your nose into it.

Cliffrose. Pale yellow flowers of this evergreen resemble a simple rose; they are highly aromatic and attract bees when the plant begins blooming in April. The leaves of the bush are very tiny and lacy. Cliffrose grows on dry, rocky hillsides from 3,500 to 8,000 ft.

Four-wing Saltbush. Growing from South Dakota to Mexico and all the way west to California, this deciduous, frosty-green plant has 1-inch linear leaves. Its name refers to its four-winged fruit, which is also green and blends in with the plant.

Fremont Mahonia. Like other members of the barberry family, this shrub has spiky, sharp, leaves that resemble small holly leaves. Its deliciously fragrant yellow flower yields tangy, edible berries in spring. The plant is named for John C. Fremont, who collected plants while exploring the region in the 1840s.

Gambel's Oak. Found in high, cool spots, this shrubby tree grows in dense thickets between 6,500 and 9,500 ft. The edible seeds and leaves attract deer, porcupine, and caterpillars, while woodpeckers, scrub jays, and chipmunks steal the acorns for winter use. The bush turns bright orange and red in fall.

Greasewood. A tough plant that grows in unfriendly environments such as alkali or saline flats, this plant has bright-green, fleshy leaves and white bark. It can reach heights of 8 ft. Wild animals forage on its young shoots and use the thorny plants as protection from predators. Livestock can also eat it, but too much is poisonous.

Greenleaf Manzanita. This easily identifiable shrub has dark-red to dark-brown bark and round, shiny, and flat evergreen leaves. In late spring it blossoms with small, white and pink urn-shaped flowers, producing edible, apple-shape berries that can be used in jams, jellies, and cider. It grows in open forests below 9,000 ft and tends to inhabit dry, sunny sites, although it prefers cooler areas. You are most likely to spot this plant in Great Basin and Bryce Canyon national parks.

Mormon Tea. This nonflowering plant grows in green, jointed stems. Native people and early pioneers made a medicinal tea from the steams and leaves, which contain pseudoephedrine, a drug commonly used in nasal decongestants and closely related to ephedrine.

Mountain Mahogany. Three species of mountain mahogany grow in canyon country: Curlleaf, Dwarf, and Alderleaf. All have dark-green, shiny leaves and reddish bark. This is good winter forage for mule deer and elk.

Rabbitbrush. In late summer and early fall you can see this plant blooming bright yellow on many roadsides throughout canyon country. It might make you sneeze and itch, as many people are allergic to it. Rabbitbrush is abundant throughout the region.

Russian Thistle. You can thank Ukrainian immigrants for the classic western scene of big tumbleweed balls blowing across sagebrush flats. They introduced Russian thistle to South Dakota in 1877 and the weed spread quickly across the Great Plains. By the early 1900s it had tumbled all the way to the Pacific coast, dispersing seeds along the way. It might get stuck under your car; it's a pest in regional yards, too.

Serviceberry. This is an inconspicuous shrub until spring, when it blooms in fragrant, white, five-petal blossoms that attract bees, butterflies, and other happy pollinators.

Its round, toothed leaves, fuzzy and with prominent veins, emerge after the flowers. Dark-purple berries, used by Native Americans in pemmican, also produced a dye.

Shadscale. Often the dominant plant in stony, alkaline soils throughout the arid West, this is an important winter browse for domestic grazing animals. It is usually less than 3 ft tall, with small, rounded leaves that are gray, often tinged with red. Closely related to four-wing saltbush, shadscale produces two-winged seeds. Spiny branches (it is also called spiny saltbush) protect the plant from some herbivores.

Snowberry. This 1–3-ft-tall shrub grows on dry, rocky slopes throughout the entire region. Closely related to the Utah honeysuckle, it produces a creamy white, pea-sized berry— a favorite of many birds and mammals—in fall. Its small, pointed leaves are deciduous and its half-inch long tubular flowers grow in groups of two.

TREES

Bristlecone Pine. This tree has been known to live for almost 5,000 years, making it the oldest living thing on earth. It usually grows in elevations between 9,000 and 11,500 ft, although specimens can be found at lower elevations. It grows on exposed, rocky sites above the timberline, where wind-blown sand and ice crystals polish the trunk and wear away sections of the tree. In protected sites the bristlecone can reach heights of 60 ft, but it survives longest where conditions are most strenuous. You can see bristlecones at Great Basin and Bryce Canyon national parks.

Douglas Fir. Growing at elevations of 6,500–9,000 ft, this tree can live up to 1,000 years. Young firs have gray, smooth bark, while older ones are dark and scaly. All have long, shiny, and pointy needles. Native Americans used the roots for basket weaving and the twigs for arrow shafts, and today it is a valuable lumber tree.

Fremont's Cottonwood. The Fremont is the most common of the three types of cottonwoods that grow in canyon country. Named for the "cotton" released by its seeds in spring, it has shiny, green leaves that turn bright yellow in fall. You'll see this tree in riparian areas near streams and rivers, where its deep roots prevent erosion and keep soil porous, allowing water to percolate down.

Pinyon Pine. Along with the Utah juniper, the pinyon pine dominates forests across much of the Colorado Plateau. Together, the two trees populate the p-j, or pygmy, forests at elevations of 5,000–7,500 ft. Very slow growing, the pinyon pine rarely exceeds 20 ft in height, even after 150 years. Its pine cones contain edible, highly nutritious nuts that are quite difficult to harvest.

Ponderosa Pine. Spacious stands of ponderosa, found at 7,000–8,500 ft, often look like man-made parks. The bark on older trees is orange or reddish in color and exudes a distinctive fragrance similar to vanilla when it heats up in the late afternoon sun. Young trees lack the orange hue and are called "blackjacks." Ponderosa can grow as tall as 100 ft; it is one of North America's most heavily harvested woods.

Quaking Aspen. The smooth, light bark of the young Aspen (it gets darker and more furrowed with age) and the tree's autumn explosion of yellow and gold foliage are a trademark of America's western mountains. This tree grows in groves, in damp places along watercourses. Its two-inch leaves are attached to twigs by long slender stalks, which accounts for the characteristic quaking produced by breezes. You'll see this tree at the higher elevations of Bryce Canyon, Mesa Verde, and Black Canyon; in Great Basin; and at the North Rim of the Grand Canyon.

Rocky Mountain Juniper. Similar to the Utah juniper, this tree prefers cooler, moister environs. Its foliage is a finer texture and appears somewhat lacy and gray. Cones are bluish when they mature.

Russian Olive. Alien to the region but now prolific, this tree has narrow, gray-green leaves and thorns. In spring it produces yellow flowers with a rather strong odor, and pollen to which many people are allergic. It often grows near cottonwoods and is so aggressive that it eventually supplants them.

Tamarisk. Also known as salt-cedar, this tree is abundant along rivers and creeks in the region. You can identify them by their scaly, thin, lacy leaves and a pungent, pink-ish flower. An invasive plant, it was introduced to the United States from the Middle East in the early 1800s for erosion control. It was sold in nurseries in California and began to appear wild in the region about 1880. The tamarisk can proliferate up river banks at a rate of 12 mi per year.

Utah Juniper. This pervasive canyon country tree grows at elevations of 3,000–8,000 ft, forming the p-j, or pygmy, forest along with the pinyon pine and sagebrush. Native Americans used the bark for torches, tobacco substitute, and woven cloth, and the nee-dles produce a tea high in vitamin C. Today the light blue berries (which are not really berries but a modified cone wrapped in a drought-resistant coating) are used for fla-voring gin.

Willow. Willows grow along streamsides along with the cottonwood and the tamarisk. They usually have long, narrow, toothed leaves and reach heights between 10 and 30 ft, depending on the species. Native Americans made a pain- and fever-reducing tea from the bark, which contains salicin. When eaten, salicin breaks down into salicylic acid, the active ingredient in aspirin.

Geology and Terrain

Anticline. Movements of the earth's crust produce an anticline when they push orig-inally horizontal rock layers upward in one spot. The anticline slopes downward from the crest.

Arch. This type of window in a rock wall forms either through erosion, when wind and sand wear away the rock face, or through the freezing action of water. When water enters spaces or joints in a rock and freezes there, the expansion of the ice can crack off chunks of rock. The parks of southern Utah contain many arches.

Badlands. A network of gullies and ridges in an area of rocky terrain is known as a badlands. Badlands form in relatively soft rocks via erosion, and are usually charac-terized by V-shape drainage ditches. Little vegetation grows in badlands because ero-sion washes away seeds and roots. The amphitheater at Bryce Canyon National Park is an example of badlands.

Basin. A basin is like a giant syncline, or dip in the earth. Within a basin there are usu-ally smaller anticlines and synclines. The Great Basin is an example of a geologic basin.

Biological soil crusts. Also known as cryptobiotic soil crust, this black, bumpy, stuff covers the ground throughout canyon country. It is composed of cyanobacteria, green algae, lichens, fungi, and mosses that form a living cover on the ground. The crust sta-bilizes the soil and allows plants to germinate and root. If it's destroyed or damaged, new plant life cannot grow. It takes an estimated 50 to 250 years for this living organ-ism to repair itself.

Bridge. If a window through a rock is created by water flowing beneath it, it is called a bridge. You can see many natural bridges in canyon country, such as Hickman Bridge at Capitol Reef National Park.

Butte. A butte is what remains when a mesa erodes. You can see good examples of this formation in Monument Valley, Arizona.

Canyon. A canyon forms when water and wind erode soft layers of the earth's rock crust. The hardness of the rock determines the shape of the canyon: A narrow, or slot, canyon generally results when the rock is the same composition all the way down and water runs through the crack. A steplike canyon such as the Grand Canyon forms when alternating soft and hard layers are eroded by wind and water, with a river cutting a narrow groove in the bottom of the canyon.

Colorado Plateau. Except for the Great Basin region, all of the parks in this chapter are located within the Colorado Plateau, a geologic area of approximately 130,000 square mi. The plateau is named for the Colorado River, the primary river that drains the area. About two billion years ago, shifts in the earth's crust (in a process called plate tectonics) caused large cracks and smaller fractures, known as faults, to form. Between 550 and 50 million years ago, as motion in the earth's crust continued, streams, seas, and wind laid down layers of sedimentary rock. More fluid than the crust below it, this rock folded and warped over the old, brittle fractures as the crustal plates keep shifting. Toward the end of this period a major disturbance in the plates lifted a massive block of sedimentary rock a mile or more above the sea level, rotated it about 90 °F, and set it back down. During that lift the block cracked, wrinkled, and crumpled, leaving behind dramatic folds, uplifts, basins, mountains and other landforms that reveal the different colors and textures of the many sedimentary layers. Today, elevations in the area range from 3,000 ft to over 14,000 ft. The process of plate tectonics is still ongoing, and along with water—especially rivers—it continues to form the land.

Desert Varnish. This dark brown or black coating seems to drip down canyon walls as if from a spilled can of paint. Windblown dust or rain containing iron and manganese creates the color. Ancestral Puebloans and other ancient Native Americans scratched drawings called petroglyphs into the desert varnish.

Great Basin. An area of approximately 200,000 square mi, this region of mountains and high desert (4,500–6,200 ft in elevation) occupies northern Nevada and much of western Utah. It was formed eons ago, when the earth's crust began to stretch in an east-west direction. Blocks of rock fractured and the pieces tilted and spread out like a row of books sliding out of place on a shelf. Some of the blocks were buried beneath sediment in the basins, while others became mountain ranges. The basin was further shaped by alpine glaciers that carved cirques (deep, hollow bowls) like the one you find beneath Wheeler Peak in Great Basin National Park.

Laccolithic Mountains. Throughout canyon country, many mountain ranges seem to rise suddenly out of the flat earth, with no transitional foothills. These ranges are generally located over faults in the earth's crust. They formed as molten rock, or magma, flowed up from below, and hardened under layers of sedimentary rock. Erosion and other geologic forces subsequently exposed the volcanic rock in the form of mountains. Among canyon country's laccolithic ranges are the La Sal Mountains near Moab, Utah; the Abajo Mountains near Canyonlands National Park's Needles District; and the La Plata and Ute mountains near Mesa Verde National Park; as well as Navajo Mountain near Monument Valley Tribal Park, Arizona.

Mesa. A mesa, or hill with a smooth, flat, tablelike top (mesa means "table" in Spanish), is a clear example of how hard rock stands higher and protects the soft rock beneath. A single mesa may cover hundreds of square miles of land. At the Island in the Sky District of Canyonlands National Park and at Mesa Verde you are standing on top of a mesa.

Monocline. The most notable geologic feature of the Colorado Plateau, a monocline is a bit like half an anticline (see above). The layers of rock on either side of a monocline are mostly level, but they bend downward like a step. Pioneers often called them "reefs" because the formations were a barrier to passage through the area. The Waterpocket Fold in Capitol Reef National Park is a most dramatic example of a monocline. Another example is the Monument Upwarp, which extends from Kayenta, Arizona, to the confluence of the Green and Colorado rivers in Canyonlands National Park. There are many smaller anticlines and synclines along the Upwarp.

Monument. This general term applies to geologic formations that are much taller than they are wide, or to formations that resemble man-made structures. You can see many examples of the first type of monument in Capitol Reef National Park's Cathedral Valley; in Monument Valley, Arizona; and in the White Rim Monument Basin area at Canyonlands National Park. Monuments that fall into the second category include the Sinking Ship in Bryce Canyon National Park and the Three Penguins at Arches National Park.

Sand Dunes. The sand dunes that you occasionally come across in canyon country have been deposited by winds. Wind blowing past rock formations will pick up grains of sand. If the wind then passes through a natural channel like a window or a slot canyon, it will lose speed when the channel ends and the sand will drop onto the ground. Plants cannot grow in these dry, windy spots, so the wind continues to deposit sand, and a dune forms. The two best examples in canyon country are at Coral Pink Sand Dunes State Park near Zion National Park, and on Route 24 near Capitol Reef National Park.

Spire. As a butte erodes, it may become one or more spires. There are many buttes and spires in Monument Valley, Arizona.

Syncline. A syncline is a troughlike downfold in the rock layers of the earth's crust, with its sides dipping in toward the axis. You can see synclines and anticlines as you drive throughout canyon country.

Window. One of the more intriguing landforms you will encounter while touring canyon country are large openings in solid rock walls. These are known as arches or bridges, depending on what created the opening. Together, the two types of form are called windows.

KODAK'S TIPS FOR TAKING GREAT PICTURES

Get Closer
- Fill the frame tightly for maximum impact
- Move closer physically or use a long lens
- Continually check the viewfinder for wasted space

Choosing a Format
- Add variety by mixing horizontal and vertical shots
- Choose the format that gives the subject greatest drama

The Rule of Thirds
- Mentally divide the frame into vertical and horizontal thirds
- Place important subjects at thirds' intersections
- Use thirds' divisions to place the horizon

Lines
- Take time to notice lines
- Let lines lead the eye to a main subject
- Use the shape of lines to establish mood

Taking Pictures Through Frames
- Use foreground frames to draw attention to a subject
- Look for frames that complement the subject
- Expose for the subject, and let the frame go dark

Patterns
- Find patterns in repeated shapes, colors, and lines
- Try close-ups or overviews
- Isolate patterns for maximum impact (use a telephoto lens)

Textures that Touch the Eyes
- Exploit the tangible qualities of subjects
- Use oblique lighting to heighten surface textures
- Compare a variety of textures within a shot

Dramatic Angles
- Try dramatic angles to make ordinary subjects exciting
- Use high angles to help organize chaos and uncover patterns, and low angles to exaggerate height

Silhouettes
- Silhouette bold shapes against bright backgrounds
- Meter and expose for the background illumination
- Don't let conflicting shapes converge

Abstract Composition
- Don't restrict yourself to realistic renderings
- Look for ideas in reflections, shapes, and colors
- Keep designs simple

Establishing Size
- Include objects of known size
- Use people for scale, where possible
- Experiment with false or misleading scale

Color
- Accentuate mood through color
- Highlight subjects or create designs through color contrasts
- Study the effects of weather and lighting

The Desert Southwest

The desert has a mystic appeal. A rare, violent rainstorm gives birth to brilliant wildflowers that burst almost overnight from dormant seeds. Damp creosote perfumes the air with a distinctive, woody aroma. The buzzing of cicadas vibrates from virtually every bush as the earth cracks under a relentless sun. Unyielding to human use, much of the arid habitat remains undisturbed. There are few power lines, fences, or grazing livestock within protected park boundaries. Rocky hillsides may be thick with twisted, thorny branches or succulent pads of prickly pear cactus. In the cool of night, oft-hidden desert creatures emerge to become the hunter or the hunted. The eerie yipping of a coyote pack and the squeal of a doomed jackrabbit announce that somewhere in the darkness nature has had its way.

In their adaptation to an arid environment, many desert plants can appear almost alien. Dagger-like tufts grace the branches of the namesake of Joshua Tree National Park in southeastern California. The saguaro cactus does not grow naturally in the U.S. outside of southern Arizona, but its stately arms silhouetted against an orange sunset have come to symbolize the deserts of the American West. Throughout the Southwest, isolated pockets of greenery surround rare desert springs. Foothills and mountains harbor scrubby pine forests where evidence from as long ago as 300 million years speaks of the lush world that once existed here. Arizona's Petrified Forest is a natural museum, with its huge, mineralized stumps and logs—remnants of a once swampy woodland—strewn across a barren landscape. Big Bend and Guadalupe Mountains national parks in west Texas, part of the northernmost extension of the Chihuahuan desert, are the only places in the U.S. where you can see certain wildlife and plant species. And when you seek refuge from the scorching desert summer, you can find cool respite underground in the damp limestone chambers and palaces of Carlsbad Caverns in southeastern New Mexico.

In This Chapter

Big Bend National Park • Carlsbad Caverns National Park • Guadalupe Mountains National Park • Joshua Tree National Park • Petrified Forest National Park • Saguaro National Park

RULES OF THE ROAD

License requirements: To drive in Arizona and Texas, you must be at least 16 years old and have a valid driver's license. In California and New Mexico, the minimum age to obtain an unrestricted driver's license is 18. Valid driver's licenses from other states and countries generally are honored.

Right turn on red: In Arizona, California, New Mexico, and Texas, you may make a right turn on red after a full stop unless there's a sign prohibiting it.

Seat belt and helmet laws: In California, seat belts are mandatory for drivers and passengers in front and rear seats, while seat belts are required only for front-seat passengers in Arizona, New Mexico, and Texas. In Arizona, a state highway patrol officer may stop a vehicle and issue a citation for a seat belt violation only if another traffic violation has been committed.

In all four states, young children (generally up to age 6) must be restrained in federally approved child safety seats. California and New Mexico mandate that young children wearing appropriate safety restraints must ride in the vehicle's back seat. Officers can stop vehicles to enforce child restraint laws in California and New Mexico.

In California, all motorcycle drivers and passengers must wear helmets that meet safety standards. Arizona and New Mexico laws require anyone under the age of 18 to wear a helmet while riding on a motorcycle. In Texas, safety helmets are required for all motorcycle drivers and passengers under age 21. Those over 21 who choose not to wear motorcycle helmets in Texas are required to complete an approved motorcycle driver training course and provide proof of health insurance coverage of at least $10,000. The motorcycle must display a sticker indicating that requirements for helmet exemption have been met.

Speed Limits: Speed limits in Arizona and New Mexico go as high as 75 mph on interstates, but remain at 55 mph in heavily traveled areas. The maximum speed limit in California and Texas is 70 mph, although laws can vary widely depending on the type of roadway. Be sure to check speed limit signs carefully and often.

For More Information: Arizona Department of Public Safety | 602/223–2000. **Arizona Motor Vehicle Department** | 602/255–0072. **California Department of Motor Vehicles** | 800/777–0133. **California Highway Patrol** | 916/657–7261. **New Mexico Department of Public Safety** | 505/827–9000. **New Mexico Motor Vehicle Division** | 888/683–4636. **Texas Department of Public Safety** | 512/424–2000. **Texas Department of Transportation** | 800/558–9368 or 512/463–8585.

Desert Southwest Driving Tour

FROM PALM SPRINGS TO SANTA FE TO LAS VEGAS

Distance: 1,700–2,150 mi   Time: 7–9 days
Breaks: Overnight in Palm Springs, CA; Tucson, AZ; El Paso and Lajitas, TX; Carlsbad and Albuquerque or Santa Fe, NM; and Holbrook, AZ

The tour description below starts at Palm Springs and proceeds counterclockwise, but you can start your trip around the loop at any point and follow it in either direction. Along the way you'll come across scores of interesting old towns and natural wonders to explore: if you've got the time, by all means extend your tour.

❶ Begin at **Palm Springs, CA,** noted for its sand dunes, agriculture, golf courses, and lavish
❷ estates. Proceed east on I-10 about 25 mi and turn at the exit to **Joshua Tree National Park** just north of the interstate. Spend about two hours exploring numerous, easy short

hikes through a landscape that transitions between the Mojave Desert and the more arid, sparsely vegetated Colorado Desert. Overnight in Palm Springs and treat yourself to a great meal.

③ Get a bright and early start from Palm Springs the next morning. A 4.5-hour, 300-mi drive east on I–10 will bring you to **Tucson, AZ,** where you will overnight on day two. Tucson is
④ flanked by the two units of **Saguaro National Park.** In the afternoon venture into the park's thick stands of tall, pale green cacti scattered like statues along the hillsides. You are now in the Sonora Desert, which you can learn more about on the morning of day three by visiting the extensive **Arizona-Sonora Desert Museum.** The museum is set up like a combination zoo and botanical garden and offers close-up views of desert wildlife and vegetation in artfully crafted habitats.

⑤ On the afternoon of day three, continue driving east on I–10 for almost five hours or 320 mi until you reach **El Paso, TX.** Spend the night in El Paso and search out one of the city's coveted Mexican restaurants such as Leo's, or drive about 20 mi east on I–10 to **Fabens** to dine on juicy slabs of steak and absorb the middle-of-nowhere, badlands bluff setting of Cattleman's Steakhouse. If you want to take a peek at Old Mexico just south of the
⑥ border, take the "Border Jumper" trolley the next day and visit **Juarez, Mexico.** Hop off at one of the shopping stops to pick up fine jewelry, leather goods, or barter for bargains at the city's mercado.

⑦ If you want to save two days you can skip Big Bend National Park and head straight from El Paso to Guadalupe Mountains National Park on day four, via U.S. 62/180 east (about 100 mi). Otherwise, head for the immense blue-sky country of west Texas by proceeding southeast on I–10 for about three hours or 220 mi, and dropping south at Kent onto Route 118. It takes about 2.5 hours to travel about 150 mi to the west entrance of **Big Bend National Park.** Before entering the park, spend the night in **Lajitas,** on Route 170 about 20 mi west of the park entrance. The charming Lajitas Resort on the Rio Grande is a good alternative to the generally indifferent lodgings closer to the park. You can also spend the night in the park at Chisos Mountains Lodge (reserve several months in advance). Pack a picnic lunch and spend the fifth day of your tour exploring the park via its mostly paved—though narrow and sometimes curving—roadways. Hike some of the trails and look for the succulent, thorny spikes of the lechuguilla, which is unique to the Chihuahuan Desert.

⑧ On day six head north from Big Bend on U.S. 385 about 40 mi to the tiny cow town of **Marathon.** Take a peek at the tiled courtyards and cool gardens of the historic Gage Hotel, then proceed west on U.S. 90 for about 30 mi to Alpine and north on Route 118 about 75 mi to I–10. Travel west on I–10 for about 40 mi or 30 minutes. Turn north onto Route 54, a slower, two-lane highway, for about 53 mi and then northeast onto U.S. 62/180 for about 2 mi to reach **Guadalupe Mountains National Park.** Including a short stop in Marathon, the drive to Guadalupe from Big Bend should take about four hours. Orient yourself at the park visitor center, where displays and a video will introduce you to this northernmost region of the Chihuahuan Desert. Spend a few hours hiking some of the easier trails and stop off at the **Frijole Ranch Museum** about 2 mi north of the park visi-
⑨ tor center. Plan on spending the night in **Carlsbad, NM,** about 55 mi northeast of the park on U.S. 62/180.

⑩ Start the next day with a visit to **Carlsbad Caverns National Park,** 27 mi southwest of town on U.S. 62/180. Plan on spending at least two hours touring the caverns. If you want some extra urban time, leave Carlsbad right after your cavern tour and proceed north to Albuquerque on U.S. 285. If another day in the country suits you, fill the afternoon with a swim in the Pecos River at **Lake Carlsbad Recreation Area** and a visit to the botanical and

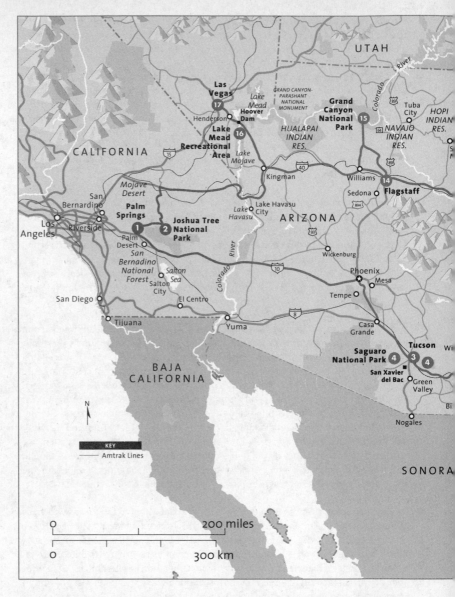

zoological displays at **Living Desert Zoo and Gardens State Park.** In summer, return to Carlsbad Caverns at sunset to witness the swirling mass exodus of bats from the cave for a night of feeding on insects. Then spend another night in Carlsbad before heading for Albuquerque.

⓫ A mostly pleasant, five-hour, 300-mi drive north on U.S. 285 brings you from Carlsbad to
⓬ **Albuquerque.** Stay the night here or in nearby **Santa Fe** and spend the afternoon and the next day touring the historic districts, adobe pueblos, art galleries, and museums of these distinctly Southwestern cities.

⓭ The following day, take I–40 west for about 230 mi (3.5 hours), into Arizona. Just past Navajo watch for the entrance to **Petrified Forest National Park.** The park's 22-mi drive winds through the almost lunar landscape, and trails lead to views of massive, mineralized logs and stumps left over from an ancient forest. Drive about 25 mi farther west on I–40 to spend the night in **Holbrook.**

⓮ From Holbrook it's about 255 mi or four hours west on I–40 to the California-Arizona state line. If you have the time, you can stop in **Flagstaff** or even head north from Williams to ⓯ **Grand Canyon National Park** on U.S. 180. You can also reach **Lake Mead National Recre-** ⓰ **ation Area** and the opulent resort hotels and casinos of **Las Vegas, NV** by detouring ⓱ northwest onto U.S. 93 at Kingman. But if you stay on I–40 it's just 125 mi west of the California-Arizona state line to the exit for Palm Springs, 12 mi south of I–40 on Rte. 111.

When to Visit the Desert Southwest

Despite the oppressive heat of the warmer months (average temperatures in the desert Southwest peak in the middle and upper 90s and low 100s to 110s in June and July), plenty of people choose to take their summer vacation in the desert. For many, the heat is an essential part of the desert experience. A hike in the late summer afternoon can be as healing as a soothing soak in a hot spring. Put on a hat, bring plenty of water, slather on the sunscreen, and let the heat's intensity permeate your clothes and body. In the evening, though, you will need a sweater or light jacket to protect against the chill. Be aware, too, that though the weather here can never really be called wet, what rain does fall tends to come in summer: Guadalupe Mountains, the wettest of the parks in this chapter, tops 3 inches of rain only in July, August, and September, and even in Joshua Tree, the driest park, rainfall creeps over the half-inch mark in September.

If you'd rather avoid the heat, one alternative is to come to the Southwest in winter. Low temperatures in the coldest months—December and January—bottom out in the 30s in most parks and dip into the 20s only at higher elevations. Many desert-lovers have learned the secret of winter in the Southwest. Among them are retirees known as snowbirds, who flock into the area, often driving RVs, to escape the gray winters of home cities that can remain snowbound for months. With increased visitation the national parks offer more interpretive programs and activities. But even here, winter springs an occasional surprise: it's not altogether unusual for a snow or ice storm to frost those scenic cacti.

Spring, especially early spring, can be a spectacular time to visit the desert, most notably following an extra wet year. The desert can be radiant with rainbows of color displayed by blooming cacti and wildflowers. Yucca plants wear a cascade of yellow blossoms on their tall stalks, while branchy ocotillo plants are brilliant with red flowers. Of course, other savvy travelers know about the joy of spring in the desert. At the height of spring blossoming, park roads that in summer are virtually empty may be clogged with vehicles. Campgrounds fill up fast and hotel rooms may be impossible to find. And the spring weather, while generally cool and pleasant, isn't always cooperative. Pervasive high winds signal the change of seasons and dreary sandstorms can ruin an outing, sometimes for days on end.

Locals often say that fall is their favorite time of year in the desert Southwest. Late September and early to mid-October is a great time for your tour of desert national parks. As temperatures drop to the comfortable 70s the sky transforms to its deepest shade of blue. The air grows still, and even desert creatures are more likely to emerge from hiding in daylight as they take advantage of the balmy weather. Fall is the time for many special events, such as harvest festivals celebrating the gathering of crops like fruit, chiles, or pecans.

What to Pack

At any time of year bright sunshine is the norm in the desert, so bring plenty of sunscreen, sunglasses, and a hat that shades your face. If you plan to do any hiking, wear jeans or other durable long pants and long-sleeved cotton shirts no matter how warm the weather. Desert plants can be as brutal as a wildcat, as you might find out in a scrape with a thorny bush or cactus. Painful thorns and cactus needles can be removed with a comb, tweezers and adhesive tape, so consider these items essential. Sharp rocks, too, can take their toll, so pack sturdy hiking shoes or boots that lend firm support to your ankles (boots also offer some protection in the unlikely event you step over or on a rattlesnake). This is a dry climate in any season, so always carry plenty of water. The general guideline is one gallon per person daily, but you actually need more than that if you exert yourself in intense summer heat.

Beyond that, because desert weather can change rather drastically in a single 24-hour period it can be exasperating to figure out how to dress and what provisions to take for a desert expedition. Summer is the most predictable season, at least in daytime, because you can almost always count on hot weather. But the dry air creates unexpectedly cool nights—it can drop as low as the 50s even after a searing hot day—so be sure to keep a light jacket or sweater on hand. You'll also need this gear if you visit Carlsbad Caverns, which is chilly and damp underground at a steady 56 degrees year-round. At all other times of the year, be prepared for virtually any eventuality in the desert. Spring and fall usually are pleasant with temperatures in the 70s or low 80s, but it's not unusual for a late or early snowstorm to dust the countryside. On the other hand, you can be bundled up for winter and experience a mild, springlike day in the middle of January. Wearing layered clothing can help you prepare for surprises.

Sand and dirt can penetrate delicate camera mechanisms, so consider bringing a dust-proof camera case. Insect repellent may be necessary if you plan to visit higher, more vegetated elevations or if you'll be spending some time next to a river, where gnats and mosquitoes prowl in early evening. Ice can disappear fast in a hot, parked vehicle, so it's a good idea to place a small block of dry ice in the bottom of your cooler and cover it with a few bags of regular ice for drinks. If you're camping, check to see if you need to bring your own firewood, since most national parks prohibit wood gathering.

BIG BEND NATIONAL PARK

WEST TEXAS

U.S. 385, 39 mi south of Marathon, Texas; Route 118, 76 mi south of Alpine, Texas; Route 170, 50 mi east of Presidio, Texas.

Miles of blue sky and desert plains, without even a fencepost to mar the view, can have a peculiar effect on those who make it to this remote park. Even some of Big Bend's first visitors, who were accustomed to open land, had mixed reactions to the unending desolation and beauty of the area, which Spanish explorers dubbed "el despoblado" (the unpopulated place). One French writer in 1885 lamented that the land, both desert and mountain, gave him a feeling of "supreme melancholy." Indeed, an urban visitor might feel uneasy at first to be surrounded by so much space: the silence alone is overpowering. But the emptiness can also be sublime. Big Bend is so remote that it receives only several hundred thousand visitors a year, among the least of any of the nation's parks, and facilities are scarce.

At 801,163 acres, this Texas park has among the biggest and best of practically every symbol of the Western outdoors. Diverse plant and animal life, sprawling spaces, mountains, desert and unending vistas constitute an immense frontier in an area the size of Rhode Island. Rare and precious water sources vary in this arid region, where water catchments may be found in hollowed rocks and natural river drainage areas. On the extreme south side of Big Bend, the muddy Rio Grande (called Rio Bravo by Mexican neighbors) twists 118 mi to create the international boundary between the U.S. and Mexico. River rafters might be seen bobbing atop the mostly tranquil currents. Depending on the time of year and extent of water runoff, some white-water churning through steep, stark cliffs can add some adventure to the river journey.

PUBLICATIONS

Naturalist's Big Bend by Roland H. Wauer gives a short history of the park, and includes detailed descriptions of plant and animal life. Color photographs of wildlife and plants illustrate *Big Bend, The Story Behind the Scenery* which provides an overview of the park's history and geology. Carol E. Sperling is the author. Publications are sold through the **Big Bend Natural History Association** (Box 196, Big Bend National Park, TX 79834 | 432/477–2236). The Natural History Association's *Road Guide on sale at park visitor centers gives detailed directions for accessing backcountry dirt roads.*

When to Visit

SCENERY AND WILDLIFE

The shy, delicately shaped white-tailed deer unique to Big Bend frequent the higher elevations of the Chisos Mountains (and are more likely to be seen at sunrise or sunset, or during cooler weather). The park also has about 450 species of birds, some found nowhere else in the U.S. Look for a flash of crimson, the vermilion flycatcher, at the picnic area of Rio Grande Village. Roadrunners are everywhere. In spring, if there has been adequate rainfall during the previous autumn, dense, breathtaking displays of wildflowers and cactus blossoms blanket virtually every hill. In winter, rare snowfall glistening across the stark desert creates alien landscapes.

HIGH AND LOW SEASON

Holiday periods (Christmas and Thanksgiving) are particularly crowded as visitors take advantage of cooler weather. During these times and also in spring when cactus flowers are blooming, you'll be unlikely to find lodging in or near the park if you don't make reservations well in advance. Campgrounds also might be full. (Spring break in particular attracts the campers.) The park is most vacant during extremely hot summer months (temperatures can range as high as 120 degrees in May and June).

Average High/Low Temperature (°F) and Monthly Precipitation (in inches)

	JAN.	FEB.	MAR.	APR.	MAY	JUNE
BIG BEND	61/35	66/38	77/45	81/52	88/59	94/65
	.46	.34	.31	.70	1.50	1.93

	JULY	AUG.	SEPT.	OCT.	NOV.	DEC.
	93/68	91/66	86/62	79/53	68/42	62/36
	2.09	2.35	2.12	2.27	.70	.57

FESTIVALS AND SEASONAL EVENTS

WINTER

Feb.: **Texas Cowboy Poetry Gathering.** The Sul Ross University campus and Museum of Big Bend in Alpine host dances, poetry, and cultural displays reflecting the true West ranching life. | 432/837–8194 | www.cowboypoetry.org.

SUMMER

June–July: **Marfa Glider Camp.** The expansive blue skies and puffy white clouds of West Texas attract many motorless flying machines that soar in air currents and updrafts. This annual event takes place at the Marfa Municipal Airport. Special sessions beginning in 2003 were to be offered at other times of the year. | 800/667–9464 | www.flygliders.com.

FALL

Sept.: **Marfa Lights Festival.** A Labor Day weekend celebration of nighttime mystery lights that have helped give this small town fame takes place with a parade, music, food booths, and live entertainment on the courthouse lawn. | 800/650–9696.

Balloon Rally. About 30 brightly splashed hot air balloons ascend into the skies of Alpine during this three-day annual Labor Day event, which also includes a "fire glow concert." | 800/561–3735.

Nearby Towns

Alpine, a town of about 6,000 people, is known for everything country from cowboy poetry to an extensive college agriculture program at Sul Ross University. This is the hub of West

Texas ranching country. An abundance of flat rock formations gave the tiny town **Lajitas** its name, which means (loosely translated) "tableland with little flat stones." Once a U.S. Cavalry outpost, it's been converted to a resort area that includes a few Old West "theme" motels and even a hardware store. **Marfa,** a middle-of-nowhere west Texas city, has some surprising national claims to fame, including its puzzling "Marfa lights" that are attributed to everything from atmospheric disturbances to imagination. Marfa also was the site of filming for the epic Hollywood film, "Giant," starring Rock Hudson, Elizabeth Taylor, and James Dean. Once the headquarters of quicksilver mining (now defunct), **Terlingua** would be a ghost town were it not for the stubborn few who still maintain residences and a few conveniences such as a dinner theater restaurant and guide services for Big Bend. The official population of the town is about 25. **Study Butte,** with a population of about 100, is 5 mi east of Terlingua and also has its roots in the old quicksilver mining industry. The town now is a tourist center, serving Big Bend.

INFORMATION

Alpine Chamber of Commerce | 106 N. 3rd St., Alpine, TX 79830 | 800/561–3735 or 432/837–2326 | www.alpinetexas.com. **Lajitas Resort** | HC 70, Box 400, Lajitas, TX 79852 | 800/944–9907 or 432/424–3471 | www.lajitas.com. **Marfa Chamber of Commerce** | 207 N. Highland St. (Box 635), Marfa, TX 79843 | 800/650–9696 | www.marfachamberofcommerce.com.

Exploring Big Bend

PARK BASICS

Contacts and Resources: Big Bend National Park | Box 129, Big Bend National Park, TX 79834 | 432/477–2251 | fax 432/477–1175 | www.nps.gov/bibe.

Hours: The park never closes. Visitor center hours are: Panther Junction, daily 8–6; Chisos Basin, daily 8–3:30 (closes for lunch hour); Persimmon Gap, daily 9–5 (open Nov.–Apr. only, closes for lunch hour); Rio Grande Village, (variable hours, closes during summer months). Most or all visitor centers may be closed Christmas Day.

Fees: It costs $15 for a noncommercial vehicle to enter at the gate. Camping fees in developed campgrounds (no round-trips in nonconcession sites) are $10 nightly and free in primitive areas (backcountry permits required).

Getting Around: Paved roads within the park have twists and turns, some very extreme in higher elevations, which also have some steep grades. For these reasons, RVs longer than 24 ft should avoid the Ross Maxwell Scenic Drive on the park's west side and the Chisos Basin road into higher elevations in the central portion of the park. Trailers longer than 20 ft also should avoid these routes. Four-wheel-drive vehicles are needed for many of the backcountry, dirt roads. Parking usually is ample at the different sites, depending on the season. However, warning signs at parking areas may advise you to take valuables with you because of the possibility of break-ins (some areas are very remote). Some outfitters also provide shuttle services in the immediate area and within the park, with varying fees depending on the area accessed, time, and requested services.

   Desert Sports Shuttle Service is among several outfitters that also offer transportation into all the Big Bend canyons. Advance reservations are advised. | Box 448, Terlingua | 888/989–6900.

Permits: Free, mandatory backcountry camping and fishing permits are available at visitor centers.

Public Telephones: Public telephones can be found at the visitor centers of Panther Junction, Chisos Basin, Persimmon Gap, and Rio Grande Village.

Rest Rooms: Public rest rooms may be found at the visitor centers of Panther Junction, Chisos Basin, Persimmon Gap, and Rio Grande Village.

BIG BEND
NATIONAL PARK

EXPLORING
ATTRACTIONS NEARBY
DINING
LODGING
CAMPING AND RV
FACILITIES
SHOPPING
ESSENTIAL
INFORMATION

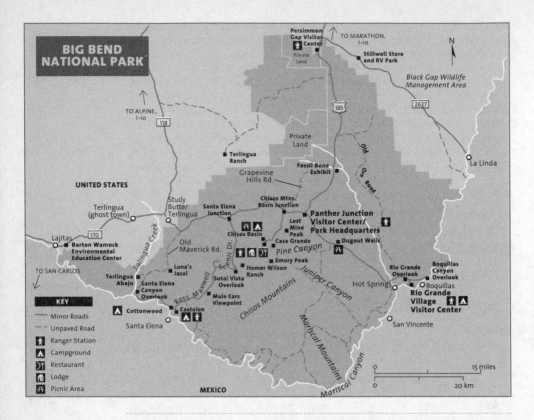

BIG BEND NATIONAL PARK

TO MARATHON, I-10

Persimmon Gap Visitor Center

Private Land

Stillwell Store and RV Park

N

Black Gap Wildlife Management Area

TO ALPINE, I-10

118

385

2627

La Linda

Private Land

Terlingua Ranch

Fossil Bone Exhibit

Old Ore Road

Grapevine Hills Rd.

UNITED STATES

Terlingua (ghost town)

Study Butte/ Terlingua

Santa Elena Junction

Chisos Mtns. Basin Junction

Panther Junction Visitor Center/ Park Headquarters

Lajitas

170

Barton Wamock Environmental Education Center

Chisos Basin

Old Maverick Rd.

Lost Mine Peak

Casa Grande

Pine Canyon

Dugout Wells

TO SAN CARLOS

Luna's Jacal

Emory Peak

Homer Wilson Ranch

Juniper Canyon

Rio Grande Overlook

Boquillas Canyon Overlook

Terlingua Abajo

Santa Elena Canyon Overlook

Sotol Vista Overlook

Mule Ears Viewpoint

Chisos Mountains

Hot Springs

Boquillas

Rio Grande Village Visitor Center

Cottonwood

Castolon

San Vincente

Santa Elena

Mariscal Mountains

Mariscal Canyon

MEXICO

KEY

— Minor Roads
- - Unpaved Road
⚑ Ranger Station
⛺ Campground
🍴 Restaurant
🏨 Lodge
⛱ Picnic Area

15 miles

20 km

Accessibility: While there are many rugged areas of the park that are not recommended for the mobility-impaired, wheelchairs can access all visitor centers along with some camp sites and rest rooms at Chisos Basin and Rio Grande Village. A TDD line (432/477–2370) is available at park headquarters at Panther Junction visitor center. Hiking trails that are wheelchair accessible include The Founder's Walk and Panther Path at Panther Junction, Window View Trail at Chisos Basin, and Rio Grande Village Nature Trail boardwalk. The Rio Grande and Chisos Basin amphitheaters, where evening slide programs often are presented, also are accessible. Some outfitters providing river float trips make provisions for mobility-impaired individuals. Brochures detailing accessibility may be obtained by writing park headquarters.

Emergencies: If you can reach a phone, dial 911 or 432/477–1188. No call boxes are available in the park and cell phones do not work in this remote location, so you must make it to the nearest occupied structure to report emergencies. Park rangers (who are law enforcement agents) can be found at visitor centers, ranger stations, and other locations. Other than first aid from qualified park staff, medical services are just outside the park in tiny communities along Route 170.

Big Bend Family Health Center | Study Butte | 432/371–2661 | Mon, Tues., Thurs., Fri. 7:30–4:30; Wed. 7:30–9:30. **Lajitas Infirmary** | Lajitas | 432/424–5111. **Terlingua Medics** | Terlingua | 432/371–2536.

Lost and Found: The park's lost-and-found is at Panther Junction visitor center.

Good Tours

BIG BEND IN ONE DAY

You'll be able to drive the paved roads of the park in one day, but you'll be missing the best part if you don't indulge in at least a few short hikes to experience big sky country.

Enter the west end of the park off Route 118, and loop southwest on unpaved **Old Maverick Road** 12.8 mi to **Santa Elena Canyon Overlook** (though unpaved, Old Maverick is easy on two–wheel drive vehicles). Take the **Santa Elena Canyon Trail** (1.7 mi round-trip). You'll have to wade Terlingua Creek, then enter the canyon where you'll see massive boulders and the Rio Grande sandwiched between sheer cliff faces. Take the **Ross Maxwell Scenic Drive** 30 mi back north and turn east at Santa Elena Junction.

Drive to the **Chisos Mountains Basin Junction** and turn south. This scenic drive will take you to the heart of Big Bend, where you can linger for a short hike (less than 0.6 mi) along the **Window View Trail.** Visit the gift shop and restaurant, or, if you brought your own lunch, settle in at one of the campground tables near the **visitor center.** Drive north back to the junction, and turn east where you will drive 23 mi to **Rio Grande Village.** Stroll through the tall, shady cottonwoods in the picnic area, and you'll likely see many varieties of birds including a few curious roadrunners. From here, drive east to the **Boquillas Canyon** overlook and view the Mexican village of Boquillas on the south side of the Rio Grande. Backtrack to Panther Junction, and turn north toward Marathon to exit the park and see a different geologic area including flats where fossils have been unearthed.

BIG BEND IN TWO DAYS

Follow the itinerary for day one, except consider staying overnight at an in-park campground, at Chisos Mountain Lodge, or at Lajitas Resort near the park's west border. Depending on the time of year and water levels of the Rio Grande, you can take a daylong guided **float trip** with one of the area outfitters. Or, consider a half-day or day-long **jeep tour** or **horseback ride** through the backcountry (also available through outfitters). The 15.6 mi (one-way) **Glenn Spring** primitive, dirt road brushes against the east side of Chisos Mountains, in a transition zone between grasslands and shrub desert. Another popular route is the 51-mi (one-way) **River Road,** a dirt route that tracks the Rio Grande from east to west across the southern boundaries of the park. You'll also pass by ruins of the old Mariscal quicksilver (mercury) mine.

Attractions

PROGRAMS AND TOURS

Big Bend Seminars. Seminars lasting one to two days cover subjects from wildflowers to geology to desert survival. Schedules vary, but seminars often are available several times monthly. Seminars are conducted at different locations throughout the park, depending on the topic and duration. | 432/477–2236 | bbnha@nps.gov | $50 per day.

Interpretive Activities. Ranger-guided activities include daily slide shows, talks, and walks on natural and cultural history. Check visitor center and campground bulletin boards for postings about scheduled events or call for more information. | 432/477–2251.

Junior Ranger Program. A program book for children is sold for $1 at all park visitor centers. Kids gain insight into the park by completing the pages after suggested short hikes. Your child is then awarded a sticker, badge, patch, and certificate. | 432/477–2251.

SCENIC DRIVES

Ross Maxwell Scenic Drive. If you don't mind a bit of a washboard gravel road, you can make this drive a loop by starting out at the west park entrance and turning southwest onto the Old Maverick Road (unpaved) for 12.8 mi to the Santa Elena Canyon overlook. Here, you'll get a taste of lowland desert amid tall stalks of yuccas. Then, turn back east and then north onto the Ross Maxwell Scenic Drive that takes you 30 mi through pyramid-shape volcanic mountains, such as Mule Ears Peaks.

★ **Chisos Basin Road.** This road leads south from Chisos Basin Junction. By driving into higher elevations (the heart of Big Bend), you're likely to spot a white-tailed deer amid juniper trees and piñon pines. You'll also see the lovely, red-barked Texas madrone along with some

**BEWARE
THE BIRDS**

*When park signs
warn you not to
feed the wildlife,
remember that
birds are included.
At the Rio Grande
Village picnic area,
you can find
yourself circled by
a flock of overly
friendly vultures if
they think you've
got a handout. This
is one familiar Old
West scene you
want to avoid.*

Chisos oaks and Douglas fir trees. Avoid this drive, however, if you are in an RV longer than 24 ft because of sharp curves.

SIGHTS TO SEE

Castolon Historic District. Lingering adobe buildings are what's left of the old farming settlement of Castolon. The Magdalena House has historical exhibits related to farming families and the U.S. military's presence in the area. You'll also find Cottonwood Campground, Castolon Ranger Station, and La Harmonia Company Store. | Southwest side of the park, at the end of the Ross Maxwell Scenic Dr. | 432/477–2225 ranger station.

★ **Chisos Basin.** Panoramic vistas and a quest for the Colima warbler (a domestic bird found only in Big Bend) await you in the forested higher park elevations. This central site also has hiking trails, a lodge, campground, grocery store, gift shop, and restaurant with scenic views. | Off Chisos Basin Rd., 7 mi southwest of Chisos Basin Junction and 9 mi southwest of Panther Junction.

Chisos Basin Visitor Center. Natural resource and geology exhibits are offered here, along with a bookstore and an interactive computer. | Off Chisos Basin Rd., 7 mi southwest of Chisos Basin Junction and 9 mi southwest of Panther Junction | 432/477–2264 | Daily 9–4:30 (varies according to time of year), closed for lunch.

Dugout Wells. A shady oasis surrounding a desert spring attracts several varieties of birds, especially white-winged doves. A picnic table is available, along with a short nature trail. | 5 mi southeast of Panther Junction.

Hot Springs. Hikers soak themselves in the 105°F waters at this historic site alongside the Rio Grande. Only evidence of a post office, motel, and bathhouse is left of this old commercial establishment that operated in the early 1900s. | 15 mi southeast of Panther Junction, near Rio Grande Village.

Panther Junction Visitor Center. This central visitor center, which has exhibits and a bookstore, is also the site of park headquarters and is a good stop for gasoline and limited groceries. | 30 mi south of U.S. 385 junction leading to north park boundary | 432/477–1158 | Daily 8–6.

Persimmon Gap Visitor Center. This visitor center, complete with exhibits and a bookstore, is the northern boundary gateway into miles of flatlands that surround the more scenic heart of Big Bend. This also is a historic route where Comanches traveled into Mexico via the Comanche Trail. Dinosaur fossils have been found in this portion of Big Bend. | North Big Bend boundary, 3 mi south of U.S. 385 junction | 432/477–2393 | Daily 9–4:30, closed for lunch. Closes during warmer season beginning May 1, often as long as six months at a time.

Rio Grande Village. A grove of giant cottonwood trees alongside the Rio Grande make this a favorite hangout of RVers, especially since this is the only area where round-trips can be found. The grassy picnic area among shade trees is highly recommended for birders. A visitor center (with a small bookstore), gasoline, and groceries are available, but don't be fooled by the name—there's no real village here. | 22 mi southeast of Panther Junction.

Rio Grande Village Visitor Center. Opening days and hours are sporadic here, but if you do find the visitor center open you can view videos of Big Bend's geologic and natural features at a mini-theater. | 22 mi southeast of Panther Junction | 432/477–2271 | Daily 8:30–4. Closes during warmer season beginning May 1.

★ **Santa Elena Canyon.** After a short round-trip hike (1.7 mi), you'll be rewarded with a spectacular view of the Rio Grande and sheer cliffs that rise 1,500 ft to create a natural box. | 30 mi southwest of Santa Elena Junction via Ross Maxwell scenic drive; 14 mi southwest of Rte. 118 via Old Maverick Rd.

Sports and Outdoor Activities

BICYCLING

Mountain biking the backcountry roads can be so solitary that you're unlikely to encounter another human being. However, the solitude also means you should be extraordinarily prepared for the unexpected with ample supplies, especially water (summer heat is brutal, and you're unlikely to find shade except in forested areas of Chisos Basin). The park has more than 100 mi of paved roads and 160 mi of backcountry, dirt roads. For a mild, easy ride on mostly level ground, try the 14-mi (one-way) unpaved Old Maverick Road on the west side of the park off Route 118. For more of a challenge, take the unpaved route known as the Old Ore Road, beginning in the north park, for 26.4 mi to near Rio Grande Village on the park's east side. For bike rentals and expeditions *see* Outfitters, *below*.

BIRD-WATCHING

Named a Globally Important Bird Area by the American Bird Conservancy, Big Bend is home to more than 450 different species. Northern extensions of the Chihuahuan Desert represent unique habitat for elusive birds such as the Colima warbler. Serious birders must visit the park to "bag" this bird and complete their checklist of U.S. sightings.

Big Bend Birding Expeditions. Custom guided and regularly scheduled tours of Big Bend are offered through Terlingua Ranch headquarters, where guides keep track of the latest spottings of rare birds such as the Colima warbler and Lawrence's goldfinch. Seminars are also given. | Box 507, Terlingua, 79852 | 888/531–2223.

Chisos Basin. You'll have to hike trails of higher elevations (5,400 ft or higher) and canyons to spy the Colima warbler, found only in Big Bend. This area also has the elusive Lucifer hummingbird. | Off Chisos Basin Rd., 9 mi southwest of Panther Junction.

★ **Rio Grande Village.** Considered the best birding habitat in Big Bend, this river wetland has summer tanagers and vermilion flycatchers among many other species. | 22 mi southeast of Panther Junction.

HIKING

The park's isolation and lack of natural water sources call for packing in plenty of provisions. Always carry enough water to provide a gallon per person for drinking daily (more in extremely hot weather).

Chihuahuan Desert Nature Trail. A windmill and spring form a desert oasis, a refreshing backdrop to a 0.5-mi, flat nature trail where wild doves are abundant. | Dugout Wells, 5 mi southeast of Panther Junction.

Chisos Basin Loop Trail. A forested area and higher elevations give you some sweeping views of the lower desert and distant volcanic mountains on this 1.6-mi round-trip. The elevation in the pass where the trail is located is 5,400 ft; the highest point on the trail is 7,825 ft. | 7 mi southwest of Chisos Basin Junction.

Hot Springs Trail. An abandoned motel and bathhouse foundation from an early 1900s resort are historic sights along this 2-mi hike leading to the Rio Grande and a natural hot spring. | 22 mi southeast of Panther Junction.

★ **Santa Elena Canyon Trail.** A 1.7-mi round-trip crosses Terlingua Creek and takes you to a view of steep cliffs jutting above the Rio Grande. | 8 mi west of Castolon, accessible via Ross Maxwell scenic drive or Old Maverick Rd.

HORSEBACK RIDING

You may camp with your horse at any of the park's primitive campsites, but not in the developed areas. Be sure you know the rules regarding feed (bring your own—grazing is not permitted) and required removal of horse manure. Some trails, such as the Santa Elena and Boquillas Canyon, are off-limits to horses. A free stock-use permit is required,

LOAN-A-BONE

Ten massive pieces of dinosaur neck bone, each weighing up to 1,000 pounds, were discovered in a park wilderness area and loaned to University of Texas at Dallas and Dallas Museum of Natural History paleontologists. The fossils, belonging to a sauropod dinosaur, are being studied at the museum.

and is available at visitor centers as long as you give 24-hours notice. A campsite with **corrals** near Panther Junction may be reserved (no longer than 10 weeks notice) by calling 432/477–1158. For guided rides outside the park, *see* Outfitters, *below.*

RAFTING

Depending on the time of year and water levels, a trip down the Rio Grande through Big Bend can be mostly a mellow experience as you gently float amid scenic canyons. A few potential white-knuckle, white-water adventures might await you, but don't expect too many thrills other than the scenery. Most outfitters are in the communities of Study Butte, Terlingua, and Lajitas just west of the park boundary, off Route 170. Lowest prices begin at about $60–$70 for a half day trip. For rafting expeditions *see* Outfitters, *below.*

Outfitters

MULTI-SPORT

Desert Sports. Besides mountain bike, boat, and equipment rentals, this multisport outfitter provides experienced guides for mountain bike touring, boating, and hiking. | Box 448, Terlingua, 79852 | 432/371–2727 or 888/989–6900 | www.desertsportstx.com.

Lajitas Stables. Lajitas Resort has many options for guided horseback riding tours outside of the park, including combinations with river rafting (offered jointly with Big Bend River Tours). Overnight trips and excursions into Old Mexico also are available. | Lajitas Resort, Lajitas, 79852 | 888/508–7667 or 432/424–3238 | www.lajitasstables.com.

Red Rock Outfitters. You can shop for all manner of outdoor equipment and clothing at this Lajitas Resort outlet, and can book excursions that include river rafting, canoeing, horseback riding, mountain biking, and interpretive tours on topics such as fossil studies and bird-watching. | Lajitas Resort, Lajitas, 79852 | 432/424–5170.

RAFTING

Big Bend River Tours. Gourmet or musical trips are among special arrangements made for rafting tours down the Rio Grande. | Lajitas Resort, Terlingua | 800/545–4240 | www.bigbendrivertours.com.

Far Flung Adventures. Various rafting trips are tailored to individual needs. Some options give you the chance to make frequent stops and explore canyons on foot. Special trips include gourmet rafting tours, with cheese and wine served on checkered tablecloths alongside the river. | Lajitas Resort, Lajitas | 800/359–4138 or 432/371–2489 | www.farflung.com/tx.

Rio Grande Adventures. Guided river raft trips take place in the various canyons; Santa Elena, Mariscal and Colorado Canyon are among them. Trips last from a half day up to a week, depending on your preference. | Box 229, Terlingua, 79852 | 800/343–1640 | www.riograndeadventures.com.

Texas River Expeditions. Specialty rafting trips can include "star parties" (we're not talking celebrities here), inspired by the vast, dark skies and brilliant constellations seen so clearly overnight. Rapids and hot springs can be part of the adventure. | Box 583, Terlingua, 79852 | 800/839–7238 | www.texasriver.com.

Attractions Nearby

Sights to See

Barton Warnock Environmental Education Center. A self-guided walking tour takes you through indoor and outdoor exhibits providing insight into cultural history and natural resources of the Big Bend area. The center, operated by Texas Parks and Wildlife, is a good way to become oriented to Chihuahuan Desert plant life before touring nearby Big Bend Ranch State Park and Big Bend National Park. A gift shop and bookstore are available. | Off Rte. 170, 1 mi east of Lajitas, between state and national Big Bend parks Terlingua 79852 | HC 70, Box 375 | 432/424–3327 | www.tpwd.state.tx.us/park/barton/barton.htm | $3 | Daily 8–4:30.

Big Bend Ranch State Park. As a southwest buffer to Big Bend National Park, this rugged desert wilderness extends along the Rio Grande across 280, 280 acres from southeast of Lajitas to Presidio. A small Texas longhorn herd roams the park, along with mountain lions and deer. You can hike, backpack, raft, and even round up longhorn steers. Various lodging and camping options are available. The eastern boundary is only several miles west of the far western extension of Big Bend National Park. | Entrance road at Fort Leaton, 4 mi southeast of Presidio off Rte. 170, Presidio 79845 | Box 2319 | 432/229–3416 | www.tpwd.state.tx.us/park/bigbend/bigbend.htm | $3 entrance fee, $3 activity fee.

Boquillas, Mexico. Concerns about terrorism have led to strict border crossing security at the Big Bend National Park boundary line. Villagers used to wait at the Rio Grande crossing with burros and pickup trucks to transport you into town just across the border. But no more. If you want to visit Boquillas, you must do so by entering official checkpoints at Del Rio or Presidio in Texas. If you try to re-enter the United States through the Big Bend park, you are now subject to fines of up to $5,000, one year's imprisonment or both. Only 25 families live in Boquillas, where there's a bed-and-breakfast and restaurant (but no electricity). Residents here greatly value and depend on tourists. | End of park access road at the Rio Grande (international boundary line), 24 mi southeast of Panther Junction, Boquillas, Mexico.

Santa Elena, Mexico. As with Boquillas (above), heightened security has ended an informal system of border crossings from the park into nearby Mexican villages. You'll no longer see a rowboat operated by villagers from Santa Elena that once ferried visitors across the Rio Grande at this crossing point near Castolon in Big Bend National Park. If you want to visit here now, you'll have to start at official border crossings in Del Rio or Presidio in Texas. And you cannot cross back over into the park from the villages, or you will risk fines of up to $5,000, one year's imprisonment or both. Santa Elena has about 250 residents along with four Mexican restaurants. Tourists here are treated cordially. | 35 mi southeast of Panther Junction, near Castolon, Santa Elena, Mexico.

Dining

In Big Bend
Chisos Mountains Lodge Restaurant. American/Casual. Views of the imposing Chisos Mountains are a pleasant accompaniment to nicely prepared (but not fancy) fare such as chicken-fried steak and hamburgers. | 7 mi southwest of Chisos Basin Junction and 9 mi southwest of Panther Junction | 432/477–2291 | $6–$14 | AE, D, DC, MC, V.

Near the Park
Candililla Cafe and Thirsty Goat Saloon. American. Steaks and scrumptious country cooking are the specialty of this restaurant with wagon wheels and Old West decor. Glass walls give you unobstructed views of glowing sunsets and the nearby golf course. The restaurant entrance is a few steps from the door to the saloon. | Lajitas Resort, off Rte. 170, 25 mi west of park entrance, Lajitas | 915/424–3471 | $5–$15 | AE, D, DC, MC, V.

Lodging

In Big Bend
Chisos Mountains Lodge. Staying in the cooler, forested section of Big Bend's higher elevations is a privilege at the only in-park lodge, but most rooms are a bit spartan though well maintained. Views of desert peaks and vistas more than make up for any lack of modern conveniences. The few motels operated near park boundaries are equally expensive and often have rooms substandard to the lodge's rooms. Make advance reservations especially before peak seasons—up to a year's lead time is not out of the question for spring cactus flower-

ing season. Checks are not accepted for deposits. TVs with video equipment for watching movie rentals are available for a $12 nightly fee. Restaurant, dining room. No room phones, no TV. Hiking. Shops. Some pets allowed. | 7 mi southwest of Chisos Basin Junction and 9 mi southwest of Panther Junction | 432/477–2291 | 72 rooms | $73–$83 | AE, D, DC, MC, V.

Near the Park
Gage Motel. Cowboy, Indian, and Hispanic cultures are reflected in room furnishings in this historic hotel, built in the 1920s in the tiny community of Marathon. The expertly crafted gardens and courtyards are worth viewing, even if you aren't a guest. Some rooms do not have private baths. A few rooms have fireplaces. Massage therapy is offered. Restaurant, bar. Some kitchenettes, some microwaves, some refrigerators. Some room phones. Pool. Massage. Shops. Some pets allowed (fee). | Off U.S. 385, 40 mi north of park boundary, Marathon | 432/386–4206 | fax 915/386–4510 | 44 rooms, 2 houses | $69–$225 | AE, D, MC, V.

Lajitas Resort. This is the nicest place to eat, shop, and overnight within 25 mi of the park. Various theme motels and lodging options are available (under the same ownership) in this revived ghost town converted into a classy, Old West–style resort community alongside the Rio Grande. Conveniences within walking distance of Lajitas include a restaurant, lounge, and golf course. Make reservations well in advance of peak seasons. 3 restaurants, bar (with entertainment). Some kitchenettes, minibars, some microwaves, some refrigerators, some in-room hot tubs. Cable TV. Pool, pond. Beauty salon, massage, spa. Golf course, tennis court. Horseback riding. Boating, bicycles. Laundry service. | Off Rte. 170, 25 mi west of park entrance, Lajitas | 432/424–3471 or (reservations) 877/525–4827 | 72 rooms, 16 suites, 2 cottages | $225–$550 | AE, D, DC, MC, V.

Camping and RV Facilities

In Big Bend
Chisos Basin Campground. A forested area in higher elevations has scenic views, mountain peaks, and cool shade. The site has no round-trips. Because of steep grades and twisting curves on the access road, trailers longer than 20 ft and RVs longer than 25 ft are not recommended. Flush toilets. Drinking water. Food service, grills, picnic tables. Public telephone. General store, ranger station. | 7 mi southwest of Chisos Basin Junction | 432/477–2251 | 65 RV and tent sites | $10 | No credit cards.

Cottonwood Campground. Twenty-two mi southwest of Santa Elena Junction, Castolon campground is next to the Rio Grande floodplain and near the Santa Elena Canyon Trail that leads to steep cliffs jutting above the river. This is also a popular bird-watching spot. The grounds are generator-free. Pit toilets. Drinking water. Grills, picnic tables. General store, ranger station. | Off Ross Maxwell Scenic Dr., Castolon | 432/477–2251 | 31 RV and tent sites | $10 | No credit cards.

★ **Rio Grande Village Campground.** A shady oasis with a store and gasoline station, the campground is the park's "hot spot" for birding because of a large grove of cottonwood trees and Rio Grande floodplain. A more informal area once used for overflow guests is now closed. Flush toilets. Dump station. Drinking water, guest laundry, showers. Grills, picnic tables. Public telephone. General store, ranger station, service station. | 22 mi southeast of Panther Junction | 432/477–2251 | 100 RV and tent sites | $10 | No credit cards.

Rio Grande Village RV Park. Popular because it's the only RV site in the park with round-trips of any kind, this campground often is full in peak seasons and no advance reservations are taken. Register at the Rio Grande Village Store (22 mi southeast of Panther Junction). You must be able to take all round-trips, and you must have a 3-inch sewer connection to stay here. Only 30 amp electrical connections are available. Flush toilets. Full round-trips, dump station. Drinking water, guest laundry. Grills, picnic tables. Electricity, public telephone. General store, ranger station, service station. | 22 mi southeast of Panther Junction | 432/477–2293 | 25 RV sites | $18 | AE, D, MC, V.

Near the Park

Big Bend Motor Inn and RV Campground. Shade trees and a scenic setting make this a nice RV roosting place within 3 mi of the west park entrance. But the motel rooms are overpriced for spartan accommodations and service can be less than cordial here and at the grocery store and restaurant near the premises. Convenience may outweigh disadvantages. Flush toilets. Full round-trips. Drinking water, guest laundry, showers. Food service, grills, picnic tables. Electricity, public telephone. General store, service station. | Hwy. 118, 3 mi west of west park entrance Study Butte | 800/848–2363 | www.texbesthotels.com/big-bend_motorinn.htm | 126 RV sites, separate informal tent area | $9 tent sites, $16 RV sites, $21 RV sites with full hookups. | AE, D, DC, MC, V.

Shopping

Chisos Mountain Lodge Gift and Photo Shop. A small gift shop with limited selections of souvenirs and books also sells photo supplies. The shop is in the park lodge lobby and restaurant area. | 7 mi south of Chisos Basin Junction | 432/477–2291.

Chisos Basin Store and Post Office. As a convenience to campers and picnickers, a few grocery items and snacks are sold here. | 7 mi south of Chisos Basin Junction | 432/477–2291 | Daily 9–9.

La Harmonia Company Store. Campers and villagers from Santa Elena, Mexico, come to this historic adobe building to buy basic grocery items and snacks. Look for the antique gas pump. | 35 mi southwest of Panther Junction at Castolon, 22 mi southwest of Santa Elena Junction | 432/477–2222 | Daily 10–1, 1:30–6.

Rio Grande Village Store. Since no food services are at this village, you might stop by for a few snacks and sandwich items and eat at the nearby picnic area. Payments (but not reservations) are taken here for RV sites with hookups. | 22 mi southeast of Panther Junction | 432/477–2293 | Daily 9–6.

Essential Information

ATMS: Quicksilver Branch Bank and ATM | Study Butte, 5 mi from west park entrance, at intersection of Rte. 118 and Rte. 170 | 432/371–2211.

AUTOMOBILE SERVICE STATIONS: Panther Junction Chevron | Panther Junction, 26 mi south of north park entrance | 432/477–2294. **Rio Grande Village Chevron** | Rio Grande Village, 22 mi southeast of Panther Junction | 432/477–2293.

POST OFFICES: Panther Junction Visitor Center | Panther Junction, 26 mi south of north park entrance, 79834 | 432/477–1158. **Chisos Basin Store.** | 7 mi southwest of Chisos Basin Junction, 79834 | 432/477–2291.

CARLSBAD CAVERNS NATIONAL PARK

SOUTHEASTERN NEW MEXICO

U.S. 62–180, 27 mi southwest of Carlsbad and 35 mi north of Guadalupe Mountains National Park. From El Paso, Texas, take U.S. 62–180 east and north 154 mi to Carlsbad Caverns.

A reverent whisper may be your tone of voice as you descend the winding, paved trail into the subterranean world of Carlsbad Caverns. Silence has existed here for eons, and the dank smell, too, is musty and old. Immense columns and distant palaces take shape in the darkness, illuminated by subtle electric lights. It seems almost pitifully inadequate to describe what is seen here only by images that are familiar to the limited human mind and experience. Yet, it is the only way. Damp formations with names like flowstone, soda straws, and draperies help set the exotic scene, yet over there, a giant "ice cream cone" is half melted. And directly ahead a whale's mouth gapes open to reveal sharp, pointed teeth. Here, shadowy inhabitants dance within a fairyland of stalactites (formations that hang from the ceiling) and stalagmites (formations that are anchored to a ground surface and grow upward).

Suddenly a chilly water drop splats upon your head, a firsthand experience of the tool that shaped the gargantuan chamber of the Big Room and the maze of passages covering more than 30 mi. The Big Room alone occupies 14 acres under towering ceilings. Rainwater percolating underground from the surface helped etch these chambers within a limestone reef, made up of organisms, plant life, and sediment that settled from a vast, ancient ocean. The process of creation that carved these chambers began about 250 million years ago. It's no wonder that people whisper, because a visit here is like touching the face of Eternity.

Carlsbad Caverns remains at a constant, chilly 56°F year-round. Public tours are limited only to developed portions of the caverns, which still offer plenty to explore. The two main touring options are a 1-mi, self-guiding Big Room Route that can be accessed by elevator. The second option is to walk down the Natural Entrance Route, which is a winding 1-mi descent of 750 ft. Once below ground, you can then stroll the 1-mi Big Room Tour on level ground. Both tours exit by way of an elevator. Pathways for both tours are paved, but baby strollers are not allowed. Electronic signals along the way trigger an optional CD-ROM audio guide—recorded commentary by park rangers, geologists, and cavers.

PUBLICATIONS

Jim White's Own Story by early explorer Jim White tells of this cowboy's exploits into the heart of Carlsbad Caverns, before it was ever developed as a national park. *Bats of Carlsbad Caverns* by various experts helps debunk myths about bats. For more publications, contact the **Carlsbad Caverns Guadalupe Mountains Association (CCGMA).** | 727 Carlsbad Caverns Hwy., Carlsbad, NM 88220 | 505/785–2232 or 505/785–2569 (bookstore) | www.ccgma.org.

When to Visit

Carlsbad Caverns National Park is open year-round. The caves are a constant temperature no matter what the weather: 56°F in Carlsbad Cavern and 62°F in Slaughter Canyon Cave. Above ground, the climate of the park is semiarid, with hot summers and mild, dry, and sunny winters. The sun shines most of the time, and humidity is generally low. Temperatures from mid-May through mid-September almost always exceed 90°F and frequently climb over 100°F. Even during the hottest periods, however, nights are comfortably cool. Winter storms, while infrequent, do occur and have been known to frost the countryside with temperatures as low as the teens.

SCENERY AND WILDLIFE

The spiraling columns of bats leaving the cave's entrance at sunset is almost as spectacular as touring the underground portion of the park. However, you must visit from about mid-May to mid-October to witness the bats, which migrate south to Mexico in winter.

One of New Mexico's best birding areas is at Rattlesnake Springs, off U.S. 62–180. Summer and fall migrations give you the best chance of spotting the most varieties of the more than 330 species of birds that come and go in the area. The golden eagle is one infrequent visitor. You might even get the thrill of glimpsing a brilliant, gray-and-crimson vermilion flycatcher found only in the southernmost reaches of Arizona, New Mexico, and Texas.

Late evening or early morning hours are the best times to spot mule deer grazing alongside highways or on the Walnut Canyon road leading to the park visitor center. If you're out walking, be wary of different rattlesnake species such as banded-rock and diamondbacks. Snakes generally appear in summer, even on trails near the visitor center. If you see one, give it a wide berth.

In spring, thick stands of yucca plants unfold yellow flowers on their tall stalks. Blossoming cacti and desert wildflowers are one of the natural wonders of the park's Walnut Canyon, particularly following an unusually wet winter or early spring. You'll see bright red blossoms adorning ocotillo plants, and sunny yellow blooms sprouting from prickly pear cactus.

HIGH AND LOW SEASON

Summer months are the most crowded, particularly because the caverns are so cool and comfortable. You'll avoid the crowds if you show up between late September and early May, except during the Christmas, New Year, and Easter holiday periods. Spring break may also attract higher than normal crowds. Some of the heaviest park usage occurs during the Fourth of July holiday, partly because nearby Carlsbad offers some extraordinary fireworks displays and other special events. You could wait in line as long as an hour to catch an elevator ride back to the surface on this day. On self-guided tours, people tend to spread out on the underground paths within massive chambers. Special tours that are arranged by reservation are limited to a certain number at any time of year.

CARLSBAD CAVERNS
NATIONAL PARK

EXPLORING
ATTRACTIONS NEARBY
DINING
LODGING
CAMPING AND RV
FACILITIES
SHOPPING
ESSENTIAL
INFORMATION

Average High/Low Temperature (°F) and Rainfall/Snowfall (in inches)

	JAN.	FEB.	MAR.	APR.	MAY	JUNE
CARLSBAD	57/27	63/32	70/38	79/47	87/56	95/64
CAVERNS	.43	.44	.30	.53	1.24	1.53
	JULY	AUG.	SEPT.	OCT.	NOV.	DEC.
	95/67	93/66	87/59	79/47	67/35	59/29
	1.73	1.96	2.34	1.24	.49	.51

FESTIVALS AND SEASONAL EVENTS
WINTER

Nov.–Dec.: **Christmas on the Pecos.** In nearby Carlsbad, dazzling Christmas displays decorate backyards and lots along a 2.5-mi stretch of the Pecos River. Fifty-minute boat tours ($10 Thurs.–Sun., $5 Mon.–Wed.) are operated from Thanksgiving night through December 31. Tickets for the event usually sell out early, so buy them in advance; they are available beginning August 1. The night breeze blowing across the water can be chilly, so dress warmly. | 505/887–6516, 505/628–0952 after Oct. 1.

SPRING

May: **Mescal Roast and Mountain Spirit Dances.** Carlsbad's Living Desert Zoo and Garden State Park celebrates the mystic connection Mescalero Apaches have long had with the Guadalupe Mountains, where mescal plants were traditionally gathered for food. | 505/887–5516.

SUMMER

July: **Independence Day Fireworks Celebration.** One of the best area fireworks displays is on the Pecos River in downtown Carlsbad, where ground and aerial lights are reflected in the water. | 505/887–6516.

Aug.: **Bat Flight Breakfast.** On the second Thursday in August, early risers gather at the entrance to Carlsbad Caverns to eat breakfast and watch tens of thousands of bats fly back into the cave after a night of feeding on insects. | 505/785–2232.

FALL

Sept.: **International Bat Festival.** Educational and family activities such as costume-judging contests take place in this three-day event staged at Carlsbad's Pecos River Village alongside the river. Interpretive programs also are offered at Carlsbad Caverns in association with the conference. | 505/785–2232.

Nearby Towns

In 1927 Charlie L. White (no relation to explorer Jim White, who was the first to explore Carlsbad Cavern) established White's Cavern Camp 7 mi east of the entrance to Carlsbad Cavern as a convenience to the ever-growing number of tourists. Now known as **White's City,** this privately owned town is the nearest place to Carlsbad Caverns to find lodging, food, and shopping facilities—plus a water park. On the Pecos River, 27 mi northeast of the park, the town of **Carlsbad** has 2.75 mi of beaches and riverside pathways, a zoo, and a museum. The rural community has plenty of hotels and restaurants to serve park visitors.

INFORMATION

Carlsbad Chamber of Commerce | 302 S. Canal St., Carlsbad, NM 88220 | 505/887–6516 | www.chamber.caverns.com. **White's City Inc.** | 17 Carlsbad Caverns Hwy., White's City, NM 88268 | 505/785–2291 or 800/228–3767 | www.whitescity.com.

Exploring Carlsbad Caverns

PARK BASICS

Contacts and Resources: Carlsbad Caverns National Park. | 3225 National Parks Hwy., Carlsbad, NM 88220 | 505/785–2232, 800/967–2283 reservations for special cave tours, 800/388–2733 cancellations | www.nps.gov/cave.

Hours: The visitor center opens daily at 8 and closes between 5 and 7, depending on the season. Tours of various caves and routes take place at appointed hours. No reservations are required for the main tours, though they are generally essential for all others. The King's Palace Tour sometimes is available without prior notice.

Fees: No fee is charged for parking or to enter the aboveground portion of the park. It costs $6 to descend into Carlsbad Cavern either by elevator or through the natural entrance. Costs for special tours range from $7 to $20 plus general admission.

Getting Around: Once you turn west on the route leading to Carlsbad Caverns visitor center, you'll have a 7-mi, scenic drive uphill on a paved two-lane road. Parking by the visitor center is ample as well as free, and a special area is set aside for recreational vehicles. The visitor center serves as the cavern entrance, so it's the starting point for most of your exploring. The 9.5-mi Walnut Canyon Desert Drive loop is one-way only. This scenic drive on a curvy, gravel road is not recommended for motor homes or trailers. Be alert for wildlife such as mule deer crossing roadways, especially during early morning or evening hours.

Permits: All hikers are advised to stop at the visitor center information desk for current information about trails; those planning overnight hikes must obtain a free backcountry permit. Trails are poorly defined but can be followed with a topographic map. Dogs are not allowed in the park, but a kennel is available at the park visitor center.

Public Telephones: Public telephones are at the visitor center.

Rest Rooms: Public rest rooms are at the park visitor center, inside the visitor center restaurant, and near the underground lunchroom.

Accessibility: Portions of the paved Big Room trails in Carlsbad Caverns are accessible to wheelchairs. A map defining appropriate routes is available at the visitor center information desk. Individuals with walkers may have difficulty accessing certain narrow and winding trails. They should ask for guidelines at the information desk. Strollers are not permitted on trails (use a baby pack instead). Individuals who may have difficulty walking should access the Big Room via elevator. From the underground lunchroom area, they should be able to step out at least a portion of a way on a trail to view some of the formations. Individuals in wheelchairs or who are otherwise mobility-impaired should not take the Natural Entrance Route because the trail is steep and winding. The TDD number is: 888/530–9796.

Emergencies: In the event of a medical emergency, dial 911, contact a park ranger, or report to the visitor center. To contact park police dial 505/785–2232, locate a park ranger, or report to the visitor center. Carlsbad Caverns has trained emergency medical technicians on duty and a first aid room. White's City has emergency medical technicians available to respond to medical emergencies. A full-service hospital is in nearby Carlsbad.

Lost and Found: The park's lost-and-found is at the **visitor center information desk.** | 505/785–2232.

Good Tours

CARLSBAD CAVERNS
NATIONAL PARK

EXPLORING
ATTRACTIONS NEARBY
DINING
LODGING
CAMPING AND RV
FACILITIES
SHOPPING
ESSENTIAL
INFORMATION

CARLSBAD CAVERNS IN ONE DAY

Begin by taking the **Natural Entrance Route Tour.** After 1.25 mi or about an hour, you'll link up with the **Big Room Route.** The underground walk extends another 1.25 mi, and takes about 1.5 hours to complete. If you have made reservations in advance or happen upon some openings, you also can take the additional **King's Palace** guided tour for 1 mi and an additional 1.5 hours. By this time, you will have spent four hours in the cave. Take the elevator back up to the top. If you haven't had enough walking by now, consider a short hike along the self-guided 0.5-mi **Desert Nature Walk** by the visitor center.

To visit **Rattlesnake Springs** picnic area, take U.S. 62–180 south from White's City 5.5 mi, and turn back west onto Route 418. You'll find old-growth shade trees, grass, picnic tables, and water. Many varieties of birds flit from tree to tree. Return to the Carlsbad Caverns entrance road and take the 9.5-mi Walnut Canyon Desert Drive loop. Leave yourself enough time to return to the **visitor center** for the evening bat flight.

CARLSBAD CAVERNS IN TWO DAYS

Follow the schedule for the first day's visit to Carlsbad Caverns. If you have an appetite for more underground adventure, head for **Slaughter Canyon Cave** early on the morning of day two (you must make a reservation several weeks in advance). It takes about two hours to tour this primitive cave, but the massive formations and pristine environment are worth the effort. Spend the afternoon on one or more of the other **special tours** at the main Carlsbad Cavern. Reservations are required for all special tours.

Attractions

Since the underground is the dominant attraction of Carlsbad Caverns, activities are not as varied as in other parks. Some hiking options are available, as well as free backpacking opportunities.

PROGRAMS AND TOURS

★ **Evening Bat Flight Program.** In the amphitheater at the Natural Cave Entrance (a short trail leads from main parking lot), a ranger discusses the park's batty residents before the creatures begin their sundown exodus. The bats aren't on any predictable schedule—so times are a little iffy. Rangers typically provide interpretive information until the bats decide it's time to rise, en masse, for a night of feeding on insects. | Natural Cave Entrance, at the visitor center | Free | Mid-May–mid-Oct., nightly at sundown.

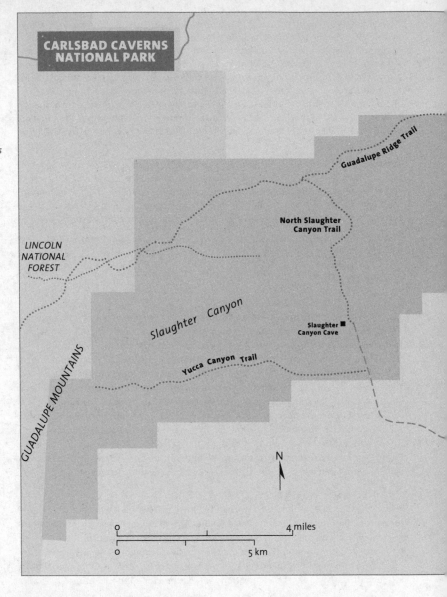

**THINGS THAT
GO BUMP IN
THE NIGHT**

*Bats use a type of
sonar system,
called
echolocation, to
orient themselves
and locate insects
to dine on while
feeding at night.
About seven species
of bats live in
Carlsbad Caverns,
although the
Mexican freetail
is the most
predominant.*

Hall of the White Giants. Plan to squirm through some tight passages for long distances to access a very remote chamber, where you'll see towering, glistening white formations that explain the name of this feature. This strenuous, ranger-led tour lasts about four hours. Steep drop-offs might make you a bit queasy. There's a special tour available for an additional charge ($20). | At the visitor center | 800/967–2283 | $6 | Tour Sat. at 1.

King's Palace. Some of the distinctive sights along this scenic detour in the main Carlsbad Caverns are the Queen's Chamber and Green Lake Room. The mile-long walk is on a paved trail, but there's one very steep hill. This ranger-guided tour lasts about 1.5 hours and gives you the chance to experience a blackout, when all lights are extinguished. While advance reservations are highly recommended, this is the one special tour that you might

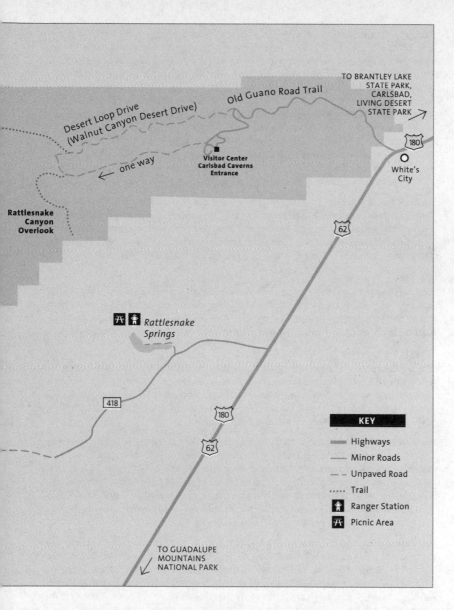

Desert Loop Drive
(Walnut Canyon Desert Drive)

Old Guano Road Trail

← one way

TO BRANTLEY LAKE
STATE PARK,
CARLSBAD,
LIVING DESERT
STATE PARK →

180

White's City

Visitor Center
Carlsbad Caverns
Entrance

Rattlesnake
Canyon
Overlook

62

Rattlesnake
Springs

418

180

62

KEY

━━━ Highways

─── Minor Roads

─ ─ Unpaved Road

····· Trail

Ranger Station

Picnic Area

TO GUADALUPE
MOUNTAINS
NATIONAL PARK

CARLSBAD CAVERNS
NATIONAL PARK

EXPLORING
ATTRACTIONS NEARBY
DINING
LODGING
CAMPING AND RV
FACILITIES
SHOPPING
ESSENTIAL
INFORMATION

be able to sign up for on the spot. | At the visitor center | 800/967–2283 | $8 | Tours Labor Day–Memorial Day, daily 10 and 2; Memorial Day–Labor Day, daily 10, 11, 2, and 3.

Left Hand Tunnel. Lantern light illuminates the easy walk on this detour in the main Carlsbad Cavern, which leads to Permian Age fossils offering evidence of the ancient reef that helped form this attraction. The guided tour over a packed, dirt trail lasts about two hours. | At the visitor center | 800/967–2283 | $7 | Tour daily at 9.

Lower Cave. Fifty-foot vertical ladders and a dirt path will take you into undeveloped portions of Carlsbad Caverns. It takes about three hours to negotiate this moderately strenuous side trip led by a knowledgeable ranger. | At the visitor center | 800/967 2283 | $20 | Reservations essential | Tour weekdays at 1.

WASHED OUT

The deserts of the Southwest experience a summer monsoon season, when shifts in wind direction over the Gulf of Mexico trigger usually brief though heavy rainstorms. Because the hard-packed soil does not absorb water easily, the cloudbursts can flood arroyos and low-lying areas. Remember that flash flooding is swift and common, and be wary of low road crossings if thunderclouds are present. Even if it hasn't rained where you are, a flash flood can appear as if from nowhere.

Slaughter Canyon Cave. One of the most popular secondary sites in the park, Slaughter Canyon Cave is about 23 mi southwest of the main Carlsbad Caverns and visitor center. From the Slaughter Canyon parking area, give yourself 45 minutes to make the steep 0.5-mi climb up a trail leading to the mouth of the cave, where you will meet your ranger guide at the appointed time. Wear hiking shoes with ankle support, and carry plenty of water. You're also expected to bring your own two D-cell flashlight. You'll find that the cave consists primarily of a single corridor, 1,140 ft long, with numerous side passages. Outstanding formations are Christmas Tree, the Monarch Room, Klansman, Tear Drop, and the China Wall. You must make reservations several weeks in advance for this tour. | End of Rte. 418, 10 mi west of U.S. 62–180 | 800/967–2283 | $15 | Reservations essential | Tours Memorial Day–Labor Day, daily 10 and 1; post-Labor Day–Dec. 31, weekends at 10; Jan. 1–Memorial Day, weekends 10 and 1.

Spider Cave. This backcountry cave is listed as "wild," a clue that you might need a similar nature to attempt viewing this one. Plan on climbing, crawling, stooping and sweating. Tight squeezes are common. Wear clothes that you don't mind getting streaked with grime. It will take you four hours to complete this ranger-led tour noted for its adventure. | Meet at visitor center | 800/967–2283 | $20 | Reservations essential | Tour Sun. at 1.

SCENIC DRIVES

Walnut Canyon Desert Drive. In late afternoon and early morning, you can enjoy the full spectrum of the desert's changing light and colors on this 9.5-mi loop. It begins 0.5 mi from the visitor center and travels along the top of the Guadalupe Ridge to the edge of Rattlesnake Canyon, then back down through upper Walnut Canyon to the main entrance road.

SIGHTS TO SEE

★ **The Big Room.** With a floor space equal to 14 football fields, this underground focal point of Carlsbad Caverns gives you the impression you could lose yourself forever. The ceiling at its highest is 255 ft (the White House could fit in one corner). The 1-mi loop walk on a mostly level, paved trail is self-guided. | At the visitor center | $6 | Memorial Day–Labor Day, daily 8:30–5; Labor Day–Memorial Day, daily 8:30 or 9–3:30.

Natural Entrance. A self-guided, paved trail leads from the natural cave entrance. The route is winding and sometimes slick from water seepage above ground. A steep descent of about 750 ft takes you about a mile through the main corridor and past features such as Bat Cave and the Boneyard. Iceberg Rock is a 200,000-ton boulder that dropped from the cave ceiling eons ago. After about a mile, you'll link up underground with the 1-mi Big Room trail and return to the surface via elevator. | At the visitor center | $6 | Memorial Day–Labor Day, daily 8:30–3:30; Labor Day–Memorial Day, daily 8:30 or 9–2.

Rattlesnake Springs. Enormous cottonwood trees shade the picnic and recreation area at this cool oasis near Black River. The rare desert wetland harbors birds, butterflies, mammals, and reptiles. Don't let its name scare you; there are no more rattlesnakes here than at any other similar site in the Southwest. Overnight camping and parking are not allowed. Take U.S. 62–180 5.5 mi south of White's City and turn west onto Route 418 for 2.5 mi. | Rte. 418.

Visitor Center. A mini-theater here offers a brief orientation video so that you can both anticipate your underground journey and also learn rules of proper cave etiquette such as staying on trails and not touching formations, which can be marred and darkened by oily skin. Exhibits explain how subterranean rooms were formed, along with park history and the life of bats. Friendly rangers staff an information desk, where tickets and maps are sold. A gift shop and bookstore also are on the premises. | 7 mi west of park entrance at White's City, off U.S. 62/180 | 505/785–2232 | Late Aug.–Memorial Day, daily 8–5; Memorial Day–late Aug., daily 8–7.

Sports and Outdoor Activities

BIRD-WATCHING

You're likely to spy an unusual species anywhere in the Carlsbad Caverns area. When at the park visitor center, ask for a checklist and then start looking for red-tailed hawks, red-winged blackbirds, white-throated swifts, northern flickers, pygmy nuthatches, yellow-billed cuckoos, roadrunners, mallards, and American coots.

Rattlesnake Springs. Rattlesnake Springs within the park is a natural wetland with old-growth cottonwoods, offering one of the better bird habitats in New Mexico. Because southern New Mexico is in the northernmost region of the Chihuahuan Desert, you're likely to see birds that can't be found anywhere else in the U.S. outside extreme southern Texas and Arizona. If you see a flash of crimson, you might have spotted a vermilion flycatcher. Wild turkeys also hang out at this oasis. | Rte. 418 2.5 mi west of U.S. 62–180, 5.5 mi south of White's City.

CAVING

By contacting the park's **Cave Resources Office** (505/785–2232 Ext. 363), you can acquire permits for about 10 backcountry caves that are open to exploration only by serious cavers (guidelines are spelled out under the park's cave management plan).

HIKING

Few trails are marked in the park. A topographical map, available at the visitor center, is helpful for finding some of the old ranch trails. Permits aren't required except for overnight backpacking, but all hikers planning long excursions are requested to register at the visitor center information desk. You should carry at least one gallon of water per person for a day's consumption, but more is actually needed on extremely hot days.

Desert Nature Walk. While waiting for the night bat flight program, try taking the 0.5-mi self-guided hike. The tagged and identified flowers and plants make this a good place to get acquainted with much of the local desert flora. | Off the cavern entrance trail, 200 yards east of the visitor center.

North Slaughter Canyon Trail. Beginning at the Slaughter Canyon parking lot, the trail traverses a heavily vegetated canyon bottom into a remote part of the park. As you begin hiking, look off to the east (to your right) to see the magnificent Elephant Back formation, the first of many dramatic limestone formations visible from the trail. The route travels 5.5 mi one way, with the last 3 mi steeply climbing onto a limestone ridge escarpment. Allow six to eight hours round-trip. | Rte. 418, 10 mi west of U.S. 62–180.

Old Guano Road Trail. An abandoned road that runs a little more than 3.5 mi one way originally was the truck and wagon route on which miners used to transported bat dung or guano (a fertilizer) from Carlsbad Cavern to Carlsbad. The terrain is mostly flat but drops sharply down to the White's City campground at the end. Because the trail follows a more direct route, it covers about half the distance of the highway to White's City. Give yourself two to three hours to complete the walk. The trailhead is at the Bat Flight Amphitheater, near the Natural Cave entrance and visitor center.

Rattlesnake Canyon Overlook Trail A 0.25-mi stroll off Walnut Canyon Desert Drive offers a nice overlook of the greenery of Rattlesnake Canyon. | Mile marker 9 on Walnut Canyon Desert Dr.

Rattlesnake Canyon Trail. This path marked with rock cairns descends from 4,570 to 3,900 ft as it winds into the canyon. Allow three to four hours to trek down into the canyon and make the somewhat strenuous climb out. The total trip is about 6 mi. | Mile marker 9 on Walnut Canyon Desert Dr.

Yucca Canyon Trail. Drive past Rattlesnake Springs and stop at the park boundary before reaching the Slaughter Canyon Cave parking lot. Turn west along the boundary fence line

CARLSBAD CAVERNS
NATIONAL PARK

EXPLORING
ATTRACTIONS NEARBY
DINING
LODGING
CAMPING AND RV
FACILITIES
SHOPPING
ESSENTIAL
INFORMATION

to the trailhead. The 6-mi round-trip begins at the mouth of Yucca Canyon, and climbs up to the top of the escarpment. Here, you'll see sweeping views of the Guadalupe Mountains and El Capitan. Most people turn around at this point; the hearty can continue along a poorly maintained route that follows the top of the ridge. The first part of the hike takes about four hours round-trip; if you continue on, add another four hours. | Rte. 418 10 mi west of U.S. 62–180.

Attractions Nearby

Brantley Lake State Park. In addition to 42,000-acre Brantley Lake, this park 13 mi north of Carlsbad offers primitive camping areas, nature trails, a visitor center, more than 51 fully equipped campsites, and fine fishing for largemouth bass, bluegill, crappie, and walleye pike. | County Rd. 30 (Capitan Reef Rd.), 5 mi off U.S. 285, Carlsbad | 505/457–2384 | www. emnrd.state.nm.us | $4 per vehicle | Open daily, year-round.

Living Desert Zoo and Gardens State Park. This nature preserve on the northwestern edge of Carlsbad focuses on the flora and fauna of the Chihuahuan Desert, including mountain lions, elk, wolves, and buffalo. Nocturnal exhibits let you in on the area's less seen residents. | 1504 Miehls, off U.S. 285, Carlsbad | 505/887–5516 | $4 | Late May–Labor Day, daily 8–8, last tour entry 6:30 PM Labor Day–late May, daily 9–5, last tour entry 3:30 PM.

Dining

In Carlsbad Caverns

Carlsbad Caverns Restaurant. American/Casual. This comfy, diner-style restaurant has the essentials—hamburgers, sandwiches, and hot roast beef. Unlike at some parks, food prices here are very reasonable. | Visitor center, 7 mi west of U.S. 62–180 at the end of the main park road | 505/785–2281 | $2–$8 | AE, D, MC, V | Closes 5 in winter, 6:30 in summer.

Rattlesnake Springs Picnic Area's old cottonwood trees shade about a dozen picnic tables and grills. Drinking water and chemical toilets are available at the site. | Rte. 418, 2.5 mi west of U.S. 62–180.

Underground Lunchroom. Fast Food. Grab a treat, soft drink or club sandwich for a quick break. | Visitor center, 7 mi west of U.S. 62–180 at the end of the main park road | 505/785– 2281 | $2–$7 | AE, D, MC, V | Closes 3:30 in winter, 5 in summer.

Near the Park

★ **Bamboo Garden Restaurant.** Chinese. Possibly the best Chinese food in southern New Mexico is right here in cowboy country. Kung Pao chicken, a dish with vegetables and peanuts stir-fried in chile pepper sauce, is among the menu items. Surroundings are pleasant but not elegant. | 1511 N. Canal St., Carlsbad | 505/887–5145 | $5–$12 | MC, V | Closed Mon.

★ **La Fonda.** Mexican. For decades, residents of Carlsbad and Roswell have driven to this modest Mexican restaurant to dine on celebrated specialties like the Guadalajara (beef, cheese, and guacamole on a corn tortilla). Artesia is 26 mi north of the park. | 206 W. Main St., Artesia | 505/746–9377 | $5–$10 | AE, D, MC, V.

Red Chimney. Barbecue. If you hanker for sweet and tangy barbecue, try this casual restaurant. Sauce from an old family recipe is slathered on chicken, pork, beef, turkey, and ham. | 817 N. Canal St., Carlsbad | 505/885–8744 | $7–$9 | MC, V | Closed weekends.

Velvet Garter Restaurant and Saloon–Jack's. American. Take your pick of these two adjoining White's City restaurants in a pueblo-style building: Jack's is a casual diner and Velvet Garter offers full service and a more comprehensive menu. | 26 Carlsbad Caverns Hwy., White's City | 505/785–2291 | $5–$15 | AE, D, DC, MC, V.

Lodging

Near the Park

Best Western Cavern Inn. The closest motel to the park offers spacious rooms, though prices are steep for the convenience. Next door is the hacienda-style Best Western Guadalupe Inn with 42 rooms and the Walnut Canyon Inn with 27 rooms. The three motels share facilities, including a water park. Mule deer often amble down from their protected haven at Carlsbad Caverns National Park. Look for the large registration sign on the south side of the road. Cable TV. 2 pools. Hot tub. Playground. Some pets allowed (fee). | 17 Carlsbad Caverns Hwy., White's City | 505/785–2291 or 800/228–3767 | fax 505/785–2283 | 63 rooms | $85–$90 | AE, D, DC, MC, V.

★ **Best Western Stevens Inn.** This is a reliable old favorite, both with tour groups and locals. The brightly colored guest rooms have mirrored vanities and modern furnishings. Some rooms have private patios. 2 restaurants, bar. Some kitchenettes. Cable TV. Pool. Playground. Laundry facilities. Some pets allowed. | 1829 S. Canal St., Carlsbad | 505/887–2851, 800/730–2851 reservations | 220 rooms | $59–$99 | AE, D, DC, MC, V.

Comfort Inn Carlsbad. The rooms of this two-story inn on the north side of Carlsbad are large and modern. The property is next to shopping outlets and downtown Lake Carlsbad Recreation Area. Pets under 20 lbs are allowed. Cable TV. Pool. Exercise Room. Playground. Laundry facilities. Some pets allowed (fee). | 2429 W. Pierce St., Carlsbad | 505/887–1994 | 54 rooms | $60–$80 | AE, D, DC, MC, V | CP.

Holiday Inn Carlsbad. This Spanish Colonial–style link in the chain has a pink stucco exterior, red-tile roofs, and portal-style balconies. Rooms are attractively decorated in deep tones from the southwest, with misty blue-and-maroon fabrics, light oak furniture, and Native American prints. 2 restaurants. Cable TV. Pool. Playground. Some pets allowed (fee). | 601 S. Canal St., Carlsbad | 505/885–8500 | 100 rooms | $75 | AE, D, DC, MC, V.

Camping and RV Facilities

In Carlsbad Caverns

No developed campsites are in the park, although backcountry primitive camping is permitted (no campfires allowed).

Near the Park

Brantley Lake State Park. The campground in this state park 13 mi north of Carlsbad is shaded with Afghan pines, Mexican elders, and desert plants. Some camping and picnic sites (with grills) have views of the 3,000-acre lake and dam—an inviting haven in this upper Chihuahuan desert region. Credit cards are accepted with advanced reservations only. Unsupervised swimming is allowed, as is with boating and fishing. Flush toilets. Full round-trips, partial round-trips, dump station. Drinking water, showers. Fire grates, grills, picnic tables. Electricity, public telephone. Ranger station. Swimming (lake). | County Rd. 30 (Capital Reef Rd.), 5 mi off U.S. 285, Carlsbad | 505/457–2384, 877/664–7787 reservations | fax 505/457–2385 | 51 RV sites, unlimited primitive sites | $8 primitive site, $14 partial round-trip, $18 full round-trip | MC, V.

Shopping

Visitor Center. The bookstore has a wide selection of titles covering specialized topics such as cave environments and area wildlife. Jewelry and souvenirs can be purchased at the gift shop. Snacks and drinks along with a limited selection of souvenirs are available at the underground lunchroom. | 7 mi west of park entrance gate at White's City, off U.S. 62/180 | 505/785–2232.

White's City. On the Western-style boardwalk of this tiny town at the park entrance gate, you'll find various souvenirs, a T-shirt shop, treats such as home-made fudge, and a small grocery store selling picnic and camping supplies. | Carlsbad Caverns Hwy., 7 mi east of park | 505/785–2291.

Essential Information

ATMS: Best Western Cavern Inn | 17 Carlsbad Caverns Hwy., White's City | 505/785–2291.

AUTOMOBILE SERVICE STATIONS: White's City 24-Hour Texaco | 17 Carlsbad Caverns Hwy., White's City | 505/785–2291.

POST OFFICES: White's City Post Office | Carlsbad Caverns Hwy., White's City, 88268 | 505/785–2220 | Weekdays 8–noon and 12:30–4:30, Sat. 8–noon.

GUADALUPE MOUNTAINS NATIONAL PARK

WEST TEXAS

Off U.S. 62–180 110 mi northeast of El Paso, TX, 40 mi southwest of Carlsbad Caverns National Park, and 55 mi southwest of Carlsbad, NM. White's City, NM is 35 mi northeast of the park on U.S. 62–180.

Looming above the desert floor, the sheered rock face of El Capitan is the most visible landmark of this isolated park, which also contains the highest point in Texas—Guadalupe Peak (8,749 ft). Such outcrops have a stark beauty, but this park is remarkably alive, too. In McKittrick Canyon a clear stream cascades through a desert woodland of bigtooth maple, walnut, ash, and oak, created by one of the arid region's few year-round springs. The park is also home to the Texas madrone tree, a lovely Ice Age relic commonly found in the wild only here and in Big Bend National Park. Then, of course, there are the Guadalupe Mountains. The lordly range began to form about 250 million years ago, from marine life and sediments deposited in an ancient, tropical ocean. After the ocean evaporated, geologic processes pushed the reef above the ground until its secrets were exposed.

Oil company geologist Wallace E. Pratt is credited with preserving what he once described as the most beautiful spot in Texas. In 1921 Pratt first explored the area in a search of likely drilling spots for what was then Humble Oil (now Exxon). He later bought 16,000 acres of an area that included McKittrick Canyon. In 1958 Pratt donated 5,632 acres of the ranch to the federal government. With other donations and the government's purchase of additional surrounding land, the 86,416-acre Guadalupe Mountains National Park was established in 1972.

PUBLICATIONS

Natural features and the history of the Guadalupe Mountains are discussed and illustrated in *The Guadalupes*, by Dan Murphy, a booklet published by the Carlsbad Caverns Guadalupe Mountains Association. Other booklets include *Trails of the Guadalupes* by Don Kurtz and William D. Goran, and *Hiking Carlsbad Caverns and Guadalupe Mountains National Parks*, by Bill Schneider. These and other publications are available at the visitor center.

When to Visit

SCENERY AND WILDLIFE

In the heat of summer, your best chance of spotting a few of the many mule deer that inhabit the park is in late evening or early morning. During other seasons, you're likely to see deer out on the trails at any time. Your best spot for seeing deer is at Dog Canyon Campground on the north park boundary.

In fall the brilliant yellows and oranges of McKittrick Canyon's fall foliage are spectacular. The yellow, red and purple blossoms of cactus and desert plants during springtime can be breathtaking, especially following an abnormally wet winter.

HIGH AND LOW SEASON

Trails here are rarely crowded, except in fall when foliage changes colors in McKittrick Canyon, and during spring break in March. Still, this is a very remote area and you'll be unlikely to find too much congestion at any time. Hikers are more apt to explore backcountry trails in spring and fall, when it's cooler but not too cold.

Average High/Low Temperature (°F) and Monthly Precipitation (in inches)

	JAN.	FEB.	MAR.	APR.	MAY	JUNE
GUADALUPE	53/30	58/35	63/38	71/46	78/55	88/63
MOUNTAINS	1.04	1.04	.87	.57	1.26	1.48
	JULY	AUG.	SEPT.	OCT.	NOV.	DEC.
	87/63	84/62	78/57	71/49	61/38	57/33
	3.08	3.77	5.22	1.41	.65	.67

FESTIVALS AND SEASONAL EVENTS

The only town with special local events in the vicinity of Guadalupe Mountains National park is Carlsbad, NM (*See* Carlsbad Cavern National Park).

Nearby Towns

Tiny **White's City, NM,** 35 mi to the northeast off U.S. 62–180, is more a crossroads than a town. Fifty-five miles northeast of the park, the town of **Carlsbad, NM,** has more amenities. For more information about both cities, including dining, lodging, and attractions, *see* Carlsbad Caverns National Park.

Exploring Guadalupe Mountains

PARK BASICS

Contacts and Resources: Headquarters Visitor Center. | HC 60, Box 400, Salt Flat, TX 79847 | 915/828–3251 | www.nps.gov/gumo.

Hours: The park is open 24 hours daily, year-round.

Fees: An admission fee of $3 is collected at the visitor's center.

Getting Around: Since about half of the Guadalupe Mountains is a designated wilderness, few roadways penetrate the park. Most sites are accessible off U.S. 62–180. Dog Canyon Campground on the north end of the park can be reached via Route 137, which traverses the woodlands of Lincoln National Forest.

Permits: For overnight backpacking trips, you must get a free permit from either Headquarters visitor center or Dog Canyon ranger station.

Public Telephones and Rest Rooms: Dog Canyon ranger station, Headquarters visitor center, McKittrick contact station, and Pine Springs campground all have public phones and rest rooms.

Accessibility: The wheelchair-accessible Headquarters visitor center has a wheelchair available for use. The 0.75-mi round-trip Pinery Trail from the visitor center to Butterfield Stage Ruins is wheelchair accessible, as is McKittrick contact station. Most other trails and sights can be difficult for those with mobility problems.

GUADALUPE
MOUNTAINS
NATIONAL PARK

EXPLORING
ATTRACTIONS NEARBY
DINING
LODGING
CAMPING AND RV
FACILITIES
SHOPPING
ESSENTIAL
INFORMATION

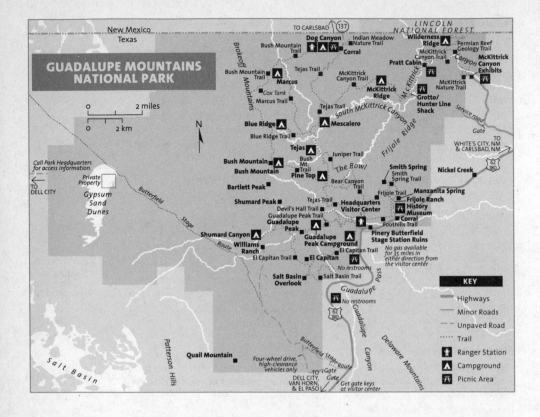

Emergencies: There are no fire boxes in this largely wilderness park, but cell phones with far-reaching service can pick up signals at key points along trails. Rangers have emergency medical technician training and are also law enforcement officers. To reach them, call 911 or contact Headquarters visitor center or Dog Canyon ranger station.

Lost and Found: The park's lost-and-found is at Headquarters visitor center.

Good Tours

GUADALUPE MOUNTAINS NATIONAL PARK IN ONE DAY

Start your tour at **Headquarters visitor center,** where exhibits and a slide show will orient you to the park's wildlife and geology. Take the short 0.75-mi round-trip **Pinery Trail** walk from the visitor center to Pinery Butterfield Stage Station ruins. Then drive to the **Frijole Ranch Museum,** where you can see the spring and grounds of an old ranch house. Drive 7 mi northeast of the visitor center on U.S. 62–180 to the turnoff to **McKittrick Canyon.** Here, you have several options for hiking in the day-use area. Making sure you've got some food and water with you, make your way to Route 137 via Rte. 62–180 and County Road 408, and drive southwest to **Dog Canyon ranger station,** a trip of about 110 mi. You have your choice of several hikes, on which you can explore meadows and a high coniferous forest. If you're not camping give yourself time for the two-hour drive back to Carlsbad, where you have plenty of lodging and dining options.

Attractions

★**Junior Ranger Program.** By participating in designated activities such as a nature walk and written exercises, youngsters can receive a certificate, badge, and patch designating them junior rangers. The program is self-guided. | Headquarters visitor center | 915/828–3251 | Free | June–Aug., daily 8–6; Sept.–May, daily 8–4:30.

SCENIC DRIVES

Williams Ranch Road. You'll see a panoramic view and get an up-close look at limestone cliffs on this 7.25-mi, one-way drive over part of what was once the Butterfield Overland Mail stage line. However, you need a high-clearance, four-wheel-drive vehicle for this trek. Obtain a gate key at the visitor center and drive west on U.S. 62–180 for 8.25 mi until you see a brown metal gate on the north side with a National Park Service sign. Drive through two locked gates (be sure to lock them behind you), and then follow the road to an abandoned ranch house. James "Dolph" Williams operated this spread with his partner, an Indian named Geronimo (no relation to the historical figure). The road is open for day trips only. Mountain bikes are permitted on this route.

SIGHTS TO SEE

Frijole Ranch Museum. Displays and photographs depicting ranch life and early park history are inside this old ranch house that's been converted to a museum. Hiking trails are adjacent to the grounds, which have a spring and shady trees. | Access road 1 mi northeast of Headquarters visitor center | 915/828–3251 | Free | Call for hours.

Headquarters Visitor Center. Exhibits and a slide show give you a quick introduction to the park, half of which is a wilderness area. Some nicely crafted exhibits depict typical wildlife and plant scenes. | U.S. 62–180, 55 mi southwest of Carlsbad, 110 mi northeast of El Paso | 915/828–3251 | fax 915/828–3269 | June–Aug., daily 8–6; Sept.–May, daily 8–4:30; closed Christmas Day.

McKittrick Canyon. A desert creek flows through this canyon, which is lined with walnut, maple, and other trees. You're also likely to spot mule deer heading for the water. | 4 mi off U.S. 62–180, about 7 mi northeast of Headquarters visitor center | Highway gate is locked at sunset.

McKittrick Contact Station. Poster-size illustrations in a shaded, outdoor patio area tell the geologic story of the Guadalupe Mountains, an area carved from an ancient sea. You can hear the recorded memoirs of oilman Wallace Pratt, who donated his ranch and surrounding scenic area to the federal government for preservation. | 4 mi off U.S. 62–180, about 7 mi northeast of Headquarters visitor center | 915/828–3251 (Headquarters visitor center) | June–Aug., daily 8–6; Sept.–May, daily 8–4:30.

★ **Pinery Butterfield Stage Station Ruins.** This was one of the stops along the old Butterfield Overland Mail stagecoach route in the mid-1800s. Passengers en route from St. Louis or San Francisco would stop for rest and refreshment. There's a paved 0.75-mi round-trip trail leading here from the visitor center, or you can drive here directly. | 1 mi northeast of Headquarters visitor center.

Sports and Outdoor Activities

BIRD-WATCHING

Look for such species as ladder-backed woodpeckers, ScottΔs oriole, SayΔs Phoebe, and white-throated swifts among the more than 300 types of birds that have been spotted in the park. Many non-native birds stop at Guadalupe during spring and fall migrations. The natural springs at the Frijole Ranch Museum make it an an excellent birding spot.

HIKING

More than 80 mi of trails give the serious hiker many options. No roads go into the park's interior, so you will definitely find solitude—but no water, so pack plenty of your own. Stop at the visitor center for details on trail conditions, and always be sure to bring plenty of water on your hike—about a gallon per day per person.

GUADALUPE
MOUNTAINS
NATIONAL PARK

EXPLORING
ATTRACTIONS NEARBY
DINING
LODGING
CAMPING AND RV
FACILITIES
SHOPPING
ESSENTIAL
INFORMATION

BACK AT THE RANCH

First established in 1876, the Frijole Ranch produced crops such as blackberries, corn, plums and figs. The site became a community gathering place for other area ranchers, and even had a schoolhouse and post office.

Dog Canyon. This area has several popular hiking options along shorter trails. | Rte. 137, 60 mi southwest of U.S. 285.

Staff at **Dog Canyon ranger station** can help you plan your hikes. | 505/981–2418.

The **Indian Meadows Nature Trail** is a very easy, mostly level 0.5-mi hike that crosses an arroyo into meadow lands. Try spending about 45 minutes savoring the countryside.

The somewhat strenuous **Lost Peak Trail** is 6.5 mi round-trip, which will take about six hours to complete if your pace is slower. It leads from Dog Canyon into a coniferous forest.

The **Bush Mountain** takes you on a moderate, 4.5-mi round-trip for a panoramic view of West Dog Canyon. Plan on about four hours for this hike.

Frijole Ranch Trailhead. From here you have access to two trails. | Access road 1 mi northeast of Headquarters visitor center.

The **Frijole/Foothills Trail** leads to the Pine Springs Campground behind Headquarters visitor center. The moderate, 5.5-mi round-trip through desert vistas takes about five hours.

The **Smith Spring Trail,** a round-trip walk of 2.3 mi, takes you through a shady oasis where you're likely to spot mule deer alongside a spring and a small waterfall. Plan on up to 1.5 hours to complete the walk.

McKittrick Canyon. The short nature loop and the trails here all start at the McKittrick contact station. | 4 mi off U.S. 62–180, about 7 mi northeast of Headquarters visitor center.

The moderate 6.75-mi round-trip to the **Grotto Picnic Area** affords views of a flowing stream and surface rock that resembles formations in an underground cave, with jagged overhangs. Plan on about five hours for a leisurely walk.

The easiest McKittrick trail is a 1-mi **nature loop.** Signs along the way explain the geologic and biological history of the area.

If you're in shape and have a serious geological bent, you may want to hike the **Permian Ridge Geology Trail.** The 8.5-mi round-trip climb heads through mainly open, expansive desert country to a forested ridge with Douglas fir and ponderosa pines. You'll have panoramic views of McKittrick Canyon and the surrounding mountain ranges. You can also see the many rock layers that built up over the eons. Set aside at least eight hours.

Along the **Pratt Lodge Trail** you can view the stream and canyon woodland area. The 4.5-mi round-trip excursion leads to the now vacant Pratt Lodge. Plan on at least two hours at a fast pace on this moderate trail. Give yourself another hour or two if you want to take your time.

Pine Springs Trailhead. From here you'll be able to embark on several different hikes. | Behind Headquarters visitor center at Pine Springs campground.

★ Cutting through forests of pine and Douglas fir, **The Bowl** is considered one of the most gorgeous trails in the park. It's a strenuous 9-mi round-trip lasting up to 10 hours, depending on your pace.

The moderate **Devil's Hall Trail** traverses 4.25 mi through a Chihuahuan desert habitat thick with spiked, succulent agave plants and prickly pear cacti amid giant, tumbled boulders. Devil's Hall is a narrow canyon about 10 ft wide and 100 ft deep. This moderate hike lasts up to five hours if you take your time.

The 8.5-mi **Guadalupe Peak Trail** is a strenuous workout over a steep grade. It offers some great views of exposed cliff face. The hike takes up to eight hours to complete.

★ The combined **El Capitan/Salt Basin Overlook Trails** are a popular loop through the low desert. El Capitan skirts the base of El Capitan peak for about 3.5 mi, leading to a junction with Salt Basin Overlook. The 4.5-mi trail has views of the stark, white salt flat below and loops back onto the El Capitan Trail. Though moderate, the 11.33-mi round-trip is not recommended in the intense heat of summer, as there is absolutely no shade.

HORSEBACK RIDING

Guadalupe Mountains National Park is a great place for a solitary ride through miles of unfenced trails, but you have to bring your own horse because rentals are not available. Most park hiking trails are open to horses; be sure to obtain proper maps so you know where you can ride. You can only bring your horse for day use, and you should obtain a free backcountry permit from either Headquarters visitor center or Dog Canyon Ranger Station. Call for reservations to corral your horse within the park, either at Frijole Ranch (915/828–3251) or at Dog Canyon Ranger Station (505/981–2418).

Dining

In Guadalupe Mountains

Picnic Areas. The park has no snack bars or restaurants, but several picnic areas are available. Wood and charcoal fires are not allowed anywhere in the park. If you want to cook a hot meal, bring a campstove.

Dog Canyon Campground. Thirteen campsites have picnic tables, with access free for day use. This is a lovely, nicely shaded area where you're very likely to see mule deer. Drinking water and rest rooms are available at the site. This area is about 2.5 hours from Headquarters visitor center. | Off Rte. 137, 65 mi southwest of Carlsbad.

Frijole Ranch Museum. This is a much cooler and shadier spot than nearby Pine Springs Campground. Two picnic tables are set up under tall trees; rest rooms are available at the ranch house–museum. | Access road 1 mi northeast of Headquarters visitor center.

Pine Springs Campground. Shade varies depending on the time of day, and it can be sparse in hot summer. You can find drinking water and rest rooms here. | Behind Headquarters visitor center.

Near the Park

For more dining options near the park, *see* Carlsbad Caverns National Park.

Nickel Creek Café. American/Casual. This tiny stop is the only dining option within 35 miles of the main park entrance (it's 5 mi northeast of Headquarters visitor center). Standard American fare is served, diner-style, but many customers are lured by the savory chile sauce accompanying the Tex-Mex dishes such as burritos and fajitas. | U.S. 62–180, 15 mi northeast of junction with Rte. 54, Pine Springs | 915/828–3295 | $4–$7 | No credit cards | Closed Sun.

Cornudas Café. American/Casual. Try owner May Carson's famous green chile hamburger amid the quirky decor. Table legs here are made to resemble those of Levi-clad cowboys. There's also a gift shop selling Mexican imports. It's 63 mi east of El Paso, Texas, and 47 mi west of Headquarters visitor center. Pull in for breakfast or lunch Monday through Wednesday. Dinner is also available the rest of the week. | U.S. 62–180, 17 mi southwest of junction with Rte. 54, Box 32, HC 60, Cornudas | 915/964–2409 | $4–$7 | AE, D, DC, MC, V.

Lodging

There is no lodging within the park. For information on lodging near the park, *see* Carlsbad Caverns National Park.

Camping and RV Facilities

In Guadalupe Mountains

The park has two developed campgrounds that charge fees and a number of designated primitive, backcountry sites where you can camp for free. Check with the visitor center

GUADALUPE
MOUNTAINS
NATIONAL PARK

EXPLORING
ATTRACTIONS NEARBY
DINING
LODGING
CAMPING AND RV
FACILITIES
SHOPPING
ESSENTIAL
INFORMATION

Early national park visitors traveled by stagecoach along simple dirt roads. These were long and dusty trips that could take more than a week. Overnight stays were in grand hotels or in immaculate tent cabins. Only those who could afford lengthy vacations and costly accommodations could tour the national parks.

about primitive camping. Throughout the park wood and charcoal fires are prohibited, but you can use your campstove.

Dog Canyon Campground. This remote campground, in a coniferous forest, is well-maintained and close to hiking trails. Flush toilets. Drinking water. Picnic tables. Public telephone. Ranger station. | 9 tent sites, 4 RV sites | Off Rte. 137, 65 mi southwest of Carlsbad | 505/981–2418 | $8 | No credit cards.

Pine Springs Campground. The sites here are set among pinyon and juniper trees at the base of a tall mountain. Flush toilets. Drinking water. Picnic tables. Public telephone. Ranger station. | 20 tent sites, 18 RV sites, 1 wheelchair accessible site (tent or RV), 2 group sites | Behind Headquarters visitor center | 915/828–3251 | $8 | No credit cards.

Near the Park

Cornudas High Desert RV Park and Motel. You can spot this pit stop by the western-style storefront of the motel building. The RV park is modestly arranged among cactus landscaping on the same grounds as the motel. This lonesome spot of Old West civilization is fun, as the series of mailboxes shaped like cattle reveals. Flush toilets. Full round-trips. Food service. Electricity, public telephone. General store, service station. | 8 sites | Off U.S. 62–180, 17 mi southwest of junction with Rte. 54, HC 60, Box 32, Cornudas | 915/964–2409 | $17 | AE, D, DC, MC, V.

Lincoln National Forest. Unlimited free primitive camping is available throughout this 1,700-square-mi stretch of mostly wild land. You can pull off almost anywhere you want and set up camp in virtual seclusion. Bring plenty of your own water. Campfires usually are allowed unless fire danger is extraordinarily high. Unless someone has been there before you, you will have to build your own fire ring. And if you don't have a self-contained RV, the bushes are your rest rooms. | Rte. 137, about 30 mi south of U.S. 285 | 505/885–4181 | Free.

Shopping

Publications are sold at the visitor center, but there are no shops within park boundaries. The closest place with a selection of snacks, groceries, and the like is White's City, 35 mi northeast of the park off U.S. 62–180. Your best selection of shops is at Carlsbad.

Essential Information

You can find more basic services in the town of Carlsbad (*see* Carlsbad Caverns National Park).

ATMS (24-HOUR): Best Western Cavern Inn | 17 Carlsbad Caverns Hwy., White's City | 505/785–2291.

AUTOMOBILE SERVICE STATIONS: White's City 24-Hour Texaco | 17 Carlsbad Caverns Hwy., White's City | 505/785–2291.

POST OFFICE: Dell City Post Office | Ranch Rd. 1437, 13 mi north of junction with Rte. 62, Dell City, TX 79837 | 915/964–2626 | Weekdays 7–11:30 and 12:30–3.

JOSHUA TREE NATIONAL PARK

SOUTHERN CALIFORNIA

West entrance: Route 62, 29 mi northeast of I–10. North entrance: Route 62, 48 mi northwest I–10. South entrance: I–10, 25 mi east of Route 111.

Ruggedly beautiful desert scenery attracts more than 1.9 million visitors each year to Joshua Tree National Park. Its mountains of jagged rock, natural cactus gardens, and lush oases shaded by tall fan palms mark the meeting place of the Mojave (high) and Colorado (low) deserts. Extensive stands of Joshua trees give the park its name, but you'll also find other exotic plants like the white yucca, red-tipped ocotillo, and cholla cactus.

Joshua Tree National Park owes its existence to the efforts of Minerva Hamilton Hoyt, a Pasadena resident who launched a campaign in the 1920s to protect the region. After years of battling bureaucracy and swaying public opinion, President Franklin D. Roosevelt established the Joshua Tree National Monument on August 10, 1936. With the 1994 passage of the California Desert Protection Act, the monument became a national park. Today the park stands at 1,239 square mi. Most of it is roadless wilderness.

PUBLICATIONS

If you want a general introduction to Joshua Tree, try *On Foot in Joshua Tree*, by Patty Furbush, which lists more than 90 hiking trails leading through the park. *A Visitor's Guide to Joshua Tree*, by Robert B. Cates, gives a history lesson on the park. Adventurers setting out to conquer the park's peaks should thumb through the *Climber's Guide to Joshua Tree* by Alan Bartlett or the *Joshua Tree Climber's Guide* by Randy Vogel. If the flora does more for you, *California Desert Wildflowers* by Philip A. Munz leads you to some of the most interesting plant life.

When to Visit

SCENERY AND WILDLIFE

Joshua Tree will shatter your notions of the desert as a vast wasteland. Life flourishes in this land of little rain, as flora and fauna have adapted to heat and drought. In most areas you'll be walking among native Joshua trees, ocotillos, and yuccas. One of the best spring desert wildflower displays in Southern California blossoms is here in March, April, and May. You'll see plenty of animals—reptiles such as the nocturnal sidewinders, birds like golden eagles or burrowing owls, and occasionally mammals like coyotes and bobcats.

HIGH AND LOW SEASON

It's cooler in the desert from October through May, when most of Joshua Tree's visitors arrive. Daytime temperatures range from the mid-70s in December and January to mid-90s in October and May. Lows can dip to near freezing in mid-winter, and in some years you may even encounter snow at the higher elevations. Summers can be torrid, with daytime temperatures reaching 110°F.

Average High/Low Temperature (°F) and Monthly Precipitation (in inches)

	JAN.	FEB.	MAR.	APR.	MAY	JUNE
JOSHUA TREE	62/32	65/37	72/40	80/50	90/55	100/65
	.38	.35	.30	.10	.06	.02

	JULY	AUG.	SEPT.	OCT.	NOV.	DEC.
	105/70	101/78	96/62	85/55	72/40	62/31
	.62	.50	.68	.32	.27	.46

FESTIVALS AND SEASONAL EVENTS

WINTER

Dec.: **Indio International Tamale Festival.** A celebration of Indio's cultural heritage with entertainment including tamale-making contests and a parade of floats decorated with corn husks. | 760/347–0676 or 800/ 444–6346.

Feb.: **Riverside County Fair and National Date Festival.** At this Arabian Nights–themed festival in Indio, people come from far and wide to witness the crowning of Queen Sheherazade. There are also camel and ostrich races and booths selling everything you can imagine. | 760/863–8247.

SPRING

May: **Pony Express Ride and Barbecue.** Step back in time for this re-enactment of the historic mail delivery service, which runs from Joshua Tree's Black Rock Canyon to Pioneertown. | 760/365–6323.

Grubstake Days. Motorcycle races, monster truck competitions, and a demolition derby are all a part of this annual celebration of Yucca Valley's past. | 760/365–6323.

FALL

Oct.:   **Pioneer Days.** Outhouse races, beard contests, and an arm-wrestling competition mark this annual celebration of frontier spirit. The festivities fill downtown Twentynine Palms. | 760/367–3445.

Dec.:   **Annual Winter Gathering Pow Wow.** Members of the Mission tribe present a festival featuring Native American dancers and drummers, arts and crafts, and traditional foods at Spotlight 29 Casino in Coachella. | 760/775–5566.

Nearby Towns

Palm Springs serves as the home base for most park visitors. This city of 43,000 has 95 golf courses, 600 tennis courts, and 30,000 swimming pools. A hideout for Hollywood stars beginning in the 1920s, Palm Springs offers a glittering array of shops, restaurants, and hotels. Stroll down Palm Canyon Drive and you're sure to run into a celebrity or two. About 9 mi north of Palm Springs is **Desert Hot Springs,** which has more than 1,000 natural hot mineral pools and 40 health spas ranging from low-key to luxurious. **Yucca Valley** is the largest and fastest growing of the communities straddling the park's northern border. The town boasts has a half dozen lodgings—perfect if you want to hit the park early. Tiny **Joshua Tree,** the closest community to the park's West Entrance, has a handful of hotels. **Twentynine Palms,** known as "two-nine" by locals, is sandwiched between the Marine Corps Air Ground Task Force Center to the north and Joshua Tree National Park to the south. Here you'll find a smattering of hip coffeehouses, antiques shops, and trendy cafés.

INFORMATION

Desert Hot Springs Chamber of Commerce | 11-711 West Dr., Desert Hot Springs, 92240 | 760/329–6403 | fax 760/329–2833 | www.deserthotsprings.com. **Joshua Tree Chamber of Commerce** | 61325 29 Palms Hwy., Suite F, Joshua Tree, 92252 | 760/366–3723 | fax 760/366–2573 | www.joshuatreechamber.org. **Palm Springs Bureau of Tourism** | 777 N. Palm Canyon Dr., Suite 201, Palm Springs, 92262 | 760/778–8415 | fax 760/323–3021 | www.palm-springs.org. **Twentynine Palms Chamber of Commerce** | 6455-A Mesquite Ave., Twentynine Palms, 92277 | 760/367–3445 | fax 760/367–3366 | www.29chamber.com. **Yucca Valley Chamber of Commerce** | 55569 29 Palms Hwy., Yucca Valley, 56711 | 760/365–6323 | fax 760/365–0763 | www.yuccavalley.org.

Exploring Joshua Tree

PARK BASICS

Contacts and Resources: Joshua Tree National Park | 74485 National Park Dr., Twentynine Palms | 760/367–5500 | fax 760/367–6392 | www.nps.gov/jotr. **Joshua Tree National Parks Association** | 74485 National Park Dr., Twentynine Palms, 92277 | 760/367–5525 | fax 760/367–5583 | www.joshuatree.org.

Hours: The park is open every day, around the clock. Oasis visitor center is open daily 8–5; Cottonwood visitor center, 8–4:40; park 24 hours.

Fees: $10 per car, $5 per person on foot. The Joshua Tree Pass, good for one year, is $25.

Permits: Required for rock-climbing, free permits are available at all the visitor centers.

Public Telephones: Pay phones are at Oasis visitor center and Black Rock Canyon Campground.

Getting Around: You might have to dodge heavy machinery and experience a few delays as improvements continue to be made on major roads and parking areas for the next few years. Call ahead for updates. Passenger cars are fine for paved areas, but you'll need four-wheel drive for many of the rugged backcountry roadways. At the park's most popular sites, free parking spaces are limited. Joshua Tree does not have public transportation.

Accessibility: Black Rock Canyon and Jumbo Rocks campgrounds each have one accessible campsite. Nature trails at Oasis of Mara, Bajada, Keys View, and Cap Rock are accessible. Some trails at roadside viewpoints can be negotiated by those with limited mobility.

Emergencies: Emergency assistance within Joshua Tree is limited. There are no telephones in the interior of the park, and cell phones don't work in most areas. Emergency-only phones are at Hidden Valley Campground and Indian Cove Campground. **Hidden Valley Campground** | North side of Park Blvd., 14 mi southeast of the West Entrance. **Indian Cove Campground** | Indian Cove Rd., south of Hwy. 62.

Lost and Found: Report any lost or found items at Oasis visitor center or Cottonwood visitor center. **Oasis visitor center** | 74485 National Park Dr. | 760/367–5500. **Cottonwood visitor center** | Pinto Basin Rd. | no phone.

Good Tours

JOSHUA TREE IN ONE DAY

If you're planning a half-day visit to Joshua Tree, enter through the North Entrance in Twentynine Palms and follow Park Boulevard south. Head to the **Oasis Visitor Center** for information on special events, then stroll through the palm-shaded **Oasis of Mara.** Stop for a picnic lunch at **Live Oak Springs,** where you'll see some interesting rock formations. Drive through **Queen Valley** where the stands of Joshua trees are particularly alluring in spring, then take a detour south to survey the entire valley from **Keys View.** Return to Park Boulevard, where you can crawl through the boulders at **Hidden Valley** before you exit through the West Entrance near Joshua Tree.

To spend a full day in the park, enter the through the North Entrance. Follow the above itinerary, arriving at Hidden Valley in time to take the 60-minute guided **Desert Queen Ranch tour.** Take the stunning desert drive through Pinto Basin, stopping at the **Cholla Cactus Garden** and at the **Ocotillo Patch.** Follow Pinto Basin Road south toward Cottonwood Springs. Refresh yourself at the visitor center, where you can explore the small museum, and exit the park onto I–10.

JOSHUA TREE IN TWO DAYS

Most visitors experience the highlights of Joshua Tree in a single day. However, if you intend to camp for one night or more, you might want to explore the sights off **Park Boulevard** on your first day, then head to those off **Pinto Basin Road** on your second day.

Attractions

PROGRAMS AND TOURS

Campfire Coffee. Bring your own mug for the coffee (or hot chocolate) served at the informative Sunday morning meetings led by rangers who answer questions and help plan your day. It's brewing at Black Rock Canyon Campground, Cottonwood Campground, and Hidden Valley Campground. | Free | Oct.–Apr. at 8 AM.

★ **Desert Queen Ranch Walking Tour.** This 60-minute ranger-led walking tour explores the homestead that once belonged to William and Frances Keys. The tour covers the 60 years

JOSHUA TREE
NATIONAL PARK

EXPLORING
ATTRACTIONS NEARBY
DINING
LODGING
CAMPING AND RV
FACILITIES
SHOPPING
ESSENTIAL
INFORMATION

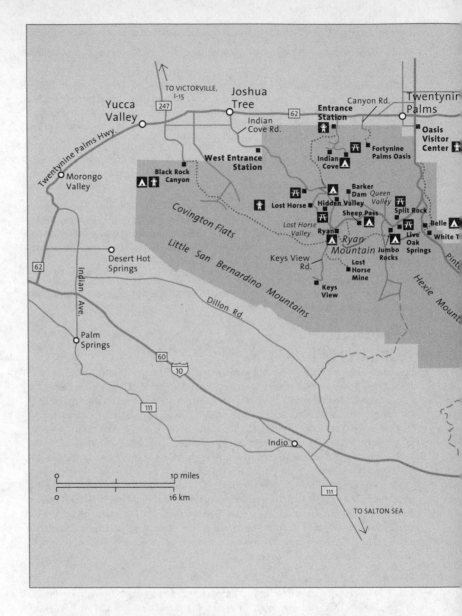

this couple spent raising five children under extreme desert conditions. The ranch—including the house, school, store, and workshop—has been restored much as it was when Bill died in 1969. | 2 mi north of Barker Dam Rd. | 760/367–5555 | Reservations essential | $5 | Oct.–May weekdays 10 and 1, weekends 10 and 1. June–Sept. Wed. and Fri. at 5:30 PM, by reservation only.

Evening Programs. Rangers present Saturday evening lectures lasting about an hour at Black Rock Canyon Nature Center, Cottonwood Amphitheater, Indian Cove Amphitheater, and Jumbo Rocks Campground. Topics range from natural history to local lore. The schedule is posted at the visitor centers. | Free | Oct.–Apr. at 7 PM; May at 8 PM.

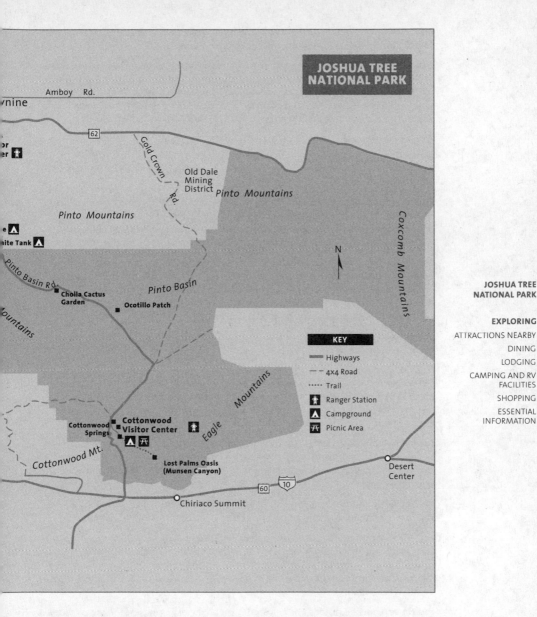

JOSHUA TREE
NATIONAL PARK

EXPLORING
ATTRACTIONS NEARBY
DINING
LODGING
CAMPING AND RV
FACILITIES
SHOPPING
ESSENTIAL
INFORMATION

SCENIC DRIVES

Park Boulevard. Traversing the most scenic portions of Joshua Tree, the well-paved Park Boulevard connects the north and west entrances in the park's high desert section. Along with some sweeping desert views, you'll see jumbles of splendid boulder formations, extensive stands of Joshua trees, and remnants of the area's wild and woolly past. Beginning at Oasis visitor center, drive south. After about 5 mi the road forks; head west toward Jumbo Rocks (clearly marked with a road sign). As you approach the high desert, keep an eye out for rock climbers.

Pinto Basin Road. Beginning at the Oasis visitor center, this paved road takes you from high desert to low desert. Take a left at the fork in the road about 5 mi from the visitor center. Continue another 9 mi to the Cholla Cactus Garden, where the sun fills the cactus needles with light. Past that is the Ocotillo Patch, filled with spindly plants with razor-sharp thorns. The only side trips from this route require a 4X4.

★ **Geology Tour Road.** Some of the park's most fascinating landscapes can be observed from this 18-mi dirt road. Parts of the journey are rough, so make sure you have a 4X4. There are 16 stops along the way, so it takes about two hours to make the round-trip. Along the way, you'll see a 100-year-old stone dam called Squaw Tank, defunct mines, and a large plain with an abundance of Joshua trees. | South of Park Blvd., west of Jumbo Rocks.

SIGHTS TO SEE

Barker Dam. Built around 1900 by ranchers and miners to hold water for cattle and mining operations, the dam now collects rainwater and is used by wildlife. | Barker Dam Rd., off Park Blvd., 14 mi south of the West Entrance.

Cholla Cactus Garden. This stand of bigelow cholla, sometimes called jumping cholla, has hooked spines that seem to jump at you as you walk past them. The cholla are best seen and photographed in late afternoon, when their backlit spiky stalks stand out against a colorful sky. | Pinto Basin Rd., 20 mi north of Cottonwood visitor center.

Cottonwood Springs Oasis. Noted for its abundant birdlife, this is an example of the palm-shaded oases that were a welcome sight to prospectors traveling through the area. The remains of an arrastra, a primitive type of gold mill, can be found nearby. Bighorn sheep frequent this area in winter. Take the 1-mi paved trail that begins at sites 13A and 13B of Cottonwood Campground. | Cottonwood visitor center.

Cottonwood Visitor Center. Exhibits in this small center, staffed by rangers and volunteers, illustrate the region's natural history. | Pinto Basin Rd. | no phone | www.nps.gov/jotr | 8–4.

Desert Queen Ranch. This 150-acre ranch, also known as Keys Ranch, illustrates one of the area's most successful attempts at homesteading. Most of the original buildings have been restored. | 2 mi north of Barker Dam Rd. | 760/367–5555 | Oct.–May weekdays 10 and 1, weekends 10, 1 and 3; June–Sept. by reservation only.

Fortynine Palms Oasis. Sights within the oasis include stands of fan palms, interesting petroglyphs, and evidence of fires built by early Native Americans. Since animals frequent this area, you may spot a coyote, bobcat, or roadrunner. | End of Canyon Rd., 4 mi west of Twentynine Palms.

Hidden Valley. This is a legendary cattle-rustlers hideout set among big boulders, where kids love to scramble over and around. | Park Blvd., 14 mi south of West Entrance.

★ **Keys View.** At 5,185 ft, this point affords a sweeping view of the Coachella Valley, the mountains of the San Bernardino National Forest, and—on a rare clear day—Signal Mountain in Mexico. Sunrise and sunset are magical times, when the light throws rocks and trees into high relief before bathing the hills in brilliant shades of red, orange, and gold. | Keys View Rd., 21 mi south of West Entrance.

Lost Horse Mine. This historic mine illustrates the gold prospecting and mining activities that took place here in the late 1800s. The site is accessed via a fairly strenuous 2-mi hike. | Keys View Rd., about 15 mi south of West Entrance.

Lost Palms Oasis. More than 100 palms comprise the largest group of the exotic plants in the park. A spring bubbles from between the boulders, but disappears into the sandy, boulder-strewn canyon. As you hike along the 4-mi trail you might spot bighorn sheep. | Cottonwood Spring visitor center.

Oasis Visitor Center. Exhibits here illustrate how Joshua Tree was formed, reveal the differences between the two types of desert within the park, and demonstrate how plants and animals eke out an existence in this arid climate. Take the 0.5-mi nature walk through the nearby Oasis of Mara, which is alive with cottonwood trees, palm trees, and mesquite shrubs. | 74485 National Park Dr., Twentynine Palms | 760/367–5500 | www.nps.gov.jotr | 8–4:30.

Sports and Outdoor Activities

BICYCLING

Mountain bikes are a great way to see Joshua Tree. With newer routes opened in backcountry areas, there are now plenty of trails waiting to be explored. Keep in mind that all except Thermal Canyon are also open to horseback riding.

Black Eagle Mountain Road. This dead-end road runs along the edge of a former lake bed, then crosses a number of dry washes before navigating several of Eagle Mountain's canyons. Several defunct mines are found along the 9-mi trail. | Off Pinto Basin Rd., 6.5 mi north of Cottonwood visitor center.

Covington Flats. This 4-mi trail leads you past some of the park's most impressive Joshua trees, as well as pinyon pines, junipers, and areas of lush desert vegetation. It's tough going toward the end, but once you reach 5,516-ft Eureka Peak you'll have great views of the Morongo Basin. | Covington Flats picnic area, La Contenta Rd., 10 mi from Rte. 62.

Old Dale Road. The first 11 mi of this 23-mi route run across Pinto Basin to the Old Dale Mining District, where several side roads head off toward dusty old shafts. Here you'll find Mission Well, dug to provide water for the area's mines and mills. The vegetation is remarkably varied, including tiny yellow chinchweed and desert willows. | Off Pinto Basin Rd., 7 mi north of Cottonwood visitor center.

Pinkham Canyon Road. Starting at Cottonwood visitor center, this challenging 20-mi trail follows Smoke Tree Wash, then descends into Pinkham Canyon. Be careful, as the route crosses some soft sand. | Cottonwood visitor center.

Thermal Canyon Bike Trail. One of the newly opened trails is this rigorous 10-mi route along a forgotten road through a rugged portion of the Cottonwood Mountains. Here you'll find some lovely views. | Off Geology Tour Rd.

Queen Valley. This 14-mi network of mostly level dirt roads winds through one of the park's most impressive groves of Joshua trees. Bike racks at the Barker Dam and Hidden Valley trailheads allow you to go hiking. | Hidden Valley Campground.

BIRD-WATCHING

Birding is a popular pastime in Joshua Tree. During the fall migration, which runs from mid-September through mid-October, there are several reliable sighting areas. At Barker Dam you might spot white-throated swifts, several types of swallows, or red-tailed hawks. Lucy's warbler, lesser goldfinches, and Anna's hummingbirds cruise around Cottonwood Spring. At Black Rock Canyon and Covington Flats, you're likely to see LaConter's thrashers, ruby crowned kinglets, and warbling vireos. Rufus hummingbirds, Pacific slope flycatchers and various warblers are frequent visitors to Indian Cove. Lists of birds found in the park, as well as information on recent sightings, are available at visitor centers.

HIKING

More than 50 mi of hiking trails in Joshua Tree range from the 0.25-mi Skull Rock Loop to the 35-mi California Riding and Hiking Trail. Many cross each other, so you can design your own desert maze. Remember that drinking water is hard to come by. You won't find water in the park except at the entrances, so make sure to bring along plenty.

Bajada All Access. Learn all about what plants do to survive in the desert on this easy 0.25-mi loop. The trail is wheelchair accessible. | South of Cottonwood visitor center, 0.5 mi from park entrance.

Boy Scout Trail. The moderately strenuous 16-mi trail runs through the westernmost edge of the Wonderland of Rocks, passing through a forest of Joshua trees, past granite

JOSHUA TREE
NATIONAL PARK

EXPLORING
ATTRACTIONS NEARBY
DINING
LODGING
CAMPING AND RV
FACILITIES
SHOPPING
ESSENTIAL
INFORMATION

POWERFUL WINDY

About 3,000 windmills churn mightily on the slopes of the Coachella Valley, generating electricity used by people all over southern California. The windmills are here, according to NASA, because this is one of the most consistently windy places on earth.

towers, and around willow-lined pools. Completing the round-trip journey requires camping along the way, so you may want to hike only part of the trail or have a car waiting at the other end. | Between Quail Springs Picnic Area and Indian Cove Campground.

California Riding and Hiking Trail. This well-traveled route stretches for 35 mi between the Black Rock Canyon Entrance and the North Entrance. No need to hike the entire trail, however. Start at any point along the way, including where it crosses major roads near Ryan Campground or Belle Campground, for hikes from 4 to 11 mi. | Trailheads at Covington Flats, Keys View, and Squaw Tank.

Cap Rock. This 0.5-mi loop, accessible to wheelchairs, winds through fascinating rock formations and has signs that explain the geology of the Mojave Desert. The trail is named after a boulder that sits like a cap atop a huge rock formation. | Junction of Park Blvd. and Keys View Rd.

Fortynine Palms Oasis Trail. Allow three hours for this moderately strenuous 3-mi trek. The trail makes a steep climb into the hills, then it drops down into a canyon where you'll find an oasis lined with fan palms. There's plenty of evidence of Native Americans in this area, from traces of cooking fires to rocks carved with petroglyphs. | End of Canyon Rd., 4 mi west of Twentynine Palms.

High View Nature Trail. This 1.3-mi loop climbs nearly to the top of 4,500-ft Summit Peak. The views of nearby Mt. San Gorgonio make the moderately steep journey worth the effort. | 0.5 mi west of Black Rock Canyon Campground.

Indian Cove Trail. Look for lizards and roadrunners along this 0.5-mi loop that follows a desert wash. This easy trail has signs with interesting facts about these and animals of the Mojave Desert. | West end of Indian Cove Campground.

Lost Horse Mine Trail. This fairly strenuous 4-mi round-trip hike follows a former mining road to a well-preserved mill that was used in the 1890s to crush gold-encrusted rock mined from the nearby mountain. The operation was one of the area's most successful, and the mine's cyanide settling tanks and stone buildings are the area's best preserved. From the mill area, a short but steep 10-minute side trip takes you to the top of a 5,278-ft peak with great views of the valley. | 1.25 mi east of Keys View Rd.

Lost Palms Oasis Trail. Allow four to six hours for the moderately strenuous, 7.5-mi round-trip, which leads to the most impressive oasis in the park. More than 100 fan palms are found here, as well as an abundance of wildflowers. | Cottonwood Spring.

★ **Mastodon Peak Trail.** Some boulder-scrambling is required on this 3-mi hike up the 3,371-ft Mastodon Peak, but the journey rewards you with stunning views of the Salton Sea. The trail passes through a region where gold was mined from 1919 to 1932, so be on the lookout for open mines. The peak draws its name from a large rock formation that early miners believed looked like the head of a prehistoric behemoth. | Cottonwood Spring Oasis.

★ **Ryan Mountain Trail.** One of the most panoramic views of Joshua Tree is the payoff for hiking to the top of 5,461-ft Ryan Mountain. From the top, you can see Mt. San Jacinto, Mt. San Gorgonio, Lost Horse Valley, and the Pinto Basin. You'll need two to three hours to complete the 3-mi round-trip. | Ryan Mountain parking area, 16 mi southeast of West Entrance or Sheep Pass, 16 mi southwest of Oasis visitor center.

Skull Rock Trail. The 0.25-mi loop guides hikers through boulder piles, desert washes, and a rocky alley. It's named for what is perhaps the park's most famous rock formation, which resembles a human head. | Jumbo Rocks Campground.

HORSEBACK RIDING

More than 200 mi of equestrian trails gradually are being added as part of a backcountry and wilderness management plan at Joshua Tree. Trail maps are available at visitor centers. Ryan and Black Rock campgrounds have designated areas for horses and mules.

ROCK CLIMBING

With an abundance of outcroppings of weathered igneous boulders, Joshua Tree is one of the world's most popular rock climbing destinations. Typically a visitor will make three to six climbs in a single day. The park offers a full menu of climbing experiences—bouldering for beginners in the Wonderland of Rocks, multiple-pitch climbs at Echo Rock and Saddle Rock, and sport climbs in Hidden Valley. A map inside the *Joshua Tree Guide* shows locations of selected wilderness and nonwilderness climbs.

Joshua Tree Rock Climbing School. The only local outfitter operating in Joshua Tree, this company offers a range of programs, from one-day introductory classes to multi-day programs for experienced climbers. The school provides all needed equipment. Beginning classes are limited to six people 13 years or over. | 6535 Park Blvd., Joshua Tree | 800/890–4745 | www.rockclimbingschool.com | $85 for beginner class | Closed July–Aug.

Vertical Adventures Climbing School. One of two climbing schools providing instruction in Joshua Tree, Vertical Adventures trains about 1,000 climbers each year. Classes meet at a designated location in the park. All equipment is provided. | Box 7548, Newport Beach, 92252 | 800/514–8785 | fax 949/854–5249 | www.verticaladventures.com | $90–$95 per class | Closed July–Aug.

Attractions Nearby

Coachella Valley Museum and Cultural Center. This former farmhouse has displays explaining how dates are harvested and ways in which the desert can be irrigated. On the grounds you'll find a smithy and an old sawmill. | 82-616 Miles Ave., Indio 92201 | 760/342–6651 | $2 | Sept.–June, Wed.–Sat. 10–4, Sun. 1–4.

Hi-Desert Nature Museum. This family-oriented museum includes a small zoo holding a number of the animals that make their home in Joshua Tree, including scorpions, snakes, ground squirrels, and chuckawalla lizards. There's also a collection of fossils from the Paleozoic era. | 57116 29 Palms Hwy., Yucca Valley 92284 | 760/369–7212 | Free | Tues.–Sun. 10–5.

Oasis of Murals. The history of Twentynine Palms is depicted in a collection of 17 murals painted on the sides of buildings. If you drive around town you can't miss them, but you can also pick up a map from the Twentynine Palms Chamber of Commerce. | 6455A Mesquite Ave., Twentynine Palms | 760/367–3445 | fax 760/367–3366 | www.oasisofmurals.com | Free.

Dining

In Joshua Tree

Picnic Areas. There are no restaurants inside Joshua Tree, so you will have to bring your own lunch. Picnic areas within the park are equipped with just the basics—tables, fire pits, and primitive rest rooms. Only those near the entrances have water.

Black Rock Canyon. Set among Joshua trees, pinyon pines, and junipers, this popular picnic area has barbecue grills and drinking water. It's one of the few with flush toilets. | End of Joshua Lane at the Black Rock Canyon Campground.

Cottonwood Spring. Shady trees make this a pleasant place to picnic. Adjacent to the visitor center, it has drinking water and rest rooms with flush toilets. | Pinto Basin Rd.

Covington Flats. This picnic area is a great place to get away from the crowds. There's just one picnic table surrounded by flat open desert dotted here and there by Joshua trees. | La Contenta Rd., 10 mi from Rte. 62.

Hidden Valley. Set among huge rock formations, Hidden Valley is one of the most pleasant places in the park to stop for lunch. The picnic tables are shaded by dense trees. | Park Blvd., 14 mi south of the West Entrance.

Indian Cove. The view here is rock formations that draw thousands of climbers to the park each year. Isolated from the rest of the park, this picnic area is reached via Twentynine Palms Highway. | End of Indian Cove Rd.

Live Oak Springs. Tucked among piles of boulders, this picnic area in the midst of interesting rock formations is near a stand of Joshua trees. | Park Blvd., east of Jumbo Rocks.

Near the Park

Arturo's. Mexican. Outside the park's West Entrance, this attractive restaurant serves traditional favorites. Try the combination burrito with moderately spicy beef-and-bean filling. | 61695 29 Palms Hwy., Joshua Tree | 760/366–2719 | Closed Mon. | $6–$15 | AE, DC, MC, V.

Edchada's. Mexican. Rock climbers gravitate to this restaurant, which has locations in Twentynine Palms and Yucca Valley. There are plenty of tacos and burritos on the menu, but locals swear by the blue corn enchiladas. | 56805 29 Palms Hwy., Yucca Valley | 760/365–7655 | 73502 Twentynine Palms Hwy., Twentynine Palms | 760/367–2131 | $5–$10 | AE, D, MC, V.

Park Rock Café. Café. Stoke up on a hearty breakfast, then order a box lunch before heading into the park. The café creates some unusual sandwiches such as nutty chicken salad or roast beef and cheddar with Ortega chiles, as well as fresh soups and salads. After a hike you can return to peruse local artwork and gift items, sip a cappuccino, or grab a late lunch before the 5 PM closing time. | 6554 Park Blvd., Joshua Tree | 760/366–3622 | fax 760/366–3288 | No dinner | $4–$6 | MC, V.

Lodging

Near the Park

Desert Hot Springs Spa. Surrounding a palm tree-filled courtyard with eight mineral-water pools, this hotel has long been popular with weekenders fleeing Los Angeles. Many rooms have balconies that overlook the San Jacinto mountains. Restaurant. Cable TV. Pool, beauty salon, hot tubs, sauna, spa. Bar. Shops. No smoking. | 10805 Palm Dr., Desert Hot Springs | 760/329–6000 or 800/808–7727 | fax 760/329–6915 | www.dhsspa.com | 50 rooms | $89–$139 | AE, D, DC, MC, V.

Homestead Inn. Run by a salt-of-the-earth innkeeper who keeps a flock of roadrunners as pets, this little lodge is set on 15 acres outside of the park. Three of the comfortable rooms have private patios; two have fireplaces and whirlpool tubs. Refrigerators, in-room VCRs (and movies). | 74153 Two Mile Rd., Twentynine Palms | 760/367–0030 or 877/367–0030 | www.joshuatreelodging.com | 6 rooms | $95–$125 | AE, MC, V.

★ **La Quinta Resort and Club.** The desert's oldest resort, opened in 1927, is still one of the area's finest accommodations. Rooms that once served as hideaways for such celebrities as Greta Garbo and Frank Capra are set in adobe casitas separated by broad expanses of lawn dotted with orange trees, while those in newer two-story units surround individual swimming pools and brilliantly colored gardens. Fireplaces, stocked refrigerators, and other amenities contribute to a discreet and sparely luxurious atmosphere. 6 restaurants. 5 golf courses, 23 tennis courts. 42 pools, health club, beauty salon, 52 hot tubs, spa. Shop. Children's programs. Business services. Some pets allowed (fee). | 618 rooms, 27 suites, 110 vacation residences | 49-499 Eisenhower Dr., La Quinta | 760/564–4111 or 800/598–3828 | fax 760/564–5768 | www.laquintaresort.com | $285–$370 | AE, D, DC, MC, V.

Mojave Rock Ranch Cabins. If peace, solitude, and stunning desert views are what you seek, try this rustic retreat. From the hammock hung on your private porch you'll see the gardens alive with barrel cactus, desert willows, and mesquite. The hilltop Bungalow has a hand-built stone-and-iron fireplace and a covered patio perfect for dining alfresco. Each cabin has an enclosed dog run. The Homesteader (available only for photo shoots) has a century-old wagon in the yard and is filled with Western antiques. hot tubs, kitchenettes, cable TV. Some pets allowed (fee). No smoking. | 64976 Starlight Rd., Joshua Tree | 760/366–8455 | fax 760/366–1996 | www.mojaverockranch.com | 4 cabins | $275–$325 | No credit cards.

★ **Roughley Manor.** No expense was spared by the wealthy pioneer who erected the stone mansion that houses this luxurious B&B. The "great room," which now serves as the dining room, was once a favorite hangout for such stars as Clark Gable and James Cagney. Elegant bedrooms are furnished with canopy beds and other antiques. The two generously proportioned suites in the main house have separate sitting rooms and wood-burning fireplaces. Kitchenettes. Outdoor hot tub. No smoking. | 74744 Joe Davis Rd., Twentynine Palms | 760/367–3238 | fax 760/367–4483 | www.roughleymanor.com | 6 rooms | $125–$150 | DC, MC, V | CP.

Camping and RV Facilities

In Joshua Tree

Camping is the best way to experience the starkly exquisite beauty of Joshua Tree. Here you have a rare opportunity to sleep outside in a semi-wilderness setting. The campgrounds, set at elevations from 3,000 to 4,500 ft, have only primitive facilities. Few have drinking water. With the exception of Black Rock and Indian Cove campgrounds, campsites are on a first-come basis. During the busy fall and spring weekends, plan to arrive early in the day to ensure a site. Temperatures can drop at night in any part of the year—bring a sweater or light jacket. If you plan to camp in late winter or early spring, be prepared for the gusty Santa Ana winds that may sweep through the park.

Backcountry camping is permitted in certain wilderness areas of Joshua Tree. You must sign in at a backcountry register board if you plan to stay overnight. For more information, stop at the visitor centers or ranger stations.

Belle Campground. This small campground is popular with families, as there are a number of boulders kids can scramble over and around. Campsites here are small and not recommended for recreational vehicles. Pit toilets. Fire pits, picnic tables. | 18 sites | 9 mi south of Oasis of Mara | 760/367–5500 | www.nps.gov.jotr | Free | Open year-round.

Black Rock Canyon Campground. Set among juniper bushes, cholla cacti, and other desert shrubs, Black Rock Canyon is one of the prettiest campgrounds in Joshua Tree. South of Yucca Valley, it's the closest campground to most of the desert communities. Located on the California Riding and Hiking Trail, it has facilities for horses and mules. Flush toilets. Dump station. Drinking water. Fire pits, picnic tables. Ranger station. | 100 sites | Joshua Lane, south of Hwy. 62 and Hwy. 247 | 760/367–5500 or (for reservations) 800/365–2267 | www.nps.gov.jotr | $10 | D, MC, V.

Cottonwood Campground. In spring this campground is surrounded by some of the best wildflower viewing in the desert. The park's southernmost campground, Cottonwood is often the last to fill up. Reservations are required for three group sites that hold up to 25 people. Flush toilets. Dump station. Drinking water. Fire pits, picnic tables. Ranger station. | 62 sites, 3 group sites | Pinto Basin Rd., 7 mi north of I–10 | 760/367–5500 | www.nps.gov.jotr | $10, $25 for groups | D, MC, V.

Hidden Valley Campground. This is the most popular campground among rock climbers, who make their way up rock formations with names like the Blob, Old Woman, and Chimney Rock. Pit toilets. Fire pits, picnic tables. | 39 sites | North side of Park Blvd., 14 mi southeast of the West Entrance | 760/367–5500 | www.nps.gov.jotr | Free | Reservations not accepted.

Indian Cove Campground. This is a very sought-after spot for rock climbers, primarily because it lies among the 50 square mi of rugged terrain at the Wonderland of Rocks. Popular climbs near the campground include Pixie Rock, Feudal Wall, and Corral Wall. Call ahead to reserve

JOSHUA TREE
NATIONAL PARK

EXPLORING
ATTRACTIONS NEARBY
DINING
LODGING
CAMPING AND RV
FACILITIES
SHOPPING
ESSENTIAL
INFORMATION

the 13 group sites. Pit toilets. Fire pits, picnic tables. | 101 sites, 13 group sites | Indian Cove Rd., south of Hwy. 62 | 760/367–5500 or (for reservations) 800/365–2267 | www.nps.gov.jotr | Free, $20–$35 for groups | Reservations essential | D, MC, V.

Jumbo Rocks. One of the most popular campgrounds in Joshua Tree, Jumbo Rocks, tucked among giant boulders, affords each campsite a bit of privacy. It's a good home base for visiting some of the park's most popular attractions, including Geology Tour Road. Pit toilets. Fire pits, picnic tables. | 125 sites | Park Blvd., 11 mi from Oasis of Mara | 760/367–5500 | www.nps.gov.jotr | Free | Reservations not accepted.

Ryan Campground. At the base of Ryan Mountain, this primitive campground is east of the turnoff leading to Keys Views and Lost Horse Mine. Although there are no facilities for them, horses are permitted here. Pit toilets. Fire pits, picnic tables. | 31 sites | 16 mi south of West Entrance | 760/367–5500 | www.nps.gov.jotr | Free | Reservations not accepted.

Sheep Pass Campground. At 4,500 ft, Sheep Pass is the highest campground in the park. As it has only six sites, all designated for groups, it is also the smallest. The campsites, set among boulders and relatively dense vegetation, are fairly private. Pit toilets. Fire pits, picnic tables. | 31 group sites | Park Blvd., 16 mi from Oasis of Mara | 760/367–5500 or (for reservations) 800/365–2267 | www.nps.gov.jotr | $20–$35 | Reservations essential | D, MC, V.

White Tank. This small, quiet campground is popular with families because a nearby trail leads to a natural arch. Campsites are small and not recommended for RVs or trailers. Pit toilets. Fire pits, picnic tables. | 15 sites | Pinto Basin Rd., 11 mi south of Oasis of Mara | 760/367–5500 | www.nps.gov.jotr | Free | Reservations not accepted.

Near the Park

Joshua Tree Lake RV and Campground. Convenient to the West Entrance to Joshua Tree, this fairly spartan park on a small lake has both tent and RV sites. Flush toilets. Dump station. Guest laundry, showers. | 49 sites | 2601 Sunfair Rd., Joshua Tree | 760/366–1213 | www.desertgold.com | $9 per space plus $2 per person | AE, MC, V.

Twentynine Palms RV Resort. Occupying a somewhat barren setting, this resort has many amenities such hot tubs, exercise rooms, horseshoe pits, shuffleboard courts, tennis courts, and a club house. It's also adjacent to a golf course. Flush toilets. Full round-trips, dump station. Drinking water, guest laundry, showers. Public telephone. Swimming (2 outdoor pools, 1 indoor pool). | 197 sites | 4949 Desert Knoll Ave., Twentynine Palms | 760/367–3320 | fax 760/367–2351 | www.29palmsgolfresort.com | $28 | MC, V.

Shopping

Black Rock Nature Center. This is a small seasonal nature center where you can pick up books, maps, and pamphlets about Joshua Tree. | 9800 Black Rock Canyon Rd. | 760/365–9585 | www.joshuatree.org | Sept.–May, daily 8–4.

Essential Information

ATMS (24-HOUR): Ultramar Gas Station | 73777 29 Palms Hwy., Twentynine Palms | 760/367–9807. **Circle K** | 61920 29 Palms Hwy., Joshua Tree | 760/366–8513.

AUTOMOBILE SERVICE STATIONS: Ultramar Gas Station | 73777 29 Palms Hwy., Twentynine Palms | 760/367–9807 | Daily 6 AM–midnight. **Circle K** | 61920 29 Palms Hwy., Joshua Tree | 760/366–8513 | Open 24 hrs.

POST OFFICES: Yucca Valley | 57280 Yucca Trail, 92284 | 800/275–8777 | Weekdays 9–5, Sat. 10–1. **Joshua Tree** | 61416 29 Palms Hwy., 92252 | 800/275–8777 | Weekdays 9–5, Sat. 9–12. **Twentynine Palms** | 73839 Gorgonio Dr., 92277 | 800/275–8777 | Weekdays 8:30–5.

JOSHUA TREE CAMPGROUNDS

	Total # of sites	# of RV sites	# of hook-ups	Drive-to sites	Hike-to sites	Flush toilets	Pit toilets	Drinking water	Showers	Fire grates/pits	Swimming	Boat access	Playground	Dump station	Ranger station	Public telephone	Reservation possible	Daily fee per site	Dates open
INSIDE THE PARK																			
Belle	18	0	0	•			•			•								Free	Y/R
Black Rock Canyon	100	100	0	•		•				•				•	•	•	•	$10	Y/R
Cottonwood	62	62	0	•		•				•				•	•		•	$10	Y/R
Hidden Valley	39	39	0	•		•				•								Free	Y/R
Indian Cove	101	101	0	•			•			•							•	Free	Y/R
Jumbo Rocks	125	125	0	•			•			•								Free	Y/R
Ryan	31	31	0	•			•			•								Free	Y/R
Sheep Pass	6	6	0	•			•			•							•	$20–35	Y/R
White Tank	15	0	0	•			•											Free	Y/R
NEAR THE PARK																			
Joshua Tree Lake	49	38	0	•		•			•					•			•	$9	Y/R
Twentynine Palms	197	197	197	•		•		•	•					•		•	•	$28	Y/R

* In summer only   ** Reservation fee charged   Y/R=Year-round
UL=Unlimited   ULP=Unlimited primitive   LD=Labor Day   MD=Memorial Day

DINOSAUR DAYS

Researchers have discovered that Petrified Forest National Park contains an incredible wealth of ancient animal fossils, including a 10-ft-long amphibian, a 6-ft-long scaled fish, a 15-ft-long crocodilelike creature, a rhinoceroslike animal with tusks and a parrotlike head, and many dinosaurs.

PETRIFIED FOREST NATIONAL PARK

EAST-CENTRAL ARIZONA

Painted Desert Entrance: I–40 exit 311, 24 mi east of Holbrook and 68 mi west of Gallup. Rainbow Forest Entrance: Route 180, 18 mi east of Holbrook and 39 mi northwest of St. Johns.

A moment of geological time more than 200 million years in the past comes to life in Petrified Forest National Park. The park's 146 square miles are covered with petrified tree trunks whose wood cells were fossilized over centuries by brightly hued mineral deposits— silica, iron oxide, manganese, aluminum, copper, lithium, and carbon. These petrified logs scattered about the landscape resemble a fairy-tale forest turned to stone. Most of the park's 93,000 acres include portions of the vast pink-hued lunarlike landscape known as the Painted Desert.

In 1984 the fossilized remains of one of the oldest dinosaurs ever unearthed—dating from the Triassic period of the Mesozoic era 225 million years ago—were discovered here. Visitors flock to the Rainbow Museum to see "Gertie," a skeleton of a phytosaur, a crocodilelike carnivore. Other plant and animal fossils in the park also date from the same period. Remnants of humans and their artifacts dating back 8,000 years have also been recovered at more than 500 sites here.

Because about 100 years ago so many looters hauled away large quantities of petrified wood, President Theodore Roosevelt made the area a national monument in 1906. Since then, it has been illegal (not to mention bad karma) to remove even a small sliver of petrified wood from the park.

PUBLICATIONS

Stop by the White Mountains ranger station in Pinetop-Lakeside and pick up a copy of the 20-page Forest Service brochure *Recreational Opportunities in the Apache Sitgreaves National Forest* for descriptions of the area's hiking, horseback riding, camping, bicycling, fishing, and boating opportunities. A similar booklet is available from the White Mountain Apaches detailing activities on nearby reservation land.

When to Visit

SCENERY AND WILDLIFE

In summer Engelmann asters, sunflowers, and other flowers bloom in the park. Past the park's scrubby brown bushes, juniper trees, cottonwoods, and willows grow along Puerco River Wash, providing shelter for all manner of wildlife. You might spot mule deer, coyotes, prairie dogs, and foxes, while other inhabitants, like porcupines and bobcats, tend to hide. Bird-watchers should keep an eye out for red-tailed and Swainson's hawks, roadrunners, swallows, mockingbirds, and many varieties of hummingbird. Try to spot all three kinds of lizards—collared, side-blotched, and southern prairie—in rock nooks and crannies. But beware of rattlesnakes, of which there are many, and don't step anywhere you can't see. The optimum time to see and photograph wildlife is early morning and just before dusk.

HIGH AND LOW SEASON

The park is rarely crowded. Weather-wise, the best time to visit is in the autumn high season, when nights are chilly, but daytime temperatures hover near 70°F. In summer temperatures reach well into the 90s, and even 100s, but half of all yearly rain falls between June and August, so spotting blooming wildflowers is possible. The park is least crowded in winter because of cold winds and occasional snow, though daytime temperatures are typically in the 50s and 60s.

Average High/Low Temperature (°F) and Monthly Precipitation (in inches)

	JAN.	FEB.	MAR.	APR.	MAY	JUNE
PETRIFIED	48/21	54/25	60/29	70/35	79/43	89/52
FOREST	.56	.53	.64	.37	.44	.34
	JULY	AUG.	SEPT.	OCT.	NOV.	DEC.
	92/60	89/59	84/52	72/40	59/28	48/22
	1.35	1.74	1.23	1.04	.67	.68

FESTIVALS AND SEASONAL EVENTS
WINTER

Dec.: **Parade of Lights.** Holbrook's nighttime Christmas parade down Hopi Boulevard the first Saturday of December often brings out the whole town. | 928/524–6558 or 800/524–2459.

Jan: **Pony Express Ride.** More than four decades of tradition are represented in this thrillling re-enactment of the Old West horse and rider method of delivering mail. | 800/524–2459.

SPRING

May: **Dog Trials.** In Alpine, working dogs compete against each other at Judd's Ranch, herding sheep over bridges and running through various obstacles. | 928/339–4330.

SUMMER

June: **Old West Celebration.** At the historic Holbrook Old West Courthouse you'll find Old West shoot-out reenactments, music, food, and children's activities. | 928/524–6558 or 800/524–2459.

June–July: **Navajo Indian Dances.** More than two dozen young people perform traditional Navajo dances at this summer event at the Old West Courthouse in Holbrook. | 928/524–6558 or 800/524–2459.

July: **Prescott Frontier Days and Rodeo.** Started in 1888, this rodeo in Prescott conducted as part of the local July 4 festivities is billed as the world's oldest—though Pecos, Texas continues to contest that point. | 928/445–2000 or 800/266–7534.

Aug.: **Annual White Mountain Bluegrass Festival.** Local and national musicians, along with food and dancing, are showcased at this festival on Show Low Lake. | 928/367–4290.

Nearby Towns

A sleepy college town of almost 60,000, **Flagstaff** is home to Northern Arizona University, and a growing destination for skiers and hikers. It's always been a popular stopping point for those traveling along I–40. There's a fascinating arboretum, an observatory, and a good symphony. And it's the closest thing to a "city" near the Petrified Forest. If you want to be closer to the park, your best bet is to stay in **Holbrook,** on historic Route 66. In 1881, when the railroad reached this area, Holbrook became part of the Aztec Land and Cattle Company. Now this ranching town of 6,000 is mostly a base for exploring the sights of northeastern Arizona. **Show Low,** the commercial center for this high-country area, has little of the charm of nearby **Pinetop-Lakeside,** but it's a good stopping point on your way to the Painted Desert or Petrified Forest. Pinetop-Lakeside, at 7,200 ft, is surrounded by the world's largest stand of Ponderosa Pines, and nearby **Alpine,** known as the "Alps of Arizona" is on the banks of the San Francisco River, purportedly along the route taken

BACKWARD TOUR

Since most people enter Petrified Forest at the north entrance, you can have the park all to yourself if you go early and enter from the south. In this direction, you'll begin with up-close views of the petrified logs themselves, moving on to scenic overlooks later in the drive, and ending with the film about the park at Painted Desert visitor center.

by Francisco Vasquez de Coronado more than 400 years ago. The small village has a variety of winter sports, and is a popular destination for hiking and fishing in summer.

INFORMATION

Alpine Chamber of Commerce | Box 410, Alpine, AZ 85920 | 928/339–4330 | www.alpine-az.com. **Flagstaff Chamber of Commerce** | 101 W. Rte. 66, Flagstaff, AZ 86001 | 928/774–4505 | www.flagstaffchamber.com. **Flagstaff Visitor Center** |,1 E. Rte. 66, Flagstaff, AZ 86001 | 928/774–9541 or 800/842–7293 | www.flagstaff.az.us. **Holbrook Chamber of Commerce** | 100 E. Arizona Ave., Holbrook, AZ 86025 | 928/524–6558 or 800/524–2459 | www.ci.holbrook.az.us. **Pinetop-Lakeside Chamber of Commerce** | 6102-C W. White Mountain Blvd., Pinetop, AZ 85929 | 928/367–4290 | www.pinetoplakesidechamber.com. **Prescott Chamber of Commerce** | 117 W. Goodwin St., Prescott, AZ 86303 | 928/445–2000 or 800/266–7534 | www.prescott.org. **Show Low Chamber of Commerce** | 81 E. Deuce of Clubs, Box 1083, Show Low, AZ 85901 | 928/537–2326 or 888/746–9569 | www.showlowchamberofcommerce.com.

Exploring Petrified Forest

PARK BASICS

Contacts and Resources: Petrified Forest National Park | 1 Park Rd. | Box 2217, Petrified Forest, AZ 86028 | 928/524–6228 | www.nps.gov/pefo.

Hours: The park is open daily 8 AM–5 PM year-round, except for Christmas Day and New Year's Day, when it's closed. Hours are extended in summer, but vary (call for information).

Fees: Entrance fees are $10 per car for seven consecutive days or $5 per person on foot, bicycle, motorcycle, or bus.

Getting Around: There are no restrictions on vehicles entering the park. Parking is free, and there's ample space at all trail heads, as well as at the visitor center and the museum. For information about road conditions call 928/524–6228.

Permits: Permits are required for backcountry hiking and camping, and are free (limit of 15 days) at the visitor center and the museum before 4 PM.

Public Telephones: The visitor center at the park's north end and the museum near the south entrance have public phones.

Rest Rooms: From north to south, you'll find rest rooms at Painted Desert Inn National Historic Landmark, Painted Desert visitor center, Chinde Point, Puerco Pueblo, Agate Bridge, and Rainbow Forest Museum.

Accessibility: The visitor center, museum, and overlooks on the scenic drive are wheelchair accessible. All trails are paved, and all are accessible except Blue Mesa, which is very steep. For more information, call the park switchboard at 928/524–6228.

Emergencies: In case of emergency, dial 911. Crystal Forest, Blue Mesa, and Puerco Pueblo have free emergency call boxes. The park switchboard (928/524–6228) can connect you with a ranger who can provide emergency medical assistance. You can also reach park police, who are located at both visitor centers, by phoning the switchboard.

Lost and Found: The lost-and-found is at Painted Desert visitor center.

A Good Tour

PETRIFIED FOREST IN ONE DAY

A drive through the park without stopping (28 mi) takes only 45 minutes, but you can spend most of a day exploring if you stop at sites along the way. Entering the park from the north, stop at **Painted Desert visitor center** and see the 20-minute film, which introduces the park highlights. At this end of the park, the **Painted Desert** is most pronounced. From almost any vantage point you can marvel at the multicolored rocks and hills, which were the home of prehistoric humans and far more ancient dinosaurs. **Painted Desert Inn visitor center,** 2 mi south of the north entrance, provides further orientation in the form of guided ranger tours. After a brief stop there, drive south 8 mi to reach **Puerco Pueblo,** a 100-room pueblo built before 1400. Continuing south you'll find Puebloan rock art petroglyphs at **Newspaper Rock** and, just beyond, **The Teepees,** cone-shaped rock formations covered with manganese and other minerals. **Blue Mesa** is roughly the mid-point of the drive and a good place to have a picnic. Follow lunch with the 1-mi, moderately steep loop hike from here that leads you around badland hills made of bentonite clay. Drive on for 5 mi until you come to **Jasper Forest,** just past **Agate Bridge,** with views of the landscape strewn with petrified logs. The next important stop is **Crystal Forest,** 18 mi south of the north entrance, named for the smoky quartz, amethyst, and citrine along the 0.8-mi loop trail. **Rainbow Forest Museum,** at the park's south entrance, has rest rooms, a bookstore, and exhibits of early reptiles, dinosaurs, and petrified wood. Just behind Rainbow Forest Museum is **Giant Logs,** a 0.4-mi loop that takes you to "Old Faithful," the largest log in the park, estimated to weigh 44 million tons.

Attractions

PROGRAMS

For information on park programs, teacher-led educational programs for elementary students, or to hire a tour guide, call the park switchboard: 928/524–6228.

Timeless Impressions. At the park's north entrance visitor center, a 20-minute educational film serves as an introduction to the park. It covers the highlights, briefly explaining the sights you'll see and their archaeological significance. The film runs continuously, starting every half hour. | Painted Desert visitor center | 928/524–6228 | Daily 8–5.

SCENIC DRIVE

Painted Desert Scenic Drive. A 28-mi one-way scenic drive takes you through the park. Entering from the north (at Painted Desert visitor center), the first 5 mi are along the edge of a high mesa, with spectacular views of Painted Desert. Beyond lies the Painted Desert Wilderness Area, a desolate, roughly carved expanse. After the 5 mi point, the road crosses I-40, then swings south toward Perco River across a landscape covered with sagebrush, saltbrush, sunflowers, and Apache plume. Past the river, the road climbs onto a narrow mesa leading to Newspaper Rock, a panel of Pueblo Indian rock art. Then the road bends southeast, enters a barren stretch, and passes teepee-shape buttes in the distance. Next you'll come to Blue Mesa, roughly the park's midpoint and a good place to stop for views of petrified logs. The next stop on the drive is Agate Bridge, really a 100-ft log over a wide wash. The remaining overlooks are Jasper Forest and Crystal Forest, which provide a further glimpse at the accumulated petrified wood. On your way out of the park, stop at the Rainbow Forest Museum for a rest and to buy a memento.

SIGHTS TO SEE

★ **Agate Bridge.** Here you'll see a 100-ft log spanning a 40-ft-wide wash. | 19 mi south of visitor center on the main park road.

Blue Mesa. This wide, flat expanse is a good place for a picnic with a view of petrified logs. | 14 mi south of visitor center on the main park road.

★ **Crystal Forest.** The fragments of petrified wood strewn here once held clear quartz and amethyst crystals. | 20 mi south of visitor center on the main park road.

★ **Giant Logs.** A short walk leads you past the park's largest log, known as "Old Faithful." It's considered the largest because of its diameter (9′ 9), as well as how tall it once was. | 28 mi south of visitor center on the main park road.

Jasper Forest. This overlook has a large concentration of petrified wood. | 17 mi south of visitor center on the main park road.

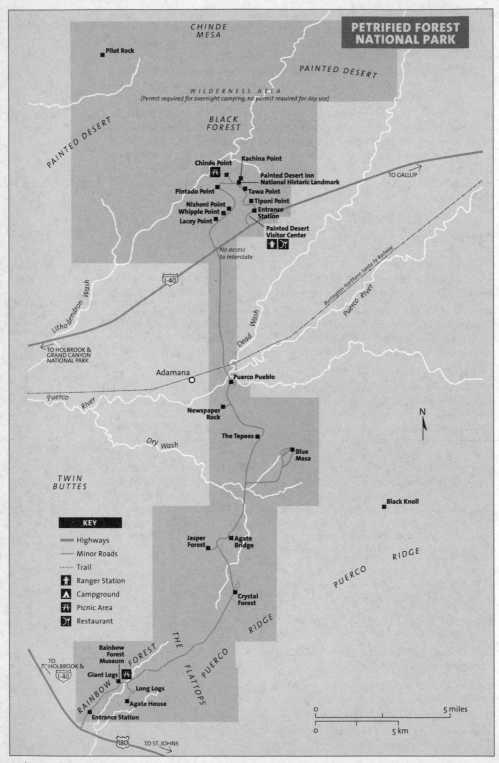

PETRIFIED FOREST NATIONAL PARK

CHINDE MESA

PAINTED DESERT

■ Pilot Rock

WILDERNESS AREA
(Permit required for overnight camping; no permit required for day use)

BLACK FOREST

PAINTED DESERT

Chinde Point ■ Kachina Point
🅰 Painted Desert Inn
National Historic Landmark
Pintado Point ■ ■ Tawa Point
Nizhoni Point ■ Tiponi Point
Whipple Point ■ Entrance Station
Lacey Point ■ Painted Desert Visitor Center

TO GALLUP

No access to Interstate

I-40

Burlington Northern Santa Fe Railway

Puerco River

Dead Wash

TO HOLBROOK & GRAND CANYON NATIONAL PARK

Adamana ○ Puerco Pueblo ■

Puerco River

Newspaper Rock ■

Dry Wash

The Tepees ■

Blue Mesa ■

N

TWIN BUTTES

Black Knoll ■

KEY
━━ Highways
── Minor Roads
······ Trail
🚹 Ranger Station
🅰 Campground
🍴 Picnic Area
🍴 Restaurant

Jasper Forest ■ ■ Agate Bridge

PUERCO RIDGE

RIDGE

Crystal Forest ■

THE FLATTOPS

PUERCO

Rainbow Forest Museum ■
TO HOLBROOK &
I-40
Giant Logs ■ 🅰
Long Logs ■
Agate House ■
Entrance Station ■

RAINBOW FOREST

180 TO ST. JOHNS

0 ━━━━ 5 miles
0 ━━━━ 5 km

Newspaper Rock. See huge boulders covered with petroglyphs carved by the Pueblo Indians more than 500 years ago. | 6 mi south of visitor center on the main park road.

Painted Desert Inn National Historic Site. You'll find cultural history exhibits, as well as the murals of Fred Kabotie, a popular 1940s artist whose work was commissioned by Mary Jane Colter. Native American crafts are displayed in this museum and mini visitor center. Check the schedule for daily events while you're here. | 2 mi north of visitor center on the main park road | 928/524–6228 | www.nps.gov/pefo | Free | Daily 8–4.

Painted Desert Visitor Center. This is the place to go for general park information and an informative 20-minute film on the park. | North entrance, off I–40, 27 mi east of Holbrook | 928/524–6228 | www.nps.gov/pefo | Daily 8–5.

Puerco Pueblo. This is a 100-room pueblo, built before 1400 and said to have housed Ancestral Pueblo people. Many visitors come to see petroglyphs, as well as a solar calendar. | 10 mi south of the visitor center on the main park road.

Rainbow Forest Museum. The museum houses artifacts of early reptiles, dinosaurs, and petrified wood. | South entrance, off U.S. 180, 18 mi southeast of Holbrook | 928/524–6228 | Free | Daily 8–5.

The Tepees. Witness the effects of time on these cone-shape rock formations colored by iron, manganese, and other minerals. | 8 mi south of visitor center on the main park road.

Sports and Outdoor Activities

BICYCLING

Bikes are allowed on the 28-mi paved drive only. There are no rentals within the park, so bring your own equipment.

HIKING

Great hiking abounds in the Petrified Forest. All trails begin off the main road, and all are clearly marked.

Agate House. A fairly flat 1-mi trip takes you to to an eight-room pueblo sitting high on a knoll. | 26 mi south of the visitor center.

Blue Mesa. Although it's only 1 mi long, Blue Mesa trail, at the park's midway point, is one of the most popular. Perhaps this is because it's significantly steeper than the rest. | 14 mi south of the visitor center.

Crystal Forest. The easy, 0.8-mi loop leads you past petrified wood that once held quartz crystals and amethyst chips. | 20 mi south of the visitor center.

Giant Logs. At 0.4 mi, Giant Logs is the park's shortest trail. The loop leads you to "Old Faithful," the park's largest log—it's 9 ft, 9 inches at its base, weighing 44 tons. | Directly behind Rainbow Forest Museum, 28 mi south of the visitor center.

Long Logs. While barren, the easy 0.6-mi loop reveals the largest concentration of wood in the park. | 26 mi south of the visitor center.

Puerco Pueblo. A relatively flat and interesting 0.5-mi trail takes you past remains of an ancestral home of the Pueblo people, built before 1400. | 10 mi south of the visitor center.

Attractions Nearby

For attractions in Flagstaff, *see* Grand Canyon National Park in Canyon Country.

SIGHTS TO SEE

Bucket of Blood Saloon. Come have a look at this classic western saloon with the gory name that has remained virtually untouched since it was built in the 1800s. Although it's not

PETRIFIED FOREST
NATIONAL PARK

EXPLORING
**ATTRACTIONS
NEARBY**
DINING
LODGING
CAMPING AND RV
FACILITIES
SHOPPING
ESSENTIAL
INFORMATION

open for inside tours, you can get a good view of the old saloon from the street. | S.E. Central St., Holbrook | 928/524–6558 | Daily (from outside only).

★ **Canyon de Chelly National Monument.** In Arizona's northeast corner, Canyon de Chelly (pronounced d'shay), is a place of spectacular beauty. Its two main gorges have dramatically red sandstone walls, some as high as 1,000 ft. Ancient pictographs adorn the cliffs. The park is also noteworthy for its ruins of Indian villages (built between AD 350 and 1300); some of the park's 7,000 archaeological sites date back 4,500 years. | 3 mi east of Chinle on Navajo Rte. 7, Chinle 86503 | Box 588 | www.nps.gov/cach | 928/674–5500 | Free | May–Sept., daily 8–6; Oct.–Apr., daily 8–5.

Homolovi Ruins State Park. Four miles northeast of Winslow off AZ 87 are four major ancestral Hopi pueblos. There are 40 ceremonial kivas dating from AD 900, and one pueblo contains more than 1,000 rooms. The Hopi hold the site to be sacred, and they welcome visitors, as they believe that each potentially brings rain. | 33 mi west of Holbrook, on AZ 87, Winslow | 928/289–4106 | $5 per vehicle up to 4 persons; additional persons $1 each | Daily 8–5.

Lyman Lake State Park. Created in 1915 by damming the Little Colorado River, the 3-mi-long Lyman Lake reservoir is popular for boating, waterskiing, windsurfing, and sailing. Designated swimming beaches accommodate those who prefer to stick closer to shore. | 55 mi southeast of Petrified Forest National Park on U.S. 180, St. Johns | 928/337–4441 | $5 per vehicle | Daily 8–5 | www.wmonline.com/attract/lymanlk.htm.

Walnut Canyon National Monument. Feel ancient life at close range when you enter a group of cliff-dwelling homes constructed by the Sinagua people between 10 and 1250. | Walnut Canyon Rd., 3 mi south of I–40, exit 204, Flagstaff | 928/526–3367 | www.nps.gov/waca | $5 | June–Aug., daily 8–6; Sept.–Nov. and March–May, daily 8–5; Dec.–Feb., daily 9–5.

Wupatki National Monument. Families from the Sinagua and other ancestral Puebloans are said to have lived together on this site between 100 and 1250. *Wupatki* means "tall house," and the original structure was, indeed, three stories high. What remains is a ruin, but rooms and recreational areas are still identifiable. | From Flagstaff, take U.S. 89 north for 12 mi, turn right at sign. The visitor center is 21 mi from this junction, Flagstaff | 928/556–7040 | www.nps.gov/wupa | $5 | Visitor Center daily 8–5.

Dining

In Petrified Forest

Painted Desert Visitor Center Cafeteria. American/Casual. This is the only place in the park where you can get a full meal. Offerings are standard cafeteria fare. | North entrance, off I–40, 27 mi east of Holbrook | 928/524–6228 | $4–$8 | MC, V.

Picnic Areas. Pack your own lunch and enjoy a meal al fresco at the park's picnic sites.
    Chinde Point Picnic Area. This small picnic area is near the north entrance and has picnic tables and rest rooms. | 2 mi north of Painted Desert visitor center.
    Rainbow Forest Museum Picnic Area. This small picnic area is near the south entrance and has picnic tables and rest rooms. | North entrance, off I–40, 27 mi east of Holbrook.

Rainbow Forest Museum Snack Bar. American/Casual. Quick snacks are available at the museum. | South entrance, Off U.S. 180, 18 mi southeast of Holbrook | 928/524–6228 | $4–$8 | MC, V.

Near the Park

For dining in Flagstaff, *see* Grand Canyon National Park in Canyon Country.

★ **Annie's Gift Shop and Tea Room.** Café. At this homey bistro across the street from the Lakeside Fire Department you can get simple lunch and breakfast fare like quiche, scones, sandwiches, and teas. | 2849 White Mountain Blvd., Lakeside | 928/368–5737 | Closed Labor Day–Memorial Day. Closed Sun. No dinner | $7–$13 | AE, D, MC, V.

Bear Wallow Café. American. In the Apache-Sitgreaves Forest, this café serves both American and Mexican cuisine, with everything from chicken-fried steak to green chili. | 42650 U.S. 180, Alpine | 928/339–4310 | $5–$9 | AE, D, MC, V.

The Chalet. American. Although its name implies Swiss food, this restaurant is best-known for its ribs and chicken. | 348 White Mountain Blvd., Alpine | 928/367–1514 | Closed Sun.–Mon. No lunch | $15–$32 | AE, D, MC, V.

Charlie Clark's Steak House. Steak. Prime rib is the house specialty at this log cabin–style restaurant. The chicken-fried steak is also deservedly popular. | 1701 White Mountain Blvd., Alpine | 928/367–4900 | $10–$19 | AE, D, MC, V.

★ **Christmas Tree.** American. Chicken and dumplings is the big draw at this down-home restaurant, but the kitchen also serves elegant dishes like lamb chops and honey duck with fried apples. The fresh fruit cobbler is a must. | Woodland Rd. and White Mountain Blvd., Lakeside | 928/367–2782 | Closed Labor Day–Memorial Day. Closed Sun. | $14–$34 | AE, D, MC, V.

High in the Pines Deli. Café. This intimate coffeehouse and sandwich shop one block east of Deuce of Clubs serves European-style charcuterie boards with fresh meats and cheeses served with baguettes, as well as a variety of specialty sandwiches. Try the garlic-pepper loin sandwich with one of the many coffee drinks. | 1201 E. Hall, Show Low | 928/537–1453 | Closed Sun. No dinner | $3–$13 | No credit cards.

PETRIFIED FOREST
NATIONAL PARK

EXPLORING
ATTRACTIONS NEARBY
DINING
LODGING
CAMPING AND RV
FACILITIES
SHOPPING
ESSENTIAL
INFORMATION

Joe and Aggies Café. Mexican. Customers keep coming back to this café, which is the oldest in town. The chiles rellenos and *chistas* (fried flour tortilla smothered in cheese and green chile sauce) are delicious. | 120 W. Hopi Dr., Holbrook | 928/524–6540 | $6–$11 | AE, D, MC, V.

Mesa Italiana. Italian. A quaint and casual spot, Mesa Italiana has tasty New Zealand baby rack of lamb and standards like *osso buco* and linguine pescatore. Lunch is a good deal. | 2318 N. Navajo Blvd., Holbrook | 928/524–6696 | $7–$20 | AE, D, MC, V.

Lacanos. Steak. Brass railings, mounted game, and Tiffany-style lamps add a touch of elegance to the four separate dining areas. Filet mignon and prime rib are top drawer. | 571 W. Deuce of Clubs Dr., Show Low | 928/537–8220 | $10–$30 | AE, D, DC, MC, V.

Plainsman Restaurant. American. With two separate dining areas and a full bar, the Plainsman is perfect for a family dinner, a romantic evening, or cocktail. The BBQ ribs, steaks, and shrimp are all popular. | 1001 W. Hopi Dr., Holbrook | 928/524–3345 | $6–$12 | AE, MC, V.

Lodging

Near the Park

For lodging in Flagstaff, *see* Grand Canyon National Park in Canyon Country.

Best Western Arizonian Inn. The rooms in this chain motel are large and spare, with standard amenities, such as AM/FM alarm clock radio and free parking. An all-night diner is steps from the parking lot. A branch in Pinetop is slightly more upscale and has a hot tub. Restaurant. Some microwaves, some refrigerators, cable TV. Pool. Some pets allowed. | 2508 E. Navajo Blvd., Holbrook | 928/524–2611 or 877/280–7300 | fax 928/524–2611 | www.bestwestern.com | 70 rooms | $58–$72 | AE, D, DC, MC, V.

Best Western Paint Pony Lodge. This is Show Low's quietest hotel, in a wooded setting farther from the main street than most. Some of the rooms have fireplaces. Rooms are otherwise standard, but optional amenities include adjoining rooms and refrigerators. Restaurant, room service. In-room data ports, some microwaves, some refrigerators, cable TV. Bar. Business services. Some pets allowed (fee). | 581 W. Deuce of Clubs Dr., Show Low | 928/537–5773 | fax 928/537–5766 | www.bestwestern.com | 50 rooms | $74–$84 | AE, D, DC, MC, V | CP.

Delaware is the only state that does not contain a site administered by the National Park Service.

Comfort Inn. This motel is across the road from the Holbrook airport and 18 mi east of Petrified Forest National Park. There's also a Lakeside branch on Route 260 in Holbrook. Rooms are standard, but new carpeting and air conditioners have erased a previously worn look. Some rooms can be noisy, though. Restaurant. Some microwaves, some refrigerators. Cable TV. Pool. Laundry facilities. Business services. Some pets allowed. | 1637 Hwy 260., Pinetop Lakeside, 85935 | 928/368–6600 or 800/843–4792 | fax 928/368–6600 | www.comfortinn.com | 54 rooms | $65 | AE, D, DC, MC, V | CP.

Econo Lodge. This chain motel is 0.5 mi from I–40 on the east side of Holbrook, next to the Comfort Inn. Rooms are standard and spartan. Restaurant, picnic area. Some refrigerators, cable TV. Pool. Laundry facilities. Some pets allowed. | 2596 E. Navajo Blvd., Holbrook | 928/524–1448 | fax 928/524–1493 | www.econolodge.com | 63 rooms | $40–$50 | AE, D, DC, MC, V | CP.

★**Hannagan Meadow Lodge.** About 22 mi south of Alpine on U.S. 191, this casual, antique-filled lodge built in 1926 has rooms with ornate brass beds in the main lodge. The self-contained log cabins, which sleep 4, are more rustic, although have modern furniture. Restaurant, bar. No room phones, no room TVs. | U.S. 191, Hanagan Meadow | 928/339–4370 | fax 928/339–4370 | www.hannaganmeadow.com | 8 rooms, 8 cabins | $55–$150 | AE, MC, V | CP.

Hon-Dah Resort. This mountain resort, at an altitude of 7,400 ft, has an extravagant lobby with a display of stuffed high-country animals, and a large fireplace and lounge area. Rooms are large, but basic, with comfortable beds and large bathrooms. Restaurant. In-room data ports, cable TV. Pool, hot tub, sauna. Bar. | 777 Hwy. 260, Pinetop | 928/369–0299 or 800/929–8744 | www.hon-dah.com. | 128 rooms | $89–$109 | AE, D, DC, MC, V.

★**Lakeview Lodge.** Antique furnishings, stone fireplaces, and rustic decor characterize this quaint inn, the oldest guest lodge in Arizona. Outside, cobblestone walkways wind through the surrounding pine forest and gardens, and a private, stocked lake is available for fishing. In-room TVs are available upon request. Restaurant, picnic area. No room phones, no TV in some rooms. | Rte. 26, Pinetop | 520/368–5253 | www.dynexgroup.com/lakeview | 9 rooms | $65–$90 | MC, V.

Motel 6. This budget motel is on the east side of town at I–40, exit 289. Rooms are standard, but quiet. Cable TV. Pool. Laundry facilities. Some pets allowed. | 2514 Navajo Blvd., Holbrook | 928/524–6101 | fax 928/524–1806 | www.motel6.com | 124 rooms | $30–$41 | AE, D, DC, MC, V.

Northwoods Resort. Surrounded by mountain pines, each of these home-style cabins has a full kitchen, covered porch, and barbecue grill. Some have in-room hot tubs; two-story cabins can accommodate up to 18 people. Picnic area. Pool, hot tub. Playground. Some pets allowed (fee). No room phones. | 165 E. White Mountain Blvd., Pinetop | 928/367–2966 or 800/813–2966 | fax 928/367–2969 | www.northwoodsaz.com | 14 cabins | $79–$349 | AE, D, MC, V.

Tal Wi Wi Lodge. Facing a lush meadow 4 mi north of Alpine, this lodge's setting is unparalleled in the area for value, quietude, and views. Rooms are simple and clean; three have wood-burning stoves. The bar has satellite TV. Restaurant. Bar. No room phones, no TV. | 40 County Rd. 2220, Alpine | 928/339–4319 or 800/476–2695 | fax 928/339–1962 | www.talwiwilodge.com | 20 rooms | $69–$99 | AE, MC, V.

Whispering Pines Resort. These cabins, at 7,200 ft, sit in a forest of conifers. Rooms are basic and clean, and all are within walking distance of hiking trails in Apache National Forest. Hot tubs, kitchenettes, microwaves, refrigerators, cable TV. Laundry facilities. Some pets allowed (fee). No room phones. | 237 E. White Mountain Blvd., Pinetop, 85935 | 928/367–4386 or 800/840–3867 | fax 928/367–3702 | www.whisperingpinesaz.com | 36 cabins | $83–$220 | AE, D, MC, V.

Wigwam Motel. This motel consists of concrete "tepees" built in the 1940s. Inside they're ordinary motel rooms. There's a small museum of Native American artifacts and local history lore. Cable TV. Some pets allowed. No room phones. | 811 W. Hopi Dr., Holbrook | 928/524-3048 | www.nephi.com/wigwam_motel.htm | 15 rooms | $33–$38 | MC, V.

Camping and RV Facilities

In Petrified Forest

There are no campgrounds in the park. Backcountry camping is allowed if you obtain a free permit at the visitor center or museum.

Near the Park

For camping in Flagstaff, *see* Grand Canyon National Park in Canyon Country.

Many of the local campgrounds are maintained by the Apache-SitGreaves National Forest, a two million acre area covering the east-central Arizona White Mountains and Mogollon Rim. **Apache-SitGreaves National Forest** | 800/280-2267 | www.fs.fed.us/r3/asnf.

Benny Creek Campground. Camping sites are in the open, under a thin canopy of Ponderosa Pine, and can accommodate tents and small trailers. The grounds are within walking distance of Greer Lake. Pit toilets. Drinking water. Fire grates. | Off Rte. 373, 2.5 mi north of Greer | 877/444-6777 | 24 tent sites | $8, $4 per each additional vehicle | May–Oct.

East Fork Recreation Area. Six adjacent campgrounds (Aspen, Buffalo Crossing, Horse Spring, Diamond Rock, Deer Creek, and Racoon Campground) form this large, popular camping area near the trout-stocked Black River, in the Apache-SitGreaves National Forest. Sites at Aspen are small, but Buffalo Crossing has large enough ones to accommodate RVs. Diamond Rock Campground has 12 Adirondack style three-sided shelters. Pit toilets. Drinking water. Fire grates. | Forest Rd. 276, 6 mi south of Forest Rd. 249, 5 mi west of U.S. 191, Alpine | 877/444-6777 | 76 tent sites, 16 RV sites | $5–$10, $3–$5 per each additional vehicle | May–Oct.

Fool Hollow Lake Recreation Area. Fool Hollow has been called "the Rolls Royce of campgrounds" and has more amenities than any other in the area, including RV round-trips and modern bathrooms. Flush toilets. Full round-trips, dump station. Drinking water, showers. Fire pits. Public telephone. Play area, swimming (lake). | Fool Hollow Lake Rd. 0.6 mi off Old Linden Rd. and Rte. 260, Show Low | 602/537-3680 | 31 tent sites, 92 RV sites with full round-trips | $10 without round-trips, $15 per night per vehicle | May–Oct.

Hannagan Meadow. A beautiful forest surrounds this group of eight adjoining campsites managed by the forest service. There are no bathing facilities, although nearby Hanagan Meadow Lodge provides hot showers for $5. Trailers under 32 ft are welcome. Pit toilets. Drinking water. | US 191, 0.25 mi south of Hanagan Meadow Lodge, Hanagan Meadow | 928/339-4384 | 8 tent sites | Free | May–Oct.

Rolfe C. Hoyer Campground. This 100-site campground in Apache-SitGreaves National Forest is popular with families and senior citizens. Most sites are suited for tent or RV and are well-maintained and shaded by tall Ponderosa pines. Flush toilets. Dump station. Drinking water, showers. Fire grates. | Rte. 373, 2 mi north of Greer, Greer | 877/444-6777 | 98 tent sites, 99 RV sites | $14 per night per vehicle, $7 per each additional vehicle | May–Oct.

South Fork Campground. The site on the Little Colorado River was once a fish hatchery and Civilian Conservation Corps camp. The popular South Fork trail no. 97 begins here. Although the grounds are open year-round, the road is not plowed in winter. Small trailers (under 32 ft) are welcome. Pit toilets. Drinking water. Fire grates. | Apache County Rd. 4124, 2 mi south of Rte. 260, South Fork | 877/444-6777 | 8 tent sites | $6 per night per vehicle, $3 per each additional vehicle | Year-round.

PETRIFIED FOREST CAMPGROUNDS

	Total # of sites	# of RV sites	# of hook-ups	Drive-to sites	Hike-to sites	Flush toilets	Pit toilets	Drinking water	Showers	Fire grates/pits	Swimming	Boat access	Playground	Dump station	Ranger station	Public telephone	Reservation possible	Daily fee per site	Dates open
NEAR THE PARK																			
Benny Creek Campground	24	0	0	•		•		•		•							•	$18	May–Oct.
East Fork Recreation Area	76	0	0	•		•		•		•							•	$5–10	May–Oct.
Fool Hollow Lake Recreation Area	123	92	92	•	•	•	•	•			•	•	•	•		•	•	$10–15	May–Oct.
Hannagan Meadow Campground	8	8	0	•			•	•									•	Free	May–Oct.
Rolfe C. Hoyer Campground	100	99	0	•		•	•	•	•	•					•		•	$14	May–Oct.
South Fork Campground	8	0	0	•		•		•		•							•	$6	YR

* In summer only   ** Reservation fee charged   Y/R=Year-round
UL=Unlimited   ULP=Unlimited primitive   LD=Labor Day   MD=Memorial Day

Shopping

McGee's Gallery. This Native American crafts shop has reasonable prices on pottery, weaving, and jewelry, among other handcrafts. | 2114 N. Navajo Blvd., Holbrook | 928/524–1977 | Weekdays 9–5:30; Sat. 9–4.

Rainbow Forest Museum. The museum houses artifacts of early reptiles, dinosaurs, and petrified wood. The shop sells books and postcards. | South entrance, Off U.S. 180, 18 mi southeast of Holbrook | 928/524–6228 | Daily 8–5.

Painted Desert Inn. This visitor center has a small book sales area. | 2 mi south of North entrance | 928/524–6228 | Daily 8–4.

Painted Desert Visitor Center. You can buy petrified wood, postcards, and books on the park for children and adults. | North entrance, Off I-40, 27 mi east of Holbrook | 928/524–6228 | www.nps.gov/pefo | Daily 8–5.

Essential Information

ATMS (24-HOUR): There are no ATMs or banks in the park, but there are many in nearby Holbrook. **Norwest Bank** | 266 Navajo Blvd., Holbrook | 928/524–6275 | Daily, 24-hrs.

AUTOMOBILE SERVICE STATIONS: Painted Desert Oasis | Near Visitor Center off I-40, 27 mi east of Holbrook | 928/524–6228 or 928/524–3756 | Daily 8–5.

POST OFFICES: Painted Desert Visitor Center | Off I-40, 27 mi east of Holbrook, Petrified Forest, 86028 | 928/524–6228 | Weekdays 11–2. **Greer Post Office** | 103 Main St., Greer, AZ 85927 | 928/735–7322 | Weekdays 8–3, Sat. 8:30–9:30.

SAGUARO NATIONAL PARK

SOUTHEASTERN ARIZONA

Rincon Mountain District (east section): off I-10 exit 257 (Speedway Boulevard) or exit 275 (Houghton Road), then east on Speedway Boulevard to Old Spanish Trail and turn right. Tucson Mountain District (west section): off I-10 exit 242 (Avra Valley Road) or exit 257, then Speedway Boulevard west to Kinney Road and turn right.

Standing sentinel in the desert, the towering saguaro cactus is perhaps the most familiar emblem of the American Southwest. These slow-growing giants are found only in the Sonoran Desert, and the world's largest concentration is in Arizona's Saguaro National Park. The Tohono O'odham people, whose reservation near Tucson is second only in size to that of the Navajo, believe that the saguaros were put on earth to inspire humans with their stalwartness and dignity. These desert dwellers celebrate the harvest of the saguaro's sweet fruit every summer, and use the plant's woody skeleton, called saguaro ribs, to build fences and building supports.

Some human interactions with the region have been less than benign. Overgrazing by cattle threatened the once-thick stands of cactus, leading President Herbert Hoover to create Saguaro National Monument in 1933. On the western side, copper, gold, and silver mining posed the greatest danger. Throughout the Tucson Mountain District you can spot remnants of some of the 100-odd shafts dug before 1961, when President John F. Kennedy signed off on this portion of the park. A bit of additional land was added to the western section when national park status was conferred in 1994. Today, the eastern side has 67,293 acres, the more-visited western side 24,034.

PUBLICATIONS

The bookshops at Saguaro National Park carry the *Tucson Hiking Guide* by Betty Leavengood, a useful and entertaining book that includes day hikes in both sections of the park. Books that give a general introduction to the park include *Saguaro National Park* by Doris

Evans and *Sonoran Desert: The Story Behind the Scenery* by Christopher L. Helms. For a poetic take by a naturalist, try Gary Nabhan's *Saguaro: A View of Saguaro National Monument and the Tucson Basin.*

When to Visit

SCENERY AND WILDLIFE

Spring is the best time to wander among the wildflowers. Mid-March through April find wildflowers at their peak, but those at higher elevations open four to eight weeks later than those on the desert floor. Some types of cactus bloom in April, while the saguaro and others wait until May or early June. The wildlife, from bobcats to jackrabbits, are most active during the early morning and at dusk. In spring and summer lizards and snakes are out and about, but keep a low profile during the mid-day heat.

HIGH AND LOW SEASON

Although Saguaro never gets overcrowded, most people visit in milder weather from December through April. In summer, the intense heat puts off most hikers, at least at lower elevations. Lodging prices are much cheaper, however–rates at top resorts in Tucson drop by as much as 70% in summer. And there's nothing like the smell of the desert after the heavy rains that normally fall in July and August.

Average High/Low Temperatures (°F) and Monthly Precipitation (in inches)

	JAN.	FEB.	MAR.	APR.	MAY	JUNE
SAGUARO	64/39	68/41	73/45	81/51	90/58	100/68
	.93	.77	.73	.30	.18	.22
	JULY	AUG.	SEPT.	OCT.	NOV.	DEC.
	99/74	97/72	94/67	85/57	73/45	66/39
	2.26	2.28	1.41	.90	.61	1.04

FESTIVALS AND SEASONAL EVENTS

WINTER

Feb.: **La Fiesta de los Vaqueros.** America's largest outdoor mid-winter rodeo takes place on the Tucson Rodeo Grounds. It's preceded by the world's largest nonmotorized parade. | 520/294–8896.

Touchstone Energy Tucson Open. This PGA golf tournament is held at the Omni Tucson. | 520/571–2271.

Tubac Festival of the Arts. High-quality arts and crafts are bought and sold at this annual show in Tubac. | 520/398–2704.

Tucson Gem and Mineral Show. This huge trade show, the largest of its kind in the world, offers everything from precious stones to geodes to beads. It's held at the Tucson Convention Center. | 520/624–1817.

SPRING

Mar.: **Welch's Fry's Championship.** More than 140 world-class women golfers compete in this LPGA tournament at the Tucson Randolph Golf Complex. | 520/791–5742.

Apr.: **Balloon Rally.** Balloon rides and special children's events are held at this annual event in Benson. | 520/586–2842.

Pima County Fair. Fire eaters, jugglers, and hypnotists entertain at the Pima County Fairgrounds. | 520/762–9100.

Yaqui Easter. On Ash Wednesday, the Yaqui people celebrate with traditional dances and ceremonies in Tucson. | 520/791–4609.

May: **Cinco de Mayo.** This festival in Nogales celebrates the region's Mexican heritage. | 520/287–3685 or 520/287–6571.

Mexican Independence Day. The town of Benson celebrates our neighbor to the south in City Park. | 520/586–2842.

SUMMER

Aug.:   **Southwest Wings Birding Festival.** Southern Arizona, noted for its abundance of bird species, particularly hummingbirds, hosts field trips, lectures, and other avian-oriented events at festivals in locales such as Sierra Vista and Bisbee. | 520/378–0233.

FALL

Oct.:   **La Fiesta de los Chiles.** Stop by the Tucson Botanical Gardens to adopt a chile plant or to enjoy the food, music, and other entertainment. | 520/326–9686.

Tucson Heritage Experience Festival. This citywide celebration focuses on the cultures of the various native peoples in the Tucson area. | 520/624–1817.

SAGUARO
NATIONAL PARK

EXPLORING
ATTRACTIONS NEARBY
DINING
LODGING
CAMPING AND RV
FACILITIES
SHOPPING
ESSENTIAL
INFORMATION

Nearby Towns

Although it's Arizona's second-largest city, **Tucson** feels like a small town—it has a sleepy mood that reminds you just how much the desert still determines the pace. Averaging 340 days of sunshine a year, Tucson is popular with golfers and nature-lovers. Those in search of culture will be enchanted by its deep Native American, Spanish, Mexican, and Old West roots. About 50 mi southeast you'll find **Benson,** which used to be a sleepy little railroad stop on the Southern Pacific line. Today this town in the heart of the San Pedro River valley is home to Kartchner Caverns State Park, a spectacular cave system. About 45 mi south of Tucson is **Tubac,** the first European settlement in Arizona. The state's first newspaper, the *Weekly Arizonian*, was printed here in 1859. Today it's a quiet artists' colony featuring over 80 galleries. You can tour the Tumacacori Mission, parts of the Spanish presidio, and the well-preserved 1855 schoolhouse. Named for the walnuts that grew along the river, **Nogales** is actually two communities—the small Arizona town and the sprawling Mexican city over the border. A little more than 60 mi south of Tucson, the Mexican side offers great food and bargains on leather, wool blankets, and tequila. Rather than driving into Mexico, park on the U.S. side and walk across the border.

INFORMATION
Benson Visitor Center | 249 E. 4th St., Benson, 85602 | 520/586–4293 | cityofbenson.com. **Metropolitan Tucson Convention and Visitors Bureau** | 110 S. Church Ave., Tucson, 85701 | 520/624–1817 or 800/638–8350 | visittucson.org. **Nogales–Santa Cruz County Chamber of Commerce** | 123 W. Kino Park Way, Nogales, 85621 | 520/287–3685. **Tubac Chamber of Commerce** | Box 1866, (40 mi south of Tucson, Exit 34 off I-19) Tubac, 85646 | 520/398–2704 | tubacaz.com.

Exploring Saguaro

PARK BASICS
Contacts and Resources: Saguaro National Park. | 3693 S. Old Spanish Trail, Tucson, AZ 85730–5699 | 520/733–5158 Saguaro West, 520/733–5153 Saguaro East | nps.gov/sagu.

Fees: Admission to the western section of the park is free. In the eastern section you'll pay $6 per car or $3 per person if you're entering by bicycle or on foot. Annual passes cost $20. Back country camping fees are $6 nightly per campsite.

Hours: The eastern district opens at 7 AM and the west district opens at 6 AM; both close at sunset. The visitor centers are open 8:30 to 5 every day except Christmas.

Getting Around: Saguaro National Park is divided into two distinct sections flanking the city of Tucson. Both districts are about a half–hour drive from central Tucson. As there is no public transportation to or within Saguaro, a car is a necessity. In the western section Bajada Loop Drive takes you through the park and to various trailheads; Cactus Forest Drive does the same for the eastern section.

Permits: Backcountry camping at designated sites in the eastern district requires a permit. You can obtain a permit for $6 nightly per campsite in person at the visitor center or by mail up to two months in advance.

Public Telephones: There are public telephones at the visitor centers.

Rest Rooms: Public rest rooms are available at the visitor centers and at all picnic areas in both sections. There is one accessible toilet at every rest room.

Accessibility: In the western section, the Red Hills visitor center and two nearby nature trails are wheelchair accessible. The 300-ft-long Cactus Garden Trail, which begins at the visitor center, acquaints you with the most common vegetation in this part of the park. A mile up the road is the Desert Discovery Trail, a more rewarding 0.5-mi paved route where you'll encounter plenty of wildlife. Shady areas with benches have been strategically placed along the path. The eastern district's visitor center is accessible, as is the Desert Ecology Trail, a paved 0.25-mi path through native vegetation. The western district visitor center is not accessible.

Emergencies: Park rangers, stationed at each visitor center, patrol the park in four-wheel-drive vehicles. To report an emergency, call 520/733–5158 or 520/733–5153. After hours, call 911.

Lost and Found: The eastern section's lost-and-found is at the **Saguaro East visitor center.** | 3693 Old Spanish Trail | 520/733–5153. Inquire about items lost on the western side at the **Red Hills visitor center.** | 2700 N. Kinney Rd. | 520/733–5158.

Good Tours

SAGUARO IN ONE DAY

Pack a lunch before setting off for either section of the park. Be sure to bring along plenty of water as well. Not only are you likely to get dehydrated in the hot, dry landscape, but you can't depend on finding water should you run out. In the western section, start out by watching the 15-minute slide show in the **Red Hills Visitor Center,** then stroll along the 0.5-mi-long **Desert Discovery Trail.** Head north along Kinney Road, then turn right onto the graded dirt **Bajada Loop Drive.** Before long you'll soon see a turnoff for the **Hugh Norris Trail** on your right. After hiking up for about 45 minutes, you'll reach a perfect spot for a picnic on the first ridge. Hike back down and drive along the Bajada Loop Drive until you reach the turnoff for **Signal Hill.** It's a short walk to the Hohokam petroglyphs. When you finish the Bajada Loop Drive you'll be back on Kinney Road.

If you're headed to the eastern section, pick up a free map of the hiking trails at the **Saguaro East Visitor Center** (it's easy to get lost, even in the most established part of the park). Drive south along the paved **Cactus Forest Drive** to the Javelina Picnic Area, where you'll see signs for the **Freeman Homestead Trail,** an easy 1-mi loop that winds through a stand of mesquite as interpretive signs describe homesteading and early inhabitants in the Tucson basin. If you're reasonably fit you might want to tackle part of the **Tanque**

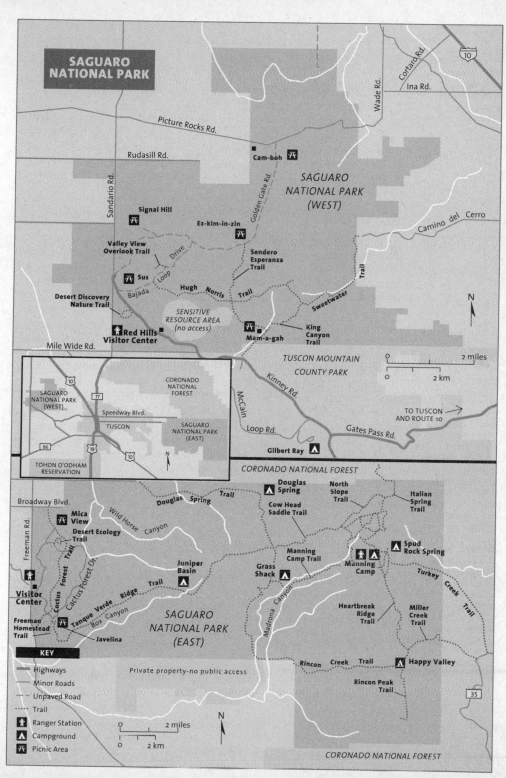

SAGUARO NATIONAL PARK

Picture Rocks Rd.

Rudasill Rd.

Wade Rd.

Cortaro Rd.

Ina Rd.

I-10

■ Cam-boh ⛺

SAGUARO NATIONAL PARK (WEST)

Golden Gate Rd.

Camino del Cerro

Sandario Rd.

Signal Hill ⛺

Ez-kim-in-zin ⛺

Valley View Overlook Trail

Sendero Esperanza Trail

Loop Drive

Sus ⛺

Bajada

Hugh Norris Trail

Sweetwater

Trail

Desert Discovery Nature Trail

SENSITIVE RESOURCE AREA (no access)

Mam-a-gah ⛺

King Canyon Trail

👤 Red Hills Visitor Center

Mile Wide Rd.

TUSCON MOUNTAIN COUNTY PARK

Kinney Rd.

0 ——— 2 miles
0 ——— 2 km

CORONADO NATIONAL FOREST

SAGUARO NATIONAL PARK (WEST)

I-10

US-77

Speedway Blvd.

TUSCON

SAGUARO NATIONAL PARK (EAST)

US-86

I-19

I-10

TOHON O'ODHAM RESERVATION

N

McCain

Loop Rd.

Gates Pass Rd.

TO TUSCON AND ROUTE 10 →

Gilbert Ray 🏕

CORONADO NATIONAL FOREST

Broadway Blvd.

Douglas Spring 🏕

Douglas Spring Trail

North Slope Trail

Italian Spring Trail

Wild Horse Canyon

Mica View ⛺

Desert Ecology Trail

Cow Head Saddle Trail

Spud Rock Spring 🏕

Cactus Forest Trail

Juniper Basin 🏕

Manning Camp Trail

Grass Shack 🏕

👤🏕 Manning Camp

Turkey Creek Trail

👤 Visitor Center

Tanque Verde Ridge Trail

Box Canyon

Heartbreak Ridge Trail

Miller Creek Trail

Freeman Homestead Trail

Javelina ⛺

SAGUARO NATIONAL PARK (EAST)

Madrona Canyon

KEY

Private property-no public access

Rincon Creek Trail

🏕 Happy Valley

Rincon Peak Trail

35

KEY
— Highways
— Minor Roads
- - - Unpaved Road
····· Trail
👤 Ranger Station
🏕 Campground
⛺ Picnic Area

Cactus Forest Dr.

Freeman Rd.

0 ——— 2 miles
0 ——— 2 km

N

CORONADO NATIONAL FOREST

SAGUARO NATIONAL PARK | 563

Verde Ridge Trail, which also begins near the Javelina Picnic Area. After about 1.5 mi you'll reach a ridge that affords excellent views of saguaro-studded hillsides. This is a good spot to stop for a picnic. There are plenty of easier trails across the lowlands. Along the northern loop of the Cactus Forest Drive you'll find **Cactus Forest Trail,** which branches off into several fairly level paths. Spend the rest of the afternoon strolling among the saguaro.

SAGUARO IN TWO OR THREE DAYS

If you have more time, follow either of the above itineraries on your first day in the park. Start your last day in the western section with a morning hike along the **King Canyon Trail.** Bring your binoculars, because you'll see many species of birds. Drive to the **Arizona-Sonora Desert Museum** for lunch. Spend the rest of the afternoon at the museum's zoo watching the animals of this region busy themselves in their ingeniously designed habitats.

Attractions

PROGRAMS AND TOURS

Orientation Programs. Both sections of the park have daily programs introducing various facets of the desert. You might find slide shows on topics such as bats, birds, or desert blooms. These presentations, as well as naturalist-led hikes and special events, change each month. No special orientation events other than films are offered in summer months. | Saguaro East visitor center | 520/733–5153 | Red Hills visitor center | 520/733–5158 | Free | Daily.

Junior Ranger Camp. Offered several times in June, this program for kids 6–11 includes daily hikes and workshops on pottery and petroglyphs. The program runs for three days in Saguaro East, two days in Saguaro West. Applications are accepted beginning mid-April on a first-come, first-served basis. In the Junior Ranger Discovery program, young visitors can pick up an activity pack and complete it within an hour or two. The self-guided programs are designed for ages 5 to 7 and 8 to 11. | Saguaro East visitor center | 520/733–5153 | Free | Daily | Red Hills visitor center | 520/733–5158 | $5–$10 | 7 AM–1 PM.

Ranger Talks. Rangers at both visitor centers talk on such topics as wildlife, geology, and archaeology. The west side also offers a monthly evening program to coincide with the full moon. Listen to stories on the patio of the visitor center as the moon illuminates the cacti. Space is limited to about 18 people, so reservations are recommended. | Saguaro East visitor center | 520/733–5153 | Red Hills visitor center | 520/733–5158 | Free | Nov.–mid-April.

Hike to Wasson Peak. A few nights before the full moon, a volunteer leads an afternoon hike on the Sendero Esperanza Trail to Wasson Peak. You'll reach the top just in time to enjoy a sunset picnic (bring your own) and then descend by the light of the moon. It's not an easy excursion, so don't be fooled by the fact that the leader is in his seventies. | Red Hills visitor center | 520/733–5158 | Free.

SCENIC DRIVES

Bajada Loop Drive. In the western section of the park, this 6-mi drive winds through thick stands of saguaros and other desert vegetation. Although the road is unpaved and moderately bumpy, it's a worthwhile trade-off for access to some of the park's densest desert growth. The road is one-way between Hugh Norris Trail and Golden Gate Road, so if you want to make the complete circuit you'll have to travel counter-clockwise.

Cactus Forest Drive. In the park's eastern section, this paved 8-mi drive provides a great overview of all Saguaro has to offer. The one-way road, which circles clockwise, also has several turnouts that make it easy to stop and linger over the scenery or find a spot for a picnic.

SIGHTS TO SEE

Manning Camp. The summer home of Levi Manning, onetime Tucson mayor, was once a popular gathering spot for the city's elite. After you reach the cabin via one of challenging high-country trails in Saguaro East you'll find it hard to imagine how they transported the family furnishings, including a piano, to this remote spot. Now used by park rangers as a working cabin, this historic site is not open to hikers. The Manning Camp campground, with six primitive campsites, sits nearby. | 12 mi from Saguaro East visitor center, on Douglas Spring Trail.

Saguaro East Visitor Center. You'll want to stop here to pick up free maps and printed materials on various aspects of the park, including maps of hiking trails and backcountry camping permits. A 15-minute slide program gives the history of the region. | 3693 S. Old Spanish Trail | 520/733–5153 | nps.gov/sagu | Daily 8:30–5.

Signal Hill. Although petroglyphs are scattered throughout both sections of the park, the most impressive ones, and the only ones with explanatory signs, are on the Bajada Loop Drive in Saguaro West. An easy 5-minute stroll from the parking area takes you to one of the largest gathering of rock carvings in the Southwest. You'll have a close-up view of the designs left by the Hohokam people between AD 900 and 1200, including large spirals some believe are astronomical markers. | 4.5 mi north of visitor center on Bajada Loop Dr.

Red Hills Visitor Center. A slide presentation (shown every half hour) offers a poetic perspective on the saguaro cactus, and a lifelike display simulates the flora and fauna of the region. Park rangers and volunteers provide maps and suggest hikes to suit your interests. | 2700 N. Kinney Rd. | 520/733–5158 | nps.gov/sagu | 8:30–5 daily.

Sports and Outdoor Activities

BICYCLING

The Cactus Forest Trail in the eastern section of the park, is the first national park trail opened specifically for mountain bikers. In the western section of the park, bicyclists are welcome on the roads, but not the hiking trails. On the two loop drives listed below, bicyclists are allowed only after the busiest hours and must be equipped with appropriate lights. Check the visitor centers for current regulations.

Bajada Loop Drive. This 6-mi dirt road, starting north of the Red Hills visitor center in Saguaro West, has "washboards" worn into the ground by seasonal drainage, which make biking a challenge. You'll share the bumpy route with cars, but most of it is one-way, and the views of saguaros set against the mountains are stunning. | Off Kinney Rd., 1.5-mi from the Red Hills visitor center.

Cactus Forest Drive. This paved 8-mi loop road with expansive vistas of saguaro-covered hills is also popular with hikers. Bicyclists are advised to go slowly during the first few hundred yards because of an unexpectedly sharp curve. Be aware that snakes, javelinas and other critters enjoy traversing the roads during cooler hours—so beware of collisions. | At Saguaro East visitor center.

Cactus Forest Trail. This 2.5-mi trail near Saguaro East visitor center is a sand single track with varied terrain. It's good for both beginning and experienced mountain bikers who don't mind sharing the path with hikers and the occasional horse. You'll see plenty of wildlife and older, larger saguaro alongside palo verde and mesquite trees. | 1 mi south of Saguaro East visitor center on Cactus Forest Dr.

BIRD-WATCHING

If you're looking for avian action within the park, focus your binoculars on the limbs of the saguaros, where many birds make their home. In general, early morning and early evening are the best times for sighting cactus wrens, hawks, quail, and many other species. Sign up for volunteer-led birding hikes in winter and spring at the visitor centers.

HIKING

To really experience the majesty of the saguaros you need to wander among these silent sentinels. Reaching them is possible even for those who cannot hike long distances. Adjacent to the visitor centers in both sections of the park are paths with signs identifying the plants you're likely to come across on longer treks. These paved paths are less than 0.25 mi each.

SAGUARO
NATIONAL PARK

EXPLORING
ATTRACTIONS NEARBY
DINING
LODGING
CAMPING AND RV
FACILITIES
SHOPPING
ESSENTIAL
INFORMATION

ROOM FOR RENT

The saguaro is like a high-rise apartment building. Many creatures can live in close quarters, and the tenants change frequently. Birds like the Gila woodpecker and gilded flicker make nest holes in the trunks and larger branches, then leave them empty for cactus wrens, screech owls, and other creatures. These homes are well-insulated, to boot.

FLOWER SHOW

Looking like clumps of tiny white party hats, saguaro blossoms appear in May and June. Each bloom opens a few hours after sunset and lasts only until the next afternoon. This spectacle repeats night after night for about four weeks until up to 100 blooms have appeared on each plant.

Desert Discovery Trail. Learn about plants and animals native to the region on this paved path in Saguaro West. The 0.5-mi loop is wheelchair accessible. | 1 mi north of the Red Hills visitor center.

Desert Ecology Trail. This 0.25-mi loop near the Mica View Picnic Area in Saguaro East has exhibits explaining how local plants and animals subsist on a limited supply of water. | 2 mi north of Saguaro East visitor center.

Douglas Spring Trail. This challenging 6-mi trail heads almost due east into the Rincon Mountains. After a half mile through a dense concentration of saguaros you reach the open desert. Farther along is Bridal Wreath Falls, worth a slight detour in early spring when melting snow creates a larger cascade. Blackened tree trunks at the Douglas Spring Campground are one of the few traces of a huge fire that swept through the area in 1989. | Eastern end of Speedway Blvd.

Freeman Homestead Trail. As its name suggests, this 1-mi loop in Saguaro East gives a bit of the history of homesteading in the region. Look for owls living in the cliffs above as you make your way through the lowland vegetation. You can also devise your own short hikes through the flatlands by consulting the trail maps available at the visitor center. | 2 mi south of Saguaro East visitor center at Javelina Picnic Area.

★ **Hugh Norris Trail.** Covering a distance of 10 mi, this trail in Saguaro West is one of the most impressive in the Southwest. Named after a former Tohono O'odham police chief, the trail leads through the Tucson Mountains, terminating at 4,687-ft Wasson Peak. It's full of switchbacks and some sections are moderately steep, but at the top you'll enjoy views of the saguaro forest spread across the *bajada* (the gently rolling hills at the base of taller mountains). | 2.5 mi north of Red Hills visitor center on Bajada Loop Drive.

King Canyon Trail. This 3.5-mi trail is the shortest, but steepest, route to the top of Wasson Peak. It meets the Hugh Norris Trail less than half a mile from the summit. The trail, which begins across from the Arizona-Sonora Desert Museum, is named after the Copper King Mine. It leads past many scars from the search for mineral wealth remain. Look for petroglyphs in this area. | 2 mi south of Red Hills visitor center.

Sendero Esperanza Trail. You'll follow a sandy mine road for the first section of this 6-mi trail in Saguaro West, then ascend via a series of switchbacks to the top of a ridge where you'll cross the Hugh Norris Trail. Descending on the other side, you'll meet up with the King Canyon Trail. The "Hope Trail" is often rocky and sometimes steep, but rewards include ruins of the Gould Mine, dating back to 1907. | 1.5 mi east of the intersection of Bajada Loop Dr. and Golden Gate Rd.

Signal Hill Trail. This 0.25-mi trail in Saguaro West is an easy, rewarding ascent to ancient petroglyphs carved a millennium ago by the Hohokam people. | 4.5 mi north of Red Hills visitor center on Bajada Loop Dr.

★ **Tanque Verde Ridge Trail.** Following its namesake, this 14-mi trail leads across Tanque Verde Ridge to Juniper Basin, one of Saguaro East's backcountry campgrounds. The hike brings you through desert scrub at the trailhead to oak, alligator juniper, and pinyon pine at the peak, where the elevation is about 6,000 ft. The views of the surrounding mountain ranges from both sides of the ridge are spectacular. | 2 mi south of Saguaro East visitor center at Javelina Picnic Area.

Valley View Overlook Trail. On clear days you can spot the distinctive slope of Picacho Peak from this 1.5-mi trail in Saguaro West. Even on an overcast day you'll be treated to splendid vistas of Avra Valley. | 3 mi north of Red Hills visitor center on Bajada Loop Dr.

HORSEBACK RIDING

Horses are permitted in both sections of the park, but are prohibited from straying from the marked trails. Most hiking trails, except for Tanque Verde Ridge Trail, are open to horses. Bring your own horse or take a ride with one of the local outfitters.

Outfitters

BICYCLING

Sabino Cycles. On the east side of Tucson, this shop offers a range of mountain and touring bikes. While the shop no longer rents cycles, you can still stock up on accessories. | 7131 E. Tanque Verde Rd. | 520/885–3666.

BIRD-WATCHING

Audubon Nature Shop. Run by the Tucson Audubon Society, this shop carries field guides, binoculars, and other items of interest to birders. It can provide a list of local independent guides who will take you out birding. The society also operates a 24-hour recorded message about sightings of rare or interesting birds. | 300 E. University Blvd., Tucson | 520/629–0510 shop, 520/798–1005 recording.

Borderlands. This organization conducts week-long birding tours about three times yearly in southeastern Arizona, with trips originating in Tucson. | 2550 W. Calle Padilla, Tucson | 520/882–7650.

Nature Conservancy. This local branch of the national organization can refer you to seasonal bird-watching trips in nature preserves. Trips range from a few hours to several days. | 1510 E. Fort Lowell Rd., Tucson | 520/622–3861.

Wild Bird Store. This shop is an excellent resource for bird-watching books, maps, and trail guides. | 3526 E. Grant Rd., Tucson | 520/322–9466.

Wings, Inc. This company leads 7–10 day ornithological expeditions in southeastern Arizona. | 1643 N. Alvernon Way, Suite 109, Tucson | 520/320–9868.

HIKING

Sierra Club. The local branch of this national organization sponsors weekend hikes around the area. | 738 N. 5th Ave., Suite 214, Tucson | 520/620–6401.

HORSEBACK RIDING

Pantano Riding Stables. This reliable operator offers guided one- and two-hour rides through saguaro-laden lowlands. | 4450 South Houghton Rd., Tucson | 520/298–8980.

Pusch Ridge Stables. In northwest Tucson, Pusch Ridge Stables offers hourly and longer horseback excursions into the foothills of the Santa Catalina Mountains. Breakfast, sunset, and children's rides are also available. | 13700 N. Oracle Rd., Tucson | 520/825–1664.

Attractions Nearby

★ **Arizona–Sonora Desert Museum.** The name "museum" is misleading; this delightful site is a beautifully planned zoo and botanical garden featuring the animals and plants of the Sonoran Desert. Hummingbirds, cactus wrens, rattlesnakes, scorpions, bighorn sheep, and prairie dogs all busy themselves in ingeniously designed habitats. The coyotes and javelinas have "invisible" fencing that separates them from humans, and the Riparian Corridor section affords great underwater views of otters and beavers. The gift shop carries an impressive selection of books about Arizona and the desert, plus jewelry and crafts. | 2021 N. Kinney Rd., Tucson | 520/883–2702 | www.desertmuseum.org | May–Oct., $9; Nov.–April, $12 | Mar.–Sept., daily 7:30–5; Oct.–Feb., daily 8:30–5. Last ticket sales 1 hr before closing | MC, V.

Catalina State Park. This 5,500-acre park 9 mi north of Tucson draws people for hiking, birding, camping, and picnicking. The park is crisscrossed with hiking trails; one of them, an easy two-hour walk, leads to the Romero Pools, a series of natural *tinajas*, or stone tanks, filled with water much of the year. | 11570 N. Oracle Rd. (Hwy. 77), Tucson | 520/628–5798 | www.azstateparks.com | $6 per vehicle | Daily 5 AM–10 PM.

SAGUARO
NATIONAL PARK

EXPLORING
**ATTRACTIONS
NEARBY**
DINING
LODGING
CAMPING AND RV
FACILITIES
SHOPPING
ESSENTIAL
INFORMATION

Room temperature or tepid water hydrates more efficiently than cold or icy water.

Colossal Cave Mountain Park. This limestone grotto 20 mi east of Tucson is the largest dry cavern in the world. Informed guides discuss the fascinating crystal formations and relate the many romantic tales surrounding the cave, including the legend that an enormous sum of money stolen in a stagecoach robbery is hidden here. Caves like this were once "mined" for bat guano, a natural adhesive used in women's eye make-up before synthetic substitutes were developed. Cave tours (sans guano) last 45 minutes and include 363 steps. Admission also buys you access to 2300 acres adjoining the park. Picnic benches give a panoramic view to the south and east. The park also includes a snack bar, gift shop, butterfly garden, bat garden, campground, and stables for horsebacking riding. | Intersection of Colossal Cave Rd. and Old Spanish Trail Rd. | 520/647–7275 or (for horseback riding stables) 520/647–3450 | colossalcave.com | $3 per car, $25 hourly rate for horseback riding | Mid-Sept.–mid-Mar., Mon.–Sat. 9–5, Sun. and holidays 9–6; mid-Mar.–mid-Sept., Mon.–Sat. 8–6, Sun. and holidays 8–7.

★ **Mission San Xavier del Bac.** The oldest Catholic church in the United States still serving the community for which it was built, San Xavier was founded in 1692 by Father Eusebio Francisco Kino, who established 22 missions in northern Mexico and southern Arizona. The current structure was constructed out of native materials by Franciscan missionaries between 1777 and 1797 and is owned by the Tohono O'odham tribe. The beauty of the mission is highlighted by the stark landscape against which it is set, inspiring an early 20th-century poet to dub it "White Dove of the Desert." Inside there's a wealth of painted statues, carvings, and frescoes. Paul Schwartzbaum, who helped restore Michelangelo's masterwork in Rome, helped supervise Tohono O'odham artisans in the restoration of the mission's artwork; he has called the mission the "Sistine Chapel of the United States." | San Xavier Rd., 9 mi southwest of Tucson on I–19 (Exit 92) | 520/294–2624 | Free | Daily 7–5; gift shop, daily 8–5.

STRANGE FRUIT

For centuries, indigenous peoples of the Sonoran Desert have harvested the fruit of the saguaro. In summer, when the cactus produces these fig-like fruits on the ends of its arms, the Tohono O'odham knock them off with long poles. The bounty is made into jam, syrup, and wine.

Sabino Canyon. Year-round, but especially in summer, locals flock to this oasis in the northeast corner of Tucson. Part of the Coronado National Forest, this is a good spot for hiking, picnicking, or enjoying the waterfalls, streams, swimming holes, and shade trees that provide a respite from the heat. No cars are allowed, but a narrated tram ride (about 45 minutes round-trip) takes you up a WPA-built road to the top of the canyon; you can hop off and on at any of the nine stops. There's also a tram ride to adjacent Bear Canyon, where you can take a much more rigorous hike to the popular Seven Falls (it'll take about 1.5 hours each way from the drop-off point, so carry plenty of water). | 5700 N. Sabino Canyon Rd. at Sunrise Dr., Tucson | 520/749–8700 | fs.fed.us/r3/coronado/scrd | Parking $5; tram $6 | Weekdays 8–4:30, weekends 8:30–4:30.

Tohono Chul Park. A 48-acre retreat designed to promote the conservation of arid regions, Tohono Chul—meaning "desert corner" in the language of the Tohono O'odham people—uses a demonstration garden, greenhouse, and geology wall to educate visitors about this unique desert area. Check out the "horizontal heliochronometer," an amazingly accurate sundial, in the garden. | 7366 N. Paseo del Norte, Tucson | 520/742–6455 | tohonochul-park.org | $5 | Daily 8–5.

Kartchner Caverns State Park. Hollow underground rooms connected by 2.75 mi of tunnel make up these spectacular caverns 9 mi south of Benson. Check out the visitor center and view the film charting the cave's discovery and subsequent preparation before taking the one-hour tour. | Rte. 90, Benson | 520/586–2283 or 520/586–4100 for reservations | pr.state.az.us | Parking $10; tours $14 | Daily 7:30–6; cave tours, daily 8:40–4:40.

Ramsey Canyon Preserve. Managed by the Nature Conservancy, this spectacular 300-acre site 6 mi south of Sierra Vista is superb for bird-watching, especially from April to October when 14 species of hummingbirds come to the area. Golden eagles have been spotted here, too. | 27 Ramsey Canyon Rd., Hereford | 520/378–2785 | www.tnc.org | $5 | Mar.–Oct., daily 8–4; Nov.–Feb., daily 9–5.

Dining

In Saguaro

Picnic Areas There are five picnic areas on the west side of the park, four of them accessible by car. In the eastern district there are two picnic areas. Each picnic area has a wheelchair-accessible pit toilet, but there's no drinking water at any of them. You'll find shade at each site, where at least some tables are under ramadas.

Cam-Boh. With its name coming from the Spanish word for "countryside," this picnic area is on the northern edge of Saguaro West, off busy Picture Rocks Road. More locals than tourists can be found at this spot with lovely views of the Tucson Mountain range. | Picture Rocks Rd. near Golden Gate Rd.

Ez-Kim-In-Zin. Named after an Apache chief, this picnic area in Saguaro West is set on a rocky hillside at the start of the Sendero Esperanza Trail, a fairly easy 1.5-mi hike to the crest of the Tucson Mountains. | 1 mi from Bajada Loop Dr. on Golden Gate Rd.

Javelina. You may not spot any javelinas, but there's a good chance some desert critters will come by begging for scraps at this popular picnic area. It's south of the Saguaro East visitor center. | 2 mi south of Saguaro East visitor center on Cactus Forest Dr.

Mam-A-Gah. Named for the deer dance of the Tohono O'odham people, this is the most isolated picnic area in Saguaro West. It's on King Canyon Trail, a good area for birding and wildflower viewing. It's about a mile walk just to reach the site, and the undeveloped trail is not wheelchair accessible. | King Canyon Trail, 1 mi from Kinney Rd.

Mica View. Talk about truth in advertising: this Saguaro East picnic area gives you an eyeful of Mica Mountain, the park's highest peak. Note that none of the tables are in the shade. | 2 mi north of Saguaro East visitor center on Cactus Forest Dr.

Signal Hill. Because of the nearby petroglyphs, Signal Hill is the most popular picnic site in Saguaro West. Its many picnic tables sprinkled around palo verde and mesquite trees and under ramadas can accommodate large groups. | 4.5 mi north of Red Hills visitor center on Bajada Loop Dr.

Sus. With a name that is short for Jésus, this Saguaro West picnic area sits at the start of the Bajada Loop drive, halfway between the Desert Discovery Nature Trail and the Valley View Overlook Trail. You'll find about 10 picnic tables, mostly shaded, at this convenient spot. | 2 mi north of Red Hills visitor center on Bajada Loop Rd.

Near the Park

★ **Arizona Inn Restaurant.** Contemporary. Chef Odell Baskerville presides over one of Tucson's most elegant eateries. Dine on the patio overlooking the grounds of this historic inn or enjoy the view from the light, airy dining room. The fire that warms the room on chilly evenings sets the stage for the slow-roasted confit of duck. Try seared Chilean sea bass with applewood-smoked bacon and crab risotto or a vegetable tart layered with herbed mozzarella and served with saffron rice. Locals come in for Sunday brunch or a civilized afternoon high tea in the library (late November–mid-April only). | 2200 E. Elm St., Tucson | 520/325–1541 | $21–$34 | AE, DC, MC, V.

....

Barrio. Contemporary. Good food and a lively atmosphere add definite zing to late-night Tucson. Try a "little plate" of crab cakes or entrées ranging from simple but delicious fish tacos to linguine with chicken, dried papaya, and mango in a chipotle chardonnay cream sauce. Save room for an elegant dessert of fresh berries in a tall glass drenched in crème anglaise. | 135 S. 6th Ave., Tucson | 520/629–0191 | No lunch Sun. | $13–$26 | AE, D, DC, MC, V.

....

Beyond Bread. Café. This bakery hasn't seen a quiet moment since it opened. Fran's Fromage (Brie, lettuce, and tomato on a baguette) or Brad's Beef (roast beef, provolone, onion, green chilies, and Russian dressing on white bread) are wonderfully satisfying meals. Eat inside or on the patio, or order take-out and munch on free bread and butter while you wait. | 3026 N. Campbell Ave., Tucson | 520/322–9965 | $3–$9 | AE, D, MC, V.

Café Poca Cosa. Mexican. Inspired by different regions of her native Mexico, Susana Davila works magic at what is arguably Tucson's most innovative Mexican restaurant. The menu, which changes daily, might include *pollo à mole* (chicken in a spicy chocolate-based sauce) or pork *pibil* (made with a tangy Yucatan barbecue seasoning). Servings are plentiful, and each table gets a stack of warm corn tortillas and bowls of beans, rice and salad to share. | 88 E. Broadway, Tucson | 520/622–6400 | Closed Sun. | $13–$18 | MC, DC, V.

Janos. Southwestern. Chef Janos Wilder was one of the first to reinvent Southwestern cuisine, and his restaurant continues to be among the finest in the West. City lights provide a sparkling backdrop as you enjoy appetizers such as the Brie and exotic mushroom *relleno* (stuffed chile pepper) and the roasted quail stuffed with chihuacle chile spoonbread on prickly pear compote. Main courses include leek-wrapped salmon stuffed with habanero pepito pesto and a pan-seared venison chop with wild mushroom and chorizo casserole and smoked tomato salsa. | 3770 E. Sunrise Dr., Tucson | 520/615–6100 | Closed Sun. No lunch | $22–$37 | AE, DC, MC, V.

★ **Le Bistro.** French. An Impressionist-style mural beckons you into one of the most elegant restaurants in town. Potted palms tower over tables covered with chic gold-and-beige striped cloths, and art nouveau-etched mirrors grace the walls. The setting is matched by the creations of Laurent Reux, a young chef whose fish and shellfish dishes are inspired by his native Brittany. Specialties include escargot cooked in garlic butter under a dome of puff pastry, chicken roulade filled with a duxelle of mushroom and artichoke hearts, and roasted quail flambéed with cognac. | 2574 N. Campbell Ave., Tucson | 520/327–3086 | www.lebistrotucson.com | No lunch weekends | $12–$23 | AE, D, MC, V.

★ **Nonie.** Cajun/Creole. Named for the owner's grandmother, this restaurant has the flamboyant style of a New Orleans bistro and the good food to match. Add sincerely friendly, fast service, a crowd of local folks, and a hopping dose of Cajun music, and you get one of the city's standouts. The delicate trout meuniére is about as staid as this place gets; the crawfish étoufée packs a punch. | 2526 E. Grant Rd., Tucson | 520/319–1965 | Closed Mon. No lunch Sat. or Sun. | $8–$20 | AE, D, MC, V.

Tony's. Delicatessens. If you're heading to Saguaro East, stop at this New York–style Italian deli to pick up some supplies—a prosciutto and provolone hero, say, accompanied by imported olives and potato salad. And if you need some comfort food after a hard day of hiking, come by for lasagna on the way back. | 6219 E. 22nd St., Tucson | 520/747–0070 | Closed Sun. | $5–$11 | AE, D, MC, V.

Ventana Room. Contemporary. This dining room in the Loews Ventana Canyon Resort is a triumph of understated elegance: muted colors, low ceilings, a see-through fireplace, and spectacular views of the lights of Tucson. The contemporary menu, which changes seasonally, has entrées such as mixed grill of game (venison, quail, and buffalo) with black barley and huckleberries and potato-wrapped striped sea bass with spinach, tomato timbale, and sweet basil beurre blanc. Can't decide? Try the four-course tasting menu. | 7000 N. Resort Dr., Tucson | 520/299–2020 | No lunch | $29–$50 | AE, D, DC, MC, V.

Vivace. Italian. Decorated in warm gold and rust tones, Vivace calls to mind a villa in the Italian countryside. The patio, overlooking the lush gardens of St. Phillip's Plaza, is even more appealing. Savor the seafood lasagnette, or try the handmade pasta with seafood and spinach filling and fresh tomato basil broth. | 4310 N. Campbell Ave., Tucson | 520/795–7221 | No lunch Sun. | $14–$21 | AE, D, MC, V.

★ **Wildflower Grill.** Contemporary. This bright restaurant is well known for its stunningly presented American fare. Warm Maine lobster salad (fresh seafood is flown in daily) with artichoke hearts and asparagus is a healthy starter, and the grilled New York strip steak cries for an accompaniment from the popular martini menu. Pan-roasted rack of lamb with a Dijon crust or meatloaf with a port wine reduction won't disappoint, either. Saturday brunch on the brick patio is a treat in any season. | 7037 N. Oracle Rd., Tucson | 520/219–4230 | $12–$24 | AE, D, DC, MC, V.

Zemam. Ethiopian. It can be hard to get a table in this popular Ethiopian eatery. The sampler plate of any three items allows you to try such dishes as *yesimir wat* (a spicy lentil-based dish) and *lega tibs* (a milder beef dish with a tomato sauce). Everything is served on a communal platter topped with *injera*, a spongy bread, and eaten with the hands. Prices are ridiculously low, considering the food quality and quantity. | 2731 E. Broadway, Tucson | 520/323–9928 | Closed Mon. | $6–$9 | MC, V.

Lodging

Near the Park

★ **Arizona Inn.** On the National Register of Historic Places, this 14-acre resort sits amid beautifully landscaped lawns and gardens that make it seem far away from it all. The individually decorated rooms are spread out in pink adobe-style casitas. Most have private patios and some have fireplaces. Two luxurious double-story private houses, each with five bedrooms and five baths, have walled gardens and heated pools. The main building houses an elegant library where complimentary high tea is sometimes served. 2 restaurants. In-room data ports. 2 tennis courts. Pool, exercise equipment, sauna. Bar, library. Laundry service, business services. | 2200 E. Elm St., Tucson | 520/325–1541 | fax 520/881–5830 | www.arizonainn.com | 70 rooms, 16 suites, 3 houses | $225 | AE, DC, MC, V.

Best Western Ghost Ranch Lodge. The bleached-out cow skulls popularized by Georgia O'Keeffe are now a Southwest cliché, but not back in 1940 when they made the neon sign that still lights up the entrance to this hotel. The Spanish tile-roof buildings are spread out over 8 acres that encompass an orange grove and cacti garden. Rooms are decorated with modern motel furnishings, but retain original brick walls and sloped wood-beam ceilings. The cottages, with a separate kitchen, sitting area, and carport, are a bargain. Restaurant. Pool, hot tub. Bar. | 72 rooms, 11 cottages | 801 W. Miracle Mile, Tucson | 520/791–7565 | fax 520/791–3898 | www.ghostranchlodge.com | $98 | AE, D, DC, MC, V.

★ **Canyon Ranch.** Drawing an international crowd of well-to-do health seekers, this superb spa is set on 70 acres in the desert foothills northeast of Tucson. There's a Health and Healing Center where dietitians, exercise physiologists, behavioral-health professionals, and medical staff attend to body and soul. Every type of physical activity is possible from yoga to guided hiking, and the food is plentiful and healthy. There's a minimum stay of four nights, and the rate includes all meals, classes, lectures, and sales tax. Dining room. 8 tennis courts. Pool, health club, beauty salon, spa, steam room. | 8600 E. Rockcliff Rd., Tucson | 520/749–9000 or 800/742–9000 | fax 520/749–1646 | www.canyonranch.com | 240 rooms | $195–$425 | AE, D, MC, V.

Casa Allegre. You'll enjoy poking around the knickknacks and antiques—everything from a hand-hewn Mexican mine shovel to an ornate 19th-century French clock—in Phyllis Florek's 1915 arts and crafts–style bungalow. The location can't be beat, as it's a straight shot west from here to the Arizona-Sonora Desert Museum and Saguaro National Park. Resting in the shade of the ramadas or taking a plunge into the pool is an ideal end to a day of sightseeing. Pool, hot tub. | 316 E. Speedway Blvd., Tucson | 520/628–1800 or 800/628–5654 | fax 520/792–1880 | www.CasaAllegreInn.com | 7 rooms | $105–$135 | D, MC, V.

Casa Tierra. Rooms in this lovely hacienda-style lodging, five minutes from the Saguaro National Park, all have private terraces. They're attractively outfitted with Mexican *equipale* chairs, cool tiled floors, and viga-beam ceilings. A central courtyard looks out onto dense desert foliage. Kitchenettes. Hot tub. | 11155 W. Calle Pima, Tucson | 520/578–3058 | casatierratucson.com | 3 rooms | $165–$195 | Closed June–mid-Sept. | No credit cards.

★ **Hacienda del Sol Guest Ranch Resort.** This 32-acre facility in the Santa Catalina foothills is part guest ranch, part resort, and entirely gracious. This former finishing school for girls attracted stars—among them Clark Gable, Katharine Hepburn, and Spencer Tracy—when it was converted to a guest ranch during World War II. Some of the one- and two-bedroom

SAGUARO
NATIONAL PARK

EXPLORING
ATTRACTIONS NEARBY
DINING
LODGING
CAMPING AND RV
FACILITIES
SHOPPING
ESSENTIAL
INFORMATION

casitas have fireplaces and private porches overlooking the Tucson Mountains. Relaxing activitiesinclude yoga, massage, and naturalist-led walks, and there's a well-stocked library with board games. Restaurant. Tennis court. Pool, Hot tub. Horseback riding. Library. | 5601 N. Hacienda del Sol Rd., Tucson | 520/299–1501 | fax 520/299–5554 | www.haciendadelsol.com | 22 rooms, 8 suites | $135–$340 | AE, D, MC, V.

Lazy K Bar Guest Ranch. At this family-oriented guest ranch in the Tucson Mountains, riders are entertained with tales of the Old West as they trot through desert landscapes bordering Saguaro West. The older stucco casitas have fireplaces and wood-beam ceilings. All of the rooms have western-themed furnishings like pigskin leather tables, brass cowboy lamps, and boot pulls. Pool. Hot tub. Horseback riding. Library. | 8401 N. Scenic Dr., Tucson | 520/744–3050 | fax 520/744–7628 | www.lazykbar.com | 24 rooms | $340 | AE, D, MC, V.

Loews Ventana Canyon Resort. One of the most luxurious of the big resorts, this desert delight with dramatic stone architecture echoes its setting. Rooms are modern and chic, furnished in muted earth tones and light woods. The center of this spectacular 93-acre property is an 80-ft waterfall that cascades down the Santa Catalina Mountains into a little lake. The Ventana Canyon hiking trail is nearby, and there's a free shuttle to nearby Sabino Canyon. 4 restaurants. Golf course, 8 tennis courts. 2 pools, exercise equipment, beauty salon, spa. Bicycles, hiking. Bar. Shops. Children's programs. Business services. | 7000 N. Resort Dr. | 520/299–2020 | fax 520/299–6832 | www.loewshotels.com | 384 rooms, 14 suites | $209–$359 | AE, D, DC, MC, V.

Rimrock West. About 7 mi north of Saguaro National Park, this B&B on 20 acres has a panoramic view of Tucson. The artwork in the adobe ranch house is all by the innkeepers and their son; their studio is on the property. Attractive rooms open onto a sunny brick courtyard; a kidney-shape pool occupies its own walled enclosure. Pool. | 3450 N. Drake Pl, Tucson | 520/749–8774 | 2 rooms, 1 cottage | $120 | No credit cards.

Hilton Tucson El Conquistador Golf & Tennis Resort. You'll know you're in the Southwest when you enter the lobby and see the huge copper mural filled with cowboys and cacti. Rooms, in private casitas or the main building, have stylish light-wood furniture with tinwork and pastel-tone spreads and curtains. Catch the colorful sunset and see if you can spot the hooting owls that inhabit the palm trees around the pool area. New to the resort are interactive fountains and fish-shaped swimming areas for children. 4 restaurants. Golf course, 31 tennis courts. 4 pools, exercise equipment, sauna. Bicycles, basketball, horseback riding, racquetball, volleyball. Bar. Business services. | 10000 N. Oracle Rd., Tucson | 520/544–5000 | fax 520/544–1224 | www.sheratonelconquistador.com | 428 rooms, 57 suites, 43 1-bedroom casitas | $244–$344 | AE, D, DC, MC, V.

★ **Tanque Verde Ranch.** The most upscale of Tucson's guest ranches, Tanque Verde rests on 640 acres in the Rincon Mountains between Coronado National Forest and Saguaro National Park. Privacy and solitude are found in tastefully furnished rooms in about 18 different buildings interspersed through the hillsides. Private casitas have patios, and some have fireplaces. The lodging price covers three meals daily, and all ranch activities—all considered, quite a bargain. 5 tennis courts. Indoor pool, outdoor pool, exercise equipment. Fishing, basketball, horseback riding, volleyball. | 14301 E. Speedway Blvd., Tucson | 520/296–6275 | fax 520/721–9426 | www.tanqueverderanch.com | 51, 23 suites, 2 houses | $350 | AE, D, MC, V.

Westin La Paloma. This dusty pink (they call it La Paloma rose) resort offers views of the Santa Catalina Mountains above and the city below. It specializes in relaxation: its golf, fitness, and beauty centers are top-notch, and its huge pool complex has Arizona's longest water slide. There's a swim-up bar and grill if you can't bear to leave the water. 4 restaurants. Golf course, 12 tennis courts. 3 pools, exercise equipment, beauty salon, 3 hot tubs, spa. Racquetball, volleyball. 2 bars. Shops. Business services. | 3800 E. Sunrise Dr., Tucson | 520/742–6000 | fax 520/577–5878 | www.westin.com | 455 rooms, 32 suites | $229–$429 | AE, D, DC, MC, V.

★ **White Stallion Ranch.** A number of scenes from *High Chaparral* were shot on this family-run ranch that sits on 3,000 acres abutting Saguaro West. Horseback rides, cattle penning, weekend rodeos, and hikes along mountain trails are among the activities here. Children enjoy the petting zoo. 2 tennis courts. Pool, hot tub. Basketball, horseback riding, volleyball. Library. Business services. | 9251 W. Twin Peaks Rd., Tucson | 520/297–0252 | fax 520/744–2786 | www.wsranch.com | 41 rooms | $245 | Closed June–Aug. | No credit cards.

Camping and RV Facilities

In Saguaro

There's no drive-up camping in the park, and backcountry camping is permitted only in Saguaro East's six designated, primitive campgrounds. All are open year-round. Pick up your free backcountry permit at the visitor center. While you're there, check out the relief map of hiking trails and the book of wilderness campground photos taken by park rangers before choosing a camping destination. You can camp in the backcountry for a maximum of 14 days. Each site can accommodate up to six people. Hikers are encouraged to set out before noon.

Douglas Spring. A fairly easy 6-mi hike on the Douglas Spring Trail brings you to the closest campground to the visitor center, where you'll encounter mostly shrubs and open terrain at an elevation of 4,800 ft. | 3 sites | 14 mi from Cactus Forest Dr. on Douglas Springs Trail | No phone | Free.

Grass Shack. This pretty campground is among juniper and small oak trees in a transitional area midway up Mica Mountain. | 3 sites | 14 mi from Cactus Forest Dr. on Manning Camp Trail | No phone | Free.

Happy Valley. Similar to Grass Shack in terrain, this campground in the southeastern corner of Saguaro East is the park's most isolated. | 3 sites | 22 mi from Cactus Forest Dr. on Rincon Creek Trail | No phone | Free.

Juniper Basin. Close to the Saguaro East visitor center, this 7-mi trail leads up the narrow and rocky Tanque Verde Ridge Trail to an elevation of 6,000 ft. Vegetation here is oaken woodland, making the expansive views worth the challenging ascent. | 3 sites | 7 mi from Cactus Forest Dr. on Tanque Verde Ridge Trail | No phone | Free.

Manning Camp. Of the park's campgrounds, only Manning Camp has water year-round, and it has to be treated. This 12-mi hike up the Douglas Spring Trail takes you through five biotic communities as you climb from desert scrub through grassland, oak and pine-oak woodland to a ponderosa pine forest at the top of Mica Mountain. | 6 sites | 15 mi from Cactus Forest Dr. on Manning Camp Trail | No phone | Free.

Spud Rock Spring. Set in the same higher elevation pine forest as Manning Camp, this campground offers a spring with intermittent water, which also must be treated. | 3 sites | 17 mi from Cactus Forest Dr. on Turkey Creek Trail | No phone | Free.

Near the Park

Catalina State Park. Although this is the closest public campground to the city of Tucson, it's about a 40-minute drive north from Saguaro West, in the scenic foothills of the Santa Catalinas. The cash-only facility operates on a first-come, first-served basis. Flush toilets. Full round-trips, dump station. Drinking water, showers. Grills, picnic tables. Electricity, public telephone. Ranger station. | 123 sites, 99 with round-trips | 11570 N. Oracle Rd., Tucson | 520/628–5798 | fax 520/628–5797 | pr.state.az.us | $6 (day use), $12 (camping), $19 (camping with round-trip) | Reservations not accepted | No credit cards.

Colossal Cave Campground. The closest nonwilderness camping to Saguaro East, this campground still *feels* like the wilderness. It has no electrical hookups, and the entrance

SAGUARO
NATIONAL PARK

EXPLORING
ATTRACTIONS NEARBY
DINING
LODGING
**CAMPING AND RV
FACILITIES**
SHOPPING
ESSENTIAL
INFORMATION

SAGUARO CAMPGROUNDS

	Total # of sites	# of RV sites	# of hook-ups	Drive-to sites	Hike-to sites	Flush toilets	Pit toilets	Drinking water	Showers	Fire grates/pits	Swimming	Boat access	Playground	Dump station	Ranger station	Public telephone	Reservation possible	Daily fee per site	Dates open
INSIDE THE PARK																			
Douglas Springs	3	0	0		•													Free	Y/R
Grass Shack	3	0	0		•													Free	Y/R
Happy Valley	3	0	0		•													Free	Y/R
Juniper Basin	3	0	0		•													Free	Y/R
Manning Camp	6	0	0		•													Free	Y/R
Spud Rock Spring	3	0	0		•													Free	Y/R
NEAR THE PARK																			
Catalina State Park	49	49	23	•			•	•	•					•	•	•		$12–19	Y/R
Colossal Cave Campground	50	0	0	•			•	•		•						•	•	$3	Y/R
Gilbert Ray Campground	130	121	121	•			•		•								•	$7–12	Y/R

* In summer only ** Reservation fee charged Y/R=Year-round
UL=Unlimited ULP=Unlimited primitive LD=Labor Day MD=Memorial Day

gates close for the night at 6 PM, but the price is right. Pit toilets. Drinking water. Fire grates, picnic tables. Public telephone. | 50 sites | Old Spanish Trail, Tucson | 520/647–7275 | fax 520/647–3299 | www.colossalcave.com | $3 parking fee.

Gilbert Ray Campground. Slumber amid saguaros at this pleasant spot 4 mi south of the park's west district and just down the road from the Arizona-Sonora Desert Museum. Flush toilets. Full round-trips. Drinking water. Grills, picnic tables. Electricity. | 130 sites | W. Kinney Rd., Tucson | 520/883–4200 | $7, $12 with round-trip.

Shopping

The visitor centers in both districts sell books, gifts, film, and single-use cameras, as well as a few necessities such as sunscreen, bug repellent, and water bottles. For other items, you'll have to drive a few miles back towards town.

Summit Hut. This is an excellent place in Tucson to pick up any hiking or camping supplies you may have forgotten. It also carries snakebite kits. | 5045 E. Speedway Blvd., Tucson | 520/325–1554 | www.summithut.com.

Essential Information

ATMS (24-HOUR): Circle K | Ajo Rd. and Kinney Rd. 5 mi south of Saguaro West, (A second Circle K with ATM is nearby at 605 E. Wetmore, 520/888–1000) Tucson | 520/883–4515. **Qwikmart** | Golf Links Rd. and Harrison Rd., 3 mi northwest of Saguaro East, Tucson | 520/298–9120. **Qwikmart** | Sandario Rd. and Picture Rocks Rd., 5 mi north of Saguaro West, Avra Valley | 520/682–7798.

AUTOMOBILE SERVICE STATIONS: Qwikmart | Golf Links Rd. and Harrison Rd., 3 mi northwest of Saguaro East, Tucson | 520/298–9120. **Qwikmart** | Sandario Rd. and Picture Rocks Rd., 5 mi north of Saguaro West, Avra Valley | 520/682–7798.

POST OFFICES: Tucson Main Post Office | 1501 Cherrybell St., 85726 | 800/275–8777 | Weekdays 8:30–8, Sat. 9–1.

SAGUARO
NATIONAL PARK

EXPLORING
ATTRACTIONS NEARBY
DINING
LODGING
CAMPING AND RV
FACILITIES
SHOPPING
**ESSENTIAL
INFORMATION**

FIELD GUIDE: DESERT SOUTHWEST

Ecological Communities

Caves. Few creatures other than bats can survive absent sunlight deep within these dark, damp subterranean worlds. Small, swooping birds known as cave swallows sometimes inhabit entryways and there are a few cave crickets and some algae, but life in general is sparse in the caves of the Southwest. The most famous cave in the region is Carlsbad Caverns, formed inside the Guadalupe Mountains when acidic surface water leaked below ground and slowly dissolved the limestone beneath. In summer, Mexican free-tail bats inhabit the caverns and fly out at night to feed on insects.

Floodplains. In the desert you may come upon mosaics of green grassland and stands of massive, old-growth trees such as cottonwoods beyond the banks of the rare stream or river. These ecological communities depend on occasional heavy rains that cause flooding when water spills into flatlands and basins. Wildlife such as doves, quail, rodents, and kit foxes congregate in the brushy cover.

High Desert. Water is scant in the higher elevations and rugged mountain regions of the desert Southwest, but life is surprisingly diverse. White-tailed or mule deer are common in some areas. Brushy forests dotted with pinyon pines and junipers form isolated habitats that are often called sky islands. Their cooler, moister environment harbors bird species such as the Mexican bluejay.

Hot Desert. The Southwest region is primarily a "hot" desert, with average annual rainfall of less than 10 inches and a landscape of sandy or hard, rocky ground. Here you will not find the frigid weather or snow and ice of "cold" deserts. Wildlife and vegetation in hot deserts have evolved to get the most out of the sparse moisture. Succulents store water reserves to survive extended droughts. The kangaroo rat and other animals metabolize water strictly from carbohydrates in food. Some dormant wildflower seeds spring to life only when it rains.

Fauna

ARACHNIDS

Tarantula. This huge dark-brown or black spider can grow as large as seven inches across and the female can live as long as 30 years. The tarantula does bite, but its venom is considered mild and it usually displays a gentle nature around humans. Some people keep tarantulas as pets. In fact, the spider is great to have around the house because it munches on crickets and cockroaches. But don't plan on taking one home with you: tarantulas are protected within park boundaries.

Vinegarroon. While this giant whip scorpion looks intimidating, the worst it does when threatened is to spray a mist of vinegary acid in warning. The dark arachnid can grow up to three inches long and wields a pair of formidable-looking pinchers.

BIRDS

Hawk. Over a dozen species of this soaring bird live in the Southwest, but don't confuse them with Turkey buzzards. The hawk usually flies alone in slow, lazy circles as it searches for an unwary rabbit or rodent below.

Quail. Several species of quail thrive in the desert Southwest, the plumed Gambel's being the most common. The birds flock in coveys as large as several hundred, and are distinguished by short bursts of low-ranging flight.

Roadrunner. New Mexico's state bird fearlessly attacks all manner of snakes and lizards. It then swallows them whole, lending some credence to the theory that birds might be descended from fierce, carnivorous dinosaurs. But this bird tends to be friendly toward humans and is known to hang out in yards and at park headquarters. As its name implies, the swift bird prefers running over walking. The birds can fly, but usually only under duress and for very short distances.

MAMMALS

Bat. About 30 different bat species live in the Southwest U.S.; probably the best-known is the Mexican-freetail bat that inhabits Carlsbad Caverns, among other places. The Mexican free-tail population has dropped drastically in recent decades, from several million to a few hundred thousand. Among the culprits is DDT contamination, which may occur south of the border during migrations or in the U.S., from residues of the now-banned substance in agricultural fields.

Carmen Mountains White-Tailed Deer. This delicate, small, and unique white-tailed deer inhabits the Chisos Mountains area of Big Bend. The species was stranded there when drought turned the land around the mountains into desert following the last Ice Age about 20,000 years ago.

Coati. This exotic, raccoon-like animal found in southern Arizona and New Mexico is distinguished by a prehensile tail. It can resemble a monkey when it wraps its tail around a tree branch for balance. The sociable creature lives in extended family units of up to several dozen. Indigenous to South American woodlands, where they are still common, coatis first migrated to the U.S. in the late 1800s, probably because increased white settlement north of the border meant better food supplies and fewer predators.

Coyote. You might glimpse a flash of grey fur and a long snout as this highly adaptable predator forages for rabbits and other food alongside roadways. The coyote is common throughout the American West and is even beginning to move into urban areas.

Jackrabbit. The jackrabbit is unmistakable for its mulelike ears and swift, bounding gait. It's extremely common in the Southwest and can induce a brief case of heart failure if you happen upon one and startle it into an explosive escape.

Javelina. Pronounced "have-ah-LEEN-ah," this collared peccary is known by locals as the javelina hog because of its pug nose and piglike appearance. In the U.S., the javelina roams southwest Texas, New Mexico, and Arizona. Prickly pear cacti are a favorite food, providing both water and nutrients.

Mountain Lion. Although relatively common in the Southwest, this shy, large cat seldom crosses the path of the casual observer. However, mountain lions overcome with curiosity have been known to follow hikers in secret. The tawny predator rarely attacks humans: its usual meal is deer, rodents, reptiles, or insects.

REPTILES

Desert Tortoise. Living as long as 70 years, this slow-moving creature generally inhabits the Sonoran and Mojave deserts of Arizona and California. It eats plants, getting most of its water from food. It is so efficient at conserving moisture that it actually urinates crystals rather than liquid.

Gila Monster. This lizard can be huge—up to 2 ft long—and can appear fearsome with its swollen head and tail. If provoked, the gila (pronounced "HEE-la") monster responds with a venomous bite that can be extremely painful though rarely fatal to humans. Its skin is beaded with colorful patterns. The lizard is found only in the Southwest and northern Mexico.

Rattlesnake. About a dozen species of rattlesnake live in the desert, where in cooler weather they enjoy sunning on rocks or coiling in other open spaces. When it's hotter, the reptile can be camouflaged by shade. It's fairly common to encounter a rattlesnake on a hot, summer day in more remote areas. It will strike only when it feels threatened, but it can deliver a serious bite. Fortunately, it often warns away possible intruders with rattles on the end of its tail that sound like dry, rustling leaves.

Flora

SHRUBS

Creosote. This rather drab-looking evergreen shrub with scant leaves is widespread throughout the Southwest. Its pleasant, woody aroma perfumes the desert after a rare rainstorm. The bush also is known by locals as greasewood because of its oily resins.

Among the oldest known living plants, this durable shrub dates back as far as 10,000 years. To reproduce, creosote clones itself, creating exact genetic copies.

Joshua Tree. The namesake of Joshua Tree National Park is not a tree at all: it belongs to the lily family. Small fibers form what appears to be its trunk, which sprouts into branches tipped with spiked tufts (its nickname is dagger tree). Common in certain desert regions of Arizona, California, Nevada, and Utah the Joshua tree can grow as tall as 35 ft and live as long as 1,000 years. Mormon settlers named it for the Bible character Joshua, possibly because of configurations that resemble outstretched arms reaching to the heavens.

Ocotillo. In spring tubular, red blossoms adorn the slim branches of this plant that grows throughout the Sonoran, Mojave, and Chihuahuan deserts. Its latticed wood stems often served as decorative building material for the fences and housing of local pioneers.

Yucca. Showy, yellow blossoms appear along the vertical stalks of this spike-leafed plant in spring. Common in the hills and on the plains of the desert Southwest, the yucca is pollinated by a small, specialized species of yucca moth. Like the Joshua tree, the yucca is a member of the lily family.

SUCCULENTS

Agave. The spiked, fleshy leaves of this plant surround tall stalks that, like those of the yucca, are sometimes covered with ornamental blossoms. A single plant may live several dozen years, but dies after producing a flower stalk. Also called mescal, the agave once was gathered by Native Americans as a food source, and it's still roasted in northern Mexico to produce alcohol.

Lechuguilla. Abundant in the Chihuahuan desert of southwest Texas, southern New Mexico, and northern Mexico, this type of agave plant has especially sharp, succulent dagger leaves that can slice deep gashes in a horse's legs. Like other agaves, the lechuguilla produces a tall stalk that blooms with flowers only once in the plant's lifetime. The plant is a food source for the javelina.

Prickly Pear Cactus. Dozens of species of prickly pear cactus plants assume distinctive forms, the most common of which produce fleshy green pads shaped like elephant ears covered with sharp spines. Local names for the plant can be colorful, ranging from "beavertails" to "Grizzly bears." The cactus produces red or purple fruits sweet enough when de-thorned to be used in jams. Like other types of cactus, the prickly pear has a waxy coating that helps prevent evaporation of precious moisture.

Saguaro Cactus. So distinctive is the strangely configured saguaro of the Sonoran Desert that it serves as a symbol of the entire desert Southwest. Found only in southern Arizona, southeasternmost California, and northern Mexico, it has an evolutionary history as unusual as its towering height and plump, thorny arms. Some scientists postulate that the saguaro was originally a tropical tree that adapted to drought conditions and began to assume its current form up to 10 million years ago. The slow-growing cactus lives as long as 300 years and can reach a weight of 10 tons. Some of the plants tower as high as 50 ft. Tucson area residents sometimes give affectionate nicknames to individual saguaros.

TREES

Texas Madrone. This evergreen with red bark is found in the northern Chihuahuan Desert, which encompasses Big Bend, Guadalupe Mountains, and Carlsbad Caverns national parks.

Geology and Terrain

Desert Pavement. High winds can scour away soil and small pebbles to leave behind bare rock, the desert pavement found in areas such as the plains of Big Bend National Park.

Fault Zones. Shifting underground land masses such as those of California's famous San Andreas Fault have helped create many of Joshua Tree National Park's upper elevations, including the Pinto Mountains on the northern border and the Little San Bernardino Mountains on the southwest side. This same geologic upheaval has shifted and cracked underground rocks, damming up the flow of groundwater and forcing it to the surface, making precious moisture available to wildlife and plants.

Fossil Reef. Much of the desert region of Texas and New Mexico shares a common geologic past, when a warm, shallow inland sea covered a large area. As the sea evaporated, a 400-mi-long limestone reef was deposited, made up of sediment, dead plants, and the skeletons of tiny sea creatures. Movement in the Earth's surface later thrust the reef upward, helping to shape the Guadalupe Mountains. One of the largest and most visible examples of fossil reef is Capitan Reef in Guadalupe Mountains National Park, which attracts geologists from around the world.

Petrified Wood. If you want to know what the desert Southwest looked like more than 200 million years ago, picture the Florida Everglades populated with giant dragonflies and smaller species of dinosaurs. Arizona's Petrified Forest offers a glimpse of the once lush, tropical world. Stumps and logs from the ancient woodland are now turned to rock because they were immersed in water and sealed away from the air, so normal decay did not occur. Instead, the preserved wood gradually hardened through the eons as silica, or sand, filtered into its porous spaces, almost like cement. Erosion and other geological processes eventually exposed the wood.

Playa. Dry, salt-encrusted lake beds known as playas commonly lie in the low points of arid Southwestern valleys. You can see examples in the Sonoran Desert near Tucson.

Spheroidal Weathering. The desert's boulder gardens, such as Joshua Tree National Park's Wonderland of Rocks, originated when molten rock seeped up from beneath the Earth's underground crust and into the fissures or joints of other types of rock. When the magma cooled and hardened, its expansion caused the rock around it to split apart. The rounded, stacked, and blocky boulders were then shaped by wind and rain into near-spheres.

Index